Butterworths New Law Guides

The Financial

Butterworths New Law Guides

The Financial Services and Markets Act 2000

Deborah A Sabalot BA, DipLib, M Lib, JD, Landwell

Richard J C Everett BSc (Hons) (Dunelm), Solicitor,
Financial Services Authority

Members of the LexisNexis Group worldwide

United Kingdom	LexisNexis Butterworths Tolley, a Division of Reed Elsevier (UK) Ltd, Halsbury House, 35 Chancery Lane, LONDON, WC2A 1EL, and 4 Hill Street, EDINBURGH EH2 3JZ
Argentina	LexisNexis Argentina, BUENOS AIRES
Australia	LexisNexis Butterworths, CHATSWOOD, New South Wales
Austria	LexisNexis Verlag ARD Orac GmbH & Co KG, VIENNA
Canada	LexisNexis Butterworths, MARKHAM, Ontario
Chile	LexisNexis Chile Ltda, SANTIAGO DE CHILE
Czech Republic	Nakladatelství Orac sro, PRAGUE
France	Editions du Juris-Classeur SA, PARIS
Germany	LexisNexis Deutschland GmbH, FRANKFURT, MUNSTER
Hong Kong	LexisNexis Butterworths, HONG KONG
Hungary	HVG-Orac, BUDAPEST
India	LexisNexis Butterworths, NEW DELHI
Ireland	LexisNexis, DUBLIN
Italy	Giuffré Editore, MILAN
Malaysia	Malayan Law Journal Sdn Bhd, KUALA LUMPUR
New Zealand	LexisNexis Butterworths, WELLINGTON
Poland	Wydawnictwo Prawnicze LexisNexis, WARSAW
Singapore	LexisNexis Butterworths, SINGAPORE
South Africa	LexisNexis Butterworths, DURBAN
Switzerland	Stämpfli Verlag AG, BERNE
USA	LexisNexis, DAYTON, Ohio

© Reed Elsevier (UK) Ltd 2004
Published by LexisNexis UK

A CIP Catalogue record for this book is available from the British Library.

Deborah Sabalot and Richard Everett, have asserted their rights under the Copyrights, Designs and Patents Act 1988 to be identified as the authors of this work.

ISBN 0 406 93141 0

Printed and bound in Great Britian by Antony Rowe Ltd, Chippenham, Wilts.

Visit LexisNexis UK at www.lexisnexis.co.uk

Foreword

With the coming into force of the Financial Services and Markets Act at midnight on 30 November 2001, the Financial Services Authority became the fully empowered single regulator of financial services that the Chancellor of the Exchequer had announced back in May 1997.

There had been much lively debate in the intervening four and a half years about the nature of the new regulator and the legal powers it was to receive. Although many of these powers had been available to the previous regulators, there were important differences, with a new emphasis on the integrity of markets, to be secured by civil sanctions for 'market abuse', which proved to be a particularly fertile area of discussion both for the legal community and for market participants. In practice, however, the new regime was introduced successfully, and the FSA approach has generally been one of incremental change, working with the grain of the markets. But there have also been some significant challenges to be met, particularly in areas affecting retail consumers, where the FSA has shown that it will not shy away from using its powers when needed.

Those powers are undoubtedly wide-ranging but as importantly they are balanced by an array of measures to ensure that it uses them sensibly and is accountable in doing so. Although some of the FSA's work has excited comment and some generalised remarks about accountability, the basic framework has stood up well The report card has shown the benefit of the long gestation period and debate before the Act came into being, as well as the considerable work on many fronts to make a reality of the original vision. The IMF's Financial System Stability Assessment, published in March 2003, reported that the UK's financial stability policy framework had been significantly strengthened and was at the forefront internationally. The CSFI's Report "Sizing up the City: London's Ranking" published in June 2003 found that respondents put London's regulatory environment at the top of a list of four major financial centres 'by a clear margin', reflecting 'a positive view both of the FSA's competence as a regulator, and the value of having an integrated regulatory structure'.

But we know how quickly conditions in the markets and the industry can change. One way of maintaining the UK's current position as a financial centre is to ensure that we both anticipate and respond to future change. When the new legislation came into force, the FSA was therefore keen to stress that it was a start rather than an end point. Much has happened since to bear this out. Changes in the scope of the regime, most significantly to bring in mortgages and general insurance, and the need to reflect the EU's Financial Services Action Plan, mean that the new legislation remains an evolving and living piece of law.

As the legislation continues to reflect changes in the external environment, the need for a guide to illustrate and illuminate the Act becomes ever more essential. I am therefore very pleased to welcome this *Butterworths New Law Guide to The Financial Services and Markets Act 2000* under the expert and well informed editorship of Deborah Sabalot and Richard Everett. I congratulate them both on this work—I am sure that it will help and inform those interested in financial services regulation for many years to come.

Andrew M Whittaker
General Counsel
The Financial Services Authority
March 2004

Preface

The Financial Services and Markets Act 2000 (FSMA 2000) has brought together under a single regulatory regime the supervision and regulation of the financial services industry in the UK. In bringing together banking, insurance, investment business and a selection of other financial institutions under one statutory regime, FSMA 2000 reflects the merging of different forms and styles of familiar regulation and supervision with wholly innovative features required by the dictates of Europe. The result is certainly greater than the sum of its parts.

This text is intended to be a practical guide to the complexities of FMSA 2000 for practitioners. By necessity, this work is limited in its scope to FSMA 2000 and the framework that the Act puts in place. It does not, therefore, deal with the substance of the regulations and rules contained in the vast amount of secondary legislation or the rules that have been made by the Financial Services Authority to implement the regime except where it has been necessary to do so to provide a better understanding of the Act's regime. It is hoped that this work will be self-standing in relation to the Act itself and will provide valuable additional information and tools for lawyers, advisers and other professionals working with FSMA 2000 to comprehend a complex and difficult piece of legislation. It must also however be read in conjunction with the orders, regulations and rules which fill out the bones of the legislation.

The magnitude of the task in trying to provide a guide to the 433 sections and 22 Schedules of the Act was certainly more than we were prepared to take on unaided. In particular a number of colleagues and friends have assisted in preparing drafts of some chapters or reviewed early drafts. We express our particular thanks to—

Brenda Sufrin, Professor of Law, University of Bristol for contributing Chapter 10 Competition scrutiny;

Joanna Gray, Solicitor and Senior Lecturer, Newcastle Law School, University of Newcastle upon Tyne for her comments in reviewing most of the chapters at some stage of their production;

Gordon Nardell, Barrister, at 39 Essex Street, London for his contributions on the Human Rights Act implications;

June Paddock, Partner, Stringer Saul for her comments on Chapter 9 The FSA as listing authority;

David Garratt, formerly General Counsel at the Financial Ombudsman Service for his comments on Chapter 14 The Ombudsman scheme.

In addition we would especially like to thank Azrine Addruse, Francesca Arcidiaco, Sandeep Bandesha, Mark Banham, Alison Barker, Jim Clarke, Nicholas Holman, Maria Kazamia, Christine Monaghan, Martin Saunders, Dan Mace and, particularly, Richard Whitehouse for their comments on one or more chapters.

Also we would like to thank colleagues and former colleagues at the FSA, Landwell/PwC and Lovells for being supportive and permitting us the time to undertake this work, as well as other friends in the world of financial services for their input and comments. We would also like to express our thanks to the Lords Sharman and Newby for having provided an opportunity to see some aspects of the legislative process as the Financial Services and Markets Bill passed through Parliament in the winter and spring of 2000. We would also like to thank the Statutory Handbooks Department at LexisNexis UK, for its patience and hard work in getting this book up and running.

Finally, we are very grateful to Andrew Whittaker, General Counsel of the Financial Services Authority, for his contribution of a foreword to this book and for lending his unique experience, having been involved with this legislation since its inception and seeing it through its difficult birth in Parliament for the FSA.

All of these individuals have been generous with their time and experience, but they have done so on a personal basis and their contributions are not and should not be construed as to be representing or on behalf of their respective firms or institutions, including the Financial Services Authority. Responsibility for the text and any errors is ours alone.

Deborah A Sabalot
Partner
Landwell

Richard J C Everett
Solicitor, General Counsel's Division
Financial Services Authority

March 2004

Contents

Table of Statutes

PARA

PARA

Table of Statutory Instruments

Table of European legislation

Table of Cases

I

1 History and background

INTRODUCTION

1.1 The Financial Services and Markets Act 2000 (FSMA 2000) is the culmination of a four-year legislative process[1] intended to take the supervision and regulation of the UK financial markets into the twenty-first century.

---

[1] From the Chancellor's first announcement of the Government's intention to reform the financial services legislation on 20 May 1997 through the Joint Committee process to passage of FSMA 2000 in May 2000, and the coming into force of its principal provisions on 'N2' (1 December 2001).

1.2 Since the enactment of its predecessors, the Banking Act 1987, the Financial Services Act 1986 (FSA 1986) and the Insurance Companies Act 1982 (ICA 1982), financial institutions have increasingly found that the regulatory framework with its compliance issues and challenges is fundamental to the operation of their businesses, both domestically and globally. In the UK, firms have faced enormous challenges during the reform of the regulatory regime, including market volatility and the dot.com collapse, the introduction of regulation of new products such as stakeholder pensions and individual pension accounts supported by the Government, and increasing globalisation of products and services.

1.3 Equally, in Europe the ever-increasing pace of change as a result of the Lamfalussy report[1] and the European Commission's Financial Services Action Plan, and the adoption of some 90 Directives which affect these areas, including the Banking Consolidation Directive,[2] the Investment Services Directive,[3] the Third Life Assurance Directive,[4] the UCITS Directive,[5] the Listing Particulars Directive,[6] the Prospectus Directive[7] and the Distance Marketing Directive,[8] have had a significant impact on the regulatory regime and on the way in which financial services firms of all descriptions conduct their business. Renewed political impetus behind the EC Financial Services Action Plan[9] for achieving a single market for financial services in Europe also requires governments and firms to keep up to date with a fast developing market and new products. Finally, e-commerce and information technology present firms with new opportunities and increased challenges in understanding both the legal and regulatory framework and the technical workings of the financial system.

[1]   Final Report of the Committee of Wise Men on the Regulation of European Securities Markets, 15 February 2001.

[2]   FSMA 2000 as printed in the Queen's Printer copy refers to the Second Banking Co-ordination Directive 89/646/EEC, which has been repealed and replaced by the Banking Consolidation Directive (European Parliament and Council Directive 2000/12/EC).

[3]   Council Directive 93/22/EC—this directive is currently under review.

[4]   Council Directive 92/96/EC.

[5]   Council Directive 85/611/EEC.

[6]   Council Directive 80/390/EEC.

[7]   Council Directive 89/298/EEC.

[8]   European Parliament and Council Directive 2002/65/EC.

[9]   'Financial Services, Europe must deliver on time', European Commission Communication, 30 November 2001, COM (2001) 712 final.

PREDECESSORS TO FSMA 2000

Insurance companies

1.4   Before FSMA 2000 came into force, insurance companies were authorised and supervised under ICA 1982 and, until January 1998, the responsibility for their supervision lay with the Department of Trade and Industry, Insurance Directorate. These responsibilities were transferred to the Treasury[1] and the day-to-day supervision contracted out by the Treasury to the Financial Services Authority (the FSA) with effect from January 1999.[2]

[1]   The Transfer of Functions (Insurance) Order 1997, SI 1997/2781.

[2]   The Contracting Out (Functions in Relation to Insurance) Order 1998, SI 1998/2842; see FSA Press Release FSA/PN/106/1998, 30 December 1998. See also FSA Information Guide: The Financial Services Authority, August 1999.

1.5   The supervision of insurance companies under ICA 1982 was limited to prudential supervision. Under FSA 1986, s 22, insurance companies and Lloyd's and underwriting agents were 'exempt' persons in respect of their investment business. However, life offices which carried on other forms of investment business were regulated by virtue of being members of one of the relevant self-regulating organisations, usually the Personal Investment Authority (PIA)[1] for their marketing of insurance products which fell within FSA 1986, Sch 1, para 10 or term life assurance and certain other types of insurance.

[1]   The successor to the Life Assurance and Unit Trust Regulatory Organisation (LAUTRO) and the Financial Intermediaries Managers and Brokers Regulatory Organisation (FIMBRA).

1.6   The Government's original reform proposals did not give the Treasury and the FSA powers over general insurance brokers.[1] However, the Government subsequently announced its intention to bring general insurance within the ambit of FSMA 2000 on 14 January 2005 when the EU Insurance Mediation Directive[2] will be brought into force.[3]

---

[1]   See Helen Liddell, HC Written Answers, 7 April 1998, col 151 and HC Written Answers, 27 July 1998, col 23.

[2]   European Parliament and Council Directive 2002/92/EC.

[3]   HM Treasury Press Release PN/140/2001, 12 December 2001. See also final timetable for introduction of mortgage and general insurance regulation, HM Treasury Press Release PN/18/2003, 11 February 2003.

1.7   The Insurance Brokers (Registration) Act 1977 (now repealed by FSMA 2000)[1] required those who called themselves insurance brokers to register with the Insurance Brokers Registration Council (the IBRC) and comply with its rules concerning investment business and its code of conduct concerning general insurance business. In May 1998, the British Insurance Brokers' Association proposed the establishment of a new self-regulatory organisation for the general insurance industry.[2] As a result, the arrangements under the IBRC became obsolete in 1998 when the FSA 'derecognised' the IBRC as a recognised professional body under FSA 1986, s 15. As a result of this derecognition, insurance brokers carrying on 'investment business' under the auspices of the IBRC were required under transitional provisions[3] made by the FSA either to become authorised by the PIA or to become appointed representatives (under FSA 1986, s 44) of authorised persons, or to cease carrying on investment business. The FSA also made interim conduct of business rules for the former IBRC firms that were essentially the same rules as those imposed by the IBRC.[4] FSMA 2000 (ss 416, 432(3) and Sch 22) repeals the Insurance Brokers Registration Act 1977 and dissolves the IBRC.[5]

---

[1]   HC Written Answers, 16 May 2000, col 106W; FSMA 2000, s 432(3), Sch 22. Certain other enactments are now repealed, or substantially repealed, including the Policyholders Protection Acts 1975–97, the Industrial Assurance Acts 1923–48: see the Financial Services and Markets Act 2000 (Consequential Amendments and Repeals) Order 2001, SI 2001/3649, art 3.

[2]   British Insurance Brokers' Association, News Release, 27 May 1998.

[3]   These transitional provisions involved IBRC member firms becoming directly regulated by the FSA for a period of six months during which they were required to become authorised, become an appointed representative or cease doing investment business. In the latter case these firms were required to withdraw formally from direct regulation under FSA 1986, s 30: see FSA, the Financial Services (IBRC Interim Authorised Persons) Rules and Regulations 1998.

[4]   See FSA Press Release FSA/PN/052/1998, 27 July 1998.

[5]   This came into force on 30 April 2001: the Financial Services and Markets Act 2000 (Commencement No 2) Order 2001, SI 2001/1282. The Financial Services and Markets Act 2000 (Dissolution of the Insurance Brokers Registration Council) (Consequential Provisions) Order 2001, SI 2001/1283 made further changes to other legislation which referred to the IBRC or the Insurance Brokers (Registration) Act 1977.

General Insurance Standards Council

1.8   After consultation with the industry, the Government proposed the establishment of the General Insurance Standards Council (the GISC), an independent non-statutory self-regulating organisation, to regulate the sales, advisory and service standards of its members (insurers and intermediaries, including brokers and agents). Its main purpose is to make sure that general insurance[1] customers are treated fairly and properly by establishing, monitoring and enforcing standards of good practice for members in all their dealings with general insurance customers, including the promulgation of rules which its members must comply with as well as maintaining an appropriate level of financial soundness and ensuring the competence of its staff.[2] The GISC will continue to have a role in the regulation of general insurance until 14 January 2005 when the FSA will take over statutory regulation of general insurance.

---

[1]   For these purposes, 'general insurance' covers such products as home insurance (buildings and contents), vehicles, caravans, boats, pets, travel insurance, private medical, dental and personal accident insurance, extended warranty and breakdown insurance, legal expenses insurance, payment protection for mortgages and other loans. However, it does not include life assurance and pensions or other forms of long term insurance contracts under ICA 1982, s 75 or the Financial Services and Markets Act 2000 (Regulated Activities) Order 2001, SI 2001/544, Sch 1, Pt I.

[2]   See GISC website at http://www.gisc.co.uk.

Other codes of conduct

1.9   Other codes of conduct also existed in the insurance industry including those promulgated by the Association of British Insurers (the ABI)[1] and the Association of Insurance Intermediaries and Brokers. However the Government's intention that GISC become the sole self-regulatory body for general insurance business has now been superseded and general insurance will fall under the statutory regulation of FSMA 2000 by early 2005.

---

[1]   The ABI General Business Code for general insurance business which was introduced in 1981 was withdrawn on 30 April 2001, when all ABI general insurer members were expected to join GISC and comply with its rules.

Lloyd's

1.10   Although regulated under ICA 1982 for prudential purposes,[1] the insurance market at Lloyd's was a largely self-regulating market within the framework of the various Lloyd's Acts.[2] It is regulated by its Council but day-to-day supervision (and enforcement) have been delegated to a Regulatory Board and Corporation of Lloyd's Regulatory Division.[3] (For further discussion of Lloyd's see Ch 17.)

1   ICA 1982, Pt IV and the Insurance (Lloyd's) Regulations 1983, SI 1983/224 as amended. These powers were delegated by the Treasury to the FSA from January 1999. See also FSA, CP 16, The future regulation of Lloyd's, November 1998.
2   Lloyd's Acts 1871, 1911, 1951 and 1982.
3   Lloyd's Regulations and Council Bye-laws.

Mutual societies

1.11   Friendly societies include a wide range of mutual and voluntary organisations, such as benevolent societies and specifically authorised societies whose main purposes are to assist members during sickness, unemployment or retirement, and to provide life assurance. (For further discussion of mutual societies see Ch 19.)

1.12   The Friendly Societies Acts of 1974 and 1992 regulated the authorisation and registration of these friendly societies in the UK and their activities were supervised by the Commission for Friendly Societies (known as the Friendly Societies Commission).[1] As part of the integration of regulation and supervision into a single regulator, the Friendly Societies Commission delegated its functions to the FSA with effect from 1 January 1999.[2]

1   See HM Treasury, Proposed Amendments to the Friendly Societies Act 1992: A Consultation Document, May 1999.
2   See FSA Press Release FSA/PN/106/1998, 30 December 1998.

Industrial and provident societies

1.13   Industrial and provident societies are also covered by FSMA 2000. These include organisations conducting an industry, business or trade either as a bona fide co-operative or for the benefit of the community. These societies were primarily governed by the Industrial and Provident Societies Act 1965, the Industrial and Provident Societies Act 1967 or the Friendly and Industrial and Provident Societies Act 1968. Day-to-day responsibility for the supervision of these bodies was transferred to the Treasury and delegated to the FSA.[1]

1   The Transfer of Functions (Insurance) Order 1997, SI 1997/2781 and the Contracting Out (Functions in Relation to Insurance) Order 1998, SI 1998/2842: see FSA Press Release FSA/PN/106/1998, 30 December 1998.

1.14   Credit unions are generally mutual savings and loan societies where members save by investing in the society's shares, thereby producing a fund from which loans can be granted to them.[1] Dividends may be paid to members from the surplus that results from lending at interest. Credit unions are subject to the Industrial and Provident Societies Act 1965 and the Credit Unions Act 1979.

---

¹ See FSA Press Release FSA/PN/036/2000, 3 March 2000.

1.15   Authorisation and regulation of credit unions was the responsibility of the Registrar of Friendly Societies but day-to-day supervision of credit unions by the Chief Registrar of Friendly Societies was delegated by contract to the FSA with effect from 1 January 1999 until the FSA assumed its statutory responsibilities under FSMA 2000 on 'N3' (2 July 2002).[1]

---

¹ See FSA Press Release FSA/PN/072/2002, 2 July 2002.

Building societies

1.16   The Building Societies Act 1986 (BSA 1986) established the regulatory framework for the authorisation of building societies whose main business is making loans that are secured on residential property. This Act defines how these building societies are to be regulated.

1.17   Building societies are mutual bodies and the loans are funded by their members. Each society has a set of rules which governs the relationship between that society and its members. In addition, building societies may carry out other forms of lending, investment, money transmission services, banking and insurance services permitted under BSA 1986.

1.18   Building societies may also follow the non-statutory voluntary Banking Code,[1] which sets minimum standards of good banking practice and customer service, and the Mortgage Code,[2] which sets out good mortgage lending practice.

---

¹ Revised March 2003. The Banking Code Standards Board is responsible for registering banks and building societies and monitoring their compliance with the Banking Code: see its website at http://www.bcsb.co.uk.

² The Mortgage Code Compliance Board establishes the Mortgage Code as a voluntary code complied with by many mortgage lenders and brokers and is responsible for registering mortgage intermediaries: see its website at http://www.mortgagecode.org.uk.

1.19   From 1 January 1999 the FSA supplied regulatory and other services under contract to the Building Societies Commission to carry out the day-to-day supervision of building societies authorised under BSA 1986 until the FSA assumed its statutory responsibilities under FSMA 2000 on N2.[1]

---

¹ See FSA Press Release FSA/PN/106/1998, 30 December 1998.

THE FINANCIAL SERVICES ACT 1986

1.20   FSA 1986 was a comprehensive attempt to regulate the activities of a broad range of firms carrying on financial services in the UK. Previous legislation had had limited effect on setting up a framework for licensing securities dealers[1] and establishing a code of conduct for broker/dealer activities.[2]

---

[1]   The Prevention of Fraud (Investments) Act 1939, re-enacted in 1958 and repealed by FSA 1986, Sch 17.
[2]   The Licensed Dealers (Conduct of Business) Rules 1960, SI 1960/1216, revoked and replaced by the Licensed Dealers (Conduct of Business) Rules 1983, SI 1983/585.

1.21   In 1981, largely as a result of a number of financial scandals and other problems in the City, Professor LCB Gower conducted a review[1] of the existing regulatory framework focusing primarily on the issue of investor protection and the need for new legislation. The resulting legislation was more wide-ranging, incorporating many of Professor Gower's recommendations but going further in establishing a framework of self-regulatory organisations as a halfway house between the rather 'laissez-faire' regime which operated under the Prevention of Fraud (Investments) Act 1958 and full statutory regulation of the industry.

---

[1]   Review of Investor Protection Report, Cmnd 9125, January 1984.

1.22   Under FSA 1986 a regulatory framework was created for all persons carrying on 'investment business' in the UK, defined as including—
   (a)   dealing or arranging deals in investments;
   (b)   managing investments for others;
   (c)   giving investment advice;
   (d)   providing safekeeping and administration of investments;
   (e)   transmitting dematerialised instructions; and
   (f)   establishing, operating or winding up collective investment schemes in the UK (FSA 1986, Sch 1, Pt II).

This definition was modified by the Investment Services Regulations 1995,[1] to include, for those firms which are credit institutions or investment firms, the provision to third parties of 'listed services' within the meaning of the Investment Services Directive.[2]

---

[1]   SI 1995/3275 (now revoked by SI 2001/3649, art 3(2)(c).
[2]   Council Directive 93/22/EC.

1.23   FSA 1986 provided that carrying on investment business in the UK without authorisation (or without being otherwise exempt under the legislation) constituted a criminal offence (FSA 1986, s 3). Under the

FSA 1986 regulatory regime, authorisation was usually obtained by firms becoming members of one of three self-regulatory bodies established under the Act.[1]

---

[1]   There were originally five self-regulating bodies recognised under FSA 1986: the Securities Authority (TSA), the Association of Futures Brokers and Dealers (AFBD), the Investment Management Regulatory Organisation (IMRO), the Life Assurance and Unit Trust Regulatory Organisation (LAUTRO) and the Financial Intermediaries, Managers and Brokers Regulatory Association (FIMBRA)) but after various mergers and consolidations this was eventually reduced to three (the Personal Investment Authority (PIA), the Securities and Futures Authority (SFA) and IMRO).

1.24   The UK self-regulatory environment was, however, highly fragmented. The previous Government's underlying thinking had been to deregulate the industry and allow market forces to determine its development. This was generally unhindered by regulatory restrictions, unless a specific issue was identified which required the legislator's intervention. This was reflected in the functional division and range of regulators and the difference in regulatory approaches which characterised the UK financial services sector until the Government's reform programme was announced in 1997 and the shaping of the new regime under FSMA 2000.

BANK OF ENGLAND ACT 1998

1.25   Until the Bank of England Act 1998 came into force on 1 June 1998, the supervision of the banking sector was a function of the Bank of England. The Banking Act 1987, as modified by the Banking Co-ordination (Second Council Directive) Regulations 1992,[1] established the framework for the authorisation and supervision of banks in the UK by the Bank of England, which focused primarily on the prudential regulation of banks with relatively little detailed regulation of the banker/customer relationship. A non-statutory 'voluntary' Banking Code[2] has, however, existed for a number of years and the regulation of banks' conduct of business vis-à-vis their customers is likely to become of greater importance in the light of European developments and the consolidated framework under FSMA 2000.

---

[1]   SI 1992/3218. Note that the Second Council Directive 89/646/EEC has been replaced by the Banking Consolidation Directive (European Parliament and Council Directive 2000/12/EC).
[2]   Revised March 2003.

REFORMING THE REGULATION OF THE FINANCIAL SERVICES INDUSTRY

1.26   The reform of the financial services regulatory regime was a central commitment of the Labour Party manifesto and one of the first legislative initiatives to be announced by the newly elected Labour Government on 20 May 1997.[1]

---

[1]   HC Debs, 20 May 1997, col 508.

1.27   Underpinning this initiative was the creation of a single regulator, the FSA, responsible for supervising and regulating the whole of the financial services industry including banking and insurance and applying a consistent approach to all sectors. It is intended that the FSA will eliminate any regulatory overlaps and end the arbitrary boundaries of the self-regulatory regime.[1]

---

[1]   FSA Policy report: A New Regulator for the New Millennium, January 2000. See also the Chancellor's Statement to the House of Commons on the Bank of England, HC Debs, 20 May 1997, col 508.

1.28   Anticipating this change, the transfer of regulatory functions to the FSA began with the enactment of the Bank of England Act 1998, which transferred banking supervision from the Bank of England to the FSA.[1] Certain other functions relating to the insurance industry were transferred by the Treasury to the new regulator[2] and the remaining regulatory bodies began to be consolidated into a de facto single authority from October 1997. The FSA has effectively brought together these former agencies (for management purposes) although the legislative framework has taken considerably longer to amend. Those agencies (designated under FSA 1986) were—

— the Securities and Investments Board (SIB);
— the three remaining Self-Regulatory Organisations (SROs), ie, the Personal Investment Authority (PIA), the Investment Management Regulatory Organisation (IMRO) and the Securities and Futures Authority (SFA);
— the Building Societies Commission;
— the Friendly Societies Commission and the Registry of Friendly Societies;
— the former Supervision and Surveillance Branch of the Bank of England; and
— the Insurance Directorate of the Treasury.

---

[1]   See para 1.25.
[2]   See paras 1.4, 1.13 and 1.19.

1.29   The new regime under which the FSA operates is based on previous financial services legislation, but extends beyond the boundaries of the pre-existing enactments. The provisions of the Credit Unions Act 1979, the Insurance Companies Act 1982, the Financial Services Act 1986, the Building Societies Act 1986, the Banking Act 1987 and the Friendly Societies Act 1992 have been coordinated, modernised and extended. FSMA 2000 repealed partially or fully several other enactments, including the Industrial Assurance Acts 1923 and 1948 and the Insurance Brokers (Registration) Act 1977. It gives the FSA new regulatory powers over the Lloyd's insurance market, except its superintendence and governance. Finally, it enables Parliament to extend the range of activities covered in order to address the changing markets, and empowers the FSA to introduce new rules and regulations in previously unregulated areas, such as mortgage regulation and long-term care.

The consultation process

1.30   The magnitude of the task before the legislators influenced the legislative procedure chosen to put FSMA 2000 on the statute book. The Government promised full and comprehensive consultation and a receptive ear aimed at smoothing the process and at dealing with additional issues and conflicting views. After a number of meetings with various sectors of the financial services industry, the Treasury published a consultation paper on the proposed draft Bill in July 1998 inviting responses by November 1998. The document, which explained the Treasury's proposed policy and included a first draft of the Financial Services and Markets Bill, attracted comments from 220 firms and organisations.[1]

---

[1]   HM Treasury, Financial Services and Markets Bill: A Consultation Document, July 1998.

1.31   At the same time the Treasury also published a number of other related consultation papers, including some drafts of secondary legislation, intended to bring into force various sections of FSMA 2000.[1] The Bill benefited also from a pre-legislative scrutiny by the Treasury Select Committee which, at the beginning of the 1998–99 Parliamentary session, embarked on an inquiry into the newly renamed FSA. It published a report[2] to which the Government responded in March 1999.[3] This report and its recommendations were considered at all subsequent stages of the legislative procedure.

---

[1]   HM Treasury, Financial Services and Markets Bill: Regulated Activities—A Consultation Document, March 1999; Draft FSMA (Regulated Activities) Order, Draft FSMA (Exemption) Order, Draft FSMA (Collective Investment Schemes) Order, and Explanatory notes on the Draft Orders, February 1999.

[2]   HM Treasury, Third Report, Financial Services Regulation: Vol I (Report and Proceedings of the Committee), HC 73-I; Vol II (Minutes of Evidence and Appendices), HC 73-II, 10 February 1999.

³ Treasury Select Committee, Fourth Special Report, Financial Services Regulation: the Government's Response to the Third Report from the Committee of Session 1998–99, HC 347, 25 March 1999.

Joint Parliamentary Committee procedure

1.32 The pre-legislative stage of the Bill included consideration by a Joint Committee of both Houses of Parliament in the early part of 1999. This innovative procedure allowed a selected number of MPs and peers to consider all aspects of the draft Bill and, more importantly, to question other interested parties at the same time as Treasury and FSA officials. This style of inquiry enabled a more effective examination of contentious issues, which were raised and justified or discussed in a multilateral dialogue between the members of the Joint Committee, with constant input from the Department in charge of the Bill (the Treasury) and its implementer (the FSA). The Joint Committee also considered the Treasury's Progress Report on the Bill, which was published in March 1999.[1] The Joint Committee published its First Report in April 1999,[2] and its Second Report, focusing on the impact on the Bill of the European Convention on Human Rights, in June 1999.[3] The Government's response to both reports was published in the same month.[4]

¹ HM Treasury, Financial Services and Markets Bill: Progress Report, March 1999.
² First Report from the Joint Committee on Financial Services and Markets, Session 1998-99: Vol I (Report and Proceedings of the Committee), HL 50-I, HC 328-I; Vol II (Minutes of Evidence and Appendices), HL 50-II, HC 328-II.
³ Second Report from the Joint Committee on Financial Services and Markets: Draft Financial Services and Markets Bill, Parts V, VI and XII in relation to the European Convention on Human Rights, HL Paper 66, HC 465, 27 May 1999.
⁴ HM Treasury, Financial Services and Markets Bill: Government Response to the Reports of the Joint Committee on Financial Services and Markets, June 1999.

The legislative procedure

1.33 The Bill was finally introduced in the House of Commons on 17 June 1999[1] and received its Second Reading on 28 June.[2] The Standing Committee Stage lasted from 6 July to 9 December 1999,[3] with the Bill thus becoming the first public bill in Parliamentary history to be carried over from one session to the next, with all-party consent. The Report Stage took place at the end of January/beginning of February 2000[4] and the Bill was passed by the House of Commons, after the Third Reading, on 9 February 2000.[5]

¹ HC 1R, 17 June 1999.
² HC 2R, 28 June 1999, col 34.
³ HC SC A, 6 July 1999, col 3; HC SC A, 9 November 1999, col 840.
⁴ HC Report Stage, 27 January 2000, col 600; HC Report Stage, 1 February 2000, col 924.
⁵ HC 3R, 9 February 2000, col 256.

1.34   The Bill was read in the House of Lords for the first time on 10 February 2000[1] and the Second Reading was on 21 February.[2] After a Committee of the whole House had examined it during the second half of March, the Report Stage took place in April/beginning of May[3] and the Third Reading was completed on 18 May 2000.[4] During this period the Treasury submitted a number of memoranda on the powers to introduce delegated legislation under this Bill. The Delegated Powers and Deregulation Committee published a number of reports[5] setting out its views on each of these documents.

[1]   HL 1R, 10 February 2000, col 775.
[2]   HL 2R, 21 February 2000, col 13.
[3]   HL Committee Stage, 16–30 March 2000; HL Report Stage, 13, 18 April 2000, 9 May 2000.
[4]   HL 3R, 18 May 2000, col 363.
[5]   Delegated Powers and Deregulation Committee Seventh Report, 16 February 2000; Eighth Report, 8 March 2000; Tenth Report, 15 March 2000; Twelfth Report, 12 April 2000; Sixteenth Report, 17 May 2000.

1.35   No one has better described this complex and lengthy procedure than Lord Saatchi on the opening day of debate in the House of Lords, when he stated—

> 'I have seen grown men weep at the sight of the Bill. It is the single biggest piece of legislation that the Government have introduced. It is 215 pages and 408 clauses long. In its epic 18-month passage through another place it attracted 1,450 amendments. A Standing Committee sat for 70 hours in 35 sessions. A fine Joint Committee of both Houses, chaired by the noble Lord, Lord Burns, prepared a set of 37 recommendations. The Bill outlasted three complete sets of ministerial teams.'[1]

This description does not, however, take into account the hundreds of Government and Lords amendments and the long sessions during both the Committee and Report Stages in the House of Lords.

[1]   HL 2R, 21 February 2000, col 18.

1.36   The Bill returned to the House of Commons for consideration of the Lords amendments on 5 June 2000,[1] and having been amended in the House of Commons was considered again by the House of Lords on 12 June 2000.[2] It received Royal Assent on 14 June 2000.[3]

[1]   HC Consideration of Lords Amendments, 5 June 2000, col 22.
[2]   HL Consideration of Commons Amendments, 12 June 2000, col 1373.
[3]   HL Royal Assent, 14 June 2000, col 1631.

Timetable for implementation

1.37 The date for commencement of FSMA 2000 was much commented on by the Treasury, who released four press releases on the subject. On 18 July 2000, shortly after FSMA 2000 received Royal Assent, the then Economic Secretary to the Treasury, Melanie Johnson, announced that commencement was planned for 'about a year's time' but recognised that the implementation of the new regime would be a complicated undertaking, and would benefit from allowing those affected to prepare properly.[1] The Economic Secretary reiterated this timetable in December 2000, when reporting on the implementation progress[2] (by which time the Treasury had issued 13 pieces of draft secondary legislation, and the FSA had published large parts of its proposed Handbook) so as to provide a balance between 'the importance of firms and consumers enjoying the benefits of the new regulatory framework as soon as practicable, and the need to give financial services firms a reasonable time to prepare' for N2.[3] On 12 July 2001, the new Economic Secretary, Ruth Kelly, 'confirmed' this commencement, announcing that N2 would be midnight at the end of 30 November 2001.[4]

---

[1] HM Treasury Press Release PN/92/2000, 18 July 2000.

[2] HM Treasury Press Release PN/150/2000, 21 December 2000 when the Economic Secretary committed to announcing a 'firm date' in the following spring and in March 2001 she announced that this would be 'no later than the end of November' of 2001 (HM Treasury Press Release PN/33/2001, 15 March 2001).

[3] HM Treasury Press Release PN/60/2001, 10 May 2001; the FSA aquired the power to make rules in June 2001 as a result of the Financial Services and Markets Act 2000 (Commencement No 3) Order 2001, SI 2001/1820.

[4] HM Treasury Press Release PN/80/2001—the notes to editors acknowledge that legally N2 would be the beginning of 1 December 2001, rather than 30 November.

1.38 One of the factors in the timing of the commencement of FSMA 2000 was the progress in making the necessary secondary legislation in the form of statutory instruments. A total of 94 statutory instruments were laid and subjected to Parliamentary scrutiny, albeit most of them subject to the negative resolution procedure, and came into force on or before N2 (some having been amended before coming into force, including the Regulated Activities Order).[1] A number of these are fundamental to the new regulatory regime—the most important of these is the Regulated Activities Order which describes in detail which activities require authorisation from the FSA under the new permissions regime.

---

[1] The Financial Services and Markets Act 2000 (Regulated Activities) Order 2001, SI 2001/544: see Ch 3.

1.39 In addition the FSA has conducted extensive consultation processes on the provisions in its Handbook, many parts of which were made as soon as its power to make rules became exercisable.[1] It has made further provisions for its Handbook since then (described in Handbook notices issued each month by the FSA). However it is unlikely that the development of the Handbook, or the making of statutory instruments, will cease merely because N2 has arrived.

---

[1]   See the FSA Handbook, Notice 1, July 2001.

TIMETABLE OF REFORM

May 1997	Chancellor's statement announcing reform of the financial services regulatory system
October 1997	Securities and Investments Board renamed and 'relaunched' as the Financial Services Authority
June 1998	Supervision of banks transferred to the FSA under the Bank of England Act 1998
July 1998	First consultation draft of the Financial Services and Markets Bill published
July 1998	IBRC derecognised as recognised professional body
January 1999	Transfer of functions relating to insurance to the Treasury
January 1999	Transfer of responsibility for supervision of insurance business to the FSA
January 1999	Delegation and integration of staff of Building Societies Commission and Registrar of Friendly Societies into the FSA
June 1999	Draft Bill introduced into Parliament
May 2000	UKLA functions transferred to the FSA (Official Listing of Securities (Change of Competent Authority) Regulations 2000)
June 2000	FSMA 2000 receives Royal Assent
June 2000	GISC promulgates Code of Conduct
1 Dec 2001 (N2)	Implementation of FSMA 2000 subject to transitional provisions
1 January 2002	Extension of FSMA 2000 to cover pre-paid funeral plans
October 2004	Extension of FSMA 2000 to regulated mortgages
January 2005	Extension of FSMA 2000 to general insurance

2 The FSA and its powers

INTRODUCTION AND HISTORICAL PERSPECTIVE

2.1 This chapter sets out the structure and powers of the Financial Services Authority (the FSA) as the single statutory regulator under the Financial Services and Markets Act 2000 (FSMA 2000).

2.2 The First Report of the Joint Committee of the Lords and Commons which considered the early stages of the Bill set out the Government's rationale for its programme of reform as follows—

> 'The existing arrangements for financial regulation involve a large number of regulators, each responsible for different parts of the industry. In recent years there has been a blurring of the distinctions between different kinds of financial services business: banks, building societies, investment firms, insurance companies and others. This has added further to the complexity of financial regulation. The Government believes the current system is costly, inefficient and confusing for both regulated firms and their consumers. It is not delivering the standard of supervision and investor protection that the public has a right to expect. We are therefore establishing a single, statutory regulator for the UK financial services industry, with clearly defined regulatory objectives and a single set of coherent functions and powers.'[1]

---

[1] Joint Committee of the Lords and Commons on Financial Services and Markets (The 'Burns Committee'), First Report, May 1999, para 99.

THE CREATION OF THE REGULATOR

2.3 FSMA 2000, s 1 specifies that the FSA has the functions conferred on it by the Act (s 1(1)). The FSA is constituted as a company limited by guarantee under the Companies Acts 1948–1981 and not as a company under the Companies Act 1985 (CA 1985).[1]

1   The FSA is the same corporate entity as the former Securities and Investments Board and later assumed functions under the Banking Act 1985 and exercised other functions under other financial services legislation on behalf of the Treasury. Explanatory Notes, para 34.

THE CONSTITUTION OF THE FSA

2.4   FSMA 2000, s 1(2) imposes various requirements for the constitution of the FSA. These are set out in Sch 1 of the Act, which also contains various provisions on the FSA's status and the exercise of certain of its functions (s 1(3)).

2.5   Schedule 1, para 2(1) provides that the FSA must have a chairman and a governing body. The members of the governing body are also directors of the company and will therefore be subject to the same statutory obligations as directors of companies under CA 1985—[1]

> 'The FSA is a private company limited by guarantee. This means that it has members, not shareholders. The members of the company are the same as the members of the Board and as such are all appointed by the Treasury. The Treasury Select Committee raised with Mr Davies[2] the reasons for this structure. Mr Davies said the answer was somewhat historical in that that was the conclusion reached in 1986 in relation to the Securities and Investment Board. The FSA had inherited that structure and adapted it to take on other responsibilities. His understanding was that "Parliament concluded that because it wanted a regulatory system which was as far as possible rooted in the markets that it regulated and funded by those markets, it should be constructed as a private company operating within those markets with private company-type corporate governance procedures and funding direct from institutions with public powers given to it. That would allow it to relate more effectively to the market place, and would allow it to employ people on broadly speaking private sector terms". The protections which people needed in relation to their ability to challenge the FSA and judicially review its decisions still applied.'[3]

1   HL Report Stage, 13 April 2000, col 291. The structure of the FSA was likened to that of the Court of the Bank of England.
2   Sir Howard Davies, Executive Chairman of the FSA.
3   Burns Committee, First Report, May 1999, para 104.

The role of the chairman

2.6   The constitution and powers of the FSA and, in particular, the role of the chairman, proved to be one of the most controversial and most debated issues during the progress of the Bill.

2.7   The Government's vision of the FSA was summed up in the Treasury's response to the Burns Committee's recommendations regarding the constitution and accountability of the FSA—

> 'The Government does not accept the Committee's recommendation that in the long term the posts of the FSA Chairman and Chief Executive should be separated . . . Under the current arrangements, there is a full time Chairman and Chief Executive and a non-executive Deputy Chairman. The Government is very happy with these arrangements and does not intend to change them. It understands the thinking behind the Committee's view that in the longer term there may be other arrangements which could work. It is however mindful of the fact that parallels with other models of corporate governance are not exact. There is also a good case for a strong line of direct accountability to Treasury Ministers from the senior executive of the regulator. These views are shared by the non-executive members of the FSA Board . . . The Government agrees with the Committee's conclusion that it would be anomalous to extend the role of the non-executive Board Members to the oversight of the role of the Board as a whole. We have considered the recommendation that their functions in relation to efficiency, internal controls and remuneration should be exercised in the form of an audit committee and a remuneration committee. It is anticipated that audit and remuneration will be important elements in the functions set out in paragraph 4(3) of Schedule 1 to the Bill. There is, however, already scope within the terms of the Bill for considerable flexibility in the way the work of the committee is organised, because specific provision is made in that paragraph for the formation of sub-committees to deal with financial controls and with remuneration, and further legislative provision is not needed to meet the Committee's suggestion.'[1]

Beyond this, the role of the chairman is not defined.

---

[1]   HM Treasury, Response to the Joint Committee's First Report, 1999, section 4.

2.8   The role and accountability of the FSA and its chairman continued to be a point of contention and a number of amendments were tabled in the House of Lords seeking to clarify the nature of the body corporate which would be the FSA. Lord Newby stated at the Bill's Report Stage that these amendments—

> ' . . . seek to clarify the structure of the FSA and make it more transparently accountable to the three groups with which it interacts; namely, those who work in the financial services sector, those who consume its products and Parliament . . .
>
> . . .
>
> [T]here is uncertainty about the exact role and powers of the directors, particularly the non-executive directors, and that needs correcting.
>
> . . .
>
> These amendments seek to square the circle by providing that there should be both a chairman and chief executive; by allowing the posts to be held by the same person; and by requiring the authority to follow the provisions of the combined code on corporate governance.'[1]

In reply, Lord McIntosh stated that while the Government recognised that combining the roles of chairman and chief executive was contrary to the recommendations of the Cadbury Committee and Combined Code, it considered that this was the best structure to enable the FSA to meet its statutory objectives. He pointed out that the FSA was different from a typical private company in three ways—

> 'First, . . . , it has no shareholders; secondly, its accountability is to Treasury Ministers; and, thirdly, it is required to take important decisions very rapidly. It is not alone in having to take decisions very rapidly, but a key difference is the potentially systemic consequences of the FSA's decisions.'

Lord McIntosh also dealt with several other opposition amendments relating to the structure and governance of the FSA, following which the amendments were withdrawn,[2] while at Third Reading further proposals to amend these provisions were defeated.[3]

---

[1]   HL Report Stage, 13 April 2000, col 291.

[2]   HL Report Stage, 13 April 2000, col 301.

[3]   HL 3R, 18 May 2000, col 377. With the appointment of Callum McCarthy as chairman and John Tiner as chief executive to succeed Sir Howard Davies on 22 September 2003, the role of chairman and chief executive has been split – both are members of the FSA's board.

The appointment of the chairman and members of the governing body

2.9   The FSA has a governing body that must include the chairman (Sch 1, para 2(1)). The chairman and each of the governing body's other members are to be appointed, and are liable to removal from office, by the Treasury (Sch 1, para 2(3)).[1]

---

[1]   See HM Treasury, Progress Report, March 1999, Section III, para B, on accountability. Members of the FSA's governing body are disqualified under the House of Commons Disqualification Act 1975 and the Northern Ireland Assembly Disqualification Act 1975 from sitting as members of these bodies (Sch 1, paras 20, 21).

Arrangements for discharging functions

2.10   In discharging its functions under FSMA 2000 the FSA has wide authority to make arrangements for any of its functions to be discharged by a committee, sub-committee, officer or member of staff of the Authority (Sch 1, para 5(1)). This provision does not apply to the FSA's legislative powers which must be exercised through the FSA's governing body (Sch 1, para 5(2)),[1] or to the non-executive functions (Sch 1, para 5(3)) which must be carried out through the FSA's non-executive committee (Sch 1, para 4(2)).

---

[1]   FSMA Explanatory Notes, paras 752–754.

2.11   The validity of the FSA's acts including its rulemaking and any other actions taken to fulfil its other functions under FSMA 2000 will not be affected by any vacancy in the office of the chairman or by any procedural defect in the appointment of any person as a member of its governing body or as chairman (Sch 1, para 2(4)).

The non-executive committee

2.12   The FSA itself must secure that the majority of the members of the governing body are non-executive members although it is not clear on the face of the legislation how this will be achieved, since the power to appoint the members of the governing body lies with the Treasury (Sch 1, para 2(3)). FSMA 2000 further requires that a non-executive committee of the governing body be established (Sch 1, para 3) and that that non-executive committee have specific functions and be regulated by a chairman, again appointed by the Treasury from among its members (Sch 1, para 3(3)). The FSA's Policy report[1] says relatively little about the governing body's role but stresses the limited 'oversight' function of the non-executive directors of the FSA—

'The Authority's powers and governance have been extensively debated in Parliament. But what will matter most to regulated firms and their customers is the way in which the FSA carries out the business of regulation from day to day, and year to year'.

---

[1]   FSA Policy report: A New Regulator for the New Millennium, January 2000, Introduction, p 3.

Functions of the non-executive committee

2.13   The non-executive functions specified in Sch 1 must be discharged by the non-executive committee. These functions are—
— keeping under review the performance of the FSA in discharging its functions in accordance with the decisions of its governing body and determining whether it is using its resources in the most efficient and economic way;
— keeping under review the FSA's internal financial controls and determining whether they secure the proper conduct of its financial affairs; and
— determining the remuneration of the FSA's chairman and the executive member of the FSA's governing body (Sch 1, para 4(3)).

2.14   Determination of remuneration for the governing body's executive members and the review of the FSA's internal financial controls may be carried out by a sub-committee (ie, a remuneration or audit committee) of the non-executive committee, which must include the chairman of the non-executive committee (Sch 1, para 4(4)). Other sub-committees of the non-executive committee may also be established, which may also include persons other than the members of the non-executive committee, presumably advisers or others on a co-opted basis to advise the non-executive committee in specialised areas (Sch 1, para 4(5)).

2.15   The non-executive committee must also prepare a report on its discharge of these functions which is to be included in the FSA's annual report to the Treasury (Sch 1, para 4(6)).

THE FSA'S LEGISLATIVE FUNCTIONS

2.16   The FSA's legislative functions are set out in FSMA 2000, Sch 1, para 1(2), as follows—
(a)   making rules;

(b)   issuing codes under s 64 or 119;
(c)   issuing statements under s 64, 69, 124 or 210;
(d)   giving directions under s 316, 318 or 328; and
(e)   issuing general guidance as defined by s 158(5).

These functions must be exercised by the FSA's governing body and these are made by legal instruments. In addition, some functions conferred by transitional provisions are also deemed to be legislative functions, in particular, the power to carry forward the FSMA 2000 rules and other provisions by designation as FSA rules.[1]

---

[1]   The Financial Services and Markets Act 2000 (Transitional Provisions and Savings) (Rules) Order 2001, SI 2001/1534, art 4(7) and the Financial Services and Markets Act 2000 (Transitional Provisions) (Reviews of Pensions Business) Order 2001, SI 2001/2512; see also the Financial Services and Markets Act 2000 (Interim Permissions) Order 2001, SI 2001/3374, art 12(3).

The FSA's arrangements for discharging its functions under FSMA 2000

2.17   The FSA has the power to appoint various persons to carry out specific functions under FSMA 2000. For example, in relation to the FSA's information gathering powers under s 165(9), an 'officer' of the FSA includes a member of the Authority's staff or an agent of the Authority.[1]

---

[1]   Investigators appointed under FSMA 2000, s 67, 168(3) and (5). See *R v IRC, ex p Davis Frankel & Mead (a firm)* [2000] STC 595, 73 TC 185 (power to require documentation may be delegated).

The FSA's monitoring arrangements

2.18   FSMA 2000, Sch 1, para 6(1) provides that the FSA must have appropriate monitoring arrangements to enable it to determine whether persons on whom the various requirements are imposed are complying with them. The FSA may delegate these monitoring functions to any body or person who is competent to perform that function (Sch 1, para 6(2))[1] but the FSA will remain responsible for ensuring that these monitoring functions are carried out (Sch 1, para 6(4)).

---

[1]   For example, the monitoring functions for the Lloyd's market: see FSA Press Releases FSA/PN/095/1998, 30 November 1998 and FSA/PN/062/1999, 30 June 1999.

The FSA's enforcement activities

2.19   The FSA is also required to maintain arrangements for enforcing the provisions of FSMA 2000 (Sch 1, para 6(3)) but these enforcement arrangements may not be delegated to any other body or person.[1]

---

[1]   FSMA Explanatory Notes, para 756.

The FSA's complaints scheme

2.20   The FSA is required to establish a complaints scheme and to arrange for the investigation of complaints[1] which arise from or in connection with the FSA's exercise of, or its failure to exercise, any of its functions under FSMA 2000 other than its legislative functions (Sch 1, para 7(1)). This covers allegations of maladminstration by the FSA or other failures to comply with the requirements of Sch 1 or the other provisions of FSMA 2000.[2] The complaints scheme does not, however, prevent the FSA from taking steps to conduct an initial investigation of any complaint made against it (Sch 1, para 8(10)).[3]

---

[1]   A 'complaint' for these purposes means any expression of dissatisfaction about the way the FSA has carried out its functions under FSMA 2000 other than its legislative functions: see the FSA Handbook, Complaints against the FSA, COAF 1.1.5G.
[2]   FSMA Explanatory Notes, para 757. See also HL Report Stage, 13 April 2000, col 314 and FSA Annual Report 2000/2001, p 4.
[3]   See COAF.

2.21   The FSA, with the approval of the Treasury, must appoint an independent person to be responsible for investigating complaints (Sch 1, para 7(1), (3)). The terms and conditions on which the investigator is to be appointed must be reasonably designed to ensure that the investigator acts independently of the FSA and without bias or favour towards it (Sch 1, para 7(4)). The investigator appointed under this provision may appoint another person to conduct the investigation on his behalf although subject to his direction (Sch 1, para 8(8)) and only if neither the investigator nor any person appointed by him is an officer or employee of the FSA (Sch 1, para 8(9)).

2.22   The complaints scheme itself must be designed to ensure as far as reasonably practicable that complaints against the FSA are investigated quickly (Sch 1, para 7(2)). The complaints scheme is not required to cover the investigation of a complaint if the FSA reasonably considers it would be more appropriately dealt with in another manner, for example, by referring the matter to the Tribunal established under FSMA 2000, s 132 or by instituting other legal proceedings (Sch 1, para 8(1)). The complaints scheme must further provide for reference to the investigator of any complaint which the FSA is investigating (Sch 1, para 8(2)(a)), and the FSA must also notify the investigator of any complaint which it decides not to investigate (Sch 1, para 8(3)).

2.23   Where the investigator has been notified of a complaint under Sch 1, para 8(3) and he believes the complaint should be investigated, he has the power to do so as if the complaint had been referred to him under the scheme (Sch 1, para 8(4)). The investigator must also have the means and authority to conduct a full investigation of the complaint, and be able to report on the result of that investigation to the FSA and to the complainant, and to publish his report (or any part of it) which he considers to be of public interest (Sch 1, para 8(2)(b)). Where the investigator has reported that the complaint made against the FSA is well founded or where he has criticised the FSA in his report, the scheme must require the FSA to inform the investigator and the complainant of the steps which it proposes to take in response to that report (Sch 1, para 8(6)). The investigator may require the FSA to publish all or part of this response (Sch 1, para 8(7)).

2.24   FSMA 2000, Sch 1, para 7(5) sets out the detailed procedure that the FSA must follow in promulgating a draft of the proposed complaints scheme and making those proposals available to the public for consultation and comment. The FSA must have regard to any representations received concerning the scheme (Sch 1, para 7(7)) and must publish a statement of the representations made and its response to them (Sch 1, para 7(8)). If the complaints scheme differs significantly from the draft published under Sch 1, para 7(5), the FSA must publish details of the difference (Sch 1, para 7(9)). Once this consultation process has been completed, the FSA is required to provide a copy of the procedures to the Treasury (Sch 1, para 7(12)) and to publish details of the complaints scheme. This must include a statement of the powers which the investigator has to investigate complaints and to recommend under Sch 1, para 8(5) either that a compensatory payment be made to the complainant, or that the FSA remedy the matter complained of (Sch 1, para 7(10)). Any proposal by the FSA to change or alter the terms of the scheme is subject to the same consultation process (Sch 1, para 7(14)).

2.25   This scheme was made by the FSA on 19 July 2001 (together with the transitional scheme made under the Financial Services and Markets Act 2000 (Transitional Provisions) (Ombudsman Scheme and Complaints Scheme) Order 2001,[1] art 18, concerning various pre-commencement matters). The first Complaints Commissioner, Rosemary Radcliffe, was appointed on 3 September 2001.[2]

---

[1]   SI 2001/2326.
[2]   See FSA Press Release FSA/PN/109/2001.

The FSA's record-keeping obligations

2.26   The FSA must maintain satisfactory arrangements for recording decisions made in the exercise of its functions under FSMA 2000 and must have in place arrangements for the safe-keeping of those documents which it considers ought to be preserved (Sch 1, para 9). The FSA is also subject to various requirements concerning data protection[1] as well as the Companies Acts. It is also expected to become subject to the provisions of the Freedom of Information Act 2000.[2]

---

[1]   HC SC A, 7 December 1999. FSA 1986, s 190 was repealed by the Data Protection Act 1998, s 74(2) which came into force on 1 March 2000. The Data Protection Act 1998, s 31(1) provides that personal data processed to discharge functions to which s 31(1) applies are exempt from subject information provisions to the extent that the application of those provisions to the data would be likely to prejudice the proper discharge of those functions. See also: *Durant v Financial Services Authority* [2003] EWCA Civ 1746.

[2]   On the Freedom of Information Act 2000, the Economic Secretary said: 'I realise that the Freedom of Information Bill does not include the FSA within the list of bodies in Schedule 1 to which it will apply. However, it is intended that an order will be laid under clause 4 of the Freedom of Information Bill, which will ensure that the FSA is subject to the new open arrangements.' HC SC A, 9 December 1999, col 1272.

THE FSA'S ANNUAL REPORT

2.27   During the debate on the FSA's accountability to the Treasury and to Parliament, attention was focused on the annual report as an appropriate mechanism for reporting on the FSA's discharge of its functions.[1]

---

[1]   HL Committee Stage, 16 March 2000, col 1774.

2.28   Under FSMA 2000, Sch 1, para 10(1), the FSA must report to the Treasury at least once a year on the discharge of its functions and the extent to which the FSA, in its opinion, has met its regulatory obligations.[1] The Treasury is required to lay this annual report before Parliament (Sch 1, para 10(3)).[2] The Treasury may require the FSA to comply with any provisions of CA 1985 about accounts and their audit which would not otherwise apply to it, or modify such provisions in relation to the FSA. This is enforceable by injunction in England, Wales or Northern Ireland or, in Scotland, by an order under the Court of Session Act 1988 (Sch 1, para 10(5)). Such proceedings, however, may only be brought by the Treasury (Sch 1, para 10(6)).

---

[1]   HC 2R, 28 June 1999, col 77.
[2]   See HL Committee Stage, 16 March 2000, col 1777.

THE FSA'S ANNUAL PUBLIC MEETING

2.29   The FSA's accountability was a highly contentious issue during the passage of the Bill through Parliament, and the mechanism of an annual public meeting was offered by the Government as a means for both regulated firms and consumers to provide feedback to the FSA on its statutory functions under FSMA 2000.[1]

---

[1]   Transcripts of these annual meetings are available on the FSA's website at http://www.fsa.gov.uk.

2.30   Under FSMA 2000, within three months of the publication of its annual report, the FSA must hold a public meeting to consider that report and provide an opportunity for general discussion of its contents and for questions to be put to the FSA on the discharge of its functions (Sch 1, para 11(1), (2)).[1] The FSA must give reasonable notice of this annual public meeting and various details must be made public including the proposed agenda (Sch 1, para 11(4), (5)). Any alterations of the published particulars of the annual meeting are subject to the same notice provisions and must be made public. Other than meeting these requirements, the FSA is free to organise and conduct the annual public meeting in a way which it considers appropriate (Sch 1, para 11(3)). One month after the annual meeting the FSA is required to publish a report of the proceedings of the meeting but FSMA 2000 does not specify any particular content for that report (Sch 1, para 12). Speaking for the Government, the Financial Secretary to the Treasury, Barbara Roche, said—

> 'The annual meeting, open to both consumers and practitioners, is seen as a valuable addition to the other accountability measures. It will give people a chance to air their views and to seek direct responses from the board of the FSA. In effect, it will deliver something similar to a shareholders' annual meeting. It will give all stakeholders a chance to be engaged with the board, and enable them to express their views and to hear the views of other stakeholders. It will also provide a test for the validity of the statements made in the annual report.'[2]

---

[1]   FSMA Explanatory Notes, para 768.
[2]   HC SC A, 13 July 1999, col 125.

THE FSA'S GENERAL DUTIES

2.31   FSMA 2000, s 2(1) prescribes the FSA's general duties and provides that in discharging its general functions the FSA must, as far as is reasonable, act in a way which is compatible with its regulatory objectives as defined in the Act and which the FSA itself considers most appropriate to meet those objectives. The FSA's general functions are set out in s 2(4) as being—

— carrying out rule-making functions under FSMA 2000;
— preparing and issuing codes under FSMA 2000;
— giving general guidance;[1] and
— determining general policy and principles for performing its particular functions under FSMA 2000.

---

[1]   For these purposes 'general guidance' is defined in s 158(5) as guidance given to persons generally or to regulated persons generally or to a class of regulated person, which is intended to have continuing effect and is given in writing or in another legible form as laid down in FSMA 2000, Pt X, Ch II.

POLICY CONSIDERATIONS FOR THE FSA'S DISCHARGE OF ITS GENERAL FUNCTIONS

2.32   In discharging its general functions, the FSA must have regard to a number of broad principles. These include—

— the need to use its resources in the most efficient and economic way;
— the principle that the burden or restriction which is imposed on any person or on the carrying on of any activity under the Act should be proportionate to the benefits which are expected to result from imposing those burdens or restrictions;
— the general desirability of facilitating innovation in connection with regulated activities in the light of the increasingly rapid environment of change in the financial services markets; and
— the responsibilities of those who manage the affairs of authorised persons, on the basis that the FSA's role is not to substitute itself for responsible management in these organisations (s 2(3)(a)–(d)).

The FSA must also have regard to certain other considerations concerning the competition between firms (s 2(3)(g)), the UK's competition position in the financial services markets (s 2(3)(e)) and the need to minimise any adverse effects on competition which may arise from the FSA's discharge of its functions (s 2(3)(f)). These are considered in more detail in Ch 10.

THE FSA'S CORPORATE GOVERNANCE OBLIGATIONS

2.33   Under FSMA 2000, s 7, the FSA must also have regard to 'such generally accepted principles of good corporate governance as it is reasonable to regard as applicable to it'.

2.34   During the passage of the Bill the Opposition parties introduced amendments proposing that the FSA should be subject to the requirements and principles of the Combined Code. It was argued that, as the listing authority for the UK, the FSA, in expecting listed companies to comply with these requirements, should at least be prepared to meet these requirements itself. The Government expressly resisted accepting the Combined Code fully as the FSA has no shareholders. Section 7 thus represents a compromise.[1]

---

[1]   See paras 2.7 and 2.8. See also HL Report Stage, 13 April 2000, col 293.

THE REGULATORY OBJECTIVES

2.35   FSMA 2000, s 2(2) defines the regulatory objectives of the FSA in broad terms as—
   —   market confidence;
   —   public awareness;
   —   the protection of consumers; and
   —   the reduction of financial crime.

Market confidence

2.36   One of the FSA's objectives is to maintain confidence in the financial system operating in the UK including the financial markets and exchanges, the carrying on of regulated activities and other activities connected with financial markets and exchanges (s 3(1), (2)). Lord McIntosh for the Government stated at the Report Stage of the Bill—

'If there was any doubt that market confidence covered systemic risk and market abuse, we would put it beyond doubt. But there is none. The market confidence objective encompasses these things, although it goes wider.'[1]

This objective provides the basis for much of the FSA's supervisory and regulatory powers including market abuse.[2]

---

[1]   HL Report Stage, 13 April 2000, col 344. See also HL Report Stage, 20 March 2000, cols 10, 11 and HL Report Stage, 16 March 2000, cols 1730–1732.
[2]   See Llewellyn, D, FSA Occasional Paper 1, The Economic Rationale for Financial Regulation, April 1999.

Public awareness

2.37   The FSA is charged with certain responsibilities in promoting public understanding of the financial system and, in particular, promoting awareness of the benefits and risks associated with different kinds of investments and other financial dealings and providing appropriate information and advice on the financial markets, exchanges, regulated activities and other activities associated with these markets (s 4). This was explained as follows—

'There is a clear risk that the very existence of a regulatory regime may lead people to expect a higher degree of protection than is achievable or desirable. Under the public awareness objective, the FSA will therefore seek to explain what it aims to achieve within the financial system, so that when failures do occur, damage to market confidence is kept to a minimum.'[1]

---

[1]   FSA Policy report: A New Regulator for the New Millennium, January 2000, para 5.

Protection of consumers

2.38   The FSA is required under FSMA 2000 to secure the appropriate degree of protection for consumers, taking into account the differing degrees of risk involved in different kinds of investment or other transaction and the different degrees of experience and expertise that consumers may have concerning different kinds of regulated activities. For these purposes the wide definition of the term 'consumers' in s 138(7) applies,[1] and also includes persons using the services of someone other than an authorised person, if they would be consumers were those services carried on by an authorised person (s 5(3)(b)).

---

[1]   Section 5(3)(a): see Appendix 1. See also FSA Policy document, Consumer Education: a strategy for promoting public understanding of the financial system, May 1999 and the earlier Consultation Paper (FSA CP 15, The FSA consults on consumer education strategy, November 1998) for the FSA's developing policy in this area.

Caveat emptor

2.39 The FSA must have regard to the needs that consumers have for advice and accurate information about regulated activities (s 5(2)(c)), subject to the general principle that consumers should take responsibility for their decisions (s 5(2)(d)). The controversial issue of the application of the principle of caveat emptor was discussed at Report Stage,[1] where it was considered that in seeking to achieve this objective FSMA 2000 must strike a balance between consumer protection and market forces. The Burns Committee stated—

> 'We recommend that the principle of caveat emptor should feature in the Bill; but that it should be redrafted in such a way that it could not be used to negate the consumer protection objective and excuse exploitation of sections of the general public'.[2]

In a speech in March 1999 the Executive Chairman of the FSA, Howard Davies, said—

> 'My own view is that it does make sense to incorporate the general principle of caveat emptor in the legislation, although it may be that the current drafting could be improved. In practice, too, we shall need to take account of this principle in different ways in relation to different consumers and markets. Consumers making long-term decisions in conditions of uncertainty, and vulnerable consumers, are clearly more in need of protection than high net worth private investors in hedge funds'.[3]

More recently the Financial Services Practitioner Panel identified as a key issue the promotion of the general principle of caveat emptor and the need for consumers to take responsible actions in their financial decision-making as well as advocating better selling practices from practitioners.[4]

---

[1] HL Committee Stage, 20 March 2000, col 30.
[2] See Burns Committee, First Report, 1999, paras 32–37. See also HC SC A, 25 November 1999.
[3] 1999 Travers Lecture, London Guildhall University Business School.
[4] Financial Services Practitioner Panel, 2002 Annual Report, February 2003, p 12.

Reduction of financial crime

2.40 The final regulatory objective of the FSA is the reduction of financial crime. This is to be achieved by reducing the extent to which it is possible for business carried on by a regulated person[1] or business carried on in contravention of the general prohibition under FSMA 2000, s 19, to be used in connection with financial crime (s 6(1)).

ๅgulated person' for these purposes includes an authorised person, a recognised
๐nt exchange or a recognised clearing house (s 6(5)). The legislation is not clear on the
of exempt persons under s 38 (exemption orders) or s 39 (exemption of appointed
representatives) in this regard. There is also a lack of clarity on the application of this objective
concerning EEA persons who are regulated persons, but the FSA has stated that the money
laundering rules will apply to incoming EEA firms that establish a branch in the UK on the basis
that the agreed approach in the EU is that money laundering is a 'host state' responsibility rather
than a fitness and properness issue: see FSA CP 46, Money Laundering: the FSA's new role, April
2000, para 4.13.

2.41 'Financial crime' is broadly defined and includes any offence
involving fraud or dishonesty, misconduct in or the misuse of
information in relation to a financial market, or the handling of the
proceeds of crime (s 6(3)).[1] An 'offence' is defined as any act or
omission which would be an offence if it had taken place in the UK
(s 6(4)). However this leaves open to question whether some 'crimes'
in other jurisdictions such as tax evasion or breaches of foreign
exchange control laws would be caught by the definition in s 6(3).

[1] The FSA has stated that there are three principal areas where it will play a significant role in
seeking to reduce financial crime, namely money laundering, fraud or dishonesty (including
e-crime and the fraudulent marketing of investments), and criminal market misconduct
(including insider dealing): see FSA Policy report, A New Regulator for the New Millennium,
January 2000, para 15.

2.42 In considering this objective, the FSA must have regard to the
desirability of regulated persons being aware of the risk of their
businesses being used for financial crime and must ensure that
regulated persons take appropriate measures to prevent financial
crime, as well as facilitating its detection and monitoring its incidence
and devote adequate resources to achieving these ends (s 6(2)).

THE FSA'S OBLIGATION TO CONSULT

2.43 Given the very general broad powers ascribed to the FSA, FSMA 2000
incorporates a consultation process (in addition to specific
consultation obligations relating to rules and guidance).[1] Under that
process the FSA must make and maintain effective arrangements for
consulting practitioners and consumers through two bodies known as
the Consumer Panel and the Practitioner Panel. The purpose of this
consultation is to ensure that the FSA's general policies and practices
are consistent with the general duties outlined in FSMA 2000, s 2
(s 8). In the legislation as originally drafted, the constitution of the
consumer and practitioner panels was less formal and their role in the

regulatory framework was far less clear. In response to criticism, the Government made these two formal statutory panels more structured and more involved in overseeing how the FSA carries out its general duties under FSMA 2000.

---

[1]   FSMA 2000, s 396.

The Consumer Panel

2.44   The Consumer Panel[1] is a panel of persons appointed by the FSA to represent the interests of consumers. It must be comprised of such consumers or persons representing the interests of consumers as the FSA considers appropriate. Given the wide definition of the term 'consumers' in s 138, it cannot be assumed that this panel will solely represent the interests of retail or individual investors, although this bias seems likely. FSMA 2000 does however require that the membership of the Panel give a fair degree of representation to those who are using or may be contemplating using services otherwise than in connection with businesses carried on by them (s 10(6)).

---

[1]   See their website at http://www.fs-cp.org.uk.

2.45   The FSA has the power to appoint one member of the Consumer Panel as its chairman (s 10(2)) but the Treasury must approve the appointment and dismissal of the chairman (s 10(3)).

2.46   The FSA must consider the representations of the Consumer Panel. If it disagrees with a view expressed or a proposal made in a representation from the Consumer Panel, it must give the Panel a statement in writing of its reasons for disagreeing (s 11).

2.47   In December 1998, in anticipation of the creation of this statutory panel under FSMA 2000, the FSA established an independent Consumer Panel of ten members appointed by the FSA to advise on the interests and concerns of consumers and to assess the FSA's effectiveness in meeting its objectives to protect consumers' interests and promote public understanding of the financial system before N2.[1] Before N2, the Consumer Panel also advised the Board of the Personal Investment Authority[2] and generally promoted the interests of consumers when considering its own research on specific topics. The stated aims of the Consumer Panel are to influence FSA policy, influence Government policy and legislation, and to understand consumer needs by commissioning research and discussion papers concerning financial issues. The Panel may also invite FSA staff to attend its meetings to discuss policy matters affecting consumers. The FSA Board also receives the Panel's views and regular reports on its work.[3]

¹   'about the panel' at http://www.fs-cp.org.uk. See also 2000 Annual Report, March 2001. See para 1.37 for further discussion of N2.
²   As successor to the PIA's Consumer Panel.
³   FSA Press Release FSA/PN/096/1998, 1 December 1998.

The Practitioner Panel

2.48   FSMA 2000, s 9(1) provides that under s 8 the FSA must establish a consultative panel to consult practitioners on the extent to which the FSA's general policies and practices are consistent with its general duties under FSMA 2000. The FSA must consider any representations made to it by the Practitioner Panel (s 9(4)). If it disagrees with the views expressed or any proposal made by the Practitioner Panel, it must give the Panel a statement in writing of its reasons (s 11(2), (3)).[1]

¹   See also HC Remaining Stages, 9 February 2000, col 366.

2.49   The FSA has the power under s 9(2) to appoint one of the members of the Practitioner Panel as its chairman. The Treasury must approve the appointment of the chairman of the Practitioner Panel (s 9(3)).

Interim arrangements: Practitioner Forum

2.50   Similar to the Consumer Panel, a Practitioner Forum was established in November 1998, comprising senior figures from regulated firms. This was intended to be a high level body which could be consulted by the FSA on policy and would communicate to the FSA views and concerns of the regulated industries in the period before N2.[1] The role of the Forum was to advise the FSA and 'to ensure that the FSA pursues its objectives in a way which is efficient and economic, facilitates innovation, and has regard to the international nature of financial services business'.[2]

¹   FSA Policy Statement, The open approach to regulation, July 1998, paras 25–27.
²   FSA Press Release FSA/PN/051/1998, 27 July 1998.

2.51   The Practitioner Forum issued two annual reports and conducted an independent survey of industry views about the financial services regulatory regime.[1] The survey, carried out in the summer of 1999, provided an overview of financial services firms' thinking about the effectiveness and past performance of the existing regulatory regime which FSMA 2000 is replacing. The statutory Practitioner Panel, which came into being on 18 June 2001, has issued two further annual reports and has continued the practice of conducting further surveys, the most recent in 2002.[2]

1   The Financial Services Practitioner Forum Annual Report 1999, January 2000 and Annual Report 2000, January 2001.
2   These reports and surveys are available from the FSA's website, www.fsa.gov.uk.

2.52   It is assumed that the Practitioner and Consumer Panels, which do not have any independent financing or other powers, will continue to operate in more or less the same form as they did before N2 within the potentially narrow remit of FSMA 2000.[1]

1   FSA, Annual General Meeting, 20 July 2000, Reports of the chairmen of the Consumer Panel and Practitioner Forum.

Other consultative groups

2.53   The FSA also consults other groups from time to time, including—
        The Collective Investment Scheme Forum: A Forum for discussion between consumers, practitioners and interested parties on unit trusts and OEICS;
        Training Advisory Panel: A Panel established to advise on development of competence and the promotion of training within regulated firms and the industry at large.[1]
        Small Business Practitioner Panel: A Panel representing a range of smaller regulated firms, with a specific focus on cost and feasibility issues.[2]

The FSA may also appoint other ad hoc groups to advise it on specific issues.[3]

1   The FSA recently announced its intention to outsource certain of its training and business ethics responsibilities to the Skills Council for Financial Services, one of the sectoral skills councils to be licensed by the Secretary of State for Education and Skills some time in early 2004. Newsletter, FSA Feedback Statement to Consultation Paper 157, July 2003.
2   See annual reports of the Small Business Practitioner Panel which are available from the FSA's website, www.fsa.gov.uk.
3   FSA Press Release FSA/PN/051/1998, 27 July 1998.

THE TREASURY'S POWER TO CONDUCT REVIEWS OF THE FSA

2.54   The Treasury has the power to appoint a person who is independent of the FSA to review the economy, efficiency and effectiveness with which the FSA uses its resources to discharge its functions under FSMA 2000 (s 12(1), (7)). The terms of reference of such a review are to be set by the Treasury (s 12(2)). However, reviews conducted under FSMA 2000, s 12 are not to be concerned with the merits of the FSA's general policy or principles which it follows in pursuing its regulatory objectives or certain other functions as listing authority under FSMA 2000, Pt VI (s 12(3)).

2.55 The person conducting a review under s 12 has the right to access at any reasonable time all documents within the FSA's custody or control which he may reasonably require for the review, and may require any person holding or accountable for such documents to provide such information and explanation as may be required for those purposes (s 13(1), (2)). An obligation to provide information or documents under s 13 is enforceable by injunction (or by an order for specific performance under the Court of Session Act 1988, s 45 in Scotland) (s 13(3)).

2.56 Having carried out a review the person appointed to carry it out must report in writing to the Treasury setting out the results and recommendations arising from that review. A copy of this report must be laid before Parliament and made public in a manner which the Treasury considers appropriate (s 12(4), (5)). The Treasury must meet the costs and expenses of carrying out a review under s 12 out of funds provided by Parliament (s 12(6)).

THE TREASURY'S POWER TO HOLD INDEPENDENT INQUIRIES

2.57 FSMA 2000 gives the Treasury the power to hold an independent inquiry in one of two cases where public interest would require it, namely that either—

(1) events have occurred in relation to a collective investment scheme or a person who is or was carrying on regulated activities (whether or not that person is an authorised person) which pose or could have posed a grave risk or caused significant damage to the financial system or the interests of consumers, and those events occurred (or the risk or damage might otherwise have been reduced), due to a serious failure in the system established under FSMA 2000 for regulating such collective investment scheme or persons carrying on regulated activities (s 14(2)); or

(2) events have occurred in relation to listed securities or an issuer of listed securities which caused or could have caused significant damage to holders of listed securities, and those

events would not have occurred or the risk or damage might otherwise have been reduced but for a serious failure in the regulatory system established under FSMA 2000, Pt VI (s 14(3)).

Definitions of terms used

2.58   For these purposes the 'financial system' means the system operating in the UK including the financial markets and exchanges, the carrying on of regulated activities and other activities connected with financial markets and exchanges (s 3(1), (2)).

2.59   'Consumers' includes those within the definition in s 138(7) and persons using the services of someone other than an authorised person if they would be consumers were those services carried on by an authorised person (s 14(5)).

2.60   'Listed securities' means anything which has been or may be admitted to the official list under FSMA 2000, Pt VI (s 14(7)).

Conduct of the inquiry

2.61   Where the Treasury exercises its powers to hold an inquiry under s 14 it may appoint any appropriate person to hold the inquiry under the terms of a direction which establishes the scope, period and conduct of the inquiry and the making of reports (s 15(1), (2)). The person has the power to require any person who, in his opinion, has any information or any document which is relevant to the inquiry, to produce that information or document. The person has the same powers as the High Court or the Court of Session in Scotland in requiring the attendance and examination of witnesses at an inquiry under s 15 (s 16(3)). The person appointed to conduct an inquiry may otherwise obtain such information and make such inquiries as he thinks fit and determine the procedure which is to be followed in conducting the inquiry (s 16(2)).

Obstruction and contempt

2.62   FSMA 2000, s 18 also provides that if any person fails to comply with any requirements for information or documentation or otherwise obstructs an inquiry under FSMA 2000, s 15, the person holding the inquiry may certify the matter to the High Court (or the Court of Session in Scotland). If the relevant court is satisfied that the person would have been in contempt of court if the inquiry had been made before the court then it may deal with him as if he had been in contempt. Directions made under s 15 may limit the nature of the inquiry to certain matters, extend it to additional matters, require its discontinuance, specify which steps are to be taken and require the person conducting it to make interim reports (s 15(3)).

Conclusion of inquiry

2.63   At the conclusion of an inquiry the person holding it must provide a written report to the Treasury setting out the results and making any recommendations he considers appropriate (s 17(1)). The Treasury may publish that report in any manner which it considers appropriate subject to certain limitations (s 17(2)), but a copy of any report published under this provision must be laid before each House of Parliament (s 17(5)). If the Treasury proposes to publish a report containing material relating to the affairs of a particular person whose interests would be seriously prejudiced by the publication of the matter, or the disclosure of that information would be incompatible with the international obligations of the UK, then the Treasury must ensure that this material is removed before publication of the report (s 17(3), (4)). The Treasury must meet the costs and expenses of conducting such an inquiry out of funds provided by Parliament (s 17(6)).

INJUNCTIONS AND RESTITUTION

The FSA's powers to obtain court orders for injunctive relief

2.64   The FSA or the Secretary of State has the power to apply to the courts[1] for an order restraining (or, in Scotland, an interdict prohibiting) contraventions of any relevant requirement[2] if it can be shown that there is a reasonable likelihood that any person will contravene such a relevant requirement or that any person has contravened a relevant requirement and there is a reasonable likelihood that the contravention will continue or be repeated (s 380(1)).

---

[1]   Jurisdiction to make orders under this section may be exercised by either the High Court or by the Court of Session (s 380(4)).

[2]   A 'relevant requirement' for these purposes is, for the FSA, a requirement which is imposed by or under FSMA 2000 or any other Act, or whose contravention it is within the FSA's power to prosecute, eg, rules made under FSMA 2000, Pt X. For the Secretary of State, it means a requirement which is imposed by or under FSMA 2000 and whose contravention constitutes an offence under which the Secretary of State has the power to prosecute, eg, a contravention of the general prohibition under FSMA 2000, s 2 (FSMA Explanatory Notes, para 663) (s 380(6)). This is modified for Scotland to the extent that a 'relevant requirement' includes one which the FSA has the power to prosecute for insider dealing or the prescribed regulations relating to money laundering which are otherwise disapplied in Scotland under s 402(1)(a) and (b). In

addition, in Scotland a relevant requirement for the Secretary of State includes any requirement which is imposed by or under FSMA 2000 and whose contravention constitutes an offence (s 380(7)). Under the Electronic Commerce Directive (Financial Services and Markets) Regulations 2002, SI 2002/1775, reg 12(2), a requirement imposed by these regulations on an authorised person carrying on incoming e-commerce activity is deemed to be a 'requirement' of FSMA 2000.

2.65   Where the FSA or the Secretary of State has applied to the court for injunctive relief and the court is satisfied that the person has contravened a relevant requirement and that there are steps which could be taken to remedy[1] (s 380(5)) the contravention, the court[2] may order that person and any other person knowingly concerned in the contravention to take such steps as it may in its order direct (s 380(2)).[3]

[1]   For the purpose of this section 'remedying' a contravention includes steps taken to mitigate its effect (s 380(5)).
[2]   Jurisdiction may be exercised by either the High Court or the Court of Session (s 380(4)).
[3]   There were transitional provisions in respect of s 380 under which certain requirements under FSA 1986, the Banking Act 1987 and the Building Societies Act 1986 were to be treated as requirements under FSMA 2000: see the Financial Services and Markets Act 2000 (Transitional Provisions and Savings) (Civil Remedies, Discipline, Criminal Offences etc) (No 2) Order 2001, SI 2001/3083 and the Financial Services and Markets Act 2000 (Transitional Provisions and Savings) (Information Requirements and Investigations) Order 2001, SI 2001/3646.

2.66   In addition, if the court is satisfied that any person has contravened a relevant requirement or has been knowingly concerned in such a contravention, it may make an order restraining (or, in Scotland, an interdict prohibiting) that person from disposing of or otherwise dealing with any assets which he is likely to dispose of or otherwise deal with (s 380(3)).

2.67   Similar provisions apply to injunctions in cases of market abuse if the court[1] is satisfied on the application of the FSA that there is a reasonable likelihood that any person will engage in market abuse, or that any person is or has engaged in market abuse, and there is a reasonable likelihood that this will continue or be repeated. In this case the court may make an order restraining (or in Scotland an interdict prohibiting) the market abuse (s 381(1)).

[1]   Jurisdiction under this section may be exercised by either the High Court or the Court of Session (s 381(5)).

2.68   Similarly, if satisfied that any person is or has engaged in market abuse and there are steps which could be taken to remedy this or mitigate its effects (s 381(6)), the court may order that person to take such steps as it may direct (s 381(2)).

2.69   The court may also make an order restraining (or in Scotland, an interdict prohibiting) any person who may be or may have been engaged in market abuse (s 381(3)) from disposing of or otherwise dealing with any of his assets which the court is satisfied that he is reasonably likely to dispose of or otherwise deal with (s 381(4)).

Restitution orders by the court—cases other than market abuse

2.70   Where a person has accrued profits as a result of a contravention of a relevant requirement under FSMA 2000 or where one or more persons have suffered a loss or otherwise been adversely affected by such a contravention, a court[1] may, on the application of the FSA or the Secretary of State, if it is satisfied that a person has contravened a relevant requirement[2] or has been knowingly concerned in the contravention of such a requirement (s 382(1)), order that person to pay to the FSA such sums as appear just to the court in restitution (s 382(2)).[3] In making a restitution order, the court should have regard to the profits which have accrued from any contravention of a relevant requirement, or the extent of the loss or other adverse effect which have arisen from that contravention (s 382(2)).

---

[1]   Both the High Court and the Court of Session may exercise jurisdiction under this section of FSMA 2000 (s 382(6)).
[2]   'Relevant requirement' is defined in s 382(9) and (10) in the same terms as noted in para 2.64, fn 2.
[3]   See also a recent succession of cases concerning the power of the court to order restitutionary damages: A-G v Blake (Jonathan Cape Ltd, third party) [1998] Ch 439, [1998] 1 All ER 883, CA, affd [2001] 1 AC 268, [2000] 4 All ER 385, HL; Alfred McAlpine Construction Ltd v Panatown Ltd [2001] 1 AC 518, [2000] 4 All ER 97.

2.71   In making any order for restitution, the court may require the person concerned to provide accounts or other information for any one or more of the following purposes—

— establishing whether and to what extent any profits accrued as a result of the contravention;

— establishing whether any persons have suffered a loss or adverse effect as a result of a contravention of a relevant requirement and the extent of that loss; and

— determining how much should be paid in restitution and to whom (s 382(4)).

The court may also require this information to be verified (s 382(5)).

2.72   Any sums paid to the FSA under this provision must be distributed by the FSA as directed by the court to those persons[1] who appear to the court to be persons to whom the profits are attributable or who suffered a loss or adverse effect as a result of the contravention (s 382(8)).

---

[1]   Defined in this section as 'qualifying persons' (s 382(8)).

2.73 Any restitution order resulting from proceedings brought by the FSA or the Secretary of State under this section does not, however, affect any other person's right to bring proceedings in relation to the matters to which this section applies, for example, the private right of action for breaches of statutory duty under FSMA 2000, s 71 (s 382(7)). However it is unlikely that this provision entitles anyone to recover the same loss twice.

Restitution orders by the court—market abuse cases

2.74 Where the FSA has made an application, the court[1] may, if it is satisfied that a person has engaged in market abuse, or has, by taking or refraining from taking any action, required or encouraged another person or persons to engage in behaviour which would amount to market abuse (s 383(1)), and that profits have accrued to that person as a result, or that one or more persons have suffered a loss or otherwise been adversely affected (s 383(2)), order the person concerned to pay to the FSA a sum which appears to the court to be just in the circumstances (s 383(4)).

---

[1] Jurisdiction under this provision may be exercised by either the High Court or the Court of Session (s 383(6)).

2.75 The court may not, however, make an order under s 383(4) if it is satisfied that the person concerned believed on reasonable grounds that his behaviour did not constitute market abuse, and that he did not take any action which required or encouraged another to engage in behaviour which would be market abuse, or that he took all reasonable precautions and exercised all due diligence to avoid so acting (s 383(3)).

2.76 Any sums paid to the FSA as a result of an order made under this section must be paid to those persons to whom the profits would have been attributable or who suffered a loss or adverse effect as a result of the action described in s 383(1) as the court may direct (s 383(5)).

2.77 Any person concerned may be required to supply the court with accounts and other information which the court may require for any one or more of the following purposes—
— establishing whether and how much profit accrued as a result of the market abuse;
— establishing whether any person or persons suffered any losses or was adversely effected as a result of that behaviour; and
— determining how much should be paid and how it should be distributed (s 383(6)).

The court may require any accounts or information provided under this provision to be verified in a manner which it directs (s 383(7)).

2.78   As with proceedings under s 382, proceedings under s 383 do not affect the right of any person other than the FSA to bring proceedings concerning any matters to which this section applies (s 383(9)).

The FSA's power to require restitution in market abuse cases

2.79   In addition to its powers to apply for a restitution order from the courts under s 383, the FSA may, in its own right, require any person it considers falls under s 384(2) and (3) to pay to affected persons or to distribute to them such amount as appears to the FSA to be just, taking into account the profits which appear to the FSA to have accrued as a result of the market abuse or the extent of the loss or other adverse effect which arose (s 384(5)).[1] If the FSA proposes to exercise its powers to order any person to pay restitution under s 384(5), it must issue a warning notice to him (s 385(1)), which must specify the amount which it proposes he should be required to pay or distribute in restitution (s 385(2)).

---

[1]   Where the FSA uses its powers under s 384(5), monies paid in restitution will be paid directly to the person or persons who suffered a loss or adverse effect as a result of the market abuse rather than the money being paid to the FSA and distributed by the FSA under a court order under s 385(2) or (3): see FSMA Explanatory Notes, para 674.

2.80   However, the FSA may not exercise these powers if, having considered any representations made to it in response to a warning notice, it is satisfied that the person concerned believed on reasonable grounds that his behaviour did not constitute market abuse or that he did not take any action (or refrain from taking any action) which required or encouraged another person to engage in behaviour which constituted market abuse, or that he took all reasonable precautions and exercised all due diligence to avoid behaviour which constituted market abuse or fell within behaviour prescribed by s 384(2) (s 384(4)).

2.81   If the FSA decides to exercise its power under s 384(5) to require a person to pay a sum in restitution, it must give that person a decision notice (s 386(1)) which must state the amount which that person is to pay and identify the person or persons to whom the amount is to be paid or among whom the amount is to be distributed, and state any other arrangements as to the payment or distribution of that amount (s 386(2)). The person in respect of whom the FSA decides to exercise its power to award restitution under s 384(5) may refer the matter to the Tribunal (s 386(3)).

The FSA's other powers to require restitution from authorised persons

2.82   The FSA may also require similar restitution[1] from any authorised person who has contravened a relevant requirement[2] or knowingly been concerned in the contravention of such a requirement and who has profited as a result of such a contravention, and one or more persons have suffered a loss or have been adversely affected by that contravention (s 384(1), (5), (6)).

---

[1] See paras 2.79–2.81.

[2] For the purposes of this section, a 'relevant requirement' is a requirement which is imposed by or under FSMA 2000 or any other Act and whose contravention constitutes an offence that the FSA has the power to prosecute under FSMA 2000 (s 384(7)). This is modified for Scotland to the extent that a 'relevant requirement' includes one which the FSA has the power to prosecute for insider dealing or the prescribed regulations relating to money laundering which are otherwise disapplied in Scotland under s 402(1)(a) and (b) (s 384(8)): see para 2.64, fn 2. Under the Electronic Commerce Directive (Financial Services and Markets) Regulations 2002, SI 2002/1775, a requirement imposed by these regulations on an authorised person on incoming e-commerce activity is deemed to be a 'requirement' of FSMA 2000.

2.83   If the FSA proposes to exercise its powers to order an authorised person to pay restitution under s 384(5), it must issue a warning notice to that person (s 385(1)). That notice must specify the amount which the FSA proposes the authorised person should be required to pay or distribute in restitution (s 385(2)).

2.84   If the FSA decides to exercise its powers under this section to require an authorised person to pay a sum in restitution, it must give the authorised person a decision notice (s 386(1)). That notice must state the amount to be paid and must identify the person or persons to whom the amount is to be paid or among whom the amount is to be distributed. It must also state any other arrangements as to the payment or distribution of that amount (s 386(2)). The authorised person in respect of whom the FSA decides to exercise its power to award restitution may refer the matter to the Tribunal (s 386(3)).

OTHER MISCELLANEOUS MATTERS

2.85   FSMA 2000 provides that, for its functions under the Act, the FSA is not to be regarded as acting on behalf of the Crown, and its members, officers and staff are not considered to be Crown servants (Sch 1, para 13).

2.86   The FSA is also exempted under FSMA 2000 from being required to use the suffix 'limited' as part of its name, although the Secretary of State may, following consultation with the Treasury, give a direction removing this exemption if he feels it appropriate to do so (Sch 1, paras 14, 15).

Exemption from liability in damages

2.87   A provision which caused some controversy during the passage of the Bill[1] was the FSA's statutory exemption from liability in damages for anything done or omitted by the FSA, its members, officers or members of staff in the discharge or purported discharge of the FSA's functions under the Act (Sch 1, para 19(1)).[2]

---

[1]   See HC SC A, 13 July 1999 and HC SC A, 28 October 1999.
[2]   This provision has been amended to include anything done by an accredited financial investigator appointed under one of the relevant provisions of the Proceeds of Crime Act 2002, Sch 11, para 38.

2.88   At the Commons Report Stage Melanie Johnson said—

'This subject has aroused considerable interest and was considered in detail by the Joint Committee, which broadly approved the immunity proposed by the Bill, subject to certain proposals to strengthen the complaints arrangements . . . It is essential that we have a structure that allows the FSA to get on with its work efficiently and effectively, . . . A strong and accountable regulator must be in the interests of the industry and consumers alike.

Immunity is vital for delivering that aim. Without it, the FSA could be frustrated by potential law suits and red tape. It would be very easy to have frivolous litigation or to distract or hinder the regulator from carrying out its duties, which could have a detrimental impact on firms as well. The absence of immunity could make the FSA more risk averse and engender a more formalistic regulatory environment . . .

. . . We want the FSA to be a dynamic regulator, and that might mean taking some difficult or finely balanced decisions in cases where the answers are not black or white. The authority should not have to run the risk of being sued as well.'[1]

---

[1]   HC Report Stage, 27 January 2000, col 629. See also *Three Rivers District Council v Bank of England* (No 3) [1996] 3 All ER 558; affd [1999] 4 All ER 800n, CA; affd in part [2000] 3 All ER 1, HL; [2001] 2 All ER 513.

2.89   This statutory exemption from liability also extends to an investigator appointed under Sch 1, para 7 to investigate a complaint against the FSA or a person appointed to conduct an investigation on his behalf under Sch 1, para 8(8).

2.90   This exemption is subject to the limitations for acts or omissions in bad faith or awards of damages for an act or omission which is unlawful by virtue of the Human Rights Act 1998 (HRA 1998), s 6(1). That section makes it unlawful for a public authority to act in a way which is incompatible with a Convention right unless, as a result of one or more provisions of primary legislation, the public authority, in this case the FSA, could not have acted differently or the legislative provisions cannot be read or given effect in a way which is compatible with the Convention rights and the FSA was acting to give effect to or enforce those provisions (Sch 1, para 19(3)).

The FSA's power to review past business

2.91   FSMA 2000, s 404 gives the Treasury the express power to make an order to establish a scheme to investigate the activities of authorised persons along the lines of those reviews which have been carried out in relation to pensions mis-selling and home equity release, and more recently, the FSA's review of issues relating to Free-Standing Additional Voluntary Contribution ("FSAVC") pension contributions.[1]

---

[1]   FSMA Explanatory Notes, para 716.

2.92   This provision is stated to apply 'whenever the failure in question occurred' (s 404(8)), thus presumably giving the Treasury the power to look into events or any failure which may have pre-dated N2.[1]

---

[1]   See para 1.37. Certain transitional provisions were made concerning the pensions mis-selling and FSAVC reviews that were being conducted under the FSA 1986 to treat these as a scheme under FSMA 2000, s 404: see the Financial Services and Markets Act 2000 (Transitional Provisions) (Reviews of Pensions Business) Order 2001, SI 2001/2512.

2.93   Under s 404, if the Treasury is satisfied that there is evidence of a widespread or regular failure on the part of authorised persons to comply with the rules relating to any type of activity[1] and, as a result of this, private persons[2] have suffered or will suffer a loss for which authorised persons are or will be liable for compensation payments, it may make regulations to establish and operate such a scheme. The purpose of this will be to establish the nature and extent of the failure and to determine the liability and amount of compensation payments (s 404(1), (2)). The scheme may also make provisions for persons acting in a fiduciary or other prescribed capacity to be treated as private persons for the purposes of these regulations (s 404(7)).

---

[1]   This power extends not only to regulated activities carried on by authorised persons but arguably also to all activities specified in the regulations made under s 404.

[2]   Regulations will define who is to be a 'private person' for the purposes of this section (s 404(10)), but it is not clear whether this will be the same as the definition of 'private persons' which may be specified for other purposes of FSMA 2000. It is possible that different markets and different circumstances could allow a wider definition of 'private person'.

2.94   An order made under this section may only be made if the FSA, having determined that such a review is an appropriate way of dealing with the failure (s 404(4)(c)), has reported the alleged failure to the Treasury setting out the FSA's proposals for such a scheme (s 404(4)(b)) and has asked the Treasury to make a scheme order (s 404(4)(a)).

2.95   The Treasury has extensive powers to adapt or modify the provisions made by or under s 404 and the scheme order may specify other provisions of or made under FSMA 2000 which would apply to such a scheme (s 404(5)).

2.96   If an authorised person does not comply with any provision of an authorised scheme, that person is to be treated as failing to comply with rules[1] made under FSMA 2000 (s 404(6)).

---

[1]   'Rules' are defined in s 417 as rules made by the FSA under FSMA 2000.

The FSA's powers in relation to a third country's decisions — Community measures

2.97   At the direction of the Treasury, the FSA may refuse an application for permission under Pt IV (s 405(1)(a)), defer its decision indefinitely (s 405(1)(b)) or give a notice of objection to a person who has acquired or notified the FSA that he proposes to acquire a 50% stake in a UK authorised person (s 405(1)(c), (d))[1] for the purpose of implementing a decision of the EC or the Council under certain provisions of the EC Single Market Directives.[2] This provision gives the Treasury the power to implement the decisions of the Council or the Commission to prohibit certain subsidiary firms from non-EEA countries from being able to become authorised persons or be controlled by persons who are the subject of a third country decision where it has been determined that EEA firms who provide financial services are not being given equivalent treatment or status in terms of competition in that third country's domestic market.[3] In certain other cases where the Council or the Commission has taken a third party decision, the Treasury may make a determination that an EFTA firm[4] does not qualify for authorisation (s 408(2))[5] where that EFTA firm is a subsidiary undertaking of a parent undertaking governed by the laws of the country to which the third country decision applies (s 408(1)).

---

[1]   FSMA 2000, s 406 defines the term 'acquirer' as including any person who has acquired a stake which meets the criteria set out in s 406(2), or any of the acquirer's associates (as defined in FSMA 2000, s 422), or the acquirer and any of his associates, and provides cross-references to certain definitions in FSMA 2000, s 422.

[2]   Those provisions are: Article 7(5) of the Investment Services Directive; Article 9(4) of the Second Banking Co-ordination Directive (now repealed and replaced by Article 23(5) of the Banking Consolidation Directive (European Parliament and Council Directive 2000/12/EC)); Article 29b(4) of the First Non-Life Insurance Directive and Article 32b(4) of the First Life Insurance Directive.

3   FSMA Explanatory Notes, para 717. As a result of World Trade Organisation (WTO) agreements on financial services, this provision only applies to those countries outside both the EEA and the WTO: FSMA Explanatory Notes, para 718.

4   Section 408(8) defines an EFTA firm as a firm, institution or undertaking which is an EEA firm within the meaning of FSMA 2000, Sch 3, para 5(a), (b) or (d) and is incorporated in or formed under the law of an EEA State which is not an EU Member State.

5   This would apply even if the firm otherwise met the criteria for authorisation under FSMA 2000, Sch 3, para 13 or 14.

2.98   If the Treasury makes a determination under s 408 concerning an EFTA firm,[1] it must notify that firm in writing (s 408(6)). Such determinations may relate to a class of firms and may be withdrawn at any time, although the subsequent withdrawal of a determination will not affect anything done in accordance with the determination before its withdrawal (s 408(3)–(5)). Any determination made under s 408 (or the withdrawal of such a determination) must be made public by the Treasury so as to bring it to the attention of anyone affected by it (s 408(7)).

1   See para 2.97, fn 4.

2.99   A direction by the Treasury under this provision may extend to any person falling within a defined class and to future applications, notices of control or acquisitions (s 405(2)). However, the Treasury may revoke an order made under s 405 at any time (s 405(3)) and such revocation does not affect the validity or otherwise of anything done in accordance with the direction before it was revoked (s 405(4)).

2.100   Where the FSA has refused an application for permission by virtue of a direction under s 405, it is not required to comply with the usual warning/decision notice procedure contained in FSMA 2000, s 52(7) and (9), but must notify the applicant and provide reasons for the refusal (s 407(1)). Similarly, if the FSA defers any application for permission as a result of a direction under s 405, the usual time limits set out in s 52(1) and (2) cease to run and the FSA must notify the applicant of the deferral and the reasons for it (s 407(2)).

2.101   If the FSA has given a person a notice of objection under s 405(1)(c) and (d), the provisions in FSMA 2000 on the acquisition of control by a person who has been given a notice of objection which would constitute an offence for the purposes of s 191(5) and the FSA's powers to impose restrictions on improperly acquired shares under s 189(1) will apply (s 407(3)(a)). The FSA must, however, state this in the notice given under s 405(1) and give its reasons for the notice (s 407(3)(b)).

Other international obligations under FSMA 2000

2.102 The Treasury also has broad powers to make a direction to prohibit—
— the FSA;
— any person exercising the functions of the competent authority under FSMA 2000, Pt VI;
— any recognised investment exchange;[1]
— any recognised clearing house;[2]
— persons subject to supervision under FSMA 2000, s 301;[3] or
— the scheme operator of the ombudsman scheme,

from taking any action which would be incompatible with any Community obligations or any other international obligations to which the UK is subject (s 410(1)).

---

[1] Excluding an overseas investment exchange (s 410(4)(c)).

[2] Excluding an overseas clearing house (s 410(4)(d)).

[3] Section 301 provides that the Treasury may make regulations extending the insolvency and market contracts regime under the Companies Act 1989, Pt VII to certain types of non-investment contracts and provide for the supervision of those persons admitted to the list maintained by the FSA for these purposes: see FSMA Explanatory Notes, paras 543–545.

2.103 A direction made under s 410 may impose on those relevant persons such supplemental or other requirements as the Treasury considers necessary or expedient. It is enforceable by the Treasury by injunction or, in Scotland, by an order for specific performance (s 410(3)).

FSMA 2000 AND THE ECHR AND HRA 1998

2.104 The regime under FSMA 2000 and the impact of the European Convention on Human Rights (ECHR) on it was one of the most contentious, or at least one of the most publicised, issues raised during the Bill's long Parliamentary process. For many years the ECHR has been applied by the European Court of Human Rights to public authorities in the UK carrying out certain regulatory functions. The current Government reinforced its commitment to the enforcement of human rights under the ECHR with the promulgation of HRA 1998 which incorporates the ECHR into UK domestic law.[1]

---

[1] Burns Committee, Second Report, 19 May 1999, para 5, note 3. HRA 1998 came fully into force on 2 October 2000 (Human Rights Act 1998 (Commencement No 2) Order 2000, SI 2000/1851).

2.105 It was clear, however, that under the regulatory regime being established by FSMA 2000, the ECHR and HRA 1998 would apply to bodies such as the FSA, the Tribunal, the Financial Services Ombudsman,[1] and any other regulatory or quasi-regulatory body established under FSMA 2000 which falls within the definition of a 'public authority'.[2]

---

[1] See Burns Committee, Second Report, 19 May 1999, para 20.

[2] HRA 1998, s 6(3) defines a 'public authority' as including a court or tribunal and any person certain of whose functions are functions of a public nature.

2.106 The ECHR and HRA 1998 may well extend to other bodies exercising quasi-supervisory or regulatory functions which are of a 'public nature' under FSMA 2000 such as recognised investment exchanges or recognised clearing houses, professional bodies carrying out functions under Pt XX and the Society of Lloyd's to the extent that these might be carrying out functions which would otherwise fall within the public statutory framework of the Act.[1]

---

[1] For the interpretation of 'public authority' see HL Debs, 5 February 1998, col 794.

2.107 Broadly speaking, it is unlawful for a public authority to act[1] in a way which is inconsistent with a Convention right, and these bodies and the procedures and processes by which they carry out their public functions under FSMA 2000 would be liable to review before the European Court of Human Rights and also justiciable in the UK courts through the application of UK domestic legislation.

---

[1] For the purposes of the HRA 1998, an 'act' includes a failure to act (HRA 1998, s 6(6)).

2.108 When the draft Bill was issued for consultation in July 1998,[1] widespread concerns were expressed[2] that the processes and procedures in the draft Bill would not withstand contest under the ECHR or under domestic law when HRA 1998 came into force. In November 1998, a Joint Committee of both Houses of Parliament was appointed to scrutinise the Bill as it then stood, and, after obtaining expert legal advice and after considerable debate, the Joint Committee made its recommendations.[3]

---

[1] HM Treasury, Financial Services and Markets Bill: A Consultation Document, July 1998.

[2] See, for example, Centre for Policy Studies, McElwee and Tyrie: Leviathan at large: the new regulator for the financial markets: 29 ways in which to improve the Financial Services and Markets Bill, 2000.

[3] Draft Financial Services and Markets Bill: First Report; House of Lords, 50 1-II, House of Commons, HC 328 1-II (29 April 1999) and Draft Financial Services and Markets Bill: Second Report; House of Lords 66, House of Commons HC 465, 2 June 1999.

2.109   The Treasury's response to this Joint Committee report was published in June 1999.[1] This debate caused the Treasury to review and ultimately to amend a number of the procedures in the Bill to make them comply with the requirements of the ECHR and HRA 1998. The FSA itself issued a consultative paper on the enforcement of the regime[2] and the FSA Handbook, Enforcement manual now indicates its policy on the inter-relationship between the civil and criminal enforcement action under FSMA 2000.[3] This paper indicates that the FSA is 'committed to exercising its powers in an appropriate, proportionate and fair manner'.

---

[1]   Reference and a further detailed history of this process is set out in the FSMA Explanatory Notes, paras 14–21.

[2]   FSA CP 25, Enforcing the New Perimeter, July 1999 and its Response Paper, December 1999. See also Speech, 'Financial Regulation and the Law', Howard Davies, Chairman, Financial Services Authority, Chancery Bar Association and Commercial Bar Spring Lecture, Lincoln's Inn, London, 3 March 1999.

[3]   See FSA Handbook, Enforcement manual, Ch 15.

2.110   The FSA acknowledges that it may, in some cases, be appropriate and necessary for the FSA to exercise both civil and criminal powers when enforcing the perimeter. However, the FSA's criminal and civil powers fulfil different functions and will be used to achieve different enforcement objectives. Civil powers in the perimeter context serve to restrain possible contraventions of the general prohibition and restriction on financial promotion and to obtain redress for customers; they are essentially preventative, protective or remedial in nature. Criminal powers, however, have a deterrent purpose. They will only be used to prosecute offenders where the evidential and public interest tests are satisfied.

2.111   Some open issues remain concerning the way in which the courts are likely to interpret FSMA 2000, the secondary legislation made under it and the processes and procedures by which the FSA and the other bodies who are made responsible under the Act discharge their various functions. These include—

— the characterisation of the civil and criminal proceedings under the Act including market abuse;[1]

— the issue of whether double jeopardy could arise in relation to certain proceedings;

— the procedures of the Tribunal concerning the right to a fair trial under ECHR, Art 6(1) including the individual's right to have an independent and impartial tribunal established by law determine his civil rights and obligations or any criminal charge against him in a fair and public hearing within a reasonable time;

— in relation to criminal charges under the Act, an individual's right to be presumed innocent until proved guilty (Art 6(2)) and

to be given legal assistance if he does not have sufficient
means to pay for it when the interests of justice so require
(Art 6(3)(c));
— jurisprudence arising from the ECHR, which gives rise to the
issue of 'equality of arms' in relation to an individual's
opportunity to make representations and to present his case
under conditions which enable him to do so fairly;
— the statutory exclusion of liability for damages granted to the
FSA under FSMA 2000;
— the right to an award of compensation/damages under HRA 1998
(and the relationship with damages under express provisions of
FSMA 2000);
— the position of restrictions on advertising/financial promotion
in relation to ECHR, Art 10 (freedom of expression);
— the individual's right to privacy in relation to the requirements
in FSMA 2000 concerning disclosure of information, and entry
and search of premises, subject to the Convention's
justification test;[2]
— the right to respect for privacy and correspondence in relation
to whether evidence can be compelled in Tribunal
proceedings;
— the right to peaceful enjoyment of one's possessions under Art 1,
First Protocol in relation to disgorgement powers;
— the right to confidentiality in the light of the FSA's information
sharing powers under s 348;[3] and
— the right of appeal to the courts and judicial review in view of
the appeals procedures under Pt IX.[4]

---

[1]   In relation to the FSA's disciplinary regime Morrison J has ruled that it was civil proceedings
for the purposes of HRA 1998 and commented that the FSMA 2000 disciplinary regime
(ignoring market abuse) was, in his view, similarly categorised (*R (on the application of
Fleurose) v Securities and Futures Authority Ltd* [2001] EWCA Admin 292, [2001] 2 All ER
(Comm) 481), [2001] EWHC Admin, 292. This was affirmed on appeal where the court held
that 'If the offence was restricted to a specific group, as was generally the case in relation to
disciplinary offences, the court would be unlikely to classify a charge under the applicable
disciplinary or regulatory code as criminal, at least unless it involved or might lead to loss of
liberty. The imposition of a substantial fine in disciplinary proceedings would not in itself render
charges criminal in nature' ([2001] All ER (D) 361 (Dec), [2001] EWCA Civ 2015).
[2]   *Funke v France* (1993) 16 EHRR 297, ECtHR.
[3]   *R v Chief Constable of the North Wales Police, ex p AB* [1999] QB 396, [1997] 4 All ER 691.
[4]   *Golder v United Kingdom* (1975) 1 EHRR 524, ECtHR.

Characterisation of proceedings and requirements of Art 6

2.112   The procedural guarantees of Art 6(1) apply wherever a
decision-making process determines a 'criminal charge' or a dispute
about 'civil rights and obligations'. The European Court of Human
Rights regards these as 'autonomous concepts'. Thus proceedings
which domestic law labels as 'civil' can be regarded as being in

substance criminal, attracting the extended guarantees of Art 6(2) and (3) (in particular the presumption of innocence and the right to legal assistance).

2.113 This principle prompted the Treasury to concede considerable changes to the original market abuse proposals. Conversely, administrative or disciplinary procedures that impinge on a party's financial interests—particularly where the right to continue trading is at stake—may count as 'civil' proceedings for Art 6 purposes, requiring at minimum a fair and public hearing before an independent body.[1] The changes made following pre-legislative scrutiny should broadly ensure that the main decision-making systems set up by FSMA 2000 are *structurally* compatible with Art 6. But that will not absolve the FSA and individual decision-makers from the responsibility of ensuring that procedures in individual cases comply with Art 6.

[1]   See *R v Securities and Futures Authority Ltd, ex p Fleurose* [2001] EWCA Civ 2015, [2002] IRLR 297, [2001] All ER (D) 361 (Dec).

The presumption of innocence: substantive law

2.114 In certain circumstances the substantive criminal law may offend Art 6(2) by imposing on an accused the burden of disproving a charge. The problem is largely confined to circumstances where the accused bears a persuasive burden in relation to an important ingredient of the offence. It does not prevent statute from creating a genuine defence and placing the burden of establishing that it applies on the accused. Hence the many provisions of FSMA 2000 that take that approach are likely to be Art 6(2) compliant.

The presumption of innocence: statements obtained by compulsion

2.115 Although Art 6 applies to the trial process rather than the preceding investigation, the prosecution's use at trial of incriminating and other statements previously obtained from the accused under compulsory powers is likely to be regarded as breaching the presumption of innocence and therefore unfair. It remains to be seen whether FSMA 2000, s 174(2), which imposes a qualified restriction on the use at trial of compulsorily obtained answers to questions, provides the accused with adequate protection in this respect.

2.116 There are in particular two potential problems. First, s 174(2) applies only to answers given to an investigator, and apparently not to answers given to a question put by notice under s 165. Second, it is not clear that the 'loss of shield' approach, which allows the prosecution to rely on material if the accused puts it in issue, is consistent with the Saunders principle.[1] Under HRA 1998, where a court or tribunal decides that s 174(2) provides insufficient protection, that body ought to deploy its discretionary power (whether under the Police and Criminal Evidence Act 1984, s 78 or otherwise) to prevent the use of the offending material. Note that *Saunders* does not prevent the indirect use of incriminating answers to fuel further investigations that uncover other, admissible evidence.[2]

---

[1] *Saunders v United Kingdom* (1996) 23 EHRR 313, ECtHR, but not necessarily so (see *Brown v Stott* [2003] 1 AC 681, 2001 SLT 59, Privy Council (on appeal from the High Court of Justiciary)). The principle is applied directly by FSMA 2000 in market abuse cases (s 174(2)— see paras 7.30–7.31).
[2] See the Second Report of the Joint Committee, 27 May 1999, para 20.

Double jeopardy

2.117 Article 3 of the Seventh Protocol to the Convention contains a specific rule against double jeopardy in criminal proceedings. That Protocol is, however, as yet unratified by the UK. The fairness requirement in Art 6 applies even where only one, or neither, set of proceedings is criminal. But the standard of protection is unlikely to be greater than provided by domestic principles of abuse of process. Under those principles, where an accused has been exonerated in one set of proceedings, a second set is abusive only if the allegations and issues are so similar to those in the first that the administration of justice would be brought into disrepute if the second set of proceedings were allowed to continue.[1]

---

[1] See *Re Barings plc (No 2)* [1999] 1 All ER 311. See the FSA Handbook, Enforcement manual, ENF 15.4.4G.

Civil liability

2.118 FSMA 2000, Sch 1, para 19(3)(b) preserves the power of a court or tribunal to award damages under HRA 1998, s 8 for an act of the FSA that has been found incompatible with a Convention right.

2.119 In certain circumstances the Convention may require a court to consider making an award of damages for an act or omission that is not itself incompatible with a Convention right but which would, but for the immunity given by Sch 1, para 19(1), involve the FSA in liability under the general law. That is because Art 6(1) imports an implied positive right of access to court to ventilate a civil claim, and that right may be restricted only so far as can be justified by reference to the principle of proportionality.

2.120   It must be said, however, that the European Court has generally taken a forgiving view of immunity provisions where the harm suffered by the would-be claimant is purely economic rather than physical.[1] But it remains to be seen whether the saving in Sch 1, para 19(3)(b) might, in an extreme case of economic harm, be found too restrictive to be compatible with Art 6(1). The comments made here also apply to the parallel provisions relating to liability of the Ombudsman Scheme.[2]

---

[1]   *Fayed v United Kingdom* (1994) 18 EHRR 393; *Osman v United Kingdom* (1998) 29 EHRR 245.
[2]   See para 14.37.

2.121   Further comment on particular Art 6 issues appears in Ch 8: The FSA's disciplinary powers, Ch 11: Market abuse, Ch 12: The Tribunal, and Ch 14: The ombudsman scheme.

3 Regulated activities and the general prohibition

INTRODUCTION

3.1 The Financial Services and Markets Act 2000 (FSMA 2000), Pts I and II establish the framework for the definition of 'regulated activities' and set out the basic scope of the Act.[1]

---

[1] Lord McIntosh, 'This Bill is about regulated activities . . .', HL Committee Stage, 27 March 2000, col 528.

THE GENERAL PROHIBITION

3.2 The core regulatory requirement of FSMA 2000 is the 'general prohibition' in s 19 which provides that no person may carry on, or purport to carry on, a regulated activity in the UK unless he is an authorised person or an exempt person.

3.3 It was the Government's broad intention to consolidate under FSMA 2000 the activities covered by the Banking Act 1987, the Insurance Companies Act 1982, the Building Societies Act 1986, the Credit Unions Act 1979, the Friendly Societies Act 1992 and the Financial Services Act 1986 (FSA 1986).[1]

---

[1] Joint Committee of the Lords and Commons ('Burns Committee'), First Report, 1999, para 66; HM Treasury, FSMA 2000: Regulated Activities—Second Consultation Document, October 2000, Pt 1, para 1.7.

3.4 Although the scope of regulation under FSMA 2000 is by and large the same in most of these areas, it has been extended in relation to certain activities including issuing electronic money,[1] regulating mortgages,[2] general insurance and insurance broking,[3] funeral plan contracts,[4] certain activities at Lloyd's[5] and establishing stakeholder pension schemes.[6]

---

[1]   The Financial Services and Markets Act 2000 (Regulated Activities) Order 2001, SI 2001/544, art 9A, as inserted by the Financial Services and Markets Act 2000 (Regulated Activities) (Amendment) Order 2002, SI 2002/682, art 3(2).
[2]   SI 2001/544, Ch XV as amended by SI 2002/1777.
[3]   With effect from January 2005—the Financial Services and Markets Act 2000 (Regulated Activities) (Amendment) (No 2) Order 2003, SI 2003/1476.
[4]   With effect from October 2004—SI 2001/544, Ch XIV.
[5]   SI 2001/544, Ch XIII.
[6]   SI 2001/544, Ch XI.

REGULATED ACTIVITIES

3.5   FSMA 2000, s 22 provides that an activity is a regulated activity for the purposes of the Act if it is an activity of a kind specified in an order made by the Treasury (the Regulated Activities Order)[1] which is carried on by way of business[2] and which relates to a specified investment or, for certain kinds of activities also specified by order, is carried on in relation to property of any kind (s 22(1), (5)).[3] 'Investment' is defined widely as any asset, right or interest specified in the order (s 22(4)).

---

[1]   The Financial Services and Markets Act 2000 (Regulated Activities) Order 2001, SI 2001/544.
[2]   FSMA 2000, s 419 enables the Treasury to make orders specifying the meaning of 'carried on by way of business': see paras 3.17–3.23.
[3]   In introducing the Regulated Activities Order for debate in the House of Commons, Melanie Johnson said: 'The boundaries of FSA regulation are to be set by Treasury Ministers accountable to this House. Although the Act provides various accountability mechanisms for the FSA, the scope of what it regulates is a matter reserved for Ministers.' HC, 10th Standing Committee on Delegated Legislation, 15 March 2001. See paras 3.17–3.23 for a discussion of the business test.

3.6   The specified activities include: accepting deposits, issuing electronic money, effecting and carrying out contracts of insurance, dealing in investments as principal, dealing in investments as agent, arranging deals in investments, managing investments, safeguarding and administering investments, sending dematerialised instructions, establishing, etc collective investment schemes, establishing, etc stakeholder pension schemes, advising on investments, advising on syndicate participation at Lloyd's, acting as Lloyd's managing agents, arranging deals in contracts of insurance written at Lloyd's, entering into funeral plan contracts and regulated mortgage contracts and agreeing to carry on certain specified kinds of activity.[1]

---

[1]   The Financial Services and Markets Act 2000 (Regulated Activities) Order 2001, SI 2001/544, as amended by SI 2001/3544, SI 2002/682, SI 2002/1310, SI 2002/1776, SI 2002/1777 and SI 2003/1476. Further amendments have been made with effect from October 2004 for mortgages and from January 2005 for general insurance mediation (SI 2003/1475 and SI 2003/1476).

Schedule 2

3.7   FSMA 2000, Sch 2 is described as making provision 'supplementing' s 22 (s 22(2)). However the activities which are outlined are intended to be merely 'indicative', and FSMA 2000 expressly provides that Sch 2 does not impose any limits on the powers conferred on the Treasury to make regulations specifying the activities which are to be regulated activities (s 22(3)). As Patricia Hewitt, Economic Secretary to the Treasury, explained in Committee Stage of consideration of the regulatory scope provisions—

> 'It might help if I explain why we are proposing to deal with the scope of regulated activities in secondary legislation rather than in the Bill itself.
>
> As hon Members have said and as we are all aware, the scope of the 1986 Act is set out in schedule 1 [of the Bill].
>
> However, fortunately, the 1986 Act allows that schedule to be amended by order. I say "fortunately" because that power has been used at least a dozen times over the past 10 years to cope with changes and developments in the marketplace.
>
> Anyone reading the 1986 Act would be misled about its scope, because what is specified in schedule 1 is significantly out of date and no longer constitutes an authoritative statement of the law. We therefore believe that a single statutory instrument comprising a definitive list of regulatory activities will avoid a great deal of the confusion that arises in respect of a provision in primary legislation that becomes increasingly out of date and must be buttressed by several supplementary regulations.
>
> . . .
>
> . . . what we are trying to achieve under the Bill [is] a single order that is kept up to date and constitutes a definitive statement of the scope of regulated activities.'[1]

Schedule 2 can, therefore, be described as largely redundant except for the supplemental provisions contained in Pt III.[2]

---

[1]   HC SC A, 22 July 1999, col 380.
[2]   See para 3.16.

Exclusions

3.8   The Regulated Activities Order[1] also includes a number of exclusions which, broadly speaking, equate to those included under the Banking Act (Exempt Transactions) Regulations 1997,[2] and under FSA 1986, Sch 1, Pts III and IV.[3] These include—

— an exclusion relating to arrangements made by trustees and personal representatives, which will not apply if the trustee receives remuneration for his activities in addition to his remuneration as trustee. However, this exclusion will not apply to the activity of managing where the assets are held for the purposes of an occupational pension scheme (art 66).

— an exclusion in respect of activities in the course of carrying on a profession or non-investment business (art 67).

— an exclusion relating to arrangements between members of a group, but limited to arrangements that are for the internal purposes of the group and not those made on behalf of the customers of a group company (art 69).

— a 'corporate finance' exclusion for activities in respect of sales of bodies corporate although the relevant shareholding percentage has been reduced from 75% (which is the figure in FSA 1986) to 50% (art 70).

— an exclusion for activities in connection with employee share schemes where members of the same group or trustees will not be deemed to be entering into transactions as principal where certain requirements are met (art 71).

— an overseas persons exclusion which is intended to have broadly the same scope as in FSA 1986, Sch 1, Pt IV. However in relation to transactions resulting from a legitimate approach under the financial promotion regime, the overseas persons exclusion will only apply (apart from dealing as principal or agent where it covers the core activity) to the activity of *agreeing* to provide custody, manage, give advice or send dematerialised instructions, and not to *doing* any of these activities (art 72).

---

[1]   SI 2001/544, Ch XVII.
[2]   SI 1997/817.
[3]   HM Treasury, FSMA 2000: Regulated Activities—Second Consultation Document, October 2000, Pt V, paras 5.13 and 5.35–5.41.

Supplementary provisions

Treasury's order-making powers

3.9   The Treasury may make orders under s 22(1) for the purposes of—
— providing for exceptions;
— conferring powers on the Treasury or the FSA;
— authorising the Treasury to make regulations or other instruments for the purposes of, or connected with, any relevant provision;
— authorising the FSA to make rules or other instruments for the purposes of or connected with any relevant provision;

—   making any other provisions in respect of any information or document which is relevant for or connected with the relevant provisions; or

—   making any consequential, transitional or supplemental provisions[1] as the Treasury consider appropriate (Sch 2, para 25(1)).

---

[1]   Provisions under Sch 2, para 25(1)(f) and (2) which empower the Treasury to make any consequential, transitional or supplemental provisions and to amend any primary or subordinate legislation including any other provision of, or made under, FSMA 2000, s 22 or Sch 2. These 'Henry VIII clauses' allow Parliament effectively to delegate the amendment or alteration of statutory provisions to the Executive. These clauses clearly allow for greater flexibility (a lack of flexibility being a principal criticism of FSA 1986) and for both primary and secondary legislation to be amended as necessary to meet changing demands. However, this power could be taken to extremes without the Parliamentary controls in FSMA 2000, Sch 2, para 26.

Parliamentary control of orders made under s 22(1)

3.10   In making the first order (Sch 2, para 26(1)) and any subsequent order which has the effect that an activity which was not previously regulated becomes regulated (Sch 2, para 26(2)), the Treasury must lay a copy of the order before Parliament after it has been made (Sch 2, para 26(3)(a)). If that order is not approved by a resolution of both the Commons and the Lords within 28 days of the date on which the order is made, it will cease to have effect on that date (Sch 2, para 26(3)(b), (4)). This process does not, however, affect anything done under the order or the power to make a new order subject to this procedure (Sch 2, para 26(3)(b)).

3.11   There was much discussion and debate regarding the breadth of the Regulated Activities Order[1] and the accountability of the Treasury and the FSA to Parliament[2] in establishing those activities that would fall to be regulated under FSMA 2000. As a result, the Government agreed that the Regulated Activities Order and certain other pieces of delegated legislation would be subject to affirmative resolution procedures. Melanie Johnson said in response to Opposition amendments—

> 'The order-making powers in the Bill have been examined and improved in the light of the House of Lords Delegated Powers and Deregulation Committee memorandum to the Joint Committee. As we stated in our response to the Joint Committee's report, we agree with the opinion expressed in that memorandum that the affirmative resolution procedure is appropriate when extending the scope of regulated activities and for the financial promotion prohibition in clauses 19 and 20. We therefore made appropriate provision in the Bill.

The way in which we have applied the affirmative and negative resolution procedures is also underpinned by the policy that Parliament should have a chance to debate any extension of the ambit of regulation. That is what lies behind [section 429] as well as section 2(3) of the Financial Services Act 1986.'

---

1   SI 2001/544.
2   HC SC A, 9 December 1999, col 1262. See also HL Committee Stage, 20 March 2000, col 123.

3.12   In the Commons, the process of affirmative resolution is carried out by the Standing Committees on Delegated Legislation which consider most of the statutory instruments requiring affirmative resolution and some of those to which the negative resolution procedure applies.[1] This affirmative resolution procedure is used most often where the powers delegated are particularly wide-ranging, for example under the Emergency Powers Act 1920 and the Human Rights Act 1998.

---

1   See The Committee System of the House of Commons, May 2003, para 16. See also First Special Report from the Select Committee on Deregulation, 24 January 2000 on the delegation of order making generally under the Deregulation and Contracting Out Act 1994.

3.13   Statutory instruments subject to affirmative resolution automatically stand referred to a standing committee unless the House of Commons otherwise orders. The Committee debates the instrument, although no amendments can be made. Debate may continue after which the instrument will be reported from a committee, either affirmatively or negatively, and the motion to approve (or reject) it will be taken 'forthwith' in the House of Commons without further debate.

3.14   The procedure in the House of Lords is for the House to resolve itself into committee[1] to consider statutory instruments requiring affirmative resolution.

---

1   Burns Committee, First Report, March 1999, Annex B, Memorandum by the House of Lords, Delegated Powers and Deregulation Committee.

3.15   Members of Parliament are able to question the Minister responsible in each of the Houses about any statutory instrument that seems to them to be unsatisfactory in some way.[1] Where, as in the case of the Regulated Activities Order,[2] the enabling Act provides that the statutory instrument is subject to an affirmative resolution of each House, such a resolution must be passed within 28 days of the order having been laid or the order will be deemed to have lapsed and have no effect after that date.

[1] The Financial Services and Markets Act 2000 (Financial Promotion) Order 2001, SI 2001/1335 (which is subject to affirmative resolution) was laid on 27 February 2001 but was withdrawn by the Government after concerns were raised in the press and in Parliament about the requirement that journalists would be required to disclose the nature of an author's financial interest (or that of a close relative) in order to take advantage of the exemption in art 20 of the order. The order was relaid with amendments before both Houses on 20 March 2001 and was subsequently amended again by the Financial Services and Markets Act 2000 (Financial Promotion) (Amendment No 2) Order 2001, SI 2001/3800, which replaced art 20, and came into force on 1 December 2001('N2').

[2] SI 2001/544.

Definitions in Sch 2

3.16 Schedule 2, para 27 contains certain defined terms,[1] but as a number of these definitions are also contained in a slightly altered form in the Regulated Activities Order[2] it is not clear what function these definitions, which relate only to Sch 2, will fulfil.

[1] These terms are drawn from the definitions in FSA 1986, Sch 1, Pt V.
[2] SI 2001/544.

THE BUSINESS TEST

3.17 The Treasury may also by means of an order made under s 419 define 'carrying on a regulated activity by way of business' for the purposes of s 22 (the 'Business Order'),[1] although FSMA 2000, s 19(1) does not specifically require such definition.[2]

[1] The Financial Services and Markets Act 2000 (Carrying on Regulated Activities by Way of Business) Order 2001, SI 2001/1177.
[2] FSMA Explanatory Notes, para 740. Orders made under s 419 are subject to affirmative resolution in both Houses of Parliament: see paras 3.12–3.15.

3.18 The Business Order specifies the circumstances where a person is or is not to be regarded as carrying on a regulated activity 'by way of business' and modifies them for different types of business (s 419(1), (2)). The Government stated that its approach was to catch, along with any mainstream activity, any activity that falls short of constituting a business in its own right but which should be regulated under FSMA 2000. The Government indicated that 'It has never been proposed that the incidental provision of financial services should generally be exempt from the authorisation requirement'.[1]

[1] HC Report Stage, 1 February 2000, col 1005.

3.19 A significant difference between the general prohibition (s 19(1)) and FSA 1986 is that the definition of 'investment business' under FSA 1986, s 1(3) included a requirement that the investment activities be carried on 'by way of business'.[1] The requirement that activities specified in the Regulated Activities Order[2] will only be 'regulated activities' if carried on 'by way of business' is also contained in the definition of 'regulated activities' (FSMA 2000, s 22(1)) and therefore allows the Treasury to adjust[3] the scope of regulated activities by defining what constitutes 'by way of business' for different activities and markets.

---

[1] See Securities and Investments Board, CP 19, March 1989, which was an attempt to define what was meant by 'by way of business' for the purposes of FSA 1986, s 1(3). This consultative paper and the guidance which it contained was never finalised and SIB/FSA did not give specific guidance as to when certain activities had to be carried on 'by way of business' in order to fall within the definition of 'investment business'.

[2] SI 2001/544.

[3] HM Treasury, FSMA 2000: Regulated Activities—Second Consultation Document, October 2000, Pt I, para 1.5.

3.20 The Government has indicated that the different tests under the various Acts being consolidated in FSMA 2000 are intended generally to have the same effect as under the previous legislation and are unlikely to exclude from regulation persons who are currently subject to regulation or to regulate persons who are currently not subject to regulation.[1]

---

[1] HM Treasury, FSMA 2000: Regulated Activities—Second Consultation Document, October 2000, Pt 1, para 1.22.

3.21 However, the Treasury recognises that the 'by way of business' test in FSMA 2000 is broader than that in FSA 1986 and that FSMA 2000 could, for example, cover employers arranging group personal pensions or companies which arrange for shareholders to sell their shares to other shareholders—activities which it is not the Treasury's intention to regulate.[1]

---

[1] HM Treasury, FSMA 2000: Regulated Activities—Second Consultation Document, October 2000, Pt 1, para 1.19.

3.22 However, the definition of 'by way of business' may be modified to meet the particular requirements of the industry. For example, the 'by way of business' test in FSMA 2000 is narrower than the business test in the Banking Act 1987 which turned on whether a person holds himself out as accepting deposits on a day-to-day basis or accepts deposits on more than specified occasions. The Business Order therefore specifies a separate business test for the acceptance of deposits.[1] That test provides that a person will not be considered as accepting deposits by way of business if he does not hold himself out as accepting deposits on a day-to-day basis and any deposits he accepts are accepted only on particular occasions, whether or not involving the issue of any securities. The order also specifies that whether a person is to be regarded as accepting deposits only on particular occasions will be determined with reference to the frequency and characteristics of those occasions.

---

[1] SI 2001/1177, art 2. See also HM Treasury, FSMA 2000: Regulated Activities—Second Consultation Document, October 2000, Pt 1, para 1.20.

3.23   The Business Order also includes other modifications of this 'by way of business' test. For example, in relation to the activity of carrying on the management of occupational pension schemes, this order may specify the circumstances in which a trustee or other relevant person will be considered to be carrying on regulated activities (art 4). This is intended broadly to reflect FSA 1986, s 191 although some changes have been made, notably the omission of overseas persons or persons who would not require authorisation to manage assets by virtue of the exclusions in FSA 1986, Sch 1, Pt IV.[1]

---

[1] HM Treasury, FSMA 2000: Regulated Activities—Second Consultation Document, October 2000, Pt 7, para 7.4. See also HM Treasury, The Financial Services and Markets Bill: Regulated Activities—A consultation document, February 1999, para 2.2.

EXEMPT PERSONS

3.24   Section 417(1) defines 'exempt persons' as those who are, in relation to a regulated activity, exempt from the general prohibition in s 19 either as a result of an exemption order made under s 38(1) or one of the specific exemption provisions under s 39(1) (appointed representatives) or s 285(2) and (3) (recognised investment exchanges and recognised clearing houses). In addition, there are further specific exemptions such as former underwriting members of Lloyd's (s 320) for carrying out contracts of insurance that have been underwritten at Lloyd's (whether or not the member is an authorised person) and professional firms carrying on exempt regulated activities under Pt XX. For the purposes of Pt XX 'exempt regulated activities' means regulated activities which may be carried on by members of a profession which is supervised and regulated by a designated professional body without breaching the general prohibition under s 19 (s 325(2)).

Exemption orders

3.25 FSMA 2000, s 38(1) provides that the Treasury may make exemption orders to exempt specific persons, or persons falling within a particular class, from the general prohibition.[1] The stated intention is that an exemption order exempts from authorisation certain 'persons who would otherwise be conducting regulated activities where regulation by the FSA would be inappropriate or unnecessary'.[2] Generally speaking the policy behind s 38 is to exempt individuals or firms rather than provide exclusions to the prescribed regulated activities. The types of person who are exempt persons include supranational persons such as the International Monetary Fund and other bodies which carry on regulated activities as a public policy function, such as Tourist Boards, and those which are subject to separate statutory control.[3] The Exemption Order consolidates and clarifies exemptions under the existing legislation, so that, broadly speaking, those who were exempt under the previous legislation do not need to seek authorisation under FSMA 2000.[4]

---

[1] The Financial Services and Markets Act 2000 (Exemption) Order 2001, SI 2001/1201 (the 'Exemption Order'), the Financial Services and Markets Act 2000 (Exemption) (Amendment) Order 2001, SI 2001/3623, the Financial Services and Markets Act 2000 (Appointed Representatives) Regulations 2001, SI 2001/1217, the Financial Services and Markets Act 2000 (Exemption) (Amendment) Order 2003, SI 2003/47, the Financial Services and Markets Act 2000 (Exemption) (Amendment) (No 2) Order 2003, SI 2003/1675. These orders are subject to affirmative resolution by both Houses of Parliament: see paras 3.12–3.15.
[2] HM Treasury, FSMA 2000: Regulated Activities—Second Consultation Document, October 2000, Pt 1, para 1.8.
[3] The Exemption Order, arts 3 and 5. See also HM Treasury, FSMA 2000: Regulated Activities—Second Consultation Document, October 2000, Pt 1, para 1.9.
[4] HM Treasury, FSMA 2000: Regulated Activities—Second Consultation Document, October 2000, Pt 1, para 1.10.

3.26 An exemption order may have the effect of exempting a person for all its regulated activities or may specify one or more regulated activities for which it will be exempt (s 38(3)(a), (b)). It may also provide that the exemption will only apply in specified circumstances or for specific functions (s 38(3)(c), (d)). The exemptions may also be subject to certain conditions (s 38(3)(e)).

3.27 However, some of these exemptions differ from those under the previous legislation as a result of changes in the regulatory framework of FSMA 2000. For example, the fact that exemption from authorisation is required only for those bodies carrying on regulated activities by way of business renders unnecessary a number of the exemptions granted under previous legislation on the basis that these bodies will not be carrying on the activities by way of business.[1]

1 HM Treasury, FSMA 2000: Regulated Activities—Second Consultation Document, October 2000, Pt 1, para 1.11.

3.28 A further difference is the removal of exemptions for persons who are authorised for some other regulated activity. FSMA 2000 specifically provides that a person cannot be an exempt person in respect of an exemption order made under s 38(1) if he has a Pt IV permission for other activities (s 38(2)).[1]

1 FSMA 2000, s 38 precludes persons holding a Pt IV permission from being exempt, while s 39 (appointed representatives) precludes authorised persons from being exempt on this basis (s 39(1)). There is, however, no bar on a recognised investment exchange or a recognised clearing house (both exempt persons) having a Part IV permission as well as an exemption.

3.29 Other exemptions have been removed as it was believed that they were no longer necessary.[1] Certain other exemptions, for example in relation to Crown bodies, have also been removed as these are not subject to the general prohibition under s 19(2).[2] In other cases, exemptions were amended to take into account the specific nature of particular segments of the financial services industry, because they were to be of limited duration or until the sector was to be brought within the scope of FSMA 2000.[3]

1 For example, nationalised industries accepting deposits from other nationalised industries (HM Treasury, FSMA 2000: Regulated Activities—Second Consultation Document, October 2000, Pt 1, para 1.11). See also HM Treasury, The Financial Services and Markets Bill: Regulated Activities—A consultation document, February 1999, para 2.14.
2 HM Treasury, FSMA 2000: Regulated Activities—Second Consultation Document, October 2000, Pt 1, para 1.11.
3 HM Treasury, FSMA 2000: Regulated Activities—Second Consultation Document, October 2000, Pt 1, para 1.12. For further discussion of N2 see para 1.37.

Definition of 'investment'

3.30 The term 'investment' is defined very broadly in FSMA 2000 as including any asset, right or interest (s 22(4)). Such a broad definition must, however, be read with the Regulated Activities Order,[1] Pt III, which specifies 'investments' for the purposes of s 22.

1 SI 2001/544.

3.31 Specified investments include deposits, electronic money, contracts of insurance, shares or stock, instruments creating or acknowledging indebtedness including debentures and bonds, government and public securities, instruments giving entitlement to investments, such as warrants, and other instruments entitling the holder to subscribe for shares, debentures or government or public securities, certificates representing certain securities such as American depositary receipts, units in a collective investment scheme, rights under a stakeholder pension scheme, options, futures, contracts for differences, etc, Lloyd's syndicate capacity and syndicate membership, rights under a funeral plan contract, rights under a regulated mortgage contract, rights to or interests in any other investment specified in the Regulated Activities Order.[1]

---

[1]   SI 2001/544, as amended by SI 2001/3544, SI 2002/682, SI 2002/1310, SI 2002/1776 and SI 2002/1777.

APPOINTED REPRESENTATIVES

3.32   The exemption for appointed representatives continues under the new regime, subject to an important change, namely that no person who holds a Pt IV permission for other activities may now be exempt for other activities by virtue of being an appointed representative (s 39(1)). Section 39(1) therefore only applies to persons other than authorised persons.

3.33   Therefore building societies and other financial institutions which have a Pt IV permission for their deposit-taking activities cannot be appointed representatives for their designated investment business activities, but need to have the appropriate Pt IV permission in their own right.

3.34   FSMA 2000, s 39 provides that a person, other than an authorised person, is exempt from the general prohibition for those regulated activities which have been prescribed in an order made by the Treasury[1] for which an authorised person (his 'principal') has accepted responsibility under a contract, the terms of which are to be prescribed by the regulations made by the Treasury (s 39(1)). The Act also provides that where a principal has accepted responsibility for the business carried on by his appointed representative, he will be responsible, as if he had expressly permitted it, for anything done or omitted to be done by the appointed representative (s 39(3)).[2] In addition, the principal will be treated as having done or having omitted anything done by its appointed representative for the purposes of determining whether the authorised person has complied with any provision (including rules made under Pt X) of FSMA 2000 (s 39(4)).

---

[1]   The Financial Services and Markets Act 2000 (Appointed Representatives) Regulations 2001, SI 2001/1217 (the 'Appointed Representative Regulations'), as amended by SI 2001/2508. See also HM Treasury, FSMA 2000: Regulated Activities—Second Consultation Document, October 2000, Pt 1, paras 1.13, 1.14.

[2]   As this exemption only applies to activities for which the principal has accepted responsibility, presumably any regulated activities for which the principal has not accepted responsibility will be outside the exemption and therefore the appointed representative could be in breach of the general prohibition under s 19.

3.35   The regulations made under s 39 (the Appointed Representative Regulations)[1] also prescribe the requirements with which contracts between appointed representatives and their principals must comply.[2] An authorised principal may, for example, impose prohibitions or restrictions on the regulated activities carried on by the appointed person on behalf of persons other than the authorised principal. In addition, the FSA may impose additional constraints on the carrying on of regulated or non-regulated activities by appointed representatives through its power under FSMA 2000 to make rules applicable to the authorised persons who take responsibility for appointed representatives.[3]

---

[1]   SI 2001/1217, as amended by SI 2001/2508.

[2]   Changes have been required to the appointed representative regime in order to implement the Insurance Mediation Directive, see the Financial Services and Markets Act 2000 (Regulated Activities) (Amendment) (No 2) Order 2003, SI 2003/1476, art 14 which comes into force on 14 January 2005.

[3]   HM Treasury, FSMA 2000: Regulated Activities—Second Consultation Document, October 2000, Pt 1, para 1.15.

NON-EXEMPT ACTIVITIES ORDER

3.36   FSMA 2000, Pt XX provides that the Treasury may make an order under s 327(6) in relation to professional firms whose regulated activities would otherwise be exempt by virtue of being regulated by professional bodies and meeting the other criteria in s 327. The Government did not intend that those providing professional services[1] should be able to carry on other mainstream financial services and rely on their exempt status under Pt XX. Therefore, the 'Non-Exempt Activities Order'[2] defines those activities for which a person who would be able to use the Pt XX exemption would have to seek separate authorisation under the Pt IV permissions regime.

---

[1]   'Professional services' is defined as services which do not constitute carrying on a regulated activity and the provision of which is supervised and regulated by a designated professional body (s 327(8)).

[2]   The Financial Services and Markets Act 2000 (Professions) (Non-Exempt Activities) Order 2001, SI 2001/1227.

3.37   The Non-Exempt Activities Order[1] provides that professional firms will not be able to set themselves up using the Pt XX arrangements as bankers,[2] insurance companies brokers or fund managers providing their own investment products for their clients, even in circumstances where they are able to show some connection between those products and the professional services which they provide.[3] The Non-Exempt Activities Order specifies the following as activities for which a person otherwise falling under Pt XX would require separate authorisation—
— accepting deposits;
— issuing electronic money;
— effecting and carrying out contracts of insurance;
— dealing in investments as principal;
— establishing collective investment schemes;
— establishing stakeholder pensions.

In addition the related activities of acting as a managing agent at Lloyd's, entering into a funeral plan contract as provider, or acting as a mortgage lender will be non-exempt. However the order does not mention 'safeguarding and administering clients' assets'.[4] Managing investments will be also be a non-exempt activity unless either all routine day-to-day decisions are taken by an authorised person or a person who is exempt in relation to that activity, or the decision is taken in accordance with the advice of an authorised person or a person who is exempt in relation to that activity.[5] Therefore, corporate finance advisory services and certain types of advice to trustees or members of occupational pension schemes are also not exempt.

---

[1] The Financial Services and Markets Act 2000 (Professions) (Non-Exempt Activities) Order 2001, SI 2001/1227, as amended by SI 2002/682.
[2] HM Treasury, FSMA 2000: Regulated Activities—Second Consultation Document, October 2000, Pt 6, para 6.2.
[3] HM Treasury, FSMA 2000: Regulated Activities—Second Consultation Document, October 2000, Pt 1, para 1.16.
[4] HM Treasury, FSMA 2000: Regulated Activities—Second Consultation Document, October 2000, Pt 6, paras 6.4 and 6.10.
[5] SI 2001/1227, art 5.

THE TERRITORIAL SCOPE OF FSMA 2000

3.38   FSMA 2000, Pt XXIX (ss 417–425) sets out various provisions for interpreting the Act including provision in relation to the scope and application of carrying out regulated activities. The wording in the general prohibition in s 19(1) establishes the broad parameters by stating that 'no person may carry on a regulated activity in the UK...'.

3.39   For these purposes 'the UK' means Great Britain and Northern Ireland
and includes England, Wales, Scotland and Northern Ireland.[1]

¹   Interpretation Act 1978, Sch 1.

3.40   In relation to Scotland, matters relating to financial services are
generally reserved to the UK Parliament under the Scotland Act 1998,
s 30, Sch 5, Pt II, although FSMA 2000 is subject to various
modifications for enforcement matters in Scotland.[1]

¹   For example, ss 130(4) and (5), 176(9).

3.41   Part XVII, Ch IV on open-ended investment companies does not,
however, apply to Northern Ireland (s 430(1)). The UK does not
include Jersey, Guernsey, the Isle of Man or any of the overseas
territories or dependencies.[1] However, s 430 provides that
FSMA 2000 may be extended by Order in Council to any of the
Channel Islands or the Isle of Man with such modifications as may be
required.

¹   See special provisions relating to Gibraltar, paras 3.50–3.52.

Outward application of FSMA 2000

3.42   Section 418 provides further interpretation of the application of
FSMA 2000 by providing five cases where a person who is carrying on
a regulated activity would not otherwise be regarded as carrying it on
in the UK—the 'so-called "outward" application [of FSMA 2000],
whereby persons based in the United Kingdom who carry on regulated
activities overseas need to be regulated in the United Kingdom'.[1]

¹   FSMA Explanatory Notes, para 738.

3.43   The first case is where the person has his registered office (or if he
does not have a registered office, his head office) in the UK and is
entitled to exercise rights under one of the single market directives[1] as
a UK firm[2] and he is carrying on a regulated activity to which that
directive applies in another EEA State (s 418(2)).

¹   The definition of 'single market directives' set out in FSMA 2000, Sch 3, para 1 has been
amended by the Banking Consolidation Directive (Consequential Amendments) Regulations 2000,
SI 2000/2952, to take into account the consolidation of the First and Second Banking
Co-ordination Directives into the Banking Consolidation Directive (2000/12/EC). See also
para 4.3, fn 1.
²   A 'UK firm' means a person whose head office is in the UK and who has an EEA right to
carry on activity in an EEA state other than the UK (Sch 3, para 10).

3.44   The second case is where a person has his registered office (or if he does not have a registered office his head office) in the UK and he is the manager of a scheme which is entitled to the rights under the relevant Community instrument for the purposes of s 264, and persons in other EEA states are invited to become participants in the scheme (s 418(3)).

3.45   The third case is where a person has his registered office (or if he does not have a registered office his head office) in the UK and the day-to-day management of the regulated activity is the responsibility of his registered office (or head office) or another establishment maintained by him in the UK (s 418(4)).

3.46   The fourth case is where a person's head office is not in the UK but the activity is carried on from an establishment maintained by that person in the UK (s 418(5)).

3.47   A fifth case has been added[1] to give effect to the Electronic Commerce Directive,[2] which provides that where the activity is an 'information society service' within the meaning of Art 2(a) of the Directive carried on in an EEA jurisdiction from an establishment in the UK, it will be regarded as carried on in the UK.

---

[1]   Section 418(5A), as inserted by the Electronic Commerce Directive (Financial Services and Markets) Regulations 2002, SI 2002/1775, reg 13.
[2]   European Parliament and Council Directive 2000/31/EC.

3.48   In all of these cases it is irrelevant where the person with whom the activity is carried on is situated (s 418(6)), and these provisions therefore open up the regulation of these activities in relation to persons located overseas.[1]

---

[1]   On this point the position under FSMA 2000 does not differ significantly from that under FSA 1986 to the extent that the FSA 1986 regime applied to business conducted in or from the UK regardless of where the customers or counterparties with whom the authorised person was dealing were resident or located.

Inward application of FSMA 2000

3.49   The 'inward' application of FSMA 2000 is implicit in s 19 (applying to regulated activities carried on by way of business in the UK), but may be restricted or expanded by order made under s 22(1).[1]

---

[1]   FSMA Explanatory Notes, para 739: see the Financial Services and Markets Act 2000 (Carrying on Regulated Activities by Way of Business) Order 2001, SI 2001/1177.

Gibraltar

3.50   The Treasury may modify FSMA 2000, Sch 3 to allow certain Gibraltar firms to qualify for authorisation in certain circumstances (s 409(1)(a)).[1] The Treasury may also modify Sch 3 to provide that UK authorised firms may exercise rights under the law of Gibraltar which correspond to EEA rights, and may modify s 264 to include collective investment schemes constituted under the law of Gibraltar (s 409(1)(b), (d)).

---

[1]   The Financial Services and Markets Act 2000 (Gibraltar) Order 2001, SI 2001/3084.

3.51   These Treasury orders may also modify FSMA 2000, Sch 4 to provide that Gibraltar firms of certain descriptions may qualify for authorisation. The orders may also provide that the FSA is able to give a notice in respect of recognised overseas schemes under s 264(2) on grounds relating to the law of Gibraltar and to provide that FSMA 2000 applies to a Gibraltar recognised scheme as if it were a recognised overseas scheme.

3.52   In introducing the relevant provisions of the Bill, Lord McIntosh of Haringey stated—

> 'This is a new clause which has been introduced to take account of several matters arising from Gibraltar's status within the European Economic Area.
>
> The provisions of the treaty relating to the right of establishment and the freedom to supply services apply to Gibraltar. However, Gibraltar is not a separate member state in its own right, but its nationals have rights to passport into other member states on the basis that it is part of the UK for these purposes.
>
> Because of this unique status, there is no Community obligation to provide the passporting mechanism between the UK and Gibraltar. However, it has been the established policy of the previous Government and of this one to provide for an "internal passport" between Gibraltar and the UK for the activities covered by the passport directives, as and when we are satisfied with the relevant regulatory standards in Gibraltar. The clause provides the necessary mechanism for this.'[1]

A 'Gibraltar firm' is defined in s 409(3) as a firm having its head office in Gibraltar or which is 'otherwise connected with Gibraltar'. This definition is wide and would permit the Treasury (under s 409) 'to enable firms from other EEA states which have exercised passport rights to branch or provide services into Gibraltar to then exercise those rights in relation to the United Kingdom proper without going through the full directive notification requirements'.[2]

1   HL Committee Stage, 30 March 2000, col 1045.
2   HL Committee Stage, 30 March 2000, col 1047.

4 Authorisation and permission

INTRODUCTION

4.1   The Financial Services and Markets Act 2000 (FSMA 2000), Pt III
(ss 31–39) and Pt IV (ss 40–55) establish and streamline the various
routes to authorisation of financial sector firms (which were
characteristic of the previous sector-based regime) into a single
functional approach, and as such provide the backbone of the Act.
The Act also prescribes various requirements (threshold conditions)
and restrictions as to the 'control' over authorised persons (Pt XII).

AUTHORISATION AND EXEMPTION

4.2   The basic requirement of FSMA 2000 (the 'general prohibition') is that
no person unless authorised or exempt may carry on regulated
activities in the UK (s 19(1)). Although the main route to authorisation
is through an application for a permission under Pt IV, s 31(1) also
lists the other persons who are authorised to carry on regulated
activities and are therefore able to carry on regulated activities
without breaching the general prohibition.[1]

---

[1]   For exemptions see paras 4.54–4.59.

Authorised persons

4.3   In addition to an application for a Pt IV permission, authorisation may
be obtained by—
—   notification by a person, who must come from or be
incorporated in, or formed under the law of, another member
State, in accordance with the relevant single market directive;[1]

— exercise, in accordance with Sch 4, of EU Treaty rights other than or beyond those governed by the single market directives;
— exercise of rights under the EC directive relating to collective investment undertakings to market in the UK collective investment schemes or product authorisation of certain open-ended investment companies (OEICs) under regulations to be made under FSMA 2000, Pt XVII, Ch IV; or
— being a person with a deemed Pt IV permission as a result of being 'grandfathered' under the transitional provisions of FSMA 2000 (ss 426, 427). This includes arrangements that 'cover persons authorised (however described) under the Banking, Financial Services, Insurance, Building Societies, Friendly Societies, Credit Unions and Lloyd's Acts (including members of self-regulating organisations and certain members of recognised professional bodies)'.[2]

---

[1]   The single market directives are the Banking Consolidation Directive (for banks and other credit institutions), the Investment Services Directive (for investment firms), and the Third Life and Third Non-life Insurance Directives (for insurance companies, including mutual insurers such as friendly societies) (Sch 3, Pt I, paras 1–4, as amended by the Banking Consolidation Directive (Consequential Amendments) Regulations 2000, SI 2000/2952). Further amendments will give effect to the Insurance Mediation Directive (2002/92/EC) and the UCITS Management Directive (2001/107/EC).
[2]   FSMA Explanatory Notes, para 79. This was given effect (other than for credit unions) for N2 by the Financial Services and Markets Act 2000 (Transitional Provisions) (Authorised Persons etc) Order 2001, SI 2001/2636 (sometimes referred to as the 'Grandfathering Order').

Partnerships and unincorporated associations

4.4   FSMA 2000 also includes specific provisions concerning the status of firms, which are defined as meaning partnerships or unincorporated associations of persons (s 32(4)).[1] Where a firm is authorised, it may carry on regulated activities in the name of the firm, and any change in the membership of that firm will not affect its authorisation (s 32(1)). This ensures that authorisation is not interrupted.[2]

---

[1]   The definition excludes a partnership which is constituted under the laws of a place outside the UK and which is a body corporate (s 32(5)). An example of this would be a US state limited liability corporation.
[2]   FSMA Explanatory Notes, para 83.

4.5   Where an authorised firm is dissolved, its authorisation will be deemed to continue to have effect in relation to any successor firm only if the members of that firm are substantially the same as those of the former firm and the successor firm has succeeded to the whole or substantially the whole of the business of the former firm (s 32(2), (3)).

ENDING OF AUTHORISATION

Withdrawal of authorisation by FSA

4.6   An authorised person will cease to be authorised if that person's Pt IV permission is cancelled and as a result he will not be permitted to carry on regulated activities (s 33(1)). Where the Financial Services Authority (the FSA) decides to withdraw a person's status as an authorised person, it must give that person a direction to that effect (s 33(2)).[1]

---

[1]   This part of the process follows the processes for cancellation of permissions in Pt IV.

EEA firms

4.7   An EEA firm[1] ceases to qualify for authorisation under Sch 3, Pt II either by having its EEA authorisation withdrawn or by ceasing to have an EEA right[2] in circumstances in which EEA authorisation is not required by that person (s 34(1)). If the EEA firm has a Pt IV permission it will not cease to be an authorised person merely because it ceases to qualify for authorisation under Sch 3, Pt II (s 34(3)). The FSA may, at the request of the EEA firm, give a direction cancelling its authorisation under Sch 3, Pt II (s 34(2)).

---

[1]   Defined in Sch 3, para 5 as a firm which does not have its head office in the UK and is either an investment firm or a credit institution which is authorised by its home state regulator, or a financial institution which fulfils the conditions set out in that paragraph, or an undertaking carrying on direct insurance within the meaning of the First Life Insurance Directive or the First Non-Life Insurance Directive which has received authorisation from its home state regulator for the purposes of the relevant single market directive.
[2]   An 'EEA right' is defined in Sch 3, para 7 as the entitlement of a person to establish a branch or to provide services in an EEA State other than that in which he has his head office in accordance with the Treaty establishing the European Community as applied in the EEA and subject to the conditions of the relevant single market directive.

EEA firms: application for permission

THRESHOLD CONDITIONS

4.8   For an EEA firm which qualifies for authorisation under Sch 3, the threshold conditions in s 41, Sch 6, paras 1, 3–5 will only apply in relation to an application for permission under FSMA 2000, Pt IV for activities for which the firm has no single market directive rights or to the FSA's powers to vary such a permission on its own initiative as set out in s 45 (Sch 6, para 6).[1]

---

[1]   See paras 4.74, 4.76, 4.77.

ESTABLISHMENT CONDITIONS

4.9   Under s 31(1)(b), an EEA firm seeking to establish a branch in the UK in exercise of an EEA right must satisfy the 'establishment conditions' (Sch 3, para 12(1)), ie, that the FSA must have received a notice from the firm's home state regulator (a 'consent notice') to the effect that the home state regulator has given the firm consent to establish such a branch in the UK (Sch 3, para 13(1)(a)).

4.10 The consent notice must have been given in accordance with the relevant single market directive, identify the activities which the EEA firm is proposing to carry on in the UK and include such other information as may be prescribed (Sch 3, para 13(1)(b)).[1]

---

[1]   The Financial Services and Markets Act 2000 (EEA Passport Rights) Regulations 2001, SI 2001/2511, reg 2 specifies the content of the consent notice which varies with the directive under which rights are being exercised. In each case the notice must identify the nature of the firm and provide certain relevant information about it.

4.11 Once the FSA has received a consent notice it must take steps to prepare for the firm's supervision, notify the firm of the applicable provisions,[1] if any, and, if the firm is undertaking direct insurance,[2] notify its home state regulator of those applicable provisions (Sch 3, para 13(2)). Such notice must be given to the firm and, if applicable, to its home state regulator, within two months of the date on which the FSA received the consent notice (Sch 3, para 13(3)).

---

[1]   'Applicable provisions' means the host state rules with which the firm must comply when carrying on a permitted activity (ie, one identified in the notice) in the UK. The host state rules are rules made in accordance with the relevant single market directive and which are the responsibility of the UK to implement and supervise compliance with (Sch 3, para 13(4)).
[2]   Within the meaning of the First Life Insurance Directive, Art 1, or the First Non-Life Insurance Directive, Art 1, which has received authorisation from its home state regulator under the relevant single market directive.

4.12 The EEA firm may establish the branch once it has been informed by the FSA of the applicable provisions or two months have elapsed from the date on which the FSA received the consent notice (Sch 3, para 13(1)(c)).

SERVICE CONDITIONS

4.13 If the EEA firm is seeking to provide services in the UK in exercise of an EEA right, it must satisfy the service conditions in order to qualify for authorisation (Sch 3, para 12(2)).

4.14 The service conditions are that the firm has given its home state regulator notice of its intention to provide services in the UK (a 'notice of intention') (Sch 3, para 14(1)(a)). If the firm is an investment firm (within the meaning of the Investment Services Directive) or an undertaking pursuing the activity of direct insurance,[1] the FSA must have received notice (a 'regulator's notice') from the home state regulator containing the information prescribed (Sch 3, para 14(1)(b)).[2] If the firm is an undertaking carrying on the activity of direct insurance, the firm must also have been informed that the regulator's notice has been sent to the FSA (Sch 3, para 14(1)(c))).

---

[1]   See para 4.11, fn 2.

[2]   The Financial Services and Markets Act 2000 (EEA Passport Rights) Regulations 2001, SI 2001/2511, reg 3 specifies the content of the regulator's notice which, as with the consent notice (see para 4.11), varies with the directive under which the rights are being exercised. For an investment firm exercising passport rights under the Investment Services Directive, the content is limited to confirmation that it is an investment firm and details of the activities it proposes to carry on in the UK. The provisions for insurers are similar but more detailed.

4.15 If the FSA has received a regulator's notice or, if no such notice is required under Sch 3, para 14(1),[1] the EEA firm has informed the FSA of its intentions to provide services in the UK, the FSA must prepare for the firm's supervision and notify it of the applicable provisions[2] with which the firm will have to comply when carrying on the activities set out either in the regulator's notice or the notice of intent under para 14(1) (Sch 3, para 14(2), (4)). This notice must be given within two months of the date on which the FSA received the regulator's notice or the date on which it was informed of the firm's intentions (Sch 3, para 14(3)).

---

[1]   Ie, in the case of credit institutions or financial institutions under the Banking Consolidation Directive (the definition of 'EEA firm' in Sch 3, para 5 has been amended by the Banking Consolidation Directive (Consequential Amendments) Regulations 2000, SI 2000/2952).

[2]   See para 4.11, fn 1.

GRANT OF PERMISSION

4.16 An EEA firm which has qualified for authorisation (having satisfied the conditions set out in Sch 3, para 12) has permission to carry on, through its UK branch or by providing services in the UK, each of the activities identified in the regulator's notice or the firm's notice of intention (Sch 3, para 15(1)). This permission is to be treated as having been given on terms equivalent to those which appear in the consent notice, the regulator's notice or the notice of intention (Sch 3, para 15(2)).

4.17 To the extent that an authorised EEA firm is carrying on a permitted activity which is Consumer Credit Act business,[1] the Consumer Credit

Act 1974 (CCA 1974), ss 21, 39(1) and 147(1) do not apply to that business unless the Director General of Fair Trading has exercised his powers under CCA 1974, s 203 (Sch 3, para 15(3)).

[1]   'Consumer Credit Act business' means consumer credit business, consumer hire business or ancillary credit business as defined in CCA 1974, s 203(10) (Sch 3, para 15(4)).

EFFECT OF CARRYING ON REGULATED ACTIVITY WHEN NOT QUALIFIED FOR AUTHORISATION

4.18   If an EEA firm is not qualified for authorisation under Sch 3, para 12, then ss 26, 27 and 29 concerning the unenforceability of agreements entered into by the firm in breach of the general prohibition are disapplied to agreements entered into by that firm (Sch 3, para 16).

CONTINUING REGULATION OF EEA FIRMS

4.19   The Treasury may make regulations which modify any of the provisions of FSMA 2000 in relation to the application of host state provisions as they would apply to an EEA firm which qualifies for authorisation.[1] They can also make provision as to any change or proposed change of a prescribed kind for EEA firms or the activities which they carry on in the UK and the procedure to be followed in such cases. Finally they can provide that the FSA may treat an EEA firm's notification that it is to cease carrying on regulated activities in the UK as a request to cancel its qualification for authorisation under Sch 3 (Sch 3, para 17).[2]

[1]   The Financial Services and Markets Act 2000 (EEA Passport Rights) Regulations 2001, SI 2001/2511, regs 4–7, 10.
[2]   See also SI 2001/2511, reg 8.

GIVING UP RIGHT TO AUTHORISATION

4.20   The Treasury may, however, make regulations which provide circumstances under which an EEA firm, which is a financial institution under the Banking Coordination Directive, may have its qualification for authorisation cancelled, and may seek to become an authorised person by applying for a Pt IV permission (Sch 3, para 18).[1]

[1]   See the Financial Services and Markets Act 2000 (EEA Passport Rights) Regulations 2001, SI 2001/2511, reg 9.

4.21   Most of the matters dealt with by the regulations relate to changes in the branch or services. The exception is in the application of the approved persons regime to passporting EEA firms.[1]

[1]   See the Financial Services and Markets Act 2000 (EEA Passport Rights) Regulations 2001, SI 2001/2511, reg 10.

4.22   An EEA firm (other than an insurance firm) exercising rights to establish a branch in the UK may not change the 'requisite details'[1] of the branch without complying with the 'relevant requirements' (reg 4(1)), but having done so its permission is treated as varied accordingly (reg 4(2)). The 'relevant requirements' are notification to both the FSA and the firm's home state regulator of the proposed changes, confirmation from the latter to the FSA, and that the firm has been informed by the FSA that it may make the changes, or one month has elapsed from the day on which the firm gave the FSA notice of the proposed changes (reg 4(4)). These are varied if the change has resulted from circumstances outside the firm's control so that the firm is obliged only to notify the FSA and its home state regulator of the relevant changes (reg 4(3), (5)). The FSA is obliged to notify the firm as soon as practicable after being notified of any changes to the 'applicable provisions' (reg 4(6)).[2]

[1]   Defined in the Financial Services and Markets Act 2000 (EEA Passport Rights) Regulations 2001, SI 2001/2511, reg 1 as particulars of the programme of operations for the branch (including a description of the activities being conducted under its passporting rights), the structural organisation of the branch, the branch address and the names of the managers of the business.
[2]   See para 4.11, fn 1.

4.23   For insurance firms the provisions are similar. The matters which may not be changed without complying with the 'relevant requirements' are all of those specified in the consent notice (regs 6(1) and 2(5)(a)–(c)). The 'relevant requirements' for insurance firms are notifications to the FSA and the home state regulator, confirmation from the home state regulator to the FSA, at least one month having elapsed since the firm gave notice to the FSA, and a further month having elapsed or the FSA having informed the home state regulator of any consequential changes in the 'applicable provisions' (reg 6(4)).[1] As with other EEA passporting firms the requirements are to notify the FSA and its home state regulator of the changes if they result from circumstances beyond the firm's control (reg 6(3), (5)).

[1]   Under reg 6(6), the FSA must do this as soon as practicable in any event, and must also acknowledge receipt of documents sent to it under the regulation.

4.24   Equivalent sorts of notification requirements are imposed before a passporting firm may change the services which it provides under the relevant EEA rights (regs 5, 7).

Treaty firms

4.25   Where a Treaty firm[1] ceases to qualify for authorisation because its home state authorisation has been withdrawn, the FSA may give a direction cancelling its Sch 4 authorisation, at the request of the Treaty firm (s 35(1), (2)). However, if the Treaty firm holds a Pt IV permission, it will not cease to be an authorised person merely because it no longer qualifies for authorisation under Sch 4 (s 35(3).[2]

---

[1]   A 'Treaty firm' means a person whose head office is situated in an EEA state other than the UK and which is recognised under the law of that State as its national (Sch 4, para 1).
[2]   See also para 4.7.

Treaty firms: qualifying for authorisation

4.26   Under s 31(1)(c), a Treaty firm qualifies for authorisation to carry on a regulated activity in the UK if it satisfies certain conditions (Sch 4, para 2).

EXERCISE OF TREATY RIGHTS

4.27   Those conditions are that the firm does not have an EEA right[1] to carry on those activities[2] and it has received authorisation[3] under the law of its home state to carry on the regulated activity.[4] In addition the relevant provisions of the home state must afford equivalent protection or satisfy the conditions laid down in a Community instrument for the co-ordination or approximation of laws, regulations or administrative provisions of member States in relation to carrying on that activity (Sch 4, para 3(1)). A Treaty firm will not, however, be deemed to have home state authorisation unless the home state regulator has notified the FSA to that effect in writing (Sch 4, para 3(2)).

---

[1]   See para 4.7, fn 2.
[2]   Either as a branch or by the provision of services on a cross-border basis.
[3]   Defined as 'home state authorisation' (Sch 4, para 3(1)(a)).
[4]   Defined as 'permitted activity' (Sch 4, para 3(1)(a)).

'EQUIVALENT PROTECTION'

4.28   'Equivalent protection', in relation to the firm's 'permitted activity', is provided by provisions which afford consumers protection at least equivalent to that which is afforded by or under FSMA 2000 for that activity (Sch 4, para 3(3)). The Treasury may issue a certificate stating that the law of a particular EEA state affords equivalent protection and this would be conclusive evidence of that fact (Sch 4, para 3(4)).

THRESHOLD CONDITIONS

4.29   A Treaty firm may also have to satisfy certain provisions of the threshold conditions set out in FSMA 2000, Sch 6, paras 1, 3–5 in relation to an application for additional permission or the exercise of the FSA's powers under s 45 to vary that permission (Sch 6, para 7).[1]

------

[1]   See paras 4.74, 4.76–4.79.

PERMISSION

4.30   A Treaty firm which has qualified for authorisation under Sch 4 has permission to carry on each permitted activity in the UK either through a branch or by providing services in the UK (Sch 4, para 4(1)). This permission is treated as being on terms which are equivalent to those imposed by virtue of its home state authorisation (Sch 4, para 4(2)).

4.31   However, if, on qualifying under Sch 4, the Treaty firm has a Pt IV permission for any permitted activity, the FSA must[1] give a direction cancelling the permission so far as it relates to that activity (Sch 4, para 4(3)).

------

[1]   The FSA is not, however, required to give a direction if it considers that there are good reasons for not doing so although the reasons are not elaborated (Sch 4, para 4(4)). Presumably the same considerations will apply as for ss 44(5) and 45(4).

NOTICE TO FSA

4.32   If a Treaty firm qualifies for authorisation but is not already carrying on regulated activities in the UK for which it has permission, it must, at least seven days before it starts to carry on those regulated activities, give the FSA a written notice of its intention to do so (Sch 4, para 5(1), (2)).[1] This notice[2] must be in such form and contain or be accompanied by such information as the FSA may direct (s 51(3)). It must also contain a statement of the regulated activity or activities which the Treaty firm proposes to carry on and for which it wishes to have permission and give the address of the place in the UK for service of any notice or other document which may be required to be served on it by or under FSMA 2000 (s 51(1)). The FSA may also require the Treaty firm to provide such other information as it may direct, or may require it to verify the information (s 51(6)).

------

[1]   See the Financial Services and Markets Act 2000 (EEA Passport Rights) Regulations 2001, SI 2001/2511. See also transitional provisions under the Financial Services and Markets Act 2000 (Consequential and Transitional Provisions) (Miscellaneous) (No 2) Order 2001, SI 2001/2659, art 3.
[2]   Section 51(1), (3) and (6) applies to a notice given by a Treaty firm as it applies to an application for a Pt IV permission (Sch 4, para 5(4)).

4.33   If the Treaty firm has already given notice under Sch 4, para 5(2) and it again qualifies for authorisation, it is not required to give notice again (Sch 4, para 5(3)).

OFFENCES UNDER SCH 4

4.34   A Treaty firm which contravenes Sch 4, para 5(2)[1] will be guilty of an offence (Sch 4, para 6(1)). It will, however, be a defence for that firm to show that it took all reasonable precautions and exercised all due diligence to avoid committing the offence (Sch 4, para 6(2)).

---

[1]   See para 4.32.

4.35   A person[1] who provides a notice under Sch 4, para 5(2) and in doing so provides information which he knows to be false or misleading in any material particular or recklessly provides information which is false or misleading in any material particular is also guilty of an offence (Sch 4, para 6(3)). On summary conviction, a person who is found guilty of either of the offences under Sch 4, para 6 may be liable to a fine not exceeding the statutory maximum or, on conviction on indictment, to a fine (Sch 4, para 6(4)).

---

[1]   A 'person' includes those persons who may commit offences under FSMA 2000, s 400 (offences by bodies corporate etc).

Persons automatically authorised under Sch 5, para 1(1)

4.36   Section 36 enables the FSA to cancel the automatic authorisation under Sch 5, para 1(1) of managers and depositaries of UCITS schemes at their request. The operator,[1] trustee[2] or depositary[3] of a collective investment scheme recognised by virtue of s 264 is deemed to be an authorised person (Sch 5, para 1(1), (2)). An authorised OEIC is also an authorised person by virtue of Sch 5 (Sch 5, para 1(3)).

---

[1]   In a unit trust scheme with a separate trustee, the 'operator' means the manager (s 237(2)).
[2]   In a unit trust scheme, the 'trustee' means the person holding the property in question on trust for the participants (s 237(2)).
[3]   In any other collective investment scheme which is not a unit trust scheme, the 'depositary' means a person to whom the property subject to the scheme is entrusted for safekeeping (s 237(2)).

4.37   An operator, trustee or depositary of a CIS scheme to which Sch 5 applies has permission to carry on any activity of the kind described in Sch 2, para 8,[1] which is appropriate to the capacity in which he acts in relation to the scheme, and any activity in connection with, or for the purposes of, the scheme to the extent that these are regulated activities (Sch 5, para 2(1)).

1   Namely the regulated activity of establishing, operating or winding up a collective investment scheme, including acting as trustee of a unit trust scheme, a depositary of a collective investment scheme other than a unit trust scheme or as sole director of a body incorporated by virtue of the regulations made under s 262.

4.38   An authorised OEIC has permission to carry on the operation of the scheme and any activity in connection with, or for the purposes of, the operation of the scheme to the extent that it is a regulated activity (Sch 5, para 2(2)).

4.39   A person who is authorised as a result of Sch 5, para 1(1) may ask the FSA to give a direction cancelling its authorisation (s 36(1)). If such a person also holds a Pt IV permission, he will not, however, cease to be an authorised person because the authorisation under Sch 5 has been cancelled (s 36(2)).

OUTWARD PASSPORT RIGHTS OF UK FIRMS

4.40   UK firms[1] may exercise their EEA rights (outward passporting) in accordance with the provisions in Sch 3, Pt III (s 37).[2]

1   A 'UK firm' is a firm whose head office is in the UK and which has an EEA right (see para 4.7, fn 2) to carry on activities in an EEA State other than the UK.
2   The relevant provisions in the FSA Handbook are contained in the Supervision manual, SUP 13.

Establishment

4.41   A UK firm may not exercise an EEA right to establish a branch in another EEA jurisdiction unless it meets three conditions (Sch 3, para 19(1)), as follows—
  — it must give the FSA notice of its intention to establish such a branch and that notice must identify the activities which it intends to carry on through that branch[1] and include any other information which the FSA may require through rules which it makes for this purpose (Sch 3, para 19(2));[2]
  — the FSA must give a consent notice in specified terms[3] to the host state regulator[4] (Sch 3, para 19(4));
  — the host state regulator must have given notice either to the firm or, in the case of passport rights under the insurance

directives, to the FSA,[5] of the applicable provisions,[6] or two months must have elapsed from the date on which the FSA gave the consent notice (Sch 3, para 19(5)).

---

[1]   This may include activities which are not 'regulated activities' (Sch 3, para 19(3)), and UK firms do not need to be authorised persons to exercise EEA passport rights. For example, a firm holding a licence under CCA 1974 (which is not a 'regulated activity') may have an EEA right to carry on Consumer Credit Act business in another EEA state: see FSMA Explanatory Notes, para 90. By the Financial Services and Markets Act 2000 (EEA Passport Rights) Regulations 2001, SI 2001/2511, reg 19, if the notice of intention identifies an activity which is not a regulated activity and the firm can carry it on in the EEA State in question without contravening any UK law, the firm is to be treated (for the purposes of its EEA rights) as authorised to carry on the activity.

[2]   Rules may specify the procedures which are to be followed in exercising its functions under Sch 3, para 19 (Sch 3, para 19(10)). The relevant provisions are set out in the FSA Handbook, Supervision manual, SUP 13.5.

[3]   The FSA must also inform the firm in writing that it has given a consent notice (Sch 3, para 19(11)): see the FSA Handbook, Supervision manual, SUP 13.3.6G.

[4]   'Host state regulator' is defined in Sch 3, para 11 as the competent authority (within the meaning of the relevant single market directive) of an EEA State other than the UK in relation to a UK firm's exercise of EEA rights there.

[5]   If, in relation to the exercise of any passport rights under the insurance directives, the FSA receives notification from the home state regulator of the applicable provisions, it must notify the firm of those provisions (Sch 3, para 19(9)).

[6]   For the purposes of Sch 3 the 'applicable provisions' are those host state rules, ie, the rules made in accordance with the relevant single market directive and which are the responsibility of the EEA State to implement and supervise compliance with, which the firm must comply with when carrying on passported business through the proposed branch (Sch 3, para 19(13), (14)).

4.42   If the passport rights which the firm intends to exercise are those which it has under the Investment Services Directive or the Banking Consolidation Directive[1] and the firm has provided the requisite notice under Sch 3, para 19(2), the FSA must give a consent notice to the host state regulator unless it has reason to doubt that the firm's financial resources or administrative structure are adequate (Sch 3, para 19(6)).

---

[1]   Schedule 3, para 19(6) is amended by the Banking Consolidation Directive (Consequential Amendment) Regulations 2000, SI 2000/2952.

4.43   If the passport rights which the firm intends to exercise derive from any of the insurance directives and the firm has provided the required notice under Sch 3, para 19(2), the FSA must give a consent notice unless it has reason to doubt the adequacy of the firm's resources or its administrative structure, or otherwise question the reputation, qualifications or experience of the directors or managers of the firm or the person proposed as the authorised agent of the branch for the purposes of those directives in relation to the business to be conducted through the proposed branch (Sch 3, para 19(7)).

4.44   If in either case the FSA proposes not to give a consent notice, it must give the firm a warning notice (Sch 3, para 19(8)).

4.45   If the FSA decides to refuse to give a consent notice, it must do so within three months of receiving the firm's notice of its intention to exercise its passport rights and it must give the firm a decision notice. The firm has the right to refer the matter to the Tribunal (Sch 3, para 19(12)).

Services

4.46   If a UK firm intends to exercise its passport rights under Sch 3, Pt III to provide services in another EEA state, it must give the FSA notice of its intention to provide those services. This notice must specify the activities which it is proposing to carry on in that state by way of the provision of services[1] and must include such other information as the FSA may specify in rules which it may make for this purpose (Sch 3, para 20(1)).

---

[1]   This notice of intent may include activities which are not regulated activities (Sch 3, para 20(2)).

4.47   If the UK firm's passport rights derive from either the banking consolidation directive[1] or the investment services directive, the FSA must send a copy of this notice of intent to the home state regulator within one month of receiving it from the firm (Sch 3, para 20(3)) and it must provide the firm with written notice that it has sent a copy to the home state regulator (Sch 3, para 20(4)).[2]

---

[1]   Schedule 3, para 20(3) is amended by the Banking Consolidation Directive (Consequential Amendments) Regulations 2000, SI 2000/2952.
[2]   Schedule 3, para 20(5) was deleted by virtue of the Financial Services (EEA Passport Rights) Regulations 2001, SI 2001/1376.

4.48   If the UK firm's passport rights derive from one of the insurance directives, within a month of receiving the notice of intent, the FSA must either send a notice in specified form to the relevant host state regulator (a consent notice) or give written notice to the firm of its refusal to do so together with its reasons for the refusal (Sch 3, para 20(3A)).[1] If the FSA gives a consent notice, it must give written notice that it has done so to the firm (Sch 3, para 20(4)). However, the firm may not provide the services covered by the notice of intent until it has received written notice of the consent notice (Sch 3, para (4B)). If the FSA notifies the firm of its refusal to give a consent notice, the firm may refer the matter to the Tribunal (Sch 3, para 20(4A)).

---

[1]   The Financial Services (EEA Passport Rights) Regulations 2001, SI 2001/1376, reg 2 amended Sch 3, para 20 by inserting para 20(3A), (4A), (4B) and (4C). Those regulations also amended para 20(4) to cover consent notices.

Offences in relation to outwardly passported business

4.49   If a firm which is not an authorised person breaches the notification requirements in Sch 3, Pt III, paras 19, 20, it will be guilty of an offence and on summary conviction, may be liable to a fine not exceeding the statutory maximum, or, on conviction on indictment to a fine. It will, however, be a defence if that firm can show that it took all reasonable precautions and exercised all due diligence to avoid committing this offence (Sch 3, para 21).

Continuing regulation of UK firms

4.50   The Treasury may make regulations in relation to a UK firm's exercise of outwardly passported EEA rights and may provide further for the application or modification or both application and modification of FSMA 2000 and any provision made under it in relation to the activities of a UK firm (Sch 3, para 22(1)). In particular, these regulations may provide for any change (or proposed change) of a prescribed kind relating to a UK firm or the type of activities which it proposes to carry on (whether through a branch or on a services basis) and the procedures with which a UK firm will have to comply (Sch 3, para 22(2)). Where such a change or proposed change requires the FSA's consent, it may only refuse consent on grounds prescribed in regulations and if the FSA decides to refuse consent, the firm may refer the matter to the Tribunal (Sch 3, para 22(3)).

4.51   The Financial Services and Markets Act 2000 (EEA Passport Rights) Regulations 2001, Pt III (regs 11–18)[1] contains the regulations made for these purposes. The changes to branches and services covered are similar to those relevant to incoming EEA firms.[2] For changes, the processes prescribed by the regulations are broadly the same as those set out for the initial exercise of the passport rights under Sch 3, Pt III. A UK firm may not carry out the change until the requirements imposed by the regulations have been complied with (a breach of this is an offence punishable by fine, unless the firm can show that it took all reasonable precautions and exercised all due diligence to avoid it (reg 18). This requires consent from the FSA for changes to branch details or to insurance services, and notice only for services under the Investment Services Directive. The grounds on which it may refuse consent are the same as under Sch 3, para 20, and if it does refuse, the firm is given the right to refer the matter to the Tribunal.

---

[1]   SI 2001/2511.
[2]   See paras 4.19, 4.21–4.24.

4.52   In relation to a firm which has a Pt IV permission and is exercising outwardly passported EEA rights in relation to carrying on Consumer

Credit Act business in another EEA State, the FSA may exercise its power under FSMA 2000, s 45[1] if it has been informed by the Director General of Fair Trading that the firm or any of its employees, agents or associates or, if the firm is a body corporate, any controller of the firm or associate of such a controller has breached any provision in CCA 1974, s 25(2)(a)–(d) (Sch 3, para 23(1), (2)).

---

[1]   Variation of a Pt IV permission on the FSA's own initiative.

4.53   In relation to a firm which is not required to have a Pt IV permission for the business which it is carrying on but is exercising its outwardly passported rights under Art 19 of the Banking Consolidation Directive[1] to carry on those activities in another EEA state, the FSA must, if it is requested by the home state regulator of that jurisdiction, impose any requirement which it could impose if the firm had a Pt IV permission and the FSA was entitled to exercise its power under s 45 to vary that permission (Sch 3, para 24).[2]

---

[1]   Sch 3, para 24(1)(b) is amended by the Banking Consolidation Directive (Consequential Amendment) Regulations 2000, SI 2000/2952.
[2]   See paras 4.84–4.86.

EXEMPTION

Exemption orders

4.54   A person will not be in breach of the general prohibition under s 19(1) if he is 'exempt' (s 19(1)(b)). This means that he falls within one of the exemptions provided for in FSMA 2000 (for example, appointed representatives under s 39 and recognised investment exchanges under s 285(2)) or in an order made under s 38(1). The Treasury has powers to make orders ('exemption orders') to provide that either specified persons or persons falling within a particular class are exempt from the general prohibition (s 38(1)).

4.55   An exemption order made under s 38 may provide for an exemption—
— for all regulated activities;
— for one or more specific regulated activities;
— only in certain circumstances;
— for certain specified functions of that person; or
— subject to conditions (s 38(3), (4)).[1]

1 Exemptions are granted under the Financial Services and Markets Act 2000 (Exemption) Order 2001, SI 2001/1201 and the Financial Services and Markets Act 2000 (Exemption) (Amendment) Order 2001, SI 2001/3623. The exemptions relate to local or national governmental bodies and certain public and multinational organisations as well as to the new electricity trading arrangements.

4.56 A person who holds a Pt IV permission may not, however, be an exempt person under an exemption order (s 38(2)).[1]

1 However, if that person then ceases to hold a Pt IV permission and the exemption from which they formerly benefited is still extant, they may benefit from it again: see FSMA Explanatory Notes, para 92.

Appointed representatives

4.57 'Appointed representatives' are a specific category of exempt persons which has been carried over from the Financial Services Act 1986 (FSA 1986) regime. Section 39(2) defines an 'appointed representative' as a person who is not an authorised person[1] and is a party to a contract with an authorised person who has accepted responsibility for his activities in writing. That contract must permit or require that person to carry on a prescribed description of business and comply with the prescribed requirements (s 39(1), (2)).[2] An appointed representative is exempt from the general prohibition in s 19(1) in relation to any regulated activity comprised in the carrying on of that business for which his principal has accepted responsibility (s 39(1)).[3]

1 Including both those persons who have authorisation by virtue of s 31 and those who have permission under FSMA 2000, Pt IV (see s 31(2)). Therefore, a bank or building society which has Pt IV permissions for its regulated activities in accepting deposits may not be an exempt person (for example, an appointed representative under s 39) but must maintain permissions appropriate to cover the whole of its regulated activities under Pt IV.
2 See para 4.58.
3 Therefore, any regulated activities which are carried on by the appointed representative in accordance with such an arrangement are the responsibility of the principal, who must therefore have permission in its own right for all the regulated activities its appointed representative carries on: see FSMA Explanatory Notes, para 94.

4.58 The Treasury has made regulations[1] specifying the type of business which the appointed representative may carry on. These regulations replace the similar provisions of FSA 1986, s 44. That section had the effect of limiting the scope of the investment business which an appointed representative could carry out in its capacity as an exempt person. The order made by the Treasury has broadly the same scope as the provision in FSA 1986 (ie, arranging and advisory activities), but not where this would be within the scope of the Investment Services Directive.[2] In addition, the Treasury has prescribed conditions which the contract between the principal and the appointed representative must meet.[3] This broadly reproduces the detailed requirements in FSA 1986, s 44(4), (5).[4]

---

[1]   The Financial Services and Markets Act 2000 (Appointed Representatives) Regulations 2001, SI 2001/1217, as amended by SI 2001/2508.
[2]   See SI 2001/1217, reg 2(2).
[3]   See the Financial Services and Markets Act 2000 (Appointed Representatives) Regulations 2001, SI 2001/1217, reg 3.
[4]   FSMA Explanatory Notes, paras 95, 96.

4.59   The principal of an appointed representative is, however, responsible for the acts and omissions of that appointed representative, for any business for which the authorised person has accepted responsibility, as if they were his own acts and omissions (s 39(3)–(5)). The FSA may take regulatory action against the principal for anything said or done (or not said or not done) by the representative in carrying on the regulated activities as if they had expressly authorised the action or inaction in question. However, nothing in s 39 would cause the knowledge or intentions of the appointed representative to be attributed to the principal or make the principal liable to prosecution for a criminal offence in place of the representative (s 39(6)). The representative may also be subject to the arrangements under Pt V concerning approved persons.[1]

---

[1]   FSMA Explanatory Notes, para 94.

PERMISSIONS REGIME

4.60   The main route for persons to obtain authorisation to conduct regulated activities is through obtaining permission under FSMA 2000, Pt IV. However, the right to apply for permission is restricted to certain classes of persons and those persons must meet the threshold conditions set out in FSMA 2000, Sch 6.

Application for permission

4.61   Under s 40(1), the following persons can become authorised by applying to the FSA for permission to carry on one or more regulated activities—
    —   an individual;
    —   a body corporate;
    —   a partnership;
    —   an unincorporated association.

An authorised person cannot apply to the FSA for permission under s 40(1) if he already has a permission which is in force and was given to him by the FSA under Pt IV or has effect as if so given (s 40(2)). This is referred to as 'a Pt IV permission' (s 40(4)).

4.62   In particular, an EEA firm cannot apply under s 40(1) for permission to carry on a regulated activity which it is or would be entitled to carry on in the UK in exercise of an EEA right, whether through the establishment of a branch in the UK or by providing services in the UK.[1]

---

[1]   See also FSMA Explanatory Notes, para 97.

PERMISSION

Giving permission

4.63   After receiving an application for permission, the FSA must consider it in the light of its duty under s 41.[1] The FSA has the discretion to decide to give permission to the applicant for all regulated activities for which he is applying or only for some of them (s 42(2)).[2] Where it gives permission, the FSA must specify the permitted regulated activity or activities, described in the manner which it considers most appropriate (s 42(6)).[3]

---

[1]   See paras 4.70–4.73.
[2]   FSMA Explanatory Notes, para 101.
[3]   It appears that the discretion granted to the FSA by FSMA 2000 would enable the FSA to have standard types of permission to be granted. However, the Act imposes no requirement on the FSA to act in this way: FSMA Explanatory Notes, para 102. In fact, the FSA has generally described the activities in the same way as the regulated activities are specified in the Financial Services and Markets Act 2000 (Regulated Activities) Order 2001, SI 2001/544, but has sub-divided some activities: see the FSA Handbook, Authorisation manual, AUTH 3.4.

4.64   If a person has applied for permission for a regulated activity, but is exempt in relation to another activity by virtue of s 39(1) or an order under s 38(1), the FSA is to treat the application as relating to all regulated activities which the person will carry on if the permission is granted (s 42(3)).

4.65   In contrast, the application is to be treated as relating only to the activity applied for if the applicant—
   —   is exempt in relation to other regulated activities by virtue of section 285(2) or (3) as a recognised investment exchange (s 42(4)); or
   —   is a person to whom, for a specific regulated activity, the general prohibition does not apply as a result of Pt XIX concerning Lloyd's (s 42(5)).

4.66   The FSA has discretion to frame the granted permission in a manner which renders the scope or description of the regulated activities different from that included in the application.[1] It may impose limitations on the regulated activity described (for example, as to circumstances in which the activity may or may not be carried out) (s 42(7)(a)), specify a narrower or wider scope of the activity described than that proposed by the applicant (s 42(7)(b)), or give permission to carry on a regulated activity which is not included among those to which the application relates (s 42(7)(c)).

---

[1]   FSMA Explanatory Notes, para 102.

Imposition of requirements

4.67   A permission granted under Pt IV can include requirements which the FSA considers appropriate, such as the requirement for an authorised person to take or refrain from taking specific action (s 43(1), (2)).[1] The requirement can extend to activities carried on by the authorised person which are not regulated activities (s 43(3)) and a requirement can be imposed by reference to the person's relationship with his group or other members of his group (s 43(4)).[2]

---

[1]   For example, the FSA might impose a limit on the amount of a certain type of business the person may conduct during the first five years after receiving the permission: FSMA Explanatory Notes, para 104.
[2]   In determining the scope of a permission the FSA might have concerns about the way in which a regulated activity might be carried on in conjunction with an unregulated activity that the person already carries on, or which he proposes to carry on: FSMA Explanatory Notes, para 105.

4.68   A requirement may be imposed in relation to an unregulated activity if, for example, the FSA considers that the manner in which the unregulated activity would be carried on in conjunction with the regulated one could pose a threat to the interests of consumers. Therefore, the FSA could limit the way in which the unregulated activity was carried on for a period after the new permission was granted to enable it to observe how the activities were carried on, or related to each other, in practice. In determining any limitations under this section, s 43(4) enables the FSA to take account of the person's membership of a wider group as defined in s 421.[1]

---

[1]   FSMA Explanatory Notes, para 105.

4.69   The FSA may specify in the permission the period during which the requirement has effect but this section does not affect the FSA's powers to vary or cancel a Pt IV permission under s 44 or 45 (s 43(5), (6)).

Threshold conditions for permissions

4.70   In giving or varying a permission, the FSA must ensure that the person satisfies, and will continue to satisfy, the threshold conditions specified in Sch 6 for all the regulated activities which he will or will have permission to carry on (s 41(1), (2)).

4.71   However this obligation does not prevent the FSA from taking action which it considers necessary to protect consumers (s 41(3)).

4.72   FSMA 2000, s 41(1) refers to the 'threshold conditions' relating to a regulated activity as the conditions which are set out in Sch 6.[1] These conditions must be satisfied by the person who holds a Pt IV permission for all the regulated activities for which this person has or will have permission. The Explanatory Notes make it clear, however, that failure to meet one of the conditions may be sufficient grounds for refusal to grant permission or for granting permission for a narrower range or definition of regulated activities than sought by the applicant. In addition, the Notes state that the fact that an applicant satisfies all the applicable conditions in Sch 6 does not confer any automatic right to permission and that the FSA retains some discretion to refuse an application even where all these conditions are satisfied.[2]

---

[1]   The Treasury has power to add to, vary or remove any of these conditions (Sch 6, para 9).
[2]   FSMA Explanatory Notes, para 800.

4.73   These threshold conditions must also be met on an ongoing basis by authorised persons. The failure of a person with a Pt IV permission to meet one of the conditions will be grounds for the FSA to exercise its power under s 45 to vary an authorised person's permission or to use its powers to withdraw an authorised person's authorisation under s 33.[1]

---

[1]   FSMA Explanatory Notes, para 801.

The conditions

4.74   *Legal status*—If the person holding the Pt IV permission is effecting or carrying out contracts of insurance that person must be a body corporate (other than a UK limited liability partnership), a registered friendly society or a member of Lloyd's (Sch 6, para 1(1)).[1] Any person carrying out the regulated activity of accepting deposits or issuing electronic money must be a body corporate or a partnership (Sch 6, para 1(2)).[2]

¹ Para 1(1), as amended by the Financial Services and Markets Act 2000 (Variation of Threshold Conditions) Order 2001, SI 2001/2507, art 2.
² Para 1(2), as amended by the Financial Services and Markets Act 2000 (Regulated Activities) (Amendment) Order 2002, SI 2002/682, art 8.

4.75   *Location of offices*—Schedule 6, para 2 provides that if the authorised person is a body corporate constituted under the law of any part of the UK, its head office and, if it has a registered office, that office, must be in the UK. If the authorised person is not a body corporate, and has its head office in the UK, it must carry on business in the UK.

4.76   *Close links*—If an authorised person or an applicant for a Pt IV permission ('the person concerned') has 'close links' with another person, the FSA must be satisfied that those close links are not likely to prevent the FSA's effective supervision of the person concerned.[1] Equally, if the person with close links to the person concerned is subject to the laws, regulations and administrative procedures of a jurisdiction which is not an EEA state, the FSA must be satisfied that those do not prevent effective supervision of the person concerned (Sch 6, para 3(1)).

¹ See European Parliament and Council Directive 95/26/EC (post-BCCI Directive). This condition has been repealed for Swiss general insurance companies by virtue of the Financial Services and Markets Act 2000 (Variation of Threshold Conditions) Order 2001, SI 2001/2507, art 3(3).

4.77   For these purposes a party has 'close links' with an authorised person or an applicant for permission if that party is—
   —   a parent undertaking of the authorised person or applicant for permission;
   —   a subsidiary undertaking[1] of that person;
   —   a parent undertaking of a subsidiary undertaking of that person;
   —   a subsidiary undertaking of a parent undertaking of that person; or
   —   the owner or controller of 20% or more of the voting rights or capital of that person;

or if the authorised person owns or controls 20% or more of the voting rights or capital of that party (Sch 6, para 3(2)).

¹ 'Subsidiary undertaking' has the meaning given to it in the Seventh Company Law Directive, Art 1(1), (2) (Sch 6, para 3(3)).

4.78   *Adequate resources*—The authorised person or applicant for permission[1] must have adequate resources for the regulated activities that he carries on or seeks to carry on (Sch 6, para 4(1)). In determining this, the FSA may take into account not only that person but the other members of that person's group, in particular, the provision which he or they make for liabilities (including contingent and future liabilities) and the means by which he or they manage the risk connected with his business (Sch 6, para 4(2)).

---

1 This condition has been repealed for Swiss general insurance companies by virtue of the Financial Services and Markets Act 2000 (Variation of Threshold Conditions) Order 2001, SI 2001/2507, art 3(3).

4.79 *Suitability*—A person who is an authorised person or an applicant for permission must satisfy the FSA that he is a fit and proper person having regard to all of the circumstances including his connection with any other person, the nature of any regulated activity which he carries on or seeks to carry on, and the need to ensure that his business is carried on soundly and prudently (Sch 6, para 5).[1]

---

1 This condition has been repealed for Swiss general insurance companies by virtue of the Financial Services and Markets Act 2000 (Variation of Threshold Conditions) Order 2001, SI 2001/2507, art 3(3).

4.80 *Additional conditions*—If a person has his head office outside the EEA and it appears to the FSA that he will be carrying on regulated activities relating to insurance business, he must satisfy specified conditions which the Treasury may make by order (Sch 6, para 8).[1]

---

1 See the Financial Services and Markets Act 2000 (Variation of Threshold Conditions) Order 2001, SI 2001/2507, art 3.

VARIATIONS AND CANCELLATION OF PERMISSION

Variation etc at request of authorised person

4.81 An authorised person may apply to the FSA for a variation to (s 44(1)), or cancellation of (s 44(2)), its permission. The FSA may decide to vary a permission by—

— adding or removing a regulated activity;
— varying the description of a regulated activity;
— varying or cancelling a requirement which had been imposed (s 44(1)).

This power is extended to enable the FSA to include in the permission any provision it could include in a wholly new permission granted in response to an application under s 40 (s 44(5)). It therefore appears that the FSA has power to impose a new requirement on the application of a firm, even though it is not expressly listed in s 44(1).

4.82   If the FSA considers that the person meets the threshold conditions for the permission resulting from the variation, it can give the variation (s 44(1)). However, it may refuse to do so if it believes that the interests of consumers or potential consumers are to be adversely affected by the resulting permission and it is therefore desirable to refuse it (s 44(3)).

4.83   If as a result of the variation of a Pt IV permission the authorised person no longer has permission to carry on any regulated activity, the FSA must cancel the Pt IV permission once it is satisfied that it is no longer necessary to keep it in force (s 44(4)). This would equate with the categories of 'former authorised institutions' under the 'FSA's Guide to Banking Supervision' where certain persons whose banking business had ceased, but who might need to maintain a deposit-taking licence until such time as all deposits had been repaid or transferred to another deposit taker. However, once a permission was no longer required, the FSA could cancel it and that person would cease to be an authorised person.

Variation etc on FSA's own initiative

4.84   The terms of a permission can also be varied or the permission cancelled at the initiative of the FSA (s 45(2)). This 'own-initiative power' (defined as such in s 45(5)) can be exercised if it appears to the FSA that—
   — the person is failing or is likely to fail to satisfy the threshold conditions;
   — the person has not used the Pt IV permission to carry on a specific regulated activity for at least one year;
   — it is desirable to exercise this power to protect the interests of consumers or potential consumers (s 45(1)).

4.85   If the variation of a Pt IV permission under s 45 results in the authorised person not having permission to carry on any regulated activities, and the FSA considers that it is not necessary for his permission to be kept in force, it must cancel it (s 45(3)).

4.86   The power to vary a Pt IV permission under s 45 again includes the power to make any provisions which the FSA could otherwise have made if the variation had been an application for permission, including the incorporation of new requirements (s 45(2), (4)).[1]

---

[1]   See paras 4.67–4.69.

Exercise of own-initiative powers: procedure

4.87   Where the FSA has decided to exercise its own-initiative powers, the FSA must give the authorised person a written notice setting out the details of the variation and when it is to take effect. The notice must also state the FSA's reasons for the variation and for its determination as to when the variation is to take effect. It must also inform the authorised person of his right to refer the matter to the Tribunal. Authorised persons may also make representations to the FSA within the period specified in the notice (whether or not they have referred the matter to the Tribunal) (s 53(4), (5)). If the notice informs the authorised person that he may refer the matter to the Tribunal it must indicate the procedures for doing so (s 53(11)).

4.88   A variation made to an authorised person's Pt IV permission under the FSA's own-initiative powers takes effect immediately (if the notice states that that is the case), on a date to be specified in the notice or, if no date is specified, when the matter is no longer open to review (s 53(2)). A variation may only be expressed to take effect immediately (or on a particular date) if the FSA considers it reasonably necessary to do so (s 53(3)).

Variation due to changes in control

4.89   Section 46 applies if a person has acquired control over a UK authorised person[1] who has a Pt IV permission but there are no grounds for the FSA to exercise its own-initiative power (s 46(1)). Section 46(2) provides that if the FSA considers the likely effect of such acquisition to be uncertain, it may vary that person's permission by imposing a s 43 requirement or varying a requirement already included in the person's permission under s 43.

---

[1]   See para 4.122.

Own-initiative variation in support of an overseas regulator

4.90   The FSA's own-initiative power to vary a permission may be exercised in support of, or at the request of, an overseas regulator if the regulator is one of a kind prescribed in regulations made by the Treasury (s 47(1)).[1]

---

[1]   The Financial Services and Markets Act 2000 (Own-initiative Power) (Overseas Regulators) Regulations 2001, SI 2001/2639, reg 2 prescribes overseas regulators whose functions correspond to any of those of the FSA under FSMA 2000 (including listing) as well as company law regulations and those investigating insider dealing offences.

4.91   If such an overseas regulator is acting in accordance with or pursuant to provisions which may be prescribed in regulations made by the Treasury,[1] the FSA must, in deciding whether to use its own-initiative power, consider whether it is necessary to do so to comply with a Community obligation (s 47(3)). If the FSA determines that this is not the case, it may take into account a number of factors including—
—   whether the country or territory would give corresponding assistance to a UK regulatory authority;
—   whether the breach or requirement in support of which the overseas regulator is requesting assistance has no close parallel in the UK or would involve the assertion of jurisdiction in an area which the UK would not recognise;
—   what the seriousness of the case and its impact on persons in the UK would be; and
—   whether it is appropriate as a matter of public interest to give the assistance requested (s 47(4)).

---

[1]   The Financial Services and Markets Act 2000 (Own-initiative Power) (Overseas Regulators) Regulations 2001, SI 2001/2639, reg 3 prescribes EEA regulators for any EEA provision (or local implementation) and the relevant supervisory authority in Switzerland for Swiss non-life insurance companies.

4.92   The FSA can exercise its own-initiative power whether or not it has other powers of intervention which can be exercised in relation to incoming firms under Pt XIII (s 47(2)).

4.93   The FSA may decide not to exercise its own-initiative power unless the overseas regulator undertakes to contribute to the costs of that exercise (s 47(5)). The FSA's discretion to so decide does not apply if the FSA considers that the exercise is necessary to comply with a Community obligation (s 47(6)).

CONNECTED PERSONS

4.94   In considering whether to vary, grant or cancel a Pt IV permission, the FSA may take into account any person who is or appears to be in a relationship with the applicant or the authorised person which is relevant (s 49(1)). In giving permission to a person who is connected with an EEA firm, or varying or cancelling the permission given to that person by the FSA, the FSA must take steps to consult the EEA firm's home state regulator (s 49(2)). A firm will be deemed to be 'connected with' an EEA firm if it is a subsidiary undertaking of the firm or if it is a subsidiary undertaking of a parent undertaking of the firm (s 49(3)).[1]

---
[1] 'Subsidiary undertaking' has the meaning given to it in the Seventh Company Law Directive, Art 1(1), (2) (s 420(1), (2)(b)).

4.95   A matter is open to review if the period during which any person may refer the matter to the Tribunal is still running, or if the matter has been referred to the Tribunal but has not been determined, or has been referred to the Tribunal and dealt with but the period for appealing against a determination by the Tribunal is still running, or if such an appeal has been brought against the Tribunal's decision but has not yet been determined (s 391(8), as applied by s 53(12)).

Extension of period for making representations

4.96   The FSA may extend the period for making representations (s 53(6)). If, having considered the representations, it decides to vary the permission as proposed or not to rescind the variation if it has already been made, the FSA must give the authorised person a further written notice (s 53(7)). This must include notice that the matter may be referred to the Tribunal and indicate the procedures for doing so (s 53(9), (11)).

Refusal to vary permission

4.97   If the FSA decides not to vary the permission in the manner proposed, or to vary it in a different way, or to rescind a variation which has already come into effect, it must provide the authorised person with a written notice to that effect (s 53(8)). This notice must comply with s 53(5) (s 58(10)).[1]

---
[1]   See para 4.87.

Additional permissions

4.98   When considering whether to grant or vary or cancel a permission under its own-initiative powers (under s 45) for an EEA firm, a Treaty firm or a person who is authorised by virtue of FSMA 2000, Sch 5, para 1(1), the FSA must take into account the home state authorisation of the authorised person, any relevant directive and the relevant provision of the Treaty constituting the European Community.

Asset requirement

4.99   The FSA has additional supplementary power to impose restrictions on authorised persons under s 48 when it imposes an 'assets requirement', whether on authorisation, on a later application for variation or when using its own-initiative powers (s 48(1)).[1]

---
[1]   See the FSA Handbook, Enforcement manual, ENF 3.2.10G.

4.100   An 'assets requirement' is a requirement under s 43 prohibiting the authorised person from disposing of or otherwise dealing with any of his assets, or restricting such disposal or dealings (s 48(3)(a)), or transferring any or all of his assets, or any assets belonging to consumers but held by him or to his order, to a trustee approved by the FSA (s 48(3)(b)).

4.101   If the FSA imposes an assets requirement and gives a notice to this effect to any institution with whom the authorised person has an account (s 48(4)), the notice has the effect that the institution who receives it will be deemed not to be acting in breach of any contract with the authorised person if that institution had been instructed by the authorised person to pay or transfer any sum or make any payment out of the authorised person's account but because of the notice refuses to do so (s 48(5)(a)). However, if the institution pays or transfers a sum in contravention of a notice given under s 48(4), the institution is liable to the FSA for an amount equal to the amount transferred or the sum paid out of the authorised person's accounts in contravention of the requirements of that notice (s 48(5)(b)).

4.102   If an order has been made to transfer an authorised person's assets to a trustee, the assets held by that trustee may be released or dealt with only with the FSA's consent (s 48(6)). A person who transfers or deals with the authorised person's assets in contravention of the requirements in s 48(6) is guilty of an offence and may be liable on summary conviction to a fine not exceeding level 5 on the standard scale (s 48(9)). Equally, if the assets have been transferred to a trustee and the authorised person creates a charge[1] over any assets of his held by the trustee, the charge (to the extent that it confers security over the assets) will be void against the liquidator or against any of the authorised person's creditors (s 48(7)).

---
[1]   Including a mortgage or, in Scotland, a security over property (s 48(10)).

4.103   Any assets held by a trustee are deemed to be held under s 48(3)(b)[1] only if the authorised person has given the trustee notice that those assets are to be held in accordance with the requirement in s 48(3)(b) or they are assets into which the assets which were held by the trustee have been transposed by the trustee on the authorised person's instructions (s 48(8)).[2]

---

[1]   See para 4.100.

[2]   This is to avoid the constructive trustee problem whereby a trustee holding on behalf of an authorised person could, if he had notice, be considered to be holding for the liquidator and/or beneficiaries/customers of the authorised person.

4.104   Section 48(6) and (8) does not, however, affect any equitable interest or remedy in favour of a person who is a beneficiary of a trust as a result of a requirement to transfer the authorised person's assets to a trustee (s 48(11)).[1]

---

[1]   This section was subject to various transitional provisions under the Financial Services and Markets Act 2000 (Consequential and Transitional Provisions) (Miscellaneous) (No 2) Order 2001, SI 2001/2659, art 3, the Financial Services and Markets Act 2000 (Permission and Applications) (Credit Unions etc) Order 2002, SI 2002/704, art 7(2) and the Financial Services and Markets Act 2000 (Transitional Provisions) (Authorised Persons etc) Order 2001, SI 2001/2636, arts 34(2)(a) and 35(4)(a).

PROCEDURE

The application process

4.105   An application for a Pt IV permission must contain a statement of the regulated activity or activities which the applicant proposes to carry on and provide an address in the UK for the service of notices and documents which are required or authorised to be served on him under FSMA 2000 (s 51(1)).

4.106   An application for variation of a permission must include a statement of the variation which is desired by the authorised person and of the regulated activity or activities which he intends to carry on if the permission is varied (s 51(2)). An application under Pt IV must be made in a manner specified by the FSA and contain or be accompanied by any information which the FSA may reasonably require (s 51(3)).[1]

---

[1]   See the FSA Handbook, Authorisation manual for new applications and the Supervision manual for variation and cancellation applications.

4.107 The FSA may require the applicant to provide additional information to it at any time between the submission of the application and its determination if that information is necessary to enable the FSA to determine the application (s 51(4)). The FSA may require the applicant to provide that information in such form as it requires or to have that information verified in a specified way (s 51(6)). Different directions may be given and different requirements may be applied to different applications (s 51(5)).

Determination of applications

4.108 The FSA must determine any application made under Pt IV within six months of the date on which it received the completed application (s 52(1)).

4.109 The FSA may also determine an incomplete application if it considers it appropriate to do so. If an application is incomplete, the FSA must in any event determine the application, including whether to grant or refuse a Pt IV permission, within twelve months of the date on which it received the original application (s 52(2)).

4.110 An applicant for a Pt IV permission may withdraw that application by giving the FSA written notice at any time before the FSA determines the application in accordance with the procedures in Pt IV (s 52(3)).

Granting of an application

4.111 If the FSA grants an application for a Pt IV permission, it must provide the applicant with written notice of that decision and state the date from which that permission takes effect (s 52(4), (5)).

Refusal of a Pt IV permission

4.112 If the FSA proposes to refuse an application for a Pt IV permission, it must give the applicant a warning notice (s 52(7)). This does not apply if the firm is an EEA firm[1] and the application has been made with a view to the applicant carrying on a regulated activity by exercising an EEA right[2] either through establishing a branch in the UK or by providing services in the UK (s 52(8)).

---

[1]   See para 4.7, fn 1.
[2]   See para 4.7, fn 2.

4.113 If the FSA proposes not to grant the application as made but to give a permission other than as applied for, it must give the applicant a warning notice (s 52(6)). If the FSA decides to refuse an application or to grant it in a narrower form or subject to limitations or requirements, it must give a decision notice (presumably taking account of any representations made in response to the warning notice under the Pt XXVI notice procedure) (s 52(9)).

Variation of a Pt IV permission

4.114 If the FSA decides to give a Pt IV permission but to exercise its powers under s 42(7)(a) or (b)[1] or any requirements under s 43(1) or to vary a Pt IV permission and to exercise its power under any of those provisions (as a result of s 44(5)), it must give the applicant a warning notice (s 52(6)).

------
[1]   See para 4.66.

4.115 If the FSA decides to vary a Pt IV permission, it must provide the applicant with written notice of that decision and state the date on which that variation of the permission takes effect (s 52(4), (5)).

Cancellation of a Pt IV permission

4.116 If the FSA proposes to cancel a Pt IV permission[1] otherwise than on an authorised person's request it must provide the authorised person with a warning notice and comply with the procedures in Pt XXVI (s 54(1)). If the FSA then decides to cancel a Pt IV permission otherwise than at the authorised person's request, it must give that person a decision notice and comply with the procedures set out in Pt XXVI (s 54(2)).

------
[1]   Under s 45(2).

REFERENCE TO THE TRIBUNAL

4.117 An applicant for permission or the variation of a permission under FSMA 2000, Pt IV who is aggrieved by the FSA's determination, or an authorised person who is aggrieved by the FSA's exercise of its own-initiative powers under Pt IV, may refer the matter to the Tribunal (s 55).

CONTROL OVER AUTHORISED PERSONS

Obligation to inform FSA

4.118 The Treasury has wide powers to make orders to provide for exemptions from the obligations to notify the acquisition, increase or reduction of control required by s 178 or 190 or to amend s 179, 180 or 181 to vary or remove any of the cases in which a person will be treated as having or having increased or having reduced control over a UK authorised person.[1] The Treasury may also by order amend the definitions in s 422 which relate to a person being treated as a controller (s 192)). The FSA must be notified of any person's intention to acquire or to increase his control over a UK authorised person[2] or to acquire an additional kind of control over such a person (s 178(1)).

[1] To the date of this publication, this has only been used to exempt acquisition of control etc for friendly societies (see the Financial Services and Markets Act 2000 (Controllers) (Exemption) Order 2001, SI 2001/2638) and building societies (see the Financial Services and Markets Act 2000 (Controllers) (Exemption) (No 2) Order 2001, SI 2001/3338).

[2] A 'UK authorised person' is an authorised person who is a body incorporated in, or an unincorporated association formed under the law of, any part of the UK and is not a person who is authorised by virtue of being a UCITS manager under FSMA 2000, Sch 5, para 1 (s 178(4)).

4.119 A 'kind of control' includes control arising as a result of—
— holding shares in the authorised person;
— holding shares in the parent undertaking of the authorised person;
— an entitlement to exercise or control the exercise of the voting power in the authorised person; or
— an entitlement to exercise or control the exercise of voting power in the parent undertaking (s 179(4)).

4.120 A 'notice of control' under s 178(1) is the responsibility of the proposed acquirer, who has the additional obligation to inform the FSA once the change in the control has taken effect and to notify the FSA of any increase in the degree of control he may hold (s 178(3), (5)). Section 191(10) provides, however, that if a person is under such a duty to notify the FSA but had no knowledge of the act or the circumstances under which that duty arose, and he subsequently became aware of that act or those circumstances, he must notify the FSA within 14 days of his becoming aware of that act or those circumstances.

4.121 If a person acquires any such control or increases control without having taken any action to that effect, he must notify the FSA of the new status within 14 days starting from the day he becomes aware he has acquired such control (s 178(2)).

Acquiring, increasing or reducing control

Acquiring control

4.122 A person acquires control over a UK authorised person (the 'acquirer') on first falling within any of the following cases—
— holding 10% or more of the shares in the authorised person;
— being able to exercise significant influence over the authorised person's management by virtue of his shareholding in that authorised person;
— holding 10% or more of the shares in a parent undertaking[1] of the authorised person;
— being able to exercise significant influence over the management of the authorised person's parent undertaking by virtue of his shareholding in that parent undertaking;
— being entitled to exercise or control the exercise of 10% or more of the voting power in the authorised person;
— being able to exercise significant influence over the authorised person's management by virtue of his voting power in that authorised person;
— being entitled to exercise or control the exercise of 10% or more of the voting power in the authorised person's parent undertaking;
— being able to exercise significant influence over the management of the authorised person's parent undertaking by virtue of his voting power in the parent undertaking (s 179(2)).

A person is an 'acquirer' in the above cases if he or any of his associates[2] or he and any of his associates acquire control (s 179(3)).[3] Thus, for example, to determine whether a person has acquired control, the percentage shareholding or voting power[4] of the person holding (or proposing to hold) shares[5] in the authorised person is aggregated with that of his associates.

---

[1] 'Parent undertaking' is defined in s 420 and in the Companies Act 1985 (CA 1985), Pt VII.
[2] An 'associate' is defined in s 422(4): see Appendix 1.
[3] For the purposes of Pt XII 'acquiring control or having control' includes acquiring or having an additional kind of control or acquiring an increase in the relevant kind of control or having increased control of a relevant kind (s 180(4)).
[4] ''Voting power' is defined in s 422(7): see Appendix 1.
[5] ''Shares' is defined in s 422(6): see Appendix 1.

Increasing control

4.123 A person who is a 'controller'[1] of a UK authorised person will be deemed to increase his control over the authorised person if—
— the percentage of shares held by him in the authorised person increases by steps as set out in s 180(2) (s 180(1)(a));

— the percentage of shares held by him in a parent undertaking[2] of the authorised person increases by those steps (s 180(1)(b));
— the percentage of voting power which he is entitled to exercise, or control the exercise of, in the authorised person increased by any of those steps (s 180(1)(c));
— the percentage of voting power which he is entitled to exercise, or control the exercise of, in the authorised person's parent undertaking increased by those steps (s 180(1)(d)); or
— he becomes a parent undertaking of the UK authorised person (s 180(1)(e)).

The steps set out in s 180(2) are—
— from below 10% to 10% or more but less than 20%;
— from below 20% to 20% or more but less than 33%;
— from below 33% to 33% or more but less than 50%;
— from 50% to 50% or more.

---

[1]   For the purposes of s 180(1)(a)–(d) a 'controller' includes the controller, any of the controller's associates or the controller and any of his associates (s 180(3)).
[2]   A 'parent undertaking' is defined in CA 1985, Pt VII and includes for these purposes an individual who would be a parent undertaking for the purposes of those provisions if he were taken to be an undertaking (s 420(1), (2)(a)).

Reducing control

4.124   A 'controller'[1] of a UK authorised person reduces his control over that authorised person if—
— the percentage of shares held by him decreases by certain prescribed changes in any of the steps set out in s 181(2) (s 181(1)(a));
— the percentage of shares held by him in a parent undertaking[2] of the UK authorised person decreases by any of those steps (s 181(1)(b));
— the percentage of voting power which he is entitled to exercise or control the exercise of in the authorised person decreases by those steps (s 181(1)(c));
— the percentage of voting power which he is entitled to exercise, or control the exercise of in the authorised person's parent undertaking decreases by those steps (s 181(1)(d)); or
— he ceases to be a parent undertaking of the authorised person (s 181(1)(e)).

Changes of this sort are not regarded as reducing control if they do not result in the controller ceasing to have the kind of control concerned (s 181(1)).

The steps set out in s 181(2) are the reverse of those that apply to the acquisition of control[3]—
— from 50% or more to 33% or more but less than 50%;

— from 33% or more to 20% or more but less than 33%;
— from 20% or more to 10% or more but less than 20%;
— from 10% or more to less than 10%.

---

[1]   For the purposes of s 181(1)(a)–(d) a 'controller' means the controller, any of his associates, or the controller and any of his associates (s 181(3)).
[2]   A 'parent undertaking' is defined in CA 1985, Pt VII and includes for these purposes an individual who would be a parent undertaking for the purposes of those provisions if he were taken to be an undertaking (s 420(1), (2)).
[3]   See para 4.123.

Notification

4.125   A notice of control must be given to the FSA in writing and include such information and be accompanied by such documentation as the FSA may require (s 182(1)). The FSA may also require the person required to give a notice of control to provide additional information or documents which the FSA considers necessary to enable it to determine what action to take concerning the notice (s 182(2)). The FSA has the power, however, to prescribe different requirements in different circumstances (s 182(3)).

FSA'S OBLIGATIONS IN RELATION TO A NOTICE OF CONTROL

4.126   Within three months from the day it received a notice of control under Pt XII, the FSA must either approve of the person having the relevant control or serve a warning notice under s 183(3) or 185(3) (s 183(1)). If the FSA proposes to give a notice of objection under s 186(1),[1] it must give a warning notice (s 183(3)).

---

[1]   See paras 4.133–4.135.

4.127   Before any action is taken, however, the FSA must comply with any requirements as to consultation with competent authorities outside the UK as may be prescribed (s 183(2)). Consultation has been prescribed in cases of proposed acquisition or change of control in relation to an investment firm or credit institution.[1] The FSA must consult with the home state regulator of each EEA investment firm or credit institution that is a proposed controller or a subsidiary (direct or indirect) of the proposed controller.[2]

---

[1]   The Financial Services and Markets Act 2000 (Consultation with Competent Authorities) Regulations 2001, SI 2001/2509.
[2]   SI 2001/2509, regs 3, 5 and 6.

Approval of acquisition of control

4.128 The FSA must notify the person in writing of its approval of the notice of control without delay (s 184(1)). If three months have passed from the date the notice was submitted, and the FSA has not communicated any decision to the person concerned, it is to be treated as having given a notice of approval at the end of this period (s 184(2)).

4.129 The FSA's approval remains valid only if the person intending to acquire the control does so before the end of the period specified in the notice or (if none is specified) before the end of a year beginning with the date either of the notice of approval, or the date on which the FSA is treated as having given that approval under s 184(2), or on the date of a decision on a reference to the Tribunal which results in the person concerned being given approval (s 184(3)).

Conditions on approval of changes of control

4.130 The FSA can give its notice of approval either unconditionally or subject to specific conditions which it considers appropriate (s 185(1)). In imposing any such conditions, the FSA must have regard to its duty under s 41 to ensure that the authorised person subject to the change of control satisfies the threshold conditions in Sch 6 (s 185(2)).[1]

---

[1]   See paras 4.70–4.80.

4.131 If the FSA proposes to impose conditions on the approval it must first provide the person concerned with a warning notice, and once it decides to impose these conditions, it must provide the person with a decision notice (s 185(3), (4)). It may on its own initiative cancel a condition it has imposed (s 185(6)).

4.132 The person subject to a condition concerning a notice of control can apply to the FSA for the condition to be varied or cancelled (s 185(5)). That person can also refer to the Tribunal the FSA's decision to impose such a condition or the FSA's decision to refuse the variation or cancellation of such a condition (s 185(7)).

Objection to acquisition of control

4.133 The FSA may object to the acquisition of new or additional control or to an increase in control, and give a decision notice to any person acquiring control if it is not satisfied that the approval requirements are met (s 186(1)). These requirements are that—

— the acquirer is a fit and proper person to have the control in question, and

— the interests of consumers[1] would not be threatened by the acquirer having the control in question (s 186(2)).

---

[1] For these purposes 'consumers' has the same meaning as for s 138 (s 186(6)): see para 5.27 on rule-making.

4.134 In deciding whether these approval requirements are met concerning the control that the acquirer has or will have over the UK authorised person if the proposed change in control is approved, the FSA must have regard to its duty under s 41 to ensure that the authorised person subject to the change of control satisfies the threshold conditions in Sch 6 for each regulated activity carried on by that authorised person (s 186(3)).

4.135 If in issuing any decision notice under this section the FSA considers that the approval requirements will be met if the person to whom a notice is given takes or refrains from taking a specific step, this step should be identified in the decision notice (s 186(4)). The person to whom a notice of objection under s 186 is given can refer the matter to the Tribunal (s 186(5)).

Objections to existing control

4.136 The FSA may issue a decision notice objecting to an existing controller if it is satisfied that the controller does not meet the approval requirements[1] and the controller did not notify the change of control as required under s 178 (s 187(1)).

---

[1] As set out in s 186: see para 4.133.

4.137 Where a controller has failed to comply with s 178(1) or (2),[1] the FSA may approve the acquisition of control as if the person had given the required notice (s 187(2)).

---

[1] See paras 4.118 and 4.121.

4.138 The FSA can also object to a person who is a controller (presumably at any time after he became a controller) by issuing a decision notice to a person if the FSA becomes aware of matters as a result of which it is satisfied that the approval requirements in s 186 are not met or that a condition imposed under s 185[1] concerning the acquisition of control has not been met (s 187(3)). In all of these cases, a controller on whom a decision notice is served may refer the matter to the Tribunal (s 187(4)).

---

[1] See paras 4.130–4.133.

Notices of objection under s 187: procedure

4.139 A notice of objection under s 187 can be given to the person concerned only if that person has been given a warning notice to that effect (s 188(1)). Before giving the warning notice, the FSA must comply with such requirements to consult with the competent authorities outside the UK as may be prescribed by regulations made by the Treasury (s 188(2)).[1]

---

[1] The Financial Services and Markets Act 2000 (Consultation with Competent Authorities) Regulations 2001, SI 2001/2509, reg 4 prescribes the same circumstances as are prescribed for the purposes of s 183: see para 4.127.

4.140 A warning notice given because of the person's failure to notify the FSA as required must be issued before the end of the three-month period beginning with the date on which the FSA became aware of the person's failure to comply with the specific obligation (s 188(3)(a)). The warning notice given to existing controllers because of their failure to meet the approval requirements must be issued before the end of the three-month period beginning with the date on which it became aware of the matters in question (s 188(3)(b)).

4.141 The FSA may require the person concerned to provide such additional information or documents as the FSA reasonably needs in each set of circumstances (s 188(4), (5)).

FSA's powers in respect of improperly acquired shares

4.142 In accordance with the requirements of the relevant EC directives, FSMA 2000 confers powers on the FSA to restrict rights deriving from improperly acquired shares. The powers may be exercised where a person acquires or continues to hold shares in contravention of a notice of objection or a condition imposed with a notice of approval (s 189(1)). In the case of an acquirer who has failed to provide the notice of control in accordance with s 178(1), s 189 applies to all of the shares—

— in the authorised person which the acquirer holds;

— held by him or an associate of his; and

— not held by him or an associate of his immediately before he became a person with control over the authorised person (s 189(7)(a)).

In the case of an acquirer who has not given the requisite notice of control and who has not notified the FSA before the end of the 14 days beginning with the day on which he became aware of having acquired such control, these powers apply to all the shares held by him or by an associate of his at the time he first became aware that he had acquired such control over the authorised person (s 189(7)(b)).

4.143 These powers also apply to all the shares of an undertaking which are held by the acquirer or any associate of his and which were not held before he became a person with control in relation to the authorised person, where that undertaking is an undertaking in which shares in the authorised person were acquired which made the acquirer a controller in relation to that authorised person (s 189(7)(c)).

4.144 The FSA may serve the person concerned with a restriction notice in writing directing that, until further notice, the shares specified in this notice are subject to one or more restrictions (s 189(2)). A copy of this notice must be served on the authorised person to whose shares it relates, and if it relates to shares held by an associate of his, to that associate as well (s 189(8)). The FSA may impose one or more of the following restrictions on the shares—
— a transfer of (or an agreement to transfer) those shares, or in the case of unissued shares any transfer of (or agreement to transfer) the right to be issued with them, is void;
— no voting rights are to be exercisable in respect of the shares;
— no further shares are to be issued in right of them or in pursuance of any offer made to their holder; and
— except in a liquidation, no payment is to be made of any sums due from the body corporate on the shares, whether in respect of capital or otherwise (s 189(2)(a)–(d)).

4.145 The FSA may also apply to the court[1] for an order directing the sale of shares to which s 189 applies, or, if the shares are subject to a restriction order, the court can order that they are to cease to be subject to such restriction (s 189(3)). However, the court cannot issue such an order if a notice of objection has been referred to the Tribunal and the Tribunal has not yet determined the case (and the reference has not been withdrawn) or if the period during which a reference to the Tribunal can be made has not expired (s 189(4)).

---

[1] The 'court' means the High Court or, in Scotland, the Court of Session (s 189(9)).

4.146 If the court makes such an order, it may, on the FSA's application, make such further order regarding the sale or transfer of the shares as it thinks appropriate (s 189(5)). If shares are sold pursuant to a court order made under s 189(3), the proceeds of sale, less the costs of the sale, must be paid into court for the benefit of the persons beneficially interested in them. Any such person may apply to the court for all or part of the proceeds to be paid to him (s 189(6)).

Reducing control: procedure

Notification

4.147 Where a controller[1] is taking a step which would reduce or cease a relevant kind of control over a UK authorised person, he must notify the FSA of his proposal (s 190(1)). If a controller of a UK authorised person ceases to have control or reduces that control without taking such a step himself, he must notify the FSA within 14 days of his becoming aware of ceasing to have that control or having reduced that control (s 190(2)).

[1] The controller who has to notify under s 190(1) must also notify the FSA when he has ceased to have such control or has reduced such control (s 190(3)).

4.148 A notice of reduction must be given to the FSA in writing and must include details of the extent of the control, if any, which the controller will continue to hold over the authorised person after the reduction in control (s 190(4)). If, however, that person who would have been under a duty to notify the FSA under s 190(1) had no knowledge of the act or the circumstances under which that duty would have arisen, but he subsequently becomes aware of that fact, he must notify the FSA within 14 days of the date on which he became aware of that fact (s 191(10)).

OFFENCES UNDER FSMA 2000, PT XII

4.149 A person who fails to comply with s 178(1) or (2)[1] or s 190(1) or (2)[2] is guilty of an offence and will be liable on summary conviction to a fine not exceeding level 5 on the standard scale (s 191(1), (2), (6)).

[1] See paras 4.118, 4.121.
[2] See paras 4.147, 4.148.

4.150 A person who has given a notice of control to the FSA will be guilty of an offence if he carries out the proposal to which that notice relates, unless the FSA has given its approval or given a warning notice under s 183(3) or 185(3) in respect of that proposal, or three months has elapsed from the date on which the FSA received the notice of control (s 191(3)). A person who has committed an offence under this section is liable on summary conviction to a fine not exceeding level 5 on the standard scale (s 191(6)).

4.151 If the FSA has issued a warning notice in respect of s 183(3) in relation to an objection to the acquisition of control and the person who has been given the notice of control acquires that control before the FSA has finally determined the matter by giving a decision notice under s 186(1), that person is guilty of an offence and is liable on summary conviction to a fine not exceeding level 5 on the standard scale (s 191(4), (6)).

4.152   A person who has received a notice of objection from the FSA and who acquires the control to which the notice applies while that notice is still in force, is guilty of an offence. He is liable on summary conviction to either a fine not exceeding one tenth of the statutory maximum for each day on which the offence continued (s 191(8)) or to a fine not exceeding the statutory maximum and, on conviction on indictment, to imprisonment for up to two years or a fine, or both imprisonment and a fine (s 191(5), (7)).

4.153   A person who has failed to notify the FSA within 14 days of his becoming aware of the act or circumstances of which he had had no knowledge which would have given rise to a duty on his part to notify the FSA under s 178(1) or 190(1) is guilty of an offence and is liable on summary conviction to a fine not exceeding level 5 on the standard scale (s 191(10), (11)).

Defences

4.154   A person who is charged with an offence under s 191(1) may as a defence show that at the time of the alleged offence he had no knowledge of the act or circumstances by virtue of which he had a duty to notify the FSA (s 191(9)).

TABLE OF OFFENCES

Person guilty of an offence	*Penalty on summary conviction*	*Penalty on indictment*
A person who fails to comply with s 178(1) or (2) or s 190(1), (2))	A fine not exceeding level 5 on the standard scale (s 191(6))	
A person who has given notice of control to the FSA and carried out the proposal to which that notice relates, unless the FSA has given its approval or given a warning notice under ss 183(3) or 185(3) in respect of that proposal, or the period of three months has elapsed from the date on which the FSA has received the notice of control (s 191(3))	A fine not exceeding level 5 on the standard scale (s 191(6))	

Person guilty of an offence	Penalty on summary conviction	Penalty on indictment
A person to whom the FSA has issued a warning notice in respect of s 183(3) in relation to an objection to the acquisition of control, and who has acquired that control before the FSA has finally determined the matter by giving a decision notice under s 186(1) (s 191(4))	A fine not exceeding level 5 on the standard scale (s 191(6))	
A person who has received a notice of objection from the FSA and who acquires the control to which the notice applies while that notice is still in force (s 191(5))	A fine not exceeding one tenth of the statutory maximum for each day on which the offence continued (s 191(8)) or to a fine not exceeding the statutory maximum (s 191(7)(a))	Imprisonment for up to two years or a fine, or both (s 191(7)(b))
A person who has failed to notify the FSA within 14 days of his becoming aware of the act or circumstances of which he had had no knowledge which would have given rise to duty on his part to notify the FSA under s 178(1) or 190(1) (s 191(10))	On summary conviction to a fine not exceeding level 5 on the standard scale (s 191(11))	

5 Conduct of regulated activities

INTRODUCTION

5.1 The integration of the rules, regulations and codes of nine former regulatory and supervisory bodies in a single handbook has been one of the most daunting tasks facing the Financial Services Authority (FSA) in its preparation for 'N2' (1 December 2001).[1] FSMA 2000, Pt V (ss 56–71) provides the framework for the standards and requirements which are to be met and sets out detailed procedures which the FSA must follow to make the regulatory process fair, flexible, and transparent, while meeting the FSA's general duties under the Financial Services and Markets Act 2000 (FSMA 2000), s 2.[2]

---

[1] See para 1.37 for further discussion of N2.
[2] See paras 2.31 and 2.32. Note also that s 2(4)(a) does not apply to listing rules, s 2(4)(c) does not apply to general guidance given in relation to FSMA 2000, Pt VI (listing), and s 2(4)(d) does not apply to functions under Pt VI (Sch 7, para 2).

5.2 The FSA has broad powers to establish the standards and requirements for both authorised persons and individuals who are approved persons, to give guidance or to give waivers or to modify those standards and requirements and to enforce those standards and modifications within the framework of FSMA 2000. The FSA also has powers, for particular circumstances, to establish standards for those who are not authorised.[1]

---

[1] Notably in relation to market abuse: see para 5.64.

APPROVED PERSONS

Approval

5.3 Authorised persons must take reasonable care to ensure that no person[1] performs a controlled function[2] unless the FSA has approved[3] that person's performance of that function (s 59(1)).[4] This is extended to include situations where the controlled function is carried on under an arrangement between the authorised person and a contractor (s 59(2)).

5.4   Section 59(1) and (2) does not apply to an arrangement[1] if the question of whether a person is a fit and proper person to perform the function is properly a matter for the home state regulator under its powers under the single market directives (s 59(8)).[2]

---

¹ See para 5.6.
² This is reflected in the controlled functions applied by the FSA to incoming EEA firms. The functions applied are the customer functions and some of the significant influence functions: see the FSA Handbook, Supervision manual, SUP 10.1.13–14R.

5.5   Rules made under s 59(3) may only include those functions which satisfy the following conditions (s 59(4))—
    —   the function is likely to enable the person carrying it out to significantly influence the conduct of the authorised person's affairs, so far as they relate to the regulated activity (s 59(5));[1]
    —   the function involves the person carrying it out dealing with customers[2] of the authorised person in a manner substantially connected with carrying on the regulated activity (s 59(6)); or
    —   the function is one which involves the person carrying it out dealing with the property of customers of the authorised person in a manner substantially connected with carrying on the regulated activity (s 59(7)).

---

¹ For example, directors, partners, senior managers and others in relation to whom the FSA may take into account the likely consequence of a failure to discharge those functions (s 59(9)). The FSA takes a risk-based approach in determining the extent of these functions and sub-divides this sort of function into governing functions, required functions and systems and controls functions when specifying them: see the FSA Handbook, Supervision manual, SUP 10.4–10.9.
² A 'customer' for these purposes means a person who is using, or who is or may be contemplating using, any of the services provided by the authorised person (s 59(11)).

Meaning of 'arrangement'

5.6   FSMA 2000, s 59(10) defines an 'arrangement' in these circumstances as any kind of arrangement for the performance of a function of the authorised person which is entered into by the authorised person or any contractor of his with another person and includes that other person's appointment to an office, or his becoming a partner or his employment by the authorised person (including employment under a contract of service or otherwise). This will, therefore, catch persons carrying out controlled functions under outsourcing agreements, consulting arrangements or secondments.[1]

---

[1] See also the FSA Handbook, Supervision manual, SUP 10.12.3–4G. The FSA includes those individuals employed by appointed representatives with customer-facing functions as being within the scope of an 'arrangement': see SUP 10.1.16R and 10.1.17R.

Applications for approval

5.7 The authorised person concerned may apply for approval (s 60(1)).[1] The application must be made in the form which, and containing such information as, the FSA directs (s 60(2)).[2] The FSA can vary this from case to case (s 60(5)), and may require the applicant to provide additional information if it reasonably requires it to determine the application (s 60(3)). The FSA may also require the applicant to provide the information in a particular form or to verify it (s 60(4)). Once made the application can only be withdrawn by the applicant before it is determined with the consent of the candidate and, if the candidate is not retained or employed by a person who is the applicant, the person who would be retaining the candidate to perform the relevant controlled function (s 61(5)).

---

[1] 'The authorised person concerned' includes an applicant for a Pt IV permission (s 60(6)).
[2] See the FSA Handbook, Supervision manual, SUP 10.

5.8 The FSA may only grant approval if it is satisfied that the person concerned, the 'candidate', is fit and proper to perform the controlled function for which the application was made (s 61(1)). In deciding this the FSA may have regard to the qualifications, training or competence of the candidate (or anyone performing a function on his behalf) (s 61(2)). The FSA has three months in which to decide whether to grant the application (s 61(3)).[1] If the FSA decides to grant the application it must give written notice of that decision to all 'interested parties' (s 62(1)).[2]

---

[1] If the FSA has required further information to be given under s 60(3), this period is suspended until the FSA has received in full the information required (s 61(4)).
[2] See para 5.9, fn 1.

5.9 If the FSA proposes to refuse an application for approval it must give a warning notice to each of the interested parties (s 62(2)).[1] If, after the warning notice procedure has been followed, the FSA decides to refuse the application, it must give a decision notice to each of the interested parties (s 62(3)), each of whom then has the right to refer the matter to the Tribunal (s 62(4)).

---

[1] 'Interested parties' for the purposes of this section are defined as the applicant, the candidate and the person by whom the candidate is to have been retained, if not the applicant (s 62(5)).

REGULATING THE CONDUCT OF APPROVED PERSONS

Statements and codes

5.10 The FSA may issue statements of principle regarding the conduct which it expects of approved persons (s 64(1)).[1] Where it issues such statements, it must also issue a code of practice to help those persons affected by a statement of principle decide whether their conduct complies with it (s 64(2)). These statements of principle and codes of practice may make different provisions for persons, cases or circumstances of different descriptions, and the power to make these statements and codes is part of the FSA's rule-making functions (s 64(11)).[2]

---

[1] 'Approved person' means a person in relation to whom the FSA has given its approval under s 59 (s 64(13)).
[2] These principles and the code are set out in the FSA Handbook, Statement of Principles and Code of Practice for Approved Persons (APER). The FSA may charge a reasonable fee for providing a copy of a statement of principles or a code (s 64(12)).

5.11 A code which is made and in force at the time when any particular conduct takes place is indicative of whether the conduct complies with a statement of principle (s 64(7)). However, if a person can show that at the time of the alleged failure to comply with a statement of principle, the statement or its associated code of practice had not been published, that person is not to be taken to have failed to comply with that statement or code (s 64(9)).

5.12 A code of practice may specify or describe the types of conduct which in the FSA's opinion comply with the principles laid down under s 64 or do not comply with those principles. The code may also set out the factors which are to be taken into account when the FSA considers whether a person has complied with a statement of principle (s 64(3)).

Procedures

5.13   Before issuing a statement or code under s 64 the FSA must publish a draft of it. The draft statement or code must be accompanied by a cost benefit analysis[1] and notice that representations may be made about it to the FSA within a specified time (s 65(1), (2)).

---

[1]   This cost benefit analysis is an estimate of the costs and an analysis of the benefits arising from the proposed new code or principles (s 65(11)). It is not required if the FSA considers that there will be no increase in costs or that any increase in costs will be of minimal significance (s 65(6), (12)).

5.14   Before issuing the statement or code the FSA must also have regard to any representations which it receives (s 65(3)). If it issues the statement or code, it must publish in general terms an account of the representations which it has received and its response to them (s 65(4)).

5.15   If the statement or code to be promulgated differs from the draft that was published by the FSA in a way which the FSA considers significant, it must also publish the details of the differences and a revised cost benefit analysis (s 65(5)).

5.16   The FSA may alter or replace a statement of principle or code at any time (s 64(4)), and must issue the altered version and publish it in a way best calculated to bring it to the attention of the public (s 64(5), (6)). The FSA must also provide a copy of any statement or code to the Treasury without delay (s 64(10)).[1]

---

[1]   The procedural requirements for making the statement of principles or the code apply also to proposals to amend or replace them (s 65(10)).

No right of action for breach of statutory duty in relation to the principles

5.17   Failure to comply with a statement of principle under s 64 does not of itself give rise to any right of action by affected persons[1] or affect the validity of any transaction (s 64(8)). However, a right of action is granted to a private person who suffers loss if an authorised person fails to take reasonable care (s 71) to ensure that controlled functions are not carried on in breach of a prohibition order or by someone not approved by the FSA.[2]

---

[1]   Contrast the position in relation to breaches of rules by authorised persons under s 150: see para 5.73.
[2]   'Private person' has its meaning set by statutory instrument and is defined as private individuals (except when carrying on regulated activities) and other persons acting otherwise than in the course of any business: see the Financial Services and Markets Act 2000 (Rights of Action) Regulations 2001, SI 2001/2256, regs 3 and 5. The rights of action may also be extended to other prescribed persons—in this case reg 5 extends the right of action to those who would be acting exclusively for the benefit of a private person as fiduciary or other representative.

WITHDRAWAL OF APPROVAL AND PROHIBITION ORDERS

5.18 If a person who performs a function in relation to a regulated activity carried on by an authorised person is found not to be fit and proper to carry out that function, the FSA may withdraw the approval for that person to carry out that function (s 63(1)).[1] The FSA may also make a prohibition order in relation to any individual who appears to it not to be fit and proper to carry on a controlled function (s 56(1), (2)).[2]

---

[1] This is an additional power to the disciplinary powers described in paras 8.8–8.11 (and see *R (on the application of Davis) v Financial Services Authority* [2003] EWCA Civ 1128, noted at para 8.10, fn 5.
[2] The power to make a prohibition order only applies to individuals and not to bodies corporate. See also the FSA Handbook, Enforcement manual, ENF 8.

Withdrawal of approval

5.19 When considering whether to withdraw its approval the FSA may take into account anything which it would be able to take into account if there was a new application for approval in relation to the same individual and function (s 63(2)). The warning and decision notice procedures apply to withdrawal of permission, and the right to refer the matter to the Tribunal applies, in the same way as to a proposal to refuse approval (s 63(3)–(5)).[1]

---

[1] See para 5.9.

Prohibition orders

5.20 A prohibition order may be in such terms as would prevent (in relation to a regulated activity carried on by an authorised person) that individual from performing either a specified[1] function, any function falling within a specified description or from performing any function at all (s 56(2)). A prohibition order may relate to a specified regulated activity, or any regulated activity falling within a specified description, or all regulated activities, and may relate to authorised persons generally or to any person within a specified class of authorised person (s 56(3)).[2]

---

[1] 'Specified' for the purposes of this section means specified in the prohibition order (s 56(9)).
[2] See CP 25 Response Paper, December 1999, paras 25–29. See also FSA press release FS/PN/039/2002.

5.21 Section 56 also applies to the performance of functions in relation to a regulated activity carried on by—

— exempt persons; and
— persons to whom, as a result of Pt XX, the general prohibition does not apply in relation to the activity;[1]

as it applies to the performance of functions in relation to a regulated activity carried on by an authorised person (s 56(8)).[2]

---

[1] The FSA has express power to make an order which would have the effect of banning persons who would otherwise be able to carry on regulated activities by virtue of being an exempt professional firm under FSMA 2000, Pt XX (s 329).

[2] These provisions are subject to transitional provisions so that a disqualification order under the Financial Services Act 1986, s 59 in relation to any person has effect from 1 December 2001 as a prohibition order made under s 56: see the Financial Services and Markets Act 2000 (Transitional Provisions) (Authorised Persons etc) Order 2001, SI 2001/2636, art 79, as amended by SI 2001/3650.

5.22 An individual who performs or agrees to perform a function in breach of a prohibition order is guilty of an offence and may be liable to a fine (s 56(4)). However, he may claim as a defence that he had taken all reasonable precautions and exercised all due diligence in seeking to avoid committing the offence (s 56(5)).

Procedure

5.23 If the FSA proposes to make a prohibition order under s 56, it must give the individual concerned a warning notice which sets out the proposed terms of the prohibition (s 57(1), (2)). If the FSA decides to make a prohibition order it must give the individual concerned a decision notice (s 57(3)) which names the individual and sets out the terms of the order (s 57(4)). A person who is the subject of a prohibition order may refer the matter to the Tribunal (s 57(5)).

Application for variation or revocation of prohibition order

5.24 On the application of the person concerned, the FSA may vary or revoke a prohibition order (s 56(7)) and if the FSA decides to grant that application for a variation or revocation, it must give the applicant written notice of its decision (s 58(1), (2)). If, however, the FSA proposes to refuse the application, it must give the applicant a warning notice (s 58(3)), and if it decides to refuse the application, a decision notice (s 58(4)). If the applicant has received a decision notice refusing the application for variation or revocation, he may refer the matter to the Tribunal (s 58(5)).

5.25 An authorised person who allows a person subject to a prohibition order to carry out a function in respect of which he is prohibited will not be committing an offence but will be subject to disciplinary action by the FSA in the same way as for breaching its Rules.[1]

1   Under FSMA 2000, Pt XIV: see paras 8.3–8.5. The authorised person will also be potentially at risk of an action for damages under FSMA 2000, s 71 by a private person who suffers loss as a result: and see para 5.17.

RULES AND GUIDANCE FOR AUTHORISED PERSONS

5.26   The FSA has the power to make general rules[1] which apply to authorised persons as it appears to be necessary or expedient to protect consumers.[2] These rules may be made in respect of activities which are regulated activities as well as activities which are not regulated activities (s 138(1)). In introducing the debate, Lord McIntosh said that—

> 'It is one of the most vital, if technical, parts of the Bill. Rules are a key instrument by which the authority will give effect at working level to its statutory objectives and the principles to which it must have regard. The role of guidance is to provide information and advice to the regulated community—with respect to rules but also on more general issues.'[3]

He went on to give an example of how this could apply to non-regulated activities—

> 'Let us suppose that an authorised person who also carried on a non-regulated coin dealing business were to operate an authorised collective investment scheme in which participants' money was pooled for the purposes of investing in coins. Operating any collective investment scheme is a regulated activity and it is perfectly lawful to operate such a scheme as long as the operator is authorised.
>
> However, it is not inconceivable that some rules might need to be applied to the coin dealing business—purely as a minimum—in order to make sure that the funds contributed by participants in the collective investment scheme—that is, the consumers of the regulated activity—are protected.
>
> A rule might be necessary to require an independent valuation of any purchase for the scheme made using investors' funds which the scheme operator makes for his coin dealing business in order to avoid any conflict of interest he might otherwise have and to ensure that the scheme participants' interests are protected. It may be arguable that the rule would touch on the running of the

non-regulated coin dealing business. However, it is clear that if he contravenes such a rule, and the coins are sold to the scheme at what turns out to be a disadvantageous price, there could be damage to the interests of the scheme participants.'[4]

---

1   See s 138(2).
2   'Consumers' is defined widely: see para 5.27.
3   HL Committee Stage, 27 March 2000, col 527.
4   HL Committee Stage, 27 March 2000, col 529.

Definition of consumers

5.27   'Consumers' is defined in s 138(7) as persons who use, have used, or are or may be contemplate using, services provided by authorised persons, or appointed representatives, rights or interests deriving from such services provided for others, or whose rights or interests may be adversely affected by the use of such services by fiduciaries or others acting on their behalf. In addition—

— a person who is or has been or may be a beneficiary of a trust where the trustee is an authorised person carrying on a regulated activity in his capacity as a trustee is to be treated as a person who is using or has used or is or may be contemplating using the authorised person's services in relation to the regulated activity (s 138(8));

— a person who deals with an authorised person is to be treated as using services provided by the authorised person (s 138(9));

and these persons would therefore fall within the wide definition of 'consumer' for the purposes of s 138.

General rule-making power

5.28   The FSA's power to make general rules is not limited by any other power which the FSA has to make regulating provisions under FSMA 2000 (s 138(3)).

5.29   General rules may include provisions which relate to any activity of other members of an authorised person's group (s 138(5)).

5.30   However they may not prohibit an EEA firm from carrying on or holding itself out as carrying on, any activity for which it had permission under FSMA 2000, Sch 3, Pt II,[1] nor may they, in respect of an EEA firm, make any provision which would otherwise be reserved to the firm's home state regulator (s 138(6)).

---

1   See paras 4.8–4.17.

5.31　The FSA's power to make general rules applying to an authorised person applies even though there is no relationship between the authorised person and the person whose interests would be protected by the rules (s 138(4)). The Explanatory Notes state that—

> 'This section confers a power on the Authority to make rules applying to authorised persons with respect to their carrying on of regulated and unregulated activities. Rules made under this section are referred to as "general rules" and can only be made to protect the interests of consumers. There need not be a direct relationship between the authorised persons to whom the rules apply and the consumers who are protected by the rules—so, for example, the Authority will be able to make rules under this section to protect the interests of beneficiaries of trusts, to further market integrity, as required by the Investment Services Directive, or to protect against systemic risk.'[1]

---

[1]　FSMA Explanatory Notes, para 253.

5.32　The general rules may also confer rights on persons to rescind agreements entered into with authorised persons or withdraw offers made to authorised persons within a specified period and to make provision that where these rights are exercised, the authorised person is required to restore the property or repay or recover any payments made in respect of those transactions (s 139(4)).[1]

---

[1]　Equivalent to the 'cancellation' or 'cooling off' rules under FSA 1986.

Clients' money rules

5.33　The FSA may make specific rules about the handling of money held by an authorised person ('clients' money') in circumstances prescribed by the rules.[1]

---

[1]　See the FSA Handbook, Client Assets sourcebook (CASS).

5.34　Clients' money rules may include provisions providing that—
   —　clients' money may be held on trust (s 139(1)(a));[1]
   —　two or more accounts may be treated as a single account[2] for specified purposes (including the distribution of money held in the accounts) (s 139(1)(b));
   —　the authorised person may retain interest accruing on clients' money (s 139(1)(c));
   —　interest which is not retained by the authorised person may be distributed (s 139(1)(d)).

---

[1]   In Scotland, references to money being held on trust are to be read as reference to its being held as agent for the person who is entitled to call for it to be paid over to him or to be paid on his direction or otherwise credited to him (s 139(3)).
[2]   The term 'account' is not defined in the legislation.

5.35   An institution with which an account is kept by an authorised person in compliance with the clients' money rules will not incur any liability as constructive trustee if money is paid into or out of that account in contravention of the clients' money rules unless the institution permitted the payment knowing that the payment was wrongful or it deliberately failed to make enquiries as to the lawfulness of the payment which a reasonable and honest person would have done (s 139(2)).

General supplementary powers

5.36   The rules may also make different provisions for different cases or circumstances and may include different provisions for different descriptions of authorised persons, activities or investments (s 156(1)). In addition, these rules may contain wide discretion for the FSA to make such incidental, supplemental, consequential or transitional provisions as it deems appropriate (s 156(2)).

SPECIFIC RULES

Authorised unit trust managers

5.37   The FSA may make rules[1] prohibiting an authorised person who has permission to act as a manager of an authorised unit trust scheme from carrying on both regulated and non-regulated activities (s 140(1), (2)).[2]

---

[1]   See the FSA Handbook, Collective Investment Schemes sourcebook, CIS.
[2]   Rules made under s 140 do not apply to incoming electronic commerce activity: see the Electronic Commerce Directive (Financial Services and Markets) Regulations 2002, SI 2002/1775, reg 4.

Insurance business rules

5.38   Where an authorised person has permission to effect or carry out contracts of insurance, the FSA may also make rules[1] prohibiting that person[2] from carrying on both regulated and non-regulated activities (s 141(1), (2)). These rules may be modified or waived under the powers set out in s 148(1)(e).

1   These are referred to as 'insurance business rules' (s 141(5)).
2   In relation to incoming electronic commerce activity see para 5.37, fn 2—the Electronic Commerce Directive (Financial Services and Markets) Regulations 2002, SI 2002/1775, reg 4.

5.39   The FSA may also, in relation to persons effecting or carrying out contracts of long-term insurance, make rules which restrict the types of property or indices of the value of property by reference to which the benefits under those contracts may be determined (s 141(3), (4)(a)). The rules may also allow for the substitution of one description of property or index of value for another in determining the benefits under such a contract (s 141(4)(b)).

Insurance business: asset identification rules

5.40   The FSA may also make rules ('asset identification rules') which require an authorised person who has permission to effect or carry out contracts of insurance to identify assets which belong to him and which are maintained in respect of particular aspects of his business (s 142(2)).[1]

1   These rules will complement the regulations made by the Treasury under s 378, ie, the Financial Services and Markets Act 2000 (Treatment of Assets of Insurers on Winding Up) Regulations 2001, SI 2001/2968: see also para 21.43.

5.41   The Treasury may also make regulations in relation to insurance business including regulations to prevent a person who is not an authorised person, but who is a parent undertaking of an authorised person who has permission to effect or carry out contracts of insurance, and falls within a prescribed class, from doing anything to lessen the effectiveness of the asset identification rules (s 142(1)).

5.42   The regulations which the Treasury make may include provisions prohibiting the payment of dividends and the creation of charges including mortgages[1] (s 142(3)(a), (b)). They may also provide that charges created in contravention of these regulations or the asset identification rules are void (s 142(3)(c), (4)). A person who contravenes these regulations commits an offence and may be subject to a fine (s 142(5)).

1   In Scotland, this includes securities over property (s 142(6)).

Endorsing rules

5.43   The FSA may make rules endorsing the City Code on Takeovers and Mergers and the Rules Governing Substantial Acquisitions of Shares (SARs) issued by the Takeover Panel (the Panel)[1] (s 143(1)).[2] These 'endorsing rules' may be made either in respect of all authorised persons or only in respect of a specified kind of authorised person (s 143(2)).

---

[1]   The relationship between the FSA and the Panel was a highly contentious issue during the passage of the Bill through the House of Lords. See HL, Amendments moved on consideration of Commons amendments, 12 Jun 2000, col 1373.
[2]   See the FSA Handbook, Market Conduct sourcebook, MAR 4. See also Panel Notice 2001/3, February 2001, for an introduction to the Takeover Code and SARs including commentary on the enforcement process.

5.44   If the FSA makes endorsing rules and if it is asked to do so by the Panel, it may exercise its powers under Pt IV (in relation to the withdrawal of permissions) or under s 66 (in relation to disciplinary proceedings against approved persons) as if a person had failed to comply with a provision of the City Code or the SARs which has been endorsed with respect to them or their activities (s 143(3)).

5.45   The FSA may also exercise its powers of intervention in respect of—
— incoming firms under Pt XIII;
— disciplinary measures under Pt XIV; and
— restitution orders under Pt XXV;

to enforce an endorsed provision against a person in respect of whom it has been endorsed (s 143(4)). A person will be deemed to have failed to comply with the relevant provision of the endorsing rules if it fails to comply with a requirement imposed or a ruling given under the City Code or the SARs (s 143(5)).

5.46   Where the provisions of the City Code or SARs have been altered, s 143(3) and (4) applies to them as altered. However, before the alteration, the FSA must have notified the Panel (and not withdrawn its notification) that it is satisfied with the consultation procedures which the Panel has carried out in relation to those changes and that that process has provided an opportunity for those persons most likely to be affected by those changes to make representations to the Panel about the proposed changes (s 143(6), (7)).

Procedure

5.47   In making or amending the endorsing rules, the FSA must, in giving any notification to the Panel under s 143,[1] publish a draft of the proposed rules in the way best calculated to bring it to the attention of the public (s 155(1)). The draft must be made available and the FSA may charge a reasonable fee for providing a copy (s 155(12)). The draft must include a notice that representations about the proposals may be made to the FSA within a specified time (s 155(2)(d)). The FSA must have regard to any representations made to it concerning the proposed endorsing rules (s 155(4)) and must publish an account of the representations which it has received and its response to them (s 155(5)). If the endorsing rules as promulgated by the FSA are different from those proposed in the draft, the FSA must publish details of the differences together with a cost benefit analysis (s 155(6)).

---

[1]   Section 155(1), (2)(d), (4), (5), (6)(a) and (12) apply with modifications to an altered proposal as they apply to a proposal to make endorsing rules (s 143(8)).

Price stabilising rules

5.48   The FSA may make rules ('price stabilising rules') concerning—
— the circumstances and manner in which;
— the conditions subject to which;
— and the time when or the period during which;

certain action may be taken to stabilise the price of investments of specific kinds (s 144(1)).[1]

---

[1]   See the FSA Handbook, Market Conduct sourcebook, MAR 2.

5.49   These rules are to apply only to authorised persons and may make different provision for different kinds of investment (s 144(2)). They provide a safe harbour, when complied with, against certain of the market manipulation offences in s 397 (s 397(4), (5)).[1]

---

[1]   See paras 8.37, 8.38.

5.50   The Treasury may however by order impose limitations on the FSA's power to make price stabilising rules (s 144(4)). These limitations may include—
— the kinds of investment to which price stabilising rules will apply;
— the actions which may be taken; or
— the time or duration of the action which may be taken for the purposes of stabilising prices (s 144(5)).

5.51   The order which the Treasury may make under s 144(5) may also impose limitations on the FSA's rule-making power including the types of investments to which the FSA's rules may apply.

Overseas stabilisation

5.52   The FSA may also make rules which provide a safe harbour in relation to certain of the market manipulation provisions contained in FSMA 2000 (s 397)[1] such that if a person acts or engages in conduct for the purpose of stabilising the price of investments and acts or engages in that conduct in conformity with rules made by an overseas body or authority which have corresponding provisions relating to the stabilisation of prices of securities,[2] that person will be treated as acting in accordance with the price stabilising rules (s 144(3)). The FSA has specified certain legislative provisions made by authorities in the United States and Japan for these purposes.[3]

---

[1]   These provisions provide a safe harbour in relation to proceedings under FSMA 2000, s 397(3), but not in relation to proceedings under FSMA 2000, s 397(2) or the Criminal Justice Act 1993, Pt V relating to insider dealing: see the FSA Handbook, Market Conduct sourcebook, MAR 2.8.1G.

[2]   The issue of the recognition of overseas price stabilising rules and practice has been a long-standing problem. The European Parliament and Council Directive on insider dealing and market manipulation (Market Abuse Directive, 2003/6/EC) seeks to harmonise common provisions on market abuse, including the safe harbour for stabilising activity. The FSA Handbook sets out those rules which have been specified as 'equivalent provisions' for the purposes of s 144(3).

[3]   See MAR 2.8.

5.53   The rules made under s 144(3) will continue to provide a safe harbour even after the provisions made by the overseas body or authority have been altered, but only if before the alteration the FSA has notified the overseas body or authority[1] that it is satisfied with its consultation procedures (s 144(6)).[2]

---

[1]   The FSA has stated that it is satisfied with the consultation procedures in relation to the United States and Japan: see the FSA Handbook, Market Conduct sourcebook, MAR 2.8.2R (5), and FSA CP 78, The Price Stabilising Rules: Feedback on CP40, December 2000.

[2]   'Consultation procedures' has the meaning given to it in s 143(7). See also para 5.46.

The financial promotion rules

5.54   FSMA 2000, s 145 provides that the FSA may make rules[1] which apply to authorised persons in relation to the communication by them, or their approval of the communication by others, of invitations or inducements to engage in investment activity[2] or to participate in a collective investment scheme (s 145(1)). These rules may specify the form and content of communications (s 145(2)).[3]

---

[1]   The Treasury has the power to impose limitations on the FSA's rule-making powers under this section (s 145(5)).

[2]   'Engage in investment activity' has the same meaning as in s 21 (s 145(4)).

[3]   See paras 6.43–6.46 for further detail about this rule-making power.

Money laundering rules

5.55   In a major shift of policy, FSMA 2000 gives the FSA the express power[1] to make rules in relation to the prevention and detection of money laundering in connection with authorised persons carrying on regulated activities (s 146).[2] The FSA also has wider powers to investigate suspected money laundering (s 168(4)(b)) and, in certain cases, to prosecute suspected cases of money laundering.[3]

---

[1] The obligation to comply with the relevant legislation and guidelines on money laundering has been relevant to the regulator's determination of whether an authorised firm is fit and proper to carry on regulated business: see the FSA Handbook, Threshold Conditions sourcebook, COND 2.5.7G (10).

[2] Even though the FSA is a 'supervisory authority' for the purposes of the Money Laundering Regulations 1993, SI 1993/1933, the rules made by the FSA relate only to regulatory requirements. Accordingly they are not 'regulatory rules or guidance' for the purposes of the criminal law under the Money Laundering Regulations 1993, reg 5(3): see the FSA Handbook, Money Laundering sourcebook, ML 1.2.4G.

[3] Section 402(1)(b) provides that, except in Scotland, the FSA may institute proceedings for an offence under prescribed regulations relating to money laundering (ie, under s 146) and in exercising this power it must comply with any conditions or restrictions imposed by the Treasury relating to those proceedings generally or in relation to particular categories of proceedings (s 402(3)): see the Financial Services and Markets Act 2000 (Regulations Relating to Money Laundering) Regulations 2001, SI 2001/1819. See also the Proceeds of Crime Act 2002 (PCA 2002). FSA staff may be appointed as accredited financial investigators under various provisions of PCA 2002: the Proceeds of Crime Act 2002 (References to Financial Investigators) Order 2003, SI 2003/172.

5.56 Only authorised firms are subject to the FSA's money laundering rules.[1] Therefore, professional firms who operate under a Pt XX exemption[2] will continue to be subject only to the Money Laundering Regulations 1993 (the 1993 Regulations)[3] and, by extension, to the Joint Money Laundering Steering Group (JMLSG) guidelines to the extent that they may be carrying on relevant financial business. The JMLSG, a collective body of trade associations in the financial sector, have issued guidance notes on the 1993 Regulations which are regarded as the relevant supervisory guidance and best practice for the purposes of the 1993 Regulations, reg 9(3). These regulations will be unaffected by the additional powers which the FSA has under FSMA 2000, s 146. Equally, the role of the National Criminal Intelligence Service, the police and other criminal enforcement agencies will not change in relation to the primary legislation on money laundering or the 1993 Regulations, but the FSA will have additional powers in respect of those firms which it regulates.

---

[1] See the FSA Handbook, Money Laundering sourcebook, ML 1.1 for application to authorised firms in relation to 'relevant regulated activities' (generally, regulated activities other than insurance: see ML 1.1.4G).

[2] FSA CP 46, Money Laundering: the FSA's new role, April 2000, para 3.7. The FSA will, however, continue to keep this area under review under its general oversight function in relation to the conduct of exempt regulated activities by the professional firms (CP 46, para 3.8).

[3] SI 1993/1933. The 1993 Regulations are to be superseded by the Money Laundering Regulations 2003, SI 2003/3075 with effect from 1 March 2004 for most purposes (reg 1(2)).

Money Laundering Regulations 1993[1]

5.57 The Money Laundering Regulations 1993, which implement the Money Laundering Directive,[2] require that those persons carrying on 'relevant financial business' maintain certain systems and controls to prevent and identify money laundering.[3]

---

[1] See para 5.56, fn 3.
[2] Council Directive 91/308/EEC.
[3] SI 1993/1933, reg 4.

5.58 The FSA also has the power to appoint investigators if there are circumstances suggesting that a person may be guilty of an offence under money laundering regulations (s 168(4)(b)). This enables the FSA to conduct investigations into possible money laundering offences regardless of where in the UK they may have been perpetrated.[1]

---

[1] See HL Committee Stage, 18 May 2000, col 425. Section 402(1)(b) does not permit the FSA to prosecute suspected breaches of money laundering regulations in Scotland.

5.59 The FSA's role under the new statutory regime in relation to money laundering comprises setting and enforcing standards on anti-money laundering systems and controls in FSA-regulated businesses. This includes requiring firms to have and maintain systems and controls to—

— take care when commencing business with a new customer;
— be alert to the possibility of money laundering by a customer or a prospective customer;
— communicate suspicions of money laundering to the criminal authorities;
— keep records which may prove significant for subsequent criminal investigations and prosecutions;
— ensure senior management monitoring and control; and
— secure and maintain the informed participation in these systems of all relevant employees of the business.[1]

---

[1] See generally the FSA Handbook, Money Laundering sourcebook, ML.

5.60 The FSA has stated that it intends to use its powers to increase confidence that existing requirements are being met consistently and effectively.[1]

---

[1] The FSA has carried out a 'money laundering theme' study assessing the industry's compliance with the Money Laundering Regulations 1993 and other requirements. These can be found on the FSA's website: http://www.fsa.gov.uk/what/ml_thematic.html.

Control of information rules

5.61 The FSA may also make rules regarding the disclosure and use of information held by an authorised person (s 147(1)) (sometimes referred to as 'Chinese walls').[1] These rules may—

— require the withholding of information from one authorised person which he would otherwise have to disclose to another person for or with whom the authorised person does business in the course of any regulated or other activity (s 147(2)(a));

— specify the circumstances in which an authorised person may withhold information which he would otherwise have to disclose to another person (s 147(2)(b));

— require an authorised person not to use for the benefit of a person information which he holds and would otherwise have to use for the benefit of that other person (s 147(2)(c));

— specify circumstances in which an authorised person may decide not to use for the benefit of a person information which he holds which he would otherwise have to use in that way (s 147(2)(d)).

In effect, if an authorised person maintains 'Chinese walls' in accordance with FSA rules made under s 147, he will not be subject to obligations as to the disclosure and use of information that would otherwise apply.

[1] See FSMA Explanatory Notes, para 271. See also the FSA Handbook, Conduct of Business sourcebook, COB 2.4.

5.62 During the debates in the House of Lords reference was made to the 1995 Law Commission report, *Fiduciary Obligations and Regulatory Rules* and its recommendation that a statutory defence should be created for any civil liability incurred by an authorised person who has acted in conformity with the FSA's 'Chinese walls' rules.[1] Following further consultation, the Government stated that it was of the view that, on balance, express provision for a defence from civil action was not necessary. Lord McIntosh said that—

'Since the Law Commission reported, and, indeed, since the consultation document published with the draft Bill, there have been developments in case law which, although not directly dealing with financial services firms, did address the issue of civil liability and procedures for dealing with conflicts of interest. The most important case here is the 1999 case of *Prince Jefri Bolkiah v KPMG*.

In the light of the statements of the Judicial Committee of this House in this case, it is the Government's firm belief that the courts would be unlikely to hold that someone could successfully sue an authorised person for breach of fiduciary duties where the authorised person has complied with FSA rules, which, of course, are made under Parliament's delegated statutory powers.

The Law Commission and many of the City Liaison Group, which includes the representatives of several City law firms, tend to agree with us that an explicit defence is not necessary here. In addition, there is concern that express provision could cast doubt on the current position in relation to rules made under the Financial Services Act 1986. Such a defence could also have implications in relation to the effect of compliance in other areas with rules made by the FSA under its statutory powers. The new clause has been recast so that rules will require an authorised firm to do various things.

Where an authorised person has no choice other than to comply with statutory rules, he cannot be subject to civil liability for anything that he does in accordance with those rules.'[2]

---

[1] See HL Report Stage, 9 May 2000, col 1405.

[2] HL Report Stage, 9 May 2000, col 1409.

5.63 These rules made under s 147 create a safe harbour in certain circumstances provided firms have established effective barriers in the form of procedures, systems, management and physical separation in order to ensure that information obtained by one part of a firm is not communicated in inappropriate circumstances to another part of the firm (for example, where it would advantage one client at the expense of another).[1]

---

[1] FSMA Explanatory Notes, para 271. This provision is similar to the provisions in FSA 1986, s 48(2)(h). The relevant provisions are set out in the FSA Handbook, Conduct of Business sourcebook, COB 2.4.

5.64 The Market Abuse Code[1] contains provisions for a safe harbour for 'behaviour not based on information' where that information is held behind an effective 'Chinese wall'. The Code indicates that both authorised and unauthorised firms may avail themselves of this safe harbour.[2] Therefore the behaviour will not amount to market abuse if the firm establishes Chinese walls arrangements, and an individual in possession of the information had no involvement in the decision to deal and either had no contact with the individual undertaking the deal, or did not behave in such a way as to influence the decision to deal (in accordance with the relevant conduct of business rules).[3] Although this wording here includes 'no contact' as a method of demonstrating that the information did not pass, it is not the only method by which to comply. If the firm can show by other methods that there was no influencing behaviour, it would not also be necessary to show that there had been no contact.[4]

---

[1]   See also Ch 11.
[2]   FSA Handbook, Market Conduct sourcebook, MAR 1.5.24.
[3]   The provisions are set out in the FSA Handbook, Conduct of Business sourcebook, COB 2.4.
[4]   FSA CP 59, Market Abuse: A Draft Code of Market Conduct, July 2000, para 6.37.

MODIFICATION OR WAIVER OF FSA RULES

5.65   Section 148 provides that many of the FSA's rules may be modified or waived on application[1] of or with the consent of an authorised person. It applies to the auditors and actuaries rules (s 340),[2] the control of information rules (s 147), the financial promotion rules (s 145), general rules (s 138(2)), the insurance business rules (s 142), the money laundering rules (s 146) and the price stabilising rules (s 144) (s 148(1)).

---

[1]   An application for waiver or modification under this section may be made in such a way as the FSA may direct (s 148(3)).
[2]   The ability to modify or waive these rules may, in practice, be limited because the obligation to comply will be on the auditor or actuary rather than on the authorised person: see further para 5.67 for the limitations on the power.

5.66   The FSA may direct[1] that all or any of these rules are not to apply to the authorised person who has applied for a modification or waiver of these rules or are to apply to that authorised person in accordance with the modifications as may be specified in the direction (s 148(2)).[2]

---

[1]   Under the Financial Services and Markets Act 2000 (Transitional Provisions and Savings) (Rules) Order 2001, SI 2001/1534, arts 8 and 51, the FSA may designate certain rules made before N2 as continuing in effect after the commencement date as if they were rules made under FSMA 2000. See also the Financial Services and Markets Act 2000 (Consequential and Transitional Provisions) (Miscellaneous) (No 2) Order 2001, SI 2001/2659, art 3 for transitional provisions relevant before N2.
[2]   Section 148(3)–(9), (11) has effect (with certain modifications) in relation to a direction by the FSA under the Open Ended Investment Companies Regulations 2001, reg 7(1), (2) to modify or waive the application of any rules made by the FSA under reg 6 of those Regulations as they have effect in relation to a direction given under s 148(2): see the Open Ended Investment Companies Regulations 2001, SI 2001/1228, reg 7(3), (4).

5.67   However, the FSA may not grant such a direction unless it is satisfied that compliance by the authorised person with the rules would be unduly burdensome or would not otherwise achieve the purpose for which the rules were made, and is satisfied that the direction would not result in undue risk to persons whose interests the rules were intended to protect (s 148(4)). A direction made under s 148 may also be made subject to conditions imposed by the FSA (s 148(5)).

5.68   The FSA must publish a direction made under s 148 in such a way as to bring the direction to the attention of those persons who are likely to be affected by it and others who may be likely to apply for a similar direction for modification or waiver of these rules (s 148(6)). The FSA need not, however, publish a direction made under s 148 if it is satisfied that it is inappropriate or unnecessary to do so (s 148(6)).

5.69   In deciding whether to publish such a direction, the FSA must take into account whether the direction relates to a rule which is actionable under the provisions regarding breach of statutory duty under s 150 (s 148(7)(a)),[1] whether the publication would unreasonably prejudice the commercial interests of the authorised person or any other member of his immediate group (s 148(7)(b)),[2] and whether its publication would be contrary to any international obligation of the UK (s 148(7)(c)). For the purposes of s 148(7)(b) and (c), the FSA must consider whether it would be possible to publish an anonymised version of the direction without disclosing the identity of the authorised person concerned (s 148(8)). Section 148(9) provides that the FSA may revoke a direction or vary it on the application, or with the consent, of the authorised person to whom it relates.

---

[1]   See para 5.73.

[2]   For the purposes of this section, 'immediate group' in relation to an authorised person means an authorised person, a parent undertaking of that authorised person, a subsidiary undertaking of that authorised person, a subsidiary undertaking of a parent undertaking of that authorised person or a parent undertaking of a subsidiary undertaking of that authorised person (s 148(11)).

5.70   The FSA may revoke a direction[1] or vary it on the application, or with the consent, of the authorised person to whom it relates (s 148(9)).

---

[1]   'Direction' means a direction under s 148(2) (s 148(10)).

CONTRAVENTION OF FSA RULES

Limit on effect of contravening rules

5.71   Section 151 provides that a person who contravenes any of the rules[1] made by the FSA under Pt X is not guilty of an offence and that the contravention of a rule made by the FSA does not render any transaction concerned void or unenforceable.

___
[1]   'Rule' is defined in s 417(1) as a rule made by the FSA under FSMA 2000.

Evidential provisions

5.72   Furthermore, the FSA can make rules,[1] contravention of which does not have any of the other consequences provided for by other provisions of FSMA 2000 (s 149(1)).[2] In these cases,[3] the rule must also provide that contravention of that rule tends to establish the contravention of another rule or that compliance with that rules tends to establish compliance with that other rule (s 149(2)).[4]

___
[1]   This provision does not apply to the FSA when it is exercising its functions as competent authority under Pt VI (Sch 7, para 4(1)).
[2]   The Financial Services and Markets Act 2000 (Transitional Provisions and Savings) (Rules) Order 2001, SI 2001/1534 provides that if the FSA has designated rules made before N2 as continuing to have effect, these rules are also subject to s 149(1).
[3]   The FSA may only make a provision under s 149(1) if it considers that it is appropriate also to include the provisions that contravention or compliance tends to establish contravention or compliance with another rule (s 149(3)).
[4]   Other provisions are made by the FSA with evidential status—see in particular the Market Abuse Code in the FSA Handbook, Market Conduct sourcebook, MAR 1.

Breach of rules: action for damages

5.73   A private person who has suffered a loss as a result of the contravention of a rule[1] by an authorised person has a right of action for damages (s 150(1)).[2] A suit brought by a private person in respect of such a contravention may be treated as quasi-strict liability and is subject to the defences applying to an action for breach of statutory duty. This right to bring an action in damages for a breach of statutory duty[3] may be extended in certain circumstances to persons who are not 'private persons' (s 150(3)). The FSA rules may, however, provide that certain rules do not give rise to an action for damages under s 150 (s 150(2)). This right is in addition to any rights the private investor may have in contract or tort or otherwise at common law.[4]

___
[1]   For the purposes of s 150 the term 'rule' does not include listing rules or a rule requiring an authorised person to have or maintain financial resources (s 150(4)).
[2]   'Private person' is defined in the Financial Services and Markets Act 2000 (Rights of Action) Regulations 2001, SI 2001/2256, reg 3. The definition includes individuals (except when conducting regulated activities) and certain others unless carrying on any business.
[3]   This is similar to FSA 1986, s 62. Similar provisions existed for friendly societies under FSA 1986, Sch 11, para 22 but there are no equivalent provisions in the Insurance Companies Act 1982 or the Banking Act 1987: see FSMA 2000: Rights of Action—A Consultation Document, 21 December 2000, paras 1.6–1.9.
[4]   *Loosemore v Financial Concepts* [2001] Lloyd's Rep PN 235.

5.74   The definition of those persons who fall within the term, 'private person' are to be prescribed by the Treasury.[1] These regulations prescribe the cases in which private (and non-private) persons may bring an action for loss suffered as a result of a breach of FSA requirements, rules and certain provisions under FSMA 2000. The regulations prescribe—

'(a)   the cases in which breach of a permission under Part IV or resulting from any other provision of FSMA is actionable by any person (section 20(3));

(b)   the definition of a 'private person' who may bring an action for breach of a duty to take reasonable care in relation to the activities of a person who is subject to a prohibition order or the performance of a controlled function (section 71(3)) and the cases in which such a breach is actionable by a person who is not a private person (section 71(2));

(c)   the definition of a 'private person' who may bring an action for breach of a rule (other than a rule relating to financial resources) (section 150(5)) and the cases in which such a breach is actionable by a person who is not a private person (section 150(3)); and

(d)   the cases in which breach of a requirement imposed by the FSA exercising its power of intervention in respect of an incoming EEA firm or Treaty firm is actionable by any person (section 202(2))'.[2]

---

[1]   See para 5.73, fn 2.

[2]   FSMA 2000: Rights of Action—A Consultation Document, 21 December 2000, para 1.1: see the Financial Services and Markets Act 2000 (Rights of Action) Regulations 2001, SI 2001/2256, reg 7.

5.75   For the purposes of s 20(3) (authorised person acting without permission) certain conditions must be met. These are that the contravention is not one of a Pt IV financial resources requirement, and the action would be brought at the suit of a private person as defined in the Rights of Action Regulations[1] or a person acting in a fiduciary or representative capacity on behalf of a private person and any remedy would be exclusively for the benefit of that private person and could not be effected through an action otherwise than at the suit of the fiduciary.[2]

---

[1]   Ie, the Financial Services and Markets Act 2000 (Rights of Action) Regulations 2001, SI 2001/2256. These conditions are similar to the restrictions in s 150.

[2]   SI 2001/2256, reg 4.

5.76   Difficulties arise over the effect of this provision in relation to certain of the rules which apply to regulated persons. In its Consultation Document the Government stated that it—

' . . . wishes to ensure that the different consequences arising from breach of a requirement, rule or other provision under FSMA do not produce perverse results. For example, it would be perverse to have a situation where, say, a right of action applied under section 20(3) of FSMA where there was a breach of a financial resources requirement imposed under section 43 of FSMA but there was no right of action by any person (private or non-private) as a result of breach of a financial resources rule by virtue of section 150(4). Since breach of a financial resources requirement is not actionable under the FS Act, the Government proposes that breach of a financial resources/capital ratio/premium income limit requirement should not be actionable by any person (private or non-private) under FSMA.

Client money is also problematic. Breach of the client money rules will give rise to a right of action by a private person under section 150(1) of FSMA but not by a non-private person except to the extent specified in regulations. But breach of a client money requirement imposed as part of a permission will be actionable by any person under section 20(3). To avoid this potentially perverse result, the Government believes that non-private persons should be able to bring an action for breach of a client money rule under section 150(3) of FSMA.'[1]

---

[1]   HM Treasury, Financial Services and Markets Act 2000: Rights of Action—A Consultation Document, 21 December 2000, paras 1.16, 1.17.

EEA and Treaty firms

5.77   Section 202(2) provides that a contravention of a requirement imposed by the FSA in respect of an incoming EEA or Treaty firm may be actionable at the suit of a person who suffers a loss as a result of the contravention subject to the defences applying to actions for breach of statutory duty.[1]

---

[1]   A right of action is available to any person who suffers loss as a result of a requirement (except a financial resources requirement): see the Financial Services and Markets Act 2000 (Rights of Action) Regulations 2001, SI 2001/2256, reg 7. While it is unlikely that the FSA would impose a financial resources requirement on a Sch 3 EEA firm, as financial resources would be a prudential matter for the home state regulator, the FSA may impose a financial resources requirement on a Sch 4 Treaty firm: see FSMA 2000: Rights of Action—A Consultation Document, 21 December 2000, para 1.23.

RULE-MAKING PROCEDURES

Notification to the Treasury

5.78 In making any rules under Pt X, the FSA must comply with the procedures set out in ss 152–155. The FSA must provide a copy of any rules which it makes to the Treasury without delay (s 152(1)), and if it revokes or amends any rules, it must give written notice to the Treasury of the change including details of any alteration (s 152(2), (3)).[1]

---

[1] 'Sunset provisions' were proposed during Parliamentary debate on FSMA 2000. These would have required the FSA to conduct a rolling review of its rules, or would have provided for the FSA's rules to expire after a set period, but these proposals were ultimately withdrawn: see HC, 1 February 2000, col 924.

Rule-making instruments

5.79 The FSA must make its rules by written instrument, and publish them in a way that brings them to the attention of the public, though it is entitled to charge a fee for providing copies of its rules (s 153(1), (4), (5)).[1]

---

[1] These provisions do not apply to the FSA in exercising its functions as competent authority under FSMA 2000, Pt VI (Sch 7, para 4(1)).

5.80 The FSA must also identify in any rule-making instrument the provision or provisions under which those rules have been made (s 153(2)), or the instrument will be void (s 153(3)). If a person is alleged to have contravened any rule made by the FSA it will be a defence if he can show that the rule-making instrument concerned had not been made available in accordance with s 153 (s 153(6)).[1]

---

[1] See para 5.79.

Verification of rules

5.81 A printed copy of a rule-making instrument which has been endorsed by a certificate signed by a member of the FSA's staff[1] (authorised by it for that purpose) which contains the required statements, is evidence[2] of the facts stated in the certificate (s 154(1)). Those statements are that—
— the instrument was made by the FSA;
— the copy is a true copy of the instrument; and
— on a specified date the instrument was made available to the public in accordance with s 153(4) (s 154(2)).[3]

A person who wishes to rely on a rule-making instrument in legal proceedings may require the FSA to endorse it in this way (s 154(4)).[4]

---

[1] The signature of a person purporting to be duly authorised to sign a certificate on behalf of the FSA is to be assumed to have been properly signed unless the contrary can be shown (s 154(3)).
[2] In Scotland, the endorsement by certificate is to be taken as 'sufficient evidence' (s 154(1)).
[3] See para 5.79.
[4] See para 5.79.

Consultation

5.82 If the FSA proposes to make any rules under FSMA 2000, it must first publish[1] a draft of the proposed rules accompanied by a cost benefit analysis (defined in s 155(10)),[2] an explanation of the purpose of the proposed rules and an explanation of the FSA's grounds for believing that the exercise of these rule-making powers is compatible with its general duties under s 2 (s 155(1), (2)(a)–(c)).[3] The FSA may charge a reasonable fee for providing copies of the draft rules to be published under s 155(1) (s 155(12)).

---

[1] Publication must be made in the way appearing to the FSA best calculated to bring the draft rules to the attention of the public (s 155(1)).
[2] 'Cost benefit analysis' is defined as an estimate of the costs together with an analysis of the benefits that will arise if the proposed rules are made, or, if the rules are different from a draft issued for consultation under s 155(1), from the rules that have been made.
[3] The requirement to publish an explanation of the FSA's reasons for believing the proposed rules are compatible with its general duties under s 2 does not apply to fee rules and guidance in relation to building societies, friendly societies, industrial and provident societies and credit unions: see the Financial Services and Markets Act 2000 (Mutual Societies) Order 2001, SI 2001/2617, art 4(3), Sch 2, paras 11(b), 14(b). In relation to the FSA's exercise of its functions as competent authority under Pt VI, s 155 is modified to the extent that the reference in s 155(2)(c) to the FSA's general duties under s 2 is to be read as a reference to its duty as competent authority under s 73 (Sch 7, para 4(2)(a)).

5.83 Any proposed rules must allow sufficient time (which must be specified when publishing the draft rules) for any representations regarding them to be made to the FSA (s 155(2)(d)).

5.84 The need to comply with the consultation process under s 155 can be overridden if the FSA considers that the delay which such consultation would cause would be prejudicial to the interests of consumers (s 155(7)).

5.85 Before making the proposed rules the FSA must have regard to the representations made to it in accordance with s 155(2)(d) (s 155(4)). If the FSA makes the proposed rules it must publish an account of the representations which have been made to it and its response to them (s 155(5)). The process adopted by the FSA of publishing a consultation paper followed by a feedback statement reflects these requirements.

5.86   If the rules differ significantly from the draft published, the FSA must (in addition to complying with s 155(5)) publish details of the difference between the draft and the final rules and a further cost benefit analysis (s 155(6)).[1] The need for a cost benefit analysis may be obviated if the FSA, making the appropriate comparison (defined in s 155(11)),[2] considers that there will be no increase in costs or that the increase of costs would be of minimal significance in relation to the rules or changes proposed (s 155(8)).

---

[1]   See para 5.82, fn 2.

[2]   The 'appropriate comparison' is a comparison between the overall position if the proposed rules are not made (if s 155(2)(a) applies—ie, on initial consultation) or a comparison between the overall position before and after the rules are made (if s 155(6)(a) applies—ie, for a further cost benefit analysis required if the rules made differ significantly from those consulted on).

5.87   A cost benefit analysis is not required where the proposed rules are to be made under—

—   s 136(2) (FSA's power to raise funds to fund the legal assistance scheme for market abuse actions before the Tribunal),[1]

—   s 213(1) (as a result of s 213(4) (the compensation scheme manager's levy raising powers));

—   s 234 (industry funding of the ombudsman scheme); or

—   Sch 1, para 17 (fees chargeable by the FSA) (s 155(9)).[2]

However, in such cases, the draft rules must be accompanied by a statement of the expected expenditure which the proposal is likely to give rise to (s 155(3)).

---

[1]   See Ch 12.

[2]   In relation to the FSA's exercise of its functions as competent authority under Pt VI, s 155(9) is modified to include reference to s 99 (fees in relation to listing) (Sch 7, para 4(2)(b)).

GUIDANCE

5.88   In addition to making rules, the FSA has wide powers to provide guidance. It may give such guidance in the form of information or advice in relation to the operation of FSMA 2000 and any of the rules made under it as it considers appropriate (s 157(1)(a)). It may also provide guidance about its functions, for the purpose of meeting its regulatory objectives or on any other matter about which the FSA considers it to be desirable to give information or advice (s (1)(b)–(d)).[1] This guidance may include recommendations made by the FSA to persons generally, to regulated persons generally or to any class of regulated person (s 157(5)).[2]

5.89 There was much debate during the passage of the Bill through its consultative and parliamentary stages about whether the FSA's procedures for issuing guidance should follow the US practice of providing 'no action letters' to firms or other persons in relation to the operation of FSMA 2000 and the rules.¹ The FSA stated its position as follows—

> 'In the UK context, routine publication of individual guidance could be expected to have serious drawbacks. It would drive relationships between regulators and firms in the direction of legalism and formalism—because, for example, firms would need to analyse previously published correspondence before approaching the FSA for guidance, and because the exchange of letters between the FSA and a firm would have to be elaborately choreographed. This in turn would impose appreciable new costs on the FSA and the regulated community. The publication of individual guidance would also mean a proliferation of detailed regulatory material, whose bulk would become increasingly unmanageable over time.'²

¹ See Burns Committee, First Report, 1999, Appendix 31, Memorandum submitted by Denton Hall. See also HC SC A, 9 November 1999 and HL 2R, 21 February 2000, col 65.
² FSA Policy Statement, The FSA's approach to giving guidance and waivers to firms, September 1999, para 21: see generally paras 5–25.

5.90 FSMA 2000 does not *require* publication of guidance to individual firms, but the FSA may publish its guidance and offer copies of it for sale for a reasonable fee (s 157(4)(a), (b)).¹ If individual guidance has been given in response to a request from any person, the FSA may make a reasonable charge for providing that guidance (s 157(4)(c)).²

¹ However, see para 5.93 on general guidance.
² Although FSMA 2000 gives the FSA the power to charge for providing guidance on an individual basis, the FSA has indicated that individual guidance will continue to be given on a 'relatively informal basis' and without charge: FSA Press Release 093/1999, 27 September 1999. The FSA has also indicated that more formal individual guidance will be available in certain circumstances: see the FSA Handbook, Supervision manual, SUP 9.

5.91 The FSA may also provide funding or other assistance to persons giving guidance in the form of information or advice of a kind which the FSA could give under s 157 (s 157(2)).

Consultation on guidance

5.92   Where the FSA proposes to give advice or guidance to regulated persons,[1] or a class of them, in relation to the FSA rules to which those persons are subject, it must consult and comply with the procedures on rules laid down in s 155 (s 157(3)).[2]

---

[1]   Under the Financial Services and Markets Act 2000 (Mutual Societies) Order 2001, SI 2001/2617, Sch 2, paras 12–17, guidance to building societies, friendly societies and industrial and provident societies generally or to a class of such societies is to be treated as if given to regulated persons regardless of whether those societies would otherwise be 'regulated persons' within the meaning of s 157(6).

[2]   See paras 5.82–5.86. This is material which will often amount to 'general guidance': see para 5.93, fn 1. As a result, much general guidance will be published during these procedures.

Notification of guidance to the Treasury

5.93   Where the FSA has given general guidance,[1] it must provide a copy of that guidance to the Treasury and where it proposes to change, alter or revoke existing guidance, it must give a written notice to the Treasury without delay (s 158(1), (2), (4)). This notice must include details of the changes to the guidance which the FSA is proposing to make (s 158(3)).[2]

---

[1]   'General guidance' means guidance given pursuant to s 157 that is given to persons generally, to regulated persons generally, or to a class of regulated person which has continuing effect and which has been given in writing or other legible form (s 158(5)). 'Regulated person' has the same meaning as for s 157: see para 5.88, fn 2.

[2]   See para 5.92, fn 1 for this provision's application to building societies, friendly societies and industrial and provident societies—the Financial Services and Markets Act 2000 (Mutual Societies) Order 2001, SI 2001/2617, Sch 2, para 12.

6 Financial promotion

INTRODUCTION

6.1   The financial promotion regime under the Financial Services and Markets Act 2000 (FSMA 2000), including the restrictions on the promotion of collective investment schemes, replaces the numerous legislative frameworks for advertisements and unsolicited calls with a single restriction and a more comprehensive set of exemptions.[1]

---

[1]   HC Report, 9 February 2000, col 276. See also HM Treasury, Financial Promotion, Third Consultation Document, October 2000, Annex C, para 5.

KEY CHANGES IN THE NEW REGIME

6.2   Although the Treasury indicated before the regime came into force that there would be no significant change in the extent of the restrictions on financial promotion,[1] there are nevertheless a number of substantive differences (both in approach and detail) under the new regime.

---

[1]   HM Treasury, Financial Promotion, Third Consultation Document, October 2000, para 1.7.

6.3   The prohibition on unlawful financial promotion set out in s 21 replaces and refines the 'investment advertisements' regime,[1] the restrictions on banking advertisements,[2] those on insurance advertisements[3] and those on unsolicited calls.[4] The financial promotion regime applies, however, to a wider range of activities than under the Financial Services Act 1986 (FSA 1986), as it now includes communications in relation to Lloyd's, the acceptance of deposits by credit unions, mortgage products and pre-paid funeral plans.[5]

---

[1]   Financial Services Act 1986, ss 57 and 58 and the orders made under those sections.
[2]   Banking Act 1987, ss 32–35 and the orders made under those sections.
[3]   FSA 1986, s 130 and the Insurance Companies Regulations 1994, SI 1994/1516, regs 35–37.
[4]   FSA 1986, s 56 and the rules made under that section.

141

[5]   HM Treasury, Financial Promotion, Third Consultation Document, October 2000, para 1.7 and Annex C, para 8. See also FSA CP 25, Enforcing the New Perimeter, July 1999 on the policy of the Financial Services Authority (FSA) regarding the enforcement of the regime in relation to unlawful financial promotions. The financial promotion regime has only applied to funeral plan contracts since 1 January 2002.

6.4   The financial promotion regime only applies to promotions made in the course of business whereas the investment advertisement regime under FSA 1986, s 57 applied to all 'investment advertisements' without restriction.[1]

[1]   See para 6.11. See also HM Treasury, Financial Promotion, Third Consultation Document, October 2000, Annex C, para 6.

6.5   Designed to 'modernise and streamline the legislative framework currently applying to financial promotion in the UK',[1] the financial promotion regime creates a generic category of 'communications' incorporating both advertising and unsolicited calls as a technologically 'neutral' media which can be interpreted broadly to allow the regulators to take account of the rapidly developing technological changes which are reshaping the promotion and delivery of financial services to both financial professionals and consumers.

[1]   See also HM Treasury, Financial Services and Markets Bill: Financial Promotion, Second Consultation Document: A new approach for the information age, October 1999, para 1.1. The Treasury consulted widely on the new financial promotion regime particularly after adverse comments from industry and lawyers on the original proposals in the July 1998 draft bill. See also HM Treasury, Financial Services and Markets Bill: Financial Promotion: Third Consultation Document, October 2000, Annex C, para 7.

6.6   The rationale behind this was explained as follows—

'In considering its approach [to financial promotion], the Government has also focused on how to address questions posed by recent developments in technology, such as the advent and increasing use of the Internet, scripted messages and multi-media communications. These have put the existing regulatory framework under some pressure, requiring ever more strained interpretations of the current legislation in order to keep pace with the changes in technology affecting the financial services industry in the UK. Accordingly, one of the Government's main aims for the new financial promotion regime is to avoid, as far as possible, discriminating between different communications media, and also to ensure that the legislation is sufficiently flexible to adapt to further technological changes.'[1]

1   HM Treasury, Financial Promotion, A Consultation Document, March 1999, para 1.3. See also HM Treasury, Financial Services and Markets Bill: Financial Promotion, Second Consultation Document: A new approach for the information age, October 1999, para 1.2 and HC SC A, 22 July 1999.

6.7   However, the new financial promotion regime will apply in some cases where it did not previously, namely in relation to certain types of solicited calls and the application of the financial promotion regime to communications (by unauthorised persons) from the UK to overseas recipients.[1]

1   HM Treasury, Financial Promotion, Third Consultation Document, October 2000, Annex C, paras 3–10.

6.8   Although 'offering' to carry out regulated activities is no longer an inchoate part of regulated activities itself,[1] under the financial promotion regime, there may be instances where a person making or communicating a financial promotion (for example, publishers, broadcasters, financial commentators, internet service providers and telemarketing companies) may be carrying out 'regulated activities' within the meaning of FSMA 2000, s 22.[2] The regulated activities which are likely to be caught in this case are giving investment advice[3] or making arrangements with a view to a transaction in investments[4] or agreeing to carry out these activities.[5]

1   Unlike the position under FSA 1986, Sch 1, Pt II.
2   FSA Handbook, Authorisation manual, AUTH App 1.23.2G and 1.23.3G.
3   The Financial Services and Markets Act 2000 (Regulated Activities) Order 2001, SI 2001/544 (the 'Regulated Activities Order'), art 53.
4   The Regulated Activities Order, art 25(1).
5   The Regulated Activities Order, art 64.

THE RESTRICTION ON FINANCIAL PROMOTIONS

6.9   FSMA 2000, s 21(1) provides that a person must not in the course of business communicate[1] an invitation or inducement[2] to engage in investment activity unless the communication is one to which certain exemptions apply under an order made under s 21(5).[3] This restriction does not apply, however, if that person is an authorised person[4] or the content of the communication is approved[5] by an authorised person for the purposes of this section (s 21(2)).

1   For the purposes of construing the provisions of Pt II 'communication' includes causing a communication to be made (s 30(9)).

[2]   See paras 6.21–6.25.

[3]   The Financial Services and Markets Act 2000 (Financial Promotion) Order 2001, SI 2001/1335 (the 'Financial Promotion Order'), as amended by SI 2001/2633, SI 2001/3650, SI 2001/3800, SI 2002/1310 and SI 2002/2157.

[4]   An 'authorised person' is defined as a person who has a Pt IV permission to carry on one or more regulated activities or an EEA firm qualifying for authorisation under Sch 3 or a Treaty firm qualifying for authorisation under Sch 4 or a person who is otherwise authorised under a provision of or made under FSMA 2000 (s 31(1)).

[5]   'Approved' for the purposes of s 21 means approved in accordance with the rules made by the FSA under s 145: see the FSA Handbook, Conduct of Business sourcebook, COB 3. Note, however, that under COB 3, authorised persons may only approve 'non-real time financial promotions' (COB 3.12.2R) and therefore 'real time' financial promotions cannot be approved for the purposes of s 21. For definition of 'non-real time' and 'real time' financial promotions, see glossary and guidance in the FSA Handbook, Authorisation manual, AUTH App 1.10.

6.10   The Act does not define a 'financial promotion' but uses the term in the context of a communication which contains an invitation or inducement to engage in investment activity.[1]

[1]   FSA Handbook, Authorisation manual, AUTH App 1.3.2G.

'In the course of business'

6.11   To fall within s 21(1) the communication must be made 'in the course of business'. The Treasury has the power to specify by regulation the circumstances where a person will be considered to be 'acting in the course of business' or 'not acting in the course of business' for the purposes of s 21.[1] To date, however, the Treasury has not used this power and therefore the phrase should be given its ordinary or natural meaning.[2]

[1]   This power to specify what constitutes 'in the course of business' is distinct from that which the Treasury has under s 419 in relation to defining what constitutes 'by way of business' for the purposes of s 22.

[2]   'We agree with Opposition Members that the financial promotion regime should catch only those promotions made in the course of business. Private communications should therefore be excluded. [Section 21(4)] will allow the Treasury to specify circumstances where a person is to be considered as acting—or not acting—in the course of business.' (HC SC A, 22 July 1999, col 349).

6.12   The FSA guidance on financial promotion indicates, however, that 'in the course of business' must include some 'commercial interest' on the part of the communicator although that interest need not be a direct pecuniary interest. The test is whether the communication is part of that person's overall business activities. For example, a holding company which proposes to sell one of its subsidiaries will be doing so 'in the course of business' even though the holding company may well not be in the business of selling subsidiaries.[1]

[1]   FSA Handbook, Authorisation manual, AUTH App 1.5.2G.

6.13   This 'commercial interest' can be construed widely, however, and the FSA Handbook states that there may be circumstances where an individual may be considered to be acting in the course of business. For example, a sole trader who is an independent financial adviser will give investment advice 'in the course of business' and so satisfies the test. An individual who is merely seeking to make personal investments will not be acting 'in the course of business' by approaching a company about investing in its shares.[1]

---

[1]   FSA Handbook, Authorisation manual, AUTH App 1.5.4G.

6.14   The FSA Handbook also points out that the communication does not need to be made by that person in the course of carrying on activities as a business in their own right, ie, meeting the test in s 22 in relation to activities carried on 'by way of business'.[1]

---

[1]   See the Financial Services and Markets Act 2000 (Carrying on Regulated Activities by Way of Business) Order 2001, SI 2001/1177, art 3.

Communication

6.15   A key difference between the financial promotion regime and the regime under FSA 1986 is that the financial promotion regime removes the distinction between advertising and unsolicited calls. The financial promotion regime includes any form of 'communication' or causing such a communication to be made (s 21(13)).

6.16   However, to fall within the regime, the communication must be one which invites or induces a person to engage in investment activity (s 21(1)). Again, questions of interpretation will no doubt arise over whether any particular communication contains or could be construed as containing those elements.[1] The Treasury Consultation Paper on the financial promotion regime stated that the prohibition should apply only to communications containing a degree of incitement and not to communications comprising purely factual information where the facts are presented in such a way that they do not also amount to an invitation or inducement.

---

[1]   See FSA Handbook, Authorisation manual, AUTH Annex.

6.17   Although recognising the difficulties the Treasury's first consultation paper on the financial promotion of collective investment schemes stated that—

> 'the Government does not believe that there is any reason to refer to intention either on the face of the Act or within the [Financial Promotion] Order. In determining whether

a particular communication constitutes an inducement, much will depend on the context of that communication. Something that would not be considered an inducement in one set of circumstances could well be so in another and that is what, if necessary, a court would consider. Even if "inducement" were qualified it would remain an issue which would require interpretation by a court. On the grounds that this issue has been fully considered, both in previous consultation and in parliamentary debate, we are not seeking further responses on this issue.'[1]

---

[1]   HM Treasury, Financial Promotion of Collective Investment Schemes, First Consultation Document, Pt II, para 2.4. See also HM .Treasury, Financial Services and Markets Bill: Financial Promotion, Second Consultation Document: A new approach for the information age, October 1999, para 4.4 and HL 3R, 18 May 2000, col 387.

6.18   The financial promotion regime intends to catch not only the person making the communication but also the person causing a communication to be made (s 21(13)), continuing the concept of 'issuing or causing to be issued' which itself derived from the English and US sedition legislation of the 18th century where not only the person responsible for 'making' the seditious statement but the 'publisher' of that statement could be prosecuted.

6.19   The FSA guidance on financial promotion indicates that a person is 'communicating' if he gives material to the recipient or where, in certain circumstances, he is responsible for transmitting the material on behalf of another person in which case both would be caught under s 21.[1] For example, a speaker at a roadshow or conference is an individual but where the individual speaks on behalf of his employer, it is the FSA's view that it will be the employer who is responsible for that communication.[2] However, where a person other than the originator of the communication (for example, a newspaper publisher) transmits a communication on the originator's behalf he is equally 'communicating' it and the originator is causing its communication. The newspaper publisher may, nonetheless, be caught by s 21 unless one of the available exemptions applies.[3]

---

[1]   FSA Handbook, Authorisation manual, AUTH App 1.6.1G.
[2]   Hence if the employer is an authorised person, the communication will have been made by an authorised person and therefore the restriction in s 21 does not apply but the authorised person would be required to comply with FSA Handbook, Conduct of Business sourcebook, COB 3.
[3]   There are exemptions, for example, 'mere conduits' (the Financial Promotion Order, art 18). See also *Godfrey v Demon Internet Ltd* [2001] QB 201, [1999] 4 All ER 342 concerning the liability of an internet service provider in relation to a defamatory statement contained in a discussion group.

6.20   Not all persons involved in the chain of creating a communication will be caught, however. The FSA Handbook indicates that an advertising agency whose sole role is assisting a company in preparing its marketing materials will not be communicating the financial promotion, nor will persons whose role is simply to print or produce material for others or those who 'place' communications.[1]

---

[1]   FSA Handbook, Authorisation manual, AUTH App 1.6.3G.

Promotional element—invitation or inducement

6.21   FSMA 2000 does not define what constitutes an 'invitation' or 'inducement' for the purpose of s 21 but assumes that these words will be given their natural meaning.[1] In introducing this provision, Patricia Hewitt for the Government said that 'The material will have to be clearly promotional, rather than simply informative.'[2] The FSA's guidance also distinguishes material which merely seeks to inform or educate consumers about the 'mechanics or risks' of investment and is therefore presumably outside the definition of a financial promotion.[3]

---

[1]   FSA Handbook, Authorisation manual, AUTH App 1.4.1G–App 1.4.7G.
[2]   HC SC A, 20 July 1999, col 326.
[3]   AUTH App 1.4.3G.

6.22   The FSA has stated an objective test for determining whether there is an invitation or inducement. The essential elements of an invitation or inducement are that the purpose or intent of the material is to lead a person to engage in investment activity and the material is promotional (ie, seeking to persuade or incite).[1]

---

[1]   FSA Handbook, Authorisation manual, AUTH App 1.4.4G.

6.23   The FSA Handbook contains further exegesis of the phrase by stating that to constitute an 'invitation' it must directly invite a person to take a step that will result in his engaging in investment activity. Examples of such an invitation are direct offer financial promotions, prospectuses with application forms and internet promotions by brokers which allow the recipient to initiate an activity by registering and dealing. It follows, therefore, in the FSA's view, that a communication may contain a statement that it is not an invitation. Furthermore, the FSA Handbook states that such 'statements may be regarded as evidence that the communication is not an invitation unless its contents indicate otherwise'. Presumably, therefore, a statement that a communication does not constitute an invitation could be regarded as a presumption of the communicator's intent unless the facts would show otherwise such as the recipient being able to act to engage in investment activity.[1] The FSA has made it clear, however, that it will consider the substance rather than the form of words and that a particular form of words which would otherwise clearly be an invitation will not change the character of the communication.

---

[1]   FSA Handbook, Authorisation manual, AUTH App 1.4.5G.

6.24   Such invitations must also meet the promotional element of the FSA's objective test and the guidance indicates that documents which would otherwise constitute a financial promotion sent to a person who had already agreed to the terms for signature would not be an 'invitation' within the meaning of s 21.[1]

---

[1]   FSA Handbook, Authorisation manual, AUTH App 1.4.6G.

6.25   Similarly, in relation to the term 'inducement' the FSA Handbook indicates that 'only those that are a significant step in persuading or inciting or seeking to persuade or incite a recipient to engage in investment activity will be inducements under section 21'.[1] The 'mere fact' that a communication may be made at a preliminary stage does not in itself, in the FSA's view, prevent that communication from being a significant step. However, a preliminary communication may simply be an inducement to contact the person making the communication to find out what he has to offer. The FSA Handbook provides as an example an advertisement which merely holds out a person as having expertise in or providing services about investment management or venture capital as not being an inducement to engage in investment activity but merely an inducement to make contact for further material rather than a significant step in the chain. However, an advertisement which claims that what the recipient should do to make his fortune is to invest in securities and that the person making the communication can provide him with the services to achieve that aim will be a significant step and will be an inducement to engage in investment activity within the meaning of s 21.[2]

---

[1]   FSA Handbook, Authorisation manual, AUTH App 1.4.7G.
[2]   AUTH App 1.4.7G.

Engaging in investment activity

6.26   For the purposes of s 21 a person is 'engaging in investment activity' if he enters or offers to enter into an agreement the making or performance of which by either party constitutes a 'controlled activity'[1] or if he exercises any rights conferred by a controlled investment[2] to acquire, dispose of, underwrite or convert a controlled investment (s 21(8)).[3]

---

[1] A 'controlled activity' is an activity which is to be specified in regulations made by the Treasury under s 21 or one which relates to a specified investment (s 21(9)).

[2] A 'controlled investment' is an investment that is to be specified in regulations made by the Treasury under s 21 (s 21(10)).

[3] Most invitations or inducements to exercise voting rights will not, in the FSA's view, constitute a financial promotion: see the FSA Handbook, Authorisation manual, AUTH 1.7.4(2)G.

6.27 An 'investment' for the purposes of this section includes any asset, right or interest (s 21(14)). Section 21(11) provides, however, that Sch 2 applies to s 21(9) and (10), and references to s 22 in that schedule are to be read as references to those subsections, with the proviso that the Treasury's power to make orders is not limited by the list of regulated activities and investments set out in Sch 2 (s 21(12)).

6.28 The Treasury has made an order under s 21(5), (9) and (10) (the Financial Promotion Order)[1] which defines the controlled activities and controlled investments.[2] Some of the exemptions contained in the Financial Promotion Order apply to all controlled activities[3] while others only apply to specific activities.[4]

---

[1] SI 2001/1335: see para 6.9, fn 3.

[2] The Financial Promotion Order, art 4.

[3] For example, communication to overseas recipients (art 12), introductions (art 15), generic promotions (art 17), mere conduits (art 18), investment professionals (art 19), communications by journalist (art 20).

[4] The Financial Promotion Order, Pt V sets out exemptions in relation to deposits and insurance and Pt VI sets out various exemptions which apply only to certain controlled activities.

6.29 In general terms, the 'controlled activities' defined in the Financial Promotion Order, Sch 1, Pt I are similar to those specified in the Regulated Activities Order. However, most of the exclusions in the Regulated Activities Order do not apply. The FSA Handbook points out certain important differences, particularly in relation to certain credit agreements[1] and funeral plans.[2] The result of this is that a person carrying on business in the UK for which authorisation is not required may nonetheless be caught by the restriction on financial promotion under s 21.

---

[1] Section 21 does not yet apply to qualifying credit agreements as defined in the Financial Promotion Order, Sch 1, para 10 but is expected to do so some time in 2004 (Financial Promotion Order, art 1(3)(b), as amended by SI 2002/1777, art 4). See also the FSA Handbook, Authorisation manual, AUTH App 1.17.

[2] See AUTH App 1.16.

6.30   Similarly, 'controlled investments' defined in the Schedule, Pt 2 mirrors certain of the investments specified in the Regulated Activities Order but there are key omissions such as electronic money, as defined in the Regulated Activities Order.[1] Electronic money is not a 'controlled investment' for the purpose of s 21 and therefore the restriction in s 21 does not apply to the communication of an invitation or inducement that concerns electronic money unless the communication is a financial promotion for some other reason.[2]

---

[1]   See SI 2001/544, art 74A, as inserted by the Financial Services and Markets Act 2000 (Regulated Activities) (Amendment) Order 2002, SI 2002/682.
[2]   FSA Handbook, Authorisation manual, AUTH App 1.7.2G.

Territorial scope

6.31   Considerable debate arose during the passage of the Bill over the scope of the financial promotion regime and, in particular, its application to both 'inward' communications, for example, financial services websites available over the internet and 'outward' communications where a communication is made by an unauthorised person exclusively to persons outside the UK.

6.32   FSMA 2000 provides that the restriction in s 21(1) only applies to communications originating outside the UK if the communication is capable of having an effect in the UK (s 21(3)). The FSA Handbook makes it clear that it is a question of whether the communication is *capable* of having an effect rather than whether it *does* have an effect, ie, whether a recipient in the UK actually engages in an investment activity.[1]

---

[1]   FSA Handbook, Authorisation manual, AUTH App 1.8.1G.

Exemptions by Treasury order

6.33   The wide-ranging restriction in s 21 does not, however, apply to authorised persons[1] or to communications where an authorised person has approved the content of the communication for the purposes of s 21 (s 21(2)).[2] In addition, the Treasury may by order specify circumstances in which the general prohibition in s 21(1) will not apply (s 21(5)).[3]

---

[1]   Authorised persons are subject to the FSA Handbook, Conduct of Business sourcebook, COB 3 and are also subject to the rules made concerning the promotion of collective investment schemes under FSMA 2000, s 238. See fn 1 to 6.43.

2   The financial promotion regime also unifies the rules for authorised persons under the FSA Handbook, COB. Under FSA 1986 there were three sets of rules relating to investment advertising: those made by the FSA under its powers, those made by the self-regulating organisations and those made by the recognised professional bodies for those members carrying on investment business.
3   The Financial Promotion Order: see para 6.9, fn 3.

6.34   The broad scope of this provision is, however, also moderated by the exemptions under the Financial Promotion Order that specifically exempts a communication to overseas recipients[1] which is made (whether from inside or outside the UK) to a person who receives the communication outside the UK or which is directed (whether from inside or outside the UK) only at persons outside the UK.[2]

1   SI 2001/1335, art 12.
2   See the Financial Promotion Order, art 6 on the distinction between a communication 'made to' and a communication 'directed at'.

6.35   Orders made under s 21(5) may also disapply the prohibition on financial promotion to communications of a specified description or those originating from a country or territory outside the UK (s 21(6)).

6.36   Other limitations may apply to the scope of s 21 for example, under the E-Commerce Directive in relation to information society services[1] or in relation to certain television broadcasts from other EEA States under the Television Without Frontiers Directive (89/552/EEC).[2]

1   See para 6.61.
2   FSA Handbook, Authorisation manual, AUTH App 1.8.3G.

6.37   The Treasury may by order repeal s 21(3) (s 21(7)). This presumably allows the Treasury flexibility to conform to the financial promotion regime in line with the plethora of European legislation which is or is about to be brought into effect in relation to communications over the internet such as the Distance Marketing Directive, the E-Commerce Directive and other harmonising pieces of EU legislation which will impact on this area.

6.38   The scope of the financial promotion regime is also wide in that it potentially catches communications which are made in the UK, into the UK from elsewhere or from the UK to another country or jurisdiction.[1] While the wording of s 21 arguably gives this very wide territorial scope to the financial promotion restriction, the Treasury has equally wide powers to grant exemptions to cut back this scope by exempting communications from individual countries or territories or from groups of countries (such as the EU). These orders may also contain provisions exempting communications which may be capable of having an effect in the UK but which are essentially covering overseas business or cutting back the application of the restrictions to promotions which are 'directed at' the UK.[2]

---

[1] FSMA Explanatory Notes, para 59.
[2] HM Treasury, Financial Promotion of Collective Investment Schemes, First Consultation Document, October 2000, para 1.10.

6.39 The issue of 'outward communications' also remains in that the Treasury intends to maintain the position which was set out in its October 1999 consultation document, namely that there be no specific exemption for financial promotions from the UK to overseas recipients, although such communications will be able to take advantage of other exemptions set out in the Financial Promotion Order. In this regard the Government acknowledges that its position on outward promotions may have the effect of extending regulation compared with the restriction on 'investment advertisements' under FSA 1986.[1]

---

[1] HM Treasury. Financial Promotion of Collective Investment Schemes, First Consultation Document, October 2000, para 2.6. See also HL 2R, 21 February 2000, col 88 where Lord McIntosh for the Government stated: 'A number of noble Lords talked about globalisation and the role of the internet. Of course we recognise that financial markets are no longer glued to a particular city or country. We recognise that globalisation means that we have to attract those markets to this country. We recognise that the availability of electronic communications increases that likelihood. What the Bill does is make our regulatory system media neutral to take full account of the opportunities and risks presented by all forms of communication, including the internet and the new global information technology generally. internet communications are treated on all fours with other forms of communication. There is no reason to believe that this provision will undermine competition or the United Kingdom's international competitiveness. On the contrary, the regulator will be required expressly to take these matters into account in meeting its regulatory objectives. We have no intention of treating websites or bulletin boards differently from any other form of communication, any more than we treat advertisements in newspapers differently. The question as to whether they are subject to control depends on their purpose and contents and the context in which they are issued.' See also para 6.64 on outgoing electronic commerce communications.

6.40 The Treasury will be able further to restrict the application of this section under the exemption orders under s 21(5) and (6).[1] Such exclusions may, in some circumstances, be subject to compliance with the financial promotion rules made by the FSA under FSMA 2000, s 145 (s 21(5)).[2]

---

[1] FSMA Explanatory Notes, para 59.
[2] FSA Handbook, Authorisation manual, AUTH App 1.9.3G. See also FSMA Explanatory Notes, para 60.

Additional restriction in relation to insurance contracts

6.41 The restriction in FSA 1986, s 130 has also been carried over into the financial promotion regime through the Financial Promotion Order, art 10, which applies to qualifying contracts of insurance. That article provides that none of the exemptions in that order apply to a communication which invites or induces a person to enter into a qualifying contract of insurance with a person who is not an authorised person, an exempt person who is exempt in relation to effecting or carrying out contracts of insurance of the class to which the communications refers or a company with its head office or a branch or agency in another EEA State and which is entitled to carry on in that country the class of insurance business being promoted or a company authorised to carry on a class of insurance business in one of the countries or territories set out in the Financial Promotion Order, Sch 2.

6.42 These countries or territories are: Guernsey, the Isle of Man, Jersey and the states of Pennsylvania and Iowa in the United States. Authorised persons are subject to the same restriction under the FSA Handbook.[1]

---

[1] Conduct of Business sourcebook, COB 3.13.1R.

FINANCIAL PROMOTION RULES

6.43 FSMA 2000, s 145 provides that the FSA may make rules[1] which apply to authorised persons in relation to the communication by them, or their approval of a communication by another person, of invitations or inducements to engage in investment activity[2] or to participate in a collective investment scheme (s 145(1)).

---

[1] The Treasury has the power to impose limitations on the FSA's rule-making powers under this section (s 145(5)).
[2] The phrase 'engage in investment activity' has the same meaning as in s 21(8) (s 145(4)): see paras 6.26–6.30.

6.44 The financial promotion rules only apply to communications which, if made by a person other than an authorised person, without the approval of an authorised person, would contravene the prohibition under s 21(1) and which may be made by an authorised person without contravening the rules made under s 238(1) in relation to the promotion of collective investment schemes (s 145(3)). The rules may specify the form and content of the communications which may be lawfully issued (s 145(2)).

6.45   The financial promotion rules may also be waived or modified in certain circumstances either at the request of an authorised person or with that person's consent (s 148(2)). The FSA however must be satisfied that compliance by the authorised person with the rules (or with the rules as unmodified) would be unduly burdensome or would not achieve the purpose for which they had been made, and that the waiver or modification would not result in undue risk for investors (s 148(4)). The FSA must publish waivers or modifications of rules made under s 148 (s 148(6)). A breach of the conditions attached to a waiver or modification by an authorised person would be the equivalent of a breach of rules.[1]

---

[1]   FSMA Explanatory Notes, para 274.

6.46   However, if an unauthorised person makes a communication and passes it on to an authorised person to be communicated by him, the s 21 restriction may nonetheless apply unless the authorised person has approved the financial promotion for the purposes of s 21 in accordance with the requirements in the FSA Handbook.[1] Conversely, if an authorised person wishes to cause an unauthorised person to communicate a financial promotion for it to third parties, it should approve its own financial promotion for the purposes of s 21.[2]

---

[1]   FSA Handbook, Conduct of Business sourcebook, COB 3.
[2]   FSA Handbook, Authorisation manual, AUTH App 1.9.3G.

RESTRICTIONS ON PROMOTION OF CERTAIN COLLECTIVE INVESTMENT SCHEMES

6.47   In addition to the general restriction on financial promotion under s 21, FSMA 2000, Pt XVII, Ch II (Restrictions on promotion) sets out additional provisions in relation to the restriction on promotion by authorised persons[1] of certain types of collective investment schemes.[2]

---

[1]   An 'authorised person' is defined as a person who has a Pt IV permission to carry on one or more regulated activities or an EEA firm qualifying for authorisation under Sch 3 or a Treaty firm qualifying for authorisation under Sch 4 or a person who is otherwise authorised under a provision of or made under FSMA 2000 (s 31(1)).

2   These restrictions do not apply in respect of 'regulated collective investment schemes' which includes authorised unit trust schemes, an investment company with variable capital, a scheme recognised under s 264 (scheme authorised in other EEA States), a scheme recognised under s 270 (scheme authorised in designated countries or territories), or a scheme recognised under s 272 (individually recognised overseas schemes).

6.48   These provisions, which apply only to authorised persons (although unauthorised persons will be subject to the general financial promotion regime under s 21), provide that an authorised person may only communicate[1] an invitation or inducement[2] to participate in a collective investment scheme to the extent permitted by ss 238 and 239 and the regulations and rules made under those sections (s 238(1), (2)).

1   For the meaning of 'communicate' see paras 6.15–6.20.
2   For the meaning of 'invitation or inducement' see paras 6.21–6.25.

6.49   In setting out the policy behind these provisions, the Economic Secretary to the Treasury, Melanie Johnson said—

'[C]hapter II of part [XVII] . . . deals with the restrictions on the promotion of collective investment schemes. That plank of investment protection is critical and [s 238] broadly continues the marketing prohibition contained in section 76 of the Financial Services Act 1986, although it has been updated in line with the proposals under [s 21] concerning financial promotion by unauthorised persons. The clause aims to be more technology-neutral than existing legislation . . .

The basic position under [s 238] is that authorised persons cannot issue an invitation to participate in a collective investment scheme unless that scheme is approved—unless, that is, it is an authorised unit trust,[1] an authorised OEIC[2] or a recognised overseas scheme. The clause also allows exemptions for other schemes to be marketed other than to the general public in circumstances to be set out in the FSA's rules. That carries forward the broad picture painted by the 1986 Act.

The one significant difference between the existing position under section 76 of the 1986 Act and the position that [s 238] will create relates to territorial scope . . .

It should be remembered that the substance of the discussion applies only to unapproved collective investment schemes; authorised unit trusts, authorised OEICs and recognised schemes[3] are exempt from the prohibitions under section 76 and will be exempt under [s 238]. We are only considering vehicles such as venture capital funds, ostrich farms and other potentially risky schemes.

Section 76 applies to advertisements issued by authorised persons that are "issued in the UK". That phrase has been widely interpreted by the market as meaning that that section applies only to promotions received in the United Kingdom. The logic behind that interpretation is that an advertisement is not issued until it is communicated or received. The view is that the current territorial scope under the section applies, first, to advertisements that originate in the United Kingdom and are sent within it and, secondly, to advertisements that originate outside the United Kingdom and are sent into it, which I shall refer to as inward promotions.

. . .

The phrase "issued in the UK" is subject to interpretation; the interpretation that I have just described is the one accepted in certain quarters . . . One important consequence of that approach would be that the collective investment scheme marketing prohibition would not cover outward promotions—those that originate in the United Kingdom but sent outside it.

By contrast, the territorial scope of [s 238] is more widely drawn and it could catch outward promotions. The only promotions that will not be caught by the prohibition—apart from those concerning approved schemes—are those that originate outside the United Kingdom and cannot have an effect here. We have proposed the same basic approach in relation to the [s 21] marketing prohibition but, as members of the Committee will recall, the Treasury has the power to make exemptions from that prohibition through secondary legislation. As the recently issued second financial promotion consultation document noted, we think that it is important to be able to restrict outward promotions issued by unauthorised persons so that the FSA can play a full role in international regulatory co-operation and the UK's reputation as a safe and clean place to do business is maintained.

Under the [s 21] prohibition relating to unauthorised persons, if an unauthorised operation were to be set up in the UK to target, say, Canadian investors, we propose that that unauthorised operation be subject to UK legislation. If the legislation were breached, the operation could, if necessary, be closed down to assist the Canadian regulator.

On further consideration, the arguments may be different in relation to the promotion by authorised persons of collective investment schemes. As [s 238] applies only to persons who are authorised and as the FSA will have authority over those persons anyway, it can, if need be, discipline them under its own rules in order to assist an overseas regulator. I agree, therefore, that the need to prohibit outward promotions in [s 238]-type cases is, arguably, much less great.'[4]

---

[1]   An 'authorised unit trust scheme' is defined in s 237(3) as a unit trust scheme which is authorised for the purposes of FSMA 2000 by an authorisation order in force under s 243.
[2]   An 'authorised open-ended investment company' is defined in s 237(3) as a body incorporated by virtue of regulations made under s 262 in respect of which an authorisation order is in force under the provisions of regulations made under s 262(2)(l).
[3]   A 'recognised scheme' is defined in s 237(3) as a scheme recognised under s 264, 270 or 272.
[4]   HC SC A, 2 December 1999, col 1083.

6.50   The Treasury may also make orders limiting or specifying the circumstances in which these restrictions are not to apply (s 238(6)).[1] In addition, under s 145 the FSA may make rules exempting from these restrictions the promotion of unregulated collective investment schemes otherwise than to the general public.[2]

---

[1]   The Financial Services and Markets Act 2000 (Promotion of Collective Investment Schemes) (Exemptions) Order 2001, SI 2001/1060, as amended by SI 2001/2633, SI 2002/1310 and SI 2002/2157.
[2]   FSA Handbook, Conduct of Business sourcebook, COB 3, Annex 5. See also s 145(1)(b) subject to s 145(3).

6.51   The combination of s 21 and s 238 therefore prohibits the promotion by unauthorised persons of unregulated collective investment schemes unless the financial promotion is approved by an authorised person or is exempt. Section 238 then precludes the promotion of an unregulated collective investment scheme by authorised persons except where:
—   an exemption has been made in an order under s 238(6);
—   the financial promotion is otherwise permitted under FSA rules made under s 238(5);
—   the scheme is a single property scheme and its promotion is exempt under s 239.

6.52   FSMA 2000, s 240, however, precludes an authorised person from approving a financial promotion for the purposes of s 21 if he would not be able to communicate it himself under s 238.

6.53   The interaction of these provisions ensures that authorised persons are able to promote unregulated collective investment schemes as widely as an unauthorised person would be permitted to do under s 21, without needing the approval of an authorised person for the content. However, authorised persons may not approve real-time financial promotions in relation to unregulated collective investment schemes for an unauthorised person who would otherwise not be caught by the restriction in s 238 and authorised persons may not approve non-real time financial promotions under the FSA Handbook.[1] The FSA's guidance on exemptions in the Financial Promotion Order will apply equally to those exemptions where they appear in the CIS Financial Promotion Order.[2] The main exception to this relates to the exemption for one-off financial promotions in the CIS Financial Promotion Order, art 15. That article provides conditions which, if met, are conclusive proof that a financial promotion is one-off. However, these do not include the condition that the identity of the product or service must be determined having regard to the recipient's circumstances.[3]

---

[1]   FSA Handbook, Conduct of Business sourcebook, COB 3.
[2]   The Financial Services and Markets Act 2000 (Promotion of Collective Investment Schemes) (Exemptions) Order 2001, SI 2001/1060.
[3]   FSA Handbook, Authorisation Manual, Auth APP 1.14.3G(2) and 1.14.4G(2).

6.54   These orders may include provisions to the effect that these restrictions do not apply to communications of a specified type, those originating in a specified country or territory or a country or territory falling within a specified description of country or territory outside the UK, or those originating outside the UK (s 238(7)).[1]

---

[1]   See paras 6.35–6.37.

6.55   For the purposes of s 238, 'promotion otherwise than to the general public' includes promotion which is designed to reduce the risk of participation by persons whose participation in the scheme would be unsuitable (s 238(10)).

6.56   In addition, these restrictions in relation to collective investment schemes mirror s 21, as s 238(3) states that the restriction applies to communications originating outside the UK only if the communication is capable of having an effect in the UK. As with s 21(3), the Treasury has the power to repeal this provision to conform with developing EU and international regulations (s 238(8)).[1]

---

[1]   See para 6.37.

Enforceability of agreements resulting from unlawful communications

6.57   FSMA 2000, s 30(2) provides that if a person has entered into a controlled agreement within the meaning of s 21(9) in consequence of an unlawful communication under s 21, that controlled agreement is unenforceable against him and he may be entitled to recover compensation for any loss sustained by him. Similarly, if a person exercises any rights in respect of a controlled investment within the meaning of s 21(10) as a result of an unlawful communication, any obligation which he may be subject to is unenforceable against him and he may be entitled to recover money or other property paid or transferred and compensation for any loss he may have otherwise suffered as a result of exercising those rights (s 30(3)).

6.58   Agreements entered into as a consequence of an unlawful communication under s 238 will not be subject to the same provisions as those made under s 21 in relation to their unenforceability. An authorised person who issues a communication in breach of the rules made under s 238 may be liable to a private investor for damages under s 150 but this does not affect the enforceability of the underlying agreement.

6.59   Compensation recoverable under s 30(2) or (3) is determined by reference to the amount agreed between the parties or, if either party applies for such a determination, an amount determined by the court (s 30(10)). If a person decides not to perform an agreement or an obligation entered into as a consequence of an unlawful communication, he must repay or return any money or other property received by him as a result (s 30(11), (12)). If any property which is to be returned under these provisions has passed to third parties, the references in s 30 should be read as an equivalent value at the time of its receipt by the person who is required to return it (s 30(13)).

6.60   However, a court may allow an agreement under s 30(2) or an obligation under s 30(3) to be enforced, or money or property retained, if it is satisfied that to do so would be just and equitable in the circumstances (s 30(4)). The court must, however, consider whether the applicant[1] made the unlawful communication in the reasonable belief that it was not unlawful, or if he did not himself make the unlawful communication, whether he knew that the agreement had been entered into in consequence of such an unlawful communication (s 30(5)–(7)).

---

[1]   Ie, the person seeking to enforce the agreement or obligation or retain the money paid or property transferred (s 30(8)).

Impact of the E-Commerce Directive on financial promotions

6.61   The Electronic Commerce Directive[1] which was implemented in August 2002[2] has made various modifications to the financial promotion regime in relation to both incoming and outgoing information society services. However, these changes do not apply to the whole of the financial promotion regime and many areas that are outside the scope of that directive will remain unaffected.[3]

---

[1]   European Parliament and Council Directive of 8 June 2000 on certain legal aspects of information society services, in particular electronic commerce in the Internal Market, Directive 2000/31/EC (the E-Commerce Directive).

[2]   The Financial Services and Markets Act 2000 (Financial Promotion) (Amendment) (Electronic Commerce Directive) Order 2002, SI 2002/2157. This order should be read in conjunction with the Electronic Commerce Directive (Financial Services and Markets) Regulations 2002, SI 2002/1775, which affect certain matters within the scope of regulation by the FSA under FSMA 2000, and the Financial Services and Markets Act 2000 (Regulated Activities) (Amendment) (No 2) Order 2002, SI 2002/1776, which amends the Regulated Activities Order. Together, these SIs implement the E-Commerce Directive.

[3]   See the FSA Handbook, Electronic Commerce Directive sourcebook, ECO 1.1.2G–1.1.5G which applies in relation to electronic commerce activities provided to a UK recipient.

6.62   The basic premise of the E-Commerce Directive is the freedom of 'information society service' providers to carry on information society services from one EEA State to another applying country of origin requirements.[1] Therefore, if a German bank is providing information society services electronically to persons in the UK, for example, over the internet, the German law will apply subject to certain consumer protection provisions. The FSA Handbook[2] provides detailed formal guidance on the scope of these provisions.[3]

---

[1]   See the FSA Handbook, Authorisation manual, AUTH App 1.1.4G from the FSA to unauthorised persons as to whether communications are subject to or comply with FSMA 2000 (AUTH App 1.1.1G).

[2]   AUTH App 1.

[3]   Guidance given under s 157 which represents the FSA's view but does not bind the courts.

6.63   The regulations implementing the E-Commerce Directive define an 'electronic commerce communication' as meaning a communication, the making of which constitutes the provision of an information society service. An incoming electronic commerce communication is therefore an electronic commerce communication made from an establishment in an EEA State other than the UK and an outgoing electronic commerce communication is an electronic commerce communication made from an establishment in the UK to a person in an EEA State other than the UK.[1]

---

[1]   The Financial Services and Markets Act 2000 (Financial Promotion) (Amendment) (Electronic Commerce Directive) Order 2002, SI 2002/2157, art 3.

6.64   The E-Commerce Directive, Art 3 provides for the regulation of information society services[1] on a 'country of origin' basis. Member States are required to ensure that providers of information society services established in their territories comply with national legal requirements and are prohibited from restricting the freedom to provide information society services from other member States.

Under the E-Commerce Directive, Art 3.2, member States are prohibited from restricting the freedom to provide information society services from other member States of the EEA in those areas which are within the 'co-ordinated field'.[2]

---

[1]   As defined in the E-Commerce Directive, Art 2(a).

[2]   The E-Commerce Directive, Art 3.3 excludes from this prohibition certain matters from the 'country of origin' approach including services consisting of the effecting or carrying out of a contract of insurance as principal, where that activity falls within the scope of any of the insurance directives (as defined in FSMA 2000, s 425, Sch 3 and listed in the Annex to the E-Commerce Directive), the advertising of their units by collective investment undertakings falling within Council Directive 85/611/EEC (the UCITS Directive), contractual obligations concerning consumer contracts, and the permissibility of unsolicited commercial communications by electronic mail. The E-Commerce Directive, Art 3.4 also creates a derogation from the country of origin approach in relation to individual information society services on public policy grounds.

6.65   The Regulated Activities Order[1] excludes from the scope of 'regulated activities' under s 22 activities constituting the provision of an information society service from an establishment in an EEA State other than the UK. Consequently, it is not necessary for persons only carrying on business by way of an information society service (an 'incoming ECA provider') to be 'authorised persons' within the meaning of FSMA 2000 before they can carry on such activities in the UK. Such persons must, however, be authorised for regulated activities carried on in the UK that do not constitute the provision of an information society service.

---

[1]   SI 2001/544, as amended by the Financial Services and Markets Act 2000 (Regulated Activities) (Amendment) (No 2) Order 2002, SI 2002/1776.

6.66   Part 2 of the Electronic Commerce Directive (Financial Services and Markets) Regulations 2002[1] modifies the FSA's functions and powers in relation to both authorised and unauthorised persons carrying on incoming electronic commerce activities including the FSA's powers under s 138 (rules to protect the interests of consumers). As a result, rules made under these provisions may apply to incoming providers who are not authorised under FSMA 2000 ('unauthorised incoming providers'). The area of application of rules made under these sections (in respect of all incoming providers, whether authorised or not) is then restricted to certain matters listed in the Annex to the E-Commerce Directive.[2]

---

[1]   SI 2002/1775.

[2]   These matters include the imposition of the information requirements specified in art 5 of the Directive ('consumer contract requirements'), communications that constitute an advertisement of its units by a collective investment undertaking authorised in accordance with the UCITS Directive, and the permissibility of unsolicited commercial communications by electronic mail. FSA Electronic Commerce Directive sourcebook, ECO 1.1.

6.67   Incoming ECA providers are not subject to the rules in the FSA Handbook, Conduct of Business sourcebook, but will apply their own home state jurisdiction's financial promotion rules subject to certain essential information which must be provided to consumers in the UK.[1]

> [1]   FSA Handbook, Electronic Commerce Directive sourcebook ECO 1.2.1R and ECO 1.2.10E provide that when it communicates a specific non-real time financial promotion which is an incoming electronic commerce communication to a UK recipient who is a consumer, an incoming ECA provider must provide the name and address of the person with whom the consumer would enter into the contract, a description of the main features of the product or service, the total price to be paid by the consumer under the contract including all related fees, charges and expenses and a description of the risks associated with the specific features of the contract.

6.68   The FSA Handbook also provides that where an authorised firm communicates a financial promotion which is an 'outgoing electronic commerce communication' the firm must comply with the FSA's rules 'as if the person to whom the communication is made or directed was in the UK'. This provision 'overrides' the scope provisions in the Conduct of Business sourcebook, COB 3.3.[1] In addition, various FSA enforcement powers will apply to incoming ECA providers even though they are not 'authorised persons'.[2]

> [1]   FSA Handbook, Electronic Commerce Directive sourcebook, ECO 2.2.3R.
> [2]   See the FSA's power in respect of incoming ECA provides (FSA Handbook, Enforcement manual, ENF 19) as well as the FSA's power to seek injunctions (ENF 6) or restitution (ENF 9) or, if the incoming ISS provider is an authorised person, to take disciplinary action under ENF 11–13.

PARLIAMENTARY SCRUTINY OF ORDERS MADE UNDER S 21

6.69   FSMA 2000, s 429[1] provides that in certain circumstances orders made under s 21 may not be made unless a draft of the order has been laid before Parliament and approved by both Houses (s 429(3)).

> [1]   These provisions which were introduced late in the legislative process were introduced to give greater parliamentary control over the broad powers given to the Treasury to prescribe the scope of financial promotion under FSMA 2000. Orders made under s 262 in relation to the promotion of collective investment schemes are also subject to the same procedure (s 429(2)).

6.70   Section 429(4) provides that if an order made under s 21—
—   is the first order to be made under s 21(4), in respect of the definition of acting in the course of business, or varies such an order so as to extend the prohibition in s 21(1);

— is the first order under s 21(5) sp
  which s 21(1) does not apply, or va
  the rules which are to apply in
  would not previously have done so;
— is the first order to be made und(
  'controlled activity' or 'controlled i\
— adds one or more activities to the li\
  one or more investment to the list of ∪

then a draft of the order must be laid before
Parliament and approved by both Houses.

INVESTIGATORY POWERS OF THE FSA IN RELATION TO BREACHES OF THE FINANCIAL PROMOTION REGIME

6.71   FSMA 2000 provides that the FSA (concurrently with the Treasury) has powers to conduct an investigation if it appears that any person has contravened s 21 or 238 (s 168(4)(e), (5)). In doing so, the FSA would use its powers as set out in the FSA Handbook.[1]

---
[1]   FSA Handbook, Enforcement manual, ENF 2.1.

6.72   In addition to its enforcement powers, the FSA as one of a number of public authorities whose access to information known as 'communications data' from providers of communications services is regulated under the Regulation of Investigatory Powers Act 2000 (RIPA). Communications data is information about the use people make of services such as the post, telephone or e-mail (RIPA 2000, s 21(4)).

6.73   The FSA is not able to intercept telephone calls, letters or e-mails but it may use its powers under RIPA to obtain details of a subscriber behind a telephone number, or when and to whom calls or e-mails were sent by particular subscribers.[1] This is particularly pertinent in relation to investigations in relation to financial promotions which may or may not be lawfully made in the UK.

---
[1]   See FSA PN 2003/95.

6.74   Bringing the FSA within the RIPA regime makes it subject to the process for the authorisation of the use of such powers, as well as providing access to a tribunal for those persons affected by these

, and administrative arrangements for independent oversight
external body. Furthermore, under FSMA 2000, s 394(7) the
is not required to disclose to third parties receiving a warning or
cision notice under FSMA 2000, Pt XXVI excluded information or
aterial upon which that warning or decision notice was based.
'Excluded material' for these purposes means material the disclosure
of which for the purposes of or in connection with any legal
proceedings is prohibited by RIPA 2000, s 17 or is a protected item as
defined in FSMA 2000, s 413.

CONTRAVENTIONS OF S 21

Sanctions

6.75 In enforcing the prohibition under s 21, the FSA may take various steps
under FSMA 2000 to prevent unlawful financial promotion including
prosecution under s 25. Section 25(1) provides that any person who
contravenes s 21(1) is guilty of an offence and liable to imprisonment
or a fine or both imprisonment and a fine. The penalty for unlawfully
breaching s 21 is, on conviction on indictment, up to two years'
imprisonment, or a fine not exceeding the statutory maximum, or both
imprisonment and a fine (s 25(1)). The FSA may also seek civil court
action, including freezing orders or orders for restitution. However, it
does not have the power to initiate compulsory insolvency proceedings
in respect of a person contravening s 21.[1]

---

[1] See FSA CP 25, Enforcing the New Perimeter, July 1999, para 2.10.

Defences

6.76 FSMA 2000 provides that it will be a defence for a person to show
that he had reasonable grounds for believing that the content of the
communication was prepared by or approved by an authorised
person for the purposes of s 21[1] or that he took all reasonable
precautions and exercised due diligence to avoid committing the
offence (s 25(2)).

---

[1] This is the 'publisher's defence' in that the person issuing the communication may be a
different person from the one who caused the communication to be issued.

PROSECUTION OF OFFENCES UNDER THE FINANCIAL PROMOTION REGIME

6.77   The FSA has the power under ss 401 and 402 to prosecute various offences under FSMA 2000.[1] In some cases, those powers are concurrent with the powers of other prosecuting authorities such as the Department of Trade and Industry, the Crown Prosecution Service or the Serious Fraud Office.[2]

---

[1]   The FSA may prosecute criminal offences in England, Wales and Northern Ireland but not in Scotland where criminal prosecutions under FSMA 2000 must be brought by the Crown Office: see the FSA Handbook, Enforcement manual, ENF 15.2.3G.
[2]   ENF 15.8.1G.

6.78   In deciding whether to prosecute for any offence under the financial promotion regime, the FSA will take into account the provisions of the Code for Crown Prosecutors[1] and will only take steps to prosecute where the 'evidential test' is met, namely that a jury or bench of magistrates would be more likely to convict than not in the circumstances.[2] In addition, the FSA will only seek to prosecute if such a prosecution is in the public interest.[3]

---

[1]   FSA Handbook, Enforcement manual, ENF 15 Annex 1G.
[2]   ENF 15.5.3G.
[3]   ENF 15.5.5G.

6.79   The FSA may decide instead to issue a caution if there is sufficient evidence to secure a conviction and the offender has admitted the offence, understands the nature of the caution and has given his informed consent to it.[1] Such cautions will not, however, be published[2] but may be taken into account in determining whether an authorised or approved person or an applicant for authorisation or approval is a fit and proper person to carry out such activities or functions.[3]

---

[1]   FSA Handbook, Enforcement manual, ENF 15.6. In deciding whether to issue a caution, the FSA will apply the Home Office guidelines on the cautioning of offenders (Home Office Circular 18/1994).
[2]   ENF 15.6.2.
[3]   FSA Handbook, The Fit and Proper test for Approved Persons, FIT 2.1.3G.

---

7 Information gathering and disclosure

THE FSA'S INFORMATION GATHERING AND INVESTIGATORY POWERS

7.1 An important part of the enhanced powers of the Financial Services Authority (FSA) is that of gathering information and appointing investigators to carry out reviews on its behalf. The relevant provisions are contained in the Financial Services and Markets Act 2000 (FSMA 2000), Pt XI (ss 165–177).

Information gathering

7.2 The FSA has the power to give notice to—
— an authorised person;
— a person who is connected with an authorised person;[1]
— an operator, trustee or depositary of a scheme recognised under s 270 or 272, who is not an authorised person;
— a recognised investment exchange; or
— a recognised clearing house,

to provide to it any specified information or information of a specified description or to produce specified documents or documents of a specified type (s 165(1), (7)). For these purposes, the term 'authorised person' includes a person who was at any time an authorised person but who has ceased to be an authorised person (s 165(8)). Section 165(4) provides that this section applies only to information and documents reasonably required in connection with the FSA's exercise of its functions under FSMA 2000.

---

[1] A person is 'connected' with an authorised person if he is or has at any relevant time been a member of the authorised person's group, a controller of the authorised person, a member of a partnership of which the authorised person is a member, or a person mentioned in FSMA 2000, Sch 15, Pt I. Schedule 15, Pt I sets out specific rules applicable to this Part of FSMA 2000 for specific bodies such as bodies corporate, partnerships, unincorporated associations, friendly societies, building societies and individuals (s 165(11)).

7.3 Any information or documents required under s 165 must be provided or produced within a reasonable period specified by the

FSA, in such form as the FSA may reasonably require and at such a place as the FSA may require in the notice (s 165(2), (5)). In addition, any officer of the FSA including a member of the FSA's staff, or an agent of the FSA, may on written authorisation from the FSA require an authorised person to produce without delay such specified[1] information or document as may be reasonably required in connection with the FSA's exercise of its functions under FSMA 2000 (s 165(3)). The FSA may also require the information provided to it[2] by the authorised person to be verified or authenticated in such manner as the FSA may reasonably require (s 165(6)).

---

[1]   'Specified' means specified in the authorisation granted by the FSA (s 165(10)(b)).

[2]   This includes information in the form of a document or otherwise: see FSMA Explanatory Notes, para 315.

The FSA's supplementary powers in relation to the production of documents

7.4   FSMA 2000, s 175 also provides that if the FSA has the power under Pt XI of the Act to require a person to produce a document but it appears that the document is in the possession of a third person, that power may also be exercised in relation to that third person (s 175(1)). In addition, any documents produced as a result of a requirement under this Part of FSMA 2000 may be copied or extracts may be taken from them by the person to whom the document has been produced and that person may require the relevant person to explain the document. The 'relevant person' is—
—   the person producing the document; or
—   any other person who has been or is or is proposed to be a director or controller of that person; or
—   a person who is or has been an auditor of that person; or
—   a person who has been or is an actuary, accountant or lawyer appointed or instructed by that person; or
—   a person who has been or is an employee of that person (s 175(2), (7)).

7.5   The FSA has further powers to require a person, who is required to produce a document and fails to do so, to state to the best of his knowledge and belief where the document is (s 175(3)). A lawyer may be required under this Part of FSMA 2000 to furnish his client's name and address (s 175(4)), although the FSA's powers do not extend to 'protected items'.[1]

---

[1]   See para 7.12.

7.6   Where a person to whom Pt XI applies owes an obligation of confidentiality by virtue of carrying on banking business, he will be obliged to disclose the information or produce a document only if—

— he is the person under investigation;

— he is a member of that person's group;

— the person to whom the obligation of confidentiality is owed is the person under investigation or a member of that person's group;

— the person to whom the obligation of confidentiality is owed consents to the disclosure of the information; or

— the FSA as the investigating authority has specifically authorised the imposition of a requirement regarding the information or the document (s 175(5)).

7.7   Where a person claims a lien on a document, the production of the document under this Part of FSMA 2000 does not affect the lien (s 175(6)).

THE FSA'S POWER TO REQUIRE REPORTS

7.8   Extending the existing regime under the Banking Act 1985, s 39 and the Building Societies Act, s 63, the FSA may give notice in writing to an authorised person or to another member of the authorised person's group or to a partnership of which the authorised person is a member, or a person who has at any relevant time fallen within any one of these categories (s 166(2)), requiring that person to provide a report on any matter about which the FSA has required or could require the provision of information or documents under s 165 (s 166(1)).

7.9   The report must be made by a person appointed or approved by the FSA and who appears to the FSA to have the skills necessary to report on the matter concerned (s 166(4)). This provision has extended the range of persons who may be appointed to provide such reports, not only to accountants, but also to any person with suitable professional qualifications such as a lawyer, actuary or, in some cases, a person with the appropriate commercial or professional experience such as a banker or those with particular information technology skills and experience.[1] A report required under s 166 must be produced in such form as the FSA may specify in the notice given under s 166(1) (s 166(3)).

---

[1]   FSMA Explanatory Notes, para 319. See also FSA CP 91, Reports by skilled persons (FSMA section 166), May 2001.

PROVISION OF INFORMATION OR DOCUMENTS BY PERSONS PROVIDING SERVICES TO A PERSON SUBJECT TO S 166

7.10 FSMA 2000, s 166(5) provides that any person who is providing or has provided services to a person to whom s 166(2) applies must provide all the assistance that the person appointed under s 166(1) may reasonably require.

7.11 The Act does not, however, define what constitutes 'services' for the purposes of this section and therefore this obligation could be construed very broadly and include any services (professional or otherwise) provided to the authorised person, any member of the authorised person's group, any other member of a partnership of which the authorised person is a member or any other person falling within the other categories specified in FSMA 2000, Sch 15, Pt 1. The Explanatory Notes to the Act narrow the application to any in-house expert working for the authorised or connected person who must co-operate with the person appointed to make a report under s 166(1). They give as an example the obligation of an authorised firm's in-house actuary to co-operate in producing the report.[1] FSMA 2000 itself, however, is arguably open to wider interpretation and could include persons providing other professional or consultancy services to the subject of the report. Furthermore, it may be assumed that nothing in this section affects the duty of an auditor or actuary to communicate matters in accordance with the relevant regulations to be made by the Treasury under FSMA 2000, Pt XXII.[2]

---

[1]   FSMA Explanatory Notes, para 320.

[2]   The Financial Services and Markets Act 2000 (Communications by Auditors) Regulations 2001, SI 2001/2587. The Financial Services and Markets Act 2000 (Communications by Actuaries) Regulations 2003, SI 2003/1294 have also been made and came into force on 1 September 2003.

Protected items

7.12 The requirement to provide information and documentation under s 166 is, however, subject to the limitations in s 413 of the Act which provides that a person may not be required to produce, disclose or permit the inspection of certain 'protected items' (s 413(1)).[1] 'Protected items' are defined for these purposes as communications between a professional legal adviser and his client or any person representing his client if the communication or item is made in connection with the giving of legal advice to the client or in connection with or in contemplation of legal proceedings and is for the purposes of those proceedings, or items which are enclosed with or referred to in such communications and are in the possession of a person entitled to be in possession of them (s 413(2), (3)). A communication or an item is not, however, protected, if it is held with the intention of furthering a criminal purpose (s 413(4)).

---

[1] This definition in essence covers the same items to which legal professional privilege is extended under the Police and Criminal Evidence Act 1984, s 10: see FSMA Explanatory Notes, para 731.

7.13 An obligation to provide information or documentation under s 166(5) is enforceable by the FSA seeking an injunction or, in Scotland, an order for specific performance under the Court of Session Act 1988, s 45 (s 166(6)).

Supplementary powers

7.14 The supplementary powers contained in s 175 apply to the power to compel the production of information or documents.[1]

---

[1] See paras 7.4–7.7.

GENERAL INVESTIGATIONS—APPOINTMENT OF INVESTIGATORS

7.15 The FSA, concurrently with the Secretary of State, has the power to appoint one or more competent persons to conduct an investigation on its behalf into—
— the nature, conduct or state of the business of an authorised person or an appointed representative or any particular aspect of that business; or
— the ownership or control of an authorised person,

if it believes there is good reason for doing so (s 167(1)). The person appointed as the investigator must report to either the FSA or the Secretary of State as the investigatory authority which appointed him under s 167 (s 170(6)).

7.16 For these purposes 'business' is not limited to regulated activities under FSMA 2000 but includes any part of the authorised person's business or the business of any person to whom this section applies by virtue of s 167(2) (s 167(5)). A person may also be appointed to investigate the affairs of the manager or trustee of any authorised unit trust scheme or the affairs of the operator, trustee or depositary of any recognised scheme regarding activities carried on in the UK or the affairs of the operator, trustee or depositary of any other collective investment scheme except an open-ended investment company incorporated under regulations made under FSMA 2000, s 262 (s 284(1)).[1]

---

[1]   See paras 15.92–15.110.

7.17   If the person appointed under s 167(1) believes it necessary for his investigation, he may also investigate the business[1] of a person who is or has been a member of the group of which the person under investigation under s 167 is part, or a partnership of which the authorised person is a member (s 167(2)). If he decides to investigate a person who may be the subject of an investigation under s 167(2), he must give that person written notice of his decision (s 167(3)).

---

[1]   See para 7.16.

7.18   These powers may also be exercised in relation to a person who has ceased to be an authorised person or an appointed representative, but only regarding business carried on by him at any time when he was an authorised person or an appointed representative or, in relation to the ownership or control of a former authorised person, at any time when he was an authorised person (s 167(4)).

Powers of investigators appointed under s 167

7.19   FSMA 2000, ss 170 and 171 set out matters relating to the conduct and the general investigatory powers of a person appointed as an 'investigator' under s 167.

7.20   The FSA or the Secretary of State as the investigatory authority under s 167 must give written notice of the appointment of an investigator to the person who is the subject of the investigation (s 170(2)) unless the investigator[1] or the investigating authority believes that such notice would be likely to result in the investigation being frustrated (s 170(3)(a)). A notice under s 170(2) must specify the provisions under which the investigator has been appointed and the reason for his appointment (s 170(4)).

---

[1]   The investigator appointed under s 167 may be a member of the investigating authority's staff (s 170(5)).

7.21   The scope of an investigation under s 167 is set out in a direction to the investigator, given by either the FSA or the Secretary of State as the relevant investigatory authority (s 170(7)). That direction may also set out—

— the period during which the investigation is to be conducted;
— other matters relating to the conduct and remit of the investigation, for example confining or extending it to particular or additional matters, or requiring the investigator to discontinue it or only to take those steps specified in the direction; and
— the form of the report or an obligation on the investigator to make such interim reports as may be required (s 170(7), (8)).

7.22   If the scope or conduct of an investigation under s 167 changes and the FSA or the Secretary of State as the investigatory authority determines that the person who is the subject of the investigation would be significantly prejudiced if not made aware of those changes, it may require a written notice of the change to be given to that person (s 170(9)).

7.23   In addition to these general powers, an investigator appointed under s 167 may require any person who is the subject of the investigation or any person connected[1] with the person under investigation to answer questions, or to otherwise provide such information as the investigator may require which is relevant to the purposes of the investigation (s 171(1), (3)).[2] The investigator may also require any person[3] to produce at a specified time and place any documents or information relevant to the purposes of the investigation which may be specified in a notice in writing to that person (s 171(2), (3), (6)).

---

[1]   A person is 'connected' to a person under investigation if that person is or has been at the relevant time a member of that person's group, a controller of that person, a partnership of which that person is or was a member, or is in the specified classes of persons mentioned in Sch 15, Pts I or II: see Sch 15, Pt II, para 8.
[2]   See paras 7.30–7.32 for the admissibility of statements made to investigators under FSMA 2000, Pt XI.
[3]   This power is not limited to those under investigation or those connected with the person (FSMA 2000, s 175).

SPECIAL INVESTIGATIONS IN PARTICULAR CASES

7.24   The FSA or the Secretary of State may also appoint one or more competent persons to conduct an investigation on their behalf in a number of particular cases. Either investigatory authority may exercise this power if it appears that there are circumstances suggesting that a person may have contravened any of the regulations made regarding insurance business under FSMA 2000, s 142 or may be guilty of an offence in relation to—

— an obligation to provide information or disclose documents under FSMA 2000, Pt XI;
— any change of control of authorised persons under Pt XII; or
— the provision of false or misleading information to an auditor or actuary under s 346, or to the FSA under s 398(1) (s 168(1), (3)).

An investigator may also be appointed in relation to offences in respect of treaty rights under Sch 4 such as the failure of a Treaty firm to notify its intention to carry on regulated business (s 168(1)(b)).

7.25   An investigator may also be appointed under these provisions if it appears that an offence has been committed in relation to any person falsely claiming to be an authorised person, or in relation to the market manipulation offence under s 397 or in contravention of the Criminal Justice Act 1993, Pt V concerning insider dealing offences (s 168(2)(a)). In addition, an investigator may be appointed if the investigatory authority considers that there may have been a breach of the general prohibition under s 23, or a contravention of s 21 in relation to financial promotion or of s 238 in relation to the promotion of collective investment schemes (s 168(2)(b), (c)), and finally, if it appears to the investigatory authority that market abuse may have taken place (s 168(2)(d)).

7.26   The FSA has additional powers to appoint an investigator to carry out an investigation on its behalf under s 168(5) if it appears to it that—
— an authorised person may have conducted regulated activities without permission, contrary to s 20;
— a person may be guilty of an offence under the Money Laundering Regulations 1993;[1]
— an authorised person may have contravened a rule made by the FSA;
— an individual may not be a fit and proper person to perform functions in relation to any regulated activity carried on by an authorised or exempt person;
— an individual may have performed or agreed to perform a function in breach of a prohibition order;
— an authorised or exempt person may have failed to comply with a prohibition order made under FSMA 2000, s 56(6);
— an authorised person has failed to obtain the FSA's approval for a person to carry out a controlled function under s 59(1) or (2);
— a person in respect of whom the FSA has given its approval under s 59 appears not to be a fit and proper person to carry out those functions to which the approval relates; or
— a person is guilty of misconduct under FSMA 2000, s 66 (s 168(4)).

¹   The Financial Services and Markets Act 2000 (Regulations Relating to Money Laundering) Regulations 2001, SI 2001/1819, prescribes the Money Laundering Regulations 1993 for the purposes of s 169(4). These Regulations are to be superseded by the Money Laundering Regulations 2003, SI 2003/3075 with effect from 1 March 2004 for most purposes (reg 1(2)).

Powers of investigators appointed under s 168 in particular cases

7.27   A person appointed under s 168(3) or (5) has the same general powers as one appointed under s 167.[1]

¹   See paras 7.19–7.23.

7.28   An investigator appointed under s 168(1) or (4) also has the power to require any person who is neither the subject of the investigation nor any person connected[1] with the person under investigation to attend to answer questions at a specified time and place or to otherwise provide such specified information[2] as the investigator may require which is necessary or expedient for the investigation (s 172(2)).

¹   For the purposes of s 172 a person is 'connected' to a person under investigation if that person is or has been at the relevant time a member of that person's group, a controller of that person, a partnership of which that person is or was a member, or is in the specified classes of persons mentioned in Sch 15, Pt I or II (s 171(4), Sch 15, Pt II, para 8).
²   'Specified' for these purposes means specified in a written notice given under s 172(2) (s 172(5)).

7.29   An investigator appointed under s 168(3) as a result of s 168(2)[1] may, if he considers that any person is or may be able to give information which is or may be relevant to the investigation, require that person to attend at a specified time and place and to answer questions or to provide such information as may be required for the purposes of the investigation (s 173(1), (2)). The investigator may also require that person to give him all assistance in connection with the investigation (s 173(4)) and to produce any specified documents or documents of a specified description which appear to the investigator to relate to any matter relevant to the investigation (s 173(3)).

¹   Ie, an investigator appointed in the circumstances described in para 7.25.

ADMISSIBILITY OF STATEMENTS MADE TO INVESTIGATORS

7.30   A statement made to an investigator appointed under s 167 or 168(3) or (5) (s 174(4)) in compliance with any requirement imposed by him under s 171, 172, 173 or 175 (s 174(5)) is admissible in evidence in any proceedings provided it also complies with any requirements in relation to the admissibility of evidence in the circumstances in question (s 174(1)).

7.31   In the case of criminal or market abuse proceedings, however, no evidence relating to the statement may be adduced and no question relating to it may be asked by or on behalf of the prosecution or the FSA unless the evidence relating to it has been adduced or the question asked in the proceedings by or on behalf of that person (s 174(2)). The restriction does not apply where a person is charged with an offence under s 177(4) in relation to breaches of FSMA 2000, Pt XI or s 398[1] or an offence in relation to false statements made under oath.[2]

---

[1]   The offence of providing false or misleading information to the FSA.
[2]   Ie, an offence under the Perjury Act 1911, s 5 or the Criminal Law (Consolidation) (Scotland) Act 1995, s 44(2) or the Perjury (Northern Ireland) Order 1979, SI 1979/1714 (NI 19), art 10.

Supplementary powers

7.32   The supplementary powers contained in s 175 apply to the power to compel the production of information or documents under FSMA 2000, Pt XI.

THE FSA'S POWERS TO PROVIDE ASSISTANCE TO OVERSEAS REGULATORS

7.33   If requested by an overseas regulator to do so, the FSA may exercise its power under s 165 or may appoint one or more competent persons to investigate any matter (s 169(1)). An investigator[1] appointed under s 169(1)(b) has the same powers as one appointed under s 168(1), (3) (s 169(2)).[2]

---

[1]   For the purposes of this section an 'investigator' is a person appointed under s 169(1)(b).
[2]   For the purposes of this section 'investigatory powers' means those powers mentioned in s 169(1).

7.34   An overseas regulator is defined in s 195 as an authority in a country or territory outside the UK which is a home state regulator[1] or one which exercises any of the following functions—
—   a function corresponding to any function of the FSA under FSMA 2000; or

— a function corresponding to any function set out in FSMA 2000, Pt VI or Sch 7 exercised by a competent authority in relation to the listing of 'shares';[2] or

— a function corresponding to any function exercised by the Secretary of State under the Companies Act 1985; or

— a function in connection with the investigation of contraventions of the insider dealing legislation or the enforcement of rules relating to such conduct; or

— a function prescribed by regulations made under this section by the Treasury relating to companies or financial services.

---

[1]   As defined in Sch 3, para 9 or Sch 4, para 1 as appropriate (s 425).

[2]   It is arguable that this should be 'securities' as defined in s 74(5). 'Shares' is defined in s 422, but that definition is not particularly relevant to the competent authority's functions under Pt VI.

7.35   In deciding whether to exercise its investigatory powers at the request of an overseas regulatory authority, the FSA must take into account whether the country or territory concerned would provide corresponding assistance to a UK regulatory authority, including, but not limited to, the FSA (s 169(4)). The FSA and the Treasury, sometimes acting together and sometimes acting separately, are parties to a number of memoranda of understanding with various overseas regulatory authorities setting out the scope and the circumstances on which such regulatory assistance might be rendered.[1]

---

[1]   The FSA has 'well over 100' memoranda of understanding (MOUs) and other information sharing agreements (FSMOUs) with other supervisory authorities worldwide: see FSA Occasional Paper 4, Plumbers and Architects: a supervisory perspective on international financial architecture, January 2000. In addition, the FSA has been an active participant in the Forum of European Securities Commissions (FESCO), a body whose Charter provides that the members 'share their experience and work together to facilitate the fair and efficient realisation of the European Single Market in financial services; . . . unite their efforts in order to develop common regulatory standards in respect of the supervision of financial activities or markets concerning aspects that are not harmonised by the existing European Directives and where a common approach is appropriate; . . . provide, to the extent permitted by law, the broadest possible mutual assistance and . . . strengthen cross-border cooperation so as to enhance market surveillance and effective enforcement against abuse.' The FSA continues to be an active member of the successor to FESCO, the Committee of European Securities Regulators (CESR) as well as IOSCO. See also FSA PN 110/2003 referring to IOSCO's multilateral memorandum of understanding on information sharing between regulators.

7.36   The FSA must also take into account whether the case involves a breach of a law or other requirement for which there are no equivalent or 'close' provisions in the UK or if the matter involves the assertion of a form of jurisdiction not recognised under UK law (s 169(4)(b)). More generally, before exercising its investigatory powers, the FSA would need to take into account the seriousness of the matter and the importance of it to persons in the UK, or whether it is otherwise appropriate in the public interest to give the assistance sought by the overseas regulator (s 169(4)(c), (d)).

7.37 Any overseas regulator making a request for the FSA to exercise its investigatory powers on its behalf may, however, have to undertake to contribute toward the costs of the exercise (s 169(5)), unless the exercise of those powers is necessary to comply with a Community obligation (s 169(6)).

7.38 If the request to the FSA to exercise its investigatory powers under s 169 is made pursuant to any Community obligation, the FSA must determine whether its exercise is necessary to comply with such an obligation (s 169(3)), but the considerations required by s 169(4) and (5) do not apply.

7.39 The FSA may also exercise its powers of intervention in support of a request from an overseas regulator under FSMA 2000, s 195.[1]

---

[1] See paras 8.52, 8.53.

7.40 An investigator appointed by the FSA pursuant to an overseas regulator's request may, if directed by the FSA to do so, permit a representative of the overseas regulator to attend and take part in any interview conducted for the purposes of the investigation (s 169(7)), subject to the terms of a statement to be published by the FSA as to its policy on these matters (s 169(9)).[1] However, the FSA may not give a direction permitting the overseas regulator's representative to obtain information or documents unless the FSA is satisfied that the information obtained is subject to safeguards equivalent to those in FSMA 2000, Pt XXIII (s 169(8)).

---

[1] The FSA must prepare this statement which the Treasury must approve and the FSA must then publish (s 169(10), (11)). No direction under s 169(7) can be given to allow an overseas regulator's representative to participate in an investigation until this policy statement has been promulgated and approved by the Treasury under these provisions (s 169(12)). The FSA's policy is set out in the FSA Handbook, Enforcement manual, ENF 2 Annex 2G.

OFFENCES IN RELATION TO INVESTIGATIONS

7.41 Where any person, other than an investigator appointed under FSMA 2000, Pt XI, fails to comply with a requirement imposed on him under Pt XI, the person imposing that requirement may certify this non-compliance in writing to the High Court or, in Scotland, to the Court of Session (s 177(1), (7)). If the court is satisfied that the person had no reasonable excuse, the court may deal with him or, if the defaulting party is a body corporate, any director or officer of that body corporate, as if he were in contempt (s 177(2)).

7.42   In addition, a person who knows or suspects that an investigation under Pt XI is being or is likely to be conducted is guilty of an offence if he falsifies, conceals, destroys or otherwise disposes of a document which he knows or suspects is or would be relevant to such an investigation (s 177(3)(a)). Such a person also commits an offence if he causes or permits the falsification, concealment, destruction or disposal of such a document (s 177(3)(b)). Offences under this section give rise on summary conviction to imprisonment for up to six months and a fine not exceeding the statutory maximum or both imprisonment and a fine, and on conviction on indictment to imprisonment for up to two years or a fine, or both imprisonment and a fine (s 177(5)).

7.43   A person who, in purported compliance with any requirement under FSMA 2000, Pt XI, provides information which he knows to be false or misleading in any material particular or which he provides recklessly which is false or misleading is also guilty of an offence which on summary conviction could lead to imprisonment for up to six months and a fine not exceeding the statutory maximum, or both imprisonment and a fine, and on conviction on indictment could lead to imprisonment for up to two years or a fine, or both imprisonment and a fine (s 177(5)).[1]

---

[1]   These offences under s 177 would presumably be to the exclusion of any offence committed in relation to misleading the FSA under FSMA 2000, s 398(2).

THE FSA'S POWER TO OBTAIN A WARRANT TO ENTER PREMISES AND SEARCH AND SEIZE DOCUMENTS

7.44   If satisfied that there are reasonable grounds for believing that certain conditions are met on information given on oath by or on behalf of the Secretary of State, the FSA or an investigator appointed under s 167 or 168(3) or (5), a justice of the peace[1] may issue a warrant authorising the entry and search of premises and the taking possession of any documents or information which appear to be relevant (s 176(1)).

---

[1]   In Scotland references to a 'justice of the peace' in this section include a justice of the peace or a sheriff and references to 'information on oath' are to be construed as references to evidence on oath (s 176(9)).

7.45   The conditions which must be met before the FSA is able to obtain a warrant from a justice of the peace, or, in Scotland, a sheriff, are that—

—   the person from whom information or documents have been required under FSMA 2000, s 165, 171, 172, 173 or 175 has failed (wholly or in part) to comply and the documents or information required is on the premises which have been specified in the warrant; or

—   the premises are those of an authorised person or an appointed representative and there are documents or information on the premises which could be required under s 165, 171, 172, 173 or 175 but if such a requirement were to be imposed it would not be complied with or the documents or information to which it related would be removed, tampered with or destroyed; or

—   in relation to an investigation under s 168 into a possible offence, the offence is one which could give rise to a sentence on conviction of two years or more and there are documents or information on the premises specified in the warrant relevant to whether that offence was committed and the documents or information could be required under s 165, 171, 172, 173 or 175 and if such a requirement were imposed it would not be complied with or the documents or information to which it related would be removed, tampered with or destroyed (s 176(2)–(4)).

7.46   If a justice of the peace grants a warrant under s 176, it authorises a constable to enter the premises set out in the warrant. The constable may search for any document or information of the kind specified in the warrant and take any other steps necessary for preserving it or otherwise preventing interference with them (s 176(5)(a), (b)). A constable may also take copies of or extracts from any documents or information appearing to be of the kind specified in the warrant or may require any person on the premises to explain any such document or information (s 176(5)(c), (d)). A constable is also authorised to use such force as may reasonably be necessary in executing the warrant (s 176(5)(e)). The constable's right to enter premises and search for documents or information under a warrant is subject to the requirements in relation to the execution of search warrants in the Police and Criminal Evidence Act 1984, ss 15(5)–(8) and 16 or in the Police and Criminal Evidence (Northern Ireland) Order 1989, arts 17(5)–(8) and 18 (s 176(6), (7)).

7.47   Any document seized under a warrant issued under s 176 may be retained for three months or, if within that three-month period proceedings to which the document may be relevant are commenced against a person for any criminal offence, until the conclusion of those proceedings (s 176(8)).[1]

---

[1]   The European Convention on Human Rights, Art 8 has resulted in the need for special caution in justices issuing warrants and for investigating authorities executing such warrants where the material to which the warrant relates is liable to include documents which are subject to legal professional privilege: see *R v Chesterfield Justices, ex p Bramley* [2000] QB 576, [2000] 1 All ER 411, CA.

THE FSA'S OBLIGATION TO MAINTAIN CERTAIN RECORDS

7.48   FSMA 2000 requires the FSA to maintain a record of every—
— authorised person;
— authorised unit trust scheme;
— authorised open-ended investment company;
— recognised scheme;
— recognised investment exchange;
— recognised clearing house;
— individual to whom a prohibition order under s 56 relates;
— approved person under s 59; and
— other person falling within any class which the FSA itself determines (s 347(1)).

The FSA has the power to remove the details of a person from the register if that person ceases to be a person to whom s 347(1) applies but the FSA has the power to retain the entry provided it makes a note to that effect in the public record and states why it considers that the person has ceased to be a person to whom this provision applies (s 347(3), (4)).

7.49   This record must include such information as the FSA deems appropriate and must include at least—
— the services which an authorised person holds himself out as able to provide and any address known to the FSA at which any notice or other document may be served on him;

— the name and address of the manager and trustee of any authorised unit trust scheme;

— the name and address of the company, the director and depositary (if any) of any authorised open-ended investment company;

— the name and address of the operator and any representative of the operator in the UK of any recognised scheme;

— the name and address of any recognised investment exchange or recognised clearing house;

— details of any prohibition order concerning an individual, who must be named, in respect of whom a prohibition order has been made under s 56;

— the name of the approved person, the name of the relevant authorised person as defined in s 66 (s 347(9)) for whom he carries out the controlled function and, if the approved person is performing the controlled function under an arrangement with a contractor, the name of that contractor (s 347(2)).

7.50 The FSA may publish the public record required under s 347[1] or any part of it and may 'exploit commercially' the information contained in the record or any part of that information (s 347(6)). The public record must, however, be made available for inspection by the public (s 347(5)(a)). The FSA must also provide a certified copy of the public record to anyone who requests it, subject to the FSA's power to impose a fee for providing a copy of the record (s 347(5)(b)).

[1]   This register is available on the FSA's website at http://www.fsa.gov.uk/register.

RESTRICTIONS ON THE DISCLOSURE OF CONFIDENTIAL INFORMATION

Restrictions on disclosure

7.51 FSMA 2000, s 348 imposes various restrictions relating to the disclosure of confidential information.[1]

[1]   'Confidential information' is defined in para 7.53.

7.52 Any person who is a 'primary recipient' of confidential information (s 348(5)) may not disclose it without the consent of the person from whom the primary recipient obtained the information and, if different, the person to whom it relates (s 348(1)).[1] Those persons who are 'primary recipients'[2] for the purposes of this section include—

— the FSA;
— any person exercising the functions of the competent authority under FSMA 2000, Pt VI;
— the Secretary of State;
— any person appointed to make a 'skilled persons' report under FSMA 2000, s 166;
— any person who is or has been employed by the FSA, a person carrying out the functions of the competent authority under Pt VI or the Secretary of State; or
— any auditor or expert, including any person appointed under FSMA 2000, s 97 or a person appointed as an investigator under Pt XI, instructed by any of those persons, or a body or person appointed by the FSA to carry out a monitoring function on its behalf under FSMA 2000, Sch 1, para 6.

---

[1] This section does not apply to 'revenue information' as defined in FSMA 2000, s 350(7) or to 'competition information' as defined under FSMA 2000, s 351(5). For disclosure of competition information see para 10.49.

[2] 'Primary recipient' includes the Bank of England for the purposes of the Financial Services and Markets Act 2000 (Confidential Information) (Bank of England) (Consequential Provisions) Order 2001, SI 2001/3648, art 3(4).

7.53   Information is 'confidential' if it relates to the business or other affairs of any person and was received by the primary recipient for the purpose of, or in the discharge of, any of the functions of the FSA, the competent authority under FSMA 2000, Pt VI or the Secretary of State under any other provision made by or under FSMA 2000 (s 348(2)). For the purposes of this section, it is immaterial whether the information was received by the primary recipient by virtue of a requirement to provide it under FSMA 2000 or for other purposes (s 348(3)). Information will not, however, be 'confidential' if it has been made publicly available by being disclosed in any circumstances in which, or for the purposes of which, disclosure was not precluded, or it is in the form of a summary or collection of information with the result that it is not capable of being identified as information relating to a particular person (s 348(4)).

Exemptions from s 348

7.54   A primary recipient is not precluded from disclosing confidential information which is made to facilitate the carrying out of a public function[1] and which is permitted by regulations made by the Treasury under FSMA 2000, s 349 (s 349(1)).[2]

---

[1] 'Public function' for the purposes of this section includes any functions conferred by or in accordance with any provision contained in any enactment (including an Act of the Scottish Parliament or Northern Ireland legislation) (s 349(6)) or subordinate legislation, or any functions

conferred by or in accordance with any provision in a Community Treaty or any Community instrument, or similar functions conferred on any person by or under provisions having similar effects in any other country or jurisdictions, and functions exercisable in relation to certain specified disciplinary proceedings (s 349(5)). 'Subordinate legislation' has the meaning given in the Interpretation Act 1978 and includes any instrument made under an Act of the Scottish Parliament or under Northern Ireland legislation (s 349(7)).

2   See the Financial Services and Markets Act 2000 (Disclosure of Confidential Information) Regulations 2001, SI 2001/2188, as amended by SI 2001/3437, SI 2001/3624, SI 2003/693, SI 2003/2174 and SI 2003/2817.

7.55   The regulations which the Treasury may make may permit the disclosure of confidential information by certain 'recipients'[1] specified in the regulations (or recipients of a particular description set out in the regulations) to any prescribed person to enable or assist the 'recipient' to carry out defined public functions (s 349(2)(a), (b)).

1   This term includes both primary recipients as defined in s 348(5) and any other person obtaining the information directly or indirectly from the primary recipient.

7.56   The Treasury has also made an order[1] under its powers under FSMA 2000, s 426 and 427 to regulate the disclosure of certain confidential information obtained by the Bank of England in pursuit of its functions as a monetary authority and its functions in relation to overseeing payment systems after the coming into force of FSMA 2000.[2] Information supplied to the Bank of England for the purpose of any of these relevant functions by an overseas regulatory authority or otherwise obtained for those purposes by the Bank, or by another person acting on its behalf in another member state, will not be subject to the restrictions on disclosure imposed by s 348(1) if it satisfies any of the criteria set out in s 348(4)(a) or (b).[3]

1   The Financial Services and Markets Act 2000 (Confidential Information) (Bank of England) (Consequential Provisions) Order 2001, SI 2001/3648. See also *Three Rivers District Council v Bank of England* (No 3) [1996] 3 All ER 558; affd [1999] 4 All ER 800n, CA; affd in part [2000] 3 All ER 1, HL; [2001] 2 All ER 513.

2   These powers previously existed under regulations made under the Banking Act 1985, s 86 and 87.

3   SI 2001/3648, art 3(1), (2).

7.57   In addition, information disclosed to the Bank under the Companies Act 1985, s 449(1) in its capacity as a competent authority under s 449(3) of that Act may be disclosed as if that information were confidential information within the meaning of FSMA 2000, s 348(2) and the Bank of England were a primary recipient of the information. However, such information may only be disclosed by the Bank or any other person with the consent of the Treasury.[1]

1   SI 2001/3648, art 5.

7.58 The regulations may also permit disclosure by the FSA to the Treasury or the Secretary of State for any purpose or by any recipient if the disclosure is with a view to or in connection with proceedings prescribed in the regulations (s 349(2)(c), (d)). Other provisions include making conditional permission to disclose confidential information (which may relate to obtaining consents to be set out in the regulations), or restricting the use to which confidential information disclosed under the regulations can be put (s 349(3)(a), (b)).

Removal of other restrictions on disclosure

7.59 FSMA 2000, s 353 also provides that the Treasury may make regulations permitting the disclosure of any information or of information of the kind prescribed in the regulations by certain specified persons for the purposes of enabling the FSA to discharge certain functions under the Act (s 353(1)). For example, these regulations may apply to the compensation scheme manager to assist him to carry out his functions under the Act. The apparent purpose of this section is to create certain information 'gateways', as it allows any person who discloses information permitted under these regulations not to be taken to have contravened any duty to which he is otherwise subject and thereby overrides other confidentiality obligations to which he might be subject (s 353(3)).[1]

---

[1] FSMA Explanatory Notes, para 627.

DISCLOSURE OF REVENUE INFORMATION

7.60 Information which is 'revenue information' may be disclosed by or under the authority of the Commissioners of Inland Revenue (s 350(2)) to the FSA or the Secretary of State if that disclosure is made to assist in an investigation under s 168 or with a view to appointing an investigator under that section (s 350(1)). Information disclosed under s 350(1) may be used only for certain limited purposes (s 350(4)), namely—

— in determining whether to appoint an investigator under s 168;
— in the conduct of an investigation under s 168;
— in criminal proceedings for insider dealing as a result of an investigation under s 168 or with a view to their institution (s 350(5));[1]
— for the purpose of taking action against a person as a result of an investigation under s 168; or

— in proceedings before a Tribunal as a result of any action taken following an investigation under s 168 or with a view to the institution of such proceedings.

---

[1] This section does not prevent the disclosure of information which was obtained by a disclosure under s 350(1) to a person to whom it could have been disclosed under that subsection (s 350(6)).

OFFENCES IN RELATION TO THE DISCLOSURE OF INFORMATION

7.61 A person who discloses information in contravention of either s 348 or 350(5) is guilty of an offence and is liable on summary conviction to imprisonment for up to three months or a fine not exceeding the statutory maximum or both imprisonment and a fine, and on conviction on indictment to imprisonment for up to two years or a fine, or both imprisonment and a fine (s 352(1), (2)). A person who uses information obtained under s 350(4) for any purposes other than those specified in that section, or uses information which has been disclosed to him under regulations made under s 349, is also guilty of an offence (s 352(3), (4)). A person guilty of an offence under s 352(3) or (4) is liable on summary conviction to imprisonment for up to three months or a fine not exceeding level 5 on the standard scale or both imprisonment and a fine.

Defence

7.62 In all of these cases the accused has a defence if he can prove he did not know and had no reason to suspect that the information was confidential information or that it had been disclosed under s 350, or that he took all reasonable precautions and exercised all due diligence to avoid committing the offence (s 352(6)).

Misleading the Director General of the OFT

7.63 The Competition Act 1998, s 44 applies in relation to any function of the Director General of Fair Trading under FSMA 2000 as if it were a function under Pt I of the 2000 Act (s 399).

Offences by bodies corporate

7.64   In certain cases, where an offence has been committed by a body corporate, certain individuals within that body corporate may also be deemed to have committed the offence and s 400 allows the FSA to pierce the corporate veil and to proceed against certain individuals. FSMA 2000 provides that the Treasury may make regulations modifying s 400 to the extent that the body corporate or unincorporated association is formed or recognised outside the UK (s 400(7)).

7.65   An offence committed under FSMA 2000 by a body corporate, if shown to have been committed with the consent or connivance of an officer of that company or to have been due to neglect on his part, is deemed to be an offence committed by that officer (s 400(1)). An officer is defined as a director, member of the committee of management, chief executive, manager, secretary or other similar officer of the company or a person who is purporting to act in one of those capacities (s 400(5)). It also includes an individual who is a controller of the company within the meaning in FSMA 2000, s 422(1).

7.66   If an offence is committed by a body corporate which is managed by its members, this will also be an offence of a member concerned in the management in the same way as if he was a director. This is limited to the acts and defaults of the member concerned which are connected with the functions of management which he carries out (s 400(2)). Similarly, an offence by a partnership which has been committed with the consent or connivance of, or is attributable to the neglect of, any partner or person purporting to act as a partner, will be deemed to be an offence committed by that person (s 400(3), (4)).

7.67   If an offence is committed by an unincorporated association with the consent or connivance of an officer of the association, or a member of its governing body, (or as a result of his neglect), the offence is considered as having been committed by that person, and the FSA can initiate proceedings against that person (s 400(6)).

THE FSA'S DUTY TO CO-OPERATE WITH OTHERS

7.68   Under FSMA 2000, s 354 the FSA has an obligation to take such steps as it considers appropriate to co-operate with other supervisory authorities, both within and outside the UK, who have functions similar to those of the FSA, or have functions in relation to the prevention or detection of financial crime (s 354(1)).[1] For the purposes of this section 'co-operation' may include sharing information (where the FSA is not otherwise prevented from disclosing that information) with those persons (s 354(2)).[2]

---

[1] 'Financial crime' is defined in FSMA 2000, s 6(3) as any offence involving fraud or dishonesty, misconduct in, or the misuse of information in relation to, a financial market, or handling the proceeds of crime.

[2] See FSA Handbook, Supervision sourcebook (SUP), 2.1.3. See also FSA Policy report: A New Regulator for the New Millennium, January 2000, p 28.

8 The FSA's disciplinary powers

INTRODUCTION

8.1 One of the criticisms levelled at some aspects of the regulatory regimes in force before the introduction of the Financial Services and Markets Act 2000 (FSMA 2000) was that the statutory regulators concerned had only a very limited range of enforcement powers. The powers in that range were regarded generally as rather drastic. For example, the Securities and Investments Board had no power to fine directly regulated firms and was limited to seeking court orders or removing authorisation. Similar issues arose in regulating banks and insurers.

8.2 The disciplinary and enforcement powers of the Financial Services Authority (FSA) under FSMA 2000 include a number of powers akin to the disciplinary powers adopted by the self-regulating organisations in relation to their members. The range and extent of the powers included in FSMA 2000 were amongst the most controversial and hotly debated topics during its passage through Parliament. The powers available to the FSA apply both to authorised persons and to individuals in relation to their conduct as approved persons. The powers are additional or alternative to the FSA's powers to remove or restrict a person's activities under FSMA 2000, Pts IV and V.[1]

---

[1] See paras 5.18–5.23 (withdrawal of approval), and 4.84–4.93 (own initiative power).

AUTHORISED PERSONS

The FSA's power to take disciplinary action

8.3 Where the FSA considers that an authorised person has contravened any requirement imposed on him by or under FSMA 2000, the FSA may publicly censure that person and publish a statement to that effect (s 205). The FSA may take action where it considers an authorised person has contravened any requirement imposed by or under FSMA 2000 and it may impose a financial penalty in respect of the contravention of an amount it considers appropriate (s 206(1)). Penalties are payable to the FSA (s 206(3)).[1] The FSA may withdraw a person's authorisation under FSMA 2000, s 33 but the Act expressly provides that the FSA may not both require an authorised person to pay a penalty and withdraw his authorisation (s 206(2)).[2]

[1] Although FSMA 2000, s 66 does not state so on its face, it is assumed that the same applies.
[2] See also para 8.9, fn 2.

The disciplinary process

8.4 Where the FSA proposes to publish a statement under s 205 or to impose a penalty under s 206 on an authorised person, it must follow the same procedures as for an approved person, subject to certain differences (ss 207, 208).[1]

[1] See para 8.10, fn 3.

Publication of statement

8.5 After the FSA publishes a statement under s 205, it must send a copy of the statement to the authorised person concerned and to any other person to whom a copy of the decision notice was given under s 393(4) (s 209).[1]

[1] Section 393(4) provides that where a decision notice relates to a matter which identifies a third party other than a person to whom the decision notice was given and, in the opinion of the FSA, is prejudicial to that third party, a copy of the decision notice must be given to the third party. Similar provisions also apply in relation to warning notices (s 393(1)).

Statement of policy

8.6 The FSA is required to prepare a statement of its policy in relation to the imposition and amount of penalties under s 206 following the same procedure as in FSMA 2000, Pt V (s 210(1), (2), (7)). This does not, however, seem to apply in relation to the publication of statements of misconduct under s 205.[1]

[1] As noted in para 8.12, fn 1, the FSA has published policy statements relating to both: see the FSA Handbook, Enforcement manual, ENF 11–13.

8.7 The FSA may alter or amend its policy on discipline following the same procedural requirements as those described in para 8.13 (ss 210(3)–(5), 211(1), (5), (7)).

APPROVED PERSONS

The FSA's power to take disciplinary action

8.8 The FSA has the power under FSMA 2000, Pt V (ss 56–71) to take disciplinary action against a person if it appears to the FSA that the person is guilty of misconduct and the FSA is satisfied that it is appropriate in all of the circumstances to take action against him (s 66(1)). For these purposes, a person is guilty of misconduct if he is or was an approved person under FSMA 2000, s 64 (s 66(6)) and while an approved person he has failed to comply with a statement of principle issued by the FSA under s 64 or has been knowingly concerned in the contravention of a requirement imposed on the relevant authorised person (s 66(2)). For these purposes 'requirement' encompasses all types of requirement imposed by or under FSMA 2000 (s 66(2)(b)), which will include, for example, breaches of permission or rule breaches.

8.9 In taking action against an approved person, the FSA may impose a penalty of such amount as it considers appropriate or publish a statement of that approved person's misconduct (s 66(3)). Presumably a penalty under s 66(3)(a) is a financial penalty, since it is expressed in terms of an 'amount' and could not therefore include an order made on an authorised person to take (or refrain from taking) any particular action.[1] It appears that the imposition of a penalty under s 66(3)(a) precludes the FSA from publishing a statement of misconduct under s 66(3)(b) and vice versa. This apparent choice between alternatives is reinforced by the procedures under FSMA 2000, s 67, which clearly split the requirements in relation to the imposition of a penalty and publication of a statement (s 67(2), (3), (5), (6)).[2] There is no provision in FSMA 2000, Pt V concerning disciplinary action against approved persons, prohibiting withdrawal of approval at the same time. It is likely therefore that it would be open to the FSA to impose a penalty under s 66 *and* to withdraw its approval of that individual to perform a controlled function under FSMA 2000, s 63.[3]

---

[1] The FSA would, however, be able to seek an injunction against an approved person under FSMA 2000, s 380.

2 Under FSMA 2000, Pt XIV (ss 205–211) it is also open to the FSA under s 206(2) to withdraw an authorised person's authorisation under FSMA 2000, s 33 but the Act expressly provides that the FSA may not both require an authorised person to pay a penalty under s 206 *and* to withdraw its authorisation under s 33 (s 206(2)).
3 The FSA has said that it will consider both discipline and withdrawal in appropriate circumstances: see the FSA Handbook, Enforcement manual, ENF 7.6.3G.

The disciplinary process

8.10 Where the FSA proposes to publish a statement under s 66(3)(b) or to impose a penalty under s 66(3)(a) on an approved person it must give that person[1] a warning notice (s 67(1)).[2] This must set out either the terms of the statement which the FSA proposes to publish or contain a statement of the amount of the penalty which it proposes to impose (s 67(2), (3)). If the FSA decides to publish a statement or to impose a penalty under s 66, it must give the approved person a decision notice.[3] The decision notice must contain the terms of the statement to be made or the amount of the penalty to be imposed (s 67(5), (6)) as well as the matters required by FSMA 2000, s 388,[4] and the approved person may refer the matter to the Tribunal under s 67(7)).[5]

1 A warning notice must also be given to any third party if the notice relates to a matter which identifies the third party and is prejudicial to it (s 393).
2 FSMA 2000, Pt XXVI applies to the notice procedures required for disciplinary action against approved persons as well as authorised persons.
3 Part V does not contain the same provisions as those set out in Pt XIV in relation to authorised persons in that s 208(1) requires that the decision notice must be provided to the authorised person 'without delay' and the form of the decision notice must be given to the authorised person whether or not it is in the same terms as any warning notice previously provided to him.
4 See para 8.19.
5 See *R (on the application of Davies) v Financial Services Authority* [2003] EWCA Civ 1128, [2003] All ER (D) 517 (Jul) which was an appeal from the refusal of Lightman J ([2002] EWHC 2997 (Admin), [2003] 1 All ER 859, [2003] 1 WLR 1284) to grant permission for judicial review of warning notices given to the applicants by the FSA under FSMA 2000, s 57. On the appeal the court held that Lightman J was right in holding that the applicants had no grounds upon which to seek judicial review and dealt with points of practical importance on the exercise of the regulatory powers of the FSA and the appropriate procedures for challenging its decisions and actions. Indeed, the Court of Appeal indicated that (other than in exceptional cases) the proper route for challenging the FSA's exercise of its powers is the Tribunal when the right of referral exists.

Publication of statement

8.11 After the FSA publishes a statement of misconduct under s 66, it must send a copy of the statement to the approved person concerned and to any other person to whom a copy of the decision notice was given (s 68).[1]

1 See para 8.5, fn 1.

Statement of policy

8.12   The FSA must prepare a statement of its policy on the imposition and amount of penalties under s 66 (s 69(1)) and, when exercising its powers under s 66, it must have regard to the statement of policy in force at the time when the misconduct in question occurred (s 69(8)).[1] In its policy, the FSA must have regard to—

— the seriousness of the misconduct in relation to the nature of the principle or requirement concerned,

— the extent to which the misconduct was deliberate or reckless, and

— whether the person on whom the penalty is to be imposed is an individual (s 69(2)).[2]

---

[1]   It appears that, in relation to approved persons, the policy statement on disciplinary matters relates to penalties under s 66, ie, both financial penalties *and* the publication of statements. This is to be contrasted with the statement of policy in relation to authorised persons where FSMA 2000, s 208(1) provides that the statement of policy *only* relates to the imposition of penalties under s 206 and *not* to the publication of statements of misconduct under s 205. The FSA has published statements of policy on all of these: see the FSA Handbook, Enforcement manual, ENF 11–13.

[2]   See *Piggott v Financial Services Authority*, FSM Tribunal, 25 March 2003 as to the production of evidence of personal financial circumstances in relation to the imposition of penalties under s 66(3).

Consultation

8.13   The FSA may alter or amend its policy on discipline but the amended or altered policy must be made publicly available (s 69(3), (4)) and the FSA must give the Treasury a copy of any statement which it publishes (s 69(5)). The FSA is also required to carry out a consultation process before publishing any statement of policy on discipline and enforcement under s 69 or any change or alteration thereto (s 70(1)). Any draft policy statement must be made publicly available and any representations in respect of it must be given due regard. The FSA must publish an account of the representations received and its response to them (s 70(2)–(4)). If, as a result of the consultation process, the FSA changes its draft policy statement, details of the differences must also be made publicly available (s 70(5)).

Limitation period for actions under s 66

8.14   An ongoing criticism of the pre-FSMA 2000 disciplinary and enforcement regime is the length of time it has taken for some disciplinary cases to be brought or to achieve closure—both from the public interest perspective and from the point of view of authorised firms. FSMA 2000 provides that the FSA may not take action under s 66 after the end of a period of two years beginning on the first day on which the FSA knew of the misconduct, unless proceedings concerning the misconduct were begun before the end of that period (s 66(4)). To determine this, the FSA is to be treated as knowing of misconduct if it has information from which misconduct can reasonably be inferred. In addition, proceedings against a person are deemed to have begun when a warning notice (rather than a decision notice) is given to the person under s 67(1) (s 66(5)).

THE FSA'S PROCEDURES FOR ISSUING NOTICES

Procedures

8.15   The FSA is required under s 395 to determine the procedure that it will follow when giving supervisory notices,[1] warning notices and decision notices but it must issue a statement of the procedure (s 395(5)) and make it available to the public (s 395(6)).[2] A copy must also be given to the Treasury (s 395(8)), and any material changes in these procedures must be published (s 395(10)).

---

[1]   A 'supervisory notice' is one given under s 53(4), (7) or (8)(b), 78(2) or (5), 197(3), (6) or (7)(b), 259(3), (8) or (9)(b), 268(3), (7)(a) or (9)(a) (as a result of sub-s (8)(b)), 282(3), (6) or (7)(b) or 321(2) or (5).
[2]   These statements have been incorporated into the FSA Handbook, Decision making manual, DEC.

Consultation on statement of procedure

8.16   The FSA must also consult on a statement of procedure under s 395 or any change to such a statement and must publish a draft of the proposed statement of procedure (s 396(1), (7)). Before issuing the statement, it must take into account any representations received and respond to them (s 396(2)–(4)). If the published form of the statement of procedure differs from the draft published under s 396(1), the FSA must publish details of the differences (s 396(5)). That procedure must be designed, however, to split the supervisory or investigatory functions of the FSA from the enforcement or disciplinary functions.[1] This is to ensure that the decision which gives rise to the obligation to give any such notice under this section of FSMA 2000 is taken by a person not directly involved in establishing the evidence on which that decision is based (s 395(2)). Section 395(3) provides that a decision to issue a supervisory notice under s 395(1) may be taken by another person if the FSA considers that it is necessary to protect the interests of consumers and the person taking the decision is of a level of authority laid down in the procedures. The level of authority required to take such decisions must be appropriate to the importance of the decision to be made (s 395(4)). If the FSA fails to follow its procedure in any particular case, the validity of the notice given is not affected (s 395(11)) but, if the subject of the notice is referred to the Tribunal, the FSA's failure to follow its published procedures under s 395 may be taken into account (s 395(12)).

---

[1]   The implementation of this separation is described in the FSA Handbook, Decision making manual, DEC4, see para 8.25, fn 1.

Notices under FSMA 2000

8.17   To establish procedures for its disciplinary powers FSMA 2000 lays down specific provisions concerning the use and format of notices given or copied under the various provisions of the Act.[1]

---

[1]   See paras 8.18–8.23.

Warning notices

8.18   FSMA 2000, s 387(1) provides that in issuing a warning notice under any provision of FSMA 2000, the FSA must state in writing the action which it proposes to take, giving its reasons for the proposed action and stating whether s 394 applies in relation to access to evidence or other material on which the proposed decision was based. If s 394 applies,[1] the FSA must state in the notice its effect and indicate whether any secondary material[2] exists, access to which the person concerned is entitled. Procedurally, a warning notice must specify a reasonable period (being at least 28 days (s 387(2))[3] within which the person to whom the warning notice has been given can make representations to the FSA. The FSA may extend this period by specifying in the notice the date by which representations must be received (s 387(3)) and must then decide within a reasonable period whether to issue the person receiving the warning notice with a decision notice (s 387(4)).

---

[1]   See s 392(a).

[2]   'Secondary material' is defined in s 394(6) as material other than material falling within s 394(1)(a) which the FSA considered in reaching the decision mentioned in that paragraph or obtained in connection with the matter to which the notice to which this section applies relates, but which it did not consider in reaching that decision.

[3]   Section 417(3) provides that any provision of FSMA 2000 authorising or requiring a person to do anything within a specified number of days takes no account of any day which is a public holiday in any part of the UK (ie, they are included in the same way as any other).

Decision notices

8.19   Any decision notice issued by the FSA under any of the provisions of FSMA 2000 must be given to the person concerned in writing (s 388(1)(a)) and must give the FSA's reasons for its decision to take the action to which the notice relates (s 388(1)(b)). The decision notice must also state whether s 394 applies (s 388(1)(c)).[1] The decision notice must also give an indication of any right which the person concerned may have to refer the matter to the Tribunal under FSMA 2000 and the procedure to be followed in making any such reference (s 388(1)(e)). Where a decision notice has been preceded by a warning notice, the action which is to be taken must be taken under the same Part of FSMA 2000 as the action proposed in the warning notice (s 388(2)).

---
[1]   See para 8.18.

8.20   If the FSA decides to take action which is different from the action previously notified under a decision notice, a further decision notice complying with these procedures must be given but only if the person to whom the original notice was given consents (s 388(3), (4)).[1] If the person who is given a further decision notice under s 388(3) had a right under the original notice to refer the matter to the Tribunal, he also has that right in respect of the further decision notice (s 388(5)).

---
[1]   The FSA may only adopt this approach if it has not yet taken the action specified in the original decision notice (s 388(3)).

Discontinuing proceedings

8.21   If the FSA decides not to take any action proposed in a warning notice under any section of FSMA 2000 or not to take the action to which a decision notice relates, it must provide a notice of discontinuance identifying the proceedings which are to be discontinued (s 389(3)) to the person[1] to whom the warning notice or decision notice were given (s 389(1)). This provision does not apply to notices given in respect of any proceedings relating to the granting of an application under FSMA 2000 (s 389(2)), for example, in relation to applications for permission under Pt IV or for approval under Pt V.

---
[1]   The FSA may publish a notice of discontinuance under s 391(2) and (3), unless that publication would be unfair or prejudicial (s 391(6)): see para 8.27.

Final notices

8.22   Where the FSA has issued a decision notice and the matter has not been referred to the Tribunal in accordance with s 133(1), the FSA must give the person to whom the decision notice was given (and any other person to whom the decision notice was copied under any provisions of FSMA 2000) a final notice (s 390(1)).[1] If the final notice relates to a statement to be published, it must set out the terms of the statement and give details about the manner in which and the date on which it is to be published (s 390(3)). If the final notice relates to an order, the notice must set out the terms of the order and the date from which it has effect (s 390(4)). If the final notice relates to a penalty, it must state the amount and the manner in which and the period within which it must be paid and details of the steps which can be taken if the penalty is not paid within that period (s 390(5)). The payment period in this case must be at least 14 days beginning on the date on which the final notice is given (s 390(8)).[2]

---

[1]   Similar requirements are imposed when the FSA is taking action in accordance with directions given by the Tribunal or the court under s 137 (s 390(2)).
[2]   See para 8.18, fn 3.

8.23   A final notice which relates to the making of a payment or distribution (in the case of a restitution order by the FSA under s 384(5)) must state the person to whom it must be made and the manner in which and the period within which it must be made (s 390(6)). Again, the payment period must be at least 14 days[1] beginning on the date on which the final notice is given (s 390(8)). In any other case, a final notice must provide details of the action being taken and must specify the date on which the action is to be taken (s 390(7)). If any payment required under a final notice under s 390(5)(b) is not paid by the date specified, the FSA may seek to recover that amount as a debt due to it (s 390(9)).

---

[1]   See para 8.18, fn 3.

8.24   If any payment required in respect of a payment or distribution (in the case of a restitution order by the FSA under s 390(6)(c)) is not made by the end of the period stated in the final notice, the obligation to make the payment is enforceable and the FSA may apply to the courts for an injunction or, in Scotland, an order under the Court of Session Act 1988, s 45 (s 390(10)).

Article 6 ECHR

8.25   The procedure following service of a warning notice will in many cases amount to a determination of civil rights and obligations within ECHR Art 6(1). It is most unlikely that the procedure leading up to a decision notice can be regarded as structurally compatible with the requirement of a fair and public hearing before an independent tribunal.[1] However, it is well established that a procedure leading to an initial decision which does not comply with Art 6 can be cured by providing a right of appeal to a tribunal that does so comply, so long as that tribunal has 'full jurisdiction' to revisit the factual and legal issues determined at first instance.[2] The right to refer a proposed decision to the Tribunal (which has power to consider afresh the merits of the FSA's proposed findings and/or penalty) therefore prevents the FSMA 2000 disciplinary machinery from falling foul of Art 6 merely because of the summary nature of the first instance procedure, as it is set out in the Act.

---

[1]   The FSA's implementation of its 'Regulatory Decisions Committee' does not cure the prima facie structural failure to comply with Art 6, because it is, in effect, a committee of the FSA board, made up of co-opted members. If the committee operates as described in the FSA Handbook, Decision making manual, the Art 6 requirements may be met in practice.
[2]   *Albert and Lecompte v Belgium* (1982) 5 EHRR 533; *Bryan v United Kingdom* (1995) 21 EHRR 342.

PUBLICATION OF NOTICES AND CONFIDENTIALITY

8.26   FSMA 2000, s 391 sets out the limitations in publishing notices under Pt XXVI of the Act. Where the FSA has issued a warning notice or a decision notice, neither the FSA nor any person to whom the notice has been given or copied may publish the notice or any details contained in it (s 391(1)).[1]

---

[1]   This, in effect, precludes publicity about a matter until the decision becomes effective or until the Tribunal hears the matter.

8.27   In the case of a notice of discontinuance the FSA may, with the consent of the person to whom the notice is given, publish such information about the matter to which the discontinued proceedings relate as it considers appropriate (s 391(2)). A copy of a notice of discontinuance must be accompanied by a statement to this effect. The same applies in respect of any person to whom the notice had been copied (s 391(3)).

8.28   The FSA must publish such information about a matter to which a final notice relates as it considers appropriate (s 391(4)). This obligation is subject to s 391(6), which provides that the FSA may not publish information which would be unfair to the person with respect to whom the action is taken or prejudicial to the interests of consumers.

Generally speaking, when it does publish information, the FSA is able to publish it in such form as it considers appropriate (s 391(7)). However it is not entitled to publish information which would, in its opinion, be unfair to the person in respect of whom the action was taken or prejudicial to the interests of consumers (s 391(6)).[1]

---

[1] 'Consumers' is defined in FSMA 2000, s 138(7).

8.29 When a supervisory notice[1] takes effect, the FSA must publish such information about the matter as it considers appropriate. In determining when a supervisory notice takes effect, a matter to which the supervisory notice relates is open to review if—

— the period during which the person affected by the notice may refer the matter to the Tribunal is still running;

— the matter has been referred to the Tribunal but has not yet been dealt with;

— the matter has been referred to the Tribunal and dealt with but the period within which an appeal may be brought is still running; or

— an appeal has been brought but has not yet been determined (s 391(8)).

---

[1] See para 8.15, fn 1.

OFFENCES UNDER FSMA 2000, PT XXVII

8.30 FSMA, Pt XXVII (ss 397–403) sets out a number of offences under FSMA 2000 which appear in the Financial Services Act 1986 (FSA 1986), the Banking Act 1987 and the Insurance Companies Act 1982. Other general provisions relate to the commission of an offence by a director or officer of a company or partnership and deal with the institution of proceedings under FSMA 2000. Part XXVII also gives the FSA power to prosecute insider dealing under the Criminal Justice Act 1993 and offences under the Money Laundering Regulations 1993,[1] as well as offences of misleading statements and practices under FSMA 2000.[2]

---

[1] SI 1993/1933.
[2] FSMA Explanatory Notes, para 699.

Misleading statements and practices

Nature of the offence

8.31   FSMA 2000, s 397 sets out the offence of making misleading statements and engaging in misleading practices as contained in FSA 1986, s 47. A person who makes a statement, promise or forecast which he knows to be misleading, false or deceptive in a material particular is guilty of an offence if he does so for the purpose of inducing, or is reckless as to whether it may induce, another person (whether or not the person to whom the statement, promise or forecast is made) to enter or offer to enter into, or to refrain from entering or offering to enter into, a relevant agreement (s 397(1)(a), (2)). For these purposes, a 'relevant agreement' means an agreement, the entering into or performance of which by either party constitutes an activity of a kind which is to be specified by order made by the Treasury or one which falls within a specified class of activity and which relates to a relevant investment (s 397(9)). A 'relevant investment' is an investment which is specified by an order made by the Treasury or falls within a class of investments so prescribed (s 397(10)).[1]

---

[1]   Section 397(11) provides that Sch 2 (except paras 25 and 26) applies to s 397(9) and (10) with references in FSMA 2000, s 22 being read as references to each of those subsections but s 397(12) provides that nothing in Sch 2, as applied by s 397(11) limits the powers of the Treasury to prescribe those investments under s 397(9) and (10). The Financial Services and Markets Act 2000 (Misleading Statements and Practices) Order 2001, SI 2001/3645 applies the offences to the same controlled activities as are specified in the Financial Promotions Order (see paras 6.29–6.30), but in relation to all investments referred to in FSMA 2000, Sch 2, Pt II. To the extent that this would include funeral plan contracts, commencement of this order was delayed until 1 January 2002 and for mortgages until such date as the Treasury may specify (see the Financial Services and Markets Act 2000 (Commencement of Mortgage Regulation) (Amendment) Order 2002, SI 2002/1777), but this is expected to be 31 October 2004.

8.32   The principal difference between FSA 1986, s 47 and FSMA 2000, s 397(1) is that the 2000 Act splits into two the offence contained in FSA 1986, s 47(1)(a). Section 397(1)(a) is broadly equivalent to FSA 1986, s 47(1)(a), but does not include the reference to a person who 'conceals any material facts' contained in s 47(1)(a). Instead a separate provision in s 397(1)(b) now refers to a situation where a person dishonestly conceals any material facts whether in connection with a statement, promise or forecast made by him or otherwise. This offence (originally incorporated in FSA 1986, s 47(1)(a)) is intended to cover situations such as a person lying about a company's financial position at a time when he is seeking to dispose of shares in that company.[1]

---

[1]   FSMA Explanatory Notes, para 701.

8.33   Thirdly, a separate offence is created where a person recklessly makes (dishonestly or otherwise) a statement, promise or forecast which is misleading, false or deceptive in a material particular and is therefore guilty of an offence under s 397(2). Again, this wording is the same as FSA 1986, s 47(1)(b) but with the change to use of the words 'material particular' (s 397(1)(c)).[1]

---

[1]   In addition, wording in FSA 1986, s 47(1) has not been carried over into s 397, namely the wording which provided that an offence arose if the person 'conceals the facts for the purpose of inducing, or is reckless as to whether it may induce, another person' (*whether or not the person to whom the statement, promise or forecast is made or from whom the facts were concealed*).

8.34   A person found guilty of an offence under s 397 may be liable to imprisonment of up to seven years or to a fine or to both imprisonment and a fine (s 397(8)).

Defence

8.35   Section 397(4) provides that it is a defence for a person against whom proceedings have been brought under s 397(2) to show that the statement, promise or forecast was made in conformity with the price stabilising rules made under s 144 or the control of information rules made under s 147. The inter-relationship between this offence and those civil offences created under s 118 (market abuse) is, however, less clear.

8.36   A person is not guilty of an offence under s 397(1) and (2), however, unless—
— the statement, promise or forecast is made in or from, or the facts are concealed in or from, the UK, or arrangements are made in or from the UK for the statement, promise or forecast to be made or the facts to be concealed;[1]
— the person on whom the inducement is intended to or may have effect is in the UK; or
— the agreement is or would be entered into or the rights are or would be exercised in the UK (s 397(6)).

---

[1]   This provision expands the scope of FSA 1986, s 47(4).

Market manipulation

8.37   The offence of market manipulation under FSA 1986, s 47(2) has been re-enacted verbatim in FSMA 2000. Section 397(3) provides that 'any person who does any act or engages in any course of conduct which creates a false or misleading impression as to the market in or the price or value of any relevant investments is guilty of an offence if he does so for the purpose of creating that impression and of thereby inducing another person to acquire, dispose of, subscribe for or underwrite those investments or to refrain from doing so or to exercise, or refrain from exercising, any rights conferred by those investments'.

8.38　Section 397(5) re-enacts the defence available under FSA 1986, s 47(3), namely that in proceedings brought against a person it is a defence for him to show that he—

— reasonably believed that his act or conduct would not create an impression which was false or misleading under s 397(3);
— acted or engaged in the conduct for the purpose of stabilising the price of investments and did so in conformity with the price stabilising rules made under s 144; or
— acted or engaged in the conduct in conformity with the control of information rules made under s 147 (s 397(4), (5)).

A person is not guilty of an offence under s 397(3) unless the act is done or the course of conduct is engaged in, in the UK or the false or misleading impression is created in the UK (s 397(7)). A person found guilty of an offence under s 397(3) may be liable to imprisonment of up to seven years or to a fine, or both imprisonment and a fine (s 397(8)).

Misleading the FSA

8.39　FSMA 2000, s 398 makes it an offence for any person who, in purported compliance with any requirement imposed by or under FSMA 2000, knowingly or recklessly gives the FSA information which is false or misleading in a material particular (s 398(1)).[1] This offence only applies to a requirement in relation to which no other provision under FSMA 2000 creates an offence in connection with the giving of information (s 398(2)) such as the offence under s 117(4) in relation to the giving of information to investigators.[2] A person guilty of an offence under this section is liable to an unlimited fine on indictment or a fine not exceeding the statutory maximum on summary conviction (s 398(3)).

---

[1]　Identical in form to FSA 1986, s 200.
[2]　FSMA Explanatory Notes, para 706.

Misleading the Office of Fair Trading (OFT)

8.40　FSMA 2000, s 399 provides that the Competition Act 1998, s 44, relating to offences connected with the provision of false or misleading information to the OFT, applies in relation to any of his functions under FSMA 2000 as if it were a function under Pt I of the 1998 Act.

Offences by bodies corporate and partnerships

8.41   If any offence under FSMA 2000 is committed by a body corporate and is shown to have been committed with the consent or connivance of an officer or is attributable to any neglect on his part, the officer as well as the body corporate is guilty of an offence and may be liable for committing an offence and proceeded against and punished accordingly (s 400(1)).[1]

---

[1]   An 'officer' for these purposes means a director, member of the committee of management, chief executive, manager, secretary or other similar officer or a person purporting to act in such a capacity and an individual who is a controller of the body (s 400(5)). See also para 8.43.

8.42   In addition, if the affairs of a body corporate are managed by its members, s 400 applies to the acts and defaults of a member in connection with his management functions as if he were a director of that body (s 400(2)). Similarly, in the case of an offence committed by a partnership, if it can be shown that the offence was committed with the consent or connivance of a partner (or anyone purporting to act as a partner) (s 400(4)) or could be attributed to any neglect on his part, he, as well as the partnership, may be guilty of the offence and liable to be proceeded against and punished accordingly (s 400(3)).

8.43   Any proceedings for an offence allegedly committed by an unincorporated association must be brought in the name of the association and not in the name of any of its members (s 403(2)). However, s 400(6) provides that if an offence is committed by an unincorporated association other than a partnership and is shown to have been committed with the consent or connivance of an officer of the association, or a member of its governing body, or to be attributed to any neglect on the part of such an officer or member, that officer or member may be guilty of an offence as well as the association and may be proceeded against and punished accordingly.

8.44   Any fine imposed on an unincorporated association on conviction of an offence under FSMA 2000 is to be paid out of the funds of the association (s 403(1)). The relevant rules of court relating to the service of documents are to have effect as if the association were a body corporate (s 403(3)). In addition, in any proceedings for an offence brought against an unincorporated association, the Criminal Justice Act 1925, s 33 and the Magistrates' Courts Act 1980, Sch 3 apply as they would in relation to a body corporate, and the Criminal Procedure (Scotland) Act 1995, s 70 applies as if the association were a body corporate. For proceedings brought against an unincorporated association in Northern Ireland, the Criminal Justice (Northern Ireland) Act 1945, s 18 and the Magistrates' Courts (Northern Ireland) Order 1981, Sch 4 apply as they would to a body corporate (s 403(4)).

8.45   All of these provisions may be modified by regulations made by the Treasury to apply to a body corporate or unincorporated associations or equivalent undertakings formed or recognised under the law of a territory outside the UK (s 400(7)).[1]

---

[1]   FSMA Explanatory Notes, para 709.

8.46   Summary proceedings for an offence under FSMA 2000[1] may be taken against a body corporate or an unincorporated association at any place at which it has a place of business and, in respect of an individual, at any place where he is for the time being (s 403(5)). These provisions do not, however, affect any jurisdiction exercisable apart from s 403 (s 403(6)).

---

[1]   Defined in s 403(7).

8.47   Section 400 is almost identical to FSA 1986, s 202 but while that provision has relatively little direct effect on most authorised persons or individuals, the scope of s 400 is potentially much greater.

The FSA's power to institute criminal proceedings under FSMA 2000

8.48   Proceedings for any offence under FSMA 2000 or any subordinate legislation[1] made under it may be instituted in England and Wales only by the FSA or the Secretary of State or by or with the consent of the Director of Public Prosecutions (s 401(2)). Similar proceedings may be instituted in Northern Ireland only by the FSA or the Secretary of State or by or with the consent of the Director of Public Prosecutions for Northern Ireland (s 401(3)), while in Scotland, the prosecution of offences is the responsibility of the Lord Advocate.[2] Proceedings for an offence under s 203 may also be brought by the OFT (except in Scotland) (s 401(4)). In exercising its power to institute proceedings under s 401, the FSA must comply with any conditions or restrictions imposed on it by the Treasury (s 401(5)). Such restrictions or conditions must be in writing and may relate to proceedings generally or to such proceedings or categories of proceedings as the Treasury may direct (s 401(6)).

---

[1]   Section 401(1) defines an 'offence' for the purposes of FSMA 2000 as an offence under FSMA 2000 or subordinate legislation made under the Act.
[2]   FSMA Explanatory Notes, para 711.

8.49   The FSA may also institute proceedings for an offence under the Criminal Justice Act 1993, Pt V in relation to offences for insider dealing or under prescribed regulations[1] in relation to money laundering (s 402(1)). In exercising its power to institute proceedings under s 402, the FSA must comply with any conditions or restrictions, such as compliance with the Code for Crown Prosecutors,[2] imposed on it by the Treasury (s 402(2)). Such restrictions or conditions must be in writing and may relate to proceedings generally or to such proceedings or categories of proceedings as the Treasury may direct (s 402(3)).[3]

---

[1]   'Prescribed' means prescribed in regulations made by the Treasury (s 417(1)).
[2]   FSMA Explanatory Notes, para 713.
[3]   The FSA has stated that it will apply the principles set out in the Code for Crown Prosecutions: see the FSA Handbook, Enforcement manual, ENF 15.5.

THE FSA'S POWER OF INTERVENTION IN RELATION TO INCOMING FIRMS

Grounds for intervention

8.50   FSMA 2000, s 196 provides that if the FSA is entitled to exercise its power of intervention in relation to an incoming firm,[1] it may impose any requirement in relation to the firm which it could impose if the firm's permission was a Pt IV permission and the FSA was entitled to exercise its power under Pt IV to vary that permission (s 196). The FSA may exercise these intervention powers under s 196 if it appears that—

— the firm has contravened or is likely to contravene a requirement imposed on it by or under FSMA 2000 in a case where the FSA is responsible for enforcing compliance in the UK; or

— the firm has, in purported compliance with any requirement (not only a Pt IV requirement) imposed by or under FSMA 2000, knowingly or recklessly given the FSA information which is false or misleading in a material particular; or

— it is desirable to exercise the power in order to protect the interests of actual or potential customers (s 194(1)).[2]

---

[1]   An 'incoming firm' is an EEA firm which is exercising or has exercised its right to carry on a regulated activity in the UK in accordance with FSMA 2000, Sch 3, or a Treaty firm which is exercising or has exercised its right to carry on a regulated activity in the UK in accordance with FSMA 2000, Sch 4 (s 193(1)).

EEA firms: consumer credit

8.51   The FSA also has these powers of intervention in respect of an incoming EEA firm falling within FSMA 2000, Sch 3, para 5(a) or (b) which is exercising an EEA right to carry on Consumer Credit Act business in the UK (s 194(2)) as defined in FSMA 2000, s 203(10). The FSA may exercise its powers of intervention if the OFT has informed it that the firm or any of its employees, agents or associates[1] (past or present), or a controller of the firm (in the case of a body corporate) has done any of the things specified in the Consumer Credit Act 1974 (CCA 1974), s 25(2) (s 194(3)).

1   'Associate' for these purposes is as defined in CCA 1974, s 25(2) by reference to CCA 1974, s 184 and includes a husband or wife or relative or former husband or wife or a reputed husband or wife. The power can be exercised therefore if the OFT informs the FSA that anyone within s 194(3) has done anything to call into question whether he is a fit person to engage in such activities. This includes committing any offence involving fraud or other dishonesty or violence or contravening any other provision of CCA 1974 or under any other enactment relating to the provision of credit to individuals or other transactions with individuals or practising discrimination on grounds of sex, colour, race or ethnic or national origins in, or in connection with the carrying on of any business or engaging in business practices which appears to the OFT to be deceptive, oppressive or otherwise unfair or improper (CCA 1974, s 25(2)).

Exercise of power in support of overseas regulator

8.52   The FSA may also exercise its powers of intervention in respect of an incoming firm at the request of or for the purpose of assisting an overseas regulator (s 195(1)). For these purposes, an 'overseas regulator' means an authority in a country or territory outside the UK which is a home state regulator[1] or which exercises any of the following functions—

   —   a function corresponding to any function of the FSA under FSMA 2000;

   —   a function corresponding to any function exercised by the competent authority under FSMA 2000, Pt VI in relation to the listing of shares;[2]

   —   a function corresponding to any function exercised by the Secretary of State under the Companies Act 1985;

   —   a function in connection with the investigation of insider dealing as prohibited by the Criminal Justice Act 1993, Pt V or the enforcement of rules (whether having the force of law or not) relating to insider dealing; or

— a function otherwise prescribed in regulations made for the purposes of s 195(4) by the Treasury which relate to companies or financial services (s 195(3), (4)).

---

1   As defined in FSMA 2000, Sch 3, para 9.
2   It is unclear whether this should be 'securities' within the meaning of s 74(5) or 'shares' as defined in s 422(6).

8.53   If a home state regulator asks the FSA to exercise its power of intervention pursuant to a Community obligation,[1] or a home state regulator has notified the FSA that an EEA firm's EEA authorisation has been withdrawn, the FSA must, in deciding whether to exercise its power of intervention, consider whether it is necessary to exercise that power to comply with a Community obligation (s 195(5)). The FSA may also decide to exercise its power of intervention only if the overseas regulator concerned undertakes to contribute to the cost of the exercise (s 195(7)) (unless the power of intervention is being exercised in order to comply with a Community obligation) (s 195(8)). In deciding in any particular case in which the FSA does not consider that the exercise of its power of intervention is necessary in order to comply with a Community obligation, it may take into account—

— whether there is reciprocity, ie, that the country or territory in question would give corresponding assistance to a UK regulatory authority;
— whether the case concerns a breach of law or requirements of which there is no close parallel in the UK or involves an assertion of jurisdiction which is not recognised in the UK;
— the seriousness of the case and its importance to persons in the UK; and
— whether the public interest otherwise demands that assistance ought to be given (s 195(6)).

---

1   The term 'Community obligation' is not defined in FSMA 2000. It has the meaning given by the European Communities Act 1972. See also Interpretation Act 1978, s 5, Sch 1.

Exercise of power of intervention

8.54   In exercising its power of intervention under s 196 any requirement imposed takes effect—

— immediately if the notice which the FSA is required to give under s 197(3) states that that is the case;
— on such date as may be specified in the notice; or
— if no date is specified, when the matter to which it relates is no longer open to review (s 197(1)).

However, such a requirement may only be given effect immediately or on a specific date if the FSA, having regard to the grounds on which it is exercising that power, considers it necessary to do so (s 197(2)). The FSA must give the incoming firm written notice (s 197(3)). The notice must set out the details of the requirement, when it takes effect, the FSA's reasons for imposing it and for the timing of when it takes effect. It must inform the incoming firm that it may make representations to the FSA within a specified period (whether or not the matter has been referred to the Tribunal) and inform the incoming firm of its right to refer the matter to the Tribunal (s 197(4)). The FSA may extend the period for representations to be made (s 197(5)) and if, having considered those representations, the FSA decides to impose the requirement proposed, or, if it has been imposed, not to rescind the requirement, it must give the incoming firm written notice which must include notification that the firm may refer the matter to the Tribunal (s 197(6), (8)).

8.55 Similarly if, having considered those representations, the FSA decides not to impose the requirement proposed, or to impose a different requirement, or to rescind a requirement which already has effect, it must give the incoming firm written notice which, if it specifies a different requirement under s 197(7)(b), must contain the same information as that specified in s 197(4) (s 197(7), (9)). Any notice to the effect that a matter may be referred to the Tribunal must also give an indication of the procedures to be followed in making such a reference (s 197(10)).[1]

---

[1] The same notice procedure applies to variations on the FSA's own initiative (s 200(3)). The warning and decision notices apply if the FSA proposes to refuse an application under s 200(1) (s 200(4), (5)).

Power to obtain an injunction in relation to certain overseas insurance companies

8.56 FSMA 2000, s 198 provides that if the FSA has received a request made in respect of an incoming EEA firm under the First Non-Life Insurance Directive, Art 20.5 or the First Life Insurance Directive, Art 24.5, it may apply to the court[1] for an injunction restraining or, in Scotland, an interdict prohibiting the incoming firm from disposing of or otherwise dealing with any of its assets (s 198(1), (2)). If the court grants an injunction (or interdiction) in accordance with s 198, it may make subsequent orders to provide for such incidental, consequential and supplementary matters as it considers necessary for the FSA to perform its functions under FSMA 2000 (s 198(3)).

---

[1] In England, Wales and Northern Ireland, the High Court or, in Scotland, the Court of Session (s 198(4)).

Additional procedure for EEA firms in certain cases

8.57   Where it appears to the FSA that its power of intervention is exercisable in relation to the contravention of a relevant requirement by an EEA firm exercising EEA rights in the UK, it must require the firm to remedy the situation, by giving it notice in writing (s 199(1), (3)). For these purposes a requirement is 'relevant' if it is imposed by the FSA under FSMA 2000[1] and if, in respect of its contravention, any of the single market directives[2] provide that a procedure of the kind set out in s 199 is to apply (s 199(2)). If, having been given notice in writing by the FSA under s 199(3), the firm fails to remedy the situation within a reasonable time, the FSA must give notice to that effect to the firm's home state regulator requesting that it take all appropriate measures to ensure that the firm remedies the matter and that it inform the FSA of the measures it proposes to take or has taken or the reasons for it not taking such measures (s 199(4)).

---

[1]   Presumably not limited to a requirement or a permission under Pt IV.

[2]   Defined in FSMA 2000, Sch 3, paras 1–4, ie, the insurance directives, the Banking Consolidation Directive and the Investment Services Directive.

8.58   If the FSA decides that it should exercise its power of intervention in relation to an incoming EEA firm as a matter of urgency to protect the interests of consumers, it may do so before it provides the notice required under s 199(3) and (4), but only where the firm's home state regulator has failed or refused to take appropriate measures or where the measures which it has taken have proved inadequate for that purpose (s 199(5)). If, however, the FSA has complied with the notice requirements and it meets the requirements of s 199(6) it may take action even where the home state regulator has not yet failed or refused to take the required measures under s 199(5) (s 199(6)). In this case, however, the FSA must at the earliest opportunity inform the firm's home state regulator and the European Commission of the action which it has taken (s 199(7)) and if the European Commission decides under any of the single market directives[1] that the FSA must rescind or vary any requirement imposed on the incoming EEA firm by the FSA in the exercise of its power of intervention, the FSA must comply (s 199(8)).[2]

---

[1]   Defined in FSMA 2000, Sch 3, paras 1–4.

[2]   It is not clear whether the provisions of s 197 would have to apply to variations required by the European Commission.

8.59   The FSA may rescind or vary a requirement imposed in exercising its power of intervention on its own initiative or on the application of the person subject to the requirements (s 200(1)). In the case of the FSA's own initiative to rescind a requirement, it must give notice in writing to the person concerned, which takes effect on the date specified in the notice (s 200(2)). If the FSA proposes to refuse an application for variation or rescission, it must provide the applicant with a warning notice (s 200(4)), and if the FSA decides to refuse such an application, it must give to the applicant a decision notice and advise him that he may refer the matter to the Tribunal (s 200(5)). Where the FSA has imposed an 'assets requirement'[1] on an incoming firm, the requirement has the same effect as it would have had in relation to an authorised person on whom it would have been imposed under FSMA 2000, s 45 (s 201). A contravention of a requirement imposed by the FSA under Pt XIII does not give rise to an offence or make any transaction void or unenforceable or give rise to any other right of action for breach of statutory duty except in certain cases prescribed by order made by the Treasury, where the contravention is actionable at the suit of a person who suffers loss as a result of the contravention. In these cases it will be subject to the defences and other 'incidents' applicable to actions for breaches of statutory duty (s 202(1), (2)).[2]

---

1   Defined in FSMA 2000, s 48(3).
2   The Financial Services and Markets Act 2000 (Rights of Action) Regulations 2001, SI 2001/2256, regs 3 and 7 prescribe cases limited to individuals (except when carrying on a regulated activity), ignoring the overseas persons exclusions in the Financial Services and Markets Act 2000 (Regulated Activities) Order 2001, SI 2001/544, art 72, and others (except when doing business) SI 2001/2256 also provides that contravention of a financial resources requirement is not actionable (regs 4, 7).

9 The FSA as listing authority

INTRODUCTION

9.1 Part VI (ss 72–103) of the Financial Services and Markets Act 2000 (FSMA 2000) is now the principal statute dealing with the official listing of securities. This Part implements the various EU Directives relating to the admission to listing and the regulation of the public offer of securities in the UK and provides a process for non-public offers and the issue of 'non-listing' prospectuses. This Part also establishes the regulatory framework for the 'competent authority' which is now the Financial Services Authority (FSA).

BACKGROUND

9.2 The Financial Services Act 1986 (FSA 1986), Pt IV implemented the provisions of the various EC listing Directives relating to the official listing of securities.[1] FSA 1986 originally provided that the competent authority for the purposes of Council Directive 79/279/EEC (Admissions to Listing Directive)[2] was the Council of The Stock Exchange. However, various changes in corporate structure in 1991 resulted in this authority being transferred to the International Stock Exchange of the UK and the Republic of Ireland Limited in 1991[3] which subsequently changed its name in 1995 to The London Stock Exchange Limited.

---

[1] Namely, the Admission to Listing Directive (79/279/EEC), the Listing Particulars Directive (80/390/EEC) and the Interim Reports Directive (82/121/EEC). In addition Pt IV partly implements the Prospectus Directive (89/298/EEC).

[2] The Admission to Listings Directive, the Listing Particulars Directive, the Major Shareholders Directive (88/627/EEC) and the Interim Reports Directive have now been consolidated in the Consolidations Admissions and Reporting Directive (2001/34/EC).

[3] Official Listing of Securities (Change of Competent Authority) Regulations 1991, SI 1991/2000.

9.3 On 4 October 1999, the Chancellor of the Exchequer, Gordon Brown, announced that it was the Government's view (and evidently also the Exchange's)[1] that the responsibilities of the competent authority should be transferred from the London Stock Exchange to the FSA. It was the Government's view that the increasing commercialisation and demutualisation of the London Stock Exchange made it inappropriate for it to continue to exercise the supervisory functions of the UK listing authority as well as those of a commercial body. The Government and the FSA emphasised first the need to have checks and balances in the system and, second, the advisability of splitting the functions of admission to listing—a fundamentally supervisory or regulatory role—and that of admission to trading—which is clearly a market role.[2]

---

[1]   FSA CP 37, The transfer of the UK Listing Authority to the FSA, December 1999, para 1.1.

[2]   HL Committee Stage, 21 March 2000, cols 185–201, HL Report Stage, 18 April 2000, cols 635–639 and HL Report Stage, 9 May 2000, col 1376 (re: IX and the proposed merger with the German Stock Exchanges); also HL Committee Stage, 29 March 2000, col 897 in relation to the then draft Official Listing of Securities (Change of Competent Authority) Regulations 2000 (now SI 2000/968) laid before Parliament, FSA CP 37, para 9.

9.4   The FSA is currently reviewing the listing regime[1] to ensure the regime remains coherent and takes into account the changing European framework for the listing of securities including the EU Prospectus Directive,[2] the Market Abuse Directive[3] and the proposed Transparency Obligations Directive.

---

[1]   FSA Feedback Statement, Review of the Listing Regime, January 2003, and see FSA Consultation Paper 203, October 2003.

[2]   Council Directive 89/298/EEC; see also Council Directive 2003/71/EC.

[3]   European Parliament and Council Directive 2003/6/EC.

THE FSA AS THE COMPETENT AUTHORITY

9.5   One of the main features of the FSMA 2000 regime is the wider range of financial instruments which may now be eligible for listing (s 74(5)) and the clearer integration of the requirements for both prospectuses for listed securities (listing particulars) and non-listing prospectuses which replace the various provisions of FSA 1986, Pt IV and the Public Offers of Securities Regulations 1995,[1] which had implemented piecemeal the various relevant EC Directives (ss 79–87).[2] FSMA 2000 also now features explicit provisions for transferring responsibilities of the competent authority to another body (s 72(3), Sch 8). FSMA 2000 establishes a policy and process for the competent authority dealing with breaches of the listing rules and the penalties which may arise as a result (ss 91–94). The FSA also has indirect responsibility for compliance with the Combined Code through the obligation imposed by the listing rules for companies to publish a statement of their compliance with the Code.

---

[1]   SI 1995/1537. The FSA is also the competent authority for the purposes of reg 11(3) of these regulations. That regulation permits the variation of the regulations relating to disclosures which must be included in non-listing prospectuses in certain circumstances: see UK Listing Authority (UKLA), LIST Issue 2, May 2003.

[2]   See also amendments to the Public Offer of Securities Regulations 1995 contained in the Financial Services and Markets Act 2000 (Consequential Amendments and Repeals) Order 2001, SI 2001/3649, arts 501–512.

Interim transfer of functions of competent authority to the FSA

9.6   In December 1999 the FSA published a consultation paper setting out its proposals for the transfer of the functions of the competent authority to it.[1] The message conveyed was very much a 'business as usual' approach to the transfer with the objective of having as little disruption as possible to the existing approach and processes.[2] The functions of the competent authority under FSA 1986, Pt IV, including the maintenance of the official list,[3] were formally transferred to the FSA by order with effect from 1 May 2000.[4] This order also transferred to the FSA all other rights and obligations of the old competent authority and the London Stock Exchange, and the Yellow Book (the listing rules for the purposes of FSA 1986, s 142(6)) has been superseded by the FSA Listing Rules.[5] Initially the London Stock Exchange retained responsibility for publishing the Official Daily List and the dissemination of information through its Regulatory News Services. However, from 15 April 2002 the mechanism by which listed companies are required to disseminate information required by the listing rules was amended and companies were given a wider choice and may choose one of seven approved primary information providers.[6]

---

[1]   FSA CP 37, The Transfer of the UK Listing Authority to the FSA, December 1999.

[2]   FSA CP 37, para 1.5.

[3]   The 'official list' is defined in FSMA 2000, s 103(1) as 'the list maintained as the official list by the Authority immediately before the coming into force of section 74 as that list has effect for the time being' under these transitional provisions.

[4]   Official Listing of Securities (Change of Competent Authority) Regulations 2000, SI 2000/968.

[5]   These are available on the FSA's website at www.fsa.gov.uk.

[6]   At the date of publication, the primary information providers are: BusinessWire, FirstSight, Hugin Announce, NewsRelease Express, PR Newswire Disclosure and the London Stock Exchange's Regulatory News Service.

Transfer of functions to the FSA under FSMA 2000

9.7   FSMA 2000 repealed and replaced FSA 1986, Pt IV and established the FSA as the competent authority for official listing purposes (s 72(1)).[1] The FSA's general functions as the competent authority[2] are—

—   making rules under FSMA 2000, Pt VI;

— giving general guidance in relation to Pt VI; and
— determining the general policy and principles under which it
performs its other functions under Pt VI (s 73(2)).

---

[1] This provision came into force on 18 June 2001 (before N2) and therefore the FSA was already the competent authority under the Official Listing of Securities (Change of Competent Authority) Regulations 2000, SI 2000/968, reg 3.
[2] Section 103(2) also provides that in relation to any function conferred on the competent authority by Pt VI any reference to 'the competent authority' should be read as a reference to the person by whom the function is for the time being exercisable.

Modifications of provisions of FSMA 2000 in relation to the FSA as competent authority

9.8 The duties and powers of the FSA as the competent authority under Pt VI have been recognised as different in substance from those general duties and powers given to the FSA as the regulator under FSMA 2000, s 1. Therefore FSMA 2000, Sch 7 sets out a number of modifications to those duties and powers.

9.9 The FSA's general functions as set out in FSMA 2000, s 2 are modified so that:
— s 2(4)(a) does not apply to listing rules made by the FSA as the competent authority (Sch 7, para 2(a))—this is because the FSA has separate powers to make listing rules under FSMA 2000, s 73(2)(a);
— s 2(4)(c) and (d) does not apply to general guidance given in relation to the provisions of Pt VI and functions under Pt VI as these are dealt with in s 73(2)(b) and (c) respectively (Sch 7, para 2(b), (c)); and
— the FSA's duty to consult with practitioners on its policies and procedures and the rules under FSMA 2000, s 8 does not apply to the FSA in its role as the competent authority because Pt VI has a separate consultation process through the Listing Authority Review Committee, which the FSA has indicated will continue to operate at least for the time being (Sch 7, para 3).

9.10 Other provisions of FSMA 2000 which do not apply to the FSA in respect of its functions as the competent authority are—
— s 149 (the use of evidential provisions in respect of rules);
— s 153 (the use of rule-making instruments in relation to any power conferred on the FSA to make rules);
— s 154 (procedures for the verification of rule-making instruments); and
— s 156 (general supplementary powers regarding rule-making) (Sch 7, para 4(1)).

Section 155 has also been modified so that the reference in s 155(2)(c) to the FSA's general duties is to be read as a reference to its duties under FSMA 2000, s 73 (Sch 7, para 4(2)).

9.11   Other provisions which have been modified by Sch 7 include the provision in Sch 1, para 5 which permits the FSA's governing body to make arrangements to delegate any of its functions except for its legislative functions (including rule-making). Schedule 7, para 5(1) applies this provision to the FSA when issuing public statements of policy in relation to penalties to be imposed for breaches of the listing rules under s 93. Consequently, this power may only be exercised by the FSA's governing body and may not be delegated. Schedule 7 also provides that Sch 1, para 1, which defines the functions of the FSA, has effect as if these powers in relation to the making of public statements of policy were included in Sch 1, para 1 (2)(d) (Sch 7, para 5(2)). In addition, the provisions in Sch 1 relating to the FSA's general powers with regard to fees and penalties do not apply to Pt VI. Sections 99 and 100 deal separately with the FSA's powers in relation to the listing rules providing for the payment of fees to the FSA as the competent authority in respect of applications for listing or other payments under s 99(1) and in relation to the payment of penalties for contravention of the listing rules or other contraventions of Pt VI (Sch 7, paras 6, 7).

Powers of the Treasury

9.12   FSMA 2000 contains provisions, however, for the functions of the competent authority to be transferred to another person (s 72(3)). The Treasury may make orders providing that any function conferred upon the FSA in its capacity as the competent authority by FSMA 2000 may be exercisable by a particular person appointed for the purpose if—

— that person has agreed in writing that the order should be made;
— the Treasury are satisfied that the transfer would significantly improve the functions being discharged; or
— the Treasury are otherwise satisfied that it is in the public interest to effect the transfer (Sch 8, para 1).

The Treasury may also make orders modifying or excluding any provision of FSMA 2000, Pts VI (listing), IX or XXVI in relation to the functions of the competent authority (Sch 8, para 2(2)(a)), and may order a review similar to that under FSMA 2000, s 12 (Sch 9, para 2(2)(b)) and impose on the new authority any of the obligations under FSMA 2000, s 152, 155 or 354 (Sch 8, para 2(2)(c)). The Treasury may also make directions to the competent authority not to take any action that is incompatible with the UK's Community obligations or its international obligations or may direct the competent authority to take action to implement those obligations (s 410(4)(b)). The Treasury also has powers to keep the regulatory provisions promulgated by the FSA as the competent authority under review from a competition perspective.[1]

---

[1]   Section 95, see paras 9.99 and 10.52.

Provision of guidance

9.13   Schedule 8, para 2(2) provides that the Treasury may also by order make further provision as to the giving of guidance by the new authority or for the delegation by the new authority of any of its transferred functions under Pt VI. These orders may also cover the transfer of any property, rights, obligations or liabilities or personnel from the previous authority to the new authority and otherwise deal with the carrying on and completion by the new authority of any acts taken by the previous authority.

9.14   The Treasury may also by order amend such other primary or secondary legislation as may be required as a consequence of this transfer of functions.[1] Furthermore, if the Treasury makes an order transferring the functions to another person under Sch 8, para 1, they may by separate order make any provision which could otherwise have been included in the transfer order (Sch 8, para 3).[2] Nothing in Sch 8 restricts the powers conferred on the FSA by FSMA 2000, s 428 (Sch 8, para 2(3)). Any such transfer or any other order made under Sch 8 does not affect anything previously done by the FSA or the previous authority in relation to the functions transferred (Sch 8, para 2(1)).

---

[1]   FSMA 2000, s 103(3) also provides that the powers under FSMA 2000, s 91 are exercisable by different persons carrying on the different functions of the competent authority as a result of orders made by the Treasury under Sch 8. However any order made under Sch 8, para 1 must be approved by both Houses of Parliament (s 429(1)).
[2]   If as a result of an order made under this paragraph different functions are conferred on different persons, the powers conferred by s 91 are exercisable by those persons in accordance with the terms of that order (s 103(3)).

The FSA's general duty as the competent authority

9.15   The FSA is acting in a separate capacity when acting as the competent authority under Pt VI but the general functions imposed on it are broadly the same as those imposed on it when acting as the regulator under FSMA 2000, s 2 except as modified by Sch 7, para 2. In discharging its general functions as the competent authority the FSA must also have regard[1] to the following—
  — the need to use its resources efficiently and economically;
  — the principle that any burden or restriction imposed by regulation should be proportionate to the resulting benefits;
  — the desirability of facilitating innovation in respect of listed securities;
  — the international character of the capital markets and the competitive position of the UK in the global market;
  — the need to minimise the adverse effects of competition on anything done in discharging its function as competent authority;
  — the desirability of facilitating competition in relation to listed securities (s 73).

The FSA in its role as the competent authority must also co-operate with other listing and regulatory authorities carrying out similar functions (s 354).

---

¹   These obligations are similar to the FSA's general duties in relation to its other functions under s 2(3) and (4).

EXEMPTION OF THE FSA FROM LIABILITY IN DAMAGES

9.16   Under FSMA 2000, s 102 the competent authority and any person who is or is acting as a member, officer or member of staff of the competent authority is exempt from liability in damages.[1] This exemption from liability applies to anything done or omitted in the discharge of or in the purported discharge of the Authority's functions under Pt VI (s 102(1)).[2] However this exemption does not apply if the act or omission is shown to have been in bad faith or so as to prevent an award of damages on the grounds that the act or omission was unlawful under the Human Rights Act 1998, s 6(1) (s 102(2)). Schedule 7 also provides that Sch 1 has effect in relation to the FSA as the competent authority as if FSMA 2000, Sch 1, para 19(1) (which relates to the exemption from liability in damages) were omitted, since this is covered separately in relation to the FSA as the competent authority by FSMA 2000, s 102.[3]

---

[1]   Section 415 provides that any proceedings against the competent authority for the purposes of Pt VI may be brought before the High Court or, in Scotland, the Court of Session.
[2]   The FSA may, however, be judicially reviewed for its decisions under the Consolidated Admissions and Reports Directive, 2001/34/EC, Art 19. See *R v International Stock Exchange of the United Kingdom and the Republic of Ireland, ex p Else (1982) Ltd* [1993] QB 534, [1993] 1 All ER 420.
[3]   Sch 7, para 8(a): Sch 7, para 8(b) also modifies Sch 1, para 19(3) to this effect but retains the Sch 1 exemption separately for investigators.

THE LISTING RULES

9.17   The FSA as the competent authority may make listing rules (s 74(4)). These rules must be made by instrument and must be published in accordance with Pt VI (s 101(3)). The FSA may make different provisions for different cases and may modify or disapply these rules in particular circumstances (s 101(1), (2)).

THE OFFICIAL LIST

9.18   The FSA must maintain the official list of securities[1] and may admit such other things as it as the competent authority may from time to time consider appropriate (s 74(1), (2)). The Treasury has the power to define those things which may not be admitted to the official list (s 74(3)). Interestingly, admission to listing is not limited to securities or investments falling within FSMA 2000, Sch 2, but could include other 'things' or choses in action unless in a category specified by the Treasury by order and admitted to the official list (s 74(3), (5)). Therefore, for the purposes of Pt VI, the term 'securities' means those things which have been admitted to the official list.

---

[1]   This official list for the purposes of s 74 is different from the London Stock Exchange's 'Daily List' which provides price information on securities traded on the Exchange.

Listing

9.19   Therefore, nothing may be admitted to the official list except by virtue of FSMA 2000, Pt VI and the term 'listing' is defined as being included in the official list according to Pt VI (s 74(5)). Admission to the official list (listing) may only be granted by the FSA on an application made in accordance with the listing rules (s 75(1)). Applications for listing must always be made by or with the consent of the issuer[1] of the securities and the FSA may not grant the application unless it is satisfied that the requirements of the listing rules and any other requirements imposed by the FSA in relation to the application have been complied with (s 75(2), (4)). Once admitted to the official list, the admission of those securities may not be called into question on the grounds that any requirement or condition has not been met (s 76(7)).[2]

---

[1]   However, the Financial Services and Markets Act 2000 (Official Listing of Securities) Regulations 2001, SI 2001/2956 prescribes certain bodies whose securities may not be considered for listing under Pt VI. These are private companies within the meaning of the Companies Act 1985 (CA 1985), s 1(3) or an old public company within the meaning of the Companies Consolidation (Consequential Provisions) Act 1985, s 1. 'Issuer' has the meaning as may be prescribed by the Treasury (s 103(1)) and SI 2001/2956, reg 4 defines an 'issuer' as the person by whom the securities have been or are to be issued and specifically provides that in relation to certificates or other instruments falling within the Regulated Activities Order, art 80, issuer means (for the purposes of FSMA 2000, Sch 11, para 16) the person by whom the certificates or instruments have been or are to be issued, and for all other purposes means the person who issued or is to issue the securities to which the certificates or instruments relate.

[2]   This provision does not affect an investor's right to compensation under s 90 for losses arising from false or misleading prospectuses.

Decision on application

9.20   The FSA as the competent authority must notify the applicant for listing in writing of its decision to grant or to refuse the application within six months from the date on which the application for listing is received (s 76(1)(a), (3), (5)). FSMA 2000 does provide, however, that this six-month period may restart if the FSA has required the applicant to provide further information in connection with the list, in which case the six-month period begins again on the date on which that information was provided (s 76(1)(b)). The FSA's failure to notify the applicant within the six-month period is deemed to be a refusal of the application (s 76(2)).

Refusal of applications for listing

9.21   If the FSA proposes to refuse an application it must give the applicant a warning notice under FSMA 2000, s 76(4) and once it has decided to refuse an application for listing it must give the applicant a decision notice under s 76(5). The applicant whose application for listing has been refused may refer the matter to the Tribunal under s 76(6).[1]

---

[1]   The Consolidated Admissions and Reports Directive 2001/34/EC specifically requires that member States provide for the judicial review of a decision to refuse a listing or the discontinuance of a listing.

9.22   The FSA may not allow listing of the securities of certain bodies which have been prescribed by order (ss 75(3), 74(3)(b)).[1]

---

[1]   See also the definition of 'securities' in s 74(5). The Financial Services and Markets Act 2000 (Official Listing of Securities) Regulations 2001, SI 2001/2956, reg 3 as amended by SI 2001/3439 and SI 2001/3439 excludes 'securities' (in the narrow sense used in the Regulated Activities Order) issued by private companies (but only where the securities in question are securities within the meaning of the Regulated Activities Order) and 'old public companies' from the scope of listing.

9.23   The FSA may also refuse an application for listing if it considers that granting listing would be detrimental to the interests of investors (s 75(5)) or if the securities to be listed are already officially listed in another EEA state and the issuer has failed to comply with any of the obligations to which he is subject as part of that listing (s 75(6)).

Fees

9.24   The FSA as the competent authority may charge fees for applications for listing or for the continued inclusion of securities in the Official List or for application to be included in the list of sponsors (s 99(1)) or for the approval of non-listing prospectuses (Sch 9, para 7). Such fees are debts due to the FSA as the competent authority and may be recovered by the FSA through civil action. FSMA 2000 provides that it may set fees that enable it to meet the expenses incurred in carrying out its functions as the competent authority and to maintain adequate reserves and to otherwise meet its funding requirements (s 99(2)). In calculating its fees, the FSA may not, however, take into account any penalties it may impose under Pt VI (s 99(3)).

PROCEDURES ON DISCONTINUANCE OR SUSPENSION OF LISTING

9.25 The FSA also has the power in accordance with the listing rules to discontinue (s 77(1)) or suspend (s 77(2)) the listing of any securities if, in the first instance, it is satisfied that there are special circumstances which would preclude 'normal regular dealings' in those securities, or it otherwise provides for suspension in the listing rules. Securities which are suspended are, however, still considered to be listed for the purposes of ss 96 and 99 (s 77(3)) and therefore s 81 still applies to suspended securities.

Notice

9.26 Notice of the FSA's intention or decision to discontinue or suspend the listing must be notified to the issuer of the securities in writing (s 78(2)). The discontinuance or suspension may take effect immediately or on such date as may be specified in the notice. This notice must specify full details, the FSA's reasons and the date on which the discontinuance or suspension took effect or will take effect (s 78(1), (3)(a), (b), (d)). The notice must also inform the issuer that he may make representations to the FSA as the competent authority (s 78(3)(c)) within a period to be specified (although this may be extended) by the FSA (s 78(4)) and that he has the right to refer the matter to the Tribunal under s 77(5) (s 78(3)(e)).

9.27 If, having considered the representations made by the issuer under s 78(4), the FSA decides to discontinue or suspend the listing or, if, having discontinued or suspended the listing, the FSA decides not to cancel the discontinuance or suspension, it must give the issuer notice in writing of its decision (s 78(5)). Any notice given under s 78(5) must also include notification to the issuer of his right to refer the matter to the Tribunal (s 78(6))[1] and an indication of the procedures to be followed on such a reference (s 78(7)).

---

[1]   See the Consolidated Admission and Reports Directives 2001/34/EC, Art 18.

9.28   Suspension of securities admitted to the official list does not, however, affect the issuer's duties in relation to its continuing obligations under s 96 or to pay the Authority's fees (s 99(1)(b)).

9.29   If the FSA decides not to discontinue or suspend the listing or to cancel the discontinuance or suspension, it must also give the issuer written notice (s 78(8)). The effect of cancelling a discontinuance is to readmit the securities to the official list without further formality (s 78(9)).

9.30   If the FSA has suspended the listing of any securities and proposes to refuse the application of the issuer to cancel that suspension order, it must give the issuer a warning notice following the procedures prescribed in s 387 (s 78(10)). Having heard the representations of the issuer, the FSA must either refuse the application for listing by a decision notice[1] or grant it by written notice of its decision (s 78(11)). If the FSA decides to refuse an application to cancel the suspension of listing, then the issuer may refer the matter to the Tribunal (s 78(12)).[2]

---

[1]   See s 388.

[2]   However, once cancellation has occurred, that listing is at an end and a fresh application is needed under s 75: see FSMA Explanatory Notes, para 168.

LISTING PARTICULARS

9.31   The listing rules promulgated by the FSA[1] as the competent authority may provide that securities of a kind specified in the listing rules (other than new issues) may not be admitted to the official list unless listing particulars have been submitted to and approved by the FSA and published (s 79(1)(a)). The listing rules may also specify other documents (other than listing particulars or prospectuses of a kind required by the listing rules) which are required to be published in relation to the admission of securities to the official list (s 79(1)(b)).

---

[1]   The Listing Rules can be found on the FSA's website at www.fsa.gov.uk.

9.32   The term 'listing particulars' is defined in FSMA 2000 as a document in such form and containing such information as the listing rules may specify (s 79(2)).[1] The definition of 'documents' includes information recorded in any form and, in relation to information recorded otherwise than in legible form, references to its production include producing a copy in legible form (s 417(1)). The precise description and form of the document is left open and thus there is the prospect of electronic prospectuses and other forms of delivery being specified in the listing rules.

[1] For the modification of these provisions for non-listing prospectuses published under s 87, see FSMA 2000, Sch 9.

Responsibility for listing particulars

9.33   FSMA 2000 provides that the Treasury may also make regulations determining the person or persons who are responsible for the listing particulars (s 79(3)).[1]

[1] The Financial Services and Markets Act 2000 (Official Listing of Securities) Regulations 2001, SI 2001/2956, Pt 3. FSMA Explanatory Notes, para 170 stated that the Treasury intended to exercise this power in relation to those persons covered by FSA 1986, s 152.

9.34   The Financial Services and Markets Act (Official Listing of Securities) Regulations 2001 provide that for the purposes of FSMA 2000, Pt VI, the persons responsible for listing particulars (including supplementary listing particulars) are—
—   the issuer of the securities to which the listing particulars relate;
—   where the issuer is a body corporate, each person who is a director of that body at the time when the listing particulars are submitted to the competent authority;
—   where the issuer is a body corporate, each person who has authorised himself to be named and is named in the listing particulars as a director or as having agreed to become a director of that body either at that time or at a future date;
—   each person who accepts and is stated in the listing particulars as accepting responsibility for the particulars; and
—   any person who has authorised the contents of the listing particulars.[1]

[1] Financial Services and Markets Act (Official Listing of Securities) Regulations 2001, SI 2001/2956, reg 6(1).

9.35   However, a director of a body corporate at the time when the particulars are submitted will not be treated as responsible for the listing particulars if they were published without his knowledge or consent and on becoming aware of their publication that person gives public notice that the particulars were published without his knowledge or consent.[1]

¹   Financial Services and Markets Act (Official Listing of Securities) Regulations 2001, SI 2001/2956, reg 6(2).

9.36   A person who accepts responsibility for listing particulars or authorises their content may limit the scope of that responsibility or authorisation only to specified parts of the particulars or only in relation to certain aspects. If this is the case, that person will only be responsible under Pt VI to the extent specified and only if the material is included in or substantially in the form and context to which he agreed.¹ A person will not, however, be construed as being responsible for any particulars by reason of giving advice as to their contents in a professional capacity.²

¹   Financial Services and Markets Act (Official Listing of Securities) Regulations 2001, SI 2001/2956, reg 6(3).
²   SI 2001/2956, reg 6(4).

General duty of disclosure in listing particulars

9.37   As a general statement of principle FSMA 2000 provides that the listing particulars must contain all such information as investors and their professional advisers would reasonably require and expect to find for the purpose of making an informed assessment of the assets and liabilities, financial position, profits and losses and prospects of the issuer and the rights attaching to the securities (s 80(1)). The person responsible for the listing particulars¹ must have regard to—

— the nature of the securities and their issuer;
— the nature of the persons likely to consider acquiring them;
— the fact that certain matters may be within the knowledge of professional advisers of a kind which persons likely to acquire the securities may reasonably be expected to consult; and
— any information available to the investor or his professional adviser as the result of any requirements imposed on the issuer by a recognised investment exchange, by the listing rules or any other relevant enactment (s 80(4)).

This obligation only applies to information within the knowledge of the person assuming responsibility for the listing particulars or which could reasonably be obtained by him by making enquiries (s 80(3)). This general principle operates in addition to any information which may be required by the listing rules or by the FSA as the competent authority as a condition for admission to the official list (s 80(2)).

¹   See the Financial Services and Markets Act 2000 (Official Listing of Securities) Regulations 2001, SI 2001/2956, reg 6(1). See also para 9.34.

Supplementary listing particulars

9.38 If the issuer as defined in s 103(1) becomes aware at any time after the preparation of listing particulars submitted in conjunction with an application for listing and before the commencement of dealings in those securities of a significant change in the information required in those listing particulars by virtue of s 80 or the listing rules, or by the competent authority, or if a significant new issue arises which would have been required for inclusion in the listing particulars, supplementary listing particulars must be prepared and submitted to the FSA as the competent authority for its approval. If such approval is received from the FSA, those supplementary listing particulars must be published accordingly (s 81(1)).

9.39 For these purposes a change is deemed to be 'significant' if it is significant in the context of investors or professional advisers making an informed assessment for the purposes of s 80(1) (s 81(2)). Section 80(5) provides that these requirements also apply in the case of any new information or matters in supplementary listing particulars which have been published under s 81.

9.40 If the issuer is not aware of the change or new matter, he is not under an obligation to comply with s 81(1) unless he has had notice of the change or new matter from the person responsible for the listing particulars (s 81(3)). If any person who is responsible for the listing particulars is or becomes aware of a change or new matter which would give rise to an obligation to prepare supplementary listing particulars, that person must give notice of it to the issuer (s 81(4)).

Exemptions from disclosure

9.41 Information otherwise required under FSMA 2000, s 80 or 81 may be omitted from listing particulars (or supplementary listing particulars) (s 82(1)) if the FSA as the competent authority authorises its omission on the basis that its disclosure would be contrary to the public interest or if the disclosure would be seriously detrimental to the issuer or the securities, or in the case of certain specified[1] types of securities its disclosure would be deemed to be unnecessary for persons who would be expected to normally buy or deal in those securities (s 82(1)). However, the FSA may not authorise an exemption from disclosure under s 82(1) on the grounds that its disclosure would be seriously detrimental to the issuer where the information concerned is essential information (s 82(2)). 'Essential information' is defined as information which a person considering acquiring the securities would be likely to need in order not to be misled about any facts

223

which it is essential for him to know in making an informed assessment (s 82(6)).

---

[1]   'Specified' in this case means specified in the listing rules (s 82(1)(c)).

9.42   If information is omitted on the basis of the disclosure being contrary to the public interest, the Secretary of State or the Treasury may issue a certificate to this effect (s 82(3)). The FSA as the competent authority is entitled to act on the basis of such a certificate if authorising an omission on these grounds (s 82(4)).

PROSPECTUSES

9.43   To comply with EC Directives the listing rules must provide that no new securities[1] for which an application for listing has been made may be admitted to the official list unless a prospectus[2] has been submitted to and approved by the FSA as the competent authority and published according to the listing rules (s 84(1)). The provisions of Pt VI also apply in relation to a non-listing prospectus (s 86(1)).

---

[1]   'New securities' are defined for these purposes as securities which are to be offered to the public in the UK for the first time before admission to the official list (s 84(2)).
[2]   A 'prospectus' is defined as a prospectus in such form and containing such information as may be specified in the listing rules (s 84(3)).

9.44   It is unlawful to offer to the public in the UK any securities to which the obligation to publish a prospectus under s 84(1) applies before that required prospectus has been published (s 85(1)).[1]

---

[1]   In FSMA 2000, Pt VI, references to listing particulars are to be read as including a reference to a prospectus and reference to supplementary listing particulars is deemed to include a supplementary prospectus (s 86(2)).

9.45   FSMA 2000, s 103 provides that a person offers securities if, and only if, as principal, he makes an offer which, if accepted, would give rise to a contract for their issue or sale either by him or by another person with whom he has an arrangement for their issue or sale, or he invites a person to make such an offer (s 103(4)).[1] 'Sale' includes any disposal for valuable consideration (s 103(7)). Interpretation of what constitutes an offer is to be determined in accordance with FSMA 2000, Sch 11 (s 103(6)).[2]

Other advertisements

9.46   If in connection with any application for listing, listing particulars are or are to be published, then any advertisement¹ or other information specified in the listing rules must be submitted to the FSA as the competent authority and the FSA must either approve the contents of those advertisements or otherwise authorise their issue without approving them (s 98(1)).² Contravention of this requirement³ is a criminal offence and any person issuing an advertisement or information is guilty of an offence and is liable to a fine not exceeding the statutory maximum or on conviction on indictment to imprisonment of up to two years or a fine or both imprisonment and a fine (s 98(2)). A person issuing an advertisement in contravention of this provision may, however, have a defence if he believed on reasonable grounds that the competent authority had approved or authorised the advertisement (s 98(3)).

¹   FSMA 2000 does not define the term 'advertisement', the phrase used in FSA 1986 but supplanted by 'communication' and 'financial promotion' under the FSMA 2000 regime.
²   The Financial Services and Markets Act 2000 (Financial Promotion) Order 2001, SI 2001/1335, art 71(1) excludes from the restriction on financial promotion non-real time communications included in documents required or permitted under the listing rules.
³   To the extent that this section is a 'relevant requirement' of FSMA 2000 for the purposes of s 380(6), the FSA may have powers to bring a court action to prevent its contravention under s 380 or to seek restitution under s 382.

9.47   However, if an advertisement or information has been approved or authorised, the person issuing it or responsible for the listing particulars¹ incurs no civil liability² by reason of any statement in or omission from the information if that information and the listing particulars would not be likely to mislead any person likely to acquire the securities.

¹   For the purposes of this section 'listing particulars' includes a prospectus required under the listing rules and in relation to non-listing prospectuses Sch 9, para 6 modifies s 98(1) to provide that the first phrase be substituted with 'If a prospectus is, or is to be, published in connection with an application for approval, then until the end of the period, during which the offer to which the prospectus relates remains open, . . .'.
²   Civil liability for these purposes includes any action a person may have to be granted any civil remedy or to repudiate or rescind the agreement (s 98(5)). Note that FSMA 2000, s 150 (action for damages) does not apply to the listing rules (s 150(4)(a)).

REGISTRATION

9.48   A copy of the listing particulars (including any supplementary listing particulars) (s 83(5)) must be delivered for registration to the relevant registrar of companies[1] on or before the date on which the listing particulars are to be published (s 83(1)). The failure to deliver listing particulars for registration constitutes an offence by the issuer of the securities in question and any other person who is a party to the publication of the listing particulars and aware of the failure to register them (s 83(3)).[2] The listing particulars must also include a statement that a copy has been delivered to the registrar (s 83(2)).

---

[1]   The 'registrar of companies' is the registrar of companies in England and Wales if the securities are or are to be issued by a company incorporated in Great Britain whose registered office is in England and Wales. If the company has its registered office in Scotland or in Northern Ireland, the registrar of companies will be the registrar of companies in Scotland or Northern Ireland respectively, or in any other case, any of those registrars (s 83(6)).
[2]   A person guilty of an offence under this section is liable on summary conviction to a fine not exceeding the statutory maximum and on conviction on indictment to a fine (s 83(4)).

Offences

9.49   Any person who contravenes s 85(1) commits a criminal offence (s 85(2)).[1] That person may also be liable for breach of statutory duty to any person who suffers a loss as a result of such a contravention (s 85(5)). Publishing a prospectus which does not fully comply with the listing rules does not constitute a breach of s 85(1) but that person may still be liable to pay compensation under s 90 (s 85(3), (4)).

---

[1]   A person guilty of an offence under this section is liable on summary conviction to imprisonment for up to three months or a fine not exceeding level 5 on the standard scale or on conviction on indictment, imprisonment for up to two years or a fine, or both imprisonment and a fine (s 85(2)).

OFFERS OF SECURITIES

9.50   For the purposes of Pt VI, a person offers securities if and only if he makes, as principal, an offer which, if accepted, would give rise to a contract for their issue or sale[1] by him or by another person with whom he has made arrangements for their issue or sale or he invites a person to make such an offer (s 103(4)).

---

[1]   For the purposes of this provision 'sale' includes any disposal for valuable consideration (s 103(7)).

9.51 FSMA 2000, Sch 11 provides detailed interpretation on what constitutes an offer of securities (s 103(6)). The general rule expressed in Sch 11, para 1 is that a person offers securities to the public in the UK[1] if, to the extent that the offer is made to persons in the UK, it is made to the public and the offer is not an exempt offer (as defined in Sch 11, para 2). An offer is regarded as being made to the public if it is made to any section of the public, including persons selected as members or debenture holders of a body corporate or clients of the person making the offer, or in any other manner (Sch 11, para 1(2)).

[1] The 'UK' means Great Britain and Northern Ireland and includes England, Wales, Scotland and Northern Ireland: see the Interpretation Act 1978, s 5 and Sch 1.

Exempt offers

9.52 Schedule 11, para 2, defines an offer as being 'exempt' if, to the extent that it is made to persons in the UK—
— one of the conditions specified in Sch 11, paras 3 to 24A[1] is satisfied; or
— the condition specified in one relevant paragraph is satisfied in relation to part, but not the whole, of the offer and, in relation to each other part of the offer the condition specified in a different relevant paragraph is satisfied.

The relevant paragraphs of Sch 11 are 3–8, 12–18 and 21, and the conditions specified in them are described in paras 9.53–9.58, 9.62–9.68 and 9.71.

[1] Para 24A was added by the Public Offers of Securities (Exemptions) Regulations, 2001, SI 2001/2955, reg 2(b).

(i) Offers for business purposes

9.53 An offer is exempt where the securities are offered to persons whose ordinary activities involve them in acquiring, holding, managing or disposing of investments (as principal or agent) for the purposes of their businesses or who it is reasonable to expect will acquire, hold, manage or dispose of investments (as principal or agent) for the purposes of their business or are otherwise offered to persons in the context of their trade, profession or occupation (Sch 11, para 3).

(ii) Offers to limited numbers

9.54 An offer is exempt where the securities are offered to no more than 50 persons (Sch 11, para 4(1)). This exemption may be aggregated with other exemptions such as the business purposes exemptions under para 3. For the purposes of this exemption the making of an offer of securities to trustees or members of a partnership in their capacity as such or the making of such an offer to any other two or more persons jointly is to be treated as making an offer to a single person (Sch 11, para 4(3)). In determining whether this condition is met, the offer is to be taken together with any other offer of the same securities which was made by the same person and was open at any time within the 12-month period ending with the date on which the offer was first made and was not an offer to the public in the UK by virtue of this condition being satisfied (Sch 11, para 4(2)).

(iii) Clubs and associations

9.55   An offer is exempt where the securities are offered to members of a club or association and the members of that club or association can reasonably be regarded as having a common interest with each other and with the club or association and in what is to be done with the proceeds of the offer (Sch 11, para 5). The club or association may be incorporated or not as the case may be. This exemption is presumably aimed at small hobby-related clubs and societies and other bodies seeking to raise money from a limited circle for specific purposes associated with the aims and interests of the club or association.

(iv) Restricted circles

9.56   An offer will be deemed to be exempt where the securities are offered to a restricted circle of investors whom the offeror reasonably believes to be sufficiently knowledgeable to understand the risks involved in accepting the offer (Sch 11, para 6). To determine whether a person is sufficiently knowledgeable to understand the risks involved, any information supplied by the person making the offer is to be disregarded apart from information about the issuer of the securities, or if the securities confer the right to acquire other securities, the issuer of those other securities (Sch 11, para 6(2)). The exemption does not set any specific definition of what constitutes a 'restricted circle' in these circumstances.

(v) Underwriting agreements

9.57   If securities are offered in connection with a genuine invitation to enter into an underwriting agreement, the offer is exempt (Sch 11, para 7).

(vi) Offers to public authorities

9.58   An offer made to a public authority is also an exempt offer (Sch 11, para 8). A 'public authority' for these purposes means the government of the UK or the government of any country or territory outside the UK and a local authority[1] in the UK or elsewhere or any international organisation the members of which include the UK or any other EEA State and any other bodies which may be specified by order made by the Treasury under Sch 11.[2]

---

[1] 'Local authority' is not defined in FSMA 2000.
[2] The National Assembly of Wales, Northern Ireland Departments and the Scottish Administration have been specified for these purposes: see the Financial Services and Markets Act 2000 (Offers of Securities) Order 2001/2958, art 4.

(vii) Maximum consideration

9.59　If the total consideration payable for the securities does not exceed 40,000 euro or an equivalent amount, the offer is exempt (Sch 11, para 9).[1] In determining whether this exemption applies, the offer is to be taken together with any other offer of the same securities which was made by the same person and which was open at any time during the 12-month period ending on the date on which the offer was first made and which was not an offer to the public in the UK by virtue of this condition having been satisfied (Sch 11, para 9(2)). In addition, an amount is deemed to be an 'equivalent amount' if it is equal in value, denominated wholly or partly in any other currency or unit of account, and calculated at the latest practicable date before the date on which the offer is first made (being not more than three days before) (Sch 11, para 9(3)).

---

[1] This exemption cannot be aggregated with other exemptions under Sch 11 (Sch 11, para 2(1)(b), (2)).

(viii) Minimum consideration

9.60　The offer will also be exempt[1] if the minimum consideration which may be paid by any person for the securities to be acquired is 40,000 euro or an equivalent amount (Sch 11, para 10(1)).[2]

---

[1] This exemption cannot be aggregated with other exemptions under Sch 11 (Sch 11, para 2(1)(b), (2)).
[2] The provision regarding the calculation of an equivalent amount set out in Sch 11, para 9(3) as detailed at para 9.59 also applies to this condition (Sch 11, para 10(2)).

(ix) Securities denominated in euro

9.61　If an offer is made[1] and the securities are denominated in amounts of at least 40,000 euro or an equivalent amount, it is an exempt offer (Sch 11, para 11(1)).[2]

[1]   This exemption cannot be aggregated with other exemptions under Sch 11 (Sch 11, para 2(1)(b), (2)).
[2]   The provision regarding the calculation of an equivalent amount set out in Sch 11, para 9(3) as detailed at para 9.59 also applies to this condition (Sch 11, para 11(2)).

(x) Takeovers

9.62   Where securities are offered in connection with a takeover offer as defined in Sch 11, para 12(2), the offer is an exempt offer (Sch 11, para 12(1)).[1] A 'takeover offer' for these purposes means an offer—

— to acquire shares[2] in a body incorporated in the UK which is a takeover offer within the meaning of CA 1985, Pt XIIIA or, in relation to Northern Ireland, the Companies (Northern Ireland) Order 1986, SI 1986/1032, Pt XIVA, or would be if those provisions applied in relation to any body corporate;

— to acquire all or substantially all of the shares, or of the shares of a particular class, in a body incorporated outside the UK; or

— made to all holders of shares or shares of a particular class in a body corporate to acquire a specified proportion of those shares (disregarding any shares which the offeror or any associate[3] of the offeror holds or has contracted to acquire: Sch 11, para 12(5)) (Sch 11, para 12(2)).

[1]   This exemption may be aggregated with other exemptions under Sch 11 (Sch 11, para 2(1)(b), (2)).
[2]   'Shares' has such meaning as may be specified in an order made by the Treasury (Sch 11, para 25) and has been defined to be the same as 'shares' in the Regulated Activities Order, art 76 by the Financial Services and Markets Act 2000 (Offers of Securities) Order 2001, SI 2001/2958, art 10.
[3]   An 'associate' is as defined in CA 1985, s 430E or, in relation to Northern Ireland, in the Companies (Northern Ireland) Order 1986, SI 1986/1032, art 423E.

(xi) Mergers

9.63   Where the securities are offered in connection with a merger as defined by the Takeover Directive[1] the offer is an exempt offer (Sch 11, para 13).

[1]   Council Directive 78/855/EEC.

(xii) Free shares

9.64   Securities which are shares and are being offered free of charge to any or all of the holders of shares in the issuer are an exempt offer (Sch 11, para 14(1)). For the purposes of this condition, the 'holders of shares' means any person who, at the close of business on a date specified in the offer and falling within the 60-day period ending on the date on which the offer was first made, were holders of such shares (Sch 11, para 14(2)).[1]

---

[1] 'Shares' has such meaning as may be specified in an order made by the Treasury (Sch 11, para 25) and has been defined to be the same as 'shares' in the Regulated Activities Order, art 76 by the Financial Services and Markets Act 2000 (Offers of Securities) Order 2001, SI 2001/2958, art 10.

(xiii) Exchange of shares

9.65   Where the securities are shares[1] or investments of a kind specified[2] as relating to shares in a body corporate and are offered in exchange for shares in the same body corporate, the offer is exempt.[3] For this condition to be fulfilled, the offer cannot result in any increase in the issued share capital of the body corporate (Sch 11, para 15).

---

[1] 'Shares' has such meaning as may be specified in an order made by the Treasury (Sch 11, para 25) and has been defined to be the same as 'shares' in the Regulated Activities Order, art 76 by the Financial Services and Markets Act 2000 (Offers of Securities) Order 2001, SI 2001/2958, art 10.

[2] 'Specified' means as may be specified in an order made by the Treasury (Sch 11, para 25).

[3] See the Financial Services and Markets Act 2000 (Offers of Securities) Order 2001, SI 2001/2958, art 5 which specifies instruments giving entitlements to investments (the Regulated Activities Order, art 79) and certificates representing securities (the Regulated Activities Order, art 80).

(xiv) Qualifying persons

9.66   Where the securities are issued by a body corporate and are offered by the issuer or by a body corporate connected with[1] the issuer or by a relevant trustee[2] only to qualifying persons the offer is an exempt offer. 'Qualifying persons' are defined as genuine employees or former employees of the issuer or employees or former employees of another body corporate in the same group,[3] or the wife, husband, widow, widower or child or stepchild under the age of 18 of such an employee or former employee (Sch 11, para 16(2)). The securities must be issued on terms that a contract to acquire the securities may be entered into only by the qualifying person to whom they were offered or, if the terms of the offer so permit, any qualifying person (Sch 11, para 16(1)).[4]

---

[1] The Financial Services and Markets Act 2000 (Offers of Securities) Order 2001, SI 2001/2958, art 11(1) defines the term 'connected with' as meaning, in relation to a body corporate, another body corporate if they are in the same group or one is entitled, either alone or with any other body corporate in the same group to exercise or control the exercise of the majority of the voting rights attributable to the share capital which are exercisable in all circumstances at a general meeting of the other body corporate or its holding company.

[2] SI 2001/2956, reg 11(2) defines a 'relevant trustee' as a person holding shares (as defined in the Regulated Activities Order, art 76) in or debentures (as defined in the Regulated Activities

Order, art 77) of a body corporate or such investments as are specified in reg 11(3)(b) and (c) of the regulations as trustee in pursuance of arrangements made by that body corporate (or by another body corporate connected with it) for the purpose of enabling or facilitating the holding of such shares or debentures by or for the benefit of qualifying persons or enabling or facilitating transaction in such shares or debentures between or for the benefit of such persons.

[3] SI 2001/2956, reg 11(4) defines 'group' as, in relation to a body corporate, that body corporate, any other body corporate which is its holding company (as defined in CA 1985, s 744) or subsidiary (as defined in CA 1985, s 736) and any other body corporate which is a subsidiary of that holding company, together with any body corporate in which a member of the group holds a qualifying capital interest. A 'qualifying capital interest' in relation to a body corporate is defined as an interest in relevant shares of the body corporate, which is held on a long-term basis for the purpose of securing a contribution to the holder's own activities by the exercise of control or influence arising from that interest. A holding of 20 per cent or more of the nominal value of a body corporate's relevant shares is presumed to be a qualifying interest unless the contrary is shown (reg 11(5)(c)). 'Relevant shares' is defined, in relation to a body corporate, as the shares comprised in the body corporate's equity share capital, of a class carrying rights to vote in all circumstances at a general meeting of that body corporate (reg 11(5)(d)).

[4] Schedule 11, para 16(2) defines the term 'qualifying person', and the terms 'connected with', 'group' and 'relevant trustee' are to have such meaning as may be prescribed by order or regulations (Sch 11, para 16(3), (4)): see SI 2001/2956, reg 11.

(xv) Convertible securities

9.67   An offer is exempt if the securities being offered result from the conversion of convertible securities and listing particulars or a prospectus relating to the convertible securities were published in the UK under Pt VI or such other provision applying in the UK as may be specified by order made by the Treasury (Sch 11, para 17(1)).[1] 'Convertible securities' means securities of a specified kind[2] which may be converted into or exchanged for, or which confer rights to acquire, other securities (Sch 11, para 17(2)).

[1] See the Financial Services and Markets Act 2000 (Offers of Securities) Order 2001, SI 2001/2958, art 6(1), which specifies CA 1985, Pt III and the Public Offer of Securities Regulations 1995, SI 1995/1537.

[2] SI 2001/2958, art 6(2) specifies debentures (the Regulated Activities Order, art 77), warrants (the Regulated Activities Order, art 79) and certificates representing securities (the Regulated Activities Order, art 80) insofar as they relate to shares (as defined in the Regulated Activities Order, art 76) though disapplying the exclusion for shares of building societies, industrial and provident societies, credit unions and equivalent bodies in other EEA states etc in the Regulated Activities Order, art 76(3).

(xvi) Charities

9.68   If the securities are issued by certain charities and the proceeds of the offer will be used for the purposes of the issuer's objectives, the offer is exempt (Sch 11, para 18). To fall within this condition the issuer of the securities must be either—

   — a charity within the meaning of the Charities Act 1993, s 96(1), or, in relation to Northern Ireland, the Charities (Northern Ireland) Act 1964, s 35;

— a recognised body within the meaning of the Law Reform (Miscellaneous Provisions) (Scotland) Act 1990, s 1(7);
— a housing association within the meaning of the Housing Act 1985, s 5(1), the Housing Associations Act 1985, s 1 or the Housing (Northern Ireland) Order 1992, SI 1992/1725, art 3;
— an industrial or provident society registered in accordance with the Industrial and Provident Societies Act 1965, s 1(2)(b) or the Industrial and Provident Societies Act 1969, s 1(2)(b); or
— a non-profit-making association or body recognised by the country or territory of which it is established with similar objectives to those bodies identified in paras (a)–(c) above.[1]

---

[1] In March 2003, the Government issued a consultation document, Enterprise for Communities: Proposals for a Community Interest Company, in relation to the establishment of a new class of community interest companies, the purpose of which is to provide an alternative corporate structure for not-for-profit enterprises. It is proposed that these CICs may issue tradeable 'preference shares' having a fixed rate of return but it is not clear from the consultation whether this exemption will be extended to cover securities issued by CIEs. The closing date for comments on these proposals was June 2003, and a Bill was introduced in the House of Lords on 3 December 2003; see the Companies (Audit, Investigations and Community Enterprise Bill).

(xvii) Building societies

9.69 Where the securities being offered are shares[1] which are issued by, or ownership of which entitles the holder to membership of or to obtain the benefits of, services provided by a UK building society or any body corporate which is an industrial or provident society or credit union incorporated under the law of or any part of the UK or a body of a similar nature established in another EEA State, the offer is exempt (Sch 11, para 19).

---

[1] 'Shares' has such meaning as may be specified in an order made by the Treasury (Sch 11, para 25) and has been defined to be the same as 'shares' in the Regulated Activities Order, art 76 by the Financial Services and Markets Act 2000 (Offers of Securities) Order 2001, SI 2001/2958, art 10.

(xviii) Euro-securities

9.70 Where the securities being offered are 'Euro-securities' and no advertisement[1] relating to the offer is issued or caused to be issued in the UK by the issuer of the Euro-securities or by any credit institution or other financial institution through which the Euro-securities may be acquired pursuant to the offer, or by any body corporate which is in the same group as the issuer or any of those institutions, the offer will be exempt (Sch 11, para 20(1)). For these purposes 'Euro-securities' means investments[2] which are to be underwritten by whatever means (Sch 11, para 20(6)) and distributed by a syndicate at least two of whose members have their registered offices in different countries or territories, and the securities are to be offered on a significant scale in one or more countries or territories other than the country or territory in which the issuer has its registered office and may be acquired pursuant to an offer only through a credit institution[3] or other financial institution (Sch 11, para 20(3)).[4]

[1]   This condition does not apply where the advertisement is of a kind prescribed by order or regulation (Sch 11, para 20(2)). The Financial Services and Markets Act 2000 (Official Listing of Securities) Regulations 2001, SI 2001/2956, reg 12 provides that the proscription in Sch 11, para 20(1) does not apply to advertisements which are only issued to investment professionals, high net worth companies and certified sophisticated investors and persons in the business of disseminating information within the meaning of the Financial Promotion Order, arts 19, 47, 49, 50.
[2]   Presumably 'investments' within the meaning of FSMA 2000, Sch 2, Pt II.
[3]   A 'credit institution' is defined as a credit institution within the meaning of the First Banking Co-ordination Directive (77/780/EEC), Art 1 (now repealed and replaced by Directive of the European Parliament and the Council 2000/12/EC, Art 67) (Sch 11, para 20(4), as amended by SI 2000/2952, reg 8(1), (6)(a) and SI 2002/765, reg 4).
[4]   A 'financial institution' is defined as a financial institution within the meaning of the Second Council Directive (89/646/EEC), Art 1 (now repealed and replaced by Banking Consolidation Directive of the European Parliament and the Council 2000/12/EC, Art 67) (Sch 11, para 20(5), as amended by SI 2000/2952, reg 8(1), (6)(b)).

(xix) Same class securities

9.71   Where the securities being offered are of the same class and were issued at the same time as securities in respect of which a prospectus had been published under FSMA 2000, Pt VI or CA 1985, Pt III or any other such provision applying in the UK as may be specified by order made by the Treasury,[1] the offer is an exempt offer (Sch 11, para 21).[2]

[1]   The provisions of the Public Offers of Securities Regulations (SI 1995/1537) have been specified for these purposes. The Financial Services and Markets Act 2000 (Offers of Securities) Order 2001, SI 2001/2958, art 7.
[2]   This exemption may not be aggregated with other exemptions under Sch 11 (Sch 11, para 2(1)(b), (2)).

(xx) Short date securities

9.72   Where the securities are debentures within the meaning of the Regulated Activities Order, art 77 with a maturity of less than one year from their date of issue, the offer is an exempt offer (Sch 11, para 22).[1] The investments which may be included in this condition may be specified by order made by the Treasury.[2]

[1]   This exemption may not be aggregated with other exemptions under Sch 11 (Sch 11, para 2(1)(b), (2)).
[2]   See the Financial Services and Markets Act 2000 (Offers of Securities) Order 2001, SI 2001/2958, art 8. See also the Public Offer of Securities Regulations 1995, SI 1995/1537, reg 3(2)(a).

(xxi) Government and public securities

9.73   Where the securities are loan stock, bonds or other instruments[1] creating or acknowledging indebtedness issued by or on behalf of a public authority[2] the offer will be an exempt offer (Sch 11, para 23).[3]

---

[1]   See the Financial Services and Markets Act 2000 (Offers of Securities) Order 2001, SI 2001/2958, art 9.
[2]   For the definition of 'public authority', see para 9.58.
[3]   This exemption may not be aggregated with other exemptions under Sch 11 (Sch 11, para 2(1)(b), (2)).

(xxii) Non-transferable securities

9.74   Where the securities are not transferable, the offer is an exempt offer (Sch 11, para 24).

(xxiii) Units in a collective investment scheme

9.75   Where the securities are units in a collective investment scheme as defined by FSMA 2000, s 237(2), the offer is an exempt offer (Sch 11, para 24A).[1] However, the marketing and promotion of units in unregulated collective investment schemes is still subject to the provisions of s 238.

---

[1]   Para 24A was added by the Public Offers of Securities (Exemptions) Regulations 2001, SI 2001/2955, reg 2(b).

NON-LISTING PROSPECTUSES

9.76   FSMA 2000 provides that the listing rules may also provide for a 'non-listing' prospectus (s 87(2)) to be submitted to and approved by the FSA as the competent authority if the securities are to be offered to the public for the first time in the UK and no application for listing of the securities has been made and the prospectus is submitted by or with the consent of the issuer of the securities (s 87(1)). The listing rules may specify the information to be contained in and the form of a non-listing prospectus (s 87(3)(a)) and the time and manner in which such a non-listing prospectus is to be published (s 87(3)(b)).[1]

---

[1]   Section 87(3)(b) is subject to any other provision or enactment which the Treasury may specify by order (s 87(4)). The Financial Services and Markets Act 2000 (Offers of Securities) Order 2001, SI 2001/2958, art 3 specifies the Public Offer of Securities Regulations 1995 for these purposes.

9.77   Generally speaking, the provisions of Pt VI apply to non-listing prospectuses including supplementary prospectuses (Sch 9, para 2) but Sch 9 also sets out a number of modifications of Pt VI which apply to non-listing prospectuses published under s 87(1).

OBLIGATIONS OF ISSUERS

9.78   The listing rules promulgated by the FSA as the competent authority may specify requirements to be complied with by issuers of listed securities and make provision for action to be taken by the FSA in the event of non-compliance (s 96(1)). The action to be taken by the FSA may include publishing information otherwise required under the listing rules if the issuer has failed to publish it (s 96(2)). This section applies whenever the listed securities are admitted to the official list (s 96(3)).

SPONSORS

9.79   The listing rules made under s 74(4) may also require that a person make arrangements for a sponsor to perform such services as the listing rules may prescribe (s 88(1)). A 'sponsor' is a person approved by the FSA as the competent authority for the purposes of these rules (s 88(2))[1] and the FSA may lay down the criteria which a person must meet to qualify to be approved as a sponsor (s 88(3)(d)). The listing rules may also provide for the FSA to maintain a list of sponsors and to specify the services which they must provide and to impose various requirements in relation to those services (s 88(3)(a)–(c)).

[1]   The FSA as UKLA maintains a list of approved sponsors on its website at www.fsa.gov.uk/ukla/SP_register.pdf.

9.80   If the FSA proposes to refuse a person's application for approval to act as a sponsor or to cancel a person's approval to act under s 88, the FSA must give him a warning notice (s 88(4)). If, after considering any representations which may be made in response to a warning notice under s 88(4), the FSA decides to grant the application or not to cancel the approval, it must give that person (and any other person who received a copy of the warning notice) a written notice of its decision (s 88(5)).

9.81   If the FSA refuses to grant the application for approval or decides to cancel the approval after considering any representations, it must give that person a decision notice under s 88(6). Any person to whom a decision notice is given under s 88(6) may refer the matter to the Tribunal (s 88(7)).

9.82   The FSA as the competent authority may also (if the listing rules so provide) publish a statement in respect of a sponsor who breaches any requirement imposed on him by the rules made under s 88(3)(c) provided it has given the sponsor a warning notice setting out the terms of the proposed statement (s 89(1), (2)). If, after having received representations regarding such a warning notice, the FSA decides to publish the statement, it must give the sponsor a decision notice setting out the terms of the statement to be published (s 89(3)) and the sponsor may refer the matter to the Tribunal under s 89(4).

INVESTIGATIONS UNDER PT VI

9.83   FSMA 2000 provides that the FSA as the competent authority under Pt VI may appoint one or more competent persons to conduct an investigation on its behalf (s 97(2)) if circumstances suggest that—
   — there may have been a breach of the listing rules;
   — a person who was at the material time a director of an issuer of listed securities was knowingly concerned in a breach of the listing rules by that issuer;
   — a person who was at the material time a director of a person applying for the admission of securities to the official list has been knowingly concerned in a breach of the listing rules by that applicant; or
   — there has otherwise been a contravention of the rules relating to the publication of listing particulars or prospectuses (s 97(1)).[1]

FSMA 2000, Pt XI (ss 165–177)[2] applies to investigations carried out under s 97(2) as if the investigator were appointed under s 167(1), references to the investigating authority in relation to that person were to the FSA as the competent authority, references to the offences in s 168 were to those mentioned in s 97(1)(a) and references to the 'authorised person' were read as references to the person under investigation (s 97(3)).

---

[1]   Referring to breaches under s 83, 85 or 98.
[2]   See paras 7.2–7.47.

PENALTIES FOR BREACH OF THE LISTING RULES

9.84   If the FSA as the competent authority[1] considers that an issuer of listed securities or an applicant for listing has contravened the listing rules it may impose a penalty of such amount as it considers appropriate (s 91(1)). Such penalties are payable to the FSA as the competent authority (s 91(5)). FSMA 2000 also imposes a time limit on the FSA so that it may not take action against any person under this section after two years beginning on the day on which the FSA knew about the contravention unless proceedings against that person were begun before the end of that period (s 91(6)). For the purposes of s 91(6) the FSA is to be treated as knowing of the contravention if it has information from which a contravention can be reasonably inferred, and the proceedings against a person are to be treated as having begun when the warning notice is given to that person under s 92 (s 91(7)).

---

[1]   If, as a result of an order having been made under Sch 8, any of the functions of the competent authority have been transferred to a different person, the powers under s 91 to impose penalties are exercisable by that person (s 103(3)).

9.85   Penalties for breaches of the listing rules can be extended to a director[1] of an issuer or applicant if at the material time that person was knowingly concerned in the contravention (s 91(2)). Alternatively, the FSA may publish a statement censuring him (s 91(3)).

---

[1]   Including a 'shadow' director, see s 417(1).

Statement of policy: procedure

9.86   The FSA must prepare and issue a policy statement setting out its policy in respect to the imposition of penalties under s 91 and the amount of those penalties (s 93(1)).[1] In determining this policy in relation to breaches under Pt VI, the FSA as the competent authority is not permitted to take account of the expenses it incurs or expects to incur in discharging its functions (s 100(1)). The FSA must consult by publishing a draft of the proposed statement and, in issuing any policy statement, must have regard to any representations made in respect of it and set out an account of the representations made and its response to them (s 94(1)–(6)). Any changes in the final policy statement must be noted and any further proposal by the FSA to alter or replace a statement will be subject to the same consultation procedure (s 94(7)).

---

[1]   See the UKLA Sourcebook, Ch 1.

Amount of penalties

9.87   In determining the amount of a penalty the FSA must have regard to the seriousness of the contravention in relation to the nature of the requirement contravened, the extent to which the contravention was deliberate or reckless and whether the penalty is being imposed on an individual rather than on a firm (s 93(2)). The FSA must also have regard to the policy statement on penalties in effect at the time of the contravention in question and may not apply subsequent statements to earlier actions or events (s 93(5)). The policy statement regarding penalties may be altered or replaced at any time but any such alteration or change must be published in a way determined to be best calculated to bring it to the attention of the public (s 93(3), (4), (6)) and the FSA must provide the Treasury with a copy of any policy statement which it publishes under s 93 (s 93(8)).

9.88   In addition, the FSA as the competent authority must prepare and operate a scheme for ensuring that monies received as penalties under FSMA 2000, Pt VI are applied for the benefit of issuers of securities admitted to the official list (s 100(2)). This scheme may make different provisions as to the different classes of issuer (s 100(3)) and the FSA must consult (s 100(7)–(10)) and promulgate the scheme details publicly (s 100(5), (6)), subject to any fee the FSA may charge for providing a copy (s 100(12)). A copy of the scheme details (ie, the document setting out up to date details of the scheme) (s 100(4)) must be sent to the Treasury (s 100(11)) and any proposal to alter or replace the scheme is subject to the same procedure (s 100(13)).

Procedures under s 91

9.89   If the FSA as the competent authority proposes to take an action against any person under s 91, it must give them a warning notice (s 92(1)) which must state the amount of the proposed penalty or, if relevant under s 91(3), set out the terms of the proposed statement (s 92(2), (3)). If the FSA decides to take action against a person under s 91 for a contravention of the listing rules, it must give him a decision notice which must state the amount of the penalty to be imposed and set out the terms of the statement which is to be published under s 91(3) (s 92(4)–(6)). Any person against whom the FSA decides to take action under s 91 may refer the matter to the Tribunal (s 92(7)).

COMPENSATION

9.90   FSMA 2000 provides that any person responsible for listing particulars under s 79(3) (or an order made under that section)[1] is liable to pay compensation to a person who has acquired securities (or any interest in them)[2] to which the listing particulars apply and who has suffered a loss in respect of them as a result of any untrue or misleading statement[3] in the listing particulars or the omission of any matter required to be included as required in the listing particulars by s 80 or 81 (s 90(1)).[4] In addition, a person failing to comply with s 81 by issuing supplementary listing particulars when so required is also liable to pay compensation to a person who has acquired[5] securities of the kind in question (or any interest in them) and has suffered a loss as a result of the failure to publish those particulars (s 90(4)). Both of these liabilities are additional to any other liability (s 90(6)) but are subject to the exemptions set out in Sch 10 (s 90(2), (5)), which are set out in s 90(8).[6]

---

[1]   The Financial Services and Markets Act 2000 (Official Listing of Securities) Regulations 2001, SI 2001/2956, reg 6.

[2]   Where an issuer of shares pays or is liable to pay compensation under this section for a loss suffered in respect of shares for which a person has subscribed, no account is to be taken of that liability or payment in determining the amount paid on subscription for those shares or the amount paid up or deemed to be paid up: see the Financial Services and Markets Act 2000 (Official Listing of Securities) Regulations, reg 6.

[3]   This also includes a failure to make a required statement about the absence of something if required by the listing rules (s 90(3)).

[4]   Section 150(4)(a) disapplies the provision that certain rules made by the FSA are actionable by private persons who have suffered a loss to the listing rules.

[5]   Or contracted to acquire them (s 90(7)).

[6]   See also paras 9.91–9.98.

Exemptions

(i) Statements believed to be true

9.91   A person will not be liable under s 90(1) for a loss resulting from a statement if he satisfies the court that at the time the listing particulars were submitted to the FSA as the competent authority he reasonably believed, having made such enquiries as were reasonable, that the statement was true and not misleading, or the matter which was omitted and caused the loss was properly omitted and that certain conditions were satisfied (Sch 10, para 1(2)). Those conditions are that—

  (a)   he continued in his belief until the securities in question were acquired;

  (b)   they were acquired before it was reasonably practicable to bring a correction to the notice of persons likely to acquire them;

(c) before they were acquired he had taken all such steps as were reasonable for him to take to bring a correction to the notice of those persons; or

(d) he continued in his belief until after the commencement of dealings in the securities and they were acquired after such a time that he ought in the circumstances to be reasonably excused (Sch 10, para 1(3)).[1]

---

[1] In relation to non-listing prospectuses, this provision is modified by Sch 9, para 5(1) such that para (d) is substituted by the following provision: '(d) the securities were acquired after such a lapse of time that he ought in the circumstances to be reasonably excused and, if the securities are dealt in on an approved exchange, he continued in that belief until after the commencement of dealings in the securities on that exchange.' An 'approved exchange' for the purposes of this provision is defined in Sch 10, para 9, as added by Sch 9, para 5(2), as being prescribed in the Financial Services and Markets Act 2000 (Official Listing of Securities) Regulations 2001, SI 2001/2956, reg 5.

(ii) Statements by experts

9.92 A person will not be liable under s 90(1) for a loss resulting from a statement if he satisfies the court that the statement included in listing particulars was made by or on the authority of an expert[1] who he reasonably believed, at the time when the particulars were submitted to the FSA, to be competent to make or authorise the statement and who had consented to its inclusion in the form and context in which it was included (Sch 10, para 2(2)). This is subject to the conditions set out in Sch 10, para 2(3), namely that—

(a) he continued in his belief until the securities in question were acquired;

(b) they were acquired before it was reasonably practicable to bring the fact that the expert was not competent, or had not consented to the inclusion of the statement, to the notice of persons likely to acquire them;

(c) before they were acquired he had taken all such steps as were reasonable for him to take to bring a correction to the notice of those persons; or

(d) he continued in his belief until after the commencement of dealings in the securities and they were acquired after such a time that he ought in the circumstances to be reasonably excused.[2]

---

[1] An 'expert' is defined as including any engineer, valuer, accountant or other person whose profession, qualifications or experience give authority to a statement made by him (Sch 10, para 8).
[2] In relation to non-listing prospectuses, this provision is modified by Sch 9, para 5(1) such that para (d) is substituted by the following provision: '(d) the securities were acquired after such a lapse of time that he ought in the circumstances to be reasonably excused and, if the securities are dealt in on an approved exchange, he continued in that belief until after the commencement of dealings in the securities on that exchange.' An 'approved exchange' for the purposes of this provision is defined in Sch 10, para 9, as added by Sch 9, para 5(2), as being prescribed in the Financial Services and Markets Act 2000 (Official Listing of Securities) Regulations 2001, SI 2001/2956, reg 5.

(iii) Correction of statements

9.93   A person will also not be liable under s 90(1) for a loss resulting from a statement if he satisfies the court that he had published any correction of that statement in a manner calculated to bring it to the attention of persons likely to acquire the securities or he took such steps as were reasonable for him to secure the publication of such a correction and reasonably believed that it would take place before the securities were acquired (Sch 10, para 3).[1]

---

[1]   This provision does not affect any exemption in Sch 10, para 1 (Sch 10, para 3(4)).

(iv) Correction of statements by experts

9.94   A person is not liable under s 90(1) for a loss resulting from a statement made by an expert[1] if before the securities in question were acquired he published the fact that the expert was not competent or had not consented to the inclusion of the statement, in a manner calculated to bring it to the attention of the persons likely to acquire the securities, or if he took all such steps as were reasonable to secure that publication and reasonably believed that it had taken place before the securities were acquired (Sch 10, para 4).[2]

---

[1]   An 'expert' is defined as including any engineer, valuer, accountant or other person whose profession, qualifications or experience give authority to a statement made by him (Sch 10, para 8).
[2]   This does not affect any exemption in Sch 10, para 2.

(v) Official statements

9.95   A person is not liable under s 90(1) for a loss resulting from a statement if it was made by an official person included in the listing particulars or was contained in a public official document which was included in the listing particulars, provided he can satisfy the court that the statement was accurately and fairly reproduced (Sch 10, para 5).[1]

---

[1]   FSMA 2000 does not define the terms 'official person' or 'public official document' for the purposes of this exemption.

(vi) False or misleading information known about

9.96   A person is not liable under s 90(1) for a loss resulting from a statement[1] if the person suffering the loss acquired the securities in question with the knowledge that the statement was false or misleading, in relation to the omitted matter or in relation to any change or new matter (Sch 10, para 6).

---

[1]   Or the omission of any matter required to be included under s 80 or 81.

(vii) Belief that supplementary listing particulars not called for

9.97 A person is not liable under s 90(4) for a loss resulting from a statement if the person responsible for the listing particulars satisfies the court that he reasonably believed that the change or new matter in question did not require supplementary listing particulars under this section (Sch 10, para 7).

(viii) Exemption under s 90(8)

9.98 Section 90(8) further provides that no person, by reason of being a promoter of a company or otherwise, is liable to pay compensation for failing to disclose information which he would not have been required to disclose in the listing particulars of the company's securities if he were responsible for those particulars or if he were responsible for them, but he was entitled to omit that information by virtue of s 82.[1]

---

[1] The reference in s 90(8) to a person who may incur liability includes a reference to any other person being entitled as against that person to be granted any civil remedy or to rescind or repudiate the agreement entered into with respect to the securities (s 90(9)).

COMPETITION SCRUTINY

9.99 Under FSMA 2000, s 95 the Treasury has the power to subject the listing rules and general guidance (its 'regulating provisions') (s 95(9)) which the FSA as the competent authority produces to competition scrutiny (s 95(1)) with a view to considering whether any of these regulating provisions or two or more of these regulating provisions taken together have or would have a significantly adverse effect on competition (s 95(2)), as defined in s 95(6).[1] If regulating provisions have, or are intended or likely to have, the effect of requiring or encouraging exploitation of the strength of a market position they are to be taken to have, or be intended or be likely to have, a significantly adverse effect on competition (s 95(7)) assuming that they are complied with (s 95(8)). An order under s 95 may include arrangements corresponding to those in Pt X, Ch III (ss 159–164) but FSMA 2000 expressly provides that this is not to be interpreted as in any way restricting the power of the Treasury to make an order in respect of s 95(1) (s 95(3), (4)).

---

[1] For determining whether any regulating provisions have any particular effect, it is to be assumed that the persons to whom the provisions concerned are addressed will act in accordance with them (s 95(8)).

10 Competition scrutiny

This Chapter has been contributed by Brenda Sufrin, Professor of Law, University of Bristol.

INTRODUCTION

10.1   The Financial Services and Markets Act 2000 (FSMA 2000), Pt X, Ch III establishes a special competition regime in respect of the regulating provisions and practices of the Financial Services Authority (FSA) itself, and also in respect of the regulatory provisions and practices of Recognised Investment Exchanges (RIEs) and Recognised Clearing Houses (RCHs) (Pt XVIII, Chs II, III). This regime involves the Office of Fair Trading (OFT),[1] the Competition Commission,[2] and the Treasury. The application of the Competition Act 1998 (CA 1998) is excluded or restricted (ss 164, 311, 312). In addition, FSMA 2000 provides for the Treasury to set up by order a competition regime for the UK Listing Authority (UKLA) (s 95). The application to financial services regulation of a special competition regime continues the policy of the Financial Services Act 1986 (FSA 1986).

---

[1]   The OFT took over the functions of the Director General of Fair Trading on 1 April 2003 pursuant to the EA 2002, ss 1 and 2: see EA 2002, s 278(1), Sch 25, para 40 and the Enterprise Act 2002 (Commencement No 2, Transitional and Transitory Provisions) Order 2003, SI 2003/766.
[2]   Previously the Monopolies and Mergers Commission. The Competition Commission took over the functions of the Monopolies and Mergers Commission on 1 April 1999: see the Competition Act 1998 (Competition Commission) Transitional, Consequential and Supplemental Provisions Order 1999, SI 1999/506.

EXCLUSION FROM THE COMPETITION ACT 1998

The Chapter I and Chapter II prohibitions

10.2   CA 1998 contains two 'prohibitions'. The Chapter I prohibition is contained in CA 1998, s 2 and prohibits agreements, concerted practices, and decisions by associations of undertakings which have as their object or effect the prevention, restriction or distortion of competition in the UK and which may affect trade in the UK. This is the UK equivalent of Art 81 (ex 85) of the Treaty of Rome (the EC Treaty). The Chapter II prohibition, which is contained in CA 1998, s 18, prohibits the abuse of a dominant position in a market if it may affect trade within the UK. It is the UK equivalent of Art 82 (ex 86) of the EC Treaty. The FSA itself, as a regulating authority not operating as a commercial entity, would not be an 'undertaking' for the purposes of CA 1998, ss 2 and 18.[1] However, the concern is that its regulating provisions and practices might operate or apply in such a way as to result in the bodies subject to them acting anti-competitively in breach of the prohibitions.

---

[1]　See the ECJ case law which is imported into the interpretation of CA 1998 by virtue of s 60 of that Act, eg, Case 30/87 *Bodson v Pompes Funèbres* [1988] ECR 2479, [1989] 4 CMLR 984; Case C-41/90 *Höfner and Elser v Macroton GmbH* [1991] ECR I-1979, [1993] 4 CMLR 306; Case 364/92 *SAT Fluggesellschaft mbH v Eurocontrol* [1994] ECR I-43, [1994] 5 CMLR 208; Case T-319/99 *FENIN v Commission* [2003] 5 CMLR 34.

Agreements, practices and conduct encouraged by the FSA's regulating provisions

10.3　CA 1998 provides that its prohibitions do not apply to agreements and conduct which are made or engaged in to comply with a legal requirement.[1] If the FSA's regulating provisions require parties to engage in anti-competitive agreements or conduct, therefore, those parties have a defence under CA 1998. It is not considered proper that parties should be penalised for acting in a way legally required of them. FSMA 2000 goes further than this by also excluding from CA 1998 agreements, practices and conduct which are 'encouraged' by the FSA's regulating provisions. FSMA 2000, s 164(1) and (2) provides that the Chapter I prohibition does not apply to agreements entered into by 'authorised persons' and persons who are otherwise subject to the FSA's regulation, or to their practices, to the extent to which the agreements or practices are encouraged by the FSA's regulating provisions.[2] Similarly, s 164(3) provides that the Chapter II prohibition does not apply to the conduct of such persons to the extent that the conduct is so encouraged.

---

[1]　CA 1998, ss 3, 19, Sch 3, para 5.
[2]　For policy background, see Whittaker, The Role of Competition in Financial Services Regulation, 27 April 2001 on the FSA website, www.fsa.gov.uk.

10.4　An 'authorised person' means a person authorised for the purposes of FSMA 2000 (ss 31, 32).[1] For the purposes of the competition provisions of FSMA 2000, 'regulating provisions' means any rules of the FSA, general guidance given by the FSA,[2] statements issued by the FSA under s 64, or code issued by the FSA under s 64 (the approved persons code) or s 119 (the market abuse code) (s 159(1)).[3] It does not include the practices adopted by the FSA in the exercise of its functions under FSMA 2000. Therefore if a person acts in a way merely encouraged by the FSA's practices it will still be subject to

CA 1998. This limitation was deliberate, as the Government considered it unfair to penalise those whose actions were encouraged by the FSA's codes and guidance, but were not prepared to go further—

> 'If people are encouraged to do something by the FSA regulatory provisions, which have been through the consultation process, and will have been the subject of cost-benefit analyses that is one thing, but where people do things as a result of FSA's practices, we do not think there should be an exclusion. It will be up to firms to decide what they do in response to practices. They are not obliged to do anything. Where they do something which is anti-competitive, there will be no protection from the Competition Act.'[4]

Nevertheless, FSMA 2000 subjects both the regulating provisions and the practices of the FSA to the special competition regime which it establishes.[5]

---

[1]　See Ch 4.

[2]　Defined in s 158(5) as guidance given by the FSA under s 157 which is given to persons generally, regulated persons generally, or a class of regulated person and is intended to have continuing effect and is given in writing or other legible form.

[3]　The FSA's functions in relation to building societies, friendly societies, industrial and provident societies and credit unions are not to be regarded as functions under FSMA 2000 nor its fee rules and guidance to be considered regulating provisions: see the Financial Services and Markets Act 2000 (Mutual Societies) Order 2001, SI 2001/2617, art 4(3), Sch 2, paras 7, 11(c), 14(c).

[4]　Lord McIntosh, HL Committee Stage, 27 March 2000, col 599.

[5]　In addition, the FSA must have regard to competition matters when exercising its general functions (primarily setting its regulatory provisions) (s 2(3)(e)–(g)).

RIEs and RCHs

10.5　There is equal concern that the rules and practices of RIEs and RCHs not result in anti-competitive agreements or conduct. A special competition regime is therefore established for them, with certain matters excluded from the normal competition rules. The exclusion from the Chapter I prohibition of CA 1998 for RIEs and RCHs deals both with bodies which are already recognised and with applicants for recognition. FSMA 2000, s 311 therefore excludes from the Chapter I prohibition—

—　an agreement for the constitution of a recognised body to the extent to which the agreement relates to that body's regulatory provisions (s 311(1));

—　an agreement for the constitution of an investment exchange or a clearing house, which is not yet a recognised body but which has applied for recognition under FSMA 2000 and whose application has not yet been determined, to the extent to which the agreement for the constitution relates to that body's regulatory provisions (s 311(2), (3));

— a recognised body's regulatory provisions (s 311(4));[1]

— a decision made by a recognised body concerning its regulatory provisions or practices (s 311(5));

— a recognised body's practices (s 311(6));

— an agreement the parties to which include a recognised body or a person subject to the rules[2] of a recognised body, in respect of provisions the inclusion of which is required or encouraged by the recognised body's regulatory provisions or practices (s 311(7)).

If an RIE or RCH has its recognition order revoked it will remain excluded from the application of CA 1998 by these provisions for six months from the date of revocation (s 311(8)).

---

[1]   Section 302 defines 'regulatory provisions' as the rules, guidance, arrangements and criteria mentioned in ss 287(3) and 288(3).
[2]   The 'rules' of a recognised body are the rules made or conditions imposed by the body regarding recognition requirements; the admission of persons to or exclusion from the use of its facilities; or matters relating to its constitution (s 313(2)).

10.6   Section 312(1) provides that the Chapter II prohibition does not apply to—

— the practices of a recognised body;

— the adoption or enforcement of a recognised body's regulatory provisions;[1]

— any conduct engaged in by a recognised body or by a person subject to the rules[2] of a recognised body to the extent to which it is encouraged or required by the body's regulatory provisions.

---

[1]   As defined in s 302(1): see para 10.29.
[2]   For the definition of 'rules' in s 303(2) see para 10.5, fn 1.

10.7   Section 311(7) excludes from the Chapter I prohibition the provisions of an agreement which are *encouraged* by a recognised body's *practices*. This can be contrasted with the exclusion in s 164, which covers matters encouraged by the FSA's regulating provisions rather than by the body's practices.[1] It is also to be contrasted with s 312 which only excludes conduct from the Chapter II prohibition if it is encouraged or required by the regulatory provisions. 'Practices' means, in this context, the practices of an RIE in its capacity as such or of an RCH in respect of its clearing arrangements (s 302(1)).

---

[1]   See para 10.4.

THE ENTERPRISE ACT 2002

The position under FSA 1986

10.8   FSA 1986, s 124 broadly exempted the financial services sector from the monopoly provisions of FTA 1973, the precursor of the market investigation reference provisions of the Enterprise Act 2002 (EA 2002). The 1973 Act provided for the investigation of scale and complex monopolies by the OFT and the Competition Commission. FSA 1986, s 124(1) provided that in determining whether a complex monopoly situation in relation to the supply of services existed[1] no account should be taken of the rules, recommendations or practices issued or required by any recognised self-regulating organisation (SRO), RIE, RCH or designated agency.[2] Section 124(3) provided that where on a monopoly reference not limited to the facts[3] the Competition Commission found that a monopoly situation existed, and that the person in whose favour it existed was an SRO, RIE, RCH, designated agency, or a person otherwise subject to those bodies, the Competition Commission was to exclude from consideration the question of whether any rules, recommendation or practices of such a person operated against the public interest.

---

[1]   By FTA 1973, s 7(1)(c), (2) a complex monopoly situation in the supply of services existed where at least one-quarter of the services of any description were supplied by a group of persons who, whether voluntarily or not, and whether by agreement or not, so conducted their respective affairs as to prevent, restrict or distort competition.

[2]   Such as the Securities and Investment Board.

[3]   By FTA 1973, a reference to the Competition Commission could either be limited to the facts (s 48) or not limited to the facts (s 49). Where the reference was not limited to the facts, the Competition Commission was concerned with whether the existence of the monopoly, or the conduct of the undertakings, was contrary to the public interest.

The position under FSMA 2000

10.9   FSA 1986, s 124 has been repealed by order under FSMA 2000, s 426.[1] FSMA 2000 contains no provision equivalent to FSA 1986, s 124. The effect of the repeal is therefore to make the financial services sector fully subject to the market investigation reference regime under the EA 2002 (Pt 4) (which replaced the monopoly provisions of FTA 1973), as well as to the special competition regime contained in FSMA 2000 itself. This means that FSMA 2000 has made a significant change to the competition scrutiny of the sector, in that the general competition law regime is not wholly disapplied.[2]

---

[1]   The Financial Services and Markets Act 2000 (Consequential Amendments and Repeals) Order 2001, SI 2001/3649, art 3. The Government signalled the application of FTA 1973 in November 1999: see Treasury Press Release 187/99, 9 November 1999.

2   On 4 November 2003 the OFT announced that it was launching an assessment of the impact on competition of FSMA 2000, as part of the Government's two year review of the Act announced by the Treasury on the same day. The OFT conducts such assessment under EA 2002, s 5.

THE 'SIGNIFICANTLY ADVERSE EFFECT ON COMPETITION' TEST UNDER FSMA 2000

10.10   The central concept of the competition regime under FSMA 2000 is that of a 'significantly adverse effect on competition' (s 302(2)). This test is applied to the regulating provisions and practices of the FSA and to the regulatory provisions and practices of RIEs and RCHs,[1] using identical terms.[2]

1   And also to the activities of the UKLA if an order is made for competition scrutiny of it under FSMA 2000, s 95: see para 10.52.
2   Although note that FSMA 2000 uses the terminology 'regulating' provision for the FSA and 'regulatory' provision for RIEs and RCHs.

10.11   Provisions and practices have a significantly adverse effect on competition if they have, or are intended or likely to have, that effect (ss 159(2)(a), 302(2)(a)) or if their effect, or their intended or likely effect, is to require or encourage behaviour which has, or is intended or likely to have, a significantly adverse effect on competition (ss 159(2)(b), 302(2)(b)). If the provisions or practices have the effect, or the intended or likely effect, of requiring or encouraging the exploitation of the strength of a market position, they are taken to have an adverse effect on competition (ss 159(3), 302(3)).

10.12   In determining these matters it may be assumed that those to whom provisions are addressed will act in accordance with them (ss 159(4), 302(4)). However, the Competition Commission must also consider whether any adverse effect is 'justified', and in doing so it must consider the compatibility of its conclusions with the obligations FSMA 2000 imposes on the FSA or on the body concerned (ss 162(6), (7), 306(8), (9)). This means that the test under FSMA 2000 is not purely concerned with 'competition' criteria.[1]

1   See further paras 10.24–10.26.

10.13   The Government decided not to replicate the terminology of CA 1998 in FSMA 2000, as the former employs that contained in EC competition law, such as 'have as their object or effect the prevention, restriction or distortion of competition'[1] and 'abuse of a dominant position'.[2] Under CA 1998, s 60, these terms in the Act are to be interpreted in line with the interpretation given to them in Community law. However, the Government were concerned to avoid any question of the applicability of the ECJ's jurisprudence in the context of FSMA 2000. The Bill originally reproduced the wording of CA 1998, but it was amended for the reasons explained by Lord McIntosh in the House of Lords—

> 'If we were to keep the current wording, there would be a danger that it might attract the European Court of Justice jurisprudence. That is particularly the case now that the Competition Act, which imports the treaty test into domestic law, has been enacted. That has never been our intention and there are two reasons why it concerns us. First, the jurisprudence has developed in the context of commercial undertakings. There is always a risk that this would have unforeseen, and possibly unwelcome, consequences if applied in a different context.
>
> Secondly, we do not want the external competition scrutiny arrangements to turn on the legal issues. While that may be appropriate under the Competition Act regime, where penalties can be imposed and legal certainty is essential, here we are dealing with questions of judgment rather than law. The key question that we want the competition regulators to address is whether the FSA, in discharging its general duties, has struck the right balance between competition and regulation. The answer to that should turn more on economic than legal arguments.'[3]

---

[1]   EC Treaty, Art 81(1) and CA 1998, s 2(1) (the Chapter I prohibition).

[2]   EC Treaty, Art 82 and CA 1998, s 18(1) (the Chapter II prohibition), (s 18(1) is worded slightly differently from Art 82, but the concept is fundamentally the same).

[3]   HL Committee Stage, 27 March 2000, col 572.

COMPETITION SCRUTINY OF THE FSA

Pt X, Ch III

10.14   FSMA 2000, Pt X, Ch III contains the provisions covering the scrutiny by the OFT, the Competition Commission and the Treasury of the FSA as a regulating authority.

Role of the OFT

10.15 The OFT is under a duty to keep the regulating provisions and practices of the FSA under review for any significantly adverse effect on competition (s 160(1)). 'Regulating provisions' for this purpose means any rules, general guidance (as defined by s 158(5)), statements issued by the FSA under s 64, or code issued by the FSA under s 64 or 119 (s 159(1)).[1] 'Practices' means practices adopted by the FSA in the exercise of functions under FSMA 2000 (s 159(1)).

---

[1]   Ie, the approved persons code and the market abuse code. See para 10.4.

10.16 If at any time the OFT considers that a regulating provision or practice, two or more regulating provisions or practices taken together, or a particular combination of regulating provisions and practices has, or have, a significantly adverse effect on competition, it must make a report to that effect (s 160(2)). The report must include details of the adverse effects on competition (s 160(4)).

10.17 The OFT may also make a report if it considers that such regulating provisions or practices do not have such an effect (s 160(3)). This covers situations where the OFT, having kept matters under review, considers that there may be adverse effects on competition, but after investigating concludes that this is not the case.[1]

---

[1]   See para 10.41.

10.18 The OFT must send a copy of any report made under s 160(2) (a finding that regulating provisions or practices have a significant adverse effect on competition) to the Treasury, the Competition Commission and the FSA (s 160(5)(a)). It must also publish the report, in the way appearing to him best calculated to bring it to public attention (s 160(5)(b)).

10.19 If the OFT makes a report under s 160(3) (a finding that regulating provisions or practices do not have a significantly adverse effect on competition), it must send a copy to the Treasury, the Competition Commission and the FSA (s 160(6)(a)). It *may* ask the Competition Commission to further consider the matter (s 162(1)(b)). Unlike a s 160(2) report, however, it does not have an obligation to publish a s 160(3) report, but it may do so (s 160(6)(b)).

10.20 The published version of a report must exclude, as far as is practicable, matters relating to the private affairs of a particular individual, or to the affairs of a particular body the publication of which, in the opinion of the OFT, would or might seriously prejudice the interests of that individual or body (s 160(7), (8)). There is, however, no obligation to exclude such matters from a report sent to the Treasury, the Competition Commission and the FSA under s 160(5)(a) or (6)(a) (s 160(9)). The OFT's reports are absolutely privileged for the purposes of defamation law (s 160(10)).

Role of the Competition Commission

10.21 If the OFT makes a report under s 160(2) or asks the Competition Commission to consider a report it has made under s 160(3), the Competition Commission must investigate the matter and make its own report,[1] unless it considers that, as a result of a change of circumstances, no useful purpose would be served by such a report (s 162(1), (2)). If it decides not to make a report on these grounds it must make a statement setting out the change of circumstances which resulted in that decision (s 162(3)).

---

[1] In considering any matter arising from a report made by the OFT under s 160, the Competition Commission must have regard to any representations made to it and to any cost benefit analysis prepared by the FSA in relation to the regulatory provisions or practice which is the subject of the report (Sch 14, para 2).

10.22 The Competition Commission's report under s 162 must state its conclusions both as to whether the regulating provisions or practices which are the subject of the report have a significantly adverse effect on competition (s 162(4)) and if so, whether it considers that that effect is justified (s 162(5)(a)). If it states that the adverse effect is not justified, the Competition Commission must give its conclusion as to what action, if any, the FSA should take (s 162(5)(b)). In deciding whether a particular adverse effect on competition is justified, the Competition Commission must ensure that so far as is reasonably possible its conclusion is compatible with the FSA's functions and obligations under FSMA 2000 (s 162(6), (7)).

10.23 Section 162 is supplemented by FSMA 2000, Sch 14,[1] which sets out the details of the Competition Commission's duties, powers and procedures for the purposes of s 162 (s 162(9)).[2] A copy of any report under s 162 must be sent to the Treasury, the FSA, and the OFT (s 162(10)). The Competition Commission's report must contain such an account of its reasons as it considers 'expedient . . . for facilitating proper understanding of [those reasons]' (s 162(8)). Reports must be made by at least a two-thirds majority and dissenting members may make reasoned statements of dissent.[3]

---

[1] As amended by EA 2002, s 278 and Sch 25.
[2] See paras 10.45–10.47. Schedule 14 also applies to the Competition Commission's role under s 306: see s 306(11).
[3] FSMA 2000, Sch 14, para 2C, as amended by EA 2002 s 278 and Sch 25.

Role of the Treasury

10.24 HM Treasury is the only body empowered to require the FSA to change its rules and practices. If a Competition Commission report under s 162 states that there is an adverse effect on competition and that it is not justified, the Treasury must (subject to s 163(3)) give a direction to the FSA as to what action to take (s 163(2)), taking into account what the Competition Commission, in its report, considered the FSA should do (s 163(4)). The Treasury must make a statement giving details of the direction (s 163(11)(a)).

10.25 However, the Treasury need not give a direction, either because it considers that such direction is unnecessary because the FSA has already taken action in response to the Competition Commission report (s 163(3)(a)), or where there are exceptional circumstances which make the giving of a direction 'inappropriate or unnecessary' (s 163(3)(b)). In these cases the Treasury can decline to follow the Competition Commission's report, but must give reasons for so doing (s 163(10)). The converse to s 163(3) also applies, in that if the Competition Commission concludes in its report that the adverse effect on competition *is* justified, the Treasury may still give the FSA a direction if they consider that exceptional circumstances require them to act (s 163(5)). The direction may require the FSA to take such specified action as the Treasury considers necessary in the light of the exceptional circumstances of the case (s 163(6)) and the Treasury must make a statement giving reasons for the direction (s 163(11)(b)).[1]

---

[1] In other cases the Treasury statement need only include details of the direction, and not the reasons for it (s 163(11)(a)).

10.26 If the Treasury is considering making a direction to the FSA, it must allow the FSA (and other persons who may be affected) an opportunity to make representations (s 163(8), (9)(a)). The Treasury must have regard to any representations made (s 163(9)(b)). The Treasury cannot require the FSA to do anything which it could not do in the absence of a direction or that would in any way be incompatible with the FSA's functions or obligations under FSMA 2000 (s 163(7)).

10.27 The effect of s 163 is that the Treasury may override the Competition Commission. However, the Treasury may give a direction only if the Competition Commission has concluded that there is a significantly adverse effect on competition. If the Competition Commission reports that there is no adverse effect, the Treasury cannot require the FSA to take any action. The Treasury's power under s 163 to depart from the conclusions of the Competition Commission (either by acting or by declining to act) applies only if an adverse effect is found. This is, nevertheless, a situation in which a political decision may be taken to override the decision of the competition authority.[1] In the Report

Stage of the Bill the Opposition expressed disquiet about this matter, describing the Competition Commission as the 'piggy-in-the-middle' in the competition regime, and complaining that if the Treasury considered there was a case for retaining a rule that protected consumers in regulatory terms it would opt for retaining it even if it were uncompetitive.[2] Melanie Johnson, Economic Secretary to the Treasury, stressed that the exercise of the override would not be common—

> 'The Competition Commission's conclusion will not be subject to routine second-guessing by Ministers. It will stand, except where the Treasury considers that exceptional circumstances cause it to reach a different view. We can envisage a Treasury override being triggered when it is necessary to meet our international obligations—for example, to give effect to European Community legislation—or when the Treasury thinks that there would be significant implications for the operation of the financial system as a whole if the changes were to be made. In the unlikely event of exercising that override, the Treasury will have to publish a statement of its reasons and lay that before Parliament.'[3]

---

[1]   In this respect the provisions are similar to the now repealed monopoly provisions of FTA 1973, Pt IV, where the action following a report of the Competition Commission was taken by the Secretary of State, who did not need to follow the Competition Commission's recommendations when it had found matters to be 'against the public interest'.
[2]   Mr Flight, HC Report Stage, 27 January 2000, col 652.
[3]   HC Report Stage, 27 January 2000, col 645.

COMPETITION SCRUTINY OF RIES AND RCHS

Pt XVIII, Chs II and III

10.28   The competition scrutiny of RIEs and RCHs deals first with the regulatory provisions of applicants for recognition under FSMA 2000, s 287 or 288,[1] and secondly with the continued competition surveillance of the regulating provisions and practices of bodies once recognised. Recognised bodies are treated differently from the FSA in that they are commercial bodies as well as being regulatory authorities, and as such they may be able to exploit their position on the market.

---

[1]   See Ch 16.

Role of the OFT in the scrutiny of applications for recognition

10.29 When an investment exchange (s 287) or a clearing house (s 288) applies to the FSA for recognition, the FSA must send a copy of its regulatory provisions to the Treasury and to the OFT (s 303(1)). 'Regulatory provisions' means the rules of the investment exchange or clearing house, any guidance issued by it, and its arrangements and criteria for its clearing services (s 302(1)).[1] The FSA must also send the OFT any information it possesses as a result of the application which it considers will assist it in considering the competition aspects of the application (s 303(2)). The OFT must then issue a report as to whether any of these regulatory provisions, or a combination of them, have a significantly adverse effect on competition (s 303(3)), giving reasons for its decision if it concludes that they do (s 303(4)). The OFT must send a copy of his report to the FSA, the Competition Commission and the Treasury (s 303(5)).

---

[1]   As mentioned in s 287(3) (investment exchanges) and s 288(3) (clearing houses). See also Ch 16.

Role of the OFT in the ongoing scrutiny of recognised bodies

10.30   The OFT has an ongoing duty to keep the regulatory provisions and practices of recognised bodies under review for significantly adverse effects on competition (s 304(1)).[1] 'Practices' means the practices of a recognised investment exchange in its capacity as such or of a recognised clearing house in respect of its clearing arrangements (s 302(1)). The provisions in s 304 setting out this duty, and the actions the OFT must take in respect of that duty, mirror those relating to the scrutiny of the FSA's regulating provisions under s 160.[2] If at any time the OFT considers that one or more regulatory provisions or practices, or a combination of them, has a significantly adverse effect on competition, it must make a report (s 304(2)), containing details of the anti-competitive effect (s 304(4)), and send a copy of it to the Treasury, the Competition Commission and the FSA (s 304(5)(a)). It must also publish it in the way best calculated to bring it to the attention of the public (s 304(5)(b)).

---

[1]   For the meaning of this term as defined in s 302(2)–(4), see paras 10.10–10.12.
[2]   See paras 10.15–10.20.

10.31 Section 304(7) is identical to s 160(7) in providing that the published report must, so far as practicable, exclude matters relating to the private affairs of an individual, publication of which, in the OFT's opinion, would or might seriously and prejudicially affect the individual's interests.[1] However, the provision in s 307(8) concerning the exclusion from publication of matters relating to the affairs of a *particular body*, publication of which might seriously prejudice it, does not include the caveat 'so far as practicable'.[2] Thus there appears to be an absolute duty on the OFT to exclude such matters. This is different from the corresponding provision in s 160(8) which *does* say that the exclusion is to be 'as far as practicable'. The absolute nature of the duty to exclude is, to some extent, diminished by leaving to 'the opinion of the OFT' the question of whether publication would be prejudicial.

---

[1]   See para 10.20.
[2]   This also differs from the provisions relating to the publication of Competition Commission reports in FSMA 2000, Sch 14, para 4, which provides for the exclusion of prejudicial material 'so far as practicable' (see para 10.46).

10.32   The OFT may also make a report at any time finding that one or more regulatory provisions or practices, or a combination of them, do *not* have a significantly adverse effect on competition (s 304(3)). If such a report is made, it must be sent to the Treasury, Competition Commission, and FSA but does not have to be published, although the OFT may choose to do so (s 304(6)). If it does make a report, the provisions as to publication of prejudicial matters apply. Any report made under s 304 is absolutely privileged for the purposes of defamation law (s 304(10)).

Role of the Competition Commission

10.33   Under s 306(1), (2) and (4) the Competition Commission must investigate and make a reasoned[1] report if the OFT sends it either a s 303(3) report concluding that the regulatory provisions of an applicant for recognition have a significantly adverse effect on competition,[2] or a s 304(2) report concluding that regulatory provisions or practices of a recognised body have such an effect.[3] Under s 306(3) and (4) the Competition Commission must also investigate and report *if asked by the OFT to do so* where the OFT—

—   sends it a s 303(3) report (on the regulatory provisions of applicants) which concludes that there is no significantly adverse effect; or

—   has chosen to make a s 304(3) report (concluding that regulatory provisions or practices of recognised bodies do *not* have a significantly adverse effect).

As under s 162(2) and (3), the Competition Commission may decline to make a report under s 306 if it considers that a report would serve no useful purpose because of a change of circumstances, in which case it must make a reasoned statement explaining this (s 306(4), (5)).

---

[1]   The Competition Commission's report must contain such an account of its reasons as in its opinion is expedient for facilitating proper understanding of them (s 306(10)). This provision is identical to s 162(8).
[2]   See para 10.29.
[3]   See para 10.30.

10.34 If the Competition Commission makes a report, it must state its conclusions as to whether the regulatory provisions or practices which are the subject of that report have a significantly adverse effect on competition (s 306(6)) and, if they do, whether that effect is justified (s 306(7)(a)). In deciding the question of justification, the Competition Commission must ensure, as far as reasonably possible, that its conclusion is compatible with the recognised body's obligations under FSMA 2000 (s 306(8), (9)). A finding that the effect is not justified must be accompanied by a conclusion as to what action, if any, the Treasury should direct the FSA to take (s 306(7)(b)). A copy of any report made by the Competition Commission under s 306 must be sent to the Treasury, the FSA and the OFT (s 306(12)). Details of the Competition Commission's duties, powers and procedures for the purposes of s 306 are set out in FSMA 2000, Sch 14,[1] which also applies to the Competition Commission's role under s 162 (s 306(11)).[2] Competition Commission reports are absolutely privileged for the purposes of the law on defamation.[3]

---

1 As amended by the EA 2002, s 278.
2 Schedule 14 is discussed at paras 10.45–10.47.
3 Schedule 14, para 2C(3), as amended by the EA 2002.

Role of the Treasury

Recognition orders

10.35 Under FSMA 2000, s 307, the Treasury's approval is required for a recognition order under s 290.[1] As explained in para 10.29, under s 303 the OFT must report on whether the regulatory provisions of an applicant body for recognition have a significantly adverse effect on competition. Although it must send a copy of this report to the Treasury, the Competition Commission and the FSA, it need not ask the Competition Commission to investigate and consider his report under s 306 if it has concluded that there is *no* significantly adverse effect on competition. This means that the Treasury may receive a report which has not been considered by the Competition Commission. In exceptional circumstances, the Treasury may, despite the findings of the OFT, refuse to approve the making of the recognition order on the grounds that it would be 'inappropriate' (s 307(2)). This power of the Treasury to refuse approval also applies if the Competition Commission *has*, under s 306, considered a report by the OFT, but concluded either that the applicant's regulatory provisions do not have a significantly adverse effect on competition or that, if they do, the effect is justified. Section 307 also provides for the reverse situation, so that the Treasury may grant approval despite a finding by the Competition Commission that the applicant's regulatory provisions do have an unjustified significantly adverse effect on competition (s 307(3), (4)).

---

[1] For recognition orders generally, see para 16.18. If the Treasury proposes to refuse approval, it must give an opportunity for representations to be made and must take account of any which are made (s 310). See also paras 10.48 and 16.67.

10.36 This power of the Treasury to override is similar to that provided for in s 163 in respect of the competition scrutiny of the FSA[1] and in s 308 in respect of the Treasury's role in the scrutiny of the regulatory provisions and practices of bodies which are already recognised. However, under s 307 the Treasury may act in respect of recognition orders even if the Competition Commission has concluded there is *no* significant adverse anti-competitive effect. The exceptional nature of the giving of Treasury approval to a recognition order where the Competition Commission has concluded that there is an unjustified anti-competitive effect is underlined by the way in which s 307(4) is worded, which is that the Treasury '*must* refuse to approve . . . *unless* they consider that the exceptional circumstances of the case make it inappropriate . . .' (emphasis added).

---

[1] See paras 10.24–10.27.

Remedial directions and statements in respect of recognised bodies

10.37 If the Competition Commission makes a report under s 306(4) (which concludes that the regulatory provisions or practices of a recognised body have a significantly adverse effect on competition which is not justified), the Treasury must (unless s 308(3) applies) give a remedial direction to the FSA (s 308(1), (2)). A remedial direction is a direction requiring the FSA to revoke a body's recognition order or to give the body concerned specified directions (s 308(8)).

10.38 The Treasury must make a statement giving details of the direction (s 309(2)(a)), publish it in the way best calculated to bring it to the attention of the public, and lay a copy before Parliament (s 309(3)). Section 308 does not impose a duty on the Treasury to follow the Competition Commission's conclusions under s 306(7)(b) as to what action the FSA should be directed to take, but under s 308(4) the Treasury should 'have regard to' those conclusions. The Treasury must also take steps to allow the recognised body and any other person to make representations about the OFT or Competition Commission's report and what the Treasury should do, and must have regard to any representations made (s 310).[1]

---

[1]   See also paras 10.48 and 16.67.

10.39 Again, however, as under ss 163 and 307, there is a power for the Treasury to override the Competition Commission. It may decline to give a direction either because it is unnecessary, since the FSA or the body concerned has already taken action in response to the Competition Commission's report (s 308(3)(a)) or because the exceptional circumstances of the case make it 'inappropriate or unnecessary' to do so (s 308(3)(b)). In either case the Treasury must publish a statement of reasons for declining to act, in the way best calculated to bring it to the attention of the public (s 309(1), (3)(a)), and must lay the statement before Parliament (s 309(3)(b)).

10.40 If the Competition Commission concludes that the adverse effect on competition *is* justified, the Treasury may still give a direction to the FSA if they consider it necessary in the light of the exceptional circumstances of the case (s 308(5), (6)). As with s 163 concerning the Treasury's role in relation to the FSA, the power to override the Competition Commission only arises if the Competition Commission has concluded that there *is* an adverse effect on competition.[1] The Treasury must publish a statement under s 309(2)(a) and (3),[2] which must explain the Treasury's reasons for giving the direction despite the Competition Commission's conclusion of justification (s 309(2)(b)).

---

[1]   But unlike the position concerning the approval of recognition orders where the Treasury may refuse approval even if the Competition Commission concludes there is no significantly adverse effect: see paras 10.35 and 10.36.

[2]   See para 10.38.

10.41 Any action the FSA is required to take under a remedial direction given by the Treasury under s 308 must be compatible with the recognition requirements of the recognised body concerned (s 308(7)(a)). A direction is enforceable by an injunction or, in Scotland, an order for specific performance under the Court of Session Act 1988.[1] A rule altered by a recognised body as a result of a direction may still subsequently be altered or revoked by the body.[2]

---

[1]   By virtue of s 308(7)(b) the direction is to be treated for these purposes as though it were a direction under FSMA 2000, s 296.

[2]   Ibid. See FSMA 2000, s 296(4).

PROCEDURAL MATTERS AND POWERS OF INVESTIGATION

Legal professional privilege

10.42 Legal professional privilege is expressly applied in relation to investigations under FSMA 2000 by virtue of s 413. Section 413 describes the protection of items from inspection or investigation in terms which reflect the provisions of the Police and Criminal Evidence Act 1984, s 10.[1] The powers of the OFT and the Competition Commission described in the following paragraphs must be read in the light of s 413.

---

[1]   See para 7.12.

Powers of the OFT to request information

10.43 Sections 161 and 305 confer on the OFT powers to require information and the production of documents in order to investigate matters with a view to making reports under s 160 (scrutiny of the FSA) and ss 303 and 304 (scrutiny of recognised bodies). The provisions of ss 161 and 305 are identical. The OFT may by notice in writing require any person to produce at a time and place specified in the notice, any specified or described document which is in that person's custody or under his control (ss 161(2), 305(2)). The OFT may also require by notice any person carrying on a business to provide such information as the notice specifies or describes (ss 161(3)(a), 305(3)(a)). The notice must specify the time within which and the manner and form in which the information is to be provided (ss 161(3)(b), 305(3)(b)). In the case of failure or refusal to comply with a notice under s 161, the OFT may certify that fact in writing to the court and the court may investigate the case (ss 161(5), 305(5)).[1] If after an enquiry into the case, including the hearing of witnesses and any other statements which may be offered in defence of the defaulting party, the court concludes that there was no reasonable excuse for the failure or refusal to comply, the court may deal with the defaulting party as if he were in contempt of court (ss 161(6), 305(6)).[2] Sections 161(4) and 305(4) make it clear that the OFT may only require documents or information 'which relate to any matters relevant to the investigation'. Lack of relevance would presumably amount to a reasonable excuse, and a dispute as to whether there was such relevance would ultimately be settled by the court in its enquiry into the case.

Misleading the OFT

10.44   Misleading the OFT by giving false and misleading information is a criminal offence as it would be under CA 1998, s 44 (s 399). A person is guilty of this offence if he knows the information is false or misleading or is reckless as to whether it is. The penalty is a fine of up to the statutory maximum on summary conviction or, on indictment, a fine or up to two years' imprisonment or both a fine and imprisonment (CA 1998, s 44).

Role of the Competition Commission

Provision of information by Treasury

10.45   Schedule 14 applies to the Competition Commission's functions under both s 162 (scrutiny of the FSA) and s 306 (scrutiny of recognised bodies).¹ Schedule 14, para 1 provides that the Treasury may give to the Competition Commission, for the purpose of its investigation, any information in its possession relating to matters within the scope of the investigation, and any other assistance. The Competition Commission must have regard to such information (Sch 14, para 1(3)). Schedule 14, para 2(a) provides that when considering a report from the OFT, the Competition Commission must have regard to any representations made to it by any person who appears to the Competition Commission to have a 'substantial interest' in the matter. When considering a report made by the OFT under s 160 (but not under s 303 or 304), the Competition Commission must also have regard to any cost benefit analysis prepared by the FSA in connection with the regulating provisions or practices under review (Sch 14, para 2(b)).

¹   Section 306(11) provides that Sch 14, except for para 2(b), also applies for the purposes of s 306.

Publication of reports

10.46   Schedule 14, para 4 contains provisions relating to the publication of Competition Commission reports under s 162. Reports must be published in a way which appears to be best calculated to bring them to public attention (Sch 14, para 4(1)). The published versions of reports (as distinct from the version sent to the Treasury, FSA and OFT under ss 162(10) and 308(12)) must exclude, as far as practicable, any matter relating to the private affairs of a particular individual or to the affairs of a particular body the publication of which, in the Competition Commission's opinion, would or might seriously and prejudicially affect his or its interests (Sch 14, para 4(2), (3)). This is the same procedure as is set out in s 160(7) and (8) in respect of reports by the OFT, and in s 304(7) in respect of OFT reports where the private affairs of an individual are concerned. It differs, however, from the procedure set out in s 304(8) regarding OFT reports where particular bodies are concerned, in that the words 'so far as practicable' do not appear.[1]

---

[1]   FSMA 2000, s 304(8): see para 10.31.

Further provisions

10.47 Certain provisions in the Enterprise Act 2002 relating to the Competition Commission apply to its functions under FSMA 2000 by virtue of Sch 14 (as amended by EA 2002, s 278 and Schs 25 and 26). These are provisions which cover—

— the attendance of witnesses and the production of documents (EA 2002, s 109), and enforcement powers over the attendance of witnesses and the production of documents (EA 2002, s 110);

— the levying of penalties for non-attendance and non-production of documents (EA 2002, s 111), the procedural requirements for levying such penalties (EA 2002, s 112), the payment of penalties and interest thereon (EA 2002, s 113), appeals in relation to penalties (EA 2002, s 114), the recovery of penalties (EA 2002, s 115); and the Commission's duty to publish a statement of policy in relation to enforcing Notices requiring production of documents or attendance of witnesses (EA 2002, 116).

The attendance of witnesses is to be secured by a notice (EA 2002, s 109(1). The Competition Commission may take evidence on oath (EA 2002, s 109(5)). Any person may be required by notice to produce specified documents (or documents falling within a specified class) which are in his custody or under his control (EA 2002, s 109(2)), and any person carrying on a business may be required to supply the Commission with specified estimates, forecasts, returns or other specified information (EA 2002, s 109(3)). Furthermore, it is an offence to knowingly or recklessly supply false or misleading information to the Competition Commission, or to another person knowing that it is to be supplied to the Commission (EA 2002, s 117).[1] Furthermore, CA 1998, Sch 7, Pt II applies to the functions of the Competition Commission under FSMA 2000, s 162.[2] These provisions govern the performance of the Commission's general functions, and cover such matters as the selection of the group of Competition Commission members to deal with any particular reference, the appointment of the chairman and matters of procedure before the Competition Commission.

1   The offence is punishable on summary conviction with a fine and on indictment by fine and
up to two years' imprisonment (EA 2002 s 117(3)).
2   This appears to be so by virtue of Sch 7 (as amended by EA 2002, s 187(3)) itself, despite the
repeal of FSMA 2000, Sch 14, para 3(2)(d) by EA 2002, s 278, Sch 26.

Procedural matters relating to the Treasury

10.48 Before the Treasury gives a remedial direction to the FSA under
s 163(2) or (6) in respect of the scrutiny of the FSA's regulating
provisions or practices, it must allow the FSA, and any other person
appearing to be affected, the opportunity to make representations,
and must have regard to such representations (s 163(8), (9)). Likewise,
if the Treasury is considering, in relation to the scrutiny of recognised
bodies, refusing approval of a recognition order under s 307, or
giving a remedial direction to the FSA under s 308(2) or (6), it must
allow the investment exchange or clearing house concerned, and any
other person appearing to be affected, the opportunity to make
representations (s 310(1), (2)). The representations may concern the
report of the OFT or of the Competition Commission and relate to
whether and how the Treasury should exercise its powers under s 307
(recognition orders) or s 308 (remedial directions), and the Treasury
must have regard to any such representations (s 310(2)).

Disclosure of information

10.49 FSMA 2000, s 351 originally included specific provisions about the
disclosure of 'competition information' provided to the competition
authorities in the exercise of their functions under the Act.
Competition information is information which relates to the affairs of
a particular individual or body, not otherwise in the public domain,
which was obtained pursuant to an order made under s 95[1] a
provision of Part X, Chapter III or Part XVIII, Chapter II (s 351 (5) and
(6)). The general provisions of FSMA 2000 about the disclosure of
information, ss 348 and 349[2] do not apply to competition information
(s 351(4)). The specific provisions[3] were repealed by EA 2002 s 247(k)
and the disclosure of competition information is now covered by the
provisions of EA 2002, ss 237–247 which cover information provided
to any 'public authority'[4] in connection with specified enactments.
FSMA 2000, Pt X, Ch III and Pt XVIII, Ch II are specified enactments
for these purposes (EA 2002, Sch 14).

10.50 The effect of the information provisions of EA 2002 is to safeguard the confidentiality of information revealed to the OFT, the CC or the Treasury in connection with their powers of competition scrutiny under FSMA 2000. EA 2002, s 237(2) prohibits disclosure of information during the lifetime of the individual to whose affairs it relates or while the undertaking to whose business it relates continues in existence. It may, however, be disclosed with consent (EA 2002, s 239). It may also be disclosed to another person if such disclosure is required for the purposes of a Community obligation (EA 2002, 240); and to persons exercising specified statutory functions[1] to facilitate the performance of those functions (EA 2002, s 241). Competition information under FSMA 2000 s 351 may *not*, however, be disclosed to overseas public authorities as it is excepted from the general provisions permitting such disclosure (EA 2002, s 243(3)(c)). Disclosure may also be made for the purposes of the investigation or the bringing of criminal proceedings (EA 2002, s 242). This may be done in respect of the enforcement of any enactment which provides for the bringing of criminal proceedings, including the cartel offence under EA 2002, s 188. Before any disclosure of information is made the authority must consider excluding disclosure on the grounds that it would be contrary to the public interest (EA 2002, s 244(2)). Further, it must consider excluding from disclosure commercial information whose disclosure would harm the legitimate business interests of the undertaking to which it relates (EA 2002, s 244(3)(a)), or information relating to an individual's private affairs where the individual's interests might be significantly harmed by disclosure (EA 2002, s 244(3)(b)).

---

[1]   Specified in Sch 15. This includes functions under FSMA 2000.

10.51 It is a criminal offence to improperly disclose information in contravention of the provisions described in paras 10.49–10.50 above. The offence is punishable on summary conviction by imprisonment for a maximum of three months and/or a fine not exceeding the statutory maximum or on indictment by up to two years imprisonment and/or a fine, on indictment (EA 2002, s 244).

OFFICIAL LISTING

10.52 The FSA took over the Stock Exchange's responsibilities as the UKLA on 1 May 2000,[1] and is the competent authority for the purposes of FSMA 2000, Pt VI, which deals with official listing.[2] FSMA 2000, s 95 allows for competition scrutiny of the competent authority by providing that the Treasury may lay down by order the details of a competition regime (s 95(1)). The competition scrutiny thus provided for would apply to the listing rules, the general guidance given by the competent authority in connection with its functions under Pt VI, and to the competent authority's practices in exercising its functions under Pt VI (s 95(1), (9)). The person charged with keeping these matters under review would be required to consider whether any regulating provisions or practices, either alone or together or in any particular combination, has or have a significantly adverse effect on competition (s 95(2)).[3] Section 95 does not state whom the Treasury should charge with keeping matters under review or what procedures should be followed by that person. However, s 95(3) provides that an order made under s 95 may include provision corresponding to that in Pt X, Ch III, which deals with the competition scrutiny of the FSA as a regulating authority. The regime set up in Pt X, Ch III, involves reports by the OFT, the Competition Commission, and directions given by the Treasury, as described above.[4]

---

[1]   The Official Listing of Securities (Change of Competent Authority) Regulations 2000, SI 2000/968.
[2]   See Ch 9.
[3]   For the circumstances in which regulations or practices have such an effect, see paras 10.10–10.12.
[4]   See paras 10.24–10.27.

10.53   The provision dealing with competition scrutiny of the UKLA was introduced so that, if the FSA's functions as the UKLA are transferred to another body,[1] the Treasury can ensure there will be competition scrutiny of the new competent authority (by statutory instrument under s 95).

---

[1]   By virtue of Sch 8: see HL Report Stage, 18 April 2000, col 658.

11 Market abuse

BACKGROUND

11.1 The Financial Services and Markets Act 2000 (FSMA 2000), Pt VIII (ss 118–131)[1] sets out the framework for the creation of new civil penalties for behaviour which would adversely affect specified UK markets. These provisions have proved to be some of the most controversial in the legislation and the most potentially far-reaching in their effect.

---

[1] These provisions in FSMA 2000 are likely to be amended in order to bring into effect the provision of the EC insider dealing and market abuse directive, Directive 2003/6/EC, which will come into force by 2005 at the latest. See also the new implementing measures contained in Commission Directive 2003/124/EC, Commission Directive 2003/125/EC and Commission Regulation 2273/2003/EC.

PURPOSE OF THE NEW REGIME

11.2 The Financial Services Authority (FSA) is required to act in a way which is compatible with and designed to meet its statutory regulatory objectives including the objective of maintaining confidence in the financial system (the 'market confidence' objective, s 3). Part of this is to ensure that the integrity of the UK markets is maintained. It must also ensure that any abusive practices which affect those markets can be dealt with. In debating these objectives Lord McIntosh of Haringey said that—

> 'The purpose of the market abuse regime is to protect the UK financial markets from the damage that can be caused to them by abuse. In order to operate effectively and efficiently, the markets rely on market users to observe expected standards of conduct, as we shall discuss when we reach that part of the Bill. If people do not do that, and if they abuse the trust of the markets, then confidence will be damaged. The markets will work less well as people seek to protect themselves from the risks of abuse by entering into transactions at higher prices or by entering into fewer transactions.

Therefore, the ground is covered by the objective on maintaining confidence in the financial system. That, of course, includes maintaining confidence in financial markets and exchanges. That is what the market abuse regime is all about. That is not to say that there is no overlap with the territory covered by the financial crime objective. However, the objectives all overlap to a certain extent; for example, market abuse will often also adversely affect consumers. For example, if people buy shares on the back of misleading information, they lose money.

It is true that some forms of more serious market abuse, such as insider dealing, criminal fraud, which is a matter for the common law, or money laundering, will also be criminal offences under this Bill or under other enactments. However, that will not always be the case. Behaviour which comes within the offences of insider dealing and market manipulation, for example, will, broadly speaking, be subsets of behaviour which can come within the market abuse regime. To that extent, the financial crime objective already covers some forms of market abuse. The matters which the FSA will have to consider as regards systems and controls in [Section] 6(2) will also be relevant to market abuse. In any event, we should expect the FSA to have an interest in systems and controls designed to detect and prevent market abuse as a result of the market confidence objective.

. . .

I believe that market abuse is adequately and properly covered by the objective on market confidence. Maintaining market confidence is at the heart of what the market abuse regime is intended to achieve. I prefer to keep that clear, as I believe it is clear under the Bill as drafted.[1]

. . .

I said at the beginning that it would be wrong to associate market abuse only with financial crime as one of the objectives. I said that that was because market abuse overlaps with a number of the objectives but is associated in particular with market confidence, although I acknowledge that there was an overlap both with financial crime and with the protection of consumers.

But the implication of that is not that it would be right to have a fifth objective—market abuse—but that the coverage of market abuse was adequately achieved by the market confidence objective . . . I said also—and it is another reason for rejecting the noble Lord's suggestion—

that market abuse is covered separately for a significant reason; that is, it is designed to apply not only to the regulated community but to everyone. It must therefore be dealt with separately from the objectives and principles which relate specifically to the regulated community.'[2]

---

[1]   HL Report Stage, 20 March 2000, col 11.
[2]   HL Report Stage, 20 March 2000, col 14.

11.3   The market abuse regime applies to both authorised and unauthorised persons where their behaviour falls within the definition of market abuse.[1] The FSA has indicated, for example, that a financial journalist dealing as an 'insider' on information that is not generally available, or publishing misleading information with a view to influencing the prices of shares would be covered by the market abuse regime and could be fined or publicly censured by the FSA.[2]

---

[1]   The market abuse may be the behaviour of a person acting alone or acting with others (s 118(9)).
[2]   FSA Press Release FSA/PN/098/2000, 25 July 2000.

DEFINITION OF 'MARKET ABUSE'

11.4   The definition of market abuse is complex and the range of behaviour which is potentially caught within the definition is deliberately wide. As the Treasury explained—

'We welcome the Joint Committee's recognition of the need to reconcile breadth with clarity. [Section 118] is deliberately drafted quite widely in order to make evasion difficult. Nonetheless our view is that the provision does also offer clarity. The underlying concept of market abuse is not a new one. Market participants have a common core understanding of the kinds of behaviour which constitute abuse of the markets as a result of well understood market conventions and expectations and particular regulatory cases. The new regime builds on this.'[1]

---

[1]   HM Treasury, Government Response to the Reports of the Joint Committee on Financial Services and Markets, Pt 2, Second Report, para 3, 19 June 1999. See also Financial Services and Markets Bill, Memorandum from HM Treasury to the Joint Committee on Pts V, VI and XII of the Bill in relation to the ECHR, 17 May 1999.

11.5 There was much debate during the passage of the Bill over the nature of these penalties and whether they should be categorised as criminal or civil. The following exchange took place in the House of Commons following the Lords Amendments to these provisions—

> '**Miss Johnson:** The right hon and learned Gentleman causes me some concern. Market abuse is a civil offence, and I am not quite sure where the criminal part of his distinction enters into the matter. My understanding is that, in United Kingdom law as proposed in the Bill, market abuse is not a criminal matter. He seemed to connect market abuse and criminality.
>
> **Sir Nicholas Lyell:** Am I not right in thinking that market abuse can lead to very large penalties?
>
> **Miss Johnson:** Yes, it can lead to large penalties, but that does not necessarily make it a criminal matter. In UK law, market abuse is a civil offence, not a criminal one.
>
> **Sir Nicholas Lyell:** The Minister cannot simply say that market abuse is called a civil offence when it has effectively criminal penalties, including unlimited fines. She cannot, like Humpty Dumpty, make words mean what she wants them to mean to that extent. Surely she recognises that the European Court of Human Rights will regard such behaviour as criminal. Perhaps she could take some advice and explain later how the Bill conforms with the convention.
>
> **Miss Johnson:** The Bill does conform. I said that market abuse was a civil offence under UK law. It may be construed as a criminal offence under the ECHR requirements, but it is a civil offence in the UK. The UK regime is non-criminal. We have introduced various protections that would be appropriate if a case was considered as a criminal matter under the ECHR only because we want to be as safe and circumspect as possible. I repeat, it is a civil offence under UK law.'[1]

---

[1] HC Consideration of Lords Amendments, 5 June 2000, col 85. See also comments by Lord Donaldson of Lymington, HL Committee Stage, 21 March 2000, col 250. The Government's approach in introducing protections which are ordinarily confined to a criminal process, including the legal assistance scheme (see Ch 12), and the comments made in debate, were confirmed by obiter remarks of Morrison J in *R (on the application of Fleurose) v Securities and Futures Authority Ltd* [2001] EWHC Admin 292, [2001] 2 All ER (Comm) 481, at first instance.

11.6 While regulators have traditionally viewed the areas of consumer protection, anti-fraud and anti-market manipulation as entirely within their remit, fragmentation amongst the regulators, and the difficulties in establishing and proving that certain behaviour is (or is not) a criminal offence under existing legislation has frustrated regulators. Consequently this area has been regarded by the regulators as a gap in their powers and purview.[1]

---

[1]   Speech, 'Financial Regulation and the Law', Howard Davies, Chairman, Financial Services Authority, Chancery Bar Association and Combar Spring Lecture, Lincoln's Inn, London, 3 March 1999.

11.7   In introducing this Part of the Bill Melanie Johnson, Economic Secretary to the Treasury, explained that—

'. . . the new regime fills a gap beneath the criminal regime covering market abuse.[1] The gap is the fact that the regulators cannot take action against unregulated market participants who damage the market. We decided not to extend the boundaries of the criminal regime to deal with that. In our view, that would not have been proportionate. However, the criminal offences will remain, and when criminal offences have been committed and the public interest and evidential tests for criminal proceedings are satisfied, they will be taken.'[2]

---

[1]   Presumably a reference to the insider dealing offences under the Criminal Justice Act 1993, Pt V.
[2]   HC SC A, 2 November 1999, col 684.

11.8   'Market abuse' is behaviour[1] which occurs in relation to qualifying investments[2] traded on[3] a market to which s 118 applies and which is likely to be regarded by a regular user[4] of that market to be a failure on the part of the person or persons concerned to observe standards of behaviour which can be reasonably expected of a person or persons in his or their position in relation to such a market and satisfies one or more of the three conditions set out in that section (s 118(1)). The markets and qualifying investments to which s 118 applies may be prescribed by orders made by the Treasury (s 118(3)).[5] In doing so, the Treasury may prescribe different investments or descriptions of investment in relation to different markets or descriptions of market (s 118(4)).

---

[1]   Which for these purposes includes both action and inaction (s 118(10)). See also the FSA Handbook, Code of Market Conduct, MAR 1.3.
[2]   The Financial Services and Markets Act 2000 (Prescribed Markets and Qualifying Investments) Order 2001, SI 2001/996, art 5 prescribes every specified investment in the Financial Services and Markets Act 2000 (Regulated Activities) Order 2001, SI 2001/544 as a qualifying investment. This identity of scope was foreshadowed in HM Treasury, Market Abuse: Prescribed Markets and Qualifying Investments, December 2000, para 7.
[3]   See HM Treasury, Market Abuse: Prescribed Markets and Qualifying Investments, December 2000, paras 5 and 6, which made it clear that following consultation, the order prescribing the markets to which s 118 applied would have the same scope as FSMA 2000 and that it would rely on the phrase 'traded on' used in s 118 itself rather than introducing a different concept, for example, of 'admitted to trading'. See also MAR 1.11.

[4] See paras 11.10 and 11.11.

[5] These are prescribed in the Financial Services and Markets Act 2000 (Prescribed Markets and Qualifying Investments) Order 2001, SI 2001/996. The prescribed markets are those established by recognised investment exchanges (art 4). This list has been amended by the addition of OFEX Limited, inserted as art 4A of this order by the Financial Services and Markets Act 2000 (Prescribed Markets and Qualifying Investments) (Amendment) Order 2001, SI 2001/3681.

11.9 The Treasury, in responding to comments raised on consultation stated—

> '8. Many of the respondents to the earlier consultation were concerned about the scope of the new regime. They also wanted the order to define the scope of the regime more clearly. In line with this, it is likely that respondents would want the current draft to specify exactly what was meant by the phrase "traded on a prescribed market". However, while section 118 of the Act gives the Treasury the power to prescribe which markets and which investments the market abuse regimes applies to, it does not give the Treasury the power to define the phrase "traded on", which is used in the Act itself. Under Section 157 of the Act the Financial Services Authority has the power to issue guidance on this issue (as on others), but in the event of any dispute final decisions on what is meant by "traded on" will be a matter for the Financial Services and Markets Tribunal.
>
> 9. We do not believe, however, that many disputes on this issue are likely. The Act does not require the behaviour itself to be behaviour that takes the form of trading on a prescribed market, and accordingly whether or not there has been trading on a prescribed market is not likely to be a central issue in most market abuse cases. The behaviour does have to be behaviour in relation to qualifying investments traded on a prescribed market, but in most cases there will be no dispute that the investments are so traded. If on the contrary there is no significant trading in the investments on a prescribed market, it seems unlikely that the behaviour would meet the tests for market abuse set out in Section 118 of the Act. The purpose of the Act is to enable action to be taken against anyone who abuses a prescribed market in a qualifying investment. However, if there is no trading in a particular investment on a prescribed market, it is difficult to see that there is much potential for abuse of the market.'[1]

[1] HM Treasury, Market Abuse: Prescribed Markets and Qualifying Investments, December 2000.

The regular user test

11.10   Central to the definition of market abuse is the effect of market abuse on the 'regular user' of the market—a reasonable person who regularly deals on that market in investments of the relevant kind (s 118(10)). At the Report Stage of the Bill, Lord McIntosh stated that—

> 'The hypothetical regular user addresses the question from the viewpoint of an impartial person who regularly uses the market. He does not decide whether there is a standard of behaviour reasonably expected of a person in the position of the alleged abuser by looking at the personal characteristics of the alleged abuser . . . He asks himself whether there is a standard of behaviour which a person in the position of the alleged abuser is reasonably expected to observe. If the answer is that there is no such standard, then the alleged abuser will not have engaged in market abuse.
>
> However, if the answer is that there is such a standard, then there will have been market abuse. But the question will turn in each case on whether an impartial regular user of the market would take the view that there is a reasonable expectation that a person in a particular position should not take advantage of that position to squeeze the market.'[1]

---

[1]   HL Report Stage, 21 March 2000, col 229.

11.11   The FSA has also reiterated its understanding of the importance of the concept of the 'regular user' of the markets as, effectively, the determinant of market abuse. As the FSA stated—

> 'A key determinant of whether or not behaviour constitutes market abuse will be the "regular user" test. This test, laid down in the Act, is a close relative of the courts' "reasonable man", or the woman on the Clapham Omnibus. The regular user is a "reasonable person who regularly deals on the market". For behaviour to count as abuse, it needs to correspond to one of the three descriptions of market abuse [specified in s 118][1] . . . and to fall below the standards reasonably expected by the regular user.'[2]

It is, therefore, important to any interpretation of Pt VIII to consider the effect that the behaviour would have on the 'regular user' of the relevant market. However, it is clear that the guidance from the FSA will be important[3] but the Tribunal will be the final arbiter of what that test means in practice.

1   See para 11.12.
2   FSA Press Release FSA/PN/098/2000, 25 July 2000. See also the FSA Handbook, Code of Market Conduct, MAR 1.2.
3   The FSA has set out its views in MAR 1.

The conditions

11.12 The conditions, one or more of which is satisfied for the behaviour to be regarded as market abuse are that—
— the behaviour is based on information which is not generally available to those using the market but which, if available to a regular user of the market would or would be likely to be regarded by him as relevant when deciding the terms on which transactions in investments should be effected (s 118(2)(a));[1]
— the behaviour is likely to give a regular user of the market a false or misleading impression as to the supply of or the demand for or as to the price or value of investments (s 118(2)(b));[2] or
— a regular user of the market would or would be likely to regard the behaviour as that which would or would be likely to distort the market in investments (s 118(2)(c)).[3]

1   See the FSA Handbook, Code of Market Conduct, MAR 1.4.
2   See MAR 1.5.
3   See MAR 1.6.

11.13 Behaviour is also within the scope of s 118 in relation to qualifying investments if it—
— occurs in relation to anything which is the subject matter or whose price or value is expressed by reference to the price or value of those qualifying investments; or
— occurs in relation to investments whose subject matter is those qualifying investments, whether or not those investments are qualifying investments (s 118(6)).

11.14 As a result, behaviour in relation to products which underlie qualifying investments, and derivatives of qualifying investments are also within the market abuse regime.[1]

1   See FSMA Explanatory Notes, para 226, and the FSA Handbook, Code of Market Conduct, MAR 1.11.6–1.11.11.

11.15 However, behaviour is not market abuse if it conforms with a rule made by the FSA which states that it does not amount to market abuse.

Generally available information

11.16 For information to be considered generally available, it must be information which can be obtained by research or analysis conducted by, or on behalf of, users of the market (s 118(7)). This is further amplified in the FSA's Market Conduct sourcebook which provides that information will be regarded as generally available if it—

(a) has been disclosed to a prescribed market through an accepted channel of information dissemination or otherwise under the rules of that market;

(b) is contained in information which is available from public records;

(c) is otherwise made public through the internet or some other publication or can be obtained by observation.[1]

---

[1] FSA Handbook, Code of Market Conduct MAR 1.4.5E.

Territorial scope

11.17 Only behaviour which occurs in the UK or which occurs in relation to qualifying instruments traded on a market to which s 118 applies situated in the UK or which is accessible electronically in the UK will be caught by the general definition in s 118 (s 118(5)). The Treasury stated that—

'. . . it is clear that the Act's aim of protecting prescribed markets in the UK would not be achieved if the market abuse provisions were confined solely to behaviour in the UK. Section 118(5) therefore makes clear that behaviour covered by the regime can include any behaviour in relation to qualifying investments traded on a prescribed market which is situated in the UK or electronically accessible in the UK.'[1]

---

[1] HM Treasury: Market Abuse: Prescribed Markets and Qualifying Investments, December 2000, para 11. See also comments, HC SC A, 2 November 1999 and the FSA Handbook, Code of Market Conduct, MAR 1.1.7.

11.18 In relation to the scope of these provisions, there was much debate regarding the markets which would be prescribed for the purposes of s 118(3) and the fact that behaviour abroad could be deemed to have an effect on a prescribed market which could lead to penalties under Pt VIII. Melanie Johnson in introducing these amendments said—

'[Section 118](3) will allow the Treasury to designate any market anywhere as a market that should be covered by the regime, although we are currently planning, as I mentioned, to prescribe only the six currently recognised UK investment exchanges. [Section 118](5) will cut back on the scope of those provisions . . . the only behaviour that will come under the scope of the regime, regardless of which markets are prescribed, is that which occurs in the UK or which has an effect on a market that is situated in the UK. If we designated an overseas market, [Section 118](5)(a) would allow us to take action when someone in the UK abused that market. That is a potentially useful power in this age of global markets and of increasing regulatory co-operation. We could not, in that situation, take action against someone overseas who abused an overseas market.

[Section 118](5)(b) involves the other side of the coin. It will allow the FSA to take action if someone overseas abuses a market that the Treasury has designated, but only when that market is situated in the UK. If someone in Monaco, for example, used privileged information to buy shares that were traded on the London Stock Exchange, he would fall within the scope of the regime.

There may be practical difficulties with taking action when a person is located overseas, but that is not a reason to exempt such behaviour. That is in line with the approach that was taken in section 47 of the Financial Services Act 1986, which relates to the criminal offence of market manipulation. It is worth noting that [our proposed changes to section 118] make it clear that if someone overseas acts in accordance with local rules, there is unlikely to be abuse. Such behaviour is likely to be in accordance with what the regular market user would expect from someone in their position in relation to the market.'[1]

---

[1]   HC SC A, 2 November 1999, col 679.

Prescribed markets

11.19   The Treasury expects the list of prescribed markets to change over time and is aware that—

'... at some future date situations will arise where a body meets the criteria for prescription but does not wish to apply for recognition as a recognised investment exchange. In those circumstances we would consider seeking to amend the order to add such a body to the list of prescribed markets.[1] The FSA is currently reviewing the regulatory requirements for alternative trading systems and when this framework is settled, we [will] consider whether the order should be extended explicitly to cover trading on such systems.'[2]

---

[1]   See the Financial Services and Markets Act 2000 (Prescribed Markets and Qualifying Investments) Order 2001, SI 2001/996, as amended by SI 2001/3681.
[2]   HM Treasury, Market Abuse: Prescribed Markets and Qualifying Investments, December 2000, para 14.

THE CODE

11.20   The backbone of the market abuse regime is the code which the FSA must prepare and issue giving guidance to those determining whether or not behaviour amounts to market abuse (s 119(1)).[1] This code may include descriptions of behaviour which, in the FSA's view, do or do not constitute market abuse and may specify the factors which are to be taken into account in determining whether market abuse has taken place (s 119(2)).

[1]   See the FSA Handbook, Code of Market Conduct, MAR 1.

11.21   The nature of the code, as opposed to provisions on the face of the Act itself, was also the subject of debate. Lord McIntosh said that—

> 'You do not need a code to tell you that buying or selling shares while in possession of inside information is likely to fall short of expected standards of behaviour unless there is a very good reason—for example, if circumstances forced the sale. Equally, you do not need a code to tell you that it is not market abuse if, say, a pension fund placing a big buy or sell order in the ordinary course of its business moves market prices. We have accepted that uncertainty exists at the margins. The purpose of the code is to provide greater certainty.
>
> Perhaps I may give the analogy of the Highway Code. The Highway Code gives people a better idea of what it means to drive with or without due care and attention. What it does not do is provide a template on which a decision can be made on whether in an individual case a charge should be brought of driving without due care and attention, or whether there should or should not be a conviction in the courts on that charge. The Highway Code provides assistance but not a definitive answer in any individual case; and it is not intended to do so.'[1]

[1]   HL Report Stage, 18 April 2000, col 682.

Effect of the code

11.22 Behaviour which the code indicates is not market abuse will not be market abuse for the purposes of FSMA 2000 (s 122(1)). Thus, where a person behaves in a manner which is described in the code (as current at the time the behaviour took place), as being behaviour which does not amount to market abuse, for the purposes of Pt VIII, that behaviour will not be taken as amounting to market abuse (s 122(1)). During the debates in the House of Lords, Lord McIntosh for the Government described the effect of s 122 as a 'safe harbour'—

> '. . . it is not, and never has been, our intention that behaviour in conformity with any completely unrelated FSA rules should protect a person against an allegation of market abuse. I do not believe that noble Lords opposite, or honourable Members of the Opposition, thought that that was the case. While we do not think that the provision would be read in this way, we are taking the opportunity to clarify the matter . . . But the protection in [Section 122] still provides a safe harbour[1] for behaviour conforming with rules such as price stabilisation rules.

> We are proposing that the protection should apply only where the rule in question states that behaviour conforming with it does not amount to market abuse. The obvious examples are rules on price stabilisation and Chinese walls, but the amendment deliberately gives the FSA the flexibility to specify other rules if that is appropriate.'[2]

---

[1]   See the FSA Handbook, Code of Market Conduct, MAR 1.1.10.
[2]   HL Committee Stage, 21 March 2000, col 228.

11.23 Beyond these 'safe harbour' provisions[1] the matters set out in the code (in force at the time of the behaviour) as indicators of the presence or absence of market abuse may be relied on as indicating whether the behaviour in question was market abuse (s 122(2)).

---

[1]   See the FSA Handbook, Code of Market Conduct, MAR 1.1.10.

Content of the code by reference to the City Code

11.24 FSMA 2000, s 120 provides that the FSA may include in the code provision that behaviour conforming with the City Code on Takeovers and Mergers (the City Code)[1] does not amount to—
 — market abuse,
 — market abuse in specific circumstances, or

— market abuse if engaged in by a specified description of person (s 120(1)).[2]

However, in doing so the FSA must obtain the Treasury's approval (s 120(2)) and must ensure that it is informed of the way in which the Panel on Takeovers and Mergers (the Takeover Panel) interprets and administers the City Code (s 120(3)).

---

[1]   As it has effect at the time of the behaviour in question (s 120(4)).

[2]   The FSA has specified safe harbours in relation to compliance with the City Code and the Substantial Acquisition Rules: see the FSA Handbook, Code of Market Conduct, MAR 1.7.4–1.7.13.

11.25 This provision, which marks a significant change in the relationship between the Takeover Panel and the FSA as principal regulator, provided one of the moments of high drama during the passage of the Bill as debate raged on the primacy of the Panel or the FSA in matters relating to market abuse. At the Commons consideration of the Lords amendments, David Heathcoat-Amory for the Opposition said—

'The key issue concerns the possible conflict—and certainly overlap—between the jurisdictions of the Financial Services Authority and the takeover panel. . . .

The FSA is charged with dealing with market abuse and the takeover panel regulates mergers and bids. . . .

The danger of overlap occurs in several areas. It must be objectionable in principle for someone to be vulnerable to double jeopardy. Someone abiding by one set of rules, published by the takeover panel, should not be vulnerable in relation to a second set of rules, published by a second regulator.

It must be bad for the market for uncertainties to develop about which regulator is responsible in each individual case. For instance, it would be dangerous if the FSA said that certain behaviour during a bid was abusive and the takeover panel said that it was not. Who would decide the outcome? If the matter went to appeal, it would certainly be very embarrassing if the court had to arbitrate between two different regulatory bodies. It is bad for the City and for the regulatory regime itself to have the possibility of conflict and overlap.

It must be recognised that parties to a bid can themselves seek to manipulate the regulatory process. Tactical litigation can be launched by the object of a bid in order to frustrate the whole process. The scope for that will be immeasurably greater if that party can appeal to the FSA outside the traditional authority of the takeover panel.

. . .

One can imagine a situation in which a hostile bidder for another company publishes a document in order to persuade independent shareholders to accept the bid. The hostile bidder might do that just before the expiry of the 60-day period. The target company might complain that the document was misleading in several material respects. At present, that issue would be considered immediately by the takeover panel, which has a reputation for dealing with such matters efficiently and swiftly, so the bid could proceed if the allegation were groundless.

However, under the Bill, the target company would be able to bring in the FSA to determine whether the behaviour in question was market abusive, and that would introduce a most unwelcome delay. Indeed, if that happened, the takeover panel might have to agree to extend the bid deadline, or, even more damagingly, one of the companies concerned could apply for judicial review, if the FSA refused to examine the issues and the particulars of the case. If that led to an injunction, it would cause unwelcome delay as well as introducing new and expensive litigation into a process that, until now, has always been dealt with swiftly and efficiently.

The Minister has not dealt with the point about delay and expense. However, she did recognise that the problem might exist. That is why, in the other place, my noble Friends succeeded in passing amendment No 180, which would provide a safe harbour. It would provide that, in a bid situation, if those concerned conformed to the City code as published by the takeover panel, that would be a safe harbour against allegations of market abuse. It is also important to recognise that, despite that provision, the FSA would remain the lead regulator and would be able to include conditions and limitations on the effect of that safe harbour. It would be the FSA that would issue a statement, modified as necessary, indicating conformity with the City code that would be a safe harbour against market abuse.'[1]

---

[1]   HC Consideration of Lords Amendments, 5 June 2000, col 91.

11.26   The code may also make different provisions for different persons, cases or circumstances (s 119(3)) and the FSA may alter or replace the code at any time (s 119(4)). The FSA must provide a copy of the code to the Treasury (s 119(7)) and also issue and publish it in a manner which will bring it to the attention of the public (s 119(5), (6)). The FSA may charge a fee for providing copies of the code (s 119(8)).

Procedures

11.27 Before issuing, altering or publishing a replacement code, the FSA must publish a draft for public consultation which must be accompanied by a cost benefit analysis and a notice that representations may be made within a specified time (s 121(1), (2), (9)).[1]

---
[1]   The FSA may charge a fee for copies of this draft (s 121(8)).

Cost benefit analysis

11.28 A cost benefit analysis means an estimate of the costs together with an analysis of the benefits which will result if the code is issued (s 121(10)).[1] A cost benefit analysis is not required if the FSA in making an appropriate comparison (as defined in s 121(11))[2] considers that the proposals will not result in increased costs or if any increase will be of minimal significance (s 121(7)).

---
[1]   This is the same test as applies for the FSA's general rule-making powers (see s 155(10)). However, in this case, the cost benefit analysis as set out in FSA CP 59, Market Abuse: A Draft Code of Market Conduct, July 2000, Annex C only dealt with matters arising from the code, whereas the Treasury published a separate cost benefit analysis in relation to the market abuse regime as a whole: see Annex B, the Financial Services and Markets Bill, Market Abuse: Prescribed Markets, HM Treasury Consultation Paper, June 1999.
[2]   This is in essence a comparison between the position without the proposals and that with them.

11.29 The FSA must take any representations made to it under s 121(2)(b) into account and if it decides to publish the code it must also give an account in general terms of the representations which it received and its response to them (s 121(3), (4)). If the code, as published, differs from that published for consultation, the FSA must publish details of the differences, with a cost benefit analysis of the proposed changes (s 121(5)).

11.30 These procedures may, however, be overridden if the FSA considers that there is an urgent need to publish or amend the code (s 121(6)).

POWER TO IMPOSE PENALTIES

11.31 If the FSA is satisfied that a person is or has engaged in market abuse, or by either taking or refraining from taking any action has required or encouraged another person to engage in behaviour which would constitute market abuse, it may impose a financial penalty on that person of an amount it thinks appropriate (s 123(1)).[1] Alternatively, it may choose to make a public statement to the effect that that person has engaged in market abuse (s 123(3)). The imposition of a penalty under Pt VIII does not, however, make any transaction void or unenforceable (s 131).

---

[1]   This section imposes no limits on the penalty, but the FSA would be required to comply with its policy on penalties set out in the FSA Handbook, Enforcement manual, ENF 14. The FSA's decision to impose a penalty would also be subject to referral to the Tribunal (see para 11.34) and would be ultimately referable to the courts by judicial review. Legal assistance would also be available to individuals for reference to the Tribunal (FSMA 2000, ss 136–138: see paras 11.54, 11.55).

11.32   However, if, after considering representations which have been made in response to a warning notice under s 126, the FSA believes that there are reasonable grounds for it to be satisfied that a person believed on reasonable grounds that his behaviour did not constitute market abuse or that he took all reasonable precautions and exercised all due diligence to avoid behaving in a manner which constituted market abuse, it may not impose a penalty on that person (s 123(2)). As Melanie Johnson commented—

> 'As I said, we believe that reasonable belief and due diligence are the right tests, and that intent and recklessness . . . are not the right tests. Let us suppose, for example, that we are dealing with a person who, not having bothered to make the inquiries that a reasonable person would have done, engages in behaviour that misleads the markets. It would be quite wrong for such a person to be given a blanket protection from the consequences of his actions, viewed from his own perspective.
>
> The appropriate question is not what a person thinks about his own actions—which, obviously, could vary widely between individuals, depending on their level of knowledge and experience—but whether the person can show reasonable grounds for believing that his action would not be regarded as abusive by a reasonable person who uses the market regularly, or that he took the precautions and displayed the diligence that a reasonable person would expect. Those are clear and proper protections.'[1]

---

[1]   HC Consideration of Lords Amendments, 5 June 2000, col 84.

WARNING NOTICES AND DECISION NOTICES

Warning notice

11.33   If the FSA proposes to impose a penalty on a person under s 123, it must serve a warning notice on that person (s 126(1)). Any warning notice given must include a statement of the amount of the proposed penalty (s 126(2)) or, if a statement is to be made instead, it must set out the terms of the proposed statement (s 126(3)).[1]

---

[1]   See para 8.10.

Decision notice

11.34   If the FSA decides to impose a penalty or issue a statement under s 123, it must give that person a decision notice (s 127(1)). This decision notice must state the amount of the penalty or set out the terms of the statement (s 127(2), (3)). The person concerned may, however, refer the matter to the Tribunal (s 127(4)).

STATEMENT OF POLICY ON PENALTIES

11.35   The FSA is required to publish a statement of its policy in relation to the imposition of penalties under s 123 and the amount of penalties to be imposed under that section (s 124(1)).[1] In deciding whether to exercise its powers under s 123, the FSA must have regard to the statement of policy under s 124 in force at the time when the behaviour concerned occurred (s 124(6)).

---

[1]   The FSA must provide a copy of any policy published under s 124 to the Treasury without delay (s 124(9)). The FSA's policy is set out in the FSA Handbook, Enforcement manual, ENF 14.

11.36   The policy adopted by the FSA must ensure that any decision on a penalty for market abuse will have regard to whether the behaviour had an adverse effect on the market in question and if so, how serious that effect was, the extent to which the behaviour was deliberate or reckless, and whether the person on whom the penalty is to be imposed is an individual (s 124(2)).

11.37   The policy statement must also contain an indication of the circumstances in which the FSA expects to regard a person as having acted in the reasonable belief that his behaviour did not amount to market abuse or as having taken reasonable precautions and exercised due diligence to avoid engaging in market abuse (s 124(3)).[1]

---

[1]   Section 123(2), which creates this defence, refers to 'all reasonable precautions' and 'all due diligence'.

Procedure

11.38   The FSA must publish a draft of the proposed statement in the way best calculated to bring it to the attention of the public, accompanied by a notice inviting representations to be made to it within the time specified (s 125(1), (2)). The FSA may charge a fee for providing copies of the draft statement to persons requesting it (s 125(6)).[1]

---

[1]   This procedure also applies to any proposals to alter or replace the statement (s 125(7)): see para 11.40.

11.39   In issuing a statement the FSA must have regard to any representations received and must publish an account of those representations and its response to them (s 125(3), (4)). If the FSA proposes to issue a statement which is significantly different from the draft which was originally published, it must, in addition to publishing this report, publish details of the differences (s 125(5)).[1]

---

[1]   This procedure also applies to any proposals to alter or replace the statement (s 125(7)): see para 11.40.

11.40   The FSA may alter or replace the statement of policy (s 124(4)) and it must be issued by the FSA in the way best calculated to bring it to the attention of the public (s 124(5), (7)). The FSA must give a copy to the Treasury (s 124(9)) and may charge a reasonable fee to persons requesting a copy of this statement (s 124(8)).

GUIDANCE

11.41   The Treasury may also from time to time issue guidance to the Secretary of State, the FSA, the Director of the Serious Fraud Office and the Director of Public Prosecutions.[1] The purpose of this guidance is to help them determine what action should be taken in cases where the behaviour is subject to the exercise of the FSA's powers under s 123 and appears to involve the commission of an offence under FSMA 2000, s 397[2] or under the Criminal Justice Act 1993, Pt V (s 130(1)).[3] Before issuing such guidance, the Treasury must, however, obtain the consent of the Attorney General and the Secretary of State (s 130(2)). In moving the Government's amendment to the Bill, Lord McIntosh said that the Government viewed this—

> 'very much [as] a reserve power. We do not envisage formal guidance being given as a matter of course for any part of the UK when the Bill comes into force. Only if the agencies concerned could not agree among themselves how to handle particular cases would we expect guidance to be given. But I stress that we have no reason to believe that such a situation is likely to arise.'[4]

[1]   Or in Northern Ireland, the Secretary of State, the FSA, the Director of the Serious Fraud Office and the Director of Public Prosecutions for Northern Ireland (s 130(3)).
[2]   In relation to false or misleading statements.
[3]   In relation to the offence of insider dealing.
[4]   HL Committee Stage, 21 March 2000, col 257.

Scotland

11.42 The Treasury power to issue guidelines in s 130 does not apply to Scotland but the Lord Advocate may consult with the Treasury and issue written guidance to help the FSA determine the action to be taken in relation to offences under s 130(1) (s 130(4), (5)).

SUSPENSION OF INVESTIGATIONS

11.43 If the FSA considers it desirable or expedient to do so because of the exercise or possible exercise of its powers to impose a penalty under s 123 or to appoint a person to investigate any alleged market abuse under s 168 in relation to market abuse, it may direct a recognised investment exchange or recognised clearing house to terminate, suspend or limit the scope of any inquiry which it may be conducting under its rules, or direct it not to conduct such an inquiry under its rules (s 128(1), (3)).[1]

[1]   See also the 'operating guidelines' between the FSA and the recognised investment exchanges on market misconduct at www.fsa.gov.uk/pubs/other/market_conduct.

11.44 A direction under s 128 must be given to the exchange or clearing house concerned in writing, and is enforceable on the application of the FSA by injunction or, in Scotland, an order made under the Court of Session Act 1988, s 45 (s 128(2)).

INJUNCTIONS

11.45 FSMA 2000, s 381 provides that the FSA may apply to the court[1] for an injunction[2] if the court is satisfied that there is a reasonable likelihood that any person will engage in market abuse or if any person is or has engaged in market abuse and that market abuse would continue or be repeated (s 381(1)).[3]

---

[1]   The 'court' means the High Court or, in Scotland, the Court of Session (s 381(5)).
[2]   A restraining order or, in Scotland, an interdict prohibiting the abuse (s 381(1)).
[3]   See paras 2.67–2.69.

11.46 The court may also make an order requiring any person who is engaging in or has engaged in market abuse, if there are steps which could be taken to remedy that market abuse or mitigate its effect (s 381(6)), to take such steps as directed (s 381(2)).

11.47 The court may also make an order[1] restraining or prohibiting any person from disposing of or dealing in assets if he may be engaged in or may have been engaged in market abuse, and the court is satisfied that he is reasonably likely to dispose of or deal with those assets (s 381(3), (4)).

---

[1]   A restraining order or, in Scotland, an interdict prohibiting such disposal or dealing.

RESTITUTION ORDERS

11.48 On the application of the FSA a court[1] may make an order under s 383(4) if a person has engaged in market abuse or has taken or refrained from taking any action which required or encouraged another person to engage in behaviour which constitutes market abuse (s 383(1)). The court may order the person to pay to the FSA such sum as appears just to the court taking into account whether profits have accrued to the person as a result of that behaviour, or a loss or other adverse effect was suffered as a result, and the court may consider the amount of those profits or the extent of the loss or other adverse effect (s 383(4)). The court may only make such a restitution order if profits have accrued to the person concerned as a result of his behaviour or if one or more persons have suffered a loss or otherwise been adversely affected by that behaviour (s 383(2)).

---

[1]   The court means the High Court or, in Scotland, the Court of Session (s 383(8)).

11.49 The making of a restitution order under s 383 does not, however, affect the rights which any person may have to bring proceedings in relation to behaviour which would constitute market abuse (s 383(9)).

11.50 The court may not, however, make such a restitution order if it is satisfied that the person believed on reasonable grounds that his behaviour did not amount to market abuse under s 383(1) or he took all reasonable precautions and exercised all due diligence to avoid behaving in a way which would amount to market abuse (s 383(3)).

11.51 Where the FSA has applied for an order under s 383, the court may require any person concerned to supply it with such accounts or other information as it may require for any one or more of the following purposes—
— establishing whether any and what profits accrued to that person;
— establishing whether any person or persons suffered a loss or adverse effect as a result of that behaviour and the extent of that loss or adverse effect; and
— determining how these amounts should be paid or distributed (s 383(6)).

The court may also require that any accounts or other information which have been provided to it under this section be verified in a manner which the court may direct (s 383(7)).

11.52 The FSA must pay any amount paid to it as a result of a restitution order made under FSMA 2000, s 383 to such persons as the court may direct, being either the person or persons to whom the profits are attributable as a result of the behaviour which amounted to market abuse, or who has suffered the loss or adverse effect as a result of such behaviour (s 383(5), (10)).

Court's power to impose penalty

11.53 Where the FSA has applied to the court under s 381 or 383, it may request the court to consider whether a penalty should be imposed on the person in respect of whom the application has been made (s 129(1)). The court may make an order requiring the person concerned to pay to the FSA a penalty of such amount as it considers appropriate (s 129(2)).

LEGAL ASSISTANCE IN MARKET ABUSE CASES

11.54 To address some of the concerns regarding the potential cost of obtaining legal assistance in matters referred to the Tribunal, and to address concerns about the impact of the European Convention on Human Rights (ECHR) on FSMA 2000, the Government proposed a stand-alone legal assistance scheme, separate from existing schemes for legal aid, which is to be administered by the Court Service.

11.55 FSMA 2000, s 134 provides that the Lord Chancellor may make regulations establishing a scheme to provide legal assistance in connection with proceedings before the Tribunal (s 134(1)).[1] Section 134(3) expressly provides that this scheme may be available to provide assistance to individuals who choose to refer a case involving a penalty for market abuse to the Tribunal (s 134(2)(a), (3)). It will, however, be subject to both a means test and an interests of justice test and eligibility under both those tests will be determined by the Tribunal.[2]

---

[1]   See paras 12.30–12.32. See also Lord Chancellor's Department CP, Financial Services and Markets Tribunal Consultation on Draft Rules, Explanatory Note, January 2001.
[2]   See HC SC A, 2 November 1999 and HL Committee Stage, 21 March 2000, cols 263, 264.

11.56 Whether proceedings are truly 'criminal' or 'civil' in character[1] for ECHR purposes may be relevant to issues other than the availability of legal assistance. If the courts were to conclude that market abuse proceedings are in substance criminal, the legal assistance scheme is likely to satisfy the extended requirements of Art 6(3).[2] But such a conclusion would raise two further, unresolved issues of compatibility with ECHR. The first is whether the 'offence' is defined with sufficient precision to satisfy the 'no punishment without law' requirement of Art 7. It is more likely than not that the 'regular user' test, supplemented by the FSA's Code of Market Conduct,[3] complies with the standard of predictability imposed on the criminal law by the European Court of Human Rights, and this is partly reinforced by the decision in *R (on the application of Fleurose) v Securities and Futures Authority Ltd* in relation to the pre-N2 SIB principles. But it could still be the subject of litigation. Secondly, the principle that a first instance procedure falling short of Art 6 standards may be saved from incompatibility by an adequate appeal process[4] is generally confined to civil cases. Where a person faces a criminal charge, the *first instance* determination of guilt or innocence should in principle satisfy the requirement of a fair and public hearing before an independent and impartial tribunal.[5] Hence there may remain a question of whether the right of appeal to the Tribunal against a 'conviction' following the paper procedure under ss 126 and 127 is adequate despite the Tribunal's broad jurisdiction.[6]

1   See paras 2.111 and 11.5.
2   To date, proceedings under the Company Directors Disqualification Act 1986 have been characterised as 'civil' despite their penal element: *Re Westminster Property Management Ltd* [2001] 1 All ER 633, [2000] 1 WLR 2230, CA, but proceedings on a 'civil' penalty for VAT evasion have been deemed criminal: *Han and Yau* v *Customs and Excise Comrs* [2000] V & DR 312.
3   FSA Handbook, Code of Market Conduct, MAR.
4   See para 8.25.
5   See for example, *Findlay* v *United Kingdom* (1997) 24 EHRR 221.
6   The English courts have suggested that the appeal process must be capable of *directly* remedying the infringement of Art 6 at first instance: see *R (on the application of Shields)* v *Crown Court at Liverpool* [2001] EWHC Admin 90, Divisional Court.

12 The Tribunal—hearings and appeals

THE FINANCIAL SERVICES AND MARKETS TRIBUNAL

12.1 A key feature of the new regulatory regime under the Financial Services and Markets Act 2000 (FSMA 2000) is the creation of the Financial Services and Markets Tribunal (the Tribunal) (s 132(1)) which is responsible for carrying out the functions in FSMA 2000, Pt IX[1] including the determination of references made to it under the various provisions of the Act.[2] The Tribunal is subject to the supervision of the Council on Tribunals under the Tribunals and Inquiries Act 1992.[3]

---

[1] References in s 132 to FSMA 2000 are to be read as including references to the Electronic Commerce Directive (Financial Services and Markets) Regulations 2002, SI 2002/1775, reg 12(3)(c).

[2] FSA CP 17 Response, July 1999, paras 2–5 set out a history of the development of the Tribunal and its procedures. See also Joint Committee, First Report, Appendix 9 and HM Treasury Response to the First Report, Pt V, on the amendments introduced by the Government concerning the Tribunal, its constitution and procedures. For further background on this Part of FSMA 2000, see also HC SC A, 4 November 1999; HL 3R, 18 May 2000, col 424; HL Report Stage, 18 April 2000, col 685.

[3] FSMA Explanatory Notes, para 240. On 11 March 2003, the Lord Chancellor's Department (now the Department of Constitutional Affairs) announced a major overhaul of the Tribunals Service. However, the Financial Services Tribunal is not one of those being included in the scheme: see Lord Chancellor's Department Press Release PN/106/03, 11 March 2003.

References to the Tribunal

12.2 A reference to the Tribunal[1] must be made before the end of a 28-day period[2] beginning with the date on which the decision notice or supervisory notice in question is given or within such other period as may be specified in rules under FSMA 2000, s 132 (s 133(1)). The rules made under s 132 may provide, however, that the Tribunal may still allow a reference made after the end of this period (s 133(2)).

---

[1] References to the Tribunal may be made under the following sections of FSMA 2000: 53(7), 55(1), (2), 57(5), 58(5), 62(4), 63(5), 67(7), 76(6), 77(5), 78(6), (12), 88(7), 89(4), 92(7), 127(4), 185(7), 186(5), 187(4), 197(8), 200(5)(b), 208(4), 245(2)(b), 252(4), 255(2), 256(5), 260(2)(b), 262, 268(4)(e), (10), 269(3), 271(3)(b), 276(2)(b), 280(2)(b), 282(3), (4), (6), (8), (10), 300(1), 320(4), 321(11), 331(9), 345(5), 386(3), 388(5), 393(9), (11) and Sch 3, para 20(4A).

EXTENSION OF THE TRIBUNAL'S FUNCTIONS IN RELATION TO DISCIPLINARY PROCEEDINGS

Recognised investment exchanges and clearing houses

12.3   The Treasury may extend the functions of the Tribunal in respect of disciplinary proceedings of recognised investment exchanges and clearing houses (s 300). In introducing this measure, Lord McIntosh set out the Government's intention as follows—

> 'If a person who is a member of a recognised investment exchange or recognised clearing house engages in behaviour which amounts to market abuse under [section 123], it is likely that this will also constitute a breach of the rules of the recognised body concerned. Rather than taking market abuse proceedings, the FSA might leave this to be dealt with as an internal disciplinary matter. In many cases, the recognised bodies might be best placed to take such action, as the bodies closest to the markets. That is right, but when it is the case, the person disciplined would not have the right to refer the matter to an independent tribunal as he would if it had been dealt with by the FSA under [section 123]. The problem with this is that it is conceivable that inconsistency might develop over time between the way such cases are dealt with by recognised bodies as compared with the tribunal. It might; I am not saying that it will but there is a possibility. . . . We are confident that all the provisions of the Bill are consistent with the provisions of the Human Rights Act 1998 and the European Convention on Human Rights. But it is possible that at some point in the future, developments in the courts' jurisprudence on these matters might require us to provide for an appeal from the internal disciplinary procedures of recognised bodies in market abuse cases to a body such as the tribunal established by the Bill.'[1]

---

1   HL 3R, 18 May 2000, col 430.

12.4   Section 300 provides that if the Treasury considers it desirable, it may by order confer powers on the Tribunal (s 300(1)). Before doing so, the Treasury must be satisfied that this is desirable to ensure that decisions taken in disciplinary proceedings relating to market abuse (s 300(4)) by a recognised investment exchange or clearing house are consistent with—

—   decisions of the Tribunal in cases arising under FSMA 2000, Pt VIII; and

—   decisions taken in other disciplinary proceedings with respect to which the Tribunal has functions (s 300(2)(a)),

or to ensure that the disciplinary proceedings are in accordance with the European Convention on Human Rights (ECHR) (s 300(2)(b)). An order made under s 300 may modify or exclude any provision made by or under FSMA 2000 with respect to Tribunal proceedings (s 300(3)).

STAY OF DECISIONS PENDING DETERMINATION OF REFERENCE

12.5   The FSA must not take the action specified in a decision notice during the period within which the matter may be referred to the Tribunal. If the matter is referred, the FSA may not take the action specified until the reference and any appeal against the Tribunal's determination have been finally disposed of (s 133(9)).[1]

---

[1]   See recent Financial Services and Markets Tribunal cases *HPA Services v Financial Services Authority*, Decision 2003/005, and *Eurosure Investment Services Ltd v Financial Services Authority*, Decision 2003/006, in relation to the Tribunal's power to stay decisions pending determination of a reference.

CONSTITUTION AND COMPOSITION OF THE TRIBUNAL

12.6   The Tribunal has the functions conferred on it by or under FSMA 2000 (s 132(2)).[1] FSMA 2000, Sch 13 sets out the constitution of and procedures to be followed by the Tribunal. However, the Lord Chancellor may generally make rules in relation to these (s 132(3)), which are not limited by the provisions set out in Sch 13 (s 132(4)).

291

The panel of chairmen and the lay panel

12.7   Members of the Tribunal are appointed by the Lord Chancellor to a panel consisting of certain persons who appear to him to be qualified by experience or otherwise to deal with the kind of matters referred to the Tribunal (Sch 13, para 3(4)). This panel is referred to as the 'lay panel' (Sch 13, para 1). There is also a separate 'panel of chairmen' (Sch 13, para 1) appointed by the Lord Chancellor for the purposes of serving as chairmen of the Tribunal (Sch 13, para 3(1)). The members of the panel of chairmen must be legally qualified persons with at least seven years' general qualification within the meaning of the Courts and Legal Services Act 1990, s 71 or must be an advocate or solicitor in Scotland, a member of the Bar of Northern Ireland or a solicitor of the Supreme Court of Northern Ireland, all of at least seven years' standing (Sch 13, para 3(2)).[1]

1   At least one member of the panel of chairmen must be qualified in this way (Sch 13, para 3(3)).

12.8   The membership of these panels appears to be flexible as FSMA 2000 allows the Lord Chancellor to define the scope and set the terms on which each member of the panel of chairmen and the lay panel is to hold or vacate office (Sch 13, para 4(1)). The Lord Chancellor may remove a member of either the panel of chairmen or the lay panel (including the President) on grounds of incapacity or misbehaviour and members of either panel may at any time resign by giving notice in writing to the Lord Chancellor. A member of either panel may be eligible for re-appointment if he ceases to hold office (Sch 13, para 4(2), (3)). The members of the panels, including the President, the Deputy President and any of the experts appointed to provide assistance to the Tribunal under Sch 13, para 7(4) are remunerated from funds held by the Lord Chancellor's Department (Sch 13, paras 5, 6(3)).

President and Deputy President

12.9   The Tribunal itself is to be presided over by a President, appointed by the Lord Chancellor from the panel of chairmen, whose role it is to preside over the discharge of the Tribunal's functions (Sch 13, para 2(1), (2)). The Lord Chancellor may also appoint a Deputy President from the panel of chairmen (Sch 13, para 2(3)). Those persons eligible for the role of President or Deputy President must be legally qualified and have at least ten years' general qualification within the meaning of the Courts and Legal Services Act 1990, s 71, be an advocate or solicitor in Scotland, a member of the Bar of Northern Ireland or a solicitor of the Supreme Court of Northern Ireland, all of at least ten years' standing (Sch 13, para 2(5)). If the President or Deputy President ceases to be a member of the panel of chairmen, he will also cease to be the President or Deputy President as the case may be (Sch 13, para 2(6)).

12.10 The Deputy President is to have responsibility for such functions in relation to the Tribunal as the President may assign to him. If the President is absent or otherwise unable to act, the functions of the President may be discharged by the Deputy President or any other person appointed from the panel of chairmen by the Lord Chancellor for that purpose (Sch 13, para 2(4), (7)). The Lord Chancellor may appoint staff for the Tribunal and their remuneration and the expenses of the Tribunal are to be met by the Lord Chancellor's Department (Sch 13, para 6).

Composition: standing arrangements for selection

12.11 When a matter is referred to the Tribunal, the persons who are to act as the members of the panel for that reference are selected from the panel of chairmen or the lay panel in accordance with the Tribunal's 'standing arrangements'. Under these at least one member of each Tribunal must be selected from the panel of chairmen (Sch 13, para 7(1), (2)). If any member of the Tribunal in respect of a specific reference becomes unable to act, then the other selected members may deal with the reference or, if a matter is being dealt with by a single member, a replacement may be selected from the panel of chairmen in accordance with the standing arrangements (Sch 13, para 7(3)).

Composition: independence and impartiality

12.12 The provisions for appointing the Tribunal and the standing arrangements for selection should be sufficient to ensure that the Tribunal complies with the requirement in ECHR, Art 6(1) of an independent tribunal for determining civil rights and obligations. Bearing in mind the Human Rights Act 1998, s 3, any purported appointment on terms failing to ensure adequate independence would probably be ultra vires. The requirement of an impartial tribunal, and the (broadly) equivalent domestic rule against bias, will apply to the selection of members under FSMA 2000, Sch 13, para 7.

TRIBUNAL PROCEDURE

12.13   The Tribunal must sit at such times and in such place as the Lord
Chancellor may direct (Sch 13, para 8). Rules made by the Lord
Chancellor under FSMA 2000, s 132 concerning the Tribunal may
include provision for—
—   the manner in which references are to be instituted;
—   the holding of hearings in private in circumstances specified in
    the rules;
—   the persons who may appear on behalf of the parties;
—   the suspension of decisions of the FSA which have taken
    effect;
—   the manner in which references may be withdrawn; and
—   the registration, publication and proof of decisions and orders
    of the Tribunal (Sch 13, para 9).

These rules may also make provision for regulating or prescribing
matters incidental to or consequential on an appeal from the Tribunal
to the courts on a point of law under FSMA 2000, s 137 (s 137(6)).
The President may also give directions as to the practice and
procedure of the Tribunal in references made to it (Sch 13, para 10).

12.14   The Financial Services and Markets Tribunal Rules 2001,[1] (the Tribunal
Rules) apply to all references to the Tribunal (r 3). They require the
reference to the Tribunal to be made in writing, stating the issues
concerning the relevant notice served by the FSA which the applicant
wishes the Tribunal to consider (r 4(1), (3)). However, the applicant is
not required to produce a full reply (though he is obliged to file a copy
of the notice to which the referral relates—r 4(5)) until after the FSA has
filed and served its statement of case in support of the action being
referred to the Tribunal (rr 5, 6). In each case the statement of case must
set out the matters relied on and be accompanied by a list of the
documents relied on by that party (rr (3), 6(3)). There are further
disclosure provisions under which the FSA is obliged to provide a
further list of documents which might reasonably be expected to
further the applicant's case (r 7(1)), and provides for certain materials to
be exempt from disclosure (r 8). Although there is no exemption from
disclosure of materials to which legal privilege attaches, they do not
have to be produced (r 8(8) applying to 'protected items' as defined by
FSMA 2000, s 413). Once a matter has been referred to the Tribunal,
the FSA must file a copy of any further notice which it gives the
applicant in relation to the referred action (r 11).

---

[1]   SI 2001/2476.

12.15   The Tribunal Rules give power to the Tribunal to give directions to
enable the parties to prepare for the hearing, to assist the Tribunal to
determine the issues and generally to ensure the just, expeditious and

economical determination of the matter (r 9(1)). Directions may be given on the application of any party (the applicant can make an application when filing the reference notice—r 4(6)) or on the Tribunal's own initiative (r 9(2)). There is provision for application notices and for representations to be made by the parties, and also for a pre-hearing review to give directions and to clarify the issues (r 9(3)–(12)), as well as particular powers for particular circumstances (see r 10).

12.16 In general the Tribunal hearings are held in public (r 17(2)), but there are occasions when they are not. In limited circumstances, notably when the parties agree or in relation to an application for directions, the Tribunal may determine all or a part of a matter which is referred to it without an oral hearing (r 16(1)). In addition r 17(3)–(5) sets out a procedure under which the parties may invite the Tribunal to direct that all or part of a hearing is to be in private. If the parties do not all apply, then the Tribunal can so direct if it is satisfied that a private hearing is necessary, having regard to public order, national security, the parties' private lives, unfairness to the application or prejudice to the interests of consumers (r 17(3)).[1] If the Tribunal does direct that a hearing is to take place in private, it may also direct that details of that hearing are not to be made available to the public through the register of references and hearings (rr 4(9), 17(10), (11)).[2] Whether or not the hearing is held in public, the Tribunal has power to exclude anyone whose conduct has disrupted or is likely to disrupt the hearing (r 17(9)).

---

[1] The Tribunal has indicated that reputational damage to the person making the reference is unlikely to be sufficient in itself to meet the 'necessary' test in the rule: *Eurolife Assurance Co Ltd v Financial Services Authority*, Decision 2002/001. Reports of Tribunal judgments can be found at www.financeandtaxtribunals.gov.uk/decisions/seldecisions/financialservices.htm.
[2] See also the power in r 10(1)(p), (9).

12.17 The Tribunal has a wide discretion about the conduct of its hearings, though, subject to directions from the Tribunal, the parties are entitled to give evidence (including expert evidence with the leave of the Tribunal), to call and question witnesses and to address the Tribunal about the evidence or otherwise on the matter referred to the Tribunal (r 19(1), (2)). At the hearing the parties are entitled to represent themselves (with assistance from any person) or to have any other person represent them, whether or not legally qualified (r 18(1)), subject to the Tribunal's power to refuse that person's presence if the Tribunal is satisfied that there are good reasons to do so (r 18(2)).

Evidence before the Tribunal

12.18 The Tribunal may consider any evidence whether or not it was available to the FSA at the material time (s 133(3)) and whether or not it would be admissible in a court of law (r 19(3)). Under FSMA 2000, the

Tribunal may summon any person to give evidence or to produce such documents as are in his custody or under his control which the Tribunal considers it necessary to examine (Sch 13, para 11(1)). Rule 12 provides for the details of the summons procedure. The rule restates the power in Sch 13, para 11 and imposes time limits for service of summonses (r 12(3)) and the tendering of expenses if the witness has to travel more than 16 kilometres from his place of residence (r 12(5)). The rule also permits witnesses not to produce documents which the Tribunal is satisfied are protected items or items subject to an exemption under r 8(1), (2) or (4) (r 12(2)), though it is not beyond doubt that the rule purports to require production of a protected item to the Tribunal to allow it to satisfy itself of the correct claim for that status, which would seem to be contrary to the absolute prohibition in FSMA 2000, s 413). Summonses must include a warning about the penalties for non-compliance (r 12(4)) but may be varied or set aside by the Tribunal (r 12(6)).

12.19   The Tribunal may also take evidence on oath and administer oaths for that purpose or require the person being examined to make and subscribe a declaration of the truth of the matters to be examined (Sch 13, para 11(2)). A person is guilty of an offence if, without reasonable excuse, he refuses or fails to attend following the issue of a summons by the Tribunal, or refuses or fails to give evidence (Sch 13, para 11(3)(a)) or alters, suppresses, conceals or destroys or refuses to produce a document which he is required to produce for the Tribunal (Sch 13, para 11(3)(b)). A person who is convicted of an offence under para 11(3)(a) may be subject to a fine, and in relation to an offence under para 11(3)(b) may be liable to a fine or imprisonment for up to two years, or both a fine and imprisonment (Sch 13, para 11(4), (5)).

Directions by the Tribunal

12.20   For each reference the Tribunal must determine what action, if any, is appropriate for the FSA to take in relation to the matter referred to the Tribunal (s 133(4)).[1] Having determined the matter the Tribunal must remit the matter to the FSA with directions for giving effect to its determination (s 133(5)). The FSA must act in accordance with the Tribunal's determination and any direction given by it, and an order made by the Tribunal may be enforced as it if were an order of a county court or, in Scotland, an order of the Court of Session (s 133(10), (11)).[2]

---

[1]   These provisions have been modified for certain references concerning banking and building society contraventions before 'N2' (1 December 2001): see the Financial Services and Markets Act 2000 (Transitional Provisions and Savings) (Civil Remedies, Discipline, Criminal Offences etc) (No 2) Order 2001, SI 2001/3083, arts 10(6) and 11(6).

[2]   Reports of Tribunal judgments can be found at: www.financeandtaxtribunals.gov.uk/decisions/seldecisions/financialservices.htm.

12.21   In the case of a reference made as a result of a decision notice the Tribunal may not direct the FSA to take any action which the FSA would not as a result of s 388(2) have had the power to take when giving the decision notice which was referred (s 133(6)).

12.22   Similarly, having determined a reference under a supervisory notice,[1] the Tribunal may not direct the FSA to take any action which would otherwise have triggered the obligation to give a decision notice (s 133(7)). In giving directions, the Tribunal may make recommendations as to the FSA's regulating provisions or its procedures (s 133(8)).

---

[1]   As defined in FSMA 2000, s 395(13), a supervisory notice is one given under s 53(4), (7) or (8)(b), 78(2) or (5), 197(3), (6) or (7)(b), 259(3), (8) or (9)(b), 268(3), 7(a) or (9)(a) (as a result of s 268(8)(b)), 282(3), (6) or (7)(b) or 321(2) or (5)).

APPEALS FROM DECISIONS OF THE TRIBUNAL

12.23   Where a party to a reference to the Tribunal has 'permission', it may appeal to the Court of Appeal or, in Scotland, to the Court of Session on a point of law arising from a decision of the Tribunal on that reference (s 137(1)). Permission may be given by the Tribunal or by the Court of Appeal or, in Scotland, by the Court of Session (s 137(2)).[1]

---

[1]   See also the Tribunal Rules, rr 23 and 24. The Tribunal also has power to review its own decisions if it is satisfied that its decision was wrongly made as a result of an error by Tribunal staff or if there is new evidence available since the hearing of the matter, the existence of which could not reasonably have been known of or foreseen (Tribunal Rules, r 22).

12.24   If the court considers that the decision of the Tribunal was wrong in law, the court may remit the matter to the Tribunal for rehearing and determination or make a determination itself (s 137(3)). An appeal may only be brought from a decision of the Court of Appeal with the leave of the Court of Appeal or the House of Lords or, if the appeal lies in respect of the Court of Session, with the leave of the Court of Session or the House of Lords.[1] Leave to appeal in these circumstances may be given on such terms as to costs, expenses or otherwise as the Court of Session or the House of Lords may determine (s 137(5)). The rules to be made by the Lord Chancellor under FSMA 2000, s 132 may also make provision for regulating or prescribing matters incidental to or consequential on an appeal under s 137 (s 137(6)).[2]

---

[1]   See *R (on the application of Davies) v Financial Services Authority* [2003] EWCA Civ 1128, [2003] All ER (D) 517 (Jul).
[2]   The Tribunal Rules themselves apply as appropriate to any remitted reference (r 25).

Judicial review

12.25   A decision of the FSA, or conceivably a decision of the Tribunal itself, might exceptionally be amenable to judicial review in a case where the statutory appeal route would for some reason be inappropriate or ineffective.[1]

---

[1]   See *R (on the application of Davies) v Financial Services Authority* [2003] EWCA Civ 1128, [2003] All ER (D) 517 (Jul), also *R v Falmouth and Truro Port Health Authority, ex p South West Water* [2001] QB 445, [2000] 3 All ER 306, CA.

Decisions

12.26   Decisions of the Tribunal may be taken by a majority (Sch 13, para 12(1)) but the decision must state whether it was unanimous or taken by a majority of the members of the relevant panel. It must be recorded in a document containing a statement of the reasons for the decision and signed and dated by the member of the panel of chairmen dealing with the reference (Sch 13, para 12(2)). Parties to a reference before the Tribunal must be informed of its decision and as soon as reasonably practical after a decision is made a copy of the decision must be sent to each party and if different, to each authorised person concerned, as well as to the Treasury (Sch 13, para 12(3), (4)).

12.27   Ordinarily the Tribunal's decisions (presumably also including the reasons for those decisions) must be pronounced in public, orally or by publishing written decisions (r 20(1)). The decisions and the reasons for them must be entered on the Tribunal register (r 20(5)). However, the Tribunal may (if all or part of the hearing was held in private) decide to take steps to restrict what is made public about the decision. The Tribunal may anonymise the decision, edit it or decline to publish all or part of it (r 20(2), (3)). Before taking any of those steps, however, it must invite the parties to the reference to make representations on the matter (r 20(4)). Similar principles apply when the Tribunal determines a reference without an oral hearing under r 16 (r 16(2)–(4)).

12.28   If a reference is withdrawn or the FSA does not oppose or withdraws its opposition to the reference, the Tribunal may determine the reference (r 14(1), (2)). The Tribunal can also determine a reference for breaches of time limits for filing statements of case without an oral hearing (r 14(3)), but may not dismiss a reference without giving the applicant an opportunity to make representations (r 14(3)).

Award of costs

12.29   The Tribunal is only able to award costs against a party to any proceedings on a reference if that party has acted 'vexatiously, frivolously or unreasonably' (Sch 13, para 13(1)). The Tribunal may also award costs against the FSA if it considers that its decision was unreasonable (Sch 13, para 13(2)). This represents a substantial change to the provisions in rulebooks of the relevant self-regulating organisations under the FSA 1986 regime which only permit recovery of costs by defendants where proceedings have been thought unnecessary. The Tribunal is not permitted to make an award of costs under these provisions without giving the party who would be required to pay an opportunity to make representations against the making of the order (r 21(2)). If it does decide to make an order, it may award a fixed sum or award costs to be assessed or taxed by an appropriate court officer on a basis which the Tribunal specifies (r 21(3)). The Tribunal may exercise its power to award costs in references which are withdrawn or unopposed or dismissed for failure to comply with time limits (r 14(4)).

THE LEGAL ASSISTANCE SCHEME

12.30 The Lord Chancellor may make regulations establishing a scheme for providing legal assistance in connection with market abuse proceedings before the Tribunal (s 134(1)). A person is only eligible for such assistance if he is an individual who has referred a matter to the Tribunal under FSMA 2000, s 127(4) and who fulfils any other criteria to be specified in the scheme under s 135 (s 134(2), (3)). Under s 135, the scheme may make provision as to—

— the kinds of legal assistance that may be provided;
— the persons by whom legal assistance may be provided;
— the manner in which applications for legal assistance are to be made;
— the criteria for determining eligibility for legal assistance;
— the persons or bodies by whom applications for legal assistance are to be determined;
— the process for appeals against refusals of applications for legal assistance;
— the revocation or variation of decisions relating to legal assistance; and
— the administration and enforcement of the scheme (s 135(1)).

In addition, the scheme rules may provide that legal assistance is provided subject to various conditions or restrictions including the making of contributions by the person to whom legal assistance is being provided (s 135(2)).[1]

---

[1] The Financial Services and Markets Tribunal (Legal Assistance) Regulations 2001, SI 2001/3632 implement the scheme for market abuse cases.

Funding the scheme

12.31 This scheme is to be funded indirectly through the industry in that under FSMA 2000 the FSA must pay to the Lord Chancellor such sums as he may direct for the anticipated or actual cost of legal assistance provided in connection with the legal assistance scheme (s 136(1)).[1] Those sums are to be paid by the Lord Chancellor into the Consolidated Fund. Out of money provided by Parliament, the Lord Chancellor's Department must fund the cost of legal assistance provided in proceedings before the Tribunal (s 136(3), (4)). The Lord Chancellor's Department may be required to make balancing payments to the FSA if over time the amount that the FSA paid to the Lord Chancellor exceeds the amount expended on the legal assistance scheme (s 136(5)(b)).

---

[1] See the Financial Services and Markets Tribunal (Legal Assistance Scheme—Costs) Regulations 2001, SI 2001/3633.

12.32 To enable it to make payments as required under s 136(1), the FSA must make rules requiring the payment to it by authorised persons or any class of authorised person of such amount or amounts calculated in a manner to be specified in rules (s 136(2)). If the FSA receives money back from the Lord Chancellor under s 136(6), it must make provision for redistributing these funds among the authorised persons on whom a levy was imposed in respect of the legal assistance scheme during that period or otherwise for reducing the amounts payable in future periods (s 136(7)).[1]

---

[1] The FSA's fee raising proposals propose to allocate the costs of the scheme so as to mirror the allocation of penalties recovered in market abuse cases, ie, allocated to all authorised firms: see FSA CP 79, Feedback statement to CP56 and second Consultation paper on the FSA's post-N2 fee-raising arrangements, December 2000, paras 5.35–5.42. No detailed provisions complementing this have yet been published.

13 The compensation scheme

INTRODUCTION

13.1 The integration of the various regulatory bodies for banking, insurance and investment business under a single statutory regulator has led to the creation of a single compensation scheme under the Financial Services and Markets Act 2000 (FSMA 2000) in the event of a default by an authorised firm. Part XV (ss 212–224) provides the framework for the scheme but the detailed provisions have been set out in rules made by the FSA to be known as the 'Financial Services Compensation Scheme' (referred to in the Act as the 'compensation scheme') (s 213(2)).[1] The Explanatory Notes explain that—

> 'The purpose of the compensation scheme is to compensate customers who suffer loss in various circumstances as a consequence of the inability of an authorised person to meet its liabilities. The scheme is not, other than in cases of the insolvency of an authorised person, intended to provide compensation for a regulatory breach (for example the mis-selling of investments), where the liability would remain with the authorised firm.'[2]

---

[1] The FSA has consulted extensively regarding the compensation scheme and its processes: see FSA CP 5, Consumer Compensation, October 1997; FSA CP 24, Consumer Consultation: A further Consultation, June 1999; FSA CP 58, Financial Services Compensation Scheme Draft Rules, July 2000; FSA CP 72, Proposed amendments to the Compensation Scheme Management Company, November 2000; FSA CP 86, Financial Services Compensation Scheme Draft Funding Rules, March 2001; FSA CP 108, Financial Services Compensation Scheme Draft Transitional Rules, September 2001; FSA CP 109, Financial Services Compensation Scheme Management Expenses Levy Limit, September 2001. See now the FSA Handbook, Compensation sourcebook (COMP).

[2] FSMA Explanatory Notes, para 421.

THE SCHEME MANAGER

13.2 Under FSMA 2000, s 212(1) the FSA is required to establish a body corporate, the 'scheme manager', to carry out the functions laid down in FSMA 2000, Pt XV, and the FSA must take such steps as are necessary to ensure that the scheme manager remains at all times capable of exercising those functions (s 212(2)). In March 2000 the FSA established a separate legal entity, the Financial Services Compensation Scheme Limited (FSCS), with a view to that body taking over the responsibilities of the scheme manager at 'N2' (1 December 2001).[1] The FSA transferred the responsibilities of the existing appointed scheme manager under FSA 1986, s 56, namely, the Investor Compensation Scheme Limited, to the FSCS before N2 to facilitate the transitional period.

---

[1]   FSA CP 72, Proposed amendments to the Compensation Scheme Management Company, November 2000, paras 1, 4. This took effect on 1 February 2001: see FSA Press Releases FSA/ PN/016/2001, 1 February 2001. FSCS also took over operation of the Deposit Protection Scheme on the same day. See also the Financial Services and Markets Act 2000 (Transitional Provisions, Repeals and Savings) (Financial Services Compensation Scheme) Order 2001, SI 2001/2967.

13.3   The Memorandum and Articles of Association of the scheme manager, together with the provisions of FSMA 2000, comprise the framework for the compensation scheme.[1] The detailed provisions are set out in the rules made by the FSA (s 213(1)).[2]

---

[1]   FSA CP 58, Financial Services Compensation Scheme Draft Rules, July 2000, para 4.6.
[2]   See the FSA Handbook, Compensation manual, COMP.

Constitution of the scheme manager

13.4   The scheme manager must have a chairman and a board (including the chairman) whose members are the scheme manager's directors (s 212(3)). The chairman and other members of the board are to be appointed by the FSA[1] but the terms of their appointment (in particular those governing removal from office) must be such that they are independent of the FSA[2] in operating the compensation scheme (s 212(4), (5)). Neither the scheme manager nor its board members, officers or staff are to be regarded as exercising functions on behalf of the Crown or as Crown servants (s 212(6), (7)).

---

[1]   The appointment of the chairman is subject to Treasury approval (s 212(4)).
[2]   See HC SC A, 30 November 1999 for debate concerning the independence of the scheme manager. FSA CP 58, Financial Services Compensation Scheme Draft Rules, July 2000, para 4.8 describes the relationship as 'independent' on a day-to-day basis but 'accountable'.

THE SCHEME

Functions of the scheme manager

13.5 The scheme manager's functions are to assess and pay compensation to claimants in relation to claims made in connection with regulated activities carried on by regulated persons (whether or not with permission), in accordance with the scheme rules (s 213(3)(a)).[1] The scheme manager has the power to impose levies on authorised persons or any class of authorised person, in order to meet its expenses[2] and recover the cost (whenever incurred) of establishing the compensation scheme (s 213(3)(b), (4)). Amounts levied under these provisions may be recovered as a debt due to the scheme manager (s 213(6)). Therefore a newly authorised firm could not claim that it was not required to pay a levy in respect of claims for compensation (or costs) which arose before it became an authorised person. However, FSMA 2000 does provide that the FSA (not the scheme manager) must take account of the desirability of ensuring that the amounts levied on a particular class of person should reflect, as far as is practicable, the amount of the claims made or likely to be made in relation to that class of authorised persons (s 213(5)).[3]

---

[1] A claimant may not claim against the compensation fund in respect of a claim against a person who should be authorised but was not (in contravention of the general prohibition under s 19): see FSMA Explanatory Notes, para 423.

[2] This includes both the costs of compensation and the scheme's administrative costs.

[3] The issue of cross-subsidisation was one which was particularly contentious in relation to the Investors Compensation Scheme under FSA 1986 and was the source of much commentary on the rather byzantine rules drawn up to ensure that different industry sectors paid into the scheme in proportion to the losses which occurred or were likely to occur in the different industries. The FSA delayed finalising these levy rules until it had consulted fully on the wider issue of its regime for regulatory fees: see FSA CP 58, Financial Services Compensation Scheme Draft Rules, July 2000, Annex B, s 13 and FSA CP 108, Financial Services Compensation Scheme Draft Transitional Rules, September 2001. The funding provisions broadly reflect the fee blocks adopted by the FSA for its own fees, but the sub-schemes operated by the FSCS will be much broader: see FSA CP 109, Financial Services Compensation Scheme Management Expenses Levy Limit, September 2001.

The operation of the compensation scheme

13.6 The compensation scheme is established to compensate persons where those persons ('relevant persons') are unable, or are likely to be unable, to satisfy claims made against them (s 213(1)).[1] The detailed provision in ss 214–217 do not, however, limit the general powers of the FSA under s 213(1) (s 213(7)). Therefore the fact that an authorised person was acting outside the scope of their Pt IV permission in breach of FSMA 2000 would not preclude a claim being made in respect of those activities if those activities were regulated activities.[2] 'Relevant person' is defined as a person who was an authorised person at the time the act or omission giving rise to the claim against him took place, or who was an appointed representative at that time. This however excludes a person who is authorised by virtue of exercising EEA passport rights under FSMA 2000, Sch 3 unless he had elected to participate in the compensation scheme in relation to those regulated activities (s 213(9), (10)).[3] Participation in the compensation scheme is therefore compulsory for authorised persons carrying on regulated activities with Pt IV permission (or authorisation under Sch 4 or Sch 5) but membership is voluntary for those who qualify for authorisation under Sch 3 and fall within a category to be prescribed in the rules.[4]

---

[1]   The scheme is intended to implement the provisions of the EC Directives on Deposit Guarantee Schemes (Directive 94/19/EC) and Investor Compensation Schemes (Directive 97/9/EC).

[2]   FSMA Explanatory Notes, para 423.

[3]   Note that the definition of 'relevant persons' is not the same as that for the purposes of ss 219, 220 and 224 (see para 13.17): see the Financial Services and Markets Act 2000 (Compensation Scheme: Electing Participants) Regulations 2001, SI 2001/1783, reg 2, which provides that EEA credit institutions and investment firms exercising passport rights are not relevant persons unless they elect to participate in the scheme.

[4]   Ie, incoming EEA firms authorised under FSMA 2000, Sch 3. The compensation scheme may provide that an incoming EEA firm can elect to participate in relation to some or all of the activities for which it has permission under Sch 3 (s 214(5)). The Financial Services and Markets Act 2000 (Compensation Scheme: Electing Participants) Regulations 2001, SI 2001/1783, reg 3 prescribes the categories of firms to which this applies: investment firms and credit institutions with UK branches.

PROVISIONS OF THE SCHEME

13.7   Generally speaking, the compensation scheme can confer on the scheme manager wide powers to determine and regulate matters relating to the scheme (s 214(3)). The scheme may impose limits on the type of claim, the type of claimants, or matters arising or events occurring in specified areas or localities (s 214(1)(f), (g), (4)). It may also make provisions as to the circumstances in which a relevant person is deemed to be unable or likely to be unable to satisfy claims made against him as well as providing for the establishment of different funds for meeting the different kinds of claims that can arise (s 214(1)(a), (b)). The compensation scheme empowers the scheme manager to impose different levies in different cases and limit the levy payable by a person in relation to a specific period,[1] and to repay funds levied as part of the scheme (s 214(1)(c)–(e)). They may also specify the scheme manager's powers in certain circumstances to make a compensation payment. These circumstances are where the claimant is entitled to receive a payment under a different compensation scheme which is comparable, or under a guarantee given by a government or other authority, and the scheme manager may seek to recover the compensation payment from that other scheme or guarantee (s 214(6)).

---

[1]   Certain relevant persons may be able to claim an exemption from the specific costs levy and the compensation costs levy under COMP 13.3 if that person does not conduct and has no reasonable likelihood of conducting business which could give rise to a protected claim by an eligible claimant.

13.8   The FSMA 2000 compensation scheme provides wide protection to consumers through three 'sub-schemes'. There are detailed rules about the availability of compensation, but the levels of cover are broadly:

— For protected deposits, 100% of the first £2,000 and 90% of the next £33,000 (ie, a maximum of £31,700).

— For general insurance, when the claim is in respect of a liability subject to compulsory insurance, 100% of the claim; in most other cases 100% of the first £2,000 and 90% of the remainder of the claim; claims are not limited by a maximum payment.

— For long-term insurance contracts, 100% of the first £2,000 and at least 90% of the remaining value of the policy (including future benefits declared before the date the relevant person is determined to be in default); again there is no maximum payment for claims brought.

— For other investment business (ie, the type of business regulated under the Financial Services Act 1986), 100% of the first £30,000 and 90% of the next £20,000 (ie, a maximum of £48,000).[1]

---

[1]   See FSA Press Releases FSA/PN/87/2000, 4 July 2000. The FSA Handbook, Compensation manual COMP 5.2 defines 'protected claims' and COMP 10.2 sets out the limits on compensation payable.

13.9   The compensation scheme may also provide for the type of claim which may be met by the scheme and the procedure which must be followed in making a claim (s 214(1)(g), (h)). The rules may also provide that the scheme manager may make interim payments in specified cases before a claim has been finally determined or limit the amount payable on a claim to a specified maximum or to a maximum calculated in a specified manner (s 214(1)(i), (j)). The rules may also provide, in certain cases, for payments to be made to persons other than the claimant (s 214(1)(k)).

13.10   The compensation scheme may also make provision as to the effect of a payment of compensation under the scheme regarding rights or obligations arising out of the claim against the relevant person (s 215(1)(a)). The right of recovery conferred on the scheme manager under s 215(1)(b) in such circumstances is, however, limited to the same rights, if any, which the claimant would have in the event of the relevant person's insolvency (s 215(2)). Thus the scheme manager can be given rights of subrogation (or equivalent) for matters on which it pays out.[1]

_____
[1]   See the FSA Handbook, Compensation manual, COMP 7.

13.11   If a person other than the scheme manager serves—
— a petition for administration in relation to a company[1] or partnership;
— a petition for the winding up of a body corporate or partnership; or
— a bankruptcy petition (as defined in s 215(7)),

the scheme manager has the same rights as the FSA has under ss 362, 371 and 374 respectively (s 215(3)–(5)).[2] Insolvency rules made under the Insolvency Act 1986 or by the Treasury (s 215(8)) may also be made to integrate any procedure for which provision is made under s 215(1) into the general procedure on the administration of a company or partnership or on a winding-up, bankruptcy or sequestration (s 215(6)).

_____
[1]   References to a company in s 215(3), (4) and (6) apply to limited liability partnerships: see the Limited Liability Partnership Regulations 2001, SI 2001/1090, reg 6.
[2]   See paras 21.15, 21.30, 21.36.

Arrangements in relation to general insurance contracts

13.12   Section 217 provides that the compensation scheme may provide for the scheme manager to take certain measures to safeguard policyholders of insurers who have permission to effect or carry out contracts of general insurance and are in financial difficulties (s 217(1), (2)).[1] These may include measures for transferring all or part of the insurer's business insofar as it constitutes carrying out contracts of insurance, or transferring any part of that business, to another authorised person (s 217(3)(a)), or providing such other assistance to enable the insurer to continue to effect or carry out contracts of insurance (s 217(3)(b)). The compensation scheme may include various supplemental provisions such as setting out the basis on which these measures should be taken by the scheme manager to safeguard eligible policyholders (s 217(4)).[2]

_____
[1]   The meaning of 'financial difficulties' is to be defined in the compensation scheme rules (s 217(8)): see the FSA Handbook, Compensation manual, COMP 3.3.
[2]   The meaning of 'eligible policyholders' is to be specified in the compensation scheme rules (s 217(8)).

13.13 The rationale behind s 217 is that due to the nature of general insurance business, claims can arise from events that happened a number of years earlier. Section 217 allows the FSA to make provision under the compensation scheme for the scheme manager to give assistance to insurance companies in financial difficulties, either by transferring the insurance business to another insurer, or by enabling the continuance of insurance business by another insurer. However, before using this power, the scheme manager must be satisfied that payments to the firm should not materially benefit other persons such as shareholders or company directors and that these measures would not cost more than the costs of compensation if the insurer were allowed to go into default.[1]

---

[1] FSMA Explanatory Notes, paras 433 and 434.

Continuity of long-term insurance policies

13.14 The compensation scheme may also include provisions for the scheme manager to make arrangements for securing continuity of insurance for policyholders if a relevant long-term insurer[1] defaults (s 216(1)).[2] The provisions of s 217 can also apply to this type of policy.[3]

---

[1] For the purposes of s 216, 'relevant long-term insurers' means relevant persons who have permission to effect or carry out contracts of long-term insurance and are unable or likely to be unable to satisfy claims against them (s 216(2)).
[2] The scheme may limit these provisions to policyholders of a specified class of insurance contract (s 216(1)).
[3] See the FSA Handbook, Compensation manual, COMP 3.3.

13.15 Those arrangements may include measures such as transferring a relevant long-term insurer's business, so far as it consists of carrying out contracts of long-term business, to another authorised person (s 216(3)(a)) or securing the issue by another authorised person to policyholders of policies in substitution for their existing policies (s 216(3)(b)). These provisions are designed to take into account the special nature of long-term insurance which means that should an insurer go into liquidation, a simple payment of compensation may not necessarily be enough to enable policyholders to find alternative cover. This may be particularly relevant, for example, if a policyholder had developed subsequent health problems.[1] The compensation scheme may also allow the scheme manager to make payments to the policyholders during a period in which he is seeking to make those arrangements or if it appears that it is not practicable for him to make such arrangements (s 216(4)). The scheme manager also has the power to impose levies to meet any expenses which he may incur as a result of making the arrangements under s 216(3) or making any payments under s 216(4) (s 216(5)).

---

[1] FSMA Explanatory Notes, para 432.

ANNUAL REPORT OF THE SCHEME MANAGER

13.16   The scheme manager must report to the FSA at least once a year on the discharge of its functions under FSMA 2000, Pt XV (s 218(1)). This report, which must be published in a manner which the scheme manager considers appropriate (s 218(3)), must include a statement of the value of each of the funds established by the compensation scheme and must comply with any other requirements imposed by the FSA (s 218(2)).

INFORMATION AND DOCUMENTS

Power to require information

13.17   In carrying out its functions the scheme manager may require relevant persons, or persons otherwise involved,[1] to provide it with information or documentation which the scheme manager considers necessary to determine fairly a claim made under the compensation scheme (s 219(1), (3)). A 'relevant person' for the purposes of s 219 is a person who was an authorised person or an appointed representative at the time the act or omission which may give rise to the liability to make a payment under the scheme took place (s 224(3)). This does not, however, include a person who was at that time authorised by virtue of FSMA 2000, Sch 3 and fell within a prescribed category unless that person had elected to participate in the compensation scheme in relation to those activities at that time (s 224(4)).[2]

---

[1]   A person is 'involved in a claim' for the purposes of the compensation scheme if he was knowingly involved in the act or omission that gave rise to the claim (s 219(10)).
[2]   The prescribed categories are credit institutions and investment firms: see the Financial Services and Markets Act 2000 (Compensation Scheme: Electing Participants) Regulations 2001, SI 2001/1783, reg 4.

13.18   The information must be produced or provided by the person before the end of a specified period and in the case of information, in a specified manner or form (s 219(2)). The scheme manager may take copies or extracts of any documents thus produced, or require the person producing the document to provide an explanation of it (s 219(4)). If the person on whom the notice was served fails to produce the document requested, the scheme manager may require that person to state where, to his best knowledge and belief, the document is (s 219(5)). Production of any document in respect of which a person claims a lien will not affect the lien (s 219(7)).

Power to inspect information held by liquidator etc

13.19 Where the relevant person[1] of whom information or documentation was requested is insolvent, the administrative receiver, administrator, liquidator or trustee in bankruptcy or permanent trustee (within the meaning of the Bankruptcy (Scotland) Act 1985) on the estate of that person (s 220(3)) must assist the scheme manager in discharging its functions (s 220(1)). They must permit a person appointed by the scheme manager to inspect relevant documents and allow them to take copies of or extracts from the document (s 220(2)).[2] However, this does not apply if the liquidator, administrator or trustee in bankruptcy of a relevant person is the Official Receiver, the Official Receiver for Northern Ireland or the Accountant in Bankruptcy as relevant (s 220(4)).[3]

[1] As defined in s 224(3), (4): see para 13.17.
[2] The scheme manager may not require the provision of information or documents under s 219 if s 220 applies to the person concerned.
[3] See para 13.21.

Powers of the court

13.20 A person who fails to produce or provide access to a document or provide the information required under a notice served under either s 219 or 220 may, on the scheme manager's application, be subject to a court[1] enquiry (s 221(1)). If the court is satisfied that the defaulter has no reasonable excuse, it may treat him as if he were in contempt of court (s 221(2)).

[1] The court for these purposes is the High Court or, in Scotland, the Court of Session (s 221(3)).

Scheme manager's power to inspect documents held by Official Receiver, etc

13.21 If documents have come into the possession of the Official Receiver, the Official Receiver for Northern Ireland or the Accountant in Bankruptcy of a relevant person,[1] those persons must permit any person authorised by the scheme manager to inspect the documents for the purpose of identifying the persons to whom he may be liable to make a payment in accordance with the compensation scheme or for the purpose of establishing the amount of any such payment (s 224(1), (5)). In addition these persons must permit a person authorised by the scheme manager to inspect the relevant documents and to take copies or extracts from them (s 224(2)).

[1] As defined in s 224(3), (4): see para 13.17.

MISCELLANEOUS

Determination of the scheme manager's management expenses

13.22 The scheme manager's ability to recover the day-to-day management expenses for the compensation scheme from sums levied under the scheme is limited to the amount fixed by the scheme as applicable to a particular period. Until this limit is fixed, the scheme manager may not, when calculating the amount of any levy, include an amount to reflect management expenses (s 223(1), (2)).[1] 'Management expenses' are defined in s 223(3) as expenses incurred by the scheme manager in connection with its functions under FSMA 2000 apart from those incurred in paying compensation or as a result of any scheme provision made by virtue of s 216(3) or (4) or s 217(1) or (6).[2]

---

[1]   See FSA CP 58, Financial Services Compensation Scheme Draft Rules, July 2000, Annex B, Section 13. See also FSA CP 86, Financial Services Compensation Scheme Draft Funding Rules, March 2001 and Policy Statement 86.
[2]   See paras 13.12–13.15.

Statutory immunity of the scheme manager

13.23 FSMA 2000, s 222 provides that neither the scheme manager nor any person who is, or is acting as, a board member, officer or member of staff of the scheme manager is liable in damages for anything done or omitted in discharging (or purportedly discharging) the functions of the scheme manager under Pt XV (s 222(1)). This statutory immunity does not apply, however, if the act or omission can be shown to have been in bad faith, or to the extent that it would prevent an award of damages on the grounds that the act or omission was unlawful by virtue of the Human Rights Act 1998, s 6(1) (s 222(2)).[1]

---

[1]   The scheme manager may be sued in the High Court or, in Scotland, the Court of Session in relation to any proceedings arising out of any act or omission under FSMA 2000 (s 415(1)(c)).

14 The Ombudsman scheme

INTRODUCTION

14.1   The framework for a unified system of consumer redress is an integral part of the FSA's statutory objective of consumer protection and a key feature of the regulatory regime under the Financial Services and Markets Act 2000 (FSMA 2000).[1]

---

[1]   FSA CP 33, Consumer Complaints and the New Single Ombudsman Scheme, November 1999, para 1.8.

14.2   As part of the integration of the nine regulatory authorities, the Government committed itself to the creation of a single ombudsman scheme out of the eight different dispute resolution schemes which existed under the regulatory regime before 'N2'.[1] The Economic Secretary stated that—

> 'It would be wrong to construe the new regime as a criticism of the efforts and achievements of existing schemes. Indeed, people in the industry have been commended for their efforts in setting up many of those schemes and for the work that has been done over a considerable period. However, the existence of so many schemes has confused consumers. It is often difficult for consumers to know where to turn if they need help to resolve a complaint. The proliferation of arrangements has not helped the schemes to bring their roles to the attention of the public. Some complaints can fall between the jurisdictions of the various schemes, while others may be covered by more than one scheme. Differences exist in the way in which the schemes operate and in the extent of their powers. Part [XVI] will establish a simple, more transparent framework for the resolution of consumer complaints. It sets out the broad details of the new single, independent and compulsory ombudsman scheme for the speedy and informal resolution of disputes between authorised firms and their customers.'[2]

The intention was to replace with a single comprehensive scheme those complaints-handling schemes already in place for most firms which would, in due course, be regulated under FSMA 2000.

¹   See para 1.37 for further discussion of N2.
²   HC SC A, 30 November 1999, col 1027. The Joint Committee, First Report, para 282 also saw this as a major benefit to consumers reducing the scope for confusion in relation to the roles and scope of the different schemes. See also HM Treasury, Financial Services and Markets Bill: Government Response to the Reports of the Joint Committee on Financial Services and Markets, Pt VII, and FSA Response to the Cruickshank Report on Competition in UK Banking, July 2000, paras 4.5 to 4.8 on points relating to the creation of the single ombudsman scheme.

14.3   This scheme therefore incorporates, broadly speaking, the previous jurisdictions of—
— the Office of the Banking Ombudsman;
— the Office of the Building Societies Ombudsman;
— the Office of the Investment Ombudsman;
— the Insurance Ombudsman Bureau;
— the Personal Investment Authority Ombudsman Bureau;
— the Personal Insurance Arbitration Services;
— the Securities and Futures Authority Complaints Bureau and Consumer Arbitration Service; and
— the FSA Complaints Unit and Independent Investigator.[1]

¹   FSA CP 33, Consumer Complaints and the New Single Ombudsman Scheme, November 1999, para 2.2. Certain schemes will continue in operation until October 2004 or January 2005 (Mortgage Code Arbitration Scheme and the General Insurance Standards Council Dispute Resolution Facility, the Finance and Leasing Conciliation and Arbitration Scheme). The Pensions Advisory Service and Pensions Ombudsman Scheme, which relate to the operation of occupational pension schemes, have continued separately. See also the arrangements for complaints against the FSA itself at paras 2.20–2.25.

14.4   The FSA consulted extensively on the handling of customer complaints and the integration of the previous schemes,[1] which varied in a number of significant respects. Some were characterised as ombudsmen and others as arbitrators; some were compulsory, others voluntary; some were established by statute, others were based in contract law; some were established by the industry, others by regulators. In addition, these predecessor schemes had significant differences in their eligibility criteria, the limits on awards, the terms of reference, the basis for awards, the procedures, and their funding and governance arrangements.[2] The integration of the predecessor schemes has created the world's largest ombudsman scheme with a staff of some 470 employees and over 10,000 firms subject, in one form or another, to its compulsory jurisdiction.[3]

¹   See FSA CP 4, Consumer Complaints, October 1997, FSA CP 33, Consumer Complaints and the New Single Ombudsman Scheme, November 1999, and FSA CP 49, Complaints Handling Arrangements: Feedback Statement on CP 33 and Draft Rules, May 2000.
²   See FSA CP4, para 17. See also FSA Press Release FSA/PN/011/1997, December 1997.
³   FSA CP 33, para 1.17. See Financial Ombudsman Service, Annual Review of 1 April 2001 to 31 March 2002. In 2002–2003, the Financial Ombudsman Service Limited (FOS) referred some 62,170 of the complaints it received to adjudication: see FOS Annual Review 2002–2003, Key Facts and Figures.

THE SCHEME

14.5   FSMA 2000, Pt XVI (ss 225–234) provides the legislative framework for the scheme and s 225(1) sets out its legislative intention, namely to resolve certain disputes quickly and with minimum formality by an independent person.[1]

---

[1]   FSMA Explanatory Notes, paras 440 and 441.

14.6   The ombudsman scheme[1] itself is administered by a body corporate[2] established by the FSA under FSMA 2000, Sch 17, para 2. The FSA is also responsible for ensuring that this body corporate is at all times capable of exercising the functions conferred on it by FSMA 2000 (Sch 17, para 2(2)). Schedule 17 sets out in detail the provisions for the constitution of the scheme operator and the jurisdiction of the scheme.

---

[1]   Although 'ombudsman scheme' is the term used in FSMA 2000, the scheme operator is given the choice of name for the scheme (s 225(3)).
[2]   Referred to in FSMA 2000 as the 'scheme operator' (s 225(2)).

14.7   The scheme operator is operationally independent of the FSA.[1] The scheme operates in accordance with the criteria for ombudsman schemes set out by the British and Irish Ombudsman Association.[2]

---

[1]   FSA CP 33, Consumer Complaints and the New Single Ombudsman Scheme, November 1999, para 1.8. See also para 14.9.
[2]   FSA CP 33, para 1.20.

Financial Ombudsman Service Limited

14.8   The Financial Ombudsman Service Limited ('FOS'—previously called the Financial Services Ombudsman Scheme Limited) is a company limited by guarantee which the FSA established for this purpose.[1] Seven out of eight of the predecessor schemes transferred their staff to FOS with effect from 1 April 2000,[2] and FOS carried out the day-to-day operation of these schemes in anticipation of the commencement of FMSA 2000.[3]

---

[1]   FSA CP 49, Complaints Handling Arrangements: Feedback Statement on CP 33 and Draft Rules, May 2000, para 1.3 and FSA CP 33, Consumer Complaints and the New Single Ombudsman Scheme, November 1999, para 1.3.
[2]   The Personal Insurance Arbitration Service continues to be operated by the Chartered Institute of Arbitrators although regulated firms providing these services became subject to the FOS scheme with effect from N2.
[3]   See FSA CP 49, Ch 1.

Constitution of the scheme operator

14.9   The scheme operator is required to have a chairman, and a board comprised of the chairman and its directors (Sch 17, para 3(1)). The members of the board are to be appointed by (and may be removed by) the FSA, while the chairman is to be appointed or removed by the FSA with the approval of the Treasury (Sch 17, para 3(2)). Despite this power to appoint and remove members of the board, the appointment of these persons must be on such terms as secure their independence from the FSA in carrying out the day-to-day operation of the scheme (Sch 17, para 3(3)).[1]

---

[1]   See HL Committee, 30 March 2000, col 920.

14.10 Certain functions of the scheme operator[1] may only be carried out by its board, including the making of voluntary jurisdiction rules as defined in FSMA 2000, s 227, and certain other functions under Sch 17, namely—

— appointing and maintaining the panel of ombudsmen (Sch 17, para 4);
— appointing the Chief Ombudsman (Sch 17, para 5);
— presenting annual reports (Sch 17, para 7);
— setting the annual budget (Sch 17, para 9); and
— making scheme rules (Sch 17, para 14) (Sch 17, para 3(4)).

The validity of any action taken by the scheme operator is not to be affected by the vacancy in the office of chairman or any defect in the appointment of the chairman, or a member of the board (Sch 17, para 3(5)).

---

[1]   The scheme operator exercising its functions under FSMA 2000 is not exercising those functions on behalf of the Crown nor are the directors, officers and staff of the scheme operator Crown servants (Sch 17, para 6(1), (2)).

Ombudsmen

14.11 The scheme operator in turn appoints a panel of persons who have the appropriate qualifications and experience to act as ombudsmen (Sch 17, para 4(1)). The terms of appointment of each ombudsman including the duration and termination of the appointment and his remuneration are to be determined by the scheme operator provided they are consistent with the independence of the person appointed and are otherwise appropriate (Sch 17, para 4(2)). The term 'ombudsman' itself refers not to a single individual but to any person who is a member of a panel established under the scheme (Sch 17, para 1).

14.12 FSMA 2000 provides that one member of the panel is to act as the Chief Ombudsman (Sch 17, para 5(1)) and is to be appointed on the terms (including duration and termination) that the scheme operator considers appropriate (Sch 17, para 5(2)).[1]

---

[1]   His only statutory function in this capacity relates to reporting to the FSA: see para 14.18.

Data Protection

14.13 FSMA 2000, s 233 amends the Data Protection Act 1998 so as to provide that the scheme operator is also to be one of those persons specified under s 31 of the 1998 Act who is not required to disclose information if that disclosure, obtained when considering a complaint brought under the scheme, would prejudice the performance of its functions.

THE DUTIES OF THE SCHEME OPERATOR

Establishing the budget

14.14 The scheme operator is responsible for establishing an annual budget that has been approved by the FSA and may vary that budget with the FSA's approval (Sch 17, para 9(1), (2)). That budget must include an indication of the resources to be employed in carrying out the scheme and any amounts of income which arise or are expected to arise from the scheme, in both cases distinguishing between its compulsory and voluntary jurisdiction (Sch 17, para 9(3)).

Funding

14.15 The issue of the funding of the ombudsman and complaints handling scheme has been controversial and the arguments against cross-subsidisation of different parts of the financial services industry has been as contentious as those debates relating to the funding of the Financial Services Compensation Scheme.[1] FSMA 2000, s 234 provides that to fund the scheme the FSA may make rules which require authorised persons or any class of authorised persons to pay specified amounts to it or to the scheme operator.[2]

---

[1]   For example, FSA CP 33, Consumer Complaints and the New Single Ombudsman Scheme, November 1999, Ch 5 discusses many of the issues relating to combining the various schemes and funding the estimated £20m running costs of the FOS.
[2]   See also para 14.44; funding is covered by the standard terms for the voluntary jurisdiction. Certain firms may be able to claim an exemption from the general levy which firms are required to pay towards the annual costs of the scheme if the firm does not conduct business with eligible complainants and has no reasonable likelihood of doing so; see DISP 1.1.7R–1.1.11G.

14.16   The scheme operator may also require the respondent in any complaint under its compulsory jurisdiction to pay a fee as specified in the scheme rules[1] although the scheme operator may have the power under those rules to—

— reduce or waive a fee;
— set different fees for different stages of the proceedings;
— refund fees in certain cases; and
— make different provisions for different types of complaint (Sch 17, para 15).

---

[1]   For 2003–2004, the standard case fee is £360 per case referred to the FOS: see the FSA Handbook, Dispute resolution: Complaints sourcebook, DISP 5.6 and DISP 5 Ann 1R, Pt 3.

Guidance

14.17   The scheme operator may publish such advice or guidance in relation to the business, operation and jurisdiction of the scheme as it considers appropriate and may elect to charge for that information or distribute it free of charge (Sch 17, para 8).

Annual reports

14.18   Both the scheme operator and the Chief Ombudsman must report to the FSA at least once a year on the discharge of their respective functions under FSMA 2000 (Sch 17, para 7(1))[1] and those reports must also be published (Sch 17, para 7(4)). The annual report must identify which matters fall within the scheme's compulsory jurisdiction and which are within its voluntary jurisdiction, and must otherwise comply with any rules laid down by the FSA concerning these reporting requirements (Sch 17, para 7(2), (3)).

---

[1]   See Financial Ombudsman Services, Annual Review at www.financial-ombudsman.org.uk.

COMPULSORY JURISDICTION OF THE SCHEME

The Authority's rules

14.19 FSMA 2000 provides that the FSA must make rules in relation to the compulsory jurisdiction of the scheme (s 226, Sch 17, para 13(1)).[1] The compulsory jurisdiction of the ombudsman scheme includes any complaint[2] which relates to an act or omission of a person carrying on activities to which the compulsory jurisdiction rules apply and which satisfies certain conditions (s 226(1)).

[1] See the FSA Handbook, Dispute resolution: Complaints sourcebook, DISP. These rules consist of—
— complaint handling rules for firms;
— jurisdiction rules under the compulsory jurisdiction of the FOS; and
— funding rules for the scheme.
Other rules may be made by the scheme operator under FSMA 2000, s 227(3) and Sch 17, paras 14 and 18(1).
[2] A complaint for the purposes of the scheme is defined widely to include any written or oral expression of dissatisfaction, whether justified or not. But only those complaints which also allege some form of financial loss, material distress or material inconvenience will fall within the scheme: see DISP 2.2.3G and DISP 3.3.1R(1). See also FSA CP 49, Complaints Handling Arrangements: Feedback Statement on CP 33 and Draft Rules, May 2000, paras 1.68 to 1.70.

Conditions for complaints

14.20 The conditions for a complaint to fall within the FOS's compulsory jurisdiction are that the complainant is eligible and wishes to have his complaint dealt with by the scheme, and that the respondent was an authorised person at the time of the act or omission to which the complaint relates, and that the act or omission occurred at a time when the compulsory jurisdiction rules were in force (s 226(2)).[1]

[1] See also the Financial Services and Markets Act 2000 (Transitional Provisions) (Ombudsman Scheme and Complaints Scheme) Order 2001, SI 2001/2326, in relation to complaints first arising before N2, or relating to acts or omissions occurring before N2.

Eligibility

14.21 The criteria for eligibility under the ombudsman scheme are specified in the compulsory jurisdiction rules (s 226(6)).[1] The rules may permit persons other than individuals (ie, businesses) to be eligible or specify that authorised persons are eligible but only in particular circumstances or for particular kinds of complaint (s 226(7)).[2] The FSA has largely limited access to the compulsory jurisdiction scheme to private individuals. However, firms (other than authorised persons) with an annual turnover of less than £1m, or trusts or charities with less than £1m in assets, will also be eligible[3] although a company which is a member of a group would only be eligible if the whole of the group met this annual turnover test.[4]

---

[1]   See the FSA Handbook, Dispute resolution: Complaints sourcebook, DISP 2.4.
[2]   The rules restrict access to small businesses (see DISP 2.4.3R(1)), and restrict access for an authorised person to matters for which it does not have permission (see DISP 2.4.3R(2)(b)).
[3]   See DISP 2.4.
[4]   See DISP 2.4.3R.

14.22   In some cases third parties (ie, persons who are not customers of the authorised persons concerned) may, nonetheless, be eligible under the compulsory jurisdiction rules.[1] However, only activities which are regulated activities or which could be made regulated activities under FSMA 2000, s 22 may be specified for the purposes of the compulsory jurisdiction rules (s 226(4)).

---

[1]   FSA Handbook, Dispute resolution: Complaints sourcebook, DISP 2.4.10R–2.4.15R.

14.23   Some activities carried on by authorised firms remain outside the scheme, such as complaints in relation to Lloyd's,[1] credit unions,[2] UCITS qualifiers[3] and authorised professional firms to the extent that the complaint relates to their non-mainstream activities.[4]

---

[1]   See the FSA Handbook, Dispute resolution: Complaints sourcebook, DISP 1.7.
[2]   See the FSA Handbook, Credit Unions sourcebook, CRED 17.
[3]   See DISP 1.1.7R.
[4]   Authorised professional firms are subject to the rules of their respective professional body in relation to such complaints.

Territorial scope

14.24   There has been some uncertainty about territorial scope of the compulsory scheme. However, the FSA has made the rules to cover every activity specified in the compulsory jurisdiction rules which is carried on by an authorised firm in or from the UK.[1] Therefore the scheme covers complaints about business carried on in or from the UK by EEA firms which have used one of the EU single market directive 'passports' to carry on regulated activities in the UK. The FSA Handbook confirms that where an EEA firm has a permanent place of business in the UK, complaints regarding its regulated activities carried on in or from the UK will fall within the scope of the compulsory jurisdiction rules.[2] However, where an EEA firm is providing services (for example, over the internet) on a cross-border basis into the UK, the compulsory jurisdiction does not arise.[3]

¹   See the FSA Handbook, Dispute resolution: Complaints sourcebook, DISP 2.7.1R. Section 226(4) provides that only activities which are regulated activities or which could be made regulated activities may be specified. However, the scope of the compulsory jurisdiction rules is wider than the scope set by the Regulated Activities Order in that it also includes certain banking and lending services (see DISP 2.6).
²   See DISP 2.7.4G.
³   See DISP 2.7.4G.

14.25   These compulsory jurisdiction rules must include a limitation period to provide that a complaint is not to be entertained by the ombudsman scheme unless it has been referred to it within a set time (Sch 17, para 13(1)). In certain circumstances, however, they may allow an ombudsman to extend that time limit (Sch 17, para 13(2)).[1] The rules may also provide that the ombudsman scheme can only consider a complaint if the complaint has been communicated to the respondent and he has been given a reasonable time to deal with it (Sch 17, para 13(3)).[2] The FSA may also require authorised persons who are subject to the compulsory jurisdiction of the scheme to have procedures for dealing with complaints.[3] Under Sch 17, para 13(4), this power to require authorised persons to establish complaints procedures relates not only to the resolution of complaints which may be referred to the scheme but also to other activities to which the FSA's powers under FSMA 2000, Pt X do not apply.

¹   See the FSA Handbook, Dispute resolution: Complaints sourcebook, DISP 2.3.
²   See DISP 2.3.1R(1)(a).
³   See DISP 1.2.1, also para 14.26.

Complaints handling rules

14.26   The part of the FSA Handbook relevant to the ombudsman scheme also imposes uniform requirements for authorised firms in respect of their complaint handling procedures.[1] In general they require all firms—

— to have written complaint handling procedures and to publish these or make them readily available to consumers;
— to investigate complaints promptly;
— to offer appropriate levels of redress where a complaint has been upheld;
— to keep a record of complaints and the actions taken to investigate and rectify them;
— to report those complaints to the FSA as the regulator; and
— to co-operate with the scheme operator in the operation and administration of the ombudsman scheme.[2]

¹   The Dispute resolution: Complaints sourcebook, DISP 1, contains these rules.
²   The FSA has suggested that firms should, as a matter of best practice, consult British Standard 8600:1999 Complaints Management Systems—Guide to Design and Implementation: see DISP 1.2.7G.

THE SCHEME OPERATOR'S RULES

14.27   The scheme operator is required to make rules setting out the procedure for its handling of complaints under the compulsory jurisdiction, known in FSMA 2000 as 'scheme rules' (Sch 17, para 14(1)).[1] The scheme operator must publish any draft scheme rules and must have regard to any representations made to it in relation to those draft scheme rules (Sch 17, para 14(4)–(6)). The FSA must approve the rules (Sch 17, para 14(7)).

---

[1]   These are also incorporated into the FSA Handbook, Dispute resolution: Complaints sourcebook, DISP: see DISP Sch 4.

14.28   FSMA 2000 provides that the scheme rules may include provisions in relation to the matters which are to be taken into account in determining whether an act or omission is fair and reasonable and the circumstances in which a complaint may be dismissed without consideration of its merits (Sch 17, para 14(2)(a), (b)). This could arise, for example, where—

— the ombudsman considers the complaint frivolous or vexatious;

— legal proceedings have been brought and the ombudsman considers those matters are best dealt with in those proceedings; or

— there are other compelling reasons why the complaint should not be dealt with under the scheme (Sch 17, para 14(3)).[1]

---

[1]   See the FSA Handbook, Dispute resolution: Complaints sourcebook, DISP 3.3.

14.29   The scheme rules may also provide for a complaint to be referred to another body for determination by someone other than an ombudsman (Sch 17, para 14(2)(c)), the basis on which evidence may be required or admitted and the consequences of failing to produce the information (whether that required under s 231 or otherwise) (Sch 17, para 14(2)(d)). The rules may also provide for different treatment of different types of complaint (Sch 17, para 14(2)(g)), and may allow an ombudsman to fix certain time limits or to extend those time limits in any proceedings, or to delegate certain activities such as the investigation or consideration of complaints to a member of the scheme operator's staff (Sch 17, para 14(2)(e), (f)). However, the determination of a complaint still rests with the ombudsman.

Determination of complaints

14.30   Complaints under the scheme's compulsory jurisdiction are to be determined by reference to what the ombudsman determines is fair and reasonable in all of the circumstances (s 228(2)).[1] The ombudsman is required to determine a complaint and to give his determination in writing to the respondent and to the complainant with reasons for his determination (s 228(3), (4)(a)).

---

[1]   See also the FSA Handbook, Dispute resolution: Complaints sourcebook, DISP 3.8.1R.

14.31   Under the terms of the written statement given by the ombudsman,[1] the complainant must give the ombudsman written notice within a specified number of days as to whether he accepts or rejects the determination (s 228(4)(c)). If the complainant accepts the determination, then it is binding on both him and the respondent and is final (s 228(5)). If the complainant has not notified the ombudsman within the specified period that he has accepted the determination, he is deemed to have rejected it (s 228(6)). The ombudsman must notify the respondent whether the complainant has accepted or rejected the determination (s 228(7)). A copy of the determination accompanied by a certificate signed by the ombudsman is deemed to be legal evidence or, in Scotland, sufficient evidence that a determination has been made (s 228(8)).[2]

---

[1]   The statement must be signed by him (s 228(4)(b)).
[2]   A certificate purporting to be signed by an ombudsman is deemed to have been duly signed unless proved otherwise (s 228(9)).

Awards under the scheme's compulsory jurisdiction

14.32   Where a determination has been made in favour of the complainant, the ombudsman may include a money award of an amount which the ombudsman considers to be fair compensation for the loss or damage suffered by the complainant (s 229(2)(a)). It may (either in addition or as an alternative) include a direction that the respondent take such steps as the ombudsman considers just and appropriate (s 229(2)(b)).[1]

---

[1]   A direction made under this section is not limited to steps that a court could order the respondent to take. See s 229(2)(b).

14.33   A money award made under s 229 may compensate for financial loss or other types of loss or damage which may be specified in the compulsory jurisdiction rules[1] (s 229(3)) up to the limit prescribed in those rules (s 229(4)). The limit is £100,000[2] although the compulsory jurisdiction rules may specify different amounts for different kinds of complaint (s 229(7)). Any award exceeding the limit specified in the rules cannot bind the respondent but the ombudsman may recommend that the respondent pay the larger amount as fair compensation (s 229(5)). Interest on a money award made under the compulsory jurisdiction rules is to accrue at a rate and as from a date specified in the award (s 229(8)(a)).

---

[1]   The rules allow an ombudsman to compensate a complainant other than for purely financial damages in that the rules would allow an award for pain and suffering, distress, inconvenience and damage to reputation: see the FSA Handbook, Dispute resolution: Complaints sourcebook, DISP 3.9.

[2]   See DISP 3.9.5R.

14.34   A direction made under s 229 may be enforced by an injunction or, in Scotland, an order under the Court of Session Act 1988, s 45 brought by the complainant only, not by the FSA or the scheme operator (s 229(9), (10)). A money award is enforceable by the complainant in the same way as a court judgment if it is registered in accordance with scheme rules (s 229(8)(b)). As a result money awards may be enforced—

— in England and Wales by execution issued from the county court as if it were payable as an order of that court;

— in Northern Ireland as a money judgment under the Judgments Enforcement (Northern Ireland) Order 1981, SI 1981/226 (NI 6); or

— as a judgment or order of the sheriff in Scotland whether or not the sheriff himself could have granted such a judgment or order (Sch 17, para 16).

Costs

14.35   The scheme operator may also make rules in relation to the award of costs against a respondent in a complaint (s 230(1)).[1] Those rules may not, however, allow an award against the complainant in respect of the respondent's costs (s 230(3)), although they may provide for the making of an award against the complainant in favour of the scheme operator for the scheme's costs if the complainant's conduct is deemed to have been improper or unreasonable or he was responsible for unreasonable delay in the matter (s 230(4)). Costs awarded against a respondent may also bear interest at a rate and as from a date specified in the order (s 230(5)).

---

[1]   Such rules must be approved by the FSA (s 230(2)).

14.36   An award in favour of the scheme operator which awards costs is recoverable as a debt due to the scheme operator. Other awards made against the respondent are to be treated in the same way as a money award.[1]

---

[1]   See para 14.34.

Statutory protections under the compulsory jurisdiction of the scheme

Limitation of liability in damages

14.37 In carrying out their functions under FSMA 2000, Pt XVI, no person, including the scheme operator, its staff and each ombudsman appointed under the scheme, is to be liable in damages for anything done in the discharge (or the purported discharge) of the scheme's compulsory jurisdiction (Sch 17, para 10(1)). This exemption does not apply, however, if the act or omission can be shown to have been committed in bad faith, or to prevent an award of damages made on the basis that the act or omission was unlawful as a result of the Human Rights Act 1998, s 6(1) (Sch 17, para 10(2)).[1] It is clear from this that this *statutory* exemption from liability in damages will only apply to actions undertaken in respect of the scheme's compulsory jurisdiction. No equivalent statutory protection is available for matters submitted to the scheme under its voluntary jurisdiction. However, the standard terms of the scheme to be established under Sch 17, para 18 may include provision to limit the liability of the scheme operator, any member of its governing body, any member of its staff or any person acting as an ombudsman under the scheme, unless that person is acting in bad faith, for anything done in the discharge or purported discharge of the scheme's voluntary jurisdiction (Sch 17, para 18(5)).[2]

---

[1] See para 2.118–2.121.
[2] See the FSA Handbook, Dispute resolution: Complaints sourcebook, DISP 4.2.7R.

Defamation

14.38 FMSA 2000 also contains express provision that for the purposes of the law relating to defamation, proceedings under the scheme's compulsory jurisdiction are to be treated as if they were proceedings before a court (Sch 17, para 11) and are therefore privileged. In addition, the defence of qualified privilege (if not absolute privilege) should apply to communications sent to FOS.[1] There is no equivalent provision in relation to proceedings under FOS's voluntary jurisdiction.

---

[1] See *Mahon v Rahn* [2000] EWCA Civ 185, which held that communications from a complainant to the financial services regulator are subject to absolute privilege.

THE SCHEME'S VOLUNTARY JURISDICTION

14.39   A complaint may also be referred to the ombudsman scheme if the act or omission is within the scope of its voluntary jurisdiction rules (s 227(1), (12)). These voluntary jurisdiction rules made by the scheme operator[1] only apply to a complaint about specified activities (s 227(3)),[2] which could not be dealt with under the scheme's compulsory jurisdiction (s 227(2)(e)). The complainant must be eligible under the terms of the voluntary jurisdiction rules[3] and wish his complaint to be handled under the scheme (s 227(2)(a)). Respondents qualify for participation in the ombudsman scheme if they are within a class of person specified in the rules in relation to the activity in question (s 227(9)). The voluntary jurisdiction is not restricted to authorised persons (s 227(10)), and can make different provision for complaints arising out of different activities (s 227(11)).

---

[1]   The rules require the FSA's approval (s 227(6)). These rules are called the 'Standard Terms': see the FSA Handbook, Dispute resolution: Complaints sourcebook, DISP 4.

[2]   These are limited to activities which are or could be specified in compulsory jurisdiction rules (s 227(4)) but can be specified individually or by category (s 227(5)).

[3]   The complainant is eligible if he falls within a class of person specified in the rules as eligible, and the potential class is not limited to individuals (s 227(7), (8)).

14.40   Ordinarily the voluntary jurisdiction can only cover complaints if, at the time of the act or omission, the respondent was a participant in the scheme and had not, at the time the complaint was referred, withdrawn from the scheme (s 227(2)(b), (c)).[1] Equally, it can generally only cover complaints if the act or omission in question occurred at a time when voluntary jurisdiction rules were in force for that activity. However, the voluntary jurisdiction can cover complaints which relate to acts or omissions occurring at a time before the rules came into force and which could have been dealt with under a scheme which has to any extent been replaced by the voluntary jurisdiction even if this would otherwise fall outside the scope of the jurisdiction (s 227(13)).[2] It can also deal with complaints which would not be eligible because the respondent was not a participant or the activities were not covered at the relevant times, but only if the respondent has agreed (s 227(14)).

---

[1]   Firms are not obliged to participate in the voluntary jurisdiction. If they do, the rules only permit them to withdraw if they provide six months' notice to the FOS and the appropriate disclosure (to be approved by the FOS) to their customers: see the FSA Handbook, Dispute resolution: Complaints sourcebook, DISP 4.2.11R.

[2]   See also the Financial Services and Markets Act 2000 (Transitional Provisions) (Ombudsman Scheme and Complaints Scheme) Order 2001, SI 2001/2326, in relation to complaints first arising before N2, or relating to acts or omissions occurring before N2.

14.41   The voluntary jurisdiction rules will cover unauthorised mortgage lenders until these activities are transferred to the scheme's compulsory jurisdiction on 31 October 2004[1] and will cover other unauthorised firms whose membership of the schemes currently provides an avenue for redress.[2]

---

[1]   FSA CP 49, Complaints Handling Arrangements: Feedback Statement on CP 33 and Draft Rules, May 2000, para 1.43. The voluntary jurisdiction of the scheme was extended to mortgage and insurance intermediaries (the FSA Handbook, Dispute resolution: Complaints sourcebook, DISP 2.6.9) with effect from 1 April 2003: see Complaints Sourcebook (Financial Services Ombudsman Voluntary Jurisdiction Mortgage and Insurance Intermediaries) Instrument 2003 made by the FOS.

[2]   See the Financial Services and Markets Act 2000 (Regulated Activities) (Amendment) (No 1) Order 2003, SI 2003/1475.

14.42   The voluntary jurisdiction rules may have retrospective effect in that a complaint which relates to an act or omission occurring before the rules come into force and which could have been dealt with under a scheme which has been replaced by the voluntary jurisdiction element of the ombudsman scheme may be dealt with under the ombudsman scheme in spite of the requirements in s 227(2) (s 227(13)). The rules can also provide for handling other complaints relating to matters that arose before the voluntary jurisdiction applied if the respondent firm agrees (s 227(14)).[1]

---

[1]   This is to be contrasted with the compulsory jurisdiction rules because the jurisdiction is voluntary/consensual rather than compulsory.

Terms of reference to the scheme

14.43   Complaints referred to the scheme under the voluntary jurisdiction are to be dealt with and determined under standard terms set by the scheme operator and approved by the FSA (Sch 17, para 18(1)). The scheme operator may not make any change to those terms without the FSA's approval (Sch 17, para 18(4)).[1]

---

[1]   See the FSA Handbook, Dispute resolution: Complaints sourcebook, DISP 4.

14.44   The standard terms may take account of different matters or different cases (Sch 17, para 18(2)) and may require participants in the scheme to make payments of such amounts as may be determined by the scheme operator or make provision for the award of costs by the scheme operator on the determination of a complaint under its voluntary jurisdiction (Sch 17, para 18(3)).

14.45   The standard terms may also include provisions which seek to limit the liability of any person acting in the discharge or purported discharge of its functions under the voluntary jurisdiction of the scheme, so that the scheme operator, any member of its governing body, any member of its staff and any person acting as an ombudsman would not be liable in damages for anything done or omitted in discharging their functions under the scheme, unless they were acting in bad faith (Sch 17, para 18(5)).[1]

---

[1]   This is a purely contractual rather than statutory exclusion of liability and there is no equivalent provision concerning privilege under Sch 17, para 11, which only applies in relation to complaints made under the scheme's compulsory jurisdiction. See also paras 14.37, 14.38.

Procedure and consultation

14.46   The scheme operator must publish a draft of any proposed rules including an explanation of the proposed rules and a statement that it will have regard to any representations received in relation to the proposed rules, within a specified time. If the final rules are significantly different to the draft rules consulted on, the scheme operator must publish a statement of the differences (Sch 17, para 22). If the scheme operator makes rules relating to its voluntary jurisdiction, it must do so in writing (Sch 17, para 20(3)), and give a copy to the FSA without delay (Sch 17, para 20(1)). Any revocation[1] of those rules must be notified to the FSA in writing, likewise without delay (Sch 17, para 20(2)). The scheme operator is required, immediately after making voluntary jurisdiction rules, to arrange for them to be printed and made available to the public (Sch 17, para 20(4)), but can charge a reasonable fee (Sch 17, para 20(5)). If the scheme operator has certified that the rules are those made by the scheme operator, that they are a true copy and that they were made available to the public as at a specified date, the rules are then considered to be verified (Sch 17, para 21).

---

[1]   Any amendment to the rules must be made by revoking the existing rules and making new rules in accordance with the procedures laid down in FSMA 2000.

Delegation by and to other schemes

14.47   The scheme operator may, subject to FSA approval (Sch 17, para 19(3)), arrange to delegate to another body any part of the scheme's voluntary jurisdiction or to assume the exercise by the scheme of any function of that other body as if it were part of the voluntary jurisdiction of the scheme (Sch 17, para 19(1)). A relevant body for these purposes is one which the scheme operator is satisfied is responsible for a broadly similar or comparable scheme for resolving disputes and exercises its jurisdiction in a way which is compatible with the way in which complaints must be handled under FSMA 2000 (Sch 17, para 19(2)).

THE OMBUDSMAN'S POWER TO REQUIRE INFORMATION

14.48   FSMA 2000, s 231 provides that where an ombudsman has given written notice to a party to a complaint that he wishes to be provided with specified information or documents or information or documents of a specified category which the ombudsman considers necessary for determining the complaint, that party must do so (s 231(1)–(3)). If it does not, the ombudsman may certify the failure to provide the required information or documents in writing to the court for it to consider the matter (s 232(1)). If the court[1] determines that the defaulter[2] does not have a reasonable excuse for failing to comply with the ombudsman's requirement, the courts may hold the defaulter in contempt (s 232(2)).

---

[1]   The High Court or, in Scotland, the Court of Session (s 232(3)).
[2]   If the defaulter is a company, this includes a director or officer of that company and if the defaulter is a limited liability company, an 'officer' means a member of the limited liability company. See the Limited Liability Partnership Regulations 2001, SI 2001/1090, Sch 5, para 21.

14.49   If information or documents are produced in accordance with a request from an ombudsman, the ombudsman may take copies or extracts or require the person producing the document to provide an explanation of the document (s 231(4)).[1] If the person fails to produce the document, the ombudsman may require him to state where the document is to the best of his knowledge and belief (s 231(5)).

---

[1]   Any lien on a document is not affected by producing it to an ombudsman under this Part of FSMA 2000 (s 231(6)).

CHALLENGES TO SCHEME DECISIONS

14.50   The scheme of FSMA 2000 provides no express appeal or review mechanism for parties dissatisfied with a determination or other decision of an ombudsman. So far as the European Convention on Human Rights is concerned, that state of affairs reflects the Government's intention to seek to ensure compliance with Art 6 of the Convention[1] within the scheme procedures themselves rather than by providing a curative appeal to a mainstream court. However, the possibility still remains that the High Court will accept jurisdiction whether by way of judicial review,[2] or, perhaps, in contract[3] to correct procedural or legal errors which prejudice a party. The court is particularly likely to intervene if it is established that the proceedings have been conducted in a way which infringes either express procedural rules or rights guaranteed by Art 6. It is also more likely to intervene at the behest of a respondent than a complainant, since the complainant is not required to accept the decision of the ombudsman (see eg, s 228(4)(c)).

---

[1]   See paras 2.104–2.111. The issue of the application of the Human Rights Act 2000 to FOS has given rise to some issues and to the position of FOS within the tribunals regime. In the 2000–2001 Annual Report of the Council on Tribunals the Council commented: 'We ourselves had not found this a wholly straightforward matter. We understand the reasons why supervision [of FOS] is not thought to be appropriate at this stage but find it disappointing that our involvement could be thought to slow down a process or to make it more formal. The Treasury expect to conduct a review of aspects of the 2000 Act two years after it comes into force. We shall be interested in that review and in particular in any further consideration that may be given to oral hearings by the FOS and indeed the experience of the FOS in this regard. We also note that the Leggatt Review recommended that we should be given supervision over the FOS.' (Sir Andrew Leggatt's report on the Tribunals system, *Tribunals for Users—One system, one service*, August 2001). Annual Report, Section 4 Finance, para 7. This debate is likely to continue in the process of constitutional reform announced by the UK Government in June 2003.

[2]   See for example, *R (on the application of Green) v Financial Ombudsman Service Ltd* [2003] EWHC 338 (Admin), [2003] All ER (D) 399 (Feb).

[3]   In relation to the voluntary jurisdiction.

15 Collective investment schemes

INTRODUCTION

15.1 The Financial Services and Markets Act 2000 (FSMA 2000), Pt XVII (Chs I–VI) defines the framework for various types of collective investment schemes and how they are to be regulated by the Financial Services Authority (FSA).

DEFINITION OF A COLLECTIVE INVESTMENT SCHEME

15.2 Part XVII, Ch I (ss 235–237) is an interpretative chapter. Section 235(1) defines a 'collective investment scheme' for the purposes of FSMA 2000 as 'any arrangements with respect to property of any description, including money, the purpose or effect of which is to enable persons taking part in the arrangements (whether by becoming owners of the property or any part of it or otherwise) to participate in or receive profits or income arising from the acquisition, holding, management or disposal of the property or sums paid out of such profits or income'.

15.3 To fall within this definition, however, the arrangements must be such that the participants in them do not have day-to-day control over the management of the property comprising the scheme, regardless of whether the participants have a right to be consulted or to give directions regarding the scheme (s 235(2)). The arrangements must also bear either or both the hallmarks of a collective investment scheme. The two hallmarks are that contributions of the participants and the profits or income are pooled and that the property is managed as a whole by or on behalf of an operator of the scheme (s 235(3)). In FSMA 2000 the term 'units' is used, in relation to collective investment schemes, to indicate the rights or interests, however described, of the participants in the scheme (s 237(2)).

15.4 If the arrangements provide for pooling of profits or income, the scheme will not constitute a single collective investment scheme unless the participants can exchange rights in one part of the scheme for rights in another (s 235(4)).

15.5   FSMA 2000 also covers both trust-based and corporate-based schemes. It defines a 'unit trust scheme' as a collective investment scheme under which the property is held on trust for the participants (s 237(1)). In this context, a trustee is the person who holds the property of the scheme on trust for the participants. If the unit trust scheme has a separate trustee, the operator of a unit trust scheme is the manager. In relation to an open-ended company,[1] the operator is the company itself (s 237(2)).

---

[1]   See paras 15.8–15.12.

Treasury exemption orders

15.6   The Treasury may also make orders that limit or restrict the scope of the definition in s 235(1) or provide that if the arrangements fall within a specified category of arrangement, they will not be collective investment schemes (s 235(5)).[1]

---

[1]   The Financial Services and Markets Act 2000 (Collective Investment Schemes) Order 2001, SI 2001/1062, as amended by SI 2001/3650.

15.7   Most of the exemptions are implemented through the Financial Services and Markets Act 2000 (Collective Investment Schemes) Order 2001.[1] They are specified in the schedule and include exemptions for individual investment management arrangements (para 1), enterprise initiative schemes (para 2), deposit taking (para 3), common accounts (para 6), employee share schemes (para 8), commercial arrangements (para 9), bodies corporate (but not including UK incorporated limited liability partnerships) (para 21). This broadly replicates the position immediately before 'N2' (1 December 2002), but the exemptions are updated to include certain funeral plan arrangements (para 18).

---

[1]   SI 2001/1062, as amended by SI 2001/3650.

OPEN-ENDED INVESTMENT COMPANIES

Definition of open-ended investment company

15.8   Section 236(1) of FSMA 2000 defines an 'open-ended investment company' (or 'OEIC') as a collective investment scheme which satisfies both the 'property condition' and the 'investment condition'.[1] However, s 236(5) allows the Treasury to make regulations to amend this definition.[2]

[1]   FSMA Explanatory Notes, para 455. Investment trusts are not however collective investment schemes as they are closed-ended bodies corporate: see the Financial Services and Markets Act 2000 (Collective Investment Schemes) Order 2001, SI 2001/1062, Schedule, para 21.
[2]   The FSA has also issued formal guidance on the definition of an OEIC: see the FSA Handbook, Authorisation manual, AUTH Appendix 2.1.

15.9   The property condition is that the property belongs beneficially to and is managed by or on behalf of a body corporate having as its purpose the investment of pooled funds with the aim of spreading investment risk and giving its members the benefit of the management of those funds by or on behalf of that body corporate (s 236(2)).

15.10   The investment condition is that, in relation to a body corporate, a reasonable investor would expect to be able to realise his investment, within a reasonable period, by reference to the value of shares in or securities of the body corporate held by him as a participant of the scheme, and that he can be satisfied that this investment would be realised on the basis of the net asset value of the property in respect of which the scheme makes arrangements (s 236(3)).[1] The investment condition will not, however, be deemed to be satisfied by any actual or potential redemption or repurchase of shares or securities[2] under the Companies Act 1985, Pt V, Ch VII, the Companies (Northern Ireland) Order 1986, Pt VI, Ch VII, corresponding provisions in any other EEA state, or those provisions in force in a country or territory other than an EEA state which the Treasury has designated for these purposes (s 236(4)).

[1]   See HC SC A, 2 December 1999, col 1115 and HL Committee, 30 March 2000, col 939. In addition see HL Report Stage, 9 May 2000, col 1494 and HC Consideration of Lords Amendment, 5 June 2000, col 121.
[2]   Companies Act 1985, Pt V, Ch VII does not define the term 'securities'.

15.11   The Treasury may make regulations to regulate OEICs and to facilitate the carrying on of collective investment by them (s 262(1)).[1] These regulations[2] may provide—
   —   for the incorporation and registration in Great Britain of bodies corporate;
   —   for the entities thus incorporated to take such form as may be specified;
   —   for the purposes for which an OEIC may exist, the investments it may issue and otherwise as to its constitution;
   —   as to the management and operation of an OEIC and the management of its property;

— as to the powers, duties, rights and liabilities of the body corporate and its directors, depositary, shareholders and persons who hold beneficial title to its shares, its auditor, and any other persons acting or purporting to act on its behalf (s 262(2)(a)–(e)).

---

[1]   FSMA 2000, s 263 amends the Companies Act 1985, s 716(1), which provides for a prohibition on the formation of companies with more than 20 members unless registered under the 1985 Act. This is now extended to include the words 'is incorporated by virtue of regulations made under section 262 of the Financial Services and Markets Act 2000'.
[2]   Before N2, the Open-Ended Investment Companies (Investment Companies with Variable Capital) Regulations 1996, SI 1996/2827 established the framework for regulating OEICs which met the definition of a UCITS under the UCITS Directive. These regulations were replaced by the Open-Ended Investment Companies Regulations 2001, SI 2001/1228.

15.12 The regulations may also specify the procedures and other matters for—
— the merger of one or more OEICs or the division of such a body corporate;
— the appointment and removal of an auditor of such an OEIC;
— the winding up or dissolution of an OEIC;
— such a body corporate or any director or depositary to be required to comply with a direction given by the FSA;
— enabling the FSA to apply to the courts for an order removing or replacing any director or depositary of an OEIC;
— carrying out investigations in relation to OEICs by the FSA or the Secretary of State; or
— corresponding to any provision in FSMA 2000, Pt XVII, Ch III (relating to unit trust schemes) including the FSA's power to make rules in respect of any such provisions (s 262(2)(f)–(l)).

These regulations may also impose criminal liability for any contravention or breach of a requirement and may confer new functions on the FSA (s 262(3)(a), (b)). They may authorise the FSA to make rules and to confer jurisdiction on any court or on the Tribunal. They may also allow the FSA to charge fees in connection with carrying out its functions under the regulations (s 262(3)(c)–(e)). They may apply, modify or exclude any primary or subordinate legislation, including any provision of or made under FSMA 2000, in relation to OEICs (s 262(3)(f)). They may also make any consequential amendments, repeals or revocations of such legislation including the power to extend or adapt any power to make subordinate legislation, or may modify or exclude any rule of law in relation to OEICs (s 262(3)(g), (h), (4)). These regulations may, in particular, revoke the Open-Ended Investment Companies (Investment Companies with Variable Capital) Regulations 1996,[1] and may provide for such other things done under or in accordance with them to be treated as if they had been done in accordance with regulations made under s 262 (s 262(5)).[2]

---

[1]   SI 1996/2827.
[2]   See the Open-Ended Investment Companies Regulations 2001, SI 2001/1228, regs 84 and 85.

AUTHORISED AND UNAUTHORISED SCHEMES

15.13 As with the pre-N2 regulatory regime, collective investment schemes can be either—

— *authorised*: an authorised unit trust scheme for the purposes of FSMA 2000, Pt XVII means a unit trust scheme which has been authorised by virtue of an authorisation order made under s 243 and similarly an authorised OEIC under the relevant regulations and for which there is an authorisation order (s 237(3));[1]

— *recognised*: a recognised scheme is a scheme organised or incorporated in another jurisdiction, which has been recognised under the procedures set out in s 264 (EEA schemes which meet the requirements of the European Directive on undertakings for collective investment in transferable securities (the 'UCITS Directive')),[2] s 270 (schemes in designated countries or territories outside the UK) or s 272 (individually recognised overseas schemes) (s 237(3));

— *unauthorised*: unauthorised unit trust schemes include a wide range of unit trusts such as certain exempt funds which do not meet the specified criteria or do not require authorisation under s 243 as well as a number of limited partnership arrangements and other arrangements which are not or do not qualify for authorisation; or

— *unrecognised*: unrecognised schemes include a range of overseas collective investment schemes which have not been recognised for the purposes of this chapter of the Act and therefore are subject to restrictions on their promotion under FSMA 2000, Pt XVII, Ch II.

---

[1] For comparison of powers under FSA 1986 and FSMA 2000 in relation to authorised unit trust schemes and OEICs see Table below.

FSA 1986 Provisions	*FSMA 2000 Provisions*
Section 81	Section 247 (trust scheme rules)
Section 85	Section 248 (scheme particulars rules)
Section 86(3)	Section 264(3) (schemes constituted in other EEA states)
Section 87(4)	Section 270(6) (designated territories schemes)
Section 87(5)	Section 278 (rules as to scheme particulars)
Section 88(10)	Section 278 (rules as to scheme particulars)
Section 90	Section 283 (facilities and information in UK)
Open-Ended Investment Companies (Investment Companies with Variable Capital) Regulations 1996	Open-Ended Investment Companies Regulations 2001, SI 2001/1228

Source: FSA CP 62, Collective Investment Schemes sourcebook, August 2000, Annex 2, para 3.
[2] Council Directive 85/611/EEC, as amended by Directive 88/220/EEC.

15.14   Under s 347(1)(b)–(d) the FSA is required, as part of its general record-keeping obligations, to keep a public record of all authorised unit trust schemes, authorised OEICs and recognised schemes.

SINGLE PROPERTY SCHEMES

15.15   FSMA 2000 also provides for specific types of schemes. Single property schemes are those schemes where the property of the scheme (apart from cash and other assets held for management purposes) is a single building or a single building with ancillary buildings managed by or on behalf of the operator of the scheme, or a group of adjacent buildings managed by him or on his behalf as a single enterprise (with or without ancillary land, furniture, fixtures or fittings or other contents) (s 239(3)). These schemes must also otherwise satisfy the requirements of regulations to be made by the Treasury exempting them from the restrictions on promotion set out in s 238(1) (s 239(1), (2)). The FSA may also make rules in respect of such schemes imposing certain duties or liabilities on the operator, trustee or depositary exempted by the Treasury regulations, and may extend the rules applicable to authorised unit trust schemes (s 239(4), (5)).

AUTHORISED UNIT TRUST SCHEMES

15.16   Unit trust schemes[1] may be authorised,[2] recognised or unregulated. If an application is made to the FSA to authorise a unit trust scheme by the manager and trustee, or proposed manager and trustee, of the scheme (who must be different: see s 242(2)), it must be in the form that the FSA may direct and must provide as much information as may be required for determining whether to grant the order for authorisation (s 242(1), (3)). The FSA may also require further information from applicants, in such form, or verified in such a way, as the FSA may require, and different directions may be given, and different requirements may be imposed, on different applications (s 242(4)–(6)). An application for authorisation may be withdrawn by the applicant at any time before it has been determined by the FSA under s 244 or 245 (s 244(3)).

---

[1]   'Unit trust scheme' is defined in ss 417(1) and 237(1).
[2]   'Authorised unit trust scheme' is defined in s 237(3).

Authorisation orders

15.17 To declare that a unit trust scheme is an authorised scheme once it has received an application, the FSA must determine first whether the unit trust scheme complies with the requirements in s 243 as follows (s 243(1)(a))—

— The manager and the trustee must each be authorised persons who have permission to carry out their respective roles and each must be a body corporate incorporated in the UK or another EEA state[1] and have a place of business in the UK. In addition each must administer their affairs in the country in which they are incorporated and be independent of one another (s 243(4), (5), (7)).

— The name of the scheme to be authorised must not be undesirable or misleading and the purposes of the scheme must be reasonably capable of being carried into effect (s 243(8), (9)).

— The scheme must allow participants to redeem their units at a price related to the net asset value of the property to which the units relate on the basis determined by the scheme (s 243(10)).

— The scheme is to be treated as complying with s 243(10) if it requires the manager to ensure that participants are able to sell their units on an investment exchange at a price not significantly different from net asset value (s 243(11)).

---

[1] If the manager of the unit trust scheme is incorporated in another EEA state, the scheme must not be one which satisfies the requirements in s 264 for recognised overseas schemes. If it does satisfy those requirements, that route to authorisation is the appropriate one (s 243(6)).

15.18 The scheme must also comply with the requirements of the trust scheme rules made by the FSA under s 247.[1] The FSA must be provided with a copy of the trust deed and with a certificate, signed by a solicitor, certifying that the scheme does so comply (s 243(1)(c)).[2]

---

[1] See the FSA Handbook, Collective Investment Schemes sourcebook, CIS 2.

[2] For example, no trust deed of an authorised unit trust scheme may contain a provision that would have the effect of exempting the manager or trustee from liability for their failure to exercise due care and diligence in discharging their functions and any such provision would be deemed to be void (s 253).

15.19 If the FSA is satisfied that the conditions set out in s 243 have been met, it may make an order declaring the unit trust scheme to be authorised (s 243(1)).[1] The FSA must provide the applicant (presumably the manager and the trustee or the proposed manager and trustee) with written notice that the authorisation order has been made (s 243(2), (3)).

---

[1]   Schemes which had been authorised under the FSA 1986 regime were treated as authorised (subject to certain conditions) under the Financial Services and Markets Act 2000 (Transitional Provisions) (Authorised Persons etc) Order 2001, SI 2001/2636, art 65.

Determination of applications

15.20   The FSA has six months beginning on the date on which it receives the completed application to determine the application under s 242 (s 244(1)). However, the FSA may also determine an incomplete application if it deems it appropriate to do so and it must do so within 12 months from the date on which the application for authorisation was first received, even if the application was not completed by then (s 244(2)).

Procedure when refusing an application

15.21   If the FSA proposes to refuse an application, it must give each of the applicants (ie, the manager and trustee) a warning notice of its intentions (s 245(1)). If it determines that it will refuse such an application, the FSA must give each of the applicants a decision notice and either applicant may refer the matter to the Tribunal (s 245(2)).[1]

---

[1]   See the FSA Handbook, Decision making manual, DEC 2 for procedures relating to warning notices and decision notices.

Certificates

15.22   If an application has been made by a manager or trustee of a unit trust scheme for a scheme which complies with the UCITS Directive, then the manager or trustee may request the FSA to issue a certificate[1] to the effect that the scheme complies with the conditions set out in the relevant directive. UCITS certificates may be issued either at the time of authorisation or at any subsequent time while the scheme is still authorised (s 246).

---

[1]   The certificate is required for a scheme to exercise its passport rights under the UCITS Directive in other EEA jurisdictions.

THE FSA'S RULE-MAKING POWERS IN RELATION TO AUTHORISED UNIT TRUST SCHEMES

Trust scheme rules

15.23   The FSA has wide-ranging powers to make rules as to the constitution, management and operation of authorised unit trust schemes, including the contents of the trust deed and any provisions to be dealt with in it (s 247(3)), the respective powers, duties, rights and liabilities of the manager and trustee of the scheme, the rights and duties of the participants and the process for winding up any such scheme (s 247(1)).[1] These trust scheme rules are directly binding on the manager, trustee and participants, and are not affected by any terms in the trust deed (s 247(4)).

---

[1]   See the FSA Handbook, Collective Investment Schemes sourcebook, CIS 2.2.8. In May 2003 the FSA issued Consultation Paper 185 (Collective Investment Schemes—a new approach) which set out the FSA's proposal for reforming the regulation of collective investment schemes including unit trusts and OEICs. The proposals include permitting a wider range of investment schemes with additional disclosure and transparency for investors. It is also proposed that there will be separate classes of 'institutional' funds available. The FSA proposes to make new rules which will come into force in 2004 and after a transitional period these new rules will apply to all UK schemes from February 2007.

15.24   The trust scheme rules may also provide for the issue and redemption of units of the scheme, the payment of expenses and the means of meeting those expenses on behalf of the scheme, the appointment, removal, powers and duties of auditors, restrictions or limits on the investment and borrowing powers, record-keeping and the preparation of periodic reports for participants and the FSA, and the amendment of the scheme (s 247(2)).[1]

---

[1]   Section 247(5) provides for the Treasury to have the power to make orders to modify these provisions if appropriate as a result of changes in the companies legislation of Great Britain or Northern Ireland which relate to a change in the rights and duties of persons holding a beneficial interest in shares in a company and it appears to the Treasury that it is expedient to modify FSA rule-making powers under this section.

Scheme particulars rules

15.25   The FSA may also make rules relating to the documentation which the manager of an authorised unit trust scheme must prepare and submit to the FSA and publish to participants or prospective participants. The documentation must include 'scheme particulars'[1] which provide information about the scheme, and any requirements specified in the rules (s 248(1)–(3)). The rules may also require that if the manager makes changes to those particulars he must update, amend and publish new scheme particulars where a significant new matter arises or the information would have previously been required under the scheme particular rules (s 248(4)).[2]

_____
[1]   See the FSA Handbook, Collective Investment Schemes sourcebook, CIS 3.5.
[2]   CIS 3.4.

15.26   The scheme particular rules made by the FSA also provide that the person responsible for the scheme particulars may be liable to pay compensation to any qualifying person[1] who has suffered a loss as a result of any untrue or misleading statement or any material omission in the scheme particulars (s 248(5)).[2] These rules do not, however, affect any other liability which a person who is responsible for the scheme particulars may have for a false or misleading statement or a material omission apart from these rules (s 248(7)).

_____
[1]   A 'qualifying person' is a person who is or will be a participant in the scheme or one who has a beneficial interest in units in the scheme (s 248(6)).
[2]   See the FSA Handbook, Collective Investment Schemes sourcebook, CIS 3.3.

Modification or waiver of the rules

15.27   The FSA may disapply or modify all or any of the trust scheme rules and the scheme particular rules in certain cases. Any person to whom the rules apply may make an application in relation to rules applicable to them, or the FSA may, on an application of, or, with the consent of the manager and trustee of a scheme acting jointly, direct[1] that all or any of the rules do not apply to that scheme, or apply with such modifications as the direction may require (s 250(1)–(3)).

_____
[1]   See the FSA Handbook, Supervision manual, SUP 8 for procedures in relation to giving such a direction.

15.28   In either case, the application for waiver or modification must be made in the form which the FSA directs but may only be granted if the FSA is satisfied that compliance with the rules would be unduly burdensome or would not achieve the purpose for which the rules were made and the modification would not result in undue risk for investors (s 148(4), as modified by s 250(4)(a), (5)(a)). Any direction waiving or modifying the trust scheme rules or the scheme particular rules may be given subject to conditions (s 148(5)) and, unless the FSA decides it is inappropriate or unnecessary to do so, the direction must be made public and brought to the attention of those persons who are likely to be affected or those who are likely to make a similar application (s 148(6)).[1] This would be the case, for example, if the rule to be waived was one, the breach of which would constitute a breach of statutory duty, or if the publicity would damage the commercial interests of the authorised person or other members of his immediate group[2] or if the publication would otherwise be contrary to any international obligation of the UK (s 148(7), as modified by s 250(4)(b), (c), (5)(b), (c)). A direction made under s 250 may be revoked or varied (s 148(9), as modified by s 250(5)(e)).

---

[1]   See the FSA Handbook, Supervision manual, SUP 8.6. Waivers are published on the FSA's website at www.fsa.gov.uk.

[2]   'Immediate group' is defined as an authorised person, its parent undertaking, a subsidiary undertaking of the authorised person, a subsidiary undertaking of a parent undertaking of the authorised person or a parent undertaking of a subsidiary undertaking of the authorised person (s 148(11)).

CHANGES TO THE SCHEME OR ITS MANAGEMENT

15.29   The manager of an authorised unit trust scheme must give the FSA written notice of any intention to alter the scheme or to replace its trustee (s 251(1)). Any notice which involves a change to the scheme's trust deed must be accompanied by a certificate from a solicitor to the effect that the change will not affect the deed's compliance with the trust scheme rules (s 251(2)).[1]

---

[1]   See the FSA Handbook, Collective Investment Schemes sourcebook, CIS 7.11 and 16.1.12G.

15.30   If the trustee of such a scheme intends to replace the manager of the scheme, he must give the FSA written notice. The proposed change must not be given effect until the FSA has approved it by written notice or one month has expired from the date on which the notice was given without the manager or the trustee having been given a warning notice under s 252 (s 251(3), (4)).

15.31   The FSA may only approve any change in the management of the scheme (ie, the replacement of the manager or trustee) if it is satisfied that the scheme will continue to comply with the requirements of s 243(4)–(7) (s 251(5)).[1]

---

[1]   See para 15.17.

Procedure when refusing approval

15.32   If the FSA proposes to refuse an application for a change of management, it must give the person who has given the notice under s 251 a warning notice.[1] If it decides to refuse an application for a change to the scheme, it must serve the warning notice[2] on both the manager and the trustee of the scheme (s 252(1), (2)). Such notices must be received by that person within one month of the date on which the proposed change was notified to the FSA (s 252(3)). Having given that person a warning notice, if the FSA decides not to approve the change, it must give that person a decision notice and that person may refer the matter to the Tribunal (s 252(4)).

---

[1] See s 387. See also the FSA Handbook, Collective Investment Schemes sourcebook, CIS 16.1.13G–16.1.15G.
[2] See s 388.

WITHDRAWAL/LOSS OF AUTHORISATION— REVOKING ORDERS

15.33 Any authorisation order made by the FSA under s 243 may be revoked if it appears to the FSA that—
— one or more of the requirements for making the order are no longer satisfied;
— the manager or the trustee has contravened a requirement imposed on him by or under FSMA 2000;
— the manager or trustee has knowingly or recklessly given the FSA information which is false or misleading in any material respect;
— no regulated activity (presumably establishing, operating or winding up collective investment schemes) has been carried on for 12 months or more; or
— the revocation is in the interests of participants or potential participants in the scheme (s 254(1)).

In determining whether the revocation of the authorisation order is in the interests of participants or potential participants, the FSA may take into account any matter relating to—
— the scheme;
— the manager or trustee;
— the persons employed by the scheme or associated with the manager or the trustee;
— any director of the manager or trustee;
— any person exercising influence over the manager or trustee;
— any body corporate in the same group as the manager or trustee;
— any director of such a group company; or
— any other person exercising influence over such a group company (s 254(2)).[1]

1   See the FSA Handbook, Enforcement manual, ENF 16.2.3G, 16.2.4G and 16.2.10G–16.2.14G.

15.34 If the FSA proposes to make a revoking order[1] it must give the manager and trustee of the authorised unit trust scheme separate warning notices and if the FSA decides to revoke authorisation it must give each of them a decision notice without delay and such a decision may be referred to the Tribunal (s 255(2)).

1   A 'revoking order' is defined as an order made under s 254 revoking authorisation (s 255(1)).

Requests for revocation of authorisation order

15.35 A revoking order may also be made at the request of the manager or trustee (s 256(1)). In this case, the FSA must give written notice to both the manager and the trustee that such an order will be made (s 256(2)). The FSA may refuse such a request, however, if it considers that it is not in the public interest to grant the request until any matter concerning the scheme has been investigated or if the revocation of authorisation would not be in the interests of participants or would otherwise be incompatible with any Community obligation (s 256(3)). If the FSA proposes to refuse a request from a manager or trustee for a revoking order, it must give separate warning notices to the manager and the trustee of the scheme and if it decides not to grant the revoking request, it must give both the manager and the trustee a decision notice, and they may refer the matter to the Tribunal (s 256(4), (5)).

POWERS OF INTERVENTION IN RELATION TO AUTHORISED UNIT TRUST SCHEMES

15.36 The FSA has broad powers to make a direction requiring the manager of an authorised unit trust scheme to cease issuing or redeeming units under the scheme or requiring the manager and trustee of the scheme to wind it up (s 257(2)) if it appears to the FSA that—

— one or more of the requirements for making an authorisation order are no longer satisfied;

— the manager or trustee has contravened or is likely to contravene any requirement imposed on him by or under FSMA 2000;

— the manager or trustee has either knowingly or recklessly provided information to the FSA which is false or misleading in any material respect; or

—   it is desirable to give a direction to protect the interests of participants or potential participants (s 257(1)).[1]

---

[1]   See the FSA Handbook, Enforcement manual, ENF 16.2.5G. Contravention of a direction can give rise to an action for damages under s 150 (s 257(5)).

15.37   If the scheme's authorisation is subsequently revoked, that revocation does not affect any direction then in force (s 257(3)). In addition, a subsequent direction may also be given under s 257 once an authorisation order has been revoked if a direction was already in force at the time the revocation was made (s 257(4)). If an application has been made by the manager or trustee for a direction to be revoked or varied by the FSA under s 257(6)[1] and the FSA proposes to vary the direction but not in accordance with the application, or to refuse to revoke or vary the direction, it must give the applicant a warning notice (s 260(1)). If the FSA subsequently decides to refuse to revoke or vary the direction in accordance with the application, it must give the applicant a decision notice and the applicant may refer the matter to the Tribunal (s 260(2)).

---

[1]   The FSA has power to revoke or vary a previously imposed direction on its own initiative (s 257(6)). See the FSA Handbook, Enforcement manual, ENF 16.2.5G–16.2.7G and 16.2.10G–16.2.14G.

15.38   A direction made under s 257 takes effect immediately if the notice states that is the case, or on such other date as may be specified in the notice (s 259(1)(a), (b)), but only if the FSA is satisfied that it is necessary for the direction to take effect immediately or on that date (s 259(2)). If no date is specified in the notice, the direction takes effect when the matter to which it relates is no longer open to review (s 259(1)(c)). Whether a matter is open to review is to be determined by reference to s 391(8) (s 259(14)). This states that a matter is still open for review if—

—   the period during which any person may refer the matter to the Tribunal is still running;

—   the matter has been referred to the Tribunal but has not been dealt with;

—   the matter has been referred to the Tribunal and dealt with but the period during which an appeal may be brought against the Tribunal's decision is running; or

—   such an appeal has been brought but has not yet been determined.

15.39   When the FSA decides to make a direction under s 257, it must give separate written notice to the manager and trustee providing details of the direction, informing those persons to whom it has been given when it takes effect and providing the reasons for making the direction and for its determination as to when it is to take effect (s 259(3), (4)(a)–(c)). It must also inform the person that representations may be made to the FSA within a specified period in relation to the direction[1] and that he has the right to refer the matter to the Tribunal (s 259(4)(d), (e)). It must also inform him of the procedures for doing so (s 259(12)).

---

[1]   The FSA may extend the period within which representation to it may be made (s 259(7)).

15.40   If, having considered any representations made by the person in respect of whom notice has been given, the FSA decides to give the direction as proposed, or if the direction has been given, not to revoke it, it must give separate written notices to the manager and trustee of the scheme (s 259(8)) including notice that the matter may be referred to the Tribunal and the procedures for such a reference (s 259(10), (12)).

15.41   However, if the FSA, after considering those representations, decides not to give the direction or to amend the terms of the direction, or to revoke a direction which has already been given effect, it must also give written notice to the manager and trustee (s 259(9)). If a notice is given to the effect that the FSA has decided to amend the terms of the direction, it must comply with the provisions of s 259(4) and (12) (s 249(11)).[1] This also applies to the variation of a direction at the FSA's own initiative (s 259(13)).

---

[1]   See para 15.39.

15.42   If the direction requires the manager to cease the issue or redemption of units of the scheme under s 257(2)(a), the notice must also state that the requirement has effect until a specified date or until a further direction is made (s 259(5)). If the direction requires the manager or trustee to wind up the scheme under s 257(2)(b), the scheme must be wound up by the date specified in the notice or, if no date is given, then as soon as practicable (s 259(6)).

15.43   A decision by the FSA to revoke a direction made under s 257 on its own initiative must be notified in writing to the manager and trustee of the authorised unit trust scheme (s 261(1)). If a direction has been made under s 257(6) to revoke or vary a direction and the FSA decides to revoke the direction or vary it in accordance with the application that has been made, the FSA must give the applicant written notice of its decision and must specify the date on which the decision takes effect (s 261(2), (3)). The FSA may also publish information about the revocation or variation in such a way as it considers appropriate (s 261(4)).

The FSA's power to obtain court orders in relation to authorised unit trust schemes

15.44   If a direction could have been made in respect of an authorised unit trust scheme under s 257,[1] the FSA may apply to the court[2] for an order removing the manager or trustee (or both) and replacing either or both with a suitable person or persons nominated by the FSA (s 258(1)).[3]

---

[1]   See para 15.36.
[2]   The court means the High Court and, in Scotland, the Court of Session (s 258(7)).
[3]   See the FSA Handbook, Enforcement manual, ENF 16.2.8G.

15.45   A person nominated under s 258(1) must meet the criteria laid down in s 243(4)–(7).[1] If no such person can be nominated, the FSA may apply to the court for an order removing the manager or trustee or both and appointing an authorised person to wind up the scheme (s 258(2), (3)).[2] The court has wide powers to make any order it deems fit under this section (s 258(4)). Where the court has made an order appointing an authorised person to wind up the scheme it may, on application from the FSA, rescind that order and substitute an order appointing a new manager or trustee or both (s 258(5)). The FSA must give written notice of making an application under s 258 to the manager and trustee of the scheme (s 258(6)).

---

[1]   See para 15.17.
[2]   See the FSA Handbook, Enforcement manual, ENF 16.2.8G–16.2.14G.

MISCELLANEOUS MATTERS RELATING TO AUTHORISED UNIT TRUST SCHEMES AND OEICs

Disqualification of auditors

15.46   If it appears to the FSA that the auditor of an authorised unit trust scheme has failed to comply with any duty imposed on him by the trust scheme rules, the FSA may disqualify that person from acting as the auditor for an authorised unit trust scheme or an authorised OEIC (s 249(1)).[1] Where the FSA proposes to make such a disqualification, it must give that person a warning notice and if it decides to disqualify him, it must give him a decision notice and that decision may be referred to the Tribunal (s 345(2), (3), (5), as applied by s 249(2)). The FSA may remove such a disqualification if it is satisfied that that person will in the future comply with any duties imposed under FSMA 2000 (s 345(4), as applied by s 249(2)).

¹   See the FSA Handbook, Enforcement manual, ENF 17.3.

RECOGNISED OVERSEAS SCHEMES: SCHEMES CONSTITUTED IN OTHER EEA STATES

15.47   To give effect to the UCITS Directive, FSMA 2000, Pt XVII, Ch V (ss 264–283) sets out the procedures for recognising collective investment schemes (including both contractual or trust schemes and corporate schemes such as OEICs (s 264(5)) established in other EEA jurisdictions. Such a scheme will be a recognised scheme if it satisfies the requirements of s 264[1] and the operator of the scheme has given the FSA the requisite notice (s 264(1)).

¹   As well as those prescribed by order (s 264(1)(a)): see the Financial Services and Markets Act 2000 (Collective Investment Schemes Constituted in Other EEA States) Regulations 2001, SI 2001/2383. Further changes take effect from February 2004 to implement the UCITS Management Directive (2001/107/EC): Collective Investment Schemes (Miscellaneous Amendments) Regulations 2003, SI 2003/2066. See also the FSA Policy Statement 'The UCITS Management Directive: Implementing the UCITS Amending Directive (2001/107/EC), August 2003.

15.48   A person who is an operator, trustee or depositary of a scheme recognised under s 264[1] will be an authorised person by virtue of s 36 and Sch 5,[2] and will be deemed to have permission to carry on any regulated activity appropriate to the capacity in which he is acting within Sch 2, para 8[3] and any other regulated activity in connection with or for the purposes of the scheme.[4]

¹   The FSA uses the term 'UCITS qualifier' in relation to such persons: see the FSA Handbook, Authorisation manual, AUTH 5.3.14G.
²   Sch 5, para 1(1).
³   Sch 5, para 2(1). See also AUTH 5.3.16G.
⁴   That paragraph defines the activity of establishing, operating or winding up a collective investment scheme including acting as the trustee of a unit trust scheme, depositary of a collective investment scheme other than a unit trust scheme or sole director of a body incorporated by virtue of regulations under FSMA 2000, s 262 (OEICs).

15.49   An authorised OEIC will also be deemed to be an authorised person[1] and will be deemed to have permission to carry on the operation of the scheme or any activity in connection with or for the purposes of the scheme.[2]

¹   Sch 5, para 1(3).
²   Sch 5, para 2(2). See also the FSA Handbook, Authorisation manual, AUTH 5.3.16G.

Notification process

15.50   At least two months before inviting persons in the UK to become participants in the scheme, the operator of the scheme must notify the FSA of his intention and advise the FSA how the invitation will be made (s 264(1)(b)).¹ That notification must include such information as the FSA may require, including information on the place of service for the operator of the scheme in the UK for notices and other documents required under FSMA 2000 (s 264(3)(b), (c)). It must also be accompanied by a certificate from the authority in the relevant EEA State that the scheme meets the requirements for compliance with any relevant EU instrument, including the UCITS Directive (s 264(3)(a)). The FSA has two months within which to consider the notice. If within that period it does not serve a notice on the operator of the scheme and the relevant regulator who has provided the certificate required under s 264(3) that the manner in which the invitation specified in the notice is to be made does not comply with UK law, the scheme will be a recognised scheme (s 264(2)).

¹   See the FSA Handbook, Collective Investment Schemes sourcebook, CIS 17.2.

15.51   If the FSA has served a notice on the operator and relevant regulator that the invitation does not comply with UK law, the notice must give the reasons for which the FSA considers that the law has not been complied with and must also provide a reasonable period (at least 28 days) within which either the operator or the regulator may make representations to the FSA (s 264(4)).

Representations from operator and references to the Tribunal

15.52   If, having served a notice under s 264(2), the FSA receives representations from the operator or the relevant regulator, it must decide, in the light of those representations, whether to withdraw that notice. If it decides to withdraw the notice, the scheme will be deemed to be a recognised scheme from the date of that withdrawal. However, if the FSA decides not to withdraw the notice, the FSA must give a decision notice to the operator, and the relevant regulator and the operator of the scheme may refer the matter to the Tribunal (s 265).

Disapplication of rules

15.53   FSMA 2000, s 266 provides that only the financial promotion rules (made under s 145) and the rules relating to facilities and information which operators of recognised schemes must maintain in the UK (made under s 283(1)) will apply to the operator, trustee or depository in relation to those regulated activities carried on by him in the UK for which he has permission.

Power of FSA to suspend promotion of scheme

15.54   If it appears to the FSA that the operator of a recognised scheme has made an invitation or communicated any other inducement in relation to the scheme in contravention of the financial promotion rules, the FSA may direct that the exemption under the financial promotion rules which would apply to such a scheme (s 238(1), (4)(c)) is not to apply and that s 238(5), which provides that the general restrictions on promotion in s 238(1) would not apply where the promotion is carried out in accordance with the FSA's rules, is not to apply to such an invitation or inducement (s 267(1), (2)).

15.55   Where the FSA has made a direction under s 267 to suspend the promotion of a scheme, it takes effect immediately[1] if the notice required states that that is the case or, if the notice specifies a date, then it takes effect on that date (s 268(1)). If no date is specified, it takes effect on the date when the matter is no longer open to review (to be determined in accordance with s 391(8)) (s 268(14)).[2] A direction under s 267(2) may have effect for a specified period, until a specified event occurs or until specified conditions are complied with (s 267(3)). The FSA must notify the operator of the scheme and inform the relevant authorities in the scheme's home state[3] that it is proposing to make such a direction (s 268(3)).

---

[1]   For the FSA to give effect to such a direction immediately or on a specified date, the FSA must consider whether it is necessary for that direction to be given such effect (s 268(2)).

[2]   See para 15.38.

[3]   The scheme's 'home state' is the EEA state in which the scheme is constituted and the competent authority is the authority responsible for authorising collective investment schemes in that jurisdiction (s 267(7)).

15.56   Notice of a direction must include the details of the direction, the date on which it is to take effect and the FSA's reasons for giving it and for its determination as to the date on which it is to take effect. The notice must inform the operator of the scheme that he may make representations to the FSA within a specified period[1] and that he has the right to refer the matter to the Tribunal (s 268(4)).

---

[1]   The FSA may extend the period allowed for the operator of the scheme to make representations (s 268(5)).

Procedure on giving, varying or revoking directions

15.57 If, after having considered any representations, the FSA decides to give the direction in the terms notified to the operator of the scheme or decides not to revoke the direction (if it has already been given), it must give the operator written notice and inform the relevant regulators in the scheme's home state (s 268(6), (7)). A notification given to the operator under this provision must also inform the operator of his right to refer the matter to the Tribunal (together with the procedures for doing so) (s 268(10), (12)). Similarly, if the FSA decides to give the direction in another form, not to give it at all, or to revoke a direction which has already come into effect, it must provide written notification to the operator of the scheme and to the relevant regulator informing them of its decision (s 268(8), (9)). Where the FSA proposes to give the direction in another form, it must include details in accordance with s 268(4),[1] including a statement that the operator may refer the matter to the Tribunal (together with the procedures for doing so) (s 268(11), (12)).

[1] See para 15.56.

15.58 Such a direction may be varied by the FSA, either on its own initiative or at the request of the operator of the scheme (s 267(4)). It may also be revoked if the FSA is satisfied that the conditions specified in the direction have been met, or it is no longer necessary for the direction to continue in force (s 267(5)). If the direction specifies that it has effect until a certain event occurs, such as imposing restrictions until a certain date, the direction will no longer have any effect once that event has taken place (s 267(6)). Where the FSA has varied a direction on its own initiative, the same procedures set out in s 268 for notifying the operator of the scheme and the relevant regulator apply (s 268(13)).[1] If the FSA decides to revoke a direction on its own initiative, it must give the operator of the scheme written notice (s 269(5)) and inform the relevant regulators of the scheme's home state (s 269(6)).

[1] See para 15.57.

15.59 Where the operator of a scheme has applied under s 267(4) or (5) to vary or revoke a direction and the FSA decides to grant the application, it must give the operator written notice of that decision (s 269(4)). If such an application is received and the FSA proposes to vary that direction otherwise than in accordance with the application or not to revoke the direction as requested, it must give the operator of the scheme a warning notice (s 269(1)). If the FSA decides to vary that direction otherwise than in accordance with the application or to refuse the application for variation or revocation, it must give the operator a decision notice (s 269(2))[1] and if the application is refused, the operator may refer the matter to the Tribunal (s 269(3)). Any notice given to an operator of a recognised scheme under s 269 must also be notified to the relevant regulator in the operator's home state (s 269(6)).

---

[1]   Having previously considered any representations made in response to the warning notice (see s 387(2)).

Withdrawal of recognised status

15.60   An operator of a recognised scheme may, on his own initiative, notify the FSA that he no longer wishes the scheme to be a recognised scheme (s 264(6)) and once such notice has been given, the scheme will cease to be a recognised scheme (s 264(7)).[1]

---

[1]   See the FSA Handbook, Collective Investment Schemes sourcebook, CIS 17.4.8G.

RECOGNISED SCHEMES IN DESIGNATED COUNTRIES OR TERRITORIES

15.61   In addition to EEA recognised schemes (which are limited to schemes constituted in other EEA states and must meet the criteria set out in s 264), FSMA 2000 provides for two further categories of recognised schemes: (1) those in designated countries or territories and (2) individually recognised overseas schemes.

15.62   Schemes in designated countries or territories are those which are managed in and authorised under the law of a country or territory outside the UK which has been designated for the purposes of s 270 by the Treasury.[1] The scheme must be of a class specified in an order made by the Treasury, where the operator has given notice to the FSA that it wishes to be recognised, and the FSA has either given its approval in writing or has not served a warning notice on the operator within two months of the operator having given such notice (s 270(1)). Where the operator of a scheme has given notice that it wishes to be recognised under s 270(1), the notice must also contain the address in the UK of a place for the service of documents on him and include such other information as the FSA may specify (s 270(6)).[2]

Procedure

15.63 The countries or territories which can be designated by the Treasury for the purposes of s 270 are limited to those in which the Treasury is satisfied that the law and practice under which collective investment schemes are authorised and supervised affords investors in the UK at least equivalent protections to that provided in relation to comparable authorised schemes (s 270(2)(a)).[1]

1 'Comparable authorised schemes' means authorised unit trust schemes, authorised OEICs or both (s 270(4)). See also para 15.62, fn 1.

15.64 In addition, the Treasury must be satisfied that adequate arrangements exist in those countries or territories for co-operation between the FSA and the relevant regulators or authorities responsible for the authorisation and supervision of collective investment schemes of the type specified in the Treasury order (s 270(2)(b), (3)). This might include the existence of a memorandum of understanding regarding the sharing of information or the co-operation between regulatory bodies. Where the Treasury has been requested to make such an order in respect of a specified country or territory, it must ask the FSA to prepare a report on the law and practice of that country or territory in relation to the authorisation and supervision of those schemes to be included in the order and on any existing or proposed co-operation agreements with that country or territory. The FSA must have regard to the Treasury's need to satisfy itself that the law and practice affords investors in the UK at least equivalent protection to that provided in relation to comparable authorised schemes and to satisfy itself on co-operation matters (s 270(5)(a)). The FSA has an obligation under FSMA 2000 to provide such a report (s 270(5)(b)) and the Treasury must have regard to that report in deciding whether to make any such order (s 270(5)(c)).[1]

1 See the Financial Services and Markets Act 2000 (Collective Investment Schemes) (Designated Countries and Territories) Order 2003, SI 2003/1181, which recites the request, the provision of, and the consideration of such a report.

15.65 If the FSA proposes not to grant an application from the operator of a scheme, it must, within two months of the date on which notice was given by the operator, give the operator a warning notice in accordance with the procedures set out in Pt XXVI (s 271(1), (2)). Having given the operator a warning notice, if the FSA decides not to grant the application, it must give the operator of the scheme a decision notice, and the operator has the right to refer the matter to the Tribunal (s 271(3)).

Rules as to scheme particulars

15.66   The FSA may make rules imposing duties or liabilities on operators of overseas schemes recognised under s 270 corresponding to those made under s 248 for the publication of scheme particulars in relation to authorised unit trust schemes (s 278).[1]

---

[1]   See the FSA Handbook, Collective Investment Schemes sourcebook, CIS 17.3.

Revocation of a designated overseas scheme

15.67   The FSA may revoke an order recognising a designated overseas scheme if it appears to the FSA that the operator, trustee or depositary of the scheme has contravened any obligation imposed on him by FSMA 2000 or has knowingly or recklessly given the FSA information which is false or misleading in any material particular or if it is in the interests of participants or potential participants (s 279(a), (b), (d)).[1]

---

[1]   See the FSA Handbook, Collective Investment Schemes sourcebook, CIS 17.4.9G.

15.68   If the FSA proposes to make a revocation order in respect of a scheme recognised under s 270, it must give a warning notice to the operator and trustee or depositary, if any, of the scheme (s 280(1)). If the FSA decides to make such an order or give a direction revoking a recognition order under s 270 it must give a decision notice to the operator and the trustee or depositary of the scheme without delay and they may refer the matter to the Tribunal (s 280(2)).

Directions in relation to recognised overseas schemes

15.69   If it appears to the FSA that the operator, trustee or depositary of a recognised scheme has contravened or is likely to contravene any requirement imposed on him by or under FSMA 2000, or has, in purported compliance with any such requirement, knowingly or recklessly provided false or misleading information which is material, or it is desirable to protect the interests of participants or potential participants in the UK, it may direct that the scheme is not to be treated as a recognised scheme for a specified period or that the scheme will not be a recognised scheme until a specified event has occurred or specified conditions set out in the direction have been complied with (s 281(2)(a), (b), (d)).

15.70 A direction made under s 281 has effect immediately if the FSA has determined it necessary and has so specified in the notice given to the operator and trustee or depositary of the scheme, or on such date as the notice may specify or (if no date is specified in the notice), when the matter is no longer open to review (s 282(1)–(3)).[1] The notice given under s 281 or a notice given under s 282, ie, which has immediate effect, must contain details of the direction and inform the persons to whom it has been given when it takes effect and state the FSA's reasons for giving it and for determining when it takes effect (s 282(4)(a)–(c)). The notice must also advise the person to whom it is addressed that he may make representations to the FSA within a specified period[2] and inform him of his right to refer the matter to the Tribunal and the procedures for doing so (s 282(4)(d), (e), (10)).

---

[1]   Section 282(12) provides that this is determined in accordance with s 391(8): see para 15.38.
[2]   The FSA may extend the period for representations to be made to it (s 282(5)).

15.71 If, having considered any representations which have been made, the FSA decides to give the direction as proposed, or, if the direction has already been given, not to revoke it, it must give separate written notice to the operator and the trustee or depositary of the scheme as relevant (s 282(6)). The FSA must inform him of his right to refer the matter to the Tribunal and the procedures for doing so (s 282(8), (10)). Alternatively, if after considering those representations the FSA decides not to give the direction as proposed, to give the direction in a manner other than that proposed in the notice or to revoke the direction if it has already been given, it must give separate written notice to the operator and the trustee or depositary concerned (s 282(7)). If the FSA decides to give the direction in a manner other than that proposed in the original notice it must provide the same details as those prescribed in s 282(4) (s 282(9)).

15.72 In cases where a direction has been made under s 270 and the FSA on its own initiative has decided to vary the terms of that direction, the same procedures apply (s 282(11)).

Facilities and information required to be maintained in the UK

15.73 Operators of schemes recognised under s 270 are subject to rules made by the FSA in relation to the facilities which they must maintain in the UK on the basis that the FSA thinks it desirable to do so in the interests of participants in those schemes (s 283(1)).[1] The FSA may give an operator of a recognised scheme a written notice which requires him to include specified explanatory information in any communication which is a communication of an invitation or inducement within the financial promotion rules, and which names the scheme (s 283(2)). A communication issued by the operator of a recognised scheme which originates outside the UK is only subject to these rules if the communication is capable of having an effect in the UK (s 283(3)).

---

[1] See the FSA Handbook, Collective Investment Schemes sourcebook, CIS 17.4.

INDIVIDUALLY RECOGNISED OVERSEAS SCHEMES

15.74 Where the FSA receives an application from the operator of a collective investment scheme which is managed in a country or territory outside the UK and it does not fulfil the criteria for being a recognised scheme either under s 264 or 270, the FSA may, if the scheme meets the criteria set out in s 272, grant the application and the scheme will be a recognised scheme (s 272(1)). If it grants the application, the FSA must give written notice to the applicant (s 275(3)).

15.75 To meet the criteria under s 272, the collective investment scheme must be an OEIC, or if it is not, the operator of the scheme must be a body corporate (s 272(7)). In addition, the operator of the scheme and any trustee or depositary of the scheme must also, if an authorised person, have permission to be the operator, trustee or depositary of such a scheme or, if not an authorised person, must be a fit and proper person to act in those capacities (s 272(8), (9)).

15.76 In determining whether these persons are 'fit and proper' the FSA may take into account any matters relating to—
— any person who is or will be employed by or associated with the operator, trustee or depositary;
— any director of the operator, trustee or depositary;
— any person exercising influence over the operator, trustee or depositary;
— any body corporate in the same group as the operator, trustee or depositary;
— any director of any such body; or
— any person exercising influence over any such body corporate (s 273).

The operator, trustee or depositary must also be willing and able to share information and to co-operate with the FSA 'in other ways' which are not specified in the legislation (s 272(10)). Additional requirements which recognised overseas schemes must meet include that—

— the name of the scheme must not be undesirable or misleading (s 272(11));
— the purposes of the scheme must be reasonably capable of being successfully carried into effect (s 272(12));
— the participants must be able to redeem their units at a price related to the net value of the property to which the units relate as determined under the scheme (s 272(13))[1] or to sell their units on an investment exchange at a price not significantly different from net asset value (s 272(14)).

---

[1]   This requirement does not mean that participants must be able to sell their units immediately on demand (s 272(15)); therefore schemes which have a lock-in period may, nonetheless, qualify for recognised status.

15.77 In approving the application from the operator of such an overseas scheme the FSA must also ensure that—
— adequate protection is afforded to participants of the scheme (s 272(2));
— the powers and duties of the operator and, if relevant, the trustee or depositary, are adequate (s 272(4)); and
— the arrangements for the scheme's constitution and management are adequate (s 272(3)).

FSMA 2000 does not define a test for determining the adequacy of these issues but provides that in making such a determination the FSA must have regard to any rule of law and any matters which are or could be the subject of rules applicable to comparable authorised schemes (s 272(5)).[1]

---

[1]   'Comparable authorised schemes' means whichever is the most appropriate (in the view of the FSA) of authorised unit trust schemes, authorised OEICs or both as the case may be (s 272(6)).

The application process for individually recognised overseas schemes

15.78 An application for recognition under s 272 must be made by the operator of the scheme in a form which the FSA directs and must contain an address in the UK for the place of service for notices and other documents required under FSMA 2000, and such other information as the FSA may require (s 274(1), (2)). Different forms of direction may be given and different requirements may be applied by the FSA in respect of applications made under s 272 (s 274(4)). The FSA may also require further information from the operator at any time after receiving the application but before making its determination (s 274(3)) and may require the applicant to provide the information in a form or to have the information verified in a manner which it specifies (s 274(5)).

Determination of applications

15.79 The FSA has six months beginning on the date on which it receives the completed application to determine the application under s 272 (s 275(1)). However, the FSA may also determine an incomplete application if it deems it appropriate to do so and it must do so within 12 months from the date on which the application for authorisation was first received, even if the application was not completed by then (s 275(2)).

15.80 The operator must notify the FSA of any change or alteration to the recognised scheme (s 277(1)). The change or alteration may only be given effect if the FSA has given its written approval or the operator has not received a written notice from the FSA stating that it has decided to refuse approval within one month of the date on which the proposed change or alteration was notified to the FSA (s 277(2)). If the operator, trustee or depositary of a recognised overseas scheme is to be replaced, notice must be given to the FSA by the outgoing operator, trustee or depositary (or the person or persons who are to replace the operator, trustee or depositary) at least one month before the date on which the replacement is to take effect (s 277(3)).

15.81 If the FSA decides to make an order under s 272(1) granting an application for recognition by an overseas scheme, it must give written notice to the applicant (s 275(3)). However, if the FSA proposes not to grant the application, it must give the applicant a warning notice and comply with the procedures set out in FSMA 2000, Pt XXVII. If the FSA has decided to refuse an application, it must give the operator[1] a decision notice, and the operator may refer the matter to the Tribunal (s 276).

---

[1]   For applications under s 272, the applicant must be the operator of the scheme (s 274(1)).

Rules as to scheme particulars

15.82 The FSA may make rules imposing duties or liabilities on operators of recognised overseas schemes corresponding to those made under s 248 for the publication of scheme particulars in relation to authorised unit trust schemes (s 278).[1]

---

[1]   See the FSA Handbook, Collective Investment Schemes sourcebook, CIS 17.3.4R.

Revocation of a recognised overseas scheme

15.83 An order made under s 272 recognising an overseas scheme may be revoked following the same procedure as an order recognising a designated overseas scheme under s 270 if the same criteria are fulfilled[1] or one or more of the requirements for making the order under s 272 is no longer satisfied (s 279).

---
[1]   See paras 15.67–15.72.

Individually recognised overseas schemes: facilities and information required to be maintained in the UK

15.84   Operators of individually recognised schemes are subject to rules made by the FSA in the same way as schemes recognised under s 270 (s 283).[1]

---
[1]   See para 15.73.

RESTRICTIONS ON THE PROMOTION OF COLLECTIVE INVESTMENT SCHEMES

15.85   A constant thread which has run through the regulatory framework for collective investment schemes since the 1950s is the limitation on the promotion of schemes which are not authorised or recognised to members of the public. During the debates there was general discussion of the territorial scope of these provisions. Melanie Johnson, Economic Secretary to the Treasury, spoke as follows—

> 'I should re-cap briefly on the position under the 1986 Act and on the Government's thinking. It should be remembered that the substance of the discussion applies only to unapproved collective investment schemes; authorised unit trusts, authorised OEICs and recognised schemes are exempt from the prohibitions under section 76 and will be exempt under [section 238]. We are only considering vehicles such as venture capital funds, ostrich farms and other potentially risky schemes.
>
> Section 76 applies to advertisements issued by authorised persons that are "issued in the UK". That phrase has been widely interpreted by the market as meaning that that section applies only to promotions received in the United Kingdom. The logic behind that interpretation is that an advertisement is not issued until it is communicated or received. The view is that the current territorial scope under the section applies, first, to advertisements that originate in the United Kingdom and are sent within it and, secondly, to advertisements that originate outside the United Kingdom and are sent into it, which I shall refer to as inward promotions.

. . . The phrase "issued in the UK" is subject to interpretation; the interpretation that I have just described is the one accepted in certain quarters. [The proposed amendments] would restrict the territorial scope of [section 238] to that which I have just described as applying to section 76. One important consequence of that approach would be that the collective investment scheme marketing prohibition would not cover outward promotions—those that originate in the United Kingdom but sent outside it.

By contrast, the territorial scope of [section 238] is more widely drawn and it could catch outward promotions. The only promotions that will not be caught by the prohibition—apart from those concerning approved schemes—are those that originate outside the United Kingdom and cannot have an effect here. We have proposed the same basic approach in relation to the [section 21] marketing prohibition but, as members of the Committee will recall, the Treasury has the power to make exemptions from that prohibition through secondary legislation. As the recently issued second financial promotion consultation document noted, we think that it is important to be able to restrict outward promotions issued by unauthorised persons so that the FSA can play a full role in international regulatory co-operation and the UK's reputation as a safe and clean place to do business is maintained.

Under the [section 21] prohibition relating to unauthorised persons, if an unauthorised operation were to be set up in the UK to target, say, Canadian investors, we propose that that unauthorised operation be subject to UK legislation. If the legislation were breached, the operation could, if necessary, be closed down to assist the Canadian regulator.

On further consideration, the arguments may be different in relation to the promotion by authorised persons of collective investment schemes. As [section 238] applies only to persons who are authorised and as the FSA will have authority over those persons anyway, it can, if need be, discipline them under its own rules in order to assist an overseas regulator. I agree, therefore, that the need to prohibit outward promotions in [section 238]-type cases is, arguably, much less great.'[1]

---

[1]   HC SC A, 2 December 1999, col 1084. See also HL Committee, 30 March 2000, col 943.

15.86 These restrictions, in FSMA 2000, s 238, which only apply to authorised persons, run in parallel with the more general restriction on financial promotion set out in FSMA 2000, s 21. Therefore a communication[1] made in the course of business regarding a collective investment scheme must—

— be made by an authorised or exempted person; or
— its contents must be approved by an authorised person; or
— an exemption must be available under s 238; or
— the regulations made under s 238 must apply,

and the scheme must either be an authorised or recognised scheme or an exception must be available under the Treasury order or the FSA's regulations.[2]

---

[1] 'Communication' is not defined but the verb 'communicate' is defined broadly in s 21 and s 238 and includes 'causing a communication to be made' (s 21(13)).
[2] See paras 15.88–15.91.

15.87 The aim of s 238 was explained in the Commons, with Barbara Roche, the Financial Secretary to the Treasury, stating that—

'It may be useful if I explain our overall intentions. The aim of the clause is to create a regime that is capable of standing up to the developments of modern technology while remaining effective against the more traditional methods of promoting financial services. There has, properly, been a great deal of discussion about new developments in technology. We all recognise that the pace of technology has advanced to such a degree over the past five years that it is difficult for legislatures to ensure that they have the right regimes in place. Therefore, our intention is to create a flexible structure that is capable of dealing with the modern world.

We are creating a framework that we want to be robust enough to deal with the different possibilities that may arise. Information technology, broadcasting and telecommunications are increasingly converging, so we need a regime that can deal with that . . .

The objective of the Bill is to set the outer boundaries of the financial promotion regime so that they are capable of encompassing those matters that should be controlled. I shall come later to some of the specific points that have been raised. Although it is true that provisions in the Bill may encompass some matters that should not be regulated, they will be taken outside the regime by secondary legislation, just as happens with the investment advertising regime under the Financial Services Act.

> We agree with Opposition Members that the financial
> promotion regime should catch only those promotions
> made in the course of business. Private communications
> should therefore be excluded.'[1]

---

[1]   HC Committee, 22 July 1999, col 348.

15.88   This broader restriction in relation to collective investment schemes is
carried through into FSMA 2000 and s 238 provides that no
authorised person may communicate or cause to be communicated[1]
an invitation or inducement to participate in a collective investment
scheme (s 238(1)), unless the scheme is an authorised unit trust
scheme, a scheme constituted as an authorised OEIC or a recognised
scheme (s 238(4)), or the authorised person so communicates within
the provisions in ss 238 and 239. The Treasury may, however, make
orders setting out other circumstances[2] where these restrictions do
not apply (s 238(6))[3] and the FSA may also make rules[4] which provide
further exemptions for the promotion of schemes otherwise than to
the general public (s 238(5)).[5] FSMA 2000 retains the prohibition on
an authorised person approving a communication for the purposes of
s 21 if he would otherwise be prohibited himself from making the
communication or causing it to be communicated (s 240(1)). An
approval given by an authorised person in contravention of s 21(1)
will be deemed not to have been given (s 240(2)) and a person issuing
a communication will be in breach of s 21(1) and so guilty of an
offence and liable to imprisonment or a fine, or both imprisonment
and a fine (s 25(1)).

---

[1]   Section 238(9).

[2]   Such an order may specify that this prohibition does not apply to communications of a
particular description or communications originating from a specific country or territory or a
category of countries or territories or originating outside the UK generally (s 238(7)): see the
Financial Services and Markets Act 2000 (Promotion of Collective Investment Schemes)
(Exemptions) Order 2001, SI 2001/1060. For the impact of the EU Distance Marketing Directive
on the promotion of collective investment schemes, see FSA CP 196, 'Implementation of the
Distance Marketing Directive: proposed rules and guidance', September 2003.

[3]   See SI 2001/1060, which includes exemptions for existing participants in an unregulated
scheme, when communications are permitted or required by statute, investment professionals,
certain high net worth individuals and sophisticated investors.

[4]   See the FSA Handbook, Conduct of Business sourcebook, COB 3.11 for these rules.

[5]   In the definition 'otherwise than to the general public' there is now included the word
'promotion' which is designed to reduce the risk, so far as is possible, of participation by
persons for whom participation in such a scheme would be unsuitable (s 238(10)). For these
purposes a 'participant' has the same meaning as that in s 235(2) (s 238(11)) and means those
persons who are to participate in the arrangements who do not have day-to-day control over the
management of the property, whether or not they may be consulted or give directions as to the
property in question.

15.89   Section 240 ensures the continued closure of a loophole which had
appeared in the original regime under FSA 1986, s 76. Until 1992

persons who were not authorised and therefore not subject to the Financial Services (Promotion of Unregulated Schemes) Regulations 1991 (such as overseas persons) could have investment advertisements under FSA 1986, s 57 approved by an authorised person and therefore comply with the advertising requirements while circumventing the more restrictive regime for collective investment schemes under s 76 which only applied to authorised persons. This loophole was closed by changes to the self-regulating organisations rules which prohibited a member of a self-regulating organisation from approving an investment advertisement for an unauthorised person if the advertisement related to an unregulated collective investment scheme.[1]

---

[1]   See the FSA Handbook, Enforcement manual, ENF 16.5.3G–16.5.5G.

15.90   If an authorised person breaches the restrictions under s 238 on the promotion of collective investment schemes or approves a communication which he himself could not otherwise communicate or cause to communicate under s 240, that breach may be actionable by a private person[1] who has suffered a loss as a result of the contravention as a breach of statutory duty by the authorised person (s 150).

---

[1]   The definition of 'private person' is specified in regulations made by the Treasury and the Treasury may, in certain cases, extend this right to other persons who are not private persons (s 150(5)): see the Financial Services and Markets Act 2000 (Rights of Action) Regulations 2001, SI 2001/2256, which confer the right on certain private investors not in the course of regulated activities or on others not in the course of any business.

15.91   FSMA 2000 also provides that these restrictions do not apply to a communication originating from outside the UK unless that communication is capable of having an effect in the UK (s 238(3)) but this provision may be repealed by a Treasury order to that effect (s 238(8)).

INVESTIGATIONS IN RELATION TO COLLECTIVE INVESTMENT SCHEMES

15.92   The FSA or the Secretary of State have wide-ranging powers to appoint one or more competent persons to investigate—
    —   the affairs of, or of the manager or trustee of, any authorised unit trust scheme;
    —   the affairs of, or the operator, trustee or depositary of, any recognised scheme (in relation to activities carried on in the UK);

— the affairs of, or of the operator, trustee or depositary of, any other collective investment scheme other than an authorised OEIC,[1]

if it appears to be a matter of public concern or in the interests of participants or potential participants to do so (s 284(1)).[2]

---

[1]   The power to investigate OEICs is not under this section but is made under FSMA 2000, s 262(2)(k) and under the Open-Ended Investment Companies Regulations 2001, SI 2001/1228, regs 23, 25 and 26.
[2]   See the FSA Handbook, Enforcement manual, ENF 2.9.1G.

15.93   A person who has been appointed by the FSA or the Secretary of State to conduct such an investigation may also, if he thinks fit, investigate the affairs of, or of the manager, trustee, operator or depositary of, any other such scheme whose manager, trustee, operator or depositary is the same as that of the scheme under investigation (s 284(2)).[1] The investigator may also, if he considers that another person is able or may be able to give information which is relevant to that investigation, require that person to produce any documents in his possession or under his control which appear to be relevant to the investigation, to attend before the investigator and otherwise to give the investigator all assistance in relation to the investigation. That person is under a statutory duty to comply with those requirements (s 284(3)).

---

[1]   This power does include the power to investigate an OEIC incorporated under s 262 and its directors and depositaries. Compare with para 15.92, fn 1.

Powers of investigators appointed under s 284

15.94   Section 284(4) provides that the procedures for conducting an investigation under s 284(1) are as set out in s 170(5)–(9).[1] The investigator appointed under s 284(1) must make his report to the investigating authority[2] which appointed him (s 170(6)) and may be a member of its staff (s 170(5)). The scope of the investigation may be controlled by direction to the investigator by either the FSA or the Secretary of State as the relevant investigatory authority (s 170(7)). That direction may set out the scope of the investigation, the period during which it is to be conducted, and other matters relating to its conduct including its remit. This could involve the investigation being confined or extended to particular or additional matters, or the requirement for the investigator to discontinue the investigation or to take only those steps specified in the direction and to specify the form of the report or to make such interim reports as may be required (s 170(7), (8)).

---

[1]   See the FSA Handbook, Enforcement manual, ENF 2.3.18G.
[2]   Ie, the FSA or the Secretary of State.

15.95   Any change in the scope or conduct of an investigation under s 284 may, if the FSA or the Secretary of State as the investigatory authority so determines, require a written notice of the change if the person who is the subject of the investigation would be significantly prejudiced if not made aware of those changes (s 170(9)).

Admissibility of statements made to investigators appointed under s 284

15.96   Section 284(5) provides that s 174 applies to a statement made by a person in compliance with a requirement imposed by that section as it applies to a statement mentioned in s 174. A statement made to an investigator under s 284 is admissible in evidence in any proceedings provided it also complies with any requirements in relation to the admissibility of evidence in the circumstances in question (s 174(1)).[1]

---

[1]   See the FSA Handbook, Enforcement manual, ENF 2.10.4G.

15.97   In the case of criminal proceedings, where a person is charged with an offence other than one under s 177(4)[1] or s 398,[2] or an offence in relation to false statements made otherwise than under oath,[3] or in proceedings in relation to any action to be taken by the FSA against that person for market abuse, no evidence relating to the statement may be adduced and no question relating to it may be asked by or on behalf of the prosecution or the FSA unless the evidence relating to it is adduced, or the question is asked, in the proceedings, by or on behalf of that person (s 174(2), (3)).

---

[1]   In relation to breaches of FSMA 2000, Pt XI.
[2]   The offence of providing false or misleading information to the FSA.
[3]   Ie, an offence under the Perjury Act 1911, s 5, the Criminal Law (Consolidation) (Scotland) Act 1995, s 44(2) or the Perjury (Northern Ireland) Order 1979, art 10.

FSA's supplementary powers in relation to the power to compel the production of information or documents under s 284

15.98   The FSA's powers to require a person to produce information or documents under s 175(2)–(4), (6) and s 177 (contained in Pt XI) apply to an investigation under s 284 as if that section were contained in Pt XI (s 284(6)).[1]

---

[1]   See the FSA Handbook, Enforcement manual, ENF 2.4.13G.

15.99   Any person to whom a document has been produced as a result of a requirement under Pt XI may take copies of or extracts from the document. That person may require the person producing the document or any other person who—

— has been or is, or is proposed to be, a director or controller of that person;
— has been or is an auditor of that person;
— has been or is an actuary, accountant or lawyer appointed or instructed by that person; or
— has been or is an employee of that person;

to provide an explanation of the document (s 175(2), (7)).

15.100 As with all its other powers under Pt XI, the FSA has the power to require a person who is required to produce a document and fails to do so to state to the best of his knowledge and belief where the document is (s 175(3)).[1] In addition, a lawyer may be required under Pt XI to furnish the name and address of his client (s 175(4)). FSMA 2000 also provides that where a person claims a lien on a document, the production of the document under Pt XI does not affect the lien (s 175(6)).

---

[1]   Subject to banking confidentiality: see the FSA Handbook, Enforcement manual, ENF 2.10.3G.

Offences in relation to investigations under Pt XVII

15.101 Where any person, other than an investigator appointed under Pt XI, fails to comply with a requirement imposed on him under Pt XI, the person imposing that requirement may certify this non-compliance in writing to the High Court or, in Scotland, to the Court of Session (s 177(1), (7)). The court may, if it is satisfied that the person in non-compliance did so without reasonable excuse, deal with him or, if the defaulting party is a body corporate, any director or officer of that body corporate, as if he were in contempt (s 177(2)).

15.102 In addition, a person who knows or suspects that an investigation under Pt XI is being or is likely to be conducted is guilty of an offence if he falsifies, conceals, destroys or otherwise disposes of a document which he knows or suspects is or would be relevant to such an investigation (s 177(3)(a)). Such a person also commits an offence if he causes or permits the falsification, concealment, destruction or disposal of such a document (s 177(3)(b)). Such an offence could give rise on summary conviction to imprisonment for up to six months or a fine not exceeding the statutory maximum or both imprisonment and a fine and on conviction on indictment to imprisonment for up to two years or a fine or both imprisonment and a fine (s 177(5)).

15.103 A person who, in purported compliance with any requirement under Pt XI, provides information which he knows to be false or misleading in any material particular or which he provides recklessly which is false or misleading would also be guilty of an offence (s 177(4)) which on summary conviction could lead to the same penalties as an offence under s 177(3)[1] (s 177(5)).[2]

15.104 Any person who intentionally obstructs the exercise of any rights conferred by a warrant issued under s 176 would also be guilty of an offence and liable on summary conviction to imprisonment for up to three months or a fine not exceeding level 5 on the standard scale, or both imprisonment and a fine (s 177(6)).

FSA's power to obtain a warrant to enter premises and search and seize documents

15.105 In conducting an investigation under s 284, the investigator appointed under this section has the broad powers under s 176 to obtain a warrant to enter premises and to search and seize documents relevant to the conduct of that investigation and s 176(1)–(9) applies as if references in that section to an investigator included references to a person appointed under s 284(1) (s 284(7)(a)).

15.106 If a justice of the peace[1] is satisfied that there are reasonable grounds for believing that certain conditions[2] are met, on information given on oath by or on behalf of the Secretary of State, the FSA or an investigator appointed under s 284(1), he may issue a warrant to enter premises (s 176(1)).

---

¹   In Scotland references to a 'justice of the peace' in this section include a justice of the peace or a sheriff and references to 'on oath' are to be construed as references to 'evidence on oath' (s 176(9)).
²   See para 15.107.

15.107 The conditions which must be met before the FSA is able to obtain a warrant from a justice of the peace (or, in Scotland, a sheriff) are that—
—   the person from whom information or documents have been required under s 175 or 284(3) has failed (wholly or in part) to comply and the documents or information required are on the premises which have been specified in the warrant;
—   the premises are those of an authorised person or an appointed representative and there are documents or information on the premises which could be required under s 175 and if such a requirement were to be imposed it would not be complied with or the documents or information to which it related would be removed, tampered with or destroyed; or
—   in relation to a special investigation under s 284(1) the offence is one which could give rise to a sentence on conviction of two years or more and there are documents or information on the premises specified in the warrant relevant to whether that offence was committed and the documents or information could be required under s 175 and if such a requirement were

imposed, it would not be complied with or the documents or information to which it related would be removed, tampered with or destroyed (s 176(2)–(4)).

15.108 If a warrant is granted by a justice of the peace under s 176(1), it authorises a constable, subject to the requirements in relation to the execution of search warrants contained in the Police and Criminal Evidence Act 1984, ss 15(5)–(8) and 16 or in the Police and Criminal Evidence (Northern Ireland) Order 1989, arts 17(5)–(8) and 18 (s 176(6), (7)) to enter the premises specified in the warrant and to search for any documents or information of the kind specified in the warrant and to take any other steps necessary for preserving them or otherwise preventing interference with them (s 176(5)(a), (b)). The constable may also take copies of or extracts from any documents or information appearing to be of the kind specified in the warrant and may require any person on the premises being searched to provide an explanation of any such document or information (s 176(5)(c), (d)). He is also authorised to use such force as may be reasonably necessary in executing the warrant (s 176(5)(e)).

15.109 Any document seized under a warrant issued under s 176 may be retained for three months or, if within that period proceedings to which the document may be relevant have been commenced, until the conclusion of those proceedings (s 176(8)).

Confidentiality

15.110 A person who is carrying on the business of banking[1] and is required to disclose information or documents under s 284 may, however, claim confidentiality for information or a document for which he owes an obligation of confidence in relation to that banking business (s 284(8)) unless—

— the person to whom the duty of confidentiality is owed consents to the disclosure or production;

— the disclosure requirement has been specifically authorised by the investigating authority; and

— if the person owing the obligation of confidentiality or to whom the obligation of confidentiality is owed is the manager, trustee, operator or depositary of the scheme which is under investigation or a director of an OEIC which is under investigation[2] or any other person whose own affairs are under investigation (s 284(9), (10)).

---

[1]   The 'business of banking' is not defined in FSMA 2000 and it is not clear whether this applies to all those who have permission or authorisation to accept deposits.

[2]   This section applies to information or documents required under FSMA 2000, s 284 and therefore presumably only applies in relation to investigations under s 284(2)(b) and not those under s 262(2)(k). FSA Enforcement manual, ENF 2.10.3G.

16 Recognised investment exchanges and clearing houses

BACKGROUND

16.1 The framework for the regulation and supervision of exchanges under the Financial Services and Markets Act 2000 (FSMA 2000) preserves many of the features of the Financial Services Act 1986 (FSA 1986) regime. However, the increasing consolidation of markets and the globalisation of trading has seen the growth of 'alternative trading systems' and this has had an impact on the approach of the FSA to supervision of the markets under FSMA 2000, Pt XVIII (ss 285–313).

16.2 As with its predecessor (FSA 1986) FSMA 2000 provides that recognised investment exchanges (RIEs), recognised clearing houses (RCHs) and certain other categories of exchanges are exempt and are not required to be authorised persons under the Act.[1] However, the new regime removes the procedural distinction between recognised exchanges (ie, those UK based exchanges which could be recognised by the SIB/FSA) and those overseas exchanges and clearing houses which had to be designated as exempt by Treasury order. The provisions under Pt XVIII give the Treasury the power to set the requirements that such bodies must meet to be recognised (the 'recognition requirements')[2] and set out the application procedures and supervisory arrangements for recognised bodies. This includes conferring powers to revoke recognition and to direct recognised bodies to take steps to meet the recognition requirements.

---

[1] Recognised bodies are entitled to be authorised by having permission under Pt IV for their regulated activities that are not activities for which they are exempt under Pt XVIII. FSMA 2000, s 38(2) only bans a combination of authorisation and exemption granted by order.

[2] These are set out in the Financial Services and Markets Act 2000 (Recognition Requirements for Investment Exchanges and Clearing Houses) Regulations 2001, SI 2001/995, and guidance on the FSA's approach to these is set out in the FSA Handbook, Recognised Investment Exchanges and Recognised Clearing Houses sourcebook, REC 2. For background see also FSA Discussion Paper, the FSA's Approach to Regulation of the Market Infrastructure, January 2000 and the Feedback Statement on it, June 2001, in particular paras 3.36–3.47. The FSA has been also an active participant in the FESCO/CESR work resulting in the FESCO consultation paper, Proposed Standards for Alternative Trading Systems, June 2001 and a new chapter has been added to the FSA's Market Conduct sourcebook setting out the framework for authorised firms operating alternative trading systems (MAR 5).

EXEMPT STATUS

16.3   An RIE is an investment exchange in respect of which a recognition order has been made under FSMA 2000, s 290 and an RCH is a clearing house in respect of which such an order has been made (s 285(1)).

16.4   An RIE is exempt in relation to the general prohibition in FSMA 2000, s 19 if it is carrying on regulated activities as part of its business of being such an exchange or for the purposes of, or in connection with, its clearing services (s 285(2)). An RCH is also exempt in relation to those regulated activities which it carries on for the purposes of, or in connection with, its provision of clearing services (s 285(3)).

Transitional provisions in relation to existing recognised bodies

16.5   For the purposes of the transition to the new regime, the Treasury provides in the Recognition Regulations,[1] reg 9 that bodies that had been recognised bodies under FSA 1986 at the time the regulations come into force were automatically recognised under the new regime. Although in an early consultation document[2] the Treasury had suggested that existing recognised bodies would be deemed to comply with the new legislation for a three-month period after it came into effect, this has not been implemented in those terms. Instead the FSA was not permitted to give notice under s 298, to impose directions under s 296[3] or to revoke the recognition order[4] for one month after N2 (ie, until 1 January 2002). Given the minimum period allowed for representations under s 298(4), this largely provides the same three-month period before the new regime could have been enforced fully against RIEs and RCHs.

---

[1]   The Financial Services and Markets Act 2000 (Recognition Requirements for Investment Exchanges and Clearing Houses) Regulations 2001, SI 2001/995.
[2]   HM Treasury, Draft Recognition Requirements for Investment Exchanges and Clearing Houses, February 1999.
[3]   See paras 16.37–16.41.
[4]   See paras 16.42 and 16.43.

16.6   The Recognition Regulations,[1] reg 9(7) provide that this is without prejudice to the FSA's power under s 298(7) to make a direction under s 296 without following the procedure laid down in Pt XVIII where it 'considers it essential to do so'. As this is an emergency power, it was presumably not felt appropriate to place any limitations on it in the regulations. The Recognition Regulations, reg 10 contains provisions relating to the transitional period. It provides that any action relating to revocation of recognition that is in progress at the point of transition can continue after 'N2' (1 December 2001).[2] However, where such revocation action continues, the FSA will not be able to rely on breach of any recognition requirement or statutory obligation which did not have an equivalent under the old regime (reg 10(7)).

---

[1] The Financial Services and Markets Act 2000 (Recognition Requirements for Investment Exchanges and Clearing Houses) Regulations 2001, SI 2001/995.
[2] See para 1.37 for further discussion of N2.

CRITERIA FOR RECOGNITION

16.7 The Treasury regulations[1] set out the requirements which must be satisfied before an investment exchange or clearing house can be recognised and which it must continue to satisfy to maintain that status (s 286(1)).[2] The Government has said[3] that—

— the new recognition requirements would not differ in substance from those under the FSA regime;
— they would all be located in one place;
— they would make explicit some matters which had been implicit;
— the linkage between an RCH and an RIE would no longer be required; and
— the regulations would provide a great degree of freedom to exchanges and clearing houses to delegate or outsource some of their functions to other 'fit and proper' bodies.

---

[1] See para 16.5, fn 1.
[2] This provision closes one of the notable loopholes under FSA 1986; under that Act there was no requirement for an RIE or RCH which had satisfied the SIB/FSA that it met the criteria in FSA 1986, Sch 4 to demonstrate that it continued to meet those requirements once the recognition order had been made. This led to the situation that once an investment exchange or clearing house had been recognised, the SIB/FSA had little power over it other than the power to de-recognise it.
[3] HM Treasury, Draft Recognition Requirements for Investment Exchanges and Clearing Houses, February 1999, para 6.

16.8 Under the Recognition Regulations,[1] an RIE must—
— have financial resources sufficient properly to perform its functions (Sch 1, para 1);
— be fit and proper to perform the functions of a recognised exchange (Sch 1, para 2);
— have adequate systems and controls (Sch 1, para 3);
— have the means of ensuring its facilities are conducted in an orderly manner and afford proper protection to investors (Sch 1, para 4);

— have procedures for disclosing information by issuers of securities (Sch 1, para 5);

— be willing and able to promote and maintain high standards of integrity and fair dealing (Sch 1, para 6);

— have procedures for making rules and consulting with users of its facilities in relation to such rule-making (Sch 1, para 7);

— have effective arrangements for enforcing its rules and disciplining users of the exchange's facilities (Sch 1, para 8);

— have effective arrangements for investigating and dealing with any complaints regarding the exchange's carrying out of its regulatory functions (Sch 1, para 9);

— have put in place margin arrangements (Sch 1, para 11);

— be willing and able to co-operate with the FSA and other regulatory and supervisory bodies (Sch 1, para 14).

---

[1] The Financial Services and Markets Act 2000 (Recognition Requirements for Investment Exchanges and Clearing Houses) Regulations 2001, SI 2001/995.

16.9 Similarly for a clearing house to be recognised it must—

— have financial resources properly to perform its functions (Sch 1, para 16);

— be fit and proper to perform the functions of a recognised clearing house (Sch 1, para 17);

— have adequate systems and controls (Sch 1, para 18);

— have the means of ensuring its facilities are conducted in an orderly manner and afford proper protection to investors (Sch 1, para 19);

— be willing and able to promote and maintain high standards of integrity and fair dealing (Sch 1, para 20);

— have procedures for making rules and consulting with users of its facilities in relation to such rule-making (Sch 1, para 21);

— have effective arrangements for monitoring and enforcing its rules and disciplining users of the clearing house's facilities (Sch 1, para 22);

— have effective arrangements for investigating and dealing with any complaints regarding the clearing house's carrying out of its regulatory functions (Sch 1, para 23);

— have put in place margin arrangements (Sch 1, para 28);

— be willing and able to co-operate with the FSA and other regulatory and supervisory bodies (Sch 1, para 27).

16.10 The regulations may contain provisions as to the default rules of an RIE or RCH or the proceedings which they may follow in the event of a default, but if they do so, the Secretary of State[1] must approve those regulations (s 286(2)).[2]

1   The Secretary of State for these purposes is the one responsible for insolvency matters (ie, the Secretary of State for Trade and Industry): see FSMA Explanatory Notes, para 520.
2   The Financial Services and Markets Act 2000 (Recognition Requirements for Investment Exchanges and Clearing Houses) Regulations 2001, SI 2001/995, Sch 1, paras 10 and 24.

16.11   'Default rules' for these purposes are rules which provide for the exchange or clearing house to be able to take action to settle market contracts[1] if an exchange or clearing house member defaults (s 286(3)). To ensure market stability, the exchanges and clearing house are expected to have powers so that market contracts can be closed out in an 'orderly and speedy' manner to prevent or limit disruption if a market participant defaults.[2]

1   'Market contract' is defined with reference to contracts to which the Companies Act 1989, Pt VII applies by virtue of s 155 of that Act or to which the Companies (No 2) (Northern Ireland) Order 1990, Pt V applies by virtue of Art 80 of that Order or any other kind of contract which may be prescribed by the Treasury (s 286(4)).
2   FSMA Explanatory Notes, para 521.

Complaints about recognised bodies

16.12   The FSA is also required to make arrangements for investigating any complaint which it considers relevant to the question of whether an RIE or RCH should remain recognised (s 299).[1]

1   The arrangements made by the FSA are set out in the FSA Handbook, Recognised Investment Exchanges and Recognised Clearing Houses sourcebook, REC 4.4.

RECOGNITION ORDERS—INVESTMENT EXCHANGES

Application for recognition

16.13   Any body corporate or unincorporated association may apply to the FSA for an order declaring it to be an RIE (s 287(1)).[1] The application must be made in a manner which the FSA may direct, accompanied by such information as the FSA may reasonably require for the purpose of determining that application,[2] a copy of the applicant's rules,[3] any guidance[4] issued by it and the required particulars[5] (s 287(2)). The FSA has not prescribed a particular form for an application but does prescribe a fee.[6]

¹   Subject to the criteria to be set out under the regulations to be made under s 286(1). Exchanges recognised under FSA 1986 were automatically recognised as if an order had been made under s 290(1) or s 292(2)(a): see the Financial Services and Markets Act 2000 (Recognition Requirements for Investment Exchanges and Clearing Houses) Regulations 2001, SI 2001/995. As at the date of publication, the recognised investment exchanges are: EDX London Ltd, LIFFE Administration and Management, London Stock Exchange plc, OM London Exchange Ltd, the International Petroleum Exchange of London Limited, the London Metal Exchange and virt-X Exchange Limited.
²   The FSA requires the provision of the information and evidence necessary to demonstrate that the recognition requirements will be met: see the FSA Handbook, Recognised Investment Exchanges and Recognised Clearing Houses sourcebook, REC 5.2.3G(3).
³   See para 16.14.
⁴   See para 16.15.
⁵   See para 16.16.
⁶   See REC 5.2.3G(4) and REC 7.

Rules

16.14   'Rules' includes any rules made or conditions imposed by the exchange with respect to recognition requirements, the admission of persons to, or the exclusion of persons from, the use of the exchange's facilities or other matters relating to its constitution (s 313(2)).

Guidance

16.15   'Guidance' is defined in s 313(3) as being any guidance issued, or any recommendation made, by an exchange, in writing or in any other legible form and intended to have continuing effect, to all or any class of its members or users, or persons seeking to become members or users. The guidance covers the recognition requirements, the admission of members or users to, or their exclusion from, the exchange's facilities, or other matters relating to its constitution (s 313(2)(a)–(c)).

Required particulars

16.16   The application for recognition must provide information about the clearing services which are to be provided in respect of transactions effected on the exchange (the 'required particulars') (s 287(2)(c), (3)(a)). If the exchange is also proposing to provide clearing services in relation to transactions which are not effected on the exchange, further particulars regarding the clearing services which are to be available must also be provided (s 287(3)(b)).

Supplementary

16.17   At any time after it has received an application for a recognition order, the FSA may require the applicant to provide such further information as the FSA deems necessary, in such a form or verified in a manner which it directs. It may give different directions, or impose different requirements in dealing with different applications (s 289).[1]

---
[1]   The FSA requires different information from overseas applicants: see the FSA Handbook, Recognised Investment Exchanges and Recognised Clearing Houses sourcebook, REC 6.

Recognition orders

16.18   In considering an application for recognition under s 287, the FSA may take into account any information which it considers relevant to the application (s 290(3)). Having reviewed this information, if it is satisfied that the applicant meets the recognition requirements, and the Treasury has given approval (s 307), the FSA may make a recognition order declaring that the applicant is an RIE (s 290(1)(a)). Such an order takes effect from the date specified in the order (s 290(4)).

Refusal to make an order: procedure

16.19   If, however, the FSA decides to refuse a recognition order, it must comply with the procedures set out in s 298 (s 290(5)).[1] Before a decision is made, the FSA must give written notice of its intention to the applicant and it must also bring the notice to the attention of the members of the applicant, and publish the notice in such a way as to bring the matter to the attention of those persons who are likely to be affected by the decision (s 298(1)). Any notice served under s 298(1) must state the reasons for the intended refusal and advise the applicant of its right to make representations to the FSA (s 298(2)). Representations in respect of a notice under s 298 must be made within two months of the date on which the notice was served on the applicant or of the date on which the notice was published if this was later, or within a longer period if the FSA permits (s 298(4)).

---
[1]   Section 290(5) does not apply where the Treasury has not approved the applicant under its powers under s 307: see para 16.64.

16.20   Representations may be made by the applicant, or any member of the applicant or any other person who is likely to be affected by the proposed refusal (s 298(3)). The FSA must have regard to any representations made to it under s 298 in relation to its decision not to grant a recognition order (s 298(5)). If after having carried out the procedures in s 298(1)–(5), the FSA decides to take a different course of action, it is not required to repeat these procedural steps (s 298(8)).

16.21   After considering the representations made to it under s 298, if the FSA decides not to grant the recognition order, it must give the applicant written notice of that decision, and take such steps as are reasonably practicable to bring the matter to the attention of the member of the applicant or any other person who, in the FSA's opinion, is likely to be affected by that decision (s 298(6)).

16.22 The FSA also has the power to make an order under s 296 without following these procedures where it considers it essential to do so even if procedures under this provision have started and the two-month period for representations has not yet elapsed (s 298(7)).

RECOGNITION ORDERS—CLEARING HOUSES

Application for recognition

16.23 Similarly, any body corporate or unincorporated association may apply for an order by the FSA declaring it to be an RCH (s 288(1)).[1]

---

[1] Provided it meets the criteria to be set out under the recognition regulations to be made under s 286(1): see the FSA Handbook, Recognised Investment Exchanges and Recognised Clearing Houses sourcebook, REC. See also para 16.2, fn 1. As at the date of publication, the recognised clearing houses are CRESTCo Limited and The London Clearing House Limited.

16.24 The application for recognition must be made in a manner which the FSA may direct and be accompanied by such information as the FSA may reasonably require to determine that application,[1] a copy of the applicant's rules[2] and any guidance[3] issued by the clearing house (s 288(2)(a), (b), (d)). The application must also provide particulars about any arrangement in respect of clearing arrangements which the applicant makes or proposes to make with an RIE. If the clearing house is proposing to provide clearing services for persons other than RIEs, further particulars are required about how the applicant will decide to whom it will provide its services (s 288(2)(c), (3)).

---

[1] See para 16.13, fn 2.
[2] See para 16.14.
[3] See para 16.25.

Guidance

16.25 'Guidance' is defined in s 313(4) as being any guidance issued, or any recommendation made, by the clearing house, in writing or in any other legible form and intended to have continuing effect, to all or any class of its members, or persons using or seeking to use its services, relating to the provision by it or its members of clearing services.

16.26 At any time after it has received an application for a recognition order, the FSA may require the applicant to provide such further information as the FSA deems necessary in such a form or verified in a manner which it directs. It may give different directions or impose different requirements in dealing with different applications (s 289).

Recognition orders: procedure

16.27 When making a recognition order under s 290 in respect of a clearing house, the procedure in s 290 applies.[1] The procedure set out in s 298 must similarly be followed if the FSA is minded to refuse an application.[2]

---

[1]   See para 16.18.
[2]   See paras 16.19–16.21.

NOTIFICATION REQUIREMENTS

16.28 Under s 293 the FSA may make rules which require any RIE or RCH to provide it with notice of such events relating to the body and such information as may be specified (s 293(1)).[1] This extends only to such notice or information as the FSA may reasonably require to exercise its functions under FSMA 2000 (s 293(3)).

---

[1]   See the rules in the FSA Handbook, Recognised Investment Exchanges and Recognised Clearing Houses sourcebook, REC 3 for UK RIEs and RCHs, and REC 6 for overseas bodies.

16.29 Any rules which the FSA makes under s 293 (or, in relation to overseas bodies, s 295) can be modified or waived by a direction of the FSA, on the application of or with the consent of an RIE or RCH (s 294(1)). The FSA's power to do so depends upon the same tests as are applicable to applications for the modification or waiver of its general rules under s 148—that compliance with the unmodified provision is unduly burdensome or does not achieve its purpose, and that modification or waiver would not result in undue risks to those whom the rule is intended to protect. As with the s 148 power the FSA may impose conditions (s 294(5)) or subsequently revoke or vary the direction it makes (on the application or with the consent of the relevant body) (s 294(6)). However, unlike s 148, s 294 does not impose any obligation to publish a direction which modifies or waives rules under s 293 (or, for overseas bodies, s 295).

16.30 If an RIE or RCH amends or revokes any of its rules or guidance as defined in FSMA 200, s 313[1] or makes new rules or guidance, it must give written notice to the FSA of those changes without delay (s 293(5)).

---

[1] See paras 16.14, 16.15 and 16.25.

16.31 If an RIE changes its arrangements for providing clearing services in relation to transactions effected on the exchange or to the criteria which it applies to the determination of the persons to whom it will provide clearing services, it must notify the FSA in writing without delay (s 293(6)). Similarly, if an RCH makes a change in the RIEs for whom it provides clearing services or the criteria which it applies in determining to whom it will provide clearing services (other than RIEs), it must give written notice to the FSA (s 293(7)).

OTHER POWERS

Supervision of certain contracts

16.32 The Secretary of State[1] and the Treasury, acting jointly, also have the power to make regulations which would apply the provisions of the Companies Act 1989, Pt VII and the Companies (No 2) (Northern Ireland) Order 1990, Pt V to 'relevant contracts'[2] as they apply to contracts connected with an RIE or RCH (s 301(1)).

---

[1] The 'Secretary of State' for these purposes is the Secretary of State for Trade and Industry.
[2] For these purposes 'relevant contracts' are those of a prescribed description in relation to which settlement arrangements are provided by a person who is admitted to a list maintained by the FSA for the purposes of s 301 (s 301(2)).

16.33 FSMA 2000, s 301(10) provides that these regulations may, in relation to a person admitted to the s 301 list, apply such provisions of, or regulations made under, FSMA 2000 as the Secretary of State and the Treasury consider appropriate and may provide for the provisions of the 1989 Act, Pt VII or the 1990 Order, Pt V to apply, and they may make such modifications, additions or exceptions as appear to them to be necessary or expedient. The power in s 301 allows the Treasury and the Secretary of State to apply any of the provisions of

FSMA 2000 and the Companies Act 1989, Pt VII (or the Companies (No 2) (Northern Ireland) Order 1990, Pt V) to a person settling contracts who is not authorised or exempt and who would otherwise be outside the scope of the Act and the FSA's regulatory remit.[1] Regulations may only be made if the Secretary of State and the Treasury are satisfied that it is appropriate for settlement arrangements to be supervised by the FSA having regard to the extent to which the relevant contracts are contracts of a kind dealt in by persons supervised by the FSA (s 301(3)).

---

[1]   These persons clearing non-investment contracts can be made subject to the FSMA regime (s 301(2)). See also FSMA Explanatory Notes, para 545.

16.34   The Treasury must approve the conditions set by the FSA for admission to the list and the arrangements for admission to and removal from it (s 301(4)). The FSA must publish this list as for the time being in force and provide a certified copy[1] of it to any person who wishes to refer to it in legal proceedings (s 301(7)). If the Treasury withdraws its approval, all regulations made under s 301 then in force are deemed to be suspended (s 301(5)). If the FSA changes the conditions or other arrangements and the Treasury gives its approval for those changes, the suspension ends on the date which the Treasury has specified in the fresh approval (s 301(6)).

---

[1]   A certified copy is deemed to be evidence or, in Scotland, sufficient evidence as to the contents of that list (s 301(8)) and a copy which purports to have been certified by or on behalf of the FSA is taken to have been duly certified unless the contrary is shown (s 301(9)).

DISCIPLINARY POWERS

16.35   The Treasury may make an order conferring on the Tribunal certain functions with respect to disciplinary proceedings[1] of one or more RIEs or RCHs in respect of which a recognition order has been made under s 290, or of all such investment exchanges or clearing houses generally (s 300(1)). An order made under s 300 may modify or exclude any of the provisions of or under FSMA 2000 with respect to proceedings before the Tribunal (s 300(3)).

---

[1]   For the purposes of this section 'disciplinary proceedings' means proceedings under the rules of the investment exchange or clearing house in relation to market abuse by a person subject to those rules (s 300(4)).

16.36 In making such an order, the Treasury must be satisfied that it is necessary to do so to ensure that the decisions taken in disciplinary proceedings with respect to which functions are to be conferred on the Tribunal are consistent with those of the Tribunal in cases arising under FSMA 2000, Pt VIII. In addition the decisions must be consistent with decisions in other disciplinary proceedings with respect to which the Tribunal may have functions as a result of an order made under s 300, and the proceedings must be in accordance with Convention rights (s 300(2)).[1] With respect to market abuse cases or cases of suspected market misconduct, the FSA has signed agreements with the UK investment exchanges to ensure a coordinated approach to enforcement actions.[2]

---

[1]   See FSMA Explanatory Notes, para 542.
[2]   A summary of these operating arrangements can be found at www.fsa.gov.uk/pubs/other/op_arrangements_overview_2.pdf. See also FSA Press Release FSA/PN/151/2002, 20 November 2001.

FSA'S POWER TO GIVE DIRECTIONS

16.37 The FSA may make a direction in respect of an RIE or RCH if it appears that it has failed or is likely to fail to satisfy the recognition requirements which apply to it[1] or it has otherwise failed to comply with any other obligation imposed on it by or under FSMA 2000 (s 296(1)).

---

[1]   Ie, those set out in recognition regulations made under FSMA 2000, s 286: see para 16.2, fn 1.

16.38 The FSA may require the RIE or RCH to take such steps as it directs to obtain that body's compliance with the recognition requirements or any other obligation of the kind in question (s 296(2)).[1]

---

[1]   'An obligation of the kind in question' is not defined but the Explanatory Notes state that these refer to other obligations under FSMA 2000, for example, those in Pt XVIII itself: see FSMA Explanatory Notes, para 536.

16.39 A direction made in respect of an RIE or RCH is enforceable on the application of the FSA by an injunction or, in Scotland, by an order for specific performance (s 296(3)).[1] If the FSA in making a direction under this provision causes a rule[2] of the RIE or RCH to be altered, this does not prevent the RIE or RCH from subsequently altering or revoking that rule (s 296(4)).

---

[1]   Under the Court of Session Act 1988, s 45.
[2]   See para 16.14.

Procedure

16.40   When giving a direction under s 296, the procedure set out in s 298 must be followed.[1]

---
[1]   See paras 16.19–16.21.

16.41   The FSA also has the power to make an order under s 296 without following the procedures in s 298, or if those procedures have started but the two-month period for representations has not yet elapsed, if it considers it essential to do so (s 298(7)).

REVOCATION OF RECOGNITION ORDER

16.42   The FSA may revoke a recognition order made in respect of an RIE or RCH at the request, or with the consent, of the RIE or RCH (s 297(1)). In addition, the FSA may act on its own initiative to revoke a recognition order in respect of an RIE or RCH if it appears to the FSA that it has failed or is failing to satisfy the recognition requirements or any other requirement imposed on it under FSMA 2000 (s 297(2)). A revocation order made in either case must specify the date on which it is to have effect (s 297(3)), which must not be earlier than the end of three months from the date on which the revocation order was made (s 297(4)). Such a revocation order may, however, be subject to such transitional provisions for the smooth winding down of transactions as the FSA deems expedient or necessary (s 297(5)).

Procedure

16.43   When giving a revocation order under s 297, the procedure set out in s 298 must be followed.[1]

---
[1]   See paras 16.19–16.21.

LIABILITY IN RELATION TO REGULATORY FUNCTIONS

16.44   FSMA 2000 extends statutory immunity to RIEs and RCHs and provides that an RIE or an RCH, its officers and staff are not to be liable in damages for anything done or omitted to be done in the discharge of its regulatory functions unless it can be shown that the act or omission was done in bad faith (s 291(1)).[1] 'Regulatory functions' are defined as functions relating to or to matters arising out of the obligations which the investment exchange or clearing house is subject to or which arise under or by virtue of FSMA 2000 (s 291(3)). This statutory immunity does not, however, extend to prevent an award of damages in relation to an act or omission which was unlawful by reason of the Human Rights Act 1998, s 6(1) (s 291(2)).

---

[1]   This is a clear departure from the position under FSA 1986.

OVERSEAS INVESTMENT EXCHANGES AND CLEARING HOUSES

16.45   The new regime under FSMA 2000 removes the difference in decision-making between UK and overseas exchanges and clearing houses. Overseas exchanges or clearing houses may apply for recognition under s 287 or 288 and will be exempt in relation to regulated activities carried on by them in the UK as an exchange or clearing house.[1] Where the applicant for a recognition order is an overseas applicant, the application for recognition must include an address in the UK for the service on the applicant of notices and other documents required or authorised to be served on it under FSMA 2000 (s 292(1)).[2]

---

[1]   As at the date of publication, the recognised overseas investment exchanges are: Cantor Financial Futures Exchange, Chicago Board of Trade, Eurex, NASDAQ LIFFE LLC Futures Exchange, NASDAQ, New York Mercantile Exchange Inc, New Zealand Futures and Options Exchange, Sydney Futures Exchange Limited, The Chicago Mercantile Exchange, the Swiss Stock Exchange and Warenterminborse Hannover.

[2]   However, the exemption for overseas recognised bodies (like UK ones) only applies to their activities as such in that s 285 applies to both UK and overseas bodies.

16.46   A recognition order may be made in respect of an overseas applicant if the FSA is satisfied that the following requirements have been met—

—   investors using that exchange or clearing house are afforded protection equivalent to that which they would be afforded if the exchange or clearing house were required to meet the recognition criteria;[1]

—   there are adequate procedures for dealing with a person who is unable or is likely to become unable to meet his obligations in respect of one or more market contracts connected with the investment exchange or clearing house;

— the applicant is able and willing to co-operate with the FSA in sharing information and in other ways; and

— there are adequate corporate arrangements in place between the FSA and those responsible for supervising the applicant in the country or territory where the applicant has its head office (s 292(3)).

[1]   See para 16.2, fn 1 and paras 16.9–16.11.

16.47   In considering whether the protections afforded are suitable and procedures are adequate, the FSA must have regard to the relevant law and practice in the country or territory in which the overseas applicant has its head office and the rules[1] and practices of the overseas applicant (s 292(4)).

[1]   See para 16.14.

Directions

16.48   In relation to making directions and revoking recognition for overseas companies the same procedures set out in ss 296–298 apply,[1] with modifications which adapt those provisions to the recognition requirements applicable under s 292(3) or (5). Sections 296(1) and 297(2) have effect as if the recognition requirements in s 292(3)(a), (b) and (c) were those mentioned in ss 296(1)(a) and 297(2)(a). For the purposes of s 297(2) the grounds on which a recognition order may be revoked in respect of an overseas investment exchange or overseas clearing house include circumstances where the arrangements for co-operation between the FSA and the relevant authority supervising the overseas investment exchange or clearing house (s 292(3)(d)) no longer exist (s 292(5)(c)).

[1]   See paras 16.19–16.21, 16.35–41.

Notification procedures

16.49   The notification requirements (including the FSA's power to make rules)[1] relating to recognised bodies contained in s 293 will also apply to overseas RIEs and RCHs,[2] although s 293(5) and (7) does not apply to overseas RIEs or RCHs (s 293(8)).

[1]   See the FSA Handbook, Recognised Investment Exchanges and Recognised Clearing Houses sourcebook, REC 6 and REC 3.2. See also paras 16.28 and 16.29.
[2]   See paras 16.28–16.30.

16.50   Every overseas investment exchange or clearing house which has been recognised by virtue of an order under s 287 or 288 must provide the FSA with an annual report. The report must contain a statement as to whether any events have occurred which are likely to affect the FSA's assessment of whether it continues to meet the criteria for recognition set out in FSMA 2000, s 292(3) or which are likely to have an effect on competition. This annual report must be copied to the Treasury and to the Office of Fair Trading (OFT) (s 295).

Competition provisions relating to exchanges and clearing houses

Role of the OFT

16.51   FSMA 2000, Pt XVIII, Ch II (ss 302–310) provides for competition scrutiny of recognised bodies (ie, RIEs and RCHs). The provisions in this chapter place a duty on the OFT[1] to monitor the competitive aspects of RIEs and RCHs and give it powers to investigate and report to the Competition Commission (CC) on any significantly adverse effects on competition of these bodies' rules, guidance and practices, or the exploitation of a strong market position. They also allow the Treasury to direct through the FSA as the recognising authority that appropriate changes should be made to the rules, guidance or practices of an exchange or clearing house which is in contravention.

---

[1]   The OFT took over the functions of the Director General of Fair Trading on 1 April 2003, pursuant to the Enterprise Act 2002, ss 1, 2. See also Ch 10 in relation to competition issues more generally under FSMA 2000.

16.52   As part of its overall responsibility for RIEs and RCHs, the FSA must send a copy of the regulatory provisions[1] it has received as part of the application process to the Treasury and the OFT (s 303(1)). It must also send to the OFT any other information which it receives as part of the application which is relevant to the OFT's consideration of the competition aspects of the proposed recognition of an investment exchange or clearing house (s 303(2)).

---

[1]   The 'regulatory provisions' are defined in s 302(1) as including the rules of the investment exchange or clearing house, any guidance issued by it and the arrangements and criteria set out in s 287(3) (for an RIE) and s 288(3) (for an RCH).

Initial report by the OFT

16.53   Having received this information, the OFT must issue a report as to whether any of these provisions or a combination of them have a significant adverse effect on competition.[1] If the OFT concludes that one or more of the provisions have an adverse effect on competition, it must include its reasons for that conclusion. Copies of this initial report must be provided to the FSA, the CC and the Treasury (s 303(3)–(5)).

[1] Section 302(2) and (3) extends this to the likely or intended effect and to circumstances in which they require or encourage behaviour with that effect (or are likely or intended to do so) or require or encourage exploitation of the strength of a market position.

Further reports by the OFT

16.54 In addition to this initial assessment, the OFT must keep all RIEs and RCHs under review (s 304(1)) and, if at any time it forms the view that any regulatory provision or practice[1] has a significantly adverse effect on competition,[2] it must make a report (s 304(2)) and provide details of the adverse effect which those provisions would have (s 304(4)). A copy of this report must be sent to the Treasury, the CC and the FSA, and the OFT must publish that report in a manner which it determines is appropriate for bringing the report to the attention of the public (s 304(5)). Reports made by the OFT are subject to absolute privilege in respect of the law of defamation (s 304(10)).

[1] The 'practices' of an investment exchange or clearing house are defined as the practices of the exchange in its capacity as such (in relation to an RIE) or in respect of its clearing arrangements (in relation to an RCH) (s 302(1)).
[2] See s 302(2) and para 16.53, fn 1.

16.55 In publishing a report under s 304, the OFT must omit from that report any matter which relates to the 'private affairs' of individuals where publication would or might seriously and prejudicially affect that person's interests (s 304(7)) or to the affairs of a particular body where publication would seriously or prejudicially affect its interests (s 304(8)). This does not apply to the copies of the report provided to the Treasury, the CC or the FSA (s 304(9)).

16.56 The OFT also has discretion to make a report if he concludes that the regulatory provisions or practices of an investment exchange or clearing house do not have an adverse effect on competition (s 304(3)). If the OFT makes a report under this subsection, it must provide a copy of the report to the Treasury, the CC and the FSA, and it may also be published (s 304(6)), subject to the provisos in s 304(7)–(10).[1]

[1] See paras 16.54 and 16.55.

Powers of investigation by the OFT

16.57 To be able to make the report required under ss 303 and 304, the OFT has certain powers to investigate matters (s 305(1)). It may request (in writing) relevant documents from any person, and request relevant information from any business within a specified time and in a specified manner and form (s 305(2), (3)). Information or documents may only be required to be produced, however, if they are relevant to the investigation (s 305(4)).[1]

---

[1]   The limitations in s 413 relating to protected items (primarily material subject to legal professional privilege) will apply.

16.58   If a person fails to produce the information or documents required under s 305, the OFT may report the matter to the court.[1] The court may enquire into the matter and, if, after hearing any witnesses or defence statements, the court is satisfied that there was no reasonable excuse for this failure, the person may be dealt with as if he were in contempt of court (s 305(5), (6)).

---

[1]   The court means the High Court or, in Scotland, the Court of Session (s 305(7)).

THE COMPETITION COMMISSION

16.59   On receipt of a report from the OFT under either s 303(2) or (3) the CC must investigate the matters set out in the report. The Explanatory Notes explain that 'the functions and duties [of the CC] are in line with those set out in the analogous provisions in s 162 in Part X',[1] and they similarly are supplemented by Sch 14[2] (the role of the Competition Commission) (s 306(11)).[3]

---

[1]   FSMA Explanatory Notes, para 552.
[2]   Section 306(11) provides that Sch 14 (except for para 2(b)) applies for the purposes of this section.
[3]   See para 10.47.

16.60   The CC must then make its own report on these matters unless it considers that, due to a change of circumstances, no useful purpose would be served by such a report being made (s 306(4)). However, if the CC decides not to make a report for that reason, it must publish a statement to that effect (s 306(5)).

16.61   If the CC makes a report, it must state its conclusions[1] as to whether the regulatory provisions or practices[2] or a combination of them have a significantly adverse effect on competition (s 306(6)). If the report concludes that there is a significantly adverse effect, it must also state whether the CC considers that effect is justified and, if it does not, what steps the Treasury ought to direct the FSA to take (s 306(7)).[3]

---

[1]   Any report made under s 306 must include an account of the CC's reasons for the purpose of 'facilitating proper understanding of them' (s 306(10)).
[2]   As defined in s 302(1): see para 16.54, fn 1.
[3]   See s 302(2) and para 16.53, fn 1.

16.62   If the report by the CC considers that the effect which the provisions and practices[1] has are justified, the CC must ensure that the conclusion which it reaches is compatible with the obligations imposed on the investment exchange or clearing house under FSMA 2000 (s 306(8), (9)).

---

[1]   As defined in s 302(1): see para 16.54, fn 1.

16.63   Any report which the CC may make under s 306 must be sent to the Treasury, the FSA and the OFT (s 306(12)). Subject to the removal of certain material,[1] the CC must publish its report (Sch 14, para 4).

---

[1]   See para 16.55.

The role of the Treasury in recognition orders

16.64   If the OFT has made an adverse initial report (under s 303) and does not ask the CC to consider that report (under s 306), or if the CC considers that the applicant's regulatory provisions do not have a significant adverse effect on competition or that the effect is justified, the Treasury may only refuse to approve the making of the recognition order if it considers that exceptional circumstances exist which make it inappropriate (s 307(1), (2)).

16.65   If, however, the CC reports that a significantly adverse effect on competition does exist, and is not justified, then the Treasury must, unless exceptional circumstances exist, refuse to approve the making of the recognition order (s 307(3), (4)).

Remedial directions by the Treasury

16.66   If an adverse report has been received from the CC under its review powers under s 306(4) (except in relation to an application for recognition), concluding that the adverse effect on competition is not justified, the Treasury must make a remedial direction to the FSA (s 308(1), (2)).[1] This requires the FSA either to revoke the recognition of the body concerned, or to direct the body to take specified steps as set out in the direction (s 308(8)).[2]

---

[1]   But see para 16.68.
[2]   In determining what steps to require the body to take, the Treasury must take into account any conclusion of the CC about possible remedial action in its report under s 306(7)(b) (s 308(4)).

16.67   In making a remedial order, the Treasury must observe the procedural steps set out in FSMA 2000, s 310. These require the Treasury to take such steps as it considers appropriate to allow the exchange or clearing house (or any other persons affected by the remedial direction) to make representations about any report made under s 303, 304 or 306 and as to whether the Treasury ought to exercise its powers under s 307 or 308, and the Treasury must have regard to such representations (s 310(2)).

16.68 The Treasury is not required to give a remedial direction either where the Treasury considers that it is not necessary as a result of action which has already been taken by the body concerned or by the FSA in response to the report, or because exceptional circumstances exist which make it inappropriate or unnecessary (s 308(3)).

16.69 If the CC's conclusion is that the adverse effect is justified but the Treasury considers that exceptional circumstances require them to act, the Treasury may make a remedial direction to the FSA requiring it to take such action as the Treasury considers appropriate in the light of those exceptional circumstances (s 308(5), (6)).

16.70 Where the remedial direction imposed by the Treasury under s 308 requires the FSA to give a direction to the body concerned, the direction must be compatible with the recognition requirements applicable to the investment exchange or clearing house and s 296(3) and (4)[1] apply as if the direction had been given under that section (s 308(7)).

---

[1] Under s 296 a direction made by the FSA is enforceable by an injunction or, in Scotland, by an order for specific performance (s 296(3)).

Statements by the Treasury in relation to competition matters

16.71 Where the Treasury has declined to give a remedial direction under s 308, it must produce a statement giving its reasons (s 309(1)). If the Treasury gives a remedial direction under s 308, it must make a statement providing the details of the direction and if the direction has been given under s 308(6) (ie, they have effectively overruled the CC where the CC held that the adverse effect on competition was justified), they must state their reasons for giving that direction (s 309(2)). Any statement under s 309 must be made publicly available and a copy of it must be laid before Parliament (s 309(3)).

The Chapter I prohibition

16.72 The prohibition of agreements preventing, restricting or distorting competition within the UK in the Competition Act 1998, Ch I (the 'Chapter I prohibition')[1] does not apply to an agreement to constitute an RIE or RCH to the extent to which the agreement relates to the regulatory provisions of that body (s 311(1)).[2] The Chapter I prohibition also does not apply to the regulatory provisions of a recognised body (s 311(4)) or to a decision in respect of its regulatory functions or practices (s 311(5), (6)), or to an agreement the parties to which include a recognised body or person subject to the rules of a recognised body to the extent that the agreement is required or encouraged by that body's regulatory provisions or practices (s 311(7)).[3]

---

[1]   Imposed by the Competition Act 1998, s 2(1).
[2]   Similarly, it does not apply to an agreement to constitute an exchange or clearing house which is not an RIE or RCH if the body has applied for a recognition order and the application has not been determined (s 311(3)).
[3]   See FSMA Explanatory Notes, para 559.

16.73 If the recognition order in respect of the investment exchange or clearing house has been revoked, s 311 continues to have effect for a further six months beginning on the day on which the revocation order took effect (s 311(8)).

The Chapter II prohibition

16.74 The prohibition of abuse of a dominant position in a market which may affect trade in the UK contained in the Competition Act 1998, Ch II, s 18(1) (the 'Chapter II prohibition') does not apply to the practices of an RIE or RCH, or to the adoption or enforcement of such a body's regulatory provisions[1] or to any conduct engaged in by that body or its members, to the extent that these are required by the body's regulatory provisions (s 312).[2]

---

[1]   As defined in s 302(1): see para 16.54.
[2]   FSMA Explanatory Notes, para 560.

17 Lloyd's

INTRODUCTION

17.1 Under the Financial Services Act 1986 (FSA 1986), the Society of Lloyd's (Lloyd's) and underwriting agents of Lloyd's were exempt persons in respect of investment business carried on by them in connection with or for the purposes of insurance business at Lloyd's (FSA 1986, s 42). The Lloyd's market, governed principally by the Lloyd's Act 1982,[1] was effectively outside the supervisory and regulatory remit of the FSA under FSA 1986 for almost all purposes. In the 1980s and 1990s concerns arose as to the regulatory position of Lloyd's as a result of the crisis in the market following the Lloyd's names litigation, and the substantial changes in the nature and structure of the market including the development of corporate membership and other integrated vehicles.

---

[1] The Lloyd's Acts of 1871 and 1982 have not been repealed by the Financial Services and Markets Act 2000 (FSMA 2000) and remain the primary statutes regarding the constitution and the management structure and rules of Lloyd's although Lloyd's announced proposed changes to the 1982 Act in 2002 which would substantially alter the structure, including the role of individual 'names' at Lloyd's. [Please check as I think these are private acts and don't show up on Is it in Force for some reason?]

17.2 In January 1998, the Government announced its intention to bring Lloyd's within the new framework for financial regulatory reform.[1] This proposed giving the FSA extensive direct and indirect regulatory responsibilities and powers in relation to Lloyd's insurance market while retaining the unique legal status of the Society of Lloyd's (the 'Society') and its members, and the functions of its Council (the 'Council') under the Lloyd's Acts 1871 to 1982.[2]

---

[1] See FSA Press Release FSA/PN/001/1998 and FSA CP 16, The Future Regulation of Lloyd's, November 1998, para 35.
[2] FSMA Explanatory Notes, para 561.

17.3 FSMA 2000 provides the FSA with a direct supervisory role in relation to the Society and its Council and an indirect role in relation to members of the Society. This flexible approach is designed to allow the FSA to utilise Lloyd's expertise and experience while retaining the power to intervene as required to monitor the market's standards of regulation.[1]

---

[1]   FSA CP 16, The Future Regulation of Lloyd's, November 1998, para 58. See also the combined arrangements between Lloyd's and the FSA for monitoring and enforcement co-operation arrangements in relation to underwriting agents. See the FSA website at www.fsa.gov.uk/lloyds/combinedarrangements.pdf.

THE FSA'S GENERAL DUTIES IN RELATION TO LLOYD'S

17.4   FSMA 2000, Pt XIX (ss 314–324) makes general provision for the regulation of Lloyd's by the FSA. Section 314 provides that the FSA must keep itself informed about the way in which the Council supervises and regulates the market at Lloyd's (s 314(1)(a)). The FSA must also keep itself informed about the way in which regulated activities are being carried on in that market (s 314(1)(b)) and must keep under review the desirability of exercising any of its powers under Pt XIX or any powers which it has in relation to the Society in the light of s 315 (s 314(2)). It was not intended that the Lloyd's market be subject to full FSA regulation as at 'N2' (1 December 2001),[1] but the framework put in place by FSMA 2000 will allow the FSA to extend its regulatory role and to take a greater degree of direct responsibility for regulating Lloyd's, should circumstances arise where the FSA considers it appropriate.[2]

---

[1]   See para 1.37 for further discussion of N2.
[2]   FSMA Explanatory Notes, para 565. See also the FSA Handbook, Lloyd's sourcebook, LLD.

THE SOCIETY OF LLOYD'S AS AN AUTHORISED PERSON

17.5   FSMA 2000, s 315(1) provides that the Society is an authorised person for the purposes of FSMA 2000 and its permission is to be treated as if it has been given on an application for permission under FSMA 2000, Pt IV (s 315(3)).[1] The Society does not therefore need to apply for permission but is deemed to have been given such permission. Under FSMA 2000 the Society has permission to carry on certain types of specified regulated activities, namely—

— arranging deals in contracts of insurance written at Lloyd's (termed 'basic market activity' for the purposes of s 315);

— arranging deals in participation in Lloyd's syndicates (termed 'secondary market activity' for these purposes); and

— any other activity carried on in connection with or for the purposes of carrying on these other market activities (s 315(2)).

---

[1]   As a result, the Society is subject to the threshold conditions set out in Sch 6, other than para 2 (s 315(5)), the approved persons regime (Pt V) and other provisions applicable to authorised firms. The FSA Handbook provisions which relate to the Society's role and its prudential supervision are in the Lloyd's sourcebook, LLD. Other provision are either the same as, or set out alongside, those applicable to firms generally. The Society and the members of Lloyd's are to be subject to the solvency requirements imposed under the relevant EC directives. Accordingly, the FSA needs, as a minimum, to require the Society and the members to meet those requirements (Explanatory Notes, para 564): see the FSA Handbook, Interim Prudential sourcebook for investment businesses, IPRU(INV) 4, and the Lloyd's sourcebook, LLD.

Definitions

17.6   For the purposes of Pt IV the term 'participation in Lloyd's syndicates', in relation to the secondary market activity referred to in para 17.5, means the investment described in Sch 2, para 21(1), ie, a person's membership (or prospective membership) of a Lloyd's syndicate (s 324(1)). The term, 'arranging deals' in relation to the investments to which Pt IV applies, has the same meaning as in Sch 2, para 3, namely—

'Making, or offering or agreeing to make—

(a) arrangements with a view to another person buying, selling, subscribing for or underwriting a particular investment;

(b) arrangements with a view to a person who participates in the arrangements buying, selling, subscribing for or underwriting investments' (s 324(1)).

FSMA 2000 also provides that any term used in Pt IV which is defined in the Lloyd's Act 1982 has the same meaning as in that Act (s 324(2)). The activities for which the Society will have permission depend on the provisions of the Regulated Activities Order[1] made by the Treasury under FSMA 2000, s 22(1).[2]

---

[1]   The Financial Services and Markets Act 2000 (Regulated Activities) Order 2001, SI 2001/544.

[2]   FSMA Explanatory Notes, para 567.

Variation or cancellation of permission

17.7   The FSA may exercise its powers under FSMA 2000, s 45 to vary or cancel the Society's Pt IV permission if it appears to the FSA that the Society as an authorised person is failing or is likely to fail to satisfy the threshold conditions[1] or has failed during a 12-month period to carry on a regulated activity for which Pt IV permission has been obtained or it is desirable to exercise that power to protect the interests of consumers or potential consumers (ss 45(1), 315(4)).

---

[1]   Section 315(5) excludes any requirements in FSMA 2000 concerning the registered office of a body corporate.

THE FSA'S POWER OF DIRECTION IN RELATION TO THE LLOYD'S MARKET

17.8   Members of Lloyd's were not, as at N2,[1] authorised persons, and s 316 provides the FSA with the power to direct the extension of the general prohibition (s 19), or, to the extent that the general prohibition is not applied, of a 'core provision'[2] to 'insurance market activity'.[3] This power may be exercised over individual members of Lloyd's (s 316(1)(a)) or over members of Lloyd's collectively (s 316(1)(b)). As a result the power enables the FSA to require members of Lloyd's to become authorised if it considers this to be appropriate.[4]

---

[1]   See para 1.37 for further discussion of N2.
[2]   These are set out in ss 316(3) and 317: see para 17.12.
[3]   Defined as 'a regulated activity relating to contracts of insurance written at Lloyd's' (s 316(3)).
[4]   FSMA Explanatory Notes, para 568.

17.9   In so far as members of Lloyd's wish to carry on any other type of regulated activity, such as giving investment advice or managing investments outside the scope of insurance market activities, they will need permission under FSMA 2000, Pt IV.[1] Equally, any person outside Lloyd's who gives advice about becoming a member of a Lloyd's syndicate must have the appropriate permissions under Pt IV to do so.[2] Managing agents and members' agents will, however, be required to be authorised by the FSA for permission to conduct Lloyd's regulated activities, and consequently will be required to satisfy the 'threshold conditions' (Sch 6) in addition to the requirements imposed by Lloyd's itself in relation to market participation.[3]

---

[1]   FSMA Explanatory Notes, para 564.
[2]   FSA CP 16 Response Paper, June 1999, para 100.
[3]   FSA CP 16 Response Paper, June 1999, paras 95 and 96.

Insurance market directions

17.10 A direction made by the FSA under s 316(1), applying the general prohibition or a core provision, is referred to as an 'insurance market direction' (s 316(2)). Insurance market directions must be in writing (s 316(5)) and must specify each core provision, class of person and kind of activity to which the direction applies (s 316(7)(a)). A direction may apply the general prohibition to different classes of person (s 316(6)) and may apply different core provisions to different classes of persons and different kinds of activity (s 316(7)(b)).[1] An insurance market direction is to have effect from the date specified in it but it cannot have retrospective effect (s 316(8)). It must be published (s 316(9))[2] and the FSA must provide the Treasury with a copy of any direction (s 316(11)). In making an insurance market direction, the FSA must have particular regard to the policyholders and potential policyholders (s 316(4)(a)). The FSA must also have regard to any failure by the Society to satisfy an obligation as a result of provisions of the law of another EEA State which gives effect to any of the insurance directives and applies to an activity carried on in that State by a person covered by this section (s 316(4)(b)). The FSA must also have regard to the need to ensure the effective exercise of its functions in relation to the Society as a result of s 315 (s 316(4)(c)).

---

[1]   See the FSA Handbook, Lloyd's sourcebook, LLD 5 in relation to the core provision applying the compulsory jurisdiction of the Ombudsman Scheme to the carrying on of insurance business by members. See also the Lloyd's Compensation Instrument 2003 (FSA 2003/75), the Lloyd's Sourcebook (Amendment No 2) Instrument 2003 (FSA 2003/32) and the Lloyd's Sourcebook (Solvency I Directive) Instrument 2003 (FSA2003/66).
[2]   The FSA may charge a reasonable fee for providing a copy of the direction, s 316(10).

Exercise of powers through Council

17.11 Under s 318(1) a direction may be given either to the Council or to the Society (acting through the Council), or both. The FSA may make such a direction as an alternative to or in addition to a direction under s 316(1) (s 318(4)).[1] Such a direction may be made in relation to the exercise of the respective powers of the Council or the Society with a view to achieving or supporting a specified objective set out in the direction (s 318(2), (3)).[2] A direction given under s 318(1) may also be given in respect of underwriting agents as if they were persons mentioned in s 316(1) (s 318(5)). A direction must be made in writing and must be published by the FSA, and a copy must be given to the

Treasury (s 318(6)(b), (9)). Such a direction does not at any time prevent the FSA from exercising any of its other powers under FSMA 2000 (s 318(6)(a)).

---

[1]   For example, the direction given in LLD 2.2.1 in relation to the Society and Council's objectives or the insurance market direction given in LLD 6.1.2 in relation to the application of the compulsory jurisdiction of the Financial Ombudsman Service to members in respect of carrying on insurance business.
[2]   FSMA Explanatory Notes, para 571.

APPLICATION OF THE CORE PROVISIONS TO THE LLOYD'S MARKET

17.12   The core provisions are defined in s 317(1) as those set out in the following parts of FSMA 2000—

Pt V—Performance of Regulated Activities
Pt X—Rules and Guidance
Pt XI—Information Gathering and Investigations
Pt XII—Control over Authorised Persons
Pt XIV—Disciplinary Measures
Pt XV—The Financial Services Compensation Scheme
Pt XVI—The Ombudsman Scheme
Pt XXII—Auditors and Actuaries
Pt XXIV—Insolvency.

In addition, ss 384–386 (restitution required by the FSA) and Pt XXVI (Notices) are also core provisions for these purposes (s 317(1)). These core provisions may be applied to members carrying on an 'insurance market activity' (s 316(1)), that is a regulated activity relating to contracts of insurance written at Lloyd's (s 316(3)).

17.13   Section 317(3) also allows the FSA to apply a core provision with modifications. This appears to be intended to enable the practical role played by the Society and underwriting agents in the day-to-day business affairs of members to be reflected in the regulatory arrangements.[1] If the FSA applies a core provision, references in it to an authorised person are treated as references to a member of the class to whom the core provision is applied (s 317(2)).

---

[1]   FSMA Explanatory Notes, para 570.

CONSULTATION PROCESS IN RELATION TO LLOYD'S

17.14 FSMA 2000, s 319 establishes a consultation process in relation to the FSA's powers over Lloyd's and for promulgating directions under ss 316 and 318 unless the FSA considers that this would result in a delay which would be prejudicial to the interests of consumers (s 319(6)). Before making a direction under either s 316 or 318, the FSA must publish a draft direction and make it available to the public (s 319(1), (9)), and may charge a reasonable fee for a copy (s 319(8)).

17.15 Any draft direction published under this provision must include a cost benefit analysis (s 319(2)(a))[1] unless the FSA considers that there will be no increase in costs or, if there will be an increase in costs, the increase will be of minimal significance (s 319(7)). It must also contain a notice that representations about the proposed direction may be made to the FSA within a specified time (s 319(2)(b)). The FSA must have regard to any representations made before making its direction (s 319(3)) and it must also publish a general account of the representations made to it in the consultation process and its response to them (s 319(4)). If the direction which is to be promulgated differs significantly from the draft which was published, the FSA must publish details of the difference and include a cost benefit analysis of those differences (s 319(5)).[2]

---

[1] A cost benefit analysis for these purposes means an estimate of the costs with an analysis of the benefits which will arise if the proposed direction or revised direction is given (s 319(10)).

[2] Subject to s 319(7).

FORMER UNDERWRITING MEMBERS

17.16 FSMA 2000, Pt XIX, ss 320–322 apply to former underwriting members of Lloyd's. Section 324(1) defines 'former underwriting member' as a person ceasing to be an underwriting member of the Society on, or at any time after, 24 December 1996. Under s 322, the FSA may make rules imposing such requirements on persons to whom the rules apply as appear to the FSA to be appropriate for protecting policyholders against the risk that former underwriting members of Lloyd's generally or a specific class of former underwriting members of Lloyd's may not be able to meet their liabilities (s 322(1), (2)). Generally speaking, Pt X (ss 138–164) does not apply to such rules (s 322(4)). Rather s 319 is applied to rules made under s 322 (s 322(3)).[1] However, ss 152–154 (the requirement for the FSA to notify the Treasury when it makes, varies or otherwise publishes its rules) do apply (s 322(4)).

---

[1]   See paras 17.14 and 17.15.

Discharge of insurance liabilities

17.17   A former underwriting member of Lloyd's (whether or not he is an authorised person)[1] may carry out each contract of insurance underwritten at Lloyd's as if he were an authorised person until such time as his insurance liabilities have been fully discharged (s 320(1)). This provision disapplies the general prohibition in relation to former members of Lloyd's in respect of contracts of insurance written by them while they were members of the Society. However, the FSA is granted the power to impose requirements on former members of Lloyd's, including members who leave in the future.[2] These requirements are in relation to the regulated activities carried on by them while they were members of Lloyd's, if it appears appropriate to do so to protect policyholders against the risk that the former underwriting member may not be able to meet his liabilities (s 320(3)). If the FSA imposes a requirement, the person concerned may refer the matter to the Tribunal (s 320(4)). A former member of Lloyd's would also need to obtain permission from and be authorised by the Authority to carry on any other regulated activities under FSMA 2000.[2]

---

[1]   If he is authorised, his Pt IV permission does not extend to activities related to insurance contracts carried out as a former underwriting member (s 320(2)).
[2]   FSMA Explanatory Notes, para 575.

Requirements imposed on former underwriting members

17.18   A requirement[1] made under s 320 on former underwriting members of Lloyd's will take effect either immediately or on such other date as may be specified in a written notice given to the person concerned (s 321(1), (2)). The notice must provide details of the requirement, state the FSA's reason for imposing it, and inform the former underwriting member that he may make representations to the FSA (within a specified period which may be extended with the FSA's agreement) (s 321(4)) with respect to the matter (whether or not he has referred the matter to the Tribunal) (s 321(3)). It must inform the former underwriting member of the date on which the requirement will take effect and inform him that he has a right to refer the matter to the Tribunal (s 321(3)). If, after receiving any representations from the former underwriting member, the FSA decides to impose the requirement or, if it has already been imposed, not to revoke it, the FSA must give the former underwriting member written notice (s 321(5)). It must also inform him of his right to refer the matter to the Tribunal, with an indication of the procedures to be followed in making such a referral (s 321(10), (12)). Equally, if the FSA decides not to impose a requirement previously published or to revoke a requirement which has been imposed, it must give the former underwriting member a written notice to that effect (s 321(6)).

---

[1] A 'requirement' made under s 320 is one in respect of which the FSA may exercise its powers under s 380 (injunctions) or s 382 (restitution) in relation to former underwriting members of Lloyd's who contravene it.

17.19 Where a former underwriting member has applied for a variation or revocation of a requirement under s 320, the FSA must, if it decides to grant the application, give him notice in writing (s 321(7)). If the former underwriting member has applied to the FSA for the variation or revocation of a requirement and the FSA proposes to refuse that application, it must give the person concerned a warning notice (s 321(8)). If, after considering any representations made to it in response to a warning notice given to the former underwriting member, the FSA decides to refuse an application to vary or revoke a requirement, it must give the former underwriting member a decision notice (s 321(9)). This must include notification that he may refer the matter to the Tribunal, with an indication of the procedure to be following in making such a referral (s 321(10)–(12)).

TRANSFERS OF BUSINESS DONE AT LLOYD'S

17.20 The Treasury may also by order provide for the application of any provision of Pt VII, which concerns the control of business transfers, to apply (with or without modification) to schemes to transfer the whole or any part of the business carried on by one or more members of the Society or former underwriting members of Lloyd's (s 323). The Treasury has applied various provisions of Pt VII to transfers of business from members (and certain former members) of Lloyd's.[1]

---

[1] The Financial Services and Markets Act 2000 (Control of Transfers of Business Done at Lloyd's) Order 2001, SI 2001/3626. The order only applies the relevant parts of Pt VII if the transfer scheme results in the business concerned being carried on from an establishment of the transferee within the EEA and if the Council has passed a resolution covering the matters specified in the order (art 4).

18 The supervision of professional firms

EXEMPTION FROM FSA AUTHORISATION

18.1   The Financial Services and Markets Act 2000 (FSMA 2000), Pt XX (ss 325–333) provides the framework within which professional firms are exempt from the requirement to obtain permission from the FSA in order to carry out certain regulated activities. Professional firms include solicitors, actuaries and accountants who are not carrying on mainstream regulated activities but are members of professional bodies designated for the purposes of Pt XX.[1]

18.2   The Economic Secretary to the Treasury, Melanie Johnson, introduced these clauses for the Government saying—

> 'Under this group of new clauses, professionals will require authorisation only when they perform investment business as their mainstream activity. The Government hope that that approach will avoid the need for precautionary authorisation—meeting the concerns of the Burns Committee, and of course others—while enabling the professions to provide an all-round service for their clients in appropriate cases.'[2]

---

[1]   See FSMA Explanatory Notes, para 579. However, even exempt professional firms must comply with certain of the FSA's Rules as set out in the Professional Firms sourcebook (PROF), PROF 1.1.1R.

[2]   See HC Report Stage, 1 February 2000, col 1007.

18.3   Approximately 15,000 firms were regulated by recognised professional bodies to carry on investment business[1] under the FSA 1986 but it is estimated that less than 2,000 of those carried on any substantive investment business activities. Even fewer (approximately 300) carried on any substantial investment business in relation to their other 'non-investment business' activities and only a very small number of major accountancy or law firms carried on a substantial amount of corporate finance activities or discretionary investment management which involves investment business.[2] As a result, a relatively small number of professional firms are now authorised persons. Firms carrying on regulated activities as mainstream business such as providing investment advice direct to clients or providing discretionary management services or substantial corporate finance advice, are not treated as exempt and have to obtain permission under FSMA 2000, Pt IV.[3]

---

[1]   See FSA CP 30 Response Paper, June 2000, para 2.3, Annex A.
[2]   FSA CP 30 Response Paper, June 2000, para 2.4.
[3]   Section 327(4) and FSA CP 30 Response Paper, June 2000, paras 1.10 and 2.14. See also para 18.5.

EXEMPT REGULATED ACTIVITIES

18.3A   FSMA 2000, s 327(1) provides that the general prohibition in FSMA 2000, s 19 will not apply to the carrying on of a regulated activity by a person if he satisfies the six conditions set out in s 327(2)–(7)[1] and no direction under s 328 or order under s 329 has been made disapplying s 327(1).

---

[1]   See paras 18.4–18.10. The FSA has stated that its view is that the conditions in s 327 do not impose any restriction on the regulated activities of an exempt professional firm outside the United Kingdom. FSA Handbook, PROF 2.1.15G.

Conditions

18.4   A person must be a member of a profession or be controlled or managed by one or more such members (s 327(2)).

18.5   The manner of the provision by a person of any service in the course of carrying on the activities must be incidental to his providing professional services (s 327(4)).[1] 'Professional services' are defined as services which are not regulated activities and the provision of which is supervised and regulated by a designated professional body (s 327(8)).[2] As the Economic Secretary to the Treasury explained—

> 'Several other hon Gentlemen have asked about the distinction between what is part of a person's normal tasks and what is incidental. The first point to be made is that, in the investment services directive, "incidental" is used to mean ancillary, perhaps subordinate. That is the sense in which we are using it, and it is a fairly common use of the word in any event. Examples of an incidental activity might be advice on investments given by an accountant for tax planning purposes, or advice on investment as part of a wider portfolio of assets given by a solicitor to a

couple who are negotiating a divorce settlement. I cited other examples in Committee, such as advice given in the course of probate.'[3]

---

[1]   FSMA 2000 does not define what is 'incidental', but the FSA Handbook provides guidance on what the FSA considers incidental and the factors that it considers relevant (PROF 2.1.10G and 2.1.14G).

[2]   The designated professional bodies are: the Law Society, the Law Society of Scotland, the Law Society of Northern Ireland, the Institute of Chartered Accountants in England and Wales, the Institute of Chartered Accountants of Scotland, the Institute of Chartered Accountants in Ireland, the Association of Chartered Certified Accountants, and the Institute of Actuaries: see the Financial Services and Markets Act 2000 (Designated Professional Bodies) Order 2001, SI 2001/1226.

[3]   HC Report Stage, 1 February 2000, col 1010. See also FSMA Explanatory Notes, para 585, which states that 'the regulated activities must be provided in a way that is incidental and complementary to the provision of professional (for example, legal, actuarial or accountancy) services'. This would also ensure that the firm was outside the scope of the Investment Services Directive, Art 2(2)(c).

18.6   **The person must not have received any pecuniary reward or other advantage, for which he does not account to his client, arising out of carrying out any of the activities (s 327(3)).[1]**

---

[1]   For example, any commission which that person received from a third party would belong to the client: see FSA CP 30 Response Paper, June 2000, para 2.9. See also FSA CP 69 Feedback Statement, May 2001, paras 3.14 and 3.15, and the FSA Handbook, PROF 2.1.12G.

18.7   **The person must not carry on or hold himself out as carrying on any regulated activity other than that for which rules have been made under s 332(3)[1] or one in relation to which he is exempt (s 327(5)).[2]**

---

[1]   See paras 18.29 and 18.30.

[2]   See para 18.11. A person carrying on exempt regulated activities under Pt XX may be exempt in other capacities, such as being an appointed representative under s 39, and, not being an authorised person, is not barred by s 38(2).

18.8   **Section 327(6) provides that the activities which that person carries on must not be of a description or relate to an investment of a description specified in an order made by the Treasury for the purposes of s 327(6).[1]**

---

[1]   The Financial Services and Markets Act 2000 (Professions) (Non-Exempt Activities) Order 2001, SI 2001/1227, arts 4–8. This order specifies the following regulated activities as being non-exempt (references are to relevant articles in the Regulated Activities Order): accepting deposits (art 5), issuing electronic money (art 9A), effecting and carrying out contracts of insurance (art 10), dealing in investments as principal (art 14), establishing, operating or winding up a collective investment scheme (art 51), establishing, operating or winding up a stakeholder pension scheme (art 52), managing the underwriting capacity of a Lloyd's syndicate (art 57), funeral plan contracts (art 59). A new art 6A was added and art 4(h) was revoked by the Financial Services and Markets Act 2000 (Miscellaneous Provisions) Order 2001, SI 2001/3650, art 3 to include activities relating to regulated mortgage contracts (art 61(1) or (2) of the Regulated Activities Order), but to exclude activities carried on by a person in his capacity as a trustee or personal representative where the borrower in question is a beneficiary under the trust, will or intestacy.

18.9   The Non-exempt Activities Order[1] specifies that deposit taking, insurance activities, dealing as principal, establishing or operating a collective investment scheme or stakeholder pension scheme and the regulated activities relating to funeral plans and mortgages[2] may not be conducted under the Pt XX exemption (art 4). The order also restricts investment management to situations where the professional firm is largely relying on the advice or decisions of an authorised person with the relevant Pt IV permission (art 5), and restricts advice which can be given (arts 6, 7).[3]

---

[1]   The Financial Services and Markets Act 2000 (Professions) (Non-Exempt Activities) Order 2001, SI 2001/1227 as amended by the Financial Services and Markets Act 2000 (Regulated Activities) (Amendment) Order 2002, SI 2002/682, art 7.
[2]   A professional person can be involved in this regulated activity if he is acting in the capacity of personal representative or trustee and the borrower under the regulated mortgage contract is a beneficiary under the trust, will or intestacy (art 6A, inserted by the Financial Services and Markets Act 2000 (Miscellaneous Provisions) Order 2001, SI 2001/3650, art 3).
[3]   Advice may not be given to private individuals if it relates to buying, selling or subscribing for investments with an investment business, or to on-exchange transactions, or to public offers for subscription, or to potential memberships of Lloyd's syndicates.

18.10   The activities must also be the only regulated activities (other than those in relation to which he is exempt) which a person carries on (s 327(7)). An exempt professional firm can not, therefore, be an authorised person and Part XX makes it clear that firms which are regulated by the FSA under FSMA 2000, Pt IV are regulated as to the whole of their activities and therefore they cannot carve out the activities which would otherwise be exempt regulated activities.[1]

---

[1]PROF 2.1.6R. See also FSA CP 30 Response Paper, June 2000, para 1.12.

18.11   However, an exempt professional firm may also be an exempt person, therefore such firms may be appointed representatives under FSMA 2000, s 39.[1]

---

[1]FN PROF 2.1.7G.

OTHERWISE EXEMPT REGULATED ACTIVITIES

18.11A The difficulties of applying the Pt XX exemption have been particularly marked in relation to those firms who, as well as activities which would otherwise be exempt regulated activities, will be carrying on 'mainstream' regulated activities such as corporate finance activities or discretionary investment management if they are carried on incidentally to their other professional services and within the conditions specified in s 327(2)–(7).

18.12   Where those firms have been required to obtain authorisation because of those mainstream activities, the whole of their regulated business would be subject to the panoply of the FSA Rules, including the Conduct of Business Rules, the Training and Competence requirements and other aspects of the authorisation regime, which similarly situated professional firms would not be subject to. To achieve a level playing field for these firms, the FSA has implemented a lighter regulatory regime for authorised firms in respect of these 'otherwise exempt regulated activities.'[1] At the Committee Stage of the Lords, Lord McIntosh said —

> 'It is only right and proper that firms carrying on mainstream investment business should require permission from the FSA to carry on those activities. It is a recipe for ineffective regulation to tie the FSA's hands so that it is unable to look at the whole of a firm's financial service business where that is appropriate. It is in the interests of consumers that an authorised firm's overall fitness to conduct financial services be assessed in the light of its activities as a whole. Such oversight by the FSA is what any firm, whether or not a professional firm, has to undergo.
>
> However, as we indicated in Committee, it does not follow that the FSA will or must necessarily apply additional burdens in respect of the non-mainstream business of authorised professional firms. The FSA will, on the contrary, be expected to act in accordance with its statutory duties, including the need to have regard to considerations of proportionality and competition. For example, any restrictions relating to the introduction by authorised firms of clients to independent financial advisers would be a matter for FSA rules—and I understand that there is no intention to make rules to that effect.
>
> We also referred in Committee to the FSA's October 1999 consultation paper on the regulation of professional firms, in which it was made clear that with regard to the provision of non-mainstream activities, in line with the degree of risk attaching to such business, a "differentiated and, where appropriate, less burdensome regime" is proposed.'[2]

---

[1]   See the FSA Handbook, Professional firms sourcebook, PROF 5, Non-mainstream regulated activities.

[2]   HL Report Stage, 18 April 2000, col 563. See also FSA CP 30 Response Paper, June 2000, Ch 3.

FSA'S GENERAL SUPERVISORY RESPONSIBILITIES

18.13   FSMA 2000 places on the FSA a general duty over the supervision of professionals carrying on regulated activities[1] and provides that it must 'keep itself informed' about the way in which these bodies supervise and regulate their members[2] who are carrying on exempt regulated activities[3] and about the way those members conduct those exempt regulated activities (s 325(1)). This is described in the Explanatory Notes as 'arms-length oversight' and will involve monitoring the effectiveness of the complaints and redress arrangements of designated professional bodies.[4] Exempt professional firms are also required to disclose their status to their clients to avoid any confusion or inference that they are authorised under FSMA 2000 or regulated by the FSA. This status disclosure must be given to clients of the exempt professional firm in writing in a manner which makes it clear, fair and not misleading and FSA suggests it be incorporated in engagement letters or client care letters.[5]

---

[1]   The FSA must keep under review the desirability of exercising any of its powers under Pt XX (s 325(3)).
[2]   'Members' for the purposes of Pt XX means persons who are entitled to practise the profession in question and who are subject to the rules of the designated professional body whether or not they are members of that body (s 325(2)).
[3]   'Exempt regulated activities' are those regulated activities which may be carried on by a member of one of the designated professional bodies without that person breaching the general prohibition in s 19 (s 325(2)).
[4]   FSMA Explanatory Notes, para 583. See also the FSA Handbook, Professional firms sourcebook, PROF 3.1.2G.
[5]   FN PROF 4.1.

18.14   FSMA 2000 also requires designated professional bodies to co-operate with the FSA in carrying out its supervisory function and to provide the FSA with such information as the FSA may require to carry out its functions under Pt XX (s 325(4)). In carrying out this supervisory function, the FSA can ban members of the professions (s 329)[1] and the FSA can also direct that the exemption be restricted.[2]

---

[1]   See also paras 18.23–18.28.
[2]   See paras 18.17–18.22.

DESIGNATED PROFESSIONAL BODIES

18.15   The Treasury has the power to designate those professional bodies[1] to which Pt XX will apply (s 326(1)), if those bodies actively regulate the provision of financial services by their members.[2] For the Treasury to designate a professional body it must be satisfied that the professional body meets the 'basic condition' and one or more of the additional conditions.[3] The basic condition is for the body to have rules applicable to its members when carrying on what would be exempt regulated activities (s 326(4)).

[1]   A body thus designated is referred to in Pt XX as a 'designated professional body' (s 326(2)).
[2]   FSMA Explanatory Notes, para 584.
[3]   See para 18.16.

18.16 The additional conditions which the Treasury may impose are that—
— the professional body has the power under any enactment[1] to regulate the practice of the profession (s 326(5)(a));
— being a member of the profession is a requirement under any enactment for exercising certain functions or holding a particular office (s 326(5)(b)); and
— the professional body has been recognised[2] for the purposes of any enactment other than FSMA 2000 and that recognition has not been withdrawn (s 326(5)(c)).

The Treasury may designate a professional body established elsewhere in the EEA, but, if it does so, the professional body must have powers corresponding to those described above in that State (s 326(5)(d)).[3]

[1]   An 'enactment' for these purposes includes an Act of the Scottish Parliament, Northern Ireland legislation and subordinate legislation (made under an Act or any Act of the Scottish Parliament or Northern Ireland legislation) (s 326(6)).
[2]   For these purposes 'recognised' means recognised by a Minister of the Crown, one of the Scottish Ministers, a Northern Ireland Minister or a Northern Ireland department or its head (s 326(7)).
[3]   The basic condition still applies (s 326(3)(a)).

DIRECTIONS IN RELATION TO THE GENERAL PROHIBITION

The direction

18.17 The FSA has the power to restrict the scope of the Pt XX exemption. It may make a direction that the exemption under Pt XX is not to apply to certain classes of professional or to different descriptions of regulated activity (s 328(1), (2)). The FSA may only exercise this power, however, where it is satisfied that it is desirable to do so to protect the interests of clients (s 328(6)).

Definition of clients

18.18 For the purposes of Pt XX 'clients' are defined as—
— persons who use, or have used, or are or may be contemplating using, any of the services provided by a member of a profession in the course of carrying on exempt regulated activities (s 328(8)(a));
— persons who have rights or interests which are derived from, or otherwise attributable to, the use of any such services by other persons (s 328(8)(b)); or
— persons who have rights or interests which may be adversely affected by the use of such services by persons acting on their behalf or in a fiduciary capacity (s 328(8)(c)).

This definition is very broad; for example, it is wider in its scope than the definition of 'client' in the Law Society's Solicitors' Practice Rules 1990. In addition, to the extent that a person carrying on exempt regulated activities is doing so in the capacity of a trustee, the persons who are, have been or may be beneficiaries of the trust are to be treated as falling within the definition of 'client' in s 328(8)(a) for the purposes of Pt XX (s 328(9)).

18.19 In making a direction under s 328 the FSA must have regard to the effectiveness of the arrangements made by a designated professional body for—
— co-operating with the FSA;[1]
— securing compliance with the rules made under s 332;
— dealing with complaints against its members in relation to exempt regulated activities; and
— offering redress to clients who have suffered or claim to have suffered a loss as a result of misconduct by its member in carrying on exempt regulated activities (s 328(7)).

---

[1]   Ie, in carrying out its supervisory functions, including the sharing of information with the FSA (s 325(4)).

18.20 A direction under s 328(1) must be made in writing (s 328(2)(a)), and a copy of the direction must be sent to the Treasury without delay (s 328(5)). It must be published in the way the FSA determines is best calculated to bring it to the attention of the public (s 328(3)). The FSA may charge a fee for providing a person with a copy (s 328(4)).

Consultation

18.21 Before making a direction under s 328, the FSA must publish a draft of the proposed direction which must be accompanied by a cost benefit analysis[1] and a notice that representations may be made to the FSA in respect of the proposed direction (s 330(1), (2)). The FSA is not required to publish a cost benefit analysis if, in making the appropriate comparison,[2] it considers there will be no increase in costs or, if there will be an increase in costs, that the increase will be of minimal significance (s 330(7)). The FSA must publish the consultation document in a way so as to ensure it is brought to the attention of the public (s 330(9)) and may charge a fee for providing copies of it (s 330(8)). The FSA is not required to consult, however, if it considers that the delay in doing so would prejudice the interests of consumers (s 330(6)).

---

[1]   Defined as an estimate of the costs together with an analysis of the benefits arising if the direction is to be or has been given (s 330(10)).

[2]   The comparison between the overall position if the direction is either given or not given, or after or before it was given (s 330(11)).

18.22   The FSA must take any representations which it received during the consultation process into account before making such a direction, and in giving the direction it must set out a summary of the representations made to it and its response to them (s 330(3), (4)). If, having taken into account the representations which it has received, the FSA decides to amend or vary the direction, it must publish a statement of the differences and set out the details of the amendment together with a cost benefit analysis if applicable (s 330(5)).

ORDERS IN RELATION TO THE GENERAL PROHIBITION

18.23   The FSA may make an order under s 329 that would have the effect of banning specified persons who are not fit and proper to do so from carrying on regulated activities.[1] If a person who would otherwise be carrying on exempt regulated activities appears to the FSA not to be a fit and proper person, the order may disapply the exemption in s 327(1) to the extent specified in the order (s 329(1), (2), (4)). This parallels the arrangements for prohibition orders in relation to individuals under s 56. The FSA may vary or revoke the order on the application of the person named in it (s 329(3)).

---

[1]   FSMA Explanatory Notes, para 587.

Partnerships

18.24   Special provisions apply to partnerships. If a partnership is named in an order made under s 329, any change in the membership of that partnership will not affect the order (s 329(5)). In addition, if the partnership named in the order is dissolved, the order continues to have effect in relation to any partnership which succeeds to its business (s 329(6)). A partnership is to be taken as having succeeded to the business of another partnership if the members of the subsequent partnership are substantially the same and the new partnership succeeds to the whole of or substantially the whole of the preceding partnership's business (s 329(7)).

Procedure on making or varying orders under s 329

18.25 If the FSA proposes to make an order under s 329, it must give the person in respect of whom the order may be made a warning notice which sets out the proposed terms of the order (s 331(1), (2)).[1]

---
[1] See paras 8.17–8.22 for procedures in relation to warning notices and decision notices.

18.26 If the FSA decides to make an order under s 329, it must give the person concerned a decision notice, which specifies the name of the person to whom the order applies and the terms on which the order has been given (s 331(3), (4)).

18.27 If, as a result of making an order under s 329, the FSA receives an application to vary or revoke the order and decides to grant the application, it must give written notice to the applicant (s 331(5), (6)). However, if it proposes not to grant the application, it must give the applicant a warning notice and, if it decides not to grant the application, it must give him a decision notice (s 331(7), (8)).

18.28 Any person who is either the subject of a proposed order under s 329 or who has made an unsuccessful application to the FSA to have such a notice varied or revoked may refer the matter to the Tribunal (s 331(9)). The referral to the Tribunal automatically stays the imposition of an order under s 329 until the period within which the matter must be referred to the Tribunal has expired and no reference to the Tribunal has been made, or, if a reference to the Tribunal has been made, until the reference has been determined (s 331(10)).

THE FSA RULE-MAKING POWERS

18.29 Although firms carrying on exempt regulated activities are subject to the rules of the relevant designated professional body, under s 332(1) the FSA may make rules in respect of professionals to whom the general prohibition does not apply by virtue of Pt XX. This power to make rules is for the purpose of requiring professionals carrying on exempt regulated activities to disclose to their clients that they are not authorised persons (s 332(2)).

18.30   FSMA 2000 imposes an express duty on the designated professional bodies to make relevant rules. The rules must apply to members of the profession who are not authorised persons, and must govern the carrying on of regulated activities by those members (other than regulated activities in relation to which they are exempt) (s 332(3)). The rules are designed to ensure that, in providing a particular professional service to a particular client, a member will only carry on regulated activities which arise out of, or are complementary to, the provision of particular professional services to a particular client (s 332(4)) although this does not extend to regulated activities conducted by professional firms as exempt persons under the Act.[1] To be effective, the rules made by the designated professional bodies must be approved by the FSA (s 332(5)). Breach of the rules is potentially serious. In introducing these clauses, Melanie Johnson explained that—

> 'If a member of a profession breaches those rules, he will be carrying on particular regulated activities in breach of the general prohibition, and therefore committing a criminal offence.'[2]

---

[1]   FSMA Explanatory Notes, para 590.
[2]   HC Report Stage, 1 February 2000, col 1008.

OFFENCES UNDER PT XX

Claims to be a person to whom the general prohibition does not apply

18.31   Section 333(1) provides that it is an offence for a person to describe himself (in whatever terms) as a person to whom the general prohibition does not apply in relation to a particular regulated activity when he is not. It also provides that it is an offence for a person to behave or otherwise hold himself out, in a manner which indicates (or which is reasonably likely to be understood as indicating) that he is such a person, when he is not.[1] A person who is found guilty of an offence under s 333 is liable on summary conviction to a maximum of six months' imprisonment or a fine not exceeding level 5 on the standard scale, or both imprisonment and a fine (s 333(3)). However, if the offence involves or includes the public display of material,[2] the maximum fine for the offence is level 5 on the standard scale multiplied by the number of days for which the display continued (s 333(4)).

---

[1]   FSMA Explanatory Notes, para 591.
[2]   Such as placing an advertisement or display card falsely making this claim.

Defence

18.32   It is a defence for a person to show that he took all reasonable precautions and exercised all due diligence to avoid committing the offence (s 333(2)).

19 Mutual societies

INTRODUCTION

19.1 The consolidation of all financial services under the single statutory regulatory body, bringing building societies, friendly societies and other forms of regulated mutual society (including industrial and provident societies) under the same regime[1] has resulted in a number of changes to the supervision of these mutual organisations. From 1 January 1999 the Financial Services Authority (FSA) began providing the necessary services in relation to supervision of these mutuals under contract to the Building Societies Commission, the Friendly Societies Commission, and the Registry of Friendly Societies. These arrangements remained in place until the Financial Services and Markets Act 2000 (FSMA 2000) came into force.

[1] There were approximately 70 building societies, 3,500 friendly societies and some 11,000 industrial and provident societies subject to supervision under the pre-FSMA regime: see HC SC A, 7 December 1999, col 1186.

19.2 The legislation relating to mutuals[1] conferred legislative powers on these bodies, often subject to the Treasury's consent, to set requirements as to the registration and constitution of such societies. These powers are exercisable by statutory instrument, and have a wholly different character from the FSA's regulatory role under FSMA 2000.[2] Accordingly it was proposed that such functions will transfer to the Treasury.[3] It was also expected that other powers and functions would transfer and have now been transferred to the FSA. [4]

[1] The Building Societies Act 1986, the Friendly Societies Act 1992, the Industrial and Provident Societies Act 1965, the Industrial and Provident Societies Act 1967, the Friendly and Industrial and Provident Societies Act 1968, the Industrial and Provident Societies Act 1975, the Industrial and Provident Societies Act 1978 and the Credit Unions Act 1979.
[2] These are more in the nature of registration requirements rather than a full regulatory framework. For example, some permit adjustment of limits in primary legislation (eg, Credit Unions Act 1979, s 5).
[3] FSMA Explanatory Notes, para 596.
[4] FSMA Explanatory Notes, para 595.

19.3 The provisions in FSMA 2000 dealing with the transfer of these functions to the FSA also include power for the Treasury to dissolve the existing bodies to take account of all their functions being transferred.[1] The Treasury was enabled to make supplemental provision, for example, to transfer the property, rights and liabilities of bodies which are being dissolved or to amend the existing legislation in the light of the transfer of functions.[2]

1   FSMA 2000, Sch 21, para 2 made certain transitional provisions concerning the position of certain self-regulating organisations (SROs) for friendly societies,[1] pending the repeal of those provisions of the Financial Services Act 1986 (FSA 1986) relating to their recognition and subsequent supervision. Schedule 21, para 2(1), (2) provided that no new application for authorisation as a friendly society may be made under FSA 1986, Sch 11, para 2, and no outstanding application made under that paragraph before the passing of FSMA 2000 (ie 14 June 2000) was permitted to continue after that date. In addition, after the date which the Treasury may specify by order (see the Financial Services and Markets (Transitional Provisions) (Designated Date for Certain Self-Regulating Organisations) Order 2000, SI 2000/1734) a recognition order for SROs for friendly societies could not be revoked under FSA 1986, Sch 11, para 5, and no application for a compliance order under FSA 1986, Sch 11, para 6 might be made in respect of such an SRO (FSMA 2000, Sch 21, para 2(3), (4)). This provision does not apply, however, to a recognised SRO which gives a notice of intention (which has not been withdrawn) to revoke its recognition order before the passing of FSMA 2000 under the 1986 Act, s 11(3). The cost of winding up a recognised SRO for friendly societies is to be borne by the FSA as part of the discharge of its functions under FSMA 2000 (Sch 21, para 2(6)). (The Financial Services and Markets (Transitional Provisions) (Designated Date for Certain Self-Regulating Organisations) Order 2000, SI 2000/1734 came into force on 25 July 2000 and provided that for the purposes of FSMA 2000, Sch 21, paras 1, 2 the designated date for (a) the Personal Investment Authority Limited and (b) the Investment Management Regulatory Organisation Limited was 25 July 2000. (These SROs, being companies limited by guarantee, have now been wound up and were dissolved on 15 January 2003.) These organisations were recognised SROs and recognised SROs for friendly societies under FSA 1986 (the Securities and Futures Authority Limited was not a recognised SRO for friendly societies).)

2   FSMA Explanatory Notes, para 597. See also HC SC A, 7 December 1999, col 1185.

19.4   The Treasury made the Financial Services and Markets Act 2000 (Mutual Societies) Order 2001[1] (the Mutuals Order) to transfer various functions (mainly legislative functions)[2] to itself, and to transfer the remainder of these functions to the FSA. These transfers came into effect at 'N2' (1 December 2001), although the Mutuals Order made provision to allow the Treasury to make regulations and orders, and the FSA to make rules and directions, before N2 so that they could come into effect at N2 (Mutuals Order, art 4).[3]

1   SI 2001/2617.
2   See the Explanatory Note to the Mutuals Order.
3   The functions which were transferred to the Treasury are set out in the Mutuals Order, Sch 1.

FRIENDLY SOCIETIES

19.5   As part of the consolidation of the supervision and regulation of financial services under the FSA, FSMA 2000 gives the Treasury the power to make an order[1] transferring any of the functions of the Friendly Societies Commission to the FSA, or transferring to the Treasury any of those functions which have not been or are not being transferred to the FSA (s 334(1)). Similarly, the Treasury may make an order transferring to the FSA any of the functions of—

— the Chief Registrar of Friendly Societies;
— any assistant registrar for the United Kingdom, the Channel Islands or the Isle of Man;[2]
— any assistant registrar for Scotland; or
— the central office of the Registry of Friendly Societies;

and any functions not so transferred may be transferred to the Treasury (s 335(1)–(3)).[3]

---

[1]   The Financial Services and Markets Act 2000 (Mutual Societies) Order 2001, SI 2001/2617, art 4, Sch 1, Pt II (the Mutuals Order).

[2]   The Friendly Societies Act 1972, s 7 is amended by FSMA 2000, Sch 18, para 2 by the substitution of the words 'in the United Kingdom, the Channel Islands or the Isle of Man' for the words 'in the central registration area or in Scotland'.

[3]   Section 334(3) and Sch 18, Pt I provide for certain amendments to the Friendly Societies Acts (1974 and 1992), and s 334(4) and Sch 18, Pt II provide for the removal of certain restrictions on the ability of incorporated friendly societies to form subsidiaries and control corporate bodies.

19.6   FSMA 2000 also provides that the Treasury may wind up the Friendly Societies Commission by making an order specifying the day on which the Commission will cease to exist (s 334(2)).[1] The Treasury may also wind up the office of the Chief Registrar of Friendly Societies, the assistant registrar for the central registration area, the central office, or the assistant registrar for Scotland. These will cease to exist on a day to be nominated or determined by the order (s 335(4)).[2]

---

[1]   The Financial Services and Markets Act 2000 (Mutual Societies) Order 2001, SI 2001/2617 (the Mutuals Order) requires the Friendly Societies Commission to report on the discharge of its functions in the period leading up to N2 both to the Treasury and to Parliament (art 10(1)). The Friendly Societies Commission must also draw up accounts for that period within seven months of N2 (art 10(2)), which the Comptroller and Auditor General must then report on (art 10(3)). On the day after that is done, the Friendly Societies Commission ceases to exist (art 10(4)).

[2]   Provisions similar to those applicable to the Friendly Societies Commission apply to the Chief Registrar, the assistant registrar for Scotland and the assistant registrars (Mutuals Order, art 12). Their reporting obligations are triggered by the dissolution of the Friendly Societies Commission rather than N2 itself (art 12(1)), and their offices cease to exist on the day after they make their report to Parliament (art 12(1), (3)).

BUILDING SOCIETIES

19.7   To bring building societies within the ambit of the FSA's supervision, FSMA 2000, s 336 makes provision for the functions of the Building Societies Commission to be transferred to the FSA and any functions which are not transferred to the FSA may be transferred to the Treasury (s 336(1)).[1] This section provides that the Treasury may make an order transferring those functions or an order providing that the Building

Societies Commission is to be deemed to cease to exist on a specified date (s 336(2)).[2] The Building Societies Investor Protection Board may also be wound up by Treasury order (s 337). Under the Mutuals Order, art 11(1)–(3), the Board must prepare a report and audited accounts, and must publish them. The Board is dissolved on the day after the report and audited accounts are published (art 11(4)).

---

[1]   See the Financial Services and Markets Act 2000 (Mutual Societies) Order 2001, SI 2001/2617 (the Mutuals Order), art 4, Sch 1, Pt III.

[2]   The Mutuals Order requires the Building Societies Commission to report on the discharge of its functions in the period leading up to N2, both to the Treasury and to Parliament (art 9(1)), in similar terms to the requirements imposed on the Friendly Societies Commission: see para 19.6, fn 1. It too is required to draw up accounts for that period within seven months of N2 (art 9(2)), which the Comptroller and Auditor General must then report on (art 9(3)). On the day after that is done, the Building Societies Commission ceases to exist (art 9(4)).

19.8   FSMA 2000, Sch 18, Pt III also amends the Building Societies Act 1986 so as to remove the obligation for obtaining initial authorisation to raise funds and borrow money and to omit various supplementary provisions relating to authorisation.

INDUSTRIAL AND PROVIDENT SOCIETIES AND CREDIT UNIONS

19.9   Similarly, the Treasury may make orders transferring to the FSA any of the functions under the following Acts—
—   the Industrial and Provident Societies Act 1965;
—   the Industrial and Provident Societies Act 1967;
—   the Friendly and Industrial and Provident Societies Act 1968;
—   the Industrial and Provident Societies Act 1975;
—   the Industrial and Provident Societies Act 1978; and
—   the Credit Unions Act 1979 (s 338(1)).[1]

The order made by the Treasury may also specify that any functions which are not transferred to the FSA may be transferred to the Treasury (s 338(2)).

---

[1]   FSA CP 77, The Regulation of Credit Unions, December 2000, p 5, para 2.1 fn 1. Credit unions in Northern Ireland have not been brought within the FSMA scheme. They are regulated under their own legislation and are exempt persons and will remain under the jurisdiction of the Registrar for Friendly Societies in Northern Ireland. (A transitional exemption in the Financial Services and Markets Act 2000 (Exemption) Order 2001, SI 2001/1201, art 6, was made permanent in respect of credit unions within the meaning of the Credit Unions (Northern Ireland) Order 1985 by the Financial Services and Markets Act 2000 (Exemption) (Amendment) Order 2001, SI 2001/3623, arts 3 and 4 which adds a new para 24A to this effect to the Schedule of SI 2001/1201.) FSMA 2000, Sch 18, Pt IV also amends the Industrial and Provident

Societies Act 1965 so as to remove references to separate registration areas for Scotland, England, Wales and the Channel Islands and to the scale of fees to be paid in respect of transactions and the inspection of documents.

19.10 Credit unions which have provided basic savings and restricted loan facilities to their members and were previously registered with the Registrar of Friendly Societies are now regulated by the FSA, thereby removing some of the more restrictive provisions of the Credit Unions Act 1979. A centralised supervisory regime protects consumers and maintain confidence in the financial system. Credit unions therefore have to meet the threshold criteria for authorisation and otherwise comply with the FSA's Principles for Businesses.[1] Certain provisions of the Credit Unions Act 1979 are also amended by FSMA 2000, Sch 18, Pt V, so as to remove restrictions as to the minimum or maximum number of members and certain provisions in relation to loans made by credit unions.[2]

---

[1] FSA CP 77, The Regulation of Credit Unions, December 2000, paras 3.2 and 3.3. The FSA has issued a separate sourcebook for credit unions (CRED) to distil those parts of the FSA Handbook which are most relevant to them.

[2] The decision to include credit unions within the FSMA regime was made two years after the reform of the regime was announced. See HM Treasury Taskforce Report, Credit Unions of the Future, November 1999. However, these provisions were brought into force in respect of credit unions seven months after N2 (on 'credit unions day', 1 July 2002), which allowed credit unions time to prepare for the new regime: see FSA CP 77, Ch 10.

SUPPLEMENTAL PROVISIONS

19.11 An order made under FSMA 2000, s 334, 335, 336 or 338 may include the power to transfer any functions of a member of the body in question or an employee (servant) or agent of that body or person, or to transfer any property, rights or liabilities held, enjoyed or incurred by that body (s 339(1)(a), (b)). It may provide for the transferee to carry on and complete any proceedings, investigations or other matters commenced by or under the authority of the transferor before the Treasury order took effect (s 339(c)). It may also amend any enactment relating to transferred functions and their exercise by or under the authority of the person to whom they are transferred, or provide for the substitution of the person to whom the functions were transferred in any instrument, contract or legal proceedings made or begun before the order took effect (s 339(1)(d), (e)). Conclusive evidence of the transfer is provided by a certificate issued by the Treasury stating that property vested in a person immediately before the order takes effect has been transferred as a result of the order (s 339(4)).

19.12 Other powers which the Treasury may exercise in making an order in relation to the winding up of the various bodies[1] may include provision—

— for the transfer of any property, right or liabilities held or enjoyed or incurred by any person in connection with the office or the body being wound up (s 339(2)(a));[2]

— for the carrying on and completion by or under the authority of a specified person of any proceedings, investigations or other matters begun before the order takes effect under the authority of the body which now ceases to exist (s 339(2)(b));

— for the amendment of any enactment which affected the office or body (s 339(2)(c));

— for the substitution by law of the FSA, the Treasury or any other body specified in the order in any instrument, contract or legal proceeding entered into by that person or body before the order took effect (s 339(2)(d)).[3]

---

[1] Ie, those powers under s 334, 335, 336 or 337. These powers are exercised in the Financial Services and Markets Act 2000 (Mutual Societies) Order 2001, SI 2001/2617 (the 'Mutuals Order'), including the various investment business compensation schemes: see the Financial Services and Markets Act 2000 (Transitional Provisions, Repeals and Savings) (Financial Services Compensation Scheme) Order 2001, SI 2001/2967, Pt 2.

[2] The conclusive certificate provision in s 339(4) applies equally to a transfer under this provision. The powers are exercised in the Mutuals Order.

[3] The Mutuals Order, art 13 and Schs 3–5 make amendments, repeals and savings consequential on the transfer of functions.

19.13 The powers under s 339(1) and (2) do not affect the powers which the Treasury may have under FSMA 2000, s 428 to make an order or to make regulations by statutory instrument (s 339(5)). The Treasury may also make any incidental, supplemental, consequential or transitional orders as are necessary to give effect to the transfer of functions under the same powers in subsequent orders (s 339(3)).

20 Auditors and actuaries

REGULATION OF AUDITORS AND ACTUARIES

20.1   The Financial Services and Markets Act 2000 (FSMA 2000), Pt XXII (ss 340–346) contains provisions relating to the auditing and actuarial oversight of firms. While the functions of auditors and actuaries are distinct, their roles in relation to authorised firms have some similarities and the provisions relating to those roles are grouped together in Pt XXII.[1]

---

[1]   FSMA Explanatory Notes, paras 599–601. Para 601 also distinguishes between the role of an auditor (or actuary) and the role of a skilled person appointed under FSMA 2000, s 166: see para 7.9.

THE APPOINTMENT OF AUDITORS AND ACTUARIES

20.2   Under the companies legislation[1] a requirement is imposed on companies to appoint auditors, and the provisions of the Companies Acts[2] form the basis of their role. However, FSMA 2000 gives power to the Financial Services Authority (FSA) to supplement these requirements by making rules which require an authorised person (or a specified class of authorised persons) to appoint auditors and actuaries, in circumstances in which the authorised person is not already under any statutory duty to do so (s 340(1)).[3] These rules can specify the qualifications and experience of the person to be appointed (s 340(6)), the manner, timing and terms of the appointment, and the remuneration, term of office, removal and resignation of the auditor or actuary, and can require notification of the appointment (s 340(4)).[4] In addition the FSA has power to make rules similar to those in the companies legislation which require the authorised person to produce periodic financial reports and to have them reported on by an auditor or actuary (s 340(2)).

---

[1]   See primarily the Companies Act 1985, s 384.
[2]   See the Companies Act 1985, Pt XI, Ch V and the Companies Act 1989, Pt II.
[3]   FSMA 2000 does not, however, include the same provisions requiring overseas businesses to appoint auditors as the Financial Services Act 1986 (FSA 1986), s 110.

4 FSA Supervision manual, SUP 3 and SUP 4, respectively. The application of these rules to authorised firms is set out in SUP 3.1 and SUP 4.1 and the accompanying tables. Certain firms may not be required to appoint an auditor under these provisions (eg certain oil and energy market participants, small personal investment firms and service companies) but may be required under other legislation (for building societies and friendly societies, see the Building Societies Act 1986, Sch 11 and the Friendly Societies Act 1992, Sch 14) such as the Companies Act 1985 to appoint auditors. See also the Companies Act 1989, Pt II in relation to qualifications.

20.3　The FSA may make rules which impose duties on auditors and actuaries of authorised persons appointed under Pt XXII (s 340(3), (5)) and give them the powers required to discharge their functions in respect of authorised persons (s 340(5)(b)). The FSA can also make rules reserving to itself a power to appoint an auditor or an actuary over the authorised person if no appointment has been made or notified to the FSA (s 340(4)(c))[1] (similar, for example, to the power given to the Secretary of State under the Companies Act 1985, s 387 in relation to companies). FSMA 2000 also imposes a statutory duty on an auditor or actuary to comply with the relevant rules made under s 340(3) (s 340(5)(a)).[2]

[1] See the FSA Handbook, Supervision manual, SUP 3.3.7R and SUP 4.3.3R respectively.
[2] The rules relating to auditors are set out in SUP 3 and the rules relating to actuaries are set out in SUP 4.

AUDITOR'S OR ACTUARY'S ACCESS TO INFORMATION, BOOKS ETC

20.4　Auditors and actuaries appointed under FSMA 2000 or provisions made under it (s 341(2)) have the right of access at all times to relevant information equivalent to that given to auditors appointed under the companies legislation.[1] FSMA 2000 gives them the right of access to the books, accounts and vouchers of an authorised person (s 341(1)(a)) and the entitlement to require the information and explanations as they reasonably consider necessary from the authorised person's officers to perform their duties as auditor or actuary (s 341(1)(b)). Although such 'books, accounts and vouchers' clearly include an authorised firm's financial records, the power is arguably wider if it can be shown that these records are reasonably necessary for the auditor's or actuary's duties under FSMA 2000. The failure of an authorised firm or its officers to comply with such a 'requirement' would allow the FSA to exercise one or more of its relevant powers, for example, its power to obtain an injunction under s 380.[2]

1   See, for example, the Companies Act 1985, s 389A(1).

2   A 'relevant requirement' for these purposes is a requirement imposed by or under FSMA 2000 or which is imposed by or under any other act and whose contravention constitutes an offence which the FSA has power to prosecute under the *Act* (or in the case of Scotland, which is imposed by or under any other Act and whose contravention constitutes an offence under Part V of the Criminal Justice Act 1993 (insider dealing) or under prescribed regulations relating to money laundering) (s 380 (6)(a), (7)(a)).

INFORMATION GIVEN BY AUDITOR OR ACTUARY TO THE FSA

20.5   Section 342 deals with the provision of information to the FSA by auditors and actuaries of authorised persons. It applies only to auditors of an authorised person appointed under a statutory provision and actuaries acting for an authorised person and appointed under or as a result of a statutory provision (s 342(1), (2)).[1] An auditor or actuary may ordinarily owe a duty of confidentiality to the person to whom his appointment relates, for example, as a matter of professional conduct imposed by the rules of their professional bodies.[2] If a statutory auditor or actuary discloses information (or an opinion) to the FSA which he reasonably believes to be relevant to any of the FSA's functions, he does not contravene any duty of confidentiality (or any other relevant duty) as long as he is acting in good faith (s 342(3)).[3] This applies whether or not he is responding to a request for information from the FSA (s 342(4)).

1   In relation to authorised persons, the relevant statutory provisions will be primarily the companies legislation (eg, the Companies Act 1985, s 384) and the rules of the FSA but these obligations are apparently not limited to those for the purposes of FSMA 2000.

2   See FSMA Explanatory Notes, para 606, although the section arguably also covers contractual and other legal duties.

3   This protection is arguably limited to actions brought in the UK. It is unlikely that these provisions would give any legal protection in other jurisdictions as such disclosure may not be 'required by law'.

20.6   The Treasury may make regulations prescribing circumstances in which auditors and actuaries[1] have a duty to pass on information to the FSA (s 342(5), (6)). This information may include matters concerning someone other than the authorised person in relation to whom the auditor or actuary was appointed (s 342(7)).[2] As far as auditors are concerned the Treasury has used this power to make the Financial Services and Markets Act 2000 (Communications by Auditors) Regulations 2001.[3] Under these regulations, an auditor must provide to the FSA information (or his opinion) on matters of which he has become aware in his capacity as an auditor. He must do so if he reasonably believes that, as regards the authorised person concerned, there has been or may be a contravention of any 'relevant requirement'[4] which may be of material significance to the FSA in determining—

— whether the FSA should exercise any of the functions conferred on it by or under FSMA 2000 (other than listing functions); and

— whether the person satisfies and will continue to satisfy the conditions set out in FSMA 2000, Sch 6 (the 'threshold conditions').

The obligation also applies where the auditor reasonably believes that the authorised person concerned is not, or may not be a going concern, if he is precluded from stating in his report on the annual accounts (or any other relevant financial reports) that they conform with the applicable legislation[5] or if he is required by that legislation to state certain facts in his report.

---

[1] This applies to both appointed and appropriate actuaries (SUP 4.5.7G).

[2] See FSMA Explanatory Notes, para 607.

[3] SI 2001/2587. See also the Financial Services and Markets Act 2000 (Communications by Actuaries) Regulations 2003, SI 2003/1294, which came into force on 1 September 2003.

[4] The 'relevant requirements' are imposed by or under FSMA 2000 in relation to authorising or carrying on a regulated activity, or are imposed by or under another enactment whose contravention the FSA has power to prosecute (reg 1).

[5] The applicable legislation is set out in reg 2(2)(d). It includes provisions in the Companies Act 1985, the Building Societies Act 1986, the Friendly Societies Act 1992 and the Friendly and Industrial and Provident Societies Act 1968, as well as FSMA 2000.

Persons with close links to authorised persons

20.7 Section 343 implements the requirements of the EC 'Post-BCCI' Directive[1] and makes particular provision, similar to s 342, about information on persons with 'close links' to an authorised person, which an auditor or actuary provides to the FSA, including the power for the Treasury to make regulations specifying occasions on which such information must be provided (s 343(1)–(7)).[2] Section 343 applies not only to auditors and actuaries subject to s 342, but also to those appointed in relation to a person with 'close links' with an authorised person (s 343(1)(b), (2)(b)).

---

[1] European Parliament and Council Directive 95/26/EC amended Directives 73/239/EEC and 92/49/EC in the field of non-life insurance, Directives 79/267/EEC and 92/96/EC in the field of life assurance, Directive 93/22/EC in the field of investment firms and Directive 85/611/EEC in the field of undertakings for collective investment in transferable securities (UCITS) with a view to reinforcing prudential supervision. There are equivalent provisions in Directive 2000/12/EC relating to the taking up and pursuit of the business of credit institutions, which are also implemented by the regulations made under s 343: see para 20.6.

[2] See para 20.6. The obligations in the Financial Services and Markets Act 2000 (Communications by Auditors) Regulations 2001, SI 2001/2587 also apply in these circumstances.

20.8   For the purposes of s 343 a person with 'close links' is—
— a parent undertaking of the authorised person;
— a subsidiary undertaking of the authorised person;
— a parent undertaking of a subsidiary undertaking of the authorised person; or
— a subsidiary undertaking of a parent undertaking of the authorised person (s 343(8)).[1]

---

[1]   Section 343(9) provides that 'subsidiary undertaking' includes all instances of a subsidiary mentioned in the Seventh Company Law Directive 89/349/EEC, Art 1(1), (2).

PROVIDING FALSE OR MISLEADING INFORMATION TO AUDITOR/ACTUARY

20.9   FSMA 2000 makes it a criminal offence for an authorised person knowingly or recklessly to give information to an appointed auditor or actuary[1] which is false or misleading in any material particular (s 346(1)). The offence is punishable by a fine or imprisonment, or both.[2] This provision applies to each officer, controller or manager of an authorised person (s 346(2)) and is similar to provisions imposed on a company's officers under the companies legislation.[3]

---

[1]   FSMA 2000 uses the phrase 'appointed auditor or actuary' which is defined in s 346(3) to mean an auditor or actuary appointed under or as a result of FSMA 2000.
[2]   On summary conviction up to six months' imprisonment or a fine not exceeding the statutory maximum or both imprisonment and a fine (s 346(1)(a)); on conviction on indictment up to two years' imprisonment or a fine or both imprisonment and a fine (s 346(1)(b)).
[3]   See, for example, the Companies Act 1985, s 389A(2).

DUTY OF RESIGNING AUDITOR OR ACTUARY TO GIVE NOTICE

20.10   FSMA 2000, s 344 requires an auditor or actuary appointed under or as a result of some statutory requirement[1] to notify the FSA without delay if he ceases to hold that appointment. The duty[2] is imposed whether he resigns, is removed or is simply not re-appointed (s 344(2)). In addition the auditor or actuary must notify the FSA without delay of anything connected to his ceasing to hold the appointment which he thinks ought to be drawn to its attention[3] or that there is nothing which he thinks should be drawn to its attention (s 344(3)).

[1] Referring to the application of s 342—again the provisions are likely to be the companies legislation and rules made by the FSA under FSMA 2000, s 340.
[2] This provision is a 'requirement' under FSMA 2000, which gives rise to certain consequences under s 380 (injunctions), s 382 (restitution) or discipline against authorised persons (ss 205, 206).
[3] Taking a similar approach to the requirements of, for example, the Companies Act 1985, s 394(1) in which auditors have responsibilities to deposit equivalent information at the registered office of the relevant company and with the companies registrar.

DISQUALIFICATION OF AUDITORS/ACTUARIES

20.11 FSMA 2000 provides the FSA with the power to disqualify an auditor or actuary who it considers has failed to comply with a duty imposed under the Act (s 345(1)).[1] It may disqualify him from his appointment as auditor or actuary, as the case may be, in relation to an authorised person or a particular class of authorised persons. If the FSA intends to disqualify an auditor or actuary, it must give that person a warning and, if it decides to disqualify that person, it must give him a decision notice (s 345(2), (3)). Because FSMA 2000, s 345 specifies this, the FSA must follow the procedures generally applicable to warning and decision notices, set out in ss 387 and 388.[2] If the FSA disqualifies a person from acting as auditor or actuary, that person has the right to refer the matter to the Tribunal (s 345(5)).[3] The FSA may remove a disqualification which it has imposed under s 345 if it is satisfied that the disqualified person will in future comply with the duty to which the disqualification related (s 345(4)).

[1] For the FSA's approach to and policy on disqualification of auditors and actuaries, see the FSA Handbook, Enforcement manual, ENF 17.
[2] See paras 8.18–8.22 in relation to the notice procedures.
[3] FSMA 2000, Pt IX makes general provision about references to the Tribunal: see s 133 and Ch 12.

21 Insolvency provisions

INTRODUCTION

21.1 The Financial Services and Markets Act 2000 (FSMA 2000), Pt XXIV (ss 355–379)[1] sets out—
- the rights and powers of the Financial Services Authority (FSA); and
- the duties of insolvency practitioners,

in relation to formal insolvency proceedings involving authorised persons,[2] except in relation to the enforceability of market contracts.[3] The provisions contained in FSMA 2000 are to be read with the principal insolvency legislation and are not free-standing. The rights, duties and powers applicable to insolvent partnership processes are (as under the Insolvent Partnerships Order 1994[4] in relation to the partnership itself) the same as for corporate bodies (adjusted appropriately).

---

[1] The Enterprise Act 2002 (EA 2002), Pt 10 revised the administration procedure with effect from 15 September 2003 and will remove the availability of the administrative receivership procedure. In addition Council Directive on the reorganisation and winding up of credit institutions (2001/24/EC) will coordinate rules for winding up proceedings to ensure that these proceedings commenced in the home State are recognised and have full effect throughout the EC; see HM Treasury Consultation Paper 'Credit Institutions Reorganisation and Winding Up Directive', November 2003.
[2] This includes within the provisions referring to a body corporate, a limited liability partnership: see the Limited Liability Partnerships Regulations 2001, SI 2001/1090, reg 6, except where the provisions of FSMA 2000 relate to insurers, which cannot be limited liability partnerships (Sch 6, para 1 as amended by SI 2001/2507).
[3] See the Companies Act 1989, Pt VII and the Financial Markets and Insolvency (Settlement Finality) Regulations 1999, SI 1999/2979. See also FSMA Explanatory Notes, para 629. The provisions relating to the interaction between insolvent firms and the compensation scheme are set out in FSMA 2000, Pt XV: see Ch 13.
[4] SI 1994/2421.

FSA'S POWERS IN INSOLVENCY PROCEEDINGS

21.2 The rights and powers of the FSA to initiate and take part in formal insolvency proceedings form part of the means which enable it to pursue its statutory objectives.[1] For example, by using its petitioning rights, where appropriate, the FSA may act to protect those doing regulated business with a person or contemplating doing regulated business with that person—whether as a user of the financial markets[2] or as a customer of the relevant person.[3] These statutory rights and powers interact with provisions in the FSA Handbook of Rules and Guidance—primarily in relation to requirements to notify the FSA of particular events[4] and to the FSA's published approach to the way in which it expects to use its statutory powers.[5]

---

[1] FSMA Explanatory Notes, para 629.
[2] See the 'market confidence objective', FSMA 2000, s 3.
[3] See the 'consumer protection objective', FSMA 2000, s 5.
[4] See the FSA Handbook, Supervision manual, SUP 15.3.21R.
[5] See the FSA Handbook, Enforcement manual, ENF 10.

21.3   The provisions build upon and develop the arrangements which were put in place under the Financial Services Act 1986 (FSA 1986) etc. In some respects they extend considerably what was in the previous legislation, for example, in relation to—

— the requirements for insolvency practitioners to report unauthorised regulated business to the FSA, and
— the FSA's rights in insolvency proceedings in relation to sole traders who are, were, or ought to have been, authorised persons.

However they do not entirely replace pre-existing provisions—

'Different arrangements apply to certain mutual societies. The arrangements under the relevant legislation, for example the Building Societies Act 1986, will continue to apply to relevant societies, with functions transferred in that case from the Building Societies Commission to the [FSA].'[1]

---

[1] FSMA Explanatory Notes, para 630. The administration procedure for building societies is not affected by EA 2002, s 249(1)(e).

EXTENDED DEFINITION OF INSOLVENCY

21.4   For the purposes of the FSA's rights to apply for administration or petition for winding up in relation to bodies corporate or partnerships[1] which are authorised persons[2] under FSMA 2000, Pt XXIV, an extended definition of insolvency applies.[3] For example, s 359 (in relation to administration applications) provides that—

'(3)   If the company or partnership is in default on an obligation to pay a sum due and payable under an agreement, it is to be treated . . . as unable to pay its debts.

(4)   "Agreement" means an agreement the making or performance of which constitutes or is part of a regulated activity carried on by the company or partnership.'

The same extended definition applies in relation to winding up by virtue of s 367. However the particular rights and obligations differ according to the nature of the insolvency proceedings and (to some degree) the nature of the regulated business undertaken—in particular they differ for insurance business.

---

1   Different provisions apply to individuals who are authorised persons, ie, sole traders: see paras 21.32–21.34.

2   Including those which were or ought to have been authorised persons.

3   This extended definition is in similar terms to that applicable to the power to present a winding-up petition under FSA 1986, ss 72, 73.

INTERPRETATION

21.5   FSMA 2000, s 355 identifies the primary insolvency legislation with which Pt XXIV is to be read, namely—

—   the Insolvency Act 1986 (IA 1986) (corporate insolvency in England and Wales and in Scotland, and individual insolvency in England and Wales);

—   the Bankruptcy (Scotland) Act 1985 (B(S)A 1985) (individual insolvency in Scotland); and

—   the Insolvency (Northern Ireland) Order 1989, SI 1989/2405 (Northern Ireland).

It also identifies the relevant court for applications relevant to Pt XXIV and makes provision for the Treasury to specify by order a particular meaning for the term 'insurer' (s 355(2)).[1]

---

1   The meaning of 'insurer' for this Part of FSMA 2000 (except s 360) is set out in the Financial Services and Markets Act 2000 (Insolvency) (Definition of 'Insurer') Order 2001, SI 2001/2634, art 2. 'Insurer' is defined as any person who is effecting or carrying out a contract of insurance apart from a friendly society, someone who is an exempt person in relation to those activities and someone doing so in the course of, or for the purposes of, a banking business (limited to certain types of contract within the Regulated Activities Order, Sch 1, paras 14–18).

VOLUNTARY ARRANGEMENTS

21.6   FSMA 2000, ss 356–358 apply both to corporate[1] and to individual voluntary arrangements, thus permitting the FSA to take part in certain court applications. Unlike the provisions relating to the court-controlled processes of administration and compulsory winding up (ss 359–362, 367–371), the FSA's rights to participate in this type of formal insolvency process only apply if the person for whom the arrangement is proposed is an authorised person.

---

[1]   Including limited liability partnerships and for these purposes partnerships in common with other aspects in which insolvency legislation applies to partnerships.

Company voluntary arrangements

21.7   The FSA is entitled under s 356(1)[1] to apply to the court to challenge an approved corporate (or partnership) voluntary arrangement by seeking a court order under IA 1986, s 6.[2] Such an order may—
— revoke or suspend approvals gained for a voluntary arrangement at meetings of the company or its creditors; and/or
— give directions about further meetings (IA 1986, s 6(4)).

Any order of the court may include supplemental directions. An application under IA 1986, s 6 may be made only on grounds of unfair prejudice to a creditor, member or contributory of the company, or on grounds of material irregularity (IA 1986, s 6(1), (6)). If any other person makes an application objecting to the voluntary arrangement under s 6, the FSA is entitled to take part in that court application (s 356(3)).

---

[1]   Section 356 was heavily amended by the Insolvency Act 2000, s 15, and this text reflects the amended provisions. The Insolvency Act 2000 introduced a new type of company voluntary arrangement with a moratorium for small companies. The Insolvency Act 2000, Sch 1, para 44 gives the FSA powers for these new form voluntary arrangements which are broadly equivalent to those for 'traditional' company voluntary arrangements.
[2]   In relation to Northern Ireland, under the Insolvency (Northern Ireland) Order 1989, SI 1989/2405, art 19 (see s 356(2)).

21.8   In addition, the FSA is entitled under s 356(1) to apply to court to challenge any act, omission or decision of the supervisor of the voluntary arrangements under IA 1986.[1] The court may—
— confirm, reverse or modify an act or decision of the supervisor;
— give directions to the supervisor; or
— make such other order as it thinks fit.[2]

The court may also appoint a replacement or additional supervisor if that is expedient and it is impracticable for the appointment to be made without a court order.[3] If any person makes an application under IA 1986, s 7, the FSA is entitled to take part in that court application (s 356(3)).

---

[1]   IA 1986, s 7 and in relation to Northern Ireland, under the Insolvency (Northern Ireland) Order 1989, SI 1989/2405, art 20: see s 356(2).
[2]   IA 1986, s 7(3).
[3]   IA 1986, s 7(5).

INDIVIDUAL VOLUNTARY ARRANGEMENTS

21.9   The FSA has rights under IA 1986 to object (and to take part in objection proceedings begun by others) to an individual voluntary arrangement on the same grounds as described in IA 1986, s 262[1] for corporate voluntary arrangements (FSMA 2000, s 357(5)(a), (6)). If an application is made under IA 1986, s 253[2] for an interim order (which can result in a stay of proceedings or other restrictions on court actions or other legal process), the FSA is entitled to be heard on that application (FSMA 2000, s 357(1)). The FSA is entitled to send a representative to attend (and speak at) a creditors' meeting summoned under IA 1986, s 257[3] to consider proposals for an individual voluntary arrangement and to receive notice of the result of the meeting (FSMA 2000, s 357(3), (4)). The FSA has additional rights to apply to court under IA 1986, s 263[4] where there is dissatisfaction with the supervisor's behaviour (and to be involved in applications to court by others) (FSMA 2000, s 357(5)(b), (6)).

---

[1]   In relation to Northern Ireland, under the Insolvency (Northern Ireland) Order 1989, SI 1989/2405, art 236.
[2]   In relation to Northern Ireland, under SI 1989/2405, art 227.
[3]   In relation to Northern Ireland, under SI 1989/2405, art 231.
[4]   In relation to Northern Ireland, under SI 1989/2405, art 237.

TRUST DEEDS FOR CREDITORS IN SCOTLAND

21.10 The individual voluntary arrangement process does not apply to proceedings in Scotland (IA 1986, s 440). The equivalent process in Scotland is a voluntary trust deed for creditors[1] as defined in B(S)A 1985, s 5(4A).[2] As with individual voluntary arrangements, FSMA 2000 gives the FSA rights similar to those enjoyed by creditors to receive notice of, attend and speak at creditors' meetings (though the FSA has no right to vote at these meetings) where an authorised person has granted a voluntary trust deed (s 358(1), (4), (5)). As soon as practicable after becoming aware that the debtor is an authorised person, the trustee must send the FSA a copy of the trust deed and other documents and information sent to creditors (s 358(2)). The FSA has the same rights to apply to the court as a creditor who has not received notice of the trust deed to seek sequestration of the debtor's estate.[3] The rights granted to the FSA by FSMA 2000 in relation to voluntary trust deeds do not affect its rights as a creditor (s 358(6)).

---

[1]   See B(S)A 1985, Sch 5, para 5(1)(c).
[2]   See FSMA Explanatory Notes, para 637.
[3]   IA 1986, Sch 5, para 11.

ADMINISTRATION ORDERS

21.11   FSMA 2000, ss 359–362A relate to the administration procedure for companies, limited liability partnerships and partnerships.[1]

---

[1]   The administration procedure has been revised as a result of EA 2002, Pt 10 (subject to relevant savings for administration orders made before 15 September 2003—see the Enterprise Act 2002 (Commencement No 4 and Transitional Provisions and Savings) Order 2003, SI 2003/2093, art 3). In particular, under FSMA 2000, s 362A, as inserted by the 2002 Act, Sch 17, para 58, the consent of the FSA must be obtained for the appointment of an administrator of a company of a kind described in s 362(1)(a)–(c) (see para 21.12).

Petitions

21.12   The FSA is entitled to apply to court for an administration order in relation to a body corporate[1] or partnership which—

'(a)   is, or has been, an authorised person;

(b)   is, or has been, an appointed representative; or

(c)   is carrying on, or has carried on, a regulated activity in contravention of the general prohibition' (s 359(1)).

The extended definition of insolvency applies to a petition by the FSA under s 359, namely that the body corporate[1] or partnership is in default on an obligation to pay a sum due under an agreement, the making or performance of which involves a regulated activity (s 359(2)–(4)). The FSA is still required to establish that the purpose of administration would be reasonably likely to be achieved, in accordance with IA 1986, Sch B1, para 11.[2]

---

[1]   For these purposes a body corporate includes a limited liability partnership formed under the Limited Liability Partnerships Act 2000.

[2]   See para 21.4.

Insurance companies

21.13   FSMA 2000, s 360 provides the Treasury with power to extend, by order, the application of the administration procedure to insurance companies.[1] Previously there was no provision for this, in contrast to the position for banks[2] or those authorised to conduct investment business under FSA 1986.

---

[1]   The Financial Services and Markets Act 2000 (Administration Orders Relating to Insurers) Order 2002, SI 2002/1242. This Order has been amended (SI 2003/2134) to take into account changes required under EA 2002. See also Treasury consultation document on this Order, 5 November 2001.

[2]   IA 1986, s 422 provides a similar power in relation to banks which is exercised through the Banks (Administration Proceedings) Order 1989, SI 1989/1276.

An administrator's duty to report to the FSA

21.14 An administrator is required to report, without delay, to the FSA if it appears to him that the body corporate[1] (or partnership) to which his appointment relates appears to be carrying on (or appears to have carried on) a regulated activity in breach of the general prohibition. This reporting requirement does apply when the administration was made by a court order on the application of the FSA (s 361(1)).[2]

---

[1] For these purposes a body corporate includes a limited liability partnership formed under the Limited Liability Partnerships Act 2000.
[2] These provisions were amended by EA 2000, s 248 with effect from 15 September 2003 but the substance of this provision remains the same.

The FSA's powers to participate in proceedings

21.15 Section 362(1) provides the FSA with rights to be involved in the administration process[1] where this applies to a body corporate[2] or partnership which is, or has been, carrying on regulated activities (or is, or was, an appointed representative), if the FSA did not apply to the court for an administration order (s 362(1)).[3] Broadly, the rights granted to the FSA are the same as those which creditors of a company have under UK insolvency legislation, namely the right to receive notices and documents, to attend (and to speak at) creditors' meetings and to apply to court (including in relation to a scheme of arrangement under the companies legislation) (s 362(3), (4), (5)(a), (c)). The FSA has the right to appear at the hearing of any administration application or petition (s 362(2)(a)) but (apparently) does not have a statutory right to receive notice of the hearing.[4] However, in practice the authorised person is required to provide the FSA with a copy of any petition or application received.[5] In some respects the FSA enjoys enhanced rights compared with those of creditors generally. In particular, its written consent is needed for an administrators' appointment by the company or its directors under IA 1986, Sch B1, para 22, and the consent is one of the documents required to be filed at court (s 362A). The FSA also has the right to be heard at any hearing in relation to the administration proceedings, and is entitled to attend (and to speak at) meetings of the creditors' committee. However, FSMA 2000 does not give the FSA any right to vote at a creditors' meeting or at a committee meeting.

---

[1] The administration procedure was rewritten for most purposes by EA 2002, s 248 with effect from 15 September 2003.
[2] For these purposes a body corporate includes a limited liability partnership formed under the Limited Liability Partnerships Act 2000.
[3] In relation to Northern Ireland, the Insolvency (Northern Ireland) Order 1989, SI 1989/2405, art 22.

4   Section 362(3) provides that the FSA is entitled to any notice sent to a creditor. However, creditors are not entitled to notice of the hearing under the Insolvency Rules 1986, SI 1986/1925, r 2.6. This should be compared with r 2.9 in relation to persons who may attend the hearing.
5   See the Notification Rules which are included in the FSA Handbook, Supervision manual, SUP 15.3.21R.

RECEIVERSHIP

21.16   FSMA 2000, ss 363 and 364[1] set out the provisions applicable to receivers appointed in relation to companies and limited liability partnerships[1] which are or were authorised persons or appointed representatives, or are carrying on or have carried on regulated activities in breach of the general prohibition (s 363(1)). The provisions apply in relation to any form of corporate receivership and not only to administrative receiverships such as those under the Law of Property Act 1925.[2]

1   The administrative receivership procedure has been revised as a result of EA 2002 and is likely to become less relevant over time in this context as a result of its replacement with the new administrative appointment procedure for administration under EA 2002, Pt 10.
2   But not, at present, to partnerships.

FSA's powers to participate in proceedings

21.17   As with administration orders, s 363 provides that the FSA is entitled to receive notices, to attend and to speak at meetings and to make applications to court in the same way as creditors of a company. In addition the FSA is entitled to be heard on applications in the receivership, and to attend and speak at any meetings of the creditors' committee.

Receiver's duty to report to FSA

21.18   A receiver must report, without delay, to the FSA if it appears to him that the body corporate[1] to which his appointment relates appears to be carrying on (or appears to have carried on) a regulated activity in breach of the general prohibition (s 364).[2] No specific penalty is provided for failing to report to the FSA under s 364.

1   For these purposes a body corporate includes a limited liability partnership formed under the Limited Liability Partnerships Act 2000.
2   This covers all receivers and not just administrative receivers. This would apply to a receiver appointed in respect of specific assets as well as one appointed in respect of the whole of a company's assets. For example, if a receiver were appointed in relation to a group of properties and it appeared that the company concerned was involved in activities which constituted establishing, operating or winding up a collective investment scheme in relation to those properties, this would be covered by s 364.

VOLUNTARY WINDING UP

21.19 FSMA 2000, ss 365 and 366 deal with the voluntary winding-up process. The provisions, as with the voluntary winding-up process itself, do not apply to partnerships.

FSA's powers to participate in voluntary winding up

21.20 The powers given to the FSA under FSMA 2000 to participate in a voluntary winding up are essentially the same as those granted in relation to administration proceedings. Again, these rights, ie, to receive reports and notices, to apply to court (including in relation to schemes of arrangement) and to attend and to speak at creditors' meetings, are the same as those granted under insolvency legislation to creditors (s 365(2), (4), (5)(a), (c), (7)), as are the rights to be heard at any court application and to attend and to speak at creditors' committee meetings (s 365(3), (5)(b), (c)).

21.21 As with its rights in relation to voluntary arrangement processes,[1] the FSA's rights in relation to voluntary liquidations only apply if the company concerned is an authorised person (s 365(1)).[2] FSMA 2000 preserves and makes explicit the FSA's right to seek a winding-up order from the court even though a voluntary liquidation may be in progress (s 365(6)).[3] Thus if the FSA is, for some reason, concerned to have the process of liquidation controlled by the court, it can still present a petition.

---

[1] See para 21.9.

[2] The special provisions relating to insurance companies which conduct long-term insurance business are described at paras 21.22 and 21.23 and see s 355(2) in relation to 'insurer' at para 21.5, fn 1.

[3] See also s 367 and para 21.26.

Insurance companies carrying on long-term insurance

21.22 The Insurance Companies Act 1982 imposed an absolute bar to voluntary windings up of insurance companies which carry out contracts of long-term insurance.[1] The FSMA Explanatory Notes state that—

> 'The reason is that if such companies went into voluntary liquidation the rights of endowment policy holders would accrue, so that they would be entitled only to the current value of their policy, and not to the terminal bonuses they would expect if their policies ran on to the end of their term.'[2]

Under FSMA 2000, these companies are now permitted to use the voluntary liquidation procedure if the FSA consents (s 366(1)). If notice of a general meeting of the company is given to its members which includes notice of a proposed winding-up resolution, a director of the company must notify the FSA as soon as practicable after he becomes aware of it (s 366(2)). Failure to do so is a criminal offence punishable by a fine (s 366(3)).

---

[1]   Insurance Companies Act 1982, s 55(2). FSMA 2000, s 424 provides that references in FSMA 2000 to contracts of long-term insurance are to be read with s 19 (general prohibition), s 22 (definition of regulated activities) and Sch 2. This presumably means as specified in the Regulated Activities Order made by the Treasury under those provisions.
[2]   FSMA Explanatory Notes, para 646.

21.23   The short notice and written resolution provisions of the companies legislation[1] do not apply to a resolution for the winding up of a company which conducts long-term insurance business (s 366(4)). In addition the company must file with the registrar of companies a certificate issued by the FSA stating that it consents to the voluntary winding up of the company at the same time as the company files a copy of the winding-up resolution (s 366(5)). Unless this is done, the resolution has no effect (s 366(7)), but if it is done, the voluntary winding up is treated as having become effective at the time the resolution was passed (s 366(6)).[2]

---

[1]   Companies Act 1985, ss 378(3), 381A; Companies (Northern Ireland) Order 1986, SI 1986/1032, arts 386(3), 389A.
[2]   It is unclear, however, what effect this provision has if the obligation to file the certificate issued by the FSA under s 366(5) is not complied with within the statutory period of 15 days under the Companies Act 1985. As the provision states that the resolution has no effect until the requirements of s 366(5) are complied with, it could result in a state of limbo during the statutory period of 15 days if a firm carrying out long-term insurance were to fail to provide the required certificate.

Liquidator's duty to report to the FSA

21.24   A liquidator is required to report, without delay, to the FSA if it appears to him that the body corporate[1] to which his appointment relates appears to be carrying on (or appears to have carried on) a regulated activity in breach of the general prohibition (s 370).[2] This is the same requirement as is imposed on liquidators in a compulsory winding up.[3]

---

[1]   For these purposes a body corporate includes a limited liability partnership formed under the Limited Liability Partnerships Act 2000.
[2]   As with s 364, there is no specific penalty for failing to report to the FSA under this provision.
[3]   See para 21.29.

COMPULSORY WINDING UP BY THE COURT

21.25 FSMA 2000, ss 367–371 relate to the compulsory winding-up process for corporate bodies and insolvent partnerships. As with administration, this is a court-supervised process and the rights given and duties imposed by FSMA 2000 in relation to the process have much in common with those given and imposed by it in relation to administration.[1]

---

[1]   See paras 21.11–21.15.

Petitions

21.26 The FSA is entitled to present a petition for a winding-up order in relation to a company, limited liability partnership or partnership which—

'(a)   is, or has been, an authorised person;

(b)   is, or has been, an appointed representative; or

(c)   is carrying on, or has carried on, a regulated activity in contravention of the general prohibition' (s 367(1)).

The court may make a winding-up order if the body corporate[1] or partnership is insolvent[2] or if the court is satisfied that it is just and equitable to make the winding-up order (s 367(3)). The extended definition of insolvency applies to a petition by the FSA under s 359(3) (ie, a company, limited liability partnership or partnership is in default on an obligation to pay a sum due and payable under an agreement, the making or performance of which involves a regulated activity carried on by the company, limited liability partnership or partnership) (s 367(4), (5)).

---

[1]   For these purposes a body corporate includes a limited liability partnership formed under the Limited Liability Partnerships Act 2000.

[2]   Within the meaning of IA 1986, s 123 or 221 or the Insolvency (Northern Ireland) Order 1989, SI 1989/2405, art 103 or 185.

EEA and Treaty firms

21.27 Section 368 restricts the FSA's right to petition for the winding up of an EEA firm[1] or a Treaty firm[2] so that the FSA may only petition if asked to do so by the relevant home state regulator (s 368).

---

[1]   As defined in s 425(1)(a) and Sch 3, para 5.

[2]   As defined in Sch 4, para 1.

Insurers

21.28 There is an express requirement in FSMA 2000, s 369 that a petitioner (other than the FSA) for the winding up of an authorised person with permission to effect or carry out contracts of insurance[1] must serve a copy of that petition on the FSA (s 369(1)).[2] Similarly if an application to appoint a provisional liquidator over such an authorised person is made by someone other than the FSA, a copy of that application must be served on the FSA (s 369(2)). This provision does not therefore apply if the relevant company is carrying out contracts of insurance in breach of its permissions from the FSA or if it is doing so in breach of the general prohibition.[3]

---

[1] This section should be read in conjunction with FSMA 2000, s 424 as noted in para 21.22, fn 1. Section 424(3) also provides that the law applicable to a contract of insurance, the effecting of which constitutes the carrying on of a regulated activity is to be determined, if it is of a prescribed description, in accordance with regulations made by the Treasury.
[2] These matters will be publicly available information and will be included in the public register of information kept by the FSA.
[3] This is restricted to authorised persons with the relevant permission. See also para 13.12–13.15 in relation to compensation provisions for insurers.

Liquidator's duty to report to the FSA

21.29 A liquidator is required to report, without delay, to the FSA if it appears to him that the corporate body[1] or partnership to which his appointment relates appears to be carrying on (or appears to have carried on) a regulated activity in breach of the general prohibition (s 370).[2] This applies where the winding-up order was made on the petition of a person other than the FSA (s 370(a)). However, the liquidator's duty to report applies irrespective of whether the winding up is compulsory or voluntary.[3]

---

[1] For these purposes a body corporate includes a limited liability partnership formed under the Limited Liability Partnerships Act 2000.
[2] As with s 364, there is no specific penalty for failing to report to the FSA under this provision.
[3] As noted in para 21.24.

FSA's powers to participate in proceedings

21.30 The powers of the FSA under FSMA 2000 to participate in a compulsory winding up are similar to those granted in relation to administration proceedings.[1] The right to receive reports and notices, to apply to court in relation to schemes of arrangement and to attend and to speak at creditors' meetings are equivalent to those granted under the insolvency legislation to creditors (s 371(3), (4)(a), (d), (5)). The FSA's right to be heard at any court application and to attend and speak at creditors' committee meetings are also equivalent to those in relation to administration orders (s 371(2), (4)). As with its powers relating to administration the FSA's powers to participate in compulsory winding-up proceedings apply in relation to companies, limited liability partnerships or partnerships which are, or were, carrying on a regulated activity (whether or not with permission) or which are, or were, appointed representatives (s 371(1)).

[1]   See paras 21.11–21.15.

BANKRUPTCY AND SEQUESTRATION PROCEEDINGS

21.31   The FSA's rights under FSMA 2000, ss 372–374 only apply if the individual[1] concerned is an authorised person in his own right (ie, a sole trader)[2] or is carrying on a regulated activity in breach of the general prohibition (s 372(7), 374(5), (6)).

[1]   FSMA Explanatory Notes, para 650 refers to s 372 as conferring power on the FSA to allow it to petition for the bankruptcy or sequestration of the estates of sole traders if they are or appear to be unable to pay their debts to consumers. The Notes also comment that this right to petition for bankruptcy/sequestration is more limited in that it only applies where the individual is unable to pay his debts and not, as with companies or partnerships, where the courts find it is 'just and equitable' to do so.

[2]   For the purposes of FSMA 2000, permission under s 40(1)(c) is granted to a partnership, not the partners individually. Therefore a partner in an authorised firm is presumably not an 'authorised person'. The FSA's right to petition for the bankruptcy or sequestration of an individual's estate under s 372 would not therefore extend to a partner of that firm although the individual partner would be an approved person for the purposes of FSMA 2000, s 59 and therefore subject to the disciplinary measures and ultimately financial penalties under the Act's regulatory regime.

Petitions by the FSA

21.32   Under FSMA 2000, s 372, the FSA has the right to petition for the bankruptcy of (or, in Scotland, for the sequestration of the estate of)[1] an individual who carries on (or has carried on) a regulated activity as an authorised person or who is in breach of the general prohibition (s 372(1), (7)). The FSA is not entitled under this section to petition against an appointed representative or an individual who is simply employed by an authorised person. The FSA's rights to petition under this section are limited to one of the two following cases, both of which are solvency tests.

[1]   See the Bankruptcy (Financial Services and Markets Act 2000) (Scotland) Rules 2001, SI 2001/3591.

21.33 The first case is where the individual appears to be unable to pay a regulated activity debt (s 372(2)(a)). This is expressed in the same terms as the extended insolvency test applied to administrations and compulsory windings up,[1] ie, that the debtor is in default on an obligation to pay a sum due and payable under an agreement, the making or performance of which constitutes or is part of a regulated activity (s 372(3), (8)).[2]

---

[1]   See paras 21.4, 21.12 and 21.26.
[2]   Note that in relation to a petition for the sequestration of an individual's estate under B(S)A 1985, s 5, FSMA 2000, s 372(6) provides that this and the case under s 372(2)(b) (see para 21.34) are treated as constituting 'apparent insolvency' and the FSA is treated as a 'qualified creditor'.

21.34 The second case is where the individual appears to have no reasonable prospect of being able to pay a regulated activity debt (s 372(2)(b)). This is established if the FSA has served a demand requiring the individual to establish to its satisfaction that there is a reasonable prospect of his ability to meet a payment obligation, and three weeks have elapsed without this demand being complied with, unless it has been set aside in accordance with the relevant insolvency rules (s 372(4), (9)). The procedure to be followed in relation to an FSA demand is set out in rules made by the Treasury.[1] The procedure prescribed in those rules follows the general approach for statutory demands, but has been adapted to take account of the fact that the FSA is not a creditor. An FSA demand must be treated under IA 1986 (or the 1989 Order)[2] as if it were a demand under s 268 of the 1986 Act or art 242 of the 1989 Order (s 372(5)).

---

[1]   The Bankruptcy (Financial Services and Markets Act 2000) Rules 2001, SI 2001/3634 and the Bankruptcy (Financial Services and Markets Act 2000) (Scotland) Rules 2001, SI 2001/3591.
[2]   Insolvency (Northern Ireland) Order 1989, SI 1989/2405.

Insolvency practitioner's duty to report to the FSA

21.35 In common with the other insolvency appointments (apart from for voluntary arrangements), an insolvency practitioner is required to report, without delay, to the FSA if it appears to him that the individual to which an appointment of his relates is carrying on (or has carried on) a regulated activity in breach of the general prohibition (s 373(1)),[1] unless the bankruptcy order or sequestration award was made on the petition of the FSA (s 373(1)(a)).

---

[1]   As with s 364, there is no specific penalty for failing to report to the FSA under this provision.

FSA's powers to participate in bankruptcy and sequestration proceedings

21.36 The FSA's rights to participate in bankruptcy and sequestration proceedings are similar to those granted to it in relation to administrations and compulsory windings up;[1] namely to be heard at the hearing of the petition or any other hearing, and to attend and to speak at creditors' and other formal meetings called under the insolvency legislation (s 374(2), (4)). These rights are broadly the same as those of creditors (though slightly extended, for example, the right to attend the creditors committee). In addition, the FSA is entitled to receive a copy of a report on a debtor's affairs prepared by an insolvency practitioner pursuant to a court order on a debtor's petition (s 374(3)).[2] These provisions apply in relation to an individual who is either an authorised person or an individual carrying on a regulated activity in breach of the general prohibition (s 374(5)). In Scotland, they are extended to the sequestration of estates belonging to or held for or jointly by the members of an 'entity', as defined in B(S)A 1985, s 6(1)[3] (s 374(1)(c), (6)).

---

[1] See paras 21.15 and 21.30.
[2] Section 374(3) refers to the reports to be made under IA 1986, s 274 (and the Insolvency (Northern Ireland) Order 1989, SI 1989/2405, art 248).
[3] For the purposes of B(S)A 1985 an 'entity' is a trust in respect of debts incurred by it, a partnership (including a dissolved partnership), a body corporate or an unincorporated body, or a limited partnership (including a dissolved partnership) within the meaning of the Limited Partnerships Act 1907 (B(S)A 1985, s 6(1)).

PROVISIONS AGAINST DEBT AVOIDANCE

21.37 The existing insolvency legislation makes a number of provisions empowering the court to set aside or adjust transactions that occurred in the period immediately before the formal insolvency, almost all of which require the relevant court application to be made by a liquidator or administrator, or trustee in bankruptcy.[1] However, IA 1986, s 423 (or the Insolvency (Northern Ireland) Order 1989, SI 1989/2405, art 367) provides that an individual creditor may apply if he is a victim of a transaction entered into at an undervalue by the debtor, the purpose of which was—

— to put assets beyond the reach of someone claiming against the debtor (or someone who may at some other time make a claim against him); or

— to prejudice otherwise the interests of a claimant or potential claimant in relation to that claim (IA 1986, s 423(3)).

---

[1] See for example the provisions relating to transactions at undervalue, preferences etc in IA 1986, ss 238–245.

FSA's right to apply for an order

21.38 Under FSMA 2000, s 375 the FSA may apply under IA 1986, s 423 (or SI 1989/2405, art 367) on behalf of all victims of the undervalue transaction (s 375(2)) where—

— at the time the transaction at an undervalue was entered into, the debtor was carrying on a regulated activity (whether or not in breach of the general prohibition); and

— a victim of the transaction is, or has been, party to an agreement with the debtor which involved the debtor in carrying on a regulated activity (s 375(1)).

Under IA 1986, s 423(2), the court may then, on the application, make such order as it thinks fit for—

(a) restoring the position to what it would have been if the transaction had not been entered into, and

(b) protecting the interests of persons who are victims of the transaction.

SUPPLEMENTAL PROVISIONS: WINDING UP OF INSURERS

Continuation of contracts of long-term insurance

21.39 Generally a liquidator is under no obligation to continue the business of the company over which he has been appointed, although he has power to do so 'so far as may be necessary for its beneficial winding up' (exercisable only with the sanction of the court or the creditors' committee in the case of a compulsory winding up) (IA 1986, ss 165, 167, Sch 4, para 5). By contrast, the Insurance Companies Act 1982, s 56(2) required the liquidator, unless the court orders otherwise, to carry on the long-term business of the company with a view to a transfer as a going concern to another insurance company. FSMA 2000, s 376 similarly obliges the liquidator to continue the business of the company (so far as it consists of carrying out contracts of long-term insurance) with a view to the transfer of that business to a party which can lawfully carry out those contracts (s 376(1), (2)).[1]

---

[1] The liquidator does not have to seek the permission of the court or the liquidation committee to apply for the approval of a transfer scheme under FSMA 2000, Pt VII (s 376(12)).

21.40 The policy behind this was stated to be that—

> 'Policyholders of long term insurers face different problems to most consumers if the company fails. They enter into agreements, for example for pensions, which are designed to last many years, and the benefits they expect to receive build up over time. Also, the terms of the contract (and importantly the premium) are set at the outset. If, for example, during the course of the contract they were to develop an illness they might not then be able to obtain alternative cover. For these reasons, it is desirable, where possible, to maintain the insurer's business as a going concern, or to find an alternative insurer to take over its policies.'[1]

---

[1]   FSMA Explanatory Notes, para 653.

21.41 In continuing the company's business, the liquidator may not effect any new contracts of insurance, but has power to agree to vary existing contracts and to seek the appointment by the court of a special manager (whose powers are contained in the court order appointing him) to assist him (s 376(3)–(7)). In addition the court is given powers to order reductions of the value of any of the company's contracts of long-term insurance and to order an actuarial report (s 376(8)–(11)).

Reducing the value of contracts instead of winding up

21.42 Section 377 gives the court power to reduce the value of any one or more of the insurer's contracts instead of winding up the company if the insurer[1] has been proved to be unable to pay its debts.[2]

---

[1]   'Insurer' for the purposes of Pt XXIV has the meaning specified in the Financial Services and Markets Act 2000 (Insolvency) (Definition of 'Insurer') Order 2001, SI 2001/2634 (s 355(2)): see para 21.5, fn 1. Section 377 does not apply to an EEA insurer by virtue of the Insurers (Reorganisation and Winding Up) Regulations 2003, SI 2003/1102, reg 4(6).
[2]   This reduction may be on such terms and subject to such conditions, if any, as the court thinks fit (s 377(3)).

Treatment of assets on winding up

21.43 FSMA 2000, s 378 provides that the Treasury may make regulations providing for the treatment of the assets of an insurer[1] on its winding up including—

— 'ringfencing' provisions[2] providing for assets representing a particular part of the insurer's business to be available only for meeting liabilities attributable to that part of the insurer's business; and

— holding separate general meetings of the creditors in respect of liabilities attributable to a particular part of the insurer's business (s 378).

---

[1] 'Insurer' has the meaning given by the Financial Services and Markets Act 2000 (Insolvency) (Definition of 'Insurer') Order 2001, SI 2001/2634: see para 21.5, fn 1.

[2] The Financial Services and Markets Act 2000 (Treatment of Assets of Insurers on Winding Up) Regulations 2001, SI 2001/2968 provide for the ringfencing of funds maintained in respect of long-term insurance from the insurer's other assets. These regulations also separate the creditors in the same class.

Winding-up rules

21.44 In addition, winding-up rules[1] may provide for determination of the amount of an insurer's liabilities to policyholders of any class or description for the purposes of proof in a winding up and generally to give effect to the provisions in FSMA 2000, Pt XXIV with respect to the winding up of insurers (s 379(1)).[2] The winding-up rules may specifically provide for all or any of the following—

— the identification of assets and liabilities;
— the apportionment of assets between different classes or descriptions;
— the determination of the amount of liabilities of a description specified in the winding-up rules;
— the application of assets for meeting liabilities of a description specified in the winding-up rules;
— the application of assets representing any excess of a description specified in the winding-up rules (s 379(2)).

Nothing in FSMA 2000, Pt XXIV otherwise affects the power of the Lord Chancellor to make winding-up rules under IA 1986 or the Insolvency (Northern Ireland) Order 1989, SI 1989/2405 (s 379(5)).

---

[1] 'Winding-up rules' means the rules made by the Lord Chancellor under IA 1986, s 411 or the Insolvency (Northern Ireland) Order 1989, SI 1989/2405, art 359 (s 379(4)).

[2] The Insurance Companies (Winding-Up) Rules 1985, SI 1985/95 have been replaced by the Insurers (Winding Up) Rules 2001, SI 2001/3635. The new rules are similar to the 1985 rules, but update them, in particular to take account of policies which have liabilities linked to the value of particular property or income. (In Scotland, see the Insurers (Winding Up) (Scotland) Rules 2001, SI 2001/4040.)

22 Business transfer schemes

INTRODUCTION

22.1 The Financial Services and Markets Act 2000 (FSMA 2000) contains both additional and new provisions for obtaining court approval of schemes to transfer banking and insurance business (s 104).[1] This may give some authorised persons the ability to use a court sanctioned process for effecting business transfers[2] which could not otherwise be undertaken without a private Act of Parliament or other formal legal process such as novation which may be impracticable or impossible to achieve by other means.[3]

---

[1] Insurance business transfer schemes were a feature of the Insurance Companies Act 1982 (ss 49–52B and Sch 2C) which implemented the EC Insurance Directive but no such schemes existed for banking business. (see para. 22.3, fn 1). However, FSMA 2000, s 104 has not been brought into effect in relation to banking business transfer schemes, as to do so would have made this the sole means by which such transfers could be effected: see the Financial Services and Markets Act 2000 (Commencement No 7) Order 2001, SI 2001/3538, art 2(2). Also HM Treasury, Control of Business Transfers (Requirements on Applicants) Regulations 2001, A Consultative Document, March 2001.

[2] Certain insurance business transfers authorised in other EEA States may also take place under the automatic process under FSMA 2000, s 116.

[3] For transitional provisions, see the Financial Services and Markets Act 2000 (Transitional Provisions and Savings) (Business Transfers) Order 2001, SI 2001/3639.

22.2 The Treasury has been given wide powers to make regulations in relation to the application (s 108)[1] and process of these business transfer schemes and may make further regulations applying to particular cases with modifications or making such amendments to FSMA 2000, Pt VII as it considers appropriate in order to make such transfers more effective (s 117).[2]

---

[1] The Financial Services and Markets Act 2000 (Control of Business Transfers) (Requirements on Applicants) Regulations 2001, SI 2001/3625. See also Explanatory Notes, para 195.

[2] Such an order has been made under s 323 in relation to insurance business transfers relating to business carried on by members at Lloyd's: see the Financial Services and Markets Act 2000 (Control of Transfers of Business Done at Lloyd's) Order 2001, SI 2001/3626. The FSA has also provided guidance on business transfers to authorised firms in SUP 18.

INSURANCE BUSINESS TRANSFERS

22.3 An insurance business transfer scheme[1] is a court ordered scheme under which the following are to be transferred to another body—

— the whole or part of the insurance business[2] carried on in one or more member States by a body which is an authorised person and which is incorporated in the UK or if an unincorporated association is formed under the law of any part of the UK (a 'UK authorised person') as defined in s 105(8) (s 105(2)(a));[3]

— the whole or part of the business which consists of reinsurance carried on in the UK through an establishment (ie, its head office or a branch) (s 105(9)) in the UK by an EEA firm exercising passport rights under FSMA 2000, Sch 3 which has permission to effect or carry out contracts of insurance (s 105(2)(b)); or

— the whole or part of the business carried on in the UK by an authorised person who is neither a UK authorised person nor an EEA firm but who has permission to effect or carry out contracts of insurance (s 105(2)(c)) which results in the business transferred being carried on from an establishment of the transferee in an EEA State.

The scheme must also not be an excluded scheme.[4]

---

[1] These provisions replace the procedures under the Insurance Companies Act 1982, ss 49–52B, Sch 2C, which were repealed when FSMA 2000 came into force: see the Financial Services and Markets Act 2000 (Consequential Amendments and Repeals) Order 2001, SI 2001/3649, art 3, subject to the savings of Sch 2C under the Financial Services and Markets Act 2000 (Transitional Provisions and Savings) (Business Transfers) Order 2001, SI 2001/3639, art 2.

[2] 'Insurance business' is business for which an authorised person has 'permission to effect or carry out contracts of insurance' (s 105(2)(a)): see the FSA Handbook, Supervision manual, SUP 18.2 and the commentary in FSA CP 110, Insurance Business and Friendly Society Transfers, September 2001.

[3] The reference to unincorporated bodies will only be relevant in relation to Lloyd's members given that insurance companies must be bodies corporate (other than limited liability partnerships) by virtue of FSMA 2000, Sch 6, para 1.

[4] See s 105(1). See also para 22.4.

Excluded schemes

22.4 Excluded schemes are those which fall into certain defined cases as set out in FSMA 2000, s 105(3), namely those where—

— the authorised person is a friendly society (s 105(3), Case 1);

— the insurance business to be transferred is carried on by a UK authorised person but the business is carried on entirely in other EEA States and not in the UK and the scheme has been approved by a court in an EEA State other than the UK or by the host state regulator (s 105(3), Case 2);

— the insurance business to be transferred is carried on by a UK authorised person but the business is carried on entirely outside the UK and the EEA and does not include policies of insurance (other than reinsurance) involving risks arising in an EEA State. In addition the scheme has been approved by a court in that country or territory or by the relevant authority responsible for supervising that business in the country or territory where it is carried on (s 105(3), Case 3);

— the insurance business to be transferred is the whole of the authorised person's business and consists solely of effecting or carrying out contracts of reinsurance or all the policyholders are controllers of the firm or of firms in the same group as the firm to which the business is to be transferred and in either case all the policyholders have consented to the transfer (s 105(3), Case 4).

However, even where the proposed transfer scheme falls within Case 2, 3 or 4, the parties to a scheme may still apply to the court for an order sanctioning the transfer scheme as if it were an insurance business transfer scheme (s 105(4)).

Compromises or arrangements under the Companies Act 1985

22.5   Where a scheme involves a compromise or arrangement falling within the Companies Act 1985 (CA 1985), s 427A or the Companies (Northern Ireland) Order 1986, art 420A, the procedures under ss 425 to 427 of CA 1985 or arts 418 to 420 of the 1986 Order apply (with modifications) to that compromise or arrangement although the procedures under FSMA 2000, Pt VII will still apply (s 105(5)–(7)).[1]

---

[1]   See the Financial Services and Markets Act 2000 (Transitional Provisions and Savings) (Business Transfers) Order 2001, SI 2001/3639, art 3.

BANKING BUSINESS TRANSFERS

22.6   Similar provisions have now been made in relation to schemes for the transfer of banking business[1] between entities. FSMA 2000, s 106 defines a banking business transfer scheme as a scheme which is not an excluded scheme (s 106(1)(c)) and under which the whole or part of the business to be transferred includes accepting deposits (s 106(1)(b)) and—

— the whole or part of the business carried on by a UK authorised person[2] who has permission to accept deposits is to be transferred (s 106(2)(a)), whether that activity is carried on in the UK or not (s 106(4)); or

— the whole or part of the business carried on in the UK by an authorised person who is not a UK authorised person but who has permission to accept deposits is transferred to another body which will carry on that business in the UK (s 106(2)(b)).

---

[1] 'Banking business' is the business of a person who has permission to accept deposits.
[2] 'UK authorised person' has the same meaning as that given in s 105 (s 106(5)). This definition is slightly different to the definition of a 'UK authorised person' in s 178(4) for the purposes of FSMA 2000, Pt XII, as defined in s 417.

22.7 For the purposes of s 106 'excluded schemes' are schemes where the authorised person is a building society[1] or credit union[2] or the scheme is a compromise or arrangement relating to the merger of divisions of public companies under CA 1985, s 427A(1) or the Companies (Northern Ireland) Order 1986, art 420A (s 106(3)).

---

[1] As defined in the Building Societies Act 1986 (FSMA 2000, s 106(6)). The FSA has issued guidance on building societies transfers in the FSA Handbook, Interim Prudential sourcebook: Building Societies, IPRU (BSOC) vol 2, ch 3.
[2] As defined in the Credit Unions Act 1979 or the Credit Unions (Northern Ireland) Order 1985 (FSMA 2000, s 106(7)). Arrangements concerning transfers from friendly societies to other bodies which are not friendly societies are governed by the Friendly Societies Act 1992, Pt VIII, Sch 15.

JURISDICTION OF THE COURT

22.8 An application made to the court[1] for an order sanctioning an insurance business transfer scheme or a banking business transfer scheme must be made by the authorised person, the transferee or both (s 107(1), (2)). In addition, if both the authorised person and the transferee have their head offices in the same jurisdiction (ie, both in Scotland or both in England or Wales), then the application for court approval must be made to the court in that jurisdiction. If the authorised person and the transferee are registered or have their head offices in different jurisdictions, application may be made to the court in either of those jurisdictions. Finally, if the transferee is not registered in the UK and does not have its head office there, the application should be made to the court which has jurisdiction over the authorised person concerned (s 107(3)).

---

[1] The 'court' means either the High Court or, in Scotland, the Court of Session (s 107(4)).

Applications for court approval

22.9   Applications for court sanctioned schemes must be made in accordance with regulations made by the Treasury (s 108(1)) and the court may not determine whether to sanction a scheme if the applicant has failed to meet the requirements prescribed in any such regulations (s 108(2)). These regulations may identify the persons to whom notice of the scheme must be given and the periods within which that notice must be given. The regulations may also enable the court to waive certain of the requirements in specified circumstances (s 108(3)). The FSA and any other person who alleges he would be adversely affected by the scheme, including an employee of the authorised person or of the transferee, has the right to participate in the court proceedings (s 110).

22.10   If the scheme is an insurance business transfer scheme, the application must be accompanied by a report setting out the terms of the scheme. That report must have been prepared by a person nominated or approved by the FSA who appears to have the necessary skills to enable him to make a proper report (s 109(1), (2)). The report required under s 109 must be prepared in a form approved by the FSA (s 109(3)).

22.11   In considering whether it will make an order in respect of an insurance business transfer scheme or a banking business transfer scheme under s 111, the court must be satisfied that in all of the circumstances it is appropriate to approve the scheme (s 111(3)). It must also ensure that the required certificates have been received, and the transferee must have (or have before the regulated business is to be transferred) the authorisation required for it to carry on the business to be transferred (s 111(2)). The transferee must deposit two copies of any order made under s 112(1) with the FSA within ten days of the date on which the order is made (s 112(10)).[1]

---

[1]   The FSA may extend this period (s 112(11)).

22.12   If an order has been made under s 111(1), the court may, at the instigation of the FSA, appoint an actuary who will report to the FSA on any reduction in the benefits payable under policies to be affected by the transfer and will investigate the business transferred under the scheme (s 113).[1]

---

[1]   Although this provision refers to orders made under s 111(1), presumably it applies only to insurance business transfer schemes.

EFFECTS OF AN ORDER MADE UNDER S 111

22.13 Once the court has made an order under s 111, it may, either in that order or in any subsequent order, make specific provision for—

— the transfer of the whole or any part of the undertaking and of any property[1] or liabilities[2] of the authorised person to the transferee;

— the allotment or appropriation by the transferee of any shares,[3] debentures,[4] policies or other interests in the transferee which are to be allotted or appropriated to or for any other person;

— the continuation by or against the transferee of any pending legal proceedings by or against the authorised person; or

— such other steps as are necessary to ensure that the scheme is fully and effectively carried out (s 112(1)).

[1] For these purposes 'property' includes any property, rights and powers of any description (s 112(12)).
[2] For these purposes 'liabilities' includes any duties (s 112(13)).
[3] For these purposes 'shares' has the same meaning as that given in CA 1985 or the Companies (Northern Ireland) Order 1986 (s 112(14)).
[4] For these purposes 'debentures' has the same meaning as that given in CA 1985 or the Companies (Northern Ireland) Order 1986 (s 112(14)).

22.14 Where an order has been made under this section, the property or liabilities are transferred to and vested in the transferee (s 112(3)). The court may also order that the property or liabilities may vest in the transferee free of any charge[1] which will, as a result of the scheme, cease to have effect (s 112(5)). However, if the property or liabilities require an instrument of transfer for the purposes of the Companies Act 1985, s 183(1) or the Companies (Northern Ireland) Order 1986, art 193(1), (2), the order is to be treated as such an instrument (s 112(6), (7)). In addition if the property or liabilities are governed by the law of a country or territory other than the UK, the order may require the authorised person to take such steps as are necessary for ensuring that the transfer to the transferee is fully effective under that law (s 112(4)).[2]

[1] For these purposes a 'charge' includes a mortgage or, in Scotland, a security over property (s 112(15)).
[2] If the order is an insurance business transfer order and the authorised person is not an EEA firm, it is immaterial under s 112(1)(a), (c), (d), (2)–(4) whether the contracts of insurance included in the transfer are under the law of an EEA State other than the UK (s 112(9)).

22.15 An order under s 111(1) may—

— transfer property or liabilities whether or not the authorised person otherwise has the capacity to effect the transfer;

— make provision in relation to the property which is held by the authorised person as trustee;

> — make provision as to the future or contingent rights or liabilities of the authorised person including the construction of instruments (including wills) under which those liabilities or rights might arise; or
>
> — otherwise make provision as to the transfer of any retirement benefits scheme operated by or on behalf of the authorised person (s 112(2)).

CERTIFICATES UNDER FSMA 2000, SCH 12: INSURANCE BUSINESS TRANSFER SCHEMES

22.16 Before the court can make an order under s 111 in relation to an insurance business transfer scheme, an appropriate certificate may be required in respect of certain specific situations.[1]

---

[1]   See Sch 12, Pt I.

Certificates as to margin of solvency

22.17 In relation to an insurance business transfer scheme, a certificate given by the relevant authority[1] in respect of non-UK authorised persons or by the FSA in respect of UK authorised persons must certify that, taking the proposed transfer into account, the transferee has the necessary margin of solvency or no necessary margin of solvency applies to him (Sch 12, paras 1(1)(a), 2).

---

[1]   The 'relevant authority' for the purposes of these provisions is, in relation to an EEA firm, the home state regulator and in relation to a Swiss general insurer, is the authority responsible in Switzerland for supervising persons who effect or carry out contracts of insurance or, in relation to any other authorised person, FSMA 2000, Sch 12, para 2(6).

Certificates as to consent

22.18 If the authorised person is a UK person who has authorisation under Art 6 of the first life insurance directive or of the first non-life insurance directive and their head office or branch from which the business is to be transferred is in an EEA State other than the UK, a certificate given by the FSA must certify that the host state regulator has been notified of the scheme and has responded to that notification or that three months have elapsed since that notification (Sch 12, paras 1(1)(b), (2), 3).

Certificates as to long-term business

22.19 If the authorised person derives its authorisation under Art 6 of the first life insurance directive and the proposed transfer relates to business which consists of effecting or carrying out contracts of long-term insurance, and, with regards to any policy which is included in the transfer and which evidences a contract of insurance (other than reinsurance), an EEA State other than the UK is the State of the commitment, a certificate given by the FSA must certify that the authority responsible for supervising persons who effect or carry out contracts of insurance in the State of the commitment has consented to the scheme or that three months have elapsed since that notification without a refusal of consent having been received (Sch 12, paras 1(1)(c), (3), 4).

Certificates as to general business

22.20 If the authorised person has received authorisation under Art 6 of the first non-life insurance directive and the business consists of effecting or carrying out contracts of general insurance and for any policy which is to be included in the transfer and which evidences a contract of insurance (other than reinsurance), the risk is situated in an EEA State outside the UK, a certificate given by the FSA must certify that the authority responsible for supervising persons who effect or carry out contracts of insurance in the State where the risk is situated has consented to the scheme or that three months have elapsed since that notification without a refusal of consent having been received (Sch 12, paras 1(1)(d), (4), 5).

Interpretation

22.21 For these purposes the 'State of the commitment' means, if the policyholder is an individual, the State in which he has his habitual residence at the date on which the commitment was entered into, or if the policyholder is not an individual, the State in which his office or branch to which the commitment relates was located at the date on which it was entered into (Sch 12, para 6(1)). 'Commitment' means a commitment represented by contracts of insurance of the prescribed class (Sch 12, para 6(2)).

22.22 References to the EEA State in which a risk is situated are—
  — if the insurance relates to a building or a building and its contents, to the EEA State where the building is located;
  — if the insurance relates to a vehicle, to the EEA State where the vehicle is registered;

— if the insurance relates to holiday or travel risk (of whatever class), to the EEA State in which the policyholder took out the policy;

— in any other case,

    (i)   if the policyholder is an individual, to the EEA State in which he has his habitual residence on the date the policy was entered into; or

    (ii) if the policyholder is not an individual, to the EEA State where his head office or branch to which the policy relates was situated at the date the policy was entered into (Sch 12, para 6(3)).

CERTIFICATES UNDER FSMA 2000, SCH 12: INSURANCE BUSINESS TRANSFERS OUTSIDE THE UK

22.23 In the case of a proposal to execute an instrument transferring the rights and obligations of a transferor under general or long-term insurance policies under equivalent provisions in another country or territory outside the UK to a UK authorised firm the FSA is given power to give certificates that the transferee has the margin of solvency which the FSA (as its supervisor) requires it to maintain to undertake this business (s 115, Sch 12, para 10(5), (6)) For this power to be exercised, one of the following conditions must be met (Sch 12, para 10(1))—

— the transferor is an EEA firm carrying on insurance business in the UK under the passport rights by virtue of Sch 3 and the transferee is an authorised person whose margin of solvency is supervised by the FSA (Sch 12, para 10(2));

— the transferor is a company authorised in another EEA State under Art 27 of the first life insurance directive or Art 23 of the first non-life insurance directive and the transferee is a UK authorised person which has received authorisation under Art 6 of either of those directives (Sch 12, para 10(3)); or

— the transferor is a Swiss general insurer and the transferee is a UK authorised person who has received authorisation under Art 6 of either the first life or first non-life insurance directives (Sch 12, para 10(4)).

Definitions

22.24 For the purpose of this type of transfer 'general policy' is a policy evidencing a contract which would have constituted the carrying on of a regulated activity by effecting contracts of general insurance if it had been effected by the transferee (Sch 12, para 10(8)). A 'long-term policy' is defined as a policy evidencing a contract which would have constituted the carrying on of a regulated activity by effecting contracts of long-term insurance if it had been effected by the transferee (Sch 12, para 10(9)). A 'Swiss general insurer' is one whose head office is in Switzerland and who has permission to carry on regulated activities relating to effecting and carrying out contracts of general insurance and whose permission is not restricted to effecting and carrying out contracts of reinsurance (Sch 12, para 2(8) and para 10(7)).

Transfers of insurance business in other EEA States

22.25 FSMA 2000 also provides for a separate process[1] to apply if, as a result of an authorised transfer of insurance business, an EEA firm which is authorised by virtue of FSMA 2000, Sch 3, para 5(d) transfers to another body all its rights and obligations under any UK policies (s 116(1)).[2] This process also applies if a company authorised in an EEA State other than the UK under Art 27 of the first life insurance directive or Art 23 of the first non-life insurance directive transfers all its rights and obligations under any UK policies (s 116(2)) to another body. If the required notice has been published, the instrument purporting to transfer all of those rights and obligations under the UK policies will be deemed to have transferred all of the transferor's rights to the transferee by operation of law (s 116(3)).

---

[1]   This process does not require court approval and provided the requirements of s 116 are complied with a transfer may be effected by operation of law without the need for agreement or consent from any party (s 116(4)).

[2]   A 'UK policy' means a policy evidencing a contract of insurance (other than a contract of reinsurance) to which the applicable law is the law of any part of the United Kingdom (s 116(6)).

Definitions

22.26 An 'authorised transfer' means, for the purposes of s 116(1), a transfer in accordance with the laws of the EEA firm's home state implementing Art 11 of the third life directive or Art 12 of the third non-life directive (s 116(5)(a)). For the purposes of s 116(2), it means a transfer in accordance with the laws of an EEA State other than the UK in accordance with Art 31a of the first life directive or Art 28a of the first non-life directive (s 116(5)(b)). An 'EEA firm' is defined in Sch 3 as meaning a firm which does not have its head office in the UK and which meets any of the following descriptions—

— an investment firm as defined in Art 1.2 of the investment services directive[1] which is authorised by its home state regulator;

— a credit institution as defined in Art 1 of the first banking co-ordination directive[2] which is authorised by its home state regulator;

— a financial institution as defined in Art 1 of the second banking co-ordination directive[3] which is a subsidiary of the kind mentioned in Art 18.2 and otherwise fulfils the conditions in Art 18 of that directive; or

— an undertaking pursuing the activity of direct insurance within the meaning of Art 1 of the first life insurance directive[4] or of the first non-life insurance directive[5] and which has been authorised by its home state regulator.

A 'UK policy' for these purposes means a policy evidencing a contract of insurance other than a contract of reinsurance to which the applicable law is the law of any part of the UK (s 116(6)).

---

[1]   Council Directive 93/22/EC.
[2]   Council Directive 77/780/EEC (now repealed and replaced by Council Directive 2000/12/EC relating to the taking up and pursuit of the business of credit institutions).
[3]   Council Directive 89/646/EEC (now repealed and replaced by Council Directive 2000/12/EC relating to the taking up and pursuit of the business of credit institutions).
[4]   Council Directive 79/267/EEC.
[5]   Council Directive 73/239/EEC.

Appropriate notice

22.27 For an instrument to be effective under these procedures, appropriate notice must be given in accordance with the law of the relevant jurisdiction (s 116(3)). 'Appropriate notice' for these purposes is defined, in the case of a UK policy evidencing a contract of insurance in relation to which an EEA State other than the UK is the State of the commitment, as notice given in accordance with the law of that State. If the UK policy evidences a contract of insurance where the risk is situated in an EEA State other than the UK, appropriate notice means notice given in accordance with the law of that State, and in any other case, it means notice given in accordance with the applicable law (s 116(7)).

22.28 If an instrument which is effective under the procedures set out in s 116 includes provisions which provide for the continuation of legal proceedings by or against the transferee in relation to those rights and obligations, this too will operate by law and the transferee will be deemed to be substituted for the transferor (s 116(3)(b)).

Definitions

22.29 For these purposes the definitions of 'State of the commitment' and the meaning of 'references to the EEA State in which a risk is situated' are as set out in paras 22.21 and 22.22.[1]

¹ Section 116(8) provides that Sch 12, para 6 applies for the purposes of this section as it applies for the purposes of that Schedule.

Specific provisions in relation to insurance business transfer schemes

22.30 If a court order is made in respect of an insurance business transfer scheme, it or any subsequent order may include provisions for—
— dealing with the interests of any person who objects to the scheme;
— dissolving without winding up the authorised person; or
— reducing, on such terms or conditions as the court deems appropriate, benefits payable under any specified type of policy or policies generally entered into by the authorised person (s 112(8)).

22.31 Where the authorised person is not an EEA firm carrying out insurance business under its passport rights and the court has made an order in relation to the scheme, and an EEA State other than the UK is concerned to the extent that policies or contracts of insurance have been written or the risk situated in that other jurisdiction, the court must ensure that the transferee publishes in that EEA State the notice of the order or the execution of any instrument required under that order giving effect to the transfer (s 114(1), (2)). That notice must specify the period during which the policyholder may exercise any rights to cancel¹ that policy (s 114(3)). The order or instrument of transfer will not affect the policyholder if the notice has not been properly published or if the policyholder cancels the policy during the period specified in the notice (s 114(4)).

¹ Whether the policyholder has a right to cancel the policy and any conditions to which such a right would be subject is a matter for the law of the EEA State in which the contract of insurance or commitment has been undertaken or the risk is situated (s 114(5)).

CERTIFICATES UNDER FSMA 2000, SCH 12: BANKING BUSINESS TRANSFER SCHEMES

22.32 For a court to make an order under s 111(1) in respect of a banking business transfer scheme, the appropriate certificates specified in Sch 12, Pt II must be obtained (s 111(2)(a)). There are two types of certificate to be issued in relation to banking business transfer schemes, namely those relating to financial resources and those confirming the consent of the FSA or the home state regulator, as relevant (Sch 12, para 7(1)).

Certificates as to financial resources

22.33 If the proposed transferee is a person with Pt IV permission or with permission under Sch 4, the court, before making an order, will need a certificate from the FSA certifying that the transferee will, either before or at the time of the transfer and taking into account the terms of the proposed transfer, have adequate financial resources to meet the home state regulator's requirements (Sch 12, para 8(1), (2)(a)).

22.34 If the authorised person or the transferee is an EEA firm carrying on regulated activities in the UK by virtue of its passport rights under Sch 3, para 5(d), the financial resources certificate required by the court before it may make an order must be given by the home state regulator (Sch 12, para 8(1), (2)(b)).

22.35 If the proposed transferee is neither a UK authorised firm nor an EEA firm falling within Sch 3, the court will need the authority who is responsible for the transferee's business in the jurisdiction where it has its head office to provide the financial resources certificate before an order may be made (Sch 12, para 8(1), (2)(c)).

Certificates as to consent of home state regulator

22.36 The second form of certificate required in relation to banking business transfers is that given by the FSA certifying that the authorised person's home state regulator has been notified and has either given its consent to the proposed transfer or three months have elapsed since it was notified (Sch 12, para 9).

Appendix 1
Financial Services and Markets Act 2000

Financial Services and Markets Act 2000

(2000 c 8)

ARRANGEMENT OF SECTIONS

PART I
THE REGULATOR

PART II
REGULATED AND PROHIBITED ACTIVITIES

PART V
PERFORMANCE OF REGULATED ACTIVITIES

Prohibition orders

PART VI
OFFICIAL LISTING

The competent authority

PART VIII
PENALTIES FOR MARKET ABUSE

Market abuse

The code

Power to impose penalties

Statement of policy

Procedure

Miscellaneous

PART IX
HEARINGS AND APPEALS

Legal assistance before the Tribunal

PART XI
INFORMATION GATHERING AND INVESTIGATIONS

Powers to gather information

Appointment of investigators

Assistance to overseas regulators

Conduct of investigations

Offences

PART XII
CONTROL OVER AUTHORISED PERSONS

Notice of control

Acquiring, increasing and reducing control

Acquiring or increasing control: procedure

Improperly acquired shares

Reducing control: procedure

CHAPTER III
AUTHORISED UNIT TRUST SCHEMES

Applications for authorisation

Applications refused

Certificates

Rules

Alterations

Exclusion clauses

Ending of authorisation

Powers of intervention

CHAPTER IV
OPEN-ENDED INVESTMENT COMPANIES

CHAPTER V
RECOGNISED OVERSEAS SCHEMES

Schemes constituted in other EEA States

PART XXV
INJUNCTIONS AND RESTITUTION

Injunctions

Restitution orders

Restitution required by Authority

PART XXVI
NOTICES

Warning notices

Decision notices

Conclusion of proceedings

Publication

An Act to make provision about the regulation of financial services and markets; to provide for the transfer of certain statutory functions relating to building societies, friendly societies, industrial and provident societies and certain other mutual societies; and for connected purposes.

[14 June 2000]

Parliamentary debates.
House of Commons:
2nd Reading 28 June 1999: 334 HC Official Report (6th series) col 34.
Committee Stage 6 July–9 November 1999, 23 November–9 December 1999: HC Official Report, SC A (Financial Services and Markets Bill).
Motion to carry over 25 October 1999: 336 HC Official Report (6th series) col 706.
Report Stage 27 January 2000: 343 HC Official Report (6th series) col 600; 1 February 2000: 343 HC Official Report (6th series) col 924.
Remaining Stages 9 February 2000: 344 HC Official Report (6th series) col 258.
Consideration of Lords Amendments 5 June 2000: 351 HC Official Report (6th series) col 38
House of Lords:
2nd Reading 21 February 2000: 610 HL Official Report (5th series) col 13.
Committee Stage 16 March 2000: 610 HL Official Report (5th series) cols 1684, 1769; 20 March 2000: 611 HL Official Report (5th series) cols 9, 88; 21 March 2000: 611 HL Official Report (5th series) cols 146, 249; 27 March 2000: 611 HL Official Report (5th series) cols 503, 526, 593; 30 March 2000: 611 HL Official Report (5th series) cols 912, 997.
Report Stage 13 April 2000: 612 HL Official Report (5th series) col 291; 18 April 2000: 612 HL Official Report (5th series) cols 561, 656; 9 May 2000: 612 HL Official Report (5th series) cols 1373, 1396, 1457.
3rd Reading 18 May 2000: 613 HL Official Report (5th series) col 363.
Consideration of Commons Amendments 12 June 2000: 613 HL Official Report (5th series) col 1373.

Limited liability partnerships: The provisions of this Act relating to companies and partnerships are applied with modifications to limited liability partnerships: see the Limited Liability Partnerships Regulations 2001, SI 2001/1090.
Transitional provisions and savings: A number of instruments have been made under this Act making transitional provisions and savings. These instruments are listed under the note "Orders under this section" to s 426 and the note "Orders under this Schedule" to Sch 21.
Transfer of functions: mutual societies: The Financial Services and Markets Act 2000 (Mutual Societies) Order 2001, SI 2001/2617, art 4(2) (made under ss 334–339, 426, 427, 428(3)) transfers to the Financial Services Authority certain functions which, immediately before 1 December 2001, were functions of: (a) the Chief Registrar of friendly societies, assistant registrars of friendly societies or the central office of the registry of friendly societies; (b) the Friendly Societies Commission; or (c) the Building Societies Commission. Sch 2 to the 2001 Order makes provisions concerning the application of this Act in relation to functions transferred (or to be transferred) to the Authority by the said art 4(2).

PART I
THE REGULATOR

1 The Financial Services Authority

(1)   The body corporate known as the Financial Services Authority ("the Authority") is to have the functions conferred on it by or under this Act.

(2)   The Authority must comply with the requirements as to its constitution set out in Schedule 1.

(3)   Schedule 1 also makes provision about the status of the Authority and the exercise of certain of its functions.

Commencement: 18 June 2001.
References: See paras 2.3, 2.4.

The Authority's general duties

2 The Authority's general duties

(1)   In discharging its general functions the Authority must, so far as is reasonably possible, act in a way—
  (a)   which is compatible with the regulatory objectives; and
  (b)   which the Authority considers most appropriate for the purpose of meeting those objectives.

(2)   The regulatory objectives are—
  (a)   market confidence;
  (b)   public awareness;
  (c)   the protection of consumers; and
  (d)   the reduction of financial crime.

(3)   In discharging its general functions the Authority must have regard to—
  (a)   the need to use its resources in the most efficient and economic way;
  (b)   the responsibilities of those who manage the affairs of authorised persons;
  (c)   the principle that a burden or restriction which is imposed on a person, or on the carrying on of an activity, should be proportionate to the benefits, considered in general terms, which are expected to result from the imposition of that burden or restriction;
  (d)   the desirability of facilitating innovation in connection with regulated activities;
  (e)   the international character of financial services and markets and the desirability of maintaining the competitive position of the United Kingdom;
  (f)   the need to minimise the adverse effects on competition that may arise from anything done in the discharge of those functions;
  (g)   the desirability of facilitating competition between those who are subject to any form of regulation by the Authority.

(4)   The Authority's general functions are—
  (a)   its function of making rules under this Act (considered as a whole);
  (b)   its function of preparing and issuing codes under this Act (considered as a whole);

  (c) its functions in relation to the giving of general guidance (considered as a whole); and

  (d) its function of determining the general policy and principles by reference to which it performs particular functions.

(5) "General guidance" has the meaning given in section 158(5).

Commencement: 18 June 2001.
References: See paras 2.31, 2.32, 2.35.

The regulatory objectives

3 Market confidence

(1) The market confidence objective is: maintaining confidence in the financial system.

(2) "The financial system" means the financial system operating in the United Kingdom and includes—

  (a) financial markets and exchanges;

  (b) regulated activities; and

  (c) other activities connected with financial markets and exchanges.

Commencement: 18 June 2001.
References: See para 2.36.

4 Public awareness

(1) The public awareness objective is: promoting public understanding of the financial system.

(2) It includes, in particular—

  (a) promoting awareness of the benefits and risks associated with different kinds of investment or other financial dealing; and

  (b) the provision of appropriate information and advice.

(3) "The financial system" has the same meaning as in section 3.

Commencement: 18 June 2001.
References: See para 2.37.

5 The protection of consumers

(1) The protection of consumers objective is: securing the appropriate degree of protection for consumers.

(2) In considering what degree of protection may be appropriate, the Authority must have regard to—

  (a) the differing degrees of risk involved in different kinds of investment or other transaction;

  (b) the differing degrees of experience and expertise that different consumers may have in relation to different kinds of regulated activity;

  (c) the needs that consumers may have for advice and accurate information; and

(d) the general principle that consumers should take responsibility for their decisions.

(3) "Consumers" means persons—
    (a) who are consumers for the purposes of section 138; or
    (b) who, in relation to regulated activities carried on otherwise than by authorised persons, would be consumers for those purposes if the activities were carried on by authorised persons.

Commencement: 18 June 2001.
References: See paras 2.38, 2.39.

6 The reduction of financial crime

(1) The reduction of financial crime objective is: reducing the extent to which it is possible for a business carried on—
    (a) by a regulated person, or
    (b) in contravention of the general prohibition,
to be used for a purpose connected with financial crime.

(2) In considering that objective the Authority must, in particular, have regard to the desirability of—
    (a) regulated persons being aware of the risk of their businesses being used in connection with the commission of financial crime;
    (b) regulated persons taking appropriate measures (in relation to their administration and employment practices, the conduct of transactions by them and otherwise) to prevent financial crime, facilitate its detection and monitor its incidence;
    (c) regulated persons devoting adequate resources to the matters mentioned in paragraph (b).

(3) "Financial crime" includes any offence involving—
    (a) fraud or dishonesty;
    (b) misconduct in, or misuse of information relating to, a financial market; or
    (c) handling the proceeds of crime.

(4) "Offence" includes an act or omission which would be an offence if it had taken place in the United Kingdom.

(5) "Regulated person" means an authorised person, a recognised investment exchange or a recognised clearing house.

Commencement: 18 June 2001.
References: See paras 2.40–2.42.

Corporate governance

7 Duty of Authority to follow principles of good governance

In managing its affairs, the Authority must have regard to such generally accepted principles of good corporate governance as it is reasonable to regard as applicable to it.

Commencement: 18 June 2001.
References: See paras 2.33, 2.34.

Arrangements for consulting practitioners and consumers

8 The Authority's general duty to consult

The Authority must make and maintain effective arrangements for consulting practitioners and consumers on the extent to which its general policies and practices are consistent with its general duties under section 2.

Commencement: 18 June 2001
References: See para 2.48.

9 The Practitioner Panel

(1)   Arrangements under section 8 must include the establishment and maintenance of a panel of persons (to be known as "the Practitioner Panel") to represent the interests of practitioners.

(2)   The Authority must appoint one of the members of the Practitioner Panel to be its chairman.

(3)   The Treasury's approval is required for the appointment or dismissal of the chairman.

(4)   The Authority must have regard to any representations made to it by the Practitioner Panel.

(5)   The Authority must appoint to the Practitioner Panel such—
      (a)   individuals who are authorised persons,
      (b)   persons representing authorised persons,
      (c)   persons representing recognised investment exchanges, and
      (d)   persons representing recognised clearing houses,
as it considers appropriate.

Commencement: 18 June 2001.
References: See paras 2.48, 2.49.

10 The Consumer Panel

(1)   Arrangements under section 8 must include the establishment and maintenance of a panel of persons (to be known as "the Consumer Panel") to represent the interests of consumers.

(2)   The Authority must appoint one of the members of the Consumer Panel to be its chairman.

(3)   The Treasury's approval is required for the appointment or dismissal of the chairman.

(4)   The Authority must have regard to any representations made to it by the Consumer Panel.

(5)   The Authority must appoint to the Consumer Panel such consumers, or persons representing the interests of consumers, as it considers appropriate.

(6)   The Authority must secure that the membership of the Consumer Panel is such as to give a fair degree of representation to those who are using, or are or may be contemplating using, services otherwise than in connection with businesses carried on by them.

(7)   "Consumers" means persons, other than authorised persons—
   (a)   who are consumers for the purposes of section 138; or
   (b)   who, in relation to regulated activities carried on otherwise than by authorised persons, would be consumers for those purposes if the activities were carried on by authorised persons.

Commencement: 18 June 2001.
References: See paras 2.44–2.47.

11 Duty to consider representations by the Panels

(1)   This section applies to a representation made, in accordance with arrangements made under section 8, by the Practitioner Panel or by the Consumer Panel.

(2)   The Authority must consider the representation.

(3)   If the Authority disagrees with a view expressed, or proposal made, in the representation, it must give the Panel a statement in writing of its reasons for disagreeing.

Commencement: 18 June 2001.
References: See paras 2.46, 2.48.

Reviews

12 Reviews

(1)   The Treasury may appoint an independent person to conduct a review of the economy, efficiency and effectiveness with which the Authority has used its resources in discharging its functions.

(2)   A review may be limited by the Treasury to such functions of the Authority (however described) as the Treasury may specify in appointing the person to conduct it.

(3)   A review is not to be concerned with the merits of the Authority's general policy or principles in pursuing regulatory objectives or in exercising functions under Part VI.

(4)   On completion of a review, the person conducting it must make a written report to the Treasury—
   (a)   setting out the result of the review; and
   (b)   making such recommendations (if any) as he considers appropriate.

(5)   A copy of the report must be—
   (a)   laid before each House of Parliament; and
   (b)   published in such manner as the Treasury consider appropriate.

(6) Any expenses reasonably incurred in the conduct of a review are to be met by the Treasury out of money provided by Parliament.

(7) "Independent" means appearing to the Treasury to be independent of the Authority.

Commencement: 1 December 2001.
References: See paras 2.54–2.56.

13 Right to obtain documents and information

(1) A person conducting a review under section 12—
  (a) has a right of access at any reasonable time to all such documents as he may reasonably require for purposes of the review; and
  (b) may require any person holding or accountable for any such document to provide such information and explanation as are reasonably necessary for that purpose.

(2) Subsection (1) applies only to documents in the custody or under the control of the Authority.

(3) An obligation imposed on a person as a result of the exercise of powers conferred by subsection (1) is enforceable by injunction or, in Scotland, by an order for specific performance under section 45 of the Court of Session Act 1988.

Commencement: 1 December 2001.
References: See para 2.55.

Inquiries

14 Cases in which the Treasury may arrange independent inquiries

(1) This section applies in two cases.

(2) The first is where it appears to the Treasury that—
  (a) events have occurred in relation to—
    (i) a collective investment scheme, or
    (ii) a person who is, or was at the time of the events, carrying on a regulated activity (whether or not as an authorised person),
  which posed or could have posed a grave risk to the financial system or caused or risked causing significant damage to the interests of consumers; and
  (b) those events might not have occurred, or the risk or damage might have been reduced, but for a serious failure in—
    (i) the system established by this Act for the regulation of such schemes or of such persons and their activities; or
    (ii) the operation of that system.

(3) The second is where it appears to the Treasury that—
  (a) events have occurred in relation to listed securities or an issuer of listed securities which caused or could have caused significant damage to holders of listed securities; and
  (b) those events might not have occurred but for a serious failure in the regulatory system established by Part VI or in its operation.

(4)   If the Treasury consider that it is in the public interest that there should be an independent inquiry into the events and the circumstances surrounding them, they may arrange for an inquiry to be held under section 15.

(5)   "Consumers" means persons—
    (a)   who are consumers for the purposes of section 138; or
    (b)   who, in relation to regulated activities carried on otherwise than by authorised persons, would be consumers for those purposes if the activities were carried on by authorised persons.

(6)   "The financial system" has the same meaning as in section 3.

(7)   "Listed securities" means anything which has been admitted to the official list under Part VI.

Commencement: 1 December 2001.
References: See paras 2.57–2.60.

15 Power to appoint person to hold an inquiry

(1)   If the Treasury decide to arrange for an inquiry to be held under this section, they may appoint such person as they consider appropriate to hold the inquiry.

(2)   The Treasury may, by a direction to the appointed person, control—
    (a)   the scope of the inquiry;
    (b)   the period during which the inquiry is to be held;
    (c)   the conduct of the inquiry; and
    (d)   the making of reports.

(3)   A direction may, in particular—
    (a)   confine the inquiry to particular matters;
    (b)   extend the inquiry to additional matters;
    (c)   require the appointed person to discontinue the inquiry or to take only such steps as are specified in the direction;
    (d)   require the appointed person to make such interim reports as are so specified.

Commencement: 1 December 2001.
References: See paras 2.61, 2.62.

16 Powers of appointed person and procedure

(1)   The person appointed to hold an inquiry under section 15 may—
    (a)   obtain such information from such persons and in such manner as he thinks fit;
    (b)   make such inquiries as he thinks fit; and
    (c)   determine the procedure to be followed in connection with the inquiry.

(2)   The appointed person may require any person who, in his opinion, is able to provide any information, or produce any document, which is relevant to the inquiry to provide any such information or produce any such document.

(3)   For the purposes of an inquiry, the appointed person has the same powers as the court in respect of the attendance and examination of witnesses (including the examination of witnesses abroad) and in respect of the production of documents.

(4)   "Court" means—
      (a)   the High Court; or
      (b)   in Scotland, the Court of Session.

Commencement: 1 December 2001.
References: See para 2.61.

17 Conclusion of inquiry

(1)   On completion of an inquiry under section 15, the person holding the inquiry must make a written report to the Treasury—
      (a)   setting out the result of the inquiry; and
      (b)   making such recommendations (if any) as he considers appropriate.

(2)   The Treasury may publish the whole, or any part, of the report and may do so in such manner as they consider appropriate.

(3)   Subsection (4) applies if the Treasury propose to publish a report but consider that it contains material—
      (a)   which relates to the affairs of a particular person whose interests would, in the opinion of the Treasury, be seriously prejudiced by publication of the material; or
      (b)   the disclosure of which would be incompatible with an international obligation of the United Kingdom.

(4)   The Treasury must ensure that the material is removed before publication.

(5)   The Treasury must lay before each House of Parliament a copy of any report or part of a report published under subsection (2).

(6)   Any expenses reasonably incurred in holding an inquiry are to be met by the Treasury out of money provided by Parliament.

Commencement: 1 December 2001.
References: See para 2.63.

18 Obstruction and contempt

(1)   If a person ("A")—
      (a)   fails to comply with a requirement imposed on him by a person holding an inquiry under section 15, or
      (b)   otherwise obstructs such an inquiry,
the person holding the inquiry may certify the matter to the High Court (or, in Scotland, the Court of Session).

(2)   The court may enquire into the matter.

(3)   If, after hearing—
      (a)   any witnesses who may be produced against or on behalf of A, and
      (b)   any statement made by or on behalf of A,
the court is satisfied that A would have been in contempt of court if the inquiry had been proceedings before the court, it may deal with him as if he were in contempt.

Commencement: 1 December 2001.
References: See para 2.62.

PART II
REGULATED AND PROHIBITED ACTIVITIES

The general prohibition

19 The general prohibition

(1)   No person may carry on a regulated activity in the United Kingdom, or purport to do so, unless he is—
>   (a)   an authorised person; or
>   (b)   an exempt person.

(2)   The prohibition is referred to in this Act as the general prohibition.

Commencement: 1 December 2001.
References: See para 3.2.

Requirement for permission

20 Authorised persons acting without permission

(1)   If an authorised person carries on a regulated activity in the United Kingdom, or purports to do so, otherwise than in accordance with permission—
>   (a)   given to him by the Authority under Part IV, or
>   (b)   resulting from any other provision of this Act,

he is to be taken to have contravened a requirement imposed on him by the Authority under this Act.

(2)   The contravention does not—
>   (a)   make a person guilty of an offence;
>   (b)   make any transaction void or unenforceable; or
>   (c)   (subject to subsection (3)) give rise to any right of action for breach of statutory duty.

(3)   In prescribed cases the contravention is actionable at the suit of a person who suffers loss as a result of the contravention, subject to the defences and other incidents applying to actions for breach of statutory duty.

Commencement: 25 February 2001 (sub-s (3), for the purpose of making orders or regulations); 1 December 2001 (remainder).
Regulations: The Financial Services and Markets Act 2000 (Rights of Action) Regulations 2001, SI 2001/2256, as amended by SI 2002/1775, SI 2002/2706.
References: See paras 5.74–5.76, 7.26.

Financial promotion

21 Restrictions on financial promotion

(1)   A person ("A") must not, in the course of business, communicate an invitation or inducement to engage in investment activity.

(2)   But subsection (1) does not apply if—
    (a)   A is an authorised person; or
    (b)   the content of the communication is approved for the purposes of this section by an authorised person.

(3)   In the case of a communication originating outside the United Kingdom, subsection (1) applies only if the communication is capable of having an effect in the United Kingdom.

(4)   The Treasury may by order specify circumstances in which a person is to be regarded for the purposes of subsection (1) as—
    (a)   acting in the course of business;
    (b)   not acting in the course of business.

(5)   The Treasury may by order specify circumstances (which may include compliance with financial promotion rules) in which subsection (1) does not apply.

(6)   An order under subsection (5) may, in particular, provide that subsection (1) does not apply in relation to communications—
    (a)   of a specified description;
    (b)   originating in a specified country or territory outside the United Kingdom;
    (c)   originating in a country or territory which falls within a specified description of country or territory outside the United Kingdom; or
    (d)   originating outside the United Kingdom.

(7)   The Treasury may by order repeal subsection (3).

(8)   "Engaging in investment activity" means—
    (a)   entering or offering to enter into an agreement the making or performance of which by either party constitutes a controlled activity; or
    (b)   exercising any rights conferred by a controlled investment to acquire, dispose of, underwrite or convert a controlled investment.

(9)   An activity is a controlled activity if—
    (a)   it is an activity of a specified kind or one which falls within a specified class of activity; and
    (b)   it relates to an investment of a specified kind, or to one which falls within a specified class of investment.

(10)   An investment is a controlled investment if it is an investment of a specified kind or one which falls within a specified class of investment.

(11)   Schedule 2 (except paragraph 26) applies for the purposes of subsections (9) and (10) with references to section 22 being read as references to each of those subsections.

(12)   Nothing in Schedule 2, as applied by subsection (11), limits the powers conferred by subsection (9) or (10).

(13)   "Communicate" includes causing a communication to be made.

(14)   "Investment" includes any asset, right or interest.

(15)   "Specified" means specified in an order made by the Treasury.

Commencement: 25 February 2001 (for the purpose of making orders or regulations); 1 December 2001 (remaining purposes).
Orders: The Financial Services and Markets Act 2000 (Financial Promotion) Order 2001, SI 2001/1335, as amended by SI 2001/2633, SI 2001/3650, SI 2001/3800, SI 2002/1310, SI 2002/1777, SI 2002/2157, SI 2003/1676; the Financial Services and Markets Act 2000 (Miscellaneous Provisions) Order 2001, SI 2001/3650, as amended by SI 2001/3771, SI 2002/1777; the Financial Services and Markets Act 2000 (Commencement of Mortgage Regulation) (Amendment) Order 2002, SI 2002/1777; the Financial Services and Markets Act 2000 (Financial Promotion) (Amendment) (Electronic Commerce Directive) Order 2002, SI 2002/2157.
References: See paras 6.9–6.42.

Regulated activities

22 The classes of activity and categories of investment

(1)   An activity is a regulated activity for the purposes of this Act if it is an activity of a specified kind which is carried on by way of business and—
  (a)   relates to an investment of a specified kind; or
  (b)   in the case of an activity of a kind which is also specified for the purposes of this paragraph, is carried on in relation to property of any kind.

(2)   Schedule 2 makes provision supplementing this section.

(3)   Nothing in Schedule 2 limits the powers conferred by subsection (1).

(4)   "Investment" includes any asset, right or interest.

(5)   "Specified" means specified in an order made by the Treasury.

Commencement: 25 February 2001.
Orders: The Financial Services and Markets Act 2000 (Regulated Activities) Order 2001, SI 2001/544, as amended by SI 2001/3544, SI 2001/3771, SI 2002/682, SI 2002/1310, SI 2002/1776, SI 2002/1777, SI 2003/1475, SI 2003/1476; the Financial Services and Markets Act 2000 (Commencement of Mortgage Regulation) (Amendment) Order 2002, SI 2002/1777; the Financial Services and Markets Act 2000 (Regulated Activities) (Amendment) (No 1) Order 2003, SI 2003/1475; the Financial Services and Markets Act 2000 (Regulated Activities) (Amendment) (No 2) Order 2003, SI 2003/1476.
References: See paras 3.5–3.16.

Offences

23 Contravention of the general prohibition

(1)   A person who contravenes the general prohibition is guilty of an offence and liable—
  (a)   on summary conviction, to imprisonment for a term not exceeding six months or a fine not exceeding the statutory maximum, or both;
  (b)   on conviction on indictment, to imprisonment for a term not exceeding two years or a fine, or both.

(2)   In this Act "an authorisation offence" means an offence under this section.

(3)   In proceedings for an authorisation offence it is a defence for the accused to show that he took all reasonable precautions and exercised all due diligence to avoid committing the offence.

Commencement: 1 December 2001.
References: See para 7.25.

24 False claims to be authorised or exempt

(1)   A person who is neither an authorised person nor, in relation to the regulated activity in question, an exempt person is guilty of an offence if he—

  (a)   describes himself (in whatever terms) as an authorised person;

  (b)   describes himself (in whatever terms) as an exempt person in relation to the regulated activity; or

  (c)   behaves, or otherwise holds himself out, in a manner which indicates (or which is reasonably likely to be understood as indicating) that he is—

  (i)   an authorised person; or

  (ii) an exempt person in relation to the regulated activity.

(2)   In proceedings for an offence under this section it is a defence for the accused to show that he took all reasonable precautions and exercised all due diligence to avoid committing the offence.

(3)   A person guilty of an offence under this section is liable on summary conviction to imprisonment for a term not exceeding six months or a fine not exceeding level 5 on the standard scale, or both.

(4)   But where the conduct constituting the offence involved or included the public display of any material, the maximum fine for the offence is level 5 on the standard scale multiplied by the number of days for which the display continued.

Commencement: 1 December 2001.

25 Contravention of section 21

(1)   A person who contravenes section 21(1) is guilty of an offence and liable—

  (a)   on summary conviction, to imprisonment for a term not exceeding six months or a fine not exceeding the statutory maximum, or both;

  (b)   on conviction on indictment, to imprisonment for a term not exceeding two years or a fine, or both.

(2)   In proceedings for an offence under this section it is a defence for the accused to show—

  (a)   that he believed on reasonable grounds that the content of the communication was prepared, or approved for the purposes of section 21, by an authorised person; or

  (b)   that he took all reasonable precautions and exercised all due diligence to avoid committing the offence.

Commencement: 1 December 2001.
References: See paras 6.75, 6.76.

Enforceability of agreements

26 Agreements made by unauthorised persons

(1)   An agreement made by a person in the course of carrying on a regulated activity in contravention of the general prohibition is unenforceable against the other party.

(2)   The other party is entitled to recover—
   (a)   any money or other property paid or transferred by him under the agreement; and
   (b)   compensation for any loss sustained by him as a result of having parted with it.

(3)   "Agreement" means an agreement—
   (a)   made after this section comes into force; and
   (b)   the making or performance of which constitutes, or is part of, the regulated activity in question.

(4)   This section does not apply if the regulated activity is accepting deposits.

Commencement: 1 December 2001.
Application to certain agreements: Sub-ss (1), (2) above apply to certain agreements entered into in contravention of the Financial Services Act 1986, s 3 (repealed by the Financial Services and Markets Act 2000 (Consequential Amendments and Repeals) Order 2001, SI 2001/3649, art 3(1)(c) (made under ss 426, 427)), or the Insurance Companies Act 1982, s 2 (repealed by art 3(1)(b) of that Order) as they apply to an agreement in contravention of the general prohibition; see the Financial Services and Markets Act 2000 (Transitional Provisions and Savings) (Civil Remedies, Discipline, Criminal Offences etc) (No 2) Order 2001, SI 2001/3083, art 5(1), (3), (4) (made under ss 426, 427, 428(3)).
References: See para 4.18.

27 Agreements made through unauthorised persons

(1)   An agreement made by an authorised person ("the provider")—
   (a)   in the course of carrying on a regulated activity (not in contravention of the general prohibition), but
   (b)   in consequence of something said or done by another person ("the third party") in the course of a regulated activity carried on by the third party in contravention of the general prohibition,

is unenforceable against the other party.

(2)   The other party is entitled to recover—
   (a)   any money or other property paid or transferred by him under the agreement; and
   (b)   compensation for any loss sustained by him as a result of having parted with it.

(3)   "Agreement" means an agreement—
   (a)   made after this section comes into force; and
   (b)   the making or performance of which constitutes, or is part of, the regulated activity in question carried on by the provider.

(4)   This section does not apply if the regulated activity is accepting deposits.

Commencement: 1 December 2001.
Application to certain agreements: Sub-ss (1), (2) above apply to certain agreements entered into in contravention of the Financial Services Act 1986, s 3 (repealed by the Financial Services and Markets Act 2000 (Consequential Amendments and Repeals) Order 2001, SI 2001/3649, art 3(1)(c) (made under ss 426, 427)) as they apply to an agreement in contravention of the general prohibition; see the Financial Services and Markets Act 2000 (Transitional Provisions and Savings) (Civil Remedies, Discipline, Criminal Offences etc) (No 2) Order 2001, SI 2001/3083, art 5(2), (3), (5) (made under ss 426, 427, 428(3)).
References: See para 4.18.

28 Agreements made unenforceable by section 26 or 27

(1)   This section applies to an agreement which is unenforceable because of section 26 or 27.

(2)   The amount of compensation recoverable as a result of that section is—
(a)   the amount agreed by the parties; or
(b)   on the application of either party, the amount determined by the court.

(3)   If the court is satisfied that it is just and equitable in the circumstances of the case, it may allow—
(a)   the agreement to be enforced; or
(b)   money and property paid or transferred under the agreement to be retained.

(4)   In considering whether to allow the agreement to be enforced or (as the case may be) the money or property paid or transferred under the agreement to be retained the court must—
(a)   if the case arises as a result of section 26, have regard to the issue mentioned in subsection (5); or
(b)   if the case arises as a result of section 27, have regard to the issue mentioned in subsection (6).

(5)   The issue is whether the person carrying on the regulated activity concerned reasonably believed that he was not contravening the general prohibition by making the agreement.

(6)   The issue is whether the provider knew that the third party was (in carrying on the regulated activity) contravening the general prohibition.

(7)   If the person against whom the agreement is unenforceable—
(a)   elects not to perform the agreement, or
(b)   as a result of this section, recovers money paid or other property transferred by him under the agreement,

he must repay any money and return any other property received by him under the agreement.

(8)   If property transferred under the agreement has passed to a third party, a reference in section 26 or 27 or this section to that property is to be read as a reference to its value at the time of its transfer under the agreement.

(9)   The commission of an authorisation offence does not make the agreement concerned illegal or invalid to any greater extent than is provided by section 26 or 27.

Commencement: 1 December 2001.
Modification: Sub-ss (5), (6) are modified in relation to certain unenforceable agreements by the Financial Services and Markets Act 2000 (Transitional Provisions and Savings) (Civil Remedies, Discipline, Criminal Offences etc) (No 2) Order 2001, SI 2001/3083, art 5(6).

---

29 Accepting deposits in breach of general prohibition

(1)   This section applies to an agreement between a person ("the depositor") and another person ("the deposit-taker") made in the course of the carrying on by the deposit-taker of accepting deposits in contravention of the general prohibition.

(2)   If the depositor is not entitled under the agreement to recover without delay any money deposited by him, he may apply to the court for an order directing the deposit-taker to return the money to him.

(3)   The court need not make such an order if it is satisfied that it would not be just and equitable for the money deposited to be returned, having regard to the issue mentioned in subsection (4).

(4)   The issue is whether the deposit-taker reasonably believed that he was not contravening the general prohibition by making the agreement.

(5)   "Agreement" means an agreement—
    (a)   made after this section comes into force; and
    (b)   the making or performance of which constitutes, or is part of, accepting deposits.

Commencement: 1 December 2001.
References: See para 4.18.

30 Enforceability of agreements resulting from unlawful communications

(1)   In this section—
    "unlawful communication" means a communication in relation to which there has been a contravention of section 21(1);
    "controlled agreement" means an agreement the making or performance of which by either party constitutes a controlled activity for the purposes of that section; and
    "controlled investment" has the same meaning as in section 21.

(2)   If in consequence of an unlawful communication a person enters as a customer into a controlled agreement, it is unenforceable against him and he is entitled to recover—
    (a)   any money or other property paid or transferred by him under the agreement; and
    (b)   compensation for any loss sustained by him as a result of having parted with it.

(3)   If in consequence of an unlawful communication a person exercises any rights conferred by a controlled investment, no obligation to which he is subject as a result of exercising them is enforceable against him and he is entitled to recover—
    (a)   any money or other property paid or transferred by him under the obligation; and
    (b)   compensation for any loss sustained by him as a result of having parted with it.

(4)   But the court may allow—
    (a)   the agreement or obligation to be enforced, or
    (b)   money or property paid or transferred under the agreement or obligation to be retained,
if it is satisfied that it is just and equitable in the circumstances of the case.

(5)   In considering whether to allow the agreement or obligation to be enforced or (as the case may be) the money or property paid or transferred under the agreement to be retained the court must have regard to the issues mentioned in subsections (6) and (7).

(6)   If the applicant made the unlawful communication, the issue is whether he reasonably believed that he was not making such a communication.

(7)   If the applicant did not make the unlawful communication, the issue is whether he knew that the agreement was entered into in consequence of such a communication.

(8)   "Applicant" means the person seeking to enforce the agreement or obligation or retain the money or property paid or transferred.

(9)   Any reference to making a communication includes causing a communication to be made.

(10)   The amount of compensation recoverable as a result of subsection (2) or (3) is—

>   (a)   the amount agreed between the parties; or
>   (b)   on the application of either party, the amount determined by the court.

(11)   If a person elects not to perform an agreement or an obligation which (by virtue of subsection (2) or (3)) is unenforceable against him, he must repay any money and return any other property received by him under the agreement.

(12)   If (by virtue of subsection (2) or (3)) a person recovers money paid or property transferred by him under an agreement or obligation, he must repay any money and return any other property received by him as a result of exercising the rights in question.

(13)   If any property required to be returned under this section has passed to a third party, references to that property are to be read as references to its value at the time of its receipt by the person required to return it.

Commencement: 1 December 2001.
References: See paras 6.57–6.60.

PART III
AUTHORISATION AND EXEMPTION

Authorisation

31 Authorised persons

(1)   The following persons are authorised for the purposes of this Act—

>   (a)   a person who has a Part IV permission to carry on one or more regulated activities;
>   (b)   an EEA firm qualifying for authorisation under Schedule 3;
>   (c)   a Treaty firm qualifying for authorisation under Schedule 4;
>   (d)   a person who is otherwise authorised by a provision of, or made under, this Act.

(2)   In this Act "authorised person" means a person who is authorised for the purposes of this Act.

Commencement: 3 September 2001 (sub-s (1)(c), for the purpose of introducing Sch 4 to the extent that it is brought into force by SI 2001/2632); 18 June 2001 (sub-s (1)(b), for the purpose of introducing Sch 3 to the extent that it is brought into force by SI 2001/1820); 25 February 2001 (sub-s (1)(b), for the purpose of introducing Sch 3 to the extent that it is brought into force by SI 2001/516); 1 December 2001 (remainder).
References: See paras 4.2, 4.9, 4.26, 4.57.

32 Partnerships and unincorporated associations

(1)   If a firm is authorised—
    (a)   it is authorised to carry on the regulated activities concerned in the name of the firm; and
    (b)   its authorisation is not affected by any change in its membership.

(2)   If an authorised firm is dissolved, its authorisation continues to have effect in relation to any firm which succeeds to the business of the dissolved firm.

(3)   For the purposes of this section, a firm is to be regarded as succeeding to the business of another firm only if—
    (a)   the members of the resulting firm are substantially the same as those of the former firm; and
    (b)   succession is to the whole or substantially the whole of the business of the former firm.

(4)   "Firm" means—
    (a)   a partnership; or
    (b)   an unincorporated association of persons.

(5)   "Partnership" does not include a partnership which is constituted under the law of any place outside the United Kingdom and is a body corporate.

Commencement: 1 December 2001.
References: See paras 4.4, 4.5.

Ending of authorisation

33 Withdrawal of authorisation by the Authority

(1)   This section applies if—
    (a)   an authorised person's Part IV permission is cancelled; and
    (b)   as a result, there is no regulated activity for which he has permission.

(2)   The Authority must give a direction withdrawing that person's status as an authorised person.

Commencement: 1 December 2001.
References: See para 4.6.

34 EEA firms

(1)   An EEA firm ceases to qualify for authorisation under Part II of Schedule 3 if it ceases to be an EEA firm as a result of—
    (a)   having its EEA authorisation withdrawn; or
    (b)   ceasing to have an EEA right in circumstances in which EEA authorisation is not required.

(2)   At the request of an EEA firm, the Authority may give a direction cancelling its authorisation under Part II of Schedule 3.

(3)   If an EEA firm has a Part IV permission, it does not cease to be an authorised person merely because it ceases to qualify for authorisation under Part II of Schedule 3.

Commencement: 1 December 2001.
References: See para 4.7.

35 Treaty firms

(1) A Treaty firm ceases to qualify for authorisation under Schedule 4 if its home State authorisation is withdrawn.

(2) At the request of a Treaty firm, the Authority may give a direction cancelling its Schedule 4 authorisation.

(3) If a Treaty firm has a Part IV permission, it does not cease to be an authorised person merely because it ceases to qualify for authorisation under Schedule 4.

Commencement: 1 December 2001.
References: See para 4.25.

36 Persons authorised as a result of paragraph 1(1) of Schedule 5

(1) At the request of a person authorised as a result of paragraph 1(1) of Schedule 5, the Authority may give a direction cancelling his authorisation as such a person.

(2) If a person authorised as a result of paragraph 1(1) of Schedule 5 has a Part IV permission, he does not cease to be an authorised person merely because he ceases to be a person so authorised.

Commencement: 1 December 2001.
References: See para 4.36–4.39.

Exercise of EEA rights by UK firms

37 Exercise of EEA rights by UK firms

Part III of Schedule 3 makes provision in relation to the exercise outside the United Kingdom of EEA rights by UK firms.

Commencement: 3 September 2001 (for the purpose of introducing Sch 3, Pt III to the extent that it is brought into force by SI 2001/2632); 18 June 2001 (for the purpose of introducing Sch 3 to the extent that it is brought into force by SI 2001/1820); 25 February 2001 (for the purpose of introducing Sch 3 to the extent that it is brought into force by SI 2001/516); 1 December 2001 (remaining purposes).
References: See para 4.40.

Exemption

38 Exemption orders

(1) The Treasury may by order ("an exemption order") provide for—
    (a) specified persons, or
    (b) persons falling within a specified class,
to be exempt from the general prohibition.

(2) But a person cannot be an exempt person as a result of an exemption order if he has a Part IV permission.

(3) An exemption order may provide for an exemption to have effect—
    (a) in respect of all regulated activities;

    (b)   in respect of one or more specified regulated activities;

    (c)   only in specified circumstances;

    (d)   only in relation to specified functions;

    (e)   subject to conditions.

(4)   "Specified" means specified by the exemption order.

Commencement: 25 February 2001.
Orders: The Financial Services and Markets Act 2000 (Exemption) Order 2001, SI 2001/1201, as amended by SI 2001/3623, SI 2002/1310, SI 2003/47, SI 2003/1675.
References: See paras 3.25–3.29, 4.54–4.56.

39 Exemption of appointed representatives

(1)   If a person (other than an authorised person)—

    (a)   is a party to a contract with an authorised person ("his principal") which—

        (i)   permits or requires him to carry on business of a prescribed description, and

        (ii)   complies with such requirements as may be prescribed, and

    (b) · is someone for whose activities in carrying on the whole or part of that business his principal has accepted responsibility in writing,

he is exempt from the general prohibition in relation to any regulated activity comprised in the carrying on of that business for which his principal has accepted responsibility.

(2)   A person who is exempt as a result of subsection (1) is referred to in this Act as an appointed representative.

(3)   The principal of an appointed representative is responsible, to the same extent as if he had expressly permitted it, for anything done or omitted by the representative in carrying on the business for which he has accepted responsibility.

(4)   In determining whether an authorised person has complied with a provision contained in or made under this Act, anything which a relevant person has done or omitted as respects business for which the authorised person has accepted responsibility is to be treated as having been done or omitted by the authorised person.

(5)   "Relevant person" means a person who at the material time is or was an appointed representative by virtue of being a party to a contract with the authorised person.

(6)   Nothing in subsection (4) is to cause the knowledge or intentions of an appointed representative to be attributed to his principal for the purpose of determining whether the principal has committed an offence, unless in all the circumstances it is reasonable for them to be attributed to him.

Commencement: 25 February 2001 (sub-s (1), for the purpose of making orders or regulations); 1 December 2001 (remainder).
Regulations: The Financial Services and Markets Act 2000 (Appointed Representatives) Regulations 2001, SI 2001/1217, as amended by SI 2001/2508, SI 2003/1475, SI 2003/1476.
References: See paras 3.32–3.35, 4.57–4.59.

PART IV
PERMISSION TO CARRY ON REGULATED ACTIVITIES

Transitional provisions: The Financial Services and Markets Act 2000 (Transitional Provisions) (Authorised Persons etc) Order 2001, SI 2001/2636, Pt II, Ch I, as amended by SI 2001/3650, (made under ss 426–428) provides that persons who are authorised or exempted from the need for authorisation under provisions of the previous regulatory regimes are treated, as from 1 December 2001, as having permission under Pt IV of this Act to carry on the activities they were lawfully able to carry on immediately before that date by reason of that authorisation or exemption. Pt II of SI 2001/2636 applies to: (a) persons authorised or exempted under the Financial Services Act 1986 (repealed by the Financial Services and Markets Act 2000 (Consequential Amendments and Repeals) Order 2001, SI 2001/3649, art 3(1)(c) (made under ss 426, 427)); (b) persons authorised under the Banking Act 1987 (repealed by SI 2001/3649, art 3(1)(d)); (c) insurance companies; (d) friendly societies; and (e) building societies.

Pt III of SI 2001/2636 provides that restrictions and prohibitions imposed under provisions of the previous regulatory regimes on authorised persons are to have effect after 1 December 2001 as if they were requirements imposed under s 43 (in relation to persons with a permission under Pt IV of this Act). Pt III of SI 2001/2636 applies to: (a) prohibitions and requirements under the Financial Services Act 1986 (repealed as noted above); (b) restrictions and directions under the Banking Act 1987 (repealed as noted above); (c) directions and requirements under the Insurance Companies Act 1982 (repealed by SI 2001/3649, art 3(1)(b)); (d) conditions and directions under the Friendly Societies Act 1992; (e) conditions and directions under the Building Societies Act 1986; and (f) prohibitions and restrictions under the Banking Coordination (Second Council Directive) Regulations 1992, SI 1992/3218 (revoked by SI 2001/3649, art 3(2)(a)) and the Investment Services Regulations 1995, SI 1995/3275 (revoked by SI 2001/3649, art 3(2)(c)).

As to transitional modifications to ss 45–48, 50, 52–55, see the Financial Services and Markets Act 2000 (Interim Permissions) Order 2001, SI 2001/3374 (made under ss 426–428).

Application for permission

40 Application for permission

(1)   An application for permission to carry on one or more regulated activities may be made to the Authority by—

    (a)   an individual;

    (b)   a body corporate;

    (c)   a partnership; or

    (d)   an unincorporated association.

(2)   An authorised person may not apply for permission under this section if he has a permission—

    (a)   given to him by the Authority under this Part, or

    (b)   having effect as if so given,

which is in force.

(3)   An EEA firm may not apply for permission under this section to carry on a regulated activity which it is, or would be, entitled to carry on in exercise of an EEA right, whether through a United Kingdom branch or by providing services in the United Kingdom.

(4)   A permission given by the Authority under this Part or having effect as if so given is referred to in this Act as "a Part IV permission".

Commencement: 3 September 2001.
References: See paras 4.61, 4.62.

41 The threshold conditions

(1)　"The threshold conditions", in relation to a regulated activity, means the conditions set out in Schedule 6.

(2)　In giving or varying permission, or imposing or varying any requirement, under this Part the Authority must ensure that the person concerned will satisfy, and continue to satisfy, the threshold conditions in relation to all of the regulated activities for which he has or will have permission.

(3)　But the duty imposed by subsection (2) does not prevent the Authority, having due regard to that duty, from taking such steps as it considers are necessary, in relation to a particular authorised person, in order to secure its regulatory objective of the protection of consumers.

Commencement: 3 September 2001 (sub-ss (2), (3)); 25 February 2001 (remainder).
References: See paras 4.70–4.73.

Permission

42 Giving permission

(1)　"The applicant" means an applicant for permission under section 40.

(2)　The Authority may give permission for the applicant to carry on the regulated activity or activities to which his application relates or such of them as may be specified in the permission.

(3)　If the applicant—
  (a)　in relation to a particular regulated activity, is exempt from the general prohibition as a result of section 39(1) or an order made under section 38(1), but
  (b)　has applied for permission in relation to another regulated activity,
the application is to be treated as relating to all the regulated activities which, if permission is given, he will carry on.

(4)　If the applicant—
  (a)　in relation to a particular regulated activity, is exempt from the general prohibition as a result of section 285(2) or (3), but
  (b)　has applied for permission in relation to another regulated activity,
the application is to be treated as relating only to that other regulated activity.

(5)　If the applicant—
  (a)　is a person to whom, in relation to a particular regulated activity, the general prohibition does not apply as a result of Part XIX, but
  (b)　has applied for permission in relation to another regulated activity,
the application is to be treated as relating only to that other regulated activity.

(6)　If it gives permission, the Authority must specify the permitted regulated activity or activities, described in such manner as the Authority considers appropriate.

(7)　The Authority may—
  (a)　incorporate in the description of a regulated activity such limitations (for example as to circumstances in which the activity may, or may not, be carried on) as it considers appropriate;

> (b) specify a narrower or wider description of regulated activity than that to which the application relates;
>
> (c) give permission for the carrying on of a regulated activity which is not included among those to which the application relates.

Commencement: 3 September 2001 (for the purposes of permissions coming into force not sooner than the day on which s 19 of this Act comes into force, and applications for such permissions); 1 December 2001 (remaining purposes).
References: See paras 4.63–4.66.

43 Imposition of requirements

(1) A Part IV permission may include such requirements as the Authority considers appropriate.

(2) A requirement may, in particular, be imposed—
  (a) so as to require the person concerned to take specified action; or
  (b) so as to require him to refrain from taking specified action.

(3) A requirement may extend to activities which are not regulated activities.

(4) A requirement may be imposed by reference to the person's relationship with—
  (a) his group; or
  (b) other members of his group.

(5) A requirement expires at the end of such period as the Authority may specify in the permission.

(6) But subsection (5) does not affect the Authority's powers under section 44 or 45.

Commencement: 3 September 2001 (for the purposes of permissions coming into force not sooner than the day on which s 19 of this Act comes into force, and applications for such permissions); 1 December 2001 (remaining purposes).
References: See paras 4.67–4.69.

Variation and cancellation of Part IV permission

44 Variation etc at request of authorised person

(1) The Authority may, on the application of an authorised person with a Part IV permission, vary the permission by—
  (a) adding a regulated activity to those for which it gives permission;
  (b) removing a regulated activity from those for which it gives permission;
  (c) varying the description of a regulated activity for which it gives permission;
  (d) cancelling a requirement imposed under section 43; or
  (e) varying such a requirement.

(2) The Authority may, on the application of an authorised person with a Part IV permission, cancel the permission.

(3)　The Authority may refuse an application under this section if it appears to it—

    (a)　that the interests of consumers, or potential consumers, would be adversely affected if the application were to be granted; and

    (b)　that it is desirable in the interests of consumers, or potential consumers, for the application to be refused.

(4)　If, as a result of a variation of a Part IV permission under this section, there are no longer any regulated activities for which the authorised person concerned has permission, the Authority must, once it is satisfied that it is no longer necessary to keep the permission in force, cancel it.

(5)　The Authority's power to vary a Part IV permission under this section extends to including any provision in the permission as varied that could be included if a fresh permission were being given in response to an application under section 40.

Commencement: 3 September 2001 (for the purposes of variations or cancellations taking effect not sooner than the day on which s 19 of this Act comes into force, and applications for such variations or cancellations); 1 December 2001 (remaining purposes).
References: See paras 4.81–4.83.

45　Variation etc on the Authority's own initiative

(1)　The Authority may exercise its power under this section in relation to an authorised person if it appears to it that—

    (a)　he is failing, or is likely to fail, to satisfy the threshold conditions;

    (b)　he has failed, during a period of at least 12 months, to carry on a regulated activity for which he has a Part IV permission; or

    (c)　it is desirable to exercise that power in order to protect the interests of consumers or potential consumers.

(2)　The Authority's power under this section is the power to vary a Part IV permission in any of the ways mentioned in section 44(1) or to cancel it.

(3)　If, as a result of a variation of a Part IV permission under this section, there are no longer any regulated activities for which the authorised person concerned has permission, the Authority must, once it is satisfied that it is no longer necessary to keep the permission in force, cancel it.

(4)　The Authority's power to vary a Part IV permission under this section extends to including any provision in the permission as varied that could be included if a fresh permission were being given in response to an application under section 40.

(5)　The Authority's power under this section is referred to in this Part as its own-initiative power.

Commencement: 3 September 2001 (for the purposes of variations or cancellations taking effect not sooner than the day on which s 19 of this Act comes into force, and applications for such variations or cancellations); 1 December 2001 (remaining purposes).
References: See paras 4.84–4.88.

---

46 Variation of permission on acquisition of control

(1)   This section applies if it appears to the Authority that—
      (a)   a person has acquired control over a UK authorised person who has a Part IV permission; but
      (b)   there are no grounds for exercising its own-initiative power.

(2)   If it appears to the Authority that the likely effect of the acquisition of control on the authorised person, or on any of its activities, is uncertain the Authority may vary the authorised person's permission by—
      (a)   imposing a requirement of a kind that could be imposed under section 43 on giving permission; or
      (b)   varying a requirement included in the authorised person's permission under that section.

(3)   Any reference to a person having acquired control is to be read in accordance with Part XII.

Commencement: 3 September 2001 (for the purposes of variations or cancellations taking effect not sooner than the day on which s 19 of this Act comes into force, and applications for such variations or cancellations); 1 December 2001 (remaining purposes).
References: See para 4.89.

---

47 Exercise of power in support of overseas regulator

(1)   The Authority's own-initiative power may be exercised in respect of an authorised person at the request of, or for the purpose of assisting, a regulator who is—
      (a)   outside the United Kingdom; and
      (b)   of a prescribed kind.

(2)   Subsection (1) applies whether or not the Authority has powers which are exercisable in relation to the authorised person by virtue of any provision of Part XIII.

(3)   If a request to the Authority for the exercise of its own-initiative power has been made by a regulator who is—
      (a)   outside the United Kingdom,
      (b)   of a prescribed kind, and
      (c)   acting in pursuance of provisions of a prescribed kind,
the Authority must, in deciding whether or not to exercise that power in response to the request, consider whether it is necessary to do so in order to comply with a Community obligation.

(4)   In deciding in any case in which the Authority does not consider that the exercise of its own-initiative power is necessary in order to comply with a Community obligation, it may take into account in particular—
      (a)   whether in the country or territory of the regulator concerned, corresponding assistance would be given to a United Kingdom regulatory authority;
      (b)   whether the case concerns the breach of a law, or other requirement, which has no close parallel in the United Kingdom or involves the assertion of a jurisdiction not recognised by the United Kingdom;
      (c)   the seriousness of the case and its importance to persons in the United Kingdom;
      (d)   whether it is otherwise appropriate in the public interest to give the assistance sought.

(5)   The Authority may decide not to exercise its own-initiative power, in response to a request, unless the regulator concerned undertakes to make such contribution towards the cost of its exercise as the Authority considers appropriate.

(6)   Subsection (5) does not apply if the Authority decides that it is necessary for it to exercise its own-initiative power in order to comply with a Community obligation.

(7)   In subsections (4) and (5) "request" means a request of a kind mentioned in subsection (1).

Commencement: 3 September 2001 (for the purposes of variations or cancellations taking effect not sooner than the day on which s 19 of this Act comes into force, and applications for such variations or cancellations); 25 February 2001 (sub-ss (1), (3), for the purpose of making orders or regulations); 1 December 2001 (remaining purposes).
Regulations: The Financial Services and Markets Act 2000 (Own-initiative Power) (Overseas Regulators) Regulations 2001, SI 2001/2639.
References: See paras 4.90–4.93.

48 Prohibitions and restrictions

(1)   This section applies if the Authority—
    (a)   on giving a person a Part IV permission, imposes an assets requirement on him; or
    (b)   varies an authorised person's Part IV permission so as to alter an assets requirement imposed on him or impose such a requirement on him.

(2)   A person on whom an assets requirement is imposed is referred to in this section as "A".

(3)   "Assets requirement" means a requirement under section 43—
    (a)   prohibiting the disposal of, or other dealing with, any of A's assets (whether in the United Kingdom or elsewhere) or restricting such disposals or dealings; or
    (b)   that all or any of A's assets, or all or any assets belonging to consumers but held by A or to his order, must be transferred to and held by a trustee approved by the Authority.

(4)   If the Authority—
    (a)   imposes a requirement of the kind mentioned in subsection (3)(a), and
    (b)   gives notice of the requirement to any institution with whom A keeps an account,
the notice has the effects mentioned in subsection (5).

(5)   Those effects are that—
    (a)   the institution does not act in breach of any contract with A if, having been instructed by A (or on his behalf) to transfer any sum or otherwise make any payment out of A's account, it refuses to do so in the reasonably held belief that complying with the instruction would be incompatible with the requirement; and
    (b)   if the institution complies with such an instruction, it is liable to pay to the Authority an amount equal to the amount transferred from, or otherwise paid out of, A's account in contravention of the requirement.

(6) If the Authority imposes a requirement of the kind mentioned in subsection (3)(b), no assets held by a person as trustee in accordance with the requirement may, while the requirement is in force, be released or dealt with except with the consent of the Authority.

(7) If, while a requirement of the kind mentioned in subsection (3)(b) is in force, A creates a charge over any assets of his held in accordance with the requirement, the charge is (to the extent that it confers security over the assets) void against the liquidator and any of A's creditors.

(8) Assets held by a person as trustee ("T") are to be taken to be held by T in accordance with a requirement mentioned in subsection (3)(b) only if—

   (a)   A has given T written notice that those assets are to be held by T in accordance with the requirement; or
   (b)   they are assets into which assets to which paragraph (a) applies have been transposed by T on the instructions of A.

(9) A person who contravenes subsection (6) is guilty of an offence and liable on summary conviction to a fine not exceeding level 5 on the standard scale.

(10) "Charge" includes a mortgage (or in Scotland a security over property).

(11) Subsections (6) and (8) do not affect any equitable interest or remedy in favour of a person who is a beneficiary of a trust as a result of a requirement of the kind mentioned in subsection (3)(b).

Commencement: 3 September 2001.
References: See paras 4.99–4.104.

Connected persons

49 Persons connected with an applicant

(1)   In considering—
   (a)   an application for a Part IV permission, or
   (b)   whether to vary or cancel a Part IV permission,

the Authority may have regard to any person appearing to it to be, or likely to be, in a relationship with the applicant or person given permission which is relevant.

(2)   Before—
   (a)   giving permission in response to an application made by a person who is connected with an EEA firm [(other than an EEA firm falling within paragraph 5(e) of Schedule 3 (insurance and reinsurance intermediaries))], or
   (b)   cancelling or varying any permission given by the Authority to such a person,

the Authority must consult the firm's home state regulator.

[(2A)   But subsection (2) does not apply to the extent that the permission in question relates to an insurance mediation activity (within the meaning given by paragraph 2(5) of Schedule 6).]

(3)   A person ("A") is connected with an EEA firm if—
   (a)   A is a subsidiary undertaking of the firm; or
   (b)   A is a subsidiary undertaking of a parent undertaking of the firm.

Commencement: 3 September 2001.
Amendments: Sub-s (2): words in square brackets in para (a) inserted by the Financial Services and Markets Act 2000 (Regulated Activities) (Amendment) (No 2) Order 2003, SI 2003/1476, art 20(1), (2), as from 31 October 2004 (in so far as relating to contracts of long-term care insurance), and as from 14 January 2005 (otherwise); for transitional provisions see arts 22–27 of that Order et seq.
Sub-s (2A): inserted by SI 2003/1476, art 20(1), (3), as from 31 October 2004 (in so far as relating to contracts of long-term care insurance), and as from 14 January 2005 (otherwise); for transitional provisions see arts 22–27 of that Order et seq.
References: See para 4.94.

Additional permissions

50 Authority's duty to consider other permissions etc

(1)   "Additional Part IV permission" means a Part IV permission which is in force in relation to an EEA firm, a Treaty firm or a person authorised as a result of paragraph 1(1) of Schedule 5.

(2)   If the Authority is considering whether, and if so how, to exercise its own-initiative power under this Part in relation to an additional Part IV permission, it must take into account—

(a)   the home State authorisation of the authorised person concerned;

(b)   any relevant directive; and

(c)   relevant provisions of the Treaty.

Commencement: 3 September 2001.

Procedure

51 Applications under this Part

(1)   An application for a Part IV permission must—

(a)   contain a statement of the regulated activity or regulated activities which the applicant proposes to carry on and for which he wishes to have permission; and

(b)   give the address of a place in the United Kingdom for service on the applicant of any notice or other document which is required or authorised to be served on him under this Act.

(2)   An application for the variation of a Part IV permission must contain a statement—

(a)   of the desired variation; and

(b)   of the regulated activity or regulated activities which the applicant proposes to carry on if his permission is varied.

(3)   Any application under this Part must—

(a)   be made in such manner as the Authority may direct; and

(b)   contain, or be accompanied by, such other information as the Authority may reasonably require.

(4)   At any time after receiving an application and before determining it, the Authority may require the applicant to provide it with such further information as it reasonably considers necessary to enable it to determine the application.

(5)   Different directions may be given, and different requirements imposed, in relation to different applications or categories of application.

(6)   The Authority may require an applicant to provide information which he is required to provide under this section in such form, or to verify it in such a way, as the Authority may direct.

Commencement: 18 June 2001 (for the purpose of giving directions or imposing requirements as mentioned in sub-s (3) above); 3 September 2001 (remaining purposes).
References: See paras 4.105–4.107.

52 Determination of applications

(1)   An application under this Part must be determined by the Authority before the end of the period of six months beginning with the date on which it received the completed application.

(2)   The Authority may determine an incomplete application if it considers it appropriate to do so; and it must in any event determine such an application within twelve months beginning with the date on which it received the application.

(3)   The applicant may withdraw his application, by giving the Authority written notice, at any time before the Authority determines it.

(4)   If the Authority grants an application for, or for variation of, a Part IV permission, it must give the applicant written notice.

(5)   The notice must state the date from which the permission, or the variation, has effect.

(6)   If the Authority proposes—
  (a)   to give a Part IV permission but to exercise its power under section 42(7)(a) or (b) or 43(1), or
  (b)   to vary a Part IV permission on the application of an authorised person but to exercise its power under any of those provisions (as a result of section 44(5)),
it must give the applicant a warning notice.

(7)   If the Authority proposes to refuse an application made under this Part, it must (unless subsection (8) applies) give the applicant a warning notice.

(8)   This subsection applies if it appears to the Authority that—
  (a)   the applicant is an EEA firm; and
  (b)   the application is made with a view to carrying on a regulated activity in a manner in which the applicant is, or would be, entitled to carry on that activity in the exercise of an EEA right whether through a United Kingdom branch or by providing services in the United Kingdom.

(9)   If the Authority decides—
  (a)   to give a Part IV permission but to exercise its power under section 42(7)(a) or (b) or 43(1),
  (b)   to vary a Part IV permission on the application of an authorised person but to exercise its power under any of those provisions (as a result of section 44(5)), or
  (c)   to refuse an application under this Part,
it must give the applicant a decision notice.

Commencement: 3 September 2001.
References: See paras 4.108–4.114.

53 Exercise of own-initiative power: procedure

(1)   This section applies to an exercise of the Authority's own-initiative power to vary an authorised person's Part IV permission.

(2)   A variation takes effect—
- (a)   immediately, if the notice given under subsection (4) states that that is the case;
- (b)   on such date as may be specified in the notice; or
- (c)   if no date is specified in the notice, when the matter to which the notice relates is no longer open to review.

(3)   A variation may be expressed to take effect immediately (or on a specified date) only if the Authority, having regard to the ground on which it is exercising its own-initiative power, reasonably considers that it is necessary for the variation to take effect immediately (or on that date).

(4)   If the Authority proposes to vary the Part IV permission, or varies it with immediate effect, it must give the authorised person written notice.

(5)   The notice must—
- (a)   give details of the variation;
- (b)   state the Authority's reasons for the variation and for its determination as to when the variation takes effect;
- (c)   inform the authorised person that he may make representations to the Authority within such period as may be specified in the notice (whether or not he has referred the matter to the Tribunal);
- (d)   inform him of when the variation takes effect; and
- (e)   inform him of his right to refer the matter to the Tribunal.

(6)   The Authority may extend the period allowed under the notice for making representations.

(7)   If, having considered any representations made by the authorised person, the Authority decides—
- (a)   to vary the permission in the way proposed, or
- (b)   if the permission has been varied, not to rescind the variation,

it must give him written notice.

(8)   If, having considered any representations made by the authorised person, the Authority decides—
- (a)   not to vary the permission in the way proposed,
- (b)   to vary the permission in a different way, or
- (c)   to rescind a variation which has effect,

it must give him written notice.

(9)   A notice given under subsection (7) must inform the authorised person of his right to refer the matter to the Tribunal.

(10)   A notice under subsection (8)(b) must comply with subsection (5).

(11)   If a notice informs a person of his right to refer a matter to the Tribunal, it must give an indication of the procedure on such a reference.

(12) For the purposes of subsection (2)(c), whether a matter is open to review is to be determined in accordance with section 391(8).

Commencement: 3 September 2001 (for the purposes of variations and cancellations taking effect not sooner than the day on which s 19 of this Act comes into force); 1 December 2001 (remaining purposes).
References: See paras 4.87, 4.88, 4.95, 4.96.

54 Cancellation of Part IV permission: procedure

(1) If the Authority proposes to cancel an authorised person's Part IV permission otherwise than at his request, it must give him a warning notice.

(2) If the Authority decides to cancel an authorised person's Part IV permission otherwise than at his request, it must give him a decision notice.

Commencement: 3 September 2001 (for the purposes of variations and cancellations taking effect not sooner than the day on which s 19 of this Act comes into force); 1 December 2001 (remaining purposes).
References: See para 4.116.

References to the Tribunal

55 Right to refer matters to the Tribunal

(1) An applicant who is aggrieved by the determination of an application made under this Part may refer the matter to the Tribunal.

(2) An authorised person who is aggrieved by the exercise of the Authority's own-initiative power may refer the matter to the Tribunal.

Commencement: 3 September 2001.
References: See para 4.116.

PART V
PERFORMANCE OF REGULATED ACTIVITIES

Prohibition orders

56 Prohibition orders

(1) Subsection (2) applies if it appears to the Authority that an individual is not a fit and proper person to perform functions in relation to a regulated activity carried on by an authorised person.

(2) The Authority may make an order ("a prohibition order") prohibiting the individual from performing a specified function, any function falling within a specified description or any function.

(3) A prohibition order may relate to—
    (a) a specified regulated activity, any regulated activity falling within a specified description or all regulated activities;
    (b) authorised persons generally or any person within a specified class of authorised person.

Financial Services and Markets Act 2000, s 57

(4)   An individual who performs or agrees to perform a function in breach of a prohibition order is guilty of an offence and liable on summary conviction to a fine not exceeding level 5 on the standard scale.

(5)   In proceedings for an offence under subsection (4) it is a defence for the accused to show that he took all reasonable precautions and exercised all due diligence to avoid committing the offence.

(6)   An authorised person must take reasonable care to ensure that no function of his, in relation to the carrying on of a regulated activity, is performed by a person who is prohibited from performing that function by a prohibition order.

(7)   The Authority may, on the application of the individual named in a prohibition order, vary or revoke it.

(8)   This section applies to the performance of functions in relation to a regulated activity carried on by—
    (a)   a person who is an exempt person in relation to that activity, and
    (b)   a person to whom, as a result of Part XX, the general prohibition does not apply in relation to that activity,

as it applies to the performance of functions in relation to a regulated activity carried on by an authorised person.

(9)   "Specified" means specified in the prohibition order.

Commencement: 3 September 2001 (for the purposes of prohibition orders coming into force not sooner than the day on which s 19 of this Act comes into force); 1 December 2001 (remaining purposes).
Transitional provisions: The Financial Services and Markets Act 2000 (Transitional Provisions) (Authorised Persons etc) Order 2001, SI 2001/2636, art 79, as amended by SI 2001/3650, provides that where, on 1 December 2001, a person is the subject of a disqualification direction made under the Financial Services Act 1986, s 59, the direction has effect after that date as a prohibition order made under this section. The 1986 Act is repealed by the Financial Services and Markets Act 2000 (Consequential Amendments and Repeals) Order 2001, SI 2001/3649, art 3(1)(c) (made under ss 426, 427).
References: See paras 5.20–5.22.

57 Prohibition orders: procedure and right to refer to Tribunal

(1)   If the Authority proposes to make a prohibition order it must give the individual concerned a warning notice.

(2)   The warning notice must set out the terms of the prohibition.

(3)   If the Authority decides to make a prohibition order it must give the individual concerned a decision notice.

(4)   The decision notice must—
    (a)   name the individual to whom the prohibition order applies;
    (b)   set out the terms of the order; and
    (c)   be given to the individual named in the order.

(5)   A person against whom a decision to make a prohibition order is made may refer the matter to the Tribunal.

Commencement: 3 September 2001 (for the purposes of prohibition orders coming into force not sooner than the day on which s 19 of this Act comes into force); 1 December 2001 (remaining purposes).
References: See para 5.23.

501

58 Applications relating to prohibitions: procedure and right to refer to Tribunal

(1)   This section applies to an application for the variation or revocation of a prohibition order.

(2)   If the Authority decides to grant the application, it must give the applicant written notice of its decision.

(3)   If the Authority proposes to refuse the application, it must give the applicant a warning notice.

(4)   If the Authority decides to refuse the application, it must give the applicant a decision notice.

(5)   If the Authority gives the applicant a decision notice, he may refer the matter to the Tribunal.

Commencement: 3 September 2001 (for the purposes of prohibition orders coming into force not sooner than the day on which s 19 of this Act comes into force); 1 December 2001 (remaining purposes).
References: See paras 5.24, 5.25.

Approval

59 Approval for particular arrangements

(1)   An authorised person ("A") must take reasonable care to ensure that no person performs a controlled function under an arrangement entered into by A in relation to the carrying on by A of a regulated activity, unless the Authority approves the performance by that person of the controlled function to which the arrangement relates.

(2)   An authorised person ("A") must take reasonable care to ensure that no person performs a controlled function under an arrangement entered into by a contractor of A in relation to the carrying on by A of a regulated activity, unless the Authority approves the performance by that person of the controlled function to which the arrangement relates.

(3)   "Controlled function" means a function of a description specified in rules.

(4)   The Authority may specify a description of function under subsection (3) only if, in relation to the carrying on of a regulated activity by an authorised person, it is satisfied that the first, second or third condition is met.

(5)   The first condition is that the function is likely to enable the person responsible for its performance to exercise a significant influence on the conduct of the authorised person's affairs, so far as relating to the regulated activity.

(6)   The second condition is that the function will involve the person performing it in dealing with customers of the authorised person in a manner substantially connected with the carrying on of the regulated activity.

(7)   The third condition is that the function will involve the person performing it in dealing with property of customers of the authorised person in a manner substantially connected with the carrying on of the regulated activity.

(8)   Neither subsection (1) nor subsection (2) applies to an arrangement which allows a person to perform a function if the question of whether he is a fit and

proper person to perform the function is reserved under any of the single market directives to an authority in a country or territory outside the United Kingdom.

(9)   In determining whether the first condition is met, the Authority may take into account the likely consequences of a failure to discharge that function properly.

(10)   "Arrangement"—

(a)   means any kind of arrangement for the performance of a function of A which is entered into by A or any contractor of his with another person; and

(b)   includes, in particular, that other person's appointment to an office, his becoming a partner or his employment (whether under a contract of service or otherwise).

(11)   "Customer", in relation to an authorised person, means a person who is using, or who is or may be contemplating using, any of the services provided by the authorised person.

Commencement: 3 September 2001 (for the purposes of approvals coming into force not sooner than the day on which s 19 of this Act comes into force, and applications for such approvals); 18 June 2001 (for the purpose of making rules); 1 December 2001 (remaining purposes).
Transitional provisions: The Financial Services and Markets Act 2000 (Transitional Provisions) (Authorised Persons etc) Order 2001, SI 2001/2636, Pt VI (made under ss 426–428), applies where a person is performing a function for another person at 1 December 2001, and provides for the continued performance of that function after that date to be taken to be approved by the Authority for the purposes of this section.
References: See paras 5.3–5.6.

60 Applications for approval

(1)   An application for the Authority's approval under section 59 may be made by the authorised person concerned.

(2)   The application must—

(a)   be made in such manner as the Authority may direct; and

(b)   contain, or be accompanied by, such information as the Authority may reasonably require.

(3)   At any time after receiving the application and before determining it, the Authority may require the applicant to provide it with such further information as it reasonably considers necessary to enable it to determine the application.

(4)   The Authority may require an applicant to present information which he is required to give under this section in such form, or to verify it in such a way, as the Authority may direct.

(5)   Different directions may be given, and different requirements imposed, in relation to different applications or categories of application.

(6)   "The authorised person concerned" includes a person who has applied for permission under Part IV and will be the authorised person concerned if permission is given.

Commencement: 3 September 2001 (for the purposes of approvals coming into force not sooner than the day on which s 19 of this Act comes into force, and applications for such approvals); 18 June 2001 (for the purpose of giving directions or imposing requirements as mentioned in sub-ss (2) or (4) above); 1 December 2001 (remaining purposes).
References: See paras 5.7–5.9.

61 Determination of applications

(1)   The Authority may grant an application made under section 60 only if it is satisfied that the person in respect of whom the application is made ("the candidate") is a fit and proper person to perform the function to which the application relates.

(2)   In deciding that question, the Authority may have regard (among other things) to whether the candidate, or any person who may perform a function on his behalf—

  (a)   has obtained a qualification,
  (b)   has undergone, or is undergoing, training, or
  (c)   possesses a level of competence,

required by general rules in relation to persons performing functions of the kind to which the application relates.

(3)   The Authority must, before the end of the period of three months beginning with the date on which it receives an application made under section 60 ("the period for consideration"), determine whether—

  (a)   to grant the application; or
  (b)   to give a warning notice under section 62(2).

(4)   If the Authority imposes a requirement under section 60(3), the period for consideration stops running on the day on which the requirement is imposed but starts running again—

  (a)   on the day on which the required information is received by the Authority; or
  (b)   if the information is not provided on a single day, on the last of the days on which it is received by the Authority.

(5)   A person who makes an application under section 60 may withdraw his application by giving written notice to the Authority at any time before the Authority determines it, but only with the consent of—

  (a)   the candidate; and
  (b)   the person by whom the candidate is to be retained to perform the function concerned, if not the applicant.

Commencement: 3 September 2001 (for the purposes of approvals coming into force not sooner than the day on which s 19 of this Act comes into force, and applications for such approvals); 1 December 2001 (remaining purposes).
References: See paras 5.7–5.9.

62 Applications for approval: procedure and right to refer to Tribunal

(1)   If the Authority decides to grant an application made under section 60 ("an application"), it must give written notice of its decision to each of the interested parties.

(2)   If the Authority proposes to refuse an application, it must give a warning notice to each of the interested parties.

(3)   If the Authority decides to refuse an application, it must give a decision notice to each of the interested parties.

(4)   If the Authority decides to refuse an application, each of the interested parties may refer the matter to the Tribunal.

(5)　"The interested parties", in relation to an application, are—
  (a)　the applicant;
  (b)　the person in respect of whom the application is made ("A"); and
  (c)　the person by whom A's services are to be retained, if not the applicant.

Commencement: 3 September 2001 (for the purposes of approvals coming into force not sooner than the day on which s 19 of this Act comes into force, and applications for such approvals); 1 December 2001 (remaining purposes).
References: See paras 5.8, 5.9.

63　Withdrawal of approval

(1)　The Authority may withdraw an approval given under section 59 if it considers that the person in respect of whom it was given is not a fit and proper person to perform the function to which the approval relates.

(2)　When considering whether to withdraw its approval, the Authority may take into account any matter which it could take into account if it were considering an application made under section 60 in respect of the performance of the function to which the approval relates.

(3)　If the Authority proposes to withdraw its approval, it must give each of the interested parties a warning notice.

(4)　If the Authority decides to withdraw its approval, it must give each of the interested parties a decision notice.

(5)　If the Authority decides to withdraw its approval, each of the interested parties may refer the matter to the Tribunal.

(6)　"The interested parties", in relation to an approval, are—
  (a)　the person on whose application it was given ("A");
  (b)　the person in respect of whom it was given ("B"); and
  (c)　the person by whom B's services are retained, if not A.

Commencement: 3 September 2001 (for the purposes of approvals coming into force not sooner than the day on which s 19 of this Act comes into force, and applications for such approvals); 1 December 2001 (remaining purposes).
References: See para 5.19.

Conduct

64　Conduct: statements and codes

(1)　The Authority may issue statements of principle with respect to the conduct expected of approved persons.

(2)　If the Authority issues a statement of principle under subsection (1), it must also issue a code of practice for the purpose of helping to determine whether or not a person's conduct complies with the statement of principle.

(3)　A code issued under subsection (2) may specify—
  (a)　descriptions of conduct which, in the opinion of the Authority, comply with a statement of principle;

> (b) descriptions of conduct which, in the opinion of the Authority, do not comply with a statement of principle;
>
> (c) factors which, in the opinion of the Authority, are to be taken into account in determining whether or not a person's conduct complies with a statement of principle.

(4)   The Authority may at any time alter or replace a statement or code issued under this section.

(5)   If a statement or code is altered or replaced, the altered or replacement statement or code must be issued by the Authority.

(6)   A statement or code issued under this section must be published by the Authority in the way appearing to the Authority to be best calculated to bring it to the attention of the public.

(7)   A code published under this section and in force at the time when any particular conduct takes place may be relied on so far as it tends to establish whether or not that conduct complies with a statement of principle.

(8)   Failure to comply with a statement of principle under this section does not of itself give rise to any right of action by persons affected or affect the validity of any transaction.

(9)   A person is not to be taken to have failed to comply with a statement of principle if he shows that, at the time of the alleged failure, it or its associated code of practice had not been published.

(10) The Authority must, without delay, give the Treasury a copy of any statement or code which it publishes under this section.

(11) The power under this section to issue statements of principle and codes of practice—

> (a) includes power to make different provision in relation to persons, cases or circumstances of different descriptions; and
>
> (b) is to be treated for the purposes of section 2(4)(a) as part of the Authority's rule-making functions.

(12) The Authority may charge a reasonable fee for providing a person with a copy of a statement or code published under this section.

(13) "Approved person" means a person in relation to whom the Authority has given its approval under section 59.

Commencement: 18 June 2001.
References: See paras 5.10–5.12.

---

65 Statements and codes: procedure

(1)   Before issuing a statement or code under section 64, the Authority must publish a draft of it in the way appearing to the Authority to be best calculated to bring it to the attention of the public.

(2)   The draft must be accompanied by—

> (a) a cost benefit analysis; and
>
> (b) notice that representations about the proposal may be made to the Authority within a specified time.

(3)   Before issuing the proposed statement or code, the Authority must have regard to any representations made to it in accordance with subsection (2)(b).

(4)   If the Authority issues the proposed statement or code it must publish an account, in general terms, of—

(a)   the representations made to it in accordance with subsection (2)(b); and

(b)   its response to them.

(5)   If the statement or code differs from the draft published under subsection (1) in a way which is, in the opinion of the Authority, significant—

(a)   the Authority must (in addition to complying with subsection (4)) publish details of the difference; and

(b)   those details must be accompanied by a cost benefit analysis.

(6)   Neither subsection (2)(a) nor subsection (5)(b) applies if the Authority considers—

(a)   that, making the appropriate comparison, there will be no increase in costs; or

(b)   that, making that comparison, there will be an increase in costs but the increase will be of minimal significance.

(7)   Subsections (1) to (6) do not apply if the Authority considers that the delay involved in complying with them would prejudice the interests of consumers.

(8)   A statement or code must state that it is issued under section 64.

(9)   The Authority may charge a reasonable fee for providing a copy of a draft published under subsection (1).

(10)   This section also applies to a proposal to alter or replace a statement or code.

(11)   "Cost benefit analysis" means an estimate of the costs together with an analysis of the benefits that will arise—

(a)   if the proposed statement or code is issued; or

(b)   if subsection (5)(b) applies, from the statement or code that has been issued.

(12)   "The appropriate comparison" means—

(a)   in relation to subsection (2)(a), a comparison between the overall position if the statement or code is issued and the overall position if it is not issued;

(b)   in relation to subsection (5)(b), a comparison between the overall position after the issuing of the statement or code and the overall position before it was issued.

Commencement: 18 June 2001.
References: See paras 5.13–5.16.

66 Disciplinary powers

(1)   The Authority may take action against a person under this section if—

(a)   it appears to the Authority that he is guilty of misconduct; and

(b)   the Authority is satisfied that it is appropriate in all the circumstances to take action against him.

(2)   A person is guilty of misconduct if, while an approved person—

    (a)   he has failed to comply with a statement of principle issued under section 64; or

    (b)   he has been knowingly concerned in a contravention by the relevant authorised person of a requirement imposed on that authorised person by or under this Act.

(3)   If the Authority is entitled to take action under this section against a person, it may—

    (a)   impose a penalty on him of such amount as it considers appropriate; or

    (b)   publish a statement of his misconduct.

(4)   The Authority may not take action under this section after the end of the period of two years beginning with the first day on which the Authority knew of the misconduct, unless proceedings in respect of it against the person concerned were begun before the end of that period.

(5)   For the purposes of subsection (4)—

    (a)   the Authority is to be treated as knowing of misconduct if it has information from which the misconduct can reasonably be inferred; and

    (b)   proceedings against a person in respect of misconduct are to be treated as begun when a warning notice is given to him under section 67(1).

(6)   "Approved person" has the same meaning as in section 64.

(7)   "Relevant authorised person", in relation to an approved person, means the person on whose application approval under section 59 was given.

Commencement: 1 December 2001.

Formerly registered individuals: As to the power of the Financial Services Authority to take action under this section in relation to persons who were formerly registered individuals (or registered persons) under the rules of a self-regulating organisation, in the case of a failure to comply with, or an act of misconduct or a contravention under, those rules, see the Financial Services and Markets Act 2000 (Transitional Provisions and Savings) (Civil Remedies, Discipline, Criminal Offences etc) (No 2) Order 2001, SI 2001/3083, art 9 (made under ss 426, 427, 428(3)).

References: See paras 8.8–8.14.

---

67 Disciplinary measures: procedure and right to refer to Tribunal

(1)   If the Authority proposes to take action against a person under section 66, it must give him a warning notice.

(2)   A warning notice about a proposal to impose a penalty must state the amount of the penalty.

(3)   A warning notice about a proposal to publish a statement must set out the terms of the statement.

(4)   If the Authority decides to take action against a person under section 66, it must give him a decision notice.

(5)   A decision notice about the imposition of a penalty must state the amount of the penalty.

(6)   A decision notice about the publication of a statement must set out the terms of the statement.

(7)   If the Authority decides to take action against a person under section 66, he may refer the matter to the Tribunal.

Commencement: 1 December 2001.
References: See paras 8.8–8.14.

68 Publication

After a statement under section 66 is published, the Authority must send a copy of it to the person concerned and to any person to whom a copy of the decision notice was given.

Commencement: 1 December 2001.
References: See para 8.11.

69 Statement of policy

(1)   The Authority must prepare and issue a statement of its policy with respect to—
    (a)   the imposition of penalties under section 66; and
    (b)   the amount of penalties under that section.

(2)   The Authority's policy in determining what the amount of a penalty should be must include having regard to—
    (a)   the seriousness of the misconduct in question in relation to the nature of the principle or requirement concerned;
    (b)   the extent to which that misconduct was deliberate or reckless; and
    (c)   whether the person on whom the penalty is to be imposed is an individual.

(3)   The Authority may at any time alter or replace a statement issued under this section.

(4)   If a statement issued under this section is altered or replaced, the Authority must issue the altered or replacement statement.

(5)   The Authority must, without delay, give the Treasury a copy of any statement which it publishes under this section.

(6)   A statement issued under this section must be published by the Authority in the way appearing to the Authority to be best calculated to bring it to the attention of the public.

(7)   The Authority may charge a reasonable fee for providing a person with a copy of the statement.

(8)   In exercising, or deciding whether to exercise, its power under section 66 in the case of any particular misconduct, the Authority must have regard to any statement of policy published under this section and in force at the time when the misconduct in question occurred.

Commencement: 18 June 2001.
References: See paras 8.12, 8.13.

70 Statements of policy: procedure

(1)   Before issuing a statement under section 69, the Authority must publish a draft of the proposed statement in the way appearing to the Authority to be best calculated to bring it to the attention of the public.

(2)   The draft must be accompanied by notice that representations about the proposal may be made to the Authority within a specified time.

(3)   Before issuing the proposed statement, the Authority must have regard to any representations made to it in accordance with subsection (2).

(4)   If the Authority issues the proposed statement it must publish an account, in general terms, of—
     (a)   the representations made to it in accordance with subsection (2); and
     (b)   its response to them.

(5)   If the statement differs from the draft published under subsection (1) in a way which is, in the opinion of the Authority, significant, the Authority must (in addition to complying with subsection (4)) publish details of the difference.

(6)   The Authority may charge a reasonable fee for providing a person with a copy of a draft published under subsection (1).

(7)   This section also applies to a proposal to alter or replace a statement.

Commencement: 18 June 2001.
References: See para 8.13.

Breach of statutory duty

71 Actions for damages

(1)   A contravention of section 56(6) or 59(1) or (2) is actionable at the suit of a private person who suffers loss as a result of the contravention, subject to the defences and other incidents applying to actions for breach of statutory duty.

(2)   In prescribed cases, a contravention of that kind which would be actionable at the suit of a private person is actionable at the suit of a person who is not a private person, subject to the defences and other incidents applying to actions for breach of statutory duty.

(3)   "Private person" has such meaning as may be prescribed.

Commencement: 25 February 2001 (sub-ss (2), (3), for the purpose of making orders or regulations); 1 December 2001 (remainder).
Regulations: The Financial Services and Markets Act 2000 (Rights of Action) Regulations 2001, SI 2001/2256, as amended by SI 2002/1775, SI 2002/2706.
References: See paras 5.17–5.74.

PART VI
OFFICIAL LISTING

Transitional provisions: See the Financial Services and Markets Act 2000 (Official Listing of Securities) (Transitional Provisions) Order 2001, SI 2001/2957.
Non-listing prospectuses: The provisions of this Part apply in relation to a non-listing prospectus as they apply in relation to listing particulars but with the modifications set out in Sch 9 to this Act: see s 87(5).

The competent authority

72 The competent authority

(1)   On the coming into force of this section, the functions conferred on the competent authority by this Part are to be exercised by the Authority.

(2)   Schedule 7 modifies this Act in its application to the Authority when it acts as the competent authority.

(3)   But provision is made by Schedule 8 allowing some or all of those functions to be transferred by the Treasury so as to be exercisable by another person.

Commencement: 18 June 2001.
Non-listing prospectuses: See note at the beginning of this Part.
References: See paras 9.5, 9.7, 9.12.

73 General duty of the competent authority

(1)   In discharging its general functions the competent authority must have regard to—
  (a)   the need to use its resources in the most efficient and economic way;
  (b)   the principle that a burden or restriction which is imposed on a person should be proportionate to the benefits, considered in general terms, which are expected to arise from the imposition of that burden or restriction;
  (c)   the desirability of facilitating innovation in respect of listed securities;
  (d)   the international character of capital markets and the desirability of maintaining the competitive position of the United Kingdom;
  (e)   the need to minimise the adverse effects on competition of anything done in the discharge of those functions;
  (f)   the desirability of facilitating competition in relation to listed securities.

(2)   The competent authority's general functions are—
  (a)   its function of making rules under this Part (considered as a whole);
  (b)   its functions in relation to the giving of general guidance in relation to this Part (considered as a whole);
  (c)   its function of determining the general policy and principles by reference to which it performs particular functions under this Part.

Commencement: 18 June 2001.
References: See para 9.15.

The official list

74 The official list

(1)   The competent authority must maintain the official list.

(2)   The competent authority may admit to the official list such securities and other things as it considers appropriate.

(3) But—

    (a) nothing may be admitted to the official list except in accordance with this Part; and

    (b) the Treasury may by order provide that anything which falls within a description or category specified in the order may not be admitted to the official list.

(4) The competent authority may make rules ("listing rules") for the purposes of this Part.

(5) In the following provisions of this Part—

    "security" means anything which has been, or may be, admitted to the official list; and

    "listing" means being included in the official list in accordance with this Part.

Commencement: 1 December 2001 (sub-ss (1)–(3)), 18 June 2001 (remainder).
References: See para 9.18.

Listing

75 Applications for listing

(1) Admission to the official list may be granted only on an application made to the competent authority in such manner as may be required by listing rules.

(2) No application for listing may be entertained by the competent authority unless it is made by, or with the consent of, the issuer of the securities concerned.

(3) No application for listing may be entertained by the competent authority in respect of securities which are to be issued by a body of a prescribed kind.

(4) The competent authority may not grant an application for listing unless it is satisfied that—

    (a) the requirements of listing rules (so far as they apply to the application), and

    (b) any other requirements imposed by the authority in relation to the application,

are complied with.

(5) An application for listing may be refused if, for a reason relating to the issuer, the competent authority considers that granting it would be detrimental to the interests of investors.

(6) An application for listing securities which are already officially listed in another EEA State may be refused if the issuer has failed to comply with any obligations to which he is subject as a result of that listing.

Commencement: 18 June 2001 (sub-s (1), for the purpose of making listing rules); 25 February 2001 (sub-s (3), for the purpose of making orders or regulations); 1 December 2001 (remainder).
Regulations: The Financial Services and Markets Act 2000 (Official Listing of Securities) Regulations 2001, SI 2001/2956, as amended by SI 2001/3439.
References: See para 9.19.

76 Decision on application

(1)   The competent authority must notify the applicant of its decision on an application for listing—
  (a)   before the end of the period of six months beginning with the date on which the application is received; or
  (b)   if within that period the authority has required the applicant to provide further information in connection with the application, before the end of the period of six months beginning with the date on which that information is provided.

(2)   If the competent authority fails to comply with subsection (1), it is to be taken to have decided to refuse the application.

(3)   If the competent authority decides to grant an application for listing, it must give the applicant written notice.

(4)   If the competent authority proposes to refuse an application for listing, it must give the applicant a warning notice.

(5)   If the competent authority decides to refuse an application for listing, it must give the applicant a decision notice.

(6)   If the competent authority decides to refuse an application for listing, the applicant may refer the matter to the Tribunal.

(7)   If securities are admitted to the official list, their admission may not be called in question on the ground that any requirement or condition for their admission has not been complied with.

Commencement: 1 December 2001.
References: See paras 9.20, 9.21.

77 Discontinuance and suspension of listing

(1)   The competent authority may, in accordance with listing rules, discontinue the listing of any securities if satisfied that there are special circumstances which preclude normal regular dealings in them.

(2)   The competent authority may, in accordance with listing rules, suspend the listing of any securities.

(3)   If securities are suspended under subsection (2) they are to be treated, for the purposes of sections 96 and 99, as still being listed.

(4)   This section applies to securities whenever they were admitted to the official list.

(5)   If the competent authority discontinues or suspends the listing of any securities, the issuer may refer the matter to the Tribunal.

Commencement: 18 June 2001 (sub-ss (1), (2), (4), for the purpose of making listing rules); 1 December 2001 (remainder).
References: See paras 9.25–9.30.

78 Discontinuance or suspension: procedure

(1)   A discontinuance or suspension takes effect—
- (a)   immediately, if the notice under subsection (2) states that that is the case;
- (b)   in any other case, on such date as may be specified in that notice.

(2)   If the competent authority—
- (a)   proposes to discontinue or suspend the listing of securities, or
- (b)   discontinues or suspends the listing of securities with immediate effect,

it must give the issuer of the securities written notice.

(3)   The notice must—
- (a)   give details of the discontinuance or suspension;
- (b)   state the competent authority's reasons for the discontinuance or suspension and for choosing the date on which it took effect or takes effect;
- (c)   inform the issuer of the securities that he may make representations to the competent authority within such period as may be specified in the notice (whether or not he has referred the matter to the Tribunal);
- (d)   inform him of the date on which the discontinuance or suspension took effect or will take effect; and
- (e)   inform him of his right to refer the matter to the Tribunal.

(4)   The competent authority may extend the period within which representations may be made to it.

(5)   If, having considered any representations made by the issuer of the securities, the competent authority decides—
- (a)   to discontinue or suspend the listing of the securities, or
- (b)   if the discontinuance or suspension has taken effect, not to cancel it,

the competent authority must give the issuer of the securities written notice.

(6)   A notice given under subsection (5) must inform the issuer of the securities of his right to refer the matter to the Tribunal.

(7)   If a notice informs a person of his right to refer a matter to the Tribunal, it must give an indication of the procedure on such a reference.

(8)   If the competent authority decides—
- (a)   not to discontinue or suspend the listing of the securities, or
- (b)   if the discontinuance or suspension has taken effect, to cancel it,

the competent authority must give the issuer of the securities written notice.

(9)   The effect of cancelling a discontinuance is that the securities concerned are to be readmitted, without more, to the official list.

(10) If the competent authority has suspended the listing of securities and proposes to refuse an application by the issuer of the securities for the cancellation of the suspension, it must give him a warning notice.

(11) The competent authority must, having considered any representations made in response to the warning notice—
- (a)   if it decides to refuse the application, give the issuer of the securities a decision notice;
- (b)   if it grants the application, give him written notice of its decision.

(12) If the competent authority decides to refuse an application for the cancellation of the suspension of listed securities, the applicant may refer the matter to the Tribunal.

(13) "Discontinuance" means a discontinuance of listing under section 77(1).

(14) "Suspension" means a suspension of listing under section 77(2).

Commencement: 1 December 2001.
References: See paras 9.25–9.30.

Listing particulars

79 Listing particulars and other documents

(1)   Listing rules may provide that securities (other than new securities) of a kind specified in the rules may not be admitted to the official list unless—

    (a)   listing particulars have been submitted to, and approved by, the competent authority and published; or

    (b)   in such cases as may be specified by listing rules, such document (other than listing particulars or a prospectus of a kind required by listing rules) as may be so specified has been published.

(2)   "Listing particulars" means a document in such form and containing such information as may be specified in listing rules.

(3)   For the purposes of this Part, the persons responsible for listing particulars are to be determined in accordance with regulations made by the Treasury.

(4)   Nothing in this section affects the competent authority's general power to make listing rules.

Commencement: 18 June 2001 (sub-ss (1), (2), (4)); 25 February 2001 (remainder).
Regulations: The Financial Services and Markets Act 2000 (Official Listing of Securities) Regulations 2001, SI 2001/2956, as amended by SI 2001/3439.
References: See paras 9.31–9.33.

80 General duty of disclosure in listing particulars

(1)   Listing particulars submitted to the competent authority under section 79 must contain all such information as investors and their professional advisers would reasonably require, and reasonably expect to find there, for the purpose of making an informed assessment of—

    (a)   the assets and liabilities, financial position, profits and losses, and prospects of the issuer of the securities; and

    (b)   the rights attaching to the securities.

(2)   That information is required in addition to any information required by—

    (a)   listing rules, or

    (b)   the competent authority,

as a condition of the admission of the securities to the official list.

(3)   Subsection (1) applies only to information—

    (a)   within the knowledge of any person responsible for the listing particulars; or

    (b)   which it would be reasonable for him to obtain by making enquiries.

(4)   In determining what information subsection (1) requires to be included in listing particulars, regard must be had (in particular) to—

(a)   the nature of the securities and their issuer;

(b)   the nature of the persons likely to consider acquiring them;

(c)   the fact that certain matters may reasonably be expected to be within the knowledge of professional advisers of a kind which persons likely to acquire the securities may reasonably be expected to consult; and

(d)   any information available to investors or their professional advisers as a result of requirements imposed on the issuer of the securities by a recognised investment exchange, by listing rules or by or under any other enactment.

Commencement: 1 December 2001.
Non-listing prospectuses: See note at the beginning of this Part for modifications in relation to non-listing prospectuses: see Sch 9, para 3.
References: See para 9.37.

81 Supplementary listing particulars

(1)   If at any time after the preparation of listing particulars which have been submitted to the competent authority under section 79 and before the commencement of dealings in the securities concerned following their admission to the official list—

(a)   there is a significant change affecting any matter contained in those particulars the inclusion of which was required by—

(i)   section 80,

(ii)   listing rules, or

(iii) the competent authority, or

(b)   a significant new matter arises, the inclusion of information in respect of which would have been so required if it had arisen when the particulars were prepared,

the issuer must, in accordance with listing rules, submit supplementary listing particulars of the change or new matter to the competent authority, for its approval and, if they are approved, publish them.

(2)   "Significant" means significant for the purpose of making an informed assessment of the kind mentioned in section 80(1).

(3)   If the issuer of the securities is not aware of the change or new matter in question, he is not under a duty to comply with subsection (1) unless he is notified of the change or new matter by a person responsible for the listing particulars.

(4)   But it is the duty of any person responsible for those particulars who is aware of such a change or new matter to give notice of it to the issuer.

(5)   Subsection (1) applies also as respects matters contained in any supplementary listing particulars previously published under this section in respect of the securities in question.

Commencement: 18 June 2001 (subs-ss (1), (5), for the purpose of making listing rules); 1 December 2001 (remainder).
Non-listing prospectuses: See note at the beginning of this Part for modifications in relation to non-listing prospectuses: see Sch 9, para 4.
References: See paras 9.38–9.40.

82 Exemptions from disclosure

(1)   The competent authority may authorise the omission from listing particulars of any information, the inclusion of which would otherwise be required by section 80 or 81, on the ground—

(a)   that its disclosure would be contrary to the public interest;

(b)   that its disclosure would be seriously detrimental to the issuer; or

(c)   in the case of securities of a kind specified in listing rules, that its disclosure is unnecessary for persons of the kind who may be expected normally to buy or deal in securities of that kind.

(2)   But—

(a)   no authority may be granted under subsection (1)(b) in respect of essential information; and

(b)   no authority granted under subsection (1)(b) extends to any such information.

(3)   The Secretary of State or the Treasury may issue a certificate to the effect that the disclosure of any information (including information that would otherwise have to be included in listing particulars for which they are themselves responsible) would be contrary to the public interest.

(4)   The competent authority is entitled to act on any such certificate in exercising its powers under subsection (1)(a).

(5)   This section does not affect any powers of the competent authority under listing rules made as a result of section 101(2).

(6)   "Essential information" means information which a person considering acquiring securities of the kind in question would be likely to need in order not to be misled about any facts which it is essential for him to know in order to make an informed assessment.

(7)   "Listing particulars" includes supplementary listing particulars.

Commencement: 18 June 2001 (subs-ss (1), (5), (7), for the purpose of making listing rules); 1 December 2001 (remainder).
References: See paras 9.41, 9.42.

---

83 Registration of listing particulars

(1)   On or before the date on which listing particulars are published as required by listing rules, a copy of the particulars must be delivered for registration to the registrar of companies.

(2)   A statement that a copy has been delivered to the registrar must be included in the listing particulars when they are published.

(3)   If there has been a failure to comply with subsection (1) in relation to listing particulars which have been published—

(a)   the issuer of the securities in question, and

(b)   any person who is a party to the publication and aware of the failure,

is guilty of an offence.

(4)   A person guilty of an offence under subsection (3) is liable—

(a)   on summary conviction, to a fine not exceeding the statutory maximum;

    (b)   on conviction on indictment, to a fine.

(5)   "Listing particulars" includes supplementary listing particulars.

(6)   "The registrar of companies" means—
    (a)   if the securities are, or are to be, issued by a company incorporated in Great Britain whose registered office is in England and Wales, the registrar of companies in England and Wales;
    (b)   if the securities are, or are to be, issued by a company incorporated in Great Britain whose registered office is in Scotland, the registrar of companies in Scotland;
    (c)   if the securities are, or are to be, issued by a company incorporated in Northern Ireland, the registrar of companies for Northern Ireland; and
    (d)   in any other case, any of those registrars.

Commencement: 1 December 2001.
References: See para 9.48.

Prospectuses

84 Prospectuses

(1)   Listing rules must provide that no new securities for which an application for listing has been made may be admitted to the official list unless a prospectus has been submitted to, and approved by, the competent authority and published.

(2)   "New securities" means securities which are to be offered to the public in the United Kingdom for the first time before admission to the official list.

(3)   "Prospectus" means a prospectus in such form and containing such information as may be specified in listing rules.

(4)   Nothing in this section affects the competent authority's general power to make listing rules.

Commencement: 18 June 2001.
References: See paras 9.43–9.45.

85 Publication of prospectus

(1)   If listing rules made under section 84 require a prospectus to be published before particular new securities are admitted to the official list, it is unlawful for any of those securities to be offered to the public in the United Kingdom before the required prospectus is published.

(2)   A person who contravenes subsection (1) is guilty of an offence and liable—
    (a)   on summary conviction, to imprisonment for a term not exceeding three months or a fine not exceeding level 5 on the standard scale;
    (b)   on conviction on indictment, to imprisonment for a term not exceeding two years or a fine, or both.

(3)   A person is not to be regarded as contravening subsection (1) merely because a prospectus does not fully comply with the requirements of listing rules as to its form or content.

(4) But subsection (3) does not affect the question whether any person is liable to pay compensation under section 90.

(5) Any contravention of subsection (1) is actionable, at the suit of a person who suffers loss as a result of the contravention, subject to the defences and other incidents applying to actions for breach of statutory duty.

Commencement: 1 December 2001.
References: See para 9.49.

86 Application of this Part to prospectuses

(1) The provisions of this Part apply in relation to a prospectus required by listing rules as they apply in relation to listing particulars.

(2) In this Part—
 (a) any reference to listing particulars is to be read as including a reference to a prospectus; and
 (b) any reference to supplementary listing particulars is to be read as including a reference to a supplementary prospectus.

Commencement: 25 February 2001.
References: See paras 9.43, 9.44.

87 Approval of prospectus where no application for listing

(1) Listing rules may provide for a prospectus to be submitted to and approved by the competent authority if—
 (a) securities are to be offered to the public in the United Kingdom for the first time;
 (b) no application for listing of the securities has been made under this Part; and
 (c) the prospectus is submitted by, or with the consent of, the issuer of the securities.

(2) "Non-listing prospectus" means a prospectus submitted to the competent authority as a result of any listing rules made under subsection (1).

(3) Listing rules made under subsection (1) may make provision—
 (a) as to the information to be contained in, and the form of, a non-listing prospectus; and
 (b) as to the timing and manner of publication of a non-listing prospectus.

(4) The power conferred by subsection (3)(b) is subject to such provision made by or under any other enactment as the Treasury may by order specify.

(5) Schedule 9 modifies provisions of this Part as they apply in relation to non-listing prospectuses.

Commencement: 18 June 2001 (sub-ss (1)–(3)); 25 February 2001 (remainder).
Orders: The Financial Services and Markets Act 2000 (Offers of Securities) Order 2001, SI 2001/2958.
References: See paras 9.76, 9.77.

Sponsors

88 Sponsors

(1)   Listing rules may require a person to make arrangements with a sponsor for the performance by the sponsor of such services in relation to him as may be specified in the rules.

(2)   "Sponsor" means a person approved by the competent authority for the purposes of the rules.

(3)   Listing rules made by virtue of subsection (1) may—
  (a)   provide for the competent authority to maintain a list of sponsors;
  (b)   specify services which must be performed by a sponsor;
  (c)   impose requirements on a sponsor in relation to the provision of services or specified services;
  (d)   specify the circumstances in which a person is qualified for being approved as a sponsor.

(4)   If the competent authority proposes—
  (a)   to refuse a person's application for approval as a sponsor, or
  (b)   to cancel a person's approval as a sponsor,
it must give him a warning notice.

(5)   If, after considering any representations made in response to the warning notice, the competent authority decides—
  (a)   to grant the application for approval, or
  (b)   not to cancel the approval,
it must give the person concerned, and any person to whom a copy of the warning notice was given, written notice of its decision.

(6)   If, after considering any representations made in response to the warning notice, the competent authority decides—
  (a)   to refuse to grant the application for approval, or
  (b)   to cancel the approval,
it must give the person concerned a decision notice.

(7)   A person to whom a decision notice is given under this section may refer the matter to the Tribunal.

Commencement: 1 December 2001 (sub-ss (4)–(7)); 18 June 2001 (remainder).
References: See paras 9.79–9.81.

89 Public censure of sponsor

(1)   Listing rules may make provision for the competent authority, if it considers that a sponsor has contravened a requirement imposed on him by rules made as a result of section 88(3)(c), to publish a statement to that effect.

(2)   If the competent authority proposes to publish a statement it must give the sponsor a warning notice setting out the terms of the proposed statement.

(3)   If, after considering any representations made in response to the warning notice, the competent authority decides to make the proposed statement, it must give the sponsor a decision notice setting out the terms of the statement.

(4)   A sponsor to whom a decision notice is given under this section may refer the matter to the Tribunal.

Commencement: 1 December 2001 (sub-ss (2)–(4)); 18 June 2001 (remainder).
References: See para 9.82.

Compensation

90 Compensation for false or misleading particulars

(1)   Any person responsible for listing particulars is liable to pay compensation to a person who has—
    (a)   acquired securities to which the particulars apply; and
    (b)   suffered loss in respect of them as a result of—
       (i)   any untrue or misleading statement in the particulars; or
      (ii)   the omission from the particulars of any matter required to be included by section 80 or 81.

(2)   Subsection (1) is subject to exemptions provided by Schedule 10.

(3)   If listing particulars are required to include information about the absence of a particular matter, the omission from the particulars of that information is to be treated as a statement in the listing particulars that there is no such matter.

(4)   Any person who fails to comply with section 81 is liable to pay compensation to any person who has—
    (a)   acquired securities of the kind in question; and
    (b)   suffered loss in respect of them as a result of the failure.

(5)   Subsection (4) is subject to exemptions provided by Schedule 10.

(6)   This section does not affect any liability which may be incurred apart from this section.

(7)   References in this section to the acquisition by a person of securities include references to his contracting to acquire them or any interest in them.

(8)   No person shall, by reason of being a promoter of a company or otherwise, incur any liability for failing to disclose information which he would not be required to disclose in listing particulars in respect of a company's securities—
    (a)   if he were responsible for those particulars; or
    (b)   if he is responsible for them, which he is entitled to omit by virtue of section 82.

(9)   The reference in subsection (8) to a person incurring liability includes a reference to any other person being entitled as against that person to be granted any civil remedy or to rescind or repudiate an agreement.

(10)   "Listing particulars", in subsection (1) and Schedule 10, includes supplementary listing particulars.

Commencement: 1 December 2001.
References: See paras 9.90–9.98.

Penalties

91 Penalties for breach of listing rules

(1)　If the competent authority considers that—

   (a)　an issuer of listed securities, or

   (b)　an applicant for listing,

has contravened any provision of listing rules, it may impose on him a penalty of such amount as it considers appropriate.

(2)　If, in such a case, the competent authority considers that a person who was at the material time a director of the issuer or applicant was knowingly concerned in the contravention, it may impose on him a penalty of such amount as it considers appropriate.

(3)　If the competent authority is entitled to impose a penalty on a person under this section in respect of a particular matter it may, instead of imposing a penalty on him in respect of that matter, publish a statement censuring him.

(4)　Nothing in this section prevents the competent authority from taking any other steps which it has power to take under this Part.

(5)　A penalty under this section is payable to the competent authority.

(6)　The competent authority may not take action against a person under this section after the end of the period of two years beginning with the first day on which it knew of the contravention unless proceedings against that person, in respect of the contravention, were begun before the end of that period.

(7)　For the purposes of subsection (6)—

   (a)　the competent authority is to be treated as knowing of a contravention if it has information from which the contravention can reasonably be inferred; and

   (b)　proceedings against a person in respect of a contravention are to be treated as begun when a warning notice is given to him under section 92.

Commencement: 1 December 2001.
References: See paras 9.84, 9.85.

92 Procedure

(1)　If the competent authority proposes to take action against a person under section 91, it must give him a warning notice.

(2)　A warning notice about a proposal to impose a penalty must state the amount of the proposed penalty.

(3)　A warning notice about a proposal to publish a statement must set out the terms of the proposed statement.

(4)　If the competent authority decides to take action against a person under section 91, it must give him a decision notice.

(5)　A decision notice about the imposition of a penalty must state the amount of the penalty.

(6)   A decision notice about the publication of a statement must set out the terms of the statement.

(7)   If the competent authority decides to take action against a person under section 91, he may refer the matter to the Tribunal.

Commencement: 1 December 2001.
References: See para 9.89.

93 Statement of policy

(1)   The competent authority must prepare and issue a statement ("its policy statement") of its policy with respect to—
    (a)   the imposition of penalties under section 91; and
    (b)   the amount of penalties under that section.

(2)   The competent authority's policy in determining what the amount of a penalty should be must include having regard to—
    (a)   the seriousness of the contravention in question in relation to the nature of the requirement contravened;
    (b)   the extent to which that contravention was deliberate or reckless; and
    (c)   whether the person on whom the penalty is to be imposed is an individual.

(3)   The competent authority may at any time alter or replace its policy statement.

(4)   If its policy statement is altered or replaced, the competent authority must issue the altered or replacement statement.

(5)   In exercising, or deciding whether to exercise, its power under section 91 in the case of any particular contravention, the competent authority must have regard to any policy statement published under this section and in force at the time when the contravention in question occurred.

(6)   The competent authority must publish a statement issued under this section in the way appearing to the competent authority to be best calculated to bring it to the attention of the public.

(7)   The competent authority may charge a reasonable fee for providing a person with a copy of the statement.

(8)   The competent authority must, without delay, give the Treasury a copy of any policy statement which it publishes under this section.

Commencement: 18 June 2001.
References: See para 9.86.

94 Statements of policy: procedure

(1)   Before issuing a statement under section 93, the competent authority must publish a draft of the proposed statement in the way appearing to the competent authority to be best calculated to bring it to the attention of the public.

(2)   The draft must be accompanied by notice that representations about the proposal may be made to the competent authority within a specified time.

(3)   Before issuing the proposed statement, the competent authority must have regard to any representations made to it in accordance with subsection (2).

(4)   If the competent authority issues the proposed statement it must publish an account, in general terms, of—
      (a)   the representations made to it in accordance with subsection (2); and
      (b)   its response to them.

(5)   If the statement differs from the draft published under subsection (1) in a way which is, in the opinion of the competent authority, significant, the competent authority must (in addition to complying with subsection (4)) publish details of the difference.

(6)   The competent authority may charge a reasonable fee for providing a person with a copy of a draft published under subsection (1).

(7)   This section also applies to a proposal to alter or replace a statement.

Commencement: 18 June 2001.
References: See para 9.86.

Competition

95 Competition scrutiny

(1)   The Treasury may by order provide for—
      (a)   regulating provisions, and
      (b)   the practices of the competent authority in exercising its functions under this Part ("practices"),
to be kept under review.

(2)   Provision made as a result of subsection (1) must require the person responsible for keeping regulating provisions and practices under review to consider—
      (a)   whether any regulating provision or practice has a significantly adverse effect on competition; or
      (b)   whether two or more regulating provisions or practices taken together have, or a particular combination of regulating provisions and practices has, such an effect.

(3)   An order under this section may include provision corresponding to that made by any provision of Chapter III of Part X.

(4)   Subsection (3) is not to be read as in any way restricting the power conferred by subsection (1).

(5)   Subsections (6) to (8) apply for the purposes of provision made by or under this section.

(6)   Regulating provisions or practices have a significantly adverse effect on competition if—
      (a)   they have, or are intended or likely to have, that effect; or
      (b)   the effect that they have, or are intended or likely to have, is to require or encourage behaviour which has, or is intended or likely to have, a significantly adverse effect on competition.

(7)   If regulating provisions or practices have, or are intended or likely to have, the effect of requiring or encouraging exploitation of the strength of a market position they are to be taken to have, or be intended or be likely to have, an adverse effect on competition.

(8)   In determining whether any of the regulating provisions or practices have, or are intended or likely to have, a particular effect, it may be assumed that the persons to whom the provisions concerned are addressed will act in accordance with them.

(9)   "Regulating provisions" means—
- (a)   listing rules,
- (b)   general guidance given by the competent authority in connection with its functions under this Part.

Commencement: 1 December 2001.
References: See paras 9.99–10.52.

Miscellaneous

96 Obligations of issuers of listed securities

(1)   Listing rules may—
- (a)   specify requirements to be complied with by issuers of listed securities; and
- (b)   make provision with respect to the action that may be taken by the competent authority in the event of non-compliance.

(2)   If the rules require an issuer to publish information, they may include provision authorising the competent authority to publish it in the event of his failure to do so.

(3)   This section applies whenever the listed securities were admitted to the official list.

Commencement: 18 June 2001.
References: See para 9.78.

97 Appointment by competent authority of persons to carry out investigations

(1)   Subsection (2) applies if it appears to the competent authority that there are circumstances suggesting that—
- (a)   there may have been a breach of listing rules;
- (b)   a person who was at the material time a director of an issuer of listed securities has been knowingly concerned in a breach of listing rules by that issuer;
- (c)   a person who was at the material time a director of a person applying for the admission of securities to the official list has been knowingly concerned in a breach of listing rules by that applicant;
- (d)   there may have been a contravention of section 83, 85 or 98.

(2)   The competent authority may appoint one or more competent persons to conduct an investigation on its behalf.

(3) Part XI applies to an investigation under subsection (2) as if—
    (a) the investigator were appointed under section 167(1);
    (b) references to the investigating authority in relation to him were to the competent authority;
    (c) references to the offences mentioned in section 168 were to those mentioned in subsection (1)(d);
    (d) references to an authorised person were references to the person under investigation.

Commencement: 1 December 2001.
References: See para 9.83.

98 Advertisements etc in connection with listing applications

(1) If listing particulars are, or are to be, published in connection with an application for listing, no advertisement or other information of a kind specified by listing rules may be issued in the United Kingdom unless the contents of the advertisement or other information have been submitted to the competent authority and that authority has—
    (a) approved those contents; or
    (b) authorised the issue of the advertisement or information without such approval.

(2) A person who contravenes subsection (1) is guilty of an offence and liable—
    (a) on summary conviction, to a fine not exceeding the statutory maximum;
    (b) on conviction on indictment, to imprisonment for a term not exceeding two years or a fine, or both.

(3) A person who issues an advertisement or other information to the order of another person is not guilty of an offence under subsection (2) if he shows that he believed on reasonable grounds that the advertisement or information had been approved, or its issue authorised, by the competent authority.

(4) If information has been approved, or its issue has been authorised, under this section, neither the person issuing it nor any person responsible for, or for any part of, the listing particulars incurs any civil liability by reason of any statement in or omission from the information if that information and the listing particulars, taken together, would not be likely to mislead persons of the kind likely to consider acquiring the securities in question.

(5) The reference in subsection (4) to a person incurring civil liability includes a reference to any other person being entitled as against that person to be granted any civil remedy or to rescind or repudiate an agreement.

Commencement: 18 June 2001 (sub-s (1), for the purpose of making listing rules); 1 December 2001 (remainder).
Non-listing prospectuses: See note at the beginning of this Part for modifications in relation to non-listing prospectuses: see Sch 9, para 6.
References: See paras 9.46, 9.47.

99 Fees

(1)   Listing rules may require the payment of fees to the competent authority in respect of—

(a)   applications for listing;

(b)   the continued inclusion of securities in the official list;

(c)   applications under section 88 for approval as a sponsor; and

(d)   continued inclusion of sponsors in the list of sponsors.

(2)   In exercising its powers under subsection (1), the competent authority may set such fees as it considers will (taking account of the income it expects as the competent authority) enable it—

(a)   to meet expenses incurred in carrying out its functions under this Part or for any incidental purpose;

(b)   to maintain adequate reserves; and

(c)   in the case of the Authority, to repay the principal of, and pay any interest on, any money which it has borrowed and which has been used for the purpose of meeting expenses incurred in relation to—

(i)   its assumption of functions from the London Stock Exchange Limited in relation to the official list; and

(ii)   its assumption of functions under this Part.

(3)   In fixing the amount of any fee which is to be payable to the competent authority, no account is to be taken of any sums which it receives, or expects to receive, by way of penalties imposed by it under this Part.

(4)   Subsection (2)(c) applies whether expenses were incurred before or after the coming into force of this Part.

(5)   Any fee which is owed to the competent authority under any provision made by or under this Part may be recovered as a debt due to it.

Commencement: 18 June 2001.
Non-listing prospectuses: See note at the beginning of this Part for modifications in relation to non-listing prospectuses: see Sch 9, para 7.
References: See para 9.24.

100 Penalties

(1)   In determining its policy with respect to the amount of penalties to be imposed by it under this Part, the competent authority must take no account of the expenses which it incurs, or expects to incur, in discharging its functions under this Part.

(2)   The competent authority must prepare and operate a scheme for ensuring that the amounts paid to it by way of penalties imposed under this Part are applied for the benefit of issuers of securities admitted to the official list.

(3)   The scheme may, in particular, make different provision with respect to different classes of issuer.

(4)   Up to date details of the scheme must be set out in a document ("the scheme details").

(5)   The scheme details must be published by the competent authority in the way appearing to it to be best calculated to bring them to the attention of the public.

(6)   Before making the scheme, the competent authority must publish a draft of the proposed scheme in the way appearing to it to be best calculated to bring it to the attention of the public.

(7)   The draft must be accompanied by notice that representations about the proposals may be made to the competent authority within a specified time.

(8)   Before making the scheme, the competent authority must have regard to any representations made to it under subsection (7).

(9)   If the competent authority makes the proposed scheme, it must publish an account, in general terms, of—

    (a)   the representations made to it in accordance with subsection (7); and

    (b)   its response to them.

(10) If the scheme differs from the draft published under subsection (6) in a way which is, in the opinion of the competent authority, significant the competent authority must (in addition to complying with subsection (9)) publish details of the difference.

(11) The competent authority must, without delay, give the Treasury a copy of any scheme details published by it.

(12) The competent authority may charge a reasonable fee for providing a person with a copy of—

    (a)   a draft published under subsection (6);

    (b)   scheme details.

(13) Subsections (6) to (10) and (12) apply also to a proposal to alter or replace the scheme.

Commencement: 18 June 2001.
References: See para 9.88.

101 Listing rules: general provisions

(1)   Listing rules may make different provision for different cases.

(2)   Listing rules may authorise the competent authority to dispense with or modify the application of the rules in particular cases and by reference to any circumstances.

(3)   Listing rules must be made by an instrument in writing.

(4)   Immediately after an instrument containing listing rules is made, it must be printed and made available to the public with or without payment.

(5)   A person is not to be taken to have contravened any listing rule if he shows that at the time of the alleged contravention the instrument containing the rule had not been made available as required by subsection (4).

(6)   The production of a printed copy of an instrument purporting to be made by the competent authority on which is endorsed a certificate signed by an officer of the authority authorised by it for that purpose and stating—

    (a)   that the instrument was made by the authority,

    (b)   that the copy is a true copy of the instrument, and

    (c)   that on a specified date the instrument was made available to the public as required by subsection (4),

is evidence (or in Scotland sufficient evidence) of the facts stated in the certificate.

(7)   A certificate purporting to be signed as mentioned in subsection (6) is to be treated as having been properly signed unless the contrary is shown.

(8)   A person who wishes in any legal proceedings to rely on a rule-making instrument may require the Authority to endorse a copy of the instrument with a certificate of the kind mentioned in subsection (6).

Commencement: 18 June 2001.
References: See para 9.17.

102 Exemption from liability in damages

(1)   Neither the competent authority nor any person who is, or is acting as, a member, officer or member of staff of the competent authority is to be liable in damages for anything done or omitted in the discharge, or purported discharge, of the authority's functions.

(2)   Subsection (1) does not apply—
  (a)   if the act or omission is shown to have been in bad faith; or
  (b)   so as to prevent an award of damages made in respect of an act or omission on the ground that the act or omission was unlawful as a result of section 6(1) of the Human Rights Act 1998.

Commencement: 18 June 2001.
References: See para 9.16.

103 Interpretation of this Part

(1)   In this Part—
  "application" means an application made under section 75;
  "issuer", in relation to anything which is or may be admitted to the official list, has such meaning as may be prescribed by the Treasury;
  "listing" has the meaning given in section 74(5);
  "listing particulars" has the meaning given in section 79(2);
  "listing rules" has the meaning given in section 74(4);
  "new securities" has the meaning given in section 84(2);
  "the official list" means the list maintained as the official list by the Authority immediately before the coming into force of section 74, as that list has effect for the time being;
  "security" (except in section 74(2)) has the meaning given in section 74(5).

(2)   In relation to any function conferred on the competent authority by this Part, any reference in this Part to the competent authority is to be read as a reference to the person by whom that function is for the time being exercisable.

(3)   If, as a result of an order under Schedule 8, different functions conferred on the competent authority by this Part are exercisable by different persons, the powers conferred by section 91 are exercisable by such person as may be determined in accordance with the provisions of the order.

(4)   For the purposes of this Part, a person offers securities if, and only if, as principal—
  (a)   he makes an offer which, if accepted, would give rise to a contract for their issue or sale by him or by another person with whom he has made arrangements for their issue or sale; or

(b)   he invites a person to make such an offer.

(5)   "Offer" and "offeror" are to be read accordingly.

(6)   For the purposes of this Part, the question whether a person offers securities to the public in the United Kingdom is to be determined in accordance with Schedule 11.

(7)   For the purposes of subsection (4) "sale" includes any disposal for valuable consideration.

Commencement: 25 February 2001.
Regulations: The Financial Services and Markets Act 2000 (Official Listing of Securities) Regulations 2001, SI 2001/2956, as amended by SI 2001/3439.
References: See Ch 9.

PART VII
CONTROL OF BUSINESS TRANSFERS

104 Control of business transfers

No insurance business transfer scheme or banking business transfer scheme is to have effect unless an order has been made in relation to it under section 111(1).

Commencement: 1 December 2001 (for the purpose of insurance business transfer schemes); to be appointed (remaining purposes).
Note: This provision has not been brought into effect in relation to banking business transfer schemes: see the Financial Services and Markets Act 2000 (Commencement No 7) Order 2001, SI 2001/3538.
References: See para 22.1.

105 Insurance business transfer schemes

(1)   A scheme is an insurance business transfer scheme if it—
    (a)   satisfies one of the conditions set out in subsection (2);
    (b)   results in the business transferred being carried on from an establishment of the transferee in an EEA State; and
    (c)   is not an excluded scheme.

(2)   The conditions are that—
    (a)   the whole or part of the business carried on in one or more member States by a UK authorised person who has permission to effect or carry out contracts of insurance ("the authorised person concerned") is to be transferred to another body ("the transferee");
    (b)   the whole or part of the business, so far as it consists of reinsurance, carried on in the United Kingdom through an establishment there by an EEA firm qualifying for authorisation under Schedule 3 which has permission to effect or carry out contracts of insurance ("the authorised person concerned") is to be transferred to another body ("the transferee");
    (c)   the whole or part of the business carried on in the United Kingdom by an authorised person who is neither a UK authorised person nor an EEA firm but who has permission to effect or carry out contracts of insurance ("the authorised person concerned") is to be transferred to another body ("the transferee").

(3)   A scheme is an excluded scheme for the purposes of this section if it falls within any of the following cases:

CASE 1

Where the authorised person concerned is a friendly society.

CASE 2

Where—
- (a)   the authorised person concerned is a UK authorised person;
- (b)   the business to be transferred under the scheme is business which consists of the effecting or carrying out of contracts of reinsurance in one or more EEA States other than the United Kingdom; and
- (c)   the scheme has been approved by a court in an EEA State other than the United Kingdom or by the host state regulator.

CASE 3

Where—
- (a)   the authorised person concerned is a UK authorised person;
- (b)   the business to be transferred under the scheme is carried on in one or more countries or territories (none of which is an EEA State) and does not include policies of insurance (other than reinsurance) against risks arising in an EEA State; and
- (c)   the scheme has been approved by a court in a country or territory other than an EEA State or by the authority responsible for the supervision of that business in a country or territory in which it is carried on.

CASE 4

Where the business to be transferred under the scheme is the whole of the business of the authorised person concerned and—
- (a)   consists solely of the effecting or carrying out of contracts of reinsurance, or
- (b)   all the policyholders are controllers of the firm or of firms within the same group as the firm which is the transferee,

and, in either case, all of the policyholders who will be affected by the transfer have consented to it.

(4)   The parties to a scheme which falls within Case 2, 3 or 4 may apply to the court for an order sanctioning the scheme as if it were an insurance business transfer scheme.

(5)   Subsection (6) applies if the scheme involves a compromise or arrangement falling within section 427A of the Companies Act 1985 (or Article 420A of the Companies (Northern Ireland) Order 1986).

(6)   Sections 425 to 427 of that Act (or Articles 418 to 420 of that Order) have effect as modified by section 427A of that Act (or Article 420A of that Order) in relation to that compromise or arrangement.

(7)   But subsection (6) does not affect the operation of this Part in relation to the scheme.

(8)   "UK authorised person" means a body which is an authorised person and which—

    (a)   is incorporated in the United Kingdom; or

    (b)   is an unincorporated association formed under the law of any part of the United Kingdom.

(9)   "Establishment" means, in relation to a person, his head office or a branch of his.

Commencement: 1 December 2001.
References: See paras 22.3–22.5.

---

106 Banking business transfer schemes

(1)   A scheme is a banking business transfer scheme if it—

    (a)   satisfies one of the conditions set out in subsection (2);

    (b)   is one under which the whole or part of the business to be transferred includes the accepting of deposits; and

    (c)   is not an excluded scheme.

(2)   The conditions are that—

    (a)   the whole or part of the business carried on by a UK authorised person who has permission to accept deposits ("the authorised person concerned") is to be transferred to another body ("the transferee");

    (b)   the whole or part of the business carried on in the United Kingdom by an authorised person who is not a UK authorised person but who has permission to accept deposits ("the authorised person concerned") is to be transferred to another body which will carry it on in the United Kingdom ("the transferee").

(3)   A scheme is an excluded scheme for the purposes of this section if—

    (a)   the authorised person concerned is a building society or a credit union; or

    (b)   the scheme is a compromise or arrangement to which section 427A(1) of the Companies Act 1985 or Article 420A of the Companies (Northern Ireland) Order 1986 (mergers and divisions of public companies) applies.

(4)   For the purposes of subsection (2)(a) it is immaterial whether or not the business to be transferred is carried on in the United Kingdom.

(5)   "UK authorised person" has the same meaning as in section 105.

(6)   "Building society" has the meaning given in the Building Societies Act 1986.

(7)   "Credit union" means a credit union within the meaning of—

    (a)   the Credit Unions Act 1979;

    (b)   the Credit Unions (Northern Ireland) Order 1985.

Commencement: 1 December 2001.
References: See paras 22.6, 22.7.

---

107 Application for order sanctioning transfer scheme

(1)   An application may be made to the court for an order sanctioning an insurance business transfer scheme or a banking business transfer scheme.

(2) An application may be made by—
  (a) the authorised person concerned;
  (b) the transferee; or
  (c) both.

(3) The application must be made—
  (a) if the authorised person concerned and the transferee are registered or have their head offices in the same jurisdiction, to the court in that jurisdiction;
  (b) if the authorised person concerned and the transferee are registered or have their head offices in different jurisdictions, to the court in either jurisdiction;
  (c) if the transferee is not registered in the United Kingdom and does not have his head office there, to the court which has jurisdiction in relation to the authorised person concerned.

(4) "Court" means—
  (a) the High Court; or
  (b) in Scotland, the Court of Session.

Commencement: 1 December 2001.
References: See para 22.8.

108 Requirements on applicants

(1) The Treasury may by regulations impose requirements on applicants under section 107.

(2) The court may not determine an application under that section if the applicant has failed to comply with a prescribed requirement.

(3) The regulations may, in particular, include provision—
  (a) as to the persons to whom, and periods within which, notice of an application must be given;
  (b) enabling the court to waive a requirement of the regulations in prescribed circumstances.

Commencement: 25 February 2001 (for the purpose of making orders or regulations); 1 December 2001 (remaining purposes).
Regulations: The Financial Services and Markets Act 2000 (Control of Business Transfers) (Requirements on Applicants) Regulations 2001, SI 2001/3625.
References: See para 22.9.

109 Scheme reports

(1) An application under section 107 in respect of an insurance business transfer scheme must be accompanied by a report on the terms of the scheme ("a scheme report").

(2) A scheme report may be made only by a person—
  (a) appearing to the Authority to have the skills necessary to enable him to make a proper report; and
  (b) nominated or approved for the purpose by the Authority.

(3) A scheme report must be made in a form approved by the Authority.

Commencement: 1 December 2001.
References: See para 22.10.

110 Right to participate in proceedings

On an application under section 107, the following are also entitled to be heard—

- (a) the Authority, and
- (b) any person (including an employee of the authorised person concerned or of the transferee) who alleges that he would be adversely affected by the carrying out of the scheme.

Commencement: 1 December 2001.
References: See para 22.9.

111 Sanction of the court for business transfer schemes

(1)　This section sets out the conditions which must be satisfied before the court may make an order under this section sanctioning an insurance business transfer scheme or a banking business transfer scheme.

(2)　The court must be satisfied that—

- (a) the appropriate certificates have been obtained (as to which see Parts I and II of Schedule 12);
- (b) the transferee has the authorisation required (if any) to enable the business, or part, which is to be transferred to be carried on in the place to which it is to be transferred (or will have it before the scheme takes effect).

(3)　The court must consider that, in all the circumstances of the case, it is appropriate to sanction the scheme.

Commencement: 25 February 2001 (sub-s (2), for the purpose of introducing Sch 12, Pt 1 to the extent that it is brought into force by SI 2001/516); 1 December 2001 (remainder).
References: See paras 22.11, 22.12.

112 Effect of order sanctioning business transfer scheme

(1)　If the court makes an order under section 111(1), it may by that or any subsequent order make such provision (if any) as it thinks fit—

- (a) for the transfer to the transferee of the whole or any part of the undertaking concerned and of any property or liabilities of the authorised person concerned;
- (b) for the allotment or appropriation by the transferee of any shares, debentures, policies or other similar interests in the transferee which under the scheme are to be allotted or appropriated to or for any other person;
- (c) for the continuation by (or against) the transferee of any pending legal proceedings by (or against) the authorised person concerned;
- (d) with respect to such incidental, consequential and supplementary matters as are, in its opinion, necessary to secure that the scheme is fully and effectively carried out.

(2)   An order under subsection (1)(a) may—

    (a)   transfer property or liabilities whether or not the authorised person concerned otherwise has the capacity to effect the transfer in question;

    (b)   make provision in relation to property which was held by the authorised person concerned as trustee;

    (c)   make provision as to future or contingent rights or liabilities of the authorised person concerned, including provision as to the construction of instruments (including wills) under which such rights or liabilities may arise;

    (d)   make provision as to the consequences of the transfer in relation to any retirement benefits scheme (within the meaning of section 611 of the Income and Corporation Taxes Act 1988) operated by or on behalf of the authorised person concerned.

(3)   If an order under subsection (1) makes provision for the transfer of property or liabilities—

    (a)   the property is transferred to and vests in, and

    (b)   the liabilities are transferred to and become liabilities of,

the transferee as a result of the order.

(4)   But if any property or liability included in the order is governed by the law of any country or territory outside the United Kingdom, the order may require the authorised person concerned, if the transferee so requires, to take all necessary steps for securing that the transfer to the transferee of the property or liability is fully effective under the law of that country or territory.

(5)   Property transferred as the result of an order under subsection (1) may, if the court so directs, vest in the transferee free from any charge which is (as a result of the scheme) to cease to have effect.

(6)   An order under subsection (1) which makes provision for the transfer of property is to be treated as an instrument of transfer for the purposes of the provisions mentioned in subsection (7) and any other enactment requiring the delivery of an instrument of transfer for the registration of property.

(7)   The provisions are—

    (a)   section 183(1) of the Companies Act 1985;

    (b)   Article 193(1) and (2) of the Companies (Northern Ireland) Order 1986.

(8)   If the court makes an order under section 111(1) in relation to an insurance business transfer scheme, it may by that or any subsequent order make such provision (if any) as it thinks fit—

    (a)   for dealing with the interests of any person who, within such time and in such manner as the court may direct, objects to the scheme;

    (b)   for the dissolution, without winding up, of the authorised person concerned;

    (c)   for the reduction, on such terms and subject to such conditions (if any) as it thinks fit, of the benefits payable under—

        (i)   any description of policy, or

        (ii)   policies generally,

entered into by the authorised person concerned and transferred as a result of the scheme.

(9)   If, in the case of an insurance business transfer scheme, the authorised person concerned is not an EEA firm, it is immaterial for the purposes of subsection (1)(a), (c) or (d) or subsection (2), (3) or (4) that the law applicable to any of the contracts of insurance included in the transfer is the law of an EEA State other than the United Kingdom.

(10)   The transferee must, if an insurance or banking business transfer scheme is sanctioned by the court, deposit two office copies of the order made under subsection (1) with the Authority within 10 days of the making of the order.

(11)   But the Authority may extend that period.

(12)   "Property" includes property, rights and powers of any description.

(13)   "Liabilities" includes duties.

(14)   "Shares" and "debentures" have the same meaning as in—
  (a)   the Companies Act 1985; or
  (b)   in Northern Ireland, the Companies (Northern Ireland) Order 1986.

(15)   "Charge" includes a mortgage (or, in Scotland, a security over property).

Commencement: 1 December 2001.
References: See paras 22.11–22.14.

113 Appointment of actuary in relation to reduction of benefits

(1)   This section applies if an order has been made under section 111(1).

(2)   The court making the order may, on the application of the Authority, appoint an independent actuary—
  (a)   to investigate the business transferred under the scheme; and
  (b)   to report to the Authority on any reduction in the benefits payable under policies entered into by the authorised person concerned that, in the opinion of the actuary, ought to be made.

Commencement: 1 December 2001.
References: See para

114 Rights of certain policyholders

(1)   This section applies in relation to an insurance business transfer scheme if—
  (a)   the authorised person concerned is an authorised person other than an EEA firm qualifying for authorisation under Schedule 3;
  (b)   the court has made an order under section 111 in relation to the scheme; and
  (c)   an EEA State other than the United Kingdom is, as regards any policy included in the transfer which evidences a contract of insurance, the State of the commitment or the EEA State in which the risk is situated ("the EEA State concerned").

(2)   The court must direct that notice of the making of the order, or the execution of any instrument, giving effect to the transfer must be published by the transferee in the EEA State concerned.

(3) A notice under subsection (2) must specify such period as the court may direct as the period during which the policyholder may exercise any right which he has to cancel the policy.

(4) The order or instrument mentioned in subsection (2) does not bind the policyholder if—

    (a)   the notice required under that subsection is not published; or

    (b)   the policyholder cancels the policy during the period specified in the notice given under that subsection.

(5) The law of the EEA State concerned governs—

    (a)   whether the policyholder has a right to cancel the policy; and

    (b)   the conditions, if any, subject to which any such right may be exercised.

(6) Paragraph 6 of Schedule 12 applies for the purposes of this section as it applies for the purposes of that Schedule.

Commencement: 1 December 2001.
References: See para 22.12.

Business transfers outside the United Kingdom

115 Certificates for purposes of insurance business transfers overseas

Part III of Schedule 12 makes provision about certificates which the Authority may issue in relation to insurance business transfers taking place outside the United Kingdom.

Commencement: 1 December 2001.
References: See para 22.23.

116 Effect of insurance business transfers authorised in other EEA States

(1) This section applies if, as a result of an authorised transfer, an EEA firm falling within paragraph 5(d) of Schedule 3 transfers to another body all its rights and obligations under any UK policies.

(2) This section also applies if, as a result of an authorised transfer, a company authorised in an EEA State other than the United Kingdom under Article 27 of the first life insurance directive, or Article 23 of the first non-life insurance directive, transfers to another body all its rights and obligations under any UK policies.

(3) If appropriate notice of the execution of an instrument giving effect to the transfer is published, the instrument has the effect in law—

    (a)   of transferring to the transferee all the transferor's rights and obligations under the UK policies to which the instrument applies, and

    (b)   if the instrument so provides, of securing the continuation by or against the transferee of any legal proceedings by or against the transferor which relate to those rights and obligations.

(4) No agreement or consent is required before subsection (3) has the effects mentioned.

(5) "Authorised transfer" means—
- (a) in subsection (1), a transfer authorised in the home State of the EEA firm in accordance with—
  - (i) Article 11 of the third life directive; or
  - (ii) Article 12 of the third non-life directive; and
- (b) in subsection (2), a transfer authorised in an EEA State other than the United Kingdom in accordance with—
  - (i) Article 31a of the first life directive; or
  - (ii) Article 28a of the first non-life directive.

(6) "UK policy" means a policy evidencing a contract of insurance (other than a contract of reinsurance) to which the applicable law is the law of any part of the United Kingdom.

(7) "Appropriate notice" means—
- (a) if the UK policy evidences a contract of insurance in relation to which an EEA State other than the United Kingdom is the State of the commitment, notice given in accordance with the law of that State;
- (b) if the UK policy evidences a contract of insurance where the risk is situated in an EEA State other than the United Kingdom, notice given in accordance with the law of that EEA State;
- (c) in any other case, notice given in accordance with the applicable law.

(8) Paragraph 6 of Schedule 12 applies for the purposes of this section as it applies for the purposes of that Schedule.

Commencement: 1 December 2001.
References: See paras 22.25–22.29.

Modifications

117 Power to modify this Part

The Treasury may by regulations—
- (a) provide for prescribed provisions of this Part to have effect in relation to prescribed cases with such modifications as may be prescribed;
- (b) make such amendments to any provision of this Part as they consider appropriate for the more effective operation of that or any other provision of this Part.

Commencement: 1 December 2001.
References: See para 22.2.

PART VIII
PENALTIES FOR MARKET ABUSE

Market abuse

118 Market abuse

(1) For the purposes of this Act, market abuse is behaviour (whether by one person alone or by two or more persons jointly or in concert)—

    (a)   which occurs in relation to qualifying investments traded on a market to which this section applies;

    (b)   which satisfies any one or more of the conditions set out in subsection (2); and

    (c)   which is likely to be regarded by a regular user of that market who is aware of the behaviour as a failure on the part of the person or persons concerned to observe the standard of behaviour reasonably expected of a person in his or their position in relation to the market.

(2)   The conditions are that—

    (a)   the behaviour is based on information which is not generally available to those using the market but which, if available to a regular user of the market, would or would be likely to be regarded by him as relevant when deciding the terms on which transactions in investments of the kind in question should be effected;

    (b)   the behaviour is likely to give a regular user of the market a false or misleading impression as to the supply of, or demand for, or as to the price or value of, investments of the kind in question;

    (c)   a regular user of the market would, or would be likely to, regard the behaviour as behaviour which would, or would be likely to, distort the market in investments of the kind in question.

(3)   The Treasury may by order prescribe (whether by name or by description)—

    (a)   the markets to which this section applies; and

    (b)   the investments which are qualifying investments in relation to those markets.

(4)   The order may prescribe different investments or descriptions of investment in relation to different markets or descriptions of market.

(5)   Behaviour is to be disregarded for the purposes of subsection (1) unless it occurs—

    (a)   in the United Kingdom; or

    (b)   in relation to qualifying investments traded on a market to which this section applies which is situated in the United Kingdom or which is accessible electronically in the United Kingdom.

(6)   For the purposes of this section, the behaviour which is to be regarded as occurring in relation to qualifying investments includes behaviour which—

    (a)   occurs in relation to anything which is the subject matter, or whose price or value is expressed by reference to the price or value, of those qualifying investments; or

    (b)   occurs in relation to investments (whether qualifying or not) whose subject matter is those qualifying investments.

(7)   Information which can be obtained by research or analysis conducted by, or on behalf of, users of a market is to be regarded for the purposes of this section as being generally available to them.

(8)   Behaviour does not amount to market abuse if it conforms with a rule which includes a provision to the effect that behaviour conforming with the rule does not amount to market abuse.

(9)   Any reference in this Act to a person engaged in market abuse is a reference to a person engaged in market abuse whether alone or with one or more other persons.

(10) In this section—
  "behaviour" includes action or inaction;
  "investment" is to be read with section 22 and Schedule 2;
  "regular user", in relation to a particular market, means a reasonable person
      who regularly deals on that market in investments of the kind in
      question.

Commencement: 1 December 2001 (sub-ss (1), (2), (5)–(9)); 25 February 2001 (remainder).
Orders: The Financial Services and Markets Act 2000 (Prescribed Markets and Qualifying Investments)
Order 2001, SI 2001/996, as amended by SI 2001/3681.
References: See paras 11.4–11.19.

The code

119 The code

(1) The Authority must prepare and issue a code containing such provisions as
the Authority considers will give appropriate guidance to those determining
whether or not behaviour amounts to market abuse.

(2) The code may among other things specify—
  (a) descriptions of behaviour that, in the opinion of the Authority,
       amount to market abuse;
  (b) descriptions of behaviour that, in the opinion of the Authority, do not
       amount to market abuse;
  (c) factors that, in the opinion of the Authority, are to be taken into
       account in determining whether or not behaviour amounts to market
       abuse.

(3) The code may make different provision in relation to persons, cases or
circumstances of different descriptions.

(4) The Authority may at any time alter or replace the code.

(5) If the code is altered or replaced, the altered or replacement code must be
issued by the Authority.

(6) A code issued under this section must be published by the Authority in the
way appearing to the Authority to be best calculated to bring it to the attention of
the public.

(7) The Authority must, without delay, give the Treasury a copy of any code
published under this section.

(8) The Authority may charge a reasonable fee for providing a person with a
copy of the code.

Commencement: 18 June 2001.
References: See paras 11.20, 11.26.

120 Provisions included in the Authority's code by reference to the City Code

(1) The Authority may include in a code issued by it under section 119 ("the
Authority's code") provision to the effect that in its opinion behaviour conforming
with the City Code—
  (a) does not amount to market abuse;

(b)   does not amount to market abuse in specified circumstances; or

(c)   does not amount to market abuse if engaged in by a specified description of person.

(2)   But the Treasury's approval is required before any such provision may be included in the Authority's code.

(3)   If the Authority's code includes provision of a kind authorised by subsection (1), the Authority must keep itself informed of the way in which the Panel on Takeovers and Mergers interprets and administers the relevant provisions of the City Code.

(4)   "City Code" means the City Code on Takeovers and Mergers issued by the Panel as it has effect at the time when the behaviour occurs.

(5)   "Specified" means specified in the Authority's code.

Commencement: 18 June 2001.
References: See para 11.24.

121 Codes: procedure

(1)   Before issuing a code under section 119, the Authority must publish a draft of the proposed code in the way appearing to the Authority to be best calculated to bring it to the attention of the public.

(2)   The draft must be accompanied by—
(a)   a cost benefit analysis; and
(b)   notice that representations about the proposal may be made to the Authority within a specified time.

(3)   Before issuing the proposed code, the Authority must have regard to any representations made to it in accordance with subsection (2)(b).

(4)   If the Authority issues the proposed code it must publish an account, in general terms, of—
(a)   the representations made to it in accordance with subsection (2)(b); and
(b)   its response to them.

(5)   If the code differs from the draft published under subsection (1) in a way which is, in the opinion of the Authority, significant—
(a)   the Authority must (in addition to complying with subsection (4)) publish details of the difference; and
(b)   those details must be accompanied by a cost benefit analysis.

(6)   Subsections (1) to (5) do not apply if the Authority considers that there is an urgent need to publish the code.

(7)   Neither subsection (2)(a) nor subsection (5)(b) applies if the Authority considers—
(a)   that, making the appropriate comparison, there will be no increase in costs; or
(b)   that, making that comparison, there will be an increase in costs but the increase will be of minimal significance.

(8)   The Authority may charge a reasonable fee for providing a person with a copy of a draft published under subsection (1).

(9)   This section also applies to a proposal to alter or replace a code.

(10)   "Cost benefit analysis" means an estimate of the costs together with an analysis of the benefits that will arise—

    (a)   if the proposed code is issued; or

    (b)   if subsection (5)(b) applies, from the code that has been issued.

(11)   "The appropriate comparison" means—

    (a)   in relation to subsection (2)(a), a comparison between the overall position if the code is issued and the overall position if it is not issued;

    (b)   in relation to subsection (5)(b), a comparison between the overall position after the issuing of the code and the overall position before it was issued.

Commencement: 18 June 2001.
References: See paras 11.27–11.30.

122 Effect of the code

(1)   If a person behaves in a way which is described (in the code in force under section 119 at the time of the behaviour) as behaviour that, in the Authority's opinion, does not amount to market abuse that behaviour of his is to be taken, for the purposes of this Act, as not amounting to market abuse.

(2)   Otherwise, the code in force under section 119 at the time when particular behaviour occurs may be relied on so far as it indicates whether or not that behaviour should be taken to amount to market abuse.

Commencement: 1 December 2001.
References: See paras 11.22, 11.23.

Power to impose penalties

123 Power to impose penalties in cases of market abuse

(1)   If the Authority is satisfied that a person ("A")—

    (a)   is or has engaged in market abuse, or

    (b)   by taking or refraining from taking any action has required or encouraged another person or persons to engage in behaviour which, if engaged in by A, would amount to market abuse,

it may impose on him a penalty of such amount as it considers appropriate.

(2)   But the Authority may not impose a penalty on a person if, having considered any representations made to it in response to a warning notice, there are reasonable grounds for it to be satisfied that—

    (a)   he believed, on reasonable grounds, that his behaviour did not fall within paragraph (a) or (b) of subsection (1), or

    (b)   he took all reasonable precautions and exercised all due diligence to avoid behaving in a way which fell within paragraph (a) or (b) of that subsection.

(3)   If the Authority is entitled to impose a penalty on a person under this section it may, instead of imposing a penalty on him, publish a statement to the effect that he has engaged in market abuse.

Commencement: 1 December 2001.
References: See paras 11.31, 11.32.

Statement of policy

124 Statement of policy

(1)   The Authority must prepare and issue a statement of its policy with respect to—

    (a)   the imposition of penalties under section 123; and

    (b)   the amount of penalties under that section.

(2)   The Authority's policy in determining what the amount of a penalty should be must include having regard to—

    (a)   whether the behaviour in respect of which the penalty is to be imposed had an adverse effect on the market in question and, if it did, how serious that effect was;

    (b)   the extent to which that behaviour was deliberate or reckless; and

    (c)   whether the person on whom the penalty is to be imposed is an individual.

(3)   A statement issued under this section must include an indication of the circumstances in which the Authority is to be expected to regard a person as—

    (a)   having a reasonable belief that his behaviour did not amount to market abuse; or

    (b)   having taken reasonable precautions and exercised due diligence to avoid engaging in market abuse.

(4)   The Authority may at any time alter or replace a statement issued under this section.

(5)   If a statement issued under this section is altered or replaced, the Authority must issue the altered or replacement statement.

(6)   In exercising, or deciding whether to exercise, its power under section 123 in the case of any particular behaviour, the Authority must have regard to any statement published under this section and in force at the time when the behaviour concerned occurred.

(7)   A statement issued under this section must be published by the Authority in the way appearing to the Authority to be best calculated to bring it to the attention of the public.

(8)   The Authority may charge a reasonable fee for providing a person with a copy of a statement published under this section.

(9)   The Authority must, without delay, give the Treasury a copy of any statement which it publishes under this section.

Commencement: 18 June 2001.
References: See paras 11.35–11.37.

125 Statement of policy: procedure

(1)   Before issuing a statement of policy under section 124, the Authority must publish a draft of the proposed statement in the way appearing to the Authority to be best calculated to bring it to the attention of the public.

(2)   The draft must be accompanied by notice that representations about the proposal may be made to the Authority within a specified time.

(3)   Before issuing the proposed statement, the Authority must have regard to any representations made to it in accordance with subsection (2).

(4)   If the Authority issues the proposed statement it must publish an account, in general terms, of—

    (a)   the representations made to it in accordance with subsection (2); and
    (b)   its response to them.

(5)   If the statement differs from the draft published under subsection (1) in a way which is, in the opinion of the Authority, significant, the Authority must (in addition to complying with subsection (4)) publish details of the difference.

(6)   The Authority may charge a reasonable fee for providing a person with a copy of a draft published under subsection (1).

(7)   This section also applies to a proposal to alter or replace a statement.

Commencement: 18 June 2001.
References: See paras 11.38–11.40.

Procedure

126 Warning notices

(1)   If the Authority proposes to take action against a person under section 123, it must give him a warning notice.

(2)   A warning notice about a proposal to impose a penalty must state the amount of the proposed penalty.

(3)   A warning notice about a proposal to publish a statement must set out the terms of the proposed statement.

Commencement: 1 December 2001.
References: See para 11.33.

127 Decision notices and right to refer to Tribunal

(1)   If the Authority decides to take action against a person under section 123, it must give him a decision notice.

(2)   A decision notice about the imposition of a penalty must state the amount of the penalty.

(3)   A decision notice about the publication of a statement must set out the terms of the statement.

(4)   If the Authority decides to take action against a person under section 123, that person may refer the matter to the Tribunal.

Commencement: 1 December 2001.
References: See para 11.34.

Miscellaneous

128 Suspension of investigations

(1)   If the Authority considers it desirable or expedient because of the exercise or possible exercise of a power relating to market abuse, it may direct a recognised investment exchange or recognised clearing house—

    (a)   to terminate, suspend or limit the scope of any inquiry which the exchange or clearing house is conducting under its rules; or

    (b)   not to conduct an inquiry which the exchange or clearing house proposes to conduct under its rules.

(2)   A direction under this section—

    (a)   must be given to the exchange or clearing house concerned by notice in writing; and

    (b)   is enforceable, on the application of the Authority, by injunction or, in Scotland, by an order under section 45 of the Court of Session Act 1988.

(3)   The Authority's powers relating to market abuse are its powers—

    (a)   to impose penalties under section 123; or

    (b)   to appoint a person to conduct an investigation under section 168 in a case falling within subsection (2)(d) of that section.

Commencement: 1 December 2001.
References: See paras 11.43, 11.44.

129 Power of court to impose penalty in cases of market abuse

(1)   The Authority may on an application to the court under section 381 or 383 request the court to consider whether the circumstances are such that a penalty should be imposed on the person to whom the application relates.

(2)   The court may, if it considers it appropriate, make an order requiring the person concerned to pay to the Authority a penalty of such amount as it considers appropriate.

Commencement: 1 December 2001.
References: See para 11.53.

130 Guidance

(1)   The Treasury may from time to time issue written guidance for the purpose of helping relevant authorities to determine the action to be taken in cases where behaviour occurs which is behaviour—

    (a)   with respect to which the power in section 123 appears to be exercisable; and

    (b)   which appears to involve the commission of an offence under section 397 of this Act or Part V of the Criminal Justice Act 1993 (insider dealing).

(2)   The Treasury must obtain the consent of the Attorney General and the Secretary of State before issuing any guidance under this section.

(3)   In this section "relevant authorities"—

    (a)   in relation to England and Wales, means the Secretary of State, the Authority, the Director of the Serious Fraud Office and the Director of Public Prosecutions;

    (b)   in relation to Northern Ireland, means the Secretary of State, the Authority, the Director of the Serious Fraud Office and the Director of Public Prosecutions for Northern Ireland.

(4)   Subsections (1) to (3) do not apply to Scotland.

(5)   In relation to Scotland, the Lord Advocate may from time to time, after consultation with the Treasury, issue written guidance for the purpose of helping the Authority to determine the action to be taken in cases where behaviour mentioned in subsection (1) occurs.

Commencement: 1 December 2001.
References: See para 11.41.

131 Effect on transactions

The imposition of a penalty under this Part does not make any transaction void or unenforceable.

Commencement: 1 December 2001.
References: See para

PART IX
HEARINGS AND APPEALS

132 The Financial Services and Markets Tribunal

(1)   For the purposes of this Act, there is to be a tribunal known as the Financial Services and Markets Tribunal (but referred to in this Act as "the Tribunal").

(2)   The Tribunal is to have the functions conferred on it by or under this Act.

(3)   The Lord Chancellor may by rules make such provision as appears to him to be necessary or expedient in respect of the conduct of proceedings before the Tribunal.

(4)   Schedule 13 is to have effect as respects the Tribunal and its proceedings (but does not limit the Lord Chancellor's powers under this section).

Commencement: 25 February 2001 (sub-s (1), for the purpose of the definition of "the Tribunal", sub-s (3) for all purposes, sub-s (4), for the purpose of introducing Sch 13 to the extent that it is brought into force by SI 2001/516); 3 September 2001 (remainder).
Rules: The Financial Services and Markets Tribunal Rules 2001, SI 2001/2476, as modified by SI 2001/3592.
References: See paras 12.1, 12.6.

133 Proceedings: general provision

(1) A reference to the Tribunal under this Act must be made before the end of—
    (a) the period of 28 days beginning with the date on which the decision notice or supervisory notice in question is given; or
    (b) such other period as may be specified in rules made under section 132.

(2) Subject to rules made under section 132, the Tribunal may allow a reference to be made after the end of that period.

(3) On a reference the Tribunal may consider any evidence relating to the subject-matter of the reference, whether or not it was available to the Authority at the material time.

(4) On a reference the Tribunal must determine what (if any) is the appropriate action for the Authority to take in relation to the matter referred to it.

(5) On determining a reference, the Tribunal must remit the matter to the Authority with such directions (if any) as the Tribunal considers appropriate for giving effect to its determination.

(6) In determining a reference made as a result of a decision notice, the Tribunal may not direct the Authority to take action which the Authority would not, as a result of section 388(2), have had power to take when giving the decision notice.

(7) In determining a reference made as a result of a supervisory notice, the Tribunal may not direct the Authority to take action which would have otherwise required the giving of a decision notice.

(8) The Tribunal may, on determining a reference, make recommendations as to the Authority's regulating provisions or its procedures.

(9) The Authority must not take the action specified in a decision notice—
    (a) during the period within which the matter to which the decision notice relates may be referred to the Tribunal; and
    (b) if the matter is so referred, until the reference, and any appeal against the Tribunal's determination, has been finally disposed of.

(10) The Authority must act in accordance with the determination of, and any direction given by, the Tribunal.

(11) An order of the Tribunal may be enforced—
    (a) as if it were an order of a county court; or
    (b) in Scotland, as if it were an order of the Court of Session.

(12) "Supervisory notice" has the same meaning as in section 395.

Commencement: 3 September 2001.
References: See paras 12.18–12.22.

Legal assistance before the Tribunal

134 Legal assistance scheme

(1) The Lord Chancellor may by regulations establish a scheme governing the provision of legal assistance in connection with proceedings before the Tribunal.

(2)   If the Lord Chancellor establishes a scheme under subsection (1), it must provide that a person is eligible for assistance only if—

(a)   he falls within subsection (3); and

(b)   he fulfils such other criteria (if any) as may be prescribed as a result of section 135(1)(d).

(3)   A person falls within this subsection if he is an individual who has referred a matter to the Tribunal under section 127(4).

(4)   In this Part of this Act "the legal assistance scheme" means any scheme in force under subsection (1).

Commencement: 25 February 2001.
Regulations: The Financial Services and Markets Tribunal (Legal Assistance) Regulations 2001, SI 2001/3632; the Financial Services and Markets Tribunal (Legal Assistance Scheme—Costs) Regulations 2001, SI 2001/3633.
References: See paras 11.55, 12.30.

135 Provisions of the legal assistance scheme

(1)   The legal assistance scheme may, in particular, make provision as to—

(a)   the kinds of legal assistance that may be provided;

(b)   the persons by whom legal assistance may be provided;

(c)   the manner in which applications for legal assistance are to be made;

(d)   the criteria on which eligibility for legal assistance is to be determined;

(e)   the persons or bodies by whom applications are to be determined;

(f)   appeals against refusals of applications;

(g)   the revocation or variation of decisions;

(h)   its administration and the enforcement of its provisions.

(2)   Legal assistance under the legal assistance scheme may be provided subject to conditions or restrictions, including conditions as to the making of contributions by the person to whom it is provided.

Commencement: 25 February 2001.
Regulations: The Financial Services and Markets Tribunal (Legal Assistance) Regulations 2001, SI 2001/3632; the Financial Services and Markets Tribunal (Legal Assistance Scheme—Costs) Regulations 2001, SI 2001/3633.
References: See para 12.30.

136 Funding of the legal assistance scheme

(1)   The Authority must pay to the Lord Chancellor such sums at such times as he may, from time to time, determine in respect of the anticipated or actual cost of legal assistance provided in connection with proceedings before the Tribunal under the legal assistance scheme.

(2)   In order to enable it to pay any sum which it is obliged to pay under subsection (1), the Authority must make rules requiring the payment to it by authorised persons or any class of authorised person of specified amounts or amounts calculated in a specified way.

(3)   Sums received by the Lord Chancellor under subsection (1) must be paid into the Consolidated Fund.

(4)   The Lord Chancellor must, out of money provided by Parliament fund the cost of legal assistance provided in connection with proceedings before the Tribunal under the legal assistance scheme.

(5)   Subsection (6) applies if, as respects a period determined by the Lord Chancellor, the amount paid to him under subsection (1) as respects that period exceeds the amount he has expended in that period under subsection (4).

(6)   The Lord Chancellor must—
  (a)   repay, out of money provided by Parliament, the excess to the Authority; or
  (b)   take the excess into account on the next occasion on which he makes a determination under subsection (1).

(7)   The Authority must make provision for any sum repaid to it under subsection (6)(a)—
  (a)   to be distributed among—
    (i)   the authorised persons on whom a levy was imposed in the period in question as a result of rules made under subsection (2); or
    (ii)   such of those persons as it may determine;
  (b)   to be applied in order to reduce any amounts which those persons, or such of them as it may determine, are or will be liable to pay to the Authority, whether under rules made under subsection (2) or otherwise; or
  (c)   to be partly so distributed and partly so applied.

(8)   If the Authority considers that it is not practicable to deal with any part of a sum repaid to it under subsection (6)(a) in accordance with provision made by it as a result of subsection (7), it may, with the consent the Lord Chancellor, apply or dispose of that part of that sum in such manner as it considers appropriate.

(9)   "Specified" means specified in the rules.

Commencement: 18 June 2001 (for the purpose of making rules); 3 September 2001 (remaining purposes).
References: See paras 12.30–12.32.

Appeals

137 Appeal on a point of law

(1)   A party to a reference to the Tribunal may with permission appeal—
  (a)   to the Court of Appeal, or
  (b)   in Scotland, to the Court of Session,
on a point of law arising from a decision of the Tribunal disposing of the reference.

(2)   "Permission" means permission given by the Tribunal or by the Court of Appeal or (in Scotland) the Court of Session.

(3)   If, on an appeal under subsection (1), the court considers that the decision of the Tribunal was wrong in law, it may—
  (a)   remit the matter to the Tribunal for rehearing and determination by it; or
  (b)   itself make a determination.

(4)   An appeal may not be brought from a decision of the Court of Appeal under subsection (3) except with the leave of—
    (a)   the Court of Appeal; or
    (b)   the House of Lords.

(5)   An appeal lies, with the leave of the Court of Session or the House of Lords, from any decision of the Court of Session under this section, and such leave may be given on such terms as to costs, expenses or otherwise as the Court of Session or the House of Lords may determine.

(6)   Rules made under section 132 may make provision for regulating or prescribing any matters incidental to or consequential on an appeal under this section.

Commencement: 3 September 2001 (sub-ss (1)–(5)); 25 February 2001 (remainder).
Rules: The Financial Services and Markets Tribunal Rules 2001, SI 2001/2476, as modified by SI 2001/3592.
References: See paras 12.13, 12.24.

PART X
RULES AND GUIDANCE

CHAPTER I
RULE-MAKING POWERS

138   General rule-making power

(1)   The Authority may make such rules applying to authorised persons—
    (a)   with respect to the carrying on by them of regulated activities, or
    (b)   with respect to the carrying on by them of activities which are not regulated activities,
as appear to it to be necessary or expedient for the purpose of protecting the interests of consumers.

(2)   Rules made under this section are referred to in this Act as the Authority's general rules.

(3)   The Authority's power to make general rules is not limited by any other power which it has to make regulating provisions.

(4)   The Authority's general rules may make provision applying to authorised persons even though there is no relationship between the authorised persons to whom the rules will apply and the persons whose interests will be protected by the rules.

(5)   General rules may contain requirements which take into account, in the case of an authorised person who is a member of a group, any activity of another member of the group.

(6)   General rules may not—
    (a)   make provision prohibiting an EEA firm from carrying on, or holding itself out as carrying on, any activity which it has permission conferred by Part II of Schedule 3 to carry on in the United Kingdom;
    (b)   make provision, as respects an EEA firm, about any matter responsibility for which is, under any of the single market directives, reserved to the firm's home state regulator.

(7) "Consumers" means persons—
- (a) who use, have used, or are or may be contemplating using, any of the services provided by—
  - (i) authorised persons in carrying on regulated activities; or
  - (ii) persons acting as appointed representatives;
- (b) who have rights or interests which are derived from, or are otherwise attributable to, the use of any such services by other persons; or
- (c) who have rights or interests which may be adversely affected by the use of any such services by persons acting on their behalf or in a fiduciary capacity in relation to them.

(8) If an authorised person is carrying on a regulated activity in his capacity as a trustee, the persons who are, have been or may be beneficiaries of the trust are to be treated as persons who use, have used or are or may be contemplating using services provided by the authorised person in his carrying on of that activity.

(9) For the purposes of subsection (7) a person who deals with an authorised person in the course of the authorised person's carrying on of a regulated activity is to be treated as using services provided by the authorised person in carrying on those activities.

Commencement: 18 June 2001.
Modification of the meaning of "Consumers": The definition of "Consumers" in sub-s (7) has been extended by the Financial Services and Markets Act 2000 (Consequential and Transitional Provisions) (Miscellaneous) Order 2001, SI 2001/1821, art 3, and the Financial Services and Markets Act 2000 (Consequential Amendments and Transitional Provisions) (Credit Unions) Order 2002, SI 2002/1501, art 4.
References: See paras 5.26–5.30.

---

139 Miscellaneous ancillary matters

(1) Rules relating to the handling of money held by an authorised person in specified circumstances ("clients' money") may—
- (a) make provision which results in that clients' money being held on trust in accordance with the rules;
- (b) treat two or more accounts as a single account for specified purposes (which may include the distribution of money held in the accounts);
- (c) authorise the retention by the authorised person of interest accruing on the clients' money; and
- (d) make provision as to the distribution of such interest which is not to be retained by him.

(2) An institution with which an account is kept in pursuance of rules relating to the handling of clients' money does not incur any liability as constructive trustee if money is wrongfully paid from the account, unless the institution permits the payment—
- (a) with knowledge that it is wrongful; or
- (b) having deliberately failed to make enquiries in circumstances in which a reasonable and honest person would have done so.

(3) In the application of subsection (1) to Scotland, the reference to money being held on trust is to be read as a reference to its being held as agent for the person who is entitled to call for it to be paid over to him or to be paid on his direction or to have it otherwise credited to him.

(4) Rules may—
   (a) confer rights on persons to rescind agreements with, or withdraw offers to, authorised persons within a specified period; and
   (b) make provision, in respect of authorised persons and persons exercising those rights, for the restitution of property and the making or recovery of payments where those rights are exercised.

(5) "Rules" means general rules.

(6) "Specified" means specified in the rules.

Commencement: 18 June 2001.
References: See paras 5.33–5.36.

140 Restriction on managers of *authorised unit trust schemes*

(1) The Authority may make rules prohibiting an authorised person who has permission to act as the manager of an authorised unit trust scheme from carrying on a specified activity.

(2) Such rules may specify an activity which is not a regulated activity.

[(3) In this section—
   (a) "authorised UCITS open-ended investment company" means an authorised open-ended investment company to which the UCITS directive applies; and
   (b) "management company" has the meaning given by Article 1a.2 of the UCITS directive.]

Commencement: 18 June 2001.
Amendments: Heading: for the words in italics there are substituted the words "certain collective investment schemes" by the Collective Investment Schemes (Miscellaneous Amendments) Regulations 2003, SI 2003/2066, reg 5(a), as from 13 February 2004.
Sub-s (1): substituted by SI 2003/2066, reg 5(b), as from 13 February 2004 as follows—

"(1) The Authority may make rules prohibiting an authorised person who has permission to act as—
   (a) the manager of an authorised unit trust scheme, or
   (b) the management company of an authorised UCITS open-ended investment company, from carrying on a specified activity.".

Sub-s (3): added by SI 2003/2066, reg 5(c), as from 13 February 2004.
References: See para 5.37.

141 Insurance business rules

(1) The Authority may make rules prohibiting an authorised person who has permission to effect or carry out contracts of insurance from carrying on a specified activity.

(2) Such rules may specify an activity which is not a regulated activity.

(3) The Authority may make rules in relation to contracts entered into by an authorised person in the course of carrying on business which consists of the effecting or carrying out of contracts of long-term insurance.

(4) Such rules may, in particular—
   (a) restrict the descriptions of property or indices of the value of property by reference to which the benefits under such contracts may be determined;

  (b) make provision, in the interests of the protection of policyholders, for the substitution of one description of property, or index of value, by reference to which the benefits under a contract are to be determined for another such description of property or index.

(5)   Rules made under this section are referred to in this Act as insurance business rules.

Commencement: 18 June 2001.
References: See paras 5.38, 5.39.

142 Insurance business: regulations supplementing Authority's rules

(1)   The Treasury may make regulations for the purpose of preventing a person who is not an authorised person but who—

  (a) is a parent undertaking of an authorised person who has permission to effect or carry out contracts of insurance, and
  (b) falls within a prescribed class,

from doing anything to lessen the effectiveness of asset identification rules.

(2)   "Asset identification rules" means rules made by the Authority which require an authorised person who has permission to effect or carry out contracts of insurance to identify assets which belong to him and which are maintained in respect of a particular aspect of his business.

(3)   The regulations may, in particular, include provision—

  (a) prohibiting the payment of dividends;
  (b) prohibiting the creation of charges;
  (c) making charges created in contravention of the regulations void.

(4)   The Treasury may by regulations provide that, in prescribed circumstances, charges created in contravention of asset identification rules are void.

(5)   A person who contravenes regulations under subsection (1) is guilty of an offence and liable on summary conviction to a fine not exceeding level 5 on the standard scale.

(6)   "Charges" includes mortgages (or in Scotland securities over property).

Commencement: 1 December 2001 (sub-s (5)); 25 February 2001 (remainder).
References: See paras 5.40–5.42.

143 Endorsement of codes etc

(1)   The Authority may make rules ("endorsing rules")—

  (a) endorsing the City Code on Takeovers and Mergers issued by the Panel on Takeovers and Mergers;
  (b) endorsing the Rules Governing Substantial Acquisitions of Shares issued by the Panel.

(2)   Endorsement may be—

  (a) as respects all authorised persons; or
  (b) only as respects a specified kind of authorised person.

(3)   At any time when endorsing rules are in force, and if asked to do so by the Panel, the Authority may exercise its powers under Part IV or section 66 as if failure to comply with an endorsed provision was a ground entitling the Authority to exercise those powers.

(4)   At any time when endorsing rules are in force and if asked to do so by the Panel, the Authority may exercise its powers under Part XIII, XIV or XXV as if the endorsed provisions were rules applying to the persons in respect of whom they are endorsed.

(5)   For the purposes of subsections (3) and (4), a failure to comply with a requirement imposed, or ruling given, under an endorsed provision is to be treated as a failure to comply with the endorsed provision under which that requirement was imposed or ruling was given.

(6)   If endorsed provisions are altered, subsections (3) and (4) apply to them as altered, but only if before the alteration the Authority has notified the Panel (and has not withdrawn its notification) that it is satisfied with the Panel's consultation procedures.

(7)   "Consultation procedures" means procedures designed to provide an opportunity for persons likely to be affected by alterations to those provisions to make representations about proposed alterations to any of those provisions.

(8)   Subsections (1), (2)(d), (4), (5), (6)(a) and (12) of section 155 apply (with the necessary modifications) to a proposal to give notification of the kind mentioned in subsection (6) as they apply to a proposal to make endorsing rules.

(9)   This section applies in relation to particular provisions of the code or rules mentioned in subsection (1) as it applies to the code or the rules.

Commencement: 18 June 2001 (for the purpose of making rules); 1 December 2001 (remaining purposes).
References: See paras 5.43–5.47.

Specific rules

144 Price stabilising rules

(1)   The Authority may make rules ("price stabilising rules") as to—
   (a)   the circumstances and manner in which,
   (b)   the conditions subject to which, and
   (c)   the time when or the period during which,
action may be taken for the purpose of stabilising the price of investments of specified kinds.

(2)   Price stabilising rules—
   (a)   are to be made so as to apply only to authorised persons;
   (b)   may make different provision in relation to different kinds of investment.

(3)   The Authority may make rules which, for the purposes of section 397(5)(b), treat a person who acts or engages in conduct—
   (a)   for the purpose of stabilising the price of investments, and

    (b)   in conformity with such provisions corresponding to price stabilising rules and made by a body or authority outside the United Kingdom as may be specified in the rules under this subsection,

as acting, or engaging in that conduct, for that purpose and in conformity with price stabilising rules.

(4) The Treasury may by order impose limitations on the power to make rules under this section.

(5) Such an order may, in particular—

    (a)   specify the kinds of investment in relation to which price stabilising rules may make provision;

    (b)   specify the kinds of investment in relation to which rules made under subsection (3) may make provision;

    (c)   provide for price stabilising rules to make provision for action to be taken for the purpose of stabilising the price of investments only in such circumstances as the order may specify;

    (d)   provide for price stabilising rules to make provision for action to be taken for that purpose only at such times or during such periods as the order may specify.

(6) If provisions specified in rules made under subsection (3) are altered, the rules continue to apply to those provisions as altered, but only if before the alteration the Authority has notified the body or authority concerned (and has not withdrawn its notification) that it is satisfied with its consultation procedures.

(7) "Consultation procedures" has the same meaning as in section 143.

Commencement: 18 June 2001 (sub-ss (1)–(3), (6), (7)); 25 February 2001 (remainder).
References: See paras 5.48–5.53.

145 Financial promotion rules

(1) The Authority may make rules applying to authorised persons about the communication by them, or their approval of the communication by others, of invitations or inducements—

    (a)   to engage in investment activity; or

    (b)   to participate in a collective investment scheme.

(2) Rules under this section may, in particular, make provision about the form and content of communications.

(3) Subsection (1) applies only to communications which—

    (a)   if made by a person other than an authorised person, without the approval of an authorised person, would contravene section 21(1);

    (b)   may be made by an authorised person without contravening section 238(1).

(4) "Engage in investment activity" has the same meaning as in section 21.

(5) The Treasury may by order impose limitations on the power to make rules under this section.

Commencement: 18 June 2001 (sub-ss (1)–(4)); 25 February 2001 (remainder).
References: See paras 5.54, 6.43, 6.44.

146 Money laundering rules

The Authority may make rules in relation to the prevention and detection of money laundering in connection with the carrying on of regulated activities by authorised persons.

Commencement: 18 June 2001.
References: See paras 5.55–5.60.

147 Control of information rules

(1)   The Authority may make rules ("control of information rules") about the disclosure and use of information held by an authorised person ("A").

(2)   Control of information rules may—
  (a)   require the withholding of information which A would otherwise have to disclose to a person ("B") for or with whom A does business in the course of carrying on any regulated or other activity;
  (b)   specify circumstances in which A may withhold information which he would otherwise have to disclose to B;
  (c)   require A not to use for the benefit of B information A holds which A would otherwise have to use in that way;
  (d)   specify circumstances in which A may decide not to use for the benefit of B information A holds which A would otherwise have to use in that way.

Commencement: 18 June 2001.
References: See paras 5.61–5.64.

Modification or waiver

148 Modification or waiver of rules

(1)   This section applies in relation to the following—
  (a)   auditors and actuaries rules;
  (b)   control of information rules;
  (c)   financial promotion rules;
  (d)   general rules;
  (e)   insurance business rules;
  (f)   money laundering rules; and
  (g)   price stabilising rules.

(2)   The Authority may, on the application or with the consent of an authorised person, direct that all or any of the rules to which this section applies—
  (a)   are not to apply to the authorised person; or
  (b)   are to apply to him with such modifications as may be specified in the direction.

(3)   An application must be made in such manner as the Authority may direct.

(4)   The Authority may not give a direction unless it is satisfied that—
  (a)   compliance by the authorised person with the rules, or with the rules as unmodified, would be unduly burdensome or would not achieve the purpose for which the rules were made; and

    (b)   the direction would not result in undue risk to persons whose interests the rules are intended to protect.

(5)   A direction may be given subject to conditions.

(6)   Unless it is satisfied that it is inappropriate or unnecessary to do so, a direction must be published by the Authority in such a way as it thinks most suitable for bringing the direction to the attention of—
    (a)   those likely to be affected by it; and
    (b)   others who may be likely to make an application for a similar direction.

(7)   In deciding whether it is satisfied as mentioned in subsection (6), the Authority must—
    (a)   take into account whether the direction relates to a rule contravention of which is actionable in accordance with section 150;
    (b)   consider whether its publication would prejudice, to an unreasonable degree, the commercial interests of the authorised person concerned or any other member of his immediate group; and
    (c)   consider whether its publication would be contrary to an international obligation of the United Kingdom.

(8)   For the purposes of paragraphs (b) and (c) of subsection (7), the Authority must consider whether it would be possible to publish the direction without either of the consequences mentioned in those paragraphs by publishing it without disclosing the identity of the authorised person concerned.

(9)   The Authority may—
    (a)   revoke a direction; or
    (b)   vary it on the application, or with the consent, of the authorised person to whom it relates.

(10)   "Direction" means a direction under subsection (2).

(11)   "Immediate group", in relation to an authorised person ("A"), means—
    (a)   A;
    (b)   a parent undertaking of A;
    (c)   a subsidiary undertaking of A;
    (d)   a subsidiary undertaking of a parent undertaking of A;
    (e)   a parent undertaking of a subsidiary undertaking of A.

Commencement: 18 June 2001 (for the purpose of giving directions as mentioned in sub-s (3) above); 3 September 2001 (remaining purposes).
Modification: Sub-ss (3)–(9), (11) above have effect, with certain modifications, in relation to a direction by the Financial Services Authority under the Open-Ended Investment Companies Regulations 2001, SI 2001/1228, reg 7(1), (2), to modify or waive the application of any rules made by the Authority under reg 6 of the 2001 Regulations, as they have effect in relation to a direction under sub-s (2) above; see the Open-Ended Investment Companies Regulations 2001, SI 2001/1228, reg 7(3), (4) (made under ss 262, 428(3)).
References: See paras 5.65–5.70, 15.28.

Contravention of rules

149 Evidential provisions

(1)   If a particular rule so provides, contravention of the rule does not give rise to any of the consequences provided for by other provisions of this Act.

(2)   A rule which so provides must also provide—

    (a)   that contravention may be relied on as tending to establish contravention of such other rule as may be specified; or

    (b)   that compliance may be relied on as tending to establish compliance with such other rule as may be specified.

(3)   A rule may include the provision mentioned in subsection (1) only if the Authority considers that it is appropriate for it also to include the provision required by subsection (2).

Commencement: 18 June 2001.
References: See para 5.72.

150 Actions for damages

(1)   A contravention by an authorised person of a rule is actionable at the suit of a private person who suffers loss as a result of the contravention, subject to the defences and other incidents applying to actions for breach of statutory duty.

(2)   If rules so provide, subsection (1) does not apply to contravention of a specified provision of those rules.

(3)   In prescribed cases, a contravention of a rule which would be actionable at the suit of a private person is actionable at the suit of a person who is not a private person, subject to the defences and other incidents applying to actions for breach of statutory duty.

(4)   In subsections (1) and (3) "rule" does not include—

    (a)   listing rules; or

    (b)   a rule requiring an authorised person to have or maintain financial resources.

(5)   "Private person" has such meaning as may be prescribed.

Commencement: 18 June 2001 (sub-ss (1), (2), for the purpose of making rules); 25 February 2001 (sub-ss (3)–(5), for the purpose of making orders or regulations); 1 December 2001 (remaining purposes).
Regulations: The Financial Services and Markets Act 2000 (Rights of Action) Regulations 2001, SI 2001/2256, as amended by SI 2002/1775, SI 2002/2706; the Financial Services and Markets Act 2000 (Fourth Motor Insurance Directive) Regulations 2002, SI 2002/2706.
References: See paras 5.73–5.76.

151 Limits on effect of contravening rules

(1)   A person is not guilty of an offence by reason of a contravention of a rule made by the Authority.

(2)   No such contravention makes any transaction void or unenforceable.

Commencement: 1 December 2001.
References: See para 5.71.

Procedural provisions

152 Notification of rules to the Treasury

(1)   If the Authority makes any rules, it must give a copy to the Treasury without delay.

(2)   If the Authority alters or revokes any rules, it must give written notice to the Treasury without delay.

(3)   Notice of an alteration must include details of the alteration.

Commencement: 18 June 2001.
References: See para 5.78.

153 Rule-making instruments

(1)   Any power conferred on the Authority to make rules is exercisable in writing.

(2)   An instrument by which rules are made by the Authority ("a rule-making instrument") must specify the provision under which the rules are made.

(3)   To the extent to which a rule-making instrument does not comply with subsection (2), it is void.

(4)   A rule-making instrument must be published by the Authority in the way appearing to the Authority to be best calculated to bring it to the attention of the public.

(5)   The Authority may charge a reasonable fee for providing a person with a copy of a rule-making instrument.

(6)   A person is not to be taken to have contravened any rule made by the Authority if he shows that at the time of the alleged contravention the rule-making instrument concerned had not been made available in accordance with this section.

Commencement: 18 June 2001.
References: See paras 5.79, 5.80.

154 Verification of rules

(1)   The production of a printed copy of a rule-making instrument purporting to be made by the Authority—

      (a)   on which is endorsed a certificate signed by a member of the Authority's staff authorised by it for that purpose, and

      (b)   which contains the required statements,

is evidence (or in Scotland sufficient evidence) of the facts stated in the certificate.

(2)   The required statements are—

      (a)   that the instrument was made by the Authority;

      (b)   that the copy is a true copy of the instrument; and

      (c)   that on a specified date the instrument was made available to the public in accordance with section 153(4).

(3)   A certificate purporting to be signed as mentioned in subsection (1) is to be taken to have been properly signed unless the contrary is shown.

(4)   A person who wishes in any legal proceedings to rely on a rule-making instrument may require the Authority to endorse a copy of the instrument with a certificate of the kind mentioned in subsection (1).

Commencement: 18 June 2001.
References: See para 5.81.

155 Consultation

(1)   If the Authority proposes to make any rules, it must publish a draft of the proposed rules in the way appearing to it to be best calculated to bring them to the attention of the public.

(2)   The draft must be accompanied by—
- (a)   a cost benefit analysis;
- (b)   an explanation of the purpose of the proposed rules;
- (c)   an explanation of the Authority's reasons for believing that making the proposed rules is compatible with its general duties under section 2; and
- (d)   notice that representations about the proposals may be made to the Authority within a specified time.

(3)   In the case of a proposal to make rules under a provision mentioned in subsection (9), the draft must also be accompanied by details of the expected expenditure by reference to which the proposal is made.

(4)   Before making the proposed rules, the Authority must have regard to any representations made to it in accordance with subsection (2)(d).

(5)   If the Authority makes the proposed rules, it must publish an account, in general terms, of—
- (a)   the representations made to it in accordance with subsection (2)(d); and
- (b)   its response to them.

(6)   If the rules differ from the draft published under subsection (1) in a way which is, in the opinion of the Authority, significant—
- (a)   the Authority must (in addition to complying with subsection (5)) publish details of the difference; and
- (b)   those details must be accompanied by a cost benefit analysis.

(7)   Subsections (1) to (6) do not apply if the Authority considers that the delay involved in complying with them would be prejudicial to the interests of consumers.

(8)   Neither subsection (2)(a) nor subsection (6)(b) applies if the Authority considers—
- (a)   that, making the appropriate comparison, there will be no increase in costs; or
- (b)   that, making that comparison, there will be an increase in costs but the increase will be of minimal significance.

(9)   Neither subsection (2)(a) nor subsection (6)(b) requires a cost benefit analysis to be carried out in relation to rules made under—
- (a)   section 136(2);
- (b)   subsection (1) of section 213 as a result of subsection (4) of that section;
- (c)   section 234;
- (d)   paragraph 17 of Schedule 1.

(10) "Cost benefit analysis" means an estimate of the costs together with an analysis of the benefits that will arise—

    (a)   if the proposed rules are made; or

    (b)   if subsection (6) applies, from the rules that have been made.

(11) "The appropriate comparison" means—

    (a)   in relation to subsection (2)(a), a comparison between the overall position if the rules are made and the overall position if they are not made;

    (b)   in relation to subsection (6)(b), a comparison between the overall position after the making of the rules and the overall position before they were made.

(12) The Authority may charge a reasonable fee for providing a person with a copy of a draft published under subsection (1).

Commencement: 18 June 2001.
References: See paras 5.82–5.87.

156 General supplementary powers

(1)   Rules made by the Authority may make different provision for different cases and may, in particular, make different provision in respect of different descriptions of authorised person, activity or investment.

(2)   Rules made by the Authority may contain such incidental, supplemental, consequential and transitional provision as the Authority considers appropriate.

Commencement: 18 June 2001.
References: See para 5.36.

CHAPTER II
GUIDANCE

157 Guidance

(1)   The Authority may give guidance consisting of such information and advice as it considers appropriate—

    (a)   with respect to the operation of this Act and of any rules made under it;

    (b)   with respect to any matters relating to functions of the Authority;

    (c)   for the purpose of meeting the regulatory objectives;

    (d)   with respect to any other matters about which it appears to the Authority to be desirable to give information or advice.

(2)   The Authority may give financial or other assistance to persons giving information or advice of a kind which the Authority could give under this section.

(3)   If the Authority proposes to give guidance to regulated persons generally, or to a class of regulated person, in relation to rules to which those persons are subject, subsections (1), (2) and (4) to (10) of section 155 apply to the proposed guidance as they apply to proposed rules.

(4)   The Authority may—

    (a)   publish its guidance;

(b) offer copies of its published guidance for sale at a reasonable price; and

(c) if it gives guidance in response to a request made by any person, make a reasonable charge for that guidance.

(5) In this Chapter, references to guidance given by the Authority include references to any recommendation made by the Authority to persons generally, to regulated persons generally or to any class of regulated person.

(6) "Regulated person" means any—
(a) authorised person;
(b) person who is otherwise subject to rules made by the Authority.

Commencement: 18 June 2001.
References: See paras 5.88–5.92.

158 Notification of guidance to the Treasury

(1) On giving any general guidance, the Authority must give the Treasury a copy of the guidance without delay.

(2) If the Authority alters any of its general guidance, it must give written notice to the Treasury without delay.

(3) The notice must include details of the alteration.

(4) If the Authority revokes any of its general guidance, it must give written notice to the Treasury without delay.

(5) "General guidance" means guidance given by the Authority under section 157 which is—
(a) given to persons generally, to regulated persons generally or to a class of regulated person;
(b) intended to have continuing effect; and
(c) given in writing or other legible form.

(6) "Regulated person" has the same meaning as in section 157.

Commencement: 18 June 2001.
References: See para 5.93.

CHAPTER III
COMPETITION SCRUTINY

159 Interpretation

(1) In this Chapter—
["OFT" means the Office of Fair Trading;]
"practices", in relation to the Authority, means practices adopted by the Authority in the exercise of functions under this Act;
"regulating provisions" means any—
(a) rules;
(b) general guidance (as defined by section 158(5));
(c) statement issued by the Authority under section 64;
(d) code issued by the Authority under section 64 or 119.

(2)   For the purposes of this Chapter, regulating provisions or practices have a significantly adverse effect on competition if—
  (a)   they have, or are intended or likely to have, that effect; or
  (b)   the effect that they have, or are intended or likely to have, is to require or encourage behaviour which has, or is intended or likely to have, a significantly adverse effect on competition.

(3)   If regulating provisions or practices have, or are intended or likely to have, the effect of requiring or encouraging exploitation of the strength of a market position they are to be taken, for the purposes of this Chapter, to have an adverse effect on competition.

(4)   In determining under this Chapter whether any of the regulating provisions have, or are likely to have, a particular effect, it may be assumed that the persons to whom the provisions concerned are addressed will act in accordance with them.

Commencement: 18 June 2001.
Amendments: Sub-s (1): definition in square brackets substituted by the Enterprise Act 2002, s 278(1), Sch 25, para 40(1), (2), as from 1 April 2003.
References: See paras 10.10–10.14.

160 Reports by [OFT]

(1)   The [OFT] must keep the regulating provisions and the Authority's practices under review.

(2)   If at any time the [OFT] considers that—
  (a)   a regulating provision or practice has a significantly adverse effect on competition, or
  (b)   two or more regulating provisions or practices taken together, or a particular combination of regulating provisions and practices, have such an effect,
[the OFT] must make a report to that effect.

(3)   If at any time the [OFT] considers that—
  (a)   a regulating provision or practice does not have a significantly adverse effect on competition, or
  (b)   two or more regulating provisions or practices taken together, or a particular combination of regulating provisions and practices, do not have any such effect,
[the OFT] may make a report to that effect.

(4)   A report under subsection (2) must include details of the adverse effect on competition.

(5)   If the [OFT] makes a report under subsection (2) [the OFT] must—
  (a)   send a copy of it to the Treasury, the Competition Commission and the Authority; and
  (b)   publish it in the way appearing to [it] to be best calculated to bring it to the attention of the public.

(6)   If the [OFT] makes a report under subsection (3)—
  (a)   [the OFT] must send a copy of it to the Treasury, the Competition Commission and the Authority; and
  (b)   [the OFT] may publish it.

(7)   Before publishing a report under this section the [OFT] must, so far as practicable, exclude any matter which relates to the private affairs of a particular individual the publication of which, in the opinion of the [OFT], would or might seriously and prejudicially affect his interests.

(8)   Before publishing such a report the [OFT] must, so far as practicable, exclude any matter which relates to the affairs of a particular body the publication of which, in the opinion of the [OFT], would or might seriously and prejudicially affect its interests.

(9)   Subsections (7) and (8) do not apply in relation to copies of a report which the [OFT] is required to send under subsection (5)(a) or (6)(a).

(10) For the purposes of the law of defamation, absolute privilege attaches to any report of the [OFT] under this section.

Commencement: 18 June 2001.
Amendments: Words in square brackets substituted by the Enterprise Act 2002, s 278(1), Sch 25, para 40(1), (3), as from 1 April 2003.
References: See paras 10.10–10.20.

---

161 Power of [OFT] to request information

(1)   For the purpose of investigating any matter with a view to its consideration under section 160, the [OFT] may exercise the powers conferred on [it] by this section.

(2)   The [OFT] may by notice in writing require any person to produce to [it] or to a person appointed by [it] for the purpose, at a time and place specified in the notice, any document which—

    (a)   is specified or described in the notice; and

    (b)   is a document in that person's custody or under his control.

(3)   The [OFT] may by notice in writing—

    (a)   require any person carrying on any business to provide [it] with such information as may be specified or described in the notice; and

    (b)   specify the time within which, and the manner and form in which, any such information is to be provided.

(4)   A requirement may be imposed under subsection (2) or (3)(a) only in respect of documents or information which relate to any matter relevant to the investigation.

(5)   If a person ("the defaulter") refuses, or otherwise fails, to comply with a notice under this section, the [OFT] may certify that fact in writing to the court and the court may enquire into the case.

(6)   If, after hearing any witness who may be produced against or on behalf of the defaulter and any statement which may be offered in defence, the court is satisfied that the defaulter did not have a reasonable excuse for refusing or otherwise failing to comply with the notice, the court may deal with the defaulter as if he were in contempt.

(7)   "Court" means—

    (a)   the High Court; or

    (b)   in relation to Scotland, the Court of Session.

Commencement: 18 June 2001.
Amendments: Words in square brackets substituted by the Enterprise Act 2002, s 278(1), Sch 25, para 40(1), (4), as from 1 April 2003.
References: See para 10.43.

162 Consideration by Competition Commission

(1)   If the [OFT]—
     (a)   makes a report under section 160(2), or
     (b)   asks the Commission to consider a report that [the OFT] has made under section 160(3),
the Commission must investigate the matter.

(2)   The Commission must then make its own report on the matter unless it considers that, as a result of a change of circumstances, no useful purpose would be served by a report.

(3)   If the Commission decides in accordance with subsection (2) not to make a report, it must make a statement setting out the change of circumstances which resulted in that decision.

(4)   A report made under this section must state the Commission's conclusion as to whether—
     (a)   the regulating provision or practice which is the subject of the report has a significantly adverse effect on competition; or
     (b)   the regulating provisions or practices, or combination of regulating provisions and practices, which are the subject of the report have such an effect.

(5)   A report under this section stating the Commission's conclusion that there is a significantly adverse effect on competition must also—
     (a)   state whether the Commission considers that that effect is justified; and
     (b)   if it states that the Commission considers that it is not justified, state its conclusion as to what action, if any, ought to be taken by the Authority.

(6)   Subsection (7) applies whenever the Commission is considering, for the purposes of this section, whether a particular adverse effect on competition is justified.

(7)   The Commission must ensure, so far as that is reasonably possible, that the conclusion it reaches is compatible with the functions conferred, and obligations imposed, on the Authority by or under this Act.

(8)   A report under this section must contain such an account of the Commission's reasons for its conclusions as is expedient, in the opinion of the Commission, for facilitating proper understanding of them.

(9)   Schedule 14 supplements this section.

(10) If the Commission makes a report under this section it must send a copy to the Treasury, the Authority and the [OFT].

Commencement: 18 June 2001.
Amendments: Sub-ss (1), (10): words in square brackets substituted by the Enterprise Act 2002, s 278(1), Sch 25, para 40(1), (5), as from 1 April 2003.
References: See paras 10.21–10.23, 10.33, 10.34.

163 Role of the Treasury

(1)   This section applies if the Competition Commission makes a report under section 162(2) which states its conclusion that there is a significantly adverse effect on competition.

(2)   If the Commission's conclusion, as stated in the report, is that the adverse effect on competition is not justified, the Treasury must give a direction to the Authority requiring it to take such action as may be specified in the direction.

(3)   But subsection (2) does not apply if the Treasury consider—

    (a)   that, as a result of action taken by the Authority in response to the Commission's report, it is unnecessary for them to give a direction; or

    (b)   that the exceptional circumstances of the case make it inappropriate or unnecessary for them to do so.

(4)   In considering the action to be specified in a direction under subsection (2), the Treasury must have regard to any conclusion of the Commission included in the report because of section 162(5)(b).

(5)   Subsection (6) applies if—

    (a)   the Commission's conclusion, as stated in its report, is that the adverse effect on competition is justified; but

    (b)   the Treasury consider that the exceptional circumstances of the case require them to act.

(6)   The Treasury may give a direction to the Authority requiring it to take such action—

    (a)   as they consider to be necessary in the light of the exceptional circumstances of the case; and

    (b)   as may be specified in the direction.

(7)   The Authority may not be required as a result of this section to take any action—

    (a)   that it would not have power to take in the absence of a direction under this section; or

    (b)   that would otherwise be incompatible with any of the functions conferred, or obligations imposed, on it by or under this Act.

(8)   Subsection (9) applies if the Treasury are considering—

    (a)   whether subsection (2) applies and, if so, what action is to be specified in a direction under that subsection; or

    (b)   whether to give a direction under subsection (6).

(9)   The Treasury must—

    (a)   do what they consider appropriate to allow the Authority, and any other person appearing to the Treasury to be affected, an opportunity to make representations; and

    (b)   have regard to any such representations.

(10) If, in reliance on subsection (3)(a) or (b), the Treasury decline to act under subsection (2), they must make a statement to that effect, giving their reasons.

(11) If the Treasury give a direction under this section they must make a statement giving—

    (a)   details of the direction; and

    (b)   if the direction is given under subsection (6), their reasons for giving it.

(12)   The Treasury must—
   (a)   publish any statement made under this section in the way appearing to them best calculated to bring it to the attention of the public; and
   (b)   lay a copy of it before Parliament.

Commencement: 18 June 2001.
References: See paras 10.24–10.27, 10.48.

164 The Competition Act 1998

(1)   The Chapter I prohibition does not apply to an agreement the parties to which consist of or include—
   (a)   an authorised person, or
   (b)   a person who is otherwise subject to the Authority's regulating provisions,
to the extent to which the agreement consists of provisions the inclusion of which in the agreement is encouraged by any of the Authority's regulating provisions.

(2)   The Chapter I prohibition does not apply to the practices of an authorised person or a person who is otherwise subject to the regulating provisions to the extent to which the practices are encouraged by any of the Authority's regulating provisions.

(3)   The Chapter II prohibition does not apply to conduct of—
   (a)   an authorised person, or
   (b)   a person who is otherwise subject to the Authority's regulating provisions,
to the extent to which the conduct is encouraged by any of the Authority's regulating provisions.

(4)   "The Chapter I prohibition" means the prohibition imposed by section 2(1) of the Competition Act 1998.

(5)   "The Chapter II prohibition" means the prohibition imposed by section 18(1) of that Act.

Commencement: 18 June 2001.
References: See para 10.3.

PART XI
INFORMATION GATHERING AND INVESTIGATIONS

Powers to gather information

165 Authority's power to require information

(1)   The Authority may, by notice in writing given to an authorised person, require him—
   (a)   to provide specified information or information of a specified description; or
   (b)   to produce specified documents or documents of a specified description.

(2)   The information or documents must be provided or produced—
   (a)   before the end of such reasonable period as may be specified; and
   (b)   at such place as may be specified.

(3)   An officer who has written authorisation from the Authority to do so may require an authorised person without delay—
   (a)   to provide the officer with specified information or information of a specified description; or
   (b)   to produce to him specified documents or documents of a specified description.

(4)   This section applies only to information and documents reasonably required in connection with the exercise by the Authority of functions conferred on it by or under this Act.

(5)   The Authority may require any information provided under this section to be provided in such form as it may reasonably require.

(6)   The Authority may require—
   (a)   any information provided, whether in a document or otherwise, to be verified in such manner, or
   (b)   any document produced to be authenticated in such manner,
as it may reasonably require.

(7)   The powers conferred by subsections (1) and (3) may also be exercised to impose requirements on—
   (a)   a person who is connected with an authorised person;
   (b)   an operator, trustee or depositary of a scheme recognised under section 270 or 272 who is not an authorised person;
   (c)   a recognised investment exchange or recognised clearing house.

(8)   "Authorised person" includes a person who was at any time an authorised person but who has ceased to be an authorised person.

(9)   "Officer" means an officer of the Authority and includes a member of the Authority's staff or an agent of the Authority.

(10)   "Specified" means—
   (a)   in subsections (1) and (2), specified in the notice; and
   (b)   in subsection (3), specified in the authorisation.

(11)   For the purposes of this section, a person is connected with an authorised person ("A") if he is or has at any relevant time been—
   (a)   a member of A's group;
   (b)   a controller of A;
   (c)   any other member of a partnership of which A is a member; or
   (d)   in relation to A, a person mentioned in Part I of Schedule 15.

Commencement: 3 September 2001.
Transitional provisions: This section and ss 166, 167 are modified by the Financial Services and Markets Act 2000 (Transitional Provisions and Savings) (Civil Remedies, Discipline, Criminal Offences etc) (No 2) Order 2001, SI 2001/3083, arts 15–17 (made under ss 426, 427, 428(3)), so that the powers conferred by ss 165–167 are exercisable in respect of any person who was, before 1 December 2001, a regulated person but who is not, and never has been, an authorised person under this Act.
References: See paras 7.2, 7.3.

166 Reports by skilled persons

(1)   The Authority may, by notice in writing given to a person to whom subsection (2) applies, require him to provide the Authority with a report on any matter about which the Authority has required or could require the provision of information or production of documents under section 165.

(2)   This subsection applies to—
    (a)   an authorised person ("A"),
    (b)   any other member of A's group,
    (c)   a partnership of which A is a member, or
    (d)   a person who has at any relevant time been a person falling within paragraph (a), (b) or (c),

who is, or was at the relevant time, carrying on a business.

(3)   The Authority may require the report to be in such form as may be specified in the notice.

(4)   The person appointed to make a report required by subsection (1) must be a person—
    (a)   nominated or approved by the Authority; and
    (b)   appearing to the Authority to have the skills necessary to make a report on the matter concerned.

(5)   It is the duty of any person who is providing (or who at any time has provided) services to a person to whom subsection (2) applies in relation to a matter on which a report is required under subsection (1) to give a person appointed to provide such a report all such assistance as the appointed person may reasonably require.

(6)   The obligation imposed by subsection (5) is enforceable, on the application of the Authority, by an injunction or, in Scotland, by an order for specific performance under section 45 of the Court of Session Act 1988.

Commencement: 3 September 2001.
Transitional provisions: See the note to s 165 ante.
References: See paras 7.8–7.13.

Appointment of investigators

167 Appointment of persons to carry out general investigations

(1)   If it appears to the Authority or the Secretary of State ("the investigating authority") that there is good reason for doing so, the investigating authority may appoint one or more competent persons to conduct an investigation on its behalf into—
    (a)   the nature, conduct or state of the business of an authorised person or of an appointed representative;
    (b)   a particular aspect of that business; or
    (c)   the ownership or control of an authorised person.

(2)   If a person appointed under subsection (1) thinks it necessary for the purposes of his investigation, he may also investigate the business of a person who is or has at any relevant time been—

     (a)   a member of the group of which the person under investigation ("A") is part; or

     (b)   a partnership of which A is a member.

(3)   If a person appointed under subsection (1) decides to investigate the business of any person under subsection (2) he must give that person written notice of his decision.

(4)   The power conferred by this section may be exercised in relation to a former authorised person (or appointed representative) but only in relation to—

     (a)   business carried on at any time when he was an authorised person (or appointed representative); or

     (b)   the ownership or control of a former authorised person at any time when he was an authorised person.

(5)   "Business" includes any part of a business even if it does not consist of carrying on regulated activities.

Commencement: 3 September 2001.
Transitional provisions: See the note to s 165 ante.
References: See paras 7.15–7.18.

168 Appointment of persons to carry out investigations in particular cases

(1)   Subsection (3) applies if it appears to an investigating authority that there are circumstances suggesting that—

     (a)   a person may have contravened any regulation made under section 142; or

     (b)   a person may be guilty of an offence under section 177, 191, 346 or 398(1) or under Schedule 4.

(2)   Subsection (3) also applies if it appears to an investigating authority that there are circumstances suggesting that—

     (a)   an offence under section 24(1) or 397 or under Part V of the Criminal Justice Act 1993 may have been committed;

     (b)   there may have been a breach of the general prohibition;

     (c)   there may have been a contravention of section 21 or 238; or

     (d)   market abuse may have taken place.

(3)   The investigating authority may appoint one or more competent persons to conduct an investigation on its behalf.

(4)   Subsection (5) applies if it appears to the Authority that there are circumstances suggesting that—

     (a)   a person may have contravened section 20;

     (b)   a person may be guilty of an offence under prescribed regulations relating to money laundering;

     (c)   an authorised person may have contravened a rule made by the Authority;

     (d)   an individual may not be a fit and proper person to perform functions in relation to a regulated activity carried on by an authorised or exempt person;

     (e)   an individual may have performed or agreed to perform a function in breach of a prohibition order;

     (f)   an authorised or exempt person may have failed to comply with section 56(6);

(g) an authorised person may have failed to comply with section 59(1) or (2);

(h) a person in relation to whom the Authority has given its approval under section 59 may not be a fit and proper person to perform the function to which that approval relates; or

(i) a person may be guilty of misconduct for the purposes of section 66.

(5) The Authority may appoint one or more competent persons to conduct an investigation on its behalf.

(6) "Investigating authority" means the Authority or the Secretary of State.

Commencement: 25 February 2001 (sub-s (4)(b), for the purpose of making orders or regulations); 3 September 2001 (remainder).
Transitional provisions: See the Financial Services and Markets Act 2000 (Transitional Provisions and Savings) (Civil Remedies, Discipline, Criminal Offences etc) (No 2) Order 2001, SI 2001/3083, art 18 (made under ss 426, 427, 428(3)).
Note: The Money Laundering Regulations 1993, SI 1993/1933 have been prescribed for the purposes of sub-s (4)(b) above by the Financial Services and Markets Act 2000 (Regulations Relating to Money Laundering Regulations 2001, SI 2001/1819.
References: See paras 7.24–7.26.

Assistance to overseas regulators

169 Investigations etc in support of overseas regulator

(1) At the request of an overseas regulator, the Authority may—
   (a) exercise the power conferred by section 165; or
   (b) appoint one or more competent persons to investigate any matter.

(2) An investigator has the same powers as an investigator appointed under section 168(3) (as a result of subsection (1) of that section).

(3) If the request has been made by a competent authority in pursuance of any Community obligation the Authority must, in deciding whether or not to exercise its investigative power, consider whether its exercise is necessary to comply with any such obligation.

(4) In deciding whether or not to exercise its investigative power, the Authority may take into account in particular—
   (a) whether in the country or territory of the overseas regulator concerned, corresponding assistance would be given to a United Kingdom regulatory authority;
   (b) whether the case concerns the breach of a law, or other requirement, which has no close parallel in the United Kingdom or involves the assertion of a jurisdiction not recognised by the United Kingdom;
   (c) the seriousness of the case and its importance to persons in the United Kingdom;
   (d) whether it is otherwise appropriate in the public interest to give the assistance sought.

(5) The Authority may decide that it will not exercise its investigative power unless the overseas regulator undertakes to make such contribution towards the cost of its exercise as the Authority considers appropriate.

(6) Subsections (4) and (5) do not apply if the Authority considers that the exercise of its investigative power is necessary to comply with a Community obligation.

(7) If the Authority has appointed an investigator in response to a request from an overseas regulator, it may direct the investigator to permit a representative of that regulator to attend, and take part in, any interview conducted for the purposes of the investigation.

(8) A direction under subsection (7) is not to be given unless the Authority is satisfied that any information obtained by an overseas regulator as a result of the interview will be subject to safeguards equivalent to those contained in Part XXIII.

(9) The Authority must prepare a statement of its policy with respect to the conduct of interviews in relation to which a direction under subsection (7) has been given.

(10) The statement requires the approval of the Treasury.

(11) If the Treasury approve the statement, the Authority must publish it.

(12) No direction may be given under subsection (7) before the statement has been published.

(13) "Overseas regulator" has the same meaning as in section 195.

(14) "Investigative power" means one of the powers mentioned in subsection (1).

(15) "Investigator" means a person appointed under subsection (1)(b).

Commencement: 18 June 2001 (for the purpose of preparing a statement of policy as mentioned in sub-s (9) above); 3 September 2001 (remaining purposes).
References: See paras 7.33–7.40.

Conduct of investigations

170 Investigations: general

(1) This section applies if an investigating authority appoints one or more competent persons ("investigators") under section 167 or 168(3) or (5) to conduct an investigation on its behalf.

(2) The investigating authority must give written notice of the appointment of an investigator to the person who is the subject of the investigation ("the person under investigation").

(3) Subsections (2) and (9) do not apply if—
- (a) the investigator is appointed as a result of section 168(1) or (4) and the investigating authority believes that the notice required by subsection (2) or (9) would be likely to result in the investigation being frustrated; or
- (b) the investigator is appointed as a result of subsection (2) of section 168.

(4) A notice under subsection (2) must—
- (a) specify the provisions under which, and as a result of which, the investigator was appointed; and
- (b) state the reason for his appointment.

(5)   Nothing prevents the investigating authority from appointing a person who is a member of its staff as an investigator.

(6)   An investigator must make a report of his investigation to the investigating authority.

(7)   The investigating authority may, by a direction to an investigator, control—
    (a)   the scope of the investigation;
    (b)   the period during which the investigation is to be conducted;
    (c)   the conduct of the investigation; and
    (d)   the reporting of the investigation.

(8)   A direction may, in particular—
    (a)   confine the investigation to particular matters;
    (b)   extend the investigation to additional matters;
    (c)   require the investigator to discontinue the investigation or to take only such steps as are specified in the direction;
    (d)   require the investigator to make such interim reports as are so specified.

(9)   If there is a change in the scope or conduct of the investigation and, in the opinion of the investigating authority, the person subject to investigation is likely to be significantly prejudiced by not being made aware of it, that person must be given written notice of the change.

(10)   "Investigating authority", in relation to an investigator, means—
    (a)   the Authority, if the Authority appointed him;
    (b)   the Secretary of State, if the Secretary of State appointed him.

Commencement: 3 September 2001.
References: See paras 7.19–7.23.

171 Powers of persons appointed under section 167

(1)   An investigator may require the person who is the subject of the investigation ("the person under investigation") or any person connected with the person under investigation—
    (a)   to attend before the investigator at a specified time and place and answer questions; or
    (b)   otherwise to provide such information as the investigator may require.

(2)   An investigator may also require any person to produce at a specified time and place any specified documents or documents of a specified description.

(3)   A requirement under subsection (1) or (2) may be imposed only so far as the investigator concerned reasonably considers the question, provision of information or production of the document to be relevant to the purposes of the investigation.

(4)   For the purposes of this section and section 172, a person is connected with the person under investigation ("A") if he is or has at any relevant time been—
    (a)   a member of A's group;
    (b)   a controller of A;
    (c)   a partnership of which A is a member; or
    (d)   in relation to A, a person mentioned in Part I or II of Schedule 15.

(5)   "Investigator" means a person conducting an investigation under section 167.

(6)   "Specified" means specified in a notice in writing.

Commencement: 3 September 2001.
References: See paras 7.19–7.23.

172 Additional power of persons appointed as a result of section 168(1) or (4)

(1)   An investigator has the powers conferred by section 171.

(2)   An investigator may also require a person who is neither the subject of the investigation ("the person under investigation") nor a person connected with the person under investigation—

(a)   to attend before the investigator at a specified time and place and answer questions; or

(b)   otherwise to provide such information as the investigator may require for the purposes of the investigation.

(3)   A requirement may only be imposed under subsection (2) if the investigator is satisfied that the requirement is necessary or expedient for the purposes of the investigation.

(4)   "Investigator" means a person appointed as a result of subsection (1) or (4) of section 168.

(5)   "Specified" means specified in a notice in writing.

Commencement: 3 September 2001.
References: See para 7.28.

173 Powers of persons appointed as a result of section 168(2)

(1)   Subsections (2) to (4) apply if an investigator considers that any person ("A") is or may be able to give information which is or may be relevant to the investigation.

(2)   The investigator may require A—

(a)   to attend before him at a specified time and place and answer questions; or

(b)   otherwise to provide such information as he may require for the purposes of the investigation.

(3)   The investigator may also require A to produce at a specified time and place any specified documents or documents of a specified description which appear to the investigator to relate to any matter relevant to the investigation.

(4)   The investigator may also otherwise require A to give him all assistance in connection with the investigation which A is reasonably able to give.

(5)   "Investigator" means a person appointed under subsection (3) of section 168 (as a result of subsection (2) of that section).

Commencement: 3 September 2001.
References: See para 7.29.

174 Admissibility of statements made to investigators

(1)   A statement made to an investigator by a person in compliance with an information requirement is admissible in evidence in any proceedings, so long as it also complies with any requirements governing the admissibility of evidence in the circumstances in question.

(2)   But in criminal proceedings in which that person is charged with an offence to which this subsection applies or in proceedings in relation to action to be taken against that person under section 123—

> (a)   no evidence relating to the statement may be adduced, and
> (b)   no question relating to it may be asked,

by or on behalf of the prosecution or (as the case may be) the Authority, unless evidence relating to it is adduced, or a question relating to it is asked, in the proceedings by or on behalf of that person.

(3)   Subsection (2) applies to any offence other than one—

> (a)   under section 177(4) or 398;
> (b)   under section 5 of the Perjury Act 1911 (false statements made otherwise than on oath);
> (c)   under section 44(2) of the Criminal Law (Consolidation) (Scotland) Act 1995 (false statements made otherwise than on oath); or
> (d)   under Article 10 of the Perjury (Northern Ireland) Order 1979.

(4)   "Investigator" means a person appointed under section 167 or 168(3) or (5).

(5)   "Information requirement" means a requirement imposed by an investigator under section 171, 172, 173 or 175.

Commencement: 3 September 2001.
References: See paras 7.30, 7.31.

175 Information and documents: supplemental provisions

(1)   If the Authority or an investigator has power under this Part to require a person to produce a document but it appears that the document is in the possession of a third person, that power may be exercised in relation to the third person.

(2)   If a document is produced in response to a requirement imposed under this Part, the person to whom it is produced may—

> (a)   take copies or extracts from the document; or
> (b)   require the person producing the document, or any relevant person, to provide an explanation of the document.

(3)   If a person who is required under this Part to produce a document fails to do so, the Authority or an investigator may require him to state, to the best of his knowledge and belief, where the document is.

(4)   A lawyer may be required under this Part to furnish the name and address of his client.

(5)   No person may be required under this Part to disclose information or produce a document in respect of which he owes an obligation of confidence by virtue of carrying on the business of banking unless—

> (a)   he is the person under investigation or a member of that person's group;

> (b) the person to whom the obligation of confidence is owed is the person under investigation or a member of that person's group;
> (c) the person to whom the obligation of confidence is owed consents to the disclosure or production; or
> (d) the imposing on him of a requirement with respect to such information or document has been specifically authorised by the investigating authority.

(6) If a person claims a lien on a document, its production under this Part does not affect the lien.

(7) "Relevant person", in relation to a person who is required to produce a document, means a person who—

> (a) has been or is or is proposed to be a director or controller of that person;
> (b) has been or is an auditor of that person;
> (c) has been or is an actuary, accountant or lawyer appointed or instructed by that person; or
> (d) has been or is an employee of that person.

(8) "Investigator" means a person appointed under section 167 or 168(3) or (5).

Commencement: 3 September 2001.
Open-ended investment companies: Sub-ss (2)–(4), (6) above have effect as if the Open-Ended Investment Companies Regulations 2001, SI 2001/1228, reg 30 (made under ss 262, 428(3)) was contained in Pt XI (ss 165–177 and Sch 15) of this Act; see reg 30(6) of the 2001 Regulations.
References: See para 7.32.

---

176 Entry of premises under warrant

(1) A justice of the peace may issue a warrant under this section if satisfied on information on oath given by or on behalf of the Secretary of State, the Authority or an investigator that there are reasonable grounds for believing that the first, second or third set of conditions is satisfied.

(2) The first set of conditions is—

> (a) that a person on whom an information requirement has been imposed has failed (wholly or in part) to comply with it; and
> (b) that on the premises specified in the warrant—
>   (i) there are documents which have been required; or
>   (ii) there is information which has been required.

(3) The second set of conditions is—

> (a) that the premises specified in the warrant are premises of an authorised person or an appointed representative;
> (b) that there are on the premises documents or information in relation to which an information requirement could be imposed; and
> (c) that if such a requirement were to be imposed—
>   (i) it would not be complied with; or
>   (ii) the documents or information to which it related would be removed, tampered with or destroyed.

(4) The third set of conditions is—

> (a) that an offence mentioned in section 168 for which the maximum sentence on conviction on indictment is two years or more has been (or is being) committed by any person;

    (b)   that there are on the premises specified in the warrant documents or information relevant to whether that offence has been (or is being) committed;

    (c)   that an information requirement could be imposed in relation to those documents or information; and

    (d)   that if such a requirement were to be imposed—

        (i)   it would not be complied with; or

        (ii)   the documents or information to which it related would be removed, tampered with or destroyed.

(5)   A warrant under this section shall authorise a constable—

    (a)   to enter the premises specified in the warrant;

    (b)   to search the premises and take possession of any documents or information appearing to be documents or information of a kind in respect of which a warrant under this section was issued ("the relevant kind") or to take, in relation to any such documents or information, any other steps which may appear to be necessary for preserving them or preventing interference with them;

    (c)   to take copies of, or extracts from, any documents or information appearing to be of the relevant kind;

    (d)   to require any person on the premises to provide an explanation of any document or information appearing to be of the relevant kind or to state where it may be found; and

    (e)   to use such force as may be reasonably necessary.

(6)   In England and Wales, sections 15(5) to (8) and section 16 of the Police and Criminal Evidence Act 1984 (execution of search warrants and safeguards) apply to warrants issued under this section.

(7)   In Northern Ireland, Articles 17(5) to (8) and 18 of the Police and Criminal Evidence (Northern Ireland) Order 1989 apply to warrants issued under this section.

(8)   Any document of which possession is taken under this section may be retained—

    (a)   for a period of three months; or

    (b)   if within that period proceedings to which the document is relevant are commenced against any person for any criminal offence, until the conclusion of those proceedings.

(9)   In the application of this section to Scotland—

    (a)   for the references to a justice of the peace substitute references to a justice of the peace or a sheriff; and

    (b)   for the references to information on oath substitute references to evidence on oath.

(10)   "Investigator" means a person appointed under section 167 or 168(3) or (5).

(11)   "Information requirement" means a requirement imposed—

    (a)   by the Authority under section 165 or 175; or

    (b)   by an investigator under section 171, 172, 173 or 175.

Commencement: 3 September 2001.
References: See paras 7.44–7.47.

Offences

177 Offences

(1)   If a person other than the investigator ("the defaulter") fails to comply with a requirement imposed on him under this Part the person imposing the requirement may certify that fact in writing to the court.

(2)   If the court is satisfied that the defaulter failed without reasonable excuse to comply with the requirement, it may deal with the defaulter (and in the case of a body corporate, any director or officer) as if he were in contempt[; and "officer", in relation to a limited liability partnership, means a member of the limited liability partnership].

(3)   A person who knows or suspects that an investigation is being or is likely to be conducted under this Part is guilty of an offence if—

  (a)   he falsifies, conceals, destroys or otherwise disposes of a document which he knows or suspects is or would be relevant to such an investigation, or

  (b)   he causes or permits the falsification, concealment, destruction or disposal of such a document,

unless he shows that he had no intention of concealing facts disclosed by the documents from the investigator.

(4)   A person who, in purported compliance with a requirement imposed on him under this Part—

  (a)   provides information which he knows to be false or misleading in a material particular, or

  (b)   recklessly provides information which is false or misleading in a material particular,

is guilty of an offence.

(5)   A person guilty of an offence under subsection (3) or (4) is liable—

  (a)   on summary conviction, to imprisonment for a term not exceeding six months or a fine not exceeding the statutory maximum, or both;

  (b)   on conviction on indictment, to imprisonment for a term not exceeding two years or a fine, or both.

(6)   Any person who intentionally obstructs the exercise of any rights conferred by a warrant under section 176 is guilty of an offence and liable on summary conviction to imprisonment for a term not exceeding three months or a fine not exceeding level 5 on the standard scale, or both.

(7)   "Court" means—

  (a)   the High Court;

  (b)   in Scotland, the Court of Session.

Commencement: 3 September 2001.
Amendments: Sub-s (2): words in square brackets added by the Limited Liability Partnerships Regulations 2001, SI 2001/1090, reg 9, Sch 5, para 21, as from 6 April 2001.
Open-ended investment companies: This section has effect as if the Open-Ended Investment Companies Regulations 2001, SI 2001/1228, reg 30 (made under ss 262, 428(3)) was contained in Pt XI (ss 165–177 and Sch 15) of this Act; see reg 30(6) of the 2001 Regulations.
References: See paras 7.41–7.43.

PART XII
CONTROL OVER AUTHORISED PERSONS

Transitional provisions: See the Financial Services and Markets Act 2000 (Transitional Provisions) (Controllers) Order 2001, SI 2001/2637, as amended by SI 2001/3650 (made under ss 426–428).

Notice of control

178 Obligation to notify the Authority

(1)   If a step which a person proposes to take would result in his acquiring—
    (a)   control over a UK authorised person,
    (b)   an additional kind of control over a UK authorised person, or
    (c)   an increase in a relevant kind of control which he already has over a UK authorised person,

he must notify the Authority of his proposal.

(2)   A person who, without himself taking any such step, acquires any such control or additional or increased control must notify the Authority before the end of the period of 14 days beginning with the day on which he first becomes aware that he has acquired it.

(3)   A person who is under the duty to notify the Authority imposed by subsection (1) must also give notice to the Authority on acquiring, or increasing, the control in question.

(4)   In this Part "UK authorised person" means an authorised person who—
    (a)   is a body incorporated in, or an unincorporated association formed under the law of, any part of the United Kingdom; and
    (b)   is not a person authorised as a result of paragraph 1 of Schedule 5.

(5)   A notice under subsection (1) or (2) is referred to in this Part as "a notice of control".

Commencement: 1 December 2001.
References: See paras 4.118–4.121.

Acquiring, increasing and reducing control

179 Acquiring control

(1)   For the purposes of this Part, a person ("the acquirer") acquires control over a UK authorised person ("A") on first falling within any of the cases in subsection (2).

(2)   The cases are where the acquirer—
    (a)   holds 10% or more of the shares in A;
    (b)   is able to exercise significant influence over the management of A by virtue of his shareholding in A;
    (c)   holds 10% or more of the shares in a parent undertaking ("P") of A;
    (d)   is able to exercise significant influence over the management of P by virtue of his shareholding in P;
    (e)   is entitled to exercise, or control the exercise of, 10% or more of the voting power in A;

(f) is able to exercise significant influence over the management of A by virtue of his voting power in A;

(g) is entitled to exercise, or control the exercise of, 10% or more of the voting power in P; or

(h) is able to exercise significant influence over the management of P by virtue of his voting power in P.

(3) In subsection (2) "the acquirer" means—

(a) the acquirer;

(b) any of the acquirer's associates; or

(c) the acquirer and any of his associates.

(4) For the purposes of this Part, each of the following is to be regarded as a kind of control—

(a) control arising as a result of the holding of shares in A;

(b) control arising as a result of the holding of shares in P;

(c) control arising as a result of the entitlement to exercise, or control the exercise of, voting power in A;

(d) control arising as a result of the entitlement to exercise, or control the exercise of, voting power in P.

(5) For the purposes of this section and sections 180 and 181, "associate", "shares" and "voting power" have the same meaning as in section 422.

Commencement: 1 December 2001.
References: See para 4.122.

180 Increasing control

(1) For the purposes of this Part, a controller of a person ("A") who is a UK authorised person increases his control over A if—

(a) the percentage of shares held by the controller in A increases by any of the steps mentioned in subsection (2);

(b) the percentage of shares held by the controller in a parent undertaking ("P") of A increases by any of the steps mentioned in subsection (2);

(c) the percentage of voting power which the controller is entitled to exercise, or control the exercise of, in A increases by any of the steps mentioned in subsection (2);

(d) the percentage of voting power which the controller is entitled to exercise, or control the exercise of, in P increases by any of the steps mentioned in subsection (2); or

(e) the controller becomes a parent undertaking of A.

(2) The steps are—

(a) from below 10% to 10% or more but less than 20%;

(b) from below 20% to 20% or more but less than 33%;

(c) from below 33% to 33% or more but less than 50%;

(d) from below 50% to 50% or more.

(3) In paragraphs (a) to (d) of subsection (1) "the controller" means—

(a) the controller;

(b) any of the controller's associates; or

(c) the controller and any of his associates.

(4)   In the rest of this Part "acquiring control" or "having control" includes—
    (a)   acquiring or having an additional kind of control; or
    (b)   acquiring an increase in a relevant kind of control, or having increased control of a relevant kind.

Commencement: 1 December 2001.
References: See para 4.123.

181 Reducing control

(1)   For the purposes of this Part, a controller of a person ("A") who is a UK authorised person reduces his control over A if—
    (a)   the percentage of shares held by the controller in A decreases by any of the steps mentioned in subsection (2),
    (b)   the percentage of shares held by the controller in a parent undertaking ("P") of A decreases by any of the steps mentioned in subsection (2),
    (c)   the percentage of voting power which the controller is entitled to exercise, or control the exercise of, in A decreases by any of the steps mentioned in subsection (2),
    (d)   the percentage of voting power which the controller is entitled to exercise, or control the exercise of, in P decreases by any of the steps mentioned in subsection (2), or
    (e)   the controller ceases to be a parent undertaking of A,
unless the controller ceases to have the kind of control concerned over A as a result.

(2)   The steps are—
    (a)   from 50% or more to 33% or more but less than 50%;
    (b)   from 33% or more to 20% or more but less than 33%;
    (c)   from 20% or more to 10% or more but less than 20%;
    (d)   from 10% or more to less than 10%.

(3)   In paragraphs (a) to (d) of subsection (1) "the controller" means—
    (a)   the controller;
    (b)   any of the controller's associates; or
    (c)   the controller and any of his associates.

Commencement: 1 December 2001.
References: See para 4.124.

Acquiring or increasing control: procedure

182 Notification

(1)   A notice of control must—
    (a)   be given to the Authority in writing; and
    (b)   include such information and be accompanied by such documents as the Authority may reasonably require.

(2)   The Authority may require the person giving a notice of control to provide such additional information or documents as it reasonably considers necessary in order to enable it to determine what action it is to take in response to the notice.

(3)   Different requirements may be imposed in different circumstances.

Commencement: 18 June 2001 (for the purpose of imposing requirements as mentioned in sub-s (1)(b) above); 1 December 2001 (remaining purposes).
References: See para 4.125.

183 Duty of Authority in relation to notice of control

(1)   The Authority must, before the end of the period of three months beginning with the date on which it receives a notice of control ("the period for consideration"), determine whether—

(a)   to approve of the person concerned having the control to which the notice relates; or

(b)   to serve a warning notice under subsection (3) or section 185(3).

(2)   Before doing so, the Authority must comply with such requirements as to consultation with competent authorities outside the United Kingdom as may be prescribed.

(3)   If the Authority proposes to give the person concerned a notice of objection under section 186(1), it must give him a warning notice.

Commencement: 25 February 2001 (sub-s (2), for the purpose of making orders or regulations); 1 December 2001 (remainder).
Regulations: The Financial Services and Markets Act 2000 (Consultation with Competent Authorities) Regulations 2001, SI 2001/2509, as amended by SI 2003/2066.
References: See paras 4.126, 4.127.

184 Approval of acquisition of control

(1)   If the Authority decides to approve of the person concerned having the control to which the notice relates it must notify that person of its approval in writing without delay.

(2)   If the Authority fails to comply with subsection (1) of section 183 it is to be treated as having given its approval and notified the person concerned at the end of the period fixed by that subsection.

(3)   The Authority's approval remains effective only if the person to whom it relates acquires the control in question—

(a)   before the end of such period as may be specified in the notice; or

(b)   if no period is specified, before the end of the period of one year beginning with the date—

(i)   of the notice of approval;

(ii)   on which the Authority is treated as having given approval under subsection (2); or

(iii)   of a decision on a reference to the Tribunal which results in the person concerned receiving approval.

Commencement: 1 December 2001.
References: See paras 4.128, 4.129.

185 Conditions attached to approval

(1)   The Authority's approval under section 184 may be given unconditionally or subject to such conditions as the Authority considers appropriate.

(2)   In imposing any conditions, the Authority must have regard to its duty under section 41.

(3)   If the Authority proposes to impose conditions on a person it must give him a warning notice.

(4)   If the Authority decides to impose conditions on a person it must give him a decision notice.

(5)   A person who is subject to a condition imposed under this section may apply to the Authority—
>   (a)   for the condition to be varied; or
>   (b)   for the condition to be cancelled.

(6)   The Authority may, on its own initiative, cancel a condition imposed under this section.

(7)   If the Authority has given its approval to a person subject to a condition, he may refer to the Tribunal—
>   (a)   the imposition of the condition; or
>   (b)   the Authority's decision to refuse an application made by him under subsection (5).

Commencement: 1 December 2001.
References: See paras 4.130–4.132.

186 Objection to acquisition of control

(1)   On considering a notice of control, the Authority may give a decision notice under this section to the person acquiring control ("the acquirer") unless it is satisfied that the approval requirements are met.

(2)   The approval requirements are that—
>   (a)   the acquirer is a fit and proper person to have the control over the authorised person that he has or would have if he acquired the control in question; and
>   (b)   the interests of consumers would not be threatened by the acquirer's control or by his acquiring that control.

(3)   In deciding whether the approval requirements are met, the Authority must have regard, in relation to the control that the acquirer—
>   (a)   has over the authorised person concerned ("A"), or
>   (b)   will have over A if the proposal to which the notice of control relates is carried into effect,

to its duty under section 41 in relation to each regulated activity carried on by A.

(4)   If the Authority gives a notice under this section but considers that the approval requirements would be met if the person to whom a notice is given were to take, or refrain from taking, a particular step, the notice must identify that step.

(5)   A person to whom a notice under this section is given may refer the matter to the Tribunal.

(6)   "Consumers" means persons who are consumers for the purposes of section 138.

Commencement: 1 December 2001.
References: See paras 4.133–4.138.

187 Objection to existing control

(1)   If the Authority is not satisfied that the approval requirements are met, it may give a decision notice under this section to a person if he has failed to comply with a duty to notify imposed by section 178.

(2)   If the failure relates to subsection (1) or (2) of that section, the Authority may (instead of giving a notice under subsection (1)) approve the acquisition of the control in question by the person concerned as if he had given it a notice of control.

(3)   The Authority may also give a decision notice under this section to a person who is a controller of a UK authorised person if the Authority becomes aware of matters as a result of which it is satisfied that—

(a)   the approval requirements are not met with respect to the controller; or

(b)   a condition imposed under section 185 required that person to do (or refrain from doing) a particular thing and the condition has been breached as a result of his failing to do (or doing) that thing.

(4)   A person to whom a notice under this section is given may refer the matter to the Tribunal.

(5)   "Approval requirements" has the same meaning as in section 186.

Commencement: 1 December 2001.
References: See paras 4.136–4.138.

188 Notices of objection under section 187: procedure

(1)   If the Authority proposes to give a notice of objection to a person under section 187, it must give him a warning notice.

(2)   Before doing so, the Authority must comply with such requirements as to consultation with competent authorities outside the United Kingdom as may be prescribed.

(3)   If the Authority decides to give a warning notice under this section, it must do so before the end of the period of three months beginning—

(a)   in the case of a notice to be given under section 187(1), with the date on which it became aware of the failure to comply with the duty in question;

(b)   in the case of a notice to be given under section 187(3), with the date on which it became aware of the matters in question.

(4)   The Authority may require the person concerned to provide such additional information or documents as it considers reasonable.

(5)   Different requirements may be imposed in different circumstances.

(6)   In this Part "notice of objection" means a notice under section 186 or 187.

Commencement: 25 February 2001 (sub-s (2), for the purpose of making orders or regulations); 1 December 2001 (remainder).
Regulations: The Financial Services and Markets Act 2000 (Consultation with Competent Authorities) Regulations 2001, SI 2001/2509, as amended by SI 2003/2066.
References: See paras 4.139–4.141.

Improperly acquired shares

189 Improperly acquired shares

(1)   The powers conferred by this section are exercisable if a person has acquired, or has continued to hold, any shares in contravention of—

    (a)   a notice of objection; or

    (b)   a condition imposed on the Authority's approval.

(2)   The Authority may by notice in writing served on the person concerned ("a restriction notice") direct that any such shares which are specified in the notice are, until further notice, subject to one or more of the following restrictions—

    (a)   a transfer of (or agreement to transfer) those shares, or in the case of unissued shares any transfer of (or agreement to transfer) the right to be issued with them, is void;

    (b)   no voting rights are to be exercisable in respect of the shares;

    (c)   no further shares are to be issued in right of them or in pursuance of any offer made to their holder;

    (d)   except in a liquidation, no payment is to be made of any sums due from the body corporate on the shares, whether in respect of capital or otherwise.

(3)   The court may, on the application of the Authority, order the sale of any shares to which this section applies and, if they are for the time being subject to any restriction under subsection (2), that they are to cease to be subject to that restriction.

(4)   No order may be made under subsection (3)—

    (a)   until the end of the period within which a reference may be made to the Tribunal in respect of the notice of objection; and

    (b)   if a reference is made, until the matter has been determined or the reference withdrawn.

(5)   If an order has been made under subsection (3), the court may, on the application of the Authority, make such further order relating to the sale or transfer of the shares as it thinks fit.

(6)   If shares are sold in pursuance of an order under this section, the proceeds of sale, less the costs of the sale, must be paid into court for the benefit of the persons beneficially interested in them; and any such person may apply to the court for the whole or part of the proceeds to be paid to him.

(7)   This section applies—

    (a)   in the case of an acquirer falling within section 178(1), to all the shares—

        (i)   in the authorised person which the acquirer has acquired;

        (ii)   which are held by him or an associate of his; and

        (iii)   which were not so held immediately before he became a person with control over the authorised person;

    (b)   in the case of an acquirer falling within section 178(2), to all the shares held by him or an associate of his at the time when he first became aware that he had acquired control over the authorised person; and

    (c)   to all the shares in an undertaking ("C")—

        (i)   which are held by the acquirer or an associate of his, and

   (ii) which were not so held before he became a person with control in relation to the authorised person,

where C is the undertaking in which shares were acquired by the acquirer (or an associate of his) and, as a result, he became a person with control in relation to that authorised person.

(8) A copy of the restriction notice must be served on—

  (a) the authorised person to whose shares it relates; and

  (b) if it relates to shares held by an associate of that authorised person, on that associate.

(9) The jurisdiction conferred by this section may be exercised by the High Court and the Court of Session.

Commencement: 1 December 2001.
References: See paras 4.142–4.146.

Reducing control: procedure

190 Notification

(1) If a step which a controller of a UK authorised person proposes to take would result in his—

  (a) ceasing to have control of a relevant kind over the authorised person, or

  (b) reducing a relevant kind of control over that person,

he must notify the Authority of his proposal.

(2) A controller of a UK authorised person who, without himself taking any such step, ceases to have that control or reduces that control must notify the Authority before the end of the period of 14 days beginning with the day on which he first becomes aware that—

  (a) he has ceased to have the control in question; or

  (b) he has reduced that control.

(3) A person who is under the duty to notify the Authority imposed by subsection (1) must also give a notice to the Authority—

  (a) on ceasing to have the control in question; or

  (b) on reducing that control.

(4) A notice under this section must—

  (a) be given to the Authority in writing; and

  (b) include details of the extent of the control (if any) which the person concerned will retain (or still retains) over the authorised person concerned.

Commencement: 1 December 2001.
References: See paras 4.147, 4.148.

Offences

191 Offences under this Part

(1) A person who fails to comply with the duty to notify the Authority imposed on him by section 178(1) or 190(1) is guilty of an offence.

(2)   A person who fails to comply with the duty to notify the Authority imposed on him by section 178(2) or 190(2) is guilty of an offence.

(3)   If a person who has given a notice of control to the Authority carries out the proposal to which the notice relates, he is guilty of an offence if—

(a)   the period of three months beginning with the date on which the Authority received the notice is still running; and

(b)   the Authority has not responded to the notice by either giving its approval or giving him a warning notice under section 183(3) or 185(3).

(4)   A person to whom the Authority has given a warning notice under section 183(3) is guilty of an offence if he carries out the proposal to which the notice relates before the Authority has decided whether to give him a notice of objection.

(5)   A person to whom a notice of objection has been given is guilty of an offence if he acquires the control to which the notice applies at a time when the notice is still in force.

(6)   A person guilty of an offence under subsection (1), (2), (3) or (4) is liable on summary conviction to a fine not exceeding level 5 on the standard scale.

(7)   A person guilty of an offence under subsection (5) is liable—

(a)   on summary conviction, to a fine not exceeding the statutory maximum; and

(b)   on conviction on indictment, to imprisonment for a term not exceeding two years or a fine, or both.

(8)   A person guilty of an offence under subsection (5) is also liable on summary conviction to a fine not exceeding one tenth of the statutory maximum for each day on which the offence has continued.

(9)   It is a defence for a person charged with an offence under subsection (1) to show that he had, at the time of the alleged offence, no knowledge of the act or circumstances by virtue of which the duty to notify the Authority arose.

(10) If a person—

(a)   was under the duty to notify the Authority imposed by section 178(1) or 190(1) but had no knowledge of the act or circumstances by virtue of which that duty arose, but

(b)   subsequently becomes aware of that act or those circumstances,

he must notify the Authority before the end of the period of 14 days beginning with the day on which he first became so aware.

(11) A person who fails to comply with the duty to notify the Authority imposed by subsection (10) is guilty of an offence and liable, on summary conviction, to a fine not exceeding level 5 on the standard scale.

Commencement: 1 December 2001.
References: See paras 4.149–4.153.

Miscellaneous

192 Power to change definitions of control etc

The Treasury may by order—

(a)   provide for exemptions from the obligations to notify imposed by sections 178 and 190;

(b)   amend section 179 by varying, or removing, any of the cases in which a person is treated as having control over a UK authorised person or by adding a case;

(c)   amend section 180 by varying, or removing, any of the cases in which a person is treated as increasing control over a UK authorised person or by adding a case;

(d)   amend section 181 by varying, or removing, any of the cases in which a person is treated as reducing his control over a UK authorised person or by adding a case;

(e)   amend section 422 by varying, or removing, any of the cases in which a person is treated as being a controller of a person or by adding a case.

Commencement: 1 December 2001 (paras (b)–(e)); 25 February 2001 (remainder).
Orders: The Financial Services and Markets Act 2000 (Controllers) (Exemption) Order 2001, SI 2001/2638; the Financial Services and Markets Act 2000 (Controllers) (Exemption) (No 2) Order 2001, SI 2001/3338; the Financial Services and Markets Act 2000 (Regulated Activities) (Amendment) (No 2) Order 2003, SI 2003/1476.
References: See para 4.118.

PART XIII
INCOMING FIRMS: INTERVENTION BY AUTHORITY

Transitional provisions: The Financial Services and Markets Act 2000 (Transitional Provisions) (Authorised Persons etc) Order 2001, SI 2001/2636, Pt III (made under ss 426–428), provides that restrictions and prohibitions imposed under provisions of the previous regulatory regimes on authorised persons are to have effect as from 1 December 2001 as if they were requirements imposed under s 196 (in relation to persons with a permission under Sch 3 or 4). As to the restrictions and prohibitions to which Pt III of the 2001 Order applies, see the second paragraph of the note "Transitional provisions" to Pt IV of this Act.

Interpretation

193 Interpretation of this Part

(1)   In this Part—
"additional procedure" means the procedure described in section 199;
"incoming firm" means—

(a)   an EEA firm which is exercising, or has exercised, its right to carry on a regulated activity in the United Kingdom in accordance with Schedule 3; or

(b)   a Treaty firm which is exercising, or has exercised, its right to carry on a regulated activity in the United Kingdom in accordance with Schedule 4; and

"power of intervention" means the power conferred on the Authority by section 196.

(2)   In relation to an incoming firm which is an EEA firm, expressions used in this Part and in Schedule 3 have the same meaning in this Part as they have in that Schedule.

Commencement: 3 September 2001.
References: See para 8.50.

194 General grounds on which power of intervention is exercisable

(1)   The Authority may exercise its power of intervention in respect of an incoming firm if it appears to it that—
    (a)   the firm has contravened, or is likely to contravene, a requirement which is imposed on it by or under this Act (in a case where the Authority is responsible for enforcing compliance in the United Kingdom);
    (b)   the firm has, in purported compliance with any requirement imposed by or under this Act, knowingly or recklessly given the Authority information which is false or misleading in a material particular; or
    (c)   it is desirable to exercise the power in order to protect the interests of actual or potential customers.

(2)   Subsection (3) applies to an incoming EEA firm falling within sub-paragraph (a) or (b) of paragraph 5 of Schedule 3 which is exercising an EEA right to carry on any Consumer Credit Act business in the United Kingdom.

(3)   The Authority may exercise its power of intervention in respect of the firm if [the Office of Fair Trading] has informed the Authority that—
    (a)   the firm,
    (b)   any of the firm's employees, agents or associates (whether past or present), or
    (c)   if the firm is a body corporate, a controller of the firm or an associate of such a controller,

has done any of the things specified in paragraphs (a) to (d) of section 25(2) of the Consumer Credit Act 1974.

(4)   "Associate", "Consumer Credit Act business" and "controller" have the same meaning as in section 203.

Commencement: 3 September 2001 (for the purposes of requirements (as mentioned in s 196) taking effect not sooner than the day on which s 19 of this Act comes into force); 1 December 2001 (remaining purposes).
Amendments: Sub-s (3): words in square brackets substituted by the Enterprise Act 2002, s 278(1), Sch 25, para 40(1), (6), as from 1 April 2003.
References: See paras 8.50, 8.51.

---

195 Exercise of power in support of overseas regulator

(1)   The Authority may exercise its power of intervention in respect of an incoming firm at the request of, or for the purpose of assisting, an overseas regulator.

(2)   Subsection (1) applies whether or not the Authority's power of intervention is also exercisable as a result of section 194.

(3)   "An overseas regulator" means an authority in a country or territory outside the United Kingdom—
    (a)   which is a home state regulator; or
    (b)   which exercises any function of a kind mentioned in subsection (4).

(4)   The functions are—
    (a)   a function corresponding to any function of the Authority under this Act;

- (b) a function corresponding to any function exercised by the competent authority under Part VI in relation to the listing of shares;
- (c) a function corresponding to any function exercised by the Secretary of State under the Companies Act 1985;
- (d) a function in connection with—
  - (i) the investigation of conduct of the kind prohibited by Part V of the Criminal Justice Act 1993 (insider dealing); or
  - (ii) the enforcement of rules (whether or not having the force of law) relating to such conduct;
- (e) a function prescribed by regulations made for the purposes of this subsection which, in the opinion of the Treasury, relates to companies or financial services.

(5) If

- (a) a request to the Authority for the exercise of its power of intervention has been made by a home state regulator in pursuance of a Community obligation, or
- (b) a home state regulator has notified the Authority that an EEA firm's EEA authorisation has been withdrawn,

the Authority must, in deciding whether or not to exercise its power of intervention, consider whether exercising it is necessary in order to comply with a Community obligation.

(6) In deciding in any case in which the Authority does not consider that the exercise of its power of intervention is necessary in order to comply with a Community obligation, it may take into account in particular—

- (a) whether in the country or territory of the overseas regulator concerned, corresponding assistance would be given to a United Kingdom regulatory authority;
- (b) whether the case concerns the breach of a law, or other requirement, which has no close parallel in the United Kingdom or involves the assertion of a jurisdiction not recognised by the United Kingdom;
- (c) the seriousness of the case and its importance to persons in the United Kingdom;
- (d) whether it is otherwise appropriate in the public interest to give the assistance sought.

(7) The Authority may decide not to exercise its power of intervention, in response to a request, unless the regulator concerned undertakes to make such contribution to the cost of its exercise as the Authority considers appropriate.

(8) Subsection (7) does not apply if the Authority decides that it is necessary for it to exercise its power of intervention in order to comply with a Community obligation.

Commencement: 3 September 2001 (for the purposes of requirements (as mentioned in s 196) taking effect not sooner than the day on which s 19 of this Act comes into force); 1 December 2001 (remaining purposes).
References: See paras 8.52, 8.53.

196 The power of intervention

If the Authority is entitled to exercise its power of intervention in respect of an incoming firm under this Part, it may impose any requirement in relation to the firm which it could impose if—

    (a)   the firm's permission was a Part IV permission; and

    (b)   the Authority was entitled to exercise its power under that Part to vary that permission.

Commencement: 3 September 2001 (for the purposes of requirements (as mentioned in s 196) taking effect not sooner than the day on which s 19 of this Act comes into force); 1 December 2001 (remaining purposes).
References: See para 8.54.

Exercise of power of intervention

197 Procedure on exercise of power of intervention

(1)   A requirement takes effect—

    (a)   immediately, if the notice given under subsection (3) states that that is the case;

    (b)   on such date as may be specified in the notice; or

    (c)   if no date is specified in the notice, when the matter to which it relates is no longer open to review.

(2)   A requirement may be expressed to take effect immediately (or on a specified date) only if the Authority, having regard to the ground on which it is exercising its power of intervention, considers that it is necessary for the requirement to take effect immediately (or on that date).

(3)   If the Authority proposes to impose a requirement under section 196 on an incoming firm, or imposes such a requirement with immediate effect, it must give the firm written notice.

(4)   The notice must—

    (a)   give details of the requirement;

    (b)   inform the firm of when the requirement takes effect;

    (c)   state the Authority's reasons for imposing the requirement and for its determination as to when the requirement takes effect;

    (d)   inform the firm that it may make representations to the Authority within such period as may be specified in the notice (whether or not it has referred the matter to the Tribunal); and

    (e)   inform it of its right to refer the matter to the Tribunal.

(5)   The Authority may extend the period allowed under the notice for making representations.

(6)   If, having considered any representations made by the firm, the Authority decides—

    (a)   to impose the requirement proposed, or

    (b)   if it has been imposed, not to rescind the requirement,

it must give it written notice.

(7)   If, having considered any representations made by the firm, the Authority decides—

    (a)   not to impose the requirement proposed,

    (b)   to impose a different requirement from that proposed, or

    (c)   to rescind a requirement which has effect,

it must give it written notice.

(8)   A notice given under subsection (6) must inform the firm of its right to refer the matter to the Tribunal.

(9)   A notice under subsection (7)(b) must comply with subsection (4).

(10) If a notice informs a person of his right to refer a matter to the Tribunal, it must give an indication of the procedure on such a reference.

Commencement: 3 September 2001 (for the purposes of requirements (as mentioned in s 196) taking effect not sooner than the day on which s 19 of this Act comes into force); 1 December 2001 (remaining purposes).
References: See paras 8.54, 8.55.

198   Power to apply to court for injunction in respect of certain overseas insurance companies

(1)   This section applies if the Authority has received a request made in respect of an incoming EEA firm in accordance with—
  (a)   Article 20.5 of the first non-life insurance directive; or
  (b)   Article 24.5 of the first life insurance directive.

(2)   The court may, on an application made to it by the Authority with respect to the firm, grant an injunction restraining (or in Scotland an interdict prohibiting) the firm disposing of or otherwise dealing with any of its assets.

(3)   If the court grants an injunction, it may by subsequent orders make provision for such incidental, consequential and supplementary matters as it considers necessary to enable the Authority to perform any of its functions under this Act.

(4)   "The court" means—
  (a)   the High Court; or
  (b)   in Scotland, the Court of Session.

Commencement: 1 December 2001.
References: See para 8.56.

199   Additional procedure for EEA firms in certain cases

(1)   This section applies if it appears to the Authority that its power of intervention is exercisable in relation to an EEA firm exercising EEA rights in the United Kingdom ("an incoming EEA firm") in respect of the contravention of a relevant requirement.

(2)   A requirement is relevant if—
  (a)   it is imposed by the Authority under this Act; and
  (b)   as respects its contravention, any of the single market directives provides that a procedure of the kind set out in the following provisions of this section is to apply.

(3)   The Authority must, in writing, require the firm to remedy the situation.

(4)   If the firm fails to comply with the requirement under subsection (3) within a reasonable time, the Authority must give a notice to that effect to the firm's home state regulator requesting it—

  (a) to take all appropriate measures for the purpose of ensuring that the firm remedies the situation which has given rise to the notice; and

  (b) to inform the Authority of the measures it proposes to take or has taken or the reasons for not taking such measures.

(5) Except as mentioned in subsection (6), the Authority may not exercise its power of intervention unless satisfied—

  (a) that the firm's home state regulator has failed or refused to take measures for the purpose mentioned in subsection (4)(a); or

  (b) that the measures taken by the home state regulator have proved inadequate for that purpose.

(6) If the Authority decides that it should exercise its power of intervention in respect of the incoming EEA firm as a matter of urgency in order to protect the interests of consumers, it may exercise that power—

  (a) before complying with subsections (3) and (4); or

  (b) where it has complied with those subsections, before it is satisfied as mentioned in subsection (5).

(7) In such a case the Authority must at the earliest opportunity inform the firm's home state regulator and the Commission.

(8) If—

  (a) the Authority has (by virtue of subsection (6)) exercised its power of intervention before complying with subsections (3) and (4) or before it is satisfied as mentioned in subsection (5), and

  (b) the Commission decides under any of the single market directives that the Authority must rescind or vary any requirement imposed in the exercise of its power of intervention,

the Authority must in accordance with the decision rescind or vary the requirement.

Commencement: 3 September 2001 (for the purposes of requirements (as mentioned in s 196) taking effect not sooner than the day on which s 19 of this Act comes into force); 1 December 2001 (remaining purposes).
References: See paras 8.57, 8.58.

Supplemental

200 Rescission and variation of requirements

(1) The Authority may rescind or vary a requirement imposed in exercise of its power of intervention on its own initiative or on the application of the person subject to the requirement.

(2) The power of the Authority on its own initiative to rescind a requirement is exercisable by written notice given by the Authority to the person concerned, which takes effect on the date specified in the notice.

(3) Section 197 applies to the exercise of the power of the Authority on its own initiative to vary a requirement as it applies to the imposition of a requirement.

(4) If the Authority proposes to refuse an application for the variation or rescission of a requirement, it must give the applicant a warning notice.

(5)   If the Authority decides to refuse an application for the variation or rescission of a requirement—

(a)   the Authority must give the applicant a decision notice; and

(b)   that person may refer the matter to the Tribunal.

Commencement: 3 September 2001.
References: See para 8.59.

201 Effect of certain requirements on other persons

If the Authority, in exercising its power of intervention, imposes on an incoming firm a requirement of a kind mentioned in subsection (3) of section 48, the requirement has the same effect in relation to the firm as it would have in relation to an authorised person if it had been imposed on the authorised person by the Authority acting under section 45.

Commencement: 3 September 2001.
References: See para 8.59.

202 Contravention of requirement imposed under this Part

(1)   Contravention of a requirement imposed by the Authority under this Part does not—

(a)   make a person guilty of an offence;

(b)   make any transaction void or unenforceable; or

(c)   (subject to subsection (2)) give rise to any right of action for breach of statutory duty.

(2)   In prescribed cases the contravention is actionable at the suit of a person who suffers loss as a result of the contravention, subject to the defences and other incidents applying to actions for breach of statutory duty.

Commencement: 25 February 2001 (sub-s (2), for the purpose of making orders or regulations); 3 September 2001 (remainder).
Regulations: The Financial Services and Markets Act 2000 (Rights of Action) Regulations 2001, SI 2001/2256, as amended by SI 2002/1775, SI 2002/2706.
References: See para 8.59.

Powers of [Office of Fair Trading]

203 Power to prohibit the carrying on of Consumer Credit Act business

(1)   If it appears to [the Office of Fair Trading ("the OFT")] that subsection (4) has been, or is likely to be, contravened as respects a consumer credit EEA firm, [it] may by written notice given to the firm impose on the firm a consumer credit prohibition.

(2)   If it appears to the [OFT] that a restriction imposed under section 204 on an EEA consumer credit firm has not been complied with, [it] may by written notice given to the firm impose a consumer credit prohibition.

(3)   "Consumer credit prohibition" means a prohibition on carrying on, or purporting to carry on, in the United Kingdom any Consumer Credit Act business which consists of or includes carrying on one or more listed activities.

(4)   This subsection is contravened as respects a firm if—

    (a)   the firm or any of its employees, agents or associates (whether past or present), or

    (b)   if the firm is a body corporate, any controller of the firm or an associate of any such controller,

does any of the things specified in paragraphs (a) to (d) of section 25(2) of the Consumer Credit Act 1974.

(5)   A consumer credit prohibition may be absolute or may be imposed—

    (a)   for such period,

    (b)   until the occurrence of such event, or

    (c)   until such conditions are complied with,

as may be specified in the notice given under subsection (1) or (2).

(6)   Any period, event or condition so specified may be varied by the [OFT] on the application of the firm concerned.

(7)   A consumer credit prohibition may be withdrawn by written notice served by the [OFT] on the firm concerned, and any such notice takes effect on such date as is specified in the notice.

(8)   Schedule 16 has effect as respects consumer credit prohibitions and restrictions under section 204.

(9)   A firm contravening a prohibition under this section is guilty of an offence and liable—

    (a)   on summary conviction, to a fine not exceeding the statutory maximum;

    (b)   on conviction on indictment, to a fine.

(10)   In this section and section 204—

    "a consumer credit EEA firm" means an EEA firm falling within any of paragraphs (a) to (c) of paragraph 5 of Schedule 3 whose EEA authorisation covers any Consumer Credit Act business;

    "Consumer Credit Act business" means consumer credit business, consumer hire business or ancillary credit business;

    "consumer credit business", "consumer hire business" and "ancillary credit business" have the same meaning as in the Consumer Credit Act 1974;

    "listed activity" means an activity listed in [Annex 1 to the banking consolidation directive] or the Annex to the investment services directive;

    "associate" has the same meaning as in section 25(2) of the Consumer Credit Act 1974;

    "controller" has the meaning given by section 189(1) of that Act.

Commencement: 1 December 2001.

Amendments: In the cross-heading preceding this section words in square brackets substituted by the Enterprise Act 2002, s 278(1), Sch 25, para 40(1), (7), as from 1 April 2003.

Sub-ss (1), (2), (6), (7): words in square brackets substituted by the Enterprise Act 2002, s 278(1), Sch 25, para 40(1), (7), as from 1 April 2003.

Sub-s (10): words in square brackets in definition "listed activity" substituted by the Banking Consolidation Directive (Consequential Amendments) Regulations 2000, SI 2000/2952, reg 8(1), (2), as from 22 November 2000.

204 Power to restrict the carrying on of Consumer Credit Act business

(1)   In this section "restriction" means a direction that a consumer credit EEA firm may not carry on in the United Kingdom, otherwise than in accordance with such condition or conditions as may be specified in the direction, any Consumer Credit Act business which—

(a)   consists of or includes carrying on any listed activity; and

(b)   is specified in the direction.

(2)   If it appears to the [OFT] that the situation as respects a consumer credit EEA firm is such that the powers conferred by section 203(1) are exercisable, the [OFT] may, instead of imposing a prohibition, impose such restriction as appears to [it] desirable.

(3)   A restriction—

(a)   may be withdrawn, or

(b)   may be varied with the agreement of the firm concerned,

by written notice served by the [OFT] on the firm, and any such notice takes effect on such date as is specified in the notice.

(4)   A firm contravening a restriction is guilty of an offence and liable—

(a)   on summary conviction, to a fine not exceeding the statutory maximum;

(b)   on conviction on indictment, to a fine.

Commencement: 1 December 2001.
Amendments: Sub-ss (2), (3): words in square brackets substituted by the Enterprise Act 2002, s 278(1), Sch 25, para 40(1), (8), as from 1 April 2003.

PART XIV
DISCIPLINARY MEASURES

205 Public censure

If the Authority considers that an authorised person has contravened a requirement imposed on him by or under this Act, the Authority may publish a statement to that effect.

Commencement: 1 December 2001.
Transitional provisions: as to the exercise of the power conferred by this section in respect of: (a) certain contraventions of the Financial Services Act 1986, before 1 December 2001; and (b) contraventions of the rules of self-regulating organisations before that date, see the Financial Services and Markets Act 2000 (Transitional Provisions and Savings) (Civil Remedies, Discipline, Criminal Offences etc) (No 2) Order 2001, SI 2001/3083, arts 6, 7 (made under ss 426, 427, 428(3)).
References: See paras 8.3–8.6.

206 Financial penalties

(1)   If the Authority considers that an authorised person has contravened a requirement imposed on him by or under this Act, it may impose on him a penalty, in respect of the contravention, of such amount as it considers appropriate.

(2)   The Authority may not in respect of any contravention both require a person to pay a penalty under this section and withdraw his authorisation under section 33.

(3)   A penalty under this section is payable to the Authority.

Commencement: 1 December 2001.
Transitional provisions: as to the exercise of the power conferred by this section in respect of contraventions of the rules of self-regulating organisations before 1 December 2001, see the Financial Services and Markets Act 2000 (Transitional Provisions and Savings) (Civil Remedies, Discipline, Criminal Offences etc) (No 2) Order 2001, SI 2001/3083, art 8 (made under ss 426, 427, 428(3)).
References: See para 8.3.

207 Proposal to take disciplinary measures

(1)   If the Authority proposes—
    (a)   to publish a statement in respect of an authorised person (under section 205), or
    (b)   to impose a penalty on an authorised person (under section 206),
it must give the authorised person a warning notice.

(2)   A warning notice about a proposal to publish a statement must set out the terms of the statement.

(3)   A warning notice about a proposal to impose a penalty, must state the amount of the penalty.

Commencement: 1 December 2001.
References: See paras 8.3, 8.4.

208 Decision notice

(1)   If the Authority decides—
    (a)   to publish a statement under section 205 (whether or not in the terms proposed), or
    (b)   to impose a penalty under section 206 (whether or not of the amount proposed),
it must without delay give the authorised person concerned a decision notice.

(2)   In the case of a statement, the decision notice must set out the terms of the statement.

(3)   In the case of a penalty, the decision notice must state the amount of the penalty.

(4)   If the Authority decides to—
    (a)   publish a statement in respect of an authorised person under section 205, or
    (b)   impose a penalty on an authorised person under section 206,
the authorised person may refer the matter to the Tribunal.

Commencement: 1 December 2001.
References: See para 8.10.

209 Publication

After a statement under section 205 is published, the Authority must send a copy of it to the authorised person and to any person on whom a copy of the decision notice was given under section 393(4).

Commencement: 1 December 2001.
References: See para 8.5.

210 Statements of policy

(1)   The Authority must prepare and issue a statement of its policy with respect to—

  (a)   the imposition of penalties under this Part; and
  (b)   the amount of penalties under this Part.

(2)   The Authority's policy in determining what the amount of a penalty should be must include having regard to—

  (a)   the seriousness of the contravention in question in relation to the nature of the requirement contravened;
  (b)   the extent to which that contravention was deliberate or reckless; and
  (c)   whether the person on whom the penalty is to be imposed is an individual.

(3)   The Authority may at any time alter or replace a statement issued under this section.

(4)   If a statement issued under this section is altered or replaced, the Authority must issue the altered or replacement statement.

(5)   The Authority must, without delay, give the Treasury a copy of any statement which it publishes under this section.

(6)   A statement issued under this section must be published by the Authority in the way appearing to the Authority to be best calculated to bring it to the attention of the public.

(7)   In exercising, or deciding whether to exercise, its power under section 206 in the case of any particular contravention, the Authority must have regard to any statement published under this section and in force at the time when the contravention in question occurred.

(8)   The Authority may charge a reasonable fee for providing a person with a copy of the statement.

Commencement: 18 June 2001.
References: See paras 8.6, 8.7.

211 Statements of policy: procedure

(1)   Before issuing a statement under section 210, the Authority must publish a draft of the proposed statement in the way appearing to the Authority to be best calculated to bring it to the attention of the public.

(2)   The draft must be accompanied by notice that representations about the proposal may be made to the Authority within a specified time.

(3)   Before issuing the proposed statement, the Authority must have regard to any representations made to it in accordance with subsection (2).

(4)   If the Authority issues the proposed statement it must publish an account, in general terms, of—
  (a)   the representations made to it in accordance with subsection (2); and
  (b)   its response to them.

(5)   If the statement differs from the draft published under subsection (1) in a way which is, in the opinion of the Authority, significant, the Authority must (in addition to complying with subsection (4)) publish details of the difference.

(6)   The Authority may charge a reasonable fee for providing a person with a copy of a draft published under subsection (1).

(7)   This section also applies to a proposal to alter or replace a statement.

Commencement: 18 June 2001.
References: See para 8.7.

PART XV
THE FINANCIAL SERVICES COMPENSATION SCHEME

The scheme manager

212 The scheme manager

(1)   The Authority must establish a body corporate ("the scheme manager") to exercise the functions conferred on the scheme manager by or under this Part.

(2)   The Authority must take such steps as are necessary to ensure that the scheme manager is, at all times, capable of exercising those functions.

(3)   The constitution of the scheme manager must provide for it to have—
  (a)   a chairman; and
  (b)   a board (which must include the chairman) whose members are the scheme manager's directors.

(4)   The chairman and other members of the board must be persons appointed, and liable to removal from office, by the Authority (acting, in the case of the chairman, with the approval of the Treasury).

(5)   But the terms of their appointment (and in particular those governing removal from office) must be such as to secure their independence from the Authority in the operation of the compensation scheme.

(6)   The scheme manager is not to be regarded as exercising functions on behalf of the Crown.

(7)   The scheme manager's board members, officers and staff are not to be regarded as Crown servants.

Commencement: 18 June 2001.
References: See paras 13.2, 13.3.

The scheme

213 The compensation scheme

(1)   The Authority must by rules establish a scheme for compensating persons in cases where relevant persons are unable, or are likely to be unable, to satisfy claims against them.

(2)   The rules are to be known as the Financial Services Compensation Scheme (but are referred to in this Act as "the compensation scheme").

(3)   The compensation scheme must, in particular, provide for the scheme manager—

> (a)   to assess and pay compensation, in accordance with the scheme, to claimants in respect of claims made in connection with regulated activities carried on (whether or not with permission) by relevant persons; and
>
> (b)   to have power to impose levies on authorised persons, or any class of authorised person, for the purpose of meeting its expenses (including in particular expenses incurred, or expected to be incurred, in paying compensation, borrowing or insuring risks).

(4)   The compensation scheme may provide for the scheme manager to have power to impose levies on authorised persons, or any class of authorised person, for the purpose of recovering the cost (whenever incurred) of establishing the scheme.

(5)   In making any provision of the scheme by virtue of subsection (3)(b), the Authority must take account of the desirability of ensuring that the amount of the levies imposed on a particular class of authorised person reflects, so far as practicable, the amount of the claims made, or likely to be made, in respect of that class of person.

(6)   An amount payable to the scheme manager as a result of any provision of the scheme made by virtue of subsection (3)(b) or (4) may be recovered as a debt due to the scheme manager.

(7)   Sections 214 to 217 make further provision about the scheme but are not to be taken as limiting the power conferred on the Authority by subsection (1).

(8)   In those sections "specified" means specified in the scheme.

(9)   In this Part (except in sections 219, 220 or 224) "relevant person" means a person who was—

> (a)   an authorised person at the time the act or omission giving rise to the claim against him took place; or
>
> (b)   an appointed representative at that time.

(10)   But a person who, at that time—

> (a)   qualified for authorisation under Schedule 3, and
>
> (b)   fell within a prescribed category,

is not to be regarded as a relevant person in relation to any activities for which he had permission as a result of any provision of, or made under, that Schedule unless he had elected to participate in the scheme in relation to those activities at that time.

Commencement: 25 February 2001 (sub-s (10), for the purpose of making orders or regulations); 18 June 2001 (remainder).
Regulations: The Financial Services and Markets Act 2000 (Compensation Scheme: Electing Participants) Regulations 2001, SI 2001/1783, as amended by SI 2003/1476, SI 2003/2066, and as modified by SI 2001/3084.
References: See paras 13.3–13.6.

Provisions of the scheme

214 General

(1) The compensation scheme may, in particular, make provision—

    (a) as to the circumstances in which a relevant person is to be taken (for the purposes of the scheme) to be unable, or likely to be unable, to satisfy claims made against him;

    (b) for the establishment of different funds for meeting different kinds of claim;

    (c) for the imposition of different levies in different cases;

    (d) limiting the levy payable by a person in respect of a specified period;

    (e) for repayment of the whole or part of a levy in specified circumstances;

    (f) for a claim to be entertained only if it is made by a specified kind of claimant;

    (g) for a claim to be entertained only if it falls within a specified kind of claim;

    (h) as to the procedure to be followed in making a claim;

    (i) for the making of interim payments before a claim is finally determined;

    (j) limiting the amount payable on a claim to a specified maximum amount or a maximum amount calculated in a specified manner;

    (k) for payment to be made, in specified circumstances, to a person other than the claimant.

(2) Different provision may be made with respect to different kinds of claim.

(3) The scheme may provide for the determination and regulation of matters relating to the scheme by the scheme manager.

(4) The scheme, or particular provisions of the scheme, may be made so as to apply only in relation to—

    (a) activities carried on,

    (b) claimants,

    (c) matters arising, or

    (d) events occurring,

in specified territories, areas or localities.

(5) The scheme may provide for a person who—

    (a) qualifies for authorisation under Schedule 3, and

    (b) falls within a prescribed category,

to elect to participate in the scheme in relation to some or all of the activities for which he has permission as a result of any provision of, or made under, that Schedule.

(6) The scheme may provide for the scheme manager to have power—

    (a) in specified circumstances,

      (b)   but only if the scheme manager is satisfied that the claimant is entitled to receive a payment in respect of his claim—

          (i)   under a scheme which is comparable to the compensation scheme, or

         (ii)   as the result of a guarantee given by a government or other authority,

to make a full payment of compensation to the claimant and recover the whole or part of the amount of that payment from the other scheme or under that guarantee.

Commencement: 25 February 2001 (sub-s (5), for the purpose of making orders or regulations); 18 June 2001 (remainder).
Regulations: The Financial Services and Markets Act 2000 (Compensation Scheme: Electing Participants) Regulations 2001, SI 2001/1783, as amended by SI 2003/1476, SI 2003/2066, and as modified by SI 2001/3084.
References: See paras 13.6–13.9.

---

215 Rights of the scheme in relevant person's insolvency

(1)   The compensation scheme may, in particular, make provision—

      (a)   as to the effect of a payment of compensation under the scheme in relation to rights or obligations arising out of the claim against a relevant person in respect of which the payment was made;

      (b)   for conferring on the scheme manager a right of recovery against that person.

(2)   Such a right of recovery conferred by the scheme does not, in the event of the relevant person's insolvency, exceed such right (if any) as the claimant would have had in that event.

(3)   If a person other than the scheme manager [makes an administration application under Schedule B1 to the 1986 Act or presents a petition under Article 22 of the 1989 Order] in relation to a company or partnership which is a relevant person, the scheme manager has the same rights as are conferred on the Authority by section 362.

[(3A) In subsection (3) the reference to making an administration application includes a reference to—

      (a)   appointing an administrator under paragraph 14 or 22 of Schedule B1 to the 1986 Act, or

      (b)   filing with the court a copy of notice of intention to appoint an administrator under either of those paragraphs.]

(4)   If a person other than the scheme manager presents a petition for the winding up of a body which is a relevant person, the scheme manager has the same rights as are conferred on the Authority by section 371.

(5)   If a person other than the scheme manager presents a bankruptcy petition to the court in relation to an individual who, or an entity which, is a relevant person, the scheme manager has the same rights as are conferred on the Authority by section 374.

(6)   Insolvency rules may be made for the purpose of integrating any procedure for which provision is made as a result of subsection (1) into the general procedure on the administration of a company or partnership or on a winding-up, bankruptcy or sequestration.

(7)   "Bankruptcy petition" means a petition to the court—
    (a)   under section 264 of the 1986 Act or Article 238 of the 1989 Order for a bankruptcy order to be made against an individual;
    (b)   under section 5 of the 1985 Act for the sequestration of the estate of an individual; or
    (c)   under section 6 of the 1985 Act for the sequestration of the estate belonging to or held for or jointly by the members of an entity mentioned in subsection (1) of that section.

(8)   "Insolvency rules" are—
    (a)   for England and Wales, rules made under sections 411 and 412 of the 1986 Act;
    (b)   for Scotland, rules made by order by the Treasury, after consultation with the Scottish Ministers, for the purposes of this section; and
    (c)   for Northern Ireland, rules made under Article 359 of the 1989 Order and section 55 of the Judicature (Northern Ireland) Act 1978.

(9)   "The 1985 Act", "the 1986 Act", "the 1989 Order" and "court" have the same meaning as in Part XXIV.

Commencement: 18 June 2001 (sub-ss (1)–(5), (7)); 25 February 2001 (remainder).
Amendments: Sub-s (3): words in square brackets substituted by the Enterprise Act 2002, s 248(3), Sch 17, paras 53, 54(1), (2), as from 15 September 2003, subject to savings in relation to special administration regimes (see s 249 of the 2003 Act) and transitional provisions in relation to cases where a petition for an administration order has been presented before 15 September 2003 (see the Enterprise Act 2002 (Commencement No 4 and Transitional Provisions and Savings) Order 2003, SI 2003/2093).
Sub-s (3A): inserted by the Enterprise Act 2002, s 248(3), Sch 17, paras 53, 54(1), (3), as from 15 September 2003, subject to savings and transitional provisions as noted to sub-s (3).
Limited liability partnerships: By virtue of the Limited Liability Partnerships Regulations 2001, SI 2001/1090, reg 6, sub-ss (3), (4) and (6) are applied with modifications to limited liability partnerships.
References: See paras 13.10, 13.11.

216 Continuity of long-term insurance policies

(1)   The compensation scheme may, in particular, include provision requiring the scheme manager to make arrangements for securing continuity of insurance for policyholders, or policyholders of a specified class, of relevant long-term insurers.

(2)   "Relevant long-term insurers" means relevant persons who—
    (a)   have permission to effect or carry out contracts of long-term insurance; and
    (b)   are unable, or likely to be unable, to satisfy claims made against them.

(3)   The scheme may provide for the scheme manager to take such measures as appear to him to be appropriate—
    (a)   for securing or facilitating the transfer of a relevant long-term insurer's business so far as it consists of the carrying out of contracts of long-term insurance, or of any part of that business, to another authorised person;
    (b)   for securing the issue by another authorised person to the policyholders concerned of policies in substitution for their existing policies.

(4)   The scheme may also provide for the scheme manager to make payments to the policyholders concerned—

    (a)   during any period while he is seeking to make arrangements mentioned in subsection (1);

    (b)   if it appears to him that it is not reasonably practicable to make such arrangements.

(5)   A provision of the scheme made by virtue of section 213(3)(b) may include power to impose levies for the purpose of meeting expenses of the scheme manager incurred in—

    (a)   taking measures as a result of any provision of the scheme made by virtue of subsection (3);

    (b)   making payments as a result of any such provision made by virtue of subsection (4).

Commencement: 18 June 2001.
References: See paras 13.14, 13.15.

217 Insurers in financial difficulties

(1)   The compensation scheme may, in particular, include provision for the scheme manager to have power to take measures for safeguarding policyholders, or policyholders of a specified class, of relevant insurers.

(2)   "Relevant insurers" means relevant persons who—

    (a)   have permission to effect or carry out contracts of insurance; and

    (b)   are in financial difficulties.

(3)   The measures may include such measures as the scheme manager considers appropriate for—

    (a)   securing or facilitating the transfer of a relevant insurer's business so far as it consists of the carrying out of contracts of insurance, or of any part of that business, to another authorised person;

    (b)   giving assistance to the relevant insurer to enable it to continue to effect or carry out contracts of insurance.

(4)   The scheme may provide—

    (a)   that if measures of a kind mentioned in subsection (3)(a) are to be taken, they should be on terms appearing to the scheme manager to be appropriate, including terms reducing, or deferring payment of, any of the things to which any of those who are eligible policyholders in relation to the relevant insurer are entitled in their capacity as such;

    (b)   that if measures of a kind mentioned in subsection (3)(b) are to be taken, they should be conditional on the reduction of, or the deferment of the payment of, the things to which any of those who are eligible policyholders in relation to the relevant insurer are entitled in their capacity as such;

    (c)   for ensuring that measures of a kind mentioned in subsection (3)(b) do not benefit to any material extent persons who were members of a relevant insurer when it began to be in financial difficulties or who had any responsibility for, or who may have profited from, the circumstances giving rise to its financial difficulties, except in specified circumstances;

(d) for requiring the scheme manager to be satisfied that any measures he proposes to take are likely to cost less than it would cost to pay compensation under the scheme if the relevant insurer became unable, or likely to be unable, to satisfy claims made against him.

(5) The scheme may provide for the Authority to have power—
(a) to give such assistance to the scheme manager as it considers appropriate for assisting the scheme manager to determine what measures are practicable or desirable in the case of a particular relevant insurer;
(b) to impose constraints on the taking of measures by the scheme manager in the case of a particular relevant insurer;
(c) to require the scheme manager to provide it with information about any particular measures which the scheme manager is proposing to take.

(6) The scheme may include provision for the scheme manager to have power—
(a) to make interim payments in respect of eligible policyholders of a relevant insurer;
(b) to indemnify any person making payments to eligible policyholders of a relevant insurer.

(7) A provision of the scheme made by virtue of section 213(3)(b) may include power to impose levies for the purpose of meeting expenses of the scheme manager incurred in—
(a) taking measures as a result of any provision of the scheme made by virtue of subsection (1);
(b) making payments or giving indemnities as a result of any such provision made by virtue of subsection (6).

(8) "Financial difficulties" and "eligible policyholders" have such meanings as may be specified.

Commencement: 18 June 2001.
References: See paras 13.12–13.15.

Annual report

218 Annual report

(1) At least once a year, the scheme manager must make a report to the Authority on the discharge of its functions.

(2) The report must—
(a) include a statement setting out the value of each of the funds established by the compensation scheme; and
(b) comply with any requirements specified in rules made by the Authority.

(3) The scheme manager must publish each report in the way it considers appropriate.

Commencement: 18 June 2001.
References: See para 13.16.

Information and documents

219 Scheme manager's power to require information

(1) The scheme manager may, by notice in writing given to the relevant person in respect of whom a claim is made under the scheme or to a person otherwise involved, require that person—

(a) to provide specified information or information of a specified description; or

(b) to produce specified documents or documents of a specified description.

(2) The information or documents must be provided or produced—

(a) before the end of such reasonable period as may be specified; and

(b) in the case of information, in such manner or form as may be specified.

(3) This section applies only to information and documents the provision or production of which the scheme manager considers—

(a) to be necessary for the fair determination of the claim; or

(b) to be necessary (or likely to be necessary) for the fair determination of other claims made (or which it expects may be made) in respect of the relevant person concerned.

(4) If a document is produced in response to a requirement imposed under this section, the scheme manager may—

(a) take copies or extracts from the document; or

(b) require the person producing the document to provide an explanation of the document.

(5) If a person who is required under this section to produce a document fails to do so, the scheme manager may require the person to state, to the best of his knowledge and belief, where the document is.

(6) If the relevant person is insolvent, no requirement may be imposed under this section on a person to whom section 220 or 224 applies.

(7) If a person claims a lien on a document, its production under this Part does not affect the lien.

(8) "Relevant person" has the same meaning as in section 224.

(9) "Specified" means specified in the notice given under subsection (1).

(10) A person is involved in a claim made under the scheme if he was knowingly involved in the act or omission giving rise to the claim.

Commencement: 1 December 2001.
References: See paras 13.17, 13.18.

220 Scheme manager's power to inspect information held by liquidator etc

(1) For the purpose of assisting the scheme manager to discharge its functions in relation to a claim made in respect of an insolvent relevant person, a person to whom this section applies must permit a person authorised by the scheme manager to inspect relevant documents.

(2)   A person inspecting a document under this section may take copies of, or extracts from, the document.

(3)   This section applies to—
      (a)   the administrative receiver, administrator, liquidator or trustee in bankruptcy of an insolvent relevant person;
      (b)   the permanent trustee, within the meaning of the Bankruptcy (Scotland) Act 1985, on the estate of an insolvent relevant person.

(4)   This section does not apply to a liquidator, administrator or trustee in bankruptcy who is—
      (a)   the Official Receiver;
      (b)   the Official Receiver for Northern Ireland; or
      (c)   the Accountant in Bankruptcy.

(5)   "Relevant person" has the same meaning as in section 224.

Commencement: 1 December 2001.
References: See paras 13.19, 13.20.

221 Powers of court where information required

(1)   If a person ("the defaulter")—
      (a)   fails to comply with a requirement imposed under section 219, or
      (b)   fails to permit documents to be inspected under section 220,
the scheme manager may certify that fact in writing to the court and the court may enquire into the case.

(2)   If the court is satisfied that the defaulter failed without reasonable excuse to comply with the requirement (or to permit the documents to be inspected), it may deal with the defaulter (and, in the case of a body corporate, any director or officer) as if he were in contempt[; and "officer", in relation to a limited liability partnership, means a member of the limited liability partnership].

(3)   "Court" means—
      (a)   the High Court;
      (b)   in Scotland, the Court of Session.

Commencement: 1 December 2001.
Amendments: Sub-s (2): words in square brackets added by the Limited Liability Partnerships Regulations 2001, SI 2001/1090, reg 9, Sch 5, para 21, as from 6 April 2001.
References: See para 13.20.

Miscellaneous

222 Statutory immunity

(1)   Neither the scheme manager nor any person who is, or is acting as, its board member, officer or member of staff is to be liable in damages for anything done or omitted in the discharge, or purported discharge, of the scheme manager's functions.

(2)   Subsection (1) does not apply—
      (a)   if the act or omission is shown to have been in bad faith; or

(b)   so as to prevent an award of damages made in respect of an act or omission on the ground that the act or omission was unlawful as a result of section 6(1) of the Human Rights Act 1998.

Commencement: 18 June 2001.
References: See para 13.23.

223 Management expenses

(1)   The amount which the scheme manager may recover, from the sums levied under the scheme, as management expenses attributable to a particular period may not exceed such amount as may be fixed by the scheme as the limit applicable to that period.

(2)   In calculating the amount of any levy to be imposed by the scheme manager, no amount may be included to reflect management expenses unless the limit mentioned in subsection (1) has been fixed by the scheme.

(3)   "Management expenses" means expenses incurred, or expected to be incurred, by the scheme manager in connection with its functions under this Act other than those incurred—
   (a)   in paying compensation;
   (b)   as a result of any provision of the scheme made by virtue of section 216(3) or (4) or 217(1) or (6).

Commencement: 18 June 2001 (for the purposes of fixing an amount by the scheme as mentioned in sub-s (1) above); 1 December 2001 (remaining purposes).
References: See para 13.22.

224 Scheme manager's power to inspect documents held by Official Receiver etc

(1)   If, as a result of the insolvency or bankruptcy of a relevant person, any documents have come into the possession of a person to whom this section applies, he must permit any person authorised by the scheme manager to inspect the documents for the purpose of establishing—
   (a)   the identity of persons to whom the scheme manager may be liable to make a payment in accordance with the compensation scheme; or
   (b)   the amount of any payment which the scheme manager may be liable to make.

(2)   A person inspecting a document under this section may take copies or extracts from the document.

(3)   In this section "relevant person" means a person who was—
   (a)   an authorised person at the time the act or omission which may give rise to the liability mentioned in subsection (1)(a) took place; or
   (b)   an appointed representative at that time.

(4)   But a person who, at that time—
   (a)   qualified for authorisation under Schedule 3, and
   (b)   fell within a prescribed category,

is not to be regarded as a relevant person for the purposes of this section in relation to any activities for which he had permission as a result of any provision of, or made under, that Schedule unless he had elected to participate in the scheme in relation to those activities at that time.

(5) This section applies to—

    (a) the Official Receiver;

    (b) the Official Receiver for Northern Ireland; and

    (c) the Accountant in Bankruptcy.

Commencement: 25 February 2001 (sub-s (4), for the purpose of making orders or regulations); 1 December 2001 (remainder).

Regulations: The Financial Services and Markets Act 2000 (Compensation Scheme: Electing Participants) Regulations 2001, SI 2001/1783, as amended by SI 2003/1476, SI 2003/2066, and as modified by SI 2001/3084.

References: See para 13.21.

PART XVI
THE OMBUDSMAN SCHEME

Transitional provisions: See the Financial Services and Markets Act 2000 (Transitional Provisions) (Ombudsman Scheme and Complaints Scheme) Order 2001, SI 2001/2326 (made under ss 426–428).

The scheme

225 The scheme and the scheme operator

(1) This Part provides for a scheme under which certain disputes may be resolved quickly and with minimum formality by an independent person.

(2) The scheme is to be administered by a body corporate ("the scheme operator").

(3) The scheme is to be operated under a name chosen by the scheme operator but is referred to in this Act as "the ombudsman scheme".

(4) Schedule 17 makes provision in connection with the ombudsman scheme and the scheme operator.

Commencement: 18 June 2001.

References: See paras 14.5–14.7.

---

226 Compulsory jurisdiction

(1) A complaint which relates to an act or omission of a person ("the respondent") in carrying on an activity to which compulsory jurisdiction rules apply is to be dealt with under the ombudsman scheme if the conditions mentioned in subsection (2) are satisfied.

(2) The conditions are that—

    (a) the complainant is eligible and wishes to have the complaint dealt with under the scheme;

    (b) the respondent was an authorised person at the time of the act or omission to which the complaint relates; and

    (c) the act or omission to which the complaint relates occurred at a time when compulsory jurisdiction rules were in force in relation to the activity in question.

(3) "Compulsory jurisdiction rules" means rules—
    (a) made by the Authority for the purposes of this section; and
    (b) specifying the activities to which they apply.

(4) Only activities which are regulated activities, or which could be made regulated activities by an order under section 22, may be specified.

(5) Activities may be specified by reference to specified categories (however described).

(6) A complainant is eligible, in relation to the compulsory jurisdiction of the ombudsman scheme, if he falls within a class of person specified in the rules as eligible.

(7) The rules—
    (a) may include provision for persons other than individuals to be eligible; but
    (b) may not provide for authorised persons to be eligible except in specified circumstances or in relation to complaints of a specified kind.

(8) The jurisdiction of the scheme which results from this section is referred to in this Act as the "compulsory jurisdiction".

Commencement: 18 June 2001 (for the purpose of the making of rules by the Authority and the scheme operator); 1 December 2001 (remaining purposes).
References: See paras 14.19–14.22.

227 Voluntary jurisdiction

(1) A complaint which relates to an act or omission of a person ("the respondent") in carrying on an activity to which voluntary jurisdiction rules apply is to be dealt with under the ombudsman scheme if the conditions mentioned in subsection (2) are satisfied.

(2) The conditions are that—
    (a) the complainant is eligible and wishes to have the complaint dealt with under the scheme;
    (b) at the time of the act or omission to which the complaint relates, the respondent was participating in the scheme;
    (c) at the time when the complaint is referred under the scheme, the respondent has not withdrawn from the scheme in accordance with its provisions;
    (d) the act or omission to which the complaint relates occurred at a time when voluntary jurisdiction rules were in force in relation to the activity in question; and
    (e) the complaint cannot be dealt with under the compulsory jurisdiction.

(3) "Voluntary jurisdiction rules" means rules—
    (a) made by the scheme operator for the purposes of this section; and
    (b) specifying the activities to which they apply.

(4) The only activities which may be specified in the rules are activities which are, or could be, specified in compulsory jurisdiction rules.

(5)   Activities may be specified by reference to specified categories (however described).

(6)   The rules require the Authority's approval.

(7)   A complainant is eligible, in relation to the voluntary jurisdiction of the ombudsman scheme, if he falls within a class of person specified in the rules as eligible.

(8)   The rules may include provision for persons other than individuals to be eligible.

(9)   A person qualifies for participation in the ombudsman scheme if he falls within a class of person specified in the rules in relation to the activity in question.

(10) Provision may be made in the rules for persons other than authorised persons to participate in the ombudsman scheme.

(11) The rules may make different provision in relation to complaints arising from different activities.

(12) The jurisdiction of the scheme which results from this section is referred to in this Act as the "voluntary jurisdiction".

(13) In such circumstances as may be specified in voluntary jurisdiction rules, a complaint—
>   (a)   which relates to an act or omission occurring at a time before the rules came into force, and
>   (b)   which could have been dealt with under a scheme which has to any extent been replaced by the voluntary jurisdiction,

is to be dealt with under the ombudsman scheme even though paragraph (b) or (d) of subsection (2) would otherwise prevent that.

(14) In such circumstances as may be specified in voluntary jurisdiction rules, a complaint is to be dealt with under the ombudsman scheme even though—
>   (a)   paragraph (b) or (d) of subsection (2) would otherwise prevent that, and
>   (b)   the complaint is not brought within the scheme as a result of subsection (13),

but only if the respondent has agreed that complaints of that kind were to be dealt with under the scheme.

Commencement: 18 June 2001 (for the purpose of the making of rules by the Authority and the scheme operator); 1 December 2001 (remaining purposes).
References: See paras 14.39–14.42.

Determination of complaints

228 Determination under the compulsory jurisdiction

(1)   This section applies only in relation to the compulsory jurisdiction.

(2)   A complaint is to be determined by reference to what is, in the opinion of the ombudsman, fair and reasonable in all the circumstances of the case.

(3)   When the ombudsman has determined a complaint he must give a written statement of his determination to the respondent and to the complainant.

(4)   The statement must—
    (a)   give the ombudsman's reasons for his determination;
    (b)   be signed by him; and
    (c)   require the complainant to notify him in writing, before a date specified in the statement, whether he accepts or rejects the determination.

(5)   If the complainant notifies the ombudsman that he accepts the determination, it is binding on the respondent and the complainant and final.

(6)   If, by the specified date, the complainant has not notified the ombudsman of his acceptance or rejection of the determination he is to be treated as having rejected it.

(7)   The ombudsman must notify the respondent of the outcome.

(8)   A copy of the determination on which appears a certificate signed by an ombudsman is evidence (or in Scotland sufficient evidence) that the determination was made under the scheme.

(9)   Such a certificate purporting to be signed by an ombudsman is to be taken to have been duly signed unless the contrary is shown.

Commencement: 1 December 2001.
References: See paras 14.30, 14.31.

229 Awards

(1)   This section applies only in relation to the compulsory jurisdiction.

(2)   If a complaint which has been dealt with under the scheme is determined in favour of the complainant, the determination may include—
    (a)   an award against the respondent of such amount as the ombudsman considers fair compensation for loss or damage (of a kind falling within subsection (3)) suffered by the complainant ("a money award");
    (b)   a direction that the respondent take such steps in relation to the complainant as the ombudsman considers just and appropriate (whether or not a court could order those steps to be taken).

(3)   A money award may compensate for—
    (a)   financial loss; or
    (b)   any other loss, or any damage, of a specified kind.

(4)   The Authority may specify the maximum amount which may be regarded as fair compensation for a particular kind of loss or damage specified under subsection (3)(b).

(5)   A money award may not exceed the monetary limit; but the ombudsman may, if he considers that fair compensation requires payment of a larger amount, recommend that the respondent pay the complainant the balance.

(6)   The monetary limit is such amount as may be specified.

(7)   Different amounts may be specified in relation to different kinds of complaint.

(8) A money award—

    (a) may provide for the amount payable under the award to bear interest at a rate and as from a date specified in the award; and

    (b) is enforceable by the complainant in accordance with Part III of Schedule 17.

(9) Compliance with a direction under subsection (2)(b)—

    (a) is enforceable by an injunction; or

    (b) in Scotland, is enforceable by an order under section 45 of the Court of Session Act 1988.

(10) Only the complainant may bring proceedings for an injunction or proceedings for an order.

(11) "Specified" means specified in compulsory jurisdiction rules.

Commencement: 18 June 2001 (for the purpose of the making of rules by the Authority and the scheme operator); 1 December 2001 (remaining purposes).
References: See paras 14.32–14.34.

230 Costs

(1) The scheme operator may by rules ("costs rules") provide for an ombudsman to have power, on determining a complaint under the compulsory jurisdiction, to award costs in accordance with the provisions of the rules.

(2) Costs rules require the approval of the Authority.

(3) Costs rules may not provide for the making of an award against the complainant in respect of the respondent's costs.

(4) But they may provide for the making of an award against the complainant in favour of the scheme operator, for the purpose of providing a contribution to resources deployed in dealing with the complaint, if in the opinion of the ombudsman—

    (a) the complainant's conduct was improper or unreasonable; or

    (b) the complainant was responsible for an unreasonable delay.

(5) Costs rules may authorise an ombudsman making an award in accordance with the rules to order that the amount payable under the award bears interest at a rate and as from a date specified in the order.

(6) An amount due under an award made in favour of the scheme operator is recoverable as a debt due to the scheme operator.

(7) Any other award made against the respondent is to be treated as a money award for the purposes of paragraph 16 of Schedule 17.

Commencement: 18 June 2001.
References: See paras 14.35, 14.36.

Information

231 Ombudsman's power to require information

(1) An ombudsman may, by notice in writing given to a party to a complaint, require that party—

> > (a) to provide specified information or information of a specified description; or
> > (b) to produce specified documents or documents of a specified description.

(2) The information or documents must be provided or produced—
> > (a) before the end of such reasonable period as may be specified; and
> > (b) in the case of information, in such manner or form as may be specified.

(3) This section applies only to information and documents the production of which the ombudsman considers necessary for the determination of the complaint.

(4) If a document is produced in response to a requirement imposed under this section, the ombudsman may—
> > (a) take copies or extracts from the document; or
> > (b) require the person producing the document to provide an explanation of the document.

(5) If a person who is required under this section to produce a document fails to do so, the ombudsman may require him to state, to the best of his knowledge and belief, where the document is.

(6) If a person claims a lien on a document, its production under this Part does not affect the lien.

(7) "Specified" means specified in the notice given under subsection (1).

Commencement: 1 December 2001.
References: See paras 14.48, 14.49.

---

232 Powers of court where information required

(1) If a person ("the defaulter") fails to comply with a requirement imposed under section 231, the ombudsman may certify that fact in writing to the court and the court may enquire into the case.

(2) If the court is satisfied that the defaulter failed without reasonable excuse to comply with the requirement, it may deal with the defaulter (and, in the case of a body corporate, any director or officer) as if he were in contempt[; and "officer", in relation to a limited liability partnership, means a member of the limited liability partnership].

(3) "Court" means—
> > (a) the High Court;
> > (b) in Scotland, the Court of Session.

Commencement: 1 December 2001.
Amendments: Sub-s (2): words in square brackets added by the Limited Liability Partnerships Regulations 2001, SI 2001/1090, reg 9, Sch 5, para 21, as from 6 April 2001.

---

233 *(Inserts the Data Protection Act 1998, s 31(4A).)*

Funding

234 Industry funding

(1)　For the purpose of funding—

    (a)　the establishment of the ombudsman scheme (whenever any relevant expense is incurred), and

    (b)　its operation in relation to the compulsory jurisdiction,

the Authority may make rules requiring the payment to it or to the scheme operator, by authorised persons or any class of authorised person of specified amounts (or amounts calculated in a specified way).

(2)　"Specified" means specified in the rules.

Commencement: 18 June 2001.
References: See para 14.15.

PART XVII
COLLECTIVE INVESTMENT SCHEMES

Transitional provisions: The Financial Services and Markets Act 2000 (Transitional Provisions) (Authorised Persons etc) Order 2001, SI 2001/2636, Pt V et seq (made under ss 426–428), provides that collective investment schemes which were authorised or recognised under the Financial Services Act 1986, Pt I, Chapter VIII immediately before 1 December 2001 are to be treated as from that date as if authorised and recognised under Pt XVII of this Act. Directions imposed on schemes under the 1986 Act have effect, as from 1 December 2001, as directions imposed under Pt XVII of this Act. The 1986 Act is repealed by the Financial Services and Markets Act 2000 (Consequential Amendments and Repeals) Order 2001, SI 2001/3649, art 3(1)(c) (made under ss 426, 427)).

CHAPTER I
INTERPRETATION

235 Collective investment schemes

(1)　In this Part "collective investment scheme" means any arrangements with respect to property of any description, including money, the purpose or effect of which is to enable persons taking part in the arrangements (whether by becoming owners of the property or any part of it or otherwise) to participate in or receive profits or income arising from the acquisition, holding, management or disposal of the property or sums paid out of such profits or income.

(2)　The arrangements must be such that the persons who are to participate ("participants") do not have day-to-day control over the management of the property, whether or not they have the right to be consulted or to give directions.

(3)　The arrangements must also have either or both of the following characteristics—

    (a)　the contributions of the participants and the profits or income out of which payments are to be made to them are pooled;

    (b)　the property is managed as a whole by or on behalf of the operator of the scheme.

(4)　If arrangements provide for such pooling as is mentioned in subsection (3)(a) in relation to separate parts of the property, the arrangements are not to be regarded as constituting a single collective investment scheme unless the participants are entitled to exchange rights in one part for rights in another.

(5)   The Treasury may by order provide that arrangements do not amount to a collective investment scheme—

      (a)   in specified circumstances; or

      (b)   if the arrangements fall within a specified category of arrangement.

Commencement: 25 February 2001.
Orders: The Financial Services and Markets Act 2000 (Collective Investment Schemes) Order 2001, SI 2001/1062, as amended by SI 2001/3650; the Financial Services and Markets Act 2000 (Miscellaneous Provisions) Order 2001, SI 2001/3650, as amended by SI 2001/3771, SI 2002/1777.
References: See paras 15.2–15.7.

236 Open-ended investment companies

(1)   In this Part "an open-ended investment company" means a collective investment scheme which satisfies both the property condition and the investment condition.

(2)   The property condition is that the property belongs beneficially to, and is managed by or on behalf of, a body corporate ("BC") having as its purpose the investment of its funds with the aim of—

      (a)   spreading investment risk; and

      (b)   giving its members the benefit of the results of the management of those funds by or on behalf of that body.

(3)   The investment condition is that, in relation to BC, a reasonable investor would, if he were to participate in the scheme—

      (a)   expect that he would be able to realize, within a period appearing to him to be reasonable, his investment in the scheme (represented, at any given time, by the value of shares in, or securities of, BC held by him as a participant in the scheme); and

      (b)   be satisfied that his investment would be realized on a basis calculated wholly or mainly by reference to the value of property in respect of which the scheme makes arrangements.

(4)   In determining whether the investment condition is satisfied, no account is to be taken of any actual or potential redemption or repurchase of shares or securities under—

      (a)   Chapter VII of Part V of the Companies Act 1985;

      (b)   Chapter VII of Part VI of the Companies (Northern Ireland) Order 1986;

      (c)   corresponding provisions in force in another EEA State; or

      (d)   provisions in force in a country or territory other than an EEA state which the Treasury have, by order, designated as corresponding provisions.

(5)   The Treasury may by order amend the definition of "an open-ended investment company" for the purposes of this Part.

Commencement: 25 February 2001.
References: See paras 15.8–15.10.

237 Other definitions

(1)   In this Part "unit trust scheme" means a collective investment scheme under which the property is held on trust for the participants.

(2)   In this Part—
"trustee", in relation to a unit trust scheme, means the person holding the property in question on trust for the participants;
"depositary", in relation to—
    (a)   a collective investment scheme which is constituted by a body incorporated by virtue of regulations under section 262, or
    (b)   any other collective investment scheme which is not a unit trust scheme,
means any person to whom the property subject to the scheme is entrusted for safekeeping;
"the operator", in relation to a unit trust scheme with a separate trustee, means the manager and in relation to an open-ended investment company, means that company;
"units" means the rights or interests (however described) of the participants in a collective investment scheme.

(3)   In this Part—
"an authorised unit trust scheme" means a unit trust scheme which is authorised for the purposes of this Act by an authorisation order in force under section 243;
"an authorised open-ended investment company" means a body incorporated by virtue of regulations under section 262 in respect of which an authorisation order is in force under any provision made in such regulations by virtue of subsection (2)(l) of that section;
"a recognised scheme" means a scheme recognised under section 264, 270 or 272.

Commencement: 25 February 2001.
References: See paras 15.3, 15.5, 15.13, 15.16.

CHAPTER II
RESTRICTIONS ON PROMOTION

238 Restrictions on promotion

(1)   An authorised person must not communicate an invitation or inducement to participate in a collective investment scheme.

(2)   But that is subject to the following provisions of this section and to section 239.

(3)   Subsection (1) applies in the case of a communication originating outside the United Kingdom only if the communication is capable of having an effect in the United Kingdom.

(4)   Subsection (1) does not apply in relation to—
    (a)   an authorised unit trust scheme;
    (b)   a scheme constituted by an authorised open-ended investment company; or
    (c)   a recognised scheme.

(5)   Subsection (1) does not apply to anything done in accordance with rules made by the Authority for the purpose of exempting from that subsection the promotion otherwise than to the general public of schemes of specified descriptions.

(6)   The Treasury may by order specify circumstances in which subsection (1) does not apply.

(7)   An order under subsection (6) may, in particular, provide that subsection (1) does not apply in relation to communications—
  (a)   of a specified description;
  (b)   originating in a specified country or territory outside the United Kingdom;
  (c)   originating in a country or territory which falls within a specified description of country or territory outside the United Kingdom; or
  (d)   originating outside the United Kingdom.

(8)   The Treasury may by order repeal subsection (3).

(9)   "Communicate" includes causing a communication to be made.

(10)   "Promotion otherwise than to the general public" includes promotion in a way designed to reduce, so far as possible, the risk of participation by persons for whom participation would be unsuitable.

(11)   "Participate", in relation to a collective investment scheme, means become a participant (within the meaning given by section 235(2)) in the scheme.

Commencement: 18 June 2001 (for the purpose of making rules); 25 February 2001 (for the purpose of making orders or regulations); 1 December 2001 (remaining purposes).
Orders: The Financial Services and Markets Act 2000 (Promotion of Collective Investment Schemes) (Exemptions) Order 2001, SI 2001/1060, as amended by SI 2001/2633, SI 2002/1310, SI 2002/2157; the Financial Services and Markets Act 2000 (Financial Promotion) (Amendment) (Electronic Commerce Directive) Order 2002, SI 2002/2157.
References: See paras 6.47–6.56, 15.85–15.88.

---

239 Single property schemes

(1)   The Treasury may by regulations make provision for exempting single property schemes from section 238(1).

(2)   For the purposes of subsection (1) a single property scheme is a scheme which has the characteristics mentioned in subsection (3) and satisfies such other requirements as are prescribed by the regulations conferring the exemption.

(3)   The characteristics are—
  (a)   that the property subject to the scheme (apart from cash or other assets held for management purposes) consists of—
    (i)   a single building (or a single building with ancillary buildings) managed by or on behalf of the operator of the scheme, or
    (ii)   a group of adjacent or contiguous buildings managed by him or on his behalf as a single enterprise,
  with or without ancillary land and with or without furniture, fittings or other contents of the building or buildings in question; and
  (b)   that the units of the participants in the scheme are either dealt in on a recognised investment exchange or offered on terms such that any agreement for their acquisition is conditional on their admission to dealings on such an exchange.

(4)   If regulations are made under subsection (1), the Authority may make rules imposing duties or liabilities on the operator and (if any) the trustee or depositary of a scheme exempted by the regulations.

(5)   The rules may include, to such extent as the Authority thinks appropriate, provision for purposes corresponding to those for which provision can be made under section 248 in relation to authorised unit trust schemes.

Commencement: 18 June 2001 (sub-ss (4), (5)); 25 February 2001 (remainder).
References: See para 15.15.

240 Restriction on approval of promotion

(1)   An authorised person may not approve for the purposes of section 21 the content of a communication relating to a collective investment scheme if he would be prohibited by section 238(1) from effecting the communication himself or from causing it to be communicated.

(2)   For the purposes of determining in any case whether there has been a contravention of section 21(1), an approval given in contravention of subsection (1) is to be regarded as not having been given.

Commencement: 1 December 2001.
References: See paras 15.88–15.90.

241 Actions for damages

If an authorised person contravenes a requirement imposed on him by section 238 or 240, section 150 applies to the contravention as it applies to a contravention mentioned in that section.

Commencement: 1 December 2001.

CHAPTER III
AUTHORISED UNIT TRUST SCHEMES

Applications for authorisation

242 Applications for authorisation of unit trust schemes

(1)   Any application for an order declaring a unit trust scheme to be an authorised unit trust scheme must be made to the Authority by the manager and trustee, or proposed manager and trustee, of the scheme.

(2)   The manager and trustee (or proposed manager and trustee) must be different persons.

(3)   The application—
    (a)   must be made in such manner as the Authority may direct; and
    (b)   must contain or be accompanied by such information as the Authority may reasonably require for the purpose of determining the application.

(4)   At any time after receiving an application and before determining it, the Authority may require the applicants to provide it with such further information as it reasonably considers necessary to enable it to determine the application.

(5)   Different directions may be given, and different requirements imposed, in relation to different applications.

(6)   The Authority may require applicants to present information which they are required to give under this section in such form, or to verify it in such a way, as the Authority may direct.

Commencement: 3 September 2001 (for the purposes of authorisation orders coming into force not sooner than the day on which s 19 of this Act comes into force, and applications for such orders); 18 June 2001 (for the purpose of giving directions or imposing requirements as mentioned in sub-s (3) above); 1 December 2001 (remaining purposes).
References: See para 15.16.

---

243 Authorisation orders

(1)   If, on an application under section 242 in respect of a unit trust scheme, the Authority—

> (a)   is satisfied that the scheme complies with the requirements set out in this section,
>
> (b)   is satisfied that the scheme complies with the requirements of the trust scheme rules, and
>
> (c)   has been provided with a copy of the trust deed and a certificate signed by a solicitor to the effect that it complies with such of the requirements of this section or those rules as relate to its contents,

the Authority may make an order declaring the scheme to be an authorised unit trust scheme.

(2)   If the Authority makes an order under subsection (1), it must give written notice of the order to the applicant.

(3)   In this Chapter "authorisation order" means an order under subsection (1).

(4)   The manager and the trustee must be persons who are independent of each other.

(5)   The manager and the trustee must each—

> (a)   be a body corporate incorporated in the United Kingdom or another EEA State, and
>
> (b)   have a place of business in the United Kingdom,

and the affairs of each must be administered in the country in which it is incorporated.

(6)   If the manager is incorporated in another EEA State, the scheme must not be one which satisfies the requirements prescribed for the purposes of section 264.

(7)   The manager and the trustee must each be an authorised person and the manager must have permission to act as manager and the trustee must have permission to act as trustee.

(8)   The name of the scheme must not be undesirable or misleading.

(9)   The purposes of the scheme must be reasonably capable of being successfully carried into effect.

(10) The participants must be entitled to have their units redeemed in accordance with the scheme at a price—

    (a)   related to the net value of the property to which the units relate; and

    (b)   determined in accordance with the scheme.

(11) But a scheme is to be treated as complying with subsection (10) if it requires the manager to ensure that a participant is able to sell his units on an investment exchange at a price not significantly different from that mentioned in that subsection.

Commencement: 3 September 2001 (for the purposes of authorisation orders coming into force not sooner than the day on which s 19 of this Act comes into force, and applications for such orders); 1 December 2001 (remaining purposes).
References: See paras 15.17–15.19.

244 Determination of applications

(1)   An application under section 242 must be determined by the Authority before the end of the period of six months beginning with the date on which it receives the completed application.

(2)   The Authority may determine an incomplete application if it considers it appropriate to do so; and it must in any event determine such an application within twelve months beginning with the date on which it first receives the application.

(3)   The applicant may withdraw his application, by giving the Authority written notice, at any time before the Authority determines it.

Commencement: 3 September 2001 (for the purposes of authorisation orders coming into force not sooner than the day on which s 19 of this Act comes into force, and applications for such orders); 1 December 2001 (remaining purposes).
References: See para 15.20.

Applications refused

245 Procedure when refusing an application

(1)   If the Authority proposes to refuse an application made under section 242 it must give each of the applicants a warning notice.

(2)   If the Authority decides to refuse the application—

    (a)   it must give each of the applicants a decision notice; and

    (b)   either applicant may refer the matter to the Tribunal.

Commencement: 3 September 2001 (for the purposes of authorisation orders coming into force not sooner than the day on which s 19 of this Act comes into force, and applications for such orders); 1 December 2001 (remaining purposes).
References: See para 15.21.

Certificates

246 Certificates

(1)   If the manager or trustee of a unit trust scheme which complies with the conditions necessary for it to enjoy the rights conferred by any relevant Community instrument so requests, the Authority may issue a certificate to the effect that the scheme complies with those conditions.

(2)   Such a certificate may be issued on the making of an authorisation order in respect of the scheme or at any subsequent time.

Commencement: 3 September 2001 (for the purposes of certificates coming into force not sooner than the day on which s 19 of this Act comes into force); 1 December 2001 (remaining purposes).
References: See para 15.22.

Rules

247 Trust scheme rules

(1)   The Authority may make rules ("trust scheme rules") as to—
- (a)   the constitution, management and operation of authorised unit trust schemes;
- (b)   the powers, duties, rights and liabilities of the manager and trustee of any such scheme;
- (c)   the rights and duties of the participants in any such scheme; and
- (d)   the winding up of any such scheme.

(2)   Trust scheme rules may, in particular, make provision—
- (a)   as to the issue and redemption of the units under the scheme;
- (b)   as to the expenses of the scheme and the means of meeting them;
- (c)   for the appointment, removal, powers and duties of an auditor for the scheme;
- (d)   for restricting or regulating the investment and borrowing powers exercisable in relation to the scheme;
- (e)   requiring the keeping of records with respect to the transactions and financial position of the scheme and for the inspection of those records;
- (f)   requiring the preparation of periodical reports with respect to the scheme and the provision of those reports to the participants and to the Authority; and
- (g)   with respect to the amendment of the scheme.

(3)   Trust scheme rules may make provision as to the contents of the trust deed, including provision requiring any of the matters mentioned in subsection (2) to be dealt with in the deed.

(4)   But trust scheme rules are binding on the manager, trustee and participants independently of the contents of the trust deed and, in the case of the participants, have effect as if contained in it.

(5)   If—
- (a)   a modification is made of the statutory provisions in force in Great Britain or Northern Ireland relating to companies,
- (b)   the modification relates to the rights and duties of persons who hold the beneficial title to any shares in a company without also holding the legal title, and
- (c)   it appears to the Treasury that, for the purpose of assimilating the law relating to authorised unit trust schemes to the law relating to companies as so modified, it is expedient to modify the rule-making powers conferred on the Authority by this section,

the Treasury may by order make such modifications of those powers as they consider appropriate.

Commencement: 18 June 2001.
References: See paras 15.23, 15.24.

248 Scheme particulars rules

(1)   The Authority may make rules ("scheme particulars rules") requiring the manager of an authorised unit trust scheme—
  (a)   to submit scheme particulars to the Authority; and
  (b)   to publish scheme particulars or make them available to the public on request.

(2)   "Scheme particulars" means particulars in such form, containing such information about the scheme and complying with such requirements, as are specified in scheme particulars rules.

(3)   Scheme particulars rules may require the manager of an authorised unit trust scheme to submit, and to publish or make available, revised or further scheme particulars if there is a significant change affecting any matter—
  (a)   which is contained in scheme particulars previously published or made available; and
  (b)   whose inclusion in those particulars was required by the rules.

(4)   Scheme particulars rules may require the manager of an authorised unit trust scheme to submit, and to publish or make available, revised or further scheme particulars if—
  (a)   a significant new matter arises; and
  (b)   the inclusion of information in respect of that matter would have been required in previous particulars if it had arisen when those particulars were prepared.

(5)   Scheme particulars rules may provide for the payment, by the person or persons who in accordance with the rules are treated as responsible for any scheme particulars, of compensation to any qualifying person who has suffered loss as a result of—
  (a)   any untrue or misleading statement in the particulars; or
  (b)   the omission from them of any matter required by the rules to be included.

(6)   "Qualifying person" means a person who—
  (a)   has become or agreed to become a participant in the scheme; or
  (b)   although not being a participant, has a beneficial interest in units in the scheme.

(7)   Scheme particulars rules do not affect any liability which any person may incur apart from the rules.

Commencement: 18 June 2001.
References: See paras 15.25, 15.26.

249 Disqualification of auditor for breach of trust scheme rules

(1)   If it appears to the Authority that an auditor has failed to comply with a duty imposed on him by trust scheme rules, it may disqualify him from being the auditor for any authorised unit trust scheme or authorised open-ended investment company.

(2)   Subsections (2) to (5) of section 345 have effect in relation to disqualification under subsection (1) as they have effect in relation to disqualification under subsection (1) of that section.

Commencement: 1 December 2001.
Open-ended investment companies: sub-s (1) above applies to a failure by an auditor to comply with a duty imposed on him by any rules made by the Financial Services Authority under the Open-Ended Investment Companies Regulations 2001, SI 2001/1228, reg 6(1) as it applies to a breach of trust scheme rules; see reg 69 of, and Sch 5, para 20 to, the 2001 Regulations (made under ss 262, 428(3)).
References: See para 15.46.

---

250 Modification or waiver of rules

(1)   In this section "rules" means—
  (a)   trust scheme rules; or
  (b)   scheme particulars rules.

(2)   The Authority may, on the application or with the consent of any person to whom any rules apply, direct that all or any of the rules—
  (a)   are not to apply to him as respects a particular scheme; or
  (b)   are to apply to him, as respects a particular scheme, with such modifications as may be specified in the direction.

(3)   The Authority may, on the application or with the consent of the manager and trustee of a particular scheme acting jointly, direct that all or any of the rules—
  (a)   are not to apply to the scheme; or
  (b)   are to apply to the scheme with such modifications as may be specified in the direction.

(4)   Subsections (3) to (9) and (11) of section 148 have effect in relation to a direction under subsection (2) as they have effect in relation to a direction under section 148(2) but with the following modifications—
  (a)   subsection (4)(a) is to be read as if the words "by the authorised person" were omitted;
  (b)   any reference to the authorised person (except in subsection (4)(a)) is to be read as a reference to the person mentioned in subsection (2); and
  (c)   subsection (7)(b) is to be read, in relation to a participant of the scheme, as if the word "commercial" were omitted.

(5)   Subsections (3) to (9) and (11) of section 148 have effect in relation to a direction under subsection (3) as they have effect in relation to a direction under section 148(2) but with the following modifications—
  (a)   subsection (4)(a) is to be read as if the words "by the authorised person" were omitted;
  (b)   subsections (7)(b) and (11) are to be read as if references to the authorised person were references to each of the manager and the trustee of the scheme;
  (c)   subsection (7)(b) is to be read, in relation to a participant of the scheme, as if the word "commercial" were omitted;
  (d)   subsection (8) is to be read as if the reference to the authorised person concerned were a reference to the scheme concerned and to its manager and trustee; and
  (e)   subsection (9) is to be read as if the reference to the authorised person were a reference to the manager and trustee of the scheme acting jointly.

Commencement: 3 September 2001.
References: See paras 15.27, 15.28.

Alterations

251 Alteration of schemes and changes of manager or trustee

(1)   The manager of an authorised unit trust scheme must give written notice to the Authority of any proposal to alter the scheme or to replace its trustee.

(2)   Any notice given in respect of a proposal to alter the scheme involving a change in the trust deed must be accompanied by a certificate signed by a solicitor to the effect that the change will not affect the compliance of the deed with the trust scheme rules.

(3)   The trustee of an authorised unit trust scheme must give written notice to the Authority of any proposal to replace the manager of the scheme.

(4)   Effect is not to be given to any proposal of which notice has been given under subsection (1) or (3) unless—
    (a)   the Authority, by written notice, has given its approval to the proposal; or
    (b)   one month, beginning with the date on which the notice was given, has expired without the manager or trustee having received from the Authority a warning notice under section 252 in respect of the proposal.

(5)   The Authority must not approve a proposal to replace the manager or the trustee of an authorised unit trust scheme unless it is satisfied that, if the proposed replacement is made, the scheme will continue to comply with the requirements of section 243(4) to (7).

Commencement: 3 September 2001 (sub-ss (1)–(3), (4)(a), (5), for the purposes of the giving of notice of any proposal to alter a scheme, or to replace its trustee or manager, not sooner than the day on which s 19 of this Act comes into force, and the giving of approval to any such proposal); 1 December 2001 (remainder).
References: See paras 15.29–15.31.

252 Procedure when refusing approval of change of manager or trustee

(1)   If the Authority proposes to refuse approval of a proposal to replace the trustee or manager of an authorised unit trust scheme, it must give a warning notice to the person by whom notice of the proposal was given under section 251(1) or (3).

(2)   If the Authority proposes to refuse approval of a proposal to alter an authorised unit trust scheme it must give separate warning notices to the manager and the trustee of the scheme.

(3)   To be valid the warning notice must be received by that person before the end of one month beginning with the date on which notice of the proposal was given.

(4)   If, having given a warning notice to a person, the Authority decides to refuse approval—

    (a)   it must give him a decision notice; and

    (b)   he may refer the matter to the Tribunal.

Commencement: 3 September 2001 (for the purposes of the giving of notice of any proposal to alter a scheme, or to replace its trustee or manager, not sooner than the day on which s 19 of this Act comes into force, and the giving of approval to any such proposal); 1 December 2001 (remainder).
References: See para 15.32.

Exclusion clauses

253 Avoidance of exclusion clauses

Any provision of the trust deed of an authorised unit trust scheme is void in so far as it would have the effect of exempting the manager or trustee from liability for any failure to exercise due care and diligence in the discharge of his functions in respect of the scheme.

Commencement: 1 December 2001.
References: See para 15.18.

Ending of authorisation

254 Revocation of authorisation order otherwise than by consent

(1)   An authorisation order may be revoked by an order made by the Authority if it appears to the Authority that—

    (a)   one or more of the requirements for the making of the order are no longer satisfied;

    (b)   the manager or trustee of the scheme concerned has contravened a requirement imposed on him by or under this Act;

    (c)   the manager or trustee of the scheme has, in purported compliance with any such requirement, knowingly or recklessly given the Authority information which is false or misleading in a material particular;

    (d)   no regulated activity is being carried on in relation to the scheme and the period of that inactivity began at least twelve months earlier; or

    (e)   none of paragraphs (a) to (d) applies, but it is desirable to revoke the authorisation order in order to protect the interests of participants or potential participants in the scheme.

(2)   For the purposes of subsection (1)(e), the Authority may take into account any matter relating to—

    (a)   the scheme;

    (b)   the manager or trustee;

    (c)   any person employed by or associated with the manager or trustee in connection with the scheme;

    (d)   any director of the manager or trustee;

    (e)   any person exercising influence over the manager or trustee;

    (f)   any body corporate in the same group as the manager or trustee;

    (g)   any director of any such body corporate;

    (h)   any person exercising influence over any such body corporate.

Commencement: 3 September 2001.
References: See paras 15.33, 15.34.

255 Procedure

(1)   If the Authority proposes to make an order under section 254 revoking an authorisation order ("a revoking order"), it must give separate warning notices to the manager and the trustee of the scheme.

(2)   If the Authority decides to make a revoking order, it must without delay give each of them a decision notice and either of them may refer the matter to the Tribunal.

Commencement: 3 September 2001.
References: See para 15.34.

256 Requests for revocation of authorisation order

(1)   An authorisation order may be revoked by an order made by the Authority at the request of the manager or trustee of the scheme concerned.

(2)   If the Authority makes an order under subsection (1), it must give written notice of the order to the manager and trustee of the scheme concerned.

(3)   The Authority may refuse a request to make an order under this section if it considers that—
- (a)   the public interest requires that any matter concerning the scheme should be investigated before a decision is taken as to whether the authorisation order should be revoked; or
- (b)   revocation would not be in the interests of the participants or would be incompatible with a Community obligation.

(4)   If the Authority proposes to refuse a request under this section, it must give separate warning notices to the manager and the trustee of the scheme.

(5)   If the Authority decides to refuse the request, it must without delay give each of them a decision notice and either of them may refer the matter to the Tribunal.

Commencement: 3 September 2001.
References: See para 15.35

Powers of intervention

257 Directions

(1)   The Authority may give a direction under this section if it appears to the Authority that—
- (a)   one or more of the requirements for the making of an authorisation order are no longer satisfied;
- (b)   the manager or trustee of an authorised unit trust scheme has contravened, or is likely to contravene, a requirement imposed on him by or under this Act;

> (c) the manager or trustee of such a scheme has, in purported compliance with any such requirement, knowingly or recklessly given the Authority information which is false or misleading in a material particular; or
>
> (d) none of paragraphs (a) to (c) applies, but it is desirable to give a direction in order to protect the interests of participants or potential participants in such a scheme.

(2) A direction under this section may—

> (a) require the manager of the scheme to cease the issue or redemption, or both the issue and redemption, of units under the scheme;
>
> (b) require the manager and trustee of the scheme to wind it up.

(3) If the authorisation order is revoked, the revocation does not affect any direction under this section which is then in force.

(4) A direction may be given under this section in relation to a scheme in the case of which the authorisation order has been revoked if a direction under this section was already in force at the time of revocation.

(5) If a person contravenes a direction under this section, section 150 applies to the contravention as it applies to a contravention mentioned in that section.

(6) The Authority may, either on its own initiative or on the application of the manager or trustee of the scheme concerned, revoke or vary a direction given under this section if it appears to the Authority—

> (a) in the case of revocation, that it is no longer necessary for the direction to take effect or continue in force;
>
> (b) in the case of variation, that the direction should take effect or continue in force in a different form.

Commencement: 3 September 2001 (for the purposes of directions coming into force not sooner than the day on which s 19 of this Act comes into force); 1 December 2001 (remaining purposes).
References: See paras 15.36, 15.37.

258 Applications to the court

(1) If the Authority could give a direction under section 257, it may also apply to the court for an order—

> (a) removing the manager or the trustee, or both the manager and the trustee, of the scheme; and
>
> (b) replacing the person or persons removed with a suitable person or persons nominated by the Authority.

(2) The Authority may nominate a person for the purposes of subsection (1)(b) only if it is satisfied that, if the order was made, the requirements of section 243(4) to (7) would be complied with.

(3) If it appears to the Authority that there is no person it can nominate for the purposes of subsection (1)(b), it may apply to the court for an order—

> (a) removing the manager or the trustee, or both the manager and the trustee, of the scheme; and
>
> (b) appointing an authorised person to wind up the scheme.

(4) On an application under this section the court may make such order as it thinks fit.

(5) The court may, on the application of the Authority, rescind any such order as is mentioned in subsection (3) and substitute such an order as is mentioned in subsection (1).

(6) The Authority must give written notice of the making of an application under this section to the manager and trustee of the scheme concerned.

(7) The jurisdiction conferred by this section may be exercised by—
 (a) the High Court;
 (b) in Scotland, the Court of Session.

Commencement: 1 December 2001.
References: See paras 15.44, 15.45.

259 Procedure on giving directions under section 257 and varying them on Authority's own initiative

(1) A direction takes effect—
 (a) immediately, if the notice given under subsection (3) states that that is the case;
 (b) on such date as may be specified in the notice; or
 (c) if no date is specified in the notice, when the matter to which it relates is no longer open to review.

(2) A direction may be expressed to take effect immediately (or on a specified date) only if the Authority, having regard to the ground on which it is exercising its power under section 257, considers that it is necessary for the direction to take effect immediately (or on that date).

(3) If the Authority proposes to give a direction under section 257, or gives such a direction with immediate effect, it must give separate written notice to the manager and the trustee of the scheme concerned.

(4) The notice must—
 (a) give details of the direction;
 (b) inform the person to whom it is given of when the direction takes effect;
 (c) state the Authority's reasons for giving the direction and for its determination as to when the direction takes effect;
 (d) inform the person to whom it is given that he may make representations to the Authority within such period as may be specified in it (whether or not he has referred the matter to the Tribunal); and
 (e) inform him of his right to refer the matter to the Tribunal.

(5) If the direction imposes a requirement under section 257(2)(a), the notice must state that the requirement has effect until—
 (a) a specified date; or
 (b) a further direction.

(6) If the direction imposes a requirement under section 257(2)(b), the scheme must be wound up—
 (a) by a date specified in the notice; or
 (b) if no date is specified, as soon as practicable.

(7)   The Authority may extend the period allowed under the notice for making representations.

(8)   If, having considered any representations made by a person to whom the notice was given, the Authority decides—

(a)   to give the direction in the way proposed, or

(b)   if it has been given, not to revoke the direction,

it must give separate written notice to the manager and the trustee of the scheme concerned.

(9)   If, having considered any representations made by a person to whom the notice was given, the Authority decides—

(a)   not to give the direction in the way proposed,

(b)   to give the direction in a way other than that proposed, or

(c)   to revoke a direction which has effect,

it must give separate written notice to the manager and the trustee of the scheme concerned.

(10)   A notice given under subsection (8) must inform the person to whom it is given of his right to refer the matter to the Tribunal.

(11)   A notice under subsection (9)(b) must comply with subsection (4).

(12)   If a notice informs a person of his right to refer a matter to the Tribunal, it must give an indication of the procedure on such a reference.

(13)   This section applies to the variation of a direction on the Authority's own initiative as it applies to the giving of a direction.

(14)   For the purposes of subsection (1)(c), whether a matter is open to review is to be determined in accordance with section 391(8).

Commencement: 3 September 2001 (for the purposes of directions coming into force not sooner than the day on which s 19 of this Act comes into force); 1 December 2001 (remaining purposes).
References: See paras 15.38–15.41.

260 Procedure: refusal to revoke or vary direction

(1)   If on an application under section 257(6) for a direction to be revoked or varied the Authority proposes—

(a)   to vary the direction otherwise than in accordance with the application, or

(b)   to refuse to revoke or vary the direction,

it must give the applicant a warning notice.

(2)   If the Authority decides to refuse to revoke or vary the direction—

(a)   it must give the applicant a decision notice; and

(b)   the applicant may refer the matter to the Tribunal.

Commencement: 3 September 2001 (for the purposes of directions coming into force not sooner than the day on which s 19 of this Act comes into force); 1 December 2001 (remaining purposes).
References: See para 15.37.

261 Procedure: revocation of direction and grant of request for variation

(1)   If the Authority decides on its own initiative to revoke a direction under section 257 it must give separate written notices of its decision to the manager and trustee of the scheme.

(2)   If on an application under section 257(6) for a direction to be revoked or varied the Authority decides to revoke the direction or vary it in accordance with the application, it must give the applicant written notice of its decision.

(3)   A notice under this section must specify the date on which the decision takes effect.

(4)   The Authority may publish such information about the revocation or variation, in such way, as it considers appropriate.

Commencement: 3 September 2001 (for the purposes of directions coming into force not sooner than the day on which s 19 of this Act comes into force); 1 December 2001 (remaining purposes).
References: See para 15.43.

CHAPTER IV
OPEN-ENDED INVESTMENT COMPANIES

262 Open-ended investment companies

(1)   The Treasury may by regulations make provision for—
    (a)   facilitating the carrying on of collective investment by means of open-ended investment companies;
    (b)   regulating such companies.

(2)   The regulations may, in particular, make provision—
    (a)   for the incorporation and registration in Great Britain of bodies corporate;
    (b)   for a body incorporated by virtue of the regulations to take such form as may be determined in accordance with the regulations;
    (c)   as to the purposes for which such a body may exist, the investments which it may issue and otherwise as to its constitution;
    (d)   as to the management and operation of such a body and the management of its property;
    (e)   as to the powers, duties, rights and liabilities of such a body and of other persons, including—
      (i)   the directors or sole director of such a body;
      (ii)   its depositary (if any);
      (iii)   its shareholders, and persons who hold the beneficial title to shares in it without holding the legal title;
      (iv)   its auditor; and
      (v)   any persons who act or purport to act on its behalf;
    (f)   as to the merger of one or more such bodies and the division of such a body;
    (g)   for the appointment and removal of an auditor for such a body;
    (h)   as to the winding up and dissolution of such a body;
    (i)   for such a body, or any director or depositary of such a body, to be required to comply with directions given by the Authority;
    (j)   enabling the Authority to apply to a court for an order removing and replacing any director or depositary of such a body;

- (k) for the carrying out of investigations by persons appointed by the Authority or the Secretary of State;
- (l) corresponding to any provision made in relation to unit trust schemes by Chapter III of this Part.

(3) Regulations under this section may—
- (a) impose criminal liability;
- (b) confer functions on the Authority;
- (c) in the case of provision made by virtue of subsection (2)(l), authorise the making of rules by the Authority;
- (d) confer jurisdiction on any court or on the Tribunal;
- (e) provide for fees to be charged by the Authority in connection with the carrying out of any of its functions under the regulations (including fees payable on a periodical basis);
- (f) modify, exclude or apply (with or without modifications) any primary or subordinate legislation (including any provision of, or made under, this Act);
- (g) make consequential amendments, repeals and revocations of any such legislation;
- (h) modify or exclude any rule of law.

(4) The provision that may be made by virtue of subsection (3)(f) includes provision extending or adapting any power to make subordinate legislation.

(5) Regulations under this section may, in particular—
- (a) revoke the Open-Ended Investment Companies (Investment Companies with Variable Capital) Regulations 1996; and
- (b) provide for things done under or in accordance with those regulations to be treated as if they had been done under or in accordance with regulations under this section.

Commencement: 25 February 2001.
Regulations: The Open-Ended Investment Companies Regulations 2001, SI 2001/1228, as amended by SI 2001/3755, SI 2003/2066.
Open-Ended Investment Companies (Investment Companies with Variable Capital) Regulations 1996: SI 1996/2827: revoked, subject to transitional provisions and savings, by the Open-Ended Investment Companies Regulations 2001, SI 2001/1228, reg 85.
References: See paras 15.11, 15.12.

263 *(Amends the Companies Act 1985, s 716.)*

CHAPTER V
RECOGNISED OVERSEAS SCHEMES

Schemes constituted in other EEA States

264 Schemes constituted in other EEA States

(1) A collective investment scheme constituted in another EEA State is a recognised scheme if—
- (a) it satisfies such requirements as are prescribed for the purposes of this section; and
- (b) not less than two months before inviting persons in the United Kingdom to become participants in the scheme, the operator of the

scheme gives notice to the Authority of his intention to do so, specifying the way in which the invitation is to be made.

(2)   But this section does not make the scheme a recognised scheme if within two months of receiving the notice under subsection (1) the Authority notifies—

   (a)   the operator of the scheme, and
   (b)   the authorities of the State in question who are responsible for the authorisation of collective investment schemes,

that the way in which the invitation is to be made does not comply with the law in force in the United Kingdom.

(3)   The notice to be given to the Authority under subsection (1)—

   (a)   must be accompanied by a certificate from the authorities mentioned in subsection (2)(b) to the effect that the scheme complies with the conditions necessary for it to enjoy the rights conferred by any relevant Community instrument;
   (b)   must contain the address of a place in the United Kingdom for the service on the operator of notices or other documents required or authorised to be served on him under this Act; and
   (c)   must contain or be accompanied by such other information and documents as may be prescribed.

(4)   A notice given by the Authority under subsection (2) must—

   (a)   give the reasons for which the Authority considers that the law in force in the United Kingdom will not be complied with; and
   (b)   specify a reasonable period (which may not be less than 28 days) within which any person to whom it is given may make representations to the Authority.

(5)   For the purposes of this section a collective investment scheme is constituted in another EEA State if—

   (a)   it is constituted under the law of that State by a contract or under a trust and is managed by a body corporate incorporated under that law; or
   (b)   it takes the form of an open-ended investment company incorporated under that law.

(6)   The operator of a recognised scheme may give written notice to the Authority that he desires the scheme to be no longer recognised by virtue of this section.

(7)   On the giving of notice under subsection (6), the scheme ceases to be a recognised scheme.

Commencement: 3 September 2001 (for the purposes of the giving of notice under sub-s (1) of intention to make invitations not sooner than the day on which s 19 of this Act comes into force; and the giving of notice under sub-ss (2) or (6)); 25 February 2001 (sub-ss (1), (3)(c), for the purpose of making orders or regulations); 1 December 2001 (remainder).
Regulations: The Financial Services and Markets Act 2000 (Collective Investment Schemes Constituted in Other EEA States) Regulations 2001, SI 2001/2383, as amended by SI 2003/2066.
References: See paras 15.47–15.50.

265 Representations and references to the Tribunal

(1)   This section applies if any representations are made to the Authority, before the period for making representations has ended, by a person to whom a notice was given by the Authority under section 264(2).

(2)   The Authority must, within a reasonable period, decide in the light of those representations whether or not to withdraw its notice.

(3)   If the Authority withdraws its notice the scheme is a recognised scheme from the date on which the notice is withdrawn.

(4)   If the Authority decides not to withdraw its notice, it must give a decision notice to each person to whom the notice under section 264(2) was given.

(5)   The operator of the scheme to whom the decision notice is given may refer the matter to the Tribunal.

Commencement: 1 December 2001 (sub-s (3)); 3 September 2001 (remainder).
References: See para 15.52.

266 Disapplication of rules

(1)   Apart from—
    (a)   financial promotion rules, and
    (b)   rules under section 283(1),

rules made by the Authority under this Act do not apply to the operator, trustee or depositary of a scheme in relation to the carrying on by him of regulated activities for which he has permission in that capacity.

[(1A) But subsection (1) does not affect the application of rules to an operator of a scheme if the operator is an EEA firm falling within paragraph 5(f) of Schedule 3 who qualifies for authorisation under that Schedule.]

(2)   "Scheme" means a scheme which is a recognised scheme by virtue of section 264.

Commencement: 18 June 2001.
Amendments: Sub-s (1A): inserted by the Collective Investment Schemes (Miscellaneous Amendments) Regulations 2003, SI 2003/2066, reg 9, as from 13 February 2004.
References: See para 15.53.

267 Power of Authority to suspend promotion of scheme

(1)   Subsection (2) applies if it appears to the Authority that the operator of a scheme has communicated an invitation or inducement in relation to the scheme in a manner contrary to financial promotion rules.

(2)   The Authority may direct that—
    (a)   the exemption from subsection (1) of section 238 provided by subsection (4)(c) of that section is not to apply in relation to the scheme; and
    (b)   subsection (5) of that section does not apply with respect to things done in relation to the scheme.

(3)   A direction under subsection (2) has effect—
    (a)   for a specified period;
    (b)   until the occurrence of a specified event; or
    (c)   until specified conditions are complied with.

(4)   The Authority may, either on its own initiative or on the application of the operator of the scheme concerned, vary a direction given under subsection (2) if it appears to the Authority that the direction should take effect or continue in force in a different form.

(5)   The Authority may, either on its own initiative or on the application of the operator of the recognised scheme concerned, revoke a direction given under subsection (2) if it appears to the Authority—

    (a)   that the conditions specified in the direction have been complied with; or

    (b)   that it is no longer necessary for the direction to take effect or continue in force.

(6)   If an event is specified, the direction ceases to have effect (unless revoked earlier) on the occurrence of that event.

(7)   For the purposes of this section and sections 268 and 269—

    (a)   the scheme's home State is the EEA State in which the scheme is constituted (within the meaning given by section 264);

    (b)   the competent authorities in the scheme's home State are the authorities in that State who are responsible for the authorisation of collective investment schemes.

(8)   "Scheme" means a scheme which is a recognised scheme by virtue of section 264.

(9)   "Specified", in relation to a direction, means specified in it.

Commencement: 1 December 2001.
References: See paras 15.54–15.59.

268 Procedure on giving directions under section 267 and varying them on Authority's own initiative

(1)   A direction under section 267 takes effect—

    (a)   immediately, if the notice given under subsection (3)(a) states that that is the case;

    (b)   on such date as may be specified in the notice; or

    (c)   if no date is specified in the notice, when the matter to which it relates is no longer open to review.

(2)   A direction may be expressed to take effect immediately (or on a specified date) only if the Authority, having regard to its reasons for exercising its power under section 267, considers that it is necessary for the direction to take effect immediately (or on that date).

(3)   If the Authority proposes to give a direction under section 267, or gives such a direction with immediate effect, it must—

    (a)   give the operator of the scheme concerned written notice; and

    (b)   inform the competent authorities in the scheme's home State of its proposal or (as the case may be) of the direction.

(4)   The notice must—

    (a)   give details of the direction;

    (b)   inform the operator of when the direction takes effect;

    (c)   state the Authority's reasons for giving the direction and for its determination as to when the direction takes effect;

    (d)   inform the operator that he may make representations to the Authority within such period as may be specified in it (whether or not he has referred the matter to the Tribunal); and

    (e)   inform him of his right to refer the matter to the Tribunal.

(5)   The Authority may extend the period allowed under the notice for making representations.

(6)   Subsection (7) applies if, having considered any representations made by the operator, the Authority decides—

    (a)   to give the direction in the way proposed, or

    (b)   if it has been given, not to revoke the direction.

(7)   The Authority must—

    (a)   give the operator of the scheme concerned written notice; and

    (b)   inform the competent authorities in the scheme's home State of the direction.

(8)   Subsection (9) applies if, having considered any representations made by a person to whom the notice was given, the Authority decides—

    (a)   not to give the direction in the way proposed,

    (b)   to give the direction in a way other than that proposed, or

    (c)   to revoke a direction which has effect.

(9)   The Authority must—

    (a)   give the operator of the scheme concerned written notice; and

    (b)   inform the competent authorities in the scheme's home State of its decision.

(10) A notice given under subsection (7)(a) must inform the operator of his right to refer the matter to the Tribunal.

(11) A notice under subsection (9)(a) given as a result of subsection (8)(b) must comply with subsection (4).

(12) If a notice informs a person of his right to refer a matter to the Tribunal, it must give an indication of the procedure on such a reference.

(13) This section applies to the variation of a direction on the Authority's own initiative as it applies to the giving of a direction.

(14) For the purposes of subsection (1)(c), whether a matter is open to review is to be determined in accordance with section 391(8).

Commencement: 1 December 2001.
References: See paras 15.55–15.58.

269 Procedure on application for variation or revocation of direction

(1)   If, on an application under subsection (4) or (5) of section 267, the Authority proposes—

    (a)   to vary a direction otherwise than in accordance with the application, or

    (b)   to refuse the application,

it must give the operator of the scheme concerned a warning notice.

(2) If, on such an application, the Authority decides—
    (a) to vary a direction otherwise than in accordance with the application, or
    (b) to refuse the application,
it must give the operator of the scheme concerned a decision notice.

(3) If the application is refused, the operator of the scheme may refer the matter to the Tribunal.

(4) If, on such an application, the Authority decides to grant the application it must give the operator of the scheme concerned written notice.

(5) If the Authority decides on its own initiative to revoke a direction given under section 267 it must give the operator of the scheme concerned written notice.

(6) The Authority must inform the competent authorities in the scheme's home State of any notice given under this section.

Commencement: 1 December 2001.
References: See paras 15.58, 15.59.

Schemes authorised in designated countries or territories

270 Schemes authorised in designated countries or territories

(1) A collective investment scheme which is not a recognised scheme by virtue of section 264 but is managed in, and authorised under the law of, a country or territory outside the United Kingdom is a recognised scheme if—
    (a) that country or territory is designated for the purposes of this section by an order made by the Treasury;
    (b) the scheme is of a class specified by the order;
    (c) the operator of the scheme has given written notice to the Authority that he wishes it to be recognised; and
    (d) either—
        (i) the Authority, by written notice, has given its approval to the scheme's being recognised; or
        (ii) two months, beginning with the date on which notice was given under paragraph (c), have expired without the operator receiving a warning notice from the Authority under section 271.

(2) The Treasury may not make an order designating any country or territory for the purposes of this section unless satisfied—
    (a) that the law and practice under which relevant collective investment schemes are authorised and supervised in that country or territory affords to investors in the United Kingdom protection at least equivalent to that provided for them by or under this Part in the case of comparable authorised schemes; and
    (b) that adequate arrangements exist, or will exist, for co-operation between the authorities of the country or territory responsible for the authorisation and supervision of relevant collective investment schemes and the Authority.

(3) "Relevant collective investment schemes" means collective investment schemes of the class or classes to be specified by the order.

(4)   "Comparable authorised schemes" means whichever of the following the Treasury consider to be the most appropriate, having regard to the class or classes of scheme to be specified by the order—

(a)   authorised unit trust schemes;
(b)   authorised open-ended investment companies;
(c)   both such unit trust schemes and such companies.

(5)   If the Treasury are considering whether to make an order designating a country or territory for the purposes of this section—

(a)   the Treasury must ask the Authority for a report—

(i)   on the law and practice of that country or territory in relation to the authorisation and supervision of relevant collective investment schemes,

(ii)   on any existing or proposed arrangements for co-operation between it and the authorities responsible in that country or territory for the authorisation and supervision of relevant collective investment schemes,

having regard to the Treasury's need to be satisfied as mentioned in subsection (2);

(b)   the Authority must provide the Treasury with such a report; and
(c)   the Treasury must have regard to it in deciding whether to make the order.

(6)   The notice to be given by the operator under subsection (1)(c)—

(a)   must contain the address of a place in the United Kingdom for the service on the operator of notices or other documents required or authorised to be served on him under this Act; and

(b)   must contain or be accompanied by such information and documents as may be specified by the Authority.

Commencement: 3 September 2001 (for the purposes of the giving of notice under sub-s (1)(c); and the giving of notice of approval under sub-s (1)(d)(i) coming into force not sooner than the day on which s 19 of this Act comes into force); 25 February 2001 (for the purpose of making orders or regulations); 1 December 2001 (remaining purposes).
Orders: The Financial Services and Markets Act 2000 (Collective Investment Schemes) (Designated Countries and Territories) Order 2003, SI 2003/1181 which supersedes SI 1988/2015, SI 1988/2148, and SI 1988/2149 (all made under FSA 1986, s 87(1)). SI 1988/2284 (also made under FSA 1986, s 87(1)) continues in force and has effect as if made under sub-s (1)(a) above by virtue of SI 2001/2636, art 67(1).
References: See paras 15.61–15.64.

271 Procedure

(1)   If the Authority proposes to refuse approval of a scheme's being a recognised scheme by virtue of section 270, it must give the operator of the scheme a warning notice.

(2)   To be valid the warning notice must be received by the operator before the end of two months beginning with the date on which notice was given under section 270(1)(c).

(3)   If, having given a warning notice, the Authority decides to refuse approval—

(a)   it must give the operator of the scheme a decision notice; and
(b)   the operator may refer the matter to the Tribunal.

Commencement: 1 December 2001 (sub-s (2)); 3 September 2001 (remainder).
References: See para 15.65.

Individually recognised overseas schemes

272 Individually recognised overseas schemes

(1)   The Authority may, on the application of the operator of a collective investment scheme which—

- (a)   is managed in a country or territory outside the United Kingdom,
- (b)   does not satisfy the requirements prescribed for the purposes of section 264,
- (c)   is not managed in a country or territory designated for the purposes of section 270 or, if it is so managed, is of a class not specified by the designation order, and
- (d)   appears to the Authority to satisfy the requirements set out in the following provisions of this section,

make an order declaring the scheme to be a recognised scheme.

(2)   Adequate protection must be afforded to participants in the scheme.

(3)   The arrangements for the scheme's constitution and management must be adequate.

(4)   The powers and duties of the operator and, if the scheme has a trustee or depositary, of the trustee or depositary must be adequate.

(5)   In deciding whether the matters mentioned in subsection (3) or (4) are adequate, the Authority must have regard to—

- (a)   any rule of law, and
- (b)   any matters which are, or could be, the subject of rules,

applicable in relation to comparable authorised schemes.

(6)   "Comparable authorised schemes" means whichever of the following the Authority considers the most appropriate, having regard to the nature of scheme in respect of which the application is made—

- (a)   authorised unit trust schemes;
- (b)   authorised open-ended investment companies;
- (c)   both such unit trust schemes and such companies.

(7)   The scheme must take the form of an open-ended investment company or (if it does not take that form) the operator must be a body corporate.

(8)   The operator of the scheme must—

- (a)   if an authorised person, have permission to act as operator;
- (b)   if not an authorised person, be a fit and proper person to act as operator.

(9)   The trustee or depositary (if any) of the scheme must—

- (a)   if an authorised person, have permission to act as trustee or depositary;
- (b)   if not an authorised person, be a fit and proper person to act as trustee or depositary.

(10) The operator and the trustee or depositary (if any) of the scheme must be able and willing to co-operate with the Authority by the sharing of information and in other ways.

(11) The name of the scheme must not be undesirable or misleading.

(12) The purposes of the scheme must be reasonably capable of being successfully carried into effect.

(13) The participants must be entitled to have their units redeemed in accordance with the scheme at a price related to the net value of the property to which the units relate and determined in accordance with the scheme.

(14) But a scheme is to be treated as complying with subsection (13) if it requires the operator to ensure that a participant is able to sell his units on an investment exchange at a price not significantly different from that mentioned in that subsection.

(15) Subsection (13) is not to be read as imposing a requirement that the participants must be entitled to have their units redeemed (or sold as mentioned in subsection (14)) immediately following a demand to that effect.

Commencement: 3 September 2001 (for the purposes of orders (and applications for orders) coming into force not sooner than the day on which s 19 of this Act comes into force); 1 December 2001 (remaining purposes).
References: See paras 15.74–15.77.

273 Matters that may be taken into account

For the purposes of subsections (8)(b) and (9)(b) of section 272, the Authority may take into account any matter relating to—

- (a) any person who is or will be employed by or associated with the operator, trustee or depositary in connection with the scheme;
- (b) any director of the operator, trustee or depositary;
- (c) any person exercising influence over the operator, trustee or depositary;
- (d) any body corporate in the same group as the operator, trustee or depositary;
- (e) any director of any such body corporate;
- (f) any person exercising influence over any such body corporate.

Commencement: 3 September 2001 (for the purposes of orders (and applications for orders) coming into force not sooner than the day on which s 19 of this Act comes into force); 1 December 2001 (remaining purposes).
References: See para 15.76.

274 Applications for recognition of individual schemes

(1) An application under section 272 for an order declaring a scheme to be a recognised scheme must be made to the Authority by the operator of the scheme.

(2) The application—

- (a) must be made in such manner as the Authority may direct;
- (b) must contain the address of a place in the United Kingdom for the service on the operator of notices or other documents required or authorised to be served on him under this Act;

    (c)   must contain or be accompanied by such information as the Authority may reasonably require for the purpose of determining the application.

(3)   At any time after receiving an application and before determining it, the Authority may require the applicant to provide it with such further information as it reasonably considers necessary to enable it to determine the application.

(4)   Different directions may be given, and different requirements imposed, in relation to different applications.

(5)   The Authority may require an applicant to present information which he is required to give under this section in such form, or to verify it in such a way, as the Authority may direct.

Commencement: 3 September 2001 (for the purposes of orders (and applications for orders) coming into force not sooner than the day on which s 19 of this Act comes into force); 18 June 2001 (for the purpose of giving directions or imposing requirements as mentioned in sub-s (2) above); 1 December 2001 (remaining purposes).
References: See para 15.78.

---

275 Determination of applications

(1)   An application under section 272 must be determined by the Authority before the end of the period of six months beginning with the date on which it receives the completed application.

(2)   The Authority may determine an incomplete application if it considers it appropriate to do so; and it must in any event determine such an application within twelve months beginning with the date on which it first receives the application.

(3)   If the Authority makes an order under section 272(1), it must give written notice of the order to the applicant.

Commencement: 3 September 2001 (for the purposes of orders (and applications for orders) coming into force not sooner than the day on which s 19 of this Act comes into force); 1 December 2001 (remaining purposes).
References: See paras 15.79, 15.81.

---

276 Procedure when refusing an application

(1)   If the Authority proposes to refuse an application made under section 272 it must give the applicant a warning notice.

(2)   If the Authority decides to refuse the application—
    (a)   it must give the applicant a decision notice; and
    (b)   the applicant may refer the matter to the Tribunal.

Commencement: 3 September 2001 (for the purposes of orders (and applications for orders) coming into force not sooner than the day on which s 19 of this Act comes into force); 1 December 2001 (remaining purposes).
References: See para 15.81.

277 Alteration of schemes and changes of operator, trustee or depositary

(1)   The operator of a scheme recognised by virtue of section 272 must give written notice to the Authority of any proposed alteration to the scheme.

(2)   Effect is not to be given to any such proposal unless—
- (a)   the Authority, by written notice, has given its approval to the proposal; or
- (b)   one month, beginning with the date on which notice was given under subsection (1), has expired without the Authority having given written notice to the operator that it has decided to refuse approval.

(3)   At least one month before any replacement of the operator, trustee or depositary of such a scheme, notice of the proposed replacement must be given to the Authority—
- (a)   by the operator, trustee or depositary (as the case may be); or
- (b)   by the person who is to replace him.

Commencement: 3 September 2001 (for the purposes of the giving of notice under sub-s (1) of any proposal to alter a scheme not sooner than the day on which s 19 of this Act comes into force, and the giving of approval to any such proposal; and the giving of notice under sub-s (3) of any proposal to replace an operator, trustee or depositary not sooner than the day on which s 19 of this Act comes into force); 1 December 2001 (remaining purposes).
References: See para 15.80.

Schemes recognised under sections 270 and 272

278 Rules as to scheme particulars

The Authority may make rules imposing duties or liabilities on the operator of a scheme recognised under section 270 or 272 for purposes corresponding to those for which rules may be made under section 248 in relation to authorised unit trust schemes.

Commencement: 18 June 2001.
References: See para 15.82.

279 Revocation of recognition

The Authority may direct that a scheme is to cease to be recognised by virtue of section 270 or revoke an order under section 272 if it appears to the Authority—
- (a)   that the operator, trustee or depositary of the scheme has contravened a requirement imposed on him by or under this Act;
- (b)   that the operator, trustee or depositary of the scheme has, in purported compliance with any such requirement, knowingly or recklessly given the Authority information which is false or misleading in a material particular;
- (c)   in the case of an order under section 272, that one or more of the requirements for the making of the order are no longer satisfied; or
- (d)   that none of paragraphs (a) to (c) applies, but it is undesirable in the interests of the participants or potential participants that the scheme should continue to be recognised.

Commencement: 3 September 2001.
References: See paras 15.67, 15.83.

280 Procedure

(1)   If the Authority proposes to give a direction under section 279 or to make an order under that section revoking a recognition order, it must give a warning notice to the operator and (if any) the trustee or depositary of the scheme.

(2)   If the Authority decides to give a direction or make an order under that section—

  (a)   it must without delay give a decision notice to the operator and (if any) the trustee or depositary of the scheme; and

  (b)   the operator or the trustee or depositary may refer the matter to the Tribunal.

Commencement: 3 September 2001.
References: See para 15.68.

281 Directions

(1)   In this section a "relevant recognised scheme" means a scheme recognised under section 270 or 272.

(2)   If it appears to the Authority that—

  (a)   the operator, trustee or depositary of a relevant recognised scheme has contravened, or is likely to contravene, a requirement imposed on him by or under this Act,

  (b)   the operator, trustee or depositary of such a scheme has, in purported compliance with any such requirement, knowingly or recklessly given the Authority information which is false or misleading in a material particular,

  (c)   one or more of the requirements for the recognition of a scheme under section 272 are no longer satisfied, or

  (d)   none of paragraphs (a) to (c) applies, but the exercise of the power conferred by this section is desirable in order to protect the interests of participants or potential participants in a relevant recognised scheme who are in the United Kingdom,

it may direct that the scheme is not to be a recognised scheme for a specified period or until the occurrence of a specified event or until specified conditions are complied with.

Commencement: 3 September 2001.
References: See paras 15.69, 15.70.

282 Procedure on giving directions under section 281 and varying them otherwise than as requested

(1)   A direction takes effect—

  (a)   immediately, if the notice given under subsection (3) states that that is the case;

  (b)   on such date as may be specified in the notice; or

  (c)   if no date is specified in the notice, when the matter to which it relates is no longer open to review.

(2) A direction may be expressed to take effect immediately (or on a specified date) only if the Authority, having regard to the ground on which it is exercising its power under section 281, considers that it is necessary for the direction to take effect immediately (or on that date).

(3) If the Authority proposes to give a direction under section 281, or gives such a direction with immediate effect, it must give separate written notice to the operator and (if any) the trustee or depositary of the scheme concerned.

(4) The notice must—
  (a) give details of the direction;
  (b) inform the person to whom it is given of when the direction takes effect;
  (c) state the Authority's reasons for giving the direction and for its determination as to when the direction takes effect;
  (d) inform the person to whom it is given that he may make representations to the Authority within such period as may be specified in it (whether or not he has referred the matter to the Tribunal); and
  (e) inform him of his right to refer the matter to the Tribunal.

(5) The Authority may extend the period allowed under the notice for making representations.

(6) If, having considered any representations made by a person to whom the notice was given, the Authority decides—
  (a) to give the direction in the way proposed, or
  (b) if it has been given, not to revoke the direction,

it must give separate written notice to the operator and (if any) the trustee or depositary of the scheme concerned.

(7) If, having considered any representations made by a person to whom the notice was given, the Authority decides—
  (a) not to give the direction in the way proposed,
  (b) to give the direction in a way other than that proposed, or
  (c) to revoke a direction which has effect,

it must give separate written notice to the operator and (if any) the trustee or depositary of the scheme concerned.

(8) A notice given under subsection (6) must inform the person to whom it is given of his right to refer the matter to the Tribunal.

(9) A notice under subsection (7)(b) must comply with subsection (4).

(10) If a notice informs a person of his right to refer a matter to the Tribunal, it must give an indication of the procedure on such a reference.

(11) This section applies to the variation of a direction on the Authority's own initiative as it applies to the giving of a direction.

(12) For the purposes of subsection (1)(c), whether a matter is open to review is to be determined in accordance with section 391(8).

Commencement: 3 September 2001.
References: See paras 15.70, 15.71.

Facilities and information in UK

283 Facilities and information in UK

(1)   The Authority may make rules requiring operators of recognised schemes to maintain in the United Kingdom, or in such part or parts of it as may be specified, such facilities as the Authority thinks desirable in the interests of participants and as are specified in rules.

(2)   The Authority may by notice in writing require the operator of any recognised scheme to include such explanatory information as is specified in the notice in any communication of his which—

(a)   is a communication of an invitation or inducement of a kind mentioned in section 21(1); and

(b)   names the scheme.

(3)   In the case of a communication originating outside the United Kingdom, subsection (2) only applies if the communication is capable of having an effect in the United Kingdom.

Commencement: 1 December 2001 (sub-ss (2), (3)); 18 June 2001 (remainder).
References: See para 15.73.

CHAPTER VI
INVESTIGATIONS

284 Power to investigate

(1)   An investigating authority may appoint one or more competent persons to investigate on its behalf—

(a)   the affairs of, or of the manager or trustee of, any authorised unit trust scheme,

(b)   the affairs of, or of the operator, trustee or depositary of, any recognised scheme so far as relating to activities carried on in the United Kingdom, or

(c)   the affairs of, or of the operator, trustee or depositary of, any other collective investment scheme except a body incorporated by virtue of regulations under section 262,

if it appears to the investigating authority that it is in the interests of the participants or potential participants to do so or that the matter is of public concern.

(2)   A person appointed under subsection (1) to investigate the affairs of, or of the manager, trustee, operator or depositary of, any scheme (scheme "A"), may also, if he thinks it necessary for the purposes of that investigation, investigate—

(a)   the affairs of, or of the manager, trustee, operator or depositary of, any other such scheme as is mentioned in subsection (1) whose manager, trustee, operator or depositary is the same person as the manager, trustee, operator or depositary of scheme A;

(b)   the affairs of such other schemes and persons (including bodies incorporated by virtue of regulations under section 262 and the directors and depositaries of such bodies) as may be prescribed.

(3)   If the person appointed to conduct an investigation under this section ("B") considers that a person ("C") is or may be able to give information which is relevant to the investigation, B may require C—

    (a)   to produce to B any documents in C's possession or under his control which appear to B to be relevant to the investigation,

    (b)   to attend before B, and

    (c)   otherwise to give B all assistance in connection with the investigation which C is reasonably able to give,

and it is C's duty to comply with that requirement.

(4)   Subsections (5) to (9) of section 170 apply if an investigating authority appoints a person under this section to conduct an investigation on its behalf as they apply in the case mentioned in subsection (1) of that section.

(5)   Section 174 applies to a statement made by a person in compliance with a requirement imposed under this section as it applies to a statement mentioned in that section.

(6)   Subsections (2) to (4) and (6) of section 175 and section 177 have effect as if this section were contained in Part XI.

(7)   Subsections (1) to (9) of section 176 apply in relation to a person appointed under subsection (1) as if—

    (a)   references to an investigator were references to a person so appointed;

    (b)   references to an information requirement were references to a requirement imposed under section 175 or under subsection (3) by a person so appointed;

    (c)   the premises mentioned in subsection (3)(a) were the premises of a person whose affairs are the subject of an investigation under this section or of an appointed representative of such a person.

(8)   No person may be required under this section to disclose information or produce a document in respect of which he owes an obligation of confidence by virtue of carrying on the business of banking unless subsection (9) or (10) applies.

(9)   This subsection applies if—

    (a)   the person to whom the obligation of confidence is owed consents to the disclosure or production; or

    (b)   the imposing on the person concerned of a requirement with respect to information or a document of a kind mentioned in subsection (8) has been specifically authorised by the investigating authority.

(10)   This subsection applies if the person owing the obligation of confidence or the person to whom it is owed is—

    (a)   the manager, trustee, operator or depositary of any collective investment scheme which is under investigation;

    (b)   the director of a body incorporated by virtue of regulations under section 262 which is under investigation;

    (c)   any other person whose own affairs are under investigation.

(11)   "Investigating authority" means the Authority or the Secretary of State.

Commencement: 25 February 2001 (sub-s (2), for the purpose of making orders or regulations); 1 December 2001 (remainder).
References: See paras 15.92–15.96.

PART XVIII
RECOGNISED INVESTMENT EXCHANGES AND CLEARING HOUSES

CHAPTER I
EXEMPTION

General

285 Exemption for recognised investment exchanges and clearing houses

(1) In this Act—

    (a) "recognised investment exchange" means an investment exchange in relation to which a recognition order is in force; and

    (b) "recognised clearing house" means a clearing house in relation to which a recognition order is in force.

(2) A recognised investment exchange is exempt from the general prohibition as respects any regulated activity—

    (a) which is carried on as a part of the exchange's business as an investment exchange; or

    (b) which is carried on for the purposes of, or in connection with, the provision of clearing services by the exchange.

(3) A recognised clearing house is exempt from the general prohibition as respects any regulated activity which is carried on for the purposes of, or in connection with, the provision of clearing services by the clearing house.

Commencement: 1 December 2001.
References: See paras 16.3–16.6.

286 Qualification for recognition

(1) The Treasury may make regulations setting out the requirements—

    (a) which must be satisfied by an investment exchange or clearing house if it is to qualify as a body in respect of which the Authority may make a recognition order under this Part; and

    (b) which, if a recognition order is made, it must continue to satisfy if it is to remain a recognised body.

(2) But if regulations contain provision as to the default rules of an investment exchange or clearing house, or as to proceedings taken under such rules by such a body, they require the approval of the Secretary of State.

(3) "Default rules" means rules of an investment exchange or clearing house which provide for the taking of action in the event of a person's appearing to be unable, or likely to become unable, to meet his obligations in respect of one or more market contracts connected with the exchange or clearing house.

(4) "Market contract" means—

    (a) a contract to which Part VII of the Companies Act 1989 applies as a result of section 155 of that Act or a contract to which Part V of the Companies (No 2) (Northern Ireland) Order 1990 applies as a result of Article 80 of that Order; and

    (b) such other kind of contract as may be prescribed.

(5) Requirements resulting from this section are referred to in this Part as "recognition requirements".

Commencement: 25 February 2001.
Regulations: The Financial Services and Markets Act 2000 (Recognition Requirements for Investment Exchanges and Clearing Houses) Regulations 2001, SI 2001/995.
References: See paras 16.7–16.11.

Applications for recognition

287 Application by an investment exchange

(1) Any body corporate or unincorporated association may apply to the Authority for an order declaring it to be a recognised investment exchange for the purposes of this Act.

(2) The application must be made in such manner as the Authority may direct and must be accompanied by—
- (a) a copy of the applicant's rules;
- (b) a copy of any guidance issued by the applicant;
- (c) the required particulars; and
- (d) such other information as the Authority may reasonably require for the purpose of determining the application.

(3) The required particulars are—
- (a) particulars of any arrangements which the applicant has made, or proposes to make, for the provision of clearing services in respect of transactions effected on the exchange;
- (b) if the applicant proposes to provide clearing services in respect of transactions other than those effected on the exchange, particulars of the criteria which the applicant will apply when determining to whom it will provide those services.

Commencement: 18 June 2001 (for the purpose of giving directions or imposing requirements as mentioned in sub-s (2) above); 3 September 2001 (remaining purposes).
References: See paras 10.28, 10.29, 16.13, 16.16.

288 Application by a clearing house

(1) Any body corporate or unincorporated association may apply to the Authority for an order declaring it to be a recognised clearing house for the purposes of this Act.

(2) The application must be made in such manner as the Authority may direct and must be accompanied by—
- (a) a copy of the applicant's rules;
- (b) a copy of any guidance issued by the applicant;
- (c) the required particulars; and
- (d) such other information as the Authority may reasonably require for the purpose of determining the application.

(3) The required particulars are—
- (a) if the applicant makes, or proposes to make, clearing arrangements with a recognised investment exchange, particulars of those arrangements;

    (b)   if the applicant proposes to provide clearing services for persons other than recognised investment exchanges, particulars of the criteria which it will apply when determining to whom it will provide those services.

Commencement: 18 June 2001 (for the purpose of giving directions or imposing requirements as mentioned in sub-s (2) above); 3 September 2001 (remaining purposes).
References: See paras 16.13, 16.16.

289 Applications: supplementary

(1)   At any time after receiving an application and before determining it, the Authority may require the applicant to provide such further information as it reasonably considers necessary to enable it to determine the application.

(2)   Information which the Authority requires in connection with an application must be provided in such form, or verified in such manner, as the Authority may direct.

(3)   Different directions may be given, or requirements imposed, by the Authority with respect to different applications.

Commencement: 3 September 2001.
References: See para 16.17.

290 Recognition orders

(1)   If it appears to the Authority that the applicant satisfies the recognition requirements applicable in its case, the Authority may make a recognition order declaring the applicant to be—
    (a)   a recognised investment exchange, if the application is made under section 287;
    (b)   a recognised clearing house, if it is made under section 288.

(2)   The Treasury's approval of the making of a recognition order is required under section 307.

(3)   In considering an application, the Authority may have regard to any information which it considers is relevant to the application.

(4)   A recognition order must specify a date on which it is to take effect.

(5)   Section 298 has effect in relation to a decision to refuse to make a recognition order—
    (a)   as it has effect in relation to a decision to revoke such an order; and
    (b)   as if references to a recognised body were references to the applicant.

(6)   Subsection (5) does not apply in a case in which the Treasury have failed to give their approval under section 307.

Commencement: 3 September 2001 (for the purposes of recognition orders coming into force not sooner than the day on which s 19 of this Act comes into force); 1 December 2001 (remaining purposes).
References: See paras 16.18, 16.19.

291 Liability in relation to recognised body's regulatory functions

(1)   A recognised body and its officers and staff are not to be liable in damages for anything done or omitted in the discharge of the recognised body's regulatory functions unless it is shown that the act or omission was in bad faith.

(2)   But subsection (1) does not prevent an award of damages made in respect of an act or omission on the ground that the act or omission was unlawful as a result of section 6(1) of the Human Rights Act 1998.

(3)   "Regulatory functions" means the functions of the recognised body so far as relating to, or to matters arising out of, the obligations to which the body is subject under or by virtue of this Act.

Commencement: 1 December 2001.
References: See para 16.44.

292 Overseas investment exchanges and overseas clearing houses

(1)   An application under section 287 or 288 by an overseas applicant must contain the address of a place in the United Kingdom for the service on the applicant of notices or other documents required or authorised to be served on it under this Act.

(2)   If it appears to the Authority that an overseas applicant satisfies the requirements of subsection (3) it may make a recognition order declaring the applicant to be—

(a)   a recognised investment exchange;

(b)   a recognised clearing house.

(3)   The requirements are that—

(a)   investors are afforded protection equivalent to that which they would be afforded if the body concerned were required to comply with recognition requirements;

(b)   there are adequate procedures for dealing with a person who is unable, or likely to become unable, to meet his obligations in respect of one or more market contracts connected with the investment exchange or clearing house;

(c)   the applicant is able and willing to co-operate with the Authority by the sharing of information and in other ways;

(d)   adequate arrangements exist for co-operation between the Authority and those responsible for the supervision of the applicant in the country or territory in which the applicant's head office is situated.

(4)   In considering whether it is satisfied as to the requirements mentioned in subsection (3)(a) and (b), the Authority is to have regard to—

(a)   the relevant law and practice of the country or territory in which the applicant's head office is situated;

(b)   the rules and practices of the applicant.

(5)   In relation to an overseas applicant and a body or association declared to be a recognised investment exchange or recognised clearing house by a recognition order made by virtue of subsection (2)—

(a)   the reference in section 313(2) to recognition requirements is to be read as a reference to matters corresponding to the matters in respect of which provision is made in the recognition requirements;

(b) sections 296(1) and 297(2) have effect as if the requirements mentioned in section 296(1)(a) and section 297(2)(a) were those of subsection (3)(a), (b), and (c) of this section;

(c) section 297(2) has effect as if the grounds on which a recognition order may be revoked under that provision included the ground that in the opinion of the Authority arrangements of the kind mentioned in subsection (3)(d) no longer exist.

Commencement: 3 September 2001 (sub-s (1), and sub-ss (2)–(5) for the purposes of recognition orders coming into force not sooner than the day on which s 19 of this Act comes into force); 1 December 2001 (remainder).
References: See paras 16.45–16.48.

Supervision

293 Notification requirements

(1) The Authority may make rules requiring a recognised body to give it—
    (a) notice of such events relating to the body as may be specified; and
    (b) such information in respect of those events as may be specified.

(2) The rules may also require a recognised body to give the Authority, at such times or in respect of such periods as may be specified, such information relating to the body as may be specified.

(3) An obligation imposed by the rules extends only to a notice or information which the Authority may reasonably require for the exercise of its functions under this Act.

(4) The rules may require information to be given in a specified form and to be verified in a specified manner.

(5) If a recognised body—
    (a) alters or revokes any of its rules or guidance, or
    (b) makes new rules or issues new guidance,
it must give written notice to the Authority without delay.

(6) If a recognised investment exchange makes a change—
    (a) in the arrangements it makes for the provision of clearing services in respect of transactions effected on the exchange, or
    (b) in the criteria which it applies when determining to whom it will provide clearing services,
it must give written notice to the Authority without delay.

(7) If a recognised clearing house makes a change—
    (a) in the recognised investment exchanges for whom it provides clearing services, or
    (b) in the criteria which it applies when determining to whom (other than recognised investment exchanges) it will provide clearing services,
it must give written notice to the Authority without delay.

(8) Subsections (5) to (7) do not apply to an overseas investment exchange or an overseas clearing house.

(9) "Specified" means specified in the Authority's rules.

Commencement: 18 June 2001 (for the purpose of making rules); 1 December 2001 (remaining purposes).
References: See paras 16.28–16.31.

294 Modification or waiver of rules

(1)   The Authority may, on the application or with the consent of a recognised body, direct that rules made under section 293 or 295—

(a)   are not to apply to the body; or

(b)   are to apply to the body with such modifications as may be specified in the direction.

(2)   An application must be made in such manner as the Authority may direct.

(3)   Subsections (4) to (6) apply to a direction given under subsection (1).

(4)   The Authority may not give a direction unless it is satisfied that—

(a)   compliance by the recognised body with the rules, or with the rules as unmodified, would be unduly burdensome or would not achieve the purpose for which the rules were made; and

(b)   the direction would not result in undue risk to persons whose interests the rules are intended to protect.

(5)   A direction may be given subject to conditions.

(6)   The Authority may—

(a)   revoke a direction; or

(b)   vary it on the application, or with the consent, of the recognised body to which it relates.

Commencement: 18 June 2001 (for the purpose of giving directions as mentioned in sub-s (2) above); 3 September 2001 (remaining purposes).
References: See para 16.29.

295 Notification: overseas investment exchanges and overseas clearing houses

(1)   At least once a year, every overseas investment exchange and overseas clearing house must provide the Authority with a report.

(2)   The report must contain a statement as to whether any events have occurred which are likely—

(a)   to affect the Authority's assessment of whether it is satisfied as to the requirements set out in section 292(3); or

(b)   to have any effect on competition.

(3)   The report must also contain such information as may be specified in rules made by the Authority.

(4)   The investment exchange or clearing house must provide the Treasury and the [OFT] with a copy of the report.

Commencement: 18 June 2001 (for the purpose of making rules); 1 December 2001 (remaining purposes).
Amendments: Sub-s (4): word in square brackets substituted by the Enterprise Act 2002, s 278(1), Sch 25, para 40(1), (9), as from 1 April 2003.
References: See para 16.50.

296 Authority's power to give directions

(1)   This section applies if it appears to the Authority that a recognised body—
     (a)   has failed, or is likely to fail, to satisfy the recognition requirements; or
     (b)   has failed to comply with any other obligation imposed on it by or under this Act.

(2)   The Authority may direct the body to take specified steps for the purpose of securing the body's compliance with—
     (a)   the recognition requirements; or
     (b)   any obligation of the kind in question.

(3)   A direction under this section is enforceable, on the application of the Authority, by an injunction or, in Scotland, by an order for specific performance under section 45 of the Court of Session Act 1988.

(4)   The fact that a rule made by a recognised body has been altered in response to a direction given by the Authority does not prevent it from being subsequently altered or revoked by the recognised body.

Commencement: 1 December 2001.
References: See para 16.39.

297 Revoking recognition

(1)   A recognition order may be revoked by an order made by the Authority at the request, or with the consent, of the recognised body concerned.

(2)   If it appears to the Authority that a recognised body—
     (a)   is failing, or has failed, to satisfy the recognition requirements, or
     (b)   is failing, or has failed, to comply with any other obligation imposed on it by or under this Act,

it may make an order revoking the recognition order for that body even though the body does not wish the order to be made.

(3)   An order under this section ("a revocation order") must specify the date on which it is to take effect.

(4)   In the case of a revocation order made under subsection (2), the specified date must not be earlier than the end of the period of three months beginning with the day on which the order is made.

(5)   A revocation order may contain such transitional provisions as the Authority thinks necessary or expedient.

Commencement: 3 September 2001.
References: See para 16.42.

298 Directions and revocation: procedure

(1)   Before giving a direction under section 296, or making a revocation order under section 297(2), the Authority must—
     (a)   give written notice of its intention to do so to the recognised body concerned;

> > (b) take such steps as it considers reasonably practicable to bring the notice to the attention of members (if any) of that body; and
> > (c) publish the notice in such manner as it thinks appropriate for bringing it to the attention of other persons who are, in its opinion, likely to be affected.
>
> (2) A notice under subsection (1) must—
> > (a) state why the Authority intends to give the direction or make the order; and
> > (b) draw attention to the right to make representations conferred by subsection (3).
>
> (3) Before the end of the period for making representations—
> > (a) the recognised body,
> > (b) any member of that body, and
> > (c) any other person who is likely to be affected by the proposed direction or revocation order,

may make representations to the Authority.

> (4) The period for making representations is—
> > (a) two months beginning—
> > > (i)   with the date on which the notice is served on the recognised body; or
> > > (ii) if later, with the date on which the notice is published; or
> > (b) such longer period as the Authority may allow in the particular case.
>
> (5) In deciding whether to—
> > (a) give a direction, or
> > (b) make a revocation order,

the Authority must have regard to any representations made in accordance with subsection (3).

> (6) When the Authority has decided whether to give a direction under section 296 or to make the proposed revocation order, it must—
> > (a) give the recognised body written notice of its decision; and
> > (b) if it has decided to give a direction or make an order, take such steps as it considers reasonably practicable for bringing its decision to the attention of members of the body or of other persons who are, in the Authority's opinion, likely to be affected.
>
> (7) If the Authority considers it essential to do so, it may give a direction under section 296—
> > (a) without following the procedure set out in this section; or
> > (b) if the Authority has begun to follow that procedure, regardless of whether the period for making representations has expired.

(8) If the Authority has, in relation to a particular matter, followed the procedure set out in subsections (1) to (5), it need not follow it again if, in relation to that matter, it decides to take action other than that specified in its notice under subsection (1).

Commencement: 3 September 2001 (for the purposes of revocation orders under s 297); 1 December 2001 (remaining purposes).
References: See paras 16.19–16.21.

299 Complaints about recognised bodies

(1)   The Authority must make arrangements for the investigation of any relevant complaint about a recognised body.

(2)   "Relevant complaint" means a complaint which the Authority considers is relevant to the question of whether the body concerned should remain a recognised body.

Commencement: 18 June 2001.
References: See para 16.12.

300 Extension of functions of Tribunal

(1)   If the Treasury are satisfied that the condition mentioned in subsection (2) is satisfied, they may by order confer functions on the Tribunal with respect to disciplinary proceedings—

> (a)   of one or more investment exchanges in relation to which a recognition order under section 290 is in force or of such investment exchanges generally, or
>
> (b)   of one or more clearing houses in relation to which a recognition order under that section is in force or of such clearing houses generally.

(2)   The condition is that it is desirable to exercise the power conferred under subsection (1) with a view to ensuring that—

> (a)   decisions taken in disciplinary proceedings with respect to which functions are to be conferred on the Tribunal are consistent with—
>> (i)   decisions of the Tribunal in cases arising under Part VIII; and
>> (ii)   decisions taken in other disciplinary proceedings with respect to which the Tribunal has functions as a result of an order under this section; or
>
> (b)   the disciplinary proceedings are in accordance with the Convention rights.

(3)   An order under this section may modify or exclude any provision made by or under this Act with respect to proceedings before the Tribunal.

(4)   "Disciplinary proceedings" means proceedings under the rules of an investment exchange or clearing house in relation to market abuse by persons subject to the rules.

(5)   "The Convention rights" has the meaning given in section 1 of the Human Rights Act 1998.

Commencement: 1 December 2001.
References: See para 16.35.

Other matters

301 Supervision of certain contracts

(1)   The Secretary of State and the Treasury, acting jointly, may by regulations provide for—

(a)   Part VII of the Companies Act 1989 (financial markets and insolvency), and

(b)   Part V of the Companies (No 2) (Northern Ireland) Order 1990,

to apply to relevant contracts as it applies to contracts connected with a recognised body.

(2)   "Relevant contracts" means contracts of a prescribed description in relation to which settlement arrangements are provided by a person for the time being included in a list ("the list") maintained by the Authority for the purposes of this section.

(3)   Regulations may be made under this section only if the Secretary of State and the Treasury are satisfied, having regard to the extent to which the relevant contracts concerned are contracts of a kind dealt in by persons supervised by the Authority, that it is appropriate for the arrangements mentioned in subsection (2) to be supervised by the Authority.

(4)   The approval of the Treasury is required for—

(a)   the conditions set by the Authority for admission to the list; and

(b)   the arrangements for admission to, and removal from, the list.

(5)   If the Treasury withdraw an approval given by them under subsection (4), all regulations made under this section and then in force are to be treated as suspended.

(6)   But if—

(a)   the Authority changes the conditions or arrangements (or both), and

(b)   the Treasury give a fresh approval under subsection (4),

the suspension of the regulations ends on such date as the Treasury may, in giving the fresh approval, specify.

(7)   The Authority must—

(a)   publish the list as for the time being in force; and

(b)   provide a certified copy of it to any person who wishes to refer to it in legal proceedings.

(8)   A certified copy of the list is evidence (or in Scotland sufficient evidence) of the contents of the list.

(9)   A copy of the list which purports to be certified by or on behalf of the Authority is to be taken to have been duly certified unless the contrary is shown.

(10)   Regulations under this section may, in relation to a person included in the list—

(a)   apply (with such exceptions, additions and modifications as appear to the Secretary of State and the Treasury to be necessary or expedient) such provisions of, or made under, this Act as they consider appropriate;

(b)   provide for the provisions of Part VII of the Companies Act 1989 and Part V of the Companies (No 2) (Northern Ireland) Order 1990 to apply (with such exceptions, additions or modifications as appear to the Secretary of State and the Treasury to be necessary or expedient).

Commencement: 1 December 2001.
References: See paras 16.32–16.34.

CHAPTER II
COMPETITION SCRUTINY

302 Interpretation

(1)   In this Chapter and Chapter III—
"practices" means—
(a)   in relation to a recognised investment exchange, the practices of the exchange in its capacity as such; and
(b)   in relation to a recognised clearing house, the practices of the clearing house in respect of its clearing arrangements;
"regulatory provisions" means—
(a)   the rules of an investment exchange or a clearing house;
(b)   any guidance issued by an investment exchange or clearing house;
(c)   in the case of an investment exchange, the arrangements and criteria mentioned in section 287(3);
(d)   in the case of a clearing house, the arrangements and criteria mentioned in section 288(3).

(2)   For the purposes of this Chapter, regulatory provisions or practices have a significantly adverse effect on competition if—
(a)   they have, or are intended or likely to have, that effect; or
(b)   the effect that they have, or are intended or likely to have, is to require or encourage behaviour which has, or is intended or likely to have, a significantly adverse effect on competition.

(3)   If regulatory provisions or practices have, or are intended or likely to have, the effect of requiring or encouraging exploitation of the strength of a market position they are to be taken, for the purposes of this Chapter, to have an adverse effect on competition.

(4)   In determining under this Chapter whether any regulatory provisions have, or are intended or likely to have, a particular effect, it may be assumed that persons to whom the provisions concerned are addressed will act in accordance with them.

Commencement: 3 September 2001.
References: See paras 10.28–10.41, 16.51–16.58.

Role of [Office of Fair Trading]

303 Initial report by [OFT]

(1)   The Authority must send to the Treasury and to the [OFT] a copy of any regulatory provisions with which it is provided on an application for recognition under section 287 or 288.

(2)   The Authority must send to the [OFT] such information in its possession as a result of the application for recognition as it considers will assist [the OFT] in discharging [its] functions in connection with the application.

(3)   The [OFT] must issue a report as to whether—
(a)   a regulatory provision of which a copy has been sent to [it] under subsection (1) has a significantly adverse effect on competition; or
(b)   a combination of regulatory provisions so copied to [it] have such an effect.

(4)   If the [OFT's] conclusion is that one or more provisions have a significantly adverse effect on competition, [it] must state [its] reasons for that conclusion.

(5)   When the [OFT] issues a report under subsection (3), [the OFT] must send a copy of it to the Authority, the Competition Commission and the Treasury.

Commencement: 3 September 2001.
Amendments: Words in square brackets substituted by the Enterprise Act 2002, s 278(1), Sch 25, para 40(1), (10), as from 1 April 2003.
References: See paras 10.29, 16.53.

304 Further reports by [OFT]

(1)   The [OFT] must keep under review the regulatory provisions and practices of recognised bodies.

(2)   If at any time the [OFT] considers that—
    (a)   a regulatory provision or practice has a significantly adverse effect on competition, or
    (b)   regulatory provisions or practices, or a combination of regulating provisions and practices have such an effect,
[the OFT] must make a report.

(3)   If at any time the [OFT] considers that—
    (a)   a regulatory provision or practice does not have a significantly adverse effect on competition, or
    (b)   regulatory provisions or practices, or a combination of regulatory provisions and practices do not have any such effect,
[the OFT] may make a report to that effect.

(4)   A report under subsection (2) must contain details of the adverse effect on competition.

(5)   If the [OFT] makes a report under subsection (2), [the OFT] must—
    (a)   send a copy of it to the Treasury, to the Competition Commission and to the Authority; and
    (b)   publish it in the way appearing to [the OFT] to be best calculated to bring it to the attention of the public.

(6)   If the [OFT] makes a report under subsection (3)—
    (a)   [the OFT] must send a copy of it to the Treasury, to the Competition Commission and to the Authority; and
    (b)   [the OFT] may publish it.

(7)   Before publishing a report under this section, the [OFT] must, so far as practicable, exclude any matter which relates to the private affairs of a particular individual the publication of which, in the opinion of the [OFT], would or might seriously and prejudicially affect his interests.

(8)   Before publishing such a report, the [OFT] must exclude any matter which relates to the affairs of a particular body the publication of which, in the opinion of the [OFT], would or might seriously and prejudicially affect its interests.

(9)   Subsections (7) and (8) do not apply to the copy of a report which the [OFT] is required to send to the Treasury, the Competition Commission and the Authority under subsection (5)(a) or (6)(a).

(10) For the purposes of the law of defamation, absolute privilege attaches to any report of the [OFT] under this section.

Commencement: 1 December 2001.
Amendments: Words in square brackets substituted by the Enterprise Act 2002, s 278(1), Sch 25, para 40(1), (11), as from 1 April 2003.
References: See paras 10.30–10.32, 16.53–16.56.

305 Investigations by [OFT]

(1)   For the purpose of investigating any matter with a view to its consideration under section 303 or 304, the [OFT] may exercise the powers conferred on [it] by this section.

(2)   The [OFT] may by notice in writing require any person to produce to [it] or to a person appointed by [it] for the purpose, at a time and place specified in the notice, any document which—
 (a)   is specified or described in the notice; and
 (b)   is a document in that person's custody or under his control.

(3)   The [OFT] may by notice in writing—
 (a)   require any person carrying on any business to provide [it] with such information as may be specified or described in the notice; and
 (b)   specify the time within which, and the manner and form in which, any such information is to be provided.

(4)   A requirement may be imposed under subsection (2) or (3)(a) only in respect of documents or information which relate to any matter relevant to the investigation.

(5)   If a person ("the defaulter") refuses, or otherwise fails, to comply with a notice under this section, the [OFT] may certify that fact in writing to the court and the court may enquire into the case.

(6)   If, after hearing any witness who may be produced against or on behalf of the defaulter and any statement which may be offered in defence, the court is satisfied that the defaulter did not have a reasonable excuse for refusing or otherwise failing to comply with the notice, the court may deal with the defaulter as if he were in contempt.

(7)   In this section, "the court" means—
 (a)   the High Court; or
 (b)   in Scotland, the Court of Session.

Commencement: 3 September 2001 (for the purposes of s 303); 1 December 2001 (remaining purposes).
Amendments: Words in square brackets substituted by the Enterprise Act 2002, s 278(1), Sch 25, para 40(1), (12), as from 1 April 2003.
References: See paras 10.43, 16.57, 16.58.

Role of Competition Commission

306 Consideration by Competition Commission

(1)   If subsection (2) or (3) applies, the Commission must investigate the matter which is the subject of the [OFT's] report.

(2)   This subsection applies if the [OFT] sends to the Competition Commission a report—

  (a)   issued by [the OFT] under section 303(3) which concludes that one or more regulatory provisions have a significantly adverse effect on competition, or

  (b)   made by [the OFT] under section 304(2).

(3)   This subsection applies if the [OFT] asks the Commission to consider a report—

  (a)   issued by [the OFT] under section 303(3) which concludes that one or more regulatory provisions do not have a significantly adverse effect on competition, or

  (b)   made by [the OFT] under section 304(3).

(4)   The Commission must then make its own report on the matter unless it considers that, as a result of a change of circumstances, no useful purpose would be served by a report.

(5)   If the Commission decides in accordance with subsection (4) not to make a report, it must make a statement setting out the change of circumstances which resulted in that decision.

(6)   A report made under this section must state the Commission's conclusion as to whether—

  (a)   the regulatory provision or practice which is the subject of the report has a significantly adverse effect on competition, or

  (b)   the regulatory provisions or practices or combination of regulatory provisions and practices which are the subject of the report have such an effect.

(7)   A report under this section stating the Commission's conclusion that there is a significantly adverse effect on competition must also—

  (a)   state whether the Commission considers that that effect is justified; and

  (b)   if it states that the Commission considers that it is not justified, state its conclusion as to what action, if any, the Treasury ought to direct the Authority to take.

(8)   Subsection (9) applies whenever the Commission is considering, for the purposes of this section, whether a particular adverse effect on competition is justified.

(9)   The Commission must ensure, so far as that is reasonably possible, that the conclusion it reaches is compatible with the obligations imposed on the recognised body concerned by or under this Act.

(10)   A report under this section must contain such an account of the Commission's reasons for its conclusions as is expedient, in the opinion of the Commission, for facilitating proper understanding of them.

(11)   The provisions of Schedule 14 (except paragraph 2(b)) apply for the purposes of this section as they apply for the purposes of section 162.

(12)   If the Commission makes a report under this section it must send a copy to the Treasury, the Authority and the [OFT].

Commencement: 3 September 2001 (for the purposes of reports issued by the Director under s 303); 1 December 2001 (remaining purposes).
Amendments: Words in square brackets substituted by the Enterprise Act 2002, s 278(1), Sch 25, para 40(1), (13), as from 1 April 2003.
References: See paras 10.33, 10.34, 16.59–16.63.

Role of the Treasury

307 Recognition orders: role of the Treasury

(1)   Subsection (2) applies if, on an application for a recognition order—
   (a)   the [OFT] makes a report under section 303 but does not ask the Competition Commission to consider it under section 306;
   (b)   the Competition Commission concludes—
      (i)   that the applicant's regulatory provisions do not have a significantly adverse effect on competition; or
      (ii)   that if those provisions do have that effect, the effect is justified.

(2)   The Treasury may refuse to approve the making of the recognition order only if they consider that the exceptional circumstances of the case make it inappropriate for them to give their approval.

(3)   Subsection (4) applies if, on an application for a recognition order, the Competition Commission concludes—
   (a)   that the applicant's regulatory provisions have a significantly adverse effect on competition; and
   (b)   that that effect is not justified.

(4)   The Treasury must refuse to approve the making of the recognition order unless they consider that the exceptional circumstances of the case make it inappropriate for them to refuse their approval.

Commencement: 3 September 2001.
Amendments: Sub-s (1): word in square brackets substituted by the Enterprise Act 2002, s 278(1), Sch 25, para 40(1), (14)(a), as from 1 April 2003.
References: See paras 10.35, 10.36, 16.64, 16.65.

308 Directions by the Treasury

(1)   This section applies if the Competition Commission makes a report under section 306(4) (other than a report on an application for a recognition order) which states the Commission's conclusion that there is a significantly adverse effect on competition.

(2)   If the Commission's conclusion, as stated in the report, is that the adverse effect on competition is not justified, the Treasury must give a remedial direction to the Authority.

(3)   But subsection (2) does not apply if the Treasury consider—
   (a)   that, as a result of action taken by the Authority or the recognised body concerned in response to the Commission's report, it is unnecessary for them to give a direction; or
   (b)   that the exceptional circumstances of the case make it inappropriate or unnecessary for them to do so.

(4)   In considering the action to be specified in a remedial direction, the Treasury must have regard to any conclusion of the Commission included in the report because of section 306(7)(b).

(5)   Subsection (6) applies if—
  (a)   the Commission's conclusion, as stated in its report, is that the adverse effect on competition is justified; but
  (b)   the Treasury consider that the exceptional circumstances of the case require them to act.

(6)   The Treasury may give a direction to the Authority requiring it to take such action—
  (a)   as they consider to be necessary in the light of the exceptional circumstances of the case; and
  (b)   as may be specified in the direction.

(7)   If the action specified in a remedial direction is the giving by the Authority of a direction—
  (a)   the direction to be given must be compatible with the recognition requirements applicable to the recognised body in relation to which it is given; and
  (b)   subsections (3) and (4) of section 296 apply to it as if it were a direction given under that section.

(8)   "Remedial direction" means a direction requiring the Authority—
  (a)   to revoke the recognition order for the body concerned; or
  (b)   to give such directions to the body concerned as may be specified in it.

Commencement: 1 December 2001.
References: See paras 10.37–10.41, 16.66–16.70.

309 Statements by the Treasury

(1)   If, in reliance on subsection (3)(a) or (b) of section 308, the Treasury decline to act under subsection (2) of that section, they must make a statement to that effect, giving their reasons.

(2)   If the Treasury give a direction under section 308 they must make a statement giving—
  (a)   details of the direction; and
  (b)   if the direction is given under subsection (6) of that section, their reasons for giving it.

(3)   The Treasury must—
  (a)   publish any statement made under this section in the way appearing to them best calculated to bring it to the attention of the public; and
  (b)   lay a copy of it before Parliament.

Commencement: 1 December 2001.
References: See paras 10.38–10.41, 16.71.

310 Procedure on exercise of certain powers by the Treasury

(1)   Subsection (2) applies if the Treasury are considering—
  (a)   whether to refuse their approval under section 307;

    (b)   whether section 308(2) applies; or

    (c)   whether to give a direction under section 308(6).

(2)   The Treasury must—

    (a)   take such steps as they consider appropriate to allow the exchange or clearing house concerned, and any other person appearing to the Treasury to be affected, an opportunity to make representations—

        (i)   about any report made by the [OFT] under section 303 or 304 or by the Competition Commission under section 306;

       (ii)   as to whether, and if so how, the Treasury should exercise their powers under section 307 or 308; and

    (b)   have regard to any such representations.

Commencement: 3 September 2001 (for the purposes of s 307); 1 December 2001 (remaining purposes).
Amendments: Sub-s (2): word in square brackets substituted by the Enterprise Act 2002, s 278(1), Sch 25, para 40(1), (14)(b), as from 1 April 2003.
References: See paras 10.48, 16.67.

CHAPTER III
EXCLUSION FROM THE COMPETITION ACT 1998

311 The Chapter I prohibition

(1)   The Chapter I prohibition does not apply to an agreement for the constitution of a recognised body to the extent to which the agreement relates to the regulatory provisions of that body.

(2)   If the conditions set out in subsection (3) are satisfied, the Chapter I prohibition does not apply to an agreement for the constitution of—

    (a)   an investment exchange which is not a recognised investment exchange, or

    (b)   a clearing house which is not a recognised clearing house,

to the extent to which the agreement relates to the regulatory provisions of that body.

(3)   The conditions are that—

    (a)   the body has applied for a recognition order in accordance with the provisions of this Act; and

    (b)   the application has not been determined.

(4)   The Chapter I prohibition does not apply to a recognised body's regulatory provisions.

(5)   The Chapter I prohibition does not apply to a decision made by a recognised body to the extent to which the decision relates to any of that body's regulatory provisions or practices.

(6)   The Chapter I prohibition does not apply to practices of a recognised body.

(7)   The Chapter I prohibition does not apply to an agreement the parties to which consist of or include—

    (a)   a recognised body, or

    (b)   a person who is subject to the rules of a recognised body,

to the extent to which the agreement consists of provisions the inclusion of which is required or encouraged by any of the body's regulatory provisions or practices.

(8)   If a recognised body's recognition order is revoked, this section is to have effect as if that body had continued to be recognised until the end of the period of six months beginning with the day on which the revocation took effect.

(9)   "The Chapter I prohibition" means the prohibition imposed by section 2(1) of the Competition Act 1998.

(10) Expressions used in this section which are also used in Part I of the Competition Act 1998 are to be interpreted in the same way as for the purposes of that Part of that Act.

Commencement: 3 September 2001.
References: See paras 10.5–10.7, 16.72, 16.73.

312 The Chapter II prohibition

(1)   The Chapter II prohibition does not apply to—
   (a)   practices of a recognised body;
   (b)   the adoption or enforcement of such a body's regulatory provisions;
   (c)   any conduct which is engaged in by such a body or by a person who is subject to the rules of such a body to the extent to which it is encouraged or required by the regulatory provisions of the body.

(2)   The Chapter II prohibition means the prohibition imposed by section 18(1) of the Competition Act 1998.

Commencement: 3 September 2001.
References: See paras 10.6, 10.7, 16.74.

CHAPTER IV

Interpretation

313 Interpretation of Part XVIII

(1)   In this Part—
   "application" means an application for a recognition order made under section 287 or 288;
   "applicant" means a body corporate or unincorporated association which has applied for a recognition order;
   ["OFT" means the Office of Fair Trading;]
   "overseas applicant" means a body corporate or association which has neither its head office nor its registered office in the United Kingdom and which has applied for a recognition order;
   "overseas investment exchange" means a body corporate or association which has neither its head office nor its registered office in the United Kingdom and in relation to which a recognition order is in force;
   "overseas clearing house" means a body corporate or association which has neither its head office nor its registered office in the United Kingdom and in relation to which a recognition order is in force;
   "recognised body" means a recognised investment exchange or a recognised clearing house;
   "recognised clearing house" has the meaning given in section 285;

"recognised investment exchange" has the meaning given in section 285;
"recognition order" means an order made under section 290 or 292;
"recognition requirements" has the meaning given by section 286;
"remedial direction" has the meaning given in section 308(8);
"revocation order" has the meaning given in section 297.

(2) References in this Part to rules of an investment exchange (or a clearing house) are to rules made, or conditions imposed, by the investment exchange (or the clearing house) with respect to—

(a) recognition requirements;
(b) admission of persons to, or their exclusion from the use of, its facilities; or
(c) matters relating to its constitution.

(3) References in this Part to guidance issued by an investment exchange are references to guidance issued, or any recommendation made, in writing or other legible form and intended to have continuing effect, by the investment exchange to—

(a) all or any class of its members or users, or
(b) persons seeking to become members of the investment exchange or to use its facilities,

with respect to any of the matters mentioned in subsection (2)(a) to (c).

(4) References in this Part to guidance issued by a clearing house are to guidance issued, or any recommendation made, in writing or other legible form and intended to have continuing effect, by the clearing house to—

(a) all or any class of its members, or
(b) persons using or seeking to use its services,

with respect to the provision by it or its members of clearing services.

Commencement: 25 February 2001.
Amendments: Sub-s (1): definition in square brackets substituted by the Enterprise Act 2002, s 278(1), Sch 25, para 40(1), (15), as from 1 April 2003.
References: See paras 16.14, 16.15.

PART XIX
LLOYD'S

General

314 Authority's general duty

(1) The Authority must keep itself informed about—
(a) the way in which the Council supervises and regulates the market at Lloyd's; and
(b) the way in which regulated activities are being carried on in that market.

(2) The Authority must keep under review the desirability of exercising—
(a) any of its powers under this Part;
(b) any powers which it has in relation to the Society as a result of section 315.

Commencement: 3 September 2001.
References: See para 17.4.

The Society

315 The Society: authorisation and permission

(1)   The Society is an authorised person.

(2)   The Society has permission to carry on a regulated activity of any of the following kinds—

(a)   arranging deals in contracts of insurance written at Lloyd's ("the basic market activity");

(b)   arranging deals in participation in Lloyd's syndicates ("the secondary market activity"); and

(c)   an activity carried on in connection with, or for the purposes of, the basic or secondary market activity.

(3)   For the purposes of Part IV, the Society's permission is to be treated as if it had been given on an application for permission under that Part.

(4)   The power conferred on the Authority by section 45 may be exercised in anticipation of the coming into force of the Society's permission (or at any other time).

(5)   The Society is not subject to any requirement of this Act concerning the registered office of a body corporate.

Commencement: 1 December 2001 (sub-ss (1), (2)); 3 September 2001 (remainder).
References: See paras 17.5, 17.7.

Power to apply Act to Lloyd's underwriting

316 Direction by Authority

(1)   The general prohibition or (if the general prohibition is not applied under this section) a core provision applies to the carrying on of an insurance market activity by—

(a)   a member of the Society, or

(b)   the members of the Society taken together,

only if the Authority so directs.

(2)   A direction given under subsection (1) which applies a core provision is referred to in this Part as "an insurance market direction".

(3)   In subsection (1)—

"core provision" means a provision of this Act mentioned in section 317; and

"insurance market activity" means a regulated activity relating to contracts of insurance written at Lloyd's.

(4)   In deciding whether to give a direction under subsection (1), the Authority must have particular regard to—

(a)   the interests of policyholders and potential policyholders;

(b)   any failure by the Society to satisfy an obligation to which it is subject as a result of a provision of the law of another EEA State which—

(i)   gives effect to any of the insurance directives; and

(ii)   is applicable to an activity carried on in that State by a person to whom this section applies;

(c)   the need to ensure the effective exercise of the functions which the Authority has in relation to the Society as a result of section 315.

(5)   A direction under subsection (1) must be in writing.

(6)   A direction under subsection (1) applying the general prohibition may apply it in relation to different classes of person.

(7)   An insurance market direction—
  (a)   must specify each core provision, class of person and kind of activity to which it applies;
  (b)   may apply different provisions in relation to different classes of person and different kinds of activity.

(8)   A direction under subsection (1) has effect from the date specified in it, which may not be earlier than the date on which it is made.

(9)   A direction under subsection (1) must be published in the way appearing to the Authority to be best calculated to bring it to the attention of the public.

(10) The Authority may charge a reasonable fee for providing a person with a copy of the direction.

(11) The Authority must, without delay, give the Treasury a copy of any direction which it gives under this section.

Commencement: 18 June 2001 (for the purpose of giving directions as mentioned in sub-s (1) coming into force not sooner than the day on which s 19 above comes into force); 1 December 2001 (remaining purposes).
References: See paras 17.8, 17.10.

317 The core provisions

(1)   The core provisions are Parts V, X, XI, XII, XIV, XV, XVI, XXII and XXIV, sections 384 to 386 and Part XXVI.

(2)   References in an applied core provision to an authorised person are (where necessary) to be read as references to a person in the class to which the insurance market direction applies.

(3)   An insurance market direction may provide that a core provision is to have effect, in relation to persons to whom the provision is applied by the direction, with modifications.

Commencement: 18 June 2001.
References: See paras 17.12, 17.13.

318 Exercise of powers through Council

(1)   The Authority may give a direction under this subsection to the Council or to the Society (acting through the Council) or to both.

(2)   A direction under subsection (1) is one given to the body concerned—
  (a)   in relation to the exercise of its powers generally with a view to achieving, or in support of, a specified objective; or

(b)   in relation to the exercise of a specified power which it has, whether in a specified manner or with a view to achieving, or in support of, a specified objective.

(3)   "Specified" means specified in the direction.

(4)   A direction under subsection (1) may be given—
    (a)   instead of giving a direction under section 316(1); or
    (b)   if the Authority considers it necessary or expedient to do so, at the same time as, or following, the giving of such a direction.

(5)   A direction may also be given under subsection (1) in respect of underwriting agents as if they were among the persons mentioned in section 316(1).

(6)   A direction under this section—
    (a)   does not, at any time, prevent the exercise by the Authority of any of its powers;
    (b)   must be in writing.

(7)   A direction under subsection (1) must be published in the way appearing to the Authority to be best calculated to bring it to the attention of the public.

(8)   The Authority may charge a reasonable fee for providing a person with a copy of the direction.

(9)   The Authority must, without delay, give the Treasury a copy of any direction which it gives under this section.

Commencement: 18 June 2001 (for the purpose of giving directions as mentioned in sub-s (1) coming into force not sooner than the day on which s 19 above comes into force); 1 December 2001 (remaining purposes).
References: See para 17.11.

319 Consultation

(1)   Before giving a direction under section 316 or 318, the Authority must publish a draft of the proposed direction.

(2)   The draft must be accompanied by—
    (a)   a cost benefit analysis; and
    (b)   notice that representations about the proposed direction may be made to the Authority within a specified time.

(3)   Before giving the proposed direction, the Authority must have regard to any representations made to it in accordance with subsection (2)(b).

(4)   If the Authority gives the proposed direction it must publish an account, in general terms, of—
    (a)   the representations made to it in accordance with subsection (2)(b); and
    (b)   its response to them.

(5)   If the direction differs from the draft published under subsection (1) in a way which is, in the opinion of the Authority, significant—
    (a)   the Authority must (in addition to complying with subsection (4)) publish details of the difference; and
    (b)   those details must be accompanied by a cost benefit analysis.

(6)   Subsections (1) to (5) do not apply if the Authority considers that the delay involved in complying with them would be prejudicial to the interests of consumers.

(7)   Neither subsection (2)(a) nor subsection (5)(b) applies if the Authority considers—

   (a)   that, making the appropriate comparison, there will be no increase in costs; or

   (b)   that, making that comparison, there will be an increase in costs but the increase will be of minimal significance.

(8)   The Authority may charge a reasonable fee for providing a person with a copy of a draft published under subsection (1).

(9)   When the Authority is required to publish a document under this section it must do so in the way appearing to it to be best calculated to bring it to the attention of the public.

(10)   "Cost benefit analysis" means an estimate of the costs together with an analysis of the benefits that will arise—

   (a)   if the proposed direction is given; or

   (b)   if subsection (5)(b) applies, from the direction that has been given.

(11)   "The appropriate comparison" means—

   (a)   in relation to subsection (2)(a), a comparison between the overall position if the direction is given and the overall position if it is not given;

   (b)   in relation to subsection (5)(b), a comparison between the overall position after the giving of the direction and the overall position before it was given.

Commencement: 18 June 2001.
References: See paras 17.14, 17.15.

Former underwriting members

320 Former underwriting members

(1)   A former underwriting member may carry out each contract of insurance that he has underwritten at Lloyd's whether or not he is an authorised person.

(2)   If he is an authorised person, any Part IV permission that he has does not extend to his activities in carrying out any of those contracts.

(3)   The Authority may impose on a former underwriting member such requirements as appear to it to be appropriate for the purpose of protecting policyholders against the risk that he may not be able to meet his liabilities.

(4)   A person on whom a requirement is imposed may refer the matter to the Tribunal.

Commencement: 3 September 2001 (sub-ss (3), (4), for the purposes of requirements taking effect not sooner than the day on which s 19 of this Act comes into force); 1 December 2001 (remainder).
References: See paras 17.16, 17.17.

321 Requirements imposed under section 320

(1) A requirement imposed under section 320 takes effect—
   (a) immediately, if the notice given under subsection (2) states that that is the case;
   (b) in any other case, on such date as may be specified in that notice.

(2) If the Authority proposes to impose a requirement on a former underwriting member ("A") under section 320, or imposes such a requirement on him which takes effect immediately, it must give him written notice.

(3) The notice must—
   (a) give details of the requirement;
   (b) state the Authority's reasons for imposing it;
   (c) inform A that he may make representations to the Authority within such period as may be specified in the notice (whether or not he has referred the matter to the Tribunal);
   (d) inform him of the date on which the requirement took effect or will take effect; and
   (e) inform him of his right to refer the matter to the Tribunal.

(4) The Authority may extend the period allowed under the notice for making representations.

(5) If, having considered any representations made by A, the Authority decides—
   (a) to impose the proposed requirement, or
   (b) if it has been imposed, not to revoke it,
it must give him written notice.

(6) If the Authority decides—
   (a) not to impose a proposed requirement, or
   (b) to revoke a requirement that has been imposed,
it must give A written notice.

(7) If the Authority decides to grant an application by A for the variation or revocation of a requirement, it must give him written notice of its decision.

(8) If the Authority proposes to refuse an application by A for the variation or revocation of a requirement it must give him a warning notice.

(9) If the Authority, having considered any representations made in response to the warning notice, decides to refuse the application, it must give A a decision notice.

(10) A notice given under—
   (a) subsection (5), or
   (b) subsection (9) in the case of a decision to refuse the application,
must inform A of his right to refer the matter to the Tribunal.

(11) If the Authority decides to refuse an application for a variation or revocation of the requirement, the applicant may refer the matter to the Tribunal.

(12) If a notice informs a person of his right to refer a matter to the Tribunal, it must give an indication of the procedure on such a reference.

Commencement: 3 September 2001 (for the purposes of requirements taking effect not sooner than the day on which s 19 of this Act comes into force); 1 December 2001 (remainder).
References: See paras 17.18, 17.19

322 Rules applicable to former underwriting members

(1)   The Authority may make rules imposing such requirements on persons to whom the rules apply as appear to it to be appropriate for protecting policyholders against the risk that those persons may not be able to meet their liabilities.

(2)   The rules may apply to—
    (a)   former underwriting members generally; or
    (b)   to a class of former underwriting member specified in them.

(3)   Section 319 applies to the making of proposed rules under this section as it applies to the giving of a proposed direction under section 316.

(4)   Part X (except sections 152 to 154) does not apply to rules made under this section.

Commencement: 18 June 2001 (for the purpose of making rules coming into force not sooner than the day on which s 19 above comes into force); 1 December 2001 (remaining purposes).
References: See para 17.16.

Transfers of business done at Lloyd's

323 Transfer schemes

The Treasury may by order provide for the application of any provision of Part VII (with or without modification) in relation to schemes for the transfer of the whole or any part of the business carried on by one or more members of the Society or former underwriting members.

Commencement: 18 June 2001.
Orders: The Financial Services and Markets Act 2000 (Control of Transfers of Business Done at Lloyd's) Order 2001, SI 2001/3626.
References: See para 17.20.

Supplemental

324 Interpretation of this Part

(1)   In this Part—
    "arranging deals", in relation to the investments to which this Part applies, has the same meaning as in paragraph 3 of Schedule 2;
    "former underwriting member" means a person ceasing to be an underwriting member of the Society on, or at any time after, 24 December 1996; and
    "participation in Lloyd's syndicates", in relation to the secondary market activity, means the investment described in sub-paragraph (1) of paragraph 21 of Schedule 2.

(2)   A term used in this Part which is defined in Lloyd's Act 1982 has the same meaning as in that Act.

Commencement: 18 June 2001.
References: See para 17.6.

PART XX
PROVISION OF FINANCIAL SERVICES BY MEMBERS OF THE PROFESSIONS

325 Authority's general duty

(1)   The Authority must keep itself informed about—
    (a)   the way in which designated professional bodies supervise and regulate the carrying on of exempt regulated activities by members of the professions in relation to which they are established;
    (b)   the way in which such members are carrying on exempt regulated activities.

(2)   In this Part—
"exempt regulated activities" means regulated activities which may, as a result of this Part, be carried on by members of a profession which is supervised and regulated by a designated professional body without breaching the general prohibition; and
"members", in relation to a profession, means persons who are entitled to practise the profession in question and, in practising it, are subject to the rules of the body designated in relation to that profession, whether or not they are members of that body.

(3)   The Authority must keep under review the desirability of exercising any of its powers under this Part.

(4)   Each designated professional body must co-operate with the Authority, by the sharing of information and in other ways, in order to enable the Authority to perform its functions under this Part.

Commencement: 1 December 2001 (sub-ss (1)–(3)); 3 September 2001 (remainder).
References: See paras 18.13, 18.14.

326 Designation of professional bodies

(1)   The Treasury may by order designate bodies for the purposes of this Part.

(2)   A body designated under subsection (1) is referred to in this Part as a designated professional body.

(3)   The Treasury may designate a body under subsection (1) only if they are satisfied that—
    (a)   the basic condition, and
    (b)   one or more of the additional conditions,
are met in relation to it.

(4)   The basic condition is that the body has rules applicable to the carrying on by members of the profession in relation to which it is established of regulated activities which, if the body were to be designated, would be exempt regulated activities.

(5)   The additional conditions are that—

(a)   the body has power under any enactment to regulate the practice of the profession;

(b)   being a member of the profession is a requirement under any enactment for the exercise of particular functions or the holding of a particular office;

(c)   the body has been recognised for the purpose of any enactment other than this Act and the recognition has not been withdrawn;

(d)   the body is established in an EEA State other than the United Kingdom and in that State—

(i)   the body has power corresponding to that mentioned in paragraph (a);

(ii)   there is a requirement in relation to the body corresponding to that mentioned in paragraph (b); or

(iii)   the body is recognised in a manner corresponding to that mentioned in paragraph (c).

(6)   "Enactment" includes an Act of the Scottish Parliament, Northern Ireland legislation and subordinate legislation (whether made under an Act, an Act of the Scottish Parliament or Northern Ireland legislation).

(7)   "Recognised" means recognised by—

(a)   a Minister of the Crown;

(b)   the Scottish Ministers;

(c)   a Northern Ireland Minister;

(d)   a Northern Ireland department or its head.

Commencement: 25 February 2001.
Orders: The Financial Services and Markets Act 2000 (Designated Professional Bodies) Order 2001, SI 2001/1226.
References: See paras 18.15, 18.16.

327 Exemption from the general prohibition

(1)   The general prohibition does not apply to the carrying on of a regulated activity by a person ("P") if—

(a)   the conditions set out in subsections (2) to (7) are satisfied; and

(b)   there is not in force—

(i)   a direction under section 328, or

(ii)   an order under section 329,

which prevents this subsection from applying to the carrying on of that activity by him.

(2)   P must be—

(a)   a member of a profession; or

(b)   controlled or managed by one or more such members.

(3)   P must not receive from a person other than his client any pecuniary reward or other advantage, for which he does not account to his client, arising out of his carrying on of any of the activities.

(4)   The manner of the provision by P of any service in the course of carrying on the activities must be incidental to the provision by him of professional services.

(5)   P must not carry on, or hold himself out as carrying on, a regulated activity other than—

    (a)   one which rules made as a result of section 332(3) allow him to carry on; or

    (b)   one in relation to which he is an exempt person.

(6)   The activities must not be of a description, or relate to an investment of a description, specified in an order made by the Treasury for the purposes of this subsection.

(7)   The activities must be the only regulated activities carried on by P (other than regulated activities in relation to which he is an exempt person).

(8)   "Professional services" means services—

    (a)   which do not constitute carrying on a regulated activity, and

    (b)   the provision of which is supervised and regulated by a designated professional body.

Commencement: 25 February 2001 (sub-s (6), for the purpose of making orders or regulations); 1 December 2001 (remainder).
Orders: The Financial Services and Markets Act 2000 (Professions) (Non-Exempt Activities) Order 2001, SI 2001/1227, as amended by SI 2001/3650, SI 2002/1777, SI 2003/1475, SI 2003/1476; the Financial Services and Markets Act 2000 (Miscellaneous Provisions) Order 2001, SI 2001/3650, as amended by SI 2001/3771, SI 2002/1777; the Financial Services and Markets Act 2000 (Commencement of Mortgage Regulation) (Amendment) Order 2002, SI 2002/1777.
References: See para 18.11A.

---

328 Directions in relation to the general prohibition

(1)   The Authority may direct that section 327(1) is not to apply to the extent specified in the direction.

(2)   A direction under subsection (1)—

    (a)   must be in writing;

    (b)   may be given in relation to different classes of person or different descriptions of regulated activity.

(3)   A direction under subsection (1) must be published in the way appearing to the Authority to be best calculated to bring it to the attention of the public.

(4)   The Authority may charge a reasonable fee for providing a person with a copy of the direction.

(5)   The Authority must, without delay, give the Treasury a copy of any direction which it gives under this section.

(6)   The Authority may exercise the power conferred by subsection (1) only if it is satisfied that it is desirable in order to protect the interests of clients.

(7)   In considering whether it is *so satisfied*, the Authority must have regard amongst other things to the effectiveness of any arrangements made by any designated professional body—

    (a)   for securing compliance with rules made under section 332(1);

    (b)   for dealing with complaints against its members in relation to the carrying on by them of exempt regulated activities;

    (c)   in order to offer redress to clients who suffer, or claim to have suffered, loss as a result of misconduct by its members in their carrying on of exempt regulated activities;

    (d)   for co-operating with the Authority under section 325(4).

(8)   In this Part "clients" means—

    (a)   persons who use, have used or are or may be contemplating using, any of the services provided by a member of a profession in the course of carrying on exempt regulated activities;

    (b)   persons who have rights or interests which are derived from, or otherwise attributable to, the use of any such services by other persons; or

    (c)   persons who have rights or interests which may be adversely affected by the use of any such services by persons acting on their behalf or in a fiduciary capacity in relation to them.

(9)   If a member of a profession is carrying on an exempt regulated activity in his capacity as a trustee, the persons who are, have been or may be beneficiaries of the trust are to be treated as persons who use, have used or are or may be contemplating using services provided by that person in his carrying on of that activity.

Commencement: 3 September 2001.
Amendments: Sub-s (6): substituted by the Insurance Mediation Directive (Miscellaneous Amendments) Regulations 2003, SI 2003/1473, reg 9(a), as from 14 January 2005 as follows—

"(6)   The Authority may exercise the power conferred by subsection (1) only if it is satisfied either—
    (a)   that it is desirable to do so in order to protect the interests of clients; or
    (b)   that it is necessary to do so in order to comply with a Community obligation imposed by the insurance mediation directive.".

Sub-s (7): for the words in italics there are substituted the words "satisfied of the matter specified in subsection (6)(a)" by SI 2003/1473, reg 9(b), as from 14 January 2005.
References: See paras 18.17–18.20.

---

329 Orders in relation to the general prohibition

(1)   Subsection (2) applies if it appears to the Authority that a person to whom, as a result of section 327(1), the general prohibition does not apply is not a fit and proper person to carry on regulated activities in accordance with that section.

(2)   The Authority may make an order disapplying section 327(1) in relation to that person to the extent specified in the order.

(3)   The Authority may, on the application of the person named in an order under subsection (1), vary or revoke it.

(4)   "Specified" means specified in the order.

(5)   If a partnership is named in an order under this section, the order is not affected by any change in its membership.

(6)   If a partnership named in an order under this section is dissolved, the order continues to have effect in relation to any partnership which succeeds to the business of the dissolved partnership.

(7)   For the purposes of subsection (6), a partnership is to be regarded as succeeding to the business of another partnership only if—

    (a)   the members of the resulting partnership are substantially the same as those of the former partnership; and

    (b)   succession is to the whole or substantially the whole of the business of the former partnership.

Commencement: 3 September 2001.
References: See paras 18.23–18.24.

330 Consultation

(1)   Before giving a direction under section 328(1), the Authority must publish a draft of the proposed direction.

(2)   The draft must be accompanied by—
    (a)   a cost benefit analysis; and
    (b)   notice that representations about the proposed direction may be made to the Authority within a specified time.

(3)   Before giving the proposed direction, the Authority must have regard to any representations made to it in accordance with subsection (2)(b).

(4)   If the Authority gives the proposed direction it must publish an account, in general terms, of—
    (a)   the representations made to it in accordance with subsection (2)(b); and
    (b)   its response to them.

(5)   If the direction differs from the draft published under subsection (1) in a way which is, in the opinion of the Authority, significant—
    (a)   the Authority must (in addition to complying with subsection (4)) publish details of the difference; and
    (b)   those details must be accompanied by a cost benefit analysis.

(6)   Subsections (1) to (5) do not apply if the Authority considers that the delay involved in complying with them would prejudice the interests of consumers.

(7)   Neither subsection (2)(a) nor subsection (5)(b) applies if the Authority considers—
    (a)   that, making the appropriate comparison, there will be no increase in costs; or
    (b)   that, making that comparison, there will be an increase in costs but the increase will be of minimal significance.

(8)   The Authority may charge a reasonable fee for providing a person with a copy of a draft published under subsection (1).

(9)   When the Authority is required to publish a document under this section it must do so in the way appearing to it to be best calculated to bring it to the attention of the public.

(10) "Cost benefit analysis" means an estimate of the costs together with an analysis of the benefits that will arise—
    (a)   if the proposed direction is given; or
    (b)   if subsection (5)(b) applies, from the direction that has been given.

(11) "The appropriate comparison" means—
    (a)   in relation to subsection (2)(a), a comparison between the overall position if the direction is given and the overall position if it is not given;
    (b)   in relation to subsection (5)(b), a comparison between the overall position after the giving of the direction and the overall position before it was given.

Commencement: 3 September 2001.
References: See paras 18.21, 18.22.

331 Procedure on making or varying orders under section 329

(1)   If the Authority proposes to make an order under section 329, it must give the person concerned a warning notice.

(2)   The warning notice must set out the terms of the proposed order.

(3)   If the Authority decides to make an order under section 329, it must give the person concerned a decision notice.

(4)   The decision notice must—
      (a)   name the person to whom the order applies;
      (b)   set out the terms of the order; and
      (c)   be given to the person named in the order.

(5)   Subsections (6) to (8) apply to an application for the variation or revocation of an order under section 329.

(6)   If the Authority decides to grant the application, it must give the applicant written notice of its decision.

(7)   If the Authority proposes to refuse the application, it must give the applicant a warning notice.

(8)   If the Authority decides to refuse the application, it must give the applicant a decision notice.

(9)   A person—
      (a)   against whom the Authority have decided to make an order under section 329, or
      (b)   whose application for the variation or revocation of such an order the Authority had decided to refuse,
may refer the matter to the Tribunal.

(10)   The Authority may not make an order under section 329 unless—
      (a)   the period within which the decision to make to the order may be referred to the Tribunal has expired and no such reference has been made; or
      (b)   if such a reference has been made, the reference has been determined.

Commencement: 3 September 2001.
References: See paras 18.25–18.28.

332 Rules in relation to persons to whom the general prohibition does not apply

(1)   The Authority may make rules applicable to persons to whom, as a result of section 327(1), the general prohibition does not apply.

(2)   The power conferred by subsection (1) is to be exercised for the purpose of ensuring that clients are aware that such persons are not authorised persons.

(3)   A designated professional body must make rules—

   (a)   applicable to members of the profession in relation to which it is established who are not authorised persons; and

   (b)   governing the carrying on by those members of regulated activities (other than regulated activities in relation to which they are exempt persons).

(4)   Rules made in compliance with subsection (3) must be designed to secure that, in providing a particular professional service to a particular client, the member carries on only regulated activities which arise out of, or are complementary to, the provision by him of that service to that client.

(5)   Rules made by a designated professional body under subsection (3) require the approval of the Authority.

Commencement: 18 June 2001.
References: See paras 18.29, 18.30.

333 False claims to be a person to whom the general prohibition does not apply

(1)   A person who—

   (a)   describes himself (in whatever terms) as a person to whom the general prohibition does not apply, in relation to a particular regulated activity, as a result of this Part, or

   (b)   behaves, or otherwise holds himself out, in a manner which indicates (or which is reasonably likely to be understood as indicating) that he is such a person,

is guilty of an offence if he is not such a person.

(2)   In proceedings for an offence under this section it is a defence for the accused to show that he took all reasonable precautions and exercised all due diligence to avoid committing the offence.

(3)   A person guilty of an offence under this section is liable on summary conviction to imprisonment for a term not exceeding six months or a fine not exceeding level 5 on the standard scale, or both.

(4)   But where the conduct constituting the offence involved or included the public display of any material, the maximum fine for the offence is level 5 on the standard scale multiplied by the number of days for which the display continued.

Commencement: 1 December 2001.
References: See paras 18.31, 18.32.

PART XXI
MUTUAL SOCIETIES

Friendly societies

334 The Friendly Societies Commission

(1)   The Treasury may by order provide—

   (a)   for any functions of the Friendly Societies Commission to be transferred to the Authority;

    (b)   for any functions of the Friendly Societies Commission which have not been, or are not being, transferred to the Authority to be transferred to the Treasury.

(2)   If the Treasury consider it appropriate to do so, they may by order provide for the Friendly Societies Commission to cease to exist on a day specified in or determined in accordance with the order.

(3)   The enactments relating to friendly societies which are mentioned in Part I of Schedule 18 are amended as set out in that Part.

(4)   Part II of Schedule 18—
    (a)   removes certain restrictions on the ability of incorporated friendly societies to form subsidiaries and control corporate bodies; and
    (b)   makes connected amendments.

Commencement: 1 December 2001 (sub-ss (3), (4)); 25 February 2001 (remainder).
Orders: The Financial Services and Markets Act 2000 (Mutual Societies) Order 2001, SI 2001/2617, as amended by SI 2001/3647, SI 2001/3649.
References: See para 19.5.

335 The Registry of Friendly Societies

(1)   The Treasury may by order provide—
    (a)   for any functions of the Chief Registrar of Friendly Societies, or of an assistant registrar of friendly societies for the central registration area, to be transferred to the Authority;
    (b)   for any of their functions which have not been, or are not being, transferred to the Authority to be transferred to the Treasury.

(2)   The Treasury may by order provide—
    (a)   for any functions of the central office of the registry of friendly societies to be transferred to the Authority;
    (b)   for any functions of that office which have not been, or are not being, transferred to the Authority to be transferred to the Treasury.

(3)   The Treasury may by order provide—
    (a)   for any functions of the assistant registrar of friendly societies for Scotland to be transferred to the Authority;
    (b)   for any functions of the assistant registrar which have not been, or are not being, transferred to the Authority to be transferred to the Treasury.

(4)   If the Treasury consider it appropriate to do so, they may by order provide for—
    (a)   the office of Chief Registrar of Friendly Societies,
    (b)   the office of assistant registrar of friendly societies for the central registration area,
    (c)   the central office, or
    (d)   the office of assistant registrar of friendly societies for Scotland,
to cease to exist on a day specified in or determined in accordance with the order.

Commencement: 25 February 2001.
Orders: The Financial Services and Markets Act 2000 (Mutual Societies) Order 2001, SI 2001/2617, as amended by SI 2001/3647, SI 2001/3649.
References: See paras 19.5, 19.6.

Building societies

336 The Building Societies Commission

(1)   The Treasury may by order provide—
- (a)   for any functions of the Building Societies Commission to be transferred to the Authority;
- (b)   for any functions of the Building Societies Commission which have not been, or are not being, transferred to the Authority to be transferred to the Treasury.

(2)   If the Treasury consider it appropriate to do so, they may by order provide for the Building Societies Commission to cease to exist on a day specified in or determined in accordance with the order.

(3)   The enactments relating to building societies which are mentioned in Part III of Schedule 18 are amended as set out in that Part.

Commencement: 1 December 2001 (sub-s (3)); 25 February 2001 (remainder).
Orders: The Financial Services and Markets Act 2000 (Mutual Societies) Order 2001, SI 2001/2617, as amended by SI 2001/3647, SI 2001/3649.
References: See para 19.7.

337 The Building Societies Investor Protection Board

The Treasury may by order provide for the Building Societies Investor Protection Board to cease to exist on a day specified in or determined in accordance with the order.

Commencement: 25 February 2001.
Orders: The Financial Services and Markets Act 2000 (Mutual Societies) Order 2001, SI 2001/2617, as amended by SI 2001/3647, SI 2001/3649.
References: See para 19.7.

Industrial and provident societies and credit unions

338 Industrial and provident societies and credit unions

(1)   The Treasury may by order provide for the transfer to the Authority of any functions conferred by—
- (a)   the Industrial and Provident Societies Act 1965;
- (b)   the Industrial and Provident Societies Act 1967;
- (c)   the Friendly and Industrial and Provident Societies Act 1968;
- (d)   the Industrial and Provident Societies Act 1975;
- (e)   the Industrial and Provident Societies Act 1978;
- (f)   the Credit Unions Act 1979.

(2)   The Treasury may by order provide for the transfer to the Treasury of any functions under those enactments which have not been, or are not being, transferred to the Authority.

(3)   The enactments relating to industrial and provident societies which are mentioned in Part IV of Schedule 18 are amended as set out in that Part.

(4)   The enactments relating to credit unions which are mentioned in Part V of Schedule 18 are amended as set out in that Part.

Commencement: 1 December 2001 (sub-ss (3), (4)); 25 February 2001 (remainder).
Orders: The Financial Services and Markets Act 2000 (Mutual Societies) Order 2001, SI 2001/2617, as amended by SI 2001/3647, SI 2001/3649.
References: See paras 19.9, 19.10.

Supplemental

339 Supplemental provisions

(1)   The additional powers conferred by section 428 on a person making an order under this Act include power for the Treasury, when making an order under section 334, 335, 336 or 338 which transfers functions, to include provision—

   (a)   for the transfer of any functions of a member of the body, or servant or agent of the body or person, whose functions are transferred by the order;

   (b)   for the transfer of any property, rights or liabilities held, enjoyed or incurred by any person in connection with transferred functions;

   (c)   for the carrying on and completion by or under the authority of the person to whom functions are transferred of any proceedings, investigations or other matters commenced, before the order takes effect, by or under the authority of the person from whom the functions are transferred;

   (d)   amending any enactment relating to transferred functions in connection with their exercise by, or under the authority of, the person to whom they are transferred;

   (e)   for the substitution of the person to whom functions are transferred for the person from whom they are transferred, in any instrument, contract or legal proceedings made or begun before the order takes effect.

(2)   The additional powers conferred by section 428 on a person making an order under this Act include power for the Treasury, when making an order under section 334(2), 335(4), 336(2) or 337, to include provision—

   (a)   for the transfer of any property, rights or liabilities held, enjoyed or incurred by any person in connection with the office or body which ceases to have effect as a result of the order;

   (b)   for the carrying on and completion by or under the authority of such person as may be specified in the order of any proceedings, investigations or other matters commenced, before the order takes effect, by or under the authority of the person whose office, or the body which, ceases to exist as a result of the order;

   (c)   amending any enactment which makes provision with respect to that office or body;

   (d)   for the substitution of the Authority, the Treasury or such other body as may be specified in the order in any instrument, contract or legal proceedings made or begun before the order takes effect.

(3)   On or after the making of an order under any of sections 334 to 338 ("the original order"), the Treasury may by order make any incidental, supplemental, consequential or transitional provision which they had power to include in the original order.

(4) A certificate issued by the Treasury that property vested in a person immediately before an order under this Part takes effect has been transferred as a result of the order is conclusive evidence of the transfer.

(5) Subsections (1) and (2) are not to be read as affecting in any way the powers conferred by section 428.

Commencement: 25 February 2001.
Orders: The Financial Services and Markets Act 2000 (Mutual Societies) Order 2001, SI 2001/2617, as amended by SI 2001/3647, SI 2001/3649; the Financial Services and Markets Act 2000 (Transitional Provisions, Repeals and Savings) (Financial Services Compensation Scheme) Order 2001, SI 2001/2967; the Financial Services and Markets Act 2000 (Consequential Amendments and Savings) (Industrial Assurance) Order 2001, SI 2001/3647.
References: See paras 19.11–19.13.

PART XXII
AUDITORS AND ACTUARIES

Appointment

340 Appointment

(1) Rules may require an authorised person, or an authorised person falling within a specified class—
    (a) to appoint an auditor, or
    (b) to appoint an actuary,
if he is not already under an obligation to do so imposed by another enactment.

(2) Rules may require an authorised person, or an authorised person falling within a specified class—
    (a) to produce periodic financial reports; and
    (b) to have them reported on by an auditor or an actuary.

(3) Rules may impose such other duties on auditors of, or actuaries acting for, authorised persons as may be specified.

(4) Rules under subsection (1) may make provision—
    (a) specifying the manner in which and time within which an auditor or actuary is to be appointed;
    (b) requiring the Authority to be notified of an appointment;
    (c) enabling the Authority to make an appointment if no appointment has been made or notified;
    (d) as to remuneration;
    (e) as to the term of office, removal and resignation of an auditor or actuary.

(5) An auditor or actuary appointed as a result of rules under subsection (1), or on whom duties are imposed by rules under subsection (3)—
    (a) must act in accordance with such provision as may be made by rules; and
    (b) is to have such powers in connection with the discharge of his functions as may be provided by rules.

(6) In subsections (1) to (3) "auditor" or "actuary" means an auditor, or actuary, who satisfies such requirements as to qualifications, experience and other matters (if any) as may be specified.

(7) "Specified" means specified in rules.

Commencement: 18 June 2001.
References: See paras 20.2, 20.3.

Information

341 Access to books etc

(1)   An appointed auditor of, or an appointed actuary acting for, an authorised person—

    (a)   has a right of access at all times to the authorised person's books, accounts and vouchers; and

    (b)   is entitled to require from the authorised person's officers such information and explanations as he reasonably considers necessary for the performance of his duties as auditor or actuary.

(2)   "Appointed" means appointed under or as a result of this Act.

Commencement: 1 December 2001.
References: See para 20.4.

342 Information given by auditor or actuary to the Authority

(1)   This section applies to a person who is, or has been, an auditor of an authorised person appointed under or as a result of a statutory provision.

(2)   This section also applies to a person who is, or has been, an actuary acting for an authorised person and appointed under or as a result of a statutory provision.

(3)   An auditor or actuary does not contravene any duty to which he is subject merely because he gives to the Authority—

    (a)   information on a matter of which he has, or had, become aware in his capacity as auditor of, or actuary acting for, the authorised person, or

    (b)   his opinion on such a matter,

if he is acting in good faith and he reasonably believes that the information or opinion is relevant to any functions of the Authority.

(4)   Subsection (3) applies whether or not the auditor or actuary is responding to a request from the Authority.

(5)   The Treasury may make regulations prescribing circumstances in which an auditor or actuary must communicate matters to the Authority as mentioned in subsection (3).

(6)   It is the duty of an auditor or actuary to whom any such regulations apply to communicate a matter to the Authority in the circumstances prescribed by the regulations.

(7)   The matters to be communicated to the Authority in accordance with the regulations may include matters relating to persons other than the authorised person concerned.

Commencement: 1 December 2001 (sub-ss (1)–(4), (6), (7)); 25 February 2001 (remainder).
Regulations: The Financial Services and Markets Act 2000 (Communications by Auditors) Regulations 2001, SI 2001/2587; the Financial Services and Markets Act 2000 (Communications by Actuaries) Regulations 2003, SI 2003/1294.
References: See paras 20.5, 20.6.

343 Information given by auditor or actuary to the Authority: persons with close links

(1)   This section applies to a person who—

    (a)   is, or has been, an auditor of an authorised person appointed under or as a result of a statutory provision; and

    (b)   is, or has been, an auditor of a person ("CL") who has close links with the authorised person.

(2)   This section also applies to a person who—

    (a)   is, or has been, an actuary acting for an authorised person and appointed under or as a result of a statutory provision; and

    (b)   is, or has been, an actuary acting for a person ("CL") who has close links with the authorised person.

(3)   An auditor or actuary does not contravene any duty to which he is subject merely because he gives to the Authority—

    (a)   information on a matter concerning the authorised person of which he has, or had, become aware in his capacity as auditor of, or actuary acting for, CL, or

    (b)   his opinion on such a matter,

if he is acting in good faith and he reasonably believes that the information or opinion is relevant to any functions of the Authority.

(4)   Subsection (3) applies whether or not the auditor or actuary is responding to a request from the Authority.

(5)   The Treasury may make regulations prescribing circumstances in which an auditor or actuary must communicate matters to the Authority as mentioned in subsection (3).

(6)   It is the duty of an auditor or actuary to whom any such regulations apply to communicate a matter to the Authority in the circumstances prescribed by the regulations.

(7)   The matters to be communicated to the Authority in accordance with the regulations may include matters relating to persons other than the authorised person concerned.

(8)   CL has close links with the authorised person concerned ("A") if CL is—

    (a)   a parent undertaking of A;

    (b)   a subsidiary undertaking of A;

    (c)   a parent undertaking of a subsidiary undertaking of A; or

    (d)   a subsidiary undertaking of a parent undertaking of A.

(9)   "Subsidiary undertaking" includes all the instances mentioned in Article 1(1) and (2) of the Seventh Company Law Directive in which an entity may be a subsidiary of an undertaking.

Commencement: 1 December 2001 (sub-ss (1)–(4), (6)–(9)); 25 February 2001 (remainder).
Regulations: The Financial Services and Markets Act 2000 (Communications by Auditors) Regulations 2001, SI 2001/2587; the Financial Services and Markets Act 2000 (Communications by Actuaries) Regulations 2003, SI 2003/1294.
References: See paras 20.7, 20.8.

---

344 Duty of auditor or actuary resigning etc to give notice

(1)   This section applies to an auditor or actuary to whom section 342 applies.

(2)   He must without delay notify the Authority if he—
  (a)   is removed from office by an authorised person;
  (b)   resigns before the expiry of his term of office with such a person; or
  (c)   is not re-appointed by such a person.

(3)   If he ceases to be an auditor of, or actuary acting for, such a person, he must without delay notify the Authority—
  (a)   of any matter connected with his so ceasing which he thinks ought to be drawn to the Authority's attention; or
  (b)   that there is no such matter.

Commencement: 1 December 2001.
References: See para 20.10.

Disqualification

345 Disqualification

(1)   If it appears to the Authority that an auditor or actuary to whom section 342 applies has failed to comply with a duty imposed on him under this Act, it may disqualify him from being the auditor of, or (as the case may be) from acting as an actuary for, any authorised person or any particular class of authorised person.

(2)   If the Authority proposes to disqualify a person under this section it must give him a warning notice.

(3)   If it decides to disqualify him it must give him a decision notice.

(4)   The Authority may remove any disqualification imposed under this section if satisfied that the disqualified person will in future comply with the duty in question.

(5)   A person who has been disqualified under this section may refer the matter to the Tribunal.

Commencement: 1 December 2001.
Transitional provisions: The Financial Services and Markets Act 2000 (Transitional Provisions) (Authorised Persons etc) Order 2001, SI 2001/2636, art 78 (made under ss 426–428), provides for the disqualification under this section of an auditor who, at 1 December 2001, has been disqualified pursuant to the Financial Services Act 1986, s 111(3) (repealed by the Financial Services and Markets Act 2000 (Consequential Amendments and Repeals) Order 2001, SI 2001/3649, art 3(1)(c) (made under ss 426, 427)) or the Insurance Companies Act 1982, s 21A(5) (repealed by art 3(1)(b) of that Order).
References: See para 20.11.

Offence

346 Provision of false or misleading information to auditor or actuary

(1)   An authorised person who knowingly or recklessly gives an appointed auditor or actuary information which is false or misleading in a material particular is guilty of an offence and liable—
  (a)   on summary conviction, to imprisonment for a term not exceeding six months or a fine not exceeding the statutory maximum, or both;

(b) on conviction on indictment, to imprisonment for a term not exceeding two years or a fine, or both.

(2) Subsection (1) applies equally to an officer, controller or manager of an authorised person.

(3) "Appointed" means appointed under or as a result of this Act.

Commencement: 1 December 2001.
References: See para 20.9.

PART XXIII
PUBLIC RECORD, DISCLOSURE OF INFORMATION AND CO-OPERATION

The public record

347 The record of authorised persons etc

(1) The Authority must maintain a record of every—
  (a) person who appears to the Authority to be an authorised person;
  (b) authorised unit trust scheme;
  (c) authorised open-ended investment company;
  (d) recognised scheme;
  (e) recognised investment exchange;
  (f) recognised clearing house;
  (g) individual to whom a prohibition order relates;
  (h) approved person; and
  (i) person falling within such other class (if any) as the Authority may determine.

(2) The record must include such information as the Authority considers appropriate and at least the following information—
  (a) in the case of a person appearing to the Authority to be an authorised person—
    (i) information as to the services which he holds himself out as able to provide; and
    (ii) any address of which the Authority is aware at which a notice or other document may be served on him;
  (b) in the case of an authorised unit trust scheme, the name and address of the manager and trustee of the scheme;
  (c) in the case of an authorised open-ended investment company, the name and address of—
    (i) the company;
    (ii) if it has only one director, the director; and
    (iii) its depositary (if any);
  (d) in the case of a recognised scheme, the name and address of—
    (i) the operator of the scheme; and
    (ii) any representative of the operator in the United Kingdom;
  (e) in the case of a recognised investment exchange or recognised clearing house, the name and address of the exchange or clearing house;

    (f)   in the case of an individual to whom a prohibition order relates—
        (i)   his name; and
        (ii)   details of the effect of the order;
    (g)   in the case of a person who is an approved person—
        (i)   his name;
        (ii)   the name of the relevant authorised person;
        (iii)   if the approved person is performing a controlled function under an arrangement with a contractor of the relevant authorised person, the name of the contractor.

(3)   If it appears to the Authority that a person in respect of whom there is an entry in the record as a result of one of the paragraphs of subsection (1) has ceased to be a person to whom that paragraph applies, the Authority may remove the entry from the record.

(4)   But if the Authority decides not to remove the entry, it must—
    (a)   make a note to that effect in the record; and
    (b)   state why it considers that the person has ceased to be a person to whom that paragraph applies.

(5)   The Authority must—
    (a)   make the record available for inspection by members of the public in a legible form at such times and in such place or places as the Authority may determine; and
    (b)   provide a certified copy of the record, or any part of it, to any person who asks for it—
        (i)   on payment of the fee (if any) fixed by the Authority; and
        (ii)   in a form (either written or electronic) in which it is legible to the person asking for it.

(6)   The Authority may—
    (a)   publish the record, or any part of it;
    (b)   exploit commercially the information contained in the record, or any part of that information.

(7)   "Authorised unit trust scheme", "authorised open-ended investment company" and "recognised scheme" have the same meaning as in Part XVII, and associated expressions are to be read accordingly.

(8)   "Approved person" means a person in relation to whom the Authority has given its approval under section 59 and "controlled function" and "arrangement" have the same meaning as in that section.

(9)   "Relevant authorised person" has the meaning given in section 66.

Commencement: 1 December 2002 (for the purpose of requiring the Authority to maintain a record of approved persons); 1 August 2002 (for the purpose of requiring the Authority to maintain a record of persons who appear to the Authority to be authorised persons who were, immediately before 1 December 2001, authorised under the Financial Services Act 1986 by virtue of holding a certificate issued for the purposes of Pt 1 of that Act by a recognised professional body (within the meaning of that Act)); 1 May 2002 (for the purpose of requiring the Authority to maintain a record of persons who appear to the Authority to be authorised persons who are EEA firms or Treaty firms); 1 December 2001 (for the purpose of enabling the Authority to maintain a record of any of the persons specified by sub-paragraphs (a) to (c) of this paragraph).
References: See paras 7.48–7.50.

Disclosure of information

348 Restrictions on disclosure of confidential information by Authority etc

(1)   Confidential information must not be disclosed by a primary recipient, or by any person obtaining the information directly or indirectly from a primary recipient, without the consent of—

> (a)   the person from whom the primary recipient obtained the information; and
>
> (b)   if different, the person to whom it relates.

(2)   In this Part "confidential information" means information which—

> (a)   relates to the business or other affairs of any person;
>
> (b)   was received by the primary recipient for the purposes of, or in the discharge of, any functions of the Authority, the competent authority for the purposes of Part VI or the Secretary of State under any provision made by or under this Act; and
>
> (c)   is not prevented from being confidential information by subsection (4).

(3)   It is immaterial for the purposes of subsection (2) whether or not the information was received—

> (a)   by virtue of a requirement to provide it imposed by or under this Act;
>
> (b)   for other purposes as well as purposes mentioned in that subsection.

(4)   Information is not confidential information if—

> (a)   it has been made available to the public by virtue of being disclosed in any circumstances in which, or for any purposes for which, disclosure is not precluded by this section; or
>
> (b)   it is in the form of a summary or collection of information so framed that it is not possible to ascertain from it information relating to any particular person.

(5)   Each of the following is a primary recipient for the purposes of this Part—

> (a)   the Authority;
>
> (b)   any person exercising functions conferred by Part VI on the competent authority;
>
> (c)   the Secretary of State;
>
> (d)   a person appointed to make a report under section 166;
>
> (e)   any person who is or has been employed by a person mentioned in paragraphs (a) to (c);
>
> (f)   any auditor or expert instructed by a person mentioned in those paragraphs.

(6)   In subsection (5)(f) "expert" includes—

> (a)   a competent person appointed by the competent authority under section 97;
>
> (b)   a competent person appointed by the Authority or the Secretary of State to conduct an investigation under Part XI;
>
> (c)   any body or person appointed under paragraph 6 of Schedule 1 to perform a function on behalf of the Authority.

Commencement: 18 June 2001.
References: See paras 7.51–7.53.

349 Exceptions from section 348

(1)   Section 348 does not prevent a disclosure of confidential information which is—

    (a)   made for the purpose of facilitating the carrying out of a public function; and

    (b)   permitted by regulations made by the Treasury under this section.

(2)   The regulations may, in particular, make provision permitting the disclosure of confidential information or of confidential information of a prescribed kind—

    (a)   by prescribed recipients, or recipients of a prescribed description, to any person for the purpose of enabling or assisting the recipient to discharge prescribed public functions;

    (b)   by prescribed recipients, or recipients of a prescribed description, to prescribed persons, or persons of prescribed descriptions, for the purpose of enabling or assisting those persons to discharge prescribed public functions;

    (c)   by the Authority to the Treasury or the Secretary of State for any purpose;

    (d)   by any recipient if the disclosure is with a view to or in connection with prescribed proceedings.

(3)   The regulations may also include provision—

    (a)   making any permission to disclose confidential information subject to conditions (which may relate to the obtaining of consents or any other matter);

    (b)   restricting the uses to which confidential information disclosed under the regulations may be put.

(4)   In relation to confidential information, each of the following is a "recipient"—

    (a)   a primary recipient;

    (b)   a person obtaining the information directly or indirectly from a primary recipient.

(5)   "Public functions" includes—

    (a)   functions conferred by or in accordance with any provision contained in any enactment or subordinate legislation;

    (b)   functions conferred by or in accordance with any provision contained in the Community Treaties or any Community instrument;

    (c)   similar functions conferred on persons by or under provisions having effect as part of the law of a country or territory outside the United Kingdom;

    (d)   functions exercisable in relation to prescribed disciplinary proceedings.

(6)   "Enactment" includes—

    (a)   an Act of the Scottish Parliament;

    (b)   Northern Ireland legislation.

(7)   "Subordinate legislation" has the meaning given in the Interpretation Act 1978 and also includes an instrument made under an Act of the Scottish Parliament or under Northern Ireland legislation.

Commencement: 25 February 2001 (for the purpose of making orders or regulations); 18 June 2001 (remaining purposes).
Transitional provisions: in relation to the Financial Services and Markets Act 2000 (Disclosure of Confidential Information) Regulations 2001, SI 2001/2188, see the Financial Services and Markets Act 2000 (Consequential and Transitional Provisions) (Miscellaneous) (No 2) Order 2001, SI 2001/2659, art 7.
Regulations: The Financial Services and Markets Act 2000 (Disclosure of Confidential Information) Regulations 2001, SI 2001/2188, as amended by SI 2001/3437, SI 2001/3624, SI 2002/1775, SI 2003/693, SI 2003/1092, SI 2003/1473, SI 2003/2066, SI 2003/2174, and modified by SI 2001/2659; the Electronic Commerce Directive (Financial Services and Markets) Regulations 2002, SI 2002/1775, as amended by SI 2002/2015.
References: See paras 7.54–7.58.

350 Disclosure of information by the Inland Revenue

(1)   No obligation as to secrecy imposed by statute or otherwise prevents the disclosure of Revenue information to—

    (a)   the Authority, or

    (b)   the Secretary of State,

if the disclosure is made for the purpose of assisting in the investigation of a matter under section 168 or with a view to the appointment of an investigator under that section.

(2)   A disclosure may only be made under subsection (1) by or under the authority of the Commissioners of Inland Revenue.

(3)   Section 348 does not apply to Revenue information.

(4)   Information obtained as a result of subsection (1) may not be used except—

    (a)   for the purpose of deciding whether to appoint an investigator under section 168;

    (b)   in the conduct of an investigation under section 168;

    (c)   in criminal proceedings brought against a person under this Act or the Criminal Justice Act 1993 as a result of an investigation under section 168;

    (d)   for the purpose of taking action under this Act against a person as a result of an investigation under section 168;

    (e)   in proceedings before the Tribunal as a result of action taken as mentioned in paragraph (d).

(5)   Information obtained as a result of subsection (1) may not be disclosed except—

    (a)   by or under the authority of the Commissioners of Inland Revenue;

    (b)   in proceedings mentioned in subsection (4)(c) or (e) or with a view to their institution.

(6)   Subsection (5) does not prevent the disclosure of information obtained as a result of subsection (1) to a person to whom it could have been disclosed under subsection (1).

(7)   "Revenue information" means information held by a person which it would be an offence under section 182 of the Finance Act 1989 for him to disclose.

Commencement: 3 September 2001 (sub-ss (1), (2), (4)–(6)); 18 June 2001 (remainder).
References: See para 7.61.

351 Competition information

(1)–(3) . . .

(4)   Section 348 does not apply to competition information.

(5)   "Competition information" means information which—
    (a)   relates to the affairs of a particular individual or body;
    (b)   is not otherwise in the public domain; and
    (c)   was obtained under or by virtue of a competition provision.

(6)   "Competition provision" means any provision of—
    (a)   an order made under section 95;
    (b)   Chapter III of Part X; or
    (c)   Chapter II of Part XVIII.

(7)   . . .

Commencement: 18 June 2001 (sub-ss (1)–(6)); 25 February 2001 (remainder).
Amendments: Sub-ss (1)–(3), (7): repealed by the Enterprise Act 2002, ss 247(k), 278(2), Sch 26, as from 20 June 2003.
References: See paras 10.49, 10.50.

352 Offences

(1)   A person who discloses information in contravention of section 348 or 350(5) is guilty of an offence.

(2)   A person guilty of an offence under subsection (1) is liable—
    (a)   on summary conviction, to imprisonment for a term not exceeding three months or a fine not exceeding the statutory maximum, or both;
    (b)   on conviction on indictment, to imprisonment for a term not exceeding two years or a fine, or both.

(3)   A person is guilty of an offence if, in contravention of any provision of regulations made under section 349, he uses information which has been disclosed to him in accordance with the regulations.

(4)   A person is guilty of an offence if, in contravention of subsection (4) of section 350, he uses information which has been disclosed to him in accordance with that section.

(5)   A person guilty of an offence under subsection (3) or (4) is liable on summary conviction to imprisonment for a term not exceeding three months or a fine not exceeding level 5 on the standard scale, or both.

(6)   In proceedings for an offence under this section it is a defence for the accused to prove—
    (a)   that he did not know and had no reason to suspect that the information was confidential information or that it had been disclosed in accordance with section 350;
    (b)   that he took all reasonable precautions and exercised all due diligence to avoid committing the offence.

Commencement: 18 June 2001 (for the purpose of any contravention of s 348); 3 September 2001 (remaining purposes).
References: See paras 7.61, 7.62.

353 Removal of other restrictions on disclosure

(1)　The Treasury may make regulations permitting the disclosure of any information, or of information of a prescribed kind—

    (a)　by prescribed persons for the purpose of assisting or enabling them to discharge prescribed functions under this Act or any rules or regulations made under it;

    (b)　by prescribed persons, or persons of a prescribed description, to the Authority for the purpose of assisting or enabling the Authority to discharge prescribed functions.

(2)　Regulations under this section may not make any provision in relation to the disclosure of confidential information by primary recipients or by any person obtaining confidential information directly or indirectly from a primary recipient.

(3)　If a person discloses any information as permitted by regulations under this section the disclosure is not to be taken as a contravention of any duty to which he is subject.

Commencement: 25 February 2001.
Regulations: The Financial Services and Markets Act 2000 (Disclosure of Information by Prescribed Persons) Regulations 2001, SI 2001/1857.
References: See para 7.59.

Co-operation

354 Authority's duty to co-operate with others

(1)　The Authority must take such steps as it considers appropriate to co-operate with other persons (whether in the United Kingdom or elsewhere) who have functions—

    (a)　similar to those of the Authority; or

    (b)　in relation to the prevention or detection of financial crime.

(2)　Co-operation may include the sharing of information which the Authority is not prevented from disclosing.

(3)　"Financial crime" has the same meaning as in section 6.

Commencement: 3 September 2001.
References: See para 7.68.

PART XXIV
INSOLVENCY

Interpretation

355 Interpretation of this Part

(1)   In this Part—
"the 1985 Act" means the Bankruptcy (Scotland) Act 1985;
"the 1986 Act" means the Insolvency Act 1986;
"the 1989 Order" means the Insolvency (Northern Ireland) Order 1989;
"body" means a body of persons—
>   (a)   over which the court has jurisdiction under any provision of, or made under, the 1986 Act (or the 1989 Order); but
>   (b)   which is not a building society, a friendly society or an industrial and provident society; and

"court" means—
>   (a)   the court having jurisdiction for the purposes of the 1985 Act or the 1986 Act; or
>   (b)   in Northern Ireland, the High Court.

(2)   In this Part "insurer" has such meaning as may be specified in an order made by the Treasury.

Commencement: 20 July 2001.
Orders: The Financial Services and Markets Act 2000 (Insolvency) (Definition of "Insurer") Order 2001, SI 2001/2634, as amended by SI 2002/1242; the Financial Services and Markets Act 2000 (Administration Orders Relating to Insurers) Order 2002, SI 2002/1242, as amended by SI 2003/2134.

Voluntary arrangements

356 Authority's powers to participate in proceedings: company voluntary arrangements

[(1)   Where a voluntary arrangement has effect under Part I of the 1986 Act in respect of a company or insolvent partnership which is an authorised person, the Authority may apply to the court under section 6 or 7 of that Act.

(2)   Where a voluntary arrangement has been approved under Part II of the 1989 Order in respect of a company or insolvent partnership which is an authorised person, the Authority may apply to the court under Article 19 or 20 of that Order.]

(3)   If a person other than the Authority makes an application to the court in relation to the company or insolvent partnership under [any] of those provisions, the Authority is entitled to be heard at any hearing relating to the application.

Commencement: 1 December 2001.
Amendments: Sub-ss (1), (2): substituted by the Insolvency Act 2000, s 15(3)(a), (b), as from 1 January 2003. Sub-s (3): word in square brackets substituted by the Insolvency Act 2000, s 15(3)(c).
Limited liability partnerships: By virtue of the Limited Liability Partnerships Regulations 2001, SI 2001/1090, reg 6, this section is applied with modifications to limited liability partnerships.
References: See paras 21.7, 21.8.

357 Authority's powers to participate in proceedings: individual voluntary arrangements

(1)   The Authority is entitled to be heard on an application by an individual who is an authorised person under section 253 of the 1986 Act (or Article 227 of the 1989 Order).

(2)   Subsections (3) to (6) apply if such an order is made on the application of such a person.

(3)   A person appointed for the purpose by the Authority is entitled to attend any meeting of creditors of the debtor summoned under section 257 of the 1986 Act (or Article 231 of the 1989 Order).

(4)   Notice of the result of a meeting so summoned is to be given to the Authority by the chairman of the meeting.

(5)   The Authority may apply to the court—
      (a)   under section 262 of the 1986 Act (or Article 236 of the 1989 Order); or
      (b)   under section 263 of the 1986 Act (or Article 237 of the 1989 Order).

(6)   If a person other than the Authority makes an application to the court under any provision mentioned in subsection (5), the Authority is entitled to be heard at any hearing relating to the application.

Commencement: 1 December 2001.
References: See para 21.9.

358 Authority's powers to participate in proceedings: trust deeds for creditors in Scotland

(1)   This section applies where a trust deed has been granted by or on behalf of a debtor who is an authorised person.

(2)   The trustee must, as soon as practicable after he becomes aware that the debtor is an authorised person, send to the Authority—
      (a)   in every case, a copy of the trust deed;
      (b)   where any other document or information is sent to every creditor known to the trustee in pursuance of paragraph 5(1)(c) of Schedule 5 to the 1985 Act, a copy of such document or information.

(3)   Paragraph 7 of that Schedule applies to the Authority as if it were a qualified creditor who has not been sent a copy of the notice as mentioned in paragraph 5(1)(c) of the Schedule.

(4)   The Authority must be given the same notice as the creditors of any meeting of creditors held in relation to the trust deed.

(5)   A person appointed for the purpose by the Authority is entitled to attend and participate in (but not to vote at) any such meeting of creditors as if the Authority were a creditor under the deed.

(6)   This section does not affect any right the Authority has as a creditor of a debtor who is an authorised person.

(7)   Expressions used in this section and in the 1985 Act have the same meaning in this section as in that Act.

Commencement: 1 December 2001.
References: See para 28.10.

Administration orders

[359 Administration order

(1)   The Authority may make an administration application under Schedule B1 to the 1986 Act (or present a petition under Article 22 of the 1989 Order) in relation to a company or insolvent partnership which—

(a)   is or has been an authorised person,

(b)   is or has been an appointed representative, or

(c)   is carrying on or has carried on a regulated activity in contravention of the general prohibition.

(2)   Subsection (3) applies in relation to an administration application made (or a petition presented) by the Authority by virtue of this section.

(3)   Any of the following shall be treated for the purpose of paragraph 11(a) of Schedule B1 to the 1986 Act (or Article 21(1)(a) of the 1989 Order) as unable to pay its debts—

(a)   a company or partnership in default on an obligation to pay a sum due and payable under an agreement, and

(b)   an authorised deposit taker in default on an obligation to pay a sum due and payable in respect of a relevant deposit.

(4)   In this section—

"agreement" means an agreement the making or performance of which constitutes or is part of a regulated activity carried on by the company or partnership,

"authorised deposit taker" means a person with a Part IV permission to accept deposits (but not a person who has a Part IV permission to accept deposits only for the purpose of carrying on another regulated activity in accordance with that permission),

"company" means a company—

(a)   in respect of which an administrator may be appointed under Schedule B1 to the 1986 Act, or

(b)   to which Article 21 of the 1989 Order applies, and

"relevant deposit" shall, ignoring any restriction on the meaning of deposit arising from the identity of the person making the deposit, be construed in accordance with—

(a)   section 22,

(b)   any relevant order under that section, and

(c)   Schedule 2.

(5)   The definition of "authorised deposit taker" in subsection (4) shall be construed in accordance with—

(a)   section 22,

(b)   any relevant order under that section, and

(c)   Schedule 2.]

Commencement: 15 September 2003.
Amendments: Substituted by the Enterprise Act 2002, s 248(3), Sch 17, paras 53, 55, as from 15 September 2003, subject to savings and transitional provisions as noted to s 215 ante.
Limited liability partnerships: by virtue of the Limited Liability Partnerships Regulations 2001, SI 2001/1090, reg 6, sub-ss (1)–(4) are applied with modifications to limited liability partnerships.
References: See para 21.12.

360 Insurers

(1)   The Treasury may by order provide that such provisions of Part II of the 1986 Act (or Part III of the 1989 Order) as may be specified are to apply in relation to insurers with such modifications as may be specified.

(2)   An order under this section—
  (a)   may provide that such provisions of this Part as may be specified are to apply in relation to the administration of insurers in accordance with the order with such modifications as may be specified; and
  (b)   requires the consent of the Secretary of State.

(3)   "Specified" means specified in the order.

Commencement: 20 July 2001.
Orders: The Financial Services and Markets Act 2000 (Administration Orders Relating to Insurers) Order 2002, SI 2002/1242, as amended by SI 2003/2134.
References: See para 21.13.

[361 Administrator's duty to report to Authority

(1)   This section applies where a company or partnership is—
  (a)   in administration within the meaning of Schedule B1 to the 1986 Act, or
  (b)   the subject of an administration order under Part III of the 1989 Order.

(2)   If the administrator thinks that the company or partnership is carrying on or has carried on a regulated activity in contravention of the general prohibition, he must report to the Authority without delay.

(3)   Subsection (2) does not apply where the administration arises out of an administration order made on an application made or petition presented by the Authority.]

Commencement: 15 September 2003.
Amendments: Substituted by the Enterprise Act 2002, s 248(3), Sch 17, paras 53, 56, as from 15 September 2003, subject to savings and transitional provisions as noted to s 215 ante.
Limited liability partnerships: by virtue of the Limited Liability Partnerships Regulations 2001, SI 2001/1090, reg 6, this section is applied with modifications to limited liability partnerships.
References: See para 21.14.

---

362 Authority's powers to participate in proceedings

(1)   This section applies if a person other than the Authority [makes an administration application under Schedule B1 to the 1986 Act (or presents a petition under Article 22 of the 1989 Order)] in relation to a company or partnership which—
  (a)   is, or has been, an authorised person;
  (b)   is, or has been, an appointed representative; or
  (c)   is carrying on, or has carried on, a regulated activity in contravention of the general prohibition.

[(1A) This section also applies in relation to—
(a) the appointment under paragraph 14 or 22 of Schedule B1 to the 1986 Act of an administrator of a company of a kind described in subsection (1)(a) to (c), or
(b) the filing with the court of a copy of notice of intention to appoint an administrator under either of those paragraphs.]

(2) The Authority is entitled to be heard—
(a) at the hearing of the [administration application or the petition]; and
(b) at any other hearing of the court in relation to the company or partnership under Part II of the 1986 Act (or Part III of the 1989 Order).

(3) Any notice or other document required to be sent to a creditor of the company or partnership must also be sent to the Authority.

[(4) The Authority may apply to the court under paragraph 74 of Schedule B1 to the 1986 Act (or Article 39 of the 1989 Order).

(4A) In respect of an application under subsection (4)—
(a) paragraph 74(1)(a) and (b) shall have effect as if for the words "harm the interests of the applicant (whether alone or in common with some or all other members or creditors)" there were substituted the words "harm the interests of some or all members or creditors", and
(b) Article 39 of the 1989 Order shall have effect with the omission of the words "(including at least himself")."]

(5) A person appointed for the purpose by the Authority is entitled—
(a) to attend any meeting of creditors of the company or partnership summoned under any enactment;
(b) to attend any meeting of a committee established under [paragraph 57 of Schedule B1 to the 1986 Act] (or Article 38 of the 1989 Order); and
(c) to make representations as to any matter for decision at such a meeting.

(6) If, during the course of the administration of a company, a compromise or arrangement is proposed between the company and its creditors, or any class of them, the Authority may apply to the court under section 425 of the Companies Act 1985 (or Article 418 of the Companies (Northern Ireland) Order 1986).

Commencement: 1 December 2001.
Amendments: Sub-s (1): words in square brackets substituted by the Enterprise Act 2002, s 248(3), Sch 17, paras 53, 57(a), as from 15 September 2003, subject to savings and transitional provisions as noted to s 215 ante.
Sub-s (1A): inserted by the Enterprise Act 2002, s 248(3), Sch 17, paras 53, 57(b), as from 15 September 2003, subject to savings and transitional provisions as noted to s 215 ante.
Sub-s (2): words in square brackets substituted by the Enterprise Act 2002, s 248(3), Sch 17, paras 53, 57(c), as from 15 September 2003, subject to savings and transitional provisions as noted to s 215 ante.
Sub-ss (4), (4A): substituted for sub-s (4) by the Enterprise Act 2002, s 248(3), Sch 17, paras 53, 57(d), as from 15 September 2003, subject to savings and transitional provisions as noted to s 215 ante.
Sub-s (5): words in square brackets substituted by the Enterprise Act 2002, s 248(3), Sch 17, paras 53, 57(e), as from 15 September 2003, subject to savings and transitional provisions as noted to s 215 ante.
Limited liability partnerships: by virtue of the Limited Liability Partnerships Regulations 2001, SI 2001/1090, reg 6, this section is applied with modifications to limited liability partnerships.
References: See para 21.15.

[362A Administrator appointed by company or directors

(1)   This section applies in relation to a company of a kind described in section 362(1)(a) to (c).

(2)   An administrator of the company may not be appointed under paragraph 22 of Schedule B1 to the 1986 Act without the consent of the Authority.

(3)   Consent under subsection (2)—
   (a)   must be in writing, and
   (b)   must be filed with the court along with the notice of intention to appoint under paragraph 27 of that Schedule.

(4)   In a case where no notice of intention to appoint is required—
   (a)   subsection (3)(b) shall not apply, but
   (b)   consent under subsection (2) must accompany the notice of appointment filed under paragraph 29 of that Schedule.]

Commencement: 15 September 2003.
Amendments: Inserted by the Enterprise Act 2002, s 248(3), Sch 17, paras 53, 58, as from 15 September 2003, subject to savings and transitional provisions as noted to s 215 ante.
References: See paras 21.11, 21.15.

Receivership

363 Authority's powers to participate in proceedings

(1)   This section applies if a receiver has been appointed in relation to a company which—
   (a)   is, or has been, an authorised person;
   (b)   is, or has been, an appointed representative; or
   (c)   is carrying on, or has carried on, a regulated activity in contravention of the general prohibition.

(2)   The Authority is entitled to be heard on an application made under section 35 or 63 of the 1986 Act (or Article 45 of the 1989 Order).

(3)   The Authority is entitled to make an application under section 41(1)(a) or 69(1)(a) of the 1986 Act (or Article 51(1)(a) of the 1989 Order).

(4)   A report under section 48(1) or 67(1) of the 1986 Act (or Article 58(1) of the 1989 Order) must be sent by the person making it to the Authority.

(5)   A person appointed for the purpose by the Authority is entitled—
   (a)   to attend any meeting of creditors of the company summoned under any enactment;
   (b)   to attend any meeting of a committee established under section 49 or 68 of the 1986 Act (or Article 59 of the 1989 Order); and
   (c)   to make representations as to any matter for decision at such a meeting.

Commencement: 1 December 2001.
Limited liability partnerships: by virtue of the Limited Liability Partnerships Regulations 2001, SI 2001/1090, reg 6, this section is applied with modifications to limited liability partnerships.
References: See para 21.17.

364 Receiver's duty to report to Authority

If—

(a) a receiver has been appointed in relation to a company, and

(b) it appears to the receiver that the company is carrying on, or has carried on, a regulated activity in contravention of the general prohibition,

the receiver must report the matter to the Authority without delay.

Commencement: 1 December 2001.
Limited liability partnerships: by virtue of the Limited Liability Partnerships Regulations 2001, SI 2001/1090, reg 6, this section is applied with modifications to limited liability partnerships.
References: See para 21.18.

Voluntary winding up

365 Authority's powers to participate in proceedings

(1) This section applies in relation to a company which—

(a) is being wound up voluntarily;

(b) is an authorised person; and

(c) is not an insurer effecting or carrying out contracts of long-term insurance.

(2) The Authority may apply to the court under section 112 of the 1986 Act (or Article 98 of the 1989 Order) in respect of the company.

(3) The Authority is entitled to be heard at any hearing of the court in relation to the voluntary winding up of the company.

(4) Any notice or other document required to be sent to a creditor of the company must also be sent to the Authority.

(5) A person appointed for the purpose by the Authority is entitled—

(a) to attend any meeting of creditors of the company summoned under any enactment;

(b) to attend any meeting of a committee established under section 101 of the 1986 Act (or Article 87 of the 1989 Order); and

(c) to make representations as to any matter for decision at such a meeting.

(6) The voluntary winding up of the company does not bar the right of the Authority to have it wound up by the court.

(7) If, during the course of the winding up of the company, a compromise or arrangement is proposed between the company and its creditors, or any class of them, the Authority may apply to the court under section 425 of the Companies Act 1985 (or Article 418 of the Companies (Northern Ireland) Order 1986).

Commencement: 1 December 2001.
Limited liability partnerships: by virtue of the Limited Liability Partnerships Regulations 2001, SI 2001/1090, reg 6, this section is applied with modifications to limited liability partnerships.
References: See paras 21.19–21.21.

---

366 Insurers effecting or carrying out long-term contracts or insurance

(1)   An insurer effecting or carrying out contracts of long-term insurance may not be wound up voluntarily without the consent of the Authority.

(2)   If notice of a general meeting of such an insurer is given, specifying the intention to propose a resolution for voluntary winding up of the insurer, a director of the insurer must notify the Authority as soon as practicable after he becomes aware of it.

(3)   A person who fails to comply with subsection (2) is guilty of an offence and liable on summary conviction to a fine not exceeding level 5 on the standard scale.

(4)   The following provisions do not apply in relation to a winding-up resolution—

> (a)   sections 378(3) and 381A of the Companies Act 1985 ("the 1985 Act"); and
> (b)   Articles 386(3) and 389A of the Companies (Northern Ireland) Order 1986 ("the 1986 Order").

(5)   A copy of a winding-up resolution forwarded to the registrar of companies in accordance with section 380 of the 1985 Act (or Article 388 of the 1986 Order) must be accompanied by a certificate issued by the Authority stating that it consents to the voluntary winding up of the insurer.

(6)   If subsection (5) is complied with, the voluntary winding up is to be treated as having commenced at the time the resolution was passed.

(7)   If subsection (5) is not complied with, the resolution has no effect.

(8)   "Winding-up resolution" means a resolution for voluntary winding up of an insurer effecting or carrying out contracts of long-term insurance.

Commencement: 1 December 2001.
References: See paras 21.22, 21.23.

Winding up by the court

367 Winding-up petitions

(1)   The Authority may present a petition to the court for the winding up of a body which—

> (a)   is, or has been, an authorised person;
> (b)   is, or has been, an appointed representative; or
> (c)   is carrying on, or has carried on, a regulated activity in contravention of the general prohibition.

(2)   In subsection (1) "body" includes any partnership.

(3)   On such a petition, the court may wind up the body if—

> (a)   the body is unable to pay its debts within the meaning of section 123 or 221 of the 1986 Act (or Article 103 or 185 of the 1989 Order); or
> (b)   the court is of the opinion that it is just and equitable that it should be wound up.

(4)   If a body is in default on an obligation to pay a sum due and payable under an agreement, it is to be treated for the purpose of subsection (3)(a) as unable to pay its debts.

(5)   "Agreement" means an agreement the making or performance of which constitutes or is part of a regulated activity carried on by the body concerned.

(6)   Subsection (7) applies if a petition is presented under subsection (1) for the winding up of a partnership—

(a)   on the ground mentioned in subsection (3)(b); or

(b)   in Scotland, on a ground mentioned in subsection (3)(a) or (b).

(7)   The court has jurisdiction, and the 1986 Act (or the 1989 Order) has effect, as if the partnership were an unregistered company as defined by section 220 of that Act (or Article 184 of that Order).

Commencement: 1 December 2001.
Limited liability partnerships: by virtue of the Limited Liability Partnerships Regulations 2001, SI 2001/1090, reg 6, this section is applied with modifications to limited liability partnerships.
Transitional provisions: as to the application of this section to a body which has been an authorised institution within the meaning of the Banking Act 1987 (repealed by the Financial Services and Markets Act 2000 (Consequential Amendments and Repeals) Order 2001, SI 2001/3649, art 3(1)(d) (made under ss 426, 427)), or which, before 1 December 2001, contravened s 3 of the 1987 Act (restriction on acceptance of deposits), see the Financial Services and Markets Act 2000 (Transitional Provisions and Savings) (Civil Remedies, Discipline, Criminal Offences etc) (No 2) Order 2001, SI 2001/3083, art 12 (made under ss 426, 427, 428(3)).
References: See paras 21.25, 21.26.

368 Winding-up petitions: EEA and Treaty firms

The Authority may not present a petition to the court under section 367 for the winding up of—

(a)   an EEA firm which qualifies for authorisation under Schedule 3, or

(b)   a Treaty firm which qualifies for authorisation under Schedule 4,

unless it has been asked to do so by the home state regulator of the firm concerned.

Commencement: 1 December 2001.
References: See para 21.27.

369 Insurers: service of petition etc on Authority

(1)   If a person other than the Authority presents a petition for the winding up of an authorised person with permission to effect or carry out contracts of insurance, the petitioner must serve a copy of the petition on the Authority.

(2)   If a person other than the Authority applies to have a provisional liquidator appointed under section 135 of the 1986 Act (or Article 115 of the 1989 Order) in respect of an authorised person with permission to effect or carry out contracts of insurance, the applicant must serve a copy of the application on the Authority.

Commencement: 1 December 2001.
References: See para 21.28.

370 Liquidator's duty to report to Authority

If—

(a) a company is being wound up voluntarily or a body is being wound up on a petition presented by a person other than the Authority, and

(b) it appears to the liquidator that the company or body is carrying on, or has carried on, a regulated activity in contravention of the general prohibition,

the liquidator must report the matter to the Authority without delay.

Commencement: 1 December 2001.
Limited liability partnerships: by virtue of the Limited Liability Partnerships Regulations 2001, SI 2001/1090, reg 6, this section is applied with modifications to limited liability partnerships.
References: See para 21.29.

371 Authority's powers to participate in proceedings

(1) This section applies if a person other than the Authority presents a petition for the winding up of a body which—

(a) is, or has been, an authorised person;

(b) is, or has been, an appointed representative; or

(c) is carrying on, or has carried on, a regulated activity in contravention of the general prohibition.

(2) The Authority is entitled to be heard—

(a) at the hearing of the petition; and

(b) at any other hearing of the court in relation to the body under or by virtue of Part IV or V of the 1986 Act (or Part V or VI of the 1989 Order).

(3) Any notice or other document required to be sent to a creditor of the body must also be sent to the Authority.

(4) A person appointed for the purpose by the Authority is entitled—

(a) to attend any meeting of creditors of the body;

(b) to attend any meeting of a committee established for the purposes of Part IV or V of the 1986 Act under section 101 of that Act or under section 141 or 142 of that Act;

(c) to attend any meeting of a committee established for the purposes of Part V or VI of the 1989 Order under Article 87 of that Order or under Article 120 of that Order; and

(d) to make representations as to any matter for decision at such a meeting.

(5) If, during the course of the winding up of a company, a compromise or arrangement is proposed between the company and its creditors, or any class of them, the Authority may apply to the court under section 425 of the Companies Act 1985 (or Article 418 of the Companies (Northern Ireland) Order 1986).

Commencement: 1 December 2001.
Limited liability partnerships: by virtue of the Limited Liability Partnerships Regulations 2001, SI 2001/1090, reg 6, this section is applied with modifications to limited liability partnerships.
References: See para 21.30.

Bankruptcy

372 Petitions

(1)   The Authority may present a petition to the court—
  (a)   under section 264 of the 1986 Act (or Article 238 of the 1989 Order) for a bankruptcy order to be made against an individual; or
  (b)   under section 5 of the 1985 Act for the sequestration of the estate of an individual.

(2)   But such a petition may be presented only on the ground that—
  (a)   the individual appears to be unable to pay a regulated activity debt; or
  (b)   the individual appears to have no reasonable prospect of being able to pay a regulated activity debt.

(3)   An individual appears to be unable to pay a regulated activity debt if he is in default on an obligation to pay a sum due and payable under an agreement.

(4)   An individual appears to have no reasonable prospect of being able to pay a regulated activity debt if—
  (a)   the Authority has served on him a demand requiring him to establish to the satisfaction of the Authority that there is a reasonable prospect that he will be able to pay a sum payable under an agreement when it falls due;
  (b)   at least three weeks have elapsed since the demand was served; and
  (c)   the demand has been neither complied with nor set aside in accordance with rules.

(5)   A demand made under subsection (4)(a) is to be treated for the purposes of the 1986 Act (or the 1989 Order) as if it were a statutory demand under section 268 of that Act (or Article 242 of that Order).

(6)   For the purposes of a petition presented in accordance with subsection (1)(b)—
  (a)   the Authority is to be treated as a qualified creditor; and
  (b)   a ground mentioned in subsection (2) constitutes apparent insolvency.

(7)   "Individual" means an individual—
  (a)   who is, or has been, an authorised person; or
  (b)   who is carrying on, or has carried on, a regulated activity in contravention of the general prohibition.

(8)   "Agreement" means an agreement the making or performance of which constitutes or is part of a regulated activity carried on by the individual concerned.

(9)   "Rules" means—
  (a)   in England and Wales, rules made under section 412 of the 1986 Act;
  (b)   in Scotland, rules made by order by the Treasury, after consultation with the Scottish Ministers, for the purposes of this section; and
  (c)   in Northern Ireland, rules made under Article 359 of the 1989 Order.

Commencement: 20 July 2001 (for the purpose of making rules); 1 December 2001 (remaining purposes).
Rules: The Bankruptcy (Financial Services and Markets Act 2000) (Scotland) Rules 2001, SI 2001/3591.
References: See paras 21.31–21.34.

373 Insolvency practitioner's duty to report to Authority

(1) If—

    (a)   a bankruptcy order or sequestration award is in force in relation to an individual by virtue of a petition presented by a person other than the Authority, and

    (b)   it appears to the insolvency practitioner that the individual is carrying on, or has carried on, a regulated activity in contravention of the general prohibition,

the insolvency practitioner must report the matter to the Authority without delay.

(2) "Bankruptcy order" means a bankruptcy order under Part IX of the 1986 Act (or Part IX of the 1989 Order).

(3) "Sequestration award" means an award of sequestration under section 12 of the 1985 Act.

(4) "Individual" includes an entity mentioned in section 374(1)(c).

Commencement: 1 December 2001.
References: See para 21.35.

374 Authority's powers to participate in proceedings

(1) This section applies if a person other than the Authority presents a petition to the court—

    (a)   under section 264 of the 1986 Act (or Article 238 of the 1989 Order) for a bankruptcy order to be made against an individual;

    (b)   under section 5 of the 1985 Act for the sequestration of the estate of an individual; or

    (c)   under section 6 of the 1985 Act for the sequestration of the estate belonging to or held for or jointly by the members of an entity mentioned in subsection (1) of that section.

(2) The Authority is entitled to be heard—

    (a)   at the hearing of the petition; and

    (b)   at any other hearing in relation to the individual or entity under—

        (i)   Part IX of the 1986 Act;

        (ii)   Part IX of the 1989 Order; or

        (iii)   the 1985 Act.

(3) A copy of the report prepared under section 274 of the 1986 Act (or Article 248 of the 1989 Order) must also be sent to the Authority.

(4) A person appointed for the purpose by the Authority is entitled—

    (a)   to attend any meeting of creditors of the individual or entity;

    (b)   to attend any meeting of a committee established under section 301 of the 1986 Act (or Article 274 of the 1989 Order);

    (c)   to attend any meeting of commissioners held under paragraph 17 or 18 of Schedule 6 to the 1985 Act; and

    (d)   to make representations as to any matter for decision at such a meeting.

(5) "Individual" means an individual who—

    (a)   is, or has been, an authorised person; or

(b)   is carrying on, or has carried on, a regulated activity in contravention of the general prohibition.

(6)   "Entity" means an entity which—
    (a)   is, or has been, an authorised person; or
    (b)   is carrying on, or has carried on, a regulated activity in contravention of the general prohibition.

Commencement: 1 December 2001.
References: See para 21.36.

Provisions against debt avoidance

375 Authority's right to apply for an order

(1)   The Authority may apply for an order under section 423 of the 1986 Act (or Article 367 of the 1989 Order) in relation to a debtor if—
    (a)   at the time the transaction at an undervalue was entered into, the debtor was carrying on a regulated activity (whether or not in contravention of the general prohibition); and
    (b)   a victim of the transaction is or was party to an agreement entered into with the debtor, the making or performance of which constituted or was part of a regulated activity carried on by the debtor.

(2)   An application made under this section is to be treated as made on behalf of every victim of the transaction to whom subsection (1)(b) applies.

(3)   Expressions which are given a meaning in Part XVI of the 1986 Act (or Article 367, 368 or 369 of the 1989 Order) have the same meaning when used in this section.

Commencement: 1 December 2001.
References: See para 21.38.

Supplemental provisions concerning insurers

376 Continuation of contracts of long-term insurance where insurer in liquidation

(1)   This section applies in relation to the winding up of an insurer which effects or carries out contracts of long-term insurance.

(2)   Unless the court otherwise orders, the liquidator must carry on the insurer's business so far as it consists of carrying out the insurer's contracts of long-term insurance with a view to its being transferred as a going concern to a person who may lawfully carry out those contracts.

(3)   In carrying on the business, the liquidator—
    (a)   may agree to the variation of any contracts of insurance in existence when the winding up order is made; but
    (b)   must not effect any new contracts of insurance.

(4)   If the liquidator is satisfied that the interests of the creditors in respect of liabilities of the insurer attributable to contracts of long-term insurance effected by it require the appointment of a special manager, he may apply to the court.

(5)   On such an application, the court may appoint a special manager to act during such time as the court may direct.

(6)   The special manager is to have such powers, including any of the powers of a receiver or manager, as the court may direct.

(7)   Section 177(5) of the 1986 Act (or Article 151(5) of the 1989 Order) applies to a special manager appointed under subsection (5) as it applies to a special manager appointed under section 177 of the 1986 Act (or Article 151 of the 1989 Order).

(8)   If the court thinks fit, it may reduce the value of one or more of the contracts of long-term insurance effected by the insurer.

(9)   Any reduction is to be on such terms and subject to such conditions (if any) as the court thinks fit.

(10) The court may, on the application of an official, appoint an independent actuary to investigate the insurer's business so far as it consists of carrying out its contracts of long-term insurance and to report to the official—
   (a)   on the desirability or otherwise of that part of the insurer's business being continued; and
   (b)   on any reduction in the contracts of long-term insurance effected by the insurer that may be necessary for successful continuation of that part of the insurer's business.

(11) "Official" means—
   (a)   the liquidator;
   (b)   a special manager appointed under subsection (5); or
   (c)   the Authority.

(12) The liquidator may make an application in the name of the insurer and on its behalf under Part VII without obtaining the permission that would otherwise be required by section 167 of, and Schedule 4 to, the 1986 Act (or Article 142 of, and Schedule 2 to, the 1989 Order).

Commencement: 1 December 2001.
References: See paras 21.39–21.41.

377   Reducing the value of contracts instead of winding up

(1)   This section applies in relation to an insurer which has been proved to be unable to pay its debts.

(2)   If the court thinks fit, it may reduce the value of one or more of the insurer's contracts instead of making a winding up order.

(3)   Any reduction is to be on such terms and subject to such conditions (if any) as the court thinks fit.

Commencement: 1 December 2001.
References: See para 21.42.

378 Treatment of assets on winding up

(1)　The Treasury may by regulations provide for the treatment of the assets of an insurer on its winding up.

(2)　The regulations may, in particular, provide for—

    (a)　assets representing a particular part of the insurer's business to be available only for meeting liabilities attributable to that part of the insurer's business;

    (b)　separate general meetings of the creditors to be held in respect of liabilities attributable to a particular part of the insurer's business.

Commencement: 20 July 2001.
Regulations: The Financial Services and Markets Act 2000 (Treatment of Assets of Insurers on Winding Up) Regulations 2001, SI 2001/2968.
References: See para 21.43.

---

379 Winding-up rules

(1)　Winding-up rules may include provision—

    (a)　for determining the amount of the liabilities of an insurer to policyholders of any class or description for the purpose of proof in a winding up; and

    (b)　generally for carrying into effect the provisions of this Part with respect to the winding up of insurers.

(2)　Winding-up rules may, in particular, make provision for all or any of the following matters—

    (a)　the identification of assets and liabilities;

    (b)　the apportionment, between assets of different classes or descriptions, of—

        (i)　the costs, charges and expenses of the winding up; and

        (ii)　any debts of the insurer of a specified class or description;

    (c)　the determination of the amount of liabilities of a specified description;

    (d)　the application of assets for meeting liabilities of a specified description;

    (e)　the application of assets representing any excess of a specified description.

(3)　"Specified" means specified in winding-up rules.

(4)　"Winding-up rules" means rules made under section 411 of the 1986 Act (or Article 359 of the 1989 Order).

(5)　Nothing in this section affects the power to make winding-up rules under the 1986 Act or the 1989 Order.

Commencement: 20 July 2001.
Rules: The Insurers (Winding Up) Rules 2001, SI 2001/3635.
References: See para 21.44.

PART XXV
INJUNCTIONS AND RESTITUTION

Injunctions

380 Injunctions

(1)   If, on the application of the Authority or the Secretary of State, the court is satisfied—

    (a)   that there is a reasonable likelihood that any person will contravene a relevant requirement, or

    (b)   that any person has contravened a relevant requirement and that there is a reasonable likelihood that the contravention will continue or be repeated,

the court may make an order restraining (or in Scotland an interdict prohibiting) the contravention.

(2)   If on the application of the Authority or the Secretary of State the court is satisfied—

    (a)   that any person has contravened a relevant requirement, and

    (b)   that there are steps which could be taken for remedying the contravention,

the court may make an order requiring that person, and any other person who appears to have been knowingly concerned in the contravention, to take such steps as the court may direct to remedy it.

(3)   If, on the application of the Authority or the Secretary of State, the court is satisfied that any person may have—

    (a)   contravened a relevant requirement, or

    (b)   been knowingly concerned in the contravention of such a requirement,

it may make an order restraining (or in Scotland an interdict prohibiting) him from disposing of, or otherwise dealing with, any assets of his which it is satisfied he is reasonably likely to dispose of or otherwise deal with.

(4)   The jurisdiction conferred by this section is exercisable by the High Court and the Court of Session.

(5)   In subsection (2), references to remedying a contravention include references to mitigating its effect.

(6)   "Relevant requirement"—

    (a)   in relation to an application by the Authority, means a requirement—

        (i)   which is imposed by or under this Act; or

        (ii)   which is imposed by or under any other Act and whose contravention constitutes an offence which the Authority has power to prosecute under this Act;

    (b)   in relation to an application by the Secretary of State, means a requirement which is imposed by or under this Act and whose contravention constitutes an offence which the Secretary of State has power to prosecute under this Act.

(7) In the application of subsection (6) to Scotland—

  (a) in paragraph (a)(ii) for "which the Authority has power to prosecute under this Act" substitute "mentioned in paragraph (a) or (b) of section 402(1)"; and

  (b) in paragraph (b) omit "which the Secretary of State has power to prosecute under this Act".

Commencement: 18 June 2001.
Transitional provisions: any requirement, condition or prohibition imposed before 1 December 2001 by or under certain specified provisions is to be treated as a relevant requirement for the purposes of sub-s (2) above, and any restriction or requirement imposed by or under certain other provisions is to be treated as a relevant requirement for the purposes of sub-s (3)(a) above; see in general, the Financial Services and Markets Act 2000 (Transitional Provisions and Savings) (Civil Remedies, Discipline, Criminal Offences etc) (No 2) Order 2001, SI 2001/3083, arts 2, 4 (made under ss 426, 427, 428(3)). The specified provisions for the purposes of sub-ss (2), (3)(a) are listed in arts 2(3), 4(3) of the 2001 order.
References: See paras 2.64–2.66.

381 Injunctions in cases of market abuse

(1) If, on the application of the Authority, the court is satisfied—

  (a) that there is a reasonable likelihood that any person will engage in market abuse, or

  (b) that any person is or has engaged in market abuse and that there is a reasonable likelihood that the market abuse will continue or be repeated,

the court may make an order restraining (or in Scotland an interdict prohibiting) the market abuse.

(2) If on the application of the Authority the court is satisfied—

  (a) that any person is or has engaged in market abuse, and

  (b) that there are steps which could be taken for remedying the market abuse,

the court may make an order requiring him to take such steps as the court may direct to remedy it.

(3) Subsection (4) applies if, on the application of the Authority, the court is satisfied that any person—

  (a) may be engaged in market abuse; or

  (b) may have been engaged in market abuse.

(4) The court make an order restraining (or in Scotland an interdict prohibiting) the person concerned from disposing of, or otherwise dealing with, any assets of his which it is satisfied that he is reasonably likely to dispose of, or otherwise deal with.

(5) The jurisdiction conferred by this section is exercisable by the High Court and the Court of Session.

(6) In subsection (2), references to remedying any market abuse include references to mitigating its effect.

Commencement: 1 December 2001.
References: See paras 2.67–2.69.

Restitution orders

382 Restitution orders

(1)   The court may, on the application of the Authority or the Secretary of State, make an order under subsection (2) if it is satisfied that a person has contravened a relevant requirement, or been knowingly concerned in the contravention of such a requirement, and—

- (a)   that profits have accrued to him as a result of the contravention; or
- (b)   that one or more persons have suffered loss or been otherwise adversely affected as a result of the contravention.

(2)   The court may order the person concerned to pay to the Authority such sum as appears to the court to be just having regard—

- (a)   in a case within paragraph (a) of subsection (1), to the profits appearing to the court to have accrued;
- (b)   in a case within paragraph (b) of that subsection, to the extent of the loss or other adverse effect;
- (c)   in a case within both of those paragraphs, to the profits appearing to the court to have accrued and to the extent of the loss or other adverse effect.

(3)   Any amount paid to the Authority in pursuance of an order under subsection (2) must be paid by it to such qualifying person or distributed by it among such qualifying persons as the court may direct.

(4)   On an application under subsection (1) the court may require the person concerned to supply it with such accounts or other information as it may require for any one or more of the following purposes—

- (a)   establishing whether any and, if so, what profits have accrued to him as mentioned in paragraph (a) of that subsection;
- (b)   establishing whether any person or persons have suffered any loss or adverse effect as mentioned in paragraph (b) of that subsection and, if so, the extent of that loss or adverse effect; and
- (c)   determining how any amounts are to be paid or distributed under subsection (3).

(5)   The court may require any accounts or other information supplied under subsection (4) to be verified in such manner as it may direct.

(6)   The jurisdiction conferred by this section is exercisable by the High Court and the Court of Session.

(7)   Nothing in this section affects the right of any person other than the Authority or the Secretary of State to bring proceedings in respect of the matters to which this section applies.

(8)   "Qualifying person" means a person appearing to the court to be someone—

- (a)   to whom the profits mentioned in subsection (1)(a) are attributable; or
- (b)   who has suffered the loss or adverse effect mentioned in subsection (1)(b).

(9)   "Relevant requirement"—

- (a)   in relation to an application by the Authority, means a requirement—
  - (i)   which is imposed by or under this Act; or

        (ii)   which is imposed by or under any other Act and whose contravention constitutes an offence which the Authority has power to prosecute under this Act;

    (b)   in relation to an application by the Secretary of State, means a requirement which is imposed by or under this Act and whose contravention constitutes an offence which the Secretary of State has power to prosecute under this Act.

(10) In the application of subsection (9) to Scotland—

    (a)   in paragraph (a)(ii) for "which the Authority has power to prosecute under this Act" substitute "mentioned in paragraph (a) or (b) of section 402(1); and

    (b)   in paragraph (b) omit "which the Secretary of State has power to prosecute under this Act".

Commencement: 18 June 2001.

Transitional provisions: any requirement, condition or prohibition imposed before 1 December 2001 by or under certain specified provisions is to be treated as a relevant requirement for the purposes of this section; see the Financial Services and Markets Act 2000 (Transitional Provisions and Savings) (Civil Remedies, Discipline, Criminal Offences etc) (No 2) Order 2001, SI 2001/3083, art 2 (made under ss 426, 427, 428(3)). The specified provisions are listed in art 2(3) of the 2001 order.

References: See paras 2.70–2.73.

---

383 Restitution orders in cases of market abuse

(1)   The court may, on the application of the Authority, make an order under subsection (4) if it is satisfied that a person ("the person concerned")—

    (a)   has engaged in market abuse, or

    (b)   by taking or refraining from taking any action has required or encouraged another person or persons to engage in behaviour which, if engaged in by the person concerned, would amount to market abuse,

and the condition mentioned in subsection (2) is fulfilled.

(2)   The condition is—

    (a)   that profits have accrued to the person concerned as a result; or

    (b)   that one or more persons have suffered loss or been otherwise adversely affected as a result.

(3)   But the court may not make an order under subsection (4) if it is satisfied that—

    (a)   the person concerned believed, on reasonable grounds, that his behaviour did not fall within paragraph (a) or (b) of subsection (1); or

    (b)   he took all reasonable precautions and exercised all due diligence to avoid behaving in a way which fell within paragraph (a) or (b) of subsection (1).

(4)   The court may order the person concerned to pay to the Authority such sum as appears to the court to be just having regard—

    (a)   in a case within paragraph (a) of subsection (2), to the profits appearing to the court to have accrued;

    (b)   in a case within paragraph (b) of that subsection, to the extent of the loss or other adverse effect;

  (c) in a case within both of those paragraphs, to the profits appearing to the court to have accrued and to the extent of the loss or other adverse effect.

(5) Any amount paid to the Authority in pursuance of an order under subsection (4) must be paid by it to such qualifying person or distributed by it among such qualifying persons as the court may direct.

(6) On an application under subsection (1) the court may require the person concerned to supply it with such accounts or other information as it may require for any one or more of the following purposes—
  (a) establishing whether any and, if so, what profits have accrued to him as mentioned in subsection (2)(a);
  (b) establishing whether any person or persons have suffered any loss or adverse effect as mentioned in subsection (2)(b) and, if so, the extent of that loss or adverse effect; and
  (c) determining how any amounts are to be paid or distributed under subsection (5).

(7) The court may require any accounts or other information supplied under subsection (6) to be verified in such manner as it may direct.

(8) The jurisdiction conferred by this section is exercisable by the High Court and the Court of Session.

(9) Nothing in this section affects the right of any person other than the Authority to bring proceedings in respect of the matters to which this section applies.

(10) "Qualifying person" means a person appearing to the court to be someone—
  (a) to whom the profits mentioned in paragraph (a) of subsection (2) are attributable; or
  (b) who has suffered the loss or adverse effect mentioned in paragraph (b) of that subsection.

Commencement: 1 December 2001.
References: See paras 2.74–2.79.

Restitution required by Authority

384 Power of Authority to require restitution

(1) The Authority may exercise the power in subsection (5) if it is satisfied that an authorised person ("the person concerned") has contravened a relevant requirement, or been knowingly concerned in the contravention of such a requirement, and—
  (a) that profits have accrued to him as a result of the contravention; or
  (b) that one or more persons have suffered loss or been otherwise adversely affected as a result of the contravention.

(2) The Authority may exercise the power in subsection (5) if it is satisfied that a person ("the person concerned")—
  (a) has engaged in market abuse, or
  (b) by taking or refraining from taking any action has required or encouraged another person or persons to engage in behaviour which, if engaged in by the person concerned, would amount to market abuse,

and the condition mentioned in subsection (3) is fulfilled,

(3)   The condition is—

    (a)   that profits have accrued to the person concerned as a result of the market abuse; or

    (b)   that one or more persons have suffered loss or been otherwise adversely affected as a result of the market abuse.

(4)   But the Authority may not exercise that power as a result of subsection (2) if, having considered any representations made to it in response to a warning notice, there are reasonable grounds for it to be satisfied that—

    (a)   the person concerned believed, on reasonable grounds, that his behaviour did not fall within paragraph (a) or (b) of that subsection; or

    (b)   he took all reasonable precautions and exercised all due diligence to avoid behaving in a way which fell within paragraph (a) or (b) of that subsection.

(5)   The power referred to in subsections (1) and (2) is a power to require the person concerned, in accordance with such arrangements as the Authority considers appropriate, to pay to the appropriate person or distribute among the appropriate persons such amount as appears to the Authority to be just having regard—

    (a)   in a case within paragraph (a) of subsection (1) or (3), to the profits appearing to the Authority to have accrued;

    (b)   in a case within paragraph (b) of subsection (1) or (3), to the extent of the loss or other adverse effect;

    (c)   in a case within paragraphs (a) and (b) of subsection (1) or (3), to the profits appearing to the Authority to have accrued and to the extent of the loss or other adverse effect.

(6)   "Appropriate person" means a person appearing to the Authority to be someone—

    (a)   to whom the profits mentioned in paragraph (a) of subsection (1) or (3) are attributable; or

    (b)   who has suffered the loss or adverse effect mentioned in paragraph (b) of subsection (1) or (3).

(7)   "Relevant requirement" means—

    (a)   a requirement imposed by or under this Act; and

    (b)   a requirement which is imposed by or under any other Act and whose contravention constitutes an offence in relation to which this Act confers power to prosecute on the Authority.

(8)   In the application of subsection (7) to Scotland, in paragraph (b) for "in relation to which this Act confers power to prosecute on the Authority" substitute "mentioned in paragraph (a) or (b) of section 402(1)".

Commencement: 1 December 2001.
Transitional provisions: as to the power of the Authority under sub-s (5) in relation to certain conduct before 1 December 2001, see the Financial Services and Markets Act 2000 (Transitional Provisions and Savings) (Civil Remedies, Discipline, Criminal Offences etc) (No 2) Order 2001, SI 2001/3083, art 3 (made under ss 426, 427, 428(3)).
References: See paras 2.79–2.82.

---

385 Warning notices

(1)   If the Authority proposes to exercise the power under section 384(5) in relation to a person, it must give him a warning notice.

(2)   A warning notice under this section must specify the amount which the Authority proposes to require the person concerned to pay or distribute as mentioned in section 384(5).

Commencement: 1 December 2001.
References: See para 2.83.

386 Decision notices

(1)   If the Authority decides to exercise the power under section 384(5), it must give a decision notice to the person in relation to whom the power is exercised.

(2)   The decision notice must—
    (a)   state the amount that he is to pay or distribute as mentioned in section 384(5);
    (b)   identify the person or persons to whom that amount is to be paid or among whom that amount is to be distributed; and
    (c)   state the arrangements in accordance with which the payment or distribution is to be made.

(3)   If the Authority decides to exercise the power under section 384(5), the person in relation to whom it is exercised may refer the matter to the Tribunal.

Commencement: 1 December 2001.
References: See para 2.84.

PART XXVI
NOTICES

Warning notices

387 Warning notices

(1)   A warning notice must—
    (a)   state the action which the Authority proposes to take;
    (b)   be in writing;
    (c)   give reasons for the proposed action;
    (d)   state whether section 394 applies; and
    (e)   if that section applies, describe its effect and state whether any secondary material exists to which the person concerned must be allowed access under it.

(2)   The warning notice must specify a reasonable period (which may not be less than 28 days) within which the person to whom it is given may make representations to the Authority.

(3)   The Authority may extend the period specified in the notice.

(4)   The Authority must then decide, within a reasonable period, whether to give the person concerned a decision notice.

Commencement: 3 September 2001.
References: See para 8.18.

Decision notices

388 Decision notices

(1)   A decision notice must—
   (a)   be in writing;
   (b)   give the Authority's reasons for the decision to take the action to which the notice relates;
   (c)   state whether section 394 applies;
   (d)   if that section applies, describe its effect and state whether any secondary material exists to which the person concerned must be allowed access under it; and
   (e)   give an indication of—
     (i)   any right to have the matter referred to the Tribunal which is given by this Act; and
     (ii)   the procedure on such a reference.

(2)   If the decision notice was preceded by a warning notice, the action to which the decision notice relates must be action under the same Part as the action proposed in the warning notice.

(3)   The Authority may, before it takes the action to which a decision notice ("the original notice") relates, give the person concerned a further decision notice which relates to different action in respect of the same matter.

(4)   The Authority may give a further decision notice as a result of subsection (3) only if the person to whom the original notice was given consents.

(5)   If the person to whom a decision notice is given under subsection (3) had the right to refer the matter to which the original decision notice related to the Tribunal, he has that right as respects the decision notice under subsection (3).

Commencement: 3 September 2001.
References: See paras 8.19, 8.20.

Conclusion of proceedings

389 Notices of discontinuance

(1)   If the Authority decides not to take—
   (a)   the action proposed in a warning notice, or
   (b)   the action to which a decision notice relates,
it must give a notice of discontinuance to the person to whom the warning notice or decision notice was given.

(2)   But subsection (1) does not apply if the discontinuance of the proceedings concerned results in the granting of an application made by the person to whom the warning or decision notice was given.

(3)   A notice of discontinuance must identify the proceedings which are being discontinued.

Commencement: 3 September 2001.
References: See para 8.21.

390 Final notices

(1)   If the Authority has given a person a decision notice and the matter was not referred to the Tribunal within the period mentioned in section 133(1), the Authority must, on taking the action to which the decision notice relates, give the person concerned and any person to whom the decision notice was copied a final notice.

(2)   If the Authority has given a person a decision notice and the matter was referred to the Tribunal, the Authority must, on taking action in accordance with any directions given by—
    (a)   the Tribunal, or
    (b)   the court under section 137,
give that person and any person to whom the decision notice was copied a final notice.

(3)   A final notice about a statement must—
    (a)   set out the terms of the statement;
    (b)   give details of the manner in which, and the date on which, the statement will be published.

(4)   A final notice about an order must—
    (a)   set out the terms of the order;
    (b)   state the date from which the order has effect.

(5)   A final notice about a penalty must—
    (a)   state the amount of the penalty;
    (b)   state the manner in which, and the period within which, the penalty is to be paid;
    (c)   give details of the way in which the penalty will be recovered if it is not paid by the date stated in the notice.

(6)   A final notice about a requirement to make a payment or distribution in accordance with section 384(5) must state—
    (a)   the persons to whom,
    (b)   the manner in which, and
    (c)   the period within which,
it must be made.

(7)   In any other case, the final notice must—
    (a)   give details of the action being taken;
    (b)   state the date on which the action is to be taken.

(8)   The period stated under subsection (5)(b) or (6)(c) may not be less than 14 days beginning with the date on which the final notice is given.

(9)   If all or any of the amount of a penalty payable under a final notice is outstanding at the end of the period stated under subsection (5)(b), the Authority may recover the outstanding amount as a debt due to it.

(10)   If all or any of a required payment or distribution has not been made at the end of a period stated in a final notice under subsection (6)(c), the obligation to

make the payment is enforceable, on the application of the Authority, by injunction or, in Scotland, by an order under section 45 of the Court of Session Act 1988.

Commencement: 3 September 2001.
References: See paras 8.22–8.24.

Publication

391 Publication

(1)   Neither the Authority nor a person to whom a warning notice or decision notice is given or copied may publish the notice or any details concerning it.

(2)   A notice of discontinuance must state that, if the person to whom the notice is given consents, the Authority may publish such information as it considers appropriate about the matter to which the discontinued proceedings related.

(3)   A copy of a notice of discontinuance must be accompanied by a statement that, if the person to whom the notice is copied consents, the Authority may publish such information as it considers appropriate about the matter to which the discontinued proceedings related, so far as relevant to that person.

(4)   The Authority must publish such information about the matter to which a final notice relates as it considers appropriate.

(5)   When a supervisory notice takes effect, the Authority must publish such information about the matter to which the notice relates as it considers appropriate.

(6)   But the Authority may not publish information under this section if publication of it would, in its opinion, be unfair to the person with respect to whom the action was taken or prejudicial to the interests of consumers.

(7)   Information is to be published under this section in such manner as the Authority considers appropriate.

(8)   For the purposes of determining when a supervisory notice takes effect, a matter to which the notice relates is open to review if—

    (a)   the period during which any person may refer the matter to the Tribunal is still running;

    (b)   the matter has been referred to the Tribunal but has not been dealt with;

    (c)   the matter has been referred to the Tribunal and dealt with but the period during which an appeal may be brought against the Tribunal's decision is still running; or

    (d)   such an appeal has been brought but has not been determined.

(9)   "Notice of discontinuance" means a notice given under section 389.

(10) "Supervisory notice" has the same meaning as in section 395.

(11) "Consumers" means persons who are consumers for the purposes of section 138.

Commencement: 3 September 2001.
References: See paras 8.26–8.29.

Third party rights and access to evidence

392 Application of sections 393 and 394

Sections 393 and 394 apply to—

  (a)   a warning notice given in accordance with section 54(1), 57(1), 63(3), 67(1), 88(4)(b), 89(2), 92(1), 126(1), 207(1), 255(1), 280(1), 331(1), 345(2) (whether as a result of subsection (1) of that section or section 249(1)) or 385(1);

  (b)   a decision notice given in accordance with section 54(2), 57(3), 63(4), 67(4), 88(6)(b), 89(3), 92(4), 127(1), 208(1), 255(2), 280(2), 331(3), 345(3) (whether as a result of subsection (1) of that section or section 249(1)) or 386(1).

Commencement: 3 September 2001.
References: See para 8.18.

393 Third party rights

  (1)   If any of the reasons contained in a warning notice to which this section applies relates to a matter which—

  (a)   identifies a person ("the third party") other than the person to whom the notice is given, and

  (b)   in the opinion of the Authority, is prejudicial to the third party,

a copy of the notice must be given to the third party.

  (2)   Subsection (1) does not require a copy to be given to the third party if the Authority—

  (a)   has given him a separate warning notice in relation to the same matter; or

  (b)   gives him such a notice at the same time as it gives the warning notice which identifies him.

  (3)   The notice copied to a third party under subsection (1) must specify a reasonable period (which may not be less than 28 days) within which he may make representations to the Authority.

  (4)   If any of the reasons contained in a decision notice to which this section applies relates to a matter which—

  (a)   identifies a person ("the third party") other than the person to whom the decision notice is given, and

  (b)   in the opinion of the Authority, is prejudicial to the third party,

a copy of the notice must be given to the third party.

  (5)   If the decision notice was preceded by a warning notice, a copy of the decision notice must (unless it has been given under subsection (4)) be given to each person to whom the warning notice was copied.

  (6)   Subsection (4) does not require a copy to be given to the third party if the Authority—

  (a)   has given him a separate decision notice in relation to the same matter; or

  (b)   gives him such a notice at the same time as it gives the decision notice which identifies him.

(7)   Neither subsection (1) nor subsection (4) requires a copy of a notice to be given to a third party if the Authority considers it impracticable to do so.

(8)   Subsections (9) to (11) apply if the person to whom a decision notice is given has a right to refer the matter to the Tribunal.

(9)   A person to whom a copy of the notice is given under this section may refer to the Tribunal—

> (a)   the decision in question, so far as it is based on a reason of the kind mentioned in subsection (4); or
>
> (b)   any opinion expressed by the Authority in relation to him.

(10) The copy must be accompanied by an indication of the third party's right to make a reference under subsection (9) and of the procedure on such a reference.

(11) A person who alleges that a copy of the notice should have been given to him, but was not, may refer to the Tribunal the alleged failure and—

> (a)   the decision in question, so far as it is based on a reason of the kind mentioned in subsection (4); or
>
> (b)   any opinion expressed by the Authority in relation to him.

(12) Section 394 applies to a third party as it applies to the person to whom the notice to which this section applies was given, in so far as the material which the Authority must disclose under that section relates to the matter which identifies the third party.

(13) A copy of a notice given to a third party under this section must be accompanied by a description of the effect of section 394 as it applies to him.

(14) Any person to whom a warning notice or decision notice was copied under this section must be given a copy of a notice of discontinuance applicable to the proceedings to which the warning notice or decision notice related.

Commencement: 3 September 2001.
References: See para 8.10.

394 Access to Authority material

(1)   If the Authority gives a person ("A") a notice to which this section applies, it must—

> (a)   allow him access to the material on which it relied in taking the decision which gave rise to the obligation to give the notice;
>
> (b)   allow him access to any secondary material which, in the opinion of the Authority, might undermine that decision.

(2)   But the Authority does not have to allow A access to material under subsection (1) if the material is excluded material or it—

> (a)   relates to a case involving a person other than A; and
>
> (b)   was taken into account by the Authority in A's case only for purposes of comparison with other cases.

(3)   The Authority may refuse A access to particular material which it would otherwise have to allow him access to if, in its opinion, allowing him access to the material—

> (a)   would not be in the public interest; or
>
> (b)   would not be fair, having regard to—

719

> > (i) the likely significance of the material to A in relation to the matter in respect of which he has been given a notice to which this section applies; and
> > (ii) the potential prejudice to the commercial interests of a person other than A which would be caused by the material's disclosure.

(4) If the Authority does not allow A access to material because it is excluded material consisting of a protected item, it must give A written notice of—

> (a) the existence of the protected item; and
> (b) the Authority's decision not to allow him access to it.

(5) If the Authority refuses under subsection (3) to allow A access to material, it must give him written notice of—

> (a) the refusal; and
> (b) the reasons for it.

(6) "Secondary material" means material, other than material falling within paragraph (a) of subsection (1) which—

> (a) was considered by the Authority in reaching the decision mentioned in that paragraph; or
> (b) was obtained by the Authority in connection with the matter to which the notice to which this section applies relates but which was not considered by it in reaching that decision.

(7) "Excluded material" means material which—

> [(a) is material the disclosure of which for the purposes of or in connection with any legal proceedings is prohibited by section 17 of the Regulation of Investigatory Powers Act 2000; or]
> (c) is a protected item (as defined in section 413).

Commencement: 3 September 2001.
Amendments: Sub-s (7): para (a) substituted for original paras (a), (b) by the Regulation of Investigatory Powers Act 2000, s 82(1), Sch 4, para 11, as from 2 October 2000.

The Authority's procedures

395 The Authority's procedures

(1) The Authority must determine the procedure that it proposes to follow in relation to the giving of—

> (a) supervisory notices; and
> (b) warning notices and decision notices.

(2) That procedure must be designed to secure, among other things, that the decision which gives rise to the obligation to give any such notice is taken by a person not directly involved in establishing the evidence on which that decision is based.

(3) But the procedure may permit a decision which gives rise to an obligation to give a supervisory notice to be taken by a person other than a person mentioned in subsection (2) if—

> (a) the Authority considers that, in the particular case, it is necessary in order to protect the interests of consumers; and

   (b)   the person taking the decision is of a level of seniority laid down by the procedure.

(4)   A level of seniority laid down by the procedure for the purposes of subsection (3)(b) must be appropriate to the importance of the decision.

(5)   The Authority must issue a statement of the procedure.

(6)   The statement must be published in the way appearing to the Authority to be best calculated to bring it to the attention of the public.

(7)   The Authority may charge a reasonable fee for providing a person with a copy of the statement.

(8)   The Authority must, without delay, give the Treasury a copy of any statement which it issues under this section.

(9)   When giving a supervisory notice, or a warning notice or decision notice, the Authority must follow its stated procedure.

(10) If the Authority changes the procedure in a material way, it must publish a revised statement.

(11) The Authority's failure in a particular case to follow its procedure as set out in the latest published statement does not affect the validity of a notice given in that case.

(12) But subsection (11) does not prevent the Tribunal from taking into account any such failure in considering a matter referred to it.

(13) "Supervisory notice" means a notice given in accordance with section—
   (a)   53(4), (7) or (8)(b);
   (b)   78(2) or (5);
   (c)   197(3), (6) or (7)(b);
   (d)   259(3), (8) or (9)(b);
   (e)   268(3), (7)(a) or (9)(a) (as a result of subsection (8)(b));
   (f)   282(3), (6) or (7)(b);
   (g)   321(2) or (5).

Commencement: 18 June 2001.
Open-ended investment companies: This section has effect as if sub-s (13) included a reference to a notice given in accordance with the Open-Ended Investment Companies Regulations 2001, SI 2001/1228, reg 27(3), (8) or (9)(b); see reg 27(15) of the 2001 Regulations (made under s 262 ante and s 428(3)).
References: See para 8.15.

396 Statements under section 395: consultation

(1)   Before issuing a statement of procedure under section 395, the Authority must publish a draft of the proposed statement in the way appearing to the Authority to be best calculated to bring it to the attention of the public.

(2)   The draft must be accompanied by notice that representations about the proposal may be made to the Authority within a specified time.

(3)   Before issuing the proposed statement of procedure, the Authority must have regard to any representations made to it in accordance with subsection (2).

(4)   If the Authority issues the proposed statement of procedure it must publish an account, in general terms, of—

    (a)   the representations made to it in accordance with subsection (2); and

    (b)   its response to them.

(5)   If the statement of procedure differs from the draft published under subsection (1) in a way which is, in the opinion of the Authority, significant, the Authority must (in addition to complying with subsection (4)) publish details of the difference.

(6)   The Authority may charge a reasonable fee for providing a person with a copy of a draft published under subsection (1).

(7)   This section also applies to a proposal to revise a statement of policy.

Commencement: 18 June 2001.
References: See para 8.16.

PART XXVII
OFFENCES

Miscellaneous offences

397 Misleading statements and practices

(1)   This subsection applies to a person who—

    (a)   makes a statement, promise or forecast which he knows to be misleading, false or deceptive in a material particular;

    (b)   dishonestly conceals any material facts whether in connection with a statement, promise or forecast made by him or otherwise; or

    (c)   recklessly makes (dishonestly or otherwise) a statement, promise or forecast which is misleading, false or deceptive in a material particular.

(2)   A person to whom subsection (1) applies is guilty of an offence if he makes the statement, promise or forecast or conceals the facts for the purpose of inducing, or is reckless as to whether it may induce, another person (whether or not the person to whom the statement, promise or forecast is made)—

    (a)   to enter or offer to enter into, or to refrain from entering or offering to enter into, a relevant agreement; or

    (b)   to exercise, or refrain from exercising, any rights conferred by a relevant investment.

(3)   Any person who does any act or engages in any course of conduct which creates a false or misleading impression as to the market in or the price or value of any relevant investments is guilty of an offence if he does so for the purpose of creating that impression and of thereby inducing another person to acquire, dispose of, subscribe for or underwrite those investments or to refrain from doing so or to exercise, or refrain from exercising, any rights conferred by those investments.

(4)   In proceedings for an offence under subsection (2) brought against a person to whom subsection (1) applies as a result of paragraph (a) of that subsection, it is a defence for him to show that the statement, promise or forecast was made in conformity with price stabilising rules or control of information rules.

(5)   In proceedings brought against any person for an offence under subsection (3) it is a defence for him to show—

    (a)   that he reasonably believed that his act or conduct would not create an impression that was false or misleading as to the matters mentioned in that subsection;

    (b)   that he acted or engaged in the conduct—

        (i)   for the purpose of stabilising the price of investments; and

        (ii)   in conformity with price stabilising rules; or

    (c)   that he acted or engaged in the conduct in conformity with control of information rules.

(6)   Subsections (1) and (2) do not apply unless—

    (a)   the statement, promise or forecast is made in or from, or the facts are concealed in or from, the United Kingdom or arrangements are made in or from the United Kingdom for the statement, promise or forecast to be made or the facts to be concealed;

    (b)   the person on whom the inducement is intended to or may have effect is in the United Kingdom; or

    (c)   the agreement is or would be entered into or the rights are or would be exercised in the United Kingdom.

(7)   Subsection (3) does not apply unless—

    (a)   the act is done, or the course of conduct is engaged in, in the United Kingdom; or

    (b)   the false or misleading impression is created there.

(8)   A person guilty of an offence under this section is liable—

    (a)   on summary conviction, to imprisonment for a term not exceeding six months or a fine not exceeding the statutory maximum, or both;

    (b)   on conviction on indictment, to imprisonment for a term not exceeding seven years or a fine, or both.

(9)   "Relevant agreement" means an agreement—

    (a)   the entering into or performance of which by either party constitutes an activity of a specified kind or one which falls within a specified class of activity; and

    (b)   which relates to a relevant investment.

(10)   "Relevant investment" means an investment of a specified kind or one which falls within a prescribed class of investment.

(11)   Schedule 2 (except paragraphs 25 and 26) applies for the purposes of subsections (9) and (10) with references to section 22 being read as references to each of those subsections.

(12)   Nothing in Schedule 2, as applied by subsection (11), limits the power conferred by subsection (9) or (10).

(13)   "Investment" includes any asset, right or interest.

(14)   "Specified" means specified in an order made by the Treasury.

Commencement: 1 December 2001 (sub-ss (1)–(8)); 25 February 2001 (remainder).
Orders: The Financial Services and Markets Act 2000 (Misleading Statements and Practices) Order 2001, SI 2001/3645, as amended by SI 2002/1777, SI 2003/1474, SI 2003/1476; the Financial Services and Markets Act 2000 (Commencement of Mortgage Regulation) (Amendment) Order 2002, SI 2002/1777.
References: See paras 8.31–8.38.

398 Misleading the Authority: residual cases

(1)   A person who, in purported compliance with any requirement imposed by or under this Act, knowingly or recklessly gives the Authority information which is false or misleading in a material particular is guilty of an offence.

(2)   Subsection (1) applies only to a requirement in relation to which no other provision of this Act creates an offence in connection with the giving of information.

(3)   A person guilty of an offence under this section is liable—
  (a)   on summary conviction, to a fine not exceeding the statutory maximum;
  (b)   on conviction on indictment, to a fine.

Commencement: 18 June 2001.
References: See para 8.39.

399 Misleading [the OFT]

Section 44 of the Competition Act 1998 (offences connected with the provision of false or misleading information) applies in relation to any function of [the Office of Fair Trading] under this Act as if it were a function under Part I of that Act.

Commencement: 18 June 2001.
Amendments: Words in square brackets substituted by the Enterprise Act 2002, s 278(1), Sch 25, para 40(1), (16), as from 1 April 2003.
References: See para 8.40.

Bodies corporate and partnerships

400 Offences by bodies corporate etc

(1)   If an offence under this Act committed by a body corporate is shown—
  (a)   to have been committed with the consent or connivance of an officer, or
  (b)   to be attributable to any neglect on his part,
the officer as well as the body corporate is guilty of the offence and liable to be proceeded against and punished accordingly.

(2)   If the affairs of a body corporate are managed by its members, subsection (1) applies in relation to the acts and defaults of a member in connection with his functions of management as if he were a director of the body.

(3)   If an offence under this Act committed by a partnership is shown—
  (a)   to have been committed with the consent or connivance of a partner, or
  (b)   to be attributable to any neglect on his part,
the partner as well as the partnership is guilty of the offence and liable to be proceeded against and punished accordingly.

(4)   In subsection (3) "partner" includes a person purporting to act as a partner.

(5)   "Officer", in relation to a body corporate, means—

(a)   a director, member of the committee of management, chief executive, manager, secretary or other similar officer of the body, or a person purporting to act in any such capacity; and

(b)   an individual who is a controller of the body.

(6)   If an offence under this Act committed by an unincorporated association (other than a partnership) is shown—

(a)   to have been committed with the consent or connivance of an officer of the association or a member of its governing body, or

(b)   to be attributable to any neglect on the part of such an officer or member,

that officer or member as well as the association is guilty of the offence and liable to be proceeded against and punished accordingly.

(7)   Regulations may provide for the application of any provision of this section, with such modifications as the Treasury consider appropriate, to a body corporate or unincorporated association formed or recognised under the law of a territory outside the United Kingdom.

Commencement: 18 June 2001.
References: See paras 8.41–8.47.

Institution of proceedings

401 Proceedings for offences

(1)   In this section "offence" means an offence under this Act or subordinate legislation made under this Act.

(2)   Proceedings for an offence may be instituted in England and Wales only—

(a)   by the Authority or the Secretary of State; or

(b)   by or with the consent of the Director of Public Prosecutions.

(3)   Proceedings for an offence may be instituted in Northern Ireland only—

(a)   by the Authority or the Secretary of State; or

(b)   by or with the consent of the Director of Public Prosecutions for Northern Ireland.

(4)   Except in Scotland, proceedings for an offence under section 203 may also be instituted by [the Office of Fair Trading].

(5)   In exercising its power to institute proceedings for an offence, the Authority must comply with any conditions or restrictions imposed in writing by the Treasury.

(6)   Conditions or restrictions may be imposed under subsection (5) in relation to—

(a)   proceedings generally; or

(b)   such proceedings, or categories of proceedings, as the Treasury may direct.

Commencement: 18 June 2001.
Amendments: Sub-s (4):words in square brackets substituted by the Enterprise Act 2002, s 278(1), Sch 25, para 40(1), (17), as from 1 April 2003.

Transitional provisions: This section and s 403 have effect as if offences committed before 1 December 2001 under certain provisions (the Insurance Companies Act 1982, the Financial Services Act 1986, the Banking Act 1987, and certain related provisions) were an offence under this Act; see the Financial Services and Markets Act 2000 (Transitional Provisions and Savings) (Civil Remedies, Discipline, Criminal Offences etc) (No 2) Order 2001, SI 2001/3083, art 13 (made under ss 426, 427, 428(3)). The 1982, 1986 and 1987 Acts are repealed by the Financial Services and Markets Act 2000 (Consequential Amendments and Repeals) Order 2001, SI 2001/3649, art 3(1)(b)–(d) (made under ss 426, 427).
References: See para 8.48.

402 Power of the Authority to institute proceedings for certain other offences

(1)   Except in Scotland, the Authority may institute proceedings for an offence under—

    (a)   Part V of the Criminal Justice Act 1993 (insider dealing); or

    (b)   prescribed regulations relating to money laundering.

(2)   In exercising its power to institute proceedings for any such offence, the Authority must comply with any conditions or restrictions imposed in writing by the Treasury.

(3)   Conditions or restrictions may be imposed under subsection (2) in relation to—

    (a)   proceedings generally; or

    (b)   such proceedings, or categories of proceedings, as the Treasury may direct.

Commencement: 25 February 2001 (sub-s (1)(b), for the purpose of making orders or regulations); 19 October 2001 (for the purposes of proceedings for offences under prescribed regulations relating to money laundering); 1 December 2001 (remainder).
Regulations: The Financial Services and Markets Act 2000 (Regulations Relating to Money Laundering) Regulations 2001, SI 2001/1819.
References: See para 8.49.

403 Jurisdiction and procedure in respect of offences

(1)   A fine imposed on an unincorporated association on its conviction of an offence is to be paid out of the funds of the association.

(2)   Proceedings for an offence alleged to have been committed by an unincorporated association must be brought in the name of the association (and not in that of any of its members).

(3)   Rules of court relating to the service of documents are to have effect as if the association were a body corporate.

(4)   In proceedings for an offence brought against an unincorporated association—

    (a)   section 33 of the Criminal Justice Act 1925 and Schedule 3 to the Magistrates' Courts Act 1980 (procedure) apply as they do in relation to a body corporate;

    (b)   section 70 of the Criminal Procedure (Scotland) Act 1995 (procedure) applies as if the association were a body corporate;

    (c)   section 18 of the Criminal Justice (Northern Ireland) Act 1945 and Schedule 4 to the Magistrates' Courts (Northern Ireland) Order 1981 (procedure) apply as they do in relation to a body corporate.

(5)   Summary proceedings for an offence may be taken—
      (a)   against a body corporate or unincorporated association at any place at which it has a place of business;
      (b)   against an individual at any place where he is for the time being.

(6)   Subsection (5) does not affect any jurisdiction exercisable apart from this section.

(7)   "Offence" means an offence under this Act.

Commencement: 18 June 2001.
Transitional provisions: See the note to s 401 ante.
References: See paras 8.43–8.46.

PART XXVIII
MISCELLANEOUS

Schemes for reviewing past business

404 Schemes for reviewing past business

(1)   Subsection (2) applies if the Treasury are satisfied that there is evidence suggesting—
      (a)   that there has been a widespread or regular failure on the part of authorised persons to comply with rules relating to a particular kind of activity; and
      (b)   that, as a result, private persons have suffered (or will suffer) loss in respect of which authorised persons are (or will be) liable to make payments ("compensation payments").

(2)   The Treasury may by order ("a scheme order") authorise the Authority to establish and operate a scheme for—
      (a)   determining the nature and extent of the failure;
      (b)   establishing the liability of authorised persons to make compensation payments; and
      (c)   determining the amounts payable by way of compensation payments.

(3)   An authorised scheme must be made so as to comply with specified requirements.

(4)   A scheme order may be made only if—
      (a)   the Authority has given the Treasury a report about the alleged failure and asked them to make a scheme order;
      (b)   the report contains details of the scheme which the Authority propose to make; and
      (c)   the Treasury are satisfied that the proposed scheme is an appropriate way of dealing with the failure.

(5)   A scheme order may provide for specified provisions of or made under this Act to apply in relation to any provision of, or determination made under, the resulting authorised scheme subject to such modifications (if any) as may be specified.

(6)   For the purposes of this Act, failure on the part of an authorised person to comply with any provision of an authorised scheme is to be treated (subject to any provision made by the scheme order concerned) as a failure on his part to comply with rules.

(7)   The Treasury may prescribe circumstances in which loss suffered by a person ("A") acting in a fiduciary or other prescribed capacity is to be treated, for the purposes of an authorised scheme, as suffered by a private person in relation to whom A was acting in that capacity.

(8)   This section applies whenever the failure in question occurred.

(9)   "Authorised scheme" means a scheme authorised by a scheme order.

(10)   "Private person" has such meaning as may be prescribed.

(11)   "Specified" means specified in a scheme order.

Commencement: 1 December 2001.
References: See paras 2.91–2.96.

Third countries

405 Directions

(1)   For the purpose of implementing a third country decision, the Treasury may direct the Authority to—

  (a)   refuse an application for permission under Part IV made by a body incorporated in, or formed under the law of, any part of the United Kingdom;

  (b)   defer its decision on such an application either indefinitely or for such period as may be specified in the direction;

  (c)   give a notice of objection to a person who has served a notice of control to the effect that he proposes to acquire a 50% stake in a UK authorised person; or

  (d)   give a notice of objection to a person who has acquired a 50% stake in a UK authorised person without having served the required notice of control.

(2)   A direction may also be given in relation to—

  (a)   any person falling within a class specified in the direction;

  (b)   future applications, notices of control or acquisitions.

(3)   The Treasury may revoke a direction at any time.

(4)   But revocation does not affect anything done in accordance with the direction before it was revoked.

(5)   "Third country decision" means a decision of the Council or the Commission under—

  (a)   Article 7(5) of the investment services directive;

  (b)   [Article 23(5) of the banking consolidation directive;]

  (c)   Article 29b(4) of the first non-life insurance directive; or

  (d)   Article 32b(4) of the first life insurance directive.

Commencement: 1 December 2001 (sub-s (1)(c), (d)); 3 September 2001 (remainder).
Amendments: Sub-s (5): words in square brackets substituted by the Banking Consolidation Directive (Consequential Amendments) Regulations 2000, SI 2000/2952, reg 8(1), (3), as from 22 November 2000.
References: See paras 2.97–2.101.

406 Interpretation of section 405

(1)   For the purposes of section 405, a person ("the acquirer") acquires a 50% stake in a UK authorised person ("A") on first falling within any of the cases set out in subsection (2).

(2)   The cases are where the acquirer—
- (a)   holds 50% or more of the shares in A;
- (b)   holds 50% or more of the shares in a parent undertaking ("P") of A;
- (c)   is entitled to exercise, or control the exercise of, 50% or more of the voting power in A; or
- (d)   is entitled to exercise, or control the exercise of, 50% or more of the voting power in P.

(3)   In subsection (2) "the acquirer" means—
- (a)   the acquirer;
- (b)   any of the acquirer's associates; or
- (c)   the acquirer and any of his associates.

(4)   "Associate", "shares" and "voting power" have the same meaning as in section 422.

Commencement: 1 December 2001.
References: See para 2.97.

407 Consequences of a direction under section 405

(1)   If the Authority refuses an application for permission as a result of a direction under section 405(1)(a)—
- (a)   subsections (7) to (9) of section 52 do not apply in relation to the refusal; but
- (b)   the Authority must notify the applicant of the refusal and the reasons for it.

(2)   If the Authority defers its decision on an application for permission as a result of a direction under section 405(1)(b)—
- (a)   the time limit for determining the application mentioned in section 52(1) or (2) stops running on the day of the deferral and starts running again (if at all) on the day the period specified in the direction (if any) ends or the day the direction is revoked; and
- (b)   the Authority must notify the applicant of the deferral and the reasons for it.

(3)   If the Authority gives a notice of objection to a person as a result of a direction under section 405(1)(c) or (d)—
- (a)   sections 189 and 191 have effect as if the notice was a notice of objection within the meaning of Part XII; and
- (b)   the Authority must state in the notice the reasons for it.

Commencement: 1 December 2001 (sub-ss (1), (2)); 3 September 2001 (remainder).
References: See paras 2.100, 2.101.

408 EFTA firms

(1)   If a third country decision has been taken, the Treasury may make a determination in relation to an EFTA firm which is a subsidiary undertaking of a parent undertaking which is governed by the law of the country to which the decision relates.

(2)   "Determination" means a determination that the firm concerned does not qualify for authorisation under Schedule 3 even if it satisfies the conditions in paragraph 13 or 14 of that Schedule.

(3)   A determination may also be made in relation to any firm falling within a class specified in the determination.

(4)   The Treasury may withdraw a determination at any time.

(5)   But withdrawal does not affect anything done in accordance with the determination before it was withdrawn.

(6)   If the Treasury make a determination in respect of a particular firm, or withdraw such a determination, they must give written notice to that firm.

(7)   The Treasury must publish notice of any determination (or the withdrawal of any determination)—

    (a)   in such a way as they think most suitable for bringing the determination (or withdrawal) to the attention of those likely to be affected by it; and

    (b)   on, or as soon as practicable after, the date of the determination (or withdrawal).

(8)   "EFTA firm" means a firm, institution or undertaking which—

    (a)   is an EEA firm as a result of paragraph 5(a), (b) or (d) of Schedule 3; and

    (b)   is incorporated in, or formed under the law of, an EEA State which is not a member State.

(9)   "Third country decision" has the same meaning as in section 405.

Commencement: 3 September 2001 (for the purposes of determinations coming into force not sooner than the day on which s 19 of this Act comes into force); 1 December 2001 (remaining purposes).
References: See paras 2.97, 2.98.

409 Gibraltar

(1)   The Treasury may by order—

    (a)   modify Schedule 3 so as to provide for Gibraltar firms of a specified description to qualify for authorisation under that Schedule in specified circumstances;

    (b)   modify Schedule 3 so as to make provision in relation to the exercise by UK firms of rights under the law of Gibraltar which correspond to EEA rights;

    (c)   modify Schedule 4 so as to provide for Gibraltar firms of a specified description to qualify for authorisation under that Schedule in specified circumstances;

    (d)   modify section 264 so as to make provision in relation to collective investment schemes constituted under the law of Gibraltar;

    (e)   provide for the Authority to be able to give notice under section 264(2) on grounds relating to the law of Gibraltar;

    (f)   provide for this Act to apply to a Gibraltar recognised scheme as if the scheme were a scheme recognised under section 264.

(2)   The fact that a firm may qualify for authorisation under Schedule 3 as a result of an order under subsection (1) does not prevent it from applying for a Part IV permission.

(3)   "Gibraltar firm" means a firm which has its head office in Gibraltar or is otherwise connected with Gibraltar.

(4)   "Gibraltar recognised scheme" means a collective investment scheme—

    (a)   constituted in an EEA State other than the United Kingdom, and

    (b)   recognised in Gibraltar under provisions which appear to the Treasury to give effect to the provisions of a relevant Community instrument.

(5)   "Specified" means specified in the order.

(6)   "UK firm" and "EEA right" have the same meaning as in Schedule 3.

Commencement: 25 February 2001.
Orders: The Financial Services and Markets Act 2000 (Gibraltar) Order 2001, SI 2001/3084.
References: See paras 3.50–3.52.

International obligations

410 International obligations

(1)   If it appears to the Treasury that any action proposed to be taken by a relevant person would be incompatible with Community obligations or any other international obligations of the United Kingdom, they may direct that person not to take that action.

(2)   If it appears to the Treasury that any action which a relevant person has power to take is required for the purpose of implementing any such obligations, they may direct that person to take that action.

(3)   A direction under this section—

    (a)   may include such supplemental or incidental requirements as the Treasury consider necessary or expedient; and

    (b)   is enforceable, on an application made by the Treasury, by injunction or, in Scotland, by an order for specific performance under section 45 of the Court of Session Act 1988.

(4)   "Relevant person" means—

    (a)   the Authority;

    (b)   any person exercising functions conferred by Part VI on the competent authority;

    (c)   any recognised investment exchange (other than one which is an overseas investment exchange);

    (d)   any recognised clearing house (other than one which is an overseas clearing house);

    (e)   a person included in the list maintained under section 301; or

    (f)   the scheme operator of the ombudsman scheme.

Commencement: 18 June 2001.
References: See paras 2.102, 2.103.

411 *(Amends the Income and Corporations Taxes Act 1988, s 76 and inserts ss 76A, 76B of that Act.)*

Gaming contracts

412 Gaming contracts

(1)   No contract to which this section applies is void or unenforceable because of—

> (a)   section 18 of the Gaming Act 1845, section 1 of the Gaming Act 1892 or Article 170 of the Betting, Gaming, Lotteries and Amusements (Northern Ireland) Order 1985; or
>
> (b)   any rule of the law of Scotland under which a contract by way of gaming or wagering is not legally enforceable.

(2)   This section applies to a contract if—

> (a)   it is entered into by either or each party by way of business;
>
> (b)   the entering into or performance of it by either party constitutes an activity of a specified kind or one which falls within a specified class of activity; and
>
> (c)   it relates to an investment of a specified kind or one which falls within a specified class of investment.

(3)   Part II of Schedule 2 applies for the purposes of subsection (2)(c), with the references to section 22 being read as references to that subsection.

(4)   Nothing in Part II of Schedule 2, as applied by subsection (3), limits the power conferred by subsection (2)(c).

(5)   "Investment" includes any asset, right or interest.

(6)   "Specified" means specified in an order made by the Treasury.

Commencement: 25 February 2001 (for the purpose of making orders or regulations); 1 December 2001 (remaining purposes).
Orders: The Financial Services and Markets Act 2000 (Gaming Contracts) Order 2001, SI 2001/2510.

Limitation on powers to require documents

413 Protected items

(1)   A person may not be required under this Act to produce, disclose or permit the inspection of protected items.

(2)   "Protected items" means—

> (a)   communications between a professional legal adviser and his client or any person representing his client which fall within subsection (3);
>
> (b)   communications between a professional legal adviser, his client or any person representing his client and any other person which fall within subsection (3) (as a result of paragraph (b) of that subsection);
>
> (c)   items which—
>
> > (i)   are enclosed with, or referred to in, such communications;
> >
> > (ii)   fall within subsection (3); and
> >
> > (iii) are in the possession of a person entitled to possession of them.

(3)   A communication or item falls within this subsection if it is made—
    (a)   in connection with the giving of legal advice to the client; or
    (b)   in connection with, or in contemplation of, legal proceedings and for the purposes of those proceedings.

(4)   A communication or item is not a protected item if it is held with the intention of furthering a criminal purpose.

Commencement: 3 September 2001.
References: See para 7.12.

Service of notices

414 Service of notices

(1)   The Treasury may by regulations make provision with respect to the procedure to be followed, or rules to be applied, when a provision of or made under this Act requires a notice, direction or document of any kind to be given or authorises the imposition of a requirement.

(2)   The regulations may, in particular, make provision—
    (a)   as to the manner in which a document must be given;
    (b)   as to the address to which a document must be sent;
    (c)   requiring, or allowing, a document to be sent electronically;
    (d)   for treating a document as having been given, or as having been received, on a date or at a time determined in accordance with the regulations;
    (e)   as to what must, or may, be done if the person to whom a document is required to be given is not an individual;
    (f)   as to what must, or may, be done if the intended recipient of a document is outside the United Kingdom.

(3)   Subsection (1) applies however the obligation to give a document is expressed (and so, in particular, includes a provision which requires a document to be served or sent).

(4)   Section 7 of the Interpretation Act 1978 (service of notice by post) has effect in relation to provisions made by or under this Act subject to any provision made by regulations under this section.

Commencement: 18 June 2001 (sub-s (4)); 25 February 2001 (remainder).
Regulations: The Financial Services and Markets Act 2000 (Service of Notices) Regulations 2001, SI 2001/1420; the Electronic Commerce Directive (Financial Services and Markets) Regulations 2002, SI 2002/1775, as amended by SI 2002/2015.

Jurisdiction

415 Jurisdiction in civil proceedings

(1)   Proceedings arising out of any act or omission (or proposed act or omission) of—
    (a)   the Authority,
    (b)   the competent authority for the purposes of Part VI,
    (c)   the scheme manager, or
    (d)   the scheme operator,

in the discharge or purported discharge of any of its functions under this Act may be brought before the High Court or the Court of Session.

(2)   The jurisdiction conferred by subsection (1) is in addition to any other jurisdiction exercisable by those courts.

Commencement: 18 June 2001.

Removal of certain unnecessary provisions

416 Provisions relating to industrial assurance and certain other enactments

(1)   The following enactments are to cease to have effect—
(a)   the Industrial Assurance Act 1923;
(b)   the Industrial Assurance and Friendly Societies Act 1948;
(c)   the Insurance Brokers (Registration) Act 1977.

(2)   The Industrial Assurance (Northern Ireland) Order 1979 is revoked.

(3)   The following bodies are to cease to exist—
(a)   the Insurance Brokers Registration Council;
(b)   the Policyholders Protection Board;
(c)   the Deposit Protection Board;
(d)   the Board of Banking Supervision.

(4)   If the Treasury consider that, as a consequence of any provision of this section, it is appropriate to do so, they may by order make any provision of a kind that they could make under this Act (and in particular any provision of a kind mentioned in section 339) with respect to anything done by or under any provision of Part XXI.

(5)   Subsection (4) is not to be read as affecting in any way any other power conferred on the Treasury by this Act.

Commencement: 2 March 2002 (sub-ss (3)(b), (c)); 1 December 2001 (sub-ss (1)(a), (b), (2), (3)(d)); 30 April 2001 (sub-ss (1)(c), (3)(a)); 25 February 2001 (remainder).
Orders: The Financial Services and Markets Act 2000 (Dissolution of the Insurance Brokers Registration Council) (Consequential Provisions) Order 2001, SI 2001/1283; the Financial Services and Markets Act 2000 (Transitional Provisions, Repeals and Savings) (Financial Services Compensation Scheme) Order 2001, SI 2001/2967; the Financial Services and Markets Act 2000 (Consequential Amendments and Savings) (Industrial Assurance) Order 2001, SI 2001/3647; the Financial Services and Markets Act 2000 (Consequential Amendments) Order 2002, SI 2002/1555.

PART XXIX
INTERPRETATION

417 Definitions

(1)   In this Act—
"appointed representative" has the meaning given in section 39(2);
"auditors and actuaries rules" means rules made under section 340;
"authorisation offence" has the meaning given in section 23(2);
"authorised open-ended investment company" has the meaning given in section 237(3);

"authorised person" has the meaning given in section 31(2);

"the Authority" means the Financial Services Authority;

"body corporate" includes a body corporate constituted under the law of a country or territory outside the United Kingdom;

"chief executive"—

    (a)   in relation to a body corporate whose principal place of business is within the United Kingdom, means an employee of that body who, alone or jointly with one or more others, is responsible under the immediate authority of the directors, for the conduct of the whole of the business of that body; and

    (b)   in relation to a body corporate whose principal place of business is outside the United Kingdom, means the person who, alone or jointly with one or more others, is responsible for the conduct of its business within the United Kingdom;

"collective investment scheme" has the meaning given in section 235;

"the Commission" means the European Commission (except in provisions relating to the Competition Commission);

"the compensation scheme" has the meaning given in section 213(2);

"control of information rules" has the meaning given in section 147(1);

"director", in relation to a body corporate, includes—

    (a)   a person occupying in relation to it the position of a director (by whatever name called); and

    (b)   a person in accordance with whose directions or instructions (not being advice given in a professional capacity) the directors of that body are accustomed to act;

"documents" includes information recorded in any form and, in relation to information recorded otherwise than in legible form, references to its production include references to producing a copy of the information in legible form[, or in a form from which it can readily be produced in visible and legible form];

["electronic commerce directive" means Directive 2000/31/EC of the European Parliament and the Council of 8 June 2000 on certain legal aspects of information society services, in particular electronic commerce, in the Internal Market (Directive on electronic commerce);]

"exempt person", in relation to a regulated activity, means a person who is exempt from the general prohibition in relation to that activity as a result of an exemption order made under section 38(1) or as a result of section 39(1) or 285(2) or (3);

"financial promotion rules" means rules made under section 145;

"friendly society" means an incorporated or registered friendly society;

"general prohibition" has the meaning given in section 19(2);

"general rules" has the meaning given in section 138(2);

"incorporated friendly society" means a society incorporated under the Friendly Societies Act 1992;

"industrial and provident society" means a society registered or deemed to be registered under the Industrial and Provident Societies Act 1965 or the Industrial and Provident Societies Act (Northern Ireland) 1969;

["information society service" means an information society service within the meaning of Article 2(a) of the electronic commerce directive;]

"market abuse" has the meaning given in section 118;

"Minister of the Crown" has the same meaning as in the Ministers of the Crown Act 1975;

"money laundering rules" means rules made under section 146;

"notice of control" has the meaning given in section 178(5);

"the ombudsman scheme" has the meaning given in section 225(3);

"open-ended investment company" has the meaning given in section 236;

"Part IV permission" has the meaning given in section 40(4);

"partnership" includes a partnership constituted under the law of a country or territory outside the United Kingdom;

"prescribed" (where not otherwise defined) means prescribed in regulations made by the Treasury;

"price stabilising rules" means rules made under section 144;

"private company" has the meaning given in section 1(3) of the Companies Act 1985 or in Article 12(3) of the Companies (Northern Ireland) Order 1986;

"prohibition order" has the meaning given in section 56(2);

"recognised clearing house" and "recognised investment exchange" have the meaning given in section 285;

"registered friendly society" means a society which is—

    (a)   a friendly society within the meaning of section 7(1)(a) of the Friendly Societies Act 1974; and

    (b)   registered within the meaning of that Act;

"regulated activity" has the meaning given in section 22;

"regulating provisions" has the meaning given in section 159(1);

"regulatory objectives" means the objectives mentioned in section 2;

"regulatory provisions" has the meaning given in section 302;

"rule" means a rule made by the Authority under this Act;

"rule-making instrument" has the meaning given in section 153;

"the scheme manager" has the meaning given in section 212(1);

"the scheme operator" has the meaning given in section 225(2);

"scheme particulars rules" has the meaning given in section 248(1);

"Seventh Company Law Directive" means the European Council Seventh Company Law Directive of 13 June 1983 on consolidated accounts (No 83/349/EEC);

"threshold conditions", in relation to a regulated activity, has the meaning given in section 41;

"the Treaty" means the treaty establishing the European Community;

"trust scheme rules" has the meaning given in section 247(1);

"UK authorised person" has the meaning given in section 178(4); and

"unit trust scheme" has the meaning given in section 237.

(2)   In the application of this Act to Scotland, references to a matter being actionable at the suit of a person are to be read as references to the matter being actionable at the instance of that person.

(3)   For the purposes of any provision of this Act authorising or requiring a person to do anything within a specified number of days no account is to be taken of any day which is a public holiday in any part of the United Kingdom.

[(4)   For the purposes of this Act—

    (a)   an information society service is provided from an EEA State if it is provided from an establishment in that State;

    (b)   an establishment, in connection with an information society service, is the place at which the provider of the service (being a national of an EEA State or a company or firm as mentioned in Article 48 of the Treaty) effectively pursues an economic activity for an indefinite period;

(c) the presence or use in a particular place of equipment or other technical means of providing an information society service does not, of itself, constitute that place as an establishment of the kind mentioned in paragraph (b);

(d) where it cannot be determined from which of a number of establishments a given information society service is provided, that service is to be regarded as provided from the establishment where the provider has the centre of his activities relating to the service.]

Commencement: 25 February 2001.
Amendments: Sub-s (1): words in square brackets in definition "documents" inserted by the Criminal Justice and Police Act 2001, s 70, Sch 2, Pt 2, para 16(1), (2)(f), as from a day to be appointed; definitions "electronic commerce directive" and "information society service" inserted by the Electronic Commerce Directive (Financial Services and Markets) Regulations 2002, SI 2002/1775, reg 13(1), (2)(a), (b) as from 21 August 2002.
Sub-s (4): added by SI 2002/1775, reg 13(1), (2)(c), as from 21 August 2002.
Seventh Company Law Directive (83/349/EEC): OJ L193, 18.7.1983, p 1.

418 Carrying on regulated activities in the United Kingdom

(1) In the [five] cases described in this section, a person who—
   (a) is carrying on a regulated activity, but
   (b) would not otherwise be regarded as carrying it on in the United Kingdom,

is, for the purposes of this Act, to be regarded as carrying it on in the United Kingdom.

(2) The first case is where—
   (a) his registered office (or if he does not have a registered office his head office) is in the United Kingdom;
   (b) he is entitled to exercise rights under a single market directive as a UK firm; and
   (c) he is carrying on in another EEA State a regulated activity to which that directive applies.

(3) The second case is where—
   (a) his registered office (or if he does not have a registered office his head office) is in the United Kingdom;
   (b) he is the manager of a scheme which is entitled to enjoy the rights conferred by an instrument which is a relevant Community instrument for the purposes of section 264; and
   (c) persons in another EEA State are invited to become participants in the scheme.

(4) The third case is where—
   (a) his registered office (or if he does not have a registered office his head office) is in the United Kingdom;
   (b) the day-to-day management of the carrying on of the regulated activity is the responsibility of—
      (i) his registered office (or head office); or
      (ii) another establishment maintained by him in the United Kingdom.

(5) The fourth case is where—
   (a) his head office is not in the United Kingdom; but

    (b)   the activity is carried on from an establishment maintained by him in the United Kingdom.

[(5A) The fifth case is any other case where the activity—
    (a)   consists of the provision of an information society service to a person or persons in one or more EEA States; and
    (b)   is carried on from an establishment in the United Kingdom.]

(6)   For the purposes of subsections (2) to [(5A)] it is irrelevant where the person with whom the activity is carried on is situated.

Commencement: 3 September 2001.
Amendments: Sub-s (1): word in square brackets substituted by the Electronic Commerce Directive (Financial Services and Markets) Regulations 2002, SI 2002/1775, reg 13(1), (3)(a), as from 21 August 2002. Sub-s (5A): inserted by SI 2002/1775, reg 13(1), (3)(b), as from 21 August 2002.
Sub-s (6): reference in square brackets substituted by SI 2002/1775, reg 13(1), (3)(c), as from 21 August 2002.
References: See paras 3.42–3.48.

419 Carrying on regulated activities by way of business

(1)   The Treasury may by order make provision—
    (a)   as to the circumstances in which a person who would otherwise not be regarded as carrying on a regulated activity by way of business is to be regarded as doing so;
    (b)   as to the circumstances in which a person who would otherwise be regarded as carrying on a regulated activity by way of business is to be regarded as not doing so.

(2)   An order under subsection (1) may be made so as to apply—
    (a)   generally in relation to all regulated activities;
    (b)   in relation to a specified category of regulated activity; or
    (c)   in relation to a particular regulated activity.

(3)   An order under subsection (1) may be made so as to apply—
    (a)   for the purposes of all provisions;
    (b)   for a specified group of provisions; or
    (c)   for a specified provision.

(4)   "Provision" means a provision of, or made under, this Act.

(5)   Nothing in this section is to be read as affecting the provisions of section 428(3).

Commencement: 25 February 2001.
Orders: The Financial Services and Markets Act 2000 (Carrying on Regulated Activities by Way of Business) Order 2001, SI 2001/1177 as amended by SI 2003/1475, SI 2003/1476.
References: See paras 3.17, 3.18.

420 Parent and subsidiary undertaking

(1)   In this Act, except in relation to an incorporated friendly society, "parent undertaking" and "subsidiary undertaking" have the same meaning as in Part VII of the Companies Act 1985 (or Part VIII of the Companies (Northern Ireland) Order 1986).

(2) But—

    (a) "parent undertaking" also includes an individual who would be a parent undertaking for the purposes of those provisions if he were taken to be an undertaking (and "subsidiary undertaking" is to be read accordingly);

    (b) "subsidiary undertaking" also includes, in relation to a body incorporated in or formed under the law of an EEA State other than the United Kingdom, an undertaking which is a subsidiary undertaking within the meaning of any rule of law in force in that State for purposes connected with implementation of the Seventh Company Law Directive (and "parent undertaking" is to be read accordingly).

(3) In this Act "subsidiary undertaking", in relation to an incorporated friendly society, means a body corporate of which the society has control within the meaning of section 13(9)(a) or (aa) of the Friendly Societies Act 1992 (and "parent undertaking" is to be read accordingly).

Commencement: 25 February 2001.
References: See paras 4.123, 4.124.

---

421 Group

(1) In this Act "group", in relation to a person ("A"), means A and any person who is—

    (a) a parent undertaking of A;
    (b) a subsidiary undertaking of A;
    (c) a subsidiary undertaking of a parent undertaking of A;
    (d) a parent undertaking of a subsidiary undertaking of A;
    (e) an undertaking in which A or an undertaking mentioned in paragraph (a), (b), (c) or (d) has a participating interest;
    (f) if A or an undertaking mentioned in paragraph (a) or (d) is a building society, an associated undertaking of the society; or
    (g) if A or an undertaking mentioned in paragraph (a) or (d) is an incorporated friendly society, a body corporate of which the society has joint control (within the meaning of section 13(9)(c) or (cc) of the Friendly Societies Act 1992).

(2) "Participating interest" has the same meaning as in Part VII of the Companies Act 1985 or Part VIII of the Companies (Northern Ireland) Order 1986; but also includes an interest held by an individual which would be a participating interest for the purposes of those provisions if he were taken to be an undertaking.

(3) "Associated undertaking" has the meaning given in section 119(1) of the Building Societies Act 1986.

Commencement: 25 February 2001.
References: See para 4.68.

---

422 Controller

(1) In this Act "controller", in relation to an undertaking ("A"), means a person who falls within any of the cases in subsection (2).

(2) The cases are where the person—
    (a) holds 10% or more of the shares in A;
    (b) is able to exercise significant influence over the management of A by virtue of his shareholding in A;
    (c) holds 10% or more of the shares in a parent undertaking ("P") of A;
    (d) is able to exercise significant influence over the management of P by virtue of his shareholding in P;
    (e) is entitled to exercise, or control the exercise of, 10% or more of the voting power in A;
    (f) is able to exercise significant influence over the management of A by virtue of his voting power in A;
    (g) is entitled to exercise, or control the exercise of, 10% or more of the voting power in P; or
    (h) is able to exercise significant influence over the management of P by virtue of his voting power in P.

(3) In subsection (2) "the person" means—
    (a) the person;
    (b) any of the person's associates; or
    (c) the person and any of his associates.

(4) "Associate", in relation to a person ("H") holding shares in an undertaking ("C") or entitled to exercise or control the exercise of voting power in relation to another undertaking ("D"), means—
    (a) the spouse of H;
    (b) a child or stepchild of H (if under 18);
    (c) the trustee of any settlement under which H has a life interest in possession (or in Scotland a life interest);
    (d) an undertaking of which H is a director;
    (e) a person who is an employee or partner of H;
    (f) if H is an undertaking—
        (i) a director of H;
        (ii) a subsidiary undertaking of H;
        (iii) a director or employee of such a subsidiary undertaking; and
    (g) if H has with any other person an agreement or arrangement with respect to the acquisition, holding or disposal of shares or other interests in C or D or under which they undertake to act together in exercising their voting power in relation to C or D, that other person.

(5) "Settlement", in subsection (4)(c), includes any disposition or arrangement under which property is held on trust (or subject to a comparable obligation).

(6) "Shares"—
    (a) in relation to an undertaking with a share capital, means allotted shares;
    (b) in relation to an undertaking with capital but no share capital, means rights to share in the capital of the undertaking;
    (c) in relation to an undertaking without capital, means interests—
        (i) conferring any right to share in the profits, or liability to contribute to the losses, of the undertaking; or
        (ii) giving rise to an obligation to contribute to the debts or expenses of the undertaking in the event of a winding up.

(7)   "Voting power", in relation to an undertaking which does not have general meetings at which matters are decided by the exercise of voting rights, means the right under the constitution of the undertaking to direct the overall policy of the undertaking or alter the terms of its constitution.

Commencement: 25 February 2001.
References: See para 4.122.

423 Manager

(1)   In this Act, except in relation to a unit trust scheme or a registered friendly society, "manager" means an employee who—

    (a)   under the immediate authority of his employer is responsible, either alone or jointly with one or more other persons, for the conduct of his employer's business; or

    (b)   under the immediate authority of his employer or of a person who is a manager by virtue of paragraph (a) exercises managerial functions or is responsible for maintaining accounts or other records of his employer.

(2)   If the employer is not an individual, references in subsection (1) to the authority of the employer are references to the authority—

    (a)   in the case of a body corporate, of the directors;

    (b)   in the case of a partnership, of the partners; and

    (c)   in the case of an unincorporated association, of its officers or the members of its governing body.

(3)   "Manager", in relation to a body corporate, means a person (other than an employee of the body) who is appointed by the body to manage any part of its business and includes an employee of the body corporate (other than the chief executive) who, under the immediate authority of a director or chief executive of the body corporate, exercises managerial functions or is responsible for maintaining accounts or other records of the body corporate.

Commencement: 25 February 2001.

424 Insurance

(1)   In this Act, references to—

    (a)   contracts of insurance,

    (b)   reinsurance,

    (c)   contracts of long-term insurance,

    (d)   contracts of general insurance,

are to be read with section 22 and Schedule 2.

(2)   In this Act "policy" and "policyholder", in relation to a contract of insurance, have such meaning as the Treasury may by order specify.

(3)   The law applicable to a contract of insurance, the effecting of which constitutes the carrying on of a regulated activity, is to be determined, if it is of a prescribed description, in accordance with regulations made by the Treasury.

Commencement: 25 February 2001 (sub-ss (1), (2), and sub-s (3) for the purpose of making orders or regulations)); 1 December 2001 (remaining purposes).
Regulations: The Financial Services and Markets Act 2000 (Law Applicable to Contracts of Insurance) Regulations 2001, SI 2001/2635, as amended by SI 2001/3542.
Orders: The Financial Services and Markets Act 2000 (Meaning of "Policy" and "Policyholder") Order 2001, SI 2001/2361.
References: See paras 21.22, 21.28.

425 Expressions relating to authorisation elsewhere in the single market

(1)   In this Act—
  (a)   "EEA authorisation", "EEA firm", "EEA right", "EEA State", "first life insurance directive", "first non-life insurance directive", "insurance directives", ["insurance mediation directive",] "investment services directive", "single market directives" and ["banking consolidation directive"] have the meaning given in Schedule 3; and
  (b)   "home state regulator", in relation to an EEA firm, has the meaning given in Schedule 3.

(2)   In this Act—
  (a)   "home state authorisation" has the meaning given in Schedule 4;
  (b)   "Treaty firm" has the meaning given in Schedule 4; and
  (c)   "home state regulator", in relation to a Treaty firm, has the meaning given in Schedule 4.

Commencement: 25 February 2001.
Amendments: Sub-s (1): para (a) substituted by the Collective Investment Schemes (Miscellaneous Amendments) Regulations 2003, SI 2003/2066, reg 2(1), as from 13 February 2004 as follows—
  "(a) "banking consolidation directive", "EEA authorisation", "EEA firm", "EEA right", "EEA State", "first life insurance directive", "first non-life insurance directive", "insurance directives", "insurance mediation directive", "investment services directive", "single market directives" and "UCITS directive" have the meaning given in Schedule 3; and".
Words in first pair of square brackets inserted by the Insurance Mediation Directive (Miscellaneous Amendments) Regulations 2003, SI 2003/1473, reg 2(1), as from 14 January 2005; words in second pair of square brackets substituted by the Banking Consolidation Directive (Consequential Amendments) Regulations 2000, SI 2000/2952, reg 8(1), (4).

PART XXX
SUPPLEMENTAL

426 Consequential and supplementary provision

(1)   A Minister of the Crown may by order make such incidental, consequential, transitional or supplemental provision as he considers necessary or expedient for the general purposes, or any particular purpose, of this Act or in consequence of any provision made by or under this Act or for giving full effect to this Act or any such provision.

(2)   An order under subsection (1) may, in particular, make provision—
  (a)   for enabling any person by whom any powers will become exercisable, on a date set by or under this Act, by virtue of any

provision made by or under this Act to take before that date any steps which are necessary as a preliminary to the exercise of those powers;

(b) for applying (with or without modifications) or amending, repealing or revoking any provision of or made under an Act passed before this Act or in the same Session;

(c) dissolving any body corporate established by any Act passed, or instrument made, before the passing of this Act;

(d) for making savings, or additional savings, from the effect of any repeal or revocation made by or under this Act.

(3) Amendments made under this section are additional, and without prejudice, to those made by or under any other provision of this Act.

(4) No other provision of this Act restricts the powers conferred by this section.

Commencement: 25 February 2001.

Modification: This section shall have effect as if the provisions referred to in sub-s (2)(b) above included the provisions of the Criminal Justice and Police Act 2001, Pt 2: see Sch 2, Pt 2, para 26 to the 2001 Act.

Regulations: The Financial Services and Markets Act 2000 (Recognition Requirements for Investment Exchanges and Clearing Houses) Regulations 2001, SI 2001/995; the Financial Services and Markets Act 2000 (Disclosure of Confidential Information) Regulations 2001, SI 2001/2188, as amended by SI 2001/3437, SI 2001/3624, SI 2002/1775, SI 2003/693, SI 2003/1473, SI 2003/2066. SI 2003/2174; the Financial Services and Markets Act 2000 (EEA Passport Rights) Regulations 2001, SI 2001/2511, as amended by SI 2002/765, SI 2003/1473, SI 2003/2066, and modified by SI 2001/3084.

Orders: The Financial Services and Markets Act 2000 (Regulated Activities) Order 2001, SI 2001/544, as amended by SI 2001/3554, SI 2001/3771, SI 2002/682, SI 2002/1310, SI 2002/1776, SI 2002/1777, SI 2003/1475, SI 2003/1476; the Financial Services and Markets Act 2000 (Transitional Provisions and Savings) (Rules) Order 2001, SI 2001/1534; the Financial Services and Markets Act 2000 (Consequential and Transitional Provisions) (Miscellaneous) Order 2001, SI 2001/1821; the Financial Services and Markets Act 2000 (Transitional Provisions) (Ombudsman Scheme and Complaints Scheme) Order 2001, SI 2001/2326; the Financial Services and Markets Act 2000 (Transitional Provisions) (Reviews of Pensions Business) Order 2001, SI 2001/2512; the Financial Services and Markets Act 2000 (Mutual Societies) Order 2001, SI 2001/2617, as amended by SI 2001/3647, SI 2001/3649; the Financial Services and Markets Act 2000 (Transitional Provisions) (Authorised Persons etc) Order 2001, SI 2001/2636, as amended by SI 2001/3650; the Financial Services and Markets Act 2000 (Transitional Provisions) (Controllers) Order 2001, SI 2001/2637, as amended by SI 2001/3650; the Financial Services and Markets Act 2000 (Consequential and Transitional Provisions) (Miscellaneous) (No 2) Order 2001, SI 2001/2659, as amended by SI 2001/3083; the Financial Services and Markets Act 2000 (Official Listing of Securities) (Transitional Provisions) Order 2001, SI 2001/2957; the Financial Services and Markets Act 2000 (Consequential Amendments) (Pre-Commencement Modifications) Order 2001, SI 2001/2966; the Financial Services and Markets Act 2000 (Transitional Provisions, Repeals and Savings) (Financial Services Compensation Scheme) Order 2001, SI 2001/2967; the Financial Services and Markets Act 2000 (Transitional Provisions and Savings) (Civil Remedies, Discipline, Criminal Offences etc) (No 2) Order 2001, SI 2001/3083; the Financial Services and Markets Act 2000 (Interim Permissions) Order 2001, SI 2001/3374; the Financial Services and Markets Act 2000 (Dissolution of the Board of Banking Supervision) (Transitional Provisions) Order 2001, SI 2001/3582; the Financial Services and Markets Act 2000 (Transitional Provisions) (Partly Completed Procedures) Order 2001, SI 2001/3592; the Financial Services and Markets Act 2000 (Consequential Amendments) (Taxes) Order 2001, SI 2001/3629; the Financial Services and Markets Act 2000 (Transitional Provisions and Savings) (Business Transfers) Order 2001, SI 2001/3639; the Financial Services and Markets Act 2000 (Savings, Modifications and Consequential Provisions) (Rehabilitation of Offenders) (Scotland) Order 2001, SI 2001/3640; the Financial Services and Markets Act 2000 (Transitional Provisions and Savings) (Information Requirements and Investigations) Order 2001, SI 2001/3646; the Financial Services and Markets Act 2000 (Consequential Amendments and Savings) (Industrial Assurance) Order 2001, SI 2001/3647; the Financial Services and Markets Act 2000 (Confidential Information) (Bank of England) (Consequential Provisions) Order 2001, SI 2001/3648; the Financial Services and Markets Act 2000 (Miscellaneous Provisions) Order 2001, SI 2001/3650, as amended by SI 2001/3771, SI 2002/1777; the Financial Services and Markets Act 2000 (Scope of Permission Notices) Order 2001, SI 2001/3771; the Financial Services and Markets Act 2000 (Consequential Amendments) (No 2) Order 2001, SI 2001/3801; the Financial Services and Markets Act 2000 (Permission and Applications) (Credit Unions etc) Order 2002, SI 2002/704, as amended by SI 2002/1501; the Financial Services and Markets Act 2000 (Administration Orders Relating to Insurers) Order 2002, SI 2002/1242, as amended by SI 2003/2134; the Financial Services and Markets Act 2000 (Consequential Amendments) (Taxes)

Order 2002, SI 2002/1409; the Financial Services and Markets Act 2000 (Consequential Amendments and Transitional Provisions) (Credit Unions) Order 2002, SI 2002/1501; the Financial Services and Markets Act 2000 (Consequential Amendments) Order 2002, SI 2002/1555; the Financial Services and Markets Act 2000 (Collective Investment Schemes) (Designated Countries and Territories) Order 2003, SI 2003/1181; the Financial Services and Markets Act 2000 (Regulated Activities) (Amendment) (No 1) Order 2003, SI 2003/1475; the Financial Services and Markets Act 2000 (Regulated Activities) (Amendment) (No 2) Order 2003, SI 2003/1476.

427 Transitional provisions

(1)   Subsections (2) and (3) apply to an order under section 426 which makes transitional provisions or savings.

(2)   The order may, in particular—

    (a)   if it makes provision about the authorisation and permission of persons who before commencement were entitled to carry on any activities, also include provision for such persons not to be treated as having any authorisation or permission (whether on an application to the Authority or otherwise);

    (b)   make provision enabling the Authority to require persons of such descriptions as it may direct to re-apply for permissions having effect by virtue of the order;

    (c)   make provision for the continuation as rules of such provisions (including primary and subordinate legislation) as may be designated in accordance with the order by the Authority, including provision for the modification by the Authority of provisions designated;

    (d)   make provision about the effect of requirements imposed, liabilities incurred and any other things done before commencement, including provision for and about investigations, penalties and the taking or continuing of any other action in respect of contraventions;

    (e)   make provision for the continuation of disciplinary and other proceedings begun before commencement, including provision about the decisions available to bodies before which such proceedings take place and the effect of their decisions;

    (f)   make provision as regards the Authority's obligation to maintain a record under section 347 as respects persons in relation to whom provision is made by the order.

(3)   The order may—

    (a)   confer functions on the Treasury, the Secretary of State, the Authority, the scheme manager, the scheme operator, members of the panel established under paragraph 4 of Schedule 17, the Competition Commission or [the Office of Fair Trading];

    (b)   confer jurisdiction on the Tribunal;

    (c)   provide for fees to be charged in connection with the carrying out of functions conferred under the order;

    (d)   modify, exclude or apply (with or without modifications) any primary or subordinate legislation (including any provision of, or made under, this Act).

(4)   In subsection (2) "commencement" means the commencement of such provisions of this Act as may be specified by the order.

Commencement: 25 February 2001.
Amendments: Sub-s (3):words in square brackets substituted by the Enterprise Act 2002, s 278(1), Sch 25, para 40(1), (18), as from 1 April 2003.

428 Regulations and orders

(1)   Any power to make an order which is conferred on a Minister of the Crown by this Act and any power to make regulations which is conferred by this Act is exercisable by statutory instrument.

(2)   The Lord Chancellor's power to make rules under section 132 is exercisable by statutory instrument.

(3)   Any statutory instrument made under this Act may—
   (a)   contain such incidental, supplemental, consequential and transitional provision as the person making it considers appropriate; and
   (b)   make different provision for different cases.

Commencement: 14 June 2000.

429 Parliamentary control of statutory instruments

(1)   No order is to be made under—
   (a)   section 144(4), 192(b) or (e), 236(5), 404 or 419, or
   (b)   paragraph 1 of Schedule 8,

unless a draft of the order has been laid before Parliament and approved by a resolution of each House.

(2)   No regulations are to be made under section 262 unless a draft of the regulations has been laid before Parliament and approved by a resolution of each House.

(3)   An order to which, if it is made, subsection (4) or (5) will apply is not to be made unless a draft of the order has been laid before Parliament and approved by a resolution of each House.

(4)   This subsection applies to an order under section 21 if—
   (a)   it is the first order to be made, or to contain provisions made, under section 21(4);
   (b)   it varies an order made under section 21(4) so as to make section 21(1) apply in circumstances in which it did not previously apply;
   (c)   it is the first order to be made, or to contain provision made, under section 21(5);
   (d)   it varies a previous order made under section 21(5) so as to make section 21(1) apply in circumstances in which it did not, as a result of that previous order, apply;
   (e)   it is the first order to be made, or to contain provisions made, under section 21(9) or (10);
   (f)   it adds one or more activities to those that are controlled activities for the purposes of section 21; or
   (g)   it adds one or more investments to those which are controlled investments for the purposes of section 21.

(5) This subsection applies to an order under section 38 if—
  (a) it is the first order to be made, or to contain provisions made, under that section; or
  (b) it contains provisions restricting or removing an exemption provided by an earlier order made under that section.

(6) An order containing a provision to which, if the order is made, subsection (7) will apply is not to be made unless a draft of the order has been laid before Parliament and approved by a resolution of each House.

(7) This subsection applies to a provision contained in an order if—
  (a) it is the first to be made in the exercise of the power conferred by subsection (1) of section 326 or it removes a body from those for the time being designated under that subsection; or
  (b) it is the first to be made in the exercise of the power conferred by subsection (6) of section 327 or it adds a description of regulated activity or investment to those for the time being specified for the purposes of that subsection.

(8) Any other statutory instrument made under this Act, apart from one made under section 431(2) or to which paragraph 26 of Schedule 2 applies, shall be subject to annulment in pursuance of a resolution of either House of Parliament.

Commencement: 25 February 2001.
References: See paras 6.69, 6.70.

430 Extent

(1) This Act, except Chapter IV of Part XVII, extends to Northern Ireland.

(2) Except where Her Majesty by Order in Council provides otherwise, the extent of any amendment or repeal made by or under this Act is the same as the extent of the provision amended or repealed.

(3) Her Majesty may by Order in Council provide for any provision of or made under this Act relating to a matter which is the subject of other legislation which extends to any of the Channel Islands or the Isle of Man to extend there with such modifications (if any) as may be specified in the Order.

Commencement: 14 June 2000.

431 Commencement

(1) The following provisions come into force on the passing of this Act—
  (a) this section;
  (b) sections 428, 430 and 433;
  (c) paragraphs 1 and 2 of Schedule 21.

(2) The other provisions of this Act come into force on such day as the Treasury may by order appoint; and different days may be appointed for different purposes.

Commencement: 14 June 2000.
Orders: The Financial Services and Markets Act 2000 (Commencement No 1) Order 2001, SI 2001/516; the Financial Services and Markets Act 2000 (Commencement No 2) Order 2001, SI 2001/1282; the Financial Services and Markets Act 2000 (Commencement No 3) Order 2001, SI 2001/1820; the

Financial Services and Markets Act 2000 (Commencement No 4 and Transitional Provision) Order 2001, SI 2001/2364; the Financial Services and Markets Act 2000 (Commencement No 5) Order 2001, SI 2001/2632; the Financial Services and Markets Act 2000 (Commencement No 6) Order 2001, SI 2001/3436; the Financial Services and Markets Act 2000 (Commencement No 7) Order 2001, SI 2001/3538.

432 Minor and consequential amendments, transitional provisions and repeals

(1)   Schedule 20 makes minor and consequential amendments.

(2)   Schedule 21 makes transitional provisions.

(3)   The enactments set out in Schedule 22 are repealed.

Commencement: 3 September 2001 (for the purposes of introducing Sch 20 so far as brought into force by SI 2001/2632); 3 July 2001 (sub-s (1), for the purpose of introducing amendments to the Tribunals and Inquiries Act 1992); 30 April 2001 (sub-s (3), for the purpose of repealing the Insurance Brokers (Registration) Act 1977 (see Sch 22)); 1 December 2001 (remainder).

433 Short title

This Act may be cited as the Financial Services and Markets Act 2000.

Commencement: 14 June 2000.

SCHEDULES

SCHEDULE 1

Section 1

THE FINANCIAL SERVICES AUTHORITY

PART I
GENERAL

Interpretation

1.—(1)   In this Schedule—
"the 1985 Act" means the Companies Act 1985;
"non-executive committee" means the committee maintained under paragraph 3;
"functions", in relation to the Authority, means functions conferred on the Authority by or under any provision of this Act.

(2)   For the purposes of this Schedule, the following are the Authority's legislative functions—
(a)   making rules;
(b)   issuing codes under section 64 or 119;
(c)   issuing statements under section 64, 69, 124 or 210;
(d)   giving directions under section 316, 318 or 328;
(e)   issuing general guidance (as defined by section 158(5)).

Constitution

2.—(1)   The constitution of the Authority must continue to provide for the Authority to have—

(a)   a chairman; and

      (b)   a governing body.

(2)   The governing body must include the chairman.

(3)   The chairman and other members of the governing body must be appointed, and be liable to removal from office, by the Treasury.

(4)   The validity of any act of the Authority is not affected—
      (a)   by a vacancy in the office of chairman; or
      (b)   by a defect in the appointment of a person as a member of the governing body or as chairman.

Non-executive members of the governing body

3.—(1)   The Authority must secure—
      (a)   that the majority of the members of its governing body are non-executive members; and
      (b)   that a committee of its governing body, consisting solely of the non-executive members, is set up and maintained for the purposes of discharging the functions conferred on the committee by this Schedule.

(2)   The members of the non-executive committee are to be appointed by the Authority.

(3)   The non-executive committee is to have a chairman appointed by the Treasury from among its members.

Functions of the non-executive committee

4.—(1)   In this paragraph "the committee" means the non-executive committee.

(2)   The non-executive functions are functions of the Authority but must be discharged by the committee.

(3)   The non-executive functions are—
      (a)   keeping under review the question whether the Authority is, in discharging its functions in accordance with decisions of its governing body, using its resources in the most efficient and economic way;
      (b)   keeping under review the question whether the Authority's internal financial controls secure the proper conduct of its financial affairs; and
      (c)   determining the remuneration of—
         (i)   the chairman of the Authority's governing body; and
        (ii)   the executive members of that body.

(4)   The function mentioned in sub-paragraph (3)(b) and those mentioned in sub-paragraph (3)(c) may be discharged on behalf of the committee by a sub-committee.

(5)   Any sub-committee of the committee—
      (a)   must have as its chairman the chairman of the committee; but
      (b)   may include persons other than members of the committee.

(6)   The committee must prepare a report on the discharge of its functions for inclusion in the Authority's annual report to the Treasury under paragraph 10.

(7)   The committee's report must relate to the same period as that covered by the Authority's report.

Arrangements for discharging functions

5.—(1)   The Authority may make arrangements for any of its functions to be discharged by a committee, sub-committee, officer or member of staff of the Authority.

(2)   But in exercising its legislative functions, the Authority must act through its governing body.

(3)   Sub-paragraph (1) does not apply to the non-executive functions.

Monitoring and enforcement

6.—(1)   The Authority must maintain arrangements designed to enable it to determine whether persons on whom requirements are imposed by or under this Act are complying with them.

(2)   Those arrangements may provide for functions to be performed on behalf of the Authority by any body or person who, in its opinion, is competent to perform them.

(3)   The Authority must also maintain arrangements for enforcing the provisions of, or made under, this Act.

(4)   Sub-paragraph (2) does not affect the Authority's duty under sub-paragraph (1).

Arrangements for the investigation of complaints

7.—(1)   The Authority must—
    (a)   make arrangements ("the complaints scheme") for the investigation of complaints arising in connection with the exercise of, or failure to exercise, any of its functions (other than its legislative functions); and
    (b)   appoint an independent person ("the investigator") to be responsible for the conduct of investigations in accordance with the complaints scheme.

(2)   The complaints scheme must be designed so that, as far as reasonably practicable, complaints are investigated quickly.

(3)   The Treasury's approval is required for the appointment or dismissal of the investigator.

(4)   The terms and conditions on which the investigator is appointed must be such as, in the opinion of the Authority, are reasonably designed to secure—
    (a)   that he will be free at all times to act independently of the Authority; and
    (b)   that complaints will be investigated under the complaints scheme without favouring the Authority.

(5)   Before making the complaints scheme, the Authority must publish a draft of the proposed scheme in the way appearing to the Authority best calculated to bring it to the attention of the public.

(6)   The draft must be accompanied by notice that representations about it may be made to the Authority within a specified time.

(7)   Before making the proposed complaints scheme, the Authority must have regard to any representations made to it in accordance with sub-paragraph (6).

(8)   If the Authority makes the proposed complaints scheme, it must publish an account, in general terms, of—
    (a)   the representations made to it in accordance with sub-paragraph (6); and
    (b)   its response to them.

(9)   If the complaints scheme differs from the draft published under sub-paragraph (5) in a way which is, in the opinion of the Authority, significant the Authority must (in addition to complying with sub-paragraph (8)) publish details of the difference.

(10)   The Authority must publish up-to-date details of the complaints scheme including, in particular, details of—
    (a)   the provision made under paragraph 8(5); and
    (b)   the powers which the investigator has to investigate a complaint.

(11)   Those details must be published in the way appearing to the Authority to be best calculated to bring them to the attention of the public.

(12)   The Authority must, without delay, give the Treasury a copy of any details published by it under this paragraph.

(13)   The Authority may charge a reasonable fee for providing a person with a copy of—
    (a)   a draft published under sub-paragraph (5);
    (b)   details published under sub-paragraph (10).

(14) Sub-paragraphs (5) to (9) and (13)(a) also apply to a proposal to alter or replace the complaints scheme.

Investigation of complaints

8.—(1)   The Authority is not obliged to investigate a complaint in accordance with the complaints scheme which it reasonably considers would be more appropriately dealt with in another way (for example by referring the matter to the Tribunal or by the institution of other legal proceedings).

(2)   The complaints scheme must provide—
- (a)   for reference to the investigator of any complaint which the Authority is investigating; and
- (b)   for him—
  - (i)   to have the means to conduct a full investigation of the complaint;
  - (ii)   to report on the result of his investigation to the Authority and the complainant; and
  - (iii)   to be able to publish his report (or any part of it) if he considers that it (or the part) ought to be brought to the attention of the public.

(3)   If the Authority has decided not to investigate a complaint, it must notify the investigator.

(4)   If the investigator considers that a complaint of which he has been notified under sub-paragraph (3) ought to be investigated, he may proceed as if the complaint had been referred to him under the complaints scheme.

(5)   The complaints scheme must confer on the investigator the power to recommend, if he thinks it appropriate, that the Authority—
- (a)   makes a compensatory payment to the complainant,
- (b)   remedies the matter complained of,

or takes both of those steps.

(6)   The complaints scheme must require the Authority, in a case where the investigator—
- (a)   has reported that a complaint is well-founded, or
- (b)   has criticised the Authority in his report,

to inform the investigator and the complainant of the steps which it proposes to take in response to the report.

(7)   The investigator may require the Authority to publish the whole or a specified part of the response.

(8)   The investigator may appoint a person to conduct the investigation on his behalf but subject to his direction.

(9)   Neither an officer nor an employee of the Authority may be appointed under sub-paragraph (8).

(10) Sub-paragraph (2) is not to be taken as preventing the Authority from making arrangements for the initial investigation of a complaint to be conducted by the Authority.

Records

9. The Authority must maintain satisfactory arrangements for—
- (a)   recording decisions made in the exercise of its functions; and
- (b)   the safe-keeping of those records which it considers ought to be preserved.

Annual report

10.—(1)   At least once a year the Authority must make a report to the Treasury on—
- (a)   the discharge of its functions;
- (b)   the extent to which, in its opinion, the regulatory objectives have been met;
- (c)   its consideration of the matters mentioned in section 2(3); and
- (d)   such other matters as the Treasury may from time to time direct.

(2)   The report must be accompanied by—
>   (a)   the report prepared by the non-executive committee under paragraph 4(6); and
>   (b)   such other reports or information, prepared by such persons, as the Treasury may from time to time direct.

(3)   The Treasury must lay before Parliament a copy of each report received by them under this paragraph.

(4)   The Treasury may—
>   (a)   require the Authority to comply with any provisions of the 1985 Act about accounts and their audit which would not otherwise apply to it; or
>   (b)   direct that any such provision of that Act is to apply to the Authority with such modifications as are specified in the direction.

(5)   Compliance with any requirement imposed under sub-paragraph (4)(a) or (b) is enforceable by injunction or, in Scotland, an order under section 45(b) of the Court of Session Act 1988.

(6)   Proceedings under sub-paragraph (5) may be brought only by the Treasury.

Annual public meeting

11.—(1)   Not later than three months after making a report under paragraph 10, the Authority must hold a public meeting ("the annual meeting") for the purposes of enabling that report to be considered.

(2)   The Authority must organise the annual meeting so as to allow—
>   (a)   a general discussion of the contents of the report which is being considered; and
>   (b)   a reasonable opportunity for those attending the meeting to put questions to the Authority about the way in which it discharged, or failed to discharge, its functions during the period to which the report relates.

(3)   But otherwise the annual meeting is to be organised and conducted in such a way as the Authority considers appropriate.

(4)   The Authority must give reasonable notice of its annual meeting.

(5)   That notice must—
>   (a)   give details of the time and place at which the meeting is to be held;
>   (b)   set out the proposed agenda for the meeting;
>   (c)   indicate the proposed duration of the meeting;
>   (d)   give details of the Authority's arrangements for enabling persons to attend; and
>   (e)   be published by the Authority in the way appearing to it to be most suitable for bringing the notice to the attention of the public.

(6)   If the Authority proposes to alter any of the arrangements which have been included in the notice given under sub-paragraph (4) it must—
>   (a)   give reasonable notice of the alteration; and
>   (b)   publish that notice in the way appearing to the Authority to be best calculated to bring it to the attention of the public.

Report of annual meeting

12.   Not later than one month after its annual meeting, the Authority must publish a report of the proceedings of the meeting.

Commencement: 19 July 2001 (paras 7, 8, for the purpose of enabling the Authority to make the complaints scheme and appoint the investigator); 3 September 2001 (paras 7, 8, remaining purposes); 18 June 2001 (remainder).
Authority's functions: The reference to the Authority's functions includes its functions as a designated agency under the Financial Services Act 1986 (repealed by the Financial Services and Markets Act 2000 (Consequential Amendments and Repeals) Order 2001, SI 2001/3649, art 3(1)(c) (made under ss 426,

427 ante)) and the reference to the Authority's legislative functions includes its functions of issuing statements of principle, rules, regulations and codes of practice under that Act; see the Financial Services and Markets Act 2000 (Consequential and Transitional Provisions) (Miscellaneous) Order 2001, SI 2001/1821, art 2(1)(b), (c) (made under ss 426–428 ante).
References: See paras 2.9–2.30.

PART II
STATUS

13. In relation to any of its functions—
    (a)the Authority is not to be regarded as acting on behalf of the Crown; and
    (b)its members, officers and staff are not to be regarded as Crown servants.

Exemption from requirement of "limited" in Authority's name

14. The Authority is to continue to be exempt from the requirements of the 1985 Act relating to the use of "limited" as part of its name.

15. If the Secretary of State is satisfied that any action taken by the Authority makes it inappropriate for the exemption given by paragraph 14 to continue he may, after consulting the Treasury, give a direction removing it.

Commencement: 18 June 2001.
Authority's functions: The reference to the Authority's functions includes its functions as a designated agency under the Financial Services Act 1986 (repealed by the Financial Services and Markets Act 2000 (Consequential Amendments and Repeals) Order 2001, SI 2001/3649, art 3(1)(c) (made under ss 426, 427 ante)) and the reference to the Authority's legislative functions includes its functions of issuing statements of principle, rules, regulations and codes of practice under that Act; see the Financial Services and Markets Act 2000 (Consequential and Transitional Provisions) (Miscellaneous) Order 2001, SI 2001/1821, art 2(1)(b), (c) (made under ss 426–428 ante).
References: See paras 2.85, 2.86.

PART III
PENALTIES AND FEES

Penalties

16.—(1) In determining its policy with respect to the amounts of penalties to be imposed by it under this Act, the Authority must take no account of the expenses which it incurs, or expects to incur, in discharging its functions.

(2) The Authority must prepare and operate a scheme for ensuring that the amounts paid to the Authority by way of penalties imposed under this Act are applied for the benefit of authorised persons.

(3) The scheme may, in particular, make different provision with respect to different classes of authorised person.

(4) Up to date details of the scheme must be set out in a document ("the scheme details").

(5) The scheme details must be published by the Authority in the way appearing to it to be best calculated to bring them to the attention of the public.

(6) Before making the scheme, the Authority must publish a draft of the proposed scheme in the way appearing to the Authority to be best calculated to bring it to the attention of the public.

(7) The draft must be accompanied by notice that representations about the proposals may be made to the Authority within a specified time.

(8) Before making the scheme, the Authority must have regard to any representations made to it in accordance with sub-paragraph (7).

(9)   If the Authority makes the proposed scheme, it must publish an account, in general terms, of—

(a)   the representations made to it in accordance with sub-paragraph (7); and

(b)   its response to them.

(10)   If the scheme differs from the draft published under sub-paragraph (6) in a way which is, in the opinion of the Authority, significant the Authority must (in addition to complying with sub-paragraph (9)) publish details of the difference.

(11)   The Authority must, without delay, give the Treasury a copy of any scheme details published by it.

(12)   The Authority may charge a reasonable fee for providing a person with a copy of—

(a)   a draft published under sub-paragraph (6);

(b)   scheme details.

(13)   Sub-paragraphs (6) to (10) and (12)(a) also apply to a proposal to alter or replace the complaints scheme.

Fees

17.—(1)   The Authority may make rules providing for the payment to it of such fees, in connection with the discharge of any of its functions under or as a result of this Act, as it considers will (taking account of its expected income from fees and charges provided for by any other provision of this Act) enable it—

(a)   to meet expenses incurred in carrying out its functions or for any incidental purpose;

(b)   to repay the principal of, and pay any interest on, any money which it has borrowed and which has been used for the purpose of meeting expenses incurred in relation to its assumption of functions under this Act or the Bank of England Act 1998; and

(c)   to maintain adequate reserves.

(2)   In fixing the amount of any fee which is to be payable to the Authority, no account is to be taken of any sums which the Authority receives, or expects to receive, by way of penalties imposed by it under this Act.

(3)   Sub-paragraph (1)(b) applies whether expenses were incurred before or after the coming into force of this Act or the Bank of England Act 1998.

(4)   Any fee which is owed to the Authority under any provision made by or under this Act may be recovered as a debt due to the Authority.

Services for which fees may not be charged

18.   The power conferred by paragraph 17 may not be used to require—

(a)   a fee to be paid in respect of the discharge of any of the Authority's functions under paragraphs 13, 14, 19 or 20 of Schedule 3; or

(b)   a fee to be paid by any person whose application for approval under section 59 has been granted.

Commencement: 18 June 2001.

Authority's functions: The reference to the Authority's functions includes its functions as a designated agency under the Financial Services Act 1986 (repealed by the Financial Services and Markets Act 2000 (Consequential Amendments and Repeals) Order 2001, SI 2001/3649, art 3(1)(c) (made under ss 426, 427 ante)) and the reference to the Authority's legislative functions includes its functions of issuing statements of principle, rules, regulations and codes of practice under that Act; see the Financial Services and Markets Act 2000 (Consequential and Transitional Provisions) (Miscellaneous) Order 2001, SI 2001/1821, art 2(1)(b), (c) (made under ss 426–428 ante).

PART IV
MISCELLANEOUS

Exemption from liability in damages

19.—(1)   Neither the Authority nor any person who is, or is acting as, a member, officer or member of staff of the Authority is to be liable in damages for anything done or omitted in the discharge, or purported discharge, of the Authority's functions.

(2)   Neither the investigator appointed under paragraph 7 nor a person appointed to conduct an investigation on his behalf under paragraph 8(8) is to be liable in damages for anything done or omitted in the discharge, or purported discharge, of his functions in relation to the investigation of a complaint.

(3)   Neither sub-paragraph (1) nor sub-paragraph (2) applies—

    (a)   if the act or omission is shown to have been in bad faith; or
    (b)   so as to prevent an award of damages made in respect of an act or omission on the ground that the act or omission was unlawful as a result of section 6(1) of the Human Rights Act 1998.

[19A.   For the purposes of this Act anything done by an accredited financial investigator within the meaning of the Proceeds of Crime Act 2002 who is—

    (a)   a member of the staff of the Authority, or
    (b)   a person appointed by the Authority under section 97, 167 or 168 to conduct an investigation,

must be treated as done in the exercise or discharge of a function of the Authority.]

20, 21 . . .

Commencement: 18 June 2001.
Amendments: Para 19A: inserted by the Proceeds of Crime Act 2002, s 456, Sch 11, para 38, as from 24 February 2003.
Para 20: amends the House of Commons Disqualification Act 1975, Sch 1, Pt III.
Para 21: amends the Northern Ireland Assembly Disqualification Act 1975, Sch 1, Pt III.
Authority's functions: The reference to the Authority's functions includes its functions as a designated agency under the Financial Services Act 1986 (repealed by the Financial Services and Markets Act 2000 (Consequential Amendments and Repeals) Order 2001, SI 2001/3649, art 3(1)(c) (made under ss 426, 427 ante)) and the reference to the Authority's legislative functions includes its functions of issuing statements of principle, rules, regulations and codes of practice under that Act; see the Financial Services and Markets Act 2000 (Consequential and Transitional Provisions) (Miscellaneous) Order 2001, SI 2001/1821, art 2(1)(b), (c) (made under ss 426–428 ante).

SCHEDULE 2

Section 22(2)

REGULATED ACTIVITIES

Regulated activities: The regulated activities for the purposes of s 22 of this Act are set out in the Financial Services and Markets Act 2000 (Regulated Activities) Order 2001, SI 2001/544, as amended by SI 2001/3554, SI 2002/682, SI 2002/1310.

PART I
REGULATED ACTIVITIES

General

1.   The matters with respect to which provision may be made under section 22(1) in respect of activities include, in particular, those described in general terms in this Part of this Schedule.

Dealing in investments

2.—(1)   Buying, selling, subscribing for or underwriting investments or offering or agreeing to do so, either as a principal or as an agent.

(2)   In the case of an investment which is a contract of insurance, that includes carrying out the contract.

Arranging deals in investments

3. Making, or offering or agreeing to make—
> (a)   arrangements with a view to another person buying, selling, subscribing for or underwriting a particular investment;
> (b)   arrangements with a view to a person who participates in the arrangements buying, selling, subscribing for or underwriting investments.

Deposit taking

4. Accepting deposits.

Safekeeping and administration of assets

5.—(1)   Safeguarding and administering assets belonging to another which consist of or include investments or offering or agreeing to do so.

(2)   Arranging for the safeguarding and administration of assets belonging to another, or offering or agreeing to do so.

Managing investments

6. Managing, or offering or agreeing to manage, assets belonging to another person where—
> (a)   the assets consist of or include investments; or
> (b)   the arrangements for their management are such that the assets may consist of or include investments at the discretion of the person managing or offering or agreeing to manage them.

Investment advice

7. Giving or offering or agreeing to give advice to persons on—
> (a)   buying, selling, subscribing for or underwriting an investment; or
> (b)   exercising any right conferred by an investment to acquire, dispose of, underwrite or convert an investment.

Establishing collective investment schemes

8. Establishing, operating or winding up a collective investment scheme, including acting as—
> (a)   trustee of a unit trust scheme;
> (b)   depositary of a collective investment scheme other than a unit trust scheme; or
> (c)   sole director of a body incorporated by virtue of regulations under section 262.

Using computer-based systems for giving investment instructions

9.—(1)   Sending on behalf of another person instructions relating to an investment by means of a computer-based system which enables investments to be transferred without a written instrument.

(2)   Offering or agreeing to send such instructions by such means on behalf of another person.

(3)   Causing such instructions to be sent by such means on behalf of another person.

(4)   Offering or agreeing to cause such instructions to be sent by such means on behalf of another person.

Commencement: 25 February 2001.
References: See para 3.7.

PART II
INVESTMENTS

General

10. The matters with respect to which provision may be made under section 22(1) in respect of investments include, in particular, those described in general terms in this Part of this Schedule.

Securities

11.—(1)   Shares or stock in the share capital of a company.

  (2)   "Company" includes—
      (a)   any body corporate (wherever incorporated), and
      (b)   any unincorporated body constituted under the law of a country or territory outside the United Kingdom,
other than an open-ended investment company.

Instruments creating or acknowledging indebtedness

12.   Any of the following—
      (a)debentures;
      (b)debenture stock;
      (c)   loan stock;
      (d)   bonds;
      (e)   certificates of deposit;
      (f)   any other instruments creating or acknowledging a present or future indebtedness.

Government and public securities

13.—(1)   Loan stock, bonds and other instruments—
      (a)   creating or acknowledging indebtedness; and
      (b)   issued by or on behalf of a government, local authority or public authority.

  (2)   "Government, local authority or public authority" means—
      (a)   the government of the United Kingdom, of Northern Ireland, or of any country or territory outside the United Kingdom;
      (b)   a local authority in the United Kingdom or elsewhere;
      (c)   any international organisation the members of which include the United Kingdom or another member State.

Instruments giving entitlement to investments

14.—(1)   Warrants or other instruments entitling the holder to subscribe for any investment.

  (2)   It is immaterial whether the investment is in existence or identifiable.

Certificates representing securities

15.   Certificates or other instruments which confer contractual or property rights—
      (a)   in respect of any investment held by someone other than the person on whom the rights are conferred by the certificate or other instrument; and
      (b)   the transfer of which may be effected without requiring the consent of that person.

Units in collective investment schemes

16.—(1)   Shares in or securities of an open-ended investment company.

(2)   Any right to participate in a collective investment scheme.

Options

17. Options to acquire or dispose of property.

Futures

18. Rights under a contract for the sale of a commodity or property of any other description under which delivery is to be made at a future date.

Contracts for differences

19. Rights under—
(a) a contract for differences; or
(b) any other contract the purpose or pretended purpose of which is to secure a profit or avoid a loss by reference to fluctuations in—
(i)   the value or price of property of any description; or
(ii) an index or other factor designated for that purpose in the contract.

Contracts of insurance

20. Rights under a contract of insurance, including rights under contracts falling within head C of Schedule 2 to the Friendly Societies Act 1992.

Participation in Lloyd's syndicates

21.—(1)   The underwriting capacity of a Lloyd's syndicate.

(2)   A person's membership (or prospective membership) of a Lloyd's syndicate.

Deposits

22. Rights under any contract under which a sum of money (whether or not denominated in a currency) is paid on terms under which it will be repaid, with or without interest or a premium, and either on demand or at a time or in circumstances agreed by or on behalf of the person making the payment and the person receiving it.

Loans secured on land

23.—(1)   Rights under any contract under which—
(a)   one person provides another with credit; and
(b)   the obligation of the borrower to repay is secured on land.

(2)   "Credit" includes any cash loan or other financial accommodation.

(3)   "Cash" includes money in any form.

Rights in investments

24. Any right or interest in anything which is an investment as a result of any other provision made under section 22(1).

Commencement: 25 February 2001.
Modifications to para 12(e): (i) A reference to a certificate of deposit includes a reference to uncertificated units of an eligible debt security where the issue of those units corresponds, in accordance with the current terms of issue of the security, to the issue of a certificate of deposit which is a certificate of deposit for the purposes of that enactment; (ii) a reference to an amount stated in a certificate of deposit includes a reference to a principal amount stated in, or determined in accordance with, the current terms of issue of an eligible debt security of the kind referred to in (i) above; see the Uncertificated Securities (Amendment) (Eligible Debt Securities) Regulations 2003, SI 2003/1633, reg 15, Sch 2, para 6.

Modifications to para 12(f): The reference to securities, instruments or investments creating or acknowledging indebtedness (or creating or acknowledging a present or future indebtedness) includes a reference to uncertificated units of eligible debt securities; see the Uncertificated Securities (Amendment) (Eligible Debt Securities) Regulations 2003, SI 2003/1633, reg 15, Sch 2, para 8.

PART III
SUPPLEMENTAL PROVISIONS

The order-making power

25.—(1) An order under section 22(1) may—
- (a) provide for exemptions;
- (b) confer powers on the Treasury or the Authority;
- (c) authorise the making of regulations or other instruments by the Treasury for purposes of, or connected with, any relevant provision;
- (d) authorise the making of rules or other instruments by the Authority for purposes of, or connected with, any relevant provision;
- (e) make provision in respect of any information or document which, in the opinion of the Treasury or the Authority, is relevant for purposes of, or connected with, any relevant provision;
- (f) make such consequential, transitional or supplemental provision as the Treasury consider appropriate for purposes of, or connected with, any relevant provision.

(2) Provision made as a result of sub-paragraph (1)(f) may amend any primary or subordinate legislation, including any provision of, or made under, this Act.

(3) "Relevant provision" means any provision—
- (a) of section 22 or this Schedule; or
- (b) made under that section or this Schedule.

Parliamentary control

26.—(1) This paragraph applies to the first order made under section 22(1).

(2) This paragraph also applies to any subsequent order made under section 22(1) which contains a statement by the Treasury that, in their opinion, the effect (or one of the effects) of the proposed order would be that an activity which is not a regulated activity would become a regulated activity.

(3) An order to which this paragraph applies—
- (a) must be laid before Parliament after being made; and
- (b) ceases to have effect at the end of the relevant period unless before the end of that period the order is approved by a resolution of each House of Parliament (but without that affecting anything done under the order or the power to make a new order).

(4) "Relevant period" means a period of twenty-eight days beginning with the day on which the order is made.

(5) In calculating the relevant period no account is to be taken of any time during which Parliament is dissolved or prorogued or during which both Houses are adjourned for more than four days.

Interpretation

27.—(1) In this Schedule—
　"buying" includes acquiring for valuable consideration;
　"offering" includes inviting to treat;
　"property" includes currency of the United Kingdom or any other country or territory; and
　"selling" includes disposing for valuable consideration.

(2) In sub-paragraph (1) "disposing" includes—
    (a) in the case of an investment consisting of rights under a contract—
        (i) surrendering, assigning or converting those rights; or
        (ii) assuming the corresponding liabilities under the contract;
    (b) in the case of an investment consisting of rights under other arrangements, assuming the corresponding liabilities under the contract or arrangements;
    (c) in the case of any other investment, issuing or creating the investment or granting the rights or interests of which it consists.

(3) In this Schedule references to an instrument include references to any record (whether or not in the form of a document).

Commencement: 25 February 2001.
Orders: The Financial Services and Markets Act 2000 (Miscellaneous Provisions) Order 2001, SI 2001/3650, as amended by SI 2001/3771.
References: See paras 3.9–3.16.

SCHEDULE 3

Sections 31(1)(b) and 37

EEA PASSPORT RIGHTS ·

Transitional provisions: The Financial Services and Markets Act 2000 (Transitional Provisions) (Authorised Persons etc) Order 2001, SI 2001/2636, Pt II, Ch II (made under ss 426–428 ante), provides that EEA firms with "passports" before 1 December 2001 under the Insurance Companies Act 1982, the Banking Coordination (Second Council Directive) Regulations 1992, SI 1992/3218, or the Investment Services Regulations 1995, SI 1995/3275, are to be treated after that date as having complied with the procedures in this Schedule. In relation to UK firms with "passports" before 1 December 2001, see art 77 of the 2001 Order. The 1982 Act is repealed, and SI 1992/3218 and SI 1995/3275 are revoked, by the Financial Services and Markets Act 2000 (Consequential Amendments and Repeals) Order 2001, SI 2001/3649, art 3(1)(b), (2)(a), (c) (made under ss 426, 427 ante).

PART I
DEFINED TERMS

The single market directives

1. "The single market directives" means—
    [(a) the banking consolidation directive;]
    (c) the insurance directives; *and*
    (d) the investment services directive[; *and*
    (e) the insurance mediation directive][; and
    (f) the UCITS directive.]

The banking [consolidation directive]

[2. "The banking consolidation directive" means Directive 2000/12/EC of the European Parliament and of the Council of 20 March 2000 relating to the taking up and pursuit of the business of credit institutions.]

The insurance directives

3.—(1) "The insurance directives" means the first, second and third non-life insurance directives and the first, second and third life insurance directives.

(2) "First non-life insurance directive" means the Council Directive of 24 July 1973 on the co-ordination of laws, regulations and administrative provisions relating to the taking up and pursuit of the business of direct insurance other than life assurance (No 73/239/EEC).

(3) "Second non-life insurance directive" means the Council Directive of 22 June 1988 on the co-ordination of laws, etc, and laying down provisions to facilitate the effective exercise of freedom to provide services and amending Directive 73/239/EEC (No 88/357/EEC).

(4) "Third non-life insurance directive" means the Council Directive of 18 June 1992 on the co-ordination of laws, etc, and amending Directives 73/239/EEC and 88/357/EEC (No 92/49/EEC).

(5) "First life insurance directive" means the Council Directive of 5 March 1979 on the co-ordination of laws, regulations and administrative provisions relating to the taking up and pursuit of the business of direct life assurance (No 79/267/EEC).

(6) "Second life insurance directive" means the Council Directive of 8 November 1990 on the co-ordination of laws, etc, and laying down provisions to facilitate the effective exercise of freedom to provide services and amending Directive 79/267/EEC (No 90/619/EEC).

(7) "Third life insurance directive" means the Council Directive of 10 November 1992 on the co-ordination of laws, etc, and amending Directives 79/267/EEC and 90/619/EEC (No 92/96/EEC).

The investment services directive

4. "The investment services directive" means the Council Directive of 10 May 1993 on investment services in the securities field (No 93/22/EEC).

[The insurance mediation directive

4A. "The insurance mediation directive" means the European Parliament and Council Directive of 9th December 2002 on insurance mediation (No 2002/92/EC).]

[The UCITS directive

4B. "The UCITS directive" means the Council Directive of 20 December 1985 on the coordination of laws, regulations and administrative provisions relating to undertakings for collective investment in transferable securities (No 85/611/EEC).]

EEA firm

5. "EEA firm" means any of the following if it does not have its *head office* in the United Kingdom—

    (a)   an investment firm (as defined in Article 1.2 of the investment services directive) which is authorised (within the meaning of Article 3) by its home state regulator;

    [(b)   a credit institution (as defined in Article 1 of the banking consolidation directive) which is authorised (within the meaning of Article 1) by its home state regulator;

    (c)   a financial institution (as defined in Article 1 of the banking consolidation directive) which is a subsidiary of the kind mentioned in Article 19 and which fulfils the conditions in Articles 18 and 19; or]

    (d)   an undertaking pursuing the activity of direct insurance (within the meaning of Article 1 of the first life insurance directive or of the first non-life insurance directive) which has received authorisation under Article 6 from its home state regulator[; or

    (e)   an insurance intermediary (as defined in Article 2.5 of the insurance mediation directive), or a reinsurance intermediary (as defined in Article 2.6) which is registered with its home state regulator under Article 3][; or

    (f)   a management company (as defined in Article 1a.2 of the UCITS directive) which is authorised (within the meaning of Article 5) by its home state regulator.]

[5A. In paragraph 5, "relevant office" means—
    (a)   in relation to a firm falling within sub-paragraph (e) of that paragraph which has a registered office, its registered office;
    (b)   in relation to any other firm, its head office.]

EEA authorisation

6. "EEA authorisation" means authorisation granted to an EEA firm by its home state regulator for the purpose of the relevant single market directive.

EEA right

7. "EEA right" means the entitlement of a person to establish a branch, or provide services, in an EEA State other than that in which he has his *head office*—
    (a)   in accordance with the Treaty as applied in the EEA; and
    (b)   subject to the conditions of the relevant single market directive.

[7A. In paragraph 7, "relevant office" means—
    (a)   in relation to a person who has a registered office and whose entitlement is subject to the conditions of the insurance mediation directive, his registered office;
    (b)   in relation to any other person, his head office.]

EEA State

8. "EEA State" means a State which is a contracting party to the agreement on the European Economic Area signed at Oporto on 2 May 1992 as it has effect for the time being.

Home state regulator

9. "Home state regulator" means the competent authority (within the meaning of the relevant single market directive) of an EEA State (other than the United Kingdom) in relation to the EEA firm concerned.

UK firm

10. "UK firm" means a person whose *head office* is in the UK and who has an EEA right to carry on activity in an EEA State other than the United Kingdom.

[10A.In paragraph 10, "relevant office" means—
    (a)   in relation to a firm whose EEA right derives from the insurance mediation directive and which has a registered office, its registered office;
    (b)   in relation to any other firm, its head office.]

11. "Host state regulator" means the competent authority (within the meaning of the relevant single market directive) of an EEA State (other than the United Kingdom) in relation to a UK firm's exercise of EEA rights there.

Commencement: 25 February 2001 (for the purpose of making orders or regulations); 18 June 2001 (for the purposes of making rules); 1 December 2001 (remaining purposes).
Amendments: Para 1: sub-para (a) substituted, for original sub-paras (a), (b), by the Banking Consolidation Directive (Consequential Amendments) Regulations 2000, SI 2000/2952, reg 8(1), (5)(a); word in italics in sub-para (c) repealed, and sub-para (e) and the word immediately preceding it inserted, by the Insurance Mediation Directive (Miscellaneous Amendments) Regulations 2003, SI 2003/1473, reg 2(2)(a), as from 14 January 2005; word in italics in sub-para (d) repealed, and sub-para (f) and the word immediately preceding it inserted, by the Collective Investment Schemes (Miscellaneous Amendments) Regulations 2003, SI 2003/2066, reg 2(2)(a), as from 13 February 2004.
Para 2: words in square brackets in cross-heading substituted by virtue of, and para 2 substituted by, SI 2000/2952, reg 8(1), (5)(b).
Paras 4A, 5A, 7A, 10A: inserted by SI 2003/1473, reg 2(2)(b), (d), (g), (i), as from 14 January 2005.
Para 4B: inserted by SI 2003/2066, reg 2(2)(b), as from 13 February 2004.
Para 5: sub-paras (b), (c) substituted by SI 2000/2952, reg 8(1), (5)(c); for the first words in italics there are substituted the words "relevant office", the word in italics in sub-para (c) is repealed, and sub-para (e) and the word immediately preceding it is inserted, by SI 2003/1473, reg 2(2)(c), as from

14 January 2005; word in italics in sub-para (d) repealed, and sub-para (f) and the word immediately preceding it inserted, by SI 2003/2066, reg 2(2)(c), as from 13 February 2004.
Para 6: substituted by SI 2003/1473, reg 2(2)(e), as from 14 January 2005, as follows—

"6.   "EEA authorisation" means—
    (a)   in relation to an EEA firm falling within paragraph 5(e), registration with its home state regulator under Article 3 of the insurance mediation directive;
    (b)   in relation to any other EEA firm, authorisation granted to an EEA firm by its home state regulator for the purpose of the relevant single market directive.".

Paras 7, 10: for the words in italics there are substituted the words "relevant office" by SI 2003/1473, reg 2(2)(f), (h), as from 14 January 2005.
Directive 2000/12/EC of the European Parliament and of the Council: OJ L126, 26.5.2000, p 1.
Council Directive 73/239/EEC: OJ L228, 16.8.1973, p 3.
Council Directive 88/357/EEC: OJ L172, 4.7.1988, p 1.
Council Directive 92/49/EEC: OJ L228,11.8.1992, p 1.
Council Directive 79/267/EEC: OJ L63, 13.3.1979, p 1.
Council Directive 90/619/EEC: OJ L330, 29.11.1990, p 50.
Council Directive 92/96/EEC: OJ L360, 9.12.1992, p 1.
Council Directive 93/22/EEC: OJ L141, 11.6.1993, p 27.
References: See paras 3.43, 4.3, 4.7, 4.41, 8.51, 8.52, 8.57, 8.58, 22.25.

PART II
EXERCISE OF PASSPORT RIGHTS BY EEA FIRMS

Firms qualifying for authorisation

12.—(1)   Once an EEA firm which is seeking to establish a branch in the United Kingdom in exercise of an EEA right satisfies the establishment conditions, it qualifies for authorisation.

(2)   Once an EEA firm which is seeking to provide services in the United Kingdom in exercise of an EEA right satisfies the service conditions, it qualifies for authorisation.

Establishment

13.—(1)   [If the firm falls within paragraph 5(a), (b), *(c)* or *(d)*,] The establishment conditions are that—
    (a)   the Authority has received notice ("a consent notice") from the firm's home state regulator that it has given the firm consent to establish a branch in the United Kingdom;
    (b)   the consent notice—
        (i)   is given in accordance with the relevant single market directive;
        (ii)   identifies the activities to which consent relates; and
        (iii)   includes such other information as may be prescribed; and
    (c)   the firm has been informed of the applicable provisions or two months have elapsed beginning with the date when the Authority received the consent notice.

[(1A)   If the firm falls within paragraph 5(e), the establishment conditions are that—
    (a)   the firm has given its home state regulator notice of its intention to establish a branch in the United Kingdom;
    (b)   the Authority has received notice ("a regulator's notice") from the firm's home state regulator that the firm intends to establish a branch in the United Kingdom;
    (c)   the firm's home state regulator has informed the firm that the regulator's notice has been sent to the Authority; and
    (d)   one month has elapsed beginning with the date on which the firm's home state regulator informed the firm that the regulator's notice has been sent to the Authority.]

(2)   If the Authority has received a consent notice, it must—
    (a)   prepare for the firm's supervision;
    (b)   notify the firm of the applicable provisions (if any); and

      (c)   if the firm falls within paragraph 5(d), notify its home state regulator of the applicable provisions (if any).

(3)   A notice under sub-paragraph (2)(b) or (c) must be given before the end of the period of two months beginning with the day on which the Authority received the consent notice.

(4)   For the purposes of this paragraph—
    "applicable provisions" means the host state rules with which the firm is required to comply when carrying on a permitted activity through a branch in the United Kingdom;
    "host state rules" means rules—
        (a)   made in accordance with the relevant single market directive; and
        (b)   which are the responsibility of the United Kingdom (both as to implementation and as to supervision of compliance) in accordance with that directive; and
    "permitted activity" means an activity identified in the consent notice [or regulator's notice, as the case may be].

Services

14.—(1)   The service conditions are that—
        (a)   the firm has given its home state regulator notice of its intention to provide services in the United Kingdom ("a notice of intention");
        (b)   if the firm falls within *paragraph 5(a) or (d)*, the Authority has received notice ("a regulator's notice") from the firm's home state regulator containing such information as may be prescribed; *and*
        (c)   if the firm falls within *paragraph 5(d)*, its home state regulator has informed it that the regulator's notice has been sent to the Authority[; and
        (d)   if the firm falls within paragraph 5(e), one month has elapsed beginning with the date on which the firm's home state regulator informed the firm that the regulator's notice has been sent to the Authority].

(2)   If the Authority has received a regulator's notice or, where none is required by sub-paragraph (1), has been informed of the firm's intention to provide services in the United Kingdom, it must[, unless the firm falls within paragraph 5(e),]—
        (a)   prepare for the firm's supervision; and
        (b)   notify the firm of the applicable provisions (if any).

(3)   A notice under sub-paragraph (2)(b) must be given before the end of the period of two months beginning on the day on which the Authority received the regulator's notice, or was informed of the firm's intention.

(4)   For the purposes of this paragraph—
    "applicable provisions" means the host state rules with which the firm is required to comply when carrying on a permitted activity by providing services in the United Kingdom;
    "host state rules" means rules—
        (a)   made in accordance with the relevant single market directive; and
        (b)   which are the responsibility of the United Kingdom (both as to implementation and as to supervision of compliance) in accordance with that directive; and
    "permitted activity" means an activity identified in—
        (a)   the regulator's notice; or
        (b)   where none is required by sub-paragraph (1), the notice of intention.

Grant of permission

15.—(1)   On qualifying for authorisation as a result of paragraph 12, a firm has, in respect of each permitted activity which is a regulated activity, permission to carry it on through its United Kingdom branch (if it satisfies the establishment conditions) or by providing services in the United Kingdom (if it satisfies the service conditions).

[(1A) Sub-paragraph (1) is to be read subject to paragraph 15A(3).]

(2)   The permission is to be treated as being on terms equivalent to those appearing from the consent notice, regulator's notice or notice of intention.

(3)   Sections 21, 39(1) and 147(1) of the Consumer Credit Act 1974 (business requiring a licence under that Act) do not apply in relation to the carrying on of a permitted activity which is Consumer Credit Act business by a firm which qualifies for authorisation as a result of paragraph 12, unless [the Office of Fair Trading] has exercised the power conferred on [it] by section 203 in relation to the firm.

(4)   "Consumer Credit Act business" has the same meaning as in section 203.

[Power to Restrict Permission of Management Companies

15A.—(1) Sub-paragraph (2) applies if—
   (a)   a firm falling within paragraph 5(f) qualifies for authorisation as a result of paragraph 12(1) (establishment conditions satisfied); but
   (b)   the Authority determines that the way in which the firm intends to invite persons in the United Kingdom to become participants in any collective investment scheme which that firm manages does not comply with the law in force in the United Kingdom.

(2)   The Authority may give a notice to the firm and the firm's home state regulator of the Authority's determination under sub-paragraph (1)(b).

(3)   Paragraph 15(1) does not give a firm to which the Authority has given (and not withdrawn) a notice under sub-paragraph (2) permission to carry on through the firm's United Kingdom branch the regulated activity of dealing in units in the collective investment schemes which the firm manages.

(4)   Any notice given under sub-paragraph (2) must be given before the end of the period of two months beginning with the day on which the Authority received the consent notice.

(5)   Sections 264(4) and 265(1), (2) and (4) apply to a notice given under sub-paragraph (2) as they apply to a notice given by the Authority under section 264(2).

(6)   If a decision notice is given to the firm under section 265(4), by virtue of sub-paragraph (5), the firm may refer the matter to the Tribunal.

(7)   In sub-paragraph (3)—
   (a)   "units" has the meaning given by section 237(2); and
   (b)   the reference to "dealing in" units in a collective investment scheme must be read with—
      (i)   section 22;
      (ii)   any relevant order under that section; and
      (iii)   Schedule 2.]

Effect of carrying on regulated activity when not qualified for authorisation

16.—(1)   This paragraph applies to an EEA firm which is not qualified for authorisation under paragraph 12.

(2)   Section 26 does not apply to an agreement entered into by the firm.

(3)   Section 27 does not apply to an agreement in relation to which the firm is a third party for the purposes of that section.

(4)   Section 29 does not apply to an agreement in relation to which the firm is the deposit-taker.

Continuing regulation of EEA firms

17. Regulations may—
   (a)   modify any provision of this Act which is an applicable provision (within the meaning of paragraph 13 or 14) in its application to an EEA firm qualifying for authorisation;

(b)   make provision as to any change (or proposed change) of a prescribed kind relating to an EEA firm or to an activity that it carries on in the United Kingdom and as to the procedure to be followed in relation to such cases;

(c)   provide that the Authority may treat an EEA firm's notification that it is to cease to carry on regulated activity in the United Kingdom as a request for cancellation of its qualification for authorisation under this Schedule.

Giving up right to authorisation

18. Regulations may provide that in prescribed circumstances an EEA firm falling within paragraph 5(c) may, on following the prescribed procedure—

(a)   have its qualification for authorisation under this Schedule cancelled; and

(b)   seek to become an authorised person by applying for a Part IV permission.

Commencement: 25 February 2001 (for the purpose of making orders or regulations); 18 June 2001 (for the purposes of making rules); 1 December 2001 (remaining purposes).
Amendments: Para 13: words in square brackets in sub-paras (1), (4), and the whole of sub-para (1A), inserted by the Insurance Mediation Directive (Miscellaneous Amendments) Regulations 2003, SI 2003/1473, reg 3, as from 14 January 2005; for the words in italics in sub-para (1) there are substituted the words "(c), (d) or (f)" by the Collective Investment Schemes (Miscellaneous Amendments) Regulations 2003, SI 2003/2066, reg 3(1)(a), as from 13 February 2004.
Para 14: for the first words in italics in sub-para (1)(b) there are substituted the words "paragraph 5(a), (d) or (e)", the second word in italics in sub-para (1)(b) is repealed, for the words in italics in sub-para (1)(c) there are substituted the words "paragraph 5(d) or (e)", sub-para (1)(d) and the word immediately preceding it is inserted, and the words in square brackets in sub-para (2) are inserted, by SI 2003/1473, reg 4, as from 14 January 2005; for the words "(d) or "(e)" in sub-para (1)(b) (as substituted by SI 2003/1473) there are substituted the words "(d), (e) or (f)" by SI 2003/2066, reg 3(1)(b), as from 13 February 2004.
Para 15: sub-para (1A) inserted by SI 2003/2066, reg 3(1)(c), as from 13 February 2004; words in square brackets in sub-para (3) substituted by the Enterprise Act 2002, s 278(1), Sch 25, para 40(1), (19)(a).
Para 15A: inserted by SI 2003/2066, reg 3(1)(d), as from 13 February 2004.
Regulations: The Financial Services and Markets Act 2000 (EEA Passport Rights) Regulations 2001, SI 2001/2511, as amended by SI 2002/765, SI 2003/1473, SI 2003/2066, and modified by SI 2001/3084.
References: See paras 4.9–4.24.

PART III
EXERCISE OF PASSPORT RIGHTS BY UK FIRMS

Establishment

19.—(1) [Subject to sub-paragraph (5A),] A UK firm may not exercise an EEA right to establish a branch unless three conditions are satisfied.

(2)   The first is that the firm has given the Authority, in the specified way, notice of its intention to establish a branch ("a notice of intention") which—

(a)   identifies the activities which it seeks to carry on through the branch; and

(b)   includes such other information as may be specified.

(3)   The activities identified in a notice of intention may include activities which are not regulated activities.

(4)   The second is that the Authority has given notice in specified terms ("a consent notice") to the host state regulator.

(5)   The third is that—

(a)   the host state regulator has notified the firm (or, where the EEA right in question derives from any of the insurance directives, the Authority) of the applicable provisions; or

(b)   two months have elapsed beginning with the date on which the Authority gave the consent notice.

[(5A) If—
    (a)   the EEA right in question derives from the insurance mediation directive, and
    (b)   the EEA State in which the firm intends to establish a branch has not notified the Commission, in accordance with Article 6(2) of that directive, of its wish to be informed of the intention of any UK firm to establish a branch in its territory,

the second and third conditions do not apply (and so the firm may establish the branch to which its notice of intention relates as soon as the first condition is satisfied).]

(6)   If the firm's EEA right derives from *the investment services directive or the [banking consolidation directive]* and the first condition is satisfied, the Authority must give a consent notice to the host state regulator unless it has reason to doubt the adequacy of the firm's resources or its administrative structure.

(7)   If the firm's EEA right derives from any of the insurance directives and the first condition is satisfied, the Authority must give a consent notice unless it has reason—
    (a)   to doubt the adequacy of the firm's resources or its administrative structure, or
    (b)   to question the reputation, qualifications or experience of the directors or managers of the firm or the person proposed as the branch's authorised agent for the purposes of those directives,

in relation to the business to be conducted through the proposed branch.

[(7A) If—
    (a)   the firm's EEA right derives from the insurance mediation directive,
    (b)   the first condition is satisfied, and
    (c)   the second condition applies,

the Authority must give a consent notice, and must do so within one month beginning with the date on which it received the firm's notice of intention.]

(8)   If the Authority proposes to refuse to give a consent notice it must give the firm concerned a warning notice.

(9)   If the firm's EEA right derives from any of the insurance directives and the host state regulator has notified it of the applicable provisions, the Authority must inform the firm of those provisions.

(10)   Rules may specify the procedure to be followed by the Authority in exercising its functions under this paragraph.

(11)   If the Authority gives a consent notice it must give written notice that it has done so to the firm concerned.

(12)   If the Authority decides to refuse to give a consent notice—
    (a)   it must, *within three months beginning with the date when it received the notice of intention*, give the person who gave that notice a decision notice to that effect; and
    (b)   that person may refer the matter to the Tribunal.

[(12A) In sub-paragraph (12), "the relevant period" means—
    (a)   if the firm's EEA right derives from the UCITS directive, two months beginning with the date on which the Authority received the notice of intention;
    (b)   in any other case, three months beginning with that date.]

(13)   In this paragraph, "applicable provisions" means the host state rules with which the firm will be required to comply when conducting business through the proposed branch in the EEA State concerned.

(14)   In sub-paragraph (13), "host state rules" means rules—
    (a)   made in accordance with the relevant single market directive; and
    (b)   which are the responsibility of the EEA State concerned (both as to implementation and as to supervision of compliance) in accordance with that directive.

(15)   "Specified" means specified in rules.

Services

20.—(1) A UK firm may not exercise an EEA right to provide services unless the firm has given the Authority, in the specified way, notice of its intention to provide services ("a notice of intention") which—

> (a) identifies the activities which it seeks to carry out by way of provision of services; and

> (b) includes such other information as may be specified.

(2) The activities identified in a notice of intention may include activities which are not regulated activities.

(3) If the firm's EEA right derives from *the investment services directive or [the banking consolidation directive]*, the Authority must, within one month of receiving a notice of intention, send a copy of it to the host state regulator [with such other information as may be specified].

[(3A) If the firm's EEA right derives from any of the insurance directives, the Authority must, within one month of receiving the notice of intention—

> (a) give notice in specified terms ("a consent notice") to the host state regulator; or

> (b) give written notice to the firm of—

> > (i) its refusal to give a consent notice; and

> > (ii) its reasons for that refusal.]

[(3B) If the firm's EEA right derives from the insurance mediation directive and the EEA State in which the firm intends to provide services has notified the Commission, in accordance with Article 6(2) of that directive, of its wish to be informed of the intention of any UK firm to provide services in its territory—

> (a) the Authority must, within one month of receiving the notice of intention, send a copy of it to the host state regulator;

> (b) the Authority, when it sends the copy in accordance with sub-paragraph (a), must give written notice to the firm concerned that it has done so; and

> (c) the firm concerned must not provide the services to which its notice of intention relates until one month, beginning with the date on which it receives the notice under sub-paragraph (b), has elapsed.]

(4) When the Authority sends the copy under sub-paragraph (3) [or gives a consent notice], it must give written notice to the firm concerned.

[(4A) If the firm is given notice under sub-paragraph (3A)(b), it may refer the matter to the Tribunal.

(4B) If the firm's EEA right derives from any of the insurance directives, it must not provide the services to which its notice of intention relates until it has received written notice under sub-paragraph (4).

(4C) Rules may specify the procedure to be followed by the Authority under this paragraph.]

(5) . . .

(6) "Specified" means specified in rules.

Offence relating to exercise of passport rights

21.—(1) If a UK firm which is not an authorised person contravenes the prohibition imposed by—

> (a) sub-paragraph (1) of paragraph 19, or

> (b) *sub-paragraph (1) or [(4B)]* of paragraph 20,

it is guilty of an offence.

(2) A firm guilty of an offence under sub-paragraph (1) is liable—

> (a) on summary conviction, to a fine not exceeding the statutory maximum; or

> (b) on conviction on indictment, to a fine.

(3)   In proceedings for an offence under sub-paragraph (1), it is a defence for the firm to show that it took all reasonable precautions and exercised all due diligence to avoid committing the offence.

Continuing regulation of UK firms

22.—(1)   Regulations may make such provision as the Treasury consider appropriate in relation to a UK firm's exercise of EEA rights, and may in particular provide for the application (with or without modification) of any provision of, or made under, this Act in relation to an activity of a UK firm.

(2)   Regulations may—
   (a)   make provision as to any change (or proposed change) of a prescribed kind relating to a UK firm or to an activity that it carries on and as to the procedure to be followed in relation to such cases;
   (b)   make provision with respect to the consequences of the firm's failure to comply with a provision of the regulations.

(3)   Where a provision of the kind mentioned in sub-paragraph (2) requires the Authority's consent to a change (or proposed change)—
   (a)   consent may be refused only on prescribed grounds; and
   (b)   if the Authority decides to refuse consent, the firm concerned may refer the matter to the Tribunal.

23.—(1)   Sub-paragraph (2) applies if a UK firm—
   (a)   has a Part IV permission; and
   (b)   is exercising an EEA right to carry on any Consumer Credit Act business in an EEA State other than the United Kingdom.

(2)   The Authority may exercise its power under section 45 in respect of the firm if [the Office of Fair Trading] has informed the Authority that—
   (a)   the firm,
   (b)   any of the firm's employees, agents or associates (whether past or present), or
   (c)   if the firm is a body corporate, a controller of the firm or an associate of such a controller,
has done any of the things specified in paragraphs (a) to (d) of section 25(2) of the Consumer Credit Act 1974.

(3)   "Associate", "Consumer Credit Act business" and "controller" have the same meaning as in section 203.

24.—(1)   Sub-paragraph (2) applies if a UK firm—
   (a)   is not required to have a Part IV permission in relation to the business which it is carrying on; and
   (b)   is exercising the right conferred by [Article 19 of the banking consolidation directive] to carry on that business in an EEA State other than the United Kingdom.

(2)   If requested to do so by the host state regulator in the EEA State in which the UK firm's business is being carried on, the Authority may impose any requirement in relation to the firm which it could impose if—
   (a)   the firm had a Part IV permission in relation to the business which it is carrying on; and
   (b)   the Authority was entitled to exercise its power under that Part to vary that permission.

[Information to be included in the public record

25. The Authority must include in the record that it maintains under section 347 in relation to any UK firm whose EEA right derives from the insurance mediation directive information as to each EEA State in which the UK firm, in accordance with such a right—
   (a)   has established a branch; or
   (b)   is providing services.]

Commencement: 25 February 2001 (for the purpose of making orders or regulations); 18 June 2001 (for the purposes of making rules); 3 September 2001 (para 19, for the purposes of the giving of notice under sub-para (2) of intention to establish a branch not sooner than 1 December 2001; para 20, for the purposes of the giving of notice under sub-para (1) of intention to provide services not sooner than 1 December 2001); 1 December 2001 (remainder).

Amendments: Para 19: for the words in italics in sub-para (6) there are substituted the words "the banking consolidation directive, the investment services directive or the UCITS directive"; for the words in italics in sub-para (12)(a) there are substituted the words "within the relevant period", and sub-para (12A) inserted, by the Collective Investment Schemes (Miscellaneous Amendments) Regulations 2003, SI 2003/2066, reg 4(1)(a), as from 13 February 2004; words in square brackets in sub-para (6) substituted by the Banking Consolidation Directive (Consequential Amendments) Regulations 2000, SI 2000/2952, reg 8(1), (5)(d); words in square brackets in sub-para (1), and the whole of sub-paras (5A), (7A) inserted, and for sub-para (5) there is substituted the following paragraph by the Insurance Mediation Directive (Miscellaneous Amendments) Regulations 2003, SI 2003/1473, reg 5, as from 14 January 2005—

"(5) The third is—

(a) if the EEA right in question derives from the insurance mediation directive, that one month has elapsed beginning with the date on which the firm received notice, in accordance with sub-paragraph (11), that the Authority has given a consent notice;

(b) in any other case, that either—

(i) the host state regulator has notified the firm (or, where the EEA right in question derives from any of the insurance directives, the Authority) of the applicable provisions; or

(ii) two months have elapsed beginning with the date on which the Authority gave the consent notice.".

Para 20: for the words in italics in sub-para (3) there are substituted the words "the banking consolidation directive, the investment services directive or the UCITS directive", and words in second pair of square brackets in sub-para (3) added, by SI 2003/2066, reg 4(1)(b), as from 13 February 2004; words in first pair of square brackets in sub-para (3) substituted by SI 2000/2952, reg 8(1), (5)(e); sub-paras (3A), (4A)–(4C) inserted, words in square brackets in sub-para (4) inserted, and sub-para (5) repealed, by the Financial Services (EEA Passport Rights) Regulations 2001, SI 2001/1376, reg 2(1)–(5); sub-para (3B) inserted by SI 2003/1473, reg 6(1), as from 14 January 2005.

Para 21: figure in square brackets substituted by SI 2001/1376, reg 2(1), (6); for the words in italics there are substituted the words "sub-paragraph (1), (3B)(c) or (4B)" by SI 2003/1473, reg 6(2), as from 14 January 2005.

Para 23: words in square brackets substituted by the Enterprise Act 2002, s 278(1), Sch 25, para 40(1), (19)(b).

Para 24: words in square brackets substituted by the Banking Consolidation Directive (Consequential Amendments) Regulations 2000, SI 2000/2952, reg 8(1), (5)(f).

Para 25: inserted, together with preceding heading, by SI 2003/1473, reg 7, as from 14 January 2005.

Regulations: The Financial Services and Markets Act 2000 (EEA Passport Rights) Regulations 2001, SI 2001/2511, as amended by SI 2002/765, SI 2003/1473, SI 2003/2066, and modified by SI 2001/3084.

References: See paras 4.41–4.53.

SCHEDULE 4

Section 31(1)(c)

TREATY RIGHTS

Transitional provisions: The Financial Services and Markets Act 2000 (Transitional Provisions) (Authorised Persons etc) Order 2001, SI 2001/2636, Pt II, Chapter III (made under ss 426–428 ante), provides that treaty firms authorised before 1 December 2001 under the Financial Services Act 1986, s 31 and certain treaty firms which were authorised insurance companies before that date are to be treated after 1 December 2001 as having complied with the procedures of this Schedule. The 1986 Act is repealed by the Financial Services and Markets Act 2000 (Consequential Amendments and Repeals) Order 2001, SI 2001/3649, art 3(1)(c) (made under ss 426, 427 ante).

Definitions

1. In this Schedule—

"consumers" means persons who are consumers for the purposes of section 138;

"Treaty firm" means a person—
   (a)   whose head office is situated in an EEA State (its "home state") other than the United Kingdom; and
   (b)   which is recognised under the law of that State as its national; and
"home state regulator", in relation to a Treaty firm, means the competent authority of the firm's home state for the purpose of its home state authorisation (as to which see paragraph 3(1)(a)).

Firms qualifying for authorisation

2.   Once a Treaty firm which is seeking to carry on a regulated activity satisfies the conditions set out in paragraph 3(1), it qualifies for authorisation.

Exercise of Treaty rights

3.—(1)   The conditions are that—
   (a)   the firm has received authorisation ("home state authorisation") under the law of its home state to carry on the regulated activity in question ("the permitted activity");
   (b)   the relevant provisions of the law of the firm's home state—
        (i)   afford equivalent protection; or
        (ii) satisfy the conditions laid down by a Community instrument for the co-ordination or approximation of laws, regulations or administrative provisions of member States relating to the carrying on of that activity; and
   (c)   the firm has no EEA right to carry on that activity in the manner in which it is seeking to carry it on.

   (2)   A firm is not to be regarded as having home state authorisation unless its home state regulator has so informed the Authority in writing.

   (3)   Provisions afford equivalent protection if, in relation to the firm's carrying on of the permitted activity, they afford consumers protection which is at least equivalent to that afforded by or under this Act in relation to that activity.

   (4)   A certificate issued by the Treasury that the provisions of the law of a particular EEA State afford equivalent protection in relation to the activities specified in the certificate is conclusive evidence of that fact.

Permission

4.—(1)   On qualifying for authorisation under this Schedule, a Treaty firm has permission to carry on each permitted activity through its United Kingdom branch or by providing services in the United Kingdom.

   (2)   The permission is to be treated as being on terms equivalent to those to which the firm's home state authorisation is subject.

   (3)   If, on qualifying for authorisation under this Schedule, a firm has a Part IV permission which includes permission to carry on a permitted activity, the Authority must give a direction cancelling the permission so far as it relates to that activity.

   (4)   The Authority need not give a direction under sub-paragraph (3) if it considers that there are good reasons for not doing so.

Notice to Authority

5.—(1)   Sub-paragraph (2) applies to a Treaty firm which—
   (a)   qualifies for authorisation under this Schedule, but
   (b)   is not carrying on in the United Kingdom the regulated activity, or any of the regulated activities, which it has permission to carry on there.

   (2)   At least seven days before it begins to carry on such a regulated activity, the firm must give the Authority written notice of its intention to do so.

(3)   If a Treaty firm to which sub-paragraph (2) applies has given notice under that sub-paragraph, it need not give such a notice if it again becomes a firm to which that sub-paragraph applies.

(4)   Subsections (1), (3) and (6) of section 51 apply to a notice under sub-paragraph (2) as they apply to an application for a Part IV permission.

Offences

6.—(1)   A person who contravenes paragraph 5(2) is guilty of an offence.

(2)   In proceedings against a person for an offence under sub-paragraph (1) it is a defence for him to show that he took all reasonable precautions and exercised all due diligence to avoid committing the offence.

(3)   A person is guilty of an offence if in, or in connection with, a notice given by him under paragraph 5(2) he—
  (a)   provides information which he knows to be false or misleading in a material particular; or
  (b)   recklessly provides information which is false or misleading in a material particular.

(4)   A person guilty of an offence under this paragraph is liable—
  (a)   on summary conviction, to a fine not exceeding the statutory maximum;
  (b)   on conviction on indictment, to a fine.

Commencement: 3 September 2001 (para 1, and para 3 for the purposes of issuing certificates under sub-para (4), and para 5 for the purposes of the giving of notice under sub-para (2) of intention to carry on regulated activities not sooner than the day on which s 19 of this Act comes into force); 1 December 2001 (remainder).
References: See paras 4.25–4.35.

SCHEDULE 5

Section 36

PERSONS CONCERNED IN COLLECTIVE INVESTMENT SCHEMES

Authorisation

1.—(1)   A person who for the time being is an operator, trustee or depositary of a recognised collective investment scheme is an authorised person.

(2)   "Recognised" means recognised by virtue of section 264.

(3)   An authorised open-ended investment company is an authorised person.

[(4)   A body—
  (a)   incorporated by virtue of regulations made under section 1 of the Open-Ended Investment Companies Act (Northern Ireland) 2002 in respect of which an authorisation order is in force, and
  (b)   to which the UCITS directive applies,
is an authorised person.

(5)   "Authorisation order" means an order made under (or having effect as made under) any provision of those regulations which is made by virtue of section 1(2)(1) of that Act (provision corresponding to Chapter 3 of Part 17 of the Act).]

Permission

2.—(1)   A person authorised as a result of paragraph 1(1) has permission to carry on, so far as it is a regulated activity—
  (a)   any activity, appropriate to the capacity in which he acts in relation to the scheme, of the kind described in paragraph 8 of Schedule 2;
  (b)   any activity in connection with, or for the purposes of, the scheme.

(2)   A person authorised as a result of paragraph 1(3) [or(4)] has permission to carry on, so far as it is a regulated activity—

(a)   the operation of the scheme;

(b)   any activity in connection with, or for the purposes of, the operation of the scheme.

Commencement: 1 December 2001.
Amendments: Para 1: sub-paras (4), (5) added by the Collective Investment Schemes (Miscellaneous Amendments) Regulations 2003, SI 2003/2066, reg 10(a), as from 13 February 2004.
Para 2: words in square brackets inserted by SI 2003/2066, reg 10(b), as from 13 February 2004.
References: See paras 4.36–4.39, 15.48.

SCHEDULE 6

Section 41

THRESHOLD CONDITIONS

PART I
PART IV PERMISSION

Legal status

1.—(1)   If the regulated activity concerned is the effecting or carrying out of contracts of insurance the authorised person must be a body corporate [(other than a limited liability partnership)], a registered friendly society or a member of Lloyd's.

(2)   If the person concerned appears to the Authority to be seeking to carry on, or to be carrying on, a regulated activity constituting accepting deposits [or issuing electronic money], it must be—

(a)   a body corporate; or

(b)   a partnership.

Location of offices

2.—(1)   [Subject to sub-paragraph (3),] If the person concerned is a body corporate constituted under the law of any part of the United Kingdom—

(a)   its head office, and

(b)   if it has a registered office, that office,

must be in the United Kingdom.

(2)   If the person concerned has its head office in the United Kingdom but is not a body corporate, it must carry on business in the United Kingdom.

[(3)   If the regulated activity concerned is an insurance mediation activity, sub-paragraph (1) does not apply.

(4)   If the regulated activity concerned is an insurance mediation activity, the person concerned—

(a)   if he is a body corporate constituted under the law of any part of the United Kingdom, must have its registered office, or if it has no registered office, its head office, in the United Kingdom;

(b)   if he is a natural person, is to be treated for the purposes of sub-paragraph (2), as having his head office in the United Kingdom if his residence is situated there.

(5)   "Insurance mediation activity" means any of the following activities—

(a)   dealing in rights under a contract of insurance as agent;

(b)   arranging deals in rights under a contract of insurance;

(c)   assisting in the administration and performance of a contract of insurance;

(d)   advising on buying or selling rights under a contract of insurance;

(e)   agreeing to do any of the activities specified in sub-paragraph (a) to (d).

(6) Paragraph (5) must be read with—
    (a) section 22;
    (b) any relevant order under that section; and
    (c) Schedule 2.]

[Appointment of claims representatives

2A.—(1) If it appears to the Authority that—
    (a) the regulated activity that the person concerned is carrying on, or is seeking to carry on, is the effecting or carrying out of contracts of insurance, and
    (b) contracts of insurance against damage arising out of or in connection with the use of motor vehicles on land (other than carrier's liability) are being, or will be, effected or carried out by the person concerned,

that person must have a claims representative in each EEA State other than the United Kingdom.

(2) For the purposes of sub-paragraph (1)(b), contracts of reinsurance are to be disregarded.

(3) A claims representative is a person with responsibility for handling and settling claims arising from accidents of the kind mentioned in Article 1(2) of the fourth motor insurance directive.

(4) In this paragraph "fourth motor insurance directive" means Directive 2000/26/EC of the European Parliament and of the Council of 16th May 2000 on the approximation of the laws of the Member States relating to insurance against civil liability in respect of the use of motor vehicles and amending Council Directives 73/239/EEC and 88/357/EEC.]

Close links

3.—(1) If the person concerned ("A") has close links with another person ("CL") the Authority must be satisfied—
    (a) that those links are not likely to prevent the Authority's effective supervision of A; and
    (b) if it appears to the Authority that CL is subject to the laws, regulations or administrative provisions of a territory which is not an EEA State ("the foreign provisions"), that neither the foreign provisions, nor any deficiency in their enforcement, would prevent the Authority's effective supervision of A.

(2) A has close links with CL if—
    (a) CL is a parent undertaking of A;
    (b) CL is a subsidiary undertaking of A;
    (c) CL is a parent undertaking of a subsidiary undertaking of A;
    (d) CL is a subsidiary undertaking of a parent undertaking of A;
    (e) CL owns or controls 20% or more of the voting rights or capital of A; or
    (f) A owns or controls 20% or more of the voting rights or capital of CL.

(3) "Subsidiary undertaking" includes all the instances mentioned in Article 1(1) and (2) of the Seventh Company Law Directive in which an entity may be a subsidiary of an undertaking.

Adequate resources

4.—(1) The resources of the person concerned must, in the opinion of the Authority, be adequate in relation to the regulated activities that he seeks to carry on, or carries on.

(2) In reaching that opinion, the Authority may—
    (a) take into account the person's membership of a group and any effect which that membership may have; and
    (b) have regard to—
        (i) the provision he makes and, if he is a member of a group, which other members of the group make in respect of liabilities (including contingent and future liabilities); and

      (ii)   the means by which he manages and, if he is a member of a group, which other members of the group manage the incidence of risk in connection with his business.

Suitability

5. The person concerned must satisfy the Authority that he is a fit and proper person having regard to all the circumstances, including—

      (a)   his connection with any person;

      (b)   the nature of any regulated activity that he carries on or seeks to carry on; and

      (c)   the need to ensure that his affairs are conducted soundly and prudently.

Commencement: 3 September 2001.

Amendments: Para 1: words in first pair of square brackets inserted by the Financial Services and Markets Act 2000 (Variation of Threshold Conditions) Order 2001, SI 2001/2507, art 2, as from 3 September 2001; words in second pair of square brackets inserted by the Financial Services and Markets Act 2000 (Regulated Activities) (Amendment) Order 2002, SI 2002/682, art 8, as from 27 April 2002.

Para 2: words in square brackets in sub-para (1), and the whole of sub-paras (3)–(6) inserted by the Financial Services and Markets Act 2000 (Regulated Activities) (Amendment) (No 2) Order 2003, SI 2003/1476, art 19, as from 31 October 2004 (in so far as relating to contracts of long-term care insurance), and as from 14 January 2005 (otherwise) (subject to transitional provisions in arts 22–27 thereto).

Para 2A: inserted by the Financial Services and Markets Act 2000 (Variation of Threshold Conditions) Order 2002, SI 2002/2707, art 2, as from 19 January 2003.

Swiss general insurance companies: Paras 3–5 have been repealed in relation to a Swiss general insurance company by virtue of the Financial Services and Markets Act 2000 (Variation of Threshold Conditions) Order 2001, SI 2001/2507, art 3(3).

References: See paras 4.8, 4.9, 4.74, 4.76–4.79.

PART II
AUTHORISATION

Authorisation under Schedule 3

6. In relation to an EEA firm qualifying for authorisation under Schedule 3, the conditions set out in paragraphs 1 and 3 to 5 apply, so far as relevant, to—

      (a)   an application for permission under Part IV;

      (b)   exercise of the Authority's own-initiative power under section 45 in relation to a Part IV permission.

Authorisation under Schedule 4

7. In relation to a person who qualifies for authorisation under Schedule 4, the conditions set out in paragraphs 1 and 3 to 5 apply, so far as relevant, to—

      (a)   an application for an additional permission;

      (b)   the exercise of the Authority's own-initiative power under section 45 in relation to additional permission.

Commencement: 3 September 2001.

References: See paras 4.8, 4.29.

PART III
ADDITIONAL CONDITIONS

8.—(1)   If this paragraph applies to the person concerned, he must, for the purposes of such provisions of this Act as may be specified, satisfy specified additional conditions.

  (2)   This paragraph applies to a person who—

      (a)   has his head office outside the EEA; and

    (b)   appears to the Authority to be seeking to carry on a regulated activity relating to insurance business.

(3)   "Specified" means specified in, or in accordance with, an order made by the Treasury.

9. The Treasury may by order—
    (a)   vary or remove any of the conditions set out in Parts I and II;
    (b)   add to those conditions.

Commencement: 25 February 2001 (for the purpose of making orders or regulations); 3 September 2001 (remaining purposes).
Orders: The Financial Services and Markets Act 2000 (Variation of Threshold Conditions) Order 2001, SI 2001/2507; the Financial Services and Markets Act 2000 (Variation of Threshold Conditions) Order 2002, SI 2002/2707.
References: See para 4.80.

SCHEDULE 7

Section 72(2)

THE AUTHORITY AS COMPETENT AUTHORITY FOR PART VI

General

1. This Act applies in relation to the Authority when it is exercising functions under Part VI as the competent authority subject to the following modifications.

The Authority's general functions

2. In section 2—
    (a)   subsection (4)(a) does not apply to listing rules;
    (b)   subsection (4)(c) does not apply to general guidance given in relation to Part VI; and
    (c)   subsection (4)(d) does not apply to functions under Part VI.

Duty to consult

3. Section 8 does not apply.

Rules

4.—(1)   Sections 149, 153, 154 and 156 do not apply.

    (2)   Section 155 has effect as if—
    (a)   the reference in subsection (2)(c) to the general duties of the Authority under section 2 were a reference to its duty under section 73; and
    (b)   section 99 were included in the provisions referred to in subsection (9).

Statements of policy

5.—(1)   Paragraph 5 of Schedule 1 has effect as if the requirement to act through the Authority's governing body applied also to the exercise of its functions of publishing statements under section 93.

    (2)   Paragraph 1 of Schedule 1 has effect as if section 93 were included in the provisions referred to in sub-paragraph (2)(d).

Penalties

6. Paragraph 16 of Schedule 1 does not apply in relation to penalties under Part VI (for which separate provision is made by section 100).

7. Paragraph 17 of Schedule 1 does not apply in relation to fees payable under Part VI (for which separate provision is made by section 99).

Exemption from liability in damages

8. Schedule 1 has effect as if—
   - (a) sub-paragraph (1) of paragraph 19 were omitted (similar provision being made in relation to the competent authority by section 102); and
   - (b) for the words from the beginning to "(a)" in sub-paragraph (3) of that paragraph, there were substituted "Sub-paragraph (2) does not apply".

Commencement: 18 June 2001.
References: See paras 9.9, 9.10.

SCHEDULE 8

Section 72(3)

TRANSFER OF FUNCTIONS UNDER PART VI

The power to transfer

1.—(1) The Treasury may by order provide for any function conferred on the competent authority which is exercisable for the time being by a particular person to be transferred so as to be exercisable by another person.

(2) An order may be made under this paragraph only if—
   - (a) the person from whom the relevant functions are to be transferred has agreed in writing that the order should be made;
   - (b) the Treasury are satisfied that the manner in which, or efficiency with which, the functions are discharged would be significantly improved if they were transferred to the transferee; or
   - (c) the Treasury are satisfied that it is otherwise in the public interest that the order should be made.

Supplemental

2.—(1) An order under this Schedule does not affect anything previously done by any person ("the previous authority") in the exercise of functions which are transferred by the order to another person ("the new authority").

(2) Such an order may, in particular, include provision—
   - (a) modifying or excluding any provision of Part VI, IX or XXVI in its application to any such functions;
   - (b) for reviews similar to that made, in relation to the Authority, by section 12;
   - (c) imposing on the new authority requirements similar to those imposed, in relation to the Authority, by sections 152, 155 and 354;
   - (d) as to the giving of guidance by the new authority;
   - (e) for the delegation by the new authority of the exercise of functions under Part VI and as to the consequences of delegation;
   - (f) for the transfer of any property, rights or liabilities relating to any such functions from the previous authority to the new authority;
   - (g) for the carrying on and completion by the new authority of anything in the process of being done by the previous authority when the order takes effect;
   - (h) for the substitution of the new authority for the previous authority in any instrument, contract or legal proceedings;
   - (i) for the transfer of persons employed by the previous authority to the new authority and as to the terms on which they are to transfer;

(j) making such amendments to any primary or subordinate legislation (including any provision of, or made under, this Act) as the Treasury consider appropriate in consequence of the transfer of functions effected by the order.

(3) Nothing in this paragraph is to be taken as restricting the powers conferred by section 428.

3. If the Treasury have made an order under paragraph 1 ("the transfer order") they may, by a separate order made under this paragraph, make any provision of a kind that could have been included in the transfer order.

Commencement: 18 June 2001.
References: See paras 9.12–9.14.

SCHEDULE 9

Section 87(5)

NON-LISTING PROSPECTUSES

General application of Part VI

1. The provisions of Part VI apply in relation to a non-listing prospectus as they apply in relation to listing particulars but with the modifications made by this Schedule.

References to listing particulars

2.—(1) Any reference to listing particulars is to be read as a reference to a prospectus.

(2) Any reference to supplementary listing particulars is to be read as a reference to a supplementary prospectus.

General duty of disclosure

3.—(1) In section 80(1), for "section 79" substitute "section 87".

(2) In section 80(2), omit "as a condition of the admission of the securities to the official list".

Supplementary prospectuses

4. In section 81(1), for "section 79 and before the commencement of dealings in the securities concerned following their admission to the official list" substitute "section 87 and before the end of the period during which the offer to which the prospectus relates remains open".

Exemption from liability for compensation

5.—(1) In paragraphs 1(3) and 2(3) of Schedule 10, for paragraph (d) substitute—
"(d) the securities were acquired after such a lapse of time that he ought in the circumstances to be reasonably excused and, if the securities are dealt in on an approved exchange, he continued in that belief until after the commencement of dealings in the securities on that exchange."

(2) After paragraph 8 of that Schedule, insert—

"Meaning of "approved exchange"

9. "Approved exchange" has such meaning as may be prescribed."

Advertisements

6. In section 98(1), for "If listing particulars are, or are to be, published in connection with an application for listing," substitute "If a prospectus is, or is to be, published in connection

with an application for approval, then, until the end of the period during which the offer to which the prospectus relates remains open,".

Fees

7. Listing rules made under section 99 may require the payment of fees to the competent authority in respect of a prospectus submitted for approval under section 87.

Commencement: 18 June 2001 (para 7); 25 February 2001 (remainder).
Regulations: The Financial Services and Markets Act 2000 (Official Listing of Securities) Regulations 2001, SI 2001/2956, as amended by SI 2001/3439 (made under para 9 of Sch 10 as inserted by para 5(2) above).
References: See paras 9.24, 9.47, 9.77, 9.91, 9.92.

SCHEDULE 10

Section 90(2) and (5)

COMPENSATION: EXEMPTIONS

Statements believed to be true

1.—(1) In this paragraph "statement" means—
- (a) any untrue or misleading statement in listing particulars; or
- (b) the omission from listing particulars of any matter required to be included by section 80 or 81.

(2) A person does not incur any liability under section 90(1) for loss caused by a statement if he satisfies the court that, at the time when the listing particulars were submitted to the competent authority, he reasonably believed (having made such enquiries, if any, as were reasonable) that—
- (a) the statement was true and not misleading, or
- (b) the matter whose omission caused the loss was properly omitted,

and that one or more of the conditions set out in sub-paragraph (3) are satisfied.

(3) The conditions are that—
- (a) he continued in his belief until the time when the securities in question were acquired;
- (b) they were acquired before it was reasonably practicable to bring a correction to the attention of persons likely to acquire them;
- (c) before the securities were acquired, he had taken all such steps as it was reasonable for him to have taken to secure that a correction was brought to the attention of those persons;
- (d) he continued in his belief until after the commencement of dealings in the securities following their admission to the official list and they were acquired after such a lapse of time that he ought in the circumstances to be reasonably excused.

Statements by experts

2.—(1) In this paragraph "statement" means a statement included in listing particulars which—
- (a) purports to be made by, or on the authority of, another person as an expert; and
- (b) is stated to be included in the listing particulars with that other person's consent.

(2) A person does not incur any liability under section 90(1) for loss in respect of any securities caused by a statement if he satisfies the court that, at the time when the listing particulars were submitted to the competent authority, he reasonably believed that the other person—
- (a) was competent to make or authorise the statement, and

> (b) had consented to its inclusion in the form and context in which it was included,

and that one or more of the conditions set out in sub-paragraph (3) are satisfied.

(3) The conditions are that—

> (a) he continued in his belief until the time when the securities were acquired;
>
> (b) they were acquired before it was reasonably practicable to bring the fact that the expert was not competent, or had not consented, to the attention of persons likely to acquire the securities in question;
>
> (c) before the securities were acquired he had taken all such steps as it was reasonable for him to have taken to secure that that fact was brought to the attention of those persons;
>
> (d) he continued in his belief until after the commencement of dealings in the securities following their admission to the official list and they were acquired after such a lapse of time that he ought in the circumstances to be reasonably excused.

Corrections of statements

3.—(1) In this paragraph "statement" has the same meaning as in paragraph 1.

(2) A person does not incur liability under section 90(1) for loss caused by a statement if he satisfies the court—

> (a) that before the securities in question were acquired, a correction had been published in a manner calculated to bring it to the attention of persons likely to acquire the securities; or
>
> (b) that he took all such steps as it was reasonable for him to take to secure such publication and reasonably believed that it had taken place before the securities were acquired.

(3) Nothing in this paragraph is to be taken as affecting paragraph 1.

Corrections of statements by experts

4.—(1) In this paragraph "statement" has the same meaning as in paragraph 2.

(2) A person does not incur liability under section 90(1) for loss caused by a statement if he satisfies the court—

> (a) that before the securities in question were acquired, the fact that the expert was not competent or had not consented had been published in a manner calculated to bring it to the attention of persons likely to acquire the securities; or
>
> (b) that he took all such steps as it was reasonable for him to take to secure such publication and reasonably believed that it had taken place before the securities were acquired.

(3) Nothing in this paragraph is to be taken as affecting paragraph 2.

Official statements

5. A person does not incur any liability under section 90(1) for loss resulting from—

> (a) a statement made by an official person which is included in the listing particulars, or
>
> (b) a statement contained in a public official document which is included in the listing particulars,

if he satisfies the court that the statement is accurately and fairly reproduced.

False or misleading information known about

6. A person does not incur any liability under section 90(1) or (4) if he satisfies the court that the person suffering the loss acquired the securities in question with knowledge—

> (a) that the statement was false or misleading,

    (b) of the omitted matter, or
    (c) of the change or new matter,
as the case may be.

Belief that supplementary listing particulars not called for

7. A person does not incur any liability under section 90(4) if he satisfies the court that he reasonably believed that the change or new matter in question was not such as to call for supplementary listing particulars.

Meaning of "expert"

8. "Expert" includes any engineer, valuer, accountant or other person whose profession, qualifications or experience give authority to a statement made by him.

Commencement: 1 December 2001.
Non-listing prospectuses: This Schedule has been modified in relation to non-listing prospectuses by Sch 9, para 5(2) of this Act as follows—
Paras 1(3)(d) and para 2(3)(d) are substituted with the following—
    "(d) the securities were acquired after such a lapse of time that he ought in the circumstances to be reasonably excused and, if the securities are dealt in on an approved exchange, he continued in that belief until after the commencement of dealings in the securities on that exchange."
After para 8 the following is added—

"Meaning of "approved exchange"

9. "Approved exchange" has such meaning as may be prescribed."

Regulations: The Financial Services and Markets Act 2000 (Official Listing of Securities) Regulations 2001, SI 2001/2956, as amended by SI 2001/3439 (made under para 9 of this Schedule as inserted as noted above).
References: See paras 9.90–9.98.

SCHEDULE 11

Section 103(6)

OFFERS OF SECURITIES

The general rule

1.—(1) A person offers securities to the public in the United Kingdom if—
    (a) to the extent that the offer is made to persons in the United Kingdom, it is made to the public; and
    (b) the offer is not an exempt offer.

    (2) For this purpose, an offer which is made to any section of the public, whether selected—
    (a) as members or debenture holders of a body corporate,
    (b) as clients of the person making the offer, or
    (c) in any other manner,
is to be regarded as made to the public.

Exempt offers

2.—(1) For the purposes of this Schedule, an offer of securities is an "exempt offer" if, to the extent that the offer is made to persons in the United Kingdom—
    (a) the condition specified in any of paragraphs 3 to [24A] is satisfied in relation to the offer; or
    (b) the condition specified in one relevant paragraph is satisfied in relation to part, but not the whole, of the offer and, in relation to each other part of the offer, the condition specified in a different relevant paragraph is satisfied.

(2)   The relevant paragraphs are 3 to 8, 12 to 18 and 21.

Offers for business purposes

3. The securities are offered to persons—
>   (a)   whose ordinary activities involve them in acquiring, holding, managing or disposing of investments (as principal or agent) for the purposes of their businesses, or
>   (b)   who it is reasonable to expect will acquire, hold, manage or dispose of investments (as principal or agent) for the purposes of their businesses,

or are otherwise offered to persons in the context of their trades, professions or occupations.

Offers to limited numbers

4.—(1)   The securities are offered to no more than fifty persons.

(2)   In determining whether this condition is satisfied, the offer is to be taken together with any other offer of the same securities which was—
>   (a)   made by the same person;
>   (b)   open at any time within the period of 12 months ending with the date on which the offer is first made; and
>   (c)   not an offer to the public in the United Kingdom by virtue of this condition being satisfied.

(3)   For the purposes of this paragraph—
>   (a)   the making of an offer of securities to trustees or members of a partnership in their capacity as such, or
>   (b)   the making of such an offer to any other two or more persons jointly,

is to be treated as the making of an offer to a single person.

Clubs and associations

5. The securities are offered to the members of a club or association (whether or not incorporated) and the members can reasonably be regarded as having a common interest with each other and with the club or association in the affairs of the club or association and in what is to be done with the proceeds of the offer.

Restricted circles

6.—(1)   The securities are offered to a restricted circle of persons whom the offeror reasonably believes to be sufficiently knowledgeable to understand the risks involved in accepting the offer.

(2)   In determining whether a person is sufficiently knowledgeable to understand the risks involved in accepting an offer of securities, any information supplied by the person making the offer is to be disregarded, apart from information about—
>   (a)   the issuer of the securities; or
>   (b)   if the securities confer the right to acquire other securities, the issuer of those other securities.

Underwriting agreements

7. The securities are offered in connection with a genuine invitation to enter into an underwriting agreement with respect to them.

Offers to public authorities

8.—(1)   The securities are offered to a public authority.

(2)   "Public authority" means—
>   (a)   the government of the United Kingdom;
>   (b)   the government of any country or territory outside the United Kingdom;
>   (c)   a local authority in the United Kingdom or elsewhere;

    (d)   any international organisation the members of which include the United Kingdom or another EEA State; and

    (e)   such other bodies, if any, as may be specified.

Maximum consideration

9.—(1)   The total consideration payable for the securities cannot exceed 40,000 euros (or an equivalent amount).

(2)   In determining whether this condition is satisfied, the offer is to be taken together with any other offer of the same securities which was—

    (a)   made by the same person;

    (b)   open at any time within the period of 12 months ending with the date on which the offer is first made; and

    (c)   not an offer to the public in the United Kingdom by virtue of this condition being satisfied.

(3)   An amount (in relation to an amount denominated in euros) is an "equivalent amount" if it is an amount of equal value, calculated at the latest practicable date before (but in any event not more than 3 days before) the date on which the offer is first made, denominated wholly or partly in another currency or unit of account.

Minimum consideration

10.—(1)   The minimum consideration which may be paid by any person for securities acquired by him pursuant to the offer is at least 40,000 euros (or an equivalent amount).

(2)   Paragraph 9(3) also applies for the purposes of this paragraph.

Securities denominated in euros

11.—(1)   The securities are denominated in amounts of at least 40,000 euros (or an equivalent amount).

(2)   Paragraph 9(3) also applies for the purposes of this paragraph.

Takeovers

12.—(1)   The securities are offered in connection with a takeover offer.

(2)   "Takeover offer" means—

    (a)   an offer to acquire shares in a body incorporated in the United Kingdom which is a takeover offer within the meaning of the takeover provisions (or would be such an offer if those provisions applied in relation to any body corporate);

    (b)   an offer to acquire all or substantially all of the shares, or of the shares of a particular class, in a body incorporated outside the United Kingdom; or

    (c)   an offer made to all the holders of shares, or of shares of a particular class, in a body corporate to acquire a specified proportion of those shares.

(3)   "The takeover provisions" means—

    (a)   Part XIIIA of the Companies Act 1985; or

    (b)   in relation to Northern Ireland, Part XIVA of the Companies (Northern Ireland) Order 1986.

(4)   For the purposes of sub-paragraph (2)(b), any shares which the offeror or any associate of his holds or has contracted to acquire are to be disregarded.

(5)   For the purposes of sub-paragraph (2)(c), the following are not to be regarded as holders of the shares in question—

    (a)   the offeror;

    (b)   any associate of the offeror; and

    (c)   any person whose shares the offeror or any associate of the offeror has contracted to acquire.

(6)   "Associate" has the same meaning as in—

    (a)   section 430E of the Companies Act 1985; or

    (b)   in relation to Northern Ireland, Article 423E of the Companies (Northern Ireland) Order 1986.

Mergers

13. The securities are offered in connection with a merger (within the meaning of Council Directive No 78/855/EEC).

Free shares

14.—(1)   The securities are shares and are offered free of charge to any or all of the holders of shares in the issuer.

   (2)   "Holders of shares" means the persons who at the close of business on a date—

    (a)   specified in the offer, and

    (b)   falling within the period of 60 days ending with the date on which the offer is first made,

were holders of such shares.

Exchange of shares

15. The securities—

    (a)   are shares, or investments of a specified kind relating to shares, in a body corporate, and

    (b)   are offered in exchange for shares in the same body corporate,

and the offer cannot result in any increase in the issued share capital of the body corporate.

Qualifying persons

16.—(1)   The securities are issued by a body corporate and are offered—

    (a)   by the issuer, by a body corporate connected with the issuer or by a relevant trustee;

    (b)   only to qualifying persons; and

    (c)   on terms that a contract to acquire any such securities may be entered into only by the qualifying person to whom they were offered or, if the terms of the offer so permit, any qualifying person.

   (2)   A person is a "qualifying person", in relation to an issuer, if he is a genuine employee or former employee of the issuer or of another body corporate in the same group or the wife, husband, widow, widower or child or stepchild under the age of eighteen of such an employee or former employee.

   (3)   In relation to an issuer of securities, "connected with" has such meaning as may be prescribed.

   (4)   "Group" and "relevant trustee" have such meaning as may be prescribed.

Convertible securities

17.—(1)   The securities result from the conversion of convertible securities and listing particulars (or a prospectus) relating to the convertible securities were (or was) published in the United Kingdom under or by virtue of Part VI or such other provisions applying in the United Kingdom as may be specified.

   (2)   "Convertible securities" means securities of a specified kind which can be converted into, or exchanged for, or which confer rights to acquire, other securities.

   (3)   "Conversion" means conversion into or exchange for, or the exercise of rights conferred by the securities to acquire, other securities.

Charities

18. The securities are issued by—
      (a)   a charity within the meaning of—
           (i)   section 96(1) of the Charities Act 1993, or
          (ii)   section 35 of the Charities Act (Northern Ireland) 1964,
      (b)   a recognised body within the meaning of section 1(7) of the Law Reform (Miscellaneous Provisions) (Scotland) Act 1990,
      (c)   a housing association within the meaning of—
           (i)   section 5(1) of the Housing Act 1985,
          (ii)   section 1 of the Housing Associations Act 1985, or
         (iii)   Article 3 of the Housing (Northern Ireland) Order 1992,
      (d)   an industrial or provident society registered in accordance with—
           (i)   section 1(2)(b) of the Industrial and Provident Societies Act 1965, or
          (ii)   section 1(2)(b) of the Industrial and Provident Societies Act 1969, or
      (e)   a non-profit making association or body, recognised by the country or territory in which it is established, with objectives similar to those of a body falling within any of paragraphs (a) to (c),

and the proceeds of the offer will be used for the purposes of the issuer's objectives.

Building societies etc

19. The securities offered are shares which are issued by, or ownership of which entitles the holder to membership of or to obtain the benefit of services provided by—
      (a)   a building society incorporated under the law of, or of any part of, the United Kingdom;
      (b)   any body incorporated under the law of, or of any part of, the United Kingdom relating to industrial and provident societies or credit unions; or
      (c)   a body of a similar nature established in another EEA State.

Euro-securities

20.—(1)The securities offered are Euro-securities and no advertisement relating to the offer is issued in the United Kingdom, or is caused to be so issued—
      (a)   by the issuer of the Euro-securities;
      (b)   by any credit institution or other financial institution through which the Euro-securities may be acquired pursuant to the offer; or
      (c)   by any body corporate which is a member of the same group as the issuer or any of those institutions.

(2)   But sub-paragraph (1) does not apply to an advertisement of a prescribed kind.

(3)   "Euro-securities" means investments which—
      (a)   are to be underwritten and distributed by a syndicate at least two of the members of which have their registered offices in different countries or territories;
      (b)   are to be offered on a significant scale in one or more countries or territories, other than the country or territory in which the issuer has its registered office; and
      (c)   may be acquired pursuant to the offer only through a credit institution or other financial institution.

(4)   "Credit institution" means a credit institution as defined in [Article 1(1)(a)] of [the banking consolidation directive].

(5)   "Financial institution" means a financial institution as defined in Article 1 of [the banking consolidation directive].

(6) "Underwritten" means underwritten by whatever means, including by acquisition or subscription, with a view to resale.

Same class securities

21. The securities are of the same class, and were issued at the same time, as securities in respect of which a prospectus has been published under or by virtue of—
    (a) Part VI;
    (b) Part III of the Companies Act 1985; or
    (c) such other provisions applying in the United Kingdom as may be specified.

Short date securities

22. The securities are investments of a specified kind with a maturity of less than one year from their date of issue.

Government and public securities

23.—(1) The securities are investments of a specified kind creating or acknowledging indebtedness issued by or on behalf of a public authority.

(2) "Public authority" means—
    (a) the government of the United Kingdom;
    (b) the government of any country or territory outside the United Kingdom;
    (c) a local authority in the United Kingdom or elsewhere;
    (d) any international organisation the members of which include the United Kingdom or another EEA State; and
    (e) such other bodies, if any, as may be specified.

Non-transferable securities

24. The securities are not transferable.

[Units in a collective investment scheme

24A. The securities are units (as defined by section 237(2)) in a collective investment scheme.]

General definitions

25. For the purposes of this Schedule—
    "shares" has such meaning as may be specified; and
    "specified" means specified in an order made by the Treasury.

Commencement: 25 February 2001.
Amendments: Para 2: figure in square brackets in sub-para (1) substituted by the Public Offers of Securities (Exemptions) Regulations 2001, SI 2001/2955, reg 2(a), as from 14 September 2001.
Para 20: words in first pair of square brackets in sub-para (4) substituted by the Electronic Money (Miscellaneous Amendments) Regulations 2002, SI 2002/765, reg 4, as from 27 April 2002, words in second pair of square brackets substituted by the Banking Consolidation Directive (Consequential Amendments) Regulations 2000, SI 2000/2952, reg 8(1), (6)(a), as from 22 November 2000; words in square brackets in sub-para (5) substituted by SI 2000/2952, reg 8(1), (6)(b), as from 22 November 2000. Para 24A: inserted, together with preceding cross-heading, by SI 2001/2955, reg 2(b), as from 14 September 2001.
Council Directive 78/855/EEC: OJ L295, 20.10.1978, p 36.
Regulations: The Financial Services and Markets Act 2000 (Official Listing of Securities) Regulations 2001, SI 2001/2956, as amended by SI 2001/3439 (made under paras 16(3), (4), 20(2)).
Orders: The Financial Services and Markets Act 2000 (Offers of Securities) Order 2001, SI 2001/2958 (made under paras 8(2), 15, 17, 21, 22, 23 and 25).
References: See paras 9.51–9.75.

SCHEDULE 12

TRANSFER SCHEMES: CERTIFICATES

PART I
INSURANCE BUSINESS TRANSFER SCHEMES

1.—(1)   For the purposes of section 111(2) the appropriate certificates, in relation to an insurance business transfer scheme, are—

    (a)   a certificate under paragraph 2;

    (b)   if sub-paragraph (2) applies, a certificate under paragraph 3;

    (c)   if sub-paragraph (3) applies, a certificate under paragraph 4;

    (d)   if sub-paragraph (4) applies, a certificate under paragraph 5.

(2)   This sub-paragraph applies if—

    (a)   the authorised person concerned is a UK authorised person which has received authorisation under Article 6 of the first life insurance directive or of the first non-life insurance directive from the Authority; and

    (b)   the establishment from which the business is to be transferred under the proposed insurance business transfer scheme is in an EEA State other than the United Kingdom.

(3)   This sub-paragraph applies if—

    (a)   the authorised person concerned has received authorisation under Article 6 of the first life insurance directive from the Authority;

    (b)   the proposed transfer relates to business which consists of the effecting or carrying out of contracts of long-term insurance; and

    (c)   as regards any policy which is included in the proposed transfer and which evidences a contract of insurance (other than reinsurance), an EEA State other than the United Kingdom is the State of the commitment.

(4)   This sub-paragraph applies if—

    (a)   the authorised person concerned has received authorisation under Article 6 of the first non-life insurance directive from the Authority;

    (b)   the business to which the proposed insurance business transfer scheme relates is business which consists of the effecting or carrying out of contracts of general insurance; and

    (c)   as regards any policy which is included in the proposed transfer and which evidences a contract of insurance (other than reinsurance), the risk is situated in an EEA State other than the United Kingdom.

Certificates as to margin of solvency

2.—(1)   A certificate under this paragraph is to be given—

    (a)   by the relevant authority; or

    (b)   in a case in which there is no relevant authority, by the Authority.

(2)   A certificate given under sub-paragraph (1)(a) is one certifying that, taking the proposed transfer into account—

    (a)   the transferee possesses, or will possess before the scheme takes effect, the necessary margin of solvency; or

    (b)   there is no necessary margin of solvency applicable to the transferee.

(3)   A certificate under sub-paragraph (1)(b) is one certifying that the Authority has received from the authority which it considers to be the authority responsible for supervising persons who effect or carry out contracts of insurance in the place to which the business is to be transferred that, taking the proposed transfer into account—

    (a)   the transferee possesses or will possess before the scheme takes effect the margin of solvency required under the law applicable in that place; or

    (b)   there is no such margin of solvency applicable to the transferee.

(4)   "Necessary margin of solvency" means the margin of solvency required in relation to the transferee, taking the proposed transfer into account, under the law which it is the responsibility of the relevant authority to apply.

(5)   "Margin of solvency" means the excess of the value of the assets of the transferee over the amount of its liabilities.

(6)   "Relevant authority" means—

    (a)   if the transferee is an EEA firm falling within paragraph 5(d) of Schedule 3, its home state regulator;

    (b)   if the transferee is a Swiss general insurer, the authority responsible in Switzerland for supervising persons who effect or carry out contracts of insurance;

    (c)   if the transferee is an authorised person not falling within paragraph (a) or (b), the Authority.

(7)   In sub-paragraph (6), any reference to a transferee of a particular description includes a reference to a transferee who will be of that description if the proposed scheme takes effect.

(8)   "Swiss general insurer" means a body—

    (a)   whose head office is in Switzerland;

    (b)   which has permission to carry on regulated activities consisting of the effecting and carrying out of contracts of general insurance; and

    (c)   whose permission is not restricted to the effecting or carrying out of contracts of reinsurance.

Certificates as to consent

3.   A certificate under this paragraph is one given by the Authority and certifying that the host State regulator has been notified of the proposed scheme and that—

    (a)   that regulator has responded to the notification; or

    (b)   that it has not responded but the period of three months beginning with the notification has elapsed.

Certificates as to long-term business

4.   A certificate under this paragraph is one given by the Authority and certifying that the authority responsible for supervising persons who effect or carry out contracts of insurance in the State of the commitment has been notified of the proposed scheme and that—

    (a)   that authority has consented to the proposed scheme; or

    (b)   the period of three months beginning with the notification has elapsed and that authority has not refused its consent.

Certificates as to general business

5.   A certificate under this paragraph is one given by the Authority and certifying that the authority responsible for supervising persons who effect or carry out contracts of insurance in the EEA State in which the risk is situated has been notified of the proposed scheme and that—

    (a)   that authority has consented to the proposed scheme; or

    (b)   the period of three months beginning with the notification has elapsed and that authority has not refused its consent.

Interpretation of Part I

6.—(1)   "State of the commitment", in relation to a commitment entered into at any date, means—

    (a)   if the policyholder is an individual, the State in which he had his habitual residence at that date;

      (b)   if the policyholder is not an individual, the State in which the establishment of the policyholder to which the commitment relates was situated at that date.

(2)   "Commitment" means a commitment represented by contracts of insurance of a prescribed class.

(3)   References to the EEA State in which a risk is situated are—

      (a)   if the insurance relates to a building or to a building and its contents (so far as the contents are covered by the same policy), to the EEA State in which the building is situated;

      (b)   if the insurance relates to a vehicle of any type, to the EEA State of registration;

      (c)   in the case of policies of a duration of four months or less covering travel or holiday risks (whatever the class concerned), to the EEA State in which the policyholder took out the policy;

      (d)   in a case not covered by paragraphs (a) to (c)—

          (i)   if the policyholder is an individual, to the EEA State in which he has his habitual residence at the date when the contract is entered into; and

         (ii)   otherwise, to the EEA State in which the establishment of the policyholder to which the policy relates is situated at that date.

Commencement: 25 February 2001 (para 6(2)); 1 December 2001 (remainder).
Regulations: The Financial Services and Markets Act 2000 (Control of Business Transfers) (Requirements on Applicants) Regulations 2001, SI 2001/3625 (made under para 6).
References: See paras 22.16–22.22.

PART II
BANKING BUSINESS TRANSFER SCHEMES

7.—(1)   For the purposes of section 111(2) the appropriate certificates, in relation to a banking business transfer scheme, are—

      (a)   a certificate under paragraph 8; and

      (b)   if sub-paragraph (2) applies, a certificate under paragraph 9.

(2)   This sub-paragraph applies if the authorised person concerned or the transferee is an EEA firm falling within paragraph 5(b) of Schedule 3.

Certificates as to financial resources

8.—(1)   A certificate under this paragraph is one given by the relevant authority and certifying that, taking the proposed transfer into account, the transferee possesses, or will possess before the scheme takes effect, adequate financial resources.

(2)   "Relevant authority" means—

      (a)   if the transferee is a person with a Part IV permission or with permission under Schedule 4, the Authority;

      (b)   if the transferee is an EEA firm falling within paragraph 5(b) of Schedule 3, its home state regulator;

      (c)   if the transferee does not fall within paragraph (a) or (b), the authority responsible for the supervision of the transferee's business in the place in which the transferee has its head office.

(3)   In sub-paragraph (2), any reference to a transferee of a particular description of person includes a reference to a transferee who will be of that description if the proposed banking business transfer scheme takes effect.

Certificates as to consent of home state regulator

9.   A certificate under this paragraph is one given by the Authority and certifying that the home State regulator of the authorised person concerned or of the transferee has been notified of the proposed scheme and that—

(a)   the home State regulator has responded to the notification; or

(b)   the period of three months beginning with the notification has elapsed.

Commencement: 1 December 2001.
References: See paras 22.32–22.36.

PART III
INSURANCE BUSINESS TRANSFERS EFFECTED OUTSIDE THE UNITED KINGDOM

10.—(1)   This paragraph applies to a proposal to execute under provisions corresponding to Part VII in a country or territory other than the United Kingdom an instrument transferring all the rights and obligations of the transferor under general or long-term insurance policies, or under such descriptions of such policies as may be specified in the instrument, to the transferee if any of the conditions in sub-paragraphs (2), (3) or (4) is met in relation to it.

(2)   The transferor is an EEA firm falling within paragraph 5(d) of Schedule 3 and the transferee is an authorised person whose margin of solvency is supervised by the Authority.

(3)   The transferor is a company authorised in an EEA State other than the United Kingdom under Article 27 of the first life insurance directive, or Article 23 of the first non-life insurance directive and the transferee is a UK authorised person which has received authorisation under Article 6 of either of those directives.

(4)   The transferor is a Swiss general insurer and the transferee is a UK authorised person which has received authorisation under Article 6 of the first life insurance directive or the first non-life insurance directive.

(5)   In relation to a proposed transfer to which this paragraph applies, the Authority may, if it is satisfied that the transferee possesses the necessary margin of solvency, issue a certificate to that effect.

(6)   "Necessary margin of solvency" means the margin of solvency which the transferee, taking the proposed transfer into account, is required by the Authority to maintain.

(7)   "Swiss general insurer" has the same meaning as in paragraph 2.

(8)   "General policy" means a policy evidencing a contract which, if it had been effected by the transferee, would have constituted the carrying on of a regulated activity consisting of the effecting of contracts of general insurance.

(9)   "Long-term policy" means a policy evidencing a contract which, if it had been effected by the transferee, would have constituted the carrying on of a regulated activity consisting of the effecting of contracts of long-term insurance.

Commencement: 1 December 2001.
References: See paras 22.23–22.31.

SCHEDULE 13

Section 132(4)

THE FINANCIAL SERVICES AND MARKETS TRIBUNAL

PART I
GENERAL

Interpretation

1.   In this Schedule—
   "panel of chairmen" means the panel established under paragraph 3(1);
   "lay panel" means the panel established under paragraph 3(4);
   "rules" means rules made by the Lord Chancellor under section 132.

Commencement: 3 September 2001.
References: See para 12.7.

PART II
THE TRIBUNAL

President

2.—(1)   The Lord Chancellor must appoint one of the members of the panel of chairmen to preside over the discharge of the Tribunal's functions.

(2)   The member so appointed is to be known as the President of the Financial Services and Markets Tribunal (but is referred to in this Act as "the President").

(3)   The Lord Chancellor may appoint one of the members of the panel of chairmen to be Deputy President.

(4)   The Deputy President is to have such functions in relation to the Tribunal as the President may assign to him.

(5)   The Lord Chancellor may not appoint a person to be the President or Deputy President unless that person—

    (a)   has a ten year general qualification within the meaning of section 71 of the Courts and Legal Services Act 1990;

    (b)   is an advocate or solicitor in Scotland of at least ten years' standing; or

    (c)   is—

        (i)   a member of the Bar of Northern Ireland of at least ten years' standing; or

        (ii)   a solicitor of the Supreme Court of Northern Ireland of at least ten years' standing.

(6)   If the President (or Deputy President) ceases to be a member of the panel of chairmen, he also ceases to be the President (or Deputy President).

(7)   The functions of the President may, if he is absent or is otherwise unable to act, be discharged—

    (a)   by the Deputy President; or

    (b)   if there is no Deputy President or he too is absent or otherwise unable to act, by a person appointed for that purpose from the panel of chairmen by the Lord Chancellor.

Panels

3.—(1)   The Lord Chancellor must appoint a panel of persons for the purposes of serving as chairmen of the Tribunal.

(2)   A person is qualified for membership of the panel of chairmen if—

    (a)   he has a seven year general qualification within the meaning of section 71 of the Courts and Legal Services Act 1990;

    (b)   he is an advocate or solicitor in Scotland of at least seven years' standing; or

    (c)   he is—

        (i)   a member of the Bar of Northern Ireland of at least seven years' standing; or

        (ii)   a solicitor of the Supreme Court of Northern Ireland of at least seven years' standing.

(3)   The panel of chairmen must include at least one member who is a person of the kind mentioned in sub-paragraph (2)(b).

(4)   The Lord Chancellor must also appoint a panel of persons who appear to him to be qualified by experience or otherwise to deal with matters of the kind that may be referred to the Tribunal.

Terms of office etc

4.—(1)   Subject to the provisions of this Schedule, each member of the panel of chairmen and the lay panel is to hold and vacate office in accordance with the terms of his appointment.

(2)   The Lord Chancellor may remove a member of either panel (including the President) on the ground of incapacity or misbehaviour.

(3)   A member of either panel—
   (a)   may at any time resign office by notice in writing to the Lord Chancellor;
   (b)   is eligible for re-appointment if he ceases to hold office.

Remuneration and expenses

5.   The Lord Chancellor may pay to any person, in respect of his service—
   (a)   as a member of the Tribunal (including service as the President or Deputy President), or
   (b)   as a person appointed under paragraph 7(4),
such remuneration and allowances as he may determine.

Staff

6.—(1)   The Lord Chancellor may appoint such staff for the Tribunal as he may determine.

(2)   The remuneration of the Tribunal's staff is to be defrayed by the Lord Chancellor.

(3)   Such expenses of the Tribunal as the Lord Chancellor may determine are to be defrayed by the Lord Chancellor.

Commencement: 3 September 2001.
References: See paras 12.7–12.10.

PART III
CONSTITUTION OF TRIBUNAL

7.—(1)   On a reference to the Tribunal, the persons to act as members of the Tribunal for the purposes of the reference are to be selected from the panel of chairmen or the lay panel in accordance with arrangements made by the President for the purposes of this paragraph ("the standing arrangements").

(2)   The standing arrangements must provide for at least one member to be selected from the panel of chairmen.

(3)   If while a reference is being dealt with, a person serving as member of the Tribunal in respect of the reference becomes unable to act, the reference may be dealt with by—
   (a)   the other members selected in respect of that reference; or
   (b)   if it is being dealt with by a single member, such other member of the panel of chairmen as may be selected in accordance with the standing arrangements for the purposes of the reference.

(4)   If it appears to the Tribunal that a matter before it involves a question of fact of special difficulty, it may appoint one or more experts to provide assistance.

Commencement: 3 September 2001.
References: See paras 12.11, 12.12.

PART IV
TRIBUNAL PROCEDURE

8.   For the purpose of dealing with references, or any matter preliminary or incidental to a reference, the Tribunal must sit at such times and in such place or places as the Lord Chancellor may direct.

9. Rules made by the Lord Chancellor under section 132 may, in particular, include provision—

    (a)   as to the manner in which references are to be instituted;

    (b)   for the holding of hearings in private in such circumstances as may be specified in the rules;

    (c)   as to the persons who may appear on behalf of the parties;

    (d)   for a member of the panel of chairmen to hear and determine interlocutory matters arising on a reference;

    (e)   for the suspension of decisions of the Authority which have taken effect;

    (f)   as to the withdrawal of references;

    (g)   as to the registration, publication and proof of decisions and orders.

Practice directions

10. The President of the Tribunal may give directions as to the practice and procedure to be followed by the Tribunal in relation to references to it.

Evidence

11.—(1) The Tribunal may by summons require any person to attend, at such time and place as is specified in the summons, to give evidence or to produce any document in his custody or under his control which the Tribunal considers it necessary to examine.

    (2)   The Tribunal may—

    (a)   take evidence on oath and for that purpose administer oaths; or

    (b)   instead of administering an oath, require the person examined to make and subscribe a declaration of the truth of the matters in respect of which he is examined.

    (3)   A person who without reasonable excuse—

    (a)   refuses or fails—

        (i)   to attend following the issue of a summons by the Tribunal, or

        (ii)   to give evidence, or

    (b)   alters, suppresses, conceals or destroys, or refuses to produce a document which he may be required to produce for the purposes of proceedings before the Tribunal,

is guilty of an offence.

    (4)   A person guilty of an offence under sub-paragraph (3)(a) is liable on summary conviction to a fine not exceeding the statutory maximum.

    (5)   A person guilty of an offence under sub-paragraph (3)(b) is liable—

    (a)   on summary conviction, to a fine not exceeding the statutory maximum;

    (b)   on conviction on indictment, to imprisonment for a term not exceeding two years or a fine or both.

Decisions of Tribunal

12.—(1) A decision of the Tribunal may be taken by a majority.

    (2)   The decision must—

    (a)   state whether it was unanimous or taken by a majority;

    (b)   be recorded in a document which—

        (i)   contains a statement of the reasons for the decision; and

        (ii)   is signed and dated by the member of the panel of chairmen dealing with the reference.

    (3)   The Tribunal must—

    (a)   inform each party of its decision; and

    (b)   as soon as reasonably practicable, send to each party and, if different, to any authorised person concerned, a copy of the document mentioned in sub-paragraph (2).

    (4)   The Tribunal must send the Treasury a copy of its decision.

Costs

13.—(1)   If the Tribunal considers that a party to any proceedings on a reference has acted vexatiously, frivolously or unreasonably it may order that party to pay to another party to the proceedings the whole or part of the costs or expenses incurred by the other party in connection with the proceedings.

(2)   If, in any proceedings on a reference, the Tribunal considers that a decision of the Authority which is the subject of the reference was unreasonable it may order the Authority to pay to another party to the proceedings the whole or part of the costs or expenses incurred by the other party in connection with the proceedings.

Commencement: 3 September 2001 (paras 8, 10–13); 25 February 2001 (remainder).
Rules: The Financial Services and Markets Tribunal Rules 2001, SI 2001/2476, as modified by SI 2001/3592.
References: See paras 12.13, 12.18, 12.19, 12.26, 12.29.

SCHEDULE 14

Section 162

ROLE OF THE COMPETITION COMMISSION

Provision of information by Treasury

1.—(1)   The Treasury's powers under this paragraph are to be exercised only for the purpose of assisting the Commission in carrying out an investigation under section 162.

(2)   The Treasury may give to the Commission—
  (a)   any information in their possession which relates to matters falling within the scope of the investigation; and
  (b)   other assistance in relation to any such matters.

(3)   In carrying out an investigation under section 162, the Commission must have regard to any information given to it under this paragraph.

Consideration of matters arising on a report

2.   In considering any matter arising from a report made by the [OFT] under section 160, the Commission must have regard to—
  (a)   any representations made to [the Commission] in connection with the matter by any person appearing to the Commission to have a substantial interest in the matter; and
  (b)   any cost benefit analysis prepared by the Authority (at any time) in connection with the regulatory provision or practice, or any of the regulatory provisions or practices, which are the subject of the report.

[Investigations under section 162: application of Enterprise Act 2002

2A.—(1)   The following sections of Part 3 of the Enterprise Act 2002 shall apply, with the modifications mentioned in sub-paragraphs (2) and (3), for the purposes of any investigation by the Commission under section 162 of this Act as they apply for the purposes of references under that Part—
  (a)   section 109 (attendance of witnesses and production of documents etc);
  (b)   section 110 (enforcement of powers under section 109: general);
  (c)   section 111 (penalties);
  (d)   section 112 (penalties: main procedural requirements);
  (e)   section 113 (payments and interest by instalments);
  (f)   section 114 (appeals in relation to penalties);
  (g)   section 115 (recovery of penalties); and
  (h)   section 116 (statement of policy).

(2)   Section 110 shall, in its application by virtue of sub-paragraph (1), have effect as if—
  (a)   subsection (2) were omitted; and

(b) in subsection (9) the words from "or section" to "section 65(3))" were omitted.

(3) Section 111(5)(b) shall, in its application by virtue of sub-paragraph (1), have effect as if for sub-paragraph (ii) there were substituted—

"(ii) if earlier, the day on which the report of the Commission on the investigation concerned is made or, if the Commission decides not to make a report, the day on which the Commission makes the statement required by section 162(3) of the Financial Services and Markets Act 2000."

(4) Section 117 of the Enterprise Act 2002 (false or misleading information) shall apply in relation to functions of the Commission in connection with an investigation under section 162 of this Act as it applies in relation to its functions under Part 3 of that Act but as if, in subsections (1)(a) and (2), the words *"the OFT,"* and "or the Secretary of State" were omitted.

(5) Provisions of Part 3 of the Enterprise Act 2002 which have effect for the purposes of sections 109 to 117 of that Act (including, in particular, provisions relating to offences and the making of orders) shall, for the purposes of the application of those sections by virtue of sub-paragraph (1) or (4) above, have effect in relation to those sections as applied by virtue of those sub-paragraphs.

(6) Accordingly, corresponding provisions of this Act shall not have effect in relation to those sections as applied by virtue of those sub-paragraphs.

Section 162: modification of Schedule 7 to the Competition Act 1998

2B. For the purposes of its application in relation to the function of the Commission of deciding in accordance with section 162(2) of this Act not to make a report, paragraph 15(7) of Schedule 7 to the Competition Act 1998 (power of the Chairman to act on his own while a group is being constituted) has effect as if, after paragraph (a), there were inserted

"; or

(aa) in the case of an investigation under section 162 of the Financial Services and Markets Act 2000, decide not to make a report in accordance with subsection (2) of that section (decision not to make a report where no useful purpose would be served)."

Reports under section 162: further provision

2C.—(1) For the purposes of section 163 of this Act, a conclusion contained in a report of the Commission is to be disregarded if the conclusion is not that of at least two-thirds of the members of the group constituted in connection with the investigation concerned in pursuance of paragraph 15 of Schedule 7 to the Competition Act 1998.

(2) If a member of a group so constituted disagrees with any conclusions contained in a report made under section 162 of this Act as the conclusions of the Commission, the report shall, if the member so wishes, include a statement of his disagreement and of his reasons for disagreeing.

(3) For the purposes of the law relating to defamation, absolute privilege attaches to any report made by the Commission under section 162.]

. . .

3. . . .

Publication of reports

4.—(1) If the Commission makes a report under section 162, it must publish it in such a way as appears to it to be best calculated to bring it to the attention of the public.

(2)   Before publishing the report the Commission must, so far as practicable, exclude any matter which relates to the private affairs of a particular individual the publication of which, in the opinion of the Commission, would or might seriously and prejudicially affect his interests.

(3)   Before publishing the report the Commission must, so far as practicable, also exclude any matter which relates to the affairs of a particular body the publication of which, in the opinion of the Commission, would or might seriously and prejudicially affect its interests.

(4)   Sub-paragraphs (2) and (3) do not apply in relation to copies of a report which the Commission is required to send under section 162(10).

Commencement: 18 June 2001.
Amendments: Para 2: words in square brackets substituted by the Enterprise Act 2002, s 278(1), Sch 25, para 40(1), (20)(a), as from 1 April 2003.
Paras 2A–2C: inserted by the Enterprise Act 2002, s 278(1), Sch 25, para 40(1), (20)(b), as from 20 June 2003, except in relation to any investigation commenced before that date under s 162 or 306 of this Act; for the words in italics in para 2A(4) there are substituted the words ""the OFT, OFCOM,"" by the Communications Act 2003, s 389, Sch 16, para 5, as from a day to be appointed (subject to transitional provisions in Sch 18 thereto).
Para 3: repealed by the Enterprise Act 2002, s 278, Sch 25, para 40(1), (20)(c), Sch 26, as from 20 June 2003, except in relation to any investigation commenced before that date under s 162 or 306 of this Act.
Orders: The Competition Commission (Penalties) Order 2003, SI 2003/1371.
References: See paras 10.21–10.23, 10.33, 10.34, 10.45–10.47.

SCHEDULE 15

Sections 165(11) and 171(4)

INFORMATION AND INVESTIGATIONS: CONNECTED PERSONS

PART I
RULES FOR SPECIFIC BODIES

Corporate bodies

1. If the authorised person ("BC") is a body corporate, a person who is or has been—
    (a)   an officer or manager of BC or of a parent undertaking of BC;
    (b)   an employee of BC;
    (c)   an agent of BC or of a parent undertaking of BC.

Partnerships

2. If the authorised person ("PP") is a partnership, a person who is or has been a member, manager, employee or agent of PP.

Unincorporated associations

3. If the authorised person ("UA") is an unincorporated association of persons which is neither a partnership nor an unincorporated friendly society, a person who is or has been an officer, manager, employee or agent of UA.

Friendly societies

4.—(1)   If the authorised person ("FS") is a friendly society, a person who is or has been an officer, manager or employee of FS.

(2)   In relation to FS, "officer" and "manager" have the same meaning as in section 119(1) of the Friendly Societies Act 1992.

Building societies

5.—(1)   If the authorised person ("BS") is a building society, a person who is or has been an officer or employee of BS.

(2)   In relation to BS, "officer" has the same meaning as it has in section 119(1) of the Building Societies Act 1986.

Individuals

6. If the authorised person ("IP") is an individual, a person who is or has been an employee or agent of IP.

Application to sections 171 and 172

7. For the purposes of sections 171 and 172, if the person under investigation is not an authorised person the references in this Part of this Schedule to an authorised person are to be taken to be references to the person under investigation.

Commencement: 3 September 2001.

PART II
ADDITIONAL RULES

8. A person who is, or at the relevant time was, the partner, manager, employee, agent, appointed representative, banker, auditor, actuary or solicitor of—
    (a)   the person under investigation ("A");
    (b)   a parent undertaking of A;
    (c)   a subsidiary undertaking of A;
    (d)   a subsidiary undertaking of a parent undertaking of A; or
    (e)   a parent undertaking of a subsidiary undertaking of A.

Commencement: 3 September 2001.
References: See paras 7.2, 7.11, 7.23, 7.28.

SCHEDULE 16

Section 203(8)

PROHIBITIONS AND RESTRICTIONS IMPOSED BY [OFFICE OF FAIR TRADING]

Preliminary

1. In this Schedule—
    "appeal period" has the same meaning as in the Consumer Credit Act 1974;
    "prohibition" means a consumer credit prohibition under section 203;
    "restriction" means a restriction under section 204.

Notice of prohibition or restriction

2.—(1)   This paragraph applies if the [OFT] proposes, in relation to a firm—
    (a)   to impose a prohibition;
    (b)   to impose a restriction; or
    (c)   to vary a restriction otherwise than with the agreement of the firm.

(2)   The [OFT] must by notice—
    (a)   inform the firm of [its] proposal, stating [its] reasons; and
    (b)   invite the firm to submit representations in accordance with paragraph 4.

(3)   If [the OFT] imposes the prohibition or restriction or varies the restriction, the [OFT] may give directions authorising the firm to carry into effect agreements made before the coming into force of the prohibition, restriction or variation.

(4)   A prohibition, restriction or variation is not to come into force before the end of the appeal period.

(5)   If the [OFT] imposes a prohibition or restriction or varies a restriction, [the OFT] must serve a copy of the prohibition, restriction or variation—

  (a)   on the Authority; and

  (b)   on the firm's home state regulator.

Application to revoke prohibition or restriction

3.—(1)   This paragraph applies if the [OFT] proposes to refuse an application made by a firm for the revocation of a prohibition or restriction.

(2)   The [OFT] must by notice—

  (a)   inform the firm of the proposed refusal, stating [its] reasons; and

  (b)   invite the firm to submit representations in accordance with paragraph 4.

Representations to [OFT]

4.—(1)   If this paragraph applies to an invitation to submit representations, the [OFT] must invite the firm, within 21 days after the notice containing the invitation is given to it or such longer period as [the OFT] may allow—

  (a)   to submit its representations in writing to [the OFT]; and

  (b)   to give notice to [the OFT], if the firm thinks fit, that it wishes to make representations orally.

(2)   If notice is given under sub-paragraph (1)(b), the [OFT] must arrange for the oral representations to be heard.

(3)   The [OFT] must give the firm notice of [its] determination.

Appeals

5. Section 41 of the Consumer Credit Act 1974 (appeals to the Secretary of State) has effect as if—

  (a)   the following determinations were mentioned in column 1 of the table set out at the end of that section—

    (i)   imposition of a prohibition or restriction or the variation of a restriction; and

    (ii)   refusal of an application for the revocation of a prohibition or restriction; and

  (b)   the firm concerned were mentioned in column 2 of that table in relation to those determinations.

Commencement: 1 December 2001.

Amendments: Words in square brackets substituted by the Enterprise Act 2002, s 278(1), Sch 25, para 40(1), (21), as from 1 April 2003.

SCHEDULE 17

Section 225(4)

THE OMBUDSMAN SCHEME

PART I
GENERAL

Interpretation

1. In this Schedule—

  "ombudsman" means a person who is a member of the panel; and

  "the panel" means the panel established under paragraph 4.

Commencement: 18 June 2001.
References: See para 14.11.

PART II
THE SCHEME OPERATOR

Establishment by the Authority

2.—(1)   The Authority must establish a body corporate to exercise the functions conferred on the scheme operator by or under this Act.

(2)   The Authority must take such steps as are necessary to ensure that the scheme operator is, at all times, capable of exercising those functions.

Constitution

3.—(1)   The constitution of the scheme operator must provide for it to have—
(a)   a chairman; and
(b)   a board (which must include the chairman) whose members are the scheme operator's directors.

(2)   The chairman and other members of the board must be persons appointed, and liable to removal from office, by the Authority (acting, in the case of the chairman, with the approval of the Treasury).

(3)   But the terms of their appointment (and in particular those governing removal from office) must be such as to secure their independence from the Authority in the operation of the scheme.

(4)   The function of making voluntary jurisdiction rules under section 227 and the functions conferred by paragraphs 4, 5, 7, 9 or 14 may be exercised only by the board.

(5)   The validity of any act of the scheme operator is unaffected by—
(a)   a vacancy in the office of chairman; or
(b)   a defect in the appointment of a person as chairman or as a member of the board.

The panel of ombudsmen

4.—(1)   The scheme operator must appoint and maintain a panel of persons, appearing to it to have appropriate qualifications and experience, to act as ombudsmen for the purposes of the scheme.

(2)   A person's appointment to the panel is to be on such terms (including terms as to the duration and termination of his appointment and as to remuneration) as the scheme operator considers—
(a)   consistent with the independence of the person appointed; and
(b)   otherwise appropriate.

The Chief Ombudsman

5.—(1)   The scheme operator must appoint one member of the panel to act as Chief Ombudsman.

(2)   The Chief Ombudsman is to be appointed on such terms (including terms as to the duration and termination of his appointment) as the scheme operator considers appropriate.

Status

6.—(1)   The scheme operator is not to be regarded as exercising functions on behalf of the Crown.

(2)   The scheme operator's board members, officers and staff are not to be regarded as Crown servants.

(3)　Appointment as Chief Ombudsman or to the panel or as a deputy ombudsman does not confer the status of Crown servant.

Annual reports

7.—(1)　At least once a year—
- (a)　the scheme operator must make a report to the Authority on the discharge of its functions; and
- (b)　the Chief Ombudsman must make a report to the Authority on the discharge of his functions.

(2)　Each report must distinguish between functions in relation to the scheme's compulsory jurisdiction and functions in relation to its voluntary jurisdiction.

(3)　Each report must also comply with any requirements specified in rules made by the Authority.

(4)　The scheme operator must publish each report in the way it considers appropriate.

Guidance

8.　The scheme operator may publish guidance consisting of such information and advice as it considers appropriate and may charge for it or distribute it free of charge.

Budget

9.—(1)　The scheme operator must, before the start of each of its financial years, adopt an annual budget which has been approved by the Authority.

(2)　The scheme operator may, with the approval of the Authority, vary the budget for a financial year at any time after its adoption.

(3)　The annual budget must include an indication of—
- (a)　the distribution of resources deployed in the operation of the scheme, and
- (b)　the amounts of income of the scheme operator arising or expected to arise from the operation of the scheme,

distinguishing between the scheme's compulsory and voluntary jurisdiction.

Exemption from liability in damages

10.—(1)　No person is to be liable in damages for anything done or omitted in the discharge, or purported discharge, of any functions under this Act in relation to the compulsory jurisdiction.

(2)　Sub-paragraph (1) does not apply—
- (a)　if the act or omission is shown to have been in bad faith; or
- (b)　so as to prevent an award of damages made in respect of an act or omission on the ground that the act or omission was unlawful as a result of section 6(1) of the Human Rights Act 1998.

Privilege

11.　For the purposes of the law relating to defamation, proceedings in relation to a complaint which is subject to the compulsory jurisdiction are to be treated as if they were proceedings before a court.

Commencement: 18 June 2001.
Scheme operator's budget: Para 9(3) above does not apply to the scheme operator's first budget (ie its budget for the financial year during which 18 June 2001 occurs); see the Financial Services and Markets Act 2000 (Consequential and Transitional Provisions) (Miscellaneous) Order 2001, SI 2001/1821, art 4 (made under ss 426–428 ante).
References: See paras 14.16–14.18.

PART III
THE COMPULSORY JURISDICTION

Introduction

12. This Part of this Schedule applies only in relation to the compulsory jurisdiction.

Authority's procedural rules

13.—(1)   The Authority must make rules providing that a complaint is not to be entertained unless the complainant has referred it under the ombudsman scheme before the applicable time limit (determined in accordance with the rules) has expired.

(2)   The rules may provide that an ombudsman may extend that time limit in specified circumstances.

(3)   The Authority may make rules providing that a complaint is not to be entertained (except in specified circumstances) if the complainant has not previously communicated its substance to the respondent and given him a reasonable opportunity to deal with it.

(4)   The Authority may make rules requiring an authorised person who may become subject to the compulsory jurisdiction as a respondent to establish such procedures as the Authority considers appropriate for the resolution of complaints which—

(a)   may be referred to the scheme; and

(b)   arise out of activity to which the Authority's powers under Part X do not apply.

The scheme operator's rules

14.—(1)   The scheme operator must make rules, to be known as "scheme rules", which are to set out the procedure for reference of complaints and for their investigation, consideration and determination by an ombudsman.

(2)   Scheme rules may, among other things—

(a)   specify matters which are to be taken into account in determining whether an act or omission was fair and reasonable;

(b)   provide that a complaint may, in specified circumstances, be dismissed without consideration of its merits;

(c)   provide for the reference of a complaint, in specified circumstances and with the consent of the complainant, to another body with a view to its being determined by that body instead of by an ombudsman;

(d)   make provision as to the evidence which may be required or admitted, the extent to which it should be oral or written and the consequences of a person's failure to produce any information or document which he has been required (under section 231 or otherwise) to produce;

(e)   allow an ombudsman to fix time limits for any aspect of the proceedings and to extend a time limit;

(f)   provide for certain things in relation to the reference, investigation or consideration (but not determination) of a complaint to be done by a member of the scheme operator's staff instead of by an ombudsman;

(g)   make different provision in relation to different kinds of complaint.

(3)   The circumstances specified under sub-paragraph (2)(b) may include the following—

(a)   the ombudsman considers the complaint frivolous or vexatious;

(b)   legal proceedings have been brought concerning the subject-matter of the complaint and the ombudsman considers that the complaint is best dealt with in those proceedings; or

(c)   the ombudsman is satisfied that there are other compelling reasons why it is inappropriate for the complaint to be dealt with under the ombudsman scheme.

(4)   If the scheme operator proposes to make any scheme rules it must publish a draft of the proposed rules in the way appearing to it to be best calculated to bring them to the attention of persons appearing to it to be likely to be affected.

(5)   The draft must be accompanied by a statement that representations about the proposals may be made to the scheme operator within a time specified in the statement.

(6)   Before making the proposed scheme rules, the scheme operator must have regard to any representations made to it under sub-paragraph (5).

(7)   The consent of the Authority is required before any scheme rules may be made.

Fees

15.—(1)   Scheme rules may require a respondent to pay to the scheme operator such fees as may be specified in the rules.

(2)   The rules may, among other things—
    (a)   provide for the scheme operator to reduce or waive a fee in a particular case;
    (b)   set different fees for different stages of the proceedings on a complaint;
    (c)   provide for fees to be refunded in specified circumstances;
    (d)   make different provision for different kinds of complaint.

Enforcement of money awards

16. A money award, including interest, which has been registered in accordance with scheme rules may—
    (a)   if a county court so orders in England and Wales, be recovered by execution issued from the county court (or otherwise) as if it were payable under an order of that court;
    (b)   be enforced in Northern Ireland as a money judgment under the Judgments Enforcement (Northern Ireland) Order 1981;
    (c)   be enforced in Scotland by the sheriff, as if it were a judgment or order of the sheriff and whether or not the sheriff could himself have granted such judgment or order.

Commencement: 18 June 2001.
References: See paras 14.19–14.38.

PART IV
THE VOLUNTARY JURISDICTION

Introduction

17. This Part of this Schedule applies only in relation to the voluntary jurisdiction.

Terms of reference to the scheme

18.—(1)   Complaints are to be dealt with and determined under the voluntary jurisdiction on standard terms fixed by the scheme operator with the approval of the Authority.

(2)   Different standard terms may be fixed with respect to different matters or in relation to different cases.

(3)   The standard terms may, in particular—
    (a)   require the making of payments to the scheme operator by participants in the scheme of such amounts, and at such times, as may be determined by the scheme operator;
    (b)   make provision as to the award of costs on the determination of a complaint.

(4)   The scheme operator may not vary any of the standard terms or add or remove terms without the approval of the Authority.

(5)   The standard terms may include provision to the effect that (unless acting in bad faith) none of the following is to be liable in damages for anything done or omitted in the discharge or purported discharge of functions in connection with the voluntary jurisdiction—

    (a)   the scheme operator;
    (b)   any member of its governing body;
    (c)   any member of its staff;
    (d)   any person acting as an ombudsman for the purposes of the scheme.

Delegation by and to other schemes

19.—(1)   The scheme operator may make arrangements with a relevant body—

    (a)   for the exercise by that body of any part of the voluntary jurisdiction of the ombudsman scheme on behalf of the scheme; or
    (b)   for the exercise by the scheme of any function of that body as if it were part of the voluntary jurisdiction of the scheme.

(2)   A "relevant body" is one which the scheme operator is satisfied—

    (a)   is responsible for the operation of a broadly comparable scheme (whether or not established by statute) for the resolution of disputes; and
    (b)   in the case of arrangements under sub-paragraph (1)(a), will exercise the jurisdiction in question in a way compatible with the requirements imposed by or under this Act in relation to complaints of the kind concerned.

(3)   Such arrangements require the approval of the Authority.

Voluntary jurisdiction rules: procedure

20.—(1)   If the scheme operator makes voluntary jurisdiction rules, it must give a copy to the Authority without delay.

(2)   If the scheme operator revokes any such rules, it must give written notice to the Authority without delay.

(3)   The power to make voluntary jurisdiction rules is exercisable in writing.

(4)   Immediately after making voluntary jurisdiction rules, the scheme operator must arrange for them to be printed and made available to the public.

(5)   The scheme operator may charge a reasonable fee for providing a person with a copy of any voluntary jurisdiction rules.

Verification of the rules

21.—(1)   The production of a printed copy of voluntary jurisdiction rules purporting to be made by the scheme operator—

    (a)   on which is endorsed a certificate signed by a member of the scheme operator's staff authorised by the scheme operator for that purpose, and
    (b)   which contains the required statements,

is evidence (or in Scotland sufficient evidence) of the facts stated in the certificate.

(2)   The required statements are—

    (a)   that the rules were made by the scheme operator;
    (b)   that the copy is a true copy of the rules; and
    (c)   that on a specified date the rules were made available to the public in accordance with paragraph 20(4).

(3)   A certificate purporting to be signed as mentioned in sub-paragraph (1) is to be taken to have been duly signed unless the contrary is shown.

Consultation

22.—(1)   If the scheme operator proposes to make voluntary jurisdiction rules, it must publish a draft of the proposed rules in the way appearing to it to be best calculated to bring them to the attention of the public.

(2)   The draft must be accompanied by—

    (a)   an explanation of the proposed rules; and

    (b)   a statement that representations about the proposals may be made to the scheme operator within a specified time.

(3)   Before making any voluntary jurisdiction rules, the scheme operator must have regard to any representations made to it in accordance with sub-paragraph (2)(b).

(4)   If voluntary jurisdiction rules made by the scheme operator differ from the draft published under sub-paragraph (1) in a way which the scheme operator considers significant, the scheme operator must publish a statement of the difference.

Commencement: 18 June 2001.
References: See paras 14.43–14.47.

SCHEDULE 18

Sections 334, 336 and 338

MUTUALS

PART I
FRIENDLY SOCIETIES

The Friendly Societies Act 1974 (c 46)

1. Omit sections 4 (provision for separate registration areas) and 10 (societies registered in one registration area carrying on business in another).

2. In section 7 (societies which may be registered), in subsection (2)(b), for "in the central registration area or in Scotland" substitute "in the United Kingdom, the Channel Islands or the Isle of Man".

3. In section 11 (additional registration requirements for societies with branches), omit "and where any such society has branches in more than one registration area, section 10 above shall apply to that society".

4. In section 99(4) (punishment of fraud etc and recovery of property misapplied), omit "in the central registration area".

The Friendly Societies Act 1992 (c 40)

5. Omit sections 31 to 36A (authorisation of friendly societies business).

6. In section 37 (restrictions on combinations of business), omit subsections (1), (1A) and (7A) to (9).

7. Omit sections 38 to 43 (restrictions on business of certain authorised societies).

8. Omit sections 44 to 50 (regulation of friendly societies business).

Commencement: 1 December 2001.
References: See paras 19.5, 19.6.

PART II
FRIENDLY SOCIETIES: SUBSIDIARIES AND CONTROLLED BODIES

Interpretation

9. In this Part of this Schedule—

    "the 1992 Act" means the Friendly Societies Act 1992; and

    "section 13" means section 13 of that Act.

Qualifying bodies

10.—(1) Subsections (2) to (5) of section 13 (incorporated friendly societies allowed to form or acquire control or joint control only of qualifying bodies) cease to have effect.

(2) As a result, omit—

    (a) subsections (8) and (11) of that section, and

    (b) Schedule 7 to the 1992 Act (activities which may be carried on by a subsidiary of, or body jointly controlled by, an incorporated friendly society).

Bodies controlled by societies

11. In section 13(9) (defined terms), after paragraph (a) insert—

    "(aa) an incorporated friendly society also has control of a body corporate if the body corporate is itself a body controlled in one of the ways mentioned in paragraph (a)(i), (ii) or (iii) by a body corporate of which the society has control;".

Joint control by societies

12. In section 13(9), after paragraph (c) insert—

    "(cc) an incorporated friendly society also has joint control of a body corporate if—

        (i) a subsidiary of the society has joint control of the body corporate in a way mentioned in paragraph (c)(i), (ii) or (iii);

        (ii) a body corporate of which the society has joint control has joint control of the body corporate in such a way; or

        (iii) the body corporate is controlled in a way mentioned in paragraph (a)(i), (ii) or (iii) by a body corporate of which the society has joint control;".

Acquisition of joint control

13. In section 13(9), in the words following paragraph (d), after "paragraph (c)" insert "or (cc)".

Amendment of Schedule 8 to the 1992 Act

14.—(1) Schedule 8 to the 1992 Act (provisions supplementing section 13) is amended as follows.

(2) Omit paragraph 3(2).

(3) After paragraph 3 insert—

"3A.—(1)A body is to be treated for the purposes of section 13(9) as having the right to appoint to a directorship if—

    (a) a person's appointment to the directorship follows necessarily from his appointment as an officer of that body; or

    (b) the directorship is held by the body itself.

(2) A body ("B") and some other person ("P") together are to be treated, for the purposes of section 13(9), as having the right to appoint to a directorship if—

    (a) P is a body corporate which has directors and a person's appointment to the directorship follows necessarily from his appointment both as an officer of B and a director of P;

    (b) P is a body corporate which does not have directors and a person's appointment to the directorship follows necessarily from his appointment both as an officer of B and as a member of P's managing body; or

    (c) the directorship is held jointly by B and P.

(3) For the purposes of section 13(9), a right to appoint (or remove) which is exercisable only with the consent or agreement of another person must be left out of account unless no other person has a right to appoint (or remove) in relation to that directorship.

(4) Nothing in this paragraph is to be read as restricting the effect of section 13(9)."

(4) In paragraph 9 (exercise of certain rights under instruction by, or in the interests of, incorporated friendly society) insert at the end "or in the interests of any body over which the society has joint control".

Consequential amendments

15.—(1) Section 52 of the 1992 Act is amended as follows.

(2) In subsection (2), omit paragraph (d).

(3) In subsection (3), for "(4) below" substitute "(2)".

(4) For subsection (4) substitute—

"(4) A court may not make an order under subsection (5) unless it is satisfied that one or more of the conditions mentioned in subsection (2) are satisfied."

(5) In subsection (5), omit the words from "or, where" to the end.

References in other enactments

16. References in any provision of, or made under, any enactment to subsidiaries of, or bodies jointly controlled by, an incorporated friendly society are to be read as including references to bodies which are such subsidiaries or bodies as a result of any provision of this Part of this Schedule.

Commencement: 1 December 2001.
References: See paras 19.5, 19.6.

PART III
BUILDING SOCIETIES

The Building Societies Act 1986 (c 53)

17. Omit section 9 (initial authorisation to raise funds and borrow money).

18. Omit Schedule 3 (supplementary provisions about authorisation).

Commencement: 1 December 2001.
References: See para 19.8.

PART IV
INDUSTRIAL AND PROVIDENT SOCIETIES

The Industrial and Provident Societies Act 1965 (c 12)

19. Omit section 8 (provision for separate registration areas for Scotland and for England, Wales and the Channel Islands).

20. Omit section 70 (scale of fees to be paid in respect of transactions and inspection of documents).

Commencement: 1 December 2001.
References: See para 19.9.

PART V
CREDIT UNIONS

The Credit Unions Act 1979 (c 34)

21. In section 6 (minimum and maximum number of members), omit subsections (2) to (6).

22. In section 11 (loans), omit subsections (2) and (6).

23. Omit sections 11B (loans approved by credit unions), 11C (grant of certificates of approval) and 11D (withdrawal of certificates of approval).

24. In section 12, omit subsections (4) and (5).

25. In section 14, omit subsections (2), (3), (5) and (6).

26. In section 28 (offences), omit subsection (2).

Commencement: 2 July 2002.
References: See para 19.10.

(*Schedule 19 repealed by the Enterprise Act 2002, ss 247(k), 278(2), Sch 26, as from 20 June 2003.*)

SCHEDULE 20

Section 432(1)

MINOR AND CONSEQUENTIAL AMENDMENTS

The House of Commons Disqualification Act 1975 (c 24)

1. In Part III of Schedule 1 to the House of Commons Disqualification Act 1975 (disqualifying offices)—
    (a)   omit—

    "Any member of the Financial Services Tribunal in receipt of remuneration"; and

    (b)   at the appropriate place, insert—

    "Any member, in receipt of remuneration, of a panel of persons who may be selected to act as members of the Financial Services and Markets Tribunal".

The Northern Ireland Assembly Disqualification Act 1975 (c 25)

2. In Part III of Schedule 1 to the Northern Ireland Assembly Disqualification Act 1975 (disqualifying offices)—
    (a)   omit—

    "Any member of the Financial Services Tribunal in receipt of remuneration"; and

    (b)   at the appropriate place, insert—

    "Any member, in receipt of remuneration, of a panel of persons who may be selected to act as members of the Financial Services and Markets Tribunal".

The Civil Jurisdiction and Judgments Act 1982 (c 27)

3. In paragraph 10 of Schedule 5 to the Civil Jurisdiction and Judgments Act 1982 (proceedings excluded from the operation of Schedule 4 to that Act), for "section 188 of the Financial Services Act 1986" substitute "section 415 of the Financial Services and Markets Act 2000".

The Income and Corporation Taxes Act 1988 (c 1)

4.—(1)   The Income and Corporation Taxes Act 1988 is amended as follows.

    (2)   In section 76 (expenses of management: insurance companies), in subsection (8), omit the definitions of—
        "the 1986 Act";

"authorised person";
"investment business";
"investor";
"investor protection scheme";
"prescribed"; and
"recognised self-regulating organisation".

(3)   In section 468 (authorised unit trusts), in subsections (6) and (8), for "78 of the Financial Services Act 1986" substitute "243 of the Financial Services and Markets Act 2000".

(4)   In section 469(7) (other unit trust schemes), for "Financial Services Act 1986" substitute "Financial Services and Markets Act 2000".

(5)   In section 728 (information in relation to transfers of securities), in subsection (7)(a), for "Financial Services Act 1986" substitute "Financial Services and Markets Act 2000".

(6)   In section 841(3) (power to apply certain provisions of the Tax Acts to recognised investment exchange), for "Financial Services Act 1986" substitute "Financial Services and Markets Act 2000".

The Finance Act 1991 (c 31)

5.—(1)   The Finance Act 1991 is amended as follows.

(2)   In section 47 (investor protection schemes), omit subsections (1), (2) and (4).

(3)   In section 116 (investment exchanges and clearing houses: stamp duty), in subsection (4)(b), for "Financial Services Act 1986" substitute "Financial Services and Markets Act 2000".

The Tribunals and Inquiries Act 1992 (c 53)

6.—(1)   The Tribunals and Inquiries Act 1992 is amended as follows.

(2)   In Schedule 1 (tribunals under supervision of the Council on Tribunals), for the entry relating to financial services and paragraph 18, substitute—

"Financial services and markets

18.   The Financial Services and Markets Tribunal."

The Judicial Pensions and Retirement Act 1993 (c 8)

7.—(1)   The Judicial Pensions and Retirement Act 1993 is amended as follows.

(2)   In Schedule 1 (offices which may be qualifying offices), in Part II, after the entry relating to the President or chairman of the Transport Tribunal insert—

"President or Deputy President of the Financial Services and Markets Tribunal"

(3)   In Schedule 5 (relevant offices in relation to retirement provisions)—
        (a)   omit the entry—

"Member of the Financial Services Tribunal appointed by the Lord Chancellor"; and

        (b)   at the end insert—

"Member of the Financial Services and Markets Tribunal".

Commencement: 3 September 2001 (paras 1(b), 2(b), 3, 7(1), (2), (3)(b)); 3 July 2001 (para 6); 1 December 2001 (remainder).

SCHEDULE 21

Section 432(2)

TRANSITIONAL PROVISIONS AND SAVINGS

Self-regulating organisations

1.—(1)   No new application under section 9 of the 1986 Act (application for recognition) may be entertained.

(2)   No outstanding application made under that section before the passing of this Act may continue to be entertained.

(3)   After the date which is the designated date for a recognised self-regulating organisation—

   (a)   the recognition order for that organisation may not be revoked under section 11 of the 1986 Act (revocation of recognition);

   (b)   no application may be made to the court under section 12 of the 1986 Act (compliance orders) with respect to that organisation.

(4)   The powers conferred by section 13 of the 1986 Act (alteration of rules for protection of investors) may not be exercised.

(5)   "Designated date" means such date as the Treasury may by order designate.

(6)   Sub-paragraph (3) does not apply to a recognised self-regulating organisation in respect of which a notice of intention to revoke its recognition order was given under section 11(3) of the 1986 Act before the passing of this Act if that notice has not been withdrawn.

(7)   Expenditure incurred by the Authority in connection with the winding up of any body which was, immediately before the passing of this Act, a recognised self-regulating organisation is to be treated as having been incurred in connection with the discharge by the Authority of functions under this Act.

(8)   "Recognised self-regulating organisation" means an organisation which, immediately before the passing of this Act, was such an organisation for the purposes of the 1986 Act.

(9)   "The 1986 Act" means the Financial Services Act 1986.

Self-regulating organisations for friendly societies

2.—(1)   No new application under paragraph 2 of Schedule 11 to the 1986 Act (application for recognition) may be entertained.

(2)   No outstanding application made under that paragraph before the passing of this Act may continue to be entertained.

(3)   After the date which is the designated date for a recognised self-regulating organisation for friendly societies—

   (a)   the recognition order for that organisation may not be revoked under paragraph 5 of Schedule 11 to the 1986 Act (revocation of recognition);

   (b)   no application may be made to the court under paragraph 6 of that Schedule (compliance orders) with respect to that organisation.

(4)   "Designated date" means such date as the Treasury may by order designate.

(5)   Sub-paragraph (3) does not apply to a recognised self-regulating organisation for friendly societies in respect of which a notice of intention to revoke its recognition order was given under section 11(3) of the 1986 Act (as applied by paragraph 5(2) of that Schedule) before the passing of this Act if that notice has not been withdrawn.

(6)   Expenditure incurred by the Authority in connection with the winding up of any body which was, immediately before the passing of this Act, a recognised self-regulating organisation for friendly societies is to be treated as having been incurred in connection with the discharge by the Authority of functions under this Act.

(7)   "Recognised self-regulating organisation for friendly societies" means an organisation which, immediately before the passing of this Act, was such an organisation for the purposes of the 1986 Act.

(8)   "The 1986 Act" means the Financial Services Act 1986.

Commencement: 14 June 2000.
Financial Services Act 1986: Repealed by the Financial Services and Markets Act 2000 (Consequential Amendments and Repeals) Order 2001, SI 2001/3649, art 3(1)(c) (made under ss 426, 427 ante).
Orders: The Financial Services and Markets (Transitional Provisions) (Designated Date for Certain Self-Regulating Organisations) Order 2000, SI 2000/1734, art 2, provides that for the purposes of paras 1, 2 of this Schedule, 25 July 2000 shall be the designated date for the Personal Investment Authority Limited an3d the Investment Management Regulatory Organisation Limited; the Financial Services and Markets (Transitional Provisions) (Designated Date for The Securities and Futures Authority) Order 2001, SI 2001/2255, art 2, provides that for the purposes of para 1(5) of this Schedule, 13 July 2001 shall be the designated date for The Securities and Futures Authority Limited.

SCHEDULE 22

Section 432(3)

REPEALS

Chapter	Short title	Extent of repeal
1923 c 8	The Industrial Assurance Act 1923.	The whole Act.
1948 c 39	The Industrial Assurance and Friendly Societies Act 1948.	The whole Act.
1965 c 12	The Industrial and Provident Societies Act 1965.	Section 8. Section 70.
1974 c 46	The Friendly Societies Act 1974.	Section 4.
		Section 10.
		In section 11, from "and where" to "that society".
		In section 99(4), "in the central registration area".
1975 c 24	The House of Commons Disqualification Act 1975.	In Schedule 1, in Part III, "Any member of the Financial Services Tribunal in receipt of remuneration".
1975 c 25	The Northern Ireland Assembly Disqualification Act 1975.	In Schedule 1, in Part III, "Any member of the Financial Services Tribunal in receipt of remuneration".
1977 c 46	The Insurance Brokers (Registration) Act 1977.	The whole Act.
1979 c 34	The Credit Unions Act 1979.	Section 6(2) to (6).
		Section 11(2) and (6).
		Sections 11B, 11C and 11D.
		Section 12(4) and (5).
		In section 14, subsections (2), (3), (5) and (6).
		Section 28(2).

Chapter	Short title	Extent of repeal
1986 c 53	The Building Societies Act 1986.	Section 9.
		Schedule 3.
1988 c 1	The Income and Corporation Taxes Act 1988.	In section 76, in subsection (8), the definitions of "the 1986 Act", "authorised person", "investment business", "investor", "investor protection scheme", "prescribed" and "recognised self-regulating organisation".
1991 c 31	The Finance Act 1991.	In section 47, subsections (1), (2) and (4).
1992 c 40	The Friendly Societies Act 1992.	In section 13, subsections (2) to (5), (8) and (11).
		Sections 31 to 36.
		In section 37, subsections (1), (1A) and (7A) to (9).
		Sections 38 to 50.
		In section 52, subsection (2)(d) and, in subsection (5), the words from "or where" to the end.
		Schedule 7.
		In Schedule 8, paragraph 3(2).
1993 c 8	The Judicial Pensions and Retirement Act 1993.	In Schedule 5, "Member of the Financial Services Tribunal appointed by the Lord Chancellor".

Commencement: 2 July 2002 (so far as repeals the Credit Unions Act 1979); 30 April 2001 (so far as repeals the Insurance Brokers (Registration) Act 1977); 1 December 2001 (remainder).

Financial Services and Markets Act 2000

Commencement Dates

Royal Assent: 14 June 2000.
Commencement provisions: s 431.
Commencement Orders: Financial Services and Markets Act 2000 (Commencement No 1) Order 2001, SI 2001/516.
Financial Services and Markets Act 2000 (Commencement No 2) Order 2001, SI 2001/1282.
Financial Services and Markets Act 2000 (Commencement No 3) Order 2001, SI 2001/1820.
Financial Services and Markets Act 2000 (Commencement No 4 and Transitional Provisions) Order 2001, SI 2001/2364.*
Financial Services and Markets Act 2000 (Commencement No 5) Order 2001, SI 2001/2632.
Financial Services and Markets Act 2000 (Commencement No 6) Order 2001, SI 2001/3436.
Financial Services and Markets Act 2000 (Commencement No 7) Order 2001, SI 2001/3538.

Section			Commencement date
1–11			18 Jun 2001 (SI 2001/1820)
12–19			1 Dec 2001 (SI 2001/3538)
20	(1), (2)		1 Dec 2001 (SI 2001/3538)
	(3)		25 Feb 2001 (for the purpose of making orders or regulations) (SI 2001/516)
			1 Dec 2001 (otherwise) (SI 2001/3538)
21			25 Feb 2001 (for the purpose of making orders or regulations) (SI 2001/516)
			1 Dec 2001 (otherwise) (SI 2001/3538)
22			25 Feb 2001 (SI 2001/516)
23–30			1 Dec 2001 (SI 2001/3538)
31	(1)	(a)	1 Dec 2001 (SI 2001/3538)
		(b)	See Sch 3 below
		(c)	See Sch 4 below
		(d)	1 Dec 2001 (SI 2001/3538)
	(2)		1 Dec 2001 (SI 2001/3538)
32–36			1 Dec 2001 (SI 2001/3538)
37			See Sch 3 below
38			25 Feb 2001 (SI 2001/516)
39	(1)		25 Feb 2001 (for the purpose of making orders or regulations) (SI 2001/516)
			1 Dec 2001 (otherwise) (SI 2001/3538)
	(2)–(6)		1 Dec 2001 (SI 2001/3538)
40			3 Sep 2001 (SI 2001/2632)
41	(1)		25 Feb 2001 (SI 2001/516)
	(2), (3)		3 Sep 2001 (SI 2001/2632)

Section		Commencement date
42, 43		3 Sep 2001 (for the purposes of permissions coming into force not sooner than the day on which s 19 of this Act comes into force, and applications for such permissions)
		1 Dec 2001 (otherwise) (SI 2001/3538)
44–46		3 Sep 2001 (for the purposes of variations or cancellations taking effect not sooner than the day on which s 19 of this Act comes into force, and applications for such variations or cancellations) (SI 2001/2632)
		1 Dec 2001 (otherwise) (SI 2001/3538)
47	(1)	25 Feb 2001 (for the purpose of making orders or regulations) (SI 2001/516)
		3 Sep 2001 (for the purposes of variations or cancellations taking effect not sooner than the day on which s 19 of this Act comes into force, and applications for such variations or cancellations) (SI 2001/2632)
		1 Dec 2001 (otherwise) (SI 2001/3538)
	(2)	3 Sep 2001 (for the purposes of variations or cancellations taking effect not sooner than the day on which s 19 of this Act comes into force, and applications for such variations or cancellations) (SI 2001/2632)
		1 Dec 2001 (otherwise) (SI 2001/3538)
	(3)	25 Feb 2001 (for the purpose of making orders or regulations) (SI 2001/516)
		3 Sep 2001 (for the purposes of variations or cancellations taking effect not sooner than the day on which s 19 of this Act comes into force, and applications for such variations or cancellations) (SI 2001/2632)
		1 Dec 2001 (otherwise) (SI 2001/3538)
	(4)–(7)	3 Sep 2001 (for the purposes of variations or cancellations taking effect not sooner than the day on which s 19 of this Act comes into force, and applications for such variations or cancellations) (SI 2001/2632)
		1 Dec 2001 (otherwise) (SI 2001/3538)
48–50		3 Sep 2001 (SI 2001/2632)
51		18 Jun 2001 (for the purpose of giving directions or imposing requirements as mentioned in sub-s (3)) (SI 2001/1820)
		3 Sep 2001 (otherwise) (SI 2001/2632)
52		3 Sep 2001 (SI 2001/2632)

Section		Commencement date
53, 54		3 Sep 2001 (for the purposes of variations and cancellations taking effect not sooner than the day on which s 19 of this Act comes into force) (SI 2001/2632)
		1 Dec 2001 (otherwise) (SI 2001/3538)
55		3 Sep 2001 (SI 2001/2632)
56–58		3 Sep 2001 (for the purposes of prohibition orders coming into force not sooner than the day on which s 19 of this Act comes into force) (SI 2001/2632)
		1 Dec 2001 (otherwise) (SI 2001/3538)
59		18 Jun 2001 (for the purpose of making rules) (SI 2001/1820)
		3 Sep 2001 (for the purposes of approvals coming into force not sooner than the day on which s 19 of this Act comes into force, and applications for such approvals) (SI 2001/2632)
		1 Dec 2001 (otherwise) (SI 2001/3538)
60		18 Jun 2001 (for the purpose of giving directions or imposing requirements as mentioned in sub-s (2) or (4)) (SI 2001/1820)
		3 Sep 2001 (for the purposes of approvals coming into force not sooner than the day on which s 19 of this Act comes into force, and applications for such approvals) (SI 2001/2632)
		1 Dec 2001 (otherwise) (SI 2001/3538)
61–63		3 Sep 2001 (for the purposes of approvals coming into force not sooner than the day on which s 19 of this Act comes into force, and applications for such approvals) (SI 2001/2632)
		1 Dec 2001 (otherwise) (SI 2001/3538)
64, 65		18 Jun 2001 (SI 2001/1820)
66–68		1 Dec 2001 (SI 2001/3538)
69, 70		18 Jun 2001 (SI 2001/1820)
71	(1)	1 Dec 2001 (SI 2001/3538)
	(2), (3)	25 Feb 2001 (for the purpose of making orders or regulations) (SI 2001/516)
		1 Dec 2001 (otherwise) (SI 2001/3538)
72, 73		18 Jun 2001 (SI 2001/1820)
74	(1)–(3)	1 Dec 2001 (SI 2001/3538)
	(4), (5)	18 Jun 2001 (SI 2001/1820)
75	(1)	18 Jun 2001 (for the purpose of making listing rules) (SI 2001/1820)
		1 Dec 2001 (otherwise) (SI 2001/3538)
	(2)	1 Dec 2001 (SI 2001/3538)

Section		Commencement date
75	(3)	25 Feb 2001 (for the purpose of making orders or regulations) (SI 2001/516)
		1 Dec 2001 (otherwise) (SI 2001/3538)
	(4)–(6)	1 Dec 2001 (SI 2001/3538)
76		1 Dec 2001 (SI 2001/3538)
77	(1), (2)	18 Jun 2001 (for the purpose of making listing rules) (SI 2001/1820)
		1 Dec 2001 (otherwise) (SI 2001/3538)
	(3)	1 Dec 2001 (SI 2001/3538)
	(4)	18 Jun 2001 (for the purpose of making listing rules) (SI 2001/1820)
		1 Dec 2001 (otherwise) (SI 2001/3538)
	(5)	1 Dec 2001 (SI 2001/3538)
78		1 Dec 2001 (SI 2001/3538)
79	(1), (2)	18 Jun 2001 (SI 2001/1820)
	(3)	25 Feb 2001 (SI 2001/516)
	(4)	18 Jun 2001 (SI 2001/1820)
80		1 Dec 2001 (SI 2001/3538)
81	(1)	18 Jun 2001 (for the purpose of making listing rules) (SI 2001/1820)
		1 Dec 2001 (otherwise) (SI 2001/3538)
	(2)–(4)	1 Dec 2001 (SI 2001/3538)
	(5)	18 Jun 2001 (for the purpose of making listing rules) (SI 2001/1820)
		1 Dec 2001 (otherwise) (SI 2001/3538)
82	(1)	18 Jun 2001 (for the purpose of making listing rules) (SI 2001/1820)
		1 Dec 2001 (otherwise) (SI 2001/3538)
	(2)–(4)	1 Dec 2001 (SI 2001/3538)
	(5)	18 Jun 2001 (for the purpose of making listing rules) (SI 2001/1820)
		1 Dec 2001 (otherwise) (SI 2001/3538)
	(6)	1 Dec 2001 (SI 2001/3538)
	(7)	18 Jun 2001 (for the purpose of making listing rules) (SI 2001/1820)
		1 Dec 2001 (otherwise) (SI 2001/3538)
83		1 Dec 2001 (SI 2001/3538)
84		18 Jun 2001 (SI 2001/1820)
85		1 Dec 2001 (SI 2001/3538)
86		25 Feb 2001 (SI 2001/516)
87	(1)–(3)	18 Jun 2001 (SI 2001/1820)
	(4), (5)	25 Feb 2001 (SI 2001/516)

Section		Commencement date
88	(1)–(3)	18 Jun 2001 (SI 2001/1820)
	(4)–(7)	1 Dec 2001 (SI 2001/3538)
89	(1)	18 Jun 2001 (SI 2001/1820)
	(2)–(4)	1 Dec 2001 (SI 2001/3538)
90–92		1 Dec 2001 (SI 2001/3538)
93, 94		18 Jun 2001 (SI 2001/1820)
95		1 Dec 2001 (SI 2001/3538)
96		18 Jun 2001 (SI 2001/1820)
97		1 Dec 2001 (SI 2001/3538)
98	(1)	18 Jun 2001 (for the purpose of making listing rules) (SI 2001/1820)
		1 Dec 2001 (otherwise) (SI 2001/3538)
	(2)–(5)	1 Dec 2001 (SI 2001/3538)
99–102		18 Jun 2001 (SI 2001/1820)
103		25 Feb 2001 (SI 2001/516)
104		1 Dec 2001 (for the purpose of insurance business transfer schemes only) (SI 2001/3538)
		Not in force (otherwise)
105–107		1 Dec 2001 (SI 2001/3538)
108		25 Feb 2001 (for the purpose of making orders or regulations) (SI 2001/516)
		1 Dec 2001 (otherwise) (SI 2001/3538)
109, 110		1 Dec 2001 (SI 2001/3538)
111	(1)	1 Dec 2001 (SI 2001/3538)
	(2)	25 Feb 2001 (for the purpose of introducing Sch12, Pt I to the extent brought into force by SI 2001/516) (SI 2001/516)
		1 Dec 2001 (otherwise) (SI 2001/3538)
	(3)	1 Dec 2001 (SI 2001/3538)
112–117		1 Dec 2001 (SI 2001/3538)
118	(1), (2)	1 Dec 2001 (SI 2001/3538)
	(3), (4)	25 Feb 2001 (SI 2001/516)
	(5)–(9)	1 Dec 2001 (SI 2001/3538)
	(10)	25 Feb 2001 (SI 2001/516)
119–121		18 Jun 2001 (SI 2001/1820)
122, 123		1 Dec 2001 (SI 2001/3538)
124, 125		18 Jun 2001 (SI 2001/1820)
126–131		1 Dec 2001 (SI 2001/3538)
132	(1)	25 Feb 2001 (for the purpose of the definition "the Tribunal") (SI 2001/516)
		3 Sep 2001 (otherwise) (SI 2001/2632)

Section			Commencement date
132	(2)		3 Sep 2001 (SI 2001/2632)
	(3)		25 Feb 2001 (SI 2001/516)
	(4)		See Sch 13 below
133			3 Sep 2001 (SI 2001/2632)
134, 135			25 Feb 2001 (SI 2001/516)
136			18 Jun 2001 (for the purpose of making rules) (SI 2001/1820)
			3 Sep 2001 (otherwise) (SI 2001/2632)
137	(1)–(5)		3 Sep 2001 (SI 2001/2632)
	(6)		25 Feb 2001 (SI 2001/516)
138–141			18 Jun 2001 (SI 2001/1820)
142	(1)–(4)		25 Feb 2001 (SI 2001/516)
	(5)		1 Dec 2001 (SI 2001/3538)
	(6)		25 Feb 2001 (SI 2001/516)
143			18 Jun 2001 (for the purpose of making rules) (SI 2001/1820)
			1 Dec 2001 (otherwise) (SI 2001/3538)
144	(1)–(3)		18 Jun 2001 (SI 2001/1820)
	(4), (5)		25 Feb 2001 (SI 2001/516)
	(6), (7)		18 Jun 2001 (SI 2001/1820)
145	(1)–(4)		18 Jun 2001 (SI 2001/1820)
	(5)		25 Feb 2001 (SI 2001/516)
146, 147			18 Jun 2001 (SI 2001/1820)
148			18 Jun 2001 (for the purpose of giving directions as mentioned in sub-s (3)) (SI 2001/1820)
			3 Sep 2001 (otherwise) (SI 2001/2632)
149			18 Jun 2001 (SI 2001/1820)
150	(1), (2)		18 Jun 2001 (for the purpose of making rules) (SI 2001/1820)
			1 Dec 2001 (otherwise) (SI 2001/3538)
	(3)–(5)		25 Feb 2001 (for the purpose of making orders or regulations) (SI 2001/516)
			18 Jun 2001 (for the purpose of making rules) (SI 2001/1820)
			1 Dec 2001 (otherwise) (SI 2001/3538)
151			1 Dec 2001 (SI 2001/3538)
152–164			18 Jun 2001 (SI 2001/1820)
165–167			3 Sep 2001 (SI 2001/2632)
168	(1)–(3)		3 Sep 2001 (SI 2001/2632)
	(4)	(a)	3 Sep 2001 (SI 2001/2632)

Section		Commencement date
168	(b)	25 Feb 2001 (for the purpose of making orders or regulations) (SI 2001/516)
		3 Sep 2001 (otherwise) (SI 2001/2632)
	(c)–(i)	3 Sep 2001 (SI 2001/2632)
	(5), (6)	3 Sep 2001 (SI 2001/2632)
169		18 Jun 2001 (for the purpose of preparing a statement of policy as mentioned in sub-s (9)) (SI 2001/1820)
		3 Sep 2001 (otherwise) (SI 2001/2632)
170–177		3 Sep 2001 (SI 2001/2632)
178–181		1 Dec 2001 (SI 2001/3538)
182		18 Jun 2001 (for the purpose of imposing requirements as mentioned in sub-s (1)(b)) (SI 2001/1820)
		1 Dec 2001 (otherwise) (SI 2001/3538)
183	(1)	1 Dec 2001 (SI 2001/3538)
	(2)	25 Feb 2001 (for the purpose of making orders or regulations) (SI 2001/516)
		1 Dec 2001 (otherwise) (SI 2001/3538)
	(3)	1 Dec 2001 (SI 2001/3538)
184–187		1 Dec 2001 (SI 2001/3538)
188	(1)	1 Dec 2001 (SI 2001/3538)
	(2)	25 Feb 2001 (for the purpose of making orders or regulations) (SI 2001/516)
		1 Dec 2001 (otherwise) (SI 2001/3538)
	(3)–(6)	1 Dec 2001 (SI 2001/3538)
189–191		1 Dec 2001 (SI 2001/3538)
192	(a)	25 Feb 2001 (SI 2001/516)
	(b)–(e)	1 Dec 2001 (SI 2001/3538)
193		3 Sep 2001 (SI 2001/2632)
194–197		3 Sep 2001 (for the purposes of requirements (as mentioned in s 196) taking effect not sooner than the day on which s 19 of this Act comes into force) (SI 2001/2632)
		1 Dec 2001 (otherwise) (SI 2001/3538)
198		1 Dec 2001 (SI 2001/3538)
199		3 Sep 2001 (for the purposes of requirements (as mentioned in s 196) taking effect not sooner than the day on which s 19 of this Act comes into force) (SI 2001/2632)
		1 Dec 2001 (otherwise) (SI 2001/3538)
200, 201		3 Sep 2001 (SI 2001/2632)
202	(1)	3 Sep 2001 (SI 2001/2632)

Section		Commencement date
202	(2)	25 Feb 2001 (for the purpose of making orders or regulations) (SI 2001/516)
		3 Sep 2001 (otherwise) (SI 2001/2632)
203–209		1 Dec 2001 (SI 2001/3538)
210–212		18 Jun 2001 (SI 2001/1820)
213	(1)–(9)	18 Jun 2001 (SI 2001/1820)
	(10)	25 Feb 2001 (for the purpose of making orders or regulations) (SI 2001/516)
		18 Jun 2001 (otherwise) (SI 2001/1820)
214	(1)–(4)	18 Jun 2001 (SI 2001/1820)
	(5)	25 Feb 2001 (for the purpose of making orders or regulations) (SI 2001/516)
		18 Jun 2001 (otherwise) (SI 2001/1820)
	(6)	18 Jun 2001 (SI 2001/1820)
215	(1)–(5)	18 Jun 2001 (SI 2001/1820)
	(6)	25 Feb 2001 (SI 2001/516)
	(7)	18 Jun 2001 (SI 2001/1820)
	(8), (9)	25 Feb 2001 (SI 2001/516)
216–218		18 Jun 2001 (SI 2001/1820)
219–221		1 Dec 2001 (SI 2001/3538)
222		18 Jun 2001 (SI 2001/1820)
223		18 Jun 2001 (for the purpose of fixing an amount by the scheme as mentioned in sub-s (1)) (SI 2001/1820)
		1 Dec 2001 (otherwise) (SI 2001/3538)
224	(1)–(3)	1 Dec 2001 (SI 2001/3538)
	(4)	25 Feb 2001 (for the purpose of making orders or regulations) (SI 2001/516)
		1 Dec 2001 (otherwise) (SI 2001/3538)
	(5)	1 Dec 2001 (SI 2001/3538)
225		18 Jun 2001 (SI 2001/1820)
226, 227		18 Jun 2001 (for the purpose of the making of rules by the Authority and the scheme operator) (SI 2001/1820)
		1 Dec 2001 (otherwise) (SI 2001/3538)
228		1 Dec 2001 (SI 2001/3538)
229		18 Jun 2001 (for the purpose of the making of rules by the Authority and the scheme operator) (SI 2001/1820)
		1 Dec 2001 (otherwise) (SI 2001/3538)
230		18 Jun 2001 (SI 2001/1820)
231–233		1 Dec 2001 (SI 2001/3538)

Section		Commencement date
234		18 Jun 2001 (SI 2001/1820)
235–237		25 Feb 2001 (SI 2001/516)
238		25 Feb 2001 (for the purpose of making orders or regulations) (SI 2001/516)
		18 Jun 2001 (for the purpose of making rules) (SI 2001/1820)
		1 Dec 2001 (otherwise) (SI 2001/3538)
239	(1)–(3)	25 Feb 2001 (SI 2001/516)
	(4), (5)	18 Jun 2001 (SI 2001/1820)
240, 241		1 Dec 2001 (SI 2001/3538)
242		18 Jun 2001 (for the purpose of giving directions or imposing requirements as mentioned in sub-s (3)) (SI 2001/1820)
		3 Sep 2001 (for the purposes of authorisation orders coming into force not sooner than the day on which s 19 of this Act comes into force) (SI 2001/2632)
		1 Dec 2001 (otherwise) (SI 2001/3538)
243–245		3 Sep 2001 (for the purposes of authorisation orders coming into force not sooner than the day on which s 19 of this Act comes into force) (SI 2001/2632)
		1 Dec 2001 (otherwise) (SI 2001/3538)
246		3 Sep 2001 (for the purposes of certificates coming into force not sooner than the day on which s 19 of this Act comes into force) (SI 2001/2632)
		1 Dec 2001 (otherwise) (SI 2001/3538)
247, 248		18 Jun 2001 (SI 2001/1820)
249		1 Dec 2001 (SI 2001/3538)
250		3 Sep 2001 (SI 2001/2632)
251	(1)–(3)	3 Sep 2001 (for the purposes of the giving of notice of any proposal to alter a scheme, or to replace its trustee or manager, not sooner than the day on which s 19 of this Act comes into force, and the giving of approval to any such proposal) (SI 2001/2632)
		1 Dec 2001 (otherwise) (SI 2001/3538)
	(4)(a)	3 Sep 2001 (for the purposes of the giving of notice of any proposal to alter a scheme, or to replace its trustee or manager, not sooner than the day on which s 19 of this Act comes into force, and the giving of approval to any such proposal) (SI 2001/2632)
		1 Dec 2001 (otherwise) (SI 2001/3538)
	(4)(b)	1 Dec 2001 (SI 2001/3538)

Section	Commencement date
251 (5)	3 Sep 2001 (for the purposes of the giving of notice of any proposal to alter a scheme, or to replace its trustee or manager, not sooner than the day on which s 19 of this Act comes into force, and the giving of approval to any such proposal) (SI 2001/2632)
	1 Dec 2001 (otherwise) (SI 2001/3538)
252	3 Sep 2001 (for the purposes of the giving of notice of any proposal to alter a scheme, or to replace its trustee or manager, not sooner than the day on which s 19 of this Act comes into force, and the giving of approval to any such proposal) (SI 2001/2632)
	1 Dec 2001 (otherwise) (SI 2001/3538)
253	1 Dec 2001 (SI 2001/3538)
254–256	3 Sep 2001 (SI 2001/2632)
257	3 Sep 2001 (for the purposes of directions coming into force not sooner than the day on which s 19 of this Act comes into force) (SI 2001/2632)
	1 Dec 2001 (otherwise) (SI 2001/3538)
258	1 Dec 2001 (SI 2001/3538)
259–261	3 Sep 2001 (for the purposes of directions coming into force not sooner than the day on which s 19 of this Act comes into force) (SI 2001/2632)
	1 Dec 2001 (otherwise) (SI 2001/3538)
262	25 Feb 2001 (SI 2001/516)
263	1 Dec 2001 (SI 2001/3538)
264 (1)	25 Feb 2001 (for the purpose of making orders or regulations) (SI 2001/516)
	3 Sep 2001 (for the purposes of— (a) the giving of notice under sub-s (1) of intention to make invitations not sooner than the day on which s 19 of this Act comes into force; and (b) the giving of notice under sub-ss (2) or (6)) (SI 2001/2632)
	1 Dec 2001 (otherwise) (SI 2001/3538)
(2)	3 Sep 2001 (for the purposes of— (a) the giving of notice under sub-s (1) of intention to make invitations not sooner than the day on which s 19 of this Act comes into force; and (b) the giving of notice under sub-ss (2) or (6)) (SI 2001/2632)
	1 Dec 2001 (otherwise) (SI 2001/3538)

Section			Commencement date
264	(3)	(a), (b)	3 Sep 2001 (for the purposes of— (a) the giving of notice under sub-s (1) of intention to make invitations not sooner than the day on which s 19 of this Act comes into force; and (b) the giving of notice under sub-ss (2) or (6)) (SI 2001/2632)
			1 Dec 2001 (otherwise) (SI 2001/3538)
		(c)	25 Feb 2001 (for the purpose of making orders or regulations) (SI 2001/516)
			3 Sep 2001 (for the purposes of— (a) the giving of notice under sub-s (1) of intention to make invitations not sooner than the day on which s 19 of this Act comes into force; and (b) the giving of notice under sub-ss (2) or (6)) (SI 2001/2632)
			1 Dec 2001 (otherwise) (SI 2001/3538)
	(4)–(7)		3 Sep 2001 (for the purposes of— (a) the giving of notice under sub-s (1) of intention to make invitations not sooner than the day on which s 19 of this Act comes into force; and (b) the giving of notice under sub-ss (2) or (6)) (SI 2001/2632)
			1 Dec 2001 (otherwise) (SI 2001/3538)
265	(1), (2)		3 Sep 2001 (SI 2001/2632)
	(3)		1 Dec 2001 (SI 2001/3538)
	(4), (5)		3 Sep 2001 (SI 2001/2632)
266			18 Jun 2001 (SI 2001/1820)
267–269			1 Dec 2001 (SI 2001/3538)
270			25 Feb 2001 (for the purpose of making orders or regulations) (SI 2001/516)
			3 Sep 2001 (for the purposes of— (a) the giving of notices under sub-s (1)(c); and (b) the giving of notice of approval under sub-s (1)(d)(i) coming into force not sooner than the day on which s 19 of this Act comes into force) (SI 2001/2632)
			1 Dec 2001 (otherwise) (SI 2001/3538)
271	(1)		3 Sep 2001 (SI 2001/2632)
	(2)		1 Dec 2001 (SI 2001/3538)
	(3)		3 Sep 2001 (SI 2001/2632)
272, 273			3 Sep 2001 (for the purposes of orders (and applications for orders) coming into force not sooner than the day on which s 19 of this Act comes into force) (SI 2001/2632)
			1 Dec 2001 (otherwise) (SI 2001/3538)

Section			Commencement date
274			18 Jun 2001 (for the purpose of giving directions or imposing requirements as mentioned in sub-s (2)) (SI 2001/1820)
			3 Sep 2001 (for the purposes of orders (and applications for orders) coming into force not sooner than the day on which s 19 of this Act comes into force) (SI 2001/2632)
			1 Dec 2001 (otherwise) (SI 2001/3538)
275, 276			3 Sep 2001 (for the purposes of orders (and applications for orders) coming into force not sooner than the day on which s 19 of this Act comes into force) (SI 2001/2632)
			1 Dec 2001 (otherwise) (SI 2001/3538)
277	(1)		3 Sep 2001 (for the purposes of— (a) the giving of notice under sub-s (1) of any proposal to alter a scheme not sooner than the day on which s 19 of this Act comes into force, and the giving of approval to any such proposal; and (b) the giving of notice under sub-s (3) of any proposal to replace an operator, trustee or depositary not sooner than the day on which s 19 of this Act comes into force) (SI 2001/2632)
			1 Dec 2001 (otherwise) (SI 2001/3538)
	(2)	(a)	3 Sep 2001 (for the purposes of— (a) the giving of notice under sub-s (1) of any proposal to alter a scheme not sooner than the day on which s 19 of this Act comes into force, and the giving of approval to any such proposal; and (b) the giving of notice under sub-s (3) of any proposal to replace an operator, trustee or depositary not sooner than the day on which s 19 of this Act comes into force) (SI 2001/2632)
			1 Dec 2001 (otherwise) (SI 2001/3538)
		(b)	1 Dec 2001 (SI 2001/3538)
	(3)		3 Sep 2001 (for the purposes of— (a) the giving of notice under sub-s (1) of any proposal to alter a scheme not sooner than the day on which s 19 of this Act comes into force, and the giving of approval to any such proposal; and (b) the giving of notice under sub-s (3) of any proposal to replace an operator, trustee or depositary not sooner than the day on which s 19 of this Act comes into force) (SI 2001/2632)
			1 Dec 2001 (otherwise) (SI 2001/3538)
278			18 Jun 2001 (SI 2001/1820)
279–282			3 Sep 2001 (SI 2001/2632)
283	(1)		18 Jun 2001 (SI 2001/1820)
	(2), (3)		1 Dec 2001 (SI 2001/3538)
284	(1)		1 Dec 2001 (SI 2001/3538)

Section		Commencement date
284	(2)	25 Feb 2001 (for the purpose of making orders or regulations) (SI 2001/516)
		1 Dec 2001 (otherwise) (SI 2001/3538)
	(3)–(11)	1 Dec 2001 (SI 2001/3538)
285		1 Dec 2001 (SI 2001/3538)
286		25 Feb 2001 (SI 2001/516)
287, 288		18 Jun 2001 (for the purpose of giving directions or imposing requirements as mentioned in sub-s (2)) (SI 2001/1820)
		3 Sep 2001 (otherwise) (SI 2001/2632)
289		3 Sep 2001 (SI 2001/2632)
290		3 Sep 2001 (for the purposes of recognition orders coming into force not sooner than the day on which s 19 of this Act comes into force) (SI 2001/2632)
		1 Dec 2001 (otherwise) (SI 2001/3538)
291		1 Dec 2001 (SI 2001/3538)
292	(1)	3 Sep 2001 (SI 2001/2632)
	(2)–(5)	3 Sep 2001 (for the purposes of recognition orders coming into force not sooner than the day on which s 19 of this Act comes into force) (SI 2001/2632)
		1 Dec 2001 (otherwise) (SI 2001/3538)
293		18 Jun 2001 (for the purpose of making rules) (SI 2001/1820)
		1 Dec 2001 (otherwise) (SI 2001/3538)
294		18 Jun 2001 (for the purpose of giving directions as mentioned in sub-s (2)) (SI 2001/1820)
		3 Sep 2001 (otherwise) (SI 2001/2632)
295		18 Jun 2001 (for the purpose of making rules) (SI 2001/1820)
		1 Dec 2001 (otherwise) (SI 2001/3538)
296		1 Dec 2001 (SI 2001/3538)
297		3 Sep 2001 (SI 2001/2632)
298		3 Sep 2001 (for the purposes of revocation orders under s 297) (SI 2001/2632)
		1 Dec 2001 (otherwise) (SI 2001/3538)
299		18 Jun 2001 (SI 2001/1820)
300, 301		1 Dec 2001 (SI 2001/3538)
302, 303		3 Sep 2001 (SI 2001/2632)
304		1 Dec 2001 (SI 2001/3538)
305		3 Sep 2001 (for the purposes of s 303) (SI 2001/2632)
		1 Dec 2001 (otherwise) (SI 2001/3538)
306		3 Sep 2001 (for the purposes of reports issued by the Director under s 303) (SI 2001/2632)
		1 Dec 2001 (otherwise) (SI 2001/3538)

Section		Commencement date
307		3 Sep 2001 (SI 2001/2632)
308, 309		1 Dec 2001 (SI 2001/3538)
310		3 Sep 2001 (for the purposes of s 307) (SI 2001/2632)
		1 Dec 2001 (otherwise) (SI 2001/3538)
311, 312		3 Sep 2001 (SI 2001/2632)
313		25 Feb 2001 (SI 2001/516)
314		3 Sep 2001 (SI 2001/2632)
315	(1), (2)	1 Dec 2001 (SI 2001/3538)
	(3)–(5)	3 Sep 2001 (SI 2001/2632)
316		18 Jun 2001 (for the purpose of giving directions as mentioned in sub-s (1) coming into force not sooner than the day on which s 19 of the Act comes into force) (SI 2001/1820)
		1 Dec 2001 (otherwise) (SI 2001/3538)
317		18 Jun 2001 (SI 2001/1820)
318		18 Jun 2001 (for the purpose of giving directions as mentioned in sub-s (1) coming into force not sooner than the day on which s 19 of the Act comes into force) (SI 2001/1820)
		1 Dec 2001 (otherwise) (SI 2001/3538)
319		18 Jun 2001 (SI 2001/1820)
320	(1), (2)	1 Dec 2001 (SI 2001/3538)
	(3), (4)	3 Sep 2001 (for the purposes of requirements taking effect not sooner than the day on which s 19 of this Act comes into force) (SI 2001/2632)
		1 Dec 2001 (otherwise) (SI 2001/3538)
321		3 Sep 2001 (for the purposes of requirements taking effect not sooner than the day on which s 19 of this Act comes into force) (SI 2001/2632)
		1 Dec 2001 (otherwise) (SI 2001/3538)
322		18 Jun 2001 (for the purpose of making rules coming into force not sooner than the day on which s 19 of the Act comes into force) (SI 2001/1820)
		1 Dec 2001 (otherwise) (SI 2001/3538)
323, 324		18 Jun 2001 (SI 2001/1820)
325	(1)–(3)	1 Dec 2001 (SI 2001/3538)
	(4)	3 Sep 2001 (SI 2001/2632)
326		25 Feb 2001 (SI 2001/516)
327	(1)–(5)	1 Dec 2001 (SI 2001/3538)
	(6)	25 Feb 2001 (for the purpose of making orders or regulations) (SI 2001/516)
		1 Dec 2001 (otherwise) (SI 2001/3538)
	(7), (8)	1 Dec 2001 (SI 2001/3538)
328–331		3 Sep 2001 (SI 2001/2632)

Section			Commencement date
332			18 Jun 2001 (SI 2001/1820)
333			1 Dec 2001 (SI 2001/3538)
334	(1), (2)		25 Feb 2001 (SI 2001/516)
	(3), (4)		1 Dec 2001 (SI 2001/3538)
335			25 Feb 2001 (SI 2001/516)
336	(1), (2)		25 Feb 2001 (SI 2001/516)
	(3)		1 Dec 2001 (SI 2001/3538)
337			25 Feb 2001 (SI 2001/516)
338	(1), (2)		25 Feb 2001 (SI 2001/516)
	(3), (4)		1 Dec 2001 (SI 2001/3538)
339			25 Feb 2001 (SI 2001/516)
340			18 Jun 2001 (SI 2001/1820)
341			1 Dec 2001 (SI 2001/3538)
342	(1)–(4)		1 Dec 2001 (SI 2001/3538)
	(5)		25 Feb 2001 (SI 2001/516)
	(6), (7)		1 Dec 2001 (SI 2001/3538)
343	(1)–(4)		1 Dec 2001 (SI 2001/3538)
	(5)		25 Feb 2001 (SI 2001/516)
	(6)–(9)		1 Dec 2001 (SI 2001/3538)
344–346			1 Dec 2001 (SI 2001/3538)
347	(1)	(a)	1 Dec 2001 (for the purpose of enabling the Authority to maintain a record of the approved persons listed below) (SI 2001/3538)
			1 May 2002 (for the purpose of requiring the Authority to maintain a record of persons who appear to the Authority to be authorised persons who are EEA firms or Treaty firms) (SI 2001/3538)
			1 Aug 2002 (for the purpose of requiring the Authority to maintain a record of persons who appear to the Authority to be authorised persons who were immediately before the appointed day, authorised under Financial Services Act 1986 by virtue of holding a certificate issued for the purposes of Part I of that Act by a recognised professional body, within the meaning of that Act) (SI 2001/3538)
		(b)–(g)	1 Dec 2001 (SI 2001/3538)
		(h)	1 Dec 2001 (for the purpose of enabling the Authority to maintain a record of approved persons) (SI 2001/3538)
			1 Dec 2002 (for the purpose of requiring the Authority to maintain a record of approved persons) (SI 2001/3538)
		(i)	1 Dec 2001 (SI 2001/3538)

Section			Commencement date
347	(2)	(a)	1 Dec 2001 (for the purpose of enabling the Authority to maintain a record of the approved persons listed below) (SI 2001/3538)
			1 May 2002 (for the purpose of requiring the Authority to maintain a record of persons who appear to the Authority to be authorised persons who are EEA firms or Treaty firms) (SI 2001/3538)
			1 Aug 2002 (for the purpose of requiring the Authority to maintain a record of persons who appear to the Authority to be authorised persons who were immediately before the appointed day, authorised under Financial Services Act 1986 by virtue of holding a certificate issued for the purposes of Part I of that Act by a recognised professional body (within the meaning of that Act) (SI 2001/3538)
	(2)	(b)–(f)	1 Dec 2001 (SI 2001/3538)
		(g)	1 Dec 2001 (for the purpose of enabling the Authority to maintain a record of approved persons) (SI 2001/3538)
			1 Dec 2002 (for the purpose of requiring the Authority to maintain a record of approved persons) (SI 2001/3538)
	(3)–(9)		1 Dec 2001 (SI 2001/3538)
348			18 Jun 2001 (SI 2001/1820)
349			25 Feb 2001 (for the purpose of making orders or regulations) (SI 2001/516)
			18 Jun 2001 (otherwise) (SI 2001/1820)
350	(1), (2)		3 Sep 2001 (SI 2001/2632)
	(3)		18 Jun 2001 (SI 2001/1820)
	(4)–(6)		3 Sep 2001 (SI 2001/2632)
	(7)		18 Jun 2001 (SI 2001/1820)
351	(1)–(6)		18 Jun 2001 (SI 2001/1820)
	(7)		25 Feb 2001 (SI 2001/516)
352			18 Jun 2001 (for the purpose of any contravention of s 348) (SI 2001/1820)
			3 Sep 2001 (otherwise) (SI 2001/2632)
353			25 Feb 2001 (SI 2001/516)
354			3 Sep 2001 (SI 2001/2632)
355			20 Jul 2001 (SI 2001/2632)
356–359			1 Dec 2001 (SI 2001/3538)
360			20 Jul 2001 (SI 2001/2632)
361–371			1 Dec 2001 (SI 2001/3538)
372			20 Jul 2001 (for the purpose of making rules[†]) (SI 2001/2632)
			1 Dec 2001 (otherwise) (SI 2001/3538)
373–377			1 Dec 2001 (SI 2001/3538)
378, 379			20 Jul 2001 (SI 2001/2632)

Section			Commencement date
380			18 Jun 2001 (SI 2001/1820)
381			1 Dec 2001 (SI 2001/3538)
382			18 Jun 2001 (SI 2001/1820)
383–386			1 Dec 2001 (SI 2001/3538)
387–394			3 Sep 2001 (SI 2001/2632)
395, 396			18 Jun 2001 (SI 2001/1820)
397	(1)–(8)		1 Dec 2001 (SI 2001/3538)
	(9)–(14)		25 Feb 2001 (SI 2001/516)
398–401			18 Jun 2001 (SI 2001/1820)
402	(1)	(a)	1 Dec 2001 (SI 2001/3538)
		(b)	25 Feb 2001 (for the purpose of making orders or regulations) (SI 2001/516)
			19 Oct 2001 (for the purposes of proceedings for offences under prescribed regulations relating to money laundering) (SI 2001/3436)
	(2), (3)		19 Oct 2001 (for the purposes of proceedings for offences under prescribed regulations relating to money laundering) (SI 2001/3436)
			1 Dec 2001 (otherwise) (SI 2001/3538)
403			18 Jun 2001 (SI 2001/1820)
404			1 Dec 2001 (SI 2001/3538)
405	(1)	(a), (b)	3 Sep 2001 (SI 2001/2632)
		(c), (d)	1 Dec 2001 (SI 2001/3538)
	(2)–(5)		3 Sep 2001 (SI 2001/2632)
406			1 Dec 2001 (SI 2001/3538)
407	(1), (2)		3 Sep 2001 (SI 2001/2632)
	(3)		1 Dec 2001 (SI 2001/3538)
408			3 Sep 2001 (for the purposes of determinations coming into force not sooner than the day on which s 19 of this Act comes into force) (SI 2001/2632)
			1 Dec 2001 (otherwise) (SI 2001/3538)
409			25 Feb 2001 (SI 2001/516)
410			18 Jun 2001 (SI 2001/1820)
411			1 Dec 2001 (SI 2001/3538)
412			25 Feb 2001 (for the purpose of making orders or regulations) (SI 2001/516)
			1 Dec 2001 (otherwise) (SI 2001/3538)
413			3 Sep 2001 (SI 2001/2632)
414	(1)–(3)		25 Feb 2001 (SI 2001/516)
	(4)		18 Jun 2001 (SI 2001/1820)
415			18 Jun 2001 (SI 2001/1820)

Section			Commencement date
416	(1)	(a), (b)	1 Dec 2001 (SI 2001/3538)
		(c)	30 Apr 2001 (SI 2001/1282)
	(2)		1 Dec 2001 (SI 2001/3538)
	(3)	(a)	30 Apr 2001 (SI 2001/1282)
		(b), (c)	2 Mar 2002 (SI 2001/3538)
		(d)	1 Dec 2001 (SI 2001/3538)
	(4), (5)		25 Feb 2001 (SI 2001/516)
417			25 Feb 2001 (SI 2001/516)
418			3 Sep 2001 (SI 2001/2632)
419–423			25 Feb 2001 (SI 2001/516)
424	(1), (2)		25 Feb 2001 (SI 2001/516)
	(3)		25 Feb 2001 (for the purpose of making orders or regulations) (SI 2001/516)
			1 Dec 2001 (otherwise) (SI 2001/3538)
425–427			25 Feb 2001 (SI 2001/516)
428			14 Jun 2000 (s 431(1))
429			25 Feb 2001 (SI 2001/516)
430, 431			14 Jun 2000 (s 431(1))
432	(1)		See Sch 20 below
	(2)		See Sch 21 below
	(3)		See Sch 22 below
433			14 Jun 2000 (s 431(1))
Schedule			
1, para	1–6		18 Jun 2001 (SI 2001/1820)
	7, 8		19 Jul 2001 (for the purpose of enabling the Authority to make the complaints scheme and appoint the investigator) (SI 2001/2364)
			3 Sep 2001 (otherwise) (SI 2001/2632)
	9–21		18 Jun 2001 (SI 2001/1820)
2			25 Feb 2001 (SI 2001/516)
3, para	1–18		25 Feb 2001 (for the purpose of making orders or regulations) (SI 2001/516)
			18 Jun 2001 (for the purpose of making rules) (SI 2001/1820)
			1 Dec 2001 (otherwise) (SI 2001/3538)
	19		25 Feb 2001 (for the purpose of making orders or regulations) (SI 2001/516)
			18 Jun 2001 (for the purpose of making rules) (SI 2001/1820)

Schedule			Commencement date
3, para	19		3 Sep 2001 (for the purposes of the giving of notice under sub-para (2) of intention to establish a branch not sooner than the day on which s 19 of this Act comes into force) (SI 2001/2632)
			1 Dec 2001 (otherwise) (SI 2001/3538)
	20		25 Feb 2001 (for the purpose of making orders or regulations) (SI 2001/516)
			18 Jun 2001 (for the purpose of making rules) (SI 2001/1820)
			3 Sep 2001 (for the purposes of the giving of notice under sub-para (1) of intention to provide services not sooner than the day on which s 19 of this Act comes into force) (SI 2001/2632)
			1 Dec 2001 (otherwise) (SI 2001/3538)
	21–24		25 Feb 2001 (for the purpose of making orders or regulations) (SI 2001/516)
			18 Jun 2001 (for the purpose of making rules) (SI 2001/1820)
			1 Dec 2001 (otherwise) (SI 2001/3538)
4, para	1		3 Sep 2001 (SI 2001/2632)
	2		1 Dec 2001 (SI 2001/3538)
	3		3 Sep 2001 (for the purposes of issuing certificates under sub-para (4)) (SI 2001/2632)
			1 Dec 2001 (otherwise) (SI 2001/3538)
	4		1 Dec 2001 (SI 2001/3538)
	5		3 Sep 2001 (for the purposes of giving notice under sub-para (2) of intention to carry on regulated activities not sooner than the day on which s 19 of this Act comes into force) (SI 2001/2632)
			1 Dec 2001 (otherwise) (SI 2001/3538)
	6		1 Dec 2001 (SI 2001/3538)
5			1 Dec 2001 (SI 2001/3538)
6, para	1–7		3 Sep 2001 (SI 2001/2632)
	8, 9		25 Feb 2001 (for the purpose of making orders or regulations) (SI 2001/516)
			3 Sep 2001 (otherwise) (SI 2001/2632)
7, 8			18 Jun 2001 (SI 2001/1820)
9, para	1–6		25 Feb 2001 (SI 2001/516)
	7		18 Jun 2001 (SI 2001/1820)
10			1 Dec 2001 (SI 2001/3538)
11			25 Feb 2001 (SI 2001/516)
12, para	1–5		1 Dec 2001 (SI 2001/3538)
	6	(1)	1 Dec 2001 (SI 2001/3538)
		(2)	25 Feb 2001 (SI 2001/516)

Schedule				Commencement date
12, para	6	(3)		1 Dec 2001 (SI 2001/3538)
	7–10			1 Dec 2001 (SI 2001/3538)
13, para	1–8			3 Sep 2001 (SI 2001/2632)
	9			25 Feb 2001 (SI 2001/516)
	10–13			3 Sep 2001 (SI 2001/2632)
14				18 Jun 2001 (SI 2001/1820)
15				3 Sep 2001 (SI 2001/2632)
16				1 Dec 2001 (SI 2001/3538)
17				18 Jun 2001 (SI 2001/1820)
18, Pt	I–IV			1 Dec 2001 (SI 2001/3538)
	V			2 Jul 2002 (SI 2001/3538)
19, Pt	I			18 Jun 2001 (SI 2001/1820)
	II, para	1–18		18 Jun 2001 (SI 2001/1820)
		19		25 Feb 2001 (for the purpose of making orders or regulations) (SI 2001/516)
				18 Jun 2001 (otherwise) (SI 2001/1820)
20, para	1	(a)		1 Dec 2001 (SI 2001/3538)
		(b)		3 Sep 2001 (SI 2001/2632)
	2	(a)		1 Dec 2001 (SI 2001/3538)
		(b)		3 Sep 2001 (SI 2001/2632)
	3			3 Sep 2001 (SI 2001/2632)
20, para	4, 5			1 Dec 2001 (SI 2001/3538)
	6			3 Jul 20011 (SI 2001/2364)
	7	(1), (2)		3 Sep 2001 (SI 2001/2632)
		(3)	(a)	1 Dec 2001 (SI 2001/3538)
			(b)	3 Sep 2001 (SI 2001/2632)
21				14 Jun 2000 (s 431(1))
22				30 Apr 2001 (repeal of Insurance Brokers (Registration) Act 1977) (SI 2001/1282)
				1 Dec 2001 (otherwise, except repeals in Credit Unions Act 1979) (SI 2001/3538)
				2 Jul 2002 (repeals in Credit Unions Act 1979) (SI 2001/3538)

* For transitional provision, see SI 2001/2364, art 3.
† Note that the Queen's Printer copy of SI 2001/2632 purports to bring s 372 into force on 20 July 2001 both for all purposes and for the purpose of making rules only; it is thought that the intention was to bring that section into force for the purpose of making rules only.

Index